American Constitutional Law

American Constitutional Law

SIXTH EDITION

Martin Shapiro

University of California School of Law, Berkeley

Rocco J. Tresolini

Late of Lehigh University

MACMILLAN PUBLISHING CO., INC.
New York

COLLIER MACMILLAN PUBLISHERS
London

PRINTED IN THE UNITED STATES OF AMERICA

MACMILLAN PUBLISHING CO., INC.
866 Third Avenue, New York, New York 10022

COLLIER MACMILLAN CANADA, INC.

Library of Congress Cataloging in Publication Data

Shapiro, Martin M.
American constitutional law.

Bibliography: p.
1. United States—Constitutional law.
I. Tresolini, Rocco J. II. Title.
KF4550.S45 1983 342.73 82–15338
ISBN 0–02–409580–1 347.302 AACR2

Printing: 2 3 4 5 6 7 8 Year: 3 4 5 6 7 8 9 0

ISBN 0-02-409580-1

Preface

As a political scientist who serves as a law professor, I constantly find myself struck by how different the needs of undergraduates are from those of law students. For instance, law students take courses in procedure before reaching a constitutional law course. Moreover, teaching about the criminal justice aspects of constitutional law has been largely shifted from their constitutional law to their criminal law courses. The paradoxical result is that an undergraduate constitutional law case book must cover more ground than its law school counterpart, for it must give its students some of the rudiments of procedure and a great deal of the detail of constitutional criminal law that law students get elsewhere.

The demands of professional education dictate that current constitutional doctrine be presented in law schools in sufficiently great detail to serve the practitioner. Inevitably this has meant that, as the amount of current doctrine has increased, historical materials have been curtailed. The normal solution has been to describe the Marshall period rather well and then move very briskly to at least 1937 before beginning thorough analysis. In undergraduate instruction we are more content to present the general contours of current doctrine rather than all the details that may help particular clients. Consequently we have more time to spend on developing the historical continuities, believing that such an investment of time comports well with the general goals of liberal arts as opposed to professional education. For better or worse we should expect the undergraduate to know more about how the law got to where it is than the law student knows and the law student to know more about the law today and less about its development than the undergraduate.

Finally, the undergraduate course typically is a course in political science, something which the law school course most definitely purports not to be. No one can teach anyone constitutional law without devoting a great deal of attention to the role of the Supreme Court in American politics. Yet that attention tends to appear intersticially in the law school courses and centrally in those in political science departments. There remains a subtle but very important difference between teaching a course about constitutional law to law students and teaching one about the Supreme Court to undergraduates. This difference is crucial even for those undergraduate instructors who are just as concerned with the constitutional law announced by the Supreme Court as they are with political science study of the Court.

Consequently nonlaw school instructors who are interested in teaching substantive constitutional law may encounter some difficulty in finding text materials that strike exactly the balance they need between the law of the Constitution and the politics of the Supreme Court. It is to be hoped that this book will be of assistance to such instructors. The sixth edition of this book, like earlier editions, is designed for courses on the Supreme Court that maintain a strong emphasis on constitutional doctrine and its historic evolution. None of the cases of the last edition have been deleted in this one. Two new cases have been added—a brief version of *Friedman* v. *Rogers,* which succinctly states the Court's new doctrine on First Amendment protection of commercial speech, and the *Fullilove* case, which is the most important of the affirmative action cases. The editing of some other cases has been somewhat tightened so that the addition of these two cases does not increase the overall case reading chores of the students. A large number of recent cases are cited in brackets in the chapter introductions in order to provide students with starting points for term papers on contemporary constitutional issues.

The final chapter on privacy is used as a general review of much earlier material and a vehicle for dealing with the whole range of cases on birth control and abortion. Chapter 5, "The Federal System," covers not only the classic materials but modern cases arising under the national civil rights statutes which present key issues of contemporary federalism. *National League of Cities* v. *Usery,* which has rekindled the classic debates over the reach of the commerce power and state sovereignty, has been included. It should serve to motivate student interest in what must now seem to them a very old New Deal controversy. At the suggestion of a number of instructors, *Barron* v. *Baltimore* has also been included.

Two chapters are devoted to equal protection and certain facets of due process that are closely brigaded with equal protection in the practice of the Court. Chapter 13 covers most of the racial discrimination cases. Chapter 14 is devoted to the "new" equal protection—the long line of recent cases that apply the logic of equal protection to issues raised in other than racial contexts. Thus, it groups together poverty, welfare, education, sexual discrimination, illegitimacy, the rights of the indigent accused, the more recent problems of reapportionment, and the access of the poor to the electoral process. In short, it deals with the whole development of the *"suspect classification,"* *"fundamental rights"* approach that the Warren Court expanded far beyond the area of race. The problem of affirmative action is presented in Chapter 14 rather than Chapter 13 because it involves sex as well as race discrimination and is best understood in the context of the Court's entire recent equal protection jurisprudence.

Chapter 15 is directed to the rights-of-accused cases. This body of constitutional law is now so detailed and complex that satisfactory teaching results cannot be attained by the "leading case" method alone. Accordingly, the introduction to the criminal procedure chapter contains a detailed primer on the development and current state of the law designed to orient the student to the leading cases that follow.

Particularly in the chapters on the new equal protection and on criminal procedure, but also in the chapters on freedom of speech, religion, and racial discrimination, special pains have been taken to compare and contrast the approaches of the Warren and Burger courts.

Chapter 16 is concerned with the intersection of constitutional due process requirements and the administrative process. In addition, introductory materials and two cases on the nonconstitutional, statutory interpretation work of the Supreme Court appear. Nonconstitutional cases are a substantial part of the Court's work load and bring to it many major issues of public policy. For instance, the concern for ecology comes to the Court as an almost purely statutory problem. The *Volpe* case illustrates this point. And some areas of the Court's statutory jurisdiction—antitrust, for instance—have far more impact in the real world than many of its lesser constitutional concerns. The *Du Pont* case is one of the major Supreme Court decisions of the twentieth century. It seems odd that it should be excluded as nonconstitutional while we continue to involve students with such topics as intergovernmental tax immunity.

Those instructors who feel strongly about preserving their constitutional purity can simply skip this chapter. The book has been quite deliberately organized to facilitate this tactic. Those who want to use the chapter but hesitate because of the unfamiliarity of the materials will find that Chapter 6 of my *Law and Politics in the Supreme Court* (New York: Free Press, 1964) presents a relatively short and simple orientation to the *Du Pont* case and that my *Supreme Court and Administrative Agencies* (New York: Free Press, 1968) provides a similar introduction to the general issues raised by *Volpe.*

I would like to thank Eve Shapiro for devoting many hours to the final stages of production for this book and apologize to her for not acknowledging her work on the last edition.

M. S.

Table of Contents

Cases

[Titles in italic capitals and figures in underscored italic type refer to opinions reprinted in the volume. Italic capital and lower case type is used for cases cited or discussed in the essays and opinions.]

American Constitutional Law

PART I

Institutional Aspects

"... But the provisions of the Constitution are not mathematical formulas having their essence in their form; they are organic living institutions transplanted from English soil. Their significance is vital, not formal; it is to be gathered not simply by taking the words and a dictionary, but by considering their origin and the line of their growth."

Oliver Wendell Holmes

In *Gompers* v. *United States,* 233 U.S. 604, 610 (1914).

CHAPTER 1

The American Constitutional System

From 1789 to the Present

The concept of a written constitution is one of the unique contributions that the United States has made to the art of government. The American Constitution, which has been in effect since 1789, is the oldest written national constitution now in use. Its long life seems even more remarkable when we consider the changes that have taken place in the United States since the Constitutional Convention of 1787.

The fifty-five delegates who attended the Philadelphia Convention came from twelve states (Rhode Island did not send a delegation) clustered along the Eastern seaboard. Each of these states was extremely jealous of its powers, and as a group they were unwilling to relinquish their powers to a central government. What was then the United States encompassed an area of about 350,000 square miles, a large portion of which was Indian country where settlers needed armed protection. To the north of this cluster of states was British Canada, to the west was Spanish territory, and the south was bounded by Spanish Florida. The total population of the United States in 1789 numbered over four million persons. The great majority of these people were of British stock, living in rural areas or small towns. Approximately 75 per cent of them were farmers, and the rest were small craftsmen, tradesmen, merchants, professional men, seamen, or slaves. The delegates to the Constitutional Convention went to Philadelphia on horseback or by stagecoach; extremely poor roads made travel risky, slow, and uncomfortable; there were no automobiles or trains; radio, television, and the telephone were still many generations away.

The role of the American state has changed drastically in the 190 years since the adoption of the Constitution. The early American conception of government, though including the notion of government support for business, particularly in the realms of finance and communication, rested heavily on the belief that government should impose as few restrictions as possible on society. There was general agreement that the function of government was to maintain law and order and to protect life, liberty, and property from both internal and external threats. The individual was to be left free to follow his own interests, in competition with other individuals. This emphasis on individual freedom was largely negative in nature. Among other things, it signified freedom from arbitrary arrest and imprisonment; freedom from executive tyranny; freedom from taxation without representation; and freedom of speech, worship, and association. Nineteenth-century Americans assumed that the purposes of law were to preserve individual natural rights from encroachment and to further such widely held interests as those in economic development, public education, and national expansion.[1]

The doctrine of individualism was particularly suited to eighteenth- and nineteenth-century America. Everywhere there was room for expansion. The frontier, with its virtually free land, beckoned to the adventuresome and the energetic. Great new areas were being opened for exploration and colonization. New inventions and discoveries created new jobs and new tools for the conquest of natural resources and the creation of new wealth. By the beginning of the twentieth century, however, this epoch was rapidly coming to an end as the result of the Industrial Revolution, the growth in population, the rise of giant industrial corporations, and numerous other factors.

The phenomenal changes that have occurred in America since 1789 could not possibly have been foreseen by the framers of the Constitution. The population has multiplied more than forty times. The simple agrarian society of 1789 has been transformed into an intricate and complex industrial one whose power and influence extend to every corner of the world. The majority of the people now dwell in urban areas and perform tasks in manufacturing, commerce, and transportation that were unknown to the Americans of 1789. Modern means of communication and transportation have knit together closely the various

[1] See Morton Horwitz, *The Transformation of American Law 1780–1860* (Cambridge: Harvard U.P., 1977).

areas of the nation. A flood of immigrants has altered drastically the original racial composition of the country. The slaves have been freed. In this transformation, the United States suffered through a terrible civil war that almost wrecked the union of states. Its power was decisively felt in two world wars during the twentieth century. Since 1939, the United States has been the leader in the development of nuclear weapons. Since World War II, the United States has maintained a complex web of international interests that have involved it in crisis situations in Berlin, Korea, Cuba, Vietnam, and the Middle East.

As Americans moved from rural areas to large urban centers and as mass production, with its early unregulated competition, replaced the artisan, a change took place in the economic life of the country. Americans began to look to the government for help. National crises engendered by two world wars and the serious economic depressions of the 1930s further stimulated the expansion of government services. Today, increasing numbers of Americans look upon government as the positive promoter of the people's general welfare. Both major political parties are now committed to programs involving social security, the maintenance of minimum health standards, minimum wages, unemployment insurance, and countless other services.

> The net effect has been a shift in political, economic, and social philosophies from individualism toward socialism, from acceptance of an economic system operating in response to the profit motive to belief in one in which government planning and direction is to play an increased role, from a social philosophy which admitted the duty of government to intervene in the distribution of income to a limited extent to one urging government to interpose for that purpose on an ever-increasing scale, and from a political and constitutional theory of rather restricted federal activity to one in which the Federal Government was assigned the major role in realizing the social objectives explicit or implicit in the new approaches to our social and economic problems.[2]

This tendency has been tempered only slightly by contemporary suspicion of big, technocratic government.

Survival of the Constitution

While these tremendous changes have been taking place, the American constitutional framework has remained essentially the same as in 1789. For some time, many people believed that the Constitution had survived so many drastic changes principally because the framers, who were looked upon as "an assembly of demigods" endowed with exceptionally perceptive powers, had created a unique instrument of government. So august an Englishman as William Gladstone called the American Constitution "the most wonderful work ever struck

[2] Henry Rottschaeffer, "The Constitution and a Planned Economy," *Michigan Law Review*, Vol. 38 (1940), pp. 1133–34.

off at a given time by the brain and purpose of man." Another Englishman, however, in a classic study of American government, arrived at a more realistic appraisal when he noted that "the American Constitution is no exception to the rule that everything which has power to win the obedience and respect of men must have its roots deep in the past and that the more slowly every institution has grown, so much the more enduring it is likely to prove. There is little in the Constitution that is absolutely new. There is much that is as old as Magna Carta." [3]

The labors and experiences of many generations of men molded the work of the Constitutional Convention. In referring to the convention, one writer stated that it is essential to know what was done and said and thought on that eventful occasion. But such behavior stemmed from "the stream of the things that had gone before." [4] This fact does not detract from the reputation of the framers, for they were a group of highly gifted and politically capable men who, of necessity, relied heavily on many previous ideas, principles, and practices of government. The men who wrote the Constitution were familiar with the operation of English and Western European governments. They were also familiar with such outstanding English documents as the Magna Carta (1215), Petition of Rights of 1628, and Bill of Rights (1689), which represented important milestones in the growth of English political institutions. They were well versed in the chief political writings of the period and were influenced most profoundly by John Locke's *Two Treatises on Government,* Montesquieu's *Spirit of the Laws,* and William Blackstone's *Commentaries on the Laws of England.* In addition, the records and experiences of the Colonial governments, of the Continental Congress, of the Articles of Confederation, and of the early state governments under their respective constitutions were important sources of many of the ideas and principles of government that were incorporated in the Constitution.[5]

If the Constitution is not, then, an original, sacrosanct document, how has it been able to survive the multiple transformations noted here? The reason is simply that it is a flexible, dynamic document that has been greatly changed and expanded through judicial interpretation, legislative enactments, custom and usage, and, to a lesser degree, by the formal process of amendment provided for in the document itself. This has been possible because important provisions of the Constitution are so vague and nebulous that room is left for growth and modification within its framework. For example, the Constitution says that Congress shall have power "to regulate Commerce with foreign nations, and among the several States, and with Indian tribes." But commerce is not specially defined. Nor does the Constitution state what actually constitutes commerce "with foreign nations" or "among the several states." Each generation interprets these phrases in its own way. Another outstanding example is the phrase "due

[3] James Bryce, *The American Commonwealth* (New York: Macmillan, 1910), Vol. I, p. 28.

[4] Conyers Read, ed., *The Constitution Reconsidered* (New York: Columbia U.P., 1938), p. xiv.

[5] On the ideas behind the Declaration of Independence see Gary Wills, *Inventing America* (Garden City, N.Y.: Doubleday, 1978).

process of law," which, as will be seen, has quite a different meaning today from what it had seventy-five years ago.

The late Charles A. Beard, the well-known historian and political scientist, referred to the Constitution as a "living thing" because it contained so many vague words and phrases that needed to be interpreted by human beings. Professor Beard listed the following expressions, among others, as being vague and indefinite: general welfare, necessary and proper, full faith and credit, republican form of government, unreasonable searches and seizures, impartial jury, cruel and unusual punishments, powers not delegated to the United States by the Constitution, and privileges and immunities.

> Each of these words or phrases covers some core of reality and justice on which a general consensus can be reached. But around the core is a huge shadow in which the good and wise can wander indefinitely without ever coming to any agreement respecting the command made by the "law." Ever since the Constitution was framed, or particular amendments were added, dispute has raged among men of strong minds and pure hearts over the meaning of these cloud-covered words and phrases. . . . Now, these vague words and phrases must be interpreted by men and women who have occasion to use them, as members of government and as citizens urging policies on government. The words and phrases cannot rise out of the Constitution and interpret themselves. Some human being, with all the parts and passions of such a creature, must undertake the task of giving them meaning in subsidiary laws and practices.[6]

Thus, the "great generalities of the Constitution have a content and a significance that vary from age to age."[7]

The ambiguous terms of the Constitution have made possible changes in interpretation to meet the demands of the times. In this process, the President and Congress, as well as the Supreme Court, have played a vital role, because each may interpret provisions of the Constitution. The Supreme Court has loomed particularly large in this process, however, because it has been thought to have "final" authority to interpret the provisions of the Constitution. Actually, there have been numerous instances in our constitutional history when Supreme Court opinions have been "overturned" or reversed either by the Court itself or in some other manner. For example, three amendments to the Constitution—the Eleventh, Thirteenth, and Sixteenth—were designed to repudiate specific Supreme Court decisions. The Eleventh Amendment reversed the decision in *Chisholm* v. *Georgia,* 2 Dall. 419 (1793), which had held that an individual could sue a state in the federal courts without the consent of the state. In the famous Dred Scott case,[8] the majority of the Court held that the Missouri Compromise, which was designed to ban slavery in the territories, was unconstitutional. Eight years later slavery was abolished throughout the United States by the Thirteenth Amendment, and the first sentence of the Fourteenth Amend-

[6] Charles A. Beard, "The Living Constitution," *The Annals,* Vol. 185 (May 1936), pp. 30–31.
[7] Benjamin N. Cardozo, *The Nature of the Judicial Process* (New Haven: Yale, 1921), p. 17.
[8] *Dred Scott* v. *Sanford,* 19 How. 393 (1857).

ment (1868) overturned the rule of citizenship declared by the Court in the Dred Scott case. The Sixteenth Amendment was ratified fewer than twenty years after the Supreme Court had decided [9] that an income tax could not be levied by Congress without apportioning it among the states according to population. Numerous instances of Supreme Court reversals of its own previous decisions could be cited. An outstanding example involved the question of child labor. In the famous case of *Hammer* v. *Dagenhart,* 247 U.S. 251 (1918), the Supreme Court held that Congress could not exclude from interstate commerce the goods manufactured by child labor. In 1941 a markedly changed Court specifically overruled [10] the Hammer case. On other occasions, both Congress and the President have initiated attempts to limit the powers of the Court.

Despite the fact that Supreme Court decisions are not final in the true sense of the word, it would be a mistake to underestimate the contribution of the Court in interpreting the Constitution. In large measure, the survival of the Constitution has been made possible by the Supreme Court's constant interpretation and reinterpretation to meet changing American social, economic, and political conditions. Many judges and legal scholars have noted that the ambiguous words and phrases of the Constitution are "empty vessels" into which a Supreme Court justice can pour almost anything he desires. In a way, the Supreme Court operates as a permanent constitutional convention. "It continues the work of the Convention of 1787 by adapting through interpretation the great charter of government, and thus its duties become political, in the highest sense of the word, as well as judicial." [11] In short, as one writer has put it, "the Supreme Court makes the Constitution march." [12] Thus, the Supreme Court has played a vital role in providing stability and permanence to the American system of government under the Constitution. But just what is the American Constitution and what are its important features?

The Constitution and Constitutional Law

THE CONSTITUTION

For practical purposes the Constitution of the United States can be referred to as the document that went into effect in 1789 as it has been amended and interpreted to the present time. To date, twenty-six amendments have been added. The first ten amendments are generally considered part of the original document, because they were approved in the first session of Congress and subsequently ratified, in 1791, by the legislatures of three fourths of the states.

[9] *Pollock* v. *Farmers' Loan and Trust Co.,* 158 U.S. 601 (1895).

[10] *U.S.* v. *Darby,* 312 U.S. 100 (1941).

[11] James M. Beck, *The Constitution of the United States* (New York: George H. Doran, 1924), p. 221.

[12] Frederick M. Davenport, *The Bacon Lectures on the Constitution of the United States* (Boston: Boston University Heffernan Press, 1939), p. 347.

The American Constitution, which is composed of an introductory part known as the Preamble, the seven articles, and the twenty-six amendments, has three major objectives:

1. It establishes the framework or structure of government.
2. It delegates or assigns powers to the government.
3. It restrains the exercise of these powers by government officials in order that certain individual rights can be preserved.

The Constitution thus serves a dual function in that it *both grants and limits powers.* The constitutional founders saw the need for establishing what was regarded in 1789 as a strong central government, but their previous political experience and knowledge had convinced them that they could not place unqualified trust in government officials. A brief perusal of some of the fundamental principles around which the Constitutional provisions are built will indicate, in part, this conflict of ideologies.

Popular Sovereignty, Limited Government, and Representation

The theories of popular sovereignty and limited government, which are perhaps the most significant concepts underlying the American constitutional system, evolved along a slow and tortuous path. From the time of Magna Carta in 1215, when King John was forced to make certain concessions to the noblemen and clergy, the idea was gradually developed that governmental power flows *from* the people. Thus, the Preamble of the Constitution states that "We the people of the United States . . . do ordain and establish this Constitution for the United States of America."

This theory of popular sovereignty was indeed a revolutionary one in an age when monarchy and sovereignty were widely viewed as synonymous. This is not to say that the Constitution initially established a political system that was democratic by present-day standards. Many persons, including those without adequate property holdings, women, and most blacks, were not qualified to vote. Senators were not elected directly by the people, and even the provision for an Electoral College reflects a certain suspicion of direct popular political expression on the part of the framers of the Constitution. Although the House was popularly elected, even it was seen as a layer of representatives lying between the people and the exercise of direct political power. The people would surely choose the best among them to represent them, and these representatives would screen and elevate public desires and moderate popular passions. But although complete democracy was not established in 1789, a sound foundation was laid for the future development of more democratic government.

In short, the American constitutional system rests on the firm conviction that governmental affairs must be conducted in accordance with the consent of the people. Americans are assumed to be capable of self-government; there is no legal limit to the power of the people. We have a limited government in the sense that government officials possess *only* such powers as have been conferred on them by the people through the Constitution.

Separation of Powers and Checks and Balances

As a further safeguard against possible tyrannical rule, the Constitution set up three institutionally distinct and theoretically equal organs of central government: legislative, executive, and judicial. These three organs were tied together in a dynamic relationship of cooperation and conflict by a system of checks and balances that, in various ways, provided for each of the three branches of government to have some check on the other two.

The rhetoric of separation of powers has always been important in political theory and in the evolution of the American constitutional system. Long before the American Revolution, many political theorists, including John Locke and Montesquieu, had incorporated this idea into their writings. The theme of divided authority runs throughout the whole body of American constitutional law. Many cases involving the meaning of the principle have been decided by the Supreme Court. A large number of cases in various chapters of this book that are classified under other subject headings are concerned with the meaning of this doctrine. As one writer puts it, "The development of the doctrine of the separation of powers in England and in this country was not worked out in the study, but in contests with the king on the field of battle, in the legislative chambers, and in the courts of law." [13] Watergate has been the latest of these contests.

In theory, the principle of separation of powers means simply that the powers of government are divided among the legislative, executive, and judicial branches. In practice, a complete separation of executive, legislative, and judicial powers has never prevailed in the United States. The framers of the Constitution, who had relied principally on the writings of Montesquieu for their conceptions of the principle of separation of powers, did not believe that *absolute* separation was possible or desirable. In *The Federalist,* No. 47, James Madison stated that Montesquieu did not favor a strict or absolute separation of powers. He noted:

> In saying, "There can be no liberty where the legislative and executive powers are united in the same person, or body of magistrates, or, if the power of judging be not separated from the legislative and executive powers," he [Montesquieu] did not mean that these departments ought to have no *partial agency* in, or no *control* over, the acts of each other. His meaning, as his own words import, and still more conclusively as illustrated by the example in his eye, can amount to no more than this, that where the *whole* power of one department is exercised by the same hands which possess the *whole* power of another department, the fundamental principles of a free constitution are subverted.[14]

Justice Holmes supported Madison's observation when he stated that "it does not seem to need argument to show that, however we may disguise it by veiling words, we do not and cannot carry out the distinction between legislative and

[13] Arthur T. Vanderbilt, *The Doctrine of the Separation of Powers and its Present-Day Significance* (Lincoln: University of Nebraska Press, 1953), p. 143.

[14] *The Federalist,* No. 47 (New York: Random, n.d., Modern Library Edition), pp. 314–15.

executive action with mathematical precision and divide the branches into water-tight compartments, were it ever so desirable to do so, which I am far from believing that it is, or that the Constitution requires." [15]

The practical experiences of the American Colonists had made them fearful of the concentration of power in despotic hands. As Madison noted in *The Federalist,* No. 47, "The accumulation of all powers, legislative, executive and judiciary, in the same hands, whether of one, a few, or many, and whether hereditary, self-appointed, or elective, may justly be pronounced as the very definition of tyranny." [16] The framers of the Constitution believed that the principle of separation of powers would make it impossible for a single group of persons to exercise too much power. Nevertheless, the principle is neither mentioned specifically in the Constitution nor explicitly adopted. Rather, it is implied from the structure of the Constitution itself, in which Article I is devoted to Congress, Article II to the President, and Article III to the federal courts.

Although the principle of separation of powers as embodied in the federal Constitution applies only to the national government, the majority of the state constitutions provide for separation by express provision or by implication.[17] The classic example of an express provision is that written into the Massachusetts Constitution of 1780, which provides as follows:

> In the government of this Commonwealth the legislative department shall never exercise the executive and the judicial powers, or either of them: the executive shall never exercise the legislative and judicial powers, or either of them: the judicial shall never exercise the legislative and executive powers, or either of them: to the end it may be a government of laws and not of men.

Perhaps it might seem at first glance that the constitutional separation of powers prescribes that the legislature possess all law-making power, the executive all administrative power, and the judiciary all power to decide individual cases under the law. In fact, whereas the Constitution gives each branch certain distinct authorities, each branch is assigned some law-making, some administrative, and some judicial tasks. Although the three departments were made separate and distinct, a system of constitutional checks and balances was devised that permits a blending of powers. A number of these provisions are noted in Ex Parte *Grossman* 267 U.S. 87 (1925), as follows:

> By affirmative action through the veto power, the Executive and one more than one third of either House may defeat all legislation. One half of the House and two thirds of the Senate may impeach and remove the members of the Judiciary. The executive can reprieve or pardon all offenses after their commission, either before trial, during trial, or after trial, by individuals, or by classes, conditionally or absolutely,

[15] Dissenting opinion in *Springer* v. *Government of Philippine Islands,* 277 U.S. 189 (1928).

[16] Loc. cit.

[17] Malcolm P. Sharp, "The Classical American Doctrine of Separation of Powers," *University of Chicago Law Review,* Vol. 2 (1935), p. 385.

and this without modification or regulation by Congress. . . . Negatively, one House of Congress can withhold all appropriations and stop the operations of government. The Senate can hold up all appointments, confirmation of which either the Constitution or a statute requires, and thus deprive the President of the necessary agents with which he is to take care that the laws be faithfully executed.

The difficulties of classifying all the functions of government into three neat pigeonholes and the necessity for the commingling of powers among the three branches of government are demonstrated well by the development and uses of contempt powers. The word *contempt* was used originally in England to denote an act committed in violation of an order or writ of the king or of any of his subordinate officers. Any such disobedience might result in an offender's quick or summary punishment without the use of any formal procedural safeguards. Despite the fact that the roots of the contempt power are found in the English executive, the courts have ruled on many occasions that the power is exclusively "inherent" in the judiciary. They have ruled that the contempt power is needed to enable courts to carry on their proceedings in an effective manner. Orderly administration of justice requires that those who persist in disturbing or slowing down judicial proceedings be punished without undue delay. On numerous occasions, the Supreme Court has ruled that summary conviction and punishment by judicial officers is consistent with the guaranties of due process of law. However, the doctrine that the contempt power is exclusively inherent in the judiciary has been weakened by the fact that legislative bodies have been allowed to use this "judicial" power. Neither the Senate nor the House of Representatives possesses express powers under the Constitution to punish for contempt except for disorderly conduct or failure to attend sessions on the part of members.[18] However, in a number of cases, Congress has been recognized to possess implied summary contempt powers under limited circumstances in order to insure the effectiveness of its legislative authority. In addition, a number of states have conferred contempt powers on administrative agencies by express constitutional provisions or by statute. Thus, a power that is supposedly judicial can be exercised by legislative officers and state executive officers as well.[19]

American political practice, too, has never followed a pattern of strict separation. One or another branch of the federal government may dominate at a particular time. For example, during the Reconstruction days which followed the Civil War, Congress was able to dominate the executive. On the other hand, Franklin D. Roosevelt's personality and his own political philosophy, together with unprecedented crisis, enabled him to dominate Congress, at least for a short time in the 1930s, with relative ease. Today we expect the President to have a legislative program and the Congress to concern itself with the efficiency of administration.

[18] Article I, Section 5, Clauses 1, 2.

[19] Much of the material in this paragraph is based on R. J. Tresolini, "The Use of Summary Contempt Powers by Administrative Agencies," *Dickinson Law Review,* Vol. 54 (1950), p. 395.

Federalism

As already noted, the Preamble states that the people established the Constitution. However, the formation of the American union may be seen as the accomplishment of the states themselves, acting as sovereign units, rather than of the whole people of the United States. The original states, being very jealous of their powers, were extremely reluctant to create a strong national government. In the light of this and other considerations, the American constitutional system was based on a division of power between the federal government and the states. This was accomplished by enumerating the powers of the national government in the body of the Constitution and leaving unspecified, residual powers to the states. The principle was confirmed by the Tenth Amendment, ratified in 1791, which provided that "the powers not delegated to the United States by the Constitution, nor prohibited by it to the states, are reserved to the States respectively, or to the people." Chapter 5 deals with some of the major constitutional problems raised by the division of powers between the national and state governments.

The Rule of Law

The classic formulation of the rule of law was set forth by A. V. Dicey, who was the foremost scholar of English constitutional law during the latter part of the nineteenth century. As will be seen, particularly in the discussion of the administrative process in Chapter 16, Dicey's rigid statement of the rule of law no longer fits the facts of modern government in either England or the United States. Nevertheless, because his theory has been influential in the development of certain aspects of American constitutional law, the most salient features of his version of the rule of law must be noted. According to Dicey, the rule of law had three distinct meanings, two of which are pertinent to this discussion.

> 1. No man is punishable or can be lawfully made to suffer in body or goods except for a distinct breach of law established in the ordinary legal manner before the ordinary courts of the land. . . .
> 2. . . . No man is above the law. . . . Every man . . . is subject to the ordinary law of the realm.[20]

The clearest expression of the rule of law in United States history is found in Article XXX of the Massachusetts Constitution of 1780, which established the separation of powers doctrine "to the end that it may be a government of laws and not of men." Although not specifically stated in the federal Constitution, the same idea is implicit in that document. Of course, the phrases "government of laws" and "government of men" have meaning only in a relative sense, because men ultimately must make and administer the laws. Yet the idea behind

[20] Albert V. Dicey, *Introduction to the Study of the Constitution* (London: Macmillan, 1939), pp. 188–95. The first edition of Dicey's book was published in 1885.

the doctrine is clear. It means that the system of laws under which we live must be applied equally to each citizen and that no person may be subject to the arbitrary decisions of government officers. Federal governmental action must be based on law—that is, it must be authorized by and not conflict with the Constitution and statutes passed by Congress, which constitute an expression of the people's sovereign will. "The difference, then, between a government of laws and a government of men (to the extent that these phrases have any real meaning) is not a difference in kind but a difference of degree only. It is nevertheless a difference of high and important degree; for it bespeaks a difference in spirit; and in government, as in most other human institutions, the spirit is often the essence." [21]

CONSTITUTIONAL AND STATUTORY LAW

As in the case of the term *constitution,* constitutional law cannot be precisely defined. In its broadest sense, the term *constitutional law* designates that branch of jurisprudence dealing with the formation, construction, and interpretation of constitutions. Because the fundamental law in the United States is the written Constitution, interpretations of that document by the President, Congress and other public officials, as well as governmental habits and customs, constitute a part of our constitutional law. However, the decisions of the courts, and especially the Supreme Court, are the principal sources of information relating to the meaning and interpretation of the Constitution. Such decisions form the chief source of our constitutional law. This fact led the late Professor Edward S. Corwin, one of the best-known students of the Constitution, to remark, "As employed in this country, Constitutional Law signifies a body of rules resulting from the interpretation by a high court of a written constitutional instrument in the course of disposing of cases in which the validity, in relation to the constitutional instrument, of some act of governmental power, State or National, has been challenged." [22]

Most of the decisions of the federal district courts and even the courts of appeal are not about constitutional but statutory law, for most of the legal rights that are of direct and immediate interest to most Americans were created by statute. The rights to receive a social security check, enter a veterans' hospital, operate a trucking business, claim an income tax deduction, or vote in a union election were created and are frequently altered by acts of Congress and administrative decisions made under the authority of such acts. They are statutory rights. About a fifth of the Supreme Court's decisions are devoted to statutory interpretation problems without any constitutional dimension. In these cases, the Court seeks to determine what a statute means and what rights it does and does not confer rather than asking whether the statute is or is not constitutional. Moreover, many Supreme Court decisions deal with the question of

[21] Howard L. McBain, *The Living Constitution* (New York: Macmillan, 1927), pp. 5–6.

[22] Edward S. Corwin, ed, *The Constitution of the United States of America* (Washington, D.C.: Legislative Reference Service, Library of Congress, 1953), p. ix.

whether someone has been deprived unconstitutionally of a right created by statute. Chapter 16 deals with statutory interpretation cases and the intersection of statutory and constitutional law.

Today there is also a large and growing body of law that lies halfway between constitutional and statutory law. Congress has passed a number of civil rights statutes that do not and could not create new constitutional rights. They do, however, provide a wide range of federal services designed to insure that individuals can adequately realize their constitutional rights. For instance, they provide for federal voting referees to oversee state election machinery where the state has previously shown a pattern of racial discrimination in the administration of its voting laws and where the discrimination appears to be continuing. They also provide for the intervention of the Justice Department in certain kinds of lawsuits in which individuals are arguing that their constitutional rights have been violated. In this way, such suits are encouraged because the government, rather than the individual whose constitutional rights have been violated, bears most of the costs of the suit. Today over three quarters of Americans—blacks and other racial minorities, those of Latin American ancestry, women, the handicapped, and the aged—enjoy special protections under the civil rights and comparable statutes. Millions of words of federal regulations, government contract provisions, and affirmative action plans are designed to implement those statutes. It is now frequently argued that those who do not fall into such statutorily favored categories, for instance, the young, healthy, white male, labor under disadvantages that may themselves be violations of the law or constitution. The civil rights laws are discussed in Chapters 5, 13, and 14.

We might divide a survey of the American constitutional system into roughly six major periods of development. This brief survey should provide the student with a background against which the cases can be read more meaningfully. Much of the material appearing in the remaining pages of this chapter is more fully developed in various other portions of the text.

THE MARSHALL ERA (1789–1835)

During this early period, the legislature was regarded as the most important branch of the national government. Most Americans firmly believed that legislatures were best suited to represent the people and their interests. Their long and difficult experience in the Colonies and their knowledge of English and Continental history had made them extremely fearful of strong executives.

At first, Americans showed very little interest in the work of the Supreme Court.[23] After the ratification of the Constitution, the state courts still handled most legal matters. The Supreme Court had no cases to decide during the first three years of its existence. The Court's lack of prestige is indicated by the fact that many outstanding persons declined appointments to the highest

[23] Julius Goebel, Jr., *History of the Supreme Court: Antecedents and Beginnings to 1801* (New York: Macmillan, 1971).

judicial tribunal in the land. The chief justiceship was refused by Patrick Henry and Alexander Hamilton. John Jay, the first Chief Justice, resigned the post to serve as Governor of New York. He refused a second appointment in 1800. Others either resigned from the Court or declined appointments in favor of state judicial positions. Unlike the executive and legislative branches, Supreme Court sessions were held in such places as basement apartments and Capitol committee rooms. It was not until 1935 that an elaborate building was provided for sessions of the Court.

Gradually, however, the Supreme Court gained in power and prestige. John Marshall, the fourth Chief Justice, who served in that post from 1801 to 1835, was responsible for the growing influence of the judiciary. He was without question the dominant justice of this period, if not of our entire history. Marshall took over the leadership of the Court during its formative period and was thus presented with the unique opportunity of directing the major lines of American constitutional development. He was more than equal to the occasion. In addition to his wide political experience, he was endowed with a fertile mind, cleverness, imagination, and courage. These great talents were used to establish clearly the supremacy of the national government.

Marshall's creed was enunciated in a number of his great decisions, such as *McCulloch* v. *Maryland* and *Gibbons* v. *Ogden,* which are considered in other portions of this book. Professor Corwin has summarized Marshall's major principles of constitutional construction:

1. Since the American Constitution is derived from the American people, it must be interpreted so as to secure to them the fullest benefit of its provisions. This idea is implicit in the "necessary and proper" clause of the Constitution, which provides that, in addition to its enumerated powers, Congress may make "all laws which shall be necessary and proper for carrying into execution the foregoing powers, and all other powers vested by this Constitution in the government of the United States, or in any department thereof."
2. The existence of the states did not limit the powers of the national government. This, according to Marshall, was implicit in the "supremacy" clause, which provides that "This Constitution, and the laws of the United States which shall be made in pursuance thereof; and all treaties made, or which shall be made, under the authority of the United States, shall be the supreme law of the land; and the judges in every state shall be bound thereby, anything in the Constitution or laws of any state to the contrary notwithstanding."
3. The Supreme Court is ultimately responsible for the interpretation of the Constitution in the interest of national supremacy. The decisions of the Supreme Court are therefore binding on the states. The principle of judicial review of legislation was enunciated in *Marbury* v. *Madison.*
4. The Constitution was designed to serve the American people for many generations. To this end, the Supreme Court must interpret the Constitution to meet the changing needs of the people in order that the Constitution may survive.[24]

[24] Edward S. Corwin, *The Twilight of the Supreme Court* (New Haven: Yale, 1934), p. 7. See Robert K. Faulkner, *The Jurisprudence of John Marshall* (Princeton: Princeton U.P., 1968).

Marshall's constitutional creed has been extremely influential in the development of American constitutional law. He looms so large that one sometimes fails to realize that there were other justices sitting with Marshall.[25]

Marshall's nationalistic interpretation of the Constitution had helped establish the Federal Government. He had used what power and prestige the Court had in supporting the nationalism of Hamilton. Marshall's influence on the constitutional system could never be erased. But the Jeffersonian theory of states' rights was still far from dead.

THE TANEY COURT (1836–1864)

Like John Marshall, Roger B. Taney (pronounced *Tawney*), Chief Justice from 1836 to 1864, was a man of wide political experience and great ability.[26] Although he had once been a strong Federalist, Taney was an ardent supporter of Andrew Jackson, who had been elected to the Presidency in 1828 and 1832. The Jacksonians, who represented the newer agrarian and pioneer elements in American politics, were suspicious of centralized powers. Although aware of the virtues of a union of states, they sought to reassert the rights of the states and local government units. Thus, Jackson, in his Second Inaugural Address, noted his readiness "to exercise my constitutional powers in arresting measures which may directly or indirectly encroach upon the rights of the States or tend to consolidate all political power in the General Government." [27]

To say that Taney became the spokesman for the Jacksonians would be to exaggerate, for the Supreme Court after 1835 did not break completely with the Marshall Court. Taney did reassert some state powers, but the principle of national supremacy was not destroyed. The Taney Court also reflected the new democratic era to some extent, showing less concern for the vested rights of property and capital and greater concern for "the people" than had the Marshall Court.

The most dramatic decision of this period was the *Dred Scott* case, which represented an unfortunate attempt by the Supreme Court to resolve the slavery issue. This case is also of importance because it extended the power of the Supreme Court. Chief Justice Hughes once called the decision one of the Court's great "self-inflicted wounds." Benjamin Wright offers a different assessment.

> The majority here attempted to transform the guarantees of civil liberties contained in the first eight amendments into positive protections to the rights of property in slaves. In arguing that the guarantees of these amendments restrict the discretionary power of Congress, Taney was making the first judicial assertion of a general supervi-

[25] Joseph Story and William Johnson were outstanding figures on the Court during this period. A distinguished biography of Johnson has thrown new light on the operation of the Marshall Court: Donald G. Morgan, *Justice William Johnson, the First Dissenter* (Columbia: U. of South Carolina Press, 1954).

[26] Carl B. Swisher, *Roger B. Taney* (New York: Macmillan, 1935).

[27] James D. Richardson, *Messages and Papers of the Presidents,* Vol. III (March 4, 1833), p. 4.

> sory jurisdiction over Congress. The Missouri Compromise Act was, furthermore, the first congressional act of any general consequence which the Court held invalid. Temporarily, the prestige of the Court suffered from the effects of the decision, but as we look back over the history of the review of congressional legislation, it is apparent that, in a long-run sense, the case was a critical victory in the campaign for judicial control.[28]

In reality, all the institutions of American politics tried and failed to resolve the slavery controversy. They all lost prestige, and their collective failure culminated in the Civil War. Perhaps all that can be said is that the Court did no worse than and recovered about as fast as did the rest of the government.

THE REVIVAL OF JUDICIAL POWER (1865–1890)

The verdict of the Civil War laid the foundation for the development of a cohesive national government. Although problems of federal versus states' rights persist to this day, the "nation of states" really ended with the Civil War; the period of rapid national growth was about to begin. The American scene changed drastically during this period: the nation's railroad system was greatly expanded, giant industrial corporations doing business on a national scale came into being, and the factory system accelerated the growth of large urban centers.

In this vast transformation, some groups were bound to perceive themselves as unfairly treated. Farmers began to demand that the railroads be regulated; the growth of the new industrial system brought vehement outcries from the ranks of labor. More and more, these and other groups turned to the national government for help in the solution of new problems. Thus, this period witnessed a definite trend toward centralization of powers in the national government. The act of 1887 establishing the Interstate Commerce Commission to deal with certain abuses of the railroads and the Sherman Antitrust Act of 1890 dealing with the monopoly problem were early examples of the now tremendous number of federal laws regulating many areas of activity.

In the years after the Civil War, the Supreme Court became more active, and federal judicial powers were greatly enlarged. During the tenure of Salmon P. Chase alone (1864–1873), the Supreme Court declared ten acts of Congress unconstitutional. It will be recalled that only two acts of Congress were held void (*Marbury* v. *Madison* and the *Dred Scott* case) in the previous seventy-four-year history of the Court. Throughout this period, many state as well as federal laws were held invalid.[29]

THE ERA OF JUDICIAL SELF-CONFIDENCE (1890–1937)

The increased activity of the Supreme Court dismayed large elements of the American population, because the legislation struck down was usually designed to aid such groups as farmers and laborers, who felt badly hurt by the

[28] Benjamin F. Wright, *The Growth of American Constitutional Law* (Boston: Houghton, 1942), pp. 76–77.

[29] Charles Fairman, *Reconstruction and Reunion 1864–88,* Vol. 1 (New York: Macmillan, 1971); *Mr. Justice Miller and the Supreme Court 1862–1890* (Cambridge: Harvard U.P., 1939).

new industrial development. The Court became an effective censor of state and federal legislation that was thought to interfere with private property. This it did by pouring the dominant economic philosophy of the day, laissez-faire capitalism, into such vague constitutional phrases as due process of law. By 1890 the Court had enunciated economic doctrines that made it an important determiner of American life and legislation. In succeeding years it would apply these doctrines to the tune of increasing controversy. At the same time, the Court was in the process of narrowly defining the provisions of the Fourteenth and Fifteenth Amendments, which were designed to guarantee basic civil rights to the newly freed Negro. By the end of this period, the Court's restricted interpretation of these amendments had made it impossible to use them effectively against racial discrimination.

In governmental affairs, the most persistent trend of the twentieth century has been the growth in the power and prestige of the executive branch in virtually every country. In the United States, neither the early fear of executive powers nor the separation of powers doctrine has prevented the rise of the executive branch to a position of predominant leadership in the affairs of state.

Many factors have been responsible for the phenomenal growth of executive powers in America. The social and economic changes brought about by industrialization inspired the intervention of the national government in a multitude of new areas. Because neither the courts nor Congress could regulate these areas adequately, these new functions came to be performed by the executive branch, largely through newly created administrative officers and bodies.[30] The powers of the executive branch were further expanded during crises of wars and depressions, which had to be fought on a national scale. The personal attitudes of "strong" presidents such as Theodore Roosevelt, Woodrow Wilson, and Franklin D. Roosevelt also resulted in the increased power and prestige of the executive branch. This growth of executive powers went hand in hand with the gradual centralization of more powers in the Federal Government.

During this period, the Supreme Court continued to invalidate much social and economic legislation demanded by large segments of the American people although its overall record is not as conservative as its liberal critics have contended. "Until 1937, Supreme Court decisions, in now advancing, now receding waves, used due process clauses and other constitutional provisions to hold back the expansion of the state and federal regulatory powers." [31] The period came to a dramatic end in the struggle between Franklin D. Roosevelt and the Court. Roosevelt had won the presidency over Hoover in a Democratic party landslide that also swept overwhelming Democratic majorities into both houses of Congress. The central election issue was the question of how to reduce the effects of the severe economic depression that had begun with the stock

[30] This development is covered in more detail in Chapter 16. The growth of executive powers from English origins is outlined in Tresolini, "The Development of Administrative Law," *University of Pittsburgh Law Review,* Vol. 12 (1951), pp. 362–80.

[31] Carl B. Swisher, *American Constitutional Development* (Boston: Houghton, 1943), p. 1019.

market collapse of 1929. Roosevelt had promised to take bold steps to deal with the Depression. To this end, his administration launched the New Deal program on taking office in 1933. This program consisted of a large number of measures designed to solve the most pressing economic problems. It was this nationwide recovery program, whose constitutionality was soon to be passed on by the Supreme Court, that precipitated the dramatic struggle with the President.

When the New Deal statutes came before the Supreme Court, that body was divided almost equally between conservative and liberal justices. It was almost a foregone conclusion that the four conservative members—James McReynolds, Pierce Butler, George Sutherland, and Willis Van Devanter—would vote against the New Deal measures. Each of these justices was thoroughly committed to the philosophy of laissez-faire and limited federal power. Justices Louis D. Brandeis, Harlan F. Stone, and Benjamin N. Cardozo were the liberals who were sympathetic to the New Deal program. Chief Justice Hughes and Owen J. Roberts, the other two members of the Court, could not be classified with either group. They held the balance of power. As it turned out, Roberts and Hughes were usually found in the conservative camp.

The first New Deal law did not come before the Court until 1935, but within the next sixteen months decisions were rendered in ten major cases involving New Deal measures. The Court invalidated eight out of the ten measures. During the sixteen-month period, the Court struck down in succession Section 9(c) of the National Industrial Recovery Act, the NRA itself, the Railroad Pension Act, the Farm Mortgage Law, the Agricultural Adjustment Act (AAA), the AAA amendments, the Bituminous Coal Act, and the Municipal Bankruptcy Act. Once these laws were declared to be unconstitutional, ". . . the basic cleavage between judicial oligarchy and popular power could no longer be concealed or circumvented. In one short term the Court had woven a tight constitutional web to bind political power at all levels. . . . By the spring of 1936 it looked as if the Court had wrecked the New Deal on the shoals and rocks of unconstitutionality." [32]

The Roosevelt administration's overwhelming victory in 1936 put the electorate's stamp of approval on the New Deal. With 60 per cent of the voters behind him, the President felt that the time had come for an assault on the Court majority, which was so hostile to his program. Early in 1937, Congress was presented with Roosevelt's famous Court-packing bill, which was designed to make sweeping changes in the federal judiciary. The bill provided for the voluntary retirement of Supreme Court justices at the age of 70. For each member of the Court who reached the age limit but failed to retire, the President would appoint an additional justice. The maximum number of Court justices was fixed at fifteen.

Although Congress failed to approve the Court-packing bill, Roosevelt had

[32] Alpheus T. Mason, *The Supreme Court: Vehicle of Revealed Truth or Power Group, 1930–1937* (Boston: Boston U.P., 1953), pp. 36–37.

"lost the battle but won the war." The temper of the Court itself had changed. The New Deal had shaken down into a firmer and more consistent set of legislative programs more acceptable to the Justices. Between 1937 and 1939 the President was able to make four new appointments that brought the Court firmly into the New Deal alliance.

During the 168 days in which Congress was considering the President's bill, the Court made the famous "switch in time which saved nine" by abandoning its opposition to the New Deal. This was made possible by a change in the previous views of Chief Justice Hughes and Justice Roberts, who may have been influenced by both the election of 1936 and the fear that continued opposition to social change would eventually wreck the Supreme Court. (Hughes denied that these considerations accounted for his change of judicial views. Roberts maintained that his views had remained consistent.) By the spring of 1937, the Court had dramatically reversed itself in a series of decisions upholding a minimum-wage statute of the state of Washington, the amended Railway Labor Act of 1934, the Farm Mortgage Act of 1935, the National Labor Relations Act of 1935, and the Social Security Act of 1935. The Court left the management of the economy to legislatures and executives.

THE NEW DEAL ERA (1937–1953)

After 1937, Supreme Court decisions followed two main lines: In the first place, the Court's constitutional decisions were not concerned greatly with the protection of traditional property rights and the maintenance of a laissez-faire system. Extensive federal regulation of many new areas became an accepted and permanent part of American life. Both major political parties were committed to programs that involved the expansion of national powers. The retreat of the Court from its 1936 position concerning the New Deal is indicated by the fact that from 1936 to 1955 only three minor pieces of federal legislation were held unconstitutional.[33]

The second major trend in Supreme Court decisions after 1937 was the increased Court protection afforded to civil liberties. While in the process of relegating many traditional property rights to a subordinate constitutional position, the Court was involved in the creation and development of elaborate new protections of other rights. Although the Court has allowed great inroads to be made on both property and personal rights during periods of national emergency, the main body of civil liberties has been preserved. During World War

[33] In *Tot* v. *United States,* 319 U.S. 463 (1943), the Court held that a section of the Federal Firearms Act, which established a presumption of guilt based on a prior conviction and present possession of a firearm, violated due process under the Fifth Amendment. In *United States* v. *Lovett,* 328 U.S. 303 (1946), a rider attached to an appropriations bill providing that three government employees were not to be paid their salaries was held to constitute a bill of attainder forbidden by the Constitution. A minor provision of the Food and Drug Act was invalidated in *United States* v. *Cardiff,* 344 U.S. 174 (1952). After 1955, however, the tempo changed, with the Court overturning some piece of federal legislation on the average of almost once a year.

II, for example, the compulsory evacuation of American citizens of Japanese ancestry from the West Coast and the complete military suppression of civil government in Hawaii were the only instances of serious infringement of individual liberty. This is not to say that the Court of the post-1937 era was consistently on the side of individual rights. Nevertheless, a long-term general change was easily discernible in the Court's attitude on matters involving civil liberties.

The new judicial attitude had its roots in a few opinions involving interpretation of World War I legislation dealing with espionage and subversion. Later, under the guiding hand of Charles Evans Hughes, who was Chief Justice from 1930 to 1941, the Court began a spirited defense of the letter and spirit of the Bill of Rights. From 1941 to 1946, under Chief Justice Harlan Stone, the Court continued to defend personal rights. When Fred M. Vinson became Chief Justice in 1946, the general expectation was that the Supreme Court would continue the defense of civil liberties. However, despite the bitter dissents of its more liberal members, the Vinson Court was reluctant to give strong support to civil liberties. Decisions unfavorable to the protection of civil liberties were rendered by the Vinson Court in the majority of such cases that it considered.[34] The Chief Justice himself and Justices Tom Clark, Stanley Reed, Sherman Minton, and usually Harold Burton and Felix Frankfurter refused to intervene in most civil liberties cases.

THE WARREN AND BURGER COURTS

Under the leadership of Earl Warren, who succeeded Vinson as Chief Justice in 1953, the Supreme Court again seemed determined to protect personal freedoms. Writing late in 1955, a well-known political observer remarked that the Supreme Court was conveying "the idea that it is remarkably united on preserving the rights of the individual, whether he be a Negro waiting for a train, or going to school, or a civil servant robbed of his pride and means of livelihood by unidentified accusers, or a businessman denied the right to travel freely about the world. . . . The Chief Justice of the United States has taken the lead in reasserting the constitutional liberties of the people. . . . After years of unparalleled aggression by the executive and legislative branches against the rights of the individual, the judiciary has stepped in to balance the scales."[35] The Warren Court's determination to preserve civil rights was indicated by the public statements of the Chief Justice himself as well as by the Court's decisions. Some two years after his appointment as Chief Justice, Warren noted that the "pursuit of justice is not the vain pursuit of a remote abstraction; it is a continuing direction of our daily conduct. Thus it is that when the generation of 1980 receives from us the Bill of Rights, the document will not have exactly the same meaning it had when we received it from our fathers. We will pass on a better Bill of Rights or a worse one, tarnished by neglect or burnished

[34] C. Herman Pritchett, *Civil Liberties and the Vinson Court* (Chicago: U. of Chicago, 1954).
[35] James Reston, *The New York Times* (Dec. 5, 1955).

by growing use. If these rights are real, they need constant and imaginative application to new situations." [36]

As will be seen more clearly in the chapters that follow, the Warren Court was often divided into two blocs. The acknowledged leader of the judicial activists was Justice Black, supported by Justices Brennan, Douglas, and the Chief Justice himself. They believed that the Court must play a positive role in the protection of individual liberties. They sought to promote social welfare and to protect American freedom from erosion by legislative bodies and executive officers. Justice Black and his supporters viewed the Court as the ultimate guardian of constitutional rights. Justice Felix Frankfurter headed another bloc on the Court that advocated a policy of "judicial self-restraint." He and his supporters believed that the primary responsibility for governing lies with the people and their duly elected officers. They felt that the Court must take a back seat to legislative bodies lest the freedom of the people to govern themselves be hampered by "judicial legislation." In short, Justice Frankfurter was wary of judicial attempts to impose justice on the community and "to deprive it of the wisdom that comes from self-inflicted wounds and the strength that grows with the burden of responsibility." [37] Justice Frankfurter was usually supported by Justice Harlan, who later became the leader of the "self-restraint" bloc, and Justices Stewart, Whittaker, and Clark. Yet on several occasions one or more of these justices voted with the civil libertarians. Justices Frankfurter and Whittaker retired in 1962 to be replaced by President Kennedy's appointees, Justices Goldberg and White. President Johnson appointed Justices Abe Fortas and Thurgood Marshall to the seats previously held by Justices Goldberg and Clark. During this period, the patterns of alliance were not always so clear. The judicial self-restraint bloc sometimes was reduced to Justice Harlan alone or in company with one other justice, with Justice Black on other occasions opposing the civil libertarians when he felt that the overzealous pursuit of political rights endangered the rule of law that guaranteed those rights.

The Warren Court embarked on four major interventions into American life: school desegregation, reapportionment, reform of criminal procedure, and the release of erotic expression from most of the constraints of obscenity laws. Each of these interventions plus the Court's ban on prayers in the public schools deeply affected many Americans. Each led to major opposition, and at least two—the segregation and obscenity decisions—actually changed the shape and tone of the daily lives of millions of people.

It is possible to argue that the Supreme Court was the major instrument of

[36] Earl Warren, "The Law and the Future," *Fortune* (Nov. 1955), p. 230.

[37] Wallace Mendelson, *Justices Black and Frankfurter: Conflict in the Court* (Chicago: U. of Chicago, 1961), p. 131. The philosophy of the judicial activists is well delineated in a series of lectures by Justices Black, Brennan, Douglas, and Chief Justice Warren in Edmond Cahn, ed., *The Great Rights* (New York: Macmillan, 1963). See also Irving Dillard, ed., *One Man's Stand for Freedom: Mr. Justice Black and the Bill of Rights* (New York: Knopf, 1963); Charles L. Black, Jr., *The People and the Court* (New York: Macmillan, 1960); and Martin Shapiro, *Freedom of Speech, the Supreme Court and Judicial Review* (Englewood Cliffs, N.J.: Prentice-Hall, 1966).

domestic reform during the 1950s and 1960s, as the Presidency had been during the 1930s. The President's power in war and foreign affairs continued to grow, and the assertions of the Presidency to absolute power in these realms grew even more absolutely than the reality, particularly during the seventies. At the same time, the Court seemed to embark on an egalitarian crusade that promised eventually to assault every invidious political, economic, and social distinction in American society.

The Court showed the way in Negro rights with Congress and the President trailing after. Basing themselves on the black parallel—or parable—every aggrieved group in American society, from prison inmates to ecologists, confidently sought judicial aid in righting their own particular perceived wrongs. The lower federal courts and many state courts, taking their lead from the top, ventured more and more boldly into every phase of public policy.[38] By the early 1970s it was almost impossible to initiate any new local, state, or federal program without a flurry of injunctions, hearings, and lawsuits following.

It is little wonder then that the courts, Supreme and otherwise, became a significant issue in American politics. For the first time since the late 1930s, the question of staffing the Supreme Court became a major item on the agendas of presidential elections. Presidential elections are rarely mandates, although the winners like to claim they are. Richard Nixon, triumphant in office, sought immediately to change the face of the Warren Court. The normal winnowing of age, plus a series of resignations by some liberal justices and the failure of others to leave the bench at times when they could have been replaced by a liberal President, gave President Nixon that opportunity.

The symbol of the change was the replacement of Chief Justice Warren by Chief Justice Burger. The new Chief Justice did reflect some of President Nixon's preferences on criminal justice, but he certainly did not return the Court to the position of minor partner in the Presidential alliance. President Nixon soon discovered that Congress had a mandate different from his when the Senate rejected two of his nominations. His failure to place Judges Haynesworth and Carswell on the Supreme Court probably reduced the possibility of its rapid realignment to that stance of conservatism and judicial inaction desired by the President. Only the appointment of Justice Rehnquist seemed to meet the President's preferences.

It is tempting to draw parallels between the Burger and the Taney Courts. In both instances, it might have been expected that the claims to political authority of their immediate predecessors would have been cut back. In both instances, it turned out that appointing strong-minded men to the Chief Justiceship is not the best tactic for those who desire a quiet Supreme Court. Chief Justice Burger and Justices Blackmun, Powell, and Stevens have somewhat different policy views from those of their Warren Court predecessors, just as the Taney Court Jacksonians differed to a degree on substantive issues from the Federalists

[38] Donald Horowitz, *The Courts and Social Policy* (Washington, D.C.: Brookings Institution, 1977).

they replaced. In both instances, however, the new justices have tended to preserve the assertions of judicial authority that they inherited. And in both they have subsequently turned them to achieve a different balance of political interests from that favored by the preceding Court.

Moreover, the basic tactic in achieving this change of direction in both instances has been to rely less (than their predecessors) on absolute and sweeping declarations of constitutional rules and more on judicial discretion to tailor discrete constitutional solutions to particular events. Judicially created absolute rules and judicial discretion both have elements of judicial activism, and both can be managed with more or less political discretion.[39] At this point it is not at all clear that the Burger Court is less active than the Warren Court. In its death penalty, abortion, presidential powers, desegregation, and campaign financing decisions, the Court continues to thrust itself or be thrust into the center of American political life. Its landmark cases are fewer than those of the Warren Court, but its overall involvement in public policy remains high.[40]

[39] Martin Shapiro, "Judicial Activism," in S. M. Lipset, ed., *The Third Century* (Chicago: University of Chicago Press, 1980). For contrasting prescriptions see Jesse Choper, *Judicial Review and the National Political Process* (Chicago: University of Chicago Press, 1980); John Hart Ely, *Democracy and Distrust: A Theory of Judicial Review* (Cambridge: Harvard U.P., 1980); and Owen Fiss, "The Forms of Justice," *Harvard Law Review*, Vol. 93 (1979), p. 1.

[40] See Stephen L. Wasby, *Continuity and Change: From the Warren Court to the Burger Court* (Pacific Palisades, Calif.: Goodyear, 1976); Richard Y. Funston, *Constitutional Counter Revolution?* (New York: Schenkman, 1977); "Symposium: The Burger Court: Reflections on the First Decade," *Law and Contemporary Problems*, Vol. 43 (1980), p. 135.

CHAPTER 2

The Federal Courts and the Law

Our federal system of government makes necessary two separate systems of law—that of the states and that of the national government. Thus, two separate and distinct sets of courts exist side by side in the United States. This dual court system is one of the most confusing aspects of American law. The state courts decide the majority of both civil and criminal cases. Yet each of the state courts has very little or no connection with the federal courts.

One might well ask why the framers of the Constitution decided to create an independent federal judiciary when they could have authorized the existing state courts to apply federal law whenever necessary. The framers' judgment that an independent system of federal courts to apply federal law would contribute to the strength of the national government certainly has been confirmed by subsequent events.

Jurisdiction of Federal Courts

Under our dual court system, the duties and jurisdiction of each system must be defined as precisely as possible. Article III of the Constitution defines specifically the jurisdiction of the federal courts. Under the Tenth Amendment, all other cases are tried in the state courts.

The cases and controversies that are subject to federal jurisdiction fall into two distinct classes: first, those that depend on the nature of the subject matter; secondly, those that depend on the nature of the parties involved without regard to subject matter. Article III enumerates nine types of cases or controversies that can be brought to the federal courts for decision:

Nature of the Subject Matter

1. All cases arising under the Constitution, federal laws, and treaties.
2. Admiralty and maritime cases.

Nature of the Parties

3. Cases affecting ambassadors, other public ministers, and consuls.
4. Controversies to which the United States is a party.
5. Controversies between two or more states.
6. Controversies between a state and citizens of another state.
7. Controversies between citizens of different states. These are known as diversity of citizenship cases.
8. Controversies between citizens of the same state claiming lands under grants of different states.
9. Controversies between a state, or citizens of a state, and a foreign government or its citizens or subjects. (This clause has been limited by judicial decisions and the Eleventh Amendment, which deprived the federal courts of jurisdiction in suits brought against a state by citizens of another state or by citizens of a foreign state.)

A case or controversy must fall within one of the classes listed here in order to be brought before a federal court. However, this does not mean that the federal courts alone may take jurisdiction in each instance. Congress may provide that some cases in the categories listed here may be tried by state as well as federal courts. An important area of such concurrent jurisdiction is suits between citizens of different states when the sum of $10,000 or more is involved. On the other hand, Congress has given the federal courts exclusive jurisdiction over some matters. For example, federal courts *must* decide disputes involving suits against ambassadors and foreign consuls; bankruptcy, copyright, and admiralty cases; and all cases involving federal criminal laws.

Organization of Federal Courts

The Constitution has very little to say about the organization of federal courts. Section I of Article III provides that the "judicial power of the United States shall be vested in one Supreme Court, and in such inferior courts as the Congress may from time to time ordain and establish." Thus, the only court provided for in the Constitution is one Supreme Court, with Congress given the responsibility for the creation of other federal courts. Neither does the Constitution say anything regarding the number of judges deemed necessary for the Supreme Court or any inferior courts that may be created by Congress. Beginning with the First Judiciary Act of 1789, Congress has enacted various laws that supplement Article III and account for the present structure and organization of the federal courts. The First Judiciary Act is of particular importance because it proved to be basic to the development of the present federal court organization. The act has been said to have three claims to greatness:

1. It set up a federal court organization which lasted almost unchanged for nearly one hundred years.
2. A section of the act empowering the Supreme Court to supervise the state courts was one of the "most important nationalizing influences" during our early history.
3. Most important, the tradition of a system of federal courts operating throughout the nation was firmly established.[1]

DISTRICT COURTS

At the bottom of the federal court system are the United States District Courts. They are courts of original jurisdiction; in other words, all cases and controversies involving federal questions, with the exception of the few disputes that start in the Supreme Court or specialized courts, are tried first in the district courts. The fifty states, together with the District of Columbia and Puerto Rico, are divided into some ninety districts, with a court in each district. The number of courts varies from time to time. Congress may create additional ones when the need arises. There is at least one federal district court in each of the states. In the larger and more heavily populated states, where there is a greater volume of work, there are more district courts. For example, New York and Texas each have four. Each district court is staffed by a number of judges.

The majority of cases in the district courts are heard by one judge. In some instances a panel of three judges must decide the issue. Two or more judges may hear cases simultaneously in different places within the same district.

The federal district courts dispose of most federal cases. In recent years, their work has increased tremendously because of the development of a large body of federal criminal, civil rights, environmental, and welfare law and the increasing number of civil cases filed each year. In recent years, three developments have further increased the work of the district courts. The rules of "standing" have been relaxed, so that far more persons than previously are entitled to bring suits in federal courts. The rules governing "class actions" have also

[1] Felix Frankfurter and James M. Landis, *The Business of the Supreme Court* (New York: Macmillan, 1928), p. 4.

been eased, so that huge classes of persons can be joined as plaintiffs in a single suit, as when all the customers of a given power or water company are brought into court as challengers of a decision by a regulatory agency that will result in increasing their bills. Thirdly, federal habeas corpus jurisdiction has been greatly expanded. (See Chapters 4 and 5.)

Like other federal judges, district judges (with the exception of those in Puerto Rico, who serve for terms of eight years) are appointed for life by the President, with the advice and consent of the Senate, and may be removed only by impeachment for misconduct.

Because the district courts are original trial courts having jurisdiction over both criminal and civil cases involving federal law, they are the only federal courts that normally use a jury. Because of their duty to enforce the reapportionment and antidiscrimination decisions of the Supreme Court, in recent years the district courts have frequently been at the center of bitter political struggles.[2]

COURTS OF APPEALS

Above the district courts are the courts of appeals. Prior to 1948, these courts were called the circuit courts of appeals. They were created in 1891 to relieve the Supreme Court of some of its appellate work. As the name suggests, these courts have only appellate jurisdiction. They hear appeals from the district courts and from important independent regulatory commissions. They are courts of final appeal in the majority of cases, because only a few of the cases they consider are carried to the Supreme Court for decision.[3]

The territory of the United States is divided into eleven numbered areas known as circuits, and in each of these areas there is a court of appeals. In addition, the District of Columbia comprises an unnumbered circuit with its own court of appeals, which is concerned principally with the large volume of litigation arising from the work of numerous federal administrative agencies in Washington. The numbered circuits encompass much larger areas. The Court of Appeals for the First Circuit, for example, disposes of cases from Maine, Massachusetts, New Hampshire, Puerto Rico, and Rhode Island; the Tenth Circuit includes Colorado, Kansas, New Mexico, Oklahoma, Utah, and Wyoming. Each of the eleven courts of appeals has from three to fourteen judges, depending on the volume of judicial work.[4] A panel of three judges usually reviews cases, with the judge who is senior in service acting as presiding officer. Until 1891, each Supreme Court justice was required to "ride the circuit"—that is, to hold court in his assigned circuit as well as to perform his duties as a member of the highest court. Although Supreme Court justices no longer

[2] See J. W. Peltason, *58 Lonely Men* (New York: Harcourt, Brace, 1961).

[3] J. W. Howard, *Courts of Appeal in the Federal Judicial System* (Princeton: Princeton U.P., 1981).

[4] For a summary and critique of the literature on the voting behavior of these judges, see Sheldon Goldman, "Voting Behavior on the United States Courts of Appeals Revisited," *American Political Science Review,* Vol. 69 (1975), p. 491.

ride the circuit, each of the justices is still assigned to particular circuits in a supervisory capacity.

SUPREME COURT

The Supreme Court of the United States is at the top of the federal court system. It consists of a Chief Justice and eight associate justices. Any six justices are necessary to constitute a quorum. The number of justices on the Court at a given time is set by Congress. The Court began with a Chief Justice and five associate justices. In 1801, the total number was reduced to five; in 1802, the number was six again; seven in 1837; and ten in 1863. In 1866 the number was fixed at seven by Congress, but the Court had not got down to the figure before Congress raised it again, in 1869, to nine. That number has remained unchanged since that date.

The Supreme Court has both original and appellate jurisdiction. Article III, Section 2, states as follows: "In all cases affecting ambassadors, other public ministers, and consuls, and those in which a State shall be party, the Supreme Court shall have original jurisdiction. In all other cases before mentioned, the Supreme Court shall have appellate jurisdiction, both as to law and fact, with such exceptions, and under such regulations, as the Congress shall make." However, for all practical purposes, the Supreme Court is an appellate court. The cases in which it has original jurisdiction are not numerous. Criminal cases involving diplomats are nonexistent because of diplomatic immunity. Nor is the constitutional grant of original jurisdiction necessarily an exclusive one, because Congress may authorize other federal courts to exercise concurrent jurisdiction. Cases are appealed to the Supreme Court from the state courts, *directly* from the district courts in some instances, from the Courts of Appeals, and occasionally from legislative courts such as the Court of Military Appeals. Courts are termed *legislative* rather than *constitutional* courts when Congress has established them under authority implied from constitutional provisions other than Article III. Because judges of legislative courts are not governed by Article III, they need not be appointed for life or good behavior or removed by impeachment. The Court of Claims was included in the legislative court category until 1953, when Congress declared it to be a court established under Article III. Similarly, Congress changed the United States Customs Court and the United States Court of Customs and Patent Appeals to constitutional courts in 1956 and 1958, respectively.

At present, the Supreme Court disposes of about 4,000 cases annually. Written opinions are handed down in about 160 of these cases each year.[5] A preliminary scrutiny of each case is made by the Court before it is placed on the calendar

[5] These figures are based on surveys of the work of the Supreme Court published each November in the *Harvard Law Review.* Justice Brennan has given an interesting insight into the workload and procedures of the Court in "The National Court of Appeals: Another Dissent," *University of Chicago Law Review,* Vol. 40 (1973), pp. 473–485.

for argument. In recent years, this sifting process has enabled the Court to dispose, without argument, of many cases coming from both the federal and state courts.

How Cases Reach the Supreme Court

Cases must reach the Supreme Court in accordance with the procedure established by Congress. At present, cases reach the Supreme Court by three principal methods: (1) by writ of certiorari, (2) by appeals and (3) by certification. The writ of error was utilized in some of the older cases in much the same way as appeal, but it was abolished for federal court usage in 1928. Relief that could be obtained in federal courts by the writ of error is now obtainable generally by appeal.

WRIT OF CERTIORARI

In 1925, Congress gave the Supreme Court almost complete power to decide what cases it would hear by allowing the Court to grant or deny petitions for writs of certiorari as it saw fit except in those limited categories of cases that are subject to appeal.

Persons who have been adversely affected by the decision of a lower court can petition for a writ of certiorari. This writ can be defined as an order to the lower court to send the entire record of the case to the higher court for review. It is granted by the Supreme Court when four justices feel that the issues raised are of sufficient public importance to merit consideration. Petitions for writs of certiorari are filed in accordance with prescribed forms, the petitioner stating why he feels the Court should grant the writ. The opposing party also may file a brief outlining the reasons why the case should not be reviewed by the Court on certiorari.[6] According to the *Revised Rules of the Supreme Court,* "a review on writ of certiorari is not a matter of right, but of sound judicial discretion, and will be granted only where there are special important reasons therefor." [7] Employing its certiorari jurisdiction, the Supreme Court may review decisions of state courts when a federal question is involved and there exists no right of appeal, decisions of the courts of appeals, and decisions of some of the legislative courts. Only a few (less than 15 per cent) of the total number of petitions for writs of certiorari filed each year are granted by the Court.

[6] Sample forms used in connection with petitions for certiorari, appeals, certification, and other writs are reproduced in Robert L. Stern and Eugene Gressman, *Supreme Court Practice* (Washington, D.C.: Bureau of National Affairs, Inc., 1976).

[7] Political scientists have done extensive research on the considerations that lead the justices to grant certiorari. This research is summarized and further advanced in Saul Brenner, "New *Certiorari* Game," *Journal of Politics,* Vol. 41 (1979), p. 649; S. Sidney Ulmer, "Selecting Cases for Supreme Court Review: An Underdog Model," *American Political Science Review,* Vol. 72 (1978), p. 902.

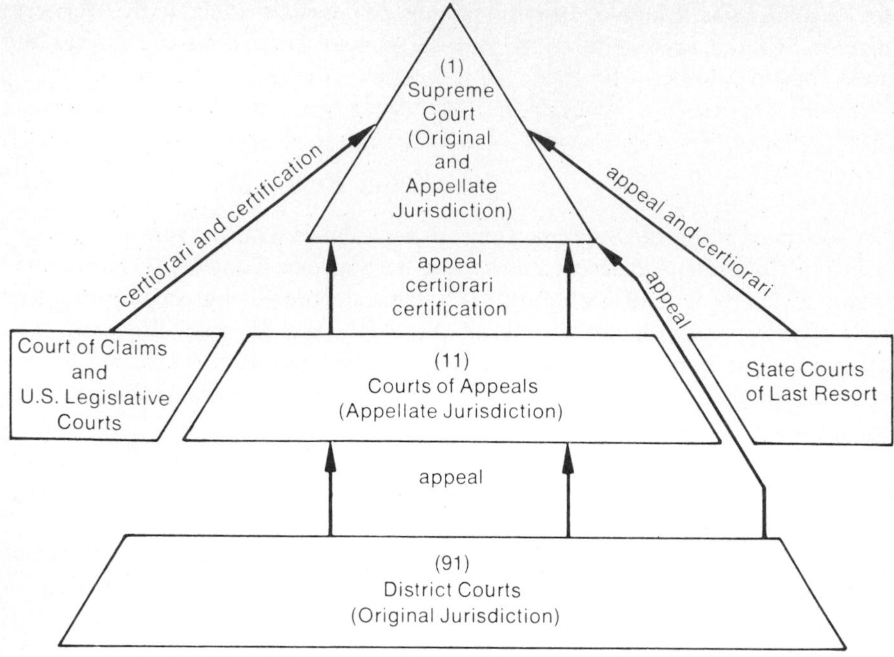

Federal Court Structure and Flow of Cases to the Supreme Court.

APPEAL

In broad terms the word *appeal* denotes any method used to bring a case to a higher court for review.[8] In the more technical sense used here, it refers to a procedure under which one of the parties may request review as a matter of right. In other words, the higher court *must* hear the case when it is brought by appeal. The Supreme Court takes appeals from state courts in two instances: (1) where the validity of a treaty or statute of the United States is questioned and the state court has held it *invalid;* (2) where the validity of a state law has been questioned on the ground that it contravenes the Constitution, treaties, or laws of the United States and the state court *sustains* its validity.

The Supreme Court takes appeals from the federal courts of appeals when a federal statute is held unconstitutional in a suit to which the United States is a party or when a state statute is held to be invalid as repugnant to the Constitution, treaties, or laws of the United States. Although the majority of district court decisions are reviewed only by a court of appeals, some causes may be carried, on *appeal,* from a district court directly to the Supreme Court.

The Supreme Court will review a case on appeal, however, only if the justices feel that a substantial federal question has been raised. For example, during one term of the Court, thirty-seven out of the fifty appeals dismissed were refused a hearing "for want of a substantial federal question. Since the Court

[8] In general see Martin Shapiro, "Appeal," *Law and Society Review,* Vol. 14 (1980), p. 630.

must pass judgment on the question of substantiality, its so-called compulsory jurisdiction has a strong element of discretion in it. The only difference between a dismissal of an appeal for lack of a substantial federal question and a denial of a petition for certiorari is that in the latter case no reason is ordinarily given, whereas in the former the Court must at least assert the absence, in its judgment, of a substantial issue." [9]

CERTIFICATION

This is a seldom-used method of appeal whereby a lower court requests that the Supreme Court answer certain questions of law so that a correct decision may be made. The Supreme Court may answer the questions, after which the lower court may reach a decision in light of the answers provided; or, in instances when a court of appeals has certified questions, the entire record of the case may be ordered up for decision by the Supreme Court itself. This method of appeal is not within the control of the litigants, because only the lower court may determine whether or not clarifications on points of law are required. Only the courts of appeals and the Court of Claims may certify questions to the Supreme Court for review.

How the Supreme Court Decides Cases

The Supreme Court's annual term usually runs from the first Monday in October to the end of the following June. After adjournment, special sessions may be called by the Chief Justice to consider questions of exceptional importance or urgency. For example, a special session was called in the summer of 1942 to deal with the case of German saboteurs. During the first week of the term, the Court usually disposes of preliminary work that has accumulated over the summer months. After that, the Court divides its time between the hearing of cases and recesses. The general pattern is for the Court to hear oral argument for two weeks and then to recess two weeks to study cases and write opinions. Most cases are disposed of in brief memorandum orders that simply note that the Court dismisses appeal or denies certiorari or affirms or reverses the decision of the court below. Such memoranda usually cite one or two previous cases as controlling, but without any further explanation of the holding. They are signed "per curiam," that is, "by the Court" rather than bearing the names of individual justices. Some per curiams are several paragraphs long and look like short opinions. Sometimes there are concurrences or dissents by individual justices to per curiam decisions. In recent years, the Court has occasionally issued a brief per curiam giving its final holding, followed

[9] David Fellman, "Constitutional Law in 1951–1952," *American Political Science Review*, Vol. 47 (March 1953), p. 127.

by individual opinions by each of the justices. (See, for instance, *New York Times Co.* v. *United States,* p. 195.)

Otherwise, the method of disposing cases by full opinion has remained substantially the same over a number of years. The procedure followed may be outlined briefly as follows:

1. Cases filed in the Supreme Court are first placed on one of three dockets. The most important of these is the *Appellate Docket,* which consists of cases from the lower courts for review. The few cases in which the original jurisdiction of the Court is invoked are placed on the *Original Docket.* The *Miscellaneous Docket,* which was created in 1945, is comprised of a wide variety of petitions, including a large number coming from prisoners who seek to challenge the legality of their convictions. Applications for the extraordinary writs, such as mandamus and habeas corpus, are also placed on the *Miscellaneous Docket.*

2. The party bringing the action before the Supreme Court must file a brief, usually within forty-five days after the case has been placed on the docket. Thirty days later an answering brief must be filed by the other contending party. When the case comes before the Court on a writ of certiorari, the party bringing the action is called the *petitioner,* with the answering party known as the *respondent.* In appeal cases, the *appellant* brings the action, with the other party being referred to as the *appellee.* Forty copies of the brief must be filed with the clerk of the Supreme Court by counsel for each party. The brief, which is filed in accordance with prescribed form, generally states the issues of the case, the questions presented, action of the lower courts, and all necessary legal arguments with the citation of cases and statutes relied on. With the permission of the Court, a brief may also be filed by a person who is not a party to the case but acts as *amicus curiae,* or friend of the court. For example, the Solicitor General of the United States may file a brief as a friend of the court if a case involves issues of direct interest or concern to the Federal Government.

3. The decision as to whether or not oral arguments need to be heard is made after the briefs and other pertinent materials have been analyzed by the Justices and/or their law clerks. The maximum time allowed for oral argument used to be one hour for each of the contending parties, but it is now usually one-half hour. During the oral presentation, the justices may ask questions or request additional data on pertinent points of the case. Many Supreme Court justices have noted the importance of the oral argument. Chief Justice Hughes remarked that "it is a great saving of time of the court, in the examination of extended records and briefs, to obtain the grasp of the case that is made possible by oral discussion and to be able more quickly to separate the wheat from the chaff." [10] Yet the quality of oral argument is often quite low.

4. After all the written and oral arguments have been presented, the justices meet in conference to vote on the case. These conferences usually are held

[10] Charles E. Hughes, *The Supreme Court of the United States* (New York: Garden City Publishing Co., 1936), p. 58.

each Friday morning while the Court is sitting. All the discussions are private, with only the members of the Court allowed in the conference room. What actually takes place at the conference can be determined only by the few comments that the justices themselves have made. However, the conference procedure is known not to vary greatly from year to year. Justice Stone described the work of the conference as follows:

> On the day before the conference each judge receives a list of cases which will be taken up at the conference, and the order in which they will be considered. This list actually includes every case which is ready for final disposition, including the cases argued the day before the conference and all pending motions and applications for certiorari.
>
> At conference each case is presented for discussion by the Chief Justice, usually by a brief statement of the facts, the questions of law involved, and with such suggestions for their disposition as he may think appropriate. No cases have been assigned to any particular judge in advance of the conference. Each justice is prepared to discuss the case at length and to give his views as to the proper solution of the questions presented. In Mr. Justice Holmes' pungent phrase, each must be ready to "recite" on the case. Each judge is requested by the Chief Justice, in the order of seniority, to give his views and the conclusions which he has reached. The discussion is of the freest character and at the end, after full opportunity has been given for each member of the Court to be heard and for the asking and answering of questions, the vote is taken and recorded in the reverse order of the discussion, the youngest, in point of service, voting first.
>
> On the same evening, after the conclusion of the conference, each member of the Court receives at his home a memorandum from the Chief Justice advising him of the assignment of cases for opinions. Opinions are written for the most part in recess, and as they are written they are printed and circulated among the justices, who make suggestions for their correlation and revision. At the next succeeding conference these suggestions are brought before the full conference and accepted or rejected as the case may be. On the following Monday the opinion is announced by the writer as the opinion of the Court.[11]

Some years ago the Court announced that it would not necessarily issue opinions only on Mondays. By the 1970s the practice of taking a formal vote in reverse order of seniority at the end of the discussion had eroded because most justices tended to reveal how they were going to vote in the course of their discussion of the case. Instead the Chief and most of the others were keeping running vote tallies as the discussion proceeded.

In addition to the majority decision of the Court, separate concurring and dissenting opinions may be written, although concurrence or dissent may be expressed without written opinion. Any justice is free to write a separate opinion if he is not satisfied with the majority opinion. A *concurring opinion* is one that agrees with the Court's decision but disagrees with the reasoning by which

[11] Harlan F. Stone, "Fifty Years' Work of the United States Supreme Court," *American Bar Association Journal,* Vol. 14 (Aug.–Sept. 1928), p. 436.

the decision was reached. *Dissenting opinions* may be written when one or more of the justices disagrees with the decision of the Court as well as with the reasoning used in reaching the decision. Important concurring and dissenting opinions are useful for the student of government, as they may help clarify the majority opinion of the Court and reveal the important political, social, and economic conflicts involved in the case. The dissenting opinion "provides an argument opposing that of the majority that may be seized on by lawyers and urged in succeeding cases with some hope of success. It calls attention to defects in the position of the majority forcing a rethinking and perhaps strengthening of that position. It further calls the majority to the bar of public opinion and enlightened legal opinion." [12] However, dissenting opinions may obscure as well as clarify the basic issues.

> The technique of the dissenter often is to exaggerate the holding of the Court beyond the meaning of the majority and then to blast away at the excess. . . . Then, too, dissenters frequently force the majority to take positions more extreme than was originally intended. The classic example is the *Dred Scott* case, in which Chief Justice Taney's extreme statements were absent in his original draft and were inserted only after Mr. Justice McLean, then a more than passive candidate for the presidency, raised the issue in dissent. The *right of dissent* is a valuable one. Wisely used on well-chosen occasions, it has been of great service to the profession and to the law. . . . The tradition of great dissents built around such names as Holmes, Brandeis, Cardozo, and Stone is not due to the frequency or multiplicity of their dissents, but to their quality and the importance of the few cases in which they carried their disagreement beyond the conference table. Also, quite contrary to the popular notion, relatively few of all dissents recorded in the Supreme Court have later become law, although some of these are of great importance.[13]

The Burger Court has been particularly prone to "purality" opinions. In such opinions fewer than a majority of those justices voting are willing to subscribe to any one opinion so there is no opinion for the Court. The outcome of the case is determined by which of the two parties receives a majority of the votes, but the legal meaning of the decision may be impossible to determine. The *Bakke* case (p. 604) is such a decision.

Sometimes Supreme Court opinions contain materials that are not pertinent to the basic issues of the case. In other words, in the course of rendering an opinion, a justice may wander away from the major points of the case and make remarks that are not essential to the reasoning or the decision. In legal terminology such remarks are known as *obiter dicta,* meaning that which was put in by the way or incidentally. Although obiter dicta do not establish principles of law, they may provide insights into a justice's personal views or indicate the development of particular judicial trends.

[12] Loren P. Beth, "Justice Harlan and the Uses of Dissent," *American Political Science Review,* Vol. 49 (Dec. 1955), p. 1104.

[13] Robert H. Jackson, *The Supreme Court in the American System of Government* (Cambridge: Harvard U.P., 1955), pp. 18–19.

Source Materials in Constitutional Law

Supreme Court opinions are available in three separate editions.

United States Reports (cited as U.S.). This is the official edition of Supreme Court cases, which is published by the Federal Government. Usually, the opinions of each term of the Court can be incorporated in four volumes of the *Reports.* Until 1875, the reports of Supreme Court decisions were cited by the name of the reporter as follows:

1789–1800	Dallas (Dall.)	4 vols.
1801–1815	Cranch (Cr.)	9 vols.
1816–1827	Wheaton (Wheat.)	12 vols.
1828–1842	Peters (Pet.)	16 vols.
1843–1860	Howard (How.)	24 vols.
1861–1862	Black (Bl.)	2 vols.
1863–1874	Wallace (Wall.)	23 vols.
1875–1882	Otto	17 vols.

The total number of volumes cited by the name of the reporter is 107. After 1882, and beginning with Volume 108, the official reports are cited by number only.

United States Supreme Court Reports, Lawyers' Edition (cited as L. Ed.). This edition is privately published by the Lawyers' Cooperative Publishing Company. Both the *Lawyers' Edition* and the *Supreme Court Reporter,* listed subsequently, contain more detailed headnotes than the official *United States Reports.* The headnotes, which appear at the beginning of the opinion, are designed to summarize the legal contents of the case. Those that appear in the two privately published editions are prepared by editorial staffs to assist lawyers in quickly obtaining comprehensive summaries of the case law in a particular subject matter. The *Lawyers' Edition* of the *Supreme Court Reports* also carries excerpts from the briefs of counsel and annotations of important cases. At the 1966 term of the Court, the *Lawyers' Edition* began a second series beginning again at Volume 1 (cited as L. Ed. 2d).

Supreme Court Reporter (cited as Sup. Ct. or S.Ct.). This edition, which is similar to the *Lawyers' Edition,* is published by West Publishing Company. It contains only those Supreme Court cases decided since 1882.

In the citing of cases, the volume number comes first, followed by the abbreviated title of the report in which the case appears and the page number, with the date in parentheses at the end. For example, the complete citation for the case of *Lochner* v. *New York,* decided in 1905, is 198 U.S. 45; 25 Sup. Ct. 539; 49 L. Ed. 937 (1905). This means that the full text of the Lochner case may be found in Volume 198 of the *United States Reports* at page 45, or in Volume 25 of the *Supreme Court Reporter* at page 539, or in Volume 49 of the *Lawyers' Edition* at page 937. The citation for *Marbury* v. *Madison* is 1

Cranch 137; 2 L. Ed. 60 (1803). The case can, therefore, be found in Volume 1 of *Cranch* at page 137 or in Volume 2 of the *Lawyers' Edition* at page 60.

One need not wait until the bound volumes appear to read the full text of a Supreme Court case. All three editions of the Supreme Court's opinions issue paperback "advance sheets" long before the bound volumes appear.

Decisions of great public significance are often reproduced in full by some leading newspapers, such as *The New York Times.* Also, the Federal Government publishes each decision in pamphlet or advance-sheet form as *Preliminary Prints.* Advance sheets and preliminary prints begin to appear about five to eight weeks after the decision is rendered. Complete opinions are available most rapidly in the *United States Law Week,* published by the Bureau of National Affairs, and in the *Supreme Court Bulletin,* published by Commerce Clearing House.

Decisions of the lower federal courts to 1924 are found in the *Federal Reporter,* which went to Volume 300, and are cited as Fed. or F. After 1924, the cases were collected in a second series known as *Federal Reporter,* second series, and cited as Fed. (2d) or F. 2d. Since 1932, the decisions of the district courts have been published separately in *Federal Supplement,* cited as F. Supp. or F.S.

Decisions rendered by the highest state courts are published in separate volumes by each state or by a commercial publisher. In addition, a regional reporting system combines the decisions of several state courts in one publication. For example, the *Atlantic Reporter* carries decisions of Connecticut, Delaware, Maine, Maryland, New Hampshire, New Jersey, Pennsylvania, Rhode Island, and Vermont since 1885. The *Southern Reporter* contains decisions of the states of Alabama, Florida, Louisiana, and Mississippi since 1887. The Northeastern, Northwestern, Pacific, Southeastern, and Southwestern *Reporters* contain the state cases of their respective areas. In the citing of state cases, the same practice is followed of giving the volume number first, the abbreviated title of the report in which the case appears, and the page number. For example, the complete citation for the Massachusetts case of *Furbush* v. *Connolly* is 318 Mass. 511, 62 N.E. 2d. 595 (1945). This means that this case, which was decided in 1945, may be found in Volume 318 of the *Massachusetts Reports* at page 511 or in Volume 62 of the *Northeastern Reporter,* second series, at page 595.

All of the cases in this volume have been edited. To read the entire decision the reporters must be consulted.

How to Read Supreme Court Cases

The title of each case is taken from the names of the two parties to the controversy. The name that appears first is the party that is bringing the action. At the trial stage, he or she is called the *plaintiff.* The *defendant* is the other party, against whom the action is taken. He or she must answer the suit brought by the plaintiff. Different terms are used in appellate proceedings. Each of the parties may be referred to as indicated in the following hypothetical case:

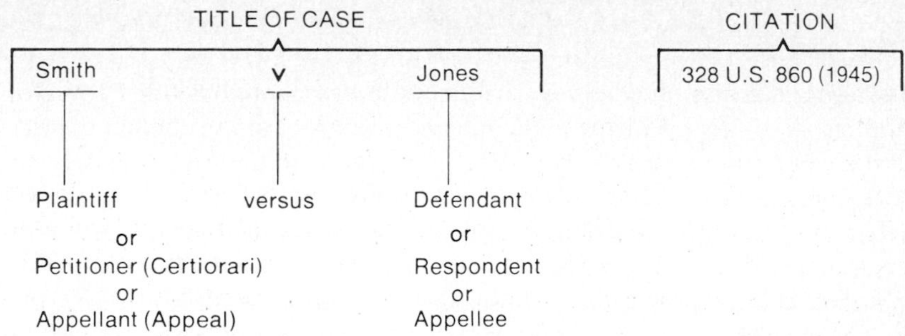

There is no one best way to read and analyze these cases. How this is done depends largely on each individual's habits and methods of study. Nevertheless, an understanding of the decision, especially during the early stages, can best be acquired by following a prescribed pattern or outline that helps to bring out the essential issues of each case. The student should read the case in its entirety at least once before attempting to use the following outline:

1. *Title and Citation.*
2. *Fact of the Case.* Here the student should make a short statement concerning the circumstances that brought about the case or controversy. The statement of facts sometimes appears in concise form at the beginning of an opinion. In other instances, the facts are found scattered throughout the case. On some occasions, the best recital of the facts is found in a dissenting opinion. Students usually obtain a better grasp of the case if the identity of the parties to the action is clearly established and if the holdings of the lower courts, if any, are understood clearly.
3. *The Law.* The student should know precisely what provisions of the Constitution and what statutes and/or administrative regulations govern a case. The constitutional provision should be precisely noted. For instance, it is not enough to categorize a case as involving "the religion clause of the First Amendment." Often it makes a great difference whether the justices treat a case as falling under the "free exercise" or "no establishment" portions of the First Amendment. As the cases in this book unfold, it will become clearer that such phenomena as theories of "incorporation" of one constitutional provision into another and the invention of new constitutional rights, such as the right of privacy, sometimes make it difficult and extremely important to specify as clearly as possible the constitutional provision under which the Court purports to be working. In dealing with state statutes, one finds the "law" is often the state statute as construed by the highest state court rather than the literal words of the statute.

Much of the law governing a case is neither a constitutional provision nor a statute as such, but a judicially created, constitutional standard, rule, test, or doctrine; or a regulation, decision, policy statement, or order issued by a government agency in the course of administering a statute. Previous decisions of the Court are an important body of law. Students should note which precedents (earlier decisions) are followed, reversed, or "distinguished" (held not applicable to the current case).

4. *Legal Question or Questions.* The question presented is often revealed by the statement of facts, which should indicate the nature of the conflict of interests that the Court must resolve. The legal question is sometimes concisely stated by the Court. For example, in *Coyle* v. *Smith,* 221 U.S. 599 (1911), the Court stated that "the only question for review by us is whether the provision of the enabling act was a valid limitation upon the power of the state after its admission, which overrides any subsequent legislation repugnant thereto."

5. *Holding.* This is the Court's answer to the question or questions presented.

6. *Opinion.* The opinion refers to the chain of legal reasoning that led the Court to its holding. The Court's line of reasoning should be outlined point by point, because an understanding of the entire case will depend largely on how well the Court's reasoning process is followed.

7. *Separate Opinion or Opinions.* Both concurring and dissenting opinions should be carefully analyzed to show major points of conflict with the majority opinion.

8. *The Decision as Precedent.* The student should note how a decision fits into earlier lines of cases. After reading subsequent cases, he or she should add notations on how the initial case was itself used as a precedent.

9. *Evaluation.* A case should be evaluated as to its internal consistency, its skill in meeting or avoiding all the relevant issues, and its fit to earlier cases. Students should ask whether the case provides a convincing explanation of why the Court should have and did decide the way it did. They should ask what other factors, not mentioned by the justices, may have actually determined the outcome. They should also evaluate the case in terms of whether it strains the political capacity of the Court to affect the behavior of others and whether the result aimed at is wise public policy.

CHAPTER 3

The Justices of the Supreme Court

The Constitution provides for the appointment of Supreme Court justices by the President by and with the advice and consent of the Senate. They serve for life "during good behavior" and may be removed by impeachment only. No member of the Court has ever been removed by the impeachment process, although Samuel Chase, who served on the Court from 1796 to 1811, was impeached by the House of Representatives but acquitted by the Senate.

Unlike the offices of President, senator, and representative, the qualifications necessary for appointment to the Court are not stipulated by the Constitution. All the justices have been lawyers. In the final analysis, only the President *really* knows why he chooses a particular person for the Court, and he may have considered so many factors that even he could not single out the determining one, so that all of the speculation and "inside information" relating to judicial appointments may well be erroneous. Nevertheless, a number of key factors considered in the selection of a justice can be isolated.

Selection of Supreme Court Justices

POLITICAL CONSIDERATIONS

Party membership and activity have always been of utmost importance in the selection of justices. Rare indeed are the instances when a President has appointed a man to the Supreme Court who is not a member of his own political party. This has been true from the beginning of the Court's history, when President Washington named ardent Federalists to the Court, to the present time. For example, when President Eisenhower named Republican Governor Earl Warren of California to be the fourteenth Chief Justice of the United States in 1953, it was the first appointment by a Republican president in more than twenty years. At that time all the members of the Court were Democrats, except Associate Justice Harold H. Burton, who was a Republican senator from Ohio when he was named to the bench by President Truman. Burton's appointment to the Court can be explained, in part, by the fact that he was a close friend of the President and had worked ably with him on a special committee investigating defense production when both men were members of the Senate.

There have been similarly sound explanations for each of the other times that a President has named a justice from outside his own party. President Hoover, for example, was all but forced to name Justice Cardozo, a New York Democrat, to replace Justice Holmes, because he was so obviously the outstanding man for the post. Two major reasons have been advanced to explain why President Eisenhower named Justice Brennan, a Roman Catholic and New Jersey Democrat, to the Court. Some observers felt that because the appointment came on the eve of the 1956 presidential election, Eisenhower was making a bid for votes from members of Brennan's party and faith in the Eastern states. Others have discounted this theory and argued that the basic reason for Brennan's appointment was the strong support he received from key Republicans and bar association leaders who were trying to persuade the President that broad judicial experience should be a prime qualification for appointment to the Court.[1] Brennan had ten years' experience as a state judge and was serving on the Supreme Court of New Jersey when appointed.

In making Supreme Court appointments, the President is, of course, interested in much more than the mere party label of a candidate. What he wants is to place people on the Court who actively share his views on the important social, political, and economic issues of the day. In brief, he wants someone who supports the policies and program of his administration. Nowhere has this been better demonstrated than in the letter President Theodore Roosevelt wrote to Senator Henry Cabot Lodge of Massachusetts when he was considering elevating

[1] Philip Yeager and John Stark, "The Supreme Court in Transition," *The New York Times Magazine* (March 10, 1957), p. 13.

Justice Holmes to the Supreme Court to replace Justice Gray. The President wrote as follows:

> In the ordinary and low sense which we attach to the words *partisan* and *politician*, a judge of the Supreme Court should be neither. But in the higher sense, the proper sense, he is not in my judgment fitted for the position unless he is a party man, a constructive statesman, constantly keeping in mind his adherence to the principles and policies under which this nation has been built up and in accordance with which it must go on; and keeping in mind also his relations with his fellow statesmen who in other branches of the government are striving in cooperation with him to advance the ends of government.
>
> *Now I should like to know that Judge Holmes was in entire sympathy with our views, that is with your views and mine and Judge Gray's . . . before I would feel justified in appointing him.* Judge Gray has been one of the most valuable members of the Court. I should hold myself as guilty of an irreparable wrong to the nation if I should put in his place any man who was not absolutely sane and sound on the great national policies for which we stand in public life.[2]

Holmes did receive the appointment but later bitterly disappointed the President when he wrote the "promonopoly" dissenting opinion in a close (5 to 4) case,[3] an opinion that went against the heart of Roosevelt's antitrust program. After that, relations between Holmes and the President were always strained. Holmes later wrote that his dissenting opinion broke up his "incipient friendship" with the President, who viewed it as a "political departure (or, I suspect, more truly, couldn't forgive anyone who stands in his way). We talked freely later but it never was the same after that, and if he had not been restrained by his friends, I am told that he would have made a fool of himself and would have excluded me from the White House."[4]

The Holmes appointment demonstrates clearly that no matter how careful he may be, a President cannot be certain that the justices he chooses will perform as expected. Chief Justice John Marshall fervently carried on the principles of the Federalists just as President John Adams thought he would, and Chief Justice Taney did not completely disappoint his good friend President Jackson. On the other hand, Justice McReynolds, chosen by the liberal President Wilson, became one of the most wrathful, hard-bitten conservatives ever to sit on the Court, whereas, much to the surprise of many of his Republican supporters, Justice Brennan quickly joined the libertarian bloc on the Warren Court.[5] Appointed by conservative President Ford, Justice Stevens has joined the liberal wing of the Court on civil liberties questions.

[2] Henry Cabot Lodge, *Selections from the Correspondence of Theodore Roosevelt and Henry Cabot Lodge, 1894–1918* (New York: Scribners, 1925), Vol. I, pp. 517–19. (Italics supplied.)

[3] *Northern Securities Co.* v. *United States,* 193 U.S. 197 (1904).

[4] *Holmes-Pollock Letters* (Cambridge: Harvard U.P., 1941), Vol. II, pp. 63–64.

[5] A case study of the appointment process is David Danelski, *A Supreme Court Justice Is Appointed* (New York: Random, 1964). A complete historical survey is Henry Abraham, *Justices and Presidents: A Political History of Appointments to the Supreme Court* (Oxford: Oxford U.P., 1974).

Nevertheless, every President will continue to name persons to the Court who appear to share his basic political views. In fact, Presidents often have appointed men to the highest bench simply as a reward for helping them obtain the nomination and win the election or for other valuable services to the party. For example, as head of the Kentucky delegation to the Republican National Convention in 1876, John Marshall Harlan took the entire delegation into the Rutherford B. Hayes camp at the crucial moment. As a result, Hayes won the nomination and subsequently became President after a bitter, hotly debated contest. Undoubtedly, this was one of the factors leading to Harlan's appointment to the Court. There are many other examples: Hugo Black was an ardent New Dealer who vigorously supported Franklin D. Roosevelt's program in the Senate before becoming the President's first appointee to the Supreme Court in 1937. Earl Warren was named Chief Justice in 1953 after his cooperation at the Republican Convention had assured Eisenhower the presidential nomination. Both Byron R. White and Arthur J. Goldberg, President Kennedy's two appointees to the Court, had actively compaigned in his behalf in the presidential election of 1960.

In a discussion of political considerations, the role of the Senate must be kept in mind. The hearings before the Senate Judiciary Committee, which first considers the qualifications of a prospective justice, indicate clearly that partisan politics plays an important part in the confirmation of a Supreme Court justice. The nomination of Louis D. Brandeis was openly opposed by many lawyers and public officers because of his alleged "radical position" on important social and economic issues and less openly because he was a Jew.

As chairman of the Senate Judiciary Committee, Senator George Norris opposed the appointment of Charles Evans Hughes to be Chief Justice because of Hughes's close association with powerful private corporations and financial interests.

Hoover was the last President until Nixon to experience a Senate rejection of one of his nominations. Most Presidents have been reluctant to risk a contest with the Senate by nominating "politically unacceptable" men for the Court. When President Nixon nominated Clement F. Haynesworth, Jr., a conservative but experienced and highly respected fourth circuit court judge from South Carolina, he apparently expected some opposition from Senate liberals but not enough to block confirmation. Some quite unanticipated evidence of possible conflict of interest stemming from Judge Haynesworth's stock holdings in companies that appeared before him as litigants seems to have swung the balance against the nomination. Whether the subsequent nomination of Judge G. Harrold Carswell, who also proved unacceptable to the Senate, was the result of shoddy staff work in the Attorney General's office or deliberate presidential defiance of the Senate is still unclear.

The risk that presidential nominations run in the Senate is also exemplified by President Johnson's attempt to move Associate Justice Fortas to the Chief Justiceship, necessitating new Senate hearings that eventually resulted in Justice Fortas's resignation from the Court—again because of evidence of possible conflict of interest.

PERSONAL FRIENDSHIP

The role of personal friendship in Supreme Court appointments is extremely difficult to measure because so many other factors (usually of a political nature) may also be present. Nevertheless, in some instances, it has been of crucial importance. President Taft, for example, believed firmly that younger men should be on the Court, but he nominated sixty-five-year-old Horace H. Lurton in 1909, principally because they had become close friends while sitting together as federal circuit court judges.[6] President Wilson was willing to risk a serious fight with the Senate to name his personal friend, Louis D. Brandeis, to the Court in 1916. Personal friendship was an important factor in each of President Truman's four Supreme Court appointments (Chief Justice Fred M. Vinson, Justices Harold H. Burton, Tom C. Clark, and Sherman Minton) and in President Kennedy's appointment of Justice White.

RELIGIOUS, RACIAL, AND SEXUAL REPRESENTATION

Again, the religious factor is ordinarily related to other considerations and is difficult to assess. However, the policy of giving broad representation to the nation's religious denominations has been an important factor in some cases. In recent years there has usually been one Catholic and one Jewish member of the Court. This has been the result in some measure of pressures from the minority denominations for representation and of the desire of the President to obtain their political support. Some observers felt that one motive in President Kennedy's choice of Arthur J. Goldberg to replace Justice Frankfurter in 1962 was the desire to maintain the modern practice (since 1916) of having at least one Jewish member on the Court, a practice continued by the appointment of Justice Fortas to replace Justice Goldberg. On the other hand, President Taft named Edward D. White to the Chief Justiceship in 1910, principally because he shared his constitutional views and not simply because he was a Catholic. Similarly, as we have seen, Justice Cardozo's superb qualifications, rather than the fact that he was Jewish, accounted for his appointment to the Court. The appointment of Justice Thurgood Marshall undoubtedly began a new tradition of black representation. President Nixon, however, announced that he would not follow the custom of ethnic and geographic representation. Since Justice Fortas's resignation, there has been no Jew on the Court. Presidents Ford and Carter had been under considerable pressure to name a woman to the Court. The appointment of Justice Stevens clearly did not recognize the claims of minority or disadvantaged groups. President Reagan's first nominee, however, was a woman who was also a political conservative with previous judicial experience, thus meeting the standard criteria for appointment by recent Republican Presidents as well as meeting the demands for a woman on the Court.

[6] Daniel S. McHargue, "President Taft's Appointments to the Court," *Journal of Politics*, Vol. 12 (1950), p. 478.

GEOGRAPHICAL AND SECTIONAL CONSIDERATIONS

During the first century of the Republic, when Supreme Court justices were required to ride the circuit, geographical and sectional considerations were of controlling importance, because it was deemed essential that the justice come from the circuit he was to serve. Thus, Samuel F. Miller was named to the Court in 1862 by President Lincoln in part because a new circuit arrangement maneuvered through Congress by Miller and his supporters created a place for him.[7]

With the end of regular circuit duties for Supreme Court justices at the turn of the century, geographical considerations became less important. However, Presidents do generally try to maintain a geographical balance on the Court. For example, the appointment of Justice Wiley B. Rutledge in 1943 was influenced by the fact that he "had geography"—that is, he was a Midwesterner who was needed on the Court to help maintain some semblance of section balance. The appointment of Justice Cardozo in 1932 demonstrates that geographical considerations can be disregarded when other factors are involved. Two New Yorkers—Chief Justice Hughes and Justice Stone—were already on the Court when Cardozo, also from New York, was nominated.

Among President Nixon's first six nominations were three Southerners and an Arizonian. President Reagan's first nominee was from Arizona. This pattern seems to have stemmed less from considerations of sectional balance than from the strategy of the Republican party, which was seeking to build a new electoral base in the Old South and the rest of the "sunshine tier"—Florida, Arizona, and California.

PRIOR JUDICIAL EXPERIENCE

Although, on the whole, prior judicial experience is of minor importance in Supreme Court appointment, it sometimes is a crucial factor. In part because of the pressure of the organized bar and of some senators and representatives, President Eisenhower showed a marked preference for experienced men. After the initial appointment of Chief Justice Warren, Eisenhower's four other nominees all had served on the bench—Justices Harlan, Brennan, Whittaker, and Stewart. Chief Justice Burger owed his appointment less to long judicial service as such than to his long record of dissent from the libertarian majority on the Court of Appeals of the District of Columbia. From time to time, bills have been introduced in Congress that would require five or even ten years' service as a judge for a Supreme Court nominee. None of these bills has been enacted, largely because most students of the Court agree with retired Justice Frankfurter that "the correlation between prior judicial experience and fitness for the Supreme Court is zero. The significance of the greatest among the justices

[7] Charles Fairman, *Mr. Justice Miller and the Supreme Court, 1862–1890* (Cambridge: Harvard U.P., 1939), pp. 40–50.

who had such experience, Holmes and Cardozo, derived not from that judicial experience but from the fact that they were Holmes and Cardozo. They were thinkers, and more particularly, legal philosophers." [8]

Prior judicial experience is not essential because of the peculiar nature of the Court's work. The Supreme Court is concerned principally with resolving major questions of public law—that is, questions arising out of broad, fundamental issues of public policy.[9] Throughout history, almost every major political issue before the country has ultimately reached the Supreme Court in the guise of litigation. What is required for the resolution of these issues is political judgment of the highest order rather than technical judicial proficiency in private law. Hence, judicial experience, although perhaps helpful, is not essential for success on the Court; in fact, if it had been a prerequisite in the past, most of the greatest Supreme Court justices, such as Marshall, Story, Taney, Miller, Hughes (first appointment), and Brandeis, would have never reached the highest bench. It is interesting to note, however, that three recent appointees, Justices Goldberg, Fortas, and Marshall, although lacking extended prior judicial experience, had previously had long and very successful records as practicing attorneys representing important clients before the Supreme Court.

MISCELLANEOUS FACTORS

Many other factors, such as age, distinguished service in high federal office, preeminence at the bar, and even chance or, as Justice Frankfurter has said, the "caprices of fortune," sometimes play an important part in Supreme Court appointments. For a variety of reasons, two of the most distinguished lower court judges in recent American history—Learned Hand of the second federal circuit and Arthur Vanderbilt of the New Jersey Supreme Court—never reached the highest bench.

That the "caprices of fortune" may well be decisive is aptly demonstrated by President Grant's nomination of Morrison R. Waite to the Chief Justiceship in 1874. Waite was by no means Grant's first choice. The President had first offered the job to one of his closest political allies, Senator Roscoe Conkling of New York, a well-known, unscrupulous machine politician, who declined because he had other unfulfilled political ambitions. Grant then reportedly offered the position to two other senators, but both declined. Grant's Secretary of State, Hamilton Fish, also declined the appointment. The next nominee was seventy-year-old Caleb Cushing of Massachusetts, who was widely known as a "political prostitute" who "never allowed principle or conscience to stand in the way of gain." The hue and cry raised against Cushing forced Grant to withdraw the nomination. Grant then named his Attorney General, George H. Williams, who had been maneuvering for the post by trying to persuade

[8] Felix Frankfurter, "The Supreme Court in the Mirror of Justices," *University of Pennsylvania Law Review,* Vol. 105 (1957), p. 781.

[9] Rocco J. Tresolini, "In Defense of the Supreme Court," *Social Science,* Vol. 36 (Jan. 1961), pp. 38–39.

the President that it would be unwise to promote any of the sitting justices to the top position. But Williams was an unfit candidate with a doubtful reputation and a scheming wife who had used her influence to obtain immunity from prosecution for various persons in return for payments of $30,000. Opposition to Williams's nomination was so strong that Grant finally withdrew his name. Grant then turned to Waite in hopes that his very obscurity would assure his confirmation. An Ohioan later remarked that "it was the queerest appointment that was ever made during Grant's two terms. Everybody was surprised and none more so than men from our own state, where he lived." Waite was confirmed by the Senate without difficulty, but his appointment aroused little enthusiasm. "The general reaction was that, while better Chief Justices could have been found, the country was lucky to get one who was at least an honest man and a competent lawyer. The Senate hastened to confirm the nomination for fear Grant might change his mind and do worse." [10]

Many disparate considerations influence the selection of justices. Although the President is alone responsible for his judicial appointments, he receives suggestions from many sources. The Attorney General of the United States is most influential in this regard. He screens candidates, maintains liaison with members of Congress and others interested in pushing a particular candidate, and, most important, makes recommendations to the President. The various bar associations are also extremely influential. In recent years, the American Bar Association (ABA) has played an increasingly important role through its Committee on the Federal Judiciary, which reports on the professional qualifications of candidates seriously considered for appointment to the Supreme Court. A negative report from this committee may eliminate a candidate from further consideration. Yet, as an outgrowth of the Haynesworth and Carswell controversies, President Nixon announced that he would not defer to ABA evaluations. The ABA remains a powerful influence, but at least for the moment it seems to have lost the battle it has waged for many years to gain a veto power at the prenomination stage of presidential consideration.[11]

The justices themselves have no official role in the selection of their associates, but there have been times when their influence has been felt. Justice Miller, for example, although he failed, used all the means at his disposal to secure an appointment for his brother-in-law. Chief Justice Taft used his influence unashamedly with the President and other key figures to secure appointments for the men he wanted. He was instrumental in the selection of both Justices Butler and Sanford. Moreover, Taft was "completely successful in keeping out men who he thought would misinterpret the Constitution or increase dissension

[10] Most of the materials in this paragraph are drawn from the *Morrison R. Waite Papers*, Manuscript Division, Library of Congress, and appeared in Rocco J. Tresolini, "Chief Justice Morrison R. Waite and the Public Interest," *Northwest Ohio Quarterly: A Journal of History and Civilization*, Vol. 34 (Summer 1962), pp. 124–37. See also C. Peter Magrath, *Morrison R. Waite: The Triumph of Character* (New York: Macmillan, 1963), Ch. 1.

[11] For an extended discussion, see Joel Grossman, *Lawyers and Judges; the ABA and the Politics of Judicial Selection* (New York: Wiley, 1965).

within the Court." [12] When considering a successor to Chief Justice Hughes in 1941, President Roosevelt followed the advice of both Hughes and Justice Frankfurter in elevating Justice Stone to the center chair.

Role of the Chief Justice

The extent of the Chief Justice's influence depends on his ability and personality. In deciding cases he has but one vote. Nevertheless, he occupies a central position because of his special administrative duties in connection with the daily work of the Court. The Chief Justice can exert great influence in carrying out the following three specific functions.

PRESIDING OFFICER

As presiding officer, the Chief Justice sets the "tone and tempo of all its proceedings. . . . The attitude of the Chief Justice is invariably reflected in the work of the other judges and in the conduct of counsel who appear before the court." [13] Certainly, a great shift in "tone and tempo" occurred with the transition from Chief Justice Warren to Chief Justice Burger. The Warren Court projected an image of questing after an ideal of human rights and social justice. The Burger Court projects an image of tough-minded day-to-day policy making.

Of course, not all of the Chief Justices have had the capacity for inspired leadership. It is sometimes argued that there was an unusual amount of squabbling on the Stone and Vinson Courts because neither Stone nor Vinson were particularly good at eliciting consensus. But when the Court faces highly divisive issues of public policy, strong disagreements among the justices will arise no matter what the personal qualities of the Chief.

Chief Justice Burger, by all accounts not a specialist at warm human relationships, has sought to further elevate the special role of the Chief Justice. He delivers an annual state of the judiciary message and has asserted a special interest and expertise in judicial administration both in his own and the lower federal courts.

Some of the great leaders on the Court never reached the higher post. Men such as Joseph Story, Oliver Wendell Holmes, Louis D. Brandeis, Stephen J. Field, and Joseph P. Bradley made much greater contributions than some Chief Justices. Chief Justice Hughes made this point well when he said that "Marshall's pre-eminence was due to the fact that he was John Marshall, not simply that he was Chief Justice." [14]

[12] Walter F. Murphy, "In His Own Image: Mr. Chief Justice Taft and Supreme Court Appointments." *The Supreme Court Review* (1961), p. 188.

[13] Merlo J. Pusey, "Chief Protector of the Constitution," *The New York Times Magazine* (Sept. 20, 1953), p. 13.

[14] Charles E. Hughes, *The Supreme Court of the United States* (New York: Columbia U.P., 1928), p. 58.

MODERATOR OF COURT CONFERENCES

Perhaps the Chief Justice's greatest opportunity for leadership comes in his role as the moderator of the Court conferences where the cases are discussed and judgments rendered. A strong Chief can influence the decision in many cases, because he is the discussion leader and has the first opportunity to state his conclusions in the conference. Chief Justice Hughes was able to dominate the Court because of his ability to conduct business in an efficient, kindly manner.

> In court and in conference he struck the pitch, as it were, for the orchestra. He guided discussion by opening up the lines for it to travel, focusing on essentials, evoking candid exchange on subtle and complex issues, and avoiding redundant talk. He never checked free debate, but the atmosphere which he created, the moral authority which he exerted, inhibited irrelevance, repetition, and fruitless discussion. He was a master of timing: he knew when discussion should be deferred and when brought to an issue. He also showed uncommon resourcefulness in drawing elements of agreement out of differences and thereby narrowing, if not always escaping, conflicts. He knew when a case was over; he had no lingering afterthoughts born of a feeling of defeat, and thereby avoided the fostering of cleavages. Intellectual issues were dealt with by him as such. As a result, differences in opinion did not arouse personal sensitiveness.[15]

ASSIGNMENT OF OPINION

The Chief Justice assigns the writing of the Court's opinion, provided he is among the majority. If he is not with the majority, the senior justice on the majority side assigns the opinion. In discharging this function, Chief Justice Hughes was "like a general deploying his army. His governing consideration was what was best for the Court as to the particular case in the particular situation. That meant disregard of self but not of the importance of the Chief Justiceship as a symbol. For there are occasions when an opinion should carry the extra weight which pronouncement by the Chief Justice gives. Selection of the Court's voice also calls for resourcefulness, so that the Court should not be denied the persuasiveness of a particular justice. . . . The grounds for assignment may not always be obvious to the outsider. Indeed, they are not always so to the members of the Court; the reasons normally remain within the breast of the Chief Justice. But these involve, if the duty is wisely discharged, perhaps the most delicate judgment demanded of the Chief Justice." [16]

Assignment politics have occasionally reached the verge of public controversy under Chief Justice Burger. When the current Chief is in the minority, the

[15] Felix Frankfurter, "The Administrative Side of Chief Justice Hughes," *Harvard Law Review*, Vol. 63 (1949), p. 3.

[16] Ibid., pp. 3, 4. The conference leadership and opinion assignment powers of the Chief Justice are examined by David Danelski in "The Influence of the Chief Justice in the Decisional Process," in Walter F. Murphy and C. Herman Pritchett, eds., *Courts, Judges, and Politics*, 3rd ed. (New York: Random House, 1979).

senior justice in length of service who would normally write the opinion himself or assign it typically was Justice Douglas before his retirement and more recently has been Justice Brennan. Both hold views very different from those of the Chief. It may be that Chief Justice Burger occasionally has voted with the majority or has construed an ambiguous statement by another justice as a vote in a particular direction for the purpose of keeping control of the initial assignment of the majority opinion.

"Influences" on the Justices

Biographical studies of the justices show that the social and economic philosophy of a justice plays important roles in how his decisions are shaped.

Perhaps even more important in indicating the impact of judicial attitudes on judicial opinions than biographical studies are those in which the techniques of social psychology are borrowed, the leading example of which is Glendon Schubert's *The Judicial Mind* (Evanston, Ill.: Northwestern U.P., 1965). Schubert and other scholars have shown that most justices vote with high levels of consistency in favor of certain classes of parties and against others. For example, Justice Douglas tended to vote for the individual and against government in conflicts between government power and civil liberties. Chief Justice Warren tended to vote for government and against business in government regulation of business cases. Furthermore, the justices' consistent voting patterns seem to reflect relatively fixed political attitudes or ideologies comparable to those found in the general population. The justices tend to divide along one dimension into economic liberals and economic conservatives and along another into civil libertarians and supporters of government authority. Within the realm of discretion left open to the justices by the ambiguities of law and the Constitution, their collective political attitudes clearly determine the outcome of many cases. To put the matter differently, when there is no clear legal solution to a problem faced by the Supreme Court, the justices must govern their decisions by what they think would be best for the country. Different justices naturally have different views of what would be best.

It is well to remember that the aphorism "no man is an island" is as applicable to Supreme Court justices as it is to men in other walks of life. Professor Paul A. Freund of the Harvard Law School has aptly written that "the law is not made by judge alone but by 'Judge and Company.' " [17] Other individuals and groups "influence" the law that judges make in various and sometimes surprising ways. However, the student must be careful not to construe the word *influence* in terms of crude threats, bribes, or string pulling. The major mode of lobbying in all political life is to seek to persuade public officials by means of reasoned argument that a proposed policy is in the public interest. The influence spoken of here is the influence of logic and reason, such as "a

[17] Paul A. Freund, *The Supreme Court of the United States, Its Business, Purposes and Performance* (Cleveland: World, 1961), p. 146.

well-reasoned and ably written brief, be it by one of the litigants or a brief *amicus curiae;* a persuasive oral argument on behalf of an issue at bar; a timely, thoughtful, and convincing book, monograph, speech, or law review article on the general or specific issue; a strategically timed use of a bona fide case"; [18] or an appeal to widely held sentiments of political and social justice. The influences on the justices can be classified as follows:

LAWYERS, LAW TEACHERS, AND LAW CLERKS

An obvious but important fact is that Supreme Court justices, "however broad and varied their past experience, are lawyers. With each other they share, to a large degree, a common background of legal knowledge and craftsmanship." [19] Thus, in varying degrees the justices continue to share the values of the legal profession, which in many subtle and sometimes subconscious ways help shape their judicial opinions.

At the same time, a justice is deeply affected by the traditions and institutional ethos of the Court itself. Justice Frankfurter once remarked that the "judicial process demands that a judge move within the framework of relevant legal rules and the covenanted modes of thought for ascertaining them. . . . *There is a good deal of shallow talk that the judicial robe does not change the man within. It does.*" [20]

More directly, the justices often borrow heavily from the briefs and arguments of counsel in the preparation of their opinions. Many of Daniel Webster's arguments, for example, found their way into the opinions of Chief Justice Marshall. John Archibald Campbell's forceful oral argument calling for economic freedom from governmental controls in the *Slaughterhouse Cases* (Chapter 10) failed to carry the Court but greatly influenced Justice Field's dissenting opinion. Relying heavily on Field's opinion, subsequent court majorities transformed the due process clause of the Fourteenth Amendment into a powerful instrument with which to implement laissez-faire economics. Another famous example of a lawyer's deep influence on the Court is the successful development of the "Brandeis brief" by Louis D. Brandeis before he was named to the Court. As noted more fully in Chapter 10, Brandeis relied on facts and statistics as well as legal arguments to show that women at that time needed protection from excessive hours of labor.

Lawyers also affect decisions of the Court in more subtle ways. The influence of great teachers of law such as Felix Frankfurter, who taught at the Harvard Law School for twenty-five years, is difficult to measure; yet certainly such

[18] Henry J. Abraham, *The Judicial Process* (New York: Oxford U.P., 1962), p. 205. See also Loren P. Beth, *Politics, the Constitution and the Supreme Court* (Evanston, Ill.: Harper, 1962), p. 67.

[19] Thomas H. Eliot, "The Teaching of Law in the Undergraduate Program," paper delivered at the annual meeting of the American Political Science Association, Washington, D.C. (Sept. 12, 1959).

[20] *Public Utilities Commission* v. *Pollak,* 343 U.S. 466–67 (1951). (Italics supplied.)

teachers help shape the law. Increasingly, articles appearing in law reviews and other legal journals may be influential in the formulation of legal doctrine.[21]

Many times law clerks (two or more for each justice), who are among the most able and intelligent of the recent law school graduates, serve as an important funnel for ideas between the justices and the law schools. The clerks do most of the preliminary work in sorting through the petitions for certiorari to determine which ones the Court should grant. In many instances, they prepare memoranda on or discuss pending decisions with the justices. Although some justices write their own opinions, today probably a majority direct their clerks to prepare at least first drafts in many cases. Although the confidential relation between justice and clerk prevents us from gathering precise data, it is clear that a substantial proportion of the words of the Court and most of the footnotes are first put on paper by the clerks.

ADMINISTRATIVE OFFICERS AND LOWER COURT JUDGES

The growth in the power of administrative officers in the twentieth century posed some serious problems for the Supreme Court. However, as administrative agencies became more firmly established and their powers more clearly defined, many aspects of the administrative process were partially insulated from the possibility of judicial review. By the 1950s, even when review did occur, the Court was generally very reluctant to overrule decisions of administrative officers.[22] The justices usually deferred to the decisions of well-established agencies and respected administrative officers. Professor Freund has wondered, for example, if the decision in *Korematsu* v. *United States* (Chapter 6) "would have been the same had the final administrative determination been made by someone whose judgment was less deeply respected than Secretary [of War] Stimson's." [23] During the 1960s and 1970s, there have been some dramatic changes in this judicial deference stance. They will be described in Chapter 16. Nevertheless, the Court continues to be greatly influenced by administrative findings of fact and policy decisions.

The deference shown by the Supreme Court to certain lower courts or individual judges may greatly influence some decisions. A classic example is Chief Justice Vinson's opinion in *Dennis* v. *United States* (Chapter 11), where he relied heavily on the court of appeals' decision written by Judge Hand. Vinson quoted extensively from Hand's opinion and adopted his rule of decision with the comment that "as articulated by Chief Judge Hand, it is as succinct and inclusive as any other we might devise at this time. It takes into consideration those factors which we deem relevant, and relates their significances. More we cannot expect from words."

[21] Chester A. Newland, "Legal Periodicals and the United States Supreme Court," *Midwest Journal of Political Science,* Vol. 3 (Feb. 1959), p. 58.

[22] Peter Woll, *Administrative Law: The Informed Process* (Berkeley and Los Angeles: University of California Press, 1963), p. 164.

[23] Freund, op. cit., pp. 146–47.

Decisions of respected courts, such as the New York Court of Appeals, with a good record of protecting individual rights are often followed by the Supreme Court with little question. Judge Henry W. Edgerton of the Federal Court of Appeals of the District of Columbia was widely respected for his careful and lucid opinions on civil liberties, and they were consistently followed by the Court; "the record of support of these opinions at the hands of the Supreme Court is most impressive evidence of Edgerton's stature as a judge." [24] Finally "one may speculate whether the decision in *Betts* v. *Brady* [overruled in *Gideon* v. *Wainwright* (see Chapter 15)], holding the appointment of counsel for indigent criminal defendants in state courts not to be an invariable constitutional requirement, would have been the same had the opinion of the court below been written by someone less highly esteemed than Chief Judge Bond of Maryland, who is referred to by name in Mr. Justice Roberts' opinion no fewer than fifteen times." [25]

Perhaps the most important influence of lower courts on the Supreme Court lies in their winnowing of cases. With the exception of a small number of cases that come to the Supreme Court directly from the federal district courts, all cases pass through at least one level of state or federal appellate courts before reaching the Supreme Court. In the process a large proportion of the "easy" cases are finally settled, leaving the more difficult ones to reach the Supreme Court. It is because state supreme courts and federal courts of appeal exist that the Supreme Court is faced almost exclusively with trouble cases—that is, cases in which the law does not clearly dictate a holding for one of the two contending parties. The ability of the Court to deal summarily with the "easy" cases that do come up to it, added to this winnowing, makes it easier to understand why the Supreme Court seems to wield such vast policy discretion. Almost none of the cases it decides with full opinions have simple, "purely legal" solutions. If they did, they would have been settled in the lower courts.

In the winnowing process, the federal courts of appeal have a special role. Quite typically, the same problem of interpreting some provision of a federal statute will show up almost simultaneously or in succession on a number of circuits. A taxpayer in Maine and one in Oregon both notice a possible loophole in a federal tax law, and both claim a deduction for their Florida vacation expenses. The Internal Revenue Service (IRS) refuses to allow the deduction. Both taxpayers go into federal district courts to challenge the Service ruling. Both lose. Both appeal. One appeal goes to the Ninth Circuit; the other, to the First. Usually, where the courts of appeal agree on how the federal statute should be interpreted, the problem never reaches the Supreme Court, because it usually refuses certiorari in statutory interpretation cases where the circuits are in agreement. Thus, the eleven courts of appeal serve as a panel of federal statutory interpreters that takes much of this burden off of the Supreme Court.

[24] Eleanor Bontecou, ed., *Freedom in the Balance: Opinions of Judge Henry W. Edgerton Relating to Civil Liberties* (Ithaca, N.Y.: Cornell U.P., 1960), p. 14.

[25] Freund, op. cit., p. 146.

Where "circuit conflict" occurs—for instance, where the Ninth Circuit allows the deduction and the First disallows it—then the problem will probably reach the Supreme Court eventually. But often the Court delays for a few terms, hoping the circuits will adjust their differences. Where a circuit conflict persists, it must be resolved by the Supreme Court if the federal law is to mean the same thing in Oregon and in Maine. Even in resolving circuit conflicts, however, the Supreme Court has the advantage of the experience, arguments, and proposed solutions offered by the various courts of appeal. Thus, circuit conflict puts the Supreme Court in the position of the head of a large organization who can tap the preliminary staff work of his subordinates to aid him in making a final decision. And in the process the Court, like the organization executive, may be deeply influenced by what subordinates have recommended even if there is disagreement among them.

Federal district courts and state trial courts also play an important role in influencing the decisions of the Supreme Court. The Supreme Court usually, but not always, accepts the findings of fact of the trial courts. Facts are frequently crucial to the outcome of Supreme Court cases. For instance, once a federal district court has found as a matter of fact that local school authorities acted with the purpose and effect of segregating students, the Supreme Court may intervene to change some details of the district court-ordered desegregation plan, but it could not rule that the school district in question need not desegregate. On the other hand, if the federal district court finds as a matter of fact that a school district had no segregatory motives and/or that the schools of the district now contain racial mixes of students comparable to the overall mix in the community, it will be very difficult for the Supreme Court to impose a desegregation plan even if it wants to.

INTERESTS, ORGANIZED AND OTHERWISE

Organized interest groups may attempt to influence decisions of the Supreme Court, principally by sponsoring and promoting test cases and by entering cases as *amici curiae.* Such attempts may be difficult to discern, because by all outward appearances a particular case may seem to be simply a contest between two private litigants. However, the two parties in the case may be sponsored and supported by conflicting interest groups who are seeking broader objectives.

> Organizations support legal action because individuals lack the necessary time, money, and skill. With no delays a case takes an average of four years to pass through two courts to the Supreme Court of the United States. A series of cases on related questions affecting the permanent interest of a group may extend over two decades or more. The constant attention that litigation demands, especially when new arguments are being advanced, makes the employment of regular counsel economical. This may be supplemented by a legal staff of some size and by volunteer lawyers of

distinction. Parties also pay court costs and meet the expense of printing the record and briefs. Organizations are better able to provide the continuity demanded in litigation than individuals. Some individuals do maintain responsibility for their own cases even at the Supreme Court level, but this is difficult under modern conditions.[26]

Two examples of interest-group activity are provided by the zealous members of a minority sect known as Jehovah's Witnesses (discussed fully in Chapter 12) and by the National Association for the Advancement of Colored People (NAACP). Beginning in 1938, the Jehovah's Witnesses brought more than fifty bona fide test cases to the Supreme Court by supporting members who had violated a local ordinance or state statute. The Witnesses concentrated on litigation for their victories because of their ". . . total helplessness in any other area. Their numbers and hence their political weight were negligible. Further impairing any appeal to the legislature or public opinion was the Witnesses' extreme unpopularity. Their offensive literature, their aggressive missionary methods, their doubtful patriotism, and their inability to advance the most reasonable argument without dragging in the iniquities of the Catholic Church, all tended to convince a large segment of the population that any Witness misfortunes were all deserved." [27]

The NAACP played a key role in preparing the way for the *Public School Desegregation Cases* (Chapter 13) and in improving generally the legal status of blacks. Since the end of World War II, the NAACP has won more than sixty cases in the Supreme Court in its attempts to secure racial equality before the law for the 25 million American blacks. "By presenting test cases to the Supreme Court, the NAACP has won successive gains protecting the right of Negroes in voting, housing, transportation, education, and service on juries. Each effort has followed the development of new theories of legal interpretation and required the preparation of specific actions in the courts to challenge existing precedent. The NAACP Legal Defense Fund has accomplished these two tasks through the cooperation of associated and allied groups." [28] That the road for the NAACP has been a long and hard one is demonstrated by its painstaking efforts to outlaw restrictive covenants. The organization brought cases to the courts for more than thirty years and spent $100,000 before winning a signal victory in the Supreme Court in the 1948 case of *Shelley* v. *Kraemer* [29] (Chapter 13). And that victory probably would not have been possible without changed social and political circumstances and the support of numerous other groups. Eighteen organizations filed briefs as *amici curiae* supporting the NAACP position in the *Shelley* case. These included such diverse groups as the American

[26] Clement E. Vose, "Litigation As a Form of Pressure Group Activity," *The Annals of the American Academy of Political and Social Science,* Vol. 319 (Sept. 1958), p. 22.

[27] David R. Manwaring, *Render Unto Caesar: The Flag Salute Controversy* (Chicago: U. of Chicago, 1962), pp. 33–34.

[28] Vose, "Litigation As a Form of Pressure Group Activity," op. cit., p. 24.

[29] Clement E. Vose, *Caucasians Only: The Supreme Court, the NAACP, and the Restrictive Covenant Cases* (Berkeley and Los Angeles: University of California Press, 1959), p. 213.

Jewish Congress, American Federation of Labor (AFL), Human Relations Commission of the Protestant Council of New York City, ACLU, and American Association for the United Nations.[30]

The Supreme Court, therefore, is sometimes a good mirror, as Justice Frankfurter once noted, of the struggles of dominant forces outside the Court. Yet a word of caution is in order when discussing the influence of interest groups. In constitutional cases, the Supreme Court is of course "aware of competing interests, and often can decide the case only by giving preference to one or the other, but not all the interests are represented by organizations or are even discernible as 'groups' in any significant sense. . . ."[31] Relatively few cases are brought to the Supreme Court by organized groups themselves.[32] Typically, a particular class of persons or economic interests is represented in court by a single litigant who may not consciously be trying to defend anyone's interests but his own. Thus in the *Bakke* litigation on affirmative action admissions programs (see Chapter 14), Bakke's lawyer insisted that his sole concern was to get Mr. Bakke into the U. C. Davis medical school, not to represent white applicants at professional schools as a class. Yet in that very case a wide range of interest groups including the NAACP, the Anti-Defamation League, and the Association of American Law Schools filed *amicus* briefs.

Quite apart from conscious group pressures, the "litigational marketplace" will assure that most important interests are heard by the Supreme Court. Most important public policies generate conflicts. When losing the conflict is costing someone more than the cost of litigating it, he will consider going to court. If he predicts that his chances of winning are good enough to justify the expenses of litigation, he will litigate. Thus, each year hundreds of thousands of individual decisions about whether or not to go to court, based on purely individual calculations of costs and benefits, will generate cases reflecting nearly every conflict of social, economic, or political interest. Indeed, only a relatively small proportion of all those who rationally ought to litigate on the basis of cost-benefit analysis need actually do so in order to generate a number of cases sufficient to introduce the Supreme Court to all the policy issues and interests of the day.

Thus, naïve pressure-group conceptions do not adequately describe the subtle intersection of political and social interests with the Supreme Court. Nor should crude analogies, which fail to take into account differing political styles and role demands, be drawn between interest-group activities in the legislative and executive spheres and those in the judicial. To say that both courts and interests are part of politics is not to say that judges respond to interest claims in exactly the same ways congressmen and administrators do.

[30] Ibid., pp. 193–97. See also the discussion in Chapter 11 of the First Amendment rights of organized groups to litigate and to anonymous association.

[31] Eliot, loc cit.

[32] See Nathan Hakman, "Lobbying the Supreme Court—An Appraisal of Political Science Folklore," *Fordham Law Review*, Vol. 35 (Oct. 1966).

PUBLIC OPINION, PARTIES, AND ELECTIONS

The study of public opinion and the Supreme Court is in its infancy, but what little we do know suggests that the Court is in about the same position as other political agencies. The general public knows almost nothing and has no opinion about almost any specific Supreme Court decision. It is possible, however, to elicit from the public a general response on whether the Supreme Court is doing a good or a bad job—although it is not clear that this response is really directed at *the* Court or at courts in general. Although general opinion on whether the Court is doing a good job probably fluctuates less violently than similar public assessments of the Presidency, the approval rate is very modest, apparently hovering around 50 per cent of the respondents. On the other hand, those segments of the public that have a strong interest in some specific issue are likely to know about, and have strong attitudes for or against, Supreme Court decisions in their area of concern. Along with these issue publics, opinion leaders—that is, the small stratum of the public that frequently talks or writes about politics—know more and have stronger opinions about the Court than the rest of the population.[33]

Thus, general public opinion is too diffuse to have much influence on individual decisions of the Court. If justices are like other politicians, they are concerned about the long-term legitimacy of their office—that is, whether people generally approve of their existence. But such long-range concerns rarely will carry much weight against the various immediate considerations surrounding the decision of the moment. In general, politicians tend to perceive whatever they wish to do now as also that course of action most likely to gain long-term approval. Most justices are likely to believe that in the long run the people will approve of "right" Court decisions—that is, the ones the justice wants to make now.

Nonetheless, it is unquestionably true that the justices think in terms of the "time having come" for some decisions and the country "not being ready" for others, even though none would admit to following public opinion polls. No doubt, issue publics and opinion leaders are influential in creating the climate of opinion that the justices perceive and to which they react in deciding cases. Occasionally, an issue becomes so salient that the general public is converted into one vast issue public on that question. By 1972, for instance, an overwhelming majority of the voters had a highly negative opinion about busing to achieve school integration. When situations such as this occur, politicians who ignore public opinion act at their peril.

One way to visualize the legal profession and lower courts in relation to the Supreme Court is as major opinion leaders who shape the attitudes of the more general public and to whom the Court is particularly responsive. Justices often get the feeling that an issue is ready for resolution or that a doctrine has had its day and is ready for change. These feelings are likely to be the

[33] See W. F. Murphy and J. Tanenhaus, "Explaining Diffuse Support for the U.S. Supreme Court," *Notre Dame Lawyer*, Vol. 49 (1974), p. 1037.

product of two factors. One is their sense of what is going on in law as reflected in the opinions of other courts and in legal writing. The other is their sense of what's going on in the world as reflected in what general opinion leaders such as news commentators, column writers, and office holders write and say.

The influence of the political parties on the Court is difficult to trace. We have already seen that there is a strong element of party partisanship in Supreme Court appointments. But most justices have tended to isolate themselves from direct party affairs once in office. More important, few issues of American politics fall neatly along party lines, with everyone in one party for, and everyone in the other against, a given policy. Thus a justice's previous party identification is not a dependable predictor of his votes on particular questions. Nor is the fact that he was appointed by a Democratic or a Republican President much of a clue as to how he will resolve specific policy issues. Where party and vote do seem partially to correspond, it is likely to be because the justices' political attitudes, as described earlier, are a good predictor of both their party and their votes. There is little to indicate that, except as a very rough and incomplete predictor of political attitudes, party identification is a significant factor in the decisions by justices.

However, the Court as an institution may react to changes in the general party structure. There is some evidence that the Supreme Court is likely to be particularly active in those historical periods when one or both of the two major parties are in the process of breaking up or reorganizing, in times of what political scientists sometimes call realigning or critical elections.[34] The two greatest pieces of early Supreme Court activism, *Marbury* v. *Madison* (Chapter 4), which established the power of judicial review, and the *Dred Scott* case (Chapter 5), which sought to resolve the slavery controversy, were decided at times of party dissolution. *Marbury* came just after the election of Jefferson signaled the end of the Federalist party as a national force. *Dred Scott* occurred when the Whig party, broken by the slavery issue, was displaced by the new Republican party. The great flurry of Supreme Court activity of the 1890s corresponded with the rise of the Populist party and the realigning election of 1898. Obviously, the Court's New Deal crisis was related to the major political realignment stimulated by the election of President Roosevelt.

Yet the judicial activism of the Warren Court came at a time of relative party stability. It can be argued that during this particular period the two major parties were both so incapable of facing the major issues on which the Court intervened—race, reapportionment, and the rights of the accused—that their stability or instability was irrelevant to judicial action.

Nevertheless, many sages tell us that the Supreme Court follows the election returns. Certainly, this is true in the sense that, in the normal course of events, a newly elected President will soon get enough appointments profoundly to affect the composition of the Court. It is also true in the sense that where a

[34] See Richard Funston, "The Supreme Court and Critical Elections," *American Political Science Review,* Vol. 69 (1975), p. 793; David Adamany, "Legitimacy, Realigning Elections, and the Supreme Court," *Wisconsin Law Review,* 1973, p. 790.

series of elections has established a firm governing coalition in Washington with a consensus on major national policies, the Court is in no position to buck the coalition successfully, at least for very long. Thus, by the 1950s, when both major parties and indeed nearly everyone in Washington had accepted both the necessity of the New Deal programs, such as Social Security, and the necessity of waging the cold war, it was inconceivable that the Court could either eject the New Deal or save the American Communists. It was precisely because a rough national consensus did exist against state laws requiring racial segregation (without the Washington coalition having as yet reached a policy consensus on what to do about it) that the Court could intervene successfully against school segregation. The Court may sometimes lead the Washington coalition, but it can rarely oppose it.[35]

PRESIDENT AND CONGRESS

Given what we have already seen about appointments, it need hardly be said that the President is a major influence on the Court. His influence, however, extends far beyond the appointment process. Presidents and presidential candidates have the power to make the Supreme Court an issue in elections as both Presidents Roosevelt and Nixon did. A President who is reluctant to enforce Supreme Court mandates, as were Presidents Jackson, Lincoln, and Eisenhower at various times, may make the Court's life quite difficult. The interaction between the President and the Court is discussed in Chapter 6.

Much of the work of the Supreme Court involves the interpretation and enforcement of federal statutes, an area in which the Court is supposed to be, and very often is, the faithful servant of the Congress that enacted the statute. When the Court interprets a statute in a way Congress does not like, Congress can pass a new statute to correct the Court's interpretation. Even when the Court declares a congressional statute unconstitutional, Congress may pass the statute again in a somewhat different form, or it may initiate a constitutional amendment to reverse the Court's decision. Congress controls the size and much of the jurisdiction of the Court and the rules under which all federal courts operate. There is a long history of congressional efforts to curb the Court, and there are differing assessments of how successful Congress has been.[36]

The problem of Court interpretation of congressional statutes is, however, much more complicated than it seems at first glance. The Court often professes

[35] Robert A. Dahl, "Decision-Making in a Democracy: The Supreme Court as a National Policy-Maker," *Journal of Public Law,* Vol. 6 (Nov. 1957), p. 284; Kenneth Dolbeare, "The Public Views the Supreme Court," in Herbert Jacob, ed., *Law, Politics and the Federal Courts* (Boston: Little, Brown, 1967); Jonathan D. Casper, "The Supreme Court and National Policy Making," *American Political Science Review,* Vol. 60 (1976), pp. 50–61.

[36] See Walter Murphy, *Congress and the Court* (Chicago: U. of Chicago, 1962); C. Herman Pritchett, *Congress Versus the Supreme Court* (Minneapolis: U. of Minnesota Press, 1961); Harry P. Stumpf, "Congressional Responses to Supreme Court Rulings," *Journal of Public Law,* Vol 14 (1966), p. 377; John R. Schmidhauser and Larry L. Berg, *The Supreme Court and Congress* (New York: Free Press, 1972).

"deference" to the will of Congress when all it is really doing is agreeing with Congress that the statute is a good one. Where the justices find a statute unsatisfactory, they may narrow its reach, change its direction, or even emasculate it by their interpretation. Often the congressional majority that coalesced to pass the statute initially has disappeared so that not enough votes can be mustered in Congress now to "correct" the Court's interpretation by passing a new statute. Often the language of a statute could mean one of several things, and some members of Congress have voted for it hoping it would mean one and others, hoping it would mean another. Indeed ambiguous language may have been chosen precisely because a majority could not agree on a single clear policy. For instance the age discrimination statute forbids discrimination in employment unless there are good business reasons for such discrimination. Clearly some Congressmen and -women wished to forbid age discrimination but not enough to get a majority for a straight prohibition. Others favored some protection for the aged but wanted to leave businesses free to preserve their efficiency. A compromise bill gained a majority for a statute that encompasses two partially conflicting policies, equality for older citizens and economic efficiency.[37] Sometimes the conflicting policies will be embodied in two different statutes, each voted by a different congressional majority. Thus the Court is frequently in a position to interpret a statute in one way or another, for instance as either prohibiting or not prohibiting mandatory retirement at age sixty-five for window washers or shirt salesmen. Or it may have to decide which of two statutes applies to a particular situation where one statute requires "sex blind" hiring and the other requires affirmative action hiring giving preference to women. No matter what it says about faithfully following the congressional command, the Court often knows that it can choose either of two rival and opposite interpretations without much chance that Congress can find the opportunity or the majority to speak out again and clearly choose one or the other interpretation. Particularly because of the extent to which various congressional civil rights statutes are now entwined with the constitutional provisions on equal protection and due process (see Chapters 13 and 14), the Court's statutory interpretation powers play a more and more important role in areas that we used to think about solely in terms of its powers to declare statutes unconstitutional. (The Court's powers of statutory interpretation where no constitutional issues are involved are discussed in Chapter 16.)

Impact of the Court's Decisions

Once the Supreme Court has made a decision, it has little or no independent means to enforce compliance with it. For it is not the Court but Congress and the President who control the budget and the armed forces and thus are in a position to buy or force obedience. The degree of compliance to Supreme

[37] Peter Schuck, "The Greying of Civil Rights Law: The Age Discrimination Act of 1975," *Yale Law Journal,* Vol. 89 (1979), p. 27.

Court decision varies greatly depending on a number of interacting factors that are not yet fully understood by political scientists. Obviously, compliance is greatest among those who want to comply. Thus local school districts that had wanted to stop having school prayers but were forced by state law to continue the practice were glad to comply with a Supreme Court order to stop the prayers. Compliance is also likely to run high where the Court's decision is in line with American values that are so dominant in the popular mind that no politician can afford to resist them. Thus when the Court announced its one person-one-vote rule, legislatures were forced to follow it even at the cost of redistricting many of their members out of office. For who could insist that "one person two votes and another person a half a vote" was the American way. Those against whom the Court can direct some immediate sanction are also highly likely to comply. A lower federal court is unlikely to resist the Supreme Court because the Supreme Court can reverse the decisions of the lower court, and judges who are reversed frequently suffer damage to their professional reputations. Often the leadership of one or a few individuals who believe that it is more important to obey the law than to resist even a "wrong" decision by the Court will bring their organizations or communities into compliance. The availability of well-organized and financed interest groups or government agencies that demand compliance and are willing to undertake further litigation to get it may be decisive.[38]

On the other hand, where the Supreme Court's decision does not trigger basic ideological support, is opposed by the dominant forces in local communities, is easily evaded because of vagueness or loopholes in its language, is not championed by those dedicated to the rule of law, and/or is not seconded by groups prepared to litigate further, then a lower level of compliance can be expected. In this connection it should be noted that local lawyers, government officials, judges, and police will typically not have read, and often will even profess to be unaware of, major Supreme Court decisions that should govern their behavior.

For students of the Supreme Court, compliance cannot be assumed. It must be investigated case by case. For instance the decisions concerning released time programs in religious education (*McCollum* v. *Board of Education* and *Zorach* v. *Clauson,* Chapter 12) were widely ignored or evaded. In the *McCollum* case the Court held 8 to 1 that the use of public school buildings for released time programs violated the separation of church and state clause of the First Amendment. Yet,

> It is no secret that after the *McCollum* decision, and despite it, many communities continued to hold released time classes in public school buildings. The most conservative estimate places noncompliance at 15 per cent of the programs, and other estimates run up to 40 to 50 per cent in some states. Five years later in the *Zorach* case the Court reaffirmed the *McCollum* ruling but offered the localities a clearly constitutional alternative: religious education off school premises. Have local religious and educational

[38] See Charles Bullock and Harrell Rodgers, *Law & Social Change: Civil Rights Laws and Their Consequences* (New York: McGraw-Hill, 1972).

> groups met the Court halfway and given up released time in the school room? The answer is "no—not entirely." In 1956 a knowledgeable authority on school law wrote that "school systems in virtually every state violate in some way the legal principle concerning religious instruction in the public schools." Some of the violations are unwitting, he wrote, but knowing violators include "some persons holding responsible church or school positions." [39]

Thus the "evidence of noncompliance with the *Zorach* ruling indicates the limited effectiveness of the Court in maintaining constitutional uniformity within the federal system. Especially in religiously homogeneous communities, where there are no dissident elements strong enough to protest or begin court action, the *McCollum* and *Zorach* rules are evaded and ignored." [40]

The most recent school prayer cases (*Engel* v. *Vitale, Abington School District* v. *Schempp, Murray* v. *Curlett,* Chapter 12) resulted in widespread verbal resistance and noncompliance. A storm of protest greeted the Court's decision in *Engel* v. *Vitale,* which held that a nondenominational prayer written by the New York Board of Regents for use in the public schools was unconstitutional. In fact, few decisions in American history have aroused such public anguish. The furor was so great that the Columbia Broadcasting Company took the unprecedented step of presenting a two-hour television program, entitled "Storm Over the Supreme Court," explaining the role of the Court in American history and exploring the issues of the school prayer decision.[41] Although the *Engel* decision had many supporters, it was loudly condemned by others.

When the Court outlawed Bible reading and the recitation of the Lord's Prayer in public schools a year later (*Abington School District* v. *Schempp, Murray* v. *Curlett*), the reaction was less violent. This was the result in part of the fact that the Court wrote a more careful series of opinions. In his long majority opinion, Justice Clark attempted to set at rest some of the public fears brought on by *Engel* v. *Vitale.* Explanatory concurring opinions by Justices Brennan and Goldberg also helped obtain acceptance of the decision. Moreover, many religious groups had anticipated the decision and had quietly urged acceptance. Nevertheless, there was still a good deal of local noncompliance, some of which continues even now.[42]

The greatest resistance by far in recent years has been to the Court's segregation decisions. Ten years after the 1954 *School Desegregation Cases,* only about 10 per cent of the South's black students were attending integrated classes. One writer has noted that the failure to obey the Court in this area "constitutes

[39] Frank J. Sorauf, "*Zorach* v. *Clauson:* The Impact of a Supreme Court Decision," *American Political Science Review,* Vol. 53 (Sept. 1959), pp. 777, 785–86. See also Gordon Patric, "The Impact of a Court Decision: Aftermath of the McCollum Case," *Journal of Public Law,* Vol. 6 (Fall 1957), p. 455.

[40] Ibid., p. 791.

[41] Presented in two parts on Feb. 20 and March 13, 1963.

[42] Three major studies of school district compliance with the Supreme Court's religious decisions have appeared: Richard Johnson, *The Dynamics of Compliance: Supreme Court Decision-Making from a New Perspective* (Evanston, Ill.: Northwestern U.P., 1968); William K. Muir, Jr., *Prayer in the Public Schools* (Chicago: U. of Chicago, 1968); and Kenneth Dolbeare and Paul Hammond, *The School Prayer Decisions* (Chicago: U. of Chicago, 1971).

the most disgraceful act of mass contempt in the history of the nation."[43] Some of the many problems that prevent the translation of printed decisions into living law in this area are examined in Chapter 13. Here we need only point out that in some areas resistance has been so great that local groups have been willing to abandon public education completely rather than to comply with the Court's order to integrate the schools.

While the compliance battle raged in the South, a series of new problems came to share the spotlight. Many Northern school districts are unwilling to end *de facto* segregation without severe judicial prodding. The Supreme Court's reapportionment decisions (see Chapter 4) for a time created major compliance problems for the state legislatures and the state and federal courts charged with their implementation. The actual impact on police practices of the Court's decisions on the rights of accused persons (see Chapter 15) remains very much in doubt.[44]

Compliance, that is direct obedience to a specific order of the Supreme Court, is only one aspect of the impact of Supreme Court decisions. More important perhaps is the general intellectual and political response to particular Supreme Court decisions, to lines or clusters of decisions that establish long-term policies and to the very existence of the Court itself.[45]

For instance, one of the most important impacts of the *School Desegregation Cases* was that they served as a catalyst for black political organization in the South. In response to the decisions and to Southern efforts to resist them, a massive civil rights movement came into existence among blacks seeking to secure their newly announced rights. This movement politically mobilized thousands of blacks who had previously been excluded from active politics. Then the spectacular clashes between the movement and local government authorities so dramatized the issues of racial segregation and discrimination that a national climate of opinion was created that resulted in congressional passage of a series of civil rights laws. One of those laws made it possible for many of the newly mobilized blacks to register and vote and to get other blacks to do so. Then followed a fundamental restructuring of politics in many places in the South as blacks became powerful voting blocks. In other words, the most immediate and significant impact of the Court's school decisions was not the integration of the schools, which has proceeded very slowly, but the stimulation of well-organized, widespread black political action, which has put blacks into political office in the South for the first time since Reconstruction and has made blacks an important political constituency that must be courted by white politicians.[46]

[43] Edward Bennett Williams, *One Man's Freedom* (New York: Atheneum, 1962), p. 300.

[44] See "Interrogations in New Haven: The Impact of Miranda," *Yale Law Journal,* Vol. 49 (July 1967), p. 1519.

[45] See Martin Shapiro, "The Impact of Supreme Court Decisions," *Journal of Legal Education,* Vol 23 (1971), p. 77.

[46] The impact literature is surveyed in Theodore Becker and Malcolm Feeley, eds., *The Impact of Supreme Court Decisions,* 2nd ed. (New York: Oxford U.P., 1972); and in Stephen L. Wasby, *The Impact of the United States Supreme Court* (Homewood, Ill.: Dorsey Press, 1970). An interesting recent study is G. Alan Tarr, *Judicial Impact and State Supreme Courts* (Lexington, Mass.: D.C. Heath, 1977).

What the Justices Do

Many justices have not read the briefs or done their own research before the initial conference. Many of them cast their votes on the basis of what they heard in oral argument and read in memoranda from their clerks. They do read many of one another's draft opinions but dissenters often do not bother specifically to reply to the arguments of the majority and vice versa. Although the final opinions sometimes constitute real debates or compromises, real collaboration or even bargaining among the justices is infrequent.

The Supreme Court is not a place where nine legal scholars exhaustively study and discuss all of the relevant issues and then write careful, principled opinions fully explaining the logical routes they have followed to their legal conclusions. Typically the justices reach their conclusions after a little reading and talking, and some more or less articulate reasoning, on the basis of

> their best guess about what resolution of the issues will be fair to the parties and promote the best public policy. . . . Like most other politicians, they confront too many problems, for most of which neither the state of our social knowledge nor the capacity of our social technology provides clear solutions. All of this is not to say that the justices act "by guess or by God" or by delegating decision making to their clerks or to the parties. Few of the issues that reach the Court are brand new. Most cases involve only a slight variation on facts and issues that have been before the Court dozens of times before.[47]

A justice who has participated in twenty automobile search cases, some of which involved cars on the streets, others cars in parking lots, and others yet cars in driveways need not ponder very hard about all the issues in deciding on how to vote in the twenty-first case which involves a car parked on a ferry boat. "Like most other government policy makers, the justices are usually confronted with choices that they can treat as incremental variations on choices that they have made in the past." [48] When big, new questions do arise, they are likely to present fundamental social dilemmas, uncertainties, or conflicts of interest, such as that between pregnant women and fetuses in the abortion cases, that cannot be resolved by conventional legal research and reasoning. In such cases the justices, like the rest of us, must rely in part on what we think we know about the world, our sense of fundamental justice and fair

[47] Martin Shapiro, "The Supreme Court: From Warren to Burger," in Anthony King, ed., *The New American Political System* (Washington, D.C.: American Enterprise Institute, 1978), p. 199.

[48] Ibid., p. 200. If read as a special kind of political novel rather than the reporting it purports to be, and if the reader can see through the dramatic, exposé style of language by which the authors seek to turn their accounts of routine, normal, and quite respectable events into big news, Bob Woodward and Scott Armstrong, *The Brethren* (New York: Simon and Schuster, 1979) provides some feel for the life of the Court at least as it is seen from the self-important perspective of the clerks who were the authors' principal sources.

play, and our guesses about what policies are likely to improve our society. To these the justices can add whatever wisdom and restraint are provided by the constitutional tradition embodied in their own previous decisions and the commentaries made upon them by others.

CHAPTER 4

The Courts and Judicial Review

As is the idea of a written constitution, the concept of judicial review is a unique American contribution to the art and practice of government. Judicial review can be defined as the power possessed by American courts to declare that legislative and executive actions are null and void if they violate the written constitution. Three branches of judicial review can be distinguished, as follows:

1. *"National" Judicial Review.* The power of all American courts from the lowest to the highest to pass upon the validity of acts of Congress under the Constitution.
2. *"Federal" Judicial Review.* The power and duty of all courts to abide by the supremacy clause of the Constitution (Article VI) in construing state constitutional provisions and statutes in conflict with the federal Constitution and laws and treaties of the United States.
3. *"State" Judicial Review.* The power of state courts to review laws of the state legislatures under the respective state constitutions.[1]

[1] Edward S. Corwin, "Judicial Review," *Encyclopedia of the Social Sciences,* Vol. 8 (1932), p. 457.

The power of judicial review is usually associated with the Supreme Court, because it renders *final* judgments in cases involving the interpretation of the federal Constitution. Cases involving only state constitutional issues are finally determined by the highest state courts.

The concept of judicial review rests on an

> extraordinarily simple foundation. Stripped to its essence, it is almost too plain for stating. The Constitution is the supreme law. It was ordained by the people, the ultimate source of all political authority. It confers limited powers on the national government. These limitations derive partly from the mere fact that these powers are enumerated—the government cannot exercise powers not granted to it—and partly from certain express prohibitions upon its powers or upon the manner of their exercise. If the government consciously or unconsciously oversteps these limitations there must be some authority competent to hold it in control, to thwart its unconstitutional attempt, and thus to vindicate and preserve inviolate the will of the people as expressed in the Constitution. This power the courts exercise. This is the beginning and the end of the theory of judicial review.[2]

The great prestige of the Supreme Court stems largely from the fact that it has final authority in the interpretation of the Constitution. In the exercise of this duty the Supreme Court acts as a superlegislature of great political powers. In the minds of the American people, the Court has been identifed almost exclusively with the function of judicial review.

Much has been written regarding the question as to whether or not the framers of the Constitution intended that the Supreme Court exercise the power of judicial review.[3] A noted historian concluded many years ago that the majority of the leading delegates to the Philadelphia Convention of 1787 favored judicial review.[4] In *The Federalist,* No. 78, Alexander Hamilton seemed to express clearly the necessity for judicial review in a constitutional system:

> The interpretation of the laws is the proper and peculiar province of the courts. A constitution is, in fact, and must be regarded by the judges, as a fundamental law. It therefore belongs to them to ascertain its meaning, as well as the meaning of any particular act proceeding from the legislative body. If there should happen to be an irreconcilable variance between the two, that which has the superior obligation and validity ought, of course, to be preferred to the statute, the intention of the people to the intention of their agents.

[2] Howard L. McBain, "Some Aspects of Judicial Review," *Bacon Lectures on the Constitution of the United States* (Boston: Boston University Heffernan Press, 1939), pp. 376–77.

[3] Compare Edward S. Corwin, *The Doctrine of Judicial Review* (Princeton, N.J.: Princeton U.P., 1914); see also by the same author, "The Constitution As Instrument and As Symbol," *American Political Science Review,* Vol. 30 (Dec. 1936), p. 1078; and Raoul Berger, *Congress v. The Supreme Court* (Cambridge: Harvard U.P., 1969) with Gary Wills, *Explaining America: The Federalist* (New York: Doubleday, 1981).

[4] Charles A. Beard, *The Supreme Court and the Constitution* (New York: Macmillan, Inc., 1912), p. 118.

Yet even Hamilton's views are not certain. The majority of the framers probably anticipated some form of judicial review, but it is quite uncertain how much and what kind. Some of the framers probably envisioned judicial review as a "self-defense" power insuring the independence of the Supreme Court—that is that the Court could invalidate only those congressional statutes that sought to limit the powers granted to the Court by Article III. Both the early attackers and defenders of review agreed that if review were to be exercised at all, it was to be only against clearly unconstitutional laws. No one at the time could have anticipated the subtle process by which the Court manages, for instance, to declare an abortion law unconstitutional because it violates a constitutional right to privacy that the justices have read into a combination of three or four clauses of the Constitution, none of which mention privacy.

Judicial review was *not* expressly granted by the Constitution. It was first asserted by Chief Justice Marshall in the famous case of *Marbury* v. *Madison* (1803). The Supreme Court had exercised the power of judicial review in earlier cases that sustained federal and state laws, but for the first time in *Marbury* v. *Madison* an act of Congress was invalidated.[5] A major state law was first held void by the Court as a violation of a provision of the Constitution in 1810.[6]

Since the decision in *Marbury* v. *Madison,* the Supreme Court has declared only some ninety acts of Congress unconstitutional. As the arbiter between the state and federal legal systems, however, the Court has declared void many more state statutes involving federal questions. Judicial review of state statutes has been extremely significant in the maintenance of the federal system. Justice Holmes once declared that he did "not think the United States would come to an end if we lost our power to declare an act of Congress void. I do think the Union would be imperiled if we could not make that declaration as to the laws of the several states." [7] And Chief Justice Hughes noted that "far more important to the development of the country than the decisions holding acts of Congress to be invalid, have been those in which the authority of Congress has been sustained and adequate national power to meet the necessities of a growing country has been found to exist within constitutional limitations." [8]

"Judicial self-restraint and judicial power seem to be the opposite sides of the same coin: it has been by judicious application of the former that the latter has been maintained. A tradition beginning with Marshall's coup in *Marbury*

[5] *Marbury* v. *Madison* was actually the second case in which a law of Congress was declared unconstitutional. In 1794, the Court held an act of Congress void in *U.S.* v. *Yale Todd,* but the decision was simply reported in a note in a much later case, *U.S.* v. *Ferreira,* 13 How. 40 (1851). Authorities disagree on the case of *Yale Todd;* some hold that to say that an act of Congress was held unconstitutional in that case is inaccurate.

[6] *Fletcher* v. *Peck,* 6 Cr. 87 (1810).

[7] Oliver W. Holmes, "Law and the Court," *Collected Legal Papers* (New York: Harcourt, 1920), p. 295.

[8] Charles E. Hughes, *The Supreme Court of the United States* (New York: Columbia U.P., 1928), pp. 96–97.

v. *Madison* . . . suggests that the Court's power has been maintained by a wise refusal to employ it in unequal combat." [9] The Court has rationalized these refusals in a number of self-declared limitations on its power of review.

CASE OR CONTROVERSY

The Supreme Court will exercise the power of judicial review only if an actual case or controversy is presented—litigation involving a real conflict of rights and interests between contending parties. The Court, therefore, cannot take the initiative in declaring laws unconstitutional. "It has no self-starting capacity and must await the action of some litigant so aggrieved as to have a justiciable case. Also, its pronouncement must await the decision in the lower courts. Often it is years after a statute is put on the books and begins to take effect before a decision on a constitutional question can be heard by the Supreme Court." [10] The *Dred Scott* case, for example, held void a law that had been enacted thirty-seven years before. The Court did not rule on the important Smith Act of 1940 until 1951.[11] Of course, what constitutes a real case or controversy must be decided by the Court, and on some occasions it has ignored this limitation by rendering decisions in test cases in which both parties seem to have wanted the same result. The Court also has refused to give advisory opinions and to decide moot cases. (A moot case is one that has ceased to have practical importance during the course of a trial or pending an appeal.)

High levels of Court activity have so eroded the cases and controversies rule, however, that one noted authority has argued that the justices have moved "away from the view that constitutional adjudication is only collateral to the essential judicial task of deciding lawsuits and towards the notion that the primary function of the Supreme Court of the United States is to ensure that other organs of government observe constitutional limitations." [12]

POLITICAL QUESTIONS

The Supreme Court will not decide "political questions," because they must be resolved by the executive or legislature. The term *political question* cannot be defined precisely, because the Court may expand or contract the definition as it sees fit. In other words, a political question is whatever the Supreme Court says it is. The political questions doctrine is discussed later in this chapter.

[9] John P. Roche, "Judicial Self-Restraint," *American Political Science Review,* Vol. 49 (Sept. 1955), p. 722.

[10] Robert H. Jackson, *The Supreme Court in the American System of Government* (Cambridge: Harvard U.P., 1955), p. 24.

[11] *Dennis* v. *United States,* 341 U.S. 494 (1951).

[12] Archibald Cox, *The Role of the Supreme Court in American Government* (New York: Oxford U.P., 1976), p. 101.

STARE DECISIS (TO STAND BY THE DECISIONS)

The rule of *stare decisis,* or precedent, theoretically limits the Supreme Court, because it means that previous decisions of the Court are binding on it in cases involving exactly the same issue. Although *stare decisis* is generally applicable to all American courts, including the Supreme Court, when they are dealing with statutes and common law, it has not even in theory been strictly applicable in the sphere of judicial review because of the duty of every judge to render "correct" constitutional decisions no matter what the errors of his predecessors. The Court has refused to follow precedent in many instances; in addition, the Court has at times expressly overruled previous decisions. Nevertheless, clearly there are instances in which the Court would have decided a case differently if it were not for the existence of controlling precedents.

AVOIDING THE CONSTITUTIONAL ISSUE

> The Court will not pass on a constitutional question, although properly presented by the record, if there is also present some other ground on which the case may be disposed of. This rule has found some varied application. Thus, if a case can be decided on either of two grounds, one involving a constitutional question, the other a question of statutory construction or general law, the Court will decide only the latter. . . . Appeals from the highest court of a state challenging its decision of a question under the federal Constitution are frequently dismissed because the judgment can be sustained on an independent state ground.[13]

PRESUMPTION OF CONSTITUTIONALITY

Justice Washington once wrote, "It is but a decent respect due to the wisdom, integrity and patriotism of the legislative body, by which any law is passed, to presume in favor of its validity, . . ." [14] The justices will normally presume that a statute is constitutional unless the opposite is clearly demonstrated. But the presumption of constitutionality is entertained by the Court much more strongly in some areas than others, and it has openly declared its particular suspicion of certain types of statutes such as those employing racial classifications and those imposing prior restraints on freedom of speech.[15] As with the cases and controversies rule, judicial activity has worn the presumption of constitutionality so thin in recent years that it is now only sporadically operative.

[13] Justice Brandeis concurring in *Ashwander* v. *Tennessee Valley Authority,* 297 U.S. 288, 346 (1936).

[14] Justice B. Washington in *Ogden* v. *Saunders,* 12 Wheat. 213 (1827).

[15] See *Korematsu* v. *United States,* 323 U.S. 214, 216 (1944); *New York Times* v. *United States,* 403 U.S. 713 (1971).

CONSTITUTIONAL STANDING

An individual has standing to challenge the constitutionality of a law only if his or her personal rights are directly affected by the operation of the statute. To have standing, one must show "not only that the statute is invalid, but that he [party invoking judicial power] has sustained or is immediately in danger of sustaining some direct injury as the result of its enforcement, and not merely that he suffers in some indefinite way in common with people generally." [16] "The Court will not pass upon the validity of a statute upon complaint of one who fails to show that he is injured by its operation." [17]

There are some very limited instances in which one may have standing to assert the constitutional rights of another.[18] Organizations may be granted standing to assert the rights of their members.[19] Until the 1970s injury alone was not enough. To have standing, a legal right had to be violated. In *Tennessee Electric Power Co.* v. *TVA,* 306 U.S. 118 (1939), the Court held that governmental action that threatens to injure an individual cannot be challenged "unless the right invaded is a legal right—one of property, one arising out of contract, one protected against tortious invasion, or one founded on a statute which confers a privilege." Today the legal right requirement has been reduced so far as to have practically disappeared. [See *Association of Data Processing Service Organizations* v. *Camp,* 397 U.S. 150 (1970).]

Although many states allow any taxpayer standing to challenge the legality of any state expenditure, taxpayers' suits have not been permitted in federal courts.[20] The Supreme Court has now opened the door somewhat, at least for challenges resting on specific guarantees of the Bill of Rights and directed at congressional expenditures under its Article I taxing and spending power. [*Flast* v. *Cohen,* 392 U.S. 83 (1968).]

That the Burger Court is not inclined to open the door on taxpayer suits any wider is to be seen in *United States* v. *Richardson,* 418 U.S. 166 (1974), in which the justices rejected for lack of standing a taxpayer's challenge to the provision of the Central Intelligence Agency Act that allows it, unlike other federal agencies, to account for its expenditures solely by the certificate of its Director. [See also *Valley Forge Christian College* v. *Americans United for Separation of Church and State, Inc.,* 102 S.Ct. 752 (1982).]

The current picture as to standing to claim rights directly under the Constitution is far from clear. (For standing under federal statutes, see Chapter 16.) Although dealing liberally with standing in many instances, particularly in cases involving birth control and abortion [see *Doe* v. *Bolton,* 410 U.S. 179 (1973)], the Burger Court has also handed down a cluster of decisions favoring a narrower

[16] *Frothingham* v. *Mellon,* 262 U.S. 447, 488 (1923).

[17] Justice Brandeis in *Ashwander* v. *TVA.*

[18] See *Barrows* v. *Jackson,* 346 U.S. 249 (1953); *Griswold* v. *Connecticut,* 381 U.S. 479 (1965); *Thornhill* v. *Alabama,* 310 U.S. 88 (1940); *Eisenstadt* v. *Baird,* 405 U.S. 438 (1972).

[19] See *NAACP v. Alabama,* 357 U.S. 449 (1958).

[20] *Massachusetts* v. *Mellon,* 262 U.S. 447 (1923).

view of standing. [See *S.* v. *D.*, 410 U.S. 614 (1973); and *Moose Lodge* v. *Irvis*, 407 U.S. 163 (1972).] One of the most notable of these is *Laird* v. *Tatum*, 408 U.S. 1 (1972), in which various activists brought suit to stop the surveillance of anti-Vietnam war protest activities by Army intelligence. In finding that the suitors had no standing, Chief Justice Burger wrote: "their claim, simply stated, is . . . that the very existence of the Army's data-gathering system produces a constitutionally impermissible chilling effect upon the exercise of their First Amendment rights. That alleged 'chilling' effect may perhaps be seen as arising from respondents' very perception of the system as inappropriate to the Army's role under our form of government, or as arising from respondents' beliefs that it is inherently dangerous for the military to be concerned with activities in the civilian sector, or as arising from respondents' less generalized yet speculative apprehensiveness that the Army may at some future date misuse the information in some way that would cause direct harm to respondents. Allegations of a subjective 'chill' are not an adequate substitute for a claim of specific present objective harm or a threat of specific future harm; . . ."

In *Schlesinger* v. *Reservists Committee to Stop the War*, 418 U.S. 208 (1974), a group of reserve officers challenged the membership of some congressmen in the armed forces reserves, citing Article I, Section 6, which provides that "no Person holding any Office under the United States, shall be a Member of either House during his continuance in Office." They alleged that because of their military obligations, the congressmen might slight their duties as representatives. The Court held that this "generalized citizen interest" in good government did not confer standing.

In a series of recent decisions, the Court has reemphasized that the cases and controversies rule of Article III and/or the "prudential standing rules" of the Court require that plaintiffs show something more than a "generalized grievance" in order to achieve standing. They must show "injury in fact" to themselves and establish that there is more than a speculative likelihood that the remedy requested will cure their own injury. Thus the Court has denied standing to poor persons who alleged that a town's zoning ordinances made it impossible for anyone to build low income housing that they might rent;[21] to indigents who sought to challenge a tax regulation that they argued encouraged private hospitals to deny free services to indigents;[22] and to blacks who sought relief from an alleged continuing pattern of racial discrimination by a local magistrate and judge in bail, sentencing, and jury fee payments.[23] In all these cases, the Court argued that the plaintiffs had not shown that they personally had been concretely injured. The poor in *Warth* had not shown that anyone proposed to build low rent housing in the town and was being denied permission to do so or that they personally would be in a position to rent the housing even if some were built. The poor in *Simon* could not show that any of them had personally been denied services by any particular hospital that they would

[21] *Warth* v. *Seldin*, 422 U.S. 490 (1975).

[22] *Simon* v. *Eastern Kentucky Welfare Rights Organization*, 426 U.S. 26 (1976).

[23] *O'Shea* v. *Littleton*, 414 U.S. 488 (1974).

have received if there had been no such tax regulation. The possibility that the black plaintiffs in *O'Shea* would at some future time be arrested and thus subjected to the practices of which they complained was, in the Court's view, purely speculative.

In *Rizzo* v. *Goode,* 423 U.S. 362 (1976), after finding that a few city police officers had committed a total of sixteen violations of citizens rights over the course of a year, a federal district court ordered city officials to draft "a comprehensive program for dealing adequately with civilian complaints" according to "guidelines" set by the court. The Supreme Court found this order improper as "an attempt by the federal judiciary to resolve a controversy between the entire citizenry of Philadelphia" and city officials about police review procedures. As to the individual plaintiffs, the Court said that their "claim to 'real and immediate' injury rests . . . upon what one of a small, unnamed minority of policemen might do to them in the future because of that unknown policeman's perception of departmental disciplinary procedures." The Court held this "attenuated hypothetical" was not enough to create standing.

Indigent, pregnant women were denied standing to challenge a statute cutting off federal funds for abortion on the ground that it violated the free exercise of religion clause of the First Amendment when they failed to show that any of them had sought an abortion for religious reasons. [*Harris* v. *McRae,* 448 U.S. 297 (1980). See also *H. L.* v. *Matheson,* 101 S.Ct. 1164 (1980).]

These decisions and others show a certain toughening in the Burger Court's attitude toward standing. It must be emphasized, however, that they occur precisely because of the recent liberalization in standing doctrines. All sorts of barely particularized complaints about the constitutionality or wisdom of various federal and state programs, which no lawyer would have dreamed of bringing into court thirty years ago, now stand a good chance of a favorable hearing by some judge somewhere. The Burger Court trims a few of the most extreme standing claims. Nevertheless, generally it allows standing to anyone injured in fact as well as to organizations whose members have been injured in fact. And once standing has been granted, the party is usually even free to plead injury to others rather than himself as the principal justification for the remedy he seeks.[24] Certainly when the Court itself is anxious to decide a constitutional question, it brushes aside standing problems. [See *Duke Power Co.* v. *North Carolina Environmental Group, Inc.,* 438 U.S. 59 (1978).]

The liberalization of the rules on class actions (see Chapter 16) and the expanded use of the declaratory judgment[25] have also allowed more interests into court to make constitutional claims and have further reduced the bite of the cases and controversies rule.

[24] See *Village of Arlington Heights* v. *Metropolitan Housing Development Corp.,* 429 U.S. 252 (1977); *Singleton* v. *Wulff,* 428 U.S. 106 (1976); *Village of Schaumburg* v. *Citizens for a Better Environment,* 444 U.S. 620 (1980).

[25] See *Katzenbach* v. *McClung,* 379 U.S. 294 (1964). Under the Federal Declaratory Judgment Act, a party threatened with enforcement of a statute, but not yet actually prosecuted under it, may sue for a declaration that the statute is unconstitutional.

Background of Marbury *v.* Madison

In *Marbury* v. *Madison,* (p. 83) Chief Justice Marshall took a court of law and "made it into an organ of government." [26] To understand fully Marshall's decision, one must know something of the historical setting in which it was decided.

John Marshall was an ardent Federalist who had seen his party, under the leadership of John Adams, barely win the Presidency in 1796. Major opposition to Federalist policies came from the Republican party, led by Jefferson. The Federalists, in accordance with the views of Hamilton, favored a strong national government and keenly distrusted the people's capacity for self-government. The Jeffersonians, on the other hand, were extremely suspicious of centralized national authority and had greater faith in the masses.

In the summer of 1798, the Adams administration pushed through Congress the drastic Alien and Sedition Acts, which were designed principally to curtail the vigorous and allegedly intemperate criticisms leveled against Federalist office-holders by the Jeffersonians. The Alien and Sedition Acts were actually composed of four separate measures. Three measures, known as the Alien Acts, dealt with the problems presented by "radical" foreigners, who were largely supporters of Jefferson, whereas the Sedition Act was specifically designed to subdue criticism of the administration by the Republican "rabble." Vigorous enforcement of the Sedition Act by Federalist judges enraged the Republicans; their resentment found expression in the Virginia and Kentucky Resolutions of 1798 (written by Madison and Jefferson), which declared that the Alien and Sedition Acts were unconstitutional and that the states should assert their rights over Congress. These resolutions were bitterly debated as part of the presidential campaign of 1800, and the unpopularity of the Alien and Sedition Acts undoubtedly contributed to the downfall of the Federalists. In the election of 1800, Jefferson and the Republican party won a decisive victory.

But the Federalists were not to be denied. They tried to maintain their influence by finding positions for loyal Federalists in the period between the election of 1800 and the inauguration of Jefferson on March 4, 1801. In January 1801, President Adams named his Secretary of State, John Marshall, to be Chief Justice of the United States. The "lame duck" Congress passed the Judiciary Act of 1801, which created a number of new judgeships in the lower courts. The act also provided that the next vacancy on the Supreme Court should not be filled, thereby reducing the membership of the Court from six to five justices and making impossible an appointment by the new Republican President. Another law of the lame duck Congress empowered President Adams to appoint forty-two new justices of the peace for the District of Columbia. Loyal Federalists, of course, were appointed. But the time was short, and some of the commissions of office for the District of Columbia were not signed by President Adams

[26] Charles P. Curtis, Jr., *Lions Under the Throne* (Boston: Houghton, 1947), p. ix.

until midnight on March 3, 1801. As a result, a number of commissions were in the office of John Marshall, the outgoing Secretary of State, awaiting delivery when Jefferson became President. Jefferson ordered his new Secretary of State, James Madison, not to deliver some of the commissions to the "midnight appointees." Thus the stage was set for the case of *Marbury* v. *Madison.*

William Marbury was one of the midnight appointees whose commissions as justices of the peace for the District of Columbia had not been delivered. He and three other appointees petitioned the Supreme Court for a writ of mandamus to compel Secretary of State Madison to deliver the commissions. (A mandamus is an ancient common law writ that originated in England. In this country it is granted by American courts in the name of the state to compel a corporation, officer, or inferior court to perform a particular duty required by law. The violation of a writ of mandamus constitutes a contempt of the court that issued it.) In December 1801, Chief Justice Marshall requested that Madison show cause (give any possible lawful reasons) why the writ of mandamus should not be issued. Madison ignored the request. The prevalent opinion was that Marshall would order Madison to deliver the commissions and thereby precipitate a struggle between the Court and the executive branch. But Marshall did no such thing. Although he scolded Madison for his failure to deliver the commissions, he held that Madison could not be compelled to act, because the statute cited by Marbury and the three other appointees was unconstitutional. Thus, Marshall established the power of the Supreme Court to declare acts of Congress unconstitutional.

REASONS FOR MARSHALL'S DECISION

Marshall actually went out of his way to declare Section 13 of the Judiciary Act void, for he might easily have avoided the issue of constitutionality in a number of ways. But *Marshall did not wish to avoid the issue of constitutionality.* His decision was largely political. When *Marbury* v. *Madison* came before the Court, the judiciary was under severe attack. In 1802, the Republican Congress had repealed the Judiciary Act of 1801. This action removed the new Federalist judges from the bench and added a new justice to the Supreme Court. Another law passed during the same year provided that the Court should hold one session, rather than two, a year. The effect of this law was to cause a lapse of almost a full year in the Court's sessions. The Republican Congress also debated the possibility of using the impeachment process to remove Federalist judges for alleged misconduct in office. In *Marbury* v. *Madison,* Marshall saw an opportunity to avoid a collision with his arch enemy, Jefferson, and at the same time strike a blow for the judiciary. He "was aware of a rising opposition to the theory of judicial control over legislation, and he no doubt concluded that the wavering opinions on federal judicial supremacy needed to be replaced by a positive and unmistakable assertion of authority." [27] And how

[27] Charles C. Haines, *The American Doctrine of Judicial Supremacy* (New York: Macmillan, 1914), p. 170.

could Jefferson and his followers effectively object, for, by refusing to order Madison to deliver the commissions, Marshall had decided in favor of the Republicans!

It is almost inconceivable that a decision that "has proved to be one of those very special occurrences that mark an epoch in the life of the Republic" [28] should emerge out of such a trivial set of circumstances. William Marbury was an obscure gentleman. The office of justice of the peace is a relatively insignificant one. And yet just such seemingly unimportant private litigations are the vehicles through which fundamental constitutional issues are ultimately determined in the United States.

Although *Marbury* v. *Madison* (p. 83) established the practice of judicial review, no statute of Congress was held invalid again until the *Dred Scott* case in 1857. There the Court held that the Missouri Compromise Act of 1820, which excluded slavery from the territories, was unconstitutional. The *Dred Scott* case represented "an important enlargement of the scope of judicial review over the doctrine of *Marbury* v. *Madison.* Marshall's early decision had held that the Court could refuse to enforce laws purporting to change its own jurisdiction when the Court believed those laws to be invalid. In the *Dred Scott* case, Taney and his colleagues go much farther. They hold that the judgment of Congress as to the scope of one of its own legislative powers, this time a power in no way concerning the Court, is wrong and that the act so passed is unconstitutional. The Court, in other words, takes on the task of determining whether Congress has exercised powers that the Constitution has not delegated to it." [29]

OPPOSITION TO MARSHALL'S DECISION

The decision in *Marbury* v. *Madison* is not classified among Marshall's great masterpieces. His reasoning is persuasive and impressive, but it can be refuted. The most effective answer to Marshall's argument was given in a dissenting opinion written by Judge Gibson of the Supreme Court of Pennsylvania in the relatively unimportant case of *Eakin* v. *Raub* (p. 87), decided in 1825. *Eakin* v. *Raub* cannot be analyzed here in conformity with the outline suggested in Chapter 2, but Judge Gibson's arguments in opposition to the doctrine of judicial review can be extracted easily.[30]

[28] Edmond Cahn, ed., *Supreme Court and Supreme Law* (Bloomington: Indiana University Press, 1954), p. 25.

[29] Robert E. Cushman, *The Role of the Supreme Court in a Democratic Nation* (Urbana: University of Illinois Press, 1938), p. 30.

[30] Twenty years later, Judge Gibson stated that he no longer subscribed to the views announced in his dissenting opinion for two reasons: "First, because a recently held state constitutional convention [Pennsylvania], by its silence on the subject, had sanctioned the right of the court to deal with the acts of the legislature; and, next, 'from the experience of the necessity of the case.'" Robert von Moschzisker, *Judicial Review of Legislation* (Washington, D.C.: National Association for Constitutional Government, 1923), p. 91.

Political Questions and Baker *v.* Carr

As one writer has said, the doctrine of political questions is a "magical formula that has the practical result of relieving a Court of the necessity of thinking further about a particular problem. It is a device for transferring the responsibility for decision of questions to another branch of the government; and it may sometimes operate to leave a problem in mid-air so that no branch decides it."[31] A number of questions have been termed *political* by the courts. These include questions arising out of the conduct of foreign relations [see *Goldwater* v. *Carter,* 444 U.S. 996 (1979)] and some questions relating to the amending process of the Constitution, as noted subsequently in this chapter in the discussion of *Coleman* v. *Miller.* Since the case of *Luther* v. *Borden* (p. 88), the Supreme Court has held consistently that what constitutes a "republican form of government" is a political question. For a long time questions involving the reapportionment of districts for congressional representation were deemed political by some of the justices. The crucial case for many years was *Colegrove* v. *Green,* 328 U.S. 549 (1946). Only seven justices voted in *Colegrove.* Justice Frankfurter wrote the opinion of the Court, joined by Justices Reed and Burton. He ruled that districting was a political question beyond the reach of the courts. Justices Black, Douglas, and Murphy dissented, arguing that the Court should declare the state apportionment statute in question unconstitutional. Justice Rutledge, the crucial seventh vote to break the 3 to 3 tie, argued that the Court did have the power to intervene, but should exercise its discretion not to do so in this particular case. (Colegrove had asked for an injunction—that is, a court order—forbidding state officials to hold an election under the old apportionment law. An injunction is an "equitable remedy." Its historical origin is not in the common law, but in the equity courts of England. Such courts had "equitable discretion" to refuse a remedy when it would do more harm than good. Modern courts inherit this discretion when dealing with equitable remedies.) Thus, if one counts Justice Rutledge's vote one way, there is a 4 to 3 majority in *Colegrove* not to intervene. If one counts it the other way, there is a 4 to 3 vote that the Court does have the power to intervene when it wants to.

In the case of *Gomillion* v. *Lightfoot,* 364 U.S. 339 (1960), the Court seemed to weaken the *Colegrove* rule, for it held unconstitutional an Alabama state law redefining the boundaries of the city of Tuskegee so as to exclude nearly all the black voters without removing a single white voter. Although the *Gomillion* case was concerned chiefly with racial discrimination rather than with reapportionment, it has been viewed as a stepping stone for the reexamination of *Colegrove* v. *Green.* This occurred in the now famous case of *Baker* v. *Carr* (p. 91), in which the federal courts were held to have jurisdiction to scrutinize the fairness of legislative apportionments under the Fourteenth

[31] John P. Frank, "Political Questions," in Cahn, ed., op. cit., p. 37.

Amendment and to take steps to assure that serious inequities are wiped out. Thus, *Baker* v. *Carr* "is not only an obviously important case. It is a critically different kind of case *because it calls upon the courts to sit in judgment on the possession and distribution of political power.* In the context of more than a century and a half of judicial review this is something distinctly new in the function of constitutional interpretation and application." [32] The *Baker* case "rests on a principle of judicial necessity to act to preserve the very essence of the democratic process. . . . It was, and remains, a very large step in the direction of close judicial scrutiny of the politics of the people. As 'an eminently realistic body of men,' it is difficult to suppose that the Court was uninfluenced by the fact of exhaustion of nonjudicial modes of relief over a period of several decades." [33]

Unlike most Supreme Court decisions, *Baker* v. *Carr* had an almost immediate impact. In fact, never before, after an assertion of expanded jurisdiction by the Court, has there been such a flurry of widespread political and judicial activity. Almost within hours of the decision, litigation was begun in state and federal courts challenging the existing schemes of legislative representation. At one time or another, nearly every state has been involved in litigation, and more than half of them have had apportionment arrangements of one sort or another overturned by the courts. In Georgia, for example, the legislature acted under pressure to modify the *county unit* system to provide fewer inequities in party primaries. The Georgia county unit scheme assigned to each county electoral votes that went to the candidate receiving the highest popular votes. It was designed principally to disfranchise the urban black population. Relying heavily on *Baker* v. *Carr,* a federal district court held that Georgia's revised county unit system violated the equal protection clause of the Fourteenth Amendment. In *Gray* v. *Sanders,* 372 U.S. 368 (1963), the Supreme Court agreed with the lower court. Moreover, the highest Court further held that the equal protection clause of the Fourteenth Amendment requires that every voter be equal to every other voter in the state when he casts his ballot in a statewide election. Speaking for the Court over the lone dissent of Justice Harlan, Justice Douglas wrote:

> Georgia gives every qualified voter one vote in a statewide election; but in counting those votes she employs the county unit system which in end result weights the rural vote more heavily than the urban vote and weights some small rural counties heavier than other larger counties. . . . How can one person be given twice or ten times the voting power of another person in a statewide election merely because he lives in a rural area or because he lives in the smallest rural county? Once the geographical unit for which a representative is chosen is designated, all who participate in

[32] Robert G. Dixon, Jr., "Reapportionment and Political Rejuvenation: A Devil's Advocate View," paper delivered at meeting of American Society for Legal History, Williamsburg, Va. (March 23, 1963).

[33] Robert G. Dixon, Jr., "Legislative Apportionment and the Federal Constitution," *Law and Contemporary Problems,* Vol. 27 (Summer 1962), p. 384. More generally, see Martin Shapiro, *Law and Politics in the Supreme Court* (New York: Free Press, 1965), Ch. 5.

the election are to have an equal vote. . . . The conception of political equality . . . can mean only one thing—one person, one vote.[34]

These decisions culminated in the Court's landmark opinion in *Wesberry* v. *Sanders* (p. 105), where it was held that, under Article I, Section 2, of the Constitution, congressional districts within each state must be roughly equal in population. Thus, for the first time since *Baker* v. *Carr,* the Court imposed a definitive yardstick on the makeup of political districts. Before delivering his stinging dissent in the case, Justice Harlan remarked from the bench: "I consider this occasion certainly the most solemn since I have been on this Court. And I think one would have to search the pages of history to find a case whose importance equals what we have decided to-day." [35]

In Georgia, where the *Wesberry* case had originated, the reaction was unbelievably swift. Four days after the decision, the state legislature, in a wild and tumultuous session, divided the heavily populated Atlanta district in two, each with its own congressman, and redrew the lines of other districts to provide units of near-equal size in terms of population. In June 1964, the Court followed the basic principle of the *Wesberry* case and held, in *Reynolds* v. *Sims,* 377 U.S. 533 (1964), that the equal protection clause requires that districts in *both* houses of a state legislature must also be substantially equal in population. In *Mahan* v. *Howell,* 410 U.S. 315 (1973), the Court accepted a state legislative apportionment involving a 16.4 per cent spread between the largest and smallest districts that resulted from respecting traditional county and city lines in constructing district boundaries. And in *Whitcomb* v. *Chavis,* 403 U.S. 124 (1971), the justices accepted Indiana state senate districting involving some single- and some multimember districts over objections that the arrangement diluted the voting power of residents of the multimember districts. (See also the discussion of *United Jewish Organizations of Williamsburgh, Inc.* v. *Carey* in Chapter 13. and the section titled "Elections" in Chapter 14.)

Another aspect of the political questions doctrine is the notion that the Court ought not to decide questions that are clearly assigned by the Constitution to other branches of government. [See *Pfizer, Inc.* v. *Government of India,* 434 U.S. 308 (1978).] Nevertheless, it has directly intervened in the seating of legislators. It declared the Georgia legislature's refusal to seat an elected candidate because of statements he had made a violation of freedom of speech guarantees in *Bond* v. *Floyd,* 385 U.S. 116 (1966). The Court also held that the power of Congress to determine the qualifications of its members extended only to those

[34] There has been a veritable flood of materials on *Baker* v. *Carr* and its aftermath. The following are among the most useful commentaries: Paul T. David and Ralph Eisenberg, *State Legislative Redistricting: Major Issues in the Wake of Judicial Decision* (Chicago: Public Administration Service, 1962); Malcolm E. Jewell, ed., *The Politics of Reapportionment* (New York: Atherton, 1962); Phil C. Neal, "*Baker* v. *Carr:* Politics in Search of Law," *Supreme Court Review* (1962), pp. 252–327; "Symposium on the Electoral Process," 2 parts, *Law and Contemporary Problems,* Vol. 27 (Spring and Summer 1962); Gordon E. Baker, *The Reapportionment Revolution* (New York: Random, 1966); Robert G. Dixon, Jr., *Democratic Representation: Reapportionment in Law and Politics* (New York: Oxford U.P., 1969).

[35] *The New York Times* (Feb. 18, 1964), p. 1.

qualifications (age, citizenship, place of residence) specifically provided in the Constitution and not to the prospective member's past behavior. However, the Court carefully preserved Congress's power to expel members as specified in Article I, Section 5.[36] In *United States* v. *Nixon* (p. 197) the President claimed that the scope of his executive privilege to withhold information was a political question assigned exclusively to the executive branch. The Court refused to treat executive privilege as a political question.

Changing the Constitution

Article V divides the procedure for formal amendment into two parts: *proposal* and *ratification.*[37] Amendments are proposed in two ways: (1) by a two-thirds vote of both houses of Congress and (2) by national constitutional conventions called by Congress upon application of two thirds of the state legislatures. All of the twenty-six amendments have been proposed by Congress. Amendments are ratified by two methods, also: (1) by the legislatures of three fourths of the states or (2) by special conventions in three fourths of the states. All of the amendments, with the exception of the Twenty-first, which repealed the Eighteenth, or Prohibition, Amendment, have been ratified by state legislatures. Congress has sole power to determine which method of ratification is to be used.[38]

A number of questions pertaining to the amending process have had to be answered by the Supreme Court. In the first case involving the procedure for amending the Constitution, the Court held that the President's approval is not required for a proposed amendment.[39] Much later, the Court held that the two-thirds vote required for proposing amendments is a "vote of two thirds of the members present—assuming the presence of a quorum, and not a vote of two thirds of the entire membership, present and absent." [40]

The Court has rendered a number of decisions on the procedure for ratification. In *Hawke* v. *Smith,* 253 U.S. 221 (1920), it held that the state of Ohio could not provide for the ratification of the Eighteenth Amendment by popular referendum, because such a procedure altered the plain language of Article V, which provides for ratification by state "legislatures" rather than by direct action of the people. The Court noted that the power to ratify a proposed amendment "has its source in the federal Constitution. The act of ratification by the state derives its authority from the federal Constitution, to which the state and its people have alike assented. . . . Any other view might lead to endless confusion in the manner of ratification of federal amendments." Despite the decision in

[36] *Powell* v. *McCormack,* 395 U.S. 486 (1969).

[37] Lester B. Orfield, *The Amending of the Federal Constitution* (Ann Arbor: University of Michigan Press, 1942), p. 1.

[38] *United States* v. *Sprague,* 282 U.S. 716 (1931).

[39] *Hollingsworth* v. *Virginia,* 3 Dall. 378 (1798). Neither is the Governor's approval required in the ratification process.

[40] *National Prohibition Cases,* 253 U.S. 350 (1920).

Hawke v. *Smith,* ratification of an amendment by specially chosen conventions in the states seems to bring about the same result as a referendum vote, if our experience with the ratification of the Twenty-first Amendment provides any lessons. In that instance, the state ratifying conventions did not act as deliberative assemblies. They simply recorded the vote of the people.

Article V does not stipulate any time limit for the ratification of amendments. When the Eighteenth Amendment was proposed, Congress, for the first time, provided that ratification was to be completed within seven years. In *Dillon* v. *Gloss,* 256 U.S. 368 (1921), the Supreme Court held that Congress had the power to impose a time limitation because Article V clearly implied that the "ratification must be within some reasonable time after the proposal." The Court felt that seven years was a reasonable limit. Congress also set a time limit of seven years for the ratification of the Twentieth, Twenty-first, and Twenty-second Amendments. Each of these was ratified long before the seven-year period expired. The Court has never decided whether a state legislature may revoke its act of ratification before enough other states have ratified to bring a proposed amendment into effect.

Until 1939, when *Coleman* v. *Miller* [307 U.S. 433 (1939)] was decided, the general assumption was that all the steps in the amending process were justiciable. But in the *Coleman* case, the Court held that *some* steps in the amending process were political questions that had to be resolved by Congress. Whether the decision of *Coleman* v. *Miller* means that the Supreme Court will not take jurisdiction in any case involving the amending process remains to be seen. In this connection, it is important to note the concurring opinion, in which four justices reasoned that Congress has *exclusive* control over the amending process. "The process itself is 'political' in its entirety, from submission until an amendment becomes part of the Constitution, and is not subject to judicial guidance, control, or interference at any point."

Federal Courts and State Law

Article III of the Constitution provides that the federal judicial power shall extend to controversies between citizens of different states. Thus, for example, if Smith, a citizen of Pennsylvania, wrecks his automobile in a collision on an Indiana highway with Jones, a citizen of Indiana, Smith may sue Jones in a federal district court rather than in an Indiana state court if the amount involved is $10,000 or more. Smith, thereby, does not suffer from any disadvantages that might result from suing in Jones's home state. Before the federal courts, both Smith and Jones stand equally regardless of their citizenship. But a federal court is then faced with the question of what law to apply. Should it apply the law of Indiana or Pennsylvania? Or is there some federal common law that may be applied?

Section 34 of the Judiciary Act of 1789 provided that "the laws of the several states, except where the Constitution, treaties, or statutes of the United States otherwise require or provide, shall be regarded as rules of decision in trials at common law, in the courts of the United States, in cases where they apply." But in *Swift* v. *Tyson,* 16 Pet. 1 (1842), the Supreme Court ruled that the federal courts could disregard state court decisions in diversity of citizenship cases involving matters of general jurisprudence and commercial law. In delivering the opinion of the Court in *Swift* v. *Tyson,* Justice Story construed the word *laws* in Section 34 of the Judiciary Act of 1789 to mean "enactments promulgated by the legislative authority" of the state only. Therefore, decisions of state courts were not binding on the federal courts, and the latter were left free to apply and expand their own common law in many fields.

"An important practical justification of Story's decision was the belief that the federal courts, headed by the Supreme Court, would bring about a uniform interpretation of the common law, which otherwise would be applied differently in different localities with great confusion as the result. The expected order was not achieved. The states continued to interpret the common law in their own way, while the federal courts added to the confusion by building up one more interpretation. Individual justices had protested from time to time against the further expansion of the rule in *Swift* v. *Tyson.*"[41] Finally, in *Erie Railroad Co.* v. *Tompkins,* the Supreme Court overruled *Swift* v. *Tyson* and, thereby, reversed a ninety-six-year-old precedent. Since the Erie Railroad decision in 1938, the federal courts have followed decisions of state courts in diversity cases. However, "the law growing out of *Erie Railroad Co.* v. *Tompkins* pertains only to litigation in the federal courts by virtue of the diversity of citizenship of the parties and involving state-created rights. Where an action is in the federal court on some other jurisdictional basis or involves rights created or protected by federal law, federal facts or policies, the doctrine of *Erie Railroad Co.* v. *Tompkins* does not apply." [42]

WILLIAM MARBURY *v.* JAMES MADISON,
Secretary of State of the United States
1 Cranch 137; 2 L. Ed. 60 (1803)

MR. JUSTICE MARSHALL delivered the opinion of the Court:

At the last term, on the affidavits then read and filed with the clerk, a rule was granted in this case, requiring the Secretary of State to show cause why a mandamus should not issue, directing him to deliver to William Marbury his commission as a justice of the peace for the county of Washington, in the District of Columbia.

No cause has been shown, and the present motion is for mandamus. The peculiar delicacy of this case, the novelty of some of its circumstances, and the real difficulty attending the points which occur in it, require a complete exposition of the principles on which the opinion to be given by the court is founded.

These principles have been, on the side of the applicant, very ably argued at the bar. In rendering the opinion of the court, there will be some departure in form, though not in substance, from the points stated in that argument.

[41] Carl B. Swisher, *American Constitutional Development* (New York: Houghton, 1943), p. 977.

[42] Herbert F. Goodrich, *Handbook of the Conflict of Laws* (St. Paul, Minn.: West Publishing Co., 1949), pp. 44–45.

In the order in which the court has viewed this subject, the following questions have been considered and decided.

1. Has the applicant a right to the commission he demands?

2. If he has a right, and that right has been violated, do the laws of his country afford him a remedy?

3. If they do afford him a remedy, is it a *mandamus* issuing from this court?

. . . It is . . . the opinion of the court,

1. That, by signing the commission of Mr. Marbury, the President of the United States appointed him a justice of peace, for the county of Washington in the District of Columbia; and that the seal of the United States, affixed thereto by the Secretary of State, is conclusive testimony of the verity of the signature, and of the completion of the appointment; and that the appointment conferred on him a legal right to the office for the space of five years.

2. That, having this legal title to the office, he has a consequent right to the commission; a refusal to deliver which, is a plain violation of that right, for which the laws of this country afford him a remedy.

It remains to be enquired whether,

3. He is entitled to the remedy for which he applies. This depends on,

1. The nature of the writ applied for and,

2. The power of this court.

. . . This, then, is a plain case for a mandamus, either to deliver the commission, or a copy of it from the record; and it only remains to be enquired, whether it can issue from this court.

The act to establish the judicial courts of the United States authorizes the Supreme Court "to issue writs of mandamus in cases warranted by the principles and usages of law, to any courts appointed, or persons holding office, under the authority of the United States."

The Secretary of State, being a person holding an office under the authority of the United States, is precisely within the letter of the description, and if this court is not authorized to issue a writ of mandamus to such an officer, it must be because the law is unconstitutional, and therefore absolutely incapable of conferring the authority, and assigning the duties which its words purport to confer and assign.

The Constitution vests the whole judicial power of the United States in one supreme court, and such inferior courts as Congress shall, from time to time, ordain and establish. This power is expressly extended to all cases arising under the laws of the United States; and, consequently, in some form, may be exercised over the present case; because the right claimed is given by a law of the United States.

In the distribution of this power it is declared that "the Supreme Court shall have original jurisdiction in all cases affecting ambassadors, other public ministers and consuls, and those in which a state shall be a party. In all other cases, the Supreme Court shall have appellate jurisdiction."

It has been insisted at the bar, that, as the original grant of jurisdiction to the Supreme and inferior courts, is general, and the clause assigning original jurisdiction to the Supreme Court contains no negative or restrictive words, the power remains to the legislature to assign original jurisdiction to that court in other cases than those specified in the article which has been recited; provided those cases belong to the judicial power of the United States.

If it had been intended to leave it in the discretion of the legislature to apportion the judicial power between the Supreme and inferior courts according to the will of that body, it would certainly have been useless to have proceeded further than to have defined the judicial power, and the tribunals in which it should be vested. The subsequent part of the section is mere surplusage, is entirely without meaning. If Congress remains at liberty to give this court appellate jurisdiction, where the Constitution has declared their jurisdiction shall be original; and original jurisdiction where the Constitution has declared it shall be appellate, the distribution of jurisdiction made in the Constitution is form without substance.

Affirmative words are often, in their operation, negative of other objects than those affirmed; and in this case, a negative or exclusive sense must be given to them, or they have no operation at all.

It cannot be presumed that any clause in the Constitution is intended to be without effect; and, therefore, such a construction is inadmissible unless the words require it.

. . . To enable this court, then to issue a mandamus, it must be shown to be an exercise of appellate jurisdiction, or to be necessary to enable them to exercise appellate jurisdiction.

It has been stated at the bar that the appellate jurisdiction may be exercised in a variety of forms, and that, if it be the will of the legislature that a mandamus should be used for that purpose, that will must be obeyed. This is true, yet the jurisdiction must be appellate, not original.

It is the essential criterion of appellate jurisdiction that it revises and corrects the proceedings in a cause already instituted, and does not create that cause. Although, therefore, a mandamus may be directed to courts, yet to issue such a writ to an officer for the delivery of a paper is in effect the same as to sustain an original action for that paper, and, therefore, seems not to belong to appellate, but to original jurisdiction. Neither is it necessary, in such a case as this, to enable the court to exercise its appellate jurisdiction.

The authority, therefore, given to the Supreme Court by the act establishing the judicial courts of the United States, to issue writs of mandamus to public officers, appears not to be warranted by the Constitution; and it becomes necessary to inquire whether a jurisdiction so conferred can be exercised.

The question, whether an act repugnant to the Constitution can become the law of the land, is a question deeply interesting to the United States; but, happily, not of an intricacy proportioned to its interest. It seems only necessary to recognize certain principles, supposed to have been long and well established, to decide it.

That the people have an original right to establish, for their future government, such principles as, in their opinion, shall most conduce to their own happiness is the basis on which the whole American fabric had been erected. The exercise of this original right is a very great exertion; nor can it, nor ought it, to be frequently repeated. The principles, therefore, so established, are deemed fundamental. And as the authority from which they proceed is supreme, and can seldom act, they are designed to be permanent.

This original and supreme will organizes the government, and assigns to different departments their respective powers. It may either stop here, or establish certain limits not to be transcended by those departments.

The government of the United States is of the latter description. The powers of the legislature are defined and limited; and that those limits may not be mistaken, or forgotten, the Constitution is written. To what purpose are powers limited, and to what purpose is that limitation committed to writing, if these limits may, at any time, be passed by those intended to be restrained? The distinction between a government with limited and unlimited powers is abolished if those limits do not confine the persons on whom they are imposed, and if acts prohibited and acts allowed are of equal obligation. It is a proposition too plain to be contested, that the Constitution controls any legislative act repugnant to it; or, that the legislature may alter the Constitution by an ordinary act.

Between these alternatives there is no middle ground. The Constitution is either a superior paramount law, unchangeable by ordinary means, or it is on a level with ordinary legislative acts, and, like other acts, is alterable when the legislature shall please to alter it.

If the former part of the alternative be true, then a legislative act contrary to the Constitution is not law: if the latter part be true, then written constitutions are absurd attempts on the part of the people to limit a power in its own nature illimitable.

Certainly all those who have framed written constitutions contemplate them as forming the fundamental and paramount law of the nation, and consequently, the theory of every such government must be, that an act of the legislature, repugnant to the constitution, is void.

This theory is essentially attached to a written constitution, and is, consequently, to be considered by this court as one of the fundamental principles of our society. It is not therefore to be lost sight of in the further consideration of this subject.

If an act of the legislature, repugnant to the Constitution, is void, does it, notwithstanding its invalidity, bind the courts, and oblige them to give it effect? Or, in other words, though it be not law, does it constitute a rule as operative as if it was a law? This would be to overthrow in fact what was established in theory; and would seem, at first view, an absurdity too gross to be insisted on. It shall, however, receive a more attentive consideration.

It is emphatically the province and duty of the judicial department to say what the law is. Those who apply the rule to particular cases must, of necessity, expound and interpret that rule. If two laws conflict with each other, the courts must decide on the operation of each.

So if a law be in opposition to the Constitution; if both the law and the Constitution apply to a particular case, so that the court must either decide that case conformably to the law, disregarding the Constitution; or conformably to the Constitution, disregarding the law; the court must determine which of these conflicting rules governs the case. This is of the very essence of judicial duty.

If, then, the courts are to regard the Constitution, and the Constitution is superior to any ordinary act of the legislature, the Constitution, and not such ordinary act, must govern the case to which they both apply.

Those, then, who controvert the principle that the Constitution is to be considered, in court, as a paramount law, are reduced to the necessity of maintaining that courts must close their eyes on the Constitution, and see only the law.

This doctrine would subvert the very foundation of all written constitutions. It would declare that an act which, according to the principles and theory of our government, is entirely void, is yet, in practice, completely obligatory. It would declare that if the legislature shall do what is expressly forbidden, such act, notwithstanding the express prohibition, is in reality effectual. It would be giving to the legislature a practical and real omnipotence, with the same breath which professes to restrict their powers within narrow limits. It is prescribing limits and declaring that those limits may be passed at pleasure.

That it thus reduces to nothing what we have deemed the greatest improvement on political institutions—a written constitution—would of itself be sufficient, in America, where written constitutions have been viewed with so much reverence, for rejecting the construction. But the peculiar expressions of the Constitution of the United States furnish additional arguments in favor of its rejection.

The judicial power of the United States is extended to all cases arising under the Constitution.

Could it be the intention of those who gave this power to say that, in using it, the Constitution should not be looked into? That a case arising under the Constitution should be decided without examining the instrument under which it rises?

This is too extravagant to be maintained.

In some cases then, the Constitution must be looked into by the judges. And if they can open it at all, what part of it are they forbidden to read or to obey?

There are many other parts of the Constitution which serve to illustrate this subject.

It is declared that "no tax or duty shall be laid on articles exported from any state." Suppose a duty on the export of cotton, of tobacco, or of flour; and a suit instituted to recover it. Ought judgment to be rendered in such a case? Ought the judges to close their eyes on the Constitution, and see only the law?

The Constitution declares that "no bill of attainder or ex post facto law shall be passed."

If, however, such a bill should be passed and a person should be prosecuted under it; must the court condemn to death those victims whom the Constitution endeavours to preserve?

"No person," says the Constitution, "shall be convicted of treason unless on the testimony of two witnesses to the same overt act, or on confession in open court."

Here the language of the Constitution is addressed especially to the courts. It prescribes, directly for them, a rule of evidence not to be departed from. If the legislature should change that rule, and declare *one* witness, or a confession *out* of court, sufficient for conviction, must the constitutional principle yield to the legislative act?

From these, and many other selections which might be made, it is apparent that the framers of the Constitution contemplated that instrument as a rule for the government of *courts,* as well as of the legislature.

Why otherwise does it direct the judges to take an oath to support it? This oath certainly applies in an especial manner to their conduct in their official character. How immoral to impose it on them, if they were to be used as the instruments, and the knowing instruments, for violating what they swear to support?

The oath of office, too, imposed by the legislature, is completely demonstrative of the legislative opinion on this subject. It is in these words: "I do solemnly swear that I will administer justice without respect to persons, and do equal right to the poor and to the rich; and that I will faithfully and impartially discharge all the duties incumbent on me as——, according to the best of my abilities and understanding agreeably to the *Constitution* and laws of the United States."

Why does a judge swear to discharge his duties agreeably to the Constitution of the United States, if that Constitution forms no rule for his government? If it is closed upon him, and cannot be inspected by him?

If such be the real state of things, this is worse than solemn mockery. To prescribe, or to take this oath, becomes equally a crime.

It is also not entirely unworthy of observation that, in declaring what shall be the *supreme* law of the land, the *Constitution* itself is first mentioned; and not the laws of the United States generally, but those only which shall be made in *pursuance* of the Constitution, have that rank.

Thus, the particular phraseology of the Constitution of the United States confirms and strengthens the principle, supposed to be essential to all written constitutions, that a law repugnant to the Constitution is void; and that *courts,* as well as other departments, are bound by that instrument.

The rule must be

Discharged.

EAKIN *v.* RAUB

12 Sergeant and Rawle (Pa. Supreme Court) 330 (1825)

JUDGE GIBSON:

I am aware that a right to declare all unconstitutional acts void . . . is generally held as a professional dogma; but I apprehend rather as a matter of faith than of reason. I admit that I once embraced the same doctrine, but without examination, and I shall therefore state the arguments that impelled me to abandon it, with great respect for those by whom it is still maintained. But I may premise, that it is not a little remarkable that, although the right in question has all along been claimed by the judiciary, no judge has ventured to discuss it, except Chief Justice Marshall, and if the argument of a jurist so distinguished for the strength of his ratiocinative powers be found inconclusive, it may fairly be set down to the weakness of the position which he attempts to defend. . . .

The ordinary and essential powers of the judiciary do not extend to the annulling of an act of the legislature. . . .

The Constitution and the right of the legislature to pass the act, may be in collision. But is that a legitimate subject for judicial determination? If it be, the judiciary must be a peculiar organ, to revise the proceedings of the legislature, and to correct its mistakes; and in what part of the Constitution are we to look for this proud pre-eminence? Viewing the matter in the opposite direction, what would be thought of an act of assembly in which it should be declared that the Supreme Court had, in a particular case, put a wrong construction on the Constitution of the United States, and that the judgment should therefore be reversed? It would doubtless be thought a usurpation of judicial power. But it is by no means clear that to declare a law void which has been enacted according to the forms prescribed in the Constitution is not a usurpation of legislative power. . . .

But it has been said to be emphatically the business of the judiciary to ascertain and pronounce what the law is; and that this necessarily involves a consideration of the Constitution. It does so; but how far? If the judiciary will inquire into anything besides the form of enactment, where shall it stop? There must be some point of limitation to such an inquiry; for no one will pretend that a judge would be justifiable in calling for the election returns, or scrutinizing the qualifications for those who composed the legislature. . . .

Everyone knows how seldom men think exactly alike on ordinary subjects; and a government constructed on the principle of assent by all its parts would be inadequate to the most simple operations. The notion of a complication of counterchecks has been carried to an extent in theory of which the framers of the Constitution never dreamt. When the entire sovereignty was separated into its elementary parts, and distributed to the appropriate branches, all things incident to the exercise of its powers were committed to each branch exclusively. The negative which each part of the legislature may exercise, in regard to the acts of the other, was thought sufficient to prevent material infractions of the restraints which were put on the power of the whole; for, had it been intended to interpose the judiciary as an additional barrier, the matter would surely not have been left in doubt. The judges would not have been left to stand on the insecure and evershifting ground of public opinion as to constructive powers; they would have been placed on the impregnable ground of an express grant. . . .

[W]hat I have in view in this inquiry, is the supposed right of the judiciary to interfere in cases where the Constitution is to be carried into effect through the instrumentality of the legislature, and where that organ must necessarily first decide on the constitutionality of its own act. The oath to support the Constitution is not peculiar to the judges, but is taken indiscriminately by every officer of the government, and is designed rather as a test of the political principles of the man, than to bind the officer in the discharge of his duty: otherwise it is difficult to determine what operation it is to have in the case of a recorder of deeds, for instance, who, in the execution of his office, has nothing to do with the Constitution. But granting it to relate to the official conduct of the judge, as well as every other officer, and not to his political principles, still it must be understood in reference to supporting the Constitution *only as far as that may be involved in his official duty;* and consequently, if his official duty does not comprehend an inquiry into the authority of the legislature, neither does his oath.

But do not the judges do a positive act in violation of the Constitution when they give effect to an unconstitutional law? Not if the law has been passed according to the forms established in the Constitution. The fallacy of the question is in supposing that the judiciary adopts the acts of the legislature as its own; whereas the enactment of a law and the interpretation of it are not concurrent acts, and as the judiciary is not required to concur in the enactment, neither is it in the breach of the Constitution which may be the consequence of the enactment. The fault is imputable to the legislature, and on it the responsibility exclusively rests. . . .

LUTHER *v.* BORDEN
7 How. 1; 12 L. Ed. 581 (1849)

[*This case grew out of an extremely unusual set of circumstances. In 1841, the constitution of Rhode Island, which was essentially the original Colonial charter of 1663 with a few minor adaptations, still strictly limited the right to vote. Although universal manhood suffrage had been generally adopted by the other states, property ownership was still a requirement for voting in Rhode Island. All attempts to broaden the franchise were defeated. In 1841, agitation for a new constitution increased. Under the leadership of a young lawyer, Thomas W. Dorr, mass meetings were held throughout the state, a constitutional convention was called, and a new constitution establishing adult manhood suffrage was written. Dorr was elected Governor under the new constitution, and he immediately tried to put the new government into operation. However, the regular government refused to recognize the new constitution and took steps to put down the "insurrection." It declared martial law, called out the state militia, and appealed to President Tyler for aid. Although no federal forces were used, the "Dorr Rebellion" was crushed. Dorr himself was captured, tried for treason, and sentenced to life imprisonment. He was later pardoned, and in 1842 the charter government yielded to popular pressures and drafted a new constitution that provided for wider electoral rights.*

Nevertheless, many of Dorr's supporters felt that the courts might hold that the new government was the rightful one, because it had the support of a majority of the people. Thus, an unimportant civil controversy between Luther and Borden was pushed to the Supreme Court. Luther, a follower of Dorr, was arrested in his home for insurrection by Borden and others, who were members of the state militia acting under orders of the charter government. Luther moved to Massachusetts in order to bring the case before the federal courts on the basis of diversity of citizenship. He sued Borden for illegal trespass on the grounds that the charter government's declaration of martial law was void because the Dorr government, supported by the majority of the people, was the rightful government. The courts were thus invited to determine which of the two governments was the lawful government of the state. A federal circuit court ruled in Borden's favor. Luther then brought the case to the Supreme Court on a writ of error.]

MR. CHIEF JUSTICE TANEY delivered the opinion of the Court:

The fourth section of the fourth article of the Constitution of the United States provides that the United States shall guarantee to every State in the Union a republican form of government, and shall protect each of them against invasion; and on the application of the legislature or of the executive (when the legislature cannot be convened) against domestic violence.

Under this article of the Constitution it rests with Congress to decide what government is the established one in a State. For as the United States guarantee to each State a republican government, Congress must necessarily decide what government is established in the State before it can determine whether it is republican or not. And when the senators and representatives of a State are admitted into the councils of the Union, the authority of the government under which they are appointed, as well as its republican character, is recognized by the proper constitutional authority. And its decision is binding on every other department of the government, and could not be questioned in a judicial tribunal. It is true that the contest in this case did not last long enough to bring the matter to this issue; and as no senators or representatives were elected under the authority of the government of which Mr. Dorr was the head, Congress was not called upon to decide the controversy. Yet the right to decide is placed there, and not in the courts.

So, too, as relates to the clause in the above-mentioned article of the Constitution, providing for cases of domestic violence. It rested with Congress, too, to determine upon the means proper to be adopted to fulfill this guarantee. They might, if they had deemed it most advisable to do so, have placed it in the power of a court to decide when the contingency had happened which required the federal government to interfere. But Congress thought otherwise, and no doubt wisely; and by the act of February 28, 1795, provided, that, "in case of an insurrection in any State against the government thereof, it shall be lawful for the President of the United States, on application of the legislature of such State or of the executive (when the legislature cannot be convened), to call forth such number of the militia of any other State or States, as may be applied for, as he may judge sufficient to suppress such insurrection."

By this act, the power of deciding whether the exigency had arisen upon which the government of the United States is bound to interfere, is given to the President. He is to act upon the application of the legislature or of the executive, and consequently he must determine what body of men constitute the legislature, and who is the governor, before he can act. The fact that both parties claim the right to the government cannot alter the case, for both cannot be entitled to it. If there is an armed conflict, like the one of which we are speaking, it is a case of domestic violence, and one of the parties must be in insurrection against the lawful government. And the President must, of necessity, decide which is the government, and which party is unlawfully arrayed against it, before he can perform the duty imposed upon him by the act of Congress.

After the President has acted and called out the militia, is a Circuit Court of the United States authorized to inquire whether his decision was right? Could the court, while the parties were actually contending in arms for the possession of the government, call witnesses before it and inquire which party represented a majority of the people? If it could, then it would become the duty of the court (provided it came to the conclusion that the President had decided incorrectly) to discharge those who were arrested or detained by the troops in the service of the United States or the government which the President was endeavoring to maintain. If the judicial power extends so far, the guarantee contained in the Constitution of the United States is a guarantee of anarchy, and not of order. Yet if this right does not reside in the courts when the conflict is raging, if the judicial power is at that time bound to follow the decision of the political, it must be equally bound when the contest is over. It cannot, when peace is restored, punish as offenses and crimes the acts which it before recognized, and was bound to recognize, as lawful.

It is true that in this case the militia were not called out by the President. But upon the application of the governor under the charter government, the President recognized him as the executive power of the State, and took measures to call out the militia to support his authority if it should be found necessary for the general government to interfere; and it is admitted in the argument, that it was the knowledge of this decision that put an end to the armed opposition to the charter government, and prevented any further efforts to establish by force the proposed constitution. The interference of the President, therefore, by announcing his determination, was as effectual as if the militia had been assembled under his orders. And it should be equally authoritative. For certainly no court of the United States, with a knowledge of this decision, would have been justified in recognizing the opposing party as the lawful government, or in treating as wrongdoers or insurgents the officers of the government which the President had recognized, and was prepared to support by an armed force. In the case of foreign nations, the government acknowledged by the President is always recognized by the courts of justice. And this principle has been applied by the act of Congress to the sovereign States of the Union.

It is said that this power in the President is dangerous to liberty, and may be abused. All power may be abused if placed in unworthy hands. But it would be difficult, we think, to point out any other hands in which this power would be more safe, and at the same time equally effectual. When citizens of the same State are in arms against each other, and the constituted authorities unable to execute the laws, the interposition of the United States must be prompt, or it is of little value. The ordinary course of proceedings in courts of justice would be utterly unfit for the crisis. And the elevated office of the President, chosen as he is by the people of the United States, and the high responsibility he could not fail to feel when acting in a case of so much moment, appear to furnish as strong safeguards against a wilful abuse of power as human prudence and foresight could well provide. At all events, it is conferred upon him by the Constitution and laws of the United States, and must therefore be respected and enforced in its judicial tribunals. . . .

Undoubtedly, if the President in exercising this power shall fall into error, or invade the rights of the people of the State, it would be in the power of Congress to apply the proper remedy. But the courts must administer the law as they find it. . . .

Much of the argument on the part of the plaintiff turned upon political rights and political questions, upon which the court has been urged to express an opinion. We decline doing so. The high power has been conferred on this court of passing judgment upon the acts of the State sovereignties, and of the legislative and executive branches of the federal government, and of determining whether they are beyond the limits of power marked out for them respectively by the Constitution of the United States. This tribunal, therefore, should be the last to overstep the boundaries which limit its own jurisdiction. And while it should always be ready to meet any question confided to it by the Constitution, it is equally its duty not to pass beyond its appropriate sphere of action, and to take care not to involve itself in discussions which properly belong to other forums. No one we believe, has ever doubted the proposition, that, according to the institutions of this country, the sovereignty in every State resides in the people of the State, and that they may alter and change their form of government at their own pleasure. But whether they have changed it or not by abolishing an old government, and establishing a new one in its place, is a question to be settled by the political power. And when that power has decided, the courts are bound to take notice of its decision, and to follow it.

The judgment of the circuit court must therefore be

Affirmed.

[MR. JUSTICE WOODBURY *wrote a dissenting opinion.*]

BAKER *v.* CARR

369 U.S. 186; 82 Sup. Ct. 691; 7 L. Ed. 2d 633 (1962)

[*The General Assembly of Tennessee consists of a Senate of thirty-three members and a House of Representatives of ninety-nine members. The constitution of Tennessee provides that representation in the legislature shall be based on the number of qualified voters residing in each county. It also provides for an apportionment of the legislators every ten years to be determined according to the federal census. In 1901, the state legislature reapportioned representation on the basis of the 1900 federal census, but despite the constitutional requirement, no subsequent reapportionment was made up to the time of* Baker v. Carr. *In the meantime, the population of Tennessee increased by 75 per cent, and many people moved from rural to urban areas. These changes resulted in extreme disparities in the number of voters in each voting district. For example, Moore County, with 2,340 voters, elected one representative, whereas Shelby County, with 312,245 voters, elected only seven. In some senatorial districts there were only 30,000 voters, whereas others had as many as 130,000. As a result of such disparities, voters in districts having only 40 per cent of the voting population could elect sixty-three of the ninety-nine representatives, and 37 per cent of the voters could elect twenty of the thirty-three members of the Senate. All attempts to reapportion in accordance with the state constitution had failed.*

In 1959, Baker and other qualified voters of Tennessee brought suit against Carr, the Tennessee Secretary of State, and other public officials, alleging deprivation of federal constitutional rights. The plaintiffs argued that the state's system of apportionment was "utterly arbitrary," thereby denying them equal protection of the laws under the Fourteenth

Amendment "by virtue of debasement of their votes." A federal district court, relying on Colegrove *v.* Green, *dismissed the complaint in 1960. The case then went to the Supreme Court on appeal.*]

MR. JUSTICE BRENNAN delivered the opinion of the Court:

I

. . . The District Court's Opinion and Order of Dismissal

Because we deal with this case on appeal from an order of dismissal granted on appellees' motions, precise identification of the issues presently confronting us demands clear exposition of the grounds upon which the District Court rested in dismissing the case. The dismissal order recited that the court sustained the appellees' grounds "(1) that the Court lacks jurisdiction of the subject matter, and (2) that the complaint fails to state a claim upon which relief can be granted. . . ."

The District Court's dismissal order . . . rested . . . upon lack of subject-matter jurisdiction and lack of justifiable cause of action without attempting to distinguish between these grounds. . . .

The court proceeded to explain its action as turning on the case's presenting a "question of the distribution of political strength for legislative purposes." For,

> "from a review of [numerous Supreme Court] . . . decisions there can be no doubt that the federal rule, as enunciated and applied by the Supreme Court, is that the federal courts, whether from a lack of jurisdiction or from the inappropriateness of the subject matter for judicial consideration, will not intervene in cases of this type to compel legislative reapportionment. . . ."

The court went on to express doubts as to the feasibility of the various possible remedies sought by the plaintiffs. . . . Then it made clear that its dismissal reflected a view not of doubt that violation of constitutional rights was alleged, but of a court's impotence to correct that violation:

> "With the plaintiff's argument that the legislature of Tennessee is guilty of a clear violation of the state constitution and of the rights of the plaintiffs the Court entirely agrees. It also agrees that the evil is a serious one which should be corrected without further delay. But even so the remedy in this situation clearly does not lie with the courts. It has long been recognized and is accepted doctrine that there are indeed some rights guaranteed by the Constitution for the violation of which the courts cannot give redress. . . ."

In light of the District Court's treatment of the case, we hold today only (a) that the court possessed jurisdiction of the subject matter; (b) that a justiciable cause of action is stated upon which appellants would be entitled to appropriate relief; and (c) because appellees raise the issue before this Court, that the appellants have standing to challenge the Tennessee apportionment statutes. Beyond noting that we have no cause at this stage to doubt the District Court will be able to fashion relief if violations of constitutional rights are found, it is improper now to consider what remedy would be most appropriate if appellants prevail at the trial.

II

Jurisdiction of the Subject Matter

The District Court was uncertain whether our cases withholding federal judicial relief rested upon a lack of federal jurisdiction or upon the inappropriateness of the subject matter for judicial consideration—what we have designated "nonjusticiability." The distinction between the two grounds is significant. In the instance of nonjusticiability, consideration of the cause is not wholly and immediately foreclosed; rather, the Court's inquiry necessarily proceeds to the point of deciding whether the duty asserted can be judicially identified and its breach judicially determined, and whether protection for the right asserted can be judicially molded. In the instance of lack of jurisdiction the cause either does not "arise under" the Federal Constitution, laws or treaties (or fall within one of the other enumerated categories of Article III, 2), or is not a "case or controversy" within the meaning of that section; or the cause is not one described by any jurisdictional statute. Our conclusion . . . that this cause presents no nonjusticiable "political question" settles the only possible doubt that it is a case or controversy. Under the present heading of "Jurisdiction of the Subject Matter" we hold only that the matter set forth in the complaint does arise under the Constitution. . . .

An unbroken line of our precedents sustains the federal courts' jurisdiction of the subject matter of federal constitutional claims of this nature. The first cases involved the redistricting of States for the purpose of electing Representatives to the Federal Congress. . . . When the Minnesota Supreme Court affirmed the dismissal of a suit to enjoin the Secretary of State of Minnesota from acting under Minnesota redistricting legislation, we reviewed the constitutional merits of the legislation and reversed the State Supreme Court. *Smiley* v. *Holm,* 285 U.S. 355 . . . When a three-judge District Court . . . permanently enjoined officers of the State of Mississippi from conducting an election of Representatives under a Mississippi redistricting act, we reviewed the federal questions on the merits and reversed the District Court. *Wood* v. *Broom,* 287 U.S. 1. . . .

The appellees refer to *Colegrove* v. *Green* . . . as authority that the District Court lacked jurisdiction of the subject matter. Appellees misconceive the holding of that case. The holding was precisely contrary to their reading of it. Seven members of the Court participated in the decision. Unlike many other cases in this field which have assumed without discussion that there was jurisdiction, all three opinions filed in *Colegrove* discussed the question. Two of the opinions expressing the views of four of the Justices, a majority, flatly held that there was jurisdiction of the subject matter. Mr. Justice Black, joined by Mr. Justice Douglas and Mr. Justice Murphy, stated: "It is my judgment that the District Court had jurisdiction. . . ." Mr. Justice Rutledge, writing separately, expressed agreement with this conclusion. . . . Indeed, it is even questionable that the opinion of Mr. Justice Frankfurter, joined by Justices Reed and Burton, doubted jurisdiction of the subject matter. . . .

Several subsequent cases similar to *Colegrove* have been decided by the Court in summary per curiam statements. None was dismissed for want of jurisdiction of the subject. . . .

Two cases decided with opinions after *Colegrove* likewise plainly imply that the subject matter of this suit is within District Court jurisdiction. In *MacDougall* v. *Green,* 335 U.S. 281, the District Court dismissed for want of jurisdiction . . . a suit to enjoin enforcement of the requirement that nominees for state-wide elections be supported by a petition signed by a minimum number of persons from at least fifty of the State's 102 counties. This Court's disagreement with that action is clear since the Court affirmed the judgment after a review of the merits and concluded that the particular claim there was without merit. In *South* v. *Peters,* 339 U.S. 276, we affirmed the dismissal of an attack on the Georgia "county unit" system but founded our action on a ground that plainly would not have been reached if the lower court lacked jurisdiction of the subject matter. . . . The express words of our holding were that "federal courts consistently refuse to exercise their equity powers in cases posing political issues arising from a state's geographical distribution of electoral strength among its political subdivisions. . . ."

We hold that the District Court has jurisdiction of the subject matter of the federal constitutional claim asserted in the complaint.

III

Standing

A federal court cannot "pronounce any statute, either of a State or of the United States, void, because irreconcilable with the Constitution, except as it is called upon to adjudge the legal rights of litigants in actual controversies. . . ." Have the appellants alleged such a personal stake in the outcome of the controversy as to assure that concrete adverseness which sharpens the presentation of issues upon which the court so largely depends for illumination of difficult constitutional questions? This is the gist of the question of standing. It is, of course, a question of federal law. . . .

We hold that the appellants do have

standing to maintain this suit. Our decisions plainly support this conclusion. Many of the cases have assumed rather than articulated the premise in deciding the merits of similar claims. And *Colegrove* v. *Green* . . . squarely held that voters who allege facts showing disadvantage to themselves as individuals have standing to sue. A number of cases decided after *Colegrove* recognized the standing of the voters there involved to bring those actions.

These appellants seek relief in order to protect or vindicate an interest of their own, and of those similarly situated. Their constitutional claim is, in substance, that the 1901 statute constitutes arbitrary and capricious state action, offensive to the Fourteenth Amendment in its irrational disregard of the standard of apportionment prescribed by the State's Constitution or of any standard, effecting a gross disproportion of representation to voting population. The injury which appellants assert is that this classification disfavors the voters in the counties in which they reside, placing them in a position of constitutionally unjustifiable inequality vis-a-vis voters in irrationally favored counties. . . .

It would not be necessary to decide whether appellants' allegations of impairment of their votes by the 1901 apportionment will, ultimately, entitle them to any relief, in order to hold that they have standing to seek it. If such impairment does produce a legally cognizable injury, they are among those who have sustained it. They are asserting "a plain, direct and adequate interest in maintaining the effectiveness of their votes," . . . not merely a claim of "the right, possessed by every citizen, to require that the Government be administered according to law. . . ."

IV

Justiciability

In holding that the subject matter of this suit was not justiciable, the District Court relied on *Colegrove* v. *Green* . . . and subsequent per curiam cases. . . . We understand the District Court to have read the cited cases as compelling the conclusion that since the appellants sought to have a legislative apportionment held unconstitutional their suit presented a "political question" and was therefor nonjusticiable. We hold that this challenge to an apportionment presents no nonjusticiable "political question." The cited cases do not hold the contrary.

Of course the mere fact that the suit seeks protection of a political right does not mean it presents a political question. Such an objection "is little more than a play upon words. . . ." Rather, it is argued that apportionment cases, whatever the actual wording of the complaint, can involve no federal constitutional right except one resting on the guaranty of a republican form of government, and that complaints based on that clause have been held to present political questions which are nonjusticiable.

We hold that the claim pleaded here neither rests upon nor implicates the Guaranty Clause and that its justiciability is therefore not foreclosed by our decisions of cases involving that clause. The District Court misinterpreted *Colegrove* v. *Green* and other decisions of this Court on which it relied. Appellants' claim that they are being denied equal protection is justiciable, and if "discrimination is sufficiently shown, the right to relief under the equal protection clause is not diminished by the fact that the discrimination relates to political rights." *Snowden* v. *Hughes,* 321 U.S. 1. . . . To show why we reject the argument based on the Guaranty Clause . . . we deem it necessary first to consider the contours of the "political question" doctrine.

Our discussion . . . requires review of a number of "political question" cases, in order to expose the attributes of the doctrine. . . . That review reveals that in the Guaranty Clause cases and in the other "political question" cases, it is the relationship between the judiciary and the coordinate branches of the Federal Government, and not the federal judiciary's relationship to the States, which gives rise to the "political question. . . ."

The nonjusticiability of a political question is primarily a function of the separation of powers. Much confusion results from the capacity of the "political question" label to obscure the need for case-by-case inquiry. Deciding whether a matter has in any measure been committed by the Constitution to another branch of government, or whether the action of that branch exceeds whatever authority has been committed, is itself a delicate exercise in constitutional interpretation, and is a responsibility of this Court as ultimate interpreter of the Constitution. . . .

Prominent on the surface of any case held to involve a political question is found a textually demonstrable constitutional commitment of the issue to a coordinate political department; or a lack of judicially discoverable and manageable standards for resolving it; or the impossibility of deciding without an initial policy determination of a kind clearly for nonjudicial discretion; or the impossibility of a court's undertaking independent resolution without expressing lack of the respect due coordinate branches of government; or an unusual need for unquestioning adherence to a political decision already made; or the potentiality of embarrassment from multifarious pronouncements by various departments on one question.

Unless one of these formulations is inextricable from the case at bar, there should be no dismissal for nonjusticiability on the ground of a political question's presence. The doctrine of which we treat is one of "political questions," not one of "political cases." The courts cannot reject as "no law suit" a bona fide controversy as to whether some action denominated "political" exceeds constitutional authority. . . .

But it is argued that this case shares the characteristics of decisions that constitute a category not yet considered, cases concerning the Constitution's guaranty, in Art. IV, Section 4, of a republican form of government. . . . [*The Court then discusses, at great length,* Luther *v.* Borden *and numerous other cases holding that the republican guaranty provision is judicially unenforceable.*]

We conclude . . . that the nonjusticiability of claims resting on the Guaranty Clause which arises from their embodiment of questions that were thought "political," can have no bearing upon the justiciability of the equal protection claim presented in this case. . . . [W]e emphasize that it is the involvement in Guaranty Clause claims of the elements thought to define "political questions," and no other feature, which could render them nonjusticiable. Specifically, we have said that such claims are not held nonjusticiable because they touch matters of state governmental organization. . . .

[O]nly last Term, in *Gomillion* v. *Lightfoot* . . . we applied the Fifteenth Amendment to strike down a redrafting of municipal boundaries which effected a discriminatory impairment of voting rights, in the face of what a majority of the Court of Appeals thought to be a sweeping commitment to state legislatures of the power to draw and redraw such boundaries. . . .

We conclude that the complaint's allegations of a denial of equal protection present a justiciable constitutional cause of action upon which appellants are entitled to a trial and a decision. The right asserted is within the reach of judicial protection under the Fourteenth Amendment.

The judgment of the District Court is reversed and the cause is remanded for further proceedings consistent with this opinion.

Reversed and remanded.

MR. JUSTICE WHITTAKER did not participate in the decision of this case.

MR. JUSTICE DOUGLAS, concurring:

While I join the opinion of the Court and, like the Court, do not reach the merits, a word of explanation is necessary. I put to one side the problems of "political" questions involving the distribution of power between this Court, the Congress, and the Chief Executive. We have here a phase of the recurring problem of the relation of the federal courts to state agencies. More particularly, the question is the extent to which a State may weight one person's vote more heavily than it does another's. . . .

The traditional test under the Equal Protection Clause has been whether a State has made "an invidious discrimination," as it does when it selects "a particular race or nationality for oppressive treatment. . . ." Universal equality is not the test; there is room for weighting. As we stated in *Williamson* v. *Lee Optical Co.,* 348 U.S. 483. . . . "The prohibition of the Equal Protection Clause goes no further than the invidious discrimination."

I agree with my Brother Clark that if the allegations in the complaint can be sustained a case for relief is established. We are told that a single vote in Moore County, Tennessee, is worth 19 votes in Hamilton County, that one vote in Stewart or in Chester County is worth nearly eight times a single vote in Shelby or Knox County. The opportunity to prove that an "invidious discrimination" exists should therefore be given the appellants. . . .

With the exceptions of *Colegrove* v. *Green,* . . . *South* v. *Peters,* . . . and the decisions they spawned, the Court has never thought that protection of voting rights was beyond judicial cognizance. Today's treatment of those cases removes the only impediment to judicial cognizance of the claims stated in the present complaint.

The justiciability of the present claims being established, any relief accorded can be fashioned in the light of well-known principles of equity.

MR. JUSTICE CLARK, concurring:

. . . The Court holds that the appellants have alleged a cause of action. However, it refuses to award relief here—although the facts are undisputed—and fails to give the District Court any guidance whatever. One dissenting opinion, bursting with words that go through so much and conclude with so little, condemns the majority action as "a massive repudiation of the experience of our whole past." Another describes the complaint as merely asserting conclusory allegations that Tennessee's apportionment is "incorrect," "arbitrary," "obsolete," and "unconstitutional." I believe it can be shown that this case is distinguishable from earlier cases dealing with the distribution of political power by a State, that a patent violation of the Equal Protection Clause of the United States Constitution has been shown, and that an appropriate remedy may be formulated.

I

I take the law of the case from *MacDougall* v. *Green* . . . which involved an attack under the Equal Protection Clause upon an Illinois election statute. The Court decided that case on its merits without hindrance from the "political question" doctrine. Although the statute under attack was upheld, it is clear that the Court based its decision upon the determination that the statute represented a rational state policy. It stated:

> "It would be strange indeed, and doctrinaire, for this Court, applying such broad constitutional concepts as due process and equal protection of the laws, to deny a State the power to assure a proper diffusion of political initiative as between its thinly populated counties and those having concentrated masses, in view of the fact that the latter have practical opportunities for exerting their political weight at the polls not available to the former. . . ."

The other cases upon which my Brethren dwell are all distinguishable or inapposite. The widely heralded case of *Colegrove* v. *Green* . . . was one not only in which the Court was bobtailed but in which there was no majority opinion. Indeed, even the "political question" point in Mr. Justice Frankfurter's opinion was no more than an alternative ground. Moreover, the appellants did not present an equal protection argument. While it has served as a Mother Hubbard to most of the subsequent cases, I feel it was in that respect illcast and for all of these reasons put it to one side. Likewise, I do not consider the Guaranty Clause cases based on Article I, Section 4, of the Constitution, because it is not invoked here and it involves different criteria, as the Courts' opinion indicates. . . . Finally, the Georgia county unit system cases, such as *South* v. *Peters,* . . . reflect the viewpoint of MacDougall, i.e., to refrain from intervening where there is some rational policy behind the State's system.

II

. . . It is true that the apportionment policy incorporated in Tennessee's Constitution, i.e., statewide numerical equality of representation with certain minor qualifications, is a rational one. On a county-by-county comparison a districting plan based thereon naturally will have disparities in representation due to the qualifications. But this to my mind does not raise constitutional problems, for the over-all policy is reasonable. However, the root of the trouble is not in Tennessee's Constitution, for admittedly its policy has not been followed.

The discrimination lies in the action of Tennessee's Assembly in allocating legislative seats to counties or districts created by it. Try as one may, Tennessee's apportionment just cannot be made to fit the pattern cut by its Constitution. This was the finding of the District Court. The policy of the Constitution referred to by the dissenters, therefore, is of no relevance here. We must examine what the Assembly has done. The frequency and magnitude of the inequalities in the present districting admit of no policy whatever; . . . [t]he apportionment picture in Tennessee is a topsy-turvical maze of gigantic proportions. . . . Tennessee's apportionment is a crazy quilt without rational basis. . . .

No one—except the dissenters advocating the Harlan "adjusted 'total representation' " formula—contends that mathematical equality among voters is required by the Equal Protection Clause. But certainly there must be some rational design to a State's districting. The discrimination here does not fit any pattern—as I have said, it is but a crazy quilt. My Brother Harlan contends that other proposed apportionment plans contain disparities. Instead of chasing those rabbits he should first pause long enough to meet appellants' proof of discrimination by showing that in fact the present plan follows a rational policy. Not being able to do this, he merely counters with such generalities as "classic legislative judgment," no "significant discrepancy," and "de minimis departures." I submit that even a casual glance at the present apportionment picture shows these conclusions to be entirely fanciful. If present representation has a policy at all, it is to maintain the status quo of invidious discrimination at any cost. . . .

III

Although I find the Tennessee apportionment statute offends the Equal Protection Clause, I would not consider intervention by this Court into so delicate a field if there were any other relief available to the people of Tennessee. But the majority of the people of Tennessee have no "practical opportunities for exerting their political weight at the polls" to correct the existing "invidious discrimination." Tennessee has no initiative and referendum. I have searched diligently for other "practical opportunities" present under the law. I find none other than through the federal courts. The majority of the voters have been caught up in a legislative strait jacket. Tennessee has an "informed, civically militant electorate" and "an aroused popular conscience," but it does not sear the "conscience of the people's representatives." This is because the legislative policy has riveted the present seats in the Assembly to their respective constituencies, and by the votes of their incumbents a reapportionment of any kind is prevented. The people have been rebuffed at the hands of the Assembly; they have tried the constitutional convention route, but since the call must originate in the Assembly it, too, has been fruitless. They have tried Tennessee courts with the same result, and Governors have fought the tide only to flounder. It is said that there is recourse in Congress and perhaps that may be, but from a practical standpoint this is without substance. To date Congress has never undertaken such a task in any State. We therefore must conclude that the people of Tennessee are stymied and without judicial intervention will be saddled with the present discrimination in the affairs of their state government.

IV

Finally, we must consider if there are any appropriate modes of effective judicial relief. The federal courts are, of course, not forums for political debates, nor should they resolve themselves into state constitutional conventions or legislative assemblies. Nor should their jurisdiction be exercised in the hope that such a declaration, as is made today, may have the direct effect of bringing on legislative action and relieving the courts of the problem of fashioning relief. To my mind this would be nothing less than blackjacking the Assembly into reapportioning the State. If judicial competence were lacking to fashion an effective decree, I would dismiss this appeal. However . . . I see no such difficulty in the position of this case. One plan might be to start with the existing assembly districts, consolidate some of them, and award the seats thus released to those counties suffering the most egregious discrimination. Other possibilities are present and might be more effective. But the plan here suggested would at least release the stranglehold now on the Assembly and permit it to redistrict itself. . . .

In view of the detailed study that the Court has given this problem, it is unfortunate that a decision is not reached on the merits. The majority appears to hold, at least sub silentio, that an invidious discrimination is present, but it remands to the three-judge court for it to make what is certain to be that formal determination. . . . [N]ot being able to muster a court to dispose of the case on the merits, I concur in the opinion of the majority and acquiesce in the decision to remand. . . .

. . . It is well for this Court to practice self-restraint and discipline in constitutional adjudication, but never in its history have those principles received sanction where the national rights of so many have been so clearly infringed for so long a time. National respect for the courts is more enhanced through the forthright enforcement of those rights rather than by rendering them nugatory through the interposition of subterfuges. In my view the ultimate decision today is in the greatest tradition of this Court.

MR. JUSTICE STEWART, concurring:

The separate writings of my dissenting and concurring Brothers stray so far from the subject of today's decision as to convey, I think, a distressingly inaccurate impression of what the Court decides. For that reason, I think it appropriate, in joining the opinion of the Court, to emphasize in a few words what the opinion does and does not say. . . .

The complaint in this case asserts that Tennessee's system of apportionment is utterly arbitrary—without any possible justification in rationality. The District Court did not reach the merits of that claim, and this Court quite properly expresses no view on the subject. Contrary to the suggestion of my Brother Harlan, the Court does not say or imply that "state legislatures must be so structured as to reflect with approximate equality the voice of every voter. . . ." The Court does not say or imply that there is anything in the Federal Constitution "to prevent a State, acting not irrationally, from choosing any electoral legislative structure it thinks best suited to the interests, temper, and custom of its people. . . ." And contrary to the suggestion of my Brother Douglas, the Court most assuredly does not decide the question. "May a State weight the vote of one county or one district more heavily than it weights the vote in another?" . . .

My Brother Clark has made a convincing prima facie showing that Tennessee's system of apportionment is in fact utterly arbitrary—without any possible justification in rationality. My Brother Harlan has, with imagination and ingenuity, hypothesized possibly rational bases for Tennessee's system. But the merits of this case are not before us now. The defendants have not yet had an opportunity to be heard in defense of the State's system of apportionment; indeed, they have not yet even filed an answer to the complaint. As in other cases, the proper place for the trial is in the trial court, not here.

MR. JUSTICE FRANKFURTER, whom MR. JUSTICE HARLAN joins, dissenting:

The Court today reverses a uniform course of decision established by a dozen cases, including one by which the very claim now sustained was unanimously rejected only five years ago. The impressive body of rulings thus cast aside reflected the equally uniform course of our political history regarding the relationship between population and legislative representation—a wholly different matter from denial of the franchise to individuals because of race, color, religion or sex. Such a massive repudiation of the experience of our whole past in asserting destructively novel judicial power demands a detailed analysis of the role of this Court in our constitutional scheme. Disregard of inherent limits in the effective exercise of the Court's "judicial Power" not only presages the futility of judicial intervention in the essentially political conflict of forces by which the relation between population and representation has time out of mind been and now is determined. It may well impair the Court's position as the ultimate organ of "the supreme Law of the Land" in that vast range of legal problems, often strongly entangled in popular feeling, on which this Court must pronounce. The Court's authority—possessed neither of the purse nor the sword—ultimately rests on sustained public confidence in its moral sanction. Such feeling must be nourished by the Court's complete detachment, in fact as in appearance, from political entanglements and by abstention from injecting itself into the clash of political forces in political settlements.

A hypothetical claim resting on abstract assumptions is now for the first time made the basis for affording illusory relief for a particular evil even though it foreshadows deeper and more pervasive difficulties in consequence. The claim is hypothetical and the assumptions are abstract because the Court does not vouchsafe the lower courts—state and federal—guidelines for formulating specific, definite, wholly unprecedented remedies for the inevitable litigations that today's umbrageous disposition is bound to stimulate in connection with politically motivated reapportionments in so many States. In such a setting, to promulgate jurisdiction in the abstract is meaningless. It is as devoid of reality as "a brooding omnipresence in the sky" for it conveys no intimation what relief, if any, a District Court is capable of affording that would not invite legislatures to play ducks and drakes with the judiciary. For this Court to direct the District Court to enforce a claim to which the Court has over the years consistently found itself required to deny legal enforcement and at the same time to find it necessary to withold any guidance to the lower court how to enforce this turnabout, new legal claim, manifests an odd—indeed an esoteric—conception of judicial propriety. One of the Court's supporting opinions, as elucidated by commentary, unwittingly affords a disheartening preview of the mathematical quagmire (apart from divers judicially inappropriate and elusive determinants), into which this Court today catapults the lower courts of the country without so much as adumbrating the basis for a legal calculus as a means of extrication. Even assuming the indispensable intellectual disinterestedness on the part of judges in such matters, they do not have accepted legal standards or criteria or even reliable analogies to draw upon for making judicial judgments. To charge courts with the task of accommodating the incommensurable factors of policy that underlie these mathematical puzzles is to attribute, however flatteringly, omnicompetence to judges. The Framers of the Constitution persistently rejected a proposal that embodied this assumption and Thomas Jefferson never entertained it.

Recent legislation, creating a district appropriately described as "an atrocity of ingenuity," is not unique. Considering the gross inequality among legislative electoral units within almost every State, the Court naturally shrinks from asserting that in districting at least substantial equality is a constitutional requirement enforceable by courts. Room continues to be allowed for weighting. This of course implies that geography, economics, urban-rural conflict, and all the other nonlegal factors which have throughout our history entered into political districting are to some extent not to be ruled out in the undefined vista now opened up by review in the federal courts of state reapportionments. To some extent—aye, there's the rub. In effect, today's decision empowers the courts of the country to devise what should constitute the proper composition of the legislatures of the fifty States. If state courts should for one reason or another find themselves unable to discharge this task, the duty of doing so is put on the federal courts or on this Court, if State views do not satisfy this Court's notion of what is proper districting.

We were soothingly told at the bar of this Court that we need not worry about the kind of remedy a court could effectively fashion once the abstract constitutional right to have courts pass on a state-wide system of electoral districting is recognized as a matter of judicial rhetoric, because legislatures would heed the Court's admonition. This is not only an euphoric hope. It implies a sorry confession of judicial impotence in place of a frank acknowledgment that there is not under our Constitution a judicial remedy for every political mischief, for every undesirable exercise of legislative power. The Framers carefully and with deliberate forethought refused so to enthrone the judiciary. In this situation, as in other of like nature, appeal for relief does not belong here. Appeal must be to an informed, civically militant electorate. In a democratic society like ours, relief must come through an aroused popular conscience that sears the conscience of the people's representatives. In any event there is nothing judicially more unseemly nor more self-defeating than for this Court to make in terrorem pronouncements, to indulge in merely empty rhetoric, sounding a word of promise to the ear, sure to be disappointing to the hope. . . .

I

In sustaining appellants' claim, based on the Fourteenth Amendment, that the District Court may entertain this suit, this Court's uniform course of decision over the years is overruled or disregarded. Explicitly it begins with *Colegrove* v. *Green* . . . but its roots run deep in the Court's historic adjudicatory process.

Colegrove held that a federal court should not entertain an action for declaratory and injunctive relief to adjudicate the constitutionality, under the Equal Protection Clause and other federal constitutional and statutory provisions, of a state statute establishing the respective districts for the State's election of Representatives to the Congress. Two opinions were written by the four Justices who composed the majority of the seven sitting members of the Court. Both opinions joining in the result in *Colegrove* v. *Green* agreed that considerations were controlling which dictated denial of jurisdiction though not in the strict sense of want of power. While the two opinions show a divergence of view regarding some of these considerations, there are important points of concurrence. Both opinions demonstrate a predominant concern, first, with avoiding federal judicial involvement; second, with respect to the difficulty—in view of the nature of the problems of apportionment and its history in this country—of drawing on or devising judicial standards for judgment, as opposed to legislative determinations, of the part which mere numerical equality among voters should play as a criterion for the allocation of political power; and, third, with problems of finding appropriate modes of relief—particularly, the problem of resolving the essentially political issue of the relative merits of at-large elections and elections held in districts of unequal population. . . .

II

The *Colegrove* doctrine, in the form in which repeated decisions have settled it, was not an innovation. It represents long judicial thought and experience. From its earliest opinions this Court has consistently recognized a class of controversies which do not lend themselves to judicial standards and judicial remedies. To classify the various instances as "political questions" is rather a form of stating this conclusion than revealing of analysis. Some of the cases so labelled have no relevance here. But from others emerge unifying considerations that are compelling. . . . [*Justice Frankfurter then reviews numerous cases involving "political questions" under the following headings: war and foreign affairs, structure and organization of state political institutions, Negro disfranchisement, and abstract questions of political power.*]

The influence of these converging considerations—the caution not to undertake decision where standards meet for judicial judgment are lacking, the reluctance to interfere with matters of state government in the absence of an unquestionable and effectively enforceable mandate, the unwillingness to make courts arbiters of the broad issues of political organization historically committed to other institutions and for whose adjustment the judicial process is ill-adapted—has been decisive of the settled line of cases, reaching back more than a century, which holds that Article IV, Section 4, of the Constitution, guaranteeing to the States "a Republican Form of Government," is not enforceable through the courts. . . .

III

The present case involves all of the elements that have made the Guarantee Clause cases nonjusticiable. It is, in effect, a Guarantee Clause claim masquerading under a different label. But it cannot make the case more fit for judicial action that appellants invoke the Fourteenth Amendment rather than Article IV, Section 4, where, in fact, the gist of their complaint is the same—unless it can be found that the Fourteenth Amendment speaks with greater particularity to their situation. . . .

What, then, is this question of legislative apportionment? Appellants invoke the right to vote and to have their votes counted. But they are permitted to vote and their votes are counted. They go to the polls, they cast their ballots, they send their representatives to the state councils. Their complaint is simply that the representatives are not sufficiently numerous or powerful—in short, that Tennessee has adopted a basis of representation with which they are dissatisfied. Talk of "debasement" or "dilution" is circular talk. One cannot speak of "debasement" or "dilution" of the value of a vote until there is first defined a standard of reference as to what a vote should be worth. What is actually asked of the Court in this case is to choose among competing bases of representation—ultimately, really among competing theories of political philosophy—in order to establish an appropriate frame of government for the State of Tennessee and thereby for all the states of the Union.

In such a matter, abstract analogies which ignore the facts of history deal in unrealities; they betray reason. This is not a case in which a State has, through a device however oblique and sophisticated, denied Negroes or Jews or red-headed persons a vote, or given them only a third or a sixth of a vote. That was *Gomillion* v. *Lightfoot*. . . . What Tennessee illustrates is an old and still widespread method of representation—representation by local geographical division, only in part respective of population—in preference to others, others, forsooth, more appealing. Appellants contest this choice and seek to make this Court the arbiter of the disagreement. They would make the Equal Protection Clause the charter of adjudication, asserting that the equality which it guarantees comports, if not the assurance of equal weight to every voter's vote, at least the basic conception that representation ought to be proportionate to population, a standard by reference to which the reasonableness of apportionment plans may be judged.

To find such a political conception legally enforceable in the broad and unspecific guarantee of equal protection is to rewrite the Constitution. . . . Certainly, "equal protection" is no more secure a foundation for judicial judgment of the permissibility of varying forms of representative governments than is "Republican Form." Indeed since "equal protection of the laws" can only mean an equality of persons standing in the same relation to whatever governmental action is challenged, the determination whether treatment is equal presupposes a determination concerning the nature of the relationship. This, with respect to apportionment, means an inquiry into the theoretic base of representation in an acceptably republican state. For a court could not determine the equal-protection issue without in fact first determining the Republican-Form issue, simply because what is reasonable for equal protection purposes will depend upon what frame of government, basically, is allowed. To divorce "equal protection" from "Republican Form" is to talk about half a question.

The notion that representation proportioned to the geographic spread of population is so universally accepted as a necessary element of equality between man and man that it must be taken to be the standard of a political equality preserved by the Fourteenth Amendment—that it is, in appellants' words "the basic principle of representative government"—is, to put it bluntly, not true. However desirable and however desired by some among the great political thinkers and framers of our government, it has never been generally practiced, today or in the past. It was not the English system, it was not the colonial system, it was not the system chosen for the national government by the Constitution, it was not the system exclusively or even predominantly practiced by the States today. Unless judges, the judges of this Court, are to make their private views of political wisdom the measure of the Constitution—views which in all honesty cannot but give the appearance, if not reflect the reality, of involvement with the business of partisan politics so inescapably a part of apportionment controversies—the Fourteenth Amendment, "itself a historical product," . . . provides no guide for judicial oversight of the representation problem. . . . [*Justice Frankfurter then deals at length with representation and apportionment practices in Great Britain, the Colonies and the Union, and the states at the time of the ratification of the Fourteenth Amendment and contemporary times.*]

Manifestly, the Equal Protection Clause supplies no clearer guide for judicial examination of apportionment methods than would the Guarantee Clause itself. Apportionment, by its character, is a subject of extraordinary complexity, involving—even after the fundamental theoretical issues concerning what is to be represented in a representative legislature have been fought out or compromised—considerations of geography, demography, electoral convenience, economic and social cohesions or divergencies among particular local groups, communications, the practical effects of political institutions like the lobby and the city machine, ancient traditions and ties of settled usage, respect for proven incumbents of long experience and senior status, mathematical mechanics, censuses compiling relevant data, and a host of others. Legislative responses throughout the country to the apportionment demands of the 1960 Census have glaringly confirmed that these are not factors that lend themselves to evaluations of a nature that are the staple of judicial determinations or for which judges are equipped to adjudicate by legal training or experience or native wit. And this is the more so true because in every strand of this complicated, intricate web of values meet the contending forces of partisan politics. The practical significance of apportionment is that the next election results may differ because of it. Apportionment battles are overwhelmingly party or intra-party contests. It will add a virulent source of friction and tension in federal-state relations to embroil the federal judiciary in them.

Appellants, however, contend that the federal courts may provide the standard which the Fourteenth Amendment lacks by reference to the provisions of the constitution of Tennessee. The argument is that although the same or greater disparities of electoral strength may be suffered to exist immune from federal judicial review in States where they result from apportionment legislation consistent with state constitutions, the Tennessee legislature may not abridge the rights which, on its face, its own constitution appears to give, without by that act denying equal protection of the laws. It is said that the law of Tennessee, as expressed by the words of its written constitution, has made the basic choice among policies in favor of representation proportioned to population, and that it is no longer open to the State to allot its voting power on other principles.

This reasoning does not bear analysis. Like claims invoking state constitutional requirements have been rejected here and for good reason. It is settled that whatever federal consequences may derive from a discrimination worked by a state statute must be the same as if the same discrimination were written into the State's fundamental law. . . . Appellants complain of a practice which, by their own allegations, has been the law of Tennessee for sixty years. They allege that the apportionment act of 1901 created unequal districts when passed and still maintains unequal districts. They allege that the Legislature has since 1901 purposefully retained unequal districts. And the Supreme Court of Tennessee has refused to invalidate the law establishing these unequal districts. . . . Tennessee's law and its policy respecting apportionment are what sixty years of practice show them to be, not what appellants cull from the unenforced and, according to its own judiciary, unenforceable words of its Constitution. . . .

In all of the apportionment cases which have come before the Court, a consideration which has been weighty in determining their non-judiciability has been the difficulty or impossibility of devising effective judicial remedies in this class of case. An injunction restraining a general election unless the legislature reapportions would paralyze the critical centers of a State's political system and threaten political dislocation whose consequences are not foreseeable. A declaration devoid of implied compulsion of injunctive or other relief would be an idle threat. Surely a Federal District Court could not itself remap the State, the same complexities which impede effective judicial review of apportionment a fortiori make impossible a court's consideration of these imponderables as an original matter. And the choice of elections at large as opposed to elections by district, however unequal the districts, is a matter of sweeping political judgment having enormous political implications, the nature and reach of which are certainly beyond the informed understanding of, and capacity for appraisal by, courts. . . .

Although the District Court had jurisdiction in the very restricted sense of power to determine whether it could adjudicate the claim, the case is of that class of political controversy which, by the nature of its subject, is unfit for federal judicial action. The judgment of the District Court, in dismissing the complaint for failure to state a claim on which relief can be granted, should therefore be affirmed.

Dissenting opinion of MR. JUSTICE HARLAN, whom MR. JUSTICE FRANKFURTER joins:

The dissenting opinion of Mr. Justice Frankfurter, in which I join, demonstrates the abrupt departure the majority makes from judicial history by putting the federal courts into this area of state concerns—an area which, in this instance, the Tennessee state courts themselves have refused to enter. . . .

It is at once essential to recognize this case for what it is. The issue here relates not to a method of state electoral apportionment by which seats in the federal House of Representatives are allocated, but solely to the right of a State to fix the basis of representation in its own legislature. Until it is first decided to what extent that right is limited by the Federal Constitution, and whether what Tennessee has done or failed to do in this instance runs afoul of any such limitations, we need not reach the issues of "justiciability" or "political question" or any of the other considerations which in such cases as *Colegrove* v. *Green* . . . led the Court to decline to adjudicate a challenge to a state apportionment affecting seats in the federal House of Representatives, in the absence of a controlling Act of Congress. . . .

The appellants' claim in this case ultimately rests entirely on the Equal Protection Clause of the Fourteenth Amendment. It is asserted that Tennessee has violated the Equal Protection Clause by maintaining in effect a system of apportionment that grossly favors in legislative representation the rural sections of the State as against its urban communities. Stripped to its essentials the complaint purports to set forth three constitutional claims of varying breadth:

1. The Equal Protection Clause requires that each vote cast in state legislative elections be given approximately equal weight.
2. Short of this, the existing apportionment of state legislators is so unreasonable as to amount to an arbitrary and capricious act of classification on the part of the Tennessee Legislature, which is offensive to the Equal Protection Clause.
3. In any event, the existing apportionment is rendered invalid under the Fourteenth Amendment because it flies in the face of the Tennessee Constitution. . . .

I

I can find nothing in the Equal Protection Clause or elsewhere in the Federal Constitution which expressly or impliedly supports the view that state legislatures must be so structured as to reflect with approximate equality the voice of every voter. Not only is that proposition refuted by history, as shown by my Brother Frankfurter, but it strikes deep into the heart of our federal system. Its acceptance would require us to turn our backs on the regard which this Court has always shown for the judgment of state legislatures and courts on matters of basically local concern.

In the last analysis, what lies at the core of this controversy is a difference of opinion as to the function of representative government. It is surely beyond argument that those who have the responsibility for devising a system of representation may permissibly consider that factors other than bare numbers should be taken into account. The existence of the United States Senate is proof enough of that. To consider that we may ignore the Tennessee Legislature's judgment in this instance because that body was the product of an asymmetrical electoral apportionment would in effect be to assume the very conclusion here disputed. Hence we must accept the present form of the Tennessee Legislature as the embodiment of the State's choice, or, more realistically, its compromise, between competing political philosophies. The federal courts have not been empowered by the Equal Protection Clause to judge whether this resolution of the State's internal political conflict is desirable or undesirable, wise or unwise. . . .

[T]here is nothing in the Federal Constitution to prevent a State, acting not irrationally, from choosing any electoral legislative structure it thinks best suited to the interests, temper, and custom of its people. . . .

A State's choice to distribute electoral strength among geographical units, rather than according to a census of population, is certainly no less a rational decision of policy than would be its choice to levy a tax on property rather than a tax on income. Both are legislative judgments entitled to equal respect from this Court.

II

The claim that Tennessee's system of apportionment is so unreasonable as to amount to a capricious classification of voting strength stands up no better under dispassionate analysis.

The Court has said time and again that the Equal Protection Clause does not demand of state enactments either mathematical identity or rigid equality. . . . All that is prohibited is "invidious discrimination" bearing no rational relation to any permissible policy of the State. . . .

What then is the basis for the claim made in this case that the distribution of state senators and representatives is the product of capriciousness or of some constitutionally prohibited policy? It is not that Tennessee has arranged its electoral districts with a deliberate purpose to dilute the voting strength of one race, cf. *Gomillion* v. *Lightfoot*, . . . or that some religious group is intentionally under-represented. Nor is it a charge that the legislature has indulged in sheer caprice by allotting representatives to each county on the basis of a throw of the dice, or of some other determinant bearing no rational relation to the question of apportionment. Rather, the claim is that the State Legislature has unreasonably retained substantially the same allocation of senators and representatives as was established by statute in 1901, refusing to recognize the great shift in the population balance between urban and rural communities that has occurred in the meantime. . . .

A Federal District Court is asked to say that the passage of time has rendered the 1901 apportionment obsolete to the point where its continuance becomes vulnerable under the Fourteenth Amendment. But is not this matter one that involves a classic legislative judgment? Surely it lies within the province of a state legislature to conclude that an existing allocation of senators and representatives constitutes a desirable balance of geographical and demographical representation, or that in the interest of stability of government it would be best to defer for some further time the redistribution of seats in the state legislature.

Indeed, I would hardly think it unconstitutional if a state legislature's expressed reason for establishing or maintaining an electoral imbalance between its rural and urban population were to protect the State's agricultural interests from the sheer weight of numbers of those residing in its cities. . . . These are matters of local policy, on the wisdom of which the federal judiciary is neither permitted nor qualified to sit in judgment. . . .

It is my view that the majority opinion has failed to point to any recognizable constitutional claim alleged in this complaint. Indeed, it is interesting to note that my Brother Stewart is at pains to disclaim for himself, and to point out that the majority opinion does not suggest, that the Federal Constitution requires of the States any particular kind of electoral apportionment, still less that they must accord to each voter approximately equal voting strength. . . . But that being so, what, may it be asked, is left of this complaint? Surely the bare allegations that the existing Tennessee apportionment is "incorrect," "arbitrary," "obsolete" and "unconstitutional"—amounting to nothing more than legal conclusions—do not themselves save the complaint from dismissal. . . .

From a reading of the majority and concurring opinions one will not find it difficult to catch the premises that underlie this decision. The fact that the appellants have been unable to obtain political redress of their asserted grievances appears to be regarded as a matter which should lead the Court to stretch to find some basis for judicial intervention. While the Equal Protection Clause is invoked, the opinion for the Court notably eschews explaining how, consonant with past decisions, the undisputed facts in this case can be considered to show a violation of that constitutional provision. The majority seems to have accepted the argument, pressed at the bar, that if this Court merely asserts authority in this field, Tennessee and other "malapportioning" States will quickly respond with appropriate political action, so that this Court need not be greatly concerned about the federal courts becoming further involved in these matters. At the same time the majority has wholly failed to reckon with what the future may hold in store if this optimistic prediction is not fulfilled. Thus, what the Court is doing reflects more an adventure in judicial experimentation than a solid piece of constitutional adjudication. . . .

In conclusion, it is appropriate to say that one need not agree, as a citizen, with what Tennessee has done or failed to do, in order to deprecate, as a judge, what the majority is doing today. Those observers of the Court who see it primarily as the last refuge for the correction of all inequality or injustice, no matter what its nature or source, will no doubt applaud this decision and its break with the past. Those who consider that continuing national respect for the Court's authority depends in large measure upon its wise exercise of self-restraint and discipline in constitutional adjudication, will view the decision with deep concern.

I would

Affirm.

WESBERRY V. SANDERS

376 U.S. 1; 84 Sup. Ct. 526; 11 L. Ed. 2d 481 (1964)

[*This important case originated in Atlanta, Georgia, when Wesberry and another qualified voter brought a suit claiming that population disparities in congressional districts deprived them of a right under the federal Constitution to have their votes for congressmen given the same weight as the votes of other Georgians. The Atlanta congressional district had 823,680 persons, as compared with the total population of 272,154 in the smallest district of the state. The average population of the ten Georgia districts was 394,312. Each district elects only one congressman.*

In his suit Wesberry asked that the Georgia districting statute be declared invalid and that Sanders, the Governor of Georgia, and the state Secretary of State be enjoined from conducting elections under it. Wesberry contended that voters in the Atlanta district were deprived of the full benefit of their right to vote in violation of the following:

1. Article I, Section 2 of the Constitution, which provides that "The House of Representatives shall be composed of members chosen every second year by the People of the several states. . . ."

2. The Due Process, Equal Protection, and Privileges and Immunities Clauses of the Fourteenth Amendment.

3. The part of Section 2 of the Fourteenth Amendment providing that "Representatives shall be opportioned among the several states according to their respective numbers. . . ."

In a 2-to-1 decision, a federal district court dismissed the complaint on the ground that challenges to apportionment of congressional districts raised only "political" questions, which are not justiciable. The district court relied on Justice Frankfurter's opinion in Colegrove *v.* Green *in reaching its decision. The dissenting district judge relied on* Baker *v.* Carr. *The case then went to the Supreme Court on appeal.*]

MR. JUSTICE BLACK delivered the opinion of the Court:

. . . *Baker* v. *Carr* . . . considered a challenge to a 1901 Tennessee statute providing for apportionment of State Representatives and Senators under the State's constitution, which called for apportionment among counties or districts "according to the number of qualified voters in each." The complaint there charged that the State's constitutional command to apportion on the basis of the number of qualified voters had not been followed in the 1901 statute and that the districts were so discriminatorily disparate in number of qualified voters that the plaintiffs and persons similarly situated were, "by virtue of the debasement of their votes," denied the equal protection of the laws guaranteed them by the Fourteenth Amendment. The cause there of the alleged "debasement" of votes for state legislators—districts containing widely varying numbers of people—was precisely that which was alleged to debase votes for Congressmen in *Colegrove* v. *Green* . . . and in the present case. The Court in *Baker* pointed out that the opinion of Mr. Justice Frankfurter in *Colegrove,* upon the reasoning of which the majority below leaned heavily in dismissing "for want of equity," was approved by only three of the seven Justices sitting. After full consideration of *Colegrove,* the Court in *Baker* held (1) that the District Court had jurisdiction of the subject matter; (2) that the qualified Tennessee voters there had standing to sue; and (3) that the plaintiffs had stated a justiciable cause of action on which relief could be granted.

The reasons which led to these conclusions in *Baker* are equally persuasive here. . . . Mr. Justice Frankfurter's *Colegrove* opinion contended that Article I, Section 4, of the Constitution had given Congress "exclusive authority" to protect the right of citizens to vote for Congressmen, but we made it clear in *Baker* that nothing in the language of that article gives support to a construction that would immunize state congressional apportionment laws which debase a citizen's right to vote from the power of courts to protect the constitutional rights of individuals from legislative destruction, a power recognized at least since our decision in *Marbury* v. *Madison.* . . . The right to vote is too important in our free society to be stripped of judicial protection by such an interpretation of Article I. This dismissal can no more be justified on the ground of "want of equity" than on the ground of "nonjusticiability." We therefore hold that the District Court erred in dismissing the complaint.

. . . We hold that, construed in its historical context, the command of Article I, Section 2, that Representatives be chosen "by the People of the several States" means that as nearly as is practicable one man's vote in a congressional election is to be worth as much as another's. This rule is followed automatically, of course, when Representatives are chosen as a group on a statewide basis, as was a widespread practice in the first fifty years of our Nation's history. It would be extraordinary to suggest that in such statewide elections the votes of inhabitants of some parts of a State . . . could be weighted at two or three times the value of the votes of people living in more populous parts of the state. . . . Cf. *Gray* v. *Sanders.* . . . We do not believe that the Framers of the Constitution intended to permit the same vote-diluting discrimination to be accomplished through the device of districts containing widely varied numbers of inhabitants. To say that a vote is worth more in one district than in another would not only run counter to our fundamental ideas of democratic government, it would cast aside the principle of a House of Representatives elected "by the People," a principle tenaciously fought for and established at the Constitutional Convention. The history of the Constitution, particularly that part of it relating to the adoption of Article I, Section 2, reveals that those who framed the Constitution meant that, no matter what the mechanics of an election, whether statewide or by districts, it was population which was to be the basis of the House of Representatives. . . . [*Justice Black then relies principally on the debates of the Constitutional Convention to show that the framers intended that every man's vote was "to count alike."*]

. . . It would defeat the principle solemnly embodied in the Great Compromise—equal representation in the House of equal numbers of people—for us to hold that, within the States, legislatures may draw the lines of congressional districts in such a way as to give some voters a greater voice in choosing a Congressman than others. The House of Representatives, the [Constitutional] Convention agreed, was to represent the people as individuals, and on a basis of complete equality for each voter. The delegates were quite aware of what Madison called the "vicious representation" in Great Britain whereby "rotten boroughs" with few inhabitants were represented in Parliament on or almost on a par with cities of greater population. [James] Wilson urged that people must escape the evils of the English system under which one man could send two members to Parliament to represent the borough of Old Sarum while London's million people sent but four. The delegates referred to rotten borough apportionments in some of the state legislatures as the kind of objectionable governmental action that the Constitution should not tolerate in the election of congressional representatives.

Madison in *The Federalist* described the system of division of States into congressional districts, the method which he and others assumed States probably would adopt: "The city of Philadelphia is supposed to contain between fifty and sixty thousand souls. It will therefore form nearly two districts for the choice of Federal Representatives." "[N]umbers," he said, not only are a suitable way to represent wealth but in any event "are the only proper scale of representation." In the state conventions, speakers urging ratification of the Constitution emphasized the theme of equal representation in the House which had permeated the debates on Philadelphia. Charles Cotesworth Pinckney told the South Carolina Convention, "the House of Representatives will be elected immediately by the people, and represent them and their personal rights individually. . . ." Speakers at the ratifying conventions emphasized that the House of Representatives was meant to be free of the malapportionment then existing in some of the state legislatures—such as those of Connecticut, Rhode Island, and South Carolina—and argued that the power given Congress in Article I, Section 4, was meant to be used to vindicate the people's right to equality of representation in the House. Congress' power, said John Steele at the North Carolina convention, was not to be used to allow Congress to create rotten boroughs; in answer to another delegate's suggestion that Congress might use its power to favor people living near the seacoast, Steele said that Congress "most probably" would "lay the State off into districts," and if it made laws "inconsistent with the Constitution, independent judges will not uphold them, nor will the people obey them."

Soon after the Constitution was adopted, James Wilson of Pennsylvania, by then as Associate Justice of this Court, gave a series of lectures at Philadelphia in which, drawing on his experience as one of the most active members of the Constitutional Convention, he said:

> "[A]ll elections ought to be equal. Elections are equal, when a given number of citizens, in one part of the state, choose as many representatives, as are chosen by the same number of citizens, in any other part of the state. In this manner, the proportion of the representatives and of the constituents will remain invariably the same."

It is in the light of such history that we must construe Article I, Section 2, of the Constitution, which, carrying out the ideas of Madison and those of like views, provides that Representatives shall be chosen "by the People of the several States" and shall be "apportioned among the several States . . . according to their respective numbers." It is not surprising that our Court has held that this Article gives persons qualified to vote a constitutional right to vote and to have their votes counted. . . . No right is more precious in a free country than that of having a voice in the election of those who make the laws under which, as good citizens, we must live. Other rights, even the most basic, are illusory if the right to vote is undermined. Our Constitution leaves no room for classification of people in a way that unnecessarily abridges this right. . . .

While it may not be possible to draw congressional districts with mathematical precision, that is no excuse for ignoring our

Constitutions' plain objective of making equal representation for equal numbers of people the fundamental goal for the House of Representatives. That is the high standard of justice and common sense which the Founders set for us.

Reversed and remanded

MR. JUSTICE CLARK, concurring in part; and dissenting in part.

Unfortunately I can join neither the opinion of the Court nor the dissent of my Brother Harlan. It is true that the opening sentence of Article I, Section 2, of the Constitution provides that Representatives are to be chosen "by the People of the several States. . . ." However, in my view, Brother Harlan has clearly demonstrated that both the historical background and language preclude a finding that Article I, Section 2, lays down the *ipse dixit* "one person, one vote" in congressional elections.

On the other hand, I agree with the majority that congressional districting is subject to judicial scrutiny. . . .

MR. JUSTICE HARLAN, dissenting:

I had not expected to witness the day when the Supreme Court of the United States would render a decision which casts grave doubt on the constitutionality of the composition of the House of Representatives. It is not an exaggeration to say that such is the effect of today's decision. The Court's holding that the Constitution requires States to select Representatives either by elections at large or by elections in districts composed "as nearly as is practicable" of equal population places in jeopardy the seats of almost all the members of the present House of Representaives.

In the last congressional election, in 1962, Representatives from forty-two States were elected from congressional districts. In all but five of those States, the difference between the populations of the largest and smallest districts exceeded 100,000 persons. A difference of this magnitude in the size of districts the average population of which in each State is less than 500,000 is presumably not equality among districts "as nearly as is practicable," although the Court does not reveal its definition of that phrase. Thus, today's decision impugns the validity of the election of 398 Representatives from thirty-seven States, leaving a "constitutional" House of thirty-seven members now sitting.

Only a demonstration which could not be avoided would justify this Court in rendering a decision the effect of which, inescapably as I see it, is to declare constitutionally defective the very composition of a coordinate branch of the Federal Government. The Court's opinion not only fails to make such a demonstration. It is unsound logically on its face and demonstrably unsound historically. . . .

Before coming to grips with the reasoning that carries such extraordinary consequences, it is important to have firmly in mind the provisions of Article I of the Constitution which controls this case:

> "Section 2. The House of Representatives shall be composed of Members chosen every second Year by the People of the several States, and the Electors in each State shall have the Qualifications requisite for Electors of the most numerous Branch of the State Legislature.
>
> "Representatives and direct Taxes shall be apportioned among the several States which may be included within this Union, according to their respective Numbers, which shall be determined by adding to the whole Number of free Persons, including those bound to Service for a Term of Years, and excluding Indians not taxed, three fifths of all other Persons. The actual Enumeration shall be made within three Years after the first Meeting of the Congress of the United States, and within every subsequent Term of ten Years, in such Manner as they shall by Law direct. The Number of Representatives shall not exceed one for every thirty Thousand, but each State shall have at Least one Representative. . . .
>
> "Section 4. The Times, Places and Manner of holding Elections for Senators and Representatives, shall be prescribed in each State by the Legislature thereof; but the Congress may at any time by Law make or alter such Regulations, except as to the Places of chusing Senators.
>
> "Section 5. Each House shall be the Judge of the Elections, Returns and

Qualifications of its own Members. . . ."

. . . [T]hese constitutional provisions and their "historical context," . . . establish:

1. That congressional Representatives are to be apportioned among the several States largely, but not entirely, according to population;
2. That the States have plenary power to select their allotted Representatives in accordance with any method of popular election they please, subject only to the supervisory power of Congress; and
3. That the supervisory power of Congress is exclusive.

In short, in the absence of legislation providing for equal districts by the Georgia Legislature or by Congress, these appellants have no right to the judicial relief which they seek. It goes without saying that it is beyond the province of this Court to decide whether equally populated districts is the preferable method for electing Representatives, whether state legislatures would have acted more fairly or wisely had they adopted such a method, or whether Congress has been derelict in not requiring state legislatures to follow that course. Once it is clear that there is no constitutional right at stake, that ends the case. . . .

Disclaiming all reliance on other provisions of the Constitution, in particular those of the Fourteenth Amendment on which the appellants relied below and in this Court, the Court holds that the provision in Article I, Section 2, for election of Representatives "by the People" means that congressional districts are to be "as nearly as is practicable" equal in population. . . . Stripped of rhetoric and a "historical context,". . . which bears little resemblance to the evidence found in the pages of history . . . the Court's opinion supports its holding only with the bland assertion that "the principle of a House of Representatives elected "by the People" would be "cast aside" if "a vote is worth more in one district than in another,". . . if congressional districts within a State, each electing a single Representative, are not equal in population. The fact is, however, that Georgia's ten Representatives are elected "by the People" of Georgia, just as Representatives from other States are elected "by the People of the several States." This is all that the Constitution requires.

Although the Court finds necessity for its artificial construction of Article I in the undoubted importance of the right to vote, that right is not involved in this case. All of the appellants do vote. The Court's talk about "debasement" and "dilution" of the vote is a model of circular reasoning, in which the premises of the argument feed on the conclusion. Moreover, by focusing exclusively on numbers in disregard of the area and shape of a congressional district as well as party affiliations within the district, the Court deals in abstractions which will be recognized even by the politically unsophisticated to have little relevance to the realities of political life.

In any event, the very sentence of Article I, Section 2, on which the Court exclusively relies confers the right to vote for Representatives only on those whom the State has found qualified to vote for members of "the most numerous Branch of the State Legislature.". . . So far as Article I is concerned, it is within the State's power to confer that right only on persons of wealth or of a particular sex or, if the State chose, living in specified areas of the State. Were Georgia to find the residents of the Fifth District unqualified to vote for Representatives to the State House of Representatives, they could not vote for Representatives to Congress, according to the express words of Article I, Section 2. Other provisions of the Constitution would, of course, be relevant, but so far as Article I, Section 2, is concerned, the disqualification would be within Georgia's power. How can it be, then that this very same sentence prevents Georgia from apportioning its Representatives as it chooses? The truth is that it does not.

The Court purports to find support for its position in the third paragraph of Article I, Section 2, which provides for the apportionment of Representatives among the States. The appearance of support in that section derives from the Court's confusion of two issues: direct election of Representatives within the States and the apportionment of Representatives among the States. Those issues are distinct, and were separately treated in the Constitution. The fallacy of the Court's reasoning in this regard is illustrated by its slide, obscured by intervening discussion . . . from the intention of the delegates at the Philadelphia Convention "that in allocating Congressmen the number assigned to each State should be determined solely by the number of the State's inhabitants,". . . to a "principle solemnly embodied in the Great Compromise—equal representation in the House of equal numbers of people,". . . The delegates did have the former intention and made clear provision for it. Although many, perhaps most, of them also believed generally—but assuredly not in the precise, formalistic way of the majority of the Court—that within the States representation should be based on population, they did not surreptitiously slip their belief into the Constitution in the phrase "by the People," to be discovered 175 years later like a Shakespearian anagram.

Far from supporting the Court, the apportionment of Representatives among the States shows how blindly the Court has marched to its decision. Representatives were to be apportioned among the States on the basis of free population plus three fifths of the slave population. Since no slave voted, the inclusion of three fifths of their number in the basis of apportionment gave the favored States representation far in excess of their voting population. If, then, slaves were intended to be without representation, Article I did exactly what the Court now says it prohibited: it "weighted" the vote of voters in the slave States. Alternatively, it might have been thought that Representatives elected by free men of a State would speak also for the slaves. But since the slaves added to the representation only of their own State, Representatives from the slave States could have been thought to speak only for the slaves of their own States, indicating both that the Convention believed it possible for a representative elected by one group to speak for another nonvoting group and that Representatives were in large degree still thought of as speaking for the whole population of a State.

There is a further basis for demonstrating the hollowness of the Court's assertion that Article I requires "one man's vote in a congressional election . . . to be worth as much as another's". . . Nothing that the Court does today will disturb the fact that although in 1960 the population of an average congressional district was 410,481, the States of Alaska, Nevada, and Wyoming each have a Representative in Congress, although their respective populations are 226,167, 285,278, and 330,066. In entire disregard of population, Article I, Section 2, guarantees each of these States and every other State "at Least one Representative." It is whimsical to assert in the face of this guarantee that an absolute principle of "equal representation in the House of equal numbers of people" is "solemnly embodied" in Article I. All that there is is a provision which bases representation in the House, generally but not entirely, on the population of the States. The provision for representation of each State in the House of Representatives is not a mere exception to the principle framed by the majority; it shows that no such principle is to be found.

Finally in this array of hurdles to its decision which the Court surmounts only by knocking them down is Section 4 of Article I. . . . The delegates were well aware of the problem of "rotten boroughs,". . . It cannot be supposed that delegates to the Convention would have labored to establish a principle of equal representation only to bury it, one would have thought beyond discovery, in Section 2, and omit all mention of it from Section 4, which deals explicitly with the conduct of elections. Section 4 states without qualification that the state legislatures shall prescribe regulations for the conduct of elections for Representatives and, equally without qualification, that Congress may make or alter such regulations. There is nothing to indicate any limitations whatsoever on this grant of plenary initial and supervisory power. The Court's holding is, of course, derogatory not only of the power of the state legislatures but also of the power of Congress, both theoretically and as they have actually exercised their power. . . . It freezes upon both, for no reason other than that it seems wise to the majority of the present Court, a particular political theory for the selection of Representatives. . . .

There is dubious propriety in turning to the "historical context" of constitutional provisions which speak so consistently and plainly. But, as one might expect when the Constitution itself is free from ambiguity, the surrounding history makes what is already clear even clearer.

As the Court repeatedly emphasizes, delegates to the Philadelphia Convention frequently expressed their view that representation should be based on population. There were also, however, many statements favoring limited monarchy and property qualifications for suffrage and expressions of disapproval for unrestricted democracy. Such expressions prove as little on one side of this case as they do on the other. Whatever the dominant political philosophy at the Convention, one thing seems clear: it is in the last degree unlikely that most or even many of the delegates would have subscribed to the principle of "one person, one vote,". . . Moreover, the statements approving population-based representation were focused on the problem of how representation should be apportioned among the States in the House of Representatives. The Great Compromise concerned representation of the States in the Congress. In all of the discussion surrounding the basis of representation of the House and all of the discussion whether Representatives should be elected by the legislatures or the people of the States, there is nothing which suggests even remotely that the delegates had in mind the problem of districting within a State.

The subject of districting within the States is discussed explicitly with reference to the provisions of Article I, Section 4, which the Court so pointedly neglects. . . . [T]he Convention understood the state legislature to have plenary power over the conduct of elections for Representatives, including the power to district well or badly, subject only to the supervisory power of Congress. How, then, can the Court hold that Article I, Section 2, prevents the state legislatures from districting as they choose? . . .

Materials supplementary to the debates are as unequivocal. In the ratifying conventions, there was no suggestion that the provisions of Article I, Section 2, restricted the power of the States to prescribe the conduct of elections conferred on them by Article I, Section 4. None of the Court's references to the ratification debates supports the view that the provision for election of Representatives "by the People" was intended to have any application to the apportionment of Representatives within the States; in each instance, the cited passage merely repeats what the Constitution itself provides: that Representatives were to be elected by the people of the States. . . . [*Justice Harlan then discusses the debates in several ratifying conventions and pertinent passages from* The Federalist *and concludes that the states, subject only to the control of Congress, could district as they chose.*]

. . . The upshot of all this is that the language of Article I, Sections 2 and 4, the surrounding text, and the relevant history are all in strong and consistent direct contradiction of the Court's holding. The constitutional scheme vests in the States plenary power to regulate the conduct of elections for Representatives, and, in order to protect the Federal Government, provides for congressional supervision of the States' exercise of their power. Within this scheme, the appellants do not have the right which they assert, in the absence of the provision for equal districts by the Georgia Legislature or the Congress. The constitutional right which the Court creates is manufactured out of whole cloth. . . .

The unstated premise of the Court's conclusion quite obviously is that the Congress has not dealt, and the Court believes it will not deal, with the problem of congressional apportionment in accordance with what the Court believes to be sound political principles. Laying aside for the moment the validity of such a consideration as a factor in constitutional interpretation, it becomes relevant to examine the history of congressional action under Article I, Section 4. This history reveals that the Court is not simply undertaking to exercise a power which the Constitution reserves to the Congress; it is also overruling congressional judgment. . . .

For a period of about fifty years . . . [*1842–1911*] Congress, by repeated legislative act, imposed on the States the requirement that congressional districts be equal in population. (This, of course, is the very requirement which the Court now declares to have been constitutionally required of the States all along without implementing legislation.) Subsequently, after giving express attention to the problem, Congress eliminated that requirement, with the intention of permitting the States to find their own solutions. Since then, despite repeated efforts to obtain congressional action again, Congress has continued to leave the problem and its solution to the States. It cannot be contended, therefore, that the Court's decision today fills a gap left by the Congress. On the contrary, the Court substitutes its own judgment for that of the Congress. . . .

Today's decision has portents for our society and the Court itself which should be recognized. This is not a case in which the Court vindicates the kind of individual rights that are assured by the Due Process Clause of the Fourteenth Amendment, whose "vague contours,". . . of course leave much room for constitutional developments necessitated by changing conditions in a dynamic society. Nor is this a case in which an emergent set of facts requires the Court to frame new principles to protect recognized constitutional rights. The claim for judicial relief in this case strikes at one of the fundamental doctrines of our system of government, the separation of powers. In upholding that claim, the Court attempts to effect reforms in a field which the Constitution, as plainly as can be, has committed exclusively to the political process.

This Court, no less than all other branches of the Government, is bound by the Constitution. The Constitution does not confer on the Court blanket authority to step into every situation where the political branch may be thought to have fallen short. The stability of this institution ultimately depends not only upon its being alert to keep the other branches of government within constitutional bounds but equally upon recognition of the limitations on the Court's own functions in the constitutional system.

What is done today saps the political process. The promise of judicial intervention in matters of this sort cannot but encourage popular inertia in efforts for political reform through the political process, with the inevitable result that the process is itself weakened. By yielding to the demand for a judicial remedy in this instance, the Court in my view does a disservice both to itself and to the broader values of our system of government.

Believing that the complaint fails to disclose a constitutional claim. I would affirm the judgment below dismissing the complaint. . . .

MR. JUSTICE STEWART:

I think it is established that "this Court has power to afford relief in a case of this type as against the objection that the issues are not justiciable," and I cannot subscribe to any possible implication to the contrary which may lurk in Mr. Justice Harlan's dissenting opinion. With this single qualification I join the dissent because I think Mr. Justice Harlan has unanswerably demonstrated that Article I, Section 2, of the Constitution gives no mandate to this Court or to any court to ordain that congressional districts within each State must be equal in population.

CHAPTER 5

The Federal System

The American constitutional system is based on a division of powers between the national government and the states; under our federal system, the powers of the national government are enumerated in the body of the constitution, whereas those powers not delegated to the national government are reserved to the states or to the people. The Tenth Amendment announces this principle of federalism.[1]

Although the words *federal* or *federation* are not used in the Constitution, the creation of a federal system of government was the natural solution for the thirteen original states.[2] The es-

[1] See Martin Shapiro, "Federalism," and Charles Lofgren, "The Origins of the Tenth Amendment: History, Sovereignty and the Problem of Constitutional Intention," in Ronald Collins, ed., *Constitutional Government in America* (Durham, N.C.: Carolina Academic Press, 1980).

[2] K. C. Wheare, *Federal Government* (London: Oxford U.P., 1951), p. 1. See also William S. Livingston, *Federalism and Constitutional Change* (Oxford: Clarendon Press, 1956), p. 1, where the author notes that "federal governments and federal constitutions do not grow simply by accident. They arise in response to certain stimuli; a federal system is consciously adopted as a means of solving the problems represented by these stimuli."

tablishment of a unitary system of government that concentrated all powers in the national government would have been impossible because of the necessity for compromise between the advocates of states' rights and the supporters of a strong central government. The framers of the Constitution "rejected summarily the advice of those few, like Hamilton, who sought to build a unitary authority, to abolish the States as autonomous units, and to provide for the appointment of governors from the national Capital. They also overruled decisively the considerably greater number who wanted to keep the union a mere confederation." [3] Instead, they created our federal system of government. "Federalism was the means and price of the formation of the Union. It was inevitable, therefore, that its basic concepts should determine much of our history." [4]

In establishing the federal system, the framers of the Constitution used three major devices:

1. The states were preserved as separate sources of authority and as organs of administration.
2. The states were given important powers in connection with the composition and selection of the national government.
3. The powers of government were distributed between the national government and the states.[5]

Distribution of Powers

POWERS OF THE NATIONAL GOVERNMENT

The national government possesses all those powers that are delegated to it by the Constitution either expressly or by implication. These powers are enumerated principally as powers of Congress in Article I, Section 8. Included among these are the power to tax, borrow and coin money, maintain armies and navies, conduct foreign relations, and regulate interstate and foreign commerce. After the enumeration of powers in Article I, Section 8, the Constitution grants Congress further authority to "make all laws which shall be necessary and proper for carrying into execution the foregoing powers, and all other powers vested by the Constitution in the government of the United States, or in any department or officer thereof." This general grant of implied powers in the "elastic" or "necessary and proper" clause of the Constitution has raised numerous questions as to the actual scope of national authority. In many instances, such questions have been resolved by the Supreme Court.

[3] *Report* of the Commission on Intergovernmental Relations (June 1955), p. 10.

[4] Herbert Wechsler, "The Political Safeguards of Federalism: The Role of the States in the Composition and Selection of the National Government," in Arthur W. Macmahon, ed., *Federalism Mature and Emergent* (Garden City, N.Y.: Doubleday, 1955), p. 97.

[5] Ibid., pp. 97–98. See also William H. Riker, "Federalism," in Fred I. Greenstein and Nelson W. Polsby, *Handbook of Political Science,* Vol. 5 (Reading, Mass: Addison-Wesley, 1975), p. 93.

Despite the fact that the states are supreme in their sphere of activities, the federal Constitution and national laws constitute the supreme law of the land when conflicts arise from attempts of both jurisdictions to govern the same subject matter. The supremacy of national authority is indicated by Article VI, clause 2, of the Constitution, which provides as follows:

> This Constitution, and and laws of the United States which shall be made in pursuance thereof; and all treaties made, or which shall be made, under the authority of the United States, shall be the supreme law of the land; and the judges in every state shall be bound thereby, any thing in the Constitution or laws of any state to the contrary notwithstanding.

POWERS OF THE STATES

The state governments possess those powers that are not given to the national government or prohibited to the states. Because the Constitution deals principally with national powers, the fact that important powers are left to the states is sometimes forgotten. Among others, the states have the power to establish schools and supervise education, regulate intrastate commerce, conduct elections, establish local government units, and borrow money. In addition, a broad and generally undefined "*police power*" enables the states to take action to protect and promote the health, safety, morals, and general welfare of their inhabitants.[6]

EXCLUSIVE AND CONCURRENT POWERS

The powers of the national and state governments are sometimes exclusive and sometimes concurrent. Most of the powers of the national government are exclusive. For example, the Federal Government alone has power to make treaties, to coin money, and to govern the District of Columbia. The states also have certain exclusive powers, such as those that relate to wills and domestic relations. When powers are shared by both the states and the national government, they are said to be concurrent. For example, both Congress and the states have the power to tax and borrow money. Both levels of government may take property for public purposes, enact bankruptcy laws, and establish courts. The only example of a constitutional provision expressly granting concurrent powers to both the Federal Government and the states is found in the Eighteenth Amendment. Section 2 of that Amendment provided that "The Congress and the several states shall have concurrent power to enforce this article by appropriate legislation."

[6] See Daniel Elazar, *American Federalism: A View from the States,* 2nd ed. (Crowell: New York, 1972).

Role of the Supreme Court in the Federal System

Of course, it was impossible for the framers of the Constitution to draw a precise line between the powers of the national government and those of the states. And even if such a line of demarcation could have been drawn at any time during our constitutional history, it would have needed revision from time to time to meet the demands of new and changing conditions. Conflicts between national and state authorities are inevitable in a federal system of government. Such conflicts must be resolved by peaceful means if the union of states is to be maintained as the servant of the American people. The Civil War may be viewed as an example of what happens when the machinery for the peaceful resolution of conflicts between the states and national authority breaks down.

Because the line of division between state and federal powers is vague and indefinite, some branch of government must resolve the inevitable clashes. Actually, the President and Congress, as well as the Supreme Court, play an important role in maintaining a working federalism. For it is often the statutes passed by the national government and the administrative regulations designed to enforce them that define the actual working relationships between federal and state agencies.

Nevertheless, although much of the shape of the federal system is left to the working of politics, the Supreme Court has played a key role in establishing the balance of power between the states and the Federal Government.[7] The Court's role as official umpire in disputes between the states and the Federal Government should be revealed clearly by the cases that follow. However, the issue of federalism also will be encountered in many other topics of constitutional law, such as the commerce and fiscal powers of Congress. (See Chapter 9.)

John Marshall's Nationalism

In the case of *McCulloch* v. *Maryland* (p. 127), the classic statement of the doctrine of implied powers is presented. One of Marshall's admirers stated that "in his opinion in this case John Marshall rose to the loftiest heights of judicial statesmanship. If his fame rested solely on this one effort, it would be secure." [8] In *McCulloch* v. *Maryland,* Marshall in effect "rewrote the fundamental law of the nation; or perhaps, it may be more accurate to say that he made a written instrument a living thing, capable of growth, capable of keeping pace with the advancement of the American people and ministering to their

[7] Compare John Schmidhauser, *The Supreme Court as Arbiter in Federal–State Relations, 1787–1957* (Chapel Hill: University of North Carolina Press, 1958) with Jesse Choper, *Judicial Review and the National Political Process* (Chicago: University of Chicago Press, 1980), who argues that the Court should not perform such a role.

[8] Albert J. Beveridge, *The Life of John Marshall* (Boston: Houghton, 1919), Vol. 4, p. 282.

changing necessities. This greatest of Marshall's treatises on government may well be entitled the 'Vitality of the Constitution.'" [9]

In the *McCulloch* case, Marshall was faced with a clear-cut issue between state and national powers, because he needed to interpret the meaning of the "necessary and proper" clause of Article I of the Constitution. Actually, his decision in *McCulloch* v. *Maryland* was clearly foreshadowed by an earlier opinion. In *United States* v. *Fisher,* 2 Cranch 358 (1805), Marshall had noted that in construing the "necessary and proper" clause "it would be incorrect and would produce endless difficulty, if the opinion should be maintained that no law was authorized which was not indispensably necessary to give effect to a specified power. Congress must possess the choice of means, and must be empowered to use any means which are in fact conducive to the exercise of a power granted by the Constitution." Nevertheless, the classic statement of the doctrine of implied powers is found in *McCulloch* v. *Maryland.*

To comprehend fully Marshall's decision in the *McCulloch* case, one must have an appreciation of the political history of that period. The First Bank of the United States, proposed by Hamilton with Federalist support, was chartered by Congress in 1791 for a period of twenty years. The bank was established over the bitter protests of Jefferson and Madison, who were opposed to the centralization of financial powers in the Federal Government. Jefferson and his strict-constructionist followers further argued that because the Constitution did not specifically grant Congress the power to charter a bank, it could not do so. Although the bank was run efficiently, it was never a popular institution. As a consequence, its charter was not renewed in 1811. Instead, the states chartered a number of new banks to take care of the financial needs of the country. But chaos rather than financial stability resulted. "When the restraining and regulating influence of that conservative and ably managed institution [First Bank of the United States] was removed altogether, local banking began a course that ended in a mad carnival of roguery, to the ruin of legitimate business and the impoverishment and bankruptcy of hundreds of thousands of the general public." [10]

President Madison's previous opposition to the bank vanished, and under his leadership the Second Bank of the United States was chartered in 1816 to avert further financial difficulties. But the Second Bank became even more unpopular than its predecessor. It was not managed as efficiently as the First Bank; and, as financial difficulties continued, a number of states passed laws or constitutional amendments designed to restrict its activities. One such state was Maryland, where inefficient management of the Baltimore branch of the Second Bank had resulted in heavy losses to a number of investors. The Maryland law, which is explained fully at the beginning of the case, is what Marshall had to deal with in *McCulloch* v. *Maryland.*

Marshall's decision was the signal for a bitter attack on the Supreme Court,

[9] Ibid., p. 308.
[10] Ibid., p. 177.

principally by the supporters of states' rights. "From his plantation the aging Jefferson called for resistance." For "behind that opinion Jefferson saw lurking the specter of consolidated government." [11] A number of newspapers throughout the country denounced Marshall and the Court. The Virginia legislature passed a resolution condemning the decision and called for a constitutional amendment that would create a "supertribunal" over the Supreme Court to decide questions involving the "powers of the general and state government." Ohio, Indiana, Illinois, and Tennessee also passed resolutions attacking Marshall's opinion. Pennsylvania proposed a constitutional amendment that would forbid Congress to establish any bank outside the District of Columbia. But these bitter attacks receded gradually as the nation became concerned increasingly with the dispute over slavery; and five years later, when Ohio attempted to defy the Supreme Court, Marshall reaffirmed the decision of *McCulloch* v. *Maryland.*[12]

In conjunction with *McCulloch* v. *Maryland,* we should consider two other opinions of John Marshall—*Gibbons* v. *Ogden* and *Cohens* v. *Virginia. Gibbons* v. *Ogden* is considered fully in Chapter 8. In *Cohens* v. *Virginia* (p. 132), Marshall held that the power of the Supreme Court was superior to that of the state courts whenever federal rights were involved.

Marshall's arguments in *Cohens* v. *Virginia* constitute, to a great extent, a restatement of Justice Story's decision in *Martin* v. *Hunter's Lessee,* 1 Wheat. 304 (1816). But Marshall's statement in *Cohens* v. *Virginia* is much more logical and persuasive. Many years later, the powerful opinion of Chief Justice Taney in *Ableman* v. *Booth,* 21 How. 506 (1859), further enhanced the power of the Supreme Court. In that case it was held that the Wisconsin Supreme Court could not grant a writ of habeas corpus to Booth, an abolitionist editor, who was being held in federal custody for the violation of a federal law. Taney held:

> No state judge or court, after they are judicially informed that the party is imprisoned under the authority of the United States, has any right to interfere with him, or to require him to be brought before them. . . . And no power is more clearly conferred by the Constitution and laws of the United States, than the power of this court [Supreme Court] to decide, ultimately and finally, all cases arising under such Constitution and laws; and for that purpose to bring here for revision . . . the judgment of a state court, where such questions have airsen, and the right claimed under them denied by the highest judicial tribunal in the State.

Like his decision in *McCulloch* v. *Maryland,* Marshall's opinion in *Cohens* v. *Virginia* was roundly denounced by the antinationalist group. Marshall himself was led to remark that his decision in *Cohens* v. *Virginia* "has been assaulted with a degree of virulence transcending what has appeared on any former occasion." [13] But Marshall and his principles endured. In six short years, from 1819 through 1824, Marshall's opinions in *McCulloch* v. *Maryland, Osborn* v.

[11] Donald G. Morgan, *Justice William Johnston, the First Dissenter* (Columbia: University of South Carolina Press, 1954), pp. 110–11.

[12] *Osborn* v. *Bank of the United States,* 9 Wheat. 738 (1824).

[13] Letter of John Marshall to Mr. Justice Story, June 15, 1821, reproduced in Erwin C. Surrency, ed., *The Marshall Reader* (New York: Oceana Publications, 1955), p. 210.

Bank of the United States, Cohens v. *Virginia,* and *Gibbons* v. *Ogden* established, for all time, the national character of the United States.

Yet Marshall ought not to be seen as an enemy of the federal system. His opinion in *Barron* v. *Baltimore* (p. 138) and his opinion in *Willson* v. *Blackbird Creek Marsh Co.,* discussed in Chapter 8, indicate his allegiance to federalism and the continuing vitality of the state governments.

Dred Scott

The nationalism furthered by Marshall received its greatest challenge from the slavery controversy and the Civil War. In the 1840s and 1850s both Congress and the Presidency worked to avert the destruction of the Union. *Dred Scott* v. *Sandford* (p. 139) was the major unsuccessful Supreme Court effort at preserving the unity of the nation. At the time, the "free soil" controversy was rending the political fabric. There was a rough balance between slave and free states in the Senate. But the western territories, such as Kansas and Missouri, were in the process of achieving statehood. Whether they entered as free or slave states would determine the balance of power in Congress. Thus, whether Southerners moving into the territories could import slavery to the prairie or whether a slave became free by virtue of stepping onto "free soil" where slavery had not previously existed became questions of crucial political concern. Congress had passed compromise legislation that, in effect, made some of the territories free and others slave, but this compromise was falling apart under political pressure. The obvious alternative compromise would have been to allow the inhabitants of each new state to decide the slavery question for themselves, thus getting the whole issue out of the national political arena where it was doing so much damage.

This was the compromise attempted in *Dred Scott,* in which the Court held that former slaves could never become citizens of the United States no matter what Congress decided, but that by state action they might become citizens of the states in which they resided. However, the Court loaded the scales somewhat on the Southern side, because it also held that Congress could not forbid the importation of slaves into the territories. The Supreme Court compromise was as roundly rejected as those of the other branches. Moreover, in order to reach it, the Court had adopted the most racist position ever officially announced by a branch of the national government. The decision resulted in the most grievous blow to the Court's prestige that it has ever suffered. *Dred Scott* was reversed by the Civil War and the Fourteenth Amendment.

Continuing Federal and State Conflicts

Controversies over the nature of federalism certainly did not end with the Civil War; nor were they confined to the commerce and tax problems that are taken up in Chapter 8. *Missouri* v. *Holland* (p. 144), which might be equally well placed in the next chapter on war and foreign affairs, involved one such controversy. Under its treaty-making power, could the central government intervene in areas—in this instance, in the control of wild game—that had traditionally been viewed as within the police powers reserved to the states? The Court's answer was yes. Although the opinion and some subsequent ones contain hints, it has never been clear just how far the treaty power overrides other constitutional provisions. For instance, could the central government enter into an international convention against racist propaganda that would allow it to censor American newspapers, thus violating the First Amendment? In *Reid* v. *Covert,* 354 U.S. 1 (1957), the Court said, "no agreement with a foreign nation can confer power on the Congress, or on any other branch of Government, which is free from the restraints of the Constitution."

In another case involving federal powers in the realm of foreign affairs and national security, the Court held a state antisedition statute unconstitutional on the grounds that federal statutes such as the Smith Act (see Chapter 11) had "occupied the field to the exclusion of parallel state legislation, that the dominant interest of the Federal Government precludes state intervention, and that administration of state acts would conflict with the operation of the federal plan, . . ." [*Pennsylvania* v. *Nelson,* 350 U.S. 497 (1956)].

The question of whether a particular federal statute "pre-empts" a field, prohibiting state regulation in the same area, continues to arise frequently. For instance, in *Goldstein* v. *California,* 412 U.S. 576 (1973), the Court held 5 to 4 that a California statute forbidding the "pirating" of records was not barred by the constitutional grant of copyright power to Congress and subsequent federal copyright laws. The closeness of the vote was no doubt due to the difficulty of harmonizing this holding with earlier decisions invalidating state statutes as precluded by the patent provisions of the Constitution and federal patent statutes. [*Sears, Roebuck & Co.* v. *Stiffel Co.,* 376 U.S. 225 (1964); and *Compco Corp.* v. *Day-Brite Lighting Inc.,* 376 U.S. 234 (1964).]

The fairly recent case of *Oregon* v. *Mitchell,* 400 U.S. 112 (1970), indicates that the classic issues of federalism are still with us. Certainly, a congressional eighteen-year-old voting statute warms the hearts of most of us. On the other hand, one can hardly think of a function more deeply imbedded in the sovereignty of the states than running their own elections for state offices. A slim majority of the Court decided that although Congress might regulate the age of voting in federal elections, it could not interfere in this way in state elections. The Twenty-sixth Amendment was necessary to overcome this continuing allegiance to federalism. Congress does have extensive powers to interfere in state elections under the Fifteenth Amendment. (See Chapters 4 and 13.)

A similarly classic issue, this time over the necessary and proper clause, arose in *United States* v. *Oregon,* 366 U.S. 643 (1961). An Oregon resident died in a federal Veteran's Administration hospital in Oregon without a will or legal heirs. Normally, matters of inheritance are firmly within the realm of state rather than federal law. Oregon law provides that the property of a person who dies without will or heirs goes to the state. But a federal statute provides that the property of a veteran who dies in a veteran's hospital without will or heirs goes to the Federal Government. The Court held that the money should go to the Federal Government. For the majority, Justice Black wrote: "Congress undoubtedly has the power—under its constitutional powers to raise armies and navies and to conduct wars—to pay pensions and to build hospitals and homes for veterans. We think it plain that the same sources of power authorize Congress to require that the personal property left by its wards when they die in government facilities shall be devoted to the comfort and recreation of other ex-service people who must depend upon the government for care. The fact that this law pertains to the devolution of property does not render it invalid. Although it is true that this is an area normally left to the states, it is not immune under the Tenth Amendment from laws passed by the Federal Government which are, as is the law here, necessary and proper to the exercise of a delegated power." In dissent, Justice Douglas said: "The power to build hospitals and homes for veterans and to pay them pensions is plainly necessary and proper to the powers to raise and support armies and navies. . . . The power to provide for the administration of the estates of veterans . . . is to me a far cry from any such power. When the Federal Government enters a field as historically local as the administration of decedents' estates, some clear relation of the asserted power to one of the delegated powers should be shown. . . . Today's decision does not square with our conception of federalism. There is nothing more deeply imbedded in the Tenth Amendment, as I read history, than the dispositon of the estates of deceased people. I do not see how a scheme for administration of decedents' estates of the kind we have here can possibly be necessary and proper to any power delegated to Congress."

In *National League of Cities* v. *Usery* (p. 146), the Court for the first time since the 1930s struck down a federal commerce regulation on grounds of federalism. *Usery* has ushered in a lively new debate on the continuing force of the Tenth Amendment as a safeguard of federalism. [See also *McCarty* v. *McCarty,* 101 S.Ct. 2728 (1981).]

In reading *Usery,* however, one should be aware that the Court has also explicitly held that Section 5 of the Fourteenth Amendment and Section 2 of the Fifteenth Amendment extend the powers of Congress to regulate state conduct beyond the powers granted it by the commerce clause. [*Fullilove* v. *Klutznick,* p. 618; *Rome* v. *United States,* 446 U.S. 156 (1980).]

A Revived Area of Federal Conflict

The Civil War amendments and the statutes flowing from them have traditionally been dealt with in the context of racial discrimination. We will return to them in this context in Chapter 13. They also raise fundamental issues of federalism—indeed, issues so fundamental as to have permanently shaped their capacity to resolve racial problems. For the vast bulk of those racial problems arose in day-to-day, common human relationships that have always fallen within the ambit of state criminal and civil law. If the Thirteenth, Fourteenth, and Fifteenth Amendments gave the national government the authority to handle all the political, social, and economic problems of the former slaves, then a fundamental breach had been created in the basic structure of federalism. For at least where Negroes were involved, the central government would be in possession of the broad mass of police powers hitherto reserved to the states. Every commercial transaction, sale of land, marriage, murder, inheritance, or road accident involving blacks might suddenly become a matter of federal rather than state law.

This prospect was enhanced by the last section of each of the amendments, which gave Congress the "power to enforce" them "by appropriate legislation"—an alarmingly broad and vague grant of new legislative authority to the central government. Congress responded with the far-reaching civil rights acts of 1866, 1870, 1871, and 1875, designed to protect the freedmen from continued coercion by their former masters.

Almost immediate judicial reaction can be seen in favor of federalism. The Fourteenth Amendment protected the privileges and immunities of "citizens of the United States." By 1873, in the *Slaughterhouse* cases (Chapter 10), the Supreme Court was already distinguishing between those rights pertaining to an individual as a citizen of the United States and those pertaining to him or her as a citizen of his or her state. Only the former, it was argued, were protected by the Fourteenth Amendment, and they were limited to such areas as travel to the nation's capital and access to her seaports. The vast mass of legal rights and relations were to remain strictly a matter of state law.

The *Civil Rights Cases* (p. 154) might fairly be viewed as sheer racism—the Supreme Court's share of the dismantling of Reconstruction in which the Congress, Presidency, and political parties were the leading participants. It might be more accurate to say that the Court's very limited sympathy for blacks was more than overcome by its allegiance to the traditions of federalism, which would have been badly strained if the various national civil rights statutes had been allowed to operate directly on individuals engaging in everyday affairs that normally had been governed by state laws.

This tendency of the Court was further demonstrated by *United States* v. *Cruikshank,* 92 U.S. 542 (1875) and *United States* v. *Harris,* 106 U.S. 629 (1882), which rendered inoperative the antilynching provisions of several federal civil rights statutes essentially because the murder of one man by another was a matter for state criminal law.

The Fourteenth Amendment says, after all, that "No *State* shall" (italics supplied). So some protection for minorities could be combined with the traditional federalism by holding that the central government could forbid the state governments from engaging in racial discrimination so long as federal actions did not touch the relationships—even discriminatory relationships—between one private individual and another that were the central focus of state law.

The extent to which this "state action" doctrine has shaped the way the justices have directly applied the Civil War amendments will be considered in Chapter 13. Here we are concerned with how it affected Court treatment of the congressional statutes passed to enforce the amendments. Although many federal provisions were struck down, two statutory characteristics had high survival value. Where a statute confined itself narrowly to the protection of specific federal constitutional rights, such as voting or petitioning the national government, and/or where its targets were confined to state officials and others acting "under color of state law," it enjoyed the best chance of receiving a friendly judicial reception—although it usually did little practical good. In other words, where the statute respected the values of federalism by confining itself to state action infringing specifically on national rights and leaving private action to state law, it would be judicially approved.

From the 1880s until the 1960s, little was heard of the early civil rights statutes. It is true that in *United States* v. *Classic,* 313 U.S. 299 (1941), one of the early acts was successfully used to prosecute state officials for ballot-box frauds. And in *Screws* v. *United States,* 325 U.S. 91 (1945), the Court reacted favorably toward a civil rights statute that made it a crime for one acting under color of state law *willfully* to deprive an individual of rights protected by the Fourteenth Amendment. Counsel for a Georgia sheriff who had killed a prisoner argued that the sheriff had not violated the federal statute because he could not have been acting "under color of state law," even though he was exercising his legal authority in arresting and holding the prisoner. For how could he have been acting under color of state law when the killing was itself a violation of state law? The Court rejected this argument. It held that the sheriff had been acting under color of state law. On the other hand, the *Screws* Court held that no violation of the federal statute could be found unless it could be proved that the sheriff had acted with *specific* intent to deprive his prisoner of his federal constitutional rights. If all he had intended to do was murder him, rather than deprive him of a fair trial, then that was a matter of state criminal law. The *Screws* decision made it almost impossible to use that civil rights statute in defense of blacks, except in those instances in which the context made it absolutely clear, as in the refusal of a state official to issue a ballot, that a federal right was the only right involved.

The decisions of the 1950s, although they evidenced some dissatisfaction with older approaches, stuck to the insistance that only state action might be forbidden by federal statutes—and then only where the state action was aimed at specific federal rights.

Then, in 1961, *Monroe* v. *Pape,* 365 U.S. 167, gave some signs of a new judicial attitude. A Chicago policeman was sued under a federal statute (42 U.S. Code 1983) for breaking into a plaintiff's house without a warrant and illegally arresting one of the family. The court allowed the suit. It again rejected the argument that a state policeman acting in his official capacity is not acting under color of state law simply because his actions are illegal under state law. It rejected the *Screws* requirement of specific intent to deprive someone of his federal constitutional rights because this was a civil rather than a criminal action and the statutory language in this instance did not require willful deprivation. Nevertheless, *Monroe* is clearly compatible with the older federalism. The offender was clearly a state officer rather than a private person, and his offense was against a specific federal constitutional right: the right against unreasonable search and seizure. (See Chapter 15.)

The new trend became even clearer in two 1966 cases, *United States* v. *Price,* 383 U.S. 787 and *United States* v. *Guest,* 383 U.S. 745. In both instances, the indictments had been dismissed by federal district courts and were reinstated by the Supreme Court. In *Price* the Court held that when the sheriff, his deputy, a policeman, and fifteen private citizens allegedly took three prisoners out of jail and murdered them, they deprived them of a specific federal constitutional right: the right to a fair trial guaranteed by the Fourteenth Amendment. In *Guest* the justices held that an alleged conspiracy to prevent certain blacks from traveling on Georgia highways was aimed at a specific federal, constitutional right: the right to travel by highway from state to state. In *Price* there was little difficulty in finding that the defendants acted under color of state law because three were state law officers and the others allegedly acted with them. In *Guest* the Court had to strain a bit but found that the indictments might possibly be charging that state officials had acted with the private conspirators. Because the Court decisions only involved reinstating the indictments and not final disposition, the justices did not have to commit themselves finally on the scope of "under color of law." Nor did they have to indicate whether the strict *Screws* requirement of specific intent needed to be maintained. But neither *Price* nor *Guest* abandon the formula of state action against national constitutional rights that preserves the barriers of federalism. Nevertheless, they represent a considerable shift from the Court of the 1950s, which had been unable to make up its mind whether Fourteenth Amendment rights were even the sort of rights that the particular statute involved in *Guest* was designed to protect.

Then, in *Griffin* v. *Breckenridge,* 403 U.S. 88 (1971), a unanimous Court held that the federal statute granting civil remedies against racially motivated conspiracies to deprive individuals of their rights was applicable to purely private conspiracies in spite of an earlier decision to the contrary. [*Collins* v. *Hardyman,* 341 U.S. 651 (1951).] The Court avoided the state-action problem of the Fourteenth Amendment entirely by basing its decision on the Thirteenth Amendment and the right to travel announced in *Guest.* It continued to insist, however, that a specific intent to deprive persons of federal constitutional rights must be shown on the part of the conspirators, rather than simply a showing that the civil rights of the plaintiffs were incidentally infringed in a course of conduct (such as assault or murder) covered by state statutes. So a strong remnant remains of the federalism barrier to direct congressional regulation of private action involving race. [See also *Dennis* v. *Sparks,* 101 S.Ct. 183 (1980), holding that a private individual has acted "under color of law" when he or she has engaged in joint action with the state or its agents.]

The reliance on the Thirteenth Amendment is significant in the light of a slightly earlier case, *Jones* v. *Alfred H. Mayer Co.* (p. 159). *Guest, Breckenridge,* and *Mayer* were all written by Justice Stewart. In *Mayer* the Court resurrects the Civil Rights Act of 1866 and discovers that it forbids "*all* discrimination against Negroes in the sale or rental of property" by private persons as well as government authorities. (Italics supplied.) And it then finds that the Thirteenth Amendment authorizes such a statute. In *McDonald* v. *Santa Fe Trail Transportation Co.,* discussed in Chapter 13, precisely the same tactic is used to allow the federal government to forbid discrimination in private employment where no "state action" is involved.

The Thirteenth Amendment is used to break through the federalism barrier and allow Congress to reach down into the sphere of property law traditionally reserved to the states and directly regulate purely private property transactions where racial discrimination is involved. The Fourteenth Amendment, with its embarrassing doctrine of state action, is entirely avoided. Justice Stewart relies on the same technique in *Runyon* v. *McCrary,* 427 U.S. 160 (1976). He holds that another section of the Act of 1866, which forbids racial discrimination in the making and enforcement of contracts, forbids private schools from excluding prospective students solely on the basis of race. For the school is denying blacks the opportunity to enter into a contract for the provision of educational services in return for the payment of tuition. [Cf. *Shelley* v. *Kraemer* (Chapter 13), in which the Court reaches a similar result in the Fourteenth Amendment context but has terrible trouble doing so.]

Although *Guest, Mayer,* and *Breckenridge* do not mean that all the old federalism barriers to congressional control of racial discrimination have toppled, they do represent a new stage in the federal balance. It seemed unlikely that the Court could long persist in the position that the Thirteenth Amendment authorizes congressional action against private discrimination but that the Fourteenth does not.

The Court has also extended the reach of the federal civil rights statutes against state and local government units. It has taken the position that the Fourteenth Amendment empowers Congress to set aside the states' Eleventh Amendment immunity from suits by its citizens. [*Fitzpatrick,* v. *Bitzer,* 427 U.S. 448 (1976).] It has also reversed that portion of *Monroe* v. *Pape* that immunized municipalities from suit under 42 U.S. Code 1983. [*Monell* v. *Dept. of Social Services,* 436 U.S. 658 (1978).] Moreover in *Maine* v. *Thiboutot,* 448 U.S. 1 (1980) it has held that Section 1983 applies to any violation of any federal law, not just civil rights laws, thus allowing individuals to sue state government officials in federal courts whenever they allege that the state official has harmed them by violating any federal law. Such "minor," "technical," "procedural" changes can have a fundamental impact on federalism. Today hundreds of federal statutes impose thousands of detailed requirements on state goverments, particularly where the states are receiving federal grants. Those federal requirements are enforced on the states by the federal executive departments. Although federal executives occasionally go to court against the states, most disputes about the meaning of federal regulations are settled by discussions between state and federal officials. As a result of the expansion of 1983, any resident of a state who believes that his state officials are not properly interpreting and complying with a federal statute, and thus denying him a right under that statute, may sue those officials in a federal court even when the federal officials enforcing the statute have no quarrel with state administrators. Thus state governments are subject to ever-increasing levels of control by federal courts. [See *Middlesex* v. *Sea Clammers,* 101 S. Ct. 2615 (1981).]

The state action doctrine does not, of course, apply to the commerce clause. The modern civil rights laws that forbid discrimination in public accommodations are grounded in the commerce clause, not the Fourteenth Amendment. They do reach private discrimination by the individual owners of hotels and restaurants. The Court has read the commerce power broadly to support such antidiscrimination laws. (See Chapters 9 and 13.) Today the federal government is the single largest provider of grants to the arts, humanities, sciences, and education and the single largest purchaser of goods and services in the United States. Invoking the taxing and spending and commerce clauses, the Court has suggested that federal laws may condition the receipt of grants or of government contracts on the fulfillment by the recipient of affirmative action goals. Here again the federal government may regulate private discrimination because Article I, not the Fourteenth Amendment, is involved. [See *Fullilove* v. *Klutznick,* p. 618.]

Finally there has always been a debate over what Section 5 of the Fourteenth Amendment means. That section specifically grants Congress the power to "enforce" the amendment "by appropriate legislation." Although the Fourteenth Amendment standing alone may apply only to state and not private discrimination, what if Congress, basing itself on Section 5, passes a statute banning private discrimination? Could such a statute be upheld as necessary and proper to the enforcement of Section 1's command that "No State shall . . . deny to any person . . . the equal protection of the laws"? There is much academic commentary and some judicial hints that Section 5 could be invoked successfully by Congress as a basis for regulating purely private discrimination. As a practical matter of working federalism, however, the issue is not a terribly important one. The state action doctrine may still place some boundaries around the power of the national Supreme Court to enforce the Fourteenth Amendment upon purely private discrimination in the absence of congressional action. It is hard to imagine, however, any significant act of private discrimination that Congress cannot legislate against today under the Court's expanded versions of the commerce and taxing and spending powers. Thus the conflict between civil rights and federalism, which was resolved in favor of federalism in the *Civil Rights Cases,* has pretty much been resolved by the contemporary Supreme Court in favor of central government control over discrimination.

This change in the position of the Supreme Court in the 1960s and 1970s is, of course, part of a far broader movement. Just as the Court largely ignored the old civil rights acts from the 1880s until the 1960s, so Congress, too, suddenly burst into new legislative activity after many years of silence. New civil rights statutes were passed in 1957, 1960, 1964, 1965, and 1968 and have since been strengthened by many new amendments. Many of their provisions dealt with voting and are considered in Chapter 13. Their public accommodations sections are dealt with in Chapter 9. Their role in employment race and sex discrimination cases are discussed in Chapters 13 and 14. The intimate interrelations between judicial and congressional action can be seen in the fact that the *Mayer* case, reading fair housing rights back into the 1866 statute, was handed down only months after the passage of the very extensive fair housing provisions of the Civil Rights Act of 1968.

Among the most significant tensions in federal-state relations today are those between federal and state courts. Much of today's law of federalism lies embedded in a mass of procedural rules that determine when a party may choose to litigate in federal rather than state court and when he or she may seek federal court intervention in state judicial proceedings.[14] For instance, *Stone* v. *Powell,* 428 U.S. 465 (1976), discussed in Chapter 15 in connection with the exclusionary rule, is also important in restricting the habeas corpus jurisdiction of the federal courts. There have been frequent complaints in recent years that federal courts use their habeas corpus powers to interfere unduly in state criminal proceedings. *Stone* severely restricts the ability of state criminal defendants to apply to federal district courts to vindicate Fourth Amendment claims that have been invoked unsuccessfully in state courts.

McCULLOCH *v.* MARYLAND
4 Wheat. 316; 4 L. Ed. 579 (1819)

[The Baltimore branch of the Second Bank of the United States was established in 1817. One year later, Maryland enacted a statute requiring that all banks not chartered by the state either pay a tax on each issuance of bank notes or make an annual payment of $15,000 to the state. McCulloch, the cashier of the Baltimore branch of the Second Bank, issued bank notes without complying with the state law. A Maryland county court and the State's highest court sustained the tax law. The bank then carried the case to the Supreme Court on a writ of error.

The lawyers for both sides in this famous case were the most distinguished of their day. Daniel Webster, William Pinckney, and William Wirt, the Attorney General of the United States, argued the case for the bank. Maryland was represented by lawyers of equal stature. The Supreme Court heard arguments for nine days, with Pinckney speaking eloquently for three days in behalf of the bank. Marshall delivered the opinion of the Court only three days after the arguments were concluded. In his opinion, Marshall relied heavily on Pinckney's three-day speech.]

[14] These problems are so complex and require so much background in the law of procedure that they are not addressed in this volume. See *Dombrowski* v. *Pfister,* 380 U.S. 479 (1965); *Younger* v. *Harris,* 401 U.S. 37 (1971); *Samuels* v. *Mackell,* 401 U.S. 66 (1971); *Steffel* v. *Thompson,* 416 U.S. 452 (1974); *Huffman* v. *Pursue, Ltd.,* 420 U.S. 592 (1975); *Hicks* v. *Miranda,* 422 U.S. 332 (1975); *Juidice* v. *Vail,* 430 U.S. 327 (1977); *Wooley* v. *Maynard,* 430 U.S. 705 (1977); *Moore* v. *Sims,* 442 U.S. 415 (1979).

MR. CHIEF JUSTICE MARSHALL delivered the opinion of the Court:

In the case now to be determined, the defendant, a sovereign State, denies the obligation of a law enacted by the legislature of the Union, and the plaintiff, on his part, contests the validity of an act which has been passed by the legislature of that State. The constitution of our country, in its most interesting and vital parts, is to be considered; the conflicting powers of the government of the Union and of its members, as marked in that constitution, are to be discussed; and an opinion given, which may essentially influence the great operations of government.

. . . The first question made in the cause is, has Congress power to incorporate a bank?

. . . If any one proposition could command the universal assent of mankind, we might expect it would be this—that the government of the Union, though limited in its powers, is supreme within its sphere of action. This would seem to result necessarily from its nature. It is the government of all; its powers are delegated by all; it represents all, and acts for all. Though any one state may be willing to control its operations, no State is willing to allow others to control them. The nation, on those subjects on which it can act, must necessarily bind its component parts. But this question is not left to mere reason: the people have, in express terms, decided it, by saying, "this Constitution, and the laws of the United States, which shall be made in pursuance thereof, shall be the supreme law of the land," and by requiring that the members of the State legislatures and the officers of the executive and judicial departments of the States, shall take the oath of fidelity of it.

The government of the United States, then, though limited in its powers, is supreme; and its laws, when made in pursuance of the Constitution, form the supreme law of the land, "any thing in the Constitution or laws of any State to the contrary notwithstanding."

Among the enumerated powers, we do not find that of establishing a bank or creating a corporation. But there is no phrase in the instrument which, like the Articles of Confederation, excludes incidental or implied powers; and which requires that every thing granted shall be expressly and minutely described. Even the Tenth Amendment, which was framed for the purpose of quieting the excessive jealousies which had been excited, omits the word "expressly," and declares only that the powers "not delegated to the United States, nor prohibited to the States, are reserved to the States or to the people"; thus leaving the question, whether the particular power which may become the subject of contest has been delegated to the one government, or prohibited to the other, to depend on a fair construction of the whole instrument. The men who drew and adopted this amendment had experienced the embarrassments resulting from the insertion of this word in the Articles of Confederation, and probably omitted it to avoid those embarassments. A constitution, to contain an accurate detail of all the subdivisions of which its great powers will admit, and of all the means by which they may be carried into execution, would partake of the prolixity of a legal code, and could scarcely be embraced by the human mind. It would probably never be understood by the public. Its nature, therefore, requires that only its great outlines should be marked, its important objects designated, and the minor ingredients which compose those objects be deduced from the nature of the objects themselves. That this idea was entertained by the framers of the American Constitution is not only to be inferred from the nature of the instrument, but from the language. Why else were some of the limitations, found in the ninth section of the first article, introduced? It is also, in some degree, warranted by their having omitted to use any restrictive term which might prevent its receiving a fair and just interpretation. In considering this question, then, we must never forget that it is *a constitution* we are expounding.

Although, among the enumerated powers of government, we do not find the word "bank" or "incorporation," we find the great powers to lay and collect taxes; to borrow money; to regulate commerce; to declare and conduct a war; and to raise and support armies and navies. The sword and the purse, all the external relations, and no inconsiderable portion of the industry of the nation, are entrusted to its government. It can never be pretended that these vast powers draw after them others of inferior importance, merely because they are inferior. Such an idea can never be advanced. But it may with great reason be contended that a government, entrusted with such ample powers, on the due execution of which the happiness and prosperity of the nation so vitally depends, must also be entrusted with ample means for their execution. The power being given, it is the interest of the nation to facilitate its execution. It can never be their interest, and cannot be presumed to have been their intention, to clog and embarrass its execution by withholding the most appropriate means. Throughout this vast republic, from the St. Croix to the Gulf of Mexico, from the Atlantic to the Pacific, revenue is to be collected and expended, armies are to be marched and supported. The exigencies of the nation may require that the treasure raised in the north should be transported to the south, *that* raised in the east conveyed to the west, or that this order should be reversed. Is that construction of the Constitution to be preferred which would render these operations difficult, hazardous, and expensive? Can we adopt that construction (unless the words imperiously require it) which would impute to the framers of that instrument, when granting these powers for the public good, the intention of impeding their exercise by withholding a choice of means? If, indeed, such be the mandate of the Constitution, we have only to obey; but that instrument does not profess to enumerate the means by which the powers it confers may be executed; nor does it prohibit the creation of a corporation, if the existence of such a being be essential to the beneficial exercise of those powers. It is, then, the subject of fair inquiry, how far such means may be employed.

. . . But the Constitution of the United States has not left the right of Congress to employ the necessary means for the execution of the powers conferred on the government to general reasoning. To its enumeration of powers is added that of making "all laws which shall be necessary and proper, for carrying into execution the foregoing powers, and all other powers vested by this Constitution, in the government of the United States, or in any department thereof."

The counsel for the State of Maryland have urged various arguments, to prove that this clause, though in terms a grant of power, is not so in effect; but is really restrictive of the general right, which might otherwise be implied, of selecting means for executing the enumerated powers.

In support of this proposition, they have found it necessary to contend that this clause was inserted for the purpose of conferring on Congress the power of making laws. That, without it, doubts might be entertained whether Congress could exercise its powers in the form of legislation.

But could this be the object for which it was inserted? A government is created by the people, having legislative, executive, and judicial powers. Its legislative powers are vested in a Congress, which is to consist of a Senate and House of Representatives. Each house may determine the rule of its proceedings; and it is declared that every bill which shall have passed both houses shall, before it becomes a law, be presented to the President of the United States. The seventh section describes the course of proceedings, by which a bill shall become a law; and, then, the eighth enumerates the powers of Congress. Could it be necessary to say that a legislature should exercise legislative powers in the shape of legislation? After allowing each house to prescribe its own course of proceeding, after describing the manner in which a bill should become a law, would it have entered into the mind of a single member of the Convention that an express power to make laws was necessary to enable the legislature to make them? That a legislature, endowed with legislative powers, can legislate, is a proposition too self-evident to have been questioned.

But the argument on which most reliance is placed is drawn from the peculiar language of this clause. Congress is not empowered by it to make all laws which may have relation to the powers conferred on the government, but such only as may be "*necessary and proper*" for carrying them into execution. The word "*necessary,*" is considered as controlling the whole sentence, and as limiting the right to pass laws for the execution of the granted powers to such as are indispensable, and without which the power would be nugatory. That it excludes the choice of means, and leaves to Congress, in each case, that only which is most direct and simple.

. . . This clause as construed by the State of Maryland, would abridge, and almost annihilate, this useful and necessary right of the legislature to select its means. That this could not be intended, is, we should think, had it not been already controverted, too apparent for controversy. We think so for the following reasons:

1. The clause is placed among the powers of Congress, not among the limitations on those powers.

2. Its terms purport to enlarge, not to diminish the powers vested in the government. It purports to be an additional power, not a restriction on those already granted. . . . Had the intention been to make this clause restrictive, it would unquestionably have been so in form as well as in effect.

The result of the most careful and attentive consideration bestowed upon this clause is, that if it does not enlarge, it cannot be construed to restrain the powers of Congress, or to impair the right of the legislature to exercise its best judgment in the selection of measures to carry into execution the constitutional powers of the government. If no other motive for its insertion can be suggested, a sufficient one is found in the desire to remove all doubts respecting the right to legislate on that vast mass of incidental powers which must be involved in the Constitution, if that instrument be not a splendid bauble.

We admit, as all must admit, that the powers of the government are limited, and that its limits are not to be transcended. But we think the sound construction of the Constitution must allow to the national legislature that discretion, with respect to the means by which the powers it confers are to be carried into execution, which will enable that body to perform the high duties assigned to it, in the manner most beneficial to the people. Let the end be legitimate, let it be within the scope of the Constitution, and all means which are appropriate, which are plainly adapted to that end, which are not prohibited, but consist with the letter and spirit of the Constitution, are constitutional.

. . . The choice of means implies a right to choose a national bank in preference to State banks, and Congress alone can make the election.

After the most deliberate consideration, it is the unanimous and decided opinion of this Court that the act to incorporate the Bank of the United States is a law made in pursuance of the Constitution, and is a part of the supreme law of the land.

The branches, proceeding from the same stock, and being conducive to the complete accomplishment of the object, are equally constitutional. It would have been unwise to locate them in the charter, and it would be unnecessarily inconvenient to employ the legislative power in making those subordinate arrangements. The great duties of the bank are prescribed; those duties require branches; and the bank itself may, we think, be safely trusted with the selection of places where those branches shall be fixed; reserving always to the government the right to require that a branch shall be located where it may be deemed necessary.

It being the opinion of the Court that the act incorporating the bank is constitutional; and that the power of establishing a branch in the State of Maryland might be properly exercised by the bank itself, we proceed to inquire. . . . Whether the State of Maryland may, without violating the Constitution, tax that branch?

That the power of taxation is one of vital importance; that it is retained by the States; that it is not abridged by the grant of a similar power to the government of the Union; that it is to be concurrently exercised by the two governments; are truths which have never been denied. But such is the paramount character of the Constitution that its capacity to withdraw any subject from the action of even this power is admitted. The States are expressly forbidden to lay any duties on imports or exports, except what may be absolutely necessary for executing their inspection laws. If the obligation of this prohibition must be conceded—if it may restrain a State from the exercise of its taxing power on imports and exports; the same paramount character would seem to restrain, as it certainly may restrain, a State from such other exercise of this power as is in its nature incompatible with, and repugnant to, the constitutional laws of the Union.

. . . That the power to tax involves the power to destroy; that the power to destroy may defeat and render useless the power to create; that there is a plain repugnance in conferring on one government a power to control the constitutional measures of another, which other, with respect to those very measures, is declared to be supreme over that which exerts the control, are propositions not to be denied.

. . . If we apply the principle for which the State of Maryland contends to the Constitution generally, we shall find it capable of changing totally the character of that instrument. We shall find it capable of arresting all the measures of the government, and of prostrating it at the foot of the States. The American people have declared their Constitution, and the laws made in pursuance thereof, to be supreme; but this principle would transfer the supremacy, in fact, to the States.

If the States may tax one instrument employed by the government in the execution of its powers, they may tax any and every other instrument. They may tax the mail; they may tax the mint; they may tax patent rights; they may tax the papers of the custom-house; they may tax judicial process; they may tax all the means employed by the government, to an excess which would defeat all the ends of government. This was not intended by the American people. They did not design to make their government dependent on the States.

. . . If the controlling power of the States be established; if their supremacy as to taxation be acknowledged; what is to restrain their exercising this control in any shape they may please to give it? Their sovereignty is not confined to taxation. That is not the only mode in which it might be displayed. The question is, in truth, a question of supremacy; and, if the right of the States to tax the means employed by the general government be conceded, the declaration that the Constitution, and the laws made in pursuance thereof, shall be the supreme law of the land, is empty and unmeaning declamation.

. . . It has also been insisted that, as the power of taxation in the general and State governments is acknowledged to be concurrent, every argument which would sustain the right of the general government to tax banks chartered by the States, will equally sustain the right of the States to tax banks chartered by the general government.

But the two cases are not on the same reason. The people of all the States have created the general government, and have conferred upon it the general power of taxation. The people of all the States, and the States themselves, are represented in Congress, and, by their representatives, exercise this power. When they tax the chartered institutions of the States, they tax their constituents; and these taxes must be uniform. But, when a State taxes the operations of the government of the United States, it acts upon institutions created, not by their own constituents, but by people over whom they claim no control. It acts upon the measures of a government created by others as well as themselves, for the benefit of others in common with themselves. The difference is that which always exists, and always must exist, between the action of the whole on a part, and the action of a part on the whole—between the laws of a government declared to be supreme, and those of a government which, when in opposition to those laws, is not supreme.

. . . [T]he States have no power, by taxation or otherwise, to retard, impede, burden, or in any manner control, the operations of the constitutional laws enacted by Congress to carry into execution the powers vested in the general government. This is, we think, the unavoidable consequence of that supremacy which the Constitution has declared.

We are unanimously of opinion, that the law passed by the legislature of Maryland imposing a tax on the Bank of the United States is unconstitutional and void. . . .

COHENS *v.* VIRGINIA
6 Wheat. 264; 5 L. Ed. 257 (1821)

[In 1802, Congress passed a law authorizing the District of Columbia to conduct lotteries. The money raised was to be used for improvements in the city of Washington that could not be brought about with available funds. Accordingly, the city passed an ordinance creating a lottery. The state of Virginia had a law prohibiting the sale of lottery tickets except for lotteries established by that state. P. J. and M. J. Cohen were arrested at their office in Norfolk, Va., for selling tickets for the Washington lottery. The borough court found them guilty and imposed a fine of $100. The case then went to the Supreme Court on a writ of error, because there was no higher state court "which could take cognizance of the case." Virginia did not object to the appeal, because it wished to force the issue of the Supreme Court's authority over state actions. The Court upheld the Cohens' conviction under the state statute on the ground that the federal statute authorizing a lottery applied only to the District of Columbia. The importance of the case lies not in the holding, however, but rather in Marshall's powerful argument that the Supreme Court had the authority to review the judgment of a state court.]

MR. CHIEF JUSTICE MARSHALL delivered the opinion of the Court:

The questions presented to the Court . . . are of great magnitude, and may be truly said vitally to affect the Union. They exclude the inquiry whether the constitution and laws of the United States have been violated by the judgment which the plaintiffs in error seek to review; and maintain that, admitting such violation, it is not in the power of the government to apply a corrective. They maintain that the nation does not possess a department capable of restraining peaceably, and by authority of law, any attempts which may be made, by a part, against the legitimate powers of the whole; and that the government is reduced to the alternative of submitting to such attempts, or of resisting them by force. They maintain that the constitution of the United States has provided no tribunal for the final construction of itself, or of the laws or treaties of the nation; but that this power may be exercised in the last resort by the Courts of every State in the Union. That the constitution, laws, and treaties, may receive as many constructions as there are States; and that this is not a mischief, or, if a mischief, is irremediable. . . .

First. The first question to be considered is, whether the jurisdiction of this Court is excluded by the character of the parties, one of them being a State, and the other a citizen of that State?

The second section of the third article of the constitution defines the extent of the judicial power of the United States. Jurisdiction is given to the Courts of the Union in two classes of cases. In the first, their jurisdiction depends on the character of the cause, whoever may be the parties. This class comprehends "all cases in law and equity arising under this constitution, the laws of the United States, and treaties made, or which shall be made, under their authority." This clause extends the jurisdiction of the Court to all the cases described, without making in its terms any exception whatever, and without any regard to the condition of the party. If there be any exception, it is to be implied against the express words of the article.

In the second class, the jurisdiction depends entirely on the character of the parties. In this are comprehended "controversies between two or more States, between a State and citizens of another State, and between a State and foreign States, citizens or subjects." If these be the parties, it is entirely unimportant what may be the subject of controversy. Be it what it may, these parties have a constitutional right to come into the Courts of the Union. . . .

If . . . a case arising under the constitution, or a law, must be one in which a party comes into Court to demand something conferred on him by the constitution or a law, we think the construction too narrow.

A case in law or equity consists of the right of the one party, as well as of the other, and may truly be said to arise under the constitution or a law of the United States, whenever its correct decision depends on the construction of either.

The jurisdiction of the Court, then, being extended by the letter of the constitution to all cases arising under it, or under the laws of the United States, it follows that those who would withdraw any cases of this description from that jurisdiction, must sustain the exemption they claim on the spirit and true meaning of the constitution, which spirit and true meaning must be so apparent as to overrule the words which its framers have employed.

The counsel for the defendant in error have undertaken to do this; and have laid down the general proposition, that a sovereign independent State is not suable, except by its own consent.

This general proposition will not be controverted. But its consent is not requisite in each particular case. It may be given in a general law. And if a State has surrendered any portion of its sovereignty, the question whether a liability to suit be a part of this portion, depends on the instrument by which the surrender is made. If, upon a just construction of that instrument, it shall appear that the State has submitted to be sued, then it has parted with this sovereign right of judging in every case on the justice of its own pretensions, and has entrusted that power to a tribunal in whose impartiality it confides.

The American States, as well as the American people, have believed a close and firm Union to be essential to their liberty and to their happiness. They have been taught by experience, that this Union cannot exist without a government for the whole; and they have been taught by the same experience that this government would be a mere shadow, that must disappoint all their hopes, unless invested with large portions of that sovereignty which belongs to independent States. Under the influence of this opinion, and thus instructed by experience, the American people, in the conventions of their respective States, adopted the present constitution.

If it could be doubted, whether from its nature, it were not supreme in all cases where it is empowered to act, that doubt would be removed by the declaration, that "this constitution, and the laws of the United States, which shall be made in pursuance thereof, and all treaties made, or which shall be made, under the authority of the United States, shall be the supreme law of the land; and the judges in every State shall be bound thereby; any thing in the constitution or laws of any State to the contrary notwithstanding."

This is the authoritative language of the American people; and, if gentlemen please, of the American States. It marks, with lines too strong to be mistaken, the characteristic distinction between the government of the Union, and those of the States. The general government, though limited as to its objects, is supreme with respect to those objects. This principle is a part of the constitution; and if there be any who deny its necessity, none can deny its authority.

To this supreme government ample powers are confided; and if it were possible to doubt the great purposes for which they were so confided, the people of the United States have declared, that they are given "in order to form a more perfect union, establish justice, ensure domestic tranquility, provide for the common defence, promote the general welfare, and secure the blessings of liberty to themselves and their posterity."

With the ample powers confided to this supreme government, for these interesting purposes, are connected many express and important limitations on the sovereignty of the States, which are made for the same purposes. The powers of the Union, on the great subjects of war, peace, and commerce and on many others, are in themselves limitations of the sovereignty of the States; but in addition to these, the sovereignty of the States is surrendered in many instances where the surrender can only operate to the benefit of the people, and where, perhaps, no other power is conferred on Congress than a conservative power to maintain the principles established in the constitution. The maintenance of these principles in their purity, is certainly among the great duties of the government. One of the instruments by which this duty may be peaceably performed, is the judicial department. It is authorized to decide all cases of every description, arising under the constitution or laws of the United States. From this general grant of jurisdiction, no exception is made of those cases in which a State may be a party. When we consider the situation of the government of the Union and of a State, in relation to each other; the nature of our constitution; the subordination of the State governments to that constitution; the great purpose for which jurisdiction over all cases arising under the constitution and laws of the United States, is confided to the judicial department; are we at liberty to insert in this general grant, an exception of those cases in which a State may be a party? Will the spirit of the constitution justify this attempt to control its words? We think it will not. We think a case arising under the constitution or laws of the United States, is cognizable in the Courts of the Union, whoever may be the parties to that case. . . .

One of the express objects, then, for which the judicial department was established, is the decision of controversies between States, and between a State and individuals. The mere circumstance, that a State is a party, gives jurisdiction to the Court. How, then, can it be contended, that the very same instrument, in the very same section, should be so construed, as that this same circumstance should withdraw a case from the jurisdiction of the Court, where the constitution or laws of the United States are supposed to have been violated? The constitution gave to every person having a claim upon a State, a right to submit his case to the Court of the nation. However unimportant his claim might be, however little the community might be interested in its decision, the framers of our constitution thought it necessary for the purposes of justice, to provide a tribunal as superior to influence as possible, in which that claim might be decided. . . .

The mischievous consequences of the construction contended for on the part of Virginia, are also entitled to great consideration. It would prostrate, it has been said, the government and its laws at the feet of every State in the Union. And would not this be its effect? What power of the government could be executed by its own means, in any State disposed to resist its execution by a course of legislation? The laws must be executed by individuals acting within the several States. If these individuals may be exposed to penalties, and if the Courts of the Union cannot correct the judgments by which these penalties, may be enforced, the course of the government may be, at any time, arrested by the will of one of its members. Each member will possess a veto on the will of the whole. . . .

These collisons may take place in times of no extraordinary commotion. But a constitution is framed for ages to come, and is designed to approach immortality as nearly as human institutions can approach it. Its course cannot always be tranquil. It is exposed to storms and tempests, and its framers must be unwise statesmen indeed, if they have not provided it, as far as its nature will permit, with the means of self-preservation from the perils it may be destined to encounter. No government ought to be so defective in its organization, as not to contain within itself the means of securing the execution of its own laws against other dangers than those which occur every day. Courts of justice are the means most usually employed; and it is reasonable to expect that a government should repose on its own Courts, rather than on others. There is certainly nothing in the circumstances under which our constitution was formed; nothing in the history of the times, which would justify the opinion that the confidence reposed in the States was so implicit as to leave in them and their tribunals the power of resisting or defeating, in the form of law, the legitimate measures of the Union. . . .

If jurisdiction depended entirely on the character of the parties, and was not given where the parties have not an original right to come into Court, that part of the second section of the third article, which extends the judicial power to all cases arising under the constitution and laws of the United States, would be mere surplusage. It is to give jurisdiction where the character of the parties would not give it, that this very important part of the clause was inserted. It may be true, that the partiality of the State tribunals, in ordinary controversies between a State and its citizens, was not apprehended, and therefore the judicial power of the Union was not extended to such cases; but this was not the sole nor the greatest object for which this department was created. A more important, a much more interesting object, was the preservation of the constitution and laws of the United States, so far as they can be preserved by judicial authority; and therefore the jurisdiction of the Courts of the Union was expressly extended to all cases arising under that constitution and those laws. If the constitution or laws may be violated by proceedings instituted by a State against its own citizens, and if that violation may be such as essentially to affect the constitution and the laws, such as to arrest the progress of government in its constitutional course, why should these cases be excepted from that provision which expressly extends the judicial power of the Union to all cases arising under the constitution and laws? . . .

It is most true that this Court will not take jurisdiction if it should not: but it is equally true, that it must take jurisdiction if it should. The judiciary cannot, as the legislature may, avoid a measure because it approaches the confines of the constitution. We cannot pass it by because it is doubtful. With whatever doubts, with whatever difficulties, a case may be attended, we must decide it, if it be brought before us. We have no more right to decline the exercise of jurisdiction which is given, than to usurp that which is not given. The one or the other would be treason to the constitution. Questions may occur which we would gladly avoid; but we cannot avoid them. All we can do is, to exercise our best judgment, and conscientiously to perform our duty. In doing this, on the present occasion, we find this tribunal invested with appellate jurisdiction in all cases arising under the constitution and laws of the United States. We find no exception to this grant and we cannot insert one. . . .

This leads to a consideration of the Eleventh Amendment.

It is in these words: "The judicial power of the United States shall not be construed to extend to any suit in law or equity commenced or prosecuted against one of the United States, by citizens of another State, or by citizens or subjects of any foreign State."

It is a part of our history, that, at the adoption of the constitution, all the States were greatly indebted; and the apprehension that these debts might be prosecuted in the federal Courts, formed a very serious objection to that instrument. Suits were instituted; and the Court maintained its jurisdiction. The alarm was general; and, to quiet the apprehensions that were so extensively entertained, this amendment was proposed in Congress, and adopted by the State legislatures. That its motive was not to maintain the sovereignty of a State from the degradation supposed to attend a compulsory appearance before the tribunal of the nation, may be inferred from the terms of the amendment. It does not comprehend controversies between two or more States, or between a State and a foreign State. The jurisdiction of the Court still extends to these cases: and in these a State may still be sued. We must ascribe the amendment, then, to some other cause than the dignity of a State. There is no difficulty in finding this cause. Those who were inhibited from commencing a suit against a State, or from prosecuting one which might be commenced before the adoption of the amendment, were persons who might probably be its creditors. There was not much reason to fear that foreign or sister States would be creditors to any considerable amount, and there was reason to retain the jurisdiction of the Court in those cases, because it might be essential to the preservation of peace. The amendment, therefore, extended to suits commenced or prosecuted by individuals, but not to those brought by States. . . .

A general interest might well be felt in leaving a State the full power of consulting its convenience in the adjustment of its debts, or of other claims upon it; but no interest could be felt in so changing the relations between the whole and its parts, as to strip the government of the means of protecting, by the instrumentality of its Courts, the constitution and laws from active violation. . . .

Under the judiciary act, the effect of a writ of error is simply to bring the record into Court, and submit the judgment of the inferior tribunal to reexamination. It does not in any manner act upon the parties; it acts only on the record. It removes the record into the supervising tribunal. Where, then, a State obtains a judgment against an individual, and the Court, rendering such judgment, overrules a defense set up under the constitution of laws of the United States, the transfer of this record into the Supreme Court, for the sole purpose of inquiring whether the judgment violates the constitution or laws of the United States, can, with no propriety, we think, be denominated a suit commenced or prosecuted against the state whose judgment is so far reexamined. Nothing is demanded from the State. No claim against it of any description is asserted or prosecuted. The party is not to be restored to the possession of any thing. Essentially, it is an appeal on a single point; and the defendant who appeals from a judgment rendered against him is never said to commence or prosecute a suit against the plaintiff who has obtained the judgment. . . .

It is, then, the opinion of the Court, that the defendant who removes a judgment rendered against him by a State Court into this Court, for the purpose of re-examining the question, whether that judgment be in violation of the constitution or laws of the United States, does not commence or prosecute a suit against the States. . . .

Second. The second objection to the jurisdiction of the Court is, that its appellate power cannot be exercised, in any case, over the judgment of a State Court.

This objection is sustained chiefly by arguments drawn from the supposed total separation of the judiciary of a State from that of the Union, and their entire independence of each other. The argument considers the federal judiciary as completely foreign to that of a State; and as being no more connected with it in any respect whatever, than the Court of a foreign State. If this hypothesis be just, the argument founded on it is equally so; but if the hypothesis be not supported by the constitution, the argument fails with it.

This hypothesis is not founded on any words in the constitution, which might seem to countenance it, but on the unreasonableness of giving a contrary construction to words which seem to require it; and on the incompatibility of the application of the appellate jurisdiction to the judgments of State Courts, with that constitutional relation which subsists between the government of the Union and the governments of those States which compose it.

Let this unreasonableness, this total incompatibilty, be examined.

That the United States form, for many, and for most important purposes, a single nation, has not yet been denied. In war, we are one people. In making peace, we are one people. In all commercial regulations, we are one and the same people. In many other respects, the American people are one; and the government which is alone capable of controlling and managing their interests in all these respects, is the government of the Union. It is their government, and in that character they have no other. America has chosen to be, in many respects, and to many purposes, a nation; and for all these purposes, her government is complete; to all these objects, it is competent. The people have declared, that in the exercise of all powers given for these objects, it is supreme. It can, then, in effecting these objects, legitimately control all individuals or governments within the American territory. The constitution and laws of a State, so far as they are repugnant to the constitution and laws of the United States, are absolutely void. These States are constituent parts of the United States. They are members of one great empire—for some purposes sovereign, for some purposes subordinate.

In a government so constituted, is it unreasonable that the judicial power should be competent to give efficacy to the constitutional laws of the legislature? The department can decide on the validity of the constitution or law of a State, if it be repugnant to the constitution or to a law of the United States. Is it unreasonable that it should also be empowered to decide on the judgment of a State tribunal enforcing such unconstitutional law? Is it so very unreasonable as to furnish a justification for controlling the words of the constitution?

We think it is not. We think that in a

government acknowledgedly supreme, with respect to objects of vital interest to the nation, there is nothing inconsistent with sound reason, nothing incompatible with the nature of government, in making all its departments supreme, so far as respects those objects, and so far as is necessary to their attainment. The exercise of the appellate power over those judgments of the State tribunals which may contravene the constitution or laws of the United States, is, we believe, essential to the attainment of those objects.

The propriety of entrusting the construction of the constitution, and laws made in pursuance thereof, to the judiciary of the Union, has not, we believe, as yet, been drawn into question. It seems to be a corollary from this political axiom, that the federal Courts should either possess exclusive jurisdiction in such cases, or a power to revise the judgment rendered in them, by the State tribunals. If the federal and State Courts have concurrent jurisdiction in all cases arising under the constitution, laws, and treaties of the United States; and if a case of this description brought in a State Court cannot be removed before judgment, nor revised after judgment, then the construction of the constitution, laws, and treaties of the United States, is not confided particularly to their judicial department, but is confided equally to that department and to the State Courts, however they may be constituted. "Thirteen independent Courts," says a very celebrated statesman (and we have now more than twenty such Courts), "of final jurisdiction over the same causes, arising upon the same laws, is a hydra in government, from which nothing but contradiction and confusion can proceed."

Dismissing the unpleasant suggestion that any motives which may not be fairly avowed, or which ought not to exist, can ever influence a State or its Courts, the necessity or uniformity, as well as correctness in expounding the constitution and laws of the United States, would itself suggest the propriety of vesting in some single tribunal the power of deciding, in the last resort, all cases in which they are involved.

We are not restrained, then, by the political relations between the general and State governments, from construing the words of the constitution, defining the judicial power, in their true sense. We are not bound to construe them more restrictively than they naturally import.

They give to the Supreme Court appellate jurisdiction in all cases arising under the constitution, laws, and treaties of the United States. The words are broad enough to comprehend all cases of this description, in whatever Court they may be decided. . . .

The framers of the constitution would naturally examine the state of things existing at the time; and their work sufficiently attests that they did so. All acknowledge that they convened for the purpose of strengthening the confederation by enlarging the powers of the government, and by giving efficacy to those which it before possessed, but could not exercise. They inform us themselves, in the instrument they presented to the American public, that one of its objects was to form a more perfect union. Under such circumstances, we certainly should not expect to find, in that instrument, a diminution of the powers of the actual government. . . .

This opinion has been already drawn out to too great a length to admit of entering into a particular consideration of the various forms in which the counsel who made this point has, with much ingenuity, presented his argument to the Court. The argument in all its forms is essentially the same. It is founded not on the words of the constitution, but on its spirit, a spirit extracted, not from the words of the instrument, but from his view of the nature of our Union, and of the great fundamental principles on which the fabric stands.

To this argument, in all its forms, the same answer may be given. Let the nature and objects of our Union be considered; let the great fundamental principles, on which the fabric stands, be examined; and we think the result must be, that there is nothing so extravagantly absurd in giving to the Court of the nation the power of revising the decisions of local tribunals on questions which affect the nation, as to require that words which import this power should be restricted by a forced construction. . . .

BARRON *v.* THE MAYOR AND CITY COUNCIL OF BALTIMORE
7 Pet. 243; 8 L. Ed. 672 (1833)

[Barron claimed that during construction work the City of Baltimore had caused the silting up of areas near his wharf so that ships could no longer dock there. He argued that this was a taking of private property for public use without compensation in violation of the Fifth Amendment.]

MR. CHIEF JUSTICE MARSHALL delivered the opinion of the Court:

The question [is], we think, of great importance, but not of much difficulty. The constitution was ordained and established by the people of the United States for themselves, for their own government, and not for the government of the individual states. Each state established a constitution for itself, and, in that constitution, provided such limitations and restrictions on the powers of its particular government as its judgment dictated. The people of the United States framed such a government for the United States as they supposed best adapted to their situation, and best calculated to promote their interests. The powers they conferred on this government were to be exercised by itself; and the limitations on power, if expressed in general terms, are naturally, and, we think, necessarily applicable to the government created by the instrument. They are limitations of power, granted in the instrument itself; not of distinct governments, framed by different persons and for different purposes. . . .

If these propositions be correct, the fifth amendment must be understood as restraining the power of the general government, not as applicable to the states. In their several constitutions they have imposed such restrictions on their respective governments as their own wisdom suggested; such as they deemed most proper for themselves. . . .

The ninth section [of Art. I] having enumerated, in the nature of a bill of rights, the limitations intended to be imposed on the powers of the general government, the tenth proceeds to enumerate those which were to operate on the state legislatures. These restrictions are brought together in the same section, and are by express words applied to the states. "No state shall enter into any treaty," &c. Perceiving that in a constitution framed by the people of the United States for the government of all, no limitation of the action of government on the people would apply to the state government, unless expressed in terms; the restrictions contained in the tenth section are in direct words so applied to the states. . . .

If the original constitution, in the ninth and tenth sections of the first article, draws this plain and marked line of discrimination between the limitations it imposes on the powers of the general government, and on those of the states; if in every inhibition intended to act on state power, words are employed which directly express that intent; some strong reason must be assigned for departing from this safe and judicious course in framing the amendments, before that departure can be assumed.

We search in vain for that reason. . . .

Had the framers of these amendments intended them to be limitations on the powers of the state governments, they would have imitated the framers of the original constitution, and have expressed that intention. Had Congress engaged in the extraordinary occupation of improving the constitutions of the several states by affording the people additional protection from the exercise of power by their own governments in matters which concerned themselves alone, they would have declared this purpose in plain and intelligible language.

But it is universally understood, it is a part of the history of the day, that the great revolution which established the constitution of the United States, was not effected without immense opposition. Serious fears were extensively entertained that those powers which the patriot statesmen, who then watched over the interests of our country, deemed essential to union, and to the attainment of those invaluable objects for which union was sought, might be exercised in a manner dangerous to liberty. In almost every convention by which the constitution was adopted, amendments to guard against the abuse of power were recommended. These amendments demanded security against the apprehended encroachments of the general government—not against those of the local governments.

In compliance with a sentiment thus generally expressed, to quiet fears thus extensively entertained, amendments were proposed by the required majority in congress, and adopted by the states. These amendments contain no expression indicating an intention to apply them to the state governments. This court cannot so apply them.

We are of opinion that the provision in the fifth amendment to the constitution, declaring that private property shall not be taken for public use without just conpensation, is intended solely as a limitation on the exercise of power by the government of the United States, and is not applicable to the legislation of the states. We are therefore of opinion that there is no repugnancy between the several acts of the general assembly of Maryland, given in evidence by the defendants at the trial of this cause, in the court of that state, and the constitution of the United States. This court, therefore, has no jurisdiction of the cause; and it is dismissed.

DRED SCOTT *v.* SANDFORD
19 How. 393; 15 L. Ed. 691 (1857)

[Every student of American history is familiar with the bitter controversy brought about by the Dred Scott *case. The report of the case occupies 240 pages, with all nine justices writing opinions. Yet the case grew out of a simple set of circumstances: Dred Scott was a slightly built, rather sickly Negro slave belonging to Dr. Emerson, a surgeon in the United States Army stationed in Missouri. In 1834, Dr. Emerson was transferred to a military post in Rock Island, Illinois, where slavery was forbidden. He took Dred Scott with him to his new post. In 1836, Scott again moved with Dr. Emerson to Fort Snelling in the territory of Upper Louisiana (now Minnesota), which was north of latitude 36° 30′ and, consequently, an area where slavery was forbidden by the terms of the Missouri Compromise of 1820. Dr. Emerson returned to Missouri with his slave in 1838. In 1846, Scott brought suit in a Missouri state court to obtain his freedom on the ground of periods of residence in free territory. Scott won the case, but the judgment was reversed by the Missouri Supreme Court. However, abolitionists and other friends of Dred Scott refused to accept defeat. They arranged for a fictitious sale of Scott to John Sandford, a citizen of New York and brother of the then widowed Mrs. Emerson, so that jurisdiction could be taken by a federal circuit court in Missouri. The federal court held that Scott and his family were Negro slaves and hence the "lawful property" of Sandford. The case then went to the Supreme Court on a writ of error.]*

MR. CHIEF JUSTICE TANEY delivered the opinion of the Court:

. . . There are two leading questions presented by the record:

1. Had the Circuit Court of the United States jurisdiction to hear and determine the case between these parties? And

2. If it had jurisdiction, is the judgment it has given erroneous or not?

The question is simply this: Can a Negro, whose ancestors were imported into this country, and sold as slaves, become a member of the political community formed and brought into existence by the Constitution of the United States, and as such become entitled to all the rights, and privileges, and immunities, guaranteed by that instrument to the citizen? One of which rights is the privilege of suing in a court of the United States in the cases specified in the Constitution. . . .

The words "people of the United States" and "citizens" are synonymous terms, and mean the same thing. They both describe the political body who, according to our republican institutions, form the sovereignty, and who hold the power and conduct the Government through their representatives. They are what we familiarly call the "sovereign people," and every citizen is one of this people, and a constituent member of this sovereignty. The question before us is, whether the class of persons described in the plea in abatement compose a portion of this people, and are constituent members of this sovereignty? We think they are not, and that they are not included, and were not intended to be included, under the word "citizens" in the Constitution, and can therefore claim none of the rights and privileges which that instrument provides for and secures to citizens of the United States. On the contrary, they were at that time considered as a subordinate and inferior class of beings, who had been subjugated by the dominant race, and, whether emancipated or not, yet remained subject to their authority, and had no rights or privileges but such as those who held the power and the government might choose to grant them. . . .

In discussing this question, we must not confound the rights of citizenship which a State may confer within its own limits and the rights of citizenship as a member of the Union. It does not by any means follow, because he has all the rights and privileges of a citizen of a State, that he must be a citizen of the United States. He may have all of the rights and privileges of the citizen of a State, and yet not be entitled to the rights and privileges of a citizen in any other State. For, previous to the adoption of the Constitution of the United States, every State had the undoubted right to confer on whomsoever it pleased the character of citizen, and to endow him with all its rights. But this character of course was confined to the boundaries of the State, and gave him no rights or privileges in other States beyond those secured to him by the laws of nations and the comity of States. Nor have the several States surrendered the power of conferring these rights and privileges by adopting the Constitution of the United States. . . .

It is very clear, therefore, that no State can, by any act or law of its own, passed since the adoption of the Constitution, introduce a new member into the political community created by the Constitution of the United States. . . .

It is true, every person, and every class and description of persons, who were at the time of the adoption of the Constitution recognized as citizens in the several States, became also citizens of this new political body; but none other; it was formed by them, and for them and their posterity, but for no one else. And the personal rights and privileges guaranteed to citizens of this new sovereignty were intended to embrace those only who were then members of the several State communities, or who would afterwards by birthright or otherwise become members, according to the provisions of the Constitution and the principles on which it was founded. . . . And it gave to each citizen rights and privileges outside of his State which he did not before possess, and placed him in every other State upon a perfect equality with its own citizens as to rights of persons and rights of property; it made him a citizen of the United States.

It becomes necessary, therefore, to determine who were citizens of the several States when the Constitution was adopted. . . . *[The Chief Justice then refers to statutes of several Northern and border states prohibiting free Negroes from marrying whites, barring them from militia service, and requiring them to carry passes.]*

The legislation of the States therefore shows, in a manner not to be mistaken, the inferior and subject condition of that race at the time the Constitution was adopted, and long afterward, throughout the thirteen States by which that instrument was framed; and it is hardly consistent with the respect due to these States, to suppose that they regarded at that time as fellow-citizens and members of the sovereignty, a class of beings whom they had thus stigmatized; whom, as we are bound, out of respect to the State sovereignties, to assume they had deemed it just and necessary thus to stigmatize, and upon whom they had impressed such deep and enduring marks of inferiority and degradation; or, that when they met in convention to form the Constitution, they looked upon them as a portion of their constituents, or deigned to include them in the provisions so carefully inserted for the security and protection of the liberties and rights of their citizens. It cannot be supposed that they intended to secure to them rights, and privileges, and rank, in the new political body throughout the Union, which every one of them denied within the limits of its own dominion. More especially, it cannot be believed that the large slaveholding States regarded them as included in the word citizens, or would have consented to a Constitution which might compel them to receive them in that character from another State. For if they were so received, and entitled to the privileges and immunities of citizens, it would exempt them from the operation of the special laws and from the police regulations which they considered to be necessary for their own safety. It would give to persons of the Negro race, who were recognised as citizens in any one State of the Union, the right to enter every other State whenever they pleased, singly or in companies, without pass or passport, and without obstruction to sojourn there as long as they pleased, to go where they pleased at every hour of the day or night without molestation, unless they committed some violation of law for which a white man would be punished; and it would give them the full liberty of speech in public and in private upon all subjects upon which its own citizens might speak; to hold public meetings upon political affairs, and to keep and carry arms wherever they went. And all of this would be done in the face of the subject race of the same color, both free and slaves, and inevitably producing discontent and insubordination among them, and endangering the peace and safety of the State. . . .

Undoubtedly, a person may be a citizen, that is, a member of the community who form the sovereignty, although he exercises no share of the political power, and is incapacitated from holding particular offices. Women and minors, who form a part of the political family, cannot vote; and when a property qualification is required to vote or hold a particular office, those who have not the necessary qualification cannot vote or hold the office, yet they are citizens.

So, too, a person may be entitled to vote by the law of the State, who is not a citizen even of the State itself. And in some of the States of the Union foreigners not naturalized are allowed to vote. And the State may give the right to free negroes and mulattoes, but that does not make them citizens of the State, and still less of the United States. And the provision in the Constitution giving privileges and immunities in other States does not apply to them.

Neither does it apply to a person who, being the citizen of a State, migrates to another State. For then he becomes subject to the laws of the State in which he lives, and he is no longer a citizen of a State from which he removed. And the State in which he resides may then, unquestionably, determine his status or condition, and place him among the class of persons who are not recognised as citizens, but belong to an inferior and subject race; and may deny him the privileges and immunities enjoyed by its citizens. . . .

No one, we presume, supposes that any change in public opinion or feeling, in relation to his unfortunate race, in the civilized nations of Europe or in this country, should induce the court to give to the words of the Constitution a more liberal construction in their favor than they were intended to bear when the instrument was framed and adopted. Such an argument would be altogether inadmissible in any tribunal called on to interpret it. If any of its provisions are deemed unjust, there is a mode prescribed in the instrument itself by which it may be amended; but while it remains unaltered, it must be construed now as it was understood at the time of its adoption. It is not only the same in words, but the same in meaning, and delegates the same powers to the Government, and reserves and secures the same rights and privileges to the citizen; and as long as it continues to exist in its present form, it speaks not only in the same words, but with the same meaning and intent with which it spoke when it came from the hands of its framers, and was voted on and adopted by the people of the United States. Any other rule of construction would abrogate the judicial character of this court, and make it the mere reflex of the popular opinion or passion of the day. This court was not created by the

Constitution for such purposes. Higher and graver trusts have been confided to it, and it must not falter in the path of duty. . . .

[T]he court is of opinion, that, . . . Dred Scott was not a citizen of Missouri within the meaning of the Constitution of the United States, and not entitled as such to sue in its courts: and, consequently, that the Circuit Court had no jurisdiction of the case. . . .

We proceed, therefore, to inquire whether the facts relied on by the plaintiff entitled him to his freedom. . . .

In considering this part of the controversy, two questions arise: (1.) Was he, together with his family, free in Missouri by reason of the stay in the territory of the United States. . . ? and (2.) If they were not, is Scott himself free by reason of his removal to Rock Island, in the State of Illinois. . . .

We proceed to examine the first question.

The act of Congress *[Missouri Compromise]* upon which the plaintiff relies, declares that slavery and involuntary servitude, except as a punishment for crime, shall be forever prohibited in all that part of the territory ceded by France, under the name of Louisiana, which lies north of 36°30′ north latitude, and not included within the limits of Missouri. And the difficulty which meets us at the threshold of this part of the inquiry is, whether Congress was authorized to pass this law under any of the powers granted to it by the Constitution; for if the authority is not given by that instrument, it is the duty of this court to declare it void and inoperative, and incapable of conferring freedom upon any one who is held as a salve under the laws of any one of the States.

The counsel for the plaintiff has laid much stress upon that article in the Constitution which confers on Congress the power "to dispose of and make all needful rules and regulations respecting the territory or other property belonging to the United States"; but, in the judgment of the court, that provision has no bearing on the present controversy, and the power there given, whatever it may be, is confined, and was intended to be confined, to the territory which at that time belonged to, or was claimed by, the United States, and was within their boundaries as settled by the treaty with Great Britain, and can have no influence upon a territory afterwards acquired from a foreign Government. It was a special provision for a known and particular territory, and to meet a present emergency, and nothing more. . . .

This brings us to examine by what provision of the Constitution the present Federal Government, under its delegated and restricted powers, is authorized to acquire territory outside of the original limits of the United States, and what powers it may exercise therein over the person of property of a citizen of the United States, while it remains a Territory, and until it shall be admitted as one of the States of the Union.

There is certainly no power given by the Constitution to the Federal Government to establish or maintain colonies bordering on the United States or at a distance, to be ruled and governed at its own pleasure; nor to enlarge its territorial limits in any way, except by the admission of new States. That power is plainly given; and if a new State is admitted, it needs no further legislation by Congress, because the Constitution itself defines the relative rights and powers, and duties of the State, and the citizens of the State, and the Federal Government. But no power is given to acquire a Territory to be held and governed permanently in that character. . . .

[It] may be safely assumed that citizens of the United States who migrate to a Territory belonging to the people of the United States, cannot be rules as mere colonists, dependent upon the will of the General Government, and to be governed by any laws it may think proper to impose. The principle upon which our Governments rest, and upon which alone they continue to exist, is the union of States, sovereign and independent within their own limits in their internal and domestic concerns, and bound together as one people by a General Government possessing certain enumerated and restricted powers, delegated to it by the people of the several States, and exercising supreme authority within the scope of the powers granted to it, throughout the dominion of the United

States. A power, therefore, in the General Government to obtain and hold colonies and dependent territories, over which they might legislate without restriction, would be inconsistent with its own existence in its present form. Whatever it acquires it acquires for the benefit of the people of the several States who created it. It is their trustee acting for them, and charged with the duty of promoting the interests of the whole people of the Union in the exercise of the powers specifically granted. . . .

. . . The Territory being a part of the United States, the Government and the citizen both enter it under the authority of the Constitution, with their respective rights defined and marked out; and the Federal Government can exercise no power over his person or property, beyond what that instrument confers, nor lawfully deny any right which it has reserved. . . .

Upon these considerations, it is the opinion of the court that the act of Congress which prohibited a citizen from holding and owning property of this kind in the territory of the United States north of the line therein mentioned, is not warranted by the Constitution, and is therefore void; and that neither Dred Scott himself, nor any of his family, were made free by being carried into this territory: even if they had been carried there by the owner, with the intention of becoming a permanent resident. . . .

But there is another point in the case which depends on State power and State law. And it is contended, on the part of the plaintiff, that he is made free by being taken to Rock Island, in the State of Illinois, independently of his residence in the territory of the United States; and being so made free, he was not again reduced to a state of slavery by being brought back to Missouri.

Our notice of this part of the case will be very brief; for the principle on which it depends was decided in this court, upon much consideration, in the case of *Strader et al.* v. *Graham,* reported in 19th Howard, 82. In that case, the slaves had been taken from Kentucky to Ohio, with the consent of the owner, and afterwards brought back to Kentucky. And this court held that their status or condition, as free or slave, depended upon the laws of Kentucky, when they were brought back into that State, and not of Ohio; and that this court had no jurisdiction to revise the judgment of a State court upon its own laws. . . .

So in this case. As Scott was a slave when taken into the State of Illinois by his owner, and was there held as such, and brought back in that character, his status, as free or slave, depended on the laws of Missouri, and not of Illinois. . . .

Upon the whole, therefore, it is the judgment of this court, that it appears by the record before us that the plaintiff in error is not a citizen of Missouri, in the sense in which that word is used in the Constitution; and that the Circuit Court of the United States, for that reason, had no jurisdiction in the case, and could give no judgment in it. Its judgment for the defendant must, consequently, be reversed, and a mandate issued, directing the suit to be dismissed for want of jurisdiction. . . .

[Justices Nelson, Grier, Daniel, Campbell and Catron concurred. Justice McLean, as well as Justice Curtis, dissented.]

MR. JUSTICE CURTIS, dissenting:

I dissent from the opinion pronounced by the Chief Justice, and from the judgment which the majority of the court think it proper to render in this case. . . .

To determine whether any free persons, descended from Africans held in slavery, were citizens of the United States under the Confederation, and consequently at the time of the adoption of the Constitution of the United States, it is only necessary to know whether any such persons were citizens of any of the States under the Confederation, at the time of the adoption of the Constitution.

Of this there can be no doubt. At the time of the ratification of the Articles of Confederation, all free native-born inhabitants of the States of New Hampshire, Massachusetts, New York, New Jersey, and North Carolina, though descended from African slaves, were not only citizens of those States, but such of them as had the other necessary qualifications possessed the franchise of electors, on equal terms with other citizens. . . .

I dissent, therefore, from that part of the opinion of the majority of the court, in which it is held that a person of African descent cannot be a citizen of the United States; and I regret I must go further, and dissent both from what I deem their assumption of authority to examine the constitutionality of the act of Congress commonly called the Missouri Compromise act, and the grounds and conclusions announced in their opinion.

Having first decided that they were bound to consider the sufficiency of the plea to the jurisdiction of the Circuit Court, and having decided that this plea showed that the Circuit Court had not jurisdiction, and consequently that this is a case to which the judicial power of the United States does not extend, they have gone on to examine the merits of the case as they appeared on the trial before the court and jury, on the issues joined on the pleas in bar, and so have reached the question of the power of Congress to pass the act of 1820. On so grave a subject as this, I feel obliged to say that, in my opinion, such an exertion of judicial power transcends the limits of the authority of the court, as described by its repeated decisions and, as I understand, acknowledged in this opinion of the majority of the court. . . .

Nor, in my judgment, will the position, that a prohibition to bring slaves into a Territory deprives any one of his property without due process of law, bear examination. . . .

MISSOURI *v.* HOLLAND, UNITED STATES GAME WARDEN
252 U.S. 346; 40 Sup. Ct. 382; 64 L. Ed. 641 (1920)

[The state of Missouri appealed from the holding of a federal district court that dismissed a bill in equity. The facts are outlined in the opinion.]

MR. JUSTICE HOLMES delivered the opinion of the Court:

This is a bill in equity, brought by the state of Missouri to prevent a game warden of the United States from attempting to enforce the Migratory Bird Treaty Act of July 3, 1918, . . . and the regulations made by the Secretary of Agriculture in pursuance of the same. The ground of the bill is that the statute is an unconstitutional interference with the rights reserved to the states by the Tenth Amendment, and that the acts of the defendant, done and threatened under that authority, invade the sovereign right of the state and contravene its will manifested in statutes. . . .

On December 8, 1916, a treaty between the United States and Great Britain was proclaimed by the President. It recited that many species of birds in the annual migrations traversed many parts of the United States and of Canada, that they were of great value as a source of food and in destroying insects injurious to vegetation, but were in danger of extermination through lack of adequate protection. It therefore provided for specified closed seasons and protection in other forms, and agreed that the two powers would take or propose to their lawmaking bodies the necessary measures for carrying the treaty out. . . . The above-mentioned Act of July 3, 1918, . . . prohibited the killing, capturing, or selling of any of the migratory birds included in the terms of the treaty except as permitted by regulations compatible with those terms, to be made by the Secretary of Agriculture. . . . [A]s we have said, the question raised is the general one whether the treaty and statute are void as an interference with the rights reserved to the states.

To answer this question, it is not enough to refer to the Tenth Amendment, reserving the powers not delegated to the United States, because by Article II, Section 2, the power to make treaties is delegated expressly, and by Article VI, treaties made under the authority of the United States, along with the Constitution and laws of the United States, made in pursuance thereof, are declared the supreme law of the land. If the treaty is valid, there can be no dispute about the validity of the statute under Article I, Section 8, as a necessary and proper means to execute the powers of the Government. The language of the Constitution as to the supremacy of treaties being general, the question before us is narrowed to an inquiry into the ground upon which the present supposed exception is placed.

It is said that a treaty cannot be valid if it infringes the Constitution; that there are limits, therefore, to the treaty-making power; and that one such limit is that what an act of Congress could not do unaided, in derogation of the powers reserved to the states, a treaty cannot do. An earlier act of Congress that attempted by itself, and not in pursuance of a treaty, to regulate the killing of migratory birds within the states, had been held bad in the district court. *United States* v. *Shauver,* 213 Fed. 154; *United States* v. *McCullagh,* 221 Fed. 288. Those decisions were supported by arguments that migratory birds were owned by the states in their sovereign capacity, for the benefit of their people, and that under cases like *Geer* v. *Connecticut,* 161 U.S. 519, this control was one that Congress had no power to displace. The same argument is supposed to apply now with equal force.

Whether the two cases cited were decided rightly or not, they cannot be accepted as a test of the treaty power. Acts of Congress are the supreme law of the land only when made in pursuance of the Constitution, while treaties are declared to be so when made under the authority of the United States. It is open to question whether the authority of the United States means more than the formal acts prescribed to make the convention. We do not mean to imply that there are no qualifications to the treaty-making power; but they must be ascertained in a different way. It is obvious that there may be matters of the sharpest exigency for the national well-being that an act of Congress could not deal with, but that a treaty followed by such an act could, and it is not lightly to be assumed that, in matters requiring national action, "a power which must belong to and somewhere reside in every civilized government" is not to be found. . . . We are not yet discussing the particular case before us, but only are considering the validity of the test proposed. With regard to that, we may add that when we are dealing with words that also are a constituent act, like the Constitution of the United States, we must realize that they have called into life a being the development of which could not have been foreseen completely by the most gifted of its begetters. It was enough for them to realize or to hope that they had created an organism; it has taken a century and has cost their successors much sweat and blood to prove that they created a nation. The case before us must be considered in the light of our whole experience, and not merely in that of what was said a hundred years ago. The treaty in question does not contravene any prohibitory words to be found in the Constitution. The only question is whether it is forbidden by some invisible radiation from the general terms of the Tenth Amendment. We must consider what this country has become in deciding what that amendment has reserved.

The state, as we have intimated, founds its claim of exclusive authority upon an assertion of title to migratory birds—an assertion that is embodied in statute. No doubt it is true that, as between a state and its inhabitants, the state may regulate the killing and sale of such birds, but it does not follow that its authority is exclusive of paramount powers. To put the claim of the state upon title is to lean upon a slender reed. Wild birds are not in the possession of anyone; and possession is the beginning of ownership. The whole foundation of the state's rights is the presence within their jurisdiction of birds that yesterday had not arrived, tomorrow may be in another state, and in a week a thousand miles away. If we are to be accurate, we cannot put the case of the state upon higher ground than that the treaty deals with creatures that for the moment are within the state borders, that it must be carried out by officers of the United States within the same territory, and that, but for the treaty, the state would be free to regulate this subject itself.

As most of the laws of the United States are carried out within the states, and as many of them deal with matters which, in the silence of such laws, the state might regulate, such general grounds are not enough to support Missouri's claim. Valid treaties, of course, "are as binding within the territorial limits of the states, as they are effective throughout the dominion of the United States. . . ." No doubt the great body of private relations usually falls within the control of the state, but a treaty may override its power. . . .

Here a national interest of very nearly the first magnitude in involved. It can be protected only by national action in concert with that of another power. The subject matter is only transitorily within the state, and has no permanent habitat therein. But for the treaty and the statute, there soon might be no birds for any powers to deal with. We see nothing in the Constitution that compels the government to sit by while a food supply is cut off and the protectors of our forests and of our crops are destroyed. It is not sufficient to rely upon the states. The reliance is vain, and were it otherwise, the question is whether the United States is forbidden to act. We are of opinion that the treaty and statute must be upheld.

MR. JUSTICE VAN DEVANTER and MR. JUSTICE PITNEY dissent.

NATIONAL LEAGUE OF CITIES *v.* USERY
426 U.S. 833; 96 S. Ct. 2465; 49 L. Ed. 2d 245 (1976)

[Various cities and the League unsuccessfully challenged in a federal district court the 1974 extension of federal wages and hours legislation to state government employees. The case then went to the Supreme Court.]

MR. JUSTICE REHNQUIST delivered the opinion for the Court:

Nearly 40 years ago Congress enacted the Fair Labor Standards Act, and required employers covered by the Act to pay their employees a minimum hourly wage and to pay them at one and one-half times their regular rate of pay for hours worked in excess of 40 during a work week.

. . . This Court unanimously upheld the Act as a valid exercise of congressional authority under the commerce power in *United States* v. *Darby*, . . .

The 1961 amendment to the Act extended its coverage to persons who were employed in "enterprises" engaged in commerce or in the production of goods for commerce. And in 1966, with the amendment of the definition of employers under the Act, the exemption heretofore extended to the States and their political subdivisions was removed with respect to employees of state hospitals, institutions, and schools. We nevertheless sustained the validity of the combined effect of these two amendments in *Maryland* v. *Wirtz*, 392 U.S. 183, . . . (1968).

By its 1974 amendments . . . Congress has now entirely removed the exemption proviously afforded States and their political subdivisions. The Act thus imposes upon almost all public employment the minimum wage and maximum hour requirements previously restricted to employees engaged in interstate commerce.

. . . the District Court . . . granted appellee Secretary of Labor's motion to dismiss the complaint . . . Upon full consideration of the question we have decided that the "far-reaching implications" of *Wirtz*, should be overruled, and that the judgment of the District Court must be reversed.

It is established beyond peradventure that the Commerce Clause of Art. I of the Constitution is a grant of plenary authority to Congress. That authority is, in the words of Chief Justice Marshall in *Gibbons* v. *Ogden*, ". . . the power to regulate; that is to prescribe the rule by which commerce is to be governed.". . .

When considering the validity of asserted applications of this power to wholly private activity, the Court had made it clear that

> "[e]ven activity that is purely intrastate in character may be regulated by Congress, where the activity, combined with like conduct by others similarly situated, affects commerce among the States or with foreign nations." *Fry* v. *United States*, 421 U.S. 542, 547, . . . (1975).

Congressional enactments which may be fully within the grant of legislative authority contained in the Commerce Clause may nonetheless be invalid because found to offend against the right to trial by jury contained in the Sixth Amendment, *United States* v. *Jackson,* 390 U.S. 570, . . . (1968), or the Due Process Clause of the Fifth Amendment, *Leary* v. *United States,* 395 U.S. 6, . . . (1969). Appellants' essential contention is that the 1974 amendments to the Act, while undoubtedly within the scope of the Commerce Clause, encounter a similar constitutional barrier because they are to be applied directly to the States and subdivisions of States as employers.

This Court has never doubted that there are limits upon the power of Congress to override state sovereignty, even when exercising its otherwise plenary powers to tax or to regulate commerce which are conferred by Art. I of the Constitution. In *Wirtz,* for example, the Court took care to assure the appellants that it had "ample power to prevent . . . 'the utter destruction of the State as a sovereign political entity,' " which they feared. . . . Appellee Secretary in this case, both in his brief and upon oral argument, has agreed that our federal system of government imposes definite limits upon the authority of Congress to regulate the activities of the States as States by means of the commerce power. . . . In *Fry, supra,* the Court recognized that an express declaration of this limitation is found in the Tenth Amendment:

> "While the Tenth Amendment has been characterized as a 'truism,' stating merely that 'all is retained which has not been surrendered,' *United States* v. *Darby,* . . . it is not without significance. The Amendment expressly declares the constitutional policy that Congress may not exercise power in a fashion that impairs the States' integrity or their ability to function effectively in a federal system. . . ."

The expressions in these more recent cases trace back to earlier decisions of this Court recognizing the essential role of the States in our federal system of government. . . . In *Texas* v. *White,* 7 Wall. 700, 725, . . . (1869), [Chief Justice Chase] declared that "[t]he Constitution, in all its provisions, looks to an indestructible Union, composed of indestructible States." In *Lane County* v. *Oregon,* 7 Wall. 71, 19 L.Ed. 101 (1869), his opinion for the Court said:

> "Both the States and the United States existed before the constitution. The people, through that instrument, established a more perfect union by substituting a national government, acting, with ample power, directly upon the citizens, instead of the Confederate government which acted with powers, greatly restricted, only upon the States. But in many Articles of the Constitution the necessary existence of the States, and, within their proper spheres, the independent authority of the States, is distinctly recognized.". . .

Appellee Secretary argues that the cases in which this Court has upheld sweeping exercises of authority by Congress, even though those exercises pre-empted state regulation of the private sector, have already curtailed the sovereignty of the States quite as much as the 1974 amendments to the Fair Labor Standards Act. We do not agree. It is one thing to recognize the authority of Congress to enact laws regulating individual businesses necessarily subject to the dual sovereignty of the government of the Nation and of the State in which they reside. It is quite another to uphold a similar exercise of congressional authority directed not to private citizens, but to the States as States. We have repeatedly recognized that there are attributes of sovereignty attaching to every state government which may not be impaired by Congress, not because Congress may lack an affirmative grant of legislative authority to reach the matter, but because the Constitution prohibits it from exercising the authority in that manner. In *Coyle* v. *Smith,* 221 U.S. 559, . . . (1911), the Court gave this example of such an attribute:

> "The power to locate its own seat of government, and to determine when and how it shall be changed from one place to another, and to appropriate its own public funds for that purpose, are essentially and peculiarly state powers. That one of the original thirteen states could now be shorn of such powers by an act

of Congress would not be for a moment entertained.". . .

One undoubted attribute of state sovereignty is the States' power to determine the wages which shall be paid to those whom they employ in order to carry out their governmental functions, what hours those persons will work, and what compensation will be provided where these employees may be called upon to work overtime. The question we must resolve in this case, then, is whether these determinations are "functions essential to separate and independent existence," *Coyle* v. *Smith, supra,* . . . so that Congress may not abrogate the States' otherwise plenary authority to make them.

In their complaint appellants advanced estimates of substantial costs which will be imposed upon them by the 1974 amendments.

Judged solely in terms of increased costs in dollars, these allegations show a significant impact on the functioning of the governmental bodies involved. The Metropolitan Government of Nashville and Davidson County, Tenn., for example, asserted that the Act will increase its costs of providing essential police and fire protection, without any increase in service or in current salary levels, by $938,000 per year. . . . The State of California, which must devote significant portions of its budget to fire suppression endeavors, estimated that application of the Act to its employment practices will necessitate an increase in its budget of between $8 million and $16 million. . . .

In its complaint in intervention, for example, California asserted that it could not comply with the overtime costs (approximately $750,000 per year) which the Act required to be paid to California Highway Patrol cadets during their academy training program. California reported that it had thus been forced to reduce its academy training program from 2,080 hours to only 960 hours, . . .

This type of forced relinquishment of important governmental activities is further reflected in the complaint's allegation that the City of Inglewood, California, has been forced to curtail its affirmative action program for providing employment opportunities for men and women interested in a career in law enforcement. . . .

Quite apart from the substantial costs imposed upon the States and their political subdivisions, the Act displaces state policies regarding the manner in which they will structure delivery of those governmental services which their citizens require. The Act, speaking directly to the States *qua* States, requires that they shall pay all but an extremely limited minority of their employees the minimum wage rates currently chosen by Congress. . . . It cannot be gainsaid that the federal requirement directly supplants the considered policy choices of the States' elected officials and administrators as to how they wish to structure pay scales in state employment. The State might wish to employ persons with little or no training, or those who wish to work on a casual basis, or those who for some other reason do not possess minimum employment requirements, and pay them less than the federally prescribed minimum wage. It may wish to offer part time or summer employment to teenagers at a figure less than the minimum wage, and if unable to do so may decline to offer such employment at all. But the Act would forbid such choices by the States. . . .

The degree to which the FLSA amendments would interfere with traditional aspects of state sovereignty can be seen even more clearly upon examining the overtime requirements of the Act. . . . The requirement imposing premium rates upon any employment in excess of what Congress has decided is appropriate for a governmental employee's workweek, for example, appears likely to have the effect of coercing the States to structure work periods in some employment areas, such as police and fire protection, in a manner substantially different from practices which have long been commonly accepted among local governments of this Nation. In addition, appellee represents that the Act will require that the premium compensation for overtime worked must be paid in cash, rather than with compensatory time off, unless such compensatory time is taken in the same pay period. . . . This too appears likely to be highly disruptive of accepted employment practices in many governmental areas where the demand for a number of employees to perform important jobs for extended periods on short notice can be both unpredictable and critical. Another example of congressional choices displacing those of the States in the area of what are without doubt essential governmental decisions may be found in the practice of using volunteer firemen, a source of manpower crucial to many of our smaller towns' existence. Under the regulations proposed by appellee, whether individuals are indeed "volunteers" rather than "employees" subject to the minimum wage provisions of the Act are questions to be decided in the courts. See Appellee's Brief, at 49 and n. 41. It goes without saying that provisions such as these contemplate a significant reduction of traditional volunteer assistance which has been in the past drawn on to complement the operation of many local governmental functions.

Our examination of the effect of the 1974 amendments, as sought to be extended to the States and their political subdivisions, satisfies us that both the minimum wage and the maximum hour provisions will impermissibly interfere with the integral governmental functions of these bodies.

. . . their application will . . . significantly alter or displace the States' abilities to structure employer-employee relationships in such areas as fire prevention, police protection, sanitation, public health, and parks and recreation. These activities are typical of those performed by state and local governments in discharging their dual functions of administering the public law and furnishing public services. Indeed, it is functions such as these which governments are created to provide, services such as these which the States have traditionally afforded their citizens. If Congress may withdraw from the States the authority to make those fundamental employment decisions upon which their systems for performance of these functions must rest, we think there would be little left of the States' "separate and independent existence." *Coyle, supra.* In so doing, Congress has sought to wield its power in a fashion that would impair the States' "ability to function effectively [with]in a federal system," *Fry, supra,* . . . This exercise of congressional authority does not comport with the federal system of government embodied in the Constitution. We hold that insofar as the challenged amendments operate to directly displace the States' freedom to structure integral operations in areas of traditional governmental functions, they are not within the authority granted Congress by Art. I, § 8, cl. 3.

One final matter requires our attention. Appellee has vigorously urged that we cannot, consistently with the Court's decisions in *Wirtz, supra,* and *Fry, supra,* rule against him here. It is important to examine this contention so that it will be clear what we hold today, and what we do not.

With regard to *Fry,* we disagree with appellee. There the Court held that the Economic Stabilization Act of 1970 was constitutional as applied to temporarily freeze the wages of state and local government employees. The Court expressly noted that the degree of intrusion upon the protected area of state sovereignty was in that case even less than that worked by the amendments to the FLSA which were before the Court in *Wirtz.* The Court recognized that the Economic Stabilization Act was "an emergency measure to counter severe inflation that threatened the national economy." 421 U.S., at 548.

We think our holding today quite consistent with *Fry.* The enactment at issue there was occasioned by an extremely serious problem which endangered the wellbeing of all the component parts of our federal system and which only collective action by the National Government might forestall. The means selected were carefully drafted so as not to interfere with the States' freedom beyond a very limited, specific period of time. The effect of the across-the-board freeze authorized by that Act, moreover, displaced no state choices as to how governmental operations should be structured nor did it force the States to remake such choices themselves. Instead, it merely required that the wage scales and employment relationships which the States themselves had chosen be maintained during the period of the emergency. Finally, the Economic Stabilization Act operated to reduce the pressures upon state budgets rather than increase them. These factors distinguish the statute in *Fry* from the provisions at issue here. The limits imposed upon the commerce power when Congress seeks to apply it to the States are not so inflexible as to preclude temporary enactments tailored to combat a national emergency. "[A]lthough an emergency may not call into life a power which has never lived, nevertheless emergency may afford a reason for the exertion of a living power already enjoyed." *Wilson* v. *News,* 243 U.S. 332, 348, . . . (1917).

With respect to the Court's decision in *Wirtz,* we reach a different conclusion. . . . In view of the conclusions expressed earlier in this opinion we do not believe the reasoning in *Wirtz* may any longer be regarded as authoritative.

Wirtz relied heavily on the Court's decision in *United States* v. *California,* 297 U.S. 175, . . . (1936). The opinion quotes the following language from that case:

> " '[We] look to the activities in which the states have traditionally engaged as marking the boundary of the restriction upon the federal taxing power. But there is no such limitation upon the plenary power to regulate commerce. The state can no more deny the power if its exercise has been authorized by Congress than can an individual.' "

But we have reaffirmed today that the States as States stand on a quite different footing than an individual or a corporation when challenging the exercise of Congress' power to regulate commerce. We think the dicta from *United States* v. *California,* simply wrong. Congress may not exercise that power so as to force directly upon the States its choices as to how essential decisions regarding the conduct of integral governmental functions are to be made. We agree that such assertions of power if unchecked, would indeed, as Mr. Justice Douglas cautioned in his dissent in *Wirtz,* allow "the National Government [to] devour the essentials of state sovereignty," . . . and would therefore transgress the bounds of the authority granted Congress under the Commerce Clause. While there are obvious differences between the schools and hospitals involved in *Wirtz,* and the fire and police departments affected here, each provides an integral portion of those governmental services which the States and their political subdivisions have traditionally afforded their citizens. We are therefore persuaded that *Wirtz* must be overruled.

The judgment of the District Court is accordingly reversed and the case is remanded for further proceedings consistent with this opinion.

So ordered.

MR. JUSTICE BLACKMUN, concurring:

. . . I do not read the opinion so despairingly as does my Brother Brennan. In my view, the result with respect to the statute under challenge here is necessarily correct. I may misinterpret the Court's opinion, but it seems to me that it adopts a balancing approach, and does not outlaw federal power in areas such as environmental protection, where the federal interest is demonstrably greater and where state facility compliance with imposed federal standards would be essential. . . . With this understanding on my part of the Court's opinion, I join it.

MR. JUSTICE BRENNAN, with whom MR. JUSTICE WHITE and MR. JUSTICE MARSHALL join, dissenting:

Only 34 years ago, *Wickard* v. *Filburn,* 317 U.S. 111, 120, . . . (1942), reaffirmed that "[a]t the beginning Chief Justice Marshall . . . made emphatic the embracing and penetrating nature of [Congress' commerce] power by warning that effective restraints on its exercise must proceed from political rather than from judicial processes."

. . . laws within the commerce power may not infringe individual liberties protected by the First Amendment, . . . the Fifth Amendment, . . . or the Sixth Amendment, . . . But there is no restraint based on state sovereignty requiring or permitting judicial enforcement anywhere expressed in the Constitution; our decisions over the last century and a half have explicitly rejected the existence of any such restraint on the commerce power.

We said in *United States* v. *California,* for example, the "[t]he sovereign power of the states is necessarily diminished to the extent of the grants of power to the federal government in the Constitution. . . . [T]he power of the state is subordinate to the constitutional exercise of the granted federal power."

My Brethren thus have today manufactured an abstraction without substance, founded neither in the words of the Constitution nor on precedent. An abstraction having such profoundly pernicious consequences is not made less so by characterizing the 1974 amendments as legislation directed against the "States *qua* States.". . .

My Brethren make no claim that the 1974 amendments are not regulations of "commerce"; rather they overrule *Wirtz* in disagreement with historic principles that *United States* v. *California, supra,* reaffirmed: "[W]hile the commerce power has limits, valid general regulations of commerce do not cease to be regulations of commerce because a State is involved. If a State is engaging in economic activities that are validly regulated by the Federal Government when engaged in by private persons, the State too may be forced to conform its activities to federal regulation." 392 U.S., at 196–197. Clearly, therefore, my Brethren are also repudiating the long line of our precedents holding that a judicial finding that Congress has not unreasonably regulated a subject matter of "commerce" brings to an end the judicial role.

The reliance of my Brethren upon the Tenth Amendment as "an express declaration of [a state sovereignty] limitation," . . . not only suggests that they overrule governing decisions of this Court that address this question but must astound scholars of the Constitution. . . .

As the Tenth Amendment's significance was . . . recently summarized:

> "The amendment states but a truism that all is retained which has not been surrendered. *There is nothing in the history of its adoption to suggest that it was more than declaratory of the relationship between the national and state governments as it had been established by the Constitution before the amendment* or that its purpose was other than to allay fears that the new national government might seek to exercise powers not granted, and that the states might not be able to exercise fully their reserved powers. . . .
>
> From the beginning and for many years the amendment has been construed as not depriving the national government of authority to resort to all means for the exercise of a granted power which are appropriate and plainly adapted to the permitted end." *United States* v. *Darby*, . . . (emphasis added).

My Brethren purport to find support for their novel state sovereignty doctrine in the concurring opinion of Chief Justice Stone in *New York* v. *United States,* 326 U.S. 572, (1946). That reliance is plainly misplaced. That case presented the question whether the Constitution either required immunity of New York State's mineral water business from federal taxation or denied to the Federal Government power to lay the tax. The Court sustained the federal tax. Chief Justice Stone observed in his concurring opinion that "a federal tax which is not discriminatory as to the subject matter may nevertheless so affect the State, merely because it is a State that is being taxed, as to interfere unduly with the State's performance of its sovereign functions of government.". . . But the Chief Justice was addressing not the question of a state sovereignty restraint upon the exercise of the commerce power, but rather the principle of implied immunity of the States and Federal Government from taxation by the other: "The counterpart of such undue interference has been recognized since Marshall's day as the implied immunity of each of the dual sovereignties of our constitutional system from taxation by the other."

In contrast, the apposite decision that Term to the question whether the Constitution implies a state sovereignty restraint upon congressional exercise of the commerce power is *Case* v. *Bowles,* 327 U.S. 92, . . . (1946). The question there was whether the Emergency Price Control Act could apply to the sale by the State of Washington to timber growing on lands granted by Congress to the State for the purport of common schools.

> "Since the Emergency Price Control Act has been sustained as a Congressional exercise of the war power, the [State's] argument is that the extent of that power as applied to state functions depends on whether these are 'essential' to the state government. The use of the same criterion in measuring the Constitutional power of Congress to tax has proved to be unworkable, and we reject

> it as a guide in the field here involved.". . .

The footnote to this statement rejected the suggested dichotomy between essential and nonessential state governmental functions as having "proved to be unworkable" by referring to "the several opinions in [*New York* v. *United States*, . . .] Even more significant for our purposes is the Court's citation of *United States* v. *California*, a case concerned with Congress' power to regulate commerce, as supporting the rejection of the State's contention that state sovereignty is a limitation on Congress' war power. *California* directly presented the question whether any state sovereignty restraint precluded application of the Federal Safety Appliance Act to a state-owned and -operated railroad. The State argued "that as the state is operating the railroad without profit, for the purpose of facilitating the commerce of the port, and is using the net proceeds of operation for harbor improvement . . . it is engaged in performing a public function in its sovereign capacity and for that reason cannot constitutionally be subjected to the provisions of the federal act." . . . Mr. Justice Stone rejected the contention in an opinion for a unanimous Court. His rationale is a complete refutation of today's holding:

> "That in operating its railroad [the State] is acting within a power reserved to the states cannot be doubted. . . . The only question we need consider is whether the exercise of that power, in whatever capacity, must be in subordination to the power to regulate interstate commerce, which has been granted specifically to the national government. The sovereign power of the states is necessarily diminished to the extent of the grants of power to the federal government in the Constitution.
>
> The analogy of the constitutional immunity of state instrumentalities from federal taxation, on which [California] relies, is not illuminating. That immunity is implied from the nature of our federal system and the relationship within it of state and national governments, and is equally a restriction on taxation by either of the instrumentalities of the other. Its nature requires that it be so construed as to allow to each government reasonable scope for its taxing power . . . which would be unduly curtailed if either by extending its activities could withdraw from the taxing power of the other subjects of taxation traditionally within it. . . . Hence we look to the activities in which the states have traditionally engaged as marking the boundary of the restriction upon the federal taxing power. *But there is no such limitation upon the plenary power to regulate commerce. The state can no more deny the power if its exercise has been authorized by Congress than can an individual.*". . .

Today's repudiation of this unbroken line of precedents that firmly reject my Brethren's ill-conceived abstraction can only be regarded as a transparent cover for invalidating a congressional judgment with which they disagree. The only analysis even remotely resembling that adopted today is found in a line of opinions dealing with the Commerce Clause and the Tenth Amendment that ultimately provoked a constitutional crisis for the Court in the 1930's. *E.g., Carter* v. *Carter Coal Co.*, . . . *United States* v. *Butler*, . . . *Hammer* v. *Dagenhart*, . . . We tend to forget that the Court invalidated legislation during the Great Depression, not solely under the Due Process Clause, but also and primarily under the Commerce Clause and the Tenth Amendment. It may have been the eventual abandonment of that overly restrictive construction of the commerce power that spelled defeat for the Court-packing plan, and preserved the integrity of this institution, . . . see, *e.g., United States* v. *Darby*, . . . *Mulford* v. *Smith*, (1939); *NLRB* v. *Jones & Laughlin Steel Corp.*, . . . but my Brethren today are transparently trying to cut back on that recognition of the scope of the commerce power. My Brethren's approach to this case is not far different from the dissenting opinions in the cases that averted the crisis. See, *e.g., Mulford* v. *Smith*, . . . (Butler, J., dissenting); *NLRB* v. *Jones & Laughlin Steel Corp.*, . . . (McReynolds, J., dissenting).

To argue, as do my Brethren, that the 1974 amendments are directed at the States *qua* States, . . . and "displace state policies regarding the manner in which they will structure delivery of those governmental services which their citizens require,". . . and therefore "directly penalize the States for choosing to hire governmental employees on terms different from those which Congress has sought to impose,". . . is only to advance precisely the unsuccessful arguments made by the State of Washington in *Case* v. *Bowles* and the State of California in *United States* v. *California.* The 1974 amendments are, however, an entirely legitimate exercise of the commerce power, not in the slightest restrained by any doctrine of state sovereignty cognizable in this Court, as *Case* v. *Bowles, United States* v. *California, Maryland* v. *Wirtz,* and our other pertinent precedents squarely and definitively establish.

I cannot recall another instance in the Court's history when the reasoning of so many decisions covering so long a span of time has been discarded roughshod. That this is done without any justification not already often advanced and consistently rejected, clearly renders today's decision an *ipse dixit* reflecting nothing but displeasure with a congressional judgment.

My Brethren's treatment of *Fry* v. *United States,* . . . further illustrates the paucity of legal reasoning or principle justifying today's result. . . .

Although my Brethren by fiat strike down the 1974 amendments without analysis of countervailing national considerations, *Fry* by contrary logic remains undisturbed because, on balance, countervailing national considerations override the interference with the State's freedom. Moreover, it is sophistry to say the Economic Stabilization Act "displaced no state choices," . . . but that the 1974 amendments do. . . . Obviously the Stabilization Act—no less than every exercise of a national power delegated to Congress by the Constitution—displaced the State's freedom. It is absurd to suggest that there is a constitutionally significant distinction between curbs against increasing wages and curbs against paying wages lower than the federal minimum. . . .

Also devoid of meaningful content is my Brethren's argument that the 1974 amendments "displace State policies.". . . The amendments neither impose policy objectives on the States nor deny the States complete freedom to fix their own objectives. My Brethren boldly assert that the decision as to wages and hours is an "undoubted attribute of state sovereignty,". . . and then never say why. . . .

My Brethren do more than turn aside longstanding constitutional jurisprudence that emphatically rejects today's conclusion. More alarming is the startling restructuring of our federal system, and the role they create therein for the federal judiciary. This Court is simply not at liberty to erect a mirror of its own conception of a desirable governmental structure. . . . It bears repeating "that effective restraints on . . . exercise [of the Commerce power] must proceed from political rather than from judicial processes." *Wickard* v. *Filburn.* . . .

It is unacceptable that the judicial process should be thought superior to the political process in this area. Under the Constitution the judiciary has no role to play beyond finding that Congress has not made an unreasonable legislative judgment respecting what is "commerce." My Brother Blackmun suggests that controlling judicial supervision of the relationship between the States and our National Government by use of a balancing approach diminishes the ominous implications of today's decision. Such an approach, however, is a thinly veiled rationalization for judicial supervision of a policy judgment that our system of government reserves to Congress.

Judicial restraint in this area merely recognizes that the political branches of our Government are structured to protect the interests of the States, as well as the Nation as a whole, and that the States are fully able to protect their own interests in the premises. Congress is constituted of representatives in both Senate and House *elected from the States.* . . . Decisions upon the extent of federal intervention under the Commerce Clause into the affairs of the States are in that sense decisions of the States themselves. Judicial redistribution of powers granted the National Government by the terms of the Constitution violates the fundamental tenet of our federalism that the extent of federal intervention into the State's affairs in the exercise of delegated powers shall be determined by the States' exercise of political power through their representatives in Congress. . . .

My Brethren's disregard for precedents

recognizing these long-settled constitutional principles is painfully obvious in their cavalier treatment of *Maryland* v. *Wirtz*. . . . The best I can make of it is that the 1966 FLSA amendments are struck down and *Wirtz* is overruled on the basis of the conceptually unworkable essential function test; and that the test is unworkable is demonstrated by my Brethren's inability to articulate any meaningful distinctions among state-operated railroads, . . . state-operated schools and hospitals, and state-operated police and fire departments. . . .

MR. JUSTICE STEVENS, dissenting:

The Court holds that the Federal Government may not interfere with a sovereign state's inherent right to pay a substandard wage to the janitor at the state capitol. The principle on which the holding rests is difficult to perceive.

The Federal Government may, I believe, require the State to act impartially when it hires or fires the janitor, to withhold taxes from his pay check, to observe safety regulations when he is performing his job, to forbid him from burning too much soft coal in the capitol furnace, from dumping untreated refuse in an adjacent waterway, from overloading a state-owned garbage truck or from driving either the truck or the governor's limousine over 55 miles an hour. Even though these and many other activities of the capitol janitor are activities of the state *qua* state, I have no doubt that they are subject to federal regulation.

I agree that it is unwise for the Federal Government to exercise its power in the ways described in the Court's opinion. For the proposition that regulation of the minimum price of a commodity—even labor—will increase the quantity consumed is not one that I can readily understand. That concern, however, applies with even greater force to the private sector of the economy where the exclusion of the marginally employable does the greatest harm and, in all events, merely reflects my views on a policy issue which has been firmly resolved by the branches of government having power to decide such questions. As far as the complexities of adjusting police and fire departments to this sort of federal control are concerned, I presume that appropriate tailor-made regulations would soon solve their most pressing problems. After all, the interests adversely affected by this legislation are not without political power.

My disagreement with the wisdom of this legislation may not, of course, affect my judgment with respect to its validity. On this issue there is no dissent from the proposition that the Federal Government's power over the labor market is adequate to embrace these employees. Since I am unable to identify a limitation on that federal power that would not also invalidate federal regulation of state activities that I consider unquestionably permissible, I am persuaded that this statute is valid. Accordingly, with respect and a great deal of sympathy for the views expressed by the Court, I dissent from its constitutional holding.

CIVIL RIGHTS CASES

109 U.S. 3; 3 Sup. Ct. 18; 27 L. Ed. 835 (1883)

[The Civil Rights Act of 1875 was designed to implement the Thirteenth and Fourteenth Amendments and thereby firmly establish the civil and legal rights of the freed Negroes. Five cases involving the Civil Rights Act of 1875 were decided together in the Civil Rights Cases. Certain persons in San Francisco, New York, and Memphis, Tennessee, were indicted for violations of the act for denying accommodation to Negroes at a hotel, admission to a theater, and admission to a ladies' car on a railway. Two of these cases went to the Supreme Court on writs of error sued out by the plaintiffs in federal circuit courts. The other three cases were certified to the Supreme Court because of a division of opinion among the lower court judges as to the constitutionality of the first and second sections of the Civil Rights Act of 1875.]

MR. JUSTICE BRADLEY delivered the opinion of the Court:

. . . It is obvious that the primary and important question in all the cases is the constitutionality of the law; for if the law is unconstitutional none of the prosecutions can stand. . . .

The essence of the law is, not to declare broadly that all persons shall be entitled to the full and equal enjoyment of the accommodation, advantages, facilities, and privileges of inns, public conveyances, and theaters; but that such enjoyment shall not be subject to any conditions applicable only to citizens of a particular race or color, or who have been in a previous condition of servitude. . . .

Has Congress constitutional power to make such a law? Of course, no one will contend that the power to pass it was contained in the Constitution before the adoption of the last three amendments. The power is sought, first, in the Fourteenth Amendment, and the views and arguments of distinguished Senators, advanced whilst the law was under consideration, claiming authority to pass it by virtue of that amendment, are the principal arguments adduced in favor of the power. . . .

The first section of the Fourteenth Amendment (which is the one relied on), after declaring who shall be citizens of the United States, and of the several States, is prohibitory in its character, and prohibitory upon the States. It declares that:

> "No State shall make or enforce any law which shall abridge the privileges or immunities of citizens of the United States; nor shall any State deprive any person of life, liberty, or property without due process of law; nor deny to any person within tis jurisdiction the equal protection of the laws."

It is State action of a particular character that is prohibited. Individual invasion of individual rights is not the subject matter of the amendment. It has a deeper and broader scope. It nullifies and makes void all State legislation, and State action of every kind, which impairs the privileges and immunities of citizens of the United States, or which injures them in life, liberty or property without due process of law, or which denies to any of them the equal protection of the laws. It not only does this, but, in order that the national will, thus declared, may not be a mere *brutum fulmen,* the last section of the amendment invests Congress with power to enforce it by appropriate legislation. To enforce what? To enforce the prohibition. To adopt appropriate legislation for correcting the effects of such prohibited State laws and State acts, and thus to render them effectually null, void, and innocuous. This is the legislative power conferred upon Congress, and this is the whole of it. It does not invest Congress with power to legislate upon subjects which are within the domain of State legislation; but to provide modes of relief against State legislation, or State action, of the kind referred to. It does not authorize Congress to create a code of municipal law for the regulation of private rights; but to provide modes of redress against the operation of State laws, and the action of State officers executive or judicial, when these are subversive of the fundamental rights specified in the amendment. Positive rights and privileges are undoubtedly secured by the Fourteenth Amendment; but they are secured by way of prohibition against State laws and State proceedings affecting those rights and privileges, and by power given to Congress to legislate for the purpose of carrying such prohibition into effect: and such legislation must necessarily be predicated upon such supposed State laws or State proceedings, and be directed to the correction of their operation and effect. . . .

[U]ntil some State law has been passed, or some State action through its officers or agents has been taken, adverse to the rights of citizens sought to be protected by the Fourteenth Amendment, no legislation of the United States under said amendment, nor any proceeding under such legislation, can be called into activity; for the prohibitions of the amendment are against State laws and acts done under State authority. Of course, legislation may, and should be, provided in advance to meet the exigency when it arises; but it should be adapted to the mischief and wrong which the amendment was intended to provide against; and this is, State laws, or State action of some kind, adverse to the rights of the citizen secured by the amendment. Such legislation cannot properly cover the whole domain of rights appertaining to life, liberty and property, defining them and providing for their vindication. That would be to establish a code of municipal law regulative of all private rights between man and man in society. It would be to make Congress take the place of the State legislatures and to supersede them. It is absurd to affirm that, because the rights of life, liberty and property (which include all civil rights that men have), are by the amendment sought to be protected against invasion on the part of the State without due process of law, Congress may therefore provide due process of law for their vindication in every case; and that, because the denial by a State to any persons, of the equal protection of the laws, is prohibited by the amendment, therefore Congress may establish laws for their equal portection. In fine, the legislation which Congress is authorized to adopt in this behalf is not general legislation upon the rights of the citizen, but corrective legislation, that is, such as may be necessary and proper for counteracting such laws as the States may adopt or enforce, and which, by the amendment, they are prohibited from making or enforcing, or such acts and proceedings as the States may commit or take, and which, by the amendment, they are prohibited from committing or taking. It is not necessary for us to state, if we could, what legislation would be proper for Congress to adopt. It is sufficient for us to examine whether the law in question is of that character.

An inspection of the law shows that it makes no reference whatever to any supposed or apprehended violation of the Fourteenth Amendment on the part of the States. It is not predicated on any such view. It proceeds *ex directo* to declare that certain acts committed by individuals shall be deemed offences, and shall be prosecuted and punished by proceedings in the courts of the United States. It does not profess to be corrective of any constitutional wrong committed by the States; it does not make its operation to depend upon any such wrong committed, it applies equally to cases arising in States which have the justest laws respecting the personal rights of citizens, and whose authorities are ever ready to enforce such laws, also to those which arise in States that may have violated the prohibition of the amendment. In other words, it steps into the domain of local jurisprudence, and lays down rules for the conduct of individuals in society towards each other, and imposes sanctions for the enforcement of those rules, without referring in any manner to any supposed action of the State or its authorities.

If this legislation is appropriate for enforcing the prohibitions of the amendment, it is difficult to see where it is to stop. Why may not Congress with equal show of authority enact a code of laws for the enforcement and vindication of all rights of life, liberty, and property? If it is supposable that the States may deprive persons of life, liberty, and property without due process of law (and the amendment itself does suppose this), why should not Congress proceed at once to prescribe due process of law for the protection of every one of these fundamental rights, in every possible case, as well as to prescribe equal privileges in inns, public conveyances and theaters? The truth is, that the implication of a power to legislate in this manner is based upon the assumption that if the States are forbidden to legislate or act in a particular way on a particular subject, and power is conferred upon Congress to enforce the prohibition, this gives Congress power to legislate generally upon that subject, and not merely power to provide modes of redress against such State legislation or action. The assumption is certainly unsound. It is repugnant to the Tenth Amendment of the Constitution, which declares that powers not delegated to the United States by the Constitution, nor prohibited by it to the States, are reserved to the States respectively or to the people. . . .

In this connection it is proper to state that civil rights, such as are guaranteed by the Constitution against State aggression, cannot be impaired by the wrongful acts of individuals, unsupported by State authority in the shape of laws, customs, or judicial or executive proceedings. The wrongful act of an individual, unsupported by any such authority, is simply a private wrong, or a crime of that individual; an invasion of the rights of the injured party, it is true, whether they affect his person, his property, or his reputation; but if not sanctioned in some way by the State, or not done under State authority, his rights remain in full force, and may presumably be vindicated by resort to the laws of the State for redress. An individual cannot deprive a man of his right to vote, to hold property, to buy and sell, to sue in the courts, or to be a witness or a juror; he may, by force or fraud, interfere with the enjoyment of the right in a particular case; he may commit an assault against the person, or commit murder, or use ruffian violence at the polls, or slander the good name of a fellow citizen; but, unless protected in these wrongful acts by some shield of State law or State authority, he cannot destroy or injure the right; he will only render himself amenable to satisfaction or punishment; and amenable therefore to the laws of the State where the wrongful acts are committed. Hence, in all those cases where the Constitution seeks to protect the rights of the citizen against discriminative and unjust laws of the State by prohibiting such laws, it is not individual offences, but abrogation and denial of rights, which it denounces, and for which it clothes the Congress with power to provide a remedy. This abrogation and denial of rights, for which the States alone were or could be responsible, was the great seminal and fundamental wrong which was intended to be remedied. And the remedy to be provided must necessarily be predicated upon that wrong. It must assume that in the case provided for, the evil or wrong actually committed rests upon some State law or State authority for its excuse and perpetration. . . .

We have discussed the question presented by the law on the assumption that a right to enjoy equal accommodation and privileges in all inns, public conveyances, and places of public amusement, is one of the essential rights of the citizen which no State can abridge or interfere with. Whether it is such a right, or not, is a different question which, in the view we have taken of the validity of the law on the ground already stated, it is not necessary to examine. . . .

But the power of Congress to adopt direct and primary, as distinguished from corrective legislation, on the subject in hand, is sought, in the second place, from the Thirteenth Amendment, which abolishes slavery. . . .

This amendment, as well as the Fourteenth, is undoubtedly self-executing without any ancillary legislation, so far as its terms are applicable to any existing state of circumstances. By its own unaided force and effect it abolished slavery, and established universal freedom. . . .

The only question under the present head, therefore, is whether the refusal to any persons of the accommodations of an inn, or a public conveyance, or a place of public amusement, by an individual, and without any sanction or support from any State law or regulation, does inflict upon such persons any manner of servitude, or form of slavery, as those terms are understood in this country? . . .

It would be running the slavery argument into the ground to make it apply to every act of discrimination which a person may see fit to make as to the guests he will entertain, or as to the people he will take into his coach or cab or car, or admit to his concert or theater, or deal with in other matters of intercourse or business. . . . On the whole we are of opinion, that no countenance of authority for the passage of the law in question can he found in either the Thirteenth or Fourteenth Amendment of the Constitution; and no other ground of authority for its passage being suggested, it must necessarily be declared void, at least so far as its operation in the several States is concerned. . . .

MR. JUSTICE HARLAN, dissenting:

The opinion in these cases proceeds, it seems to me, upon grounds entirely too narrow and artificial. I cannot resist the conclusion that the substance and spirit of the recent amendments of the Constitution have been sacrificed by a subtle and ingenious verbal criticism. . . .

There seems to be no substantial difference between my brethren and myself as to the purpose of Congress; for, they say that the essence of the law is, not to declare broadly that all persons shall be entitled to the full and equal enjoyment of the accommodation, advantages, facilities, and privileges of inns, public conveyances, and theaters; but that such enjoyment shall not be subject to conditions applicable only to citizens of a particular race or color, or who had been in a previous condition of servitude. The effect of the statute, the court says, is, that colored citizens whether formerly slaves or not, and citizens of other races, shall have the same accommodations and privileges in all inns, public conveyances, and places of amusement as are enjoyed by white persons; and vice versa.

The court adjudges, I think erroneously, that Congress is without power, under either the Thirteenth or Fourteenth Amendment, to establish such regulations and that the first and second sections of the statute are, in all their parts, unconstitutional, and void. . . .

Congress has not, in these matters, entered the domain of State control and supervision. It does not . . . assume to prescribe the general conditions and limitations under which inns, public conveyances, and places of public amusement, shall be conducted or managed. It simply declares, in effect, that since the nation has established universal freedom in this country, for all time, there shall be no discrimination, based merely upon race or color, in respect of the accommodations and advantages of public conveyances, inns, and places of public amusement.

I am of the opinion that such discrimination practised by corporations and individuals in the exercise of their public or quasi-public functions is a badge of servitude the imposition of which Congress may prevent under its power, by appropriate legislation, to enforce the Thirteenth Amendment; and, consequently, without reference to its enlarged power under the Fourteenth Amendment, the act of March 1, 1875, is not, in my judgment, repugnant to the Constitution. . . .

The assumption that this amendment [the Fourteenth] consists wholly of prohibitions upon State laws and State proceedings in hostility to its provisions, is unauthorized by its language. The first clause of the first section—"All persons born or naturalized in the United States, and subject to the jurisdiction thereof, are citizens of the United States, and of the State wherein they reside"—is of a distinctly affirmative character. In its application to the colored race, previously liberated, it created and granted, citizenship of the United States, as well as citizenship of the State in which they respectively resided. It introduced all of that race, whose ancestors had been imported and sold as slaves, at once, into the political community known as the "People of the United States." They became, instantly, citizens of the United States, and of their respective States. Further, they were brought, by this supreme act of the nation, within the direct operation of that provision of the Constitution which declares that "the citizens of each State shall be entitled to all privileges and immunities of citizens in the several States." Article 4, Section 2.

The citizenship, thus acquired, by that race, in virtue of an affirmative grant from the nation, may be protected, not alone by the judicial branch of the government, but by congressional legislation of a primary direct character; this, because the power of Congress is not restricted to the enforcement of prohibitions upon State laws or State action. It is, in terms distinct and positive, to enforce "the provisions of this article" of amendment; not simply those of a prohibitive character, but the provisions—all of the provisions—affirmative and prohibitive, of the amendment. It is, therefore, a grave misconception to suppose that the fifth section of the amendment has reference exclusively to express prohibitions upon State laws or State action. If any right was created by that amendment, the grant of power, through appropriate legislation, to enforce its provisions, authorizes Congress, by means of legislation, operating throughout the entire Union, to guard, secure, and protect the right. . . .

[G]overnment has nothing to do with social, as distinguished from technically legal, rights of individuals. No government ever has brought, or ever can bring, its people into social intercourse against their wishes. Whether one person will permit or maintain social relations with another is a matter with which government has no concern. . . . The rights which Congress, by the act of 1875, endeavored to secure and protect are legal, not social rights. The right, for instance, of a colored citizen to use the accommodations of a public highway, upon the same terms as are permitted to white citizens, is no more a social right than his right, under the law, to use the public street of a city or a town, or a turnpike road, or a public market, or a post office, or his right to sit in a public building with others, of whatever race, for the purpose of hearing the political questions of the day discussed.

The supreme law of the land has decreed that no authority shall be exercised in this country upon the basis of discrimination, in respect of civil rights, against freemen and citizens because of their race, color, or previous condition of servitude. To that decree—for the due enforcement of which, by appropriate legislation, Congress has been invested with express power—every one must bow, whatever may have been, or whatever now are, his individual views as to the wisdom or policy, either of the recent changes in the fundamental law, or of the legislation which has been enacted to give them effect.

For the reasons stated I feel constrained to withhold my assent to the opinion of the Court.

JONES *v.* ALFRED H. MAYER CO.
392 U.S. 409; 88 Sup. Ct. 2186; 20 L. Ed. 2d 1189 (1968)

[42 U.S.C. Section 1982 was originally part of Section 1 of the Civil Rights Act of 1866. It reads: "All citizens of the United States shall have the same right, in every State and Territory, as is enjoyed by white citizens thereof to inherit, purchase, lease, sell, hold, and convey real and personal property."]

On September 2, 1965, the petitioners filed a complaint . . . alleging that the respondents had refused to sell them a home in the Paddock Woods community of St. Louis County for the sole reason that petitioner Joseph Lee Jones is a Negro. Relying in part upon Section 1982, the petitioners sought injunctive and other relief. The District Court sustained the respondents' motion to dismiss the complaint, and the Court of Appeals for the Eighth Circuit affirmed, concluding that Section 1982 applies only to state action. . . .

On its face, 42 U.S.C. Section 1982 appears to prohibit *all* discrimination against Negroes in the sale or rental of property—discrimination by private owners as well as discrimination by public authorities. . . . Stressing what they consider to be the revolutionary implications of so literal a reading of Section 1982, the respondents argue that Congress cannot possibly have intended any such result. Our examination of the relevant history, however, persuades us that Congress meant exactly what it said.

Nor was the scope of the 1866 Act altered when it was reenacted in 1870, some two years after the ratification of the Fourteenth Amendment. It is quite true that some members of Congress supported the Fourteenth Amendment "in order to eliminate doubt as to the constitutional validity of the Civil Rights Act as applied to the States." But it certainly does not follow that the adoption of the Fourteenth Amendment or the subsequent readoption of the Civil Rights Act were meant somehow to *limit* its application to state action. The legislative history furnishes not the slightest factual basis for any such speculation, and the conditions prevailing in 1870 make it highly implausible. . . .

The remaining question is whether Congress has power under the Constitution to do what Section 1982 purports to do. . . . Our starting point is the Thirteenth Amendment, for it was pursuant to that constitutional provision that Congress originally enacted what is now Section 1982. . . . It has never been doubted . . . "that the power vested in Congress to enforce the article by appropriate legislation," *[Civil Rights Cases]* includes the power to enact laws "direct and primary, operating upon the acts of individuals, whether sanctioned by State legislation or not." [Ibid.] . . .

The constitutional question in this case, therefore, comes to this: Does the authority of Congress to enforce the Thirteenth Amendment "by appropriate legislation" include the power to eliminate all racial barriers to the acquisition of real and personal property? We think the answer to that question is plainly yes.

"By its own unaided force and effect," the Thirteenth Amendment "abolished slavery, and established universal freedom." *[Civil Rights Cases]* Whether or not the Amendment *itself* did any more than that—a question not involved in this case—it is at least clear that the Enabling Clause of that Amendment empowered Congress to do much more. For that clause clothed "Congress with power to pass *all laws necessary and proper for abolishing all badges and incidents of slavery in the United States.*" [Ibid.] (Italics supplied.)

Those who opposed passage of the Civil Rights Act of 1866 argued in effect that the Thirteenth Amendment merely authorized Congress to dissolve the legal bond by which the Negro slave was held to his master. Yet many had earlier opposed the Thirteenth Amendment on the very ground that it would give Congress virtually unlimited power to enact laws for the protection of Negroes in every State. And the majority leaders in Congress—who were, after all, the authors of the Thirteenth Amendment—had no doubt that its Enabling Clause contemplated the sort of positive legislation that was embodied in the 1866 Civil Rights Act. . . .

Surely Congress has the power under the Thirteenth Amendment rationally to determine what are the badges and the incidents of slavery, and the authority to translate that determination into effective legislation. Nor can we say that the determination Congress has made is an irrational one. For this Court recognized long ago that, whatever else they may have encompassed, the badges and incidents of slavery—its "burdens and disabilities"—included restraints upon "those fundamental rights which are the essence of civil freedom, namely the same right . . . to inherit, purchase, lease, sell and convey property, as is enjoyed by white citizens." *[Civil Rights Cases]* Just as the Black Codes, enacted after the Civil War to restrict the free exercise of those rights, were substitutes for the slave system, so the exclusion of Negroes from white communities became a substitute for the Black Codes. And when racial discrimination herds men into ghettos and makes their ability to buy property turn on the color of their skin, then it too is a relic of slavery.

. . . At the very least, the freedom that Congress is empowered to secure under the Thirteenth Amendment includes the freedom to buy whatever a white man can buy, the right to live wherever a white man can live. If Congress cannot say that being a free man means at least this much, then the Thirteenth Amendment made a promise the Nation cannot keep. . . .

Reversed

MR. JUSTICE HARLAN, whom MR. JUSTICE WHITE joins, dissented.

A NOTE ON INTERGOVERNMENTAL TAX IMMUNITIES

One of the most puzzling long-term problems of federalism is the capacity, or incapacity, of the Federal Government to tax the states and vice versa. Although this problem continues to generate cases involving important financial consequences, their concerns are so specialized and the doctrines so complex that they have fallen outside the mainstream of constitutional law. This note is included for those especially interested in the subject.

The power of Congress to tax is concurrent with that of the state governments. The "entire field of taxation remains open to each of the governments, national and state." The "burden of taxation of each sovereign may fall on the same persons, natural and artificial, the same property, privilege, or activity." [1] But the Constitution is silent about whether or not the states and the national government can tax the instrumentalities of one another. Hence, this question had to be settled by the Supreme Court.

It will be recalled that in *McCulloch* v. *Maryland* the Court held that the agencies and instrumentalities of the Federal Government could not be taxed by the states. Chief Justice Marshall's famous phrase in that case, "the power to tax involves the power to destroy," was the basis for establishing federal immunity from state taxation. The principle announced in *McCulloch* v. *Maryland* was broadened in *Dobbins* v. *Commissioners of Erie County,* 16 Pet. 435 (1842), where the Court held federal salaries immune from state taxation. Finally, in 1870, the Court expanded the immunity doctrine by making it applicable to federal taxation of state instrumentalities in the case of *Collector* v. *Day,* 11 Wall, 113 (1871). In that case, the Court relied on both the *McCulloch* and *Dobbins* decisions in holding that the salary of a state judge was exempt from federal taxation. Thus, "some fifty years after the Court established the immunity of federal instrumentalities from state taxation (in *McCulloch* v. *Maryland),* the immunity was made reciprocal in *Collector* v. *Day,* on the theory that 'the exception rests upon necessary implication, and is upheld by the great law of self-preservation.' " [2]

The doctrine of tax immunity enunciated in *McCulloch* v. *Maryland* had "its origin in political necessity. In a real sense, Marshall's formulation of the immunity doctrine was part of his larger struggle against state's rights." [3] In one sense, *Collector* v. *Day* was in conflict with portions of *McCulloch* v. *Maryland* and other important decisions establishing the principle of federal supremacy. For the clear implication of *Collector* v. *Day* was that the national government and the states are equal. But, as Justice Stone indicated in a later case, the state immunity from national taxation recognized in *Collector* v. *Day* was "narrowly limited to a state judicial officer engaged in the performance of a function which pertained to state governments at the time the Constitution was adopted." [4] Another important fact to remember about this case is that it was decided during the Reconstruction period, when the Court "was engaged in endeavoring to stem the tendency in Congress toward extreme centralization at the expense of state rights." [5]

[1] Owen J. Roberts, *The Court and the Constitution* (Cambridge: Harvard U.P., 1951), p. 3.

[2] David Fellman, "Ten Years of the Supreme Court: 1937–1947, Federalism," *American Political Science Review,* Vol. 41 (1947), p. 1157.

[3] Samuel J. Konefsky, *Chief Justice Stone and the Supreme Court* (New York: Macmillan, Inc., 1945), p. 42.

[4] *Helvering* v. *Gerhardt,* 304 U.S. 405 (1938). In this case the Court overruled an earlier decision [*Brush* v. *Commissioner of Internal Revenue,* 300 U.S. 352 (1937)], and held that the salaries of officers of the New York Port Authority were not immune from federal income taxation.

[5] John M. Mathews, *The American Constitutional System* (New York: McGraw-Hill, 1940), p. 259.

The doctrine of *Collector* v. *Day* was never applied widely after the Reconstruction era. And in recent years the area of the states' immunity from federal taxation has been reduced greatly. In fact, the whole doctrine of intergovernmental tax immunity has undergone considerable modification. Changes first appeared in *South Carolina* v. *United States,* 199 U.S. 437 (1905). South Carolina had taken over the business of dispensing liquor. But when the Federal Government attempted to collect the national excise tax on liquor dealers, the state claimed immunity under the doctrine of *Collector* v. *Day.* In holding that South Carolina was required to pay the tax, the Supreme Court drew a distinction between state functions that were strictly governmental and those that were business or proprietary in nature. Governmental functions were said to be immune from taxation, but when a state enters an ordinary business, such as the liquor business, as South Carolina had done, no immunity existed.

The *South Carolina* case imposed on the Court the difficult task of determining in specific cases when a particular function was or was not a governmental one. That this is extremely difficult to do is demonstrated by numerous decisions. For example, in *Brush* v. *Commissioner of Internal Revenue,* the Court held that because a waterworks is a governmental function, the salary of an employee of the Bureau of Water Supply in New York City was immune from federal income taxation. But in *Allen* v. *Regents of University of Georgia,* 304 U.S. 439 (1938), the Court held that receipts from state university athletic contests were liable to federal taxation because such contests are proprietary rather than governmental in nature. Of the *Brush* and *Allen* cases, it has been well said that "it would be interesting to see whether a Byzantine theologian could discover any genuine distinction between the two cases." [6] Thus, as Justice Jackson once remarked, "it is easy to see that the line between the taxable and the immune has been drawn with an unsteady hand." [7]

From time to time various members of the Court protested against the illogical distinction between governmental and business activities and called for a complete reexamination of the entire tax-immunity doctrine. Justice Stone took the lead in this development; he wrote the majority opinions in *Helvering* v. *Gerhardt* and *Graves* v. *New York* ex rel. *O'Keefe,* 306 U.S. 466 (1939), which modified considerably the doctrine of intergovernmental tax immunity. In the latter case, the Court upheld a nondiscriminatory state income tax on the earnings of a federal official. The Court held: "*Collector* v. *Day* [is] overruled so far as [it] recognize[s] an implied constitutional immunity from income taxation of the salaries of officers or employees of the national or a state government or their instrumentalities."

In the case of *New York* v. *United States,* 326 U.S. 572 (1946), the Court held that the sale of mineral waters by the state of New York constituted a business function that was subject to a federal tax. The case is important principally because some of the justices were willing to reject the traditional distinction

[6] Fellman, op. cit., p. 1158.

[7] *United States* v. *Allegheny County,* 322 U.S. 174 (1944).

between governmental and business activities as a basis for applying the doctrine of tax immunity. Although no new general rule was framed in the *New York* case, the Court will undoubtedly continue to search for more realistic criteria. To this end, Chief Justice Stone, who was joined by Justices Reed, Murphy, and Burton in his concurring opinion in *New York* v. *United States,* repeated what he had said in an earlier case as follows:

> Taxation by either the state or the Federal Government affects in some measure the cost of operation of the other. But neither government may destroy the other nor curtail in any substantial manner the exercise of its powers. Hence, the limitation upon the taxing power of each, so far as it affects the other, must receive a practical construction which permits both to function with the minimum of interference each with the other; and that limitation cannot be so varied or extended as seriously to impair either the taxing power of the government imposing the tax or the appropriate exercise of the functions of the government affected by it.

The latest doctrinal turns and twists can be followed in *Rohr Aircraft Corp.* v. *San Diego County,* 362 U.S. 628 (1960); *First Agric. Nat. Bank* v. *State Tax Comm'n,* 392 U.S. 339 (1968); *Mescalero Apache Tribe* v. *Jones,* 411 U.S. 145 (1973); *United States* v. *County of Fresno,* 429 U.S. 915 (1976); *Massachusetts* v. *United States,* 435 U.S. 444 (1978); and *United States* v. *New Mexico,* 102 S.Ct. 1373 (1982).[8]

[8] In general, see Laurence H. Tribe, "Intergovernmental Immunities," *Harvard Law Review,* Vol. 89 (1976), p. 682.

CHAPTER 6

War, Foreign Affairs, and the Presidency

War and foreign affairs do not fit neatly into the wording of the Constitution. About the only constitutional provision dealing with these subjects that seems precise is the one providing that Congress shall declare war. Yet, after World War II, which was declared by Congress, there was a "cold war" with the Soviet Union in the late 1940s and 1950s and a whole series of limited wars, invasions, and coups such as Vietnam and the Bay of Pigs. These actions, initiated by various Presidents and their subordinates acting alone, have made the "undeclared war" a pressing reality and the subject of an unresolved political and constitutional debate. In general, where Congress has cooperated with the President in the exercise of his vaguely defined war and foreign affairs powers, the Supreme Court has had little to say. Where the President has acted alone, and particularly where he seems to have acted in opposition to congressional policies, the Court has been slightly more bold. However, situations of outright conflict between Congress and the

President are not likely to tempt the justices to very bold action. Our constitutional tradition seems to compel the Court to define the constitutional boundaries established by Article I and Article II. Yet the Court has neither the physical nor political punch to impose its solutions to legislative-executive conflicts on its two coequal, but far more powerful, branches of the government. The Court has always been haunted by the problem of what it would or could do if it ordered the Congress or President to do something and one or the other simply refused. As a result, it has been highly reluctant to issue orders about war, foreign policy, or the presidential authority stemming from those government functions.

The Presidency

In the twentieth century, the vital role of the President in both national and international affairs can hardly be exaggerated.[1] The vast powers now exercised by modern Presidents could not have been envisioned by the framers of the Constitution. In fact, the framers were not quite sure how the executive branch should be set up. The fear of executive tyranny, coupled with a strong faith in legislative bodies, made some of the framers reluctant to confer important powers on a single executive. On the other hand, expeirence with a weak, headless government under the Articles of Confederation led others to demand a strong executive branch that could deal effectively with national problems but that, at the same time, was not so strong that it would overwhelm the other two branches. This they tried to do in Article II of the Constitution, which deals with the executive branch.

The language of Article II is very vague and indefinite when compared with Articles I and III, which define the authority of the other branches of government. Article II loosely provides that the executive power is vested in the President and that he shall take care that the laws be faithfully executed. Of course, the President was given other specific powers under Article II. He was made Commander-in-Chief of the Army and Navy. He was empowered to appoint numerous officers, to grant pardons and reprieves, to make treaties, to receive ambassadors and ministers, and to perform certain important duties in connection with Congress. Nevertheless, the Constitution does not define precisely the boundaries of executive power. Although Article II provides the base for the present-day power of the President, the scope of his authority is much broader than is indicated by the rudimentary constitutional provisions. In short, the modern Presidency is largely the product of practical political experience.[2]

[1] Arthur M. Schlesinger, Jr., *The Imperial Presidency* (Boston: Houghton Mifflin, 1973). For an exhaustive review of the powers of the President, see Vol. 2 of Bernard Schwartz, *A Commentary on the Constitution of the United States* (New York: Macmillan, Inc., 1963).

[2] Louis Fisher, *The Constitution Between Friends: Congress, the President and the Law* (New York: St. Martin's Press, 1978).

The vagueness of the Constitution virtually "invited men of will, courage, and program to build a Presidential tradition." [3] The tradition of the strong Presidency has been particularly associated with Franklin Delano Roosevelt, although his predecessors, Theodore Roosevelt and Woodrow Wilson, had much to do with it, too. Under the pressure of hostile domestic reaction to the Vietnam War—or, rather their own strained, some might say pathological, response to that hostility—Presidents Johnson and Nixon often pressed the tradition to its ultimate extremes. Both the Johnson and Nixon administrations tended to treat Congress and the people on a "need to know" basis, telling them whatever they needed to know to support the President's war. This dedication to pursuing presidential war aims, no matter what the rest of the nation might want, reached its ultimate expression at the time President Johnson continued to press the war vigorously while refusing to submit himself to a reelection campaign in which the people could pass judgment on his policy.

President Nixon and his subordinates continued this stance of presidential quasiabsolutism. Even lying to the President himself—not to mention lying to Congress and the public—as well as assorted burglaries, assaults, and acts of political espionage were defended on the ground of the paramount need to place presidential power beyond the reach of its opponents and the need to keep Mr. Nixon in the Presidency. At times the Nixon Presidency asserted an absolute constitutional right to refuse to spend money legally appropriated by Congress and to withhold any and all information about the operation of the executive branch from Congress and the people. In the heat of battle the Nixon forces occasionally asserted that impeachment was about the only constitutional limitation on the "inherent powers" of the President.

Although the Nixon position was sometimes little more than a symptom of shock caused by the tremendous blow to presidential prestige dealt by Watergate, there is no doubt that the Presidency's political powers have grown so enormously as to alter fundamentally the constitutional balance. But even in the twentieth century, the scope of this power depends to a large degree on the qualities of each individual President. Furthermore, the President is limited, first of all, by various provisions of the Constitution. For example, he must share the general power to govern with the other two branches of government. He shares the treaty-making power with the Senate. The Twenty-second Amendment establishes a flat ban on a third term. The President's powers are also restricted by specific actions of Congress and the courts, by his own or the opposing political party, and by public opinion.

The courts are the least reliable restraint upon the powers of the President. In fact, the Supreme Court has done more to expand than to contract presidential powers. For example, in the case of In re *Neagle,* 135 U.S. 1 (1890), the Court attributed powers to the President that were not specifically granted by statute or expressly mentioned in the Constitution. In that case the justices held that there was a "peace of the United States" which the President was empowered

[3] James W. Hurst, *The Growth of American Law: The Law Makers* (Boston: Little, Brown, 1950), p. 384.

to protect by armed force even though keeping the peace would seem to fall squarely within the police powers retained by the states under the Constitution. In numerous other instances, the Court has supported the strong actions of various Presidents. Although on some occasions the Court has proved to be an important restraint on presidential powers, in the long run "the Court can be expected to go on rationalizing most pretensions of most Presidents." [4] This is particularly so in periods of emergency, when the Court has been reluctant to interfere with the President in the absence of *extreme* abuses of authority.

Many Congressional statutes now contain "legislative veto" provisions that permit Congress to invalidate new regulations made by executive agencies. The constitutionality of the legislative veto is in doubt because it allows Congress to avoid subjecting some of its actions to the Presidential veto provided in Art. I, Sec. 7.

War

Not until the Civil War period did fundamental conflicts arise between constitutional limitations and claims of military necessity. One of the very first of these, involving the blockade of Southern ports, reached the Court in *The Prize Cases* (p. 177), one of the few cases in which the Court directly confronted the problem of undeclared war. President Lincoln felt strongly that private constitutional rights had to be disregarded when they interfered with the winning of the war and the preservation of the Union. As a consequence, individual rights were curtailed drastically during the Civil War by the unprecedented expansion of military powers. Among other things, military officers were authorized by the President to suspend the writ of habeas corpus, martial law was instituted in a number of areas, and military tribunals were used for trial of civilians.

The clash between judicial and executive authorities during this period can be seen in the case of Ex Parte *Merryman,* 17 Fed. Cas. 144 (No. 9487) (1861). John Merryman, a Southern agitator of wealth and position residing in Maryland, was arrested by order of the military authorities of the area for his opposition to the Union. After his confinement in Fort McHenry, Merryman petitioned Chief Justice Taney for a writ of habeas corpus. At that time, Maryland was part of the circuit over which the Chief Justice presided. Taney issued the writ, which directed the commanding general of Fort McHenry to bring Merryman before the circuit court so that the reasons for his imprisonment could be examined. The commanding general refused to comply with Taney's order and replied through a military aide that he had been authorized by the President to suspend the writ of habeas corpus. Taney thereupon ordered that the general be brought before the court, but a United States marshal was denied entrance to Fort McHenry; the general simply ignored Taney's order. Because Taney could not obtain compliance with his orders, he could do nothing but write

[4] Clinton Rossiter, *The American Presidency* (New York: Harcourt, 1960), p. 59.

his opinion, in which he stated that the President had no authority to suspend the writ of habeas corpus and that only Congress could suspend the writ. Taney decried the usurpation of power by military authorities and directed that a copy of the entire record of the case be sent to President Lincoln. He concluded that "it will then remain for that high officer, in fulfillment of his constitutional obligation to take care that the laws be faithfully executed, to determine what measures he will take to cause the civil process of the United States to be respected and enforced." President Lincoln never *directly* answered the Chief Justice. However, Merryman was later released from Fort McHenry and turned over to civilian authorities. He was subsequently indicted for treason, but the case against him was finally dropped. "This was typical of the treatment accorded such cases by the Lincoln administration. When Merryman was no longer capable of harming the Union, Lincoln, who sought no tyranny, gladly washed his hands of the Merryman controversy. But neither the President nor the Chief Justice had a change of heart, and their differences endured." [5]

The encroachment upon civil authority by the military continued throughout the Civil War, but in only one case [Ex Parte *Vallandigham,* 1 Wall. 243 (1864)] was the system of military trials challenged in the Supreme Court, and there the Court dismissed the case, stating that it was without jurisdiction to review the proceedings of a military tribunal. The dearth of cases in the Supreme Court despite the great number of trials held before military commissions can be explained by the fact that judicial review was almost impossible to obtain during this period. "Since review by certiorari was not possible, the only way to get a case before the courts was to ask the judiciary to consider the question of the constitutionality of the President's suspension of the privilege of the writ of habeas corpus. The Supreme Court was unwilling to do this until the war was over and Lincoln was dead." [6] By that time the Court was ready to place restraints upon the exercise of military powers. This it did in Ex Parte *Milligan* (p. 178) in an opinion written by Justice Davis, who had been one of Lincoln's closest friends and most ardent supporters. The *Milligan* case stands out as one of the great landmark decisions in the cause of civil supremacy. The sweeping majority opinion of Justice Davis declared that Congress had *no* authority to establish military commissions even if it chose to do so. The concurring justices, on the other hand, were unwilling to deny, categorically, the power of Congress to establish military tribunals.

By its decision in the *Milligan* case, the Court became embroiled deeply in the conflict between President Johnson and Congress over Reconstruction. The decision cast serious doubts on the efforts of the Radical Republicans to impose military rule on the Southern states and strengthened President Johnson's proposals for moderation. Leading Radical Republicans launched a violent attack on

[5] David M. Silver, *Lincoln's Supreme Court* (Urbana: University of Illinois Press, 1957), p. 36. A thorough discussion of the *Merryman* case and the *Korematsu* case (noted subsequently) are found in Rocco J. Tresolini, *Justice and the Supreme Court* (Philadelphia: Lippincott, 1963), Chs. 1 and 7.

[6] Glendon A. Schubert, *The Presidency in the Courts* (Minneapolis: University of Minnesota Press, 1957), p. 188.

the Court soon after the *Milligan* decision was rendered. In 1866, they pushed a law through Congress that reduced the number of justices from nine to seven; and when the Radical Republicans thought that the Court might hold the Reconstruction acts invalid in a pending case, Congress enacted a statute that withdrew the Court's jurisdiction over the case. The Court acquiesced and subsequently dismissed the case on the ground that it had no jurisdiction.[7]

Mississippi v. *Johnson* (p. 181) also involved the Reconstruction acts. President Johnson favored a policy of moderation, whereas the Radical Republicans in Congress wished to impose strict military control over the defeated rebellious states. The Court stayed out of the clash between the President and Congress by holding that it was without power to enjoin the President from enforcing a congressional statute.

Whatever the President's immunity from judicial control under the doctrine of *Mississippi* v. *Johnson,* it does not extend to his subordinate executive officers. The President's subordinates can be enjoined from carrying out a threatened illegal act or be compelled to perform a legal duty by a writ of mandamus. This lack of immunity on the part of the President's subordinates is demonstrated by *Youngstown Sheet and Tube Co.* v. *Sawyer* (p. 189). The President is wholly immune from civil damage suits, but his aids have only limited immunity. [*Nixon* v. *Fitzgerald,* 50 L.W. 4797; *Harlow* v. *Fitzgerald,* 50 L.W. 4815 (1982).]

WORLD WAR II

America's limited participation in World War I produced no significant conflicts between military and civil authority, but the unprecedented extensions of military powers during World War II created many new problems concerning civil-military relationships. In fact, the only two major encroachments on individual liberties during World War II resulted from military action.

Individual liberties were seriously impaired as the result of the military evacuation of some 70,000 citizens and 40,000 aliens of Japanese descent from the Pacific Coast during World War II. The details relating to the compulsory removal of these Japanese-Americans from their homes are noted subsequently in connection with *Korematsu* v. *United States* (p. 183), where the Supreme Court held that the evacuation program was constitutional. On the same day that the *Korematsu* case was decided, the Court held, in Ex Parte *Endo,* 323 U.S. 283 (1944), that a Japanese-American girl, whose loyalty to the United States had been clearly established, could not be held in a war relocation center. However, the Court evaded the major constitutional issue in the *Endo* case and refused to invalidate the entire internment program. The Court held simply that neither Congress nor the President had empowered the War Relocation Authority to *continue* the detention of Japanese-American citizens once their loyalty had been established. In the "calm perspective of hindsight," most postwar commentators have concluded that the military evacuation and confinement

[7] Ex Parte *McCardle,* 7 Wall. 506 (1869).

of Japanese-Americans constituted an unnecessary infringement of individual liberties.[8]

The second major instance of the military suppression of individual liberties during World War II occurred in Hawaii. Under the President's power as Commander-in-Chief, military government was established in Hawaii a few hours after the Japanese attack on Pearl Harbor on December 7, 1941. The writ of habeas corpus was suspended, and the civilian governor's powers were conferred upon the local army commander. The new military governor immediately closed all the regular civil and criminal courts and established military commissions to try civilians as well as military personnel. Sentences imposed by the new military courts were not subject to review by the regular federal courts. In 1943, civil government was partially restored by order of the President, but the writ of habeas corpus remained suspended and military courts were still authorized to try civilians for violations of military orders; not until October 1944 was military government in Hawaii terminated entirely. Serious objections were raised to their long-continued subordination to army control by the civil officers and inhabitants of Hawaii. They argued that military government was unnecessary in Hawaii after the battle of Midway in June 1942, because that battle had ended any danger of a Japanese invasion of the islands; federal judges maintained that the regular civilian courts were in a position to handle effectively the cases turned over to military courts.

Not until after the war, in *Duncan* v. *Kahanamoku,* 327 U.S. 304 (1946), did the Supreme Court have an opportunity to pass on the validity of the Hawaiian military government. The Court held in the *Duncan* case that Congress had not authorized the establishment of military tribunals in Hawaii to try civilians when the civil courts were open and available. Thus, the Court ruled that the military leaders had exceeded their authority in suppressing civil government in Hawaii under the provisions of the Hawaiian Organic Act of 1900. But again, as in the *Milligan* case, judicial restraints were not placed on the President as Commander-in-Chief and on the military until after the war was ended.

MILITARY JURISDICTION

In Ex Parte *Quirin,* 317 U.S. 1 (1942) and In re *Yamashita,* 327 U.S. 1 (1946), the Court held that the President had the authority to establish military commissions to try enemy combatants who were not American citizens and that such commissions were not subject to judicial review.

In addition to the cases presented by enemy nationals after the war, the Supreme Court was faced with important questions relating to court-martial jurisdiction. In a long and sometimes wavering line of cases, the Court eventually confined courts-martial to very narrow limits, holding that they could not try

[8] See, for example, Robert E. Cushman, "Civil Liberties in the Atomic Age," *The Annals,* Vol. 249 (Jan. 1947), p. 54.

civilians or discharged former members of the military at all—at least in peacetime or where civilian courts were open—and that they might try even members of the armed forces only for service-connected offenses. [*Kinsella* v. *United States ex rel. Singleton,* 361 U.S. 234 (1960); *United States ex rel. Toth* v. *Quarles,* 350 U.S. 11 (1955); *O'Callahan* v. *Parker,* 395 U.S. 258 (1969).] In *Wilson* v. *Girard,* 354 U.S. 524 (1957), Girard, an American soldier who had killed a Japanese woman, was turned over to the Japanese courts for trial under a "status-of-forces" agreement between the United States and Japan dealing with the stationing of American troops in Japan. The Court held that there are "no constitutional or statutory barriers" that prohibit surrendering American military personnel to foreign courts.

Foreign Affairs and the Inherent Powers Doctrine

The conduct of foreign affairs is primarily the responsibility of the President and his subordinates in the Department of State. Of course, the President's authority in foreign relations is shared with Congress, particularly the Senate. Through its power to appropriate money, Congress exercises important controls over foreign affairs. The President has authority to ratify treaties only after receiving the concurrence of two thirds of the Senate. His power to appoint diplomats is subject to ratification by a Senate majority. Nevertheless, the President's position in foreign relations is "paramount, if not indeed dominant." The "growth of presidential authority in this area seems to have been almost inevitable. Constitution, laws, custom, the practice of other nations, and the logic of history have combined to place the President in a dominant position." [9] That Congress may delegate vast powers to the President in the field of foreign affairs is indicated clearly by *United States* v. *Curtiss-Wright Export Corp.* (p. 186). Indeed, in resolutions connected with the Korean and Vietnamese wars, Congress delegated much of its power to declare war to the President, although serious doubts have been raised as to the constitutionality of these congressional actions. The Supreme Court repeatedly refused to decide on the constitutionality of the undeclared war in Vietnam, in spite of the openly declared desire of several of the justices to do so.

The President has freed himself from the Senate in some instances by using executive agreements rather than treaties to make international arrangements. Such agreements do not require the approval of the Senate. However, the Supreme Court ruled, in *United States* v. *Belmont,* 301 U.S. 324 (1937), that they have the same legal effect as formal treaties. The principle of the *Belmont* case was confirmed in *United States* v. *Pink,* 315 U.S. 203 (1942). Thus, the Court's holdings on the scope of the treaty power in *Missouri* v. *Holland* (p. 144) may well apply to executive agreements as well.

United States v. *Curtiss-Wright Export Corp.* introduced the doctrine of in-

[9] Rossiter, op. cit., p. 26.

herent powers—that the central government had certain sovereign powers in the realm of foreign affairs quite independent of the specific grants of authority in the Constitution. Given the central role of the President, inherent powers arguments almost inevitably become arguments for presidential capacity to exercise a vague and virtually unlimited authority derived not from specific constitutional provisions but from the aggregate of presidential responsibilities as Commander-in-Chief and chief director of foreign policy. Inherent powers arguments were raised and rejected in *Youngstown Sheet and Tube Co.* v. *Sawyer* (p. 189). They appear again in *New York Times Co.* v. *United States* (p. 195), where the Court as a body avoids them. However, they are taken up in the individual opinions of a number of the justices.[10]

"Executive privilege" is one of the aspects of the inherent powers doctrine. A privilege of the President to withhold evidence from courts that all other citizens are required to provide is nowhere mentioned in the Constitution. It derives, as do most inherent powers theories, from arguing that certain necessities arise from the President's war, foreign affairs, and general executive responsibilities. If the President is to carry out those responsibilities, so it is argued, he must be assured of full and frank interchanges with his advisers and subordinates. He could not get frank advice if those speaking to him knew that everything they said might shortly end up on the front page. Nor could he speak freely to them under such conditions. Thus the special need of the President to maintain the confidentiality of his conversations and papers.

The key issue of the Watergate scandal was not the burglaries, briberies, and other crimes and abuses of power committed by the President's subordinates, nor his own alleged ordering or foreknowledge of their offenses, but his alleged covering up of their misdeeds after they occurred. Precisely those presidential conversations that would be covered by a general claim of executive privilege would be the key evidence in proving whether the President was or was not guilty of an impeachable offense.

Throughout the Watergate affair, President Nixon offered inherent powers, separation of powers, and executive privilege arguments in such a way as to assert that the President was totally above and beyond the normal processes of law and that whether and to what extent he obeyed court orders was a matter within his own sole discretion.

In 1974 the whole issue came to a head when the Watergate special prosecutor sought presidential tape recordings as evidence in the criminal trials resulting from indictments handed down by the Watergate grand jury. *United States* v. *Nixon* (p. 197) not only resolved the issue but led directly to the resignation of President Nixon. What drew public attention in the political context of the moment was the Court's resounding rejection of presidential claims to being totally above and beyond the reach of the judicial process. The long-run significance of the decision lies more in the fact that the justices did unanimously recognize the constitutional status of executive privilege, a presidential power

[10] See Martin Shapiro, *The Pentagon Papers and the Courts* (San Francisco: Chandler Publishing Co., 1972).

which had not previously been acknowledged by the Court and which adds substantially to the President's power to put himself beyond the reach of democratic controls.

In the aftermath of Watergate, Congress passed the Presidential Recordings and Materials Preservation Act, which requires the General Services Administration to take possession of the President's papers when he or she leaves office and to make them available when they are properly subpoenaed. The Supreme Court upheld this statute against former President Nixon's claim of presidential privilege in *Nixon* v. *Administrator of General Services,* 433 U.S. 425 (1977).

Appointment and Removal of Officers

The President exerts a great deal of influence over both foreign and internal affairs through his power to appoint and remove public officers. Article II of the Constitution provides that the President shall nominate and, by and with the advice and consent of the Senate, appoint ambassadors, public ministers, consuls, judges of the Supreme Court, and other officers of the United States. The original version of the Campaign Financing Act of 1974, which is discussed at length in Chapter 11, provided for a Federal Elections Commission, two of whose members were to be appointed by the President, two by the Senate, and two by the House. In *Buckley* v. *Valeo* (p. 400) the Court declared this provision of the statute unconstitutional as a violation of Article II. Congress responded with a new statute providing that the election commissioners should be chosen through the normal process of presidential nomination and Senate advice and consent. Article II also declares that Congress may vest the appointment of inferior officers in the President alone, in the courts of law, or in the heads of departments. The Constitution does not define the term *inferior officers,* so Congress actually decides who falls into this category.

The Constitution does not provide for the removal of federal executive officers except through the cumbersome, seldom-used impeachment process. Not until 1926, in the celebrated case of *Myers* v. *United States,* 272 U.S. 52 (1926), was the Supreme Court finally forced to resolve important questions concerning the President's removal powers.

The *Myers* decision resulted in considerable controversy because of two important propositions laid down by the Court:

1. The power to remove an executive officer of the United States who has been appointed by the President by and with the advice and consent of the Senate belongs to the *President alone* under the Constitution.
2. Because the President may remove executive officers, a necessary corollary is that *all such officers may be removed at his discretion.* "The result of this ruling is to deny to Congress, which alone has power under the Constitution to create officers, any right to determine their tenure as against the removal power" of the President.[11]

[11] Edward S. Corwin, *The President's Removal Power Under the Constitution* (New York: National Municipal League, 1927), p. vi.

The *Myers* decision thus appeared to give the President unlimited power to remove all officers, with the exception of federal judges, in whose appointment he had participated. But the broad dictum of the case was limited considerably in *Humphrey's Executor* v. *United States* 295 U.S. 602 (1935). Since that decision, the President may continue to remove purely executive officers at will, but officers exercising quasijudicial and quasilegislative powers are protected by congressional limitations on the President's removal power. But because no precise definition of a purely executive officer can be given, the courts must decide in each individual case how a federal officer is to be classified. In 1941, for example, the Supreme Court denied certiorari in *Morgan* v. *United States,* 312 U.S. 701 (1938), after a lower federal court had approved President Roosevelt's removal of the chairman of the Tennessee Valley Authority (TVA). The lower court had held that the Humphrey case did not apply because the TVA "exercises predominately an executive or administrative function." It should not be "aligned with the Federal Trade Commission, the Interstate Commerce Commission or other administrative bodies mainly exercising clearly quasilegislative or quasijudicial functions—it is predominantly an administrative arm of the executive department." Nevertheless, the Humphrey case placed important restrictions on the President's removal powers during a turbulent period in the relationship between President F. D. Roosevelt and the Court.

In *Wiener* v. *United States,* 357 U.S. 349 (1958), the Court reasserted the *Humphrey's* rule prohibiting presidential removal from quasijudicial agencies even when Congress had said nothing about removal one way or the other. (See also *Elrod* v. *Burns* (1976), discussed in Chapter 11, but note that it applies only to nonpolicy-making levels of government.)

Citizenship

The constitutional dispute over citizenship is also deeply entangled with foreign policy problems. For it is often argued that the power to deprive an American of his citizenship is an important tool of foreign policy where, for instance, an American has become involved in the politics of another country or is serving in a foreign army.

The opening clause of the Fourteenth Amendment was designed principally to grant both national and state citizenship to the newly freed Negro. Under its terms, citizenship can be acquired by either birth or naturalization. With the few exceptions noted in the *Wong Kim Ark* case [169 U.S. 649 (1898)], *any* person born in the United States is a citizen regardless of his parentage. Thus, the English doctrine of *jus soli* (law of soil or place), by which citizenship is determined by place of birth, is the fundamental rule in the United States. Under the rule of *jus sanguinis* (law of blood), which is used in continental Europe, a person's citizenship is derived from the nationality of his parents regardless of the place of birth. Although the rule of *jus soli* is predominant in the United States, Congress has provided also that persons may be considered natural-born citizens under the doctrine of *jus sanguinis* in certain instances. For example, a child born abroad of American parents is an American citizen at birth under certain conditions specified by statute.

American citizenship is also acquired by naturalization. Under the Constitution (Article I, Section 8, clause 4), Congress has the power to establish rules governing the acquisition of citizenship by naturalization.

An alien's right to naturalization is largely a question of statutory rather than constitutional law. The major function of the courts in naturalization cases, therefore, is to construe the intent of Congress. Only a few such cases have reached the highest court. The most important Supreme Court decisions have involved the naturalization of pacifists or conscientious objectors.

Congress had long required that an alien seeking American citizenship must take an oath that he would support and defend the Constitution and laws of the United States against all foreign and domestic enemies. Did this mean that an applicant for naturalization had to be willing to bear arms in defense of the United States? In *United States* v. *Schwimmer,* 279 U.S. 644 (1929), an educated fifty-year-old, woman pacifist was denied citizenship because she stated that she was unwilling to fight in defense of the United States. In *Girouard* v. *United States,* 328 U.S. 61 (1946), *Schwimmer* was overruled. In the *Girouard* case, the Court granted citizenship to a Seventh Day Adventist who was willing to perform noncombatant duties in the army but would not promise to bear arms because of his religious convictions. In the majority opinion, Justice Douglas noted with approval Justice Holmes's dissent in the *Schwimmer* case and stated that "refusal to bear arms is not necessarily a sign of disloyalty or a lack of attachment to our institutions. One may serve his country faithfully and devotedly, though his religious scruples make it impossible for him to shoulder a rifle. Devotion to one's country can be as real and as enduring among noncombatants as among combatants."

The intention of Congress was clarified by legislation enacted in 1950 and 1952 that was in accord with the Supreme Court holdings in *Girouard.* The legislation provided that pacifists who base their refusal to bear arms on religious grounds may be naturalized. However, pacifists who are unwilling to fight because of political, sociological, or philosophical reasons are still barred from citizenship.

In *Perez* v. *Brownell,* 356 U.S. 44 (1958), the Supreme Court, by a 5-to-4 vote, held that under a section of the Nationality Act of 1940, Congress could deprive a person of citizenship for voting in a foreign election on the ground that this was a reasonable exercise of the power of Congress to regulate foreign affairs. On the same day, however, the Court ruled in another 5-to-4 decision [*Trop* v. *Dulles,* 356 U.S. 86 (1958)] that another section of the Nationality Act of 1940, which prescribed loss of citizenship for desertion from the armed forces during wartime, was unconstitutional because it involved cruel and unusual punishment. Then, in *Kennedy* v. *Mendoza-Martinez,* 372 U.S. 144 (1963), the Court held certain amendments to the Nationality Act "invalid because in them Congress has plainly employed the sanction of deprivation of nationality as a punishment—for the offense of leaving or remaining outside the country to evade military service—without affording the procedural safeguards guaranteed by the Fifth and Sixth Amendments." In *Schneider* v. *Rusk,* 377 U.S. 163 (1964), the Court struck down provisions for the denaturalization of naturalized citizens who subsequently resided in the country of their birth for three years or more. Finally, in *Afroyin* v. *Rusk* (p. 204), the Court overruled *Perez* v. *Brownell.*

The Burger Court has retrenched slightly on the Afroyim holding by deciding that a person granted citizenship under statutory provisions governing *jus sanguinis* can be deprived of citizenship for failing to fulfill the statutory requirement that he or she be continuously physically present in the United States for at least five years between the ages of fourteen and twenty-eight [*Rogers* v. *Bellei,* 401 U.S. 815 (1971). See also *Vance* v. *Terrazas,* 444 U.S. 252 (1980).]

Right to Travel

The argument that the actions of American citizens abroad may compromise our foreign policy has been used not only to justify statutes providing for deprivation of citizenship but also to support government refusal to allow Americans to travel abroad. In *Kent* v. *Dulles,* 357 U.S. 116 (1958), the Court announced a constitutional right to travel while confining itself to the limited holding that the Secretary of State's refusal to issue a passport to Kent had not been authorized by Congress. Then in *Aptheker* v. *Secretary of State,* 378 U.S. 500 (1964), the Court invalidated a section of the Subversive Activities Control Act of 1950, denying passports to members of a "Communist organization" on the ground that the statute did not confine itself to those persons whose travel presented a real likelihood of endangering American interests abroad. In *Zemel* v. *Rusk,* 381 U.S. 1 (1965), the Court upheld a State Department ban on travel to Cuba, holding that it was supported by "the weightiest considerations of national security." In *United States* v. *Guest,* 383 U.S. 745 (1966), the Court declared that there was a "constitutional right to travel from one state to another." [See also *Shapiro* v. *Thompson* (p. 570).] In *Hague* v. *Agee,* 101 S.Ct. 2766 (1981) the Court sharply distinguished between the "right to travel" within the United States which is "virtually unqualified" and the "freedom to travel abroad with a . . . passport" which "is subordinate to national security and foreign policy considerations." Deviating sharply from the narrow interpretation of the Passport Act it had adopted in *Kent* v. *Dulles,* the Court also held that Congress had broadly authorized the Secretary of State to withhold passports in the interests of national security. Accordingly the Court upheld the revocation of the passport of a former CIA employee who wrote and lectured abroad about the agency's secret operations and revealed the names and addresses of its agents posted around the world. [See also *Califano* v. *Aznavorian,* 439

U.S. 170 (1978) which sharply distinguishes between a domestic and an international right to travel.]

THE PRIZE CASES
2 Black 635; 17 L. Ed. 459 (1863)

[In 1861, President Lincoln declared a blockade of Confederate ports before Congress acted. The owners of ships seized as blockade runners challenged the legality of the blockade.]

MR. JUSTICE GRIER:

Whether the President in fulfilling his duties, as Commander-in-chief, is suppressing an insurrection, has met with such armed hostile resistance, and a civil war of such alarming proportions as will compel him to accord to them the character of belligerents, is a question to be decided *by him,* and this Court must be governed by the decisions and acts of the political department of the government to which this power was intrusted. He must determine what degree of force the crisis demands. The proclamation of blockade is itself official and conclusive evidence to the Court that a state of war existed which demanded and authorized a recourse to such a measure, under the circumstances peculiar to the case. . . .

It it were necessary to the technical existence of a war, that it should have a legislative sanction, we find it in almost every act passed at the extraordinary session of the legislature of 1861, which was wholly employed in enacting laws to enable the government to prosecute the war with vigor and efficiency. And finally, in 1861, we find Congress . . . passing an act "approving, legalizing, making valid all the acts, proclamations, and orders of the President, etc., as if they had been *issued and done under the previous express authority* and direction of the Congress of the United States."

. . . we are of the opinion that the President had a right, *jure belli,* to institute a blockade of ports in possession of the States in rebellion, which neutrals are bound to regard.

MR. JUSTICE NELSON, dissenting:

. . . the right of making war belongs exclusively to the supreme or sovereign power of the State.

This power in all civilized nations is regulated by the fundamental laws or municipal constitution of the country.

By our Constitution this power is lodged in Congress. Congress shall have power "to declare war, grant letters of marque and reprisal, and make rules concerning captures on land and water."

. . . before this insurrection against the established Government can be dealt with on the footing of a civil war, within the meaning of the law of nations and the Constitution of the United States, and which will draw after it belligerent rights, it must be recognized or declared by the war making power of the Government.

. . . I am compelled to the conclusion that no civil war existed between this government and the States in insurrection till recognized by the act of Congress 13th of July, 1861; that the President does not possess the power under the Constitution to declare war or recognize its existence within the meaning of the law of nations, which carries with it belligerent rights, and thus change the country and all its citizens from a state of peace to a state of war; that his power belongs exclusively to the Congress of the United States, and consequently, that the President has no power to set on foot a blockade under the law of nations, and that the capture of the vessel and cargo in this case, and in all cases before us in which capture occurred before the 13th of July 1861, . . . are illegal and void, and that the decrees of condemnation should be reversed and the vessel and cargo restored.

MR. CHIEF JUSTICE TANEY, MR. JUSTICE CATRON, *and* MR. JUSTICE CLIFFORD *concurred in the dissenting opinion of* MR. JUSTICE NELSON.

EX PARTE MILLIGAN
4 Wall. 2; 18 L. Ed. 281 (1866)

[A civilian named Lambdin P. Milligan, who resided in Indiana, was a Confederate sympathizer during the Civil War. In 1864, he was arrested by order of the commanding officer of the military district of Indiana and tried before a military commission on charges of conspiracy against the United States, affording aid and comfort to the Confederacy, inciting insurrection, disloyal practices, and violation of the laws of war. Milligan was found guilty of various specifications under each charge, such as resisting the draft and conspiracy to seize arms and ammunition stored in arsenals. He was sentenced to death by hanging. In May 1865, Milligan petitioned a circuit court for a writ of habeas corpus on the ground that the military commission had no jurisdiction over him because he was a civilian resident of a state where the ordinary civil courts were still open. He also contended that the military commission's action violated his right to trial by jury as guaranteed by the Constitution.

Congress had authorized the President to suspend the writ of habeas corpus by the Act of March 3, 1863. However, that law further provided that federal courts were to discharge prisoners where a grand jury had met and adjourned without taking any action against such persons. A grand jury was empaneled by the federal circuit court in Indiana after Milligan's sentence, but it adjourned without bringing an indictment against him; therefore, the circuit court had to consider Milligan's release. The circuit court could not reach agreement on the major questions presented and so certified them to the Supreme Court for decision. After the Court's decision, Milligan was released. He subsequently won a judgment against the commanding officer of the military district and was awarded nominal damages for unlawful imprisonment.]

MR. JUSTICE DAVIS delivered the opinion of the Court:

The controlling question in the case is this: Upon the facts stated in Milligan's petition, and the exhibits filed, had the military commission mentioned in it jurisdiction, legally, to try and sentence him? Milligan, not a resident of one of the rebellious states, or a prisoner of war, but a citizen of Indiana for twenty years past, and never in the military or naval service, is, while at his home, arrested by the military power of the United States, imprisoned, and, on certain criminal charges preferred against him, tried, convicted, and sentenced to be hanged by a military commission, organized under the direction of the military commander of the military district of Indiana. Had this tribunal the *legal* power and authority to try and punish this man?

. . . The Constitution of the United States is a law for rulers and people, equally in war and in peace, and covers with the shield of its protection all classes of men, at all times, and under all circumstances. No doctrine involving more pernicious consequences was ever invented by the wit of man than that any of its provisions can be suspended during any of the great exigencies of government. Such a doctrine leads directly to anarchy or despotism, but the theory of necessity on which it is based is false; for the government, within the Constitution, has all the powers granted to it which are necessary to preserve its existence; as has been happily proved by the result of the great effort to throw off its just authority.

Have any of the rights guaranteed by the Constitution been violated in the case of Milligan? and if so, what are they?

Every trial involves the exercise of judicial power; and from what source did the military commission that tried him derive their authority? Certainly no part of the judicial power of the country was conferred on them; because the Constitution expressly vests it "in our supreme court and such inferior courts as the Congress may from time to time ordain and establish," and it is not pretended that the commission was a court ordained and established by Congress. They cannot justify on the mandate of the President; because he is controlled by law, and has his appropriate sphere of duty, which is to execute, not to make, the laws; and there is "no unwritten criminal code to which resort can be had as a source of jurisdiction."

But it is said that the jurisdiction is complete under the "laws and usages of war."

It can serve no useful purpose to inquire what those laws and usages are, whence they originated, where found and on whom they operate; they can never be applied to citizens in states which have upheld the authority of the government, and where the courts are open and their process unobstructed. This court has judicial knowledge that in Indiana the Federal authority was always unopposed, and its courts always open to hear criminal accusations and redress grievances; and no usage of war could sanction a military trial there for any offence whatever or a citizen in civil life, in nowise connected with the military service. Congress could grant no such power; and to the honor of our national legislature be it said, it has never been provoked by the state of the country even to attempt its exercise. One of the plainest constitutional provisions was, therefore, infringed when Milligan was tried by a court not ordained and established by Congress, and not composed of judges appointed during good behavior.

Why was he not delivered to the Circuit Court of Indiana to be proceeded against according to law? No reason of necessity could be urged against it; because Congress had declared penalties against the offences charged, provided for their punishment, and directed that court to hear and determine them. And soon after this military tribunal was ended, the Circuit Court met, peacefully transacted its business, and adjourned. It needed no bayonets to protect it, and required no military aid to execute its judgments. It was held in a state, eminently distinguished for patriotism, by judges commissioned during the Rebellion, who were provided with juries, upright, intelligent, and selected by a marshal appointed by the President. The government had no right to conclude that Milligan, if guilty, would not receive in that court merited punishment; for its records disclose that it was constantly engaged in the trial of similar offences, and was never interrupted in its administration of criminal justice. If it was dangerous, in the distracted condition of affairs, to leave Milligan unrestrained of his liberty, because he "conspired against the government, afforded aid and comfort to rebels, and incited the people to insurrection," the *law* said arrest him, confine him closely, render him powerless to do further mischief; and then present his case to the grand jury of the district, with proofs of his guilt, and, if indicted, try him according to the course of the common law. If this had been done, the Constitution would have been vindicated, the law of 1863 enforced, and the securities for personal liberty preserved and defended.

Another guaranty of freedom was broken when Milligan was denied a trial by jury. . . . The Sixth Amendment affirms that "in all criminal prosecutions the accused shall enjoy the right to a speedy and public trial by an impartial jury," language broad enough to embrace all persons and cases; but the Fifth, recognizing the necessity of an indictment, or presentment, before any one can be held to answer for high crimes, "*excepts* cases arising in the land of naval forces, or in the militia, when in actual service, in time of war or public danger"; and the framers of the Constitution, doubtless, meant to limit the right of trial by jury, in the Sixth Amendment, to those persons who were subject to indictment or presentment in the Fifth.

The discipline necessary to the efficiency of the army and navy required other and swifter modes of trial than are furnished by the common-law courts; and, in pursuance of the power conferred by the Constitution, Congress has declared the kinds of trial, and the manner in which they shall be conducted, for offences committed while the party is in the military or naval service. Everyone connected with these branches of the public service is amenable to the jurisdiction which Congress has created for their government, and, while thus serving, surrenders his right to be tried by the civil courts. *All other per-*

sons, citizens of states where the courts are open, if charged with crime, are guaranteed the inestimable privilege of trial by jury. This privilege is a vital principle, underlying the whole administration of criminal justice. . . .

It is claimed that martial law covers with its broad mantle the proceedings of this military commission. The proposition is this: that in a time of war the commander of an armed force (if in his opinion the exigencies of the country demand it, and of which he is to judge), has the power, within the lines of his military district, to suspend all civil rights and their remedies, and subject citizens as well as soldiers to the role of *his will;* and in the exercise of his lawful authority cannot be restrained, except by his superior officer or the President of the United States.

If this position is sound to the extent claimed, then when war exists, foreign or domestic, and the country is subdivided into military departments for mere convenience, the commander of one of them can, if he chooses, within his limits, on the plea of necessity, with the approval of the Executive, substitute military force for and to the exclusion of the laws, and punish all persons, as he thinks right and proper, without fixed or certain rules.

The statement of this proposition shows its importance; for, if true, republican government is a failure, and there is an end of liberty regulated by law. Martial law, established on such a basis, destroys every guaranty of the Constitution, and effectually renders the "military independent of and superior to the civil power"—the attempt to do which by the King of Great Britain was deemed by our fathers such an offence, that they assigned it to the world as one of the causes which impelled them to declare their independence. Civil liberty and this kind of martial law cannot endure together; the antagonism is irreconcilable; and in the conflict, one or the other must perish.

. . . But, it is insisted that the safety of the country in time of war demands that this broad claim for martial law shall be sustained. If this were true, it could be well said that a country preserved at the sacrifice of all the cardinal principles of liberty, is not worth the cost of preservation. Happily, it is not so.

It will be borne in mind that this is not a question of the power to proclaim martial law, when war exists in a community and the courts and civil authorities are overthrown. Nor is it a question what rule a military commander, at the head of his army, can impose on states in rebellion to cripple their resources and quell the insurrection. The jurisdiction claimed is much more extensive. The necessities of the service, during the late Rebellion, required that the loyal states should be placed within the limits of certain military districts and commanders appointed in them; and, it is urged, that this, in a military sense, constituted them the theater of military operations; and, as in this case, Indiana had been and was again threatened with invasion by the enemy, the occasion was furnished to establish martial law. The conclusion does not follow from the premises. If armies were collected in Indiana, they were to be employed in another locality, where the laws were obstructed and the national authority disputed. On *her* soil there was no hostile foot; if one invaded, that invasion was at an end, and with it all pretext for martial law. Martial law cannot arise from a *threatened* invasion. The necessity must be actual and present; the invasion real, such as effectually closes the courts and deposes the civil administration.

It is difficult to see how the *safety* of the country required martial law in Indiana. If any of her citizens were plotting treason, the power of arrest could secure them, until the government was prepared for their trial, when the courts were open and ready to try them. It was as easy to protect witnesses before a civil as a military tribunal; and as there could be no wish to convict, except on sufficient legal evidence, surely an ordained and established court was better able to judge of this than a military tribunal composed of gentlemen not trained to the profession of the law.

It follows, from what has been said on this subject, that there are occasions when martial rule can be properly applied. If, in foreign invasions or civil war, the courts are actually closed, and it is impossible to administer criminal justice according to law, *then,* in the theater of active military operations, where war really prevails, there is a necessity to furnish a substitute for the civil authority, thus overthrown, to preserve the safety of the army and society; and as no power is left but the military, it is allowed to govern by martial rule until the laws can have their free course. As necessity creates the rule, so it limits its duration; for, if this government is continued *after* the courts are reinstated, it is a gross usurpation of power. Martial rule can never exist where the courts are open, and in the proper and unobstructed exercise of their jurisdiction. It is also confined to the locality of actual war. Because, during the late Rebellion it could have been enforced in Virginia, where the national authority was overturned and the courts driven out, it does not follow that it should obtain in Indiana, where that authority was never disputed, and justice was always administered. And so in the case of a foreign invasion martial rule may become a necessity in one state, when, in another, it would be "mere lawless violence.". . .

The two remaining questions in this case must be answered in the affirmative. The suspension of the privilege of the writ of habeas corpus does not suspend the writ itself. The writ issues as a matter of course; and on the return made to it the court decides whether the party applying is denied the right of proceeding any further with it.

If the military trial of Milligan was contrary to law, then he was entitled, on the facts stated in his petition, to be discharged from custody by the terms of the act of Congress of March 3d, 1863. . . .

But it is insisted that Milligan was a prisoner of war, and, therefore, excluded from the privileges of the statute. It is not easy to see how he can be treated as a prisoner of war, when he lived in Indiana for the past twenty years, was arrested there, and had not been, during the late troubles, a resident of any of the states in rebellion. If in Indiana he conspired with bad men to assist the enemy, he is punishable for it in the courts of Indiana; but, when tried for the offence, he cannot plead the rights of war; for he was not engaged in legal acts of hostility against the government, and only such persons, when captured, are prisoners of war. If he cannot enjoy the immunities attaching to the character of a prisoner of war, how can he be subject to their pains and penalties? . . .

THE CHIEF JUSTICE [CHASE] delivered the following opinion:

Four members of the Court . . . unable to concur in some important particulars with the opinion which has just been read, think it their duty to make a separate statement of their views of the whole case. . . .

The opinion . . . as we understand it, asserts not only that the military commission held in Indiana was not authorized by Congress, but that it was not in the power of Congress to authorize it; from which it may be thought to follow that Congress has no power to indemnify the officers who composed the commission against liability in civil courts for acting as members of it. We cannot agree to this. . . .

We think that Congress had power, though not exercised, to authorize the military commission which was held in Indiana. . . .

MR. JUSTICE WAYNE, MR. JUSTICE SWAYNE, and MR. JUSTICE MILLER concur with me in these views.

MISSISSIPPI *v.* JOHNSON
4 Wall. 475; 18 L. Ed. 437 (1867)

THE CHIEF JUSTICE [CHASE] delivered the opinion of the Court:

A motion was made, some days since, in behalf of the State of Mississippi, for leave to file a bill in the name of the State, praying this court perpetually to enjoin and restrain Andrew Johnson, President of the United States, and E. O. C. Ord, General commanding in the District of Mississippi and Arkansas, from executing, or in any manner carrying out, certain acts of Congress therein named.

The acts referred to are those of March 2d and March 23d, 1867, commonly known as the Reconstruction acts.

The Attorney General objected to the

leave asked for, upon the ground that no bill which makes a President a defendant, and seeks an injunction against him to restrain the performance of his duties as President, should be allowed to be filed in this court. . . .

The single point which requires consideration is this: Can the President be restrained by injunction from carrying into effect an act of Congress alleged to be unconstitutional?

It is assumed by the counsel for the State of Mississippi that the President, in the execution of the Reconstruction acts, is required to perform a mere ministerial duty. In this assumption there is, we think, a confounding of the terms ministerial and executive, which are by no means equivalent in import.

A ministerial duty, the performance of which may, in proper cases, be required of the head of a department, by judicial process, is one in respect to which nothing is left to discretion. It is a simple, definite duty, arising under conditions admitted or proved to exist, and imposed by law.

The case of *Marbury* v. *Madison* . . . furnishes an illustration. A citizen had been nominated, confirmed, and appointed a justice of the peace for the District of Columbia, and his commission had been made out, signed, and sealed. Nothing remained to be done except delivery, and the duty of delivery was imposed by law on the Secretary of State. It was held that the performance of this duty might be enforced by mandamus issuing from a court having jurisdiction. . . .

Very different is the duty of the President in the exercise of the power to see that the laws are faithfully executed, and among these laws the acts named in the bill. By the first of these acts he is required to assign generals to command in the several military districts, and to detail sufficient military force to enable such officers to discharge their duties under the law. By the supplementary act, other duties are imposed on the several commanding generals, and these duties must necessarily be performed under the supervision of the President as commander-in-chief. The duty thus imposed on the President is in no just sense ministerial. It is purely executive and political.

An attempt on the part of the judicial department of the government to enforce the performance of such duties by the President might be justly characterized, in the language of Chief Justice Marshall, as "an absurd and excessive extravagance."

It is true that in the instance before us the interposition of the court is not sought to enforce action by the Executive under constitutional legislation, but to restrain such action under legislation alleged to be unconstitutional. But we are unable to perceive that this curcumstance takes the case out of the general principles which forbid judicial interference with the exercise of Executive discretion.

It was admitted in the argument that the application now made to us is without a precedent, and this is of much weight against it.

Had it been supposed at the bar that this court would, in any case, interpose by injunction to prevent the execution of an unconstitutional act of Congress, it can hardly be doubted that applications with that object would have been heretofore addressed to it. . . .

The fact that no such application was ever before made in any case indicates the general judgment of the profession that no such application should be entertained.

It will hardly be contended that [the courts] can interpose, in any case, to restrain the enactment of an unconstitutional law; and yet how can the right to judicial interposition to prevent such an enactment, when the purpose is evident and the execution of that purpose certain, be distinguished, in principle, from the right to such interposition against the execution of such a law by the President?

The Congress is the legislative department of the government; the President is the executive department. Neither can be restrained in its action by the judicial department; though the acts of both, when performed, are, in proper cases, subject to its cognizance.

The impropriety of such interference will be clearly seen upon consideration of its possible consequences.

Suppose the bill filed and the injunction prayed for [be] allowed. If the President refuse obedience, it is needless to observe that the court is without power to enforce its process. If, on the other hand, the President complies with the order of the court and refuses to execute the acts of Congress, is it not clear that a collision may occur between the executive and legislative departments of the government? May not the House of Representatives impeach the President for such refusal? And in that case could this court interfere, in behalf of the President, thus endangered by compliance with its mandate, and restrain by injunction the Senate of the United States from sitting as a court of impeachment? Would the strange spectacle be offered to the public world of an attempt by this court to arrest proceedings in that court?

These questions answer themselves. . . .

It has been suggested that the bill contains a prayer that, if the relief sought cannot be had against Andrew Johnson as President, it may be granted against Andrew Johnson as a citizen of Tennessee. But it is plain that relief as against the execution of an act of Congress by Andrew Johnson, is relief against its execution by the President. A bill praying an injunction against the execution of an act of Congress by the incumbent of the presidential office cannot be received, whether it describes him as President or as a citizen of a State.

The motion for leave to file the bill is, therefore,

Denied.

KOREMATSU *v.* UNITED STATES
323 U.S. 214; 65 Sup. Ct. 193; 89 L. Ed. 194 (1945)

[Shortly after America's entrance into World War II, the President issued an executive order that authorized the creation of military areas from which persons might be excluded in order to prevent sabotage and espionage. Military commanders were further authorized to prescribe regulations concerning the right of persons to enter, leave, or remain in these military areas. Penalties for violations of the military regulations were provided by an act of Congress. Acting under this executive and legislative authority, the commanding general of the Western Defense Command divided the entire Pacific Coast region into two military areas. Various restrictions were then imposed on certain classes of persons living in the military districts. The commanding general first imposed a curfew that applied only to aliens and persons of Japanese ancestry. In Hirabayashi *v.* United States, *320 U.S. 81 (1943), the Supreme Court upheld the curfew order as a proper wartime measure.*

Later, the commanding general ordered the compulsory removal of all persons of Japanese ancestry to War Relocation Centers. Korematsu, who was one of the American citizens of Japanese ancestry subject to removal to relocation centers, refused to leave his home in California. He was convicted in a federal district court for knowingly violating the exclusion order. A circuit court of appeals affirmed the conviction. Korematsu then brought the case to the Supreme Court on a writ of certiorari.]

MR. JUSTICE BLACK delivered the opinion of the Court:

. . . In the light of the principles we announced in the *Hirabayashi* case, we are unable to conclude that it was beyond the war power of Congress and the Executive to exclude those of Japanese ancestry from the West Coast war area at the time they did. True, exclusion from the area in which one's home is located is a far greater deprivation than constant confinement to the home from 8 P.M. to 6 A.M. Nothing short of apprehension by the proper military authorities of the gravest imminent danger to the public safety can constitutionally justify either. But exclusion from a threatened area, no less than curfew, has a definite and close relationship to the prevention of espionage and sabotage. The military authorities, charged with the primary responsibility of defending our shores, concluded that curfew provided inadequate protection and ordered exclusion. They did so, as pointed out in our *Hirabayashi* opinion, in accordance with Congressional authority to the military to say who should, and who should not, remain in the threatened areas. . . .

Like curfew, exclusion of those of Japanese origin was deemed necessary because of the presence of an unascertained number of disloyal members of the group, most of whom we have no doubt were loyal to this country. It was because we could not reject the finding of the military authorities that it was impossible to bring about an immediate segregation of the disloyal from the loyal that we sustained the validity of the curfew order as applying to the whole group. In the instant case, temporary exclusion of the entire group was rested by the military on the same ground. The judgment that exclusion of the whole group was for the same reason a military imperative answers the contention that the exclusion was in the nature of group punishment based on antagonism to those of Japanese origin. That there were members of the group who retained loyalties to Japan had been confirmed by investigations made subsequent to the exclusion. Approximately 5,000 American citizens of Japanese ancestry refused to swear unqualified allegiance to the United States and to renounce allegiance to the Japanese Emperor, and several thousand evacuees requested repatriation to Japan.

We uphold the exclusion order as of the time it was made and when the petitioner violated it. . . . In doing so, we are not unmindful of the hardships imposed by it upon a large group of American citizens. . . . But hardships are part of war, and war is an aggregation of hardships. All citizens alike, both in and out of uniform, feel the impact of war in greater or lesser measure. Citizenship has its responsibilities as well as its privileges, and in time of war the burden is always heavier. Compulsory exclusion of large groups of citizens from their homes, except under curcumstances of direct emergency and peril, is inconsistent with our basic governmental institutions. But when under conditions of modern warfare our shores are threatened by hostile forces, the power to protect must be commensurate with the threatened danger. . . .

It is said that we are dealing here with the case of imprisonment of a citizen in a concentration camp solely because of his ancestry, without evidence or inquiry concerning his loyalty and good disposition towards the United States. Our task would be simple, our duty clear, were this a case involving the imprisonment of a loyal citizen in a concentration camp because of racial prejudice. Regardless of the true nature of the assembly and relocation centers—and we deem it unjustifiable to call them concentration camps with all the ugly connotations that term implies—we are dealing specifically with nothing but an exclusion order. To cast this case into outlines of racial prejudice, without reference to the real military dangers which were presented, merely confuses the issue. Korematsu was not excluded from the Military Area because of hostility to him or his race. He *was* excluded because we are at war with the Japanese Empire, because the properly constituted military authorities feared an invasion of our West Coast and felt constrained to take proper security measures, because they decided that the military urgency of the situation demanded that all citizens of Japanese ancestry be segregated from the West Coast temporarily, and finally, because Congress, reposing its confidence in this time of war in our military leaders—as inevitably it must—determined that they should have the power to do just this. There was evidence of disloyalty on the part of some, the military authorities considered that the need for action was great, and time was short. We cannot—by availing ourselves of the calm perspective of hindsight—now say that at that time these actions were unjustified.

Affirmed.

[MR. JUSTICE FRANKFURTER wrote a concurring opinion.]

MR. JUSTICE ROBERTS:

I dissent, because I think the indisputable facts exhibit a clear violation of constitutional rights.

This is not a case of keeping people off the streets at night as was *Hirabayashi* v. *United States* . . . nor a case of temporary exclusion of a citizen from an area for his own safety or that of the community, nor a case of offering him an opportunity to go temporarily out of an area where his presence might cause danger to himself or to his fellows. On the contrary, it is the case of convicting a citizen as a punishment for not submitting to imprisonment in a concentration camp, based on his ancestry, and solely because of his ancestry, without evidence or inquiry concerning his loyalty and good disposition towards the United States. If this be a correct statement of the facts disclosed by this record, and facts of which we take judicial notice, I need hardly labor the conclusion that Constitutional rights have been violated. . . .

MR. JUSTICE MURPHY, dissenting:

In dealing with matters relating to the prosecution and progress of a war, we must accord great respect and consideration to the judgments of the military authorities who are on the scene and who have full knowledge of the military facts. The scope of their discretion must, as a matter of necessity and common sense, be wide. And their judgments ought not to be overruled lightly by those whose training and duties ill equip them to deal intelligently with matters so vital to the physical security of the nation.

At the same time, however, it is essential that there be definite limits to military discretion, especially where martial law has not been declared. . . . "What are the allowable limits of military discretion, and whether or not they have been overstepped in a particular case, are judicial questions.". . .

The judicial test of whether the Government, on a plea of military necessity, can validly deprive an individual of any of his constitutional rights is whether the deprivation is reasonably related to a public danger that is so "immediate, imminent, and impending" as not to admit of delay and not to permit the intervention of ordinary constitutional processes to alleviate the danger. . . . Yet no reasonable relation to an "immediate, imminent, and impending" public danger is evident to support this racial restriction, which is one of the most sweeping and complete deprivations of constitutional rights in the history of this nation in the absence of martial law.

It must be conceded that the military and naval situation in the spring of 1942 was such as to generate a very real fear of invasion of the Pacific Coast, accompanied by fears of sabotage and espionage in that area. The military command was therefore justified in adopting all reasonable means necessary to combat these dangers. In adjudging the military action taken in light of the then apparent dangers, we must not erect too high or too meticulous standards, it is necessary only that the action have some reasonable relation to the removal of the dangers of invasion, sabotage, and espionage. But the exclusion, either temporarily or permanently, of all persons with Japanese blood in their veins has no such reasonable relation. And that relation is lacking because the exclusion order necessarily must rely for its reasonableness upon the assumption that *all* persons of Japanese ancestry may have a dangerous tendency to commit sabotage and espionage and to aid our Japanese enemy in other ways. It is difficult to believe that reason, logic, or experience could be marshalled in support of such an assumption.

That this forced exclusion was the result in good measure of this erroneous assumption of racial guilt rather than bona fide military necessity is evidenced by the commanding general's Final Report on the evacuation from the Pacific Coast area. In it he refers to all individuals of Japanese descent as "subversive," as belonging to "an enemy race" whose "racial strains are undiluted," and as constituting "over 112,000 potential enemies . . . at large today" along the Pacific Coast. In support of this blanket condemnation of all persons of Japanese descent, however, no reliable evidence is cited to show that such individuals were generally disloyal, or had generally so conducted themselves in this area as to constitute a special menace to defense installations or war industries, or had otherwise by their behavior furnished reasonable ground for their exclusion as a group. . . .

The military necessity which is essential to the validity of the evacuation order . . . resolves itself into a few intimations that certain individuals actively aided the enemy, from which it is inferred that the entire group of Japanese-Americans could not be trusted to be or remain loyal to the United States. No one denies, of course, that there were some disloyal persons of Japanese descent on the Pacific Coast who did all in their power to aid their ancestral land. Similar disloyal activities have been engaged in by many persons of German,

Italian, and even more pioneer stock in our country. But to infer that examples of individual disloyalty prove group disloyalty and justify discriminatory action against the entire group is to deny that under our system of law individual guilt is the sole basis for deprivation of rights. . . .

No adequate reason is given for the failure to treat these Japanese-Americans on an individual basis by holding investigations and hearings to separate the loyal from the disloyal, as was done in the case of persons of German and Italian ancestry. . . . It is asserted merely that the loyalties of this group "were unknown and time was of the essence." Yet nearly four months elapsed after Pearl Harbor before the first exclusion order was issued; nearly eight months went by until the last order was issued; and the last of these "subversive" persons was not acutally removed until almost eleven months had elapsed. Leisure and deliberation seem to have been more of the essence than speed. . . .

I dissent, therefore, from this legalization of racism. Racial discrimination in any form and in any degree has no justifiable part whatever in our democratic way of life. It is unattractive in any setting but it is utterly revolting among a free people who have embraced the principles set forth in the Constitution of the United States. All residents of this nation are kin in some way by blood or culture to a foreign land. Yet they are primarily and necessarily a part of the new and distinct civilization of the United States. They must accordingly be treated at all times as the heirs of the American experiment and as entitled to all the rights and freedoms guaranteed by the Constitution.

MR. JUSTICE JACKSON, dissenting:

. . . if we cannot confine military expedients by the Constitution, neither would I distort the Constitution to approve all that the military may deem expedient. That is what the Court appears to be doing, whether consciously or not. I cannot say, from any evidence before me, that the orders of General DeWitt were not reasonably expedient military precautions, nor could I say that they were. But even if they were permissible military procedures, I deny that it follows that they are constitutional.

. . . a judicial construction of the due process clause that will sustain this order is a far more subtle blow to liberty than the promulgation of the order itself. A military order, however unconstitutional, is not apt to last longer than the military emergency. . . . once a judicial opinion rationalizes such an order to show that it conforms to the Constitution, or rather rationalizes the Constitution to show that the Constitution sanctions such an order, the Court for all time has validated the principle of racial discrimination in criminal procedure and of transplanting American citizens. The principle then lies about like a loaded weapon ready for the hand of any authority that can bring forward a plausible claim of an urgent need. . . .

I should hold that a civil court cannot be made to enforce an order which violates constitutional limitations even if it is a reasonable exercise of military authority. The courts can exercise only the judicial power, can apply only law, and must abide by the Constitution, or they cease to be civil courts and become instruments of military policy. . . .

My duties as a justice as I see them do not require me to make a military judgment as to whether General DeWitt's evacuation and detention program was a reasonable military necessity. I do not suggest that the courts should have attempted to interfere with the Army in carrying out its task. But I do not think they may be asked to execute a military expedient that has no place in law under the Constitution. I would reverse the judgment and discharge the prisoner.

UNITED STATES *v.* CURTISS-WRIGHT EXPORT CORP. *et al.*
299 U.S. 304; 57 Sup. Ct. 216; 81 L. Ed. 255 (1936)

[A Joint Resolution of Congress approved on May 28, 1934, empowered the President to prohibit the sale of arms and munitions to Bolivia and Paraguay, who were then at war, if in his judgment such an action might restore peace. On the same day, President Franklin

D. Roosevelt issued a proclamation forbidding the sale of war materials to both countries. Violation of the presidential proclamation constituted a crime punishable by fine or imprisonment, or both. The Curtiss-Wright Corporation was charged with having conspired to sell fifteen machine guns to Bolivia in violation of the President's order. The company demurred to the indictment on the ground that the joint resolution's delegation of power to the President was invalid. After the District Court of New York sustained the demurrer, the United States appealed directly to the Supreme Court.]

MR. JUSTICE SUTHERLAND delivered the opinion of the Court:

. . . *First.* It is contended that by the Joint Resolution, the going into effect and continued operation of the resolution was conditioned (a) upon the President's judgment as to its beneficial effect upon the reestablishment of peace between the countries engaged in armed conflict in the Chaco; (b) upon the making of a proclamation, which was left to his unfettered discretion, thus constituting an attempted substitution of the President's will for that of Congress; (c) upon the making of a proclamation putting an end to the operation of the resolution, which again was left to the President's unfettered discretion; and (d) further, that the extent of its operation in particular cases was subject to limitation and exception by the President, controlled by no standard. In each of these particulars, appellees urge that Congress abdicated its essential functions and delegated them to the Executive.

Whether, if the Joint Resolution had related solely to internal affairs it would be open to the challenge that it constituted an unlawful delegation of legislative power to the Executive, we find it unnecessary to determine. The whole aim of the resolution is to affect a situation entirely external to the United States, and falling within the category of foreign affairs. The determination which we are called to make, therefore, is whether the Joint Resolution, as applied to that situation, is vulnerable to attack under the rule that forbids a delegation of the law-making power. In other words, assuming (but not deciding) that the challenged delegation, if it were confined to internal affairs, would be invalid, may it nevertheless be sustained on the ground that its exclusive aim is to afford a remedy for a hurtful condition within foreign territory?

It will contribute to the elucidation of the question if we first consider the differences between the powers of the federal government in respect of foreign or external affairs and those in respect of domestic or internal affairs. That there are differences between them, and that these differences are fundamental, may not be doubted.

The two classes of powers are different, both in respect of their origin and their nature. The broad statement that the federal government can exercise no powers except those specifically enumerated in the constitution, and such implied powers as are necessary and proper to carry into effect the enumerated powers, is categorically true only in respect of our internal affairs. In that field, the primary purpose of the Constitution was to carve from the general mass of legislative powers *then possessed by the states* such portions as it was thought desirable to vest in the federal government, leaving those not included in the enumeration still in the states. . . . That this doctrine applies only to powers which the states had, is self-evident. And since the states severally never possessed international powers, such powers could not have been carved from the mass of state powers but obviously were transmitted to the United States from some other source. During the Colonial period, those powers were possessed exclusively by and were entirely under the control of the Crown. By the Declaration of Independence, "the Representatives of the United States of America" declared the United (not the several) Colonies to be free and independent states, and as such to have "full Power to levy War, conclude Peace, contract Alliances, establish Commerce and to do all other Acts and Things which Independent States may of right do."

As a result of the separation from Great Britain by the Colonies acting as a unit, the powers of external sovereignty passed from the Crown not to the Colonies severally, but to the Colonies in their collective and corporate capacity as the United States of America. Even before the Declaration, the Colonies were a unit in foreign affairs, acting through a common agency—namely the Continental Congress, composed of delegates from the thirteen Colonies. That agency exercised the powers of war and peace, raised an army, created a navy, and finally adopted the Declaration of Independence. Rulers come and go; governments end and forms of government change; but sovereignty survives. A political society cannot endure without a supreme will somewhere. Sovereignty is never held in suspense. When, therefore, the external sovereignty of Great Britain in respect of the colonies ceased, it immediately passed to the Union. . . . That fact was given practical application almost at once. The treaty of peace, made on September 23, 1783, was concluded between his Britannic Majesty and the "United States of America. . . ."

The Union existed before the Constitution, which was ordained and established among other things to form "a more perfect Union. . . ."

It results that the investment of the federal government with the powers of external sovereignty did not depend upon the affirmative grants of the Constitution. The powers to declare and wage war, to conclude peace, to make treaties, to maintain diplomatic relation with other sovereignties, if they had never been mentioned in the Constitution, would have vested in the federal government as necessary concomitants of nationality. . . . As a member of the family of nations, the right and power of the United States in that field are equal to the right and power of the other members of the international family. Otherwise, the United States is not completely sovereign. . . .

Not only, as we have shown, is the federal power over external affairs in origin and essential character different from that over internal affairs, but participation in the exercise of the power is significantly limited. In this vast external realm, with its important, complicated, delicate and manifold problems, the President alone has the power to speak or listen as a representative of the nation. He *makes* treaties with the advice and consent of the Senate; but he alone negotiates. Into the field of negotiation the Senate cannot intrude; and Congress itself is powerless to invade it. As Marshall said. . . , "The President is the sole organ of the nation in its external relations, and its sole representative with foreign nations. . . ."

It is important to bear in mind that we are here dealing not alone with an authority vested in the President by an exertion of legislative power, but with such an authority plus the very delicate, plenary and exclusive power of the President as the sole organ of the federal government in the field of international relations—a power which does not require as a basis for its exercise an act of Congress, but which, of course, like every other government power, must be exercised in subordination to the applicable provisions of the Constitution. It is quite apparent that if, in the maintenance of our international relations, embarrassment—perhaps serious embarrassment—is to be avoided and success for our aims achieved, congressional legislation which is to be made effective through negotiation and inquiry within the international field must often accord to the President a degree of discretion and freedom from statutory restriction which would not be admissible were domestic affairs alone involved. Moreover, he, not Congress, has the better opportunity of knowing the conditions which prevail in foreign countries, and especially is this true in time of war. He has his confidential sources of information. He has his agents in the form of diplomatic, consular, and other officials. Secrecy in respect of information gathered by them may be highly necessary, and the premature disclosure of it productive of harmful results. Indeed, so clearly is this true that the first President refused to accede to a request to lay before the House of Representatives the instructions, correspondence, and documents relating to the negotiation of the Jay Treaty—a refusal the wisdom of which was recognized by the House itself and has never since been doubted. . . .

In the light of the foregoing observations, it is evident that this court should not be in haste to apply a general rule which will have the effect of condemning legislation like that under review as constituting an unlawful delegation of legislative power. The principles which justify such legislation find overwhelming support in the unbroken legislative practice which has prevailed almost from the inception of the national government to the present day. . . .

Practically every volume of the United States Statutes contains one or more acts or joint resolutions of Congress authorizing action by the President in respect of subjects, affecting foreign relations, which either leave the exercise of the power to his unrestricted judgment, or provide a standard far more general than that which has always been considered requisite with regard to domestic affairs. . . .

The result of holding that the joint resolution here under attack is void and unenforceable as constituting an unlawful delegation of legislative power would be to stamp this multitude of comparable acts and resolutions as likewise invalid. And while this court may not, and should not, hesitate to declare acts of Congress, however many times repeated, to be unconstitutional if beyond all rational doubt it finds them to be so, an impressive array of legislation such as we have just set forth, enacted by nearly every Congress from the beginning of our national existence to the present day, must be given unusual weight in the process of reaching a correct determination of the problem. A legislative practice such as we have here, evidenced not by only occasional instances, but marked by the movement of a steady stream for a century and a half of time, goes a long way in the direction of proving the presence of unassailable ground for the constitutionality of the practice, to be found in the origin and history of the power involved, or in its nature, or in both combined.

. . . [B]oth upon principle and in accordance with precedent, we conclude there is sufficient warrant for the broad discretion vested in the President to determine whether the enforcement of the statute will have a beneficial effect upon the re-establishment of peace in the affected countries; whether he shall make proclamation to bring the resolution into operation; whether and when the resolution shall cease to operate and to make proclamation accordingly; and to prescribe limitations and exceptions to which the enforcement of the resolution shall be subject. . . .

Reversed.

MR. JUSTICE MC REYNOLDS does not agree. He is of opinion that the court below reached the right conclusion and its judgment ought to be affirmed.

MR. JUSTICE STONE took no part in the consideration or decision of this case.

YOUNGSTOWN SHEET & TUBE CO. *et al.* *v.* SAWYER

343 U.S. 579; 72 Sup. Ct. 863; 96 L. Ed. 1153 (1952)

[This case, which is popularly known as the Steel Seizure case, was the climax of a long dispute between the steel companies and their employees over terms of new collective-bargaining agreements. In December 1951, the United Steelworkers of America, CIO, served notice that a strike would be called on December 31, 1951. The Federal Mediation and Conciliation Service intervened immediately but failed to negotiate a settlement. The President then referred the dispute to the Federal Wage Stabilization Board, which also failed to bring about an agreement. On April 4, 1952, the union announced that a nationwide strike would begin on April 9. A few hours before the strike deadline, President Truman issued an executive order authorizing Sawyer, the Secretary of Commerce, to seize and continue operation of the steel mills. The President's order was not based on any statutory authority. He directed the seizure because the proposed strike would have seriously jeopardized national defense. (At this time American troops were fighting in Korea.) The Secretary of Commerce issued the appropriate orders taking possession of the steel mills for the United States. President Truman reported the seizure to Congress in two separate messages,

but Congress took no action. The steel companies complied with the seizure order under protest and sought an injunction restraining Sawyer from a federal district court. On April 30, the district court issued a preliminary injunction restraining the Secretary of Commerce from "continuing the seizure and possession of the plants." On the same day the court of appeals stayed the district court's injunction. Because the dispute raised issues of vital national importance, the Supreme Court acted promptly; it granted certiorari on May 3 and heard argument on May 12. The decision was handed down on June 2, 1952.]

MR. JUSTICE BLACK delivered the opinion of the Court:

We are asked to decide whether the President was acting within his constitutional power when he issued an order directing the Secretary of Commerce to take possession of and operate most of the nation's steel mills. The mill owners argue that the President's order amounts to lawmaking, a legislative function which the Constitution has expressly confided to the Congress and not to the President. The Government's position is that the order was made on findings of the President that his action was necessary to avert a national catastrophe which would inevitably result from a stoppage of steel production, and that in meeting this grave emergency the President was acting within the aggregate of his constitutional powers as the nation's Chief Executive and the Commander-in-chief of the Armed Forces of the United States. . . .

The President's power, if any, to issue the order must stem either from an act of Congress or from the Constitution itself. There is no statute that expressly authorizes the President to take possession of property as he did here. Nor is there any act of Congress to which such a power can fairly be implied. Indeed, we do not understand the Government to rely on statutory authorization for this seizure. There are two statutes which do authorize the President to take both personal and real property under certain conditions. (The Selective Service Act of 1948 and the Defense Production Act of 1950.) However, the Government admits that these conditions were not met and that the President's order was not rooted in either of the statutes. The Government refers to the seizure provisions of one of these statutes . . . as "much too cumbersome, involved, and time-consuming for the crisis which was at hand."

Moreover, the use of the seizure technique to solve labor disputes in order to prevent work stoppages was not only unauthorized by any congressional enactment; prior to this controversy, Congress had refused to adopt that method of settling labor disputes. When the Taft-Hartley Act was under consideration in 1947, Congress rejected an amendment which would have authorized such governmental seizures in cases of emergency. Apparently it was thought that the technique of seizure, like that of compulsory arbitration, would interfere with the process of collective bargaining. Consequently, the plan Congress adopted in that Act did not provide for seizure under any circumstances. Instead, the plan sought to bring about settlements by use of the customary devices of mediation, conciliation, investigation by boards of inquiry, and public reports. In some instances temporary injunctions were authorized to provide cooling-off periods. All this failing, unions were left free to strike after a secret vote by employees as to whether they wished to accept their employers' final settlement offer.

It is clear that if the President had authority to issue the order he did, it must be found in some provision of the Constitution. And it is not claimed that express constitutional language grants this power to the President. The contention is that presidential power should be implied from the aggregate of his powers under the Constitution. Particular reliance is placed on provisions in Article II which say that "The executive Power shall be vested in a President . . ."; that "he shall take Care that the Laws be faithfully executed"; and that he "shall be Commander-in-chief of the Army and Navy of the United States."

The order cannot properly be sustained as an exercise of the President's military power as Commander-in-chief of the Armed

Forces. The Government attempts to do so by citing a number of cases upholding broad powers in military commanders engaged in day-to-day fighting in a theater of war. Such cases need not concern us here. Even though "theater of war" be an expanding concept, we cannot with faithfulness to our constitutional system hold that the Commander-in-chief of the Armed Forces has the ultimate power as such to take possession of private property in order to keep labor disputes from stopping production. This is a job for the nation's lawmakers, not for its military authorities.

Nor can the seizure order be sustained because of the several constitutional provisions that grant executive power to the President. In the framework of our Constitution, the President's power to see that the laws are faithfully executed refutes the idea that he is to be a lawmaker. The Constitution limits his functions in the lawmaking process to the recommending of laws he thinks wise and the vetoing of laws he thinks bad. And the Constitution is neither silent nor equivocal about who shall make laws which the President is to execute. The first section of the first article says that "All legislative Powers herein granted shall be vested in a Congress of the United States. . . ."

The President's order does not direct that a congressional policy be excuted in a manner prescribed by Congress—it directs that a presidential policy be executed in a manner prescribed by the President. The preamble of the order itself, like that of many statutes, sets out reasons why the President believes certain policies should be adopted, proclaims these policies as rules of conduct to be followed, and again like a statute, authorizes a government official to promulgate additional rules and regulations consistent with the policy proclaimed and needed to carry that policy into execution. The power of Congress to adopt such public policies as those proclaimed by the order is beyond question. It can authorize the taking of private property for public use. It can make laws regulating the relationships between employers and employees, prescribing rules designed to settle labor disputes, and fixing wages and working conditions in certain fields of our economy. The Constitution does not subject this lawmaking power of Congress to presidential or military supervision or control.

It is said that other Presidents without congressional authority have taken possession of private business enterprises in order to settle labor disputes. But even if this be true, Congress has not thereby lost its exclusive constitutional authority to make laws necessary and proper to carry out the powers vested by the Constitution "in the Government of the United States, or any Department or Office thereof."

The Founders of this nation entrusted the lawmaking power to the Congress alone in both good and bad times. It would do no good to recall the historical events, the fears of power and the hopes for freedom that lay behind their choice. Such a review would but confirm our holding that this seizure order cannot stand.

The judgment of the District Court is *Affirmed.*

MR. JUSTICE FRANKFURTER, concurring:

Although the considerations relevant to the legal enforcement of the principle of separation of powers seem to me more complicated and flexible than may appear from what Mr. Justice Black has written, I join his opinion because I thoroughly agree with the application of the principle to the circumstances of this case. . . .

The issue before us can be met, and therefore should be, without attempting to define the President's powers comprehensively. I shall not attempt to delineate what belongs to him by virtue of his office beyond the power even of Congress to contract; what authority belongs to him until Congress acts; what kind of problems may be dealt with either by the Congress or by the President or by both . . . ; what power must be exercised by the Congress and cannot be delegated to the President. It is as unprofitable to lump together in an undiscriminating hotch-potch past presidential actions claimed to be derived from occupancy of the office as it is to conjure up hypothetical future cases. The judiciary may, as this case proves, have to intervene in determining where authority lies as between the democratic forces in our scheme of government. But in doing so we should be wary and humble. Such is the teaching of this Court's role in the history of the country.

It is in this mood and with this perspective that the issue before the Court must be approached. We must therefore put to one side consideration of what powers the President would have had if there had been no legislation whatever bearing on the authority asserted by the seizure, or if the seizure had been only for a short, explicitly temporary period, to be terminated automatically unless Congressional approval were given. These and other questions, like or unlike, are not now here. I would exceed my authority were I to say anything about them.

The question before the Court comes in this setting. Congress has frequently—at least sixteen times since 1916—specifically provided for executive seizure of production, transportation, communications, or storage facilities. In every case it has qualified this grant of power with limitations and safeguards. This body of enactments . . . demonstrates that Congress deemed seizure so drastic a power as to require that it be carefully circumscribed whenever the President was vested with this extraordinary authority. The power to seize has uniformly been given only for a limited period or for a defined emergency, or has been repealed after a short period. Its exercise has been restricted to particular circumstances such as "time of war or when war is imminent," "the needs of public safety" or of "national security or defense," or "urgent and impending need." The period of governmental operation has been limited, as, for instance, to "sixty days after the restoration of productive efficiency." Seizure statutes usually make executive action dependent on detailed conditions: for example, (a) failure or refusal of the owner of a plant to meet governmental supply needs or (b) failure of voluntary negotiations with the owner for the use of a plant necessary for great public ends. Congress often has specified the particular executive agency which should seize or operate the plants or whose judgment would appropriately test the need for seizure. Congress also has not left to implication that just compensation be paid; it has usually legislated in detail regarding enforcement of this litigation-breeding general requirement.

Congress in 1947 was again called upon to consider whether governmental seizure should be used to avoid serious industrial shutdowns. Congress decided against conferring such power generally and in advance, without special Congressional enactment to meet each particular need. Under the urgency of telephone and coal strikes in the winter of 1946, Congress addressed itself to the problems raised by "national emergency" strikes and lockouts. The termination of wartime seizure powers on December 31, 1946, brought these matters to the attention of Congress with vivid impact. A proposal that the President be given powers to seize plants to avert a shutdown where the "health or safety" of the nation was endangered, was thoroughly canvassed by Congress and rejected. No room for doubt remains that the proponents as well as the opponents of the bill which became the Labor Management Relations Act of 1947 clearly understood that as a result of that legislation the only recourse for preventing a shutdown in any basic industry, after failure of mediation, was Congress. Authorization for seizure as an available remedy for potential dangers was unequivocally put aside. . . .

In adopting the provisions which it did, by the Labor Management Relations Act of 1947, for dealing with a "national emergency" arising out of a breakdown in peaceful industrial relations, Congress was very familiar with governmental seizure as a protective measure. On a balance of considerations, Congress chose not to lodge this power in the President. It chose not to make available in advance a remedy to which both industry and labor were fiercely hostile. In deciding that authority to seize should be given to the President only after full consideration of the particular situation should show such legislation to be necessary, Congress presumably acted on experience with similar industrial conflicts in the past. It evidently assumed that industrial shutdowns in basic industries are not instances of spontaneous generation, and that danger warnings are sufficiently plain before the event to give ample opportunity to start the legislative process into action.

In any event, nothing can be plainer than that Congress made a conscious choice of policy in a field full of perplexity and peculiarly within legislative responsibility for choice. In formulating legislation for dealing with industrial conflicts, Congress could not more clearly and emphatically have withheld authority than it did in 1947. . . .

By the Labor Management Relations Act of 1947, Congress said to the President, "You may not seize. Please report to us and ask for seizure power if you think it is needed in a specific situation. . . ."

MR. JUSTICE JACKSON, concurring:

The actual art of governing under our Constitution does not and cannot conform to judicial definitions of the power of any of its branches based on isolated clauses or even single Articles torn from context. While the Constitution diffuses power the better to secure liberty, it also contemplates that practice will integrate the dispersed powers into a workable government. It enjoins upon its branches separateness but interdependence, autonomy but reciprocity. Presidential powers are not fixed but fluctuate, depending upon their disjunction or conjunction with those of Congress. We may well begin by a somewhat oversimplified grouping of practical stituations in which a President may doubt, or others may challenge, his powers, and by distinguishing roughly the legal consequences of this factor of relativity.

1. When the President acts pursuant to an express or implied authorization of Congress, his authority is at its maximum, for it includes all that he possesses in his own right plus all that Congress can delegate. In these circumstances, and in these only, may he be said (for what it may be worth) to personify the federal sovereignty. If his act is held unconstitutional under these circumstances, it usually means that the Federal Government as an undivided whole lacks power. A seizure executed by the President pursuant to an Act of Congress would be supported by the strongest of presumptions and the widest latitude of judicial interpretation, and the burden of persuasion would rest heavily upon any who might attack it.

2. When the President acts in absence of either a congressional grant or denial of authority, he can only rely upon his own independent powers, but there is a zone of twilight in which he and Congress may have concurrent authority, or in which its distribution is uncertain. Therefore, congressional inertia, indifference or quiescence may sometimes, at least as a practical matter, enable, if not invite, measures on independent presidential responsibility. In this area, any actual test of power is likely to depend on the imperatives of events and contemporary imponderables rather than on abstract theories of law.

3. When the President takes measures incompatible with the expressed or implied will of Congress, his power is at its lowest ebb, for then he can rely only upon his own constitutional powers minus any constitutional powers of Congress over the matter. Courts can sustain exclusive presidential control in such a case only by disabling the Congress from acting upon the subject. Presidential claims to a power at once so conclusive and preclusive must be scrutinized with caution, for what is at stake is the equilibrium established by our constitutional system.

Into which of these classifications does this executive seizure of the steel industry fit? It is eliminated from the first by admission, for it is conceded that no congressional authorization exists for this seizure. That takes away also the support of the many precedents and declarations which were made in relation, and must be confined, to this category.

Can it then be defended under flexible tests available to the second category? It seems clearly eliminated from that class because Congress has not left seizure of private property an open field but has covered it by three statutory policies inconsistent with this seizure. In cases where the purpose is to supply needs of the Government itself, two courses are provided: one, seizure of a plant which fails to comply with obligatory orders placed by the Government; another, condemnation of facilities, including temporary use under the power of eminent domain. The third is applicable where it is the general economy of the country that is to be protected rather than exclusive governmental interests. None of these were invoked. In choosing a different and inconsistent way of his own, the President cannot claim that it is necessitated or invited by failure of Congress to legislate upon the occasions, grounds, and methods for seizure of industrial properties.

This leaves the current seizure to be justified only by the severe tests under the third grouping, where it can be supported only by any remainder of executive power after subtraction of such powers as Congress may have over the subject. In short, we can sustain the President only by holding that seizure of such strike-bound industries is within his domain and beyond control of Congress. Thus, this Court's first review of such seizures occurs under circumstances which leave presidential power most vulnerable to attack and in the least favorable of possible constitutional postures. . . .

MR. JUSTICE BURTON, concurring:

The controlling fact here is that Congress, within its constitutionally delegated power, has prescribed for the President specific procedures, exclusive of seizure, for his use in meeting the present type of emergency. Congress has reserved to itself the right to determine where and when to authorize the seizure of property in meeting such an emergency. Under these circumstances, the President's order of April 8 invaded the jurisdiction of Congress. It violated the essence of the principle of the separation of governmental powers. Accordingly, the injunction against its effectiveness should be sustained.

MR. JUSTICE CLARK, concurring:

I conclude that where Congress has laid down specific procedures to deal with the type of crisis confronting the President, he must follow those procedures in meeting the crisis; but that in the absence of such action by Congress, the President's independent power to act depends upon the gravity of the situation confronting the nation. I cannot sustain the seizure in question because here . . . Congress had prescribed methods to be followed by the President in meeting the emergency at hand. . . .

[MR. JUSTICE DOUGLAS *also wrote a concurring opinion.*]

MR. CHIEF JUSTICE VINSON, with whom MR. JUSTICE REED and MR. JUSTICE MINTON join, dissenting:

. . . Focusing now on the situation confronting the President on the night of April 8, 1952, we cannot but conclude that the President was performing his duty under the Constitution to "take Care that the Laws be faithfully executed"—a duty described by President Benjamin Harrison as "the central idea of the office."

The President reported to Congress the morning after the seizure that he acted because a work stoppage in steel production would immediately imperil the safety of the nation by preventing execution of the legislative programs for procurement of military equipment. And, while a shutdown could be averted by granting the price concessions requested by plaintiffs, granting such concessions would disrupt the price stabilization program also enacted by Congress. Rather than fail to execute either legislative program, the President acted to execute both. . . .

The absence of a specific statute authorizing seizure of the steel mills as a mode of executing the laws—both the military procurement program and the anti-inflation program—has not until today been thought to prevent the President from executing the laws. Unlike an administrative commission confined to the enforcement of the statute under which it was created, or the head of a department when administering a particular statute, the President is a constitutional officer charged with taking care that a "mass of legislation" be executed. Flexibility as to mode of execution to meet critical situations is a matter of practical necessity. . . .

As the District Judge stated, this is no time for "timorous" judicial action. But neither is this a time for timorous executive action. Faced with the duty of executing the defense programs which Congress had enacted and the disastrous effects that any stoppage in steel production would have on these programs, the President acted to preserve those programs by seizing the steel mills. There is no question that the possession was other than temporary in character and subject to congressional direction—either approving, disapproving, or regulating the manner in which the mills were to be administered and returned to the owners. The President immediately informed Congress of his action and clearly stated his intention to abide by the legislative will. No basis for claims of arbitrary action, unlimited powers, or dictatorial usurpation of congressional power appears from the facts of this case. On the contrary, judicial, legislative, and executive precedents throughout our history demonstrate that in this case the President acted in full conformity with his duties under the Constitution. Accordingly, we would reverse the order of the District Court.

NEW YORK TIMES CO. *v.* UNITED STATES
403 U.S. 713; 91 Sup. Ct. 2140; 29 L. Ed. 2d 822 (1971)

[The Attorney General sought court injunctions preventing publication of excerpts from "The Pentagon Papers" by The New York Times *and* The Washington Post. *The Pentagon Papers were a government staff report prepared by subordinates of the Secretaries of State and Defense. Because the injunctions would have prohibited supposedly illegal speech before it occurred rather than subjecting someone to subsequent criminal punishment after his speech, the injunction would have constituted a "prior restraint" of speech to which the Court has always been particularly opposed. (See Chapter 11.)]*

Per Curiam

Any system of prior restraints of expression comes to this Court bearing a heavy presumption against its constitutional validity. The Government thus carries a heavy burden of showing justification for the imposition of such a restraint. The district court . . . held that the government had not met that burden. We agree. . . . the case is remanded with directions to enter a judgment affirming the judgment of the district court.

MR. JUSTICE BLACK, with whom MR. JUSTICE DOUGLAS joins, concurring: (JUSTICE DOUGLAS also concurred separately.) . . . the Government argues in its brief that in spite of the First Amendment, "the authority of the Executive Department to protect the nation against publication of information whose disclosure would endanger the national security stems from two interrelated sources: the constitutional power of the President over the conduct of foreign affairs and his authority as Commander-in-chief.". . .

The Government does not even attempt to rely on any act of Congress. . . . To find that the President has "inherent power" to halt the publication of news by resort to the courts would wipe out the First Amendment and destroy the fundamental liberty and security of the very people the Government hopes to make "secure."

MR. JUSTICE BRENNAN, concurring:

. . . Our cases . . . have indicated that there is a single, extremely narrow class of cases in which the First Amendment's ban on prior judicial restraint may be overridden. Our cases have thus far indicated that such cases may arise only when the nation "is at war," during which times "no one would question but that a government might prevent actual obstruction to its recruiting service or the publication of the sailing dates of transports or the number and location of troops." Even if the present world situation were assumed to be tantamount to a time of war, or if the power of presently available armaments would justify even in peacetime the suppression of information that would set in motion a nuclear holocaust, in neither of these actions has the government presented or even alleged that publication of items from or based upon the material at issue would cause the happening of an event of that nature. . . . Thus, only governmental allegations and proof that publication must inevitably, directly, and immediately cause the occurrence of an event kindred to imperiling the safety of a transport already at sea can support even the issuance of an interim restraining order. In no event may mere conclusions be sufficient: for if the executive branch seeks judicial aid in preventing publication, it must inevitably submit the basis upon which that aid is sought to scrutiny by the judiciary. . . . Unless and until the government has clearly made out its case, the First Amendment commands that no injunction may issue.

MR. JUSTICE STEWART, with whom MR. JUSTICE WHITE joins, concurring:

In the governmental structure created by our Constitution, the executive is endowed with enormous power in the two related areas of national defense and international relations. This power, largely unchecked by the legislative and judicial branches, has been pressed to the very hilt since the advent of the nuclear missile age. For better or for worse, the simple fact is that a President of the United States possesses vastly greater constitutional independence in these two vital areas of power than does, say a prime minister. . . .

In the absence of the governmental checks and balances present in other areas of our national life, the only effective restraint upon executive policy and power in the areas of national defense and international affairs may lie in an enlightened citizenry. . . .

Yet it is elementary that the successful conduct of international diplomacy and the maintenance of an effective national defense require both confidentiality and secrecy. Other nations can hardly deal with this nation in an atmosphere of mutual trust unless they can be assured that their confidences will be kept. And within our own executive departments, the development of considered and intelligent international policies would be impossible if those charged with their formulation could not communicate with each other freely, frankly, and in confidence. In the area of basic national defense the frequent need for absolute secrecy is, of course, self-evident.

I think there can be but one answer to this dilemma, if dilemma it be. The responsibility must be where the power is. If the Constitution gives the executive a large degree of unshared power in the conduct of foreign affairs and the maintenance of our national defense, then under the Constitution the executive must have the largely unshared duty to determine and preserve the degree of internal security necessary to exercise that power successfully. . . . But be that as it may, it is clear to me that it is the constitutional duty of the executive—as a matter of sovereign prerogative and not as a matter of law as the courts know law—through the promulgation and enforcement of executive regulations, to protect the confidentiality necessary to carry out its responsibilities in the fields in international relations and national defense.

This is not to say that Congress and the courts have no role to play. Undoubtedly Congress has the power to enact specific and appropriate criminal laws to protect government property and preserve government secrets.

But in the cases before us we are asked neither to construe specific regulations nor to apply specific laws. We are asked, instead, to perform a function that the Constitution gave to the executive, not the judiciary. We are asked, quite simply, to prevent the publication by two newspapers of material that the executive branch insists should not, in the national interest, be published. I am convinced that the executive is correct with respect to some of the documents involved. But I cannot say that disclosure of any of them will surely result in direct, immediate, and irreparable damage to our nation or its people. That being so, there can under the First Amendment be but one judicial resolution of the issues before us. I join the judgments of the Court.

MR. JUSTICE WHITE, with whom MR. JUSTICE STEWART joins, concurring:

At least in the absence of legislation by Congress, based on its own investigations and findings, I am quite unable to agree that the inherent powers of the executive and the courts reach so far as to authorize remedies having such sweeping potential for inhibiting publications by the press. . . . To sustain the government in these cases would start the courts down a long and hazardous road that I am not willing to travel, at least without congressional guidance and direction. . . .

When the Espionage Act was under consideration in 1917, Congress eliminated from the bill a provision that would have given the President broad powers in time of war to proscribe, under threat of criminal penalty, the publication of various categories of information related to the national defense. Congress at that time was unwilling to clothe the President with such far-reaching powers. . . .

The Criminal Code contains numerous provisions potentially relevant to these cases. . . .

It is thus clear that Congress has addressed itself to the problems of protecting the security of the country and the national defense from unauthorized disclosure of potentially damaging information. It has not, however, authorized the injunctive remedy against threatened publication. It has apparently been satisfied to rely on criminal sanctions and their deterrent effect on the responsible as well as the irresponsible press.

MR. JUSTICE MARSHALL, concurring:

. . . The government argues that in addition to the inherent power of any government to protect itself, the President's power to conduct foreign affairs and his position as Commander-in-Chief give him authority to impose censorship on the press to protect his ability to deal effectively with foreign nations and to conduct the military affairs of the country. . . .

It would, however, be utterly inconsistent with the concept of separation of powers for this Court to use its power . . . to prevent behavior that Congress has specifically declined to prohibit. . . . The Constitution . . . did not provide for government by injunction in which the courts and the executive branch can "make law" without regard to the action of Congress.

. . . it is clear that Congress has specifically rejected passing legislation that would have clearly given the President the power he seeks here and made the current activity of the newspapers unlawful. When Congress specifically declines to make conduct unlawful it is not for this Court to redecide those issues—to overrule Congress.

MR. JUSTICE HARLAN, with whom THE CHIEF JUSTICE and MR. JUSTICE BLACKMUN, join, dissenting:

The power to evaluate the pernicious influence of premature disclosure is not, however, lodged in the executive alone. I agree that, in performance of its duty to protect the values of the First Amendment against political pressures, the judiciary must review the initial executive determination to the point of satisfying itself that the subject matter of the dispute does lie within the proper compass of the President's foreign relations power. Constitutional considerations forbid a complete abandonment of judicial control. Moreover the judiciary may properly insist that the determination that disclosure of the subject matter would irreparably impair the national security be made by the head of the executive department concerned—here the Secretary of State or the Secretary of Defense—after actual personal consideration by that officer. This safeguard is required in the analogous area of executive claims of privilege for secrets of state.

But in my judgment the judiciary may not properly go beyond these two inquiries and redetermine for itself the probable impact of disclosure on the national security. . . .

Even if there is some room for the judiciary to override the executive determination, it is plain that the scope of review must be exceedingly narrow. I can see no indication in the opinion of either the District Court or the Court of Appeals in the *Post* litigation that the conclusions of the executive were given even the deference owing to an administrative agency, much less that owing to a coequal branch of the government operating within the field of its constitutional prerogative.

Accordingly, I would vacate the judgment of the Court of Appeals for the District of Columbia on this ground and remand the case for further proceedings. . . .

[Chief Justice Burger and Justice Blackmun also dissented separately.]

UNITED STATES *v.* NIXON

418 U.S. 683; 94 Sup. Ct. 3090; 41 L. Ed. 1039 (1974)

[This case arose out of the Watergate scandals. A special prosecutor, Archibald Cox, was initially appointed to investigate the events preceding, during, and after the burglaries of the Democratic National Committee and the office of the psychiatrist of Daniel Ellsberg,

who had been responsible for providing the "Pentagon Papers" to The New York Times. *(See* New York Times Co. *v.* United States, *p. 195). A special prosecutor appointed from the outside and operating independently of the Justice Department appeared necessary because the former head of the Justice Department, John Mitchell, seemed to be implicated in the alleged offenses. Indeed it is former Attorney General Mitchell who is the criminal defendant in* United States *v.* Mitchell, *discussed in the first paragraph of the opinion that follows. When Mr. Cox sought actually to exercise his independence, the President ordered him fired. The then Attorney General, Elliot Richardson, refused to fire Cox and thus found it necessary to resign. Finally, after the second in command of the Justice Department also refused to carry out the President's order and was dismissed, the third in command fired Cox. The resulting congressional and public uproar forced the President to designate a second special prosecutor, Leon Jaworski, who was provided with very special legal powers and protections designed to ensure his independence from the presidency.* United States *v.* Nixon *was initiated by Jaworski in an attempt to get tape recordings of conversations between the President and his associates to be used as evidence in the prosecutions of those associates. Under a claim of executive privilege, the President had refused to surrender the tapes even when they were subpoenaed by the federal district judge sitting in the criminal cases. Because the President's challenge of the lawfulness of the subpoena occurred in May and the Mitchell trial was scheduled to begin in September, the Supreme Court agreed to take the case directly, without the normal hearing by a court of appeals, and extended its term beyond the traditional end-of-June closing in order to render an opinion. For the same reason it directed its mandate to be obeyed "forthwith" rather than permitting the considerable time that parties are normally allowed to bring themselves into obedience to a Supreme Court order. These considerations of time took on added significance because impeachment inquiries were then under way in the House of Representatives. After refusing to commit himself in advance on whether he would obey the Supreme Court's decision, the President did do so and the tapes began to flow into court just after the House Judiciary Committee had voted on articles of impeachment.]*

MR. CHIEF JUSTICE BURGER delivered the opinion of the Court:

These cases present for review the denial of a motion, filed on behalf of the President of the United States, in the case of *United States* v. *Mitchell et al.*, to quash a third-party subpoena duces tecum issued by the U.S. District Court for the District of Columbia, pursuant to Fed. Rule Crim. Proc. 17 c. The subpoena directed the President to produce certain tape recordings and documents relating to his conversations with aides and advisers. . . .

On March 1, 1974, a grand jury of the U.S. District Court for the District of Columbia returned an indictment charging seven named individuals with various offenses, including conspiracy to defraud the United States and to obstruct justice. Although he was not designated as such in the indictment, the grand jury named the President, among others, as an unindicted coconspirator.

On April 18, 1974, upon motion of the special prosecutor, a subpoena duces tecum was issued pursuant to Rule 17 c to the President by the U.S. District Court and made returnable on May 2, 1974. This subpoena required the production in advance of the Sept. 9 trial date, of certain tapes, memoranda, papers, transcripts, or other writings relating to certain precisely identified meetings between the President and others.

The special prosecutor was able to fix the time, place and persons present at these discussions because the White House daily logs and appointment records had been delivered to him. On April 30, the President publicly released edited transcripts of 43 conversations; portions of 20 conversations subject to subpoena in the present case were included.

On May 1, 1974, the President's counsel filed a "special appearance" and a motion to quash the subpoena, . . .

On May 20, 1974, the District Court denied the motion to quash. It further ordered "the President or any subordinate officer, official or employee with custody or control of the documents or objects subpoenaed" to deliver to the District Court, on or before May 31, 1974, the originals of all subpoenaed items, as well as an index and analysis of those items, together with tape copies of those portions of the subpoenaed recordings for which transcripts had been released to the public by the President on April 30. . . .

In the District Court, the President's counsel argued that the court lacked jurisdiction to issue the subpoena because the matter was an intrabranch dispute between a subordinate and superior officer of the executive branch and hence not subject to judicial resolution.

That argument has been renewed in this court with emphasis on the contention that the dispute does not present a "case" or "controversy" which can be adjudicated in the federal courts. The President's counsel argues that the federal courts should not intrude into areas committed to the other branches of government.

He views the present dispute as essentially a "jurisdictional" dispute within the executive branch which he analogizes to a dispute between two congressional committees. Since the executive branch has exclusive authority and absolute discretion to decide whether to prosecute a case, *Confiscation Cases,* 7 Wall. 454 (1869), it is contended that a President's decision is final in determining what evidence is to be used in a given criminal case.

Although his counsel concedes the President has delegated certain specific powers to the special prosecutor, he has not "waived nor delegated to the special prosecutor the President's duty to claim privilege as to all materials . . . which fall within the President's inherent authority to refuse to disclose to any executive officer." Brief for the President 47. The special prosecutor's demand for the items therefore presents, in the view of the President's counsel, a political question under *Baker* v. *Carr,* since it involves a "textually demonstrable" grant of power under Art. II.

The mere assertion of a claim of an "intrabranch dispute," without more, has never operated to defeat federal jurisdiction; justiciability does not depend on such a surface inquiry. In *United States* v. *ICC,* 337 U.S. 426 (1949), the court observed, "courts must look behind names that symbolize the parties to determine whether a justiciable case or controversy is presented." Id., at 430.

Our starting point is the nature of the proceeding for which the evidence is sought—here a pending criminal prosecution. It is a judicial proceeding in a federal court alleging violation of federal laws and is brought in the name of the United States as sovereign. Under the authority of Art. II, 2, Congress has vested in the attorney general the power to conduct the criminal litigation of the U.S. Government. 28 U.S.C. 516.

It has also vested in him the power to appoint subordinate officers to assist him in the discharge of his duties. 28 U.S.C. 509, 510, 515, 533. Acting pursuant to those statutes, the attorney general has delegated the authority to represent the United States in these particular matters to a special prosecutor with unique authority and tenure. The regulation gives the special prosecutor explicit power to contest the invocation of executive privilege in the process of seeking evidence deemed relevant to the performance of these specially delegated duties.

So long as this regulation is extant it has the force of law. In *Accardi* v. *Shaughnessy,* 347 U.S. 260 (1953), regulations of the attorney general delegated certain of his discretionary powers to the Board of Immigration Appeals and required that board to exercise its own discretion on appeals in deportation cases.

The court held that so long as the attorney general's regulations remained operative, he denied himself the authority to exercise the discretion delegated to the board even though the original authority was his and he could reassert it by amending the regulations. *Service* v. *Dulles,* 354 U.S. 363, 388 (1957), and *Vitarelli* v. *Seaton,* 359 U.S. 535 (1959), reaffirmed the basic holding of *Accardi.*

Here, as in *Accardi,* it is theoretically possible for the attorney general to amend or revoke the regulation defining the special prosecutor's authority. But he has not done so. So long as this regulation remains in force the executive branch is bound by it, and indeed the United States as the sovereign composed of the three branches is bound to respect and to enforce it.

Moreover, the delegation of authority to the special prosecutor in this case is not an ordinary delegation by the attorney general to a subordinate officer: with the authorization of the President, the acting attorney general provided in the regulation that the special prosecutor was not to be removed without the "consensus" of eight designated leaders of Congress.

The demand of and the resistance to the subpoena present an obvious controversy in the ordinary sense, but that alone is not sufficient to meet constitutional standards. In the constitutional sense, controversy means more than disagreement and conflict; rather it means the kind of controversy courts traditionally resolve.

Here at issue is the production or nonproduction of specified evidence deemed by the special prosecutor to be relevant and admissible in a pending criminal case. It is sought by one official government within the scope of his express authority; it is resisted by the chief executive on the ground of his duty to preserve the confidentiality of the communications of the President.

Whatever the correct answer on the merits, these issues are "of a type which are traditionally justiciable." *United States* v. *ICC,* 337 U.S., at 430. The independent special prosecutor with his asserted need for the subpoenaed material in the underlying criminal prosecution is opposed by the President with his steadfast assertion of privilege against disclosure of the material. This setting assures there is "that concrete adverseness which sharpens the presentation of issues upon which the court so largely depends for illumination of difficult constitutional questions." *Baker* v. *Carr,* 369 U.S., at 204.

Moreover, since the matter is one arising in the regular course of a federal criminal prosecution, it is within the traditional scope of Art. III power. Id., at 198.

In light of the uniqueness of the setting in which the conflict arises, the fact that both parties are officers of the executive branch cannot be viewed as a barrier to justiciability. It would be inconsistent with the applicable law and regulation, and the unique facts of this case to conclude other than that the special prosecutor has standing to bring this action and that a justiciable controversy is presented for decision. . . .

. . . we turn to the claim that the subpoena should be quashed because it demands "confidential conversations between a President and his close advisers that it would be inconsistent with the public interest to produce."

The first contention is a broad claim that the separation of powers doctrine precludes judicial review of a President's claim of privilege. The second contention is that if he does not prevail on the claim of absolute privilege, the court should hold as a matter of constitutional law that the privilege prevails over the subpoena duces tecum.

In the performance of assigned constitutional duties each branch of the government must initially interpret the Constitution, and the interpretation of its powers by any branch is due great respect from the others. The President's counsel, as we have noted, reads the Constitution as providing an absolute privilege of confidentiality for all presidential communications.

Many decisions of this Court, however, have unequivocally reaffirmed the holding of *Marbury* v. *Madison* that "it is emphatically the province and duty of the judicial department to say what the law is."

No holding of the court has defined the scope of judicial power specifically relating to the enforcement of a subpoena for confidential presidential communications for use in a criminal prosecution, but other exercises of powers by the executive branch and the legislative branch have been found invalid as in conflict with the Constitution, *Youngstown.* In a series of cases, the court interpreted the explicit immunity conferred by express provisions of the Constitution on members of the House and Senate by the Speech or Debate Clause.

Since this Court has consistently exercised the power to construe and delineate claims arising under express powers, it must follow that the Court has authority to interpret claims with respect to powers alleged to derive from enumerated powers.

Our system of government "requires that federal courts on occasion interpret the Constitution in a manner at variance with the construction given the document by another branch." *Powell* v. *McCormack.*

And in *Baker* v. *Carr,* 369 U.S. at 211, the court stated:

> "Deciding whether a matter has in any measure been committed by the Constitution to another branch of government, or whether the action of that branch exceeds whatever authority has been committed, is itself a delicate exercise in constitutional interpretation, and is a responsibility of this Court as ultimate interpreter of the Constitution."

Notwithstanding the deference each branch must accord the others, the "judicial power of the United States" vested in the federal courts by Art. III of the Constitution can no more be shared with the executive branch than the chief executive, for example, can share with the judiciary the veto power, or the Congress share with the judiciary the power to override a presidential veto.

Any other conclusion would be contrary to the basic concept of separation of powers and the checks and balances that flow from the scheme of a tripartite government. *The Federalist,* No. 47. We therefore reaffirm that it is "emphatically the province and the duty" of this court "to say what the law is" with respect to the claim of privilege presented in this case. *Marbury* v. *Madison.*

In support of his claim of absolute privilege, the President's counsel urges two grounds one of which is common to all governments and one of which is peculiar to our system of separation of powers. The first ground is the valid need for protection of communications between high government officials and those who advise and assist them in the performance of their manifold duties; . . .

Whatever the nature of the privilege of confidentiality of presidental communications in the exercise of Art. II powers the privilege can be said to derive from the supremacy of each branch within its own assigned area of constitutional duties. Certain powers and privileges flow from the nature of enumerated powers; the protection of the confidentiality of presidential communications has similar constitutional underpinnings.

The second ground asserted by the President's counsel in support of the claim of absolute privilege rests on the doctrine of separation of powers. Here it is argued that the independence of the executive branch within its own sphere [*Humphrey's Executor* v. *United States,* 295 U.S. 602, 629–630 (1935); *Kilbourn* v. *Thompson,* 103 U.S. 168, 190–191 (1880)] insulates a President from a judicial subpoena in an ongoing criminal prosecution, and thereby protects confidential presidential communications.

However, neither the doctrine of separation of powers, nor the need for confidentiality of high level communications, without more, can sustain an absolute, unqualified presidential privilege of immunity from judicial process under all circumstances. The President's need for complete candor and objectivity from advisers calls for great deference from the courts.

However, when the privilege depends solely on the broad, undifferentiated claim of public interest in the confidentiality of such conversations, a confrontation with other values arises. Absent a claim of need to protect military, diplomatic or sensitive national security secrets, we find it difficult to accept the argument that even the very important interest in confidentiality of presidential communications is significantly diminished by production of such material for in camera inspection with all the protection that a district court will be obliged to provide.

The impediment that an absolute, unqualified privilege would place in the way of the primary constitutional duty of the judicial branch to do justice in criminal prosecutions would plainly conflict with the function of the courts under Art. III. In designing the structure of our government and dividing and allocating the sovereign power among three coequal branches, the framers of the Constitution sought to provide a comprehensive system, but the separate powers were not intended to operate with absolute independence.

"While the Constitution diffuses power

the better to secure liberty, it also contemplates that practice will integrate the dispersed powers into a workable government. It enjoins upon its branches separateness but interdependence, autonomy but reciprocity." *Youngstown Sheet & Tube Co.* v. *Sawyer,* 343 U.S. 579, 635, (1952), Jackson J. concurring.

To read the Art. II powers of the President as providing an absolute privilege as against a subpoena essential to enforcement of criminal statutes on no more than a generalized claim of the public interest in confidentiality of nonmilitary and nondiplomatic discussions would upset the constitutional balance of "a workable government" and gravely impair the role of the courts under Art. III.

Since we conclude that the legitimate needs of the judicial process may outweigh presidential privilege, it is necessary to resolve those competing interests in a manner that preserves the essential functions of each branch. The right and indeed the duty to resolve that question does not free the judiciary from according high respect to the representations made on behalf of the President. *United States* v. *Burr,* 25 Fed. Cas. 187 (1807).

The expectation of a President to the confidentiality of his conversations and correspondence, like the claim of confidentiality of judicial deliberations, for example, has all the values to which we accord deference for the privacy of all citizens and added to those values the necessity for protection of the public interest in candid, objective, and even blunt or harsh opinions in presidential decision-making.

A President and those who assist him must be free to explore alternatives in the process of shaping policies and making decisions and to do so in a way many would be unwilling to express except privately. These are the considerations justifying a presumptive privilege for presidential communications.

The privilege is fundamental to the operation of government and inextricably rooted in the separation of powers under the Constitution. In *Nixon* v. *Sirica,*—U.S. App. D.C.—487 F. 2d 700 (1973), the Court of Appeals held that such presidential communications are "presumptively privileged," id., at 717, and this position is accepted by both parties in the present litigation.

We agree with Mr. Chief Justice Marshall's observation, therefore, that "in no case of this kind would a court be required to proceed against the President as against an ordinary individual." *United States* v. *Burr.*

But this presumptive privilege must be considered in light of our historic commitment to the rule of law. This is nowhere more profoundly manifest than in our view that "the twofold aim of criminal justice is that guilt shall not escape or innocence suffer." *Berger* v. *United States,* 295 U.S. 78, 88 (1935).

We have elected to employ an adversary system of criminal justice in which the parties contest all issues before a court of law. The need to develop all relevant facts in the adversary system is both fundamental and comprehensive. The ends of criminal justice would be defeated if judgments were to be founded on a partial or speculative presentation of the facts.

The very integrity of the judicial system and public confidence in the system depend on full disclosure of all the facts, within the framework of the rules of evidence. To ensure that justice is done, it is imperative to the function of courts that compulsory process be available for the production of evidence needed either by the prosecution or by the defense.

Only recently the court restated the ancient proposition of law, albeit in the context of a grand jury inquiry rather than a trial, " 'that the public . . . has a right to every man's evidence' except for those persons protected by a constitutional, common law, or statutory privilege, *United States* v. *Bryan,* 339, U.S. at 331 (1950); *Blackmer* v. *United States,* 284 U.S. 421, 438 (1932); *Branzburg* v. *Hayes,* 408 U.S. 665, 688 (1972)."

The privileges referred to by the court are designed to protect weighty and legitimate competing interests. Thus, the Fifth Amendment to the Constitution provides that no man "shall be compelled in any criminal case to be a witness against himself." And, generally, an attorney or a priest may not be required to disclose what has been revealed in professional confidence.

These and other interests are recognized in law by privileges against forced disclosure, established in the Constitution, by statute, or a common law. Whatever their origins, these exceptions to the demand for every man's evidence are not lightly created nor expansively construed, for they are in derogation of the search for truth.

In this case the President challenges a subpoena served on him as a third party requiring the production of materials for use in criminal prosecution on the claim that he has a privilege against disclosure of confidential communications. He does not place his claim of privilege on the ground they are military or diplomatic secrets. As to these areas of Art. II duties the courts have traditionally shown the utmost deference to presidential responsibilities. . . .

No case of the Court, however, has extended this high degree of deference to a President's generalized interest in confidentiality. Nowhere in the Constitution, as we have noted earlier, is there any explicit reference to a privilege of confidentiality, yet to the extent this interest relates to the effective discharge of a President's powers, it is constitutionally based.

The right to the production of all evidence at a criminal trial similarly has constitutional dimensions. The Sixth Amendment explicitly confers upon every defendant in a criminal trial the right "to be confronted with the witness against him" and "to have compulsory process for obtaining witness in his favor."

Moreover, the Fifth Amendment also guarantees that no person shall be deprived of liberty without due process of law. It is the manifest duty of the courts to vindicate those guarantees and to accomplish that it is essential that all relevant and admissible evidence be produced.

In this case we must weigh the importance of the general privilege of confidentiality of presidential communications in performance of his responsibilities against the inroads of such a privilege on the fair administration of criminal justice. The interest in preserving confidentiality is weighty indeed and entitled to great respect. However, we cannot conclude that advisers will be moved to temper the candor of their remarks by the infrequent occasions of disclosure because of the possibility that such conversations will be called for in the context of a criminal prosecution.

On the other hand, the allowance of the privilege to withhold evidence that is demonstrably relevant in a criminal trial would cut deeply into the guarantee of due process of law and gravely impair the basic function of the courts. A President's acknowledged need for confidentiality in the communications of his office is general in nature, whereas the constitutional need for production of relevant evidence in a criminal proceeding is specific and central to the fair adjudication of a particular criminal case in the administration of justice.

Without access to specific facts a criminal prosecution may be totally frustrated. The President's broad interest in confidentiality of communications will not be vitiated by disclosure of a limited number of conversations preliminarily shown to have some bearing on the pending criminal cases.

We conclude that when the ground for asserting privilege as to subpoenaed materials sought for use in a criminal trial is based only on the generalized interest in confidentiality, it cannot prevail over the fundamental demands of due process of law in the fair administration of criminal justice. The generalized assertion of privilege must yield to the demonstrated, specific need for evidence in a pending criminal trial.

We have earlier determined that the District Court did not err in authorizing the issuance of the subpoena. If a President concludes that compliance with a subpoena would be injurious to the public interest he may properly, as was done here, invoke a claim of privilege on the return of the subpoena. Upon receiving a claim of privilege from the chief executive, it became the further duty of the District Court to treat the subpoenaed material as presumptively privileged and to require the special prosecutor to demonstrate that the presidential material was "essential to the justice of the pending criminal case." *United States* v. *Burr,* at 192.

Here the District Court treated the material as presumptively privileged, proceeded to find that the special prosecutor had made a sufficient showing to rebut the presumption and ordered an in camera examination of the subpoenaed material. On the basis of our examination of the record we are unable to conclude that the District Court erred in ordering the inspection.

Accordingly we affirm the order of the District Court that subpoenaed materials be transmitted to that court. We now turn to the important question of the District Court's responsibilities in conducting the in camera examination of presidential materials or communications delivered under the compulsion of the subpoena duces tecum. . . .

"The guard, furnished to the President to protect him from being harassed by vexatious and unnecessary subpoenas, is to be looked for in the conduct of the District Court after the subpoenas have issued; not in any circumstances which is to precede their being issued." *United States* v. *Burr,* at 34. Statements that meet the test of admissibility and relevance must be isolated; all other material must be excised.

. . . it is obvious that the District Court has a very heavy responsibility to see to it that presidential conversations, which are either not relevant or not admissible, are accorded that high degree of respect due the President of the United States. Mr. Chief Justice Marshall sitting as a trial judge in the Burr case was extraordinarily careful to point out that:

> "In no case of this kind would a court be required to proceed against the President as against an ordinary individual." 191.

Marshall's statement cannot be read to mean in any sense that a President is above the law, but relates to the singularly unique role under Art. II of a President's communications and activities, related to the performance of duties under that Article. Moreover, a President's communications and activities encompass a vastly wider range of sensitive material than would be true of any "ordinary individual."

It is therefore necessary in the public interest to afford presidential confidentiality the greatest protection consistent with the fair administration of justice. The need for confidentiality even as to idle conversations with associates in which casual reference might be made concerning political leaders within the country or foreign statesmen is too obvious to call for further treatment. . . .

This burden applies with even greater force to excised material; once the decision is made to excise, the material is restored to its privileged status and should be returned under seal to its lawful custodian.

Since this matter came before the court during the pendency of a criminal prosecution, and on representations that time is of the essence, the mandate shall issue forthwith.

Affirmed.

MR. JUSTICE REHNQUIST took no part in the consideration or decision of these cases.

AFROYIM *v.* RUSK

387 U.S. 253; 87 Sup. Ct. 1660; 18 L. Ed. 2d 757 (1967)

[Afroyim was born in Poland and became a naturalized American citizen in 1926. In 1950 he voted in an Israeli election. In 1960 the State Department refused to renew his passport on the ground that Section 401 (e) of the Nationality Act of 1940 provided that a U.S. citizen shall "lose" his citizenship if he votes "in a political election in a foreign state." The District Court and Court of Appeals upheld the action of the then Secretary of State Dean Rusk in refusing the passport.]

MR. JUSTICE BLACK delivered the opinion of the Court:

. . . The fundamental issue before this Court here, as it was in [*Perez* v. *Brownell* (1958)], is whether Congress can consistently with the Fourteenth Amendment enact a law stripping an American of his citizenship which he has never voluntarily renounced or given up. The majority in *Perez* held that Congress could do this because withdrawal of citizenship is "reasonably calculated to effect the end that is within the power of Congress to achieve." That conclusion was reached by this chain of reasoning: Congress has an implied power to deal with foreign affairs as an indispensable attribute of sovereignty; this implied power, plus the Necessary and Proper Clause, empowers Congress to regulate voting by American citizens in foreign elections; involuntary expatriation is within the "ample scope" of "appropriate modes" Congress can adopt to effectuate its general regulatory power. Then, upon summarily concluding that "there is nothing . . . in the Fourteenth Amendment to warrant drawing from it a restriction upon the power otherwise possessed by Congress to withdraw citizenship," the majority specifically rejected the "notion that the power of Congress to terminate citizenship depends upon the citizen's assent."

First we reject the idea expressed in *Perez* that, aside from the Fourteenth Amendment, Congress has any general power, express or implied, to take away an American citizen's citizenship without his assent. This power cannot, as *Perez* indicated, be sutained as an implied attribute of sovereignty possessed by all nations. Other nations are governed by their own constitutions, if any, and we can draw no support from theirs. In our country the people are sovereign and the Government cannot sever its relationship to the people by taking away their citizenship. Our Constitution governs us and we must never forget that our Constitution limits the Government to those powers specifically granted or those that are necessary and proper to carry out the specifically granted ones. The Constitution, of course, grants Congress no express power to strip people of their citizenship, whether in the exercise of the implied power to regulate foreign affairs or in the exercise of any specifically granted power. And even before the adoption of the Fourteenth Amendment, views were expressed in Congress and by the Court that under the Constitution the Government was granted no power, even under its express power to pass a uniform rule of naturalization, to determine what conduct should and should not result in the loss of citizenship. On three occasions, in 1795, 1797, and 1818, Congress considered and rejected proposals to enact laws which would describe certain conduct as resulting in expatriation. . . . It is in this setting that six years later, in *Osborn* v. *Bank of the United States* (1824), this Court, speaking through Chief Justice Marshall, declared in what appears to be a mature and well-considered dictum that Congress, once a person becomes a citizen, cannot deprive him of that status:

> "[The naturalized citizen] becomes a member of the society, possessing all the right of a native citizen, and standing, in the view of the constitution, on the footing of a native. The constitution does not authorize Congress to enlarge or abridge those rights. The simple power of the national Legislature, is to prescribe a uniform rule of naturalization, and the exercise of this power exhausts it, so far as respects the individual."

Although these legislative and judicial statements may be regarded as inconclusive, . . . the Fourteenth Amendment . . . provides its own constitutional rule in language calculated completely to control the status of citizenship: "All persons born or naturalized in the United States . . . are citizens of the United States. . . ." There is no indication in these words of a fleeting citizenship, good at the moment it is acquired but subject to destruction by the Government at any time. Rather the Amendment can most reasonably be read as defining a citizenship which a citizen keeps unless he voluntarily relinquishes it. Once acquired, this Fourteenth Amendment citizenship was not to be shifted, canceled, or diluted at the will of the Federal Government, the States, or any other governmental unit.

It is true that the chief interest of the people in giving permanence and security to citizenship in the Fourteenth Amendment was the desire to protect Negroes. . . .

This undeniable purpose of the Fourteenth Amendment to make citizenship of Negroes permanent and secure would be frustrated by holding that the Government can rob a citizen of his citizenship without his consent by simply proceeding to act under an implied general power to regulate foreign affairs or some other power generally granted. Though the framers of the Amendment were not particularly concerned with the problem of expatriation, it seems undeniable from the language they used that they wanted to put citizenship beyond the power of any governmental unit to destroy. In 1868, two years after the Fourteenth Amendment had been adopted, Congress specifically considered the subject of expatriation. . . .

The entire legislative history of the 1868 Act makes it abundantly clear that there was a strong feeling in the Congress that the only way the citizenship it conferred could be lost was by the voluntary renunciation or abandonment by the citizen himself. And this was the unequivocal statement of the Court in the case of *United States* v. *Wong Kim Ark* (1898). The issues in that case were whether a person born in the United States to Chinese aliens was a citizen of the United States and whether, nevertheless, he could be excluded under the Chinese Exclusion Act. The Court first held that, within the terms of the Fourteenth Amendment, Wong Kim Ark was a citizen of the United States, and then pointed out that though he might "renounce this citizenship, and become a citizen of . . . any other country," he had never done so. The Court then held that Congress could not do anything to abridge or affect his citizenship conferred by the Fourteenth Amendment. Quoting Chief Justice Marshall's well considered and oft-repeated dictum in *Osborn* to the effect that Congress under the power of naturalization has "a power to confer citizenship, not a power to take it away," the Court said:

"Congress having no power to abridge the rights conferred by the Constitution upon those who have become naturalized citizens by virtue of acts of Congress, a fortiori no act . . . of Congress . . . can affect citizenship acquired as a birthright, by virtue of the Constitution itself. . . . The Fourteenth Amendment, while it leaves the power, where it was before, in Congress, to regulate naturalization, has conferred no authority upon Congress to restrict the effect of birth, declared by the Constitution to constitute a sufficient and complete right to citizenship."

To uphold Congress' power to take away a man's citizenship because he voted in a foreign election in violation of Section 401 (e) would be equivalent to holding that Congress has the power to "abridge," "affect," "restrict the effect of," and "take . . . away" citizenship. Because the Fourteenth Amendment prevents Congress from doing any of these things, we agree with the Chief Justice's dissent in the *Perez* case that the Government is without power to rob a citizen of his citizenship under Section 401 (e).

Because the legislative history of the Fourteenth Amendment and the expatriation proposals which preceded and followed it, like most other legislative history, contains many statements from which conflicting inferences can be drawn, our holding might be unwarranted if it rested entirely or principally upon that legislative history. But it does not. Our holding we think is the only one that can stand in view of the language and the purpose of the Fourteenth Amendment, and our construction of that Amendment, we believe, comports more nearly than *Perez* with the principles of liberty and equal justice to all that the entire Fourteenth Amendment was adopted to guarantee. Citizenship is no light trifle to be jeopardized any moment Congress decides to do so under the name of one of its general or implied grants of power. In some instances, loss of citizenship can mean that a man is left without the protection of citizenship in any country in the world—as a man without a country. Citizenship in this Nation is a part of a cooperative affair. Its citizenry is the country and the country is its citizenry. The very nature of our free government makes it completely incongruous to have a rule of law under which a group of citizens temporarily in office can deprive another group of citizens of their citizenship. We hold that the Fourteenth Amendment was designed to, and does, protect every citizen of this Nation against a congressional forcible destruction of his citizenship, whatever his creed, color, or race. Our holding does no more than to give to this citizen that which is his own, a constitutional right to remain a citizen in a free country unless he voluntarily relinquishes that citizenship.

Perez v. *Brownell* is overruled. The judgment is

Reversed.

[*Mr. Justice Harlan, whom Justices Clark, Stewart, and White joined, dissenting:*]

Ten years ago, in *Perez* v. *Brownell,* the Court upheld the constitutionality of Section 401 (e) of the Nationality Act of 1940. The section deprives of his nationality any citizen who has voted in a foreign political election. The Court reasoned that Congress derived from its power to regulate foreign affairs authority to expatriate any citizen who intentionally commits acts which may be prejudicial to the foreign relations of the United States, and which reasonably may be deemed to indicate a dilution of his allegiance to this country. Congress, it was held, could appropriately consider purposeful voting in a foreign political election to be such an act.

The Court today overrules *Perez,* and declares Section 401 (e) unconstitutional, by a remarkable process of circumlocution. First, the Court fails almost entirely to dispute the reasoning in *Perez;* it is essentially content with the conclusory and quite unsubstantiated assertion that Congress is without "any general power, express or implied," to expatriate a citizen "without his assent." * Next, the Court embarks upon a lengthy, albeit incomplete, survey of the historical power at stake here, and yet, at the end, concedes that the history is susceptible to "conflicting inferences." The Court acknowledges that its conclusions might not be warranted by that history alone, and disclaims that the decision today relies, even "principally," upon it. Finally, the Court declares that its result is bottomed upon the "language and purpose" of the Citizenship Clause of the Fourteenth Amendment; in explanation, the Court offers only the terms of the clause itself, the contention that any other result would be "completely incongruous," and the essentially arcane observation that the "citizenry is the country and the country is its citizenry."

I can find nothing in this extraordinary series of circumventions which permits, still less compels, the imposition of this constitutional constraint upon the authority of Congress. I must respectfully dissent. . . . [T]he Court relies [on] a brief obiter dictum from the lengthy opinion for the Court in *Osborn* v. *Bank of the United States,* written by Mr. Chief Justice Marshall. This use of the dictum is entirely unpersuasive, for its terms and context make quite plain that it cannot have been intended to reach the questions presented here. The central issue before the Court in *Osborn* was the right of the bank to bring its suit for equitable relief in the courts of the United States. In argument, counsel for *Osborn* had asserted that although the bank had been created by the laws of the United States, it did not necessarily follow that any cause involving the bank had arisen under those laws. Counsel urged by analogy that the naturalization of an alien might as readily be said to confer upon the new citizen a right to bring all his actions in the federal courts. Not surprisingly, the Court rejected the analogy, and remarked that an act of naturalization "does not proceed to give, to regulate, or to prescribe his capacities," since the Constitution demands that naturalized citizens must in all respects stand "on the footing of native." The Court plainly meant no more than that counsel's analogy is broken by Congress' inability to offer naturalized citizens rights or capacities which differ in any particular from those given to a native-born citizen by birth. Mr. Justice Johnson's discussion of the analogy in dissent confirms the Court's purpose. . . .

The most pertinent evidence from this period upon these questions has been en-

*. . . Whatever the Court's position, it has assumed that voluntariness is here a term of fixed meaning; in fact, of course, it has been employed to describe both a specific intent to renounce citizenship, and the uncoerced commission of an act conclusively deemed by law to be a relinquishment of citizenship. Until the Court indicates with greater precision what it means by "assent," today's opinion will surely cause still greater confusion in this area of the law.

tirely overlooked by the Court. Twice in the two years immediately prior to its passage of the Fourteenth Amendment, Congress exercised the very authority which the Court now suggests that it should have recognized was entirely lacking. In each case, a bill was debated and adopted by both Houses which included provisions to expatriate unwilling citizens.

In the spring and summer of 1864, both Houses debated intensively the Wade-Davis bill to provide reconstruction governments for the States which had seceded to form the Confederacy. Among the bill's provisions was Section 14, by which "every person who shall hereafter hold or exercise any office . . . in the rebel service . . . is hereby declared not to be a citizen of the United States." . . . The bill was not signed by President Lincoln before the adjournment of Congress, and thus failed to become law, but a subsequent statement issued by Lincoln makes quite plain that he was not troubled by any doubts of the constitutionality of Section 14. Passage of the Wade-Davis bill of itself "suffices to destroy the notion that the men who drafted the Fourteenth Amendment felt that citizenship was an 'absolute.' "

Twelve months later, and less than a year before its passage of the Fourteenth Amendment, Congress adopted a second measure which included provisions that permitted the expatriation of unwilling citizens. Section 21 of the Enrollment Act of 1865 provided that deserters from the military service of the United States "shall be deemed and taken to have voluntarily relinquished and forfeited their rights of citizenship and their rights to become citizens; . . ." The bitterness of war did not cause Congress here to neglect the requirements of the Constitution; for it was argued in both Houses that Section 21 as written was ex post facto, and thus was constitutionally impermissible. Significantly, however, it was never suggested in either debate that expatriation without a citizen's consent lay beyond Congress' authority. . . . The pertinent evidence for the period prior to the adoption of the Fourteenth Amendment can therefore be summarized as follows. The Court's conclusion today is supported only by the statements, associated at least in part with a now abandoned view of citizenship, of three individual Congressmen, and by the ambiguous and inapposite dictum from *Osborn*. Inconsistent with the Court's position are statements from individual Congressmen in 1794, and Congress' passage in 1864 and 1865 of legislation which expressly authorized the expatriation of unwilling citizens. It may be that legislation adopted in the heat of war should be discounted in part by its origins, but, even if this is done, it is surely plain that the Court's conclusion is entirely unwarranted by the available historical evidence for the period prior to the passage of the Fourteenth Amendment. The evidence suggests, to the contrary, that Congress in 1865 understood that it had authority, at least in some circumstances, to deprive a citizen of his nationality.

II

The evidence with which the Court supports its thesis that the Citizenship Clause of the Fourteenth Amendment was intended to lay at rest any doubts of Congress' inability to expatriate without the citizen's consent is no more persuasive. . . . The debate upon the clause was essentially cursory in both Houses, but there are several clear indications of its intended effect. Its sponsors evidently shared the fears of Senators Stewart and Wade that unless citizenship were defined, freedmen might, under the reasoning of the *Dred Scott* decision, be excluded by the courts from the scope of the Amendment. It was agreed that, since the "courts have stumbled on the subject," it would be prudent to remove the "doubt thrown over" it. The clause would essentially overrule *Dred Scott,* and place beyond question the freedmen's right of citizenship because of birth. . . . Nothing in the debates, however, supports the Court's assertion that the clause was intended to deny Congress its authority to expatriate unwilling citizens. The evidence indicates that its draftsmen instead expected the clause only to declare unreservedly to whom citizenship initially adhered. . . .

The narrow, essentially definitional purpose of the Citizenship Clause is reflected in the clear declarations in the debates that the clause would not revise the prevailing incidents of citizenship. . . .

Between the two brief statements from Senator Howard relied upon by the Court, Howard, in response to a question, said the following:

> "I take it for granted that after a man becomes a citizen of the United States under the Constitution he cannot cease to be a citizen, *except* by expatriation or *the commission of some crime by which his citizenship shall be forfeited.*" (Italics supplied.)

It would be difficult to imagine a more unqualified rejection of the Court's position; Senator Howard, the clause's sponsor, very plainly believed that it would leave unimpaired Congress' power to deprive unwilling citizens of their citizenship. . . .

The Citizenship Clause thus neither denies nor provides to Congress any power of expatriation; its consequences are, for present purposes, exhausted by its declaration of the classes of individuals to whom citizenship initially attaches. Once obtained, citizenship is of course protected from arbitrary withdrawal by the constraints placed around Congress' powers by the Constitution; it is not proper to create from the Citizenship Clause an additional, and entirely unwarranted, restriction upon legislative authority. The construction now placed on the Citizenship Clause rests, in the last analysis, simply on the Court's ipse dixit, evincing little more, it is quite apparent, than the present majority's own distaste for the expatriation power.

I believe that *Perez* was rightly decided, and on its authority would affirm the judgment of the Court of Appeals.

P A R T **II**

Economic Regulation in a Federal System

"Our Constitution is not a strait-jacket. It is a living organism. As such it is capable of growth—of expansion and of adaptation to new conditions. Growth implies changes, political, economic and social. Growth which is significant manifests itself rather in intellectual and moral conceptions than in material things. Because our Constitution possesses the capacity of adaptation, it has endured as the fundamental law of an ever-developing people."

Unpublished passage in Justice Brandeis's original dissenting opinion in *United States* v. *Moreland,* 258 U.S. 433 (1922). Quoted in Alexander M. Bickel, *The Least Dangerous Branch* (New York and Indianapolis: Bobbs-Merrill, 1962), p. 107.

CHAPTER 7

The Contract Clause

The Constitution (Article I, Section 10) declares that no state shall pass any law impairing the obligation of contracts. In the early case of *Sturges* v. *Crowninsheild,* 4 Wheat. 122 (1819), Chief Justice Marshall defined the key terms of the contract clause:

> A contract is an agreement in which a party undertakes to do, or not to do, a particular thing. The law binds him to perform his undertaking, and this is of course, the obligation of his contract. In the case at bar, the defendant has given his promissory note to pay the plaintiff a sum of money on or before a certain day. The contract binds him to pay that sum on that day; and this is its obligation. Any law which releases a part of this obligation, must, in the literal sense of the word, impair it. Much more must a law impair it which makes it totally invalid and entirely discharges it.

The contract clause and the monetary provisions of Article I, Section 10, were designed to protect the creditor classes. Under the Articles of Confederation, the states had passed numerous laws that interfered with the vested property rights of creditors. As indicated in *Home Building and Loan Assoc.* v. *Blaisdell* (p. 223), the contract clause was framed for the specific purpose of preventing state legislation for the relief of debtors, particularly in times of financial emergencies. Thus, the clause would help "to provide adequate safeguards for property and contracts against state legislative power." This was "one of the most important objects of the framers, if indeed it was not the most important." [1]

Expansion of the Contract Clause

The contract clause constitutes a limitation on the states *alone*. There is no corresponding restriction on the Federal Government, but the due process clause of the Fifth Amendment provides some protection against arbitrary interference with contracts from this level. Also, the framers obviously intended that the contract clause prohibit the states from interfering only with contracts between *individuals*. But Chief Justice Marshall, in a number of historic opinions, expanded the meaning of the contract clause far beyond the original intention of the framers.

In the period immediately following the adoption of the Constitution, it was hoped by many that the ex post facto clauses (Article I, Sections 9–10) would protect established property rights against legislative meddling. But in *Calder* v. *Bull*, 3 Dall. 386 (1798) the Court limited the clauses to the prohibition of retroactive penal legislation, holding that they were not designed "to secure the citizen in his private rights of either property or contracts."

Confronted by *Calder*, Marshall turned to the contract clause as a vehicle for protecting vested rights. The Supreme Court first interpreted the contract clause in *Fletcher* v. *Peck*, 6 Cranch 87 (1810), where a state statute was held void under the Constitution for the first time. The case had its origin in a Georgia statute in 1795 that granted more than 35 million acres of rich territory to four land companies. The passage of the bill was secured by wholesale bribery of the legislature.[2] Popular indignation forced the next session of the Georgia legislature to revoke the grant on the ground that it had been secured by fraud. Meanwhile, however, some of the land had been purchased by persons from other parts of the country. These buyers contested the validity of the rescinding act on the ground that the original grant was a contract that could not be impaired. In an opinion written by Chief Justice Marshall, the Court agreed unanimously with the purchasers and held that the Georgia rescinding act violated the contract clause when the land in question had passed into the hands of innocent third parties. Marshall thus expanded the meaning of the clause by making it applicable to transactions to which the state itself was a party.

[1] Edward S. Corwin, *John Marshall and the Constitution* (New Haven: Yale, 1919), p. 147.

[2] The full story is told in C. Peter Magrath, *Yazoo: Law and Politics in the New Republic* (Providence, R.I.: Brown University Press, 1966).

The contract clause now could be applied to public as well as private contracts.

Marshall extended the contract clause still further in the famous case of *Dartmouth College* v. *Woodward* (p. 216) by holding that a corporate charter is a contract protected against infringement by state legislatures. Although the case involved an educational rather than an industrial institution, it was of tremendous importance to the economic development of the nation, because it gave assurance to business corporations that they would be protected from legislative interference. The decision was announced at a time when numerous corporations "were springing up in response to the necessity for larger and more constant business units and because of the convenience and profit of such organizations. Marshall's opinion was a tremendous stimulant to this natural economic tendency. It reassured investors in corporate securities and gave confidence and steadiness to the business world." [3] "By employing a far broader conception of contract than had been prevalent in 1787 and by combining this conception with the principles of eighteenth-century natural law, he was able to make of the contract clause a mighty instrument for the protection of the rights of private property." [4]

Modification of Marshall's Contract Doctrines

Subsequent decisions of the Court modified Marshall's position. His attempt to extend the clause to protect future as well as past contracts from state laws that might impair them met with defeat in *Ogden* v. *Saunders,* 12 Wheat. 213 (1827). The Court held that a state law could not alter the terms of contracts entered into before the statute was passed but that such a law could regulate the provisions of contracts entered into in the future. For the first and only time in his judicial career, Marshall dissented on a question of constitutional law. With the decision in *Ogden* v. *Saunders,* further expansion of the contract clause as a curb on state legislation came to an end. If the case had come before the Court a few years earlier, Marshall "might have had his way and made the obligation of contract as inclusive as the later interpretation of liberty of contract under the due process clause. But by 1827 a majority of the Court was unwilling to go so far, and the first great restriction upon the scope of the clause was set forth over the stout opposition of the Chief Justice." [5]

Marshall's doctrines were limited further by the Taney Court, principally in the famous case of *Charles River Bridge Co.* v. *Warren Bridge Co.* (p. 220).

Although Marshall's contract concepts were modified by the Taney Court, they were not abandoned. The contract clause continued to be invoked for the defense of property rights in a great number of cases until 1890. In fact, the clause reached its highest point of importance during the great industrial

[3] Albert J. Beveridge, *The Life of John Marshall* (Boston: Houghton Mifflin, 1919), Vol. 4, p. 276.

[4] Benjamin F. Wright, *The Contract Clause of the Constitution* (Cambridge, Mass.: Harvard U.P., 1938), p. 28.

[5] Ibid., p. 52.

era following the Civil War. But after 1890, the contract clause as an instrument for the protection of private rights declined in significance. This decline was due principally to the expansion of the due process clause of the Fourteenth Amendment as an even more important vehicle for the protection of vested economic interests.

> The displacement of the contract clause by due process of law is but an incident in the continuous development of an idea. The former clause had become too circumscribed by judicially created or permitted limitations, and its place was gradually taken by another clause where the absence of restrictive precedent allowed freer play to judicial discretion. [But] the decline of the contract clause after 1890 cannot be taken as an indication that old-style conceptual individualism based on contract was dead. The battle was to be fought with a newer and a more deadly weapon. The contract clause was to become merely a technical provision to be applied to varying situations in the light of well-established precedents. In terms of specific cases its application did not, on that account, become less important. But is ceased to be the vehicle which conveyed new bodies of ideas into the law of the Constitution.[6]

The most important modern contract case is *Home Building and Loan Association* v. *Blaisdell,* (p. 223), decided during the depression. The Court allowed the state's police power to make certain inroads on contract rights, even though the contract clause was designed by the framers to prevent just such state laws as the one at issue in the *Blaisdell* case.

It is often assumed that the *Home Building and Loan* case ended the relevance of the contract clause. Actually, the Court has continued to hear abridgment of contract cases and occasionally decides them in favor of the property holder. [See *Allied Structural Steel Co.* v. *Spannaus,* 438 U.S. 234 (1978).] *El Paso* v. *Simmons,* 379 U.S. 497 (1965) indicates that the Court is not prepared to read the contract clause in a way that is very restrictive to state authority. *United States Trust Co. v. New Jersey,* 431 U.S. 1 (1977), a 4-to-3 opinion, suggests that the Court will be more likely to intervene when the state seeks to alter a contract to which it itself is one of the contracting parties than when the contract is between two private parties.

THE TRUSTEES OF DARTMOUTH COLLEGE *v.* WOODWARD
4 Wheat. 518; 4 L Ed. 629 (1819)

[Dartmouth College was granted a charter by the English Crown in 1769. The charter created a board of trustees of twelve members who were empowered to govern the affairs of the new college. The founder and first president of the college died in 1779, whereupon his son, John Wheelock, became president. However, Wheelock was removed from the presidency by the board of trustees after numerous unpleasant conflicts that attracted statewide attention. The two political parties in the state were also drawn into the controversy, the Federalists supporting the trustees while the Jeffersonians sided with Wheelock. In 1816, the Republican majority in the state legislature enacted three laws that amended

[6] Ibid., p. 258.

the original charter and provided for a new governing body for the institution, whose name was changed to Dartmouth University. The old trustees refused to be governed by the new law and continued to run the college with the support of loyal members of the faculty and the majority of the student body. The new "state" trustees appointed by the Governor "removed" the old trustees and reelected Wheelock to the presidency.

The old board of trustees contended that the 1816 legislation impaired the obligation of contract contained in the original charter of 1769 and brought an action in the state courts to recover possession of the college charter, records, seal, and accounts from Woodward, the secretary of the new board. (Woodward had been secretary and treasurer of the original college, but he had sided with the Wheelock faction in the dispute.) The state courts ruled against the college. The old trustees then took the case to the Supreme Court on a writ of error, and Daniel Webster argued with "emotional eloquence" in behalf of the college from which he had graduated.]

The opinion of the Court was delivered by MR. CHIEF JUSTICE MARSHALL:

. . . It can require no argument to prove that the circumstances of this case constitute a contract. An application is made to the Crown for a charter to incorporate a religious and literary institution. In the application, it is stated that large contributions have been made for the object, which will be conferred on the corporation, as soon as it shall be created. The charter is granted, and on its faith the property is conveyed. Surely in this transaction every ingredient of a complete and legitimate contract is to be found.

The points for consideration are,

1. Is this contract protected by the Constitution of the United States?

2. Is it impaired by the acts under which the defendant holds?

1. . . . The parties in this case differ less on general principles, less on the true construction of the Constitution in the abstract, than on the application of those principles to this case, and on the true construction of the charter of 1769. This is the point on which the case essentially depends. If the act of incorporation be a grant of political power, if it create a civil institution to be employed in the administration of the government, or if the funds of the college be public property, or if the State of New Hampshire, as a government, be alone interested in its transaction, the subject is one in which the legislature of the State may act according to its own judgment, unrestrained by any limitation of its power imposed by the Constitution of the United States.

But if this be a private eleemosynary institution, endowed with a capacity to take property for objects unconnected with government, whose funds are bestowed by individuals on the faith of the charter; if the donors have stipulated for the future disposition and management of those funds in the manner prescribed by themselves; there may be more difficulty in the case, although neither the persons who have made these stipulations, nor those for whose benefit they were made, should be parties to the cause. Those who are no longer interested in the property may yet retain such an interest in the preservation of their own arrangements as to have a right to insist that those arrangements shall be held sacred. Or, if they have themselves disappeared, it becomes a subject of serious and anxious inquiry, whether those whom they have legally empowered to represent them forever, may not assert all the rights which they possessed while in being; whether, if they be without personal representatives who may feel injured by a violation of the compact, the trustees be not so completely their representatives in the eye of the law as to stand in their place, not only as respects the government of the college, but also as respect the maintenance of the college charter.

It becomes then the duty of the Court most seriously to examine this charter, and to ascertain its true character.

. . . A corporation is an artifical being, invisible, intangible, and existing only in contemplation of law. Being the mere creature of law, it possesses only those properties which the charter of its creation confers upon it, either expressly, or as incidental to its very existence. These are such as are supposed best calculated to effect the object for which it was created. Among the most important are immortality, and, if the expression may be allowed, individuality; properties, by which a perpetual succession of many persons are considered as the same, and may act as a single individual. They enable a corporation to manage its own affairs, and to hold property without the perplexing intricacies, the hazardous and endless necessity, of perpetual conveyances for the purpose of transmitting it from hand to hand. It is chiefly for the purpose of clothing bodies of men, in succession, with these qualities and capacities, that corporations were invented, and are in use. By these means, a perpetual succession of individuals are capable of acting for the promotion of the particular object, like one immortal being. . . .

The objects for which a corporation is created are universally such as the government wishes to promote. They are deemed beneficial to the country; and this benefit constitutes the consideration, and, in most cases, the sole consideration of the grant. In most eleemosynary institutions, the object would be difficult, perhaps unattainable, without the aid of a charter of incorporation. Charitable, or public-spirited individuals, desirous of making permanent appropriations for charitable or other useful purposes, find it impossible to effect their design securely, and certainly, without an incorporating act. They apply to the government, state their beneficent object, and offer to advance the money necessary for its accomplishment, provided the government will confer on the instrument which is to execute their designs the capacity to execute them. . . .

[I]t appears, that Dartmouth College is an eleemosynary institution, incorporated for the purpose of perpetuating the application of the bounty of the donors, to the specified objects of that bounty; that its trustees or governors were originally named by the founder, and invested with the power of perpetuating themselves; that they are not public officers, nor is it a civil institution, participating in the administration of government; but a charity school, or a seminary of education, incorporated for the preservation of its property, and the perpetual application of that property to the objects of its creation. . . .

This is plainly a contract to which the donors, the trustees, and the Crown (to whose rights and obligations New Hampshire succeeds) were the original parties. It is a contract made on a valuable consideration. It is a contract for the security and disposition of property. It is a contract, on the faith of which real and personal estate has been conveyed to the corporation. It is then a contract within the letter of the Constitution, and within its spirit also, unless the fact that the property is invested by the donors in trustees for the promotion of religion and education, for the benefit of persons who are perpetually changing, though the objects remain the same, shall create a particular exception, taking this case out of the prohibition contained in the Constitution.

It is more than possible, that the preservation of rights of this description was not particularly in the view of the framers of the Constitution, when the clause under consideration was introduced into that instrument. It is probable, that interferences of more frequent recurrence, to which the temptation was stronger, and of which the mischief was more extensive, constituted the great motive for imposing this restriction on the State legislatures. But although a particular and a rare case may not, in itself, be of sufficient magnitude to induce a rule, yet it must be governed by the rule, when established, unless some plain and strong reason for excluding it can be given. It is not enough to say, that this particular case was not in the mind of the Convention, when the article was framed, nor of the American people, when it was adopted. It is necessary to go farther, and to say that, had this particular case been suggested, the language would have been so varied as to exclude it, or it would have been made a special exception. The case being within the words of the rule, must be within its operation likewise, unless there be something in the literal construction so obviously absurd, or mischievous, or repugnant to the general spirit of the instrument, as to justify those who expound the Constitution in making it an exception. . . .

The opinion of the Court, after mature

deliberation, is that this is a contract, the obligation of which cannot be impaired without violating the Constitution of the United States. This opinion appears to us to be equally supported by reason, and by the former decision of this Court.

2. We next proceed to the inquiry, whether its obligation has been impaired by those acts of the legislature of New Hampshire, to which the special verdict refers.

From the review of this charter which has been taken, it appears that the whole power of governing the college, of appointing and removing tutors, of fixing their salaries, of directing the course of study to be pursued by the students, and of filling up vacancies created in their own body, was vested in the trustees. On the part of the Crown it was expressly stipulated that this corporation, thus constituted, should continue forever; and that the number of trustees should forever consist of twelve, and no more. By this contrast the Crown was bound, and could have made no violent alteration in its essential terms, without impairing its obligation.

By the Revolution, the duties, as well as the powers, of government devolved on the people of New Hampshire. It is admitted that among the latter was comprehended the transcendent power of parliament, as well as that of the executive department. It is too clear to require the support of argument, that all contracts and rights respecting property remained unchanged by the revolution. The obligations then, which were created by the charter to Dartmouth College, were the same in the new, that they had been in the old government. The power of the government was also the same. A repeal of this charter at any time prior to the adoption of the present constitution of the United States would have been an extraordinary and unprecedented act of power, but one which could have been contested only by the restrictions upon the legislature to be found in the constitution of the State. But the Constitution of the United States has imposed this additional limitation, that the legislature of a State shall pass no act "impairing the obligation of contracts."

It has been already stated, that the act "to amend the charter, and enlarge and improve the corporation of Dartmouth College," increases the number of trustees to twenty-one, gives the appointment of the additional members to the executive of the State, and creates a board of overseers, to consist of twenty-five persons, of whom twenty-one are also appointed by the executive of New Hampshire, who have power to inspect and control the most important acts of the trustees.

On the effect of this law, two opinions cannot be entertained. Between acting directly, and acting through the agency of trustees and overseers, no essential difference is perceived. The whole power of governing the college is transferred from trustees appointed according to the will of the founder, expressed in the charter, to the executive of New Hampshire. The management and application of the funds of this eleemosynary institution, which are placed by the donors in the hands of trustees named in the charter, and empowered to perpetuate themselves, are placed by this act under the control of the government of the State. The will of the State is substituted for the will of the donors in every essential operation of the college. This is not an immaterial change. The founders of the college contracted, not merely for the perpetual application of the funds which they gave, to the objects for which those funds were given; they contracted also, to secure that application by the constitution of the corporation. They contracted for a system which should, as far as human foresight can provide, retain forever the government of the literary institution they had formed, in the hands of persons approved by themselves. This system is totally changed. The charter of 1769 exists no longer. It is reorganized; and reorganized in such a manner as to convert a literary institution, moulded according to the will of its founders, and placed under the control of private literary men, into a machine entirely subservient to the will of government. This may be for the advantage of literature in general; but it is not according to the will of the donors, and is subversive of that contract, on the faith of which their property was given. . . .

It results from this opinion, that the acts of the legislature of New Hampshire, which are stated in the special verdict found in this cause, are repugnant to the Constitution of the United States; and that the judgment on this special verdict ought to have been for the plaintiffs. The judgment of the State Court must, therefore, be

Reversed.

[Mr. Justice Washington and Mr. Justice Story delivered separate concurring opinions. Mr. Justice Duvall dissented.]

CHARLES RIVER BRIDGE CO. *v.* WARREN BRIDGE CO.
11 Pet. 420; 9 L. Ed. 773 (1837)

[To overcome the inconvenience of transportation by ferries, the Massachusetts legislature, in 1785, granted the Charles River Bridge Company a charter to construct a bridge between Charlestown and Boston with the power to collect tolls for forty years (later extended to seventy years). This franchise replaced an exclusive ferry right granted to Harvard College in 1650; provision was made for compensating Harvard for the impairment of its ferry franchise. The Charles River Bridge was built at considerable financial risk, but it proved to be an extremely profitable venture. However, the management of the bridge monopoly became involved in party politics, and in 1828 the state legislature authorized the Warren Bridge Company to construct another bridge very close to the old one. On the Boston side the bridges were to be 825 feet apart, whereas on the Charlestown side the distance between them was to be only 264 feet. No tolls were to be charged on the new bridge as soon as its construction had been paid for or at the end of a maximum period of six years. The Charles River Bridge Company sought an injunction to prevent the erection of the Warren bridge and then, after the bridge was built, for general relief, contending that the legislature, in authorizing the new bridge, violated the contract clause of the Constitution. The Massachusetts supreme court rejected the plaintiff company's bill for an injunction and other relief. The case then went to the Supreme Court on a writ of error.]

MR. CHIEF JUSTICE TANEY delivered the opinion of the Court:

The questions involved in this case are of the gravest character, and the court has given to them the most anxious and deliberate consideration. The value of the right claimed by the plaintiffs is large in amount; and many persons may no doubt be seriously affected in their pecuniary interests by any decision which the court may pronounce; and the questions which have been raised as to the power of the several states, in relation to the corporations they have chartered, are pregnant with important consequences; not only to the individuals who are concerned in the corporate franchises, but to the communities in which they exist. . . .

The plaintiffs in error insist, mainly upon two grounds: First. That by virtue of the grant of 1650, Harvard College was entitled, in perpetuity, to the right of keeping a ferry between Charleston and Boston; that this right was exclusive; and that the legislature had not the power to establish another ferry on the same line of travel, because it would infringe the rights of the college; and that these rights, upon the erection of the bridge in the place of the ferry, under the charter of 1785, were transferred to, and became vested in "the proprietors of the Charles River bridge"; and that under, and by virtue of this transfer of the ferry right, the rights of the bridge company were as exclusive in that line of travel, as the rights of the ferry. Second. That independently of the ferry right, the acts of the legislature of Massachusetts of 1785, and 1792, by their true construction, necessarily implied that the legislature would not authorize another bridge, and especially a free one, by the side of this, and placed in the same line of travel, whereby the franchise granted to "the proprietors of the Charles River bridge" should be rendered of no value; and the plaintiffs in error contend, that the grant of the ferry to the college, and of the charter to the proprietors of the bridge, are both contracts on the part of the state; and that the law authorizing the erection of the Warren bridge in 1828, impairs the obligation of one or both of these contracts. . . .

But upon what ground can the plaintiffs in error contend that the ferry rights of the college have been transferred to the proprietors of the bridge? If they have been thus transferred, it must be by some mode of transfer known to the law; and the evidence relied on to prove it, can be pointed out in the record. How was it transferred? It is not suggested that there ever was, in a point of fact, a deed of conveyance executed by the college to the bridge company. Is there any evidence in the record from which such a conveyance may, upon legal principle, be presumed? The testimony before the court, so far from laying the foundation for such a presumption, repels it in the most positive terms. The petition to the legislature, in 1785, on which the charter was granted, does not suggest an assignment, nor any agreement or consent on the part of the college; and the petitioners do not appear to have regarded the wishes of that institution, as by any means necessary to ensure their success. They place their application entirely on considerations of public interest and public convenience, and the superior advantages of a communication across Charles River by a bridge, instead of a ferry. . . .

This brings us to the act of the legislature of Massachusetts, of 1785, by which the plaintiffs were incorporated by the name of "The Proprietors of the Charles River Bridge"; and it is here, and in the law of 1792, prolonging their charter, that we must look for the extent and nature of the franchise conferred upon the plaintiffs.

Much has been said in the argument of the principles of construction by which this law is to be expounded, and what undertakings, on the part of the state may be implied. The court think there can be no serious difficulty on that head. It is the grant of certain franchises by the public to a private corporation, and in a matter where the public interest is concerned. The rule of construction in such cases is well settled, both in England, and by the decisions of our tribunals. . . . "[T]he rule of construction in all such cases, is now fully established to be this—that any ambiguity in the terms of the contract, must operate against the adventurers, and in favor of the public, and the plaintiffs can claim nothing that is not clearly given them by the act.". . .

[T]he object and end of all government is to promote the happiness and prosperity of the community by which it is established; and it can never be assumed, that the government intended to diminish its power of accomplishing the end for which it was created. And in a country like ours, free, active, and enterprising, continually advancing in number and wealth; new channels of communication are daily found necessary, both for travel and trade; and are essential to the comfort, convenience, and prosperity of the people. A state ought never to be presumed to surrender this power, because, like the taxing power, the whole community have an interest in preserving it undiminished. And when a corporation alleges, that a state has surrendered for seventy years, its power of improvement and public accommodation, in a great and important line of travel, along which a vast number of its citizens must daily pass; the community have a right to insist . . . "that its abandonment ought not to be presumed, in a case, in which the deliberate purpose of the state to abandon it does not appear." The continued existence of a government would be of no great value, if by implications and presumptions, it was disarmed of the powers necessary to accomplish the ends of its creation; and the functions it was designed to perform, transferred to the hands of privileged corporations. . . . No one will question that the interests of the great body of the people of the state, would, in this instance, be affected by the surrender of this great line of travel to a single corporation, with the right to exact toll, and exclude competition for seventy years. While the rights of private property are sacredly guarded, we must not forget that the community also have rights, and that the happiness and well-being of every citizen depends on their faithful preservation.

Adopting the rule of construction above stated as the settled one, we proceed to apply it to the charter of 1785, to the proprietors of the Charles River bridge. This act of incorporation is in the usual form, and the privileges such as are commonly given to corporations of that kind. It confers on them the ordinary faculties of a corporation, for the purpose of building the bridge; and establishes certain rates of toll, which the company are authorized to take. This is the whole grant. There is no exclusive privilege given to them over the waters of Charles River, above or below their bridge. No right to erect another bridge themselves, nor to prevent other persons from erecting one. No engagement from the state, that another shall not be erected; and no undertaking not to sanction competition, nor to make improvements that may diminish the amount of its income. Upon all these subjects the charter is silent; and nothing is said in it about a line of travel, so much insisted on in the argument, in which they are to have exclusive privileges. No words are used, from which an intention to grant any of these rights can be inferred. If the plaintiff is entitled to them, it must be implied, simply, from the nature of the grant; and cannot be inferred, from the words by which the grant is made.

The relative position of the Warren bridge has already been described. It does not interrupt the passage over the Charles River bridge, nor make the way to it or from it less convenient. None of the faculties or franchises granted to that corporation, have been revoked by the legislature; and its right to take the tolls granted by the charter remains unaltered. In short, all the franchises and rights of property enumerated in the charter, and there mentioned to have been granted to it, remain unimpaired. But its income is destroyed by the Warren bridge; which, being free, draws off the passengers and property which would have gone over it, and renders their franchise of no value. This is the gist of the complaint. For it is not pretended, that the erection of the Warren bridge would have done them any injury, or in any degree affected their right of property; if it had not diminished the amount of their tolls. In order then to entitle themselves to relief, it is necessary to show, that the legislature contracted not to do the act of which they complain; and that they impaired, or in other words violated that contract by the erection of the Warren bridge.

The inquiry then is, does the charter contain such a contract on the part of the state? Is there any such stipulation to be found in that instrument? It must be admitted on all hands, that there is none—no words that even relate to another bridge, or to the diminution of their tolls, or to the line of travel. If a contract on that subject can be gathered from the charter, it must be by implication; and cannot be found in the words used. Can such an agreement be implied? The rule of construction before stated is an answer to the question. In charters of this description, no rights are taken from the public, or given to the corporation, beyond those which the words of the charter, by their natural and proper construction, purport to convey. There are no words which import such a contract as the plaintiffs in error contended for, and none can be implied. . . .

Indeed, the practice and usage of almost every state in the Union, old enough to have commenced the work of internal improvement, is opposed to the doctrine contended for on the part of the plaintiffs in error. Turnpike roads have been made in succession, on the same line of travel; the later ones interfering materially with the profits of the first. These corporations have, in some instances, been utterly ruined by the introduction of newer and better modes of transportation, and travelling. In some cases, railroads have rendered the turnpike roads on the same line of travel so entirely useless, that the franchise of the turnpike corporation is not worth preserving.

Yet in none of these cases have the corporations supposed that their privileges were invaded, or any contract violated on the part of the state. Amid the multitude of cases which have occurred, and have been daily occurring for the last forty or fifty years, this is the first instance in which such an implied contract has been contended for, and this court called upon to infer it from an ordinary act of incorporation, containing nothing more than the usual stipulations and provisions to be found in every such law. The absence of any such controversy, when there must have been so many occasions to give rise to it, proves that neither states, nor individuals, nor corporations, ever imagined that such a contract could be implied from such charters. It shows that the men who voted for these laws, never imagined that they were forming such a contract; and if we maintain that they have made it, we must create it by a legal fiction, in opposition to the truth of the fact, and the obvious intention of the party. We cannot deal thus with the rights reserved to the states; and by legal intendments and mere technical reasoning, take away from them any portion of that power over their own internal police and improvement, which is so necessary to their well-being and prosperity. . . .

The judgment of the supreme judicial court of the commonwealth of Massachusetts, dismissing the plaintiffs' bill, must, therefore, be affirmed, with costs.

[Mr. Justice Mc Lean wrote an opinion urging that the bill be dismissed for lack of jurisdiction. He believed, however, that the plaintiffs' claim had merit.]

MR. JUSTICE STORY, dissenting:

. . . I maintain, that, upon the principles of common reason and legal interpretation, the present grant carries with it a necessary implication that the legislature shall do no act to destroy or essentially to impair the franchise; that (as one of the learned judges of the state court expressed it), there is an implied agreement of the state to grant the undisturbed use of the bridge and its tolls, so far as respects any acts of its own, or of any persons acting under its authority. In other words, the state, impliedly, contracts not to resume its grants, or to do any act to the prejudice or destruction of its grant. I maintain, that there is no authority or principle established in relation to the construction of crown grants, or legislative grants; which does not concede and justify this doctrine. Where the thing is given, the incidents, without which it cannot be enjoyed, are also given. . . . I maintain that a different doctrine is utterly repugnant to all the principles of the common law, applicable to all franchises of a like nature; and that we must overturn some of the best securities of the rights of property, before it can be established. . . . I maintain, that under the principles of the common law, there exists no more right in the legislature of Massachusetts, to erect the Warren bridge, to the ruin of the franchise of the Charles River bridge, than exists to transfer the latter to the former, or to authorize the former to demolish the latter. If the legislature does not mean in its grant to give any exclusive rights, let it say so, expressly; directly; and in terms admitting of no misconstruction. . . .

My judgment is formed upon the terms of the grant, its nature and objects, its design and duties; and, in its interpretation, I seek for no new principles, but I apply such as are as old as the very rudiments of the common law. . . .

Upon the whole, my judgment is, that the act of the legislature of Massachusetts granting the charter of Warren bridge, is an act impairing the obligation of the prior contract and grant to the proprietors of Charles River bridge; and, by the Constitution of the United States, it is therefore utterly void. I am for reversing the decree of the state court (dismissing the bill); and for remanding the cause to the state court for further proceedings, as to law and justice shall appertain.

[Mr. Justice Thompson concurred in this opinion.]

HOME BUILDING AND LOAN ASSOCIATION *v.* BLAISDELL
290 U.S. 398; 54 Sup. Ct. 231; 78 L. Ed. 413 (1934)

[Blaisdell and his wife owned some property in Minneapolis that they had mortgaged to the Home Building and Loan Association, the appellant. The loan company foreclosed the mortgage by reason of appellees' default. Blaisdell and his wife then sought to extend the date of redemption under the terms of the Minnesota Mortgage Moratorium Act,

which had been passed in 1933. That law provided procedures for temporarily extending the time for the redemption of real property from foreclosures and sale during the emergency produced by the economic depression. Upon Blaisdell's application, a county court extended the period of redemption from May 2, 1933, to May 1, 1935. The county court granted the extension on condition that the appellees pay a certain amount each month through the extended period to cover taxes, insurance, interest, and mortgage indebtedness. The Supreme Court of Minnesota affirmed the judgment and upheld the statute. The loan company then appealed to the Supreme Court, contending that the Minnesota law violated the contract clause and the due process and equal protection clauses of the Fourteenth Amendment.]

MR. CHIEF JUSTICE HUGHES delivered the opinion of the Court:

. . . The state court upheld the statute as an emergency measure. Although conceding that the obligations of the mortgage contract were impaired, the court decided that what it thus described as an impairment was, notwithstanding the contract clause of the Federal Constitution, within the police power of the State as that power was called into exercise by the public economic emergency which the legislature had found to exist. Attention is thus directed to the preamble and first section of the statute, which described the existing emergency in terms that were deemed to justify the temporary relief which the statute affords. The state court, declaring that it could not say that this legislative finding was without basis, supplemented that finding by its own statement of conditions of which it took judical notice. The court said: "In addition to the weight to be given the determination of the legislature that an economic emergency exists which demands relief, the court must take notice of other considerations. The members of the legislature come from every community of the state and from all the walks of life. They are familiar with conditions generally in every calling, occupation, profession, and business in the state. Not only they, but the courts must be guided by what is common knowledge. It is common knowledge that in the last few years land values have shrunk enormously. Loans made a few years ago upon the basis of the then going values cannot possibly be replaced on the basis of present values. We all know that when this law was enacted the large financial companies, which had made it their business to invest in mortgages, had ceased to do so. No bank would directly or indirectly loan on real estate mortgages. Life-insurance companies, large investors in such mortgages, had even declared a moratorium as to the loan provisions of their policy contracts. The President had closed banks temporarily. The Congress, in addition to many extraordinary measures looking to the relief of the economic emergency, had passed an act to supply funds whereby mortgagors may be able within a reasonable time to refinance their mortgages or redeem from sales where the redemption has not expired. With this knowledge the court cannot well hold that the legislature had no basis in fact for the conclusion that an economic emergency existed which called for the exercise of the police power to grant relief."

In determining whether the provision for this temporary and conditional relief exceeds the power of the State by reason of the clause in the Federal Constitution prohibiting impairment of the obligations of contracts, we must consider the relation of emergency to constitutional power, the historical setting of the contract clause, the development of the jurisprudence of this Court in the construction of that clause, and the principles of construction which we may consider to be established.

Emergency does not create power. Emergency does not increase granted power or remove or diminish the restrictions imposed upon power granted or reserved. The Constitution was adopted in a period of grave emergency. Its grants of power to the Federal Government and its limitations of the power of the States were determined in the light of emergency and they are not altered by emergency. What power was thus granted and what limitations were thus imposed are questions which have always been, and always will be, the subject of close examination under our constitutional system.

While emergency does not create power, emergency may furnish the occasion for the exercise of power. . . . The constitutional question presented in the light of an emergency is whether the power possessed embraces the particular exercise of it in response to particular conditions. Thus, the war power of the Federal Government is not created by the emergency of war, but it is a power given to meet that emergency. It is a power to wage war successfully, and thus it permits the harnessing of the entire energies of the people in a supreme cooperative effort to preserve the nation. But even the war power does not remove constitutional limitations safeguarding essential liberties. When the provisions of the Constitution, in grant or restriction, are specific, so particularized as not to admit of construction, no question is presented. Thus, emergency would not permit a State to have more than two Senators in the Congress, or permit the election of the President by a general popular vote without regard to the number of electors to which the States are respectively entitled, or permit the States to "coin money" or to "make anything but gold and silver coin a tender in payment of debts." But where constitutional grants and limitations of power are set forth in general clauses, which afford a broad outline, the process of construction is essential to fill in the details. That is true of the contract clause. . . .

In the construction of the contract clause, the debates in the Constitutional Convention are of little aid. But the reasons which led to the adoption of that clause, and of the other prohibitions of Section 10 of Article I, are not left in doubt and have frequently been described with eloquent emphasis. The widespread distress following the Revolutionary period, and the plight of debtors, had called forth in the States an ignoble array of legislative schemes for the defeat of creditors and the invasion of contractual obligations. Legislative interferences had been so numerous and extreme that the confidence essential to prosperous trade had been undermined and the utter destruction of credit was threatened. . . .

But full recognition of the occasion and general purpose of the clause does not suffice to fix its precise scope. Nor does an examination of the details of prior legislation in the States yield criteria which can be considered controlling. To ascertain the scope of the constitutional prohibition we examine the course of judicial decisions in its application. These put it beyond question that the prohibition is not an absolute one and is not to be read with literal exactness like a mathematical formula. . . .

The inescapable problems of construction have been: What is a contract? What are the obligations of contracts? What constitutes impairment of these obligations? What residuum of power is there still in the States in relation to the operation of contracts, to protect the vital interests of the community? Questions of this character, "of no small nicety and intricacy, have vexed the legislative halls, as well as the judicial tribunals, with an uncounted variety and frequency of litigation and speculation."

. . . Not only is the constitutional provision qualified by the measure of control which the State retains over remedial processes, but the State also continues to possess authority to safeguard the vital interests of its people. It does not matter that legislation appropriate to that end "has the result of modifying or abrogating contracts already in effect." . . . Not only are existing laws read into contracts in order to fix obligations as between the parties, but the reservation of essential attributes of sovereign power is also read into contracts as a postulate of the legal order. The policy of protecting contracts against impairment presupposes the maintenance of a government by virtue of which contractual relations are worthwhile—a government which retains adequate authority to secure the peace and good order of society. This principle of harmonizing the constitutional prohibition with the necessary residuum of state power has had progressive recognition in the decisions of this Court. . . .

The legislature cannot "bargain away the public health or the public morals." Thus, the constitutional provision against the impairment of contracts was held not to be violated by an amendment of the state constitution which put an end to a lottery theretofore authorized by the legislature. *Stone* v. *Mississippi,* 101 U.S. 814. . . . The lottery was a valid enterprise when established under express state authority, but the legislature in the public interest could put a stop to it. A similar rule has been applied to the control by the State of the sale of intoxicating liquors. . . . The States retain adequate power to protect the public health against the maintenance of nuisances despite insistence upon existing contracts. . . . Legislation to protect the public safety comes within the same category of reserved power. . . . This principle has had recent and noteworthy application to the regulation of the use of public highways by common carriers and "contract carriers," where the assertion of interference with existing contract rights has been without avail. . . .

The argument is pressed that in the cases we have cited the obligation of contracts was affected only incidentally. This argument proceeds upon a misconception. The question is not whether the legislative action affects contracts incidentally, or directly or indirectly, but whether the legislation is addressed to a legitimate end and the measures taken are reasonable and appropriate to that end. Another argument, which comes more closely to the point, is that the state power may be addressed directly to the prevention of the enforcement of contracts only when these are of a sort which the legislature in its discretion may denounce as being in themselves hostile to public morals, or public health, safety, or welfare, or where the prohibition is merely of injurious practices; that interference with the enforcement of other and valid contracts according to appropriate legal procedure, although the interference is temporary and for a public purpose, is not permissible. This is but to contend that in the latter case the end is not legitimate in the view that it cannot be reconciled with a fair interpretation of the constitutional provision.

Undoubtedly, whatever is reserved of state power must be consistent with the fair intent of the constitutional limitation of that power. The reserved power cannot be construed so as to destroy the limitation, nor is the limitation to be construed to destroy the reserved power in its essential aspects. They must be construed in harmony with each other. This principle precludes a construction which would permit the State to adopt as its policy the repudiation of debts or the destruction of contracts or the denial of means to enforce them. But it does not follow that conditions may not arise in which a temporary restraint of enforcement may be consistent with the spirit and purpose of the constitutional provision and thus be found to be within the range of the reserved power of the State to protect the vital interests of the community. It cannot be maintained that the constitutional prohibition should be so construed as to prevent limited and temporary interpositions with respect to the enforcement of contracts if made necessary by a great public calamity such as fire, flood, or earthquake. . . . The reservation of state power appropriate to such extraordinary conditions may be deemed to be as much a part of all contracts, as is the reservation of state power to protect the public interest in the other situations to which we have referred. And if state power exists to give temporary relief from the enforcement of contracts in the presence of disasters due to physical causes such as fire, flood, or earthquake, that power cannot be said to be nonexistent when the urgent public need demanding such relief is produced by other and economic causes. . . .

It is manifest . . . that there has been a growing appreciation of public needs and of the necessity of finding ground for a rational compromise between individual rights and public welfare. The settlement and consequent contraction of the public domain, the pressure of a constantly increasing density of population, the interrelation of the activities of our people and the complexity of our economic interests, have inevitably led to an increased use of the organization of society in order to protect the very bases of individual opportunity. Where, in earlier days, it was thought that only the concerns of individuals or of classes were involved, and that those of the State itself were touched only remotely, it has later been found that the fundamental interests of the State are directly affected;

and that the question is no longer merely that of one party to a contract as against another, but of the use of reasonable means to safeguard the economic structure upon which the good of all depends.

It is no answer to say that this public need was not apprehended a century ago, or to insist that what the provision of the Constitution meant to the vision of that day it must mean to the vision of our time. If by the statement that what the Constitution meant at the time of its adoption it means today, it is intended to say that the great clauses of the Constitution must be confined to the interpretation which the framers, with the conditions and outlook of their time, would have placed upon them, the statement carries its own refutation. It was to guard against such a narrow conception that Chief Justice Marshall uttered the memorable warning—"We must never forget that it is a *constitution* we are expounding" *(McCulloch* v. *Maryland)*—"a constitution intended to endure for ages to come, and consequently, to be adapted to the various *crises* of human affairs." . . . When we are dealing with the words of the Constitution, said this Court in *Missouri* v. *Holland,* "we must realize that they have called into life a being the development of which could not have been foreseen completely by the most gifted of its begetters. . . . The case before us must be considered in the light of our whole experience and not merely in that of what was said a hundred years ago."

Nor is it helpful to attempt to draw a fine distinction between the intended meaning of the words of the Constitution and their intended application. When we consider the contract clause and the decisions which have expounded it in harmony with the essential reserved power of the States to protect the security of their peoples, we find no warrant for the conclusion that the clause has been warped by these decisions from its proper significance or that the founders of our Government would have interpreted the clause differently had they had occasion to assume that responsibility in the conditions of the later day. The vast body of law which has been developed was unknown to the fathers, but it is believed to have preserved the essential content and the spirit of the Constitution. With a growing recognition of public needs and the relation of individual right to public security, the court has sought to prevent the perversion of the clause through its use as an instrument to throttle the capacity of the States to protect their fundamental interests. This development is a growth from the seeds which the fathers planted. . . .

Applying the criteria established by our decision we conclude:

1. An emergency existed in Minnesota which furnished a proper occasion for the exercise of the reserved power of the State to protect the vital interests of the community. The declarations of the existence of this emergency by the legislature and by the Supreme Court of Minnesota cannot be regarded as a subterfuge or as lacking in adequate basis. . . .

2. The legislation was addressed to a legitimate end, that is, the legislation was not for the mere advantage of particular individuals but for the protection of a basic interest of society.

3. In view of the nature of the contracts in question—mortgages of unquestionable validity—the relief afforded and justified by the emergency, in order not to contravene the constitutional provision, could only be of a character appropriate to that emergency and could be granted only upon reasonable conditions.

4. The conditions upon which the period of redemption is extended do not appear to be unreasonable. . . .

5. The legislation is temporary in operation. It is limited to the exigency which called it forth. . . .

We are of the opinion that the Minnesota statute as here applied does not violate the contract clause of the Federal Constitution. Whether the legislation is wise or unwise as a matter of policy is a question with which we are not concerned.

What has been said on that point is also applicable to the contention presented under the due process clause . . .

Nor do we think that the statute denies to the appellant the equal protection of the laws. The classification which the statute makes cannot be said to be an arbitrary one. . . .

Judgment

Affirmed.

MR. JUSTICE SUTHERLAND, dissenting:

. . . . A provision of the Constitution, it is hardly necessary to say, does not admit of two distinctly opposite interpretations. It does not mean one thing at one time and an entirely different thing at another time. If the contract impairment clause, when framed and adopted, meant that the terms of a contract for the payment of money could not be altered . . . by a state statute enacted for the relief of hardly pressed debtors to the end and with the effect of postponing payment or enforcement during and because of an economic or financial emergency, it is but to state the obvious to say that it means the same now. . . .

The Minnesota statute either impairs the obligation of contracts or it does not. If it does not, the occasion to which it relates becomes immaterial, since then the passage of the statute is the exercise of a normal, unrestricted, state power and requires no special occasion to render it effective. If it does, the emergency no more furnishes a proper occasion for its exercise than if the emergency were nonexistent. And so, while, in form, the suggested distinction seems to put us forward in a straight line, in reality it simply carries us back in a circle, like bewildered travelers lost in a wood, to the point where we parted company with the view of the state court. . . .

. . . The phrase, "obligation of a contract," in the constitutional sense imports a legal duty to perform the specified obligation of *that* contract, not to substitute and perform, against the will of one of the parties, a different, albeit equally valuable, obligation. And a state, under the contract impairment clause, has no more power to accomplish such a substitution than has one of the parties to the contract against the will of the other. It cannot do so either by acting directly upon the contract, or by bringing about the result under the guise of a statute in form acting only upon the remedy. If it could, the efficacy of the constitutional restriction would, in large measure, be made to disappear. . . .

I am authorized to say that MR. JUSTICE VAN DEVANTER, MR. JUSTICE MCREYNOLDS and MR. JUSTICE BUTLER concur in this opinion.

CHAPTER 8

The States and the Commerce Power

Congress did not have the power to regulate interstate and foreign commerce under the Articles of Confederation. The need for more centralized control over commerce soon became one of the "moving purposes" that brought about the Constitutional Convention in 1787. Article I, Section 8, of the Constitution provides that Congress "shall have power . . . to regulate commerce with foreign nations and among the several states and with Indian tribes." In this brief provision the framers sought to prevent the states from interfering with the regulation of commerce across state lines. They hoped to eliminate "barriers to interstate and foreign trade which the several states had erected for the purpose of collecting toll from business originating in other states or in foreign countries and for the purpose of reserving local business opportunities for the benefit of local businessmen. The commerce clause was one of a number of clauses in the Constitution by which the framers sought to remove local fetters from business and to keep them removed." [1]

[1] Carl B. Swisher, *The Growth of Constitutional Power in the United States* (Chicago: U. of Chicago, 1945), p. 79.

The constitutional meaning of the commerce clause has been developed and expanded by a great number of statutory enactments and through judicial interpretation. As a result, the clause has become one of the most important grants of authority in the Constitution. Justice Stone once said that the "commerce clause and the wise interpretation of it, perhaps more than any other contributing element, have united to bind the several states into a nation." [2] No provision of the Constitution "has been more vitally involved in the development of our national economic life and in the transitions through which our constitutional system has passed." [3] Largely through the use of the commerce power, the national government today regulates almost every conceivable aspect of American life. Of course, other powers of the Federal Government, such as the powers to tax, to spend for the public welfare, and to wage war have been used to expand national authority. Yet the commerce power is used most frequently and continues to expand to immense and fascinating proportions.

As Justice William O. Douglas has noted, the commerce clause "has a negative as well as a positive aspect. The clause not only serves to augment federal authority. By its own force it also cuts down the power of a constituent state in its exercise of what normally would be a part of its residual police power." [4] But the Constitution does not define specific spheres of state and national authority over interstate commerce. Thus, by default, the Supreme Court is given the power to decide finally what the states and the Federal Government may or may not do with respect to interstate commerce. In this process the Court again becomes the referee between the claims of national and local authorities. In choosing between competing interests, the Court thereby involves itself irrevocably in the formulation of fundamental policy in an extremely important area.

The first case under the commerce clause to reach the Supreme Court was *Gibbons* v. *Ogden* (p. 236), which involved an unpopular steamboat monopoly in New York. This first great case involved the negative rather than the positive aspects of the commerce clause. In *Gibbons* v. *Ogden,* John Marshall held simply that a state regulation affecting commerce is invalid when it is in conflict with a law of Congress. In this last of his major decisions, Marshall defined commerce and described the federal commerce power "with a breadth never yet exceeded." His broad view of the commerce power permeates the entire opinion. It made possible the development of commerce under federal, rather than state, control.

Unlike Marshall's other great decisions, the opinion in *Gibbons* v. *Ogden* was greeted with acclaim. He had at last delivered a popular opinion, largely because he had ruled against a monopoly. The public was so satisfied that "they were, for the most part, quiescent as to Marshall's assertion of nationalism in this particular case." [5] And there were important practical effects of *Gibbons* v. *Ogden.*

[2] Harlan F. Stone, "Fifty Years Work of the United States Supreme Court," *American Bar Association Journal,* Vol. 14 (Aug.–Sept. 1928), p. 430.

[3] George L. Haskins, "Marshall and the Commerce Clause of the Constitution," in W. Melville Jones, ed., *Chief Justice John Marshall* (Ithaca, N.Y.: Cornell University Press, 1956), p. 145.

[4] William O. Douglas, *We the Judges* (Garden City, N.Y.: Doubleday, 1956), p. 222.

[5] Albert J. Beveridge, *The Life of John Marshall* (Boston: Houghton, 1919), p. 446.

> Steamboat navigation of American waters increased suddenly at an incredible rate. The opening of the Hudson River and Long Island Sound to the free passage of steamboats gave immediate impetus to the growth of New York as a commercial center, while New England manufacturing was given new life because the transportation of anthracite coal became cheap and easy. From a less immediate standpoint, *Gibbons* v. *Ogden* was the needed guarantee that interstate rail, telephone and telegraph, oil and gas pipe lines might be built across state lines without the threat of local interference from state action. In short, Marshall's opinion was . . . the "emancipation proclamation of American commerce." [6]

In *Gibbons* v. *Ogden,* the Supreme Court did not answer the question as to whether or not the states had concurrent power over interstate commerce. The concurring opinion of Justice William Johnson, Jefferson's first appointee to the Supreme Court, is surprising in that he maintained that Congress had exclusive power over interstate commerce. In that opinion, which ranks as one of Johnson's best, "he was defending before the public his extreme assertion of national power." [7] But although Marshall was inclined to agree with Johnson's view, he was unwilling to hold specifically that the federal power over interstate commerce was exclusive.

Marshall was presented with an opportunity to explain his position more fully in *Willson* v. *Blackbird Creek Marsh Co.,* 2 Pet. 245 (1829). In that case he upheld a Delaware statute, enacted under the state's police power, that authorized the building of a dam across a small but navigable waterway. The dam had been erected in order to drain marshes for the protection of health and the enhancement of property values, but it had been broken by Willson's vessel, sailing under a federal coasting license. Marshall pointed out that Delaware could regulate in this instance, because Congress had not attempted to deal with the local matter involved. Speaking for the Court, he asserted: "We do not think that the act empowering the Blackbird Creek Marsh Company to place a dam across the creek, can, under all the circumstances of the case, be considered as repugnant to the power to regulate commerce in its dormant state, or as being in conflict with any law passed on the subject." But Marshall did not attempt to provide any further explanation of this statement. His decision "plainly implies that the Delaware statute falls outside the ban of the 'dormant' commerce clause, because it is not a regulation of commerce, but of 'police.' State regulations of commerce were one thing; state exercise of the police power quite another. But Marshall hardly furnished us a litmus-paper test for distinguishing one from the other. He gaves us only intimations." [8]

In the absence of a coherently expressed doctrine, the Court continued to be plagued with problems involving the validity of state laws affecting foreign or interstate commerce. The cases decided during much of the Taney era did

[6] Haskins, op. cit., pp. 152–53.

[7] Donald G. Morgan, *Justice William Johnson, the First Dissenter* (Columbia: University of South Carolina Press, 1954), p. 205.

[8] Felix Frankfurter, *The Commerce Clause Under Marshall, Taney and Waite* (Chapel Hill: University of North Carolina Press, 1937), pp. 29–30.

not clarify the state of the law. Instead, the Court vacillated in a confused and muddled way on the extent to which the commerce clause limited regulations of interstate commerce by the state legislatures.[9] Finally, in the classic case of *Cooley* v. *Board of Wardens* (p. 241), the Supreme Court fashioned a new formula that combined the exclusive and concurrent doctrines. The Court held that the commerce power is exclusive with respect to some matters and concurrent with respect to others. The principle of the *Cooley* case is still important. The majority opinion does not constitute a precise, automatic rule for deciding cases. In each case the Court must face the difficult question of whether a particular subject of commercial regulation requires uniform and thus exclusively national control or is so local in character that a state may regulate it unless and until the federal government chooses to do so.

Limitations on the Powers of the States

Decisions of the Supreme Court have made clear the doctrine that the "purpose of the commerce clause was not to preclude all state regulation of commerce crossing state lines but to prevent discrimination and the erection of barriers or obstacles to the free flow of commerce, interstate or foreign." [10] Actually, the states have passed very little legislation that is designed principally for the purpose of regulating interstate commerce. But much state legislation concerning local matters happens to affect persons or transactions in interstate commerce, and many such acts have been challenged on the ground that they place unconstitutional burdens on interstate commerce.

State burdens on commerce arise primarily out of the exercise of their police and tax powers.

Police Powers of the States. In enacting legislation for the protection of the health, safety, morals, and welfare of its inhabitants, a state may sometimes impose burdens on or affect interstate commerce. Ever since *Willson* the Court has struggled to announce clear doctrinal rules incorporating two fundamental ideas. The first is that a state statute whose purpose is to erect trade barriers between the states is unconstitutional. [*Maryland* v. *Louisiana,* 101 S.Ct. 2114 (1981).] The second is that, no matter what its purpose, a state statute that does in fact create substantial impediments to interstate trade is unconstitutional. Conversely a state statute designed to protect legitimate state interests and whose impediment to interstate commerce is economically slight is constitutional. The Court often uses the language of "unreasonable" or "direct burden" versus "indirect" or "incidental effect" on interstate commerce to express these ideas. Since the 1930s it has usually spoken more openly of balancing legitimate state purposes against adverse impact on interstate commerce. [See e.g. *Cities*

[9] *Mayor of New York* v. *Miln,* 11 Pet. 102 (1837); *License Cases,* 5 How. 504 (1847); *Passenger Cases,* 7 How. 283 (1849).

[10] Justice Stone dissenting in *Di Santo* v. *Pennsylvania,* 273 U.S. 34 (1927).

Service Co. v. *Peerless Co.,* 340 U.S. 179 (1950); *Minnesota* v. *Cloverleaf Creamery Co.,* 101 S.Ct. 715 (1981).]

Two leading cases that illustrate the issues are *Parker* v. *Brown,* 317 U.S. 341(1943) and *Hood* v. *DuMond,* 336 U.S. 525 (1949). *Parker* involved a California program to restrict the sale by farmers and maintain the price of raisins, a major crop of the state. Although most of the locally grown and sold raisins eventually were bound for interstate commerce, the Court upheld the state regulation—but largely because it harmonized with federal agricultural price-support schemes. In *Hood,* a Massachusetts milk firm seeking additional supplies for its Boston market sought to expand its milk purchases in the state of New York. The New York Commisioner of Agriculture and Markets refused Hood the necessary license under his authority to assure that New York would have adequate supplies of milk for the health of its citizens. He ruled that additional purchases by Hood would reduce the local supply and create destructive competition in the local market. The Court struck down the New York action on the grounds that the very purpose of the commerce clause was to prevent the states from establishing local markets insulated from interstate trade.

State milk regulations provide a good illustration of the Court's problems. In *Dean Milk Co.* v. *City of Madison,* 340 U.S. 349 (1951), the Court struck down a city ordinance requiring that milk be pasteurized in plants within five miles of town, on the grounds that it insulated the Madison market from interstate competition. In *Baldwin* v. *Seelig,* 294 U.S. 511 (1935), the Court struck down a state statute forbidding the sale of out-of-state milk bought at prices lower than the minimums set by the state for its own milk. And in *Polar Ice Cream & Creamery Co.* v. *Andrews,* 375 U.S. 361 (1964), the Court struck down a Florida statute whose effect was to exclude a major portion of the Florida milk market from out-of-state competition. But in *Milk Control Board* v. *Eisenberg Farm Products,* 306 U.S. 346 (1939), the Court upheld a Pennsylvania minimum-price statute aimed at stabilizing the local market—even though the regulation incidentally resulted in requiring New York firms buying in the Pennsylvania market to pay the state-set minimums.

That the task of the Court in resolving the conflict between federal and state authorities remains a difficult one is apparent in the majority and minority opinions in *Southern Pacific Company* v. *Arizona* (p. 244).

Southern Pacific, of course, deals with trains, but state highway regulations also create potential conflicts with interstate commerce. The Court has been particularly receptive to state highway safety regulations even when they impose some burden on interstate commerce. [See *South Carolina Highway Dept.* v. *Barnwell Bros.,* 303 U.S. 177 (1938).] But it struck down an Illinois statute requiring a particular kind of mud guard on truck trailers, when the result of the requirement would have been to interfere seriously with interstate truck operation. [*Bibb* v. *Navajo Freight Lines, Inc.,* 359 U.S. 520 (1959). See also *Kassel* v. *Consolidated Freightways,* 101 S.Ct. 1309 (1981).]

Edwards v. *California* (p. 249) also is concerned with the conflict between state police power and interstate commerce, but the unique facts of this case led four members of the Court to base their decision on grounds other than commerce. The position of the four justices is revealed clearly in Justice Jackson's concurring opinion, which in some ways anticipated the right to travel announced later in *United States* v. *Guest* (see Chapter 6) and *Shapiro* v. *Thompson* (Chapter 14).

In recent years the Court has struck down a number of state actions as violative of the commerce clause. [See e.g. *Pike* v. *Bruce Church, Inc.*, 397 U.S. 137 (1970); *Raymond Motor Transport, Inc.* v. *Rice*, 434 U.S. 429 (1978); *Hughes* v. *Oklahoma*, 441 U.S. 322 (1979); *Lewis* v. *BT Investment Managers, Inc.*, 447 U.S. 27 (1980). Cf. *Exxon Corp.* v. *Maryland*, 437 U.S. 117 (1978).] *Gibbons* itself is replayed in *Douglas* v. *Seacoast Products, Inc.*, 431 U.S. 265 (1977), in which Justice Thurgood Marshall invalidated a Virginia fishing regulation on the grounds that it conflicted with the current version of the federal act for "enrolling and licensing of steamboats" that played so important a role in Chief Justice John Marshall's opinion. Moreover, state environmental protection laws are likely to be challenged in federal courts both on *Gibbons* and *Cooley* grounds. Such laws may conflict with federal statutes. Or they may involve subjects that require uniform national rules. Or they may directly and unreasonably burden interstate commerce.[11] In *Hughes* v. *Alexandria Scrap Corp.*, 426 U.S. 794 (1976), the Court split badly in upholding a Maryland statute under which the state government paid Maryland scrap processors, but not those of other states, a bounty for each old auto body they destroyed. The majority focused on the purpose of the statute, which was to encourage cleaning up the environment. The dissenters argued that by discriminating in favor of its own scrap dealers, Maryland unconstitutionally burdened the interstate market in scrap. In *Philadelphia* v. *New Jersey*, 437 U.S. 617 (1978), the Court dealt with a state statute that prohibited the shipment of out-of-state garbage into the state. New Jersey was seeking to slow the pace at which its wet lands were being turned into garbage dumps. The Court struck down the statute as erecting an unconstitutional barrier to interstate commerce in garbage.

Power of the States to Tax. State tax laws sometimes have an important impact on interstate commerce.

> Forms of state taxation whose tendency is to prohibit the commerce or place it at a disadvantage as compared with or in competition with intrastate commerce, and any state tax which discriminates against the commerce, are familiar examples of the exercise of state taxing power in an unconstitutional manner, because of its obvious regulatory effect upon commerce between the states. But it was not the purpose of the commerce clause to relieve those engaged in interstate commerce of their just

[11] See *Huron Portland Cement Co.* v. *Detroit*, 362 U.S. 440 (1960), upholding a local air pollution regulation but basing itself largely on the now outdated conclusion that air pollution was "peculiarly a matter of state and local concern." See also *Ray* v. *Atlantic Richfield Co.*, 435 U.S. 151 (1978), which strikes down parts of a state statute that sought to regulate super tankers because of their dangers to the environment. Using the *Cooley* rule the Court invoked the supremacy clause against parts of the statute and upheld other parts on the grounds that Congress had not acted and the matters did not require uniform national rules.

> share of state tax burdens, merely because an incidental or consequential effect of the tax is an increase in the cost of doing the business. Not all state taxation is to be condemned because, in some manner, it has an effect upon commerce between the states, and there are many forms of tax whose burdens, when distributed through the play of economic forces, affect interstate commerce which nevertheless fall short of the regulation of the commerce which the Constitution leaves to Congress.[12]

In the early case of *Brown* v. *Maryland,* 12 Wheat. 419 (1827), Chief Justice Marshall held that a state license tax on goods imported from abroad and still in their original packages was void because it was in conflict with the powers of Congress under the commerce clause. The Maryland tax also was said to violate the express clause of the Constitution (Article I, Section 10), which prohibits the states from taxing imports and exports without the consent of Congress. Marshall further noted that "we suppose the principles laid down in this case to apply equally to importations from a sister state." In 1890, in the case of *Leisy* v. *Hardin,* 135 U.S. 100, the original package doctrine was applied to state regulation as well as state taxation of interstate commerce. In Marshall's day importers purchased many kinds of consumer goods in Europe and had them shipped to their home states in huge barrels. Marshall's ruling meant that a state might not tax such goods until the importer opened the barrel and began selling the individual items from it. This was a good, rough and ready test of when the goods had ceased to be in foreign or interstate commerce and had "come to rest" within the state and entered local commerce. But the doctrine is only a rough rule of thumb that cannot be applied precisely. As Justice Cardozo asserted in *Baldwin* v. *Seelig,* 294 U.S. 511 (1935), "the test of the 'original package' is not inflexible and final for the transactions of interstate commerce. . . . It marks a convenient boundary and one sufficiently precise save in exceptional conditions. What is ultimate is the principle that one state in its dealing with another may not place itself in a position of economic isolation."

Perhaps far more important than the original-package doctrine was Marshall's dictum in *Brown* v. *Maryland* that the commerce clause placed broad limitations on the states' powers of taxation.[13]

> At the same time, it has been recognized that the power of the states to tax in order to maintain their governments must not be unduly curtailed and that interstate commerce must pay its way. Hence there has arisen in the field of taxation the same problem of accommodating state and national interests with which Marshall was concerned in the *Ogden* and *Blackbird* cases, and the Court has repeatedly recognized the relevance of those cases to the problem of state taxation.[14]

[12] *McGoldrick* v. *Berwind-White Coal Mining Co.,* 309 U.S. 33 (1940).

[13] The original-package doctrine is no longer applied to state police power regulations of interstate commerce. However, in the field of foreign commerce it is still applied both to prevent the states from taxing imports and from prohibiting imports from abroad under the police powers.

[14] Haskins, op. cit., p. 162.

In general, "despite mechanical or artificial distinctions sometimes taken between the taxes deemed permissible and those condemned, the decisions appear to be predicated on a practical judgment as to the likelihood of the tax being used to place interstate commerce at a competitive disadvantage." [15]

The Court's current test as stated in *Complete Auto Transit, Inc.* v. *Brady,* 430 U.S. 274 (1977) and reaffirmed in *Commonwealth Edison Co.* v. *Montana,* 101 S.Ct. 2946 (1981), is that a state tax does not offend the commerce clause if it "is applied to an activity with a substantial nexus with the taxing State, is fairly apportioned, does not discriminate against interstate commerce, and is fairly related to services provided by the State."

The issues have become quite complex, particularly in relation to state taxes based on gross receipts of interstate corporations operating within their boundaries and property taxes directed at equipment like jet aircraft that are sometimes in one state and sometimes in another. Most of the issues are canvassed in such cases as *Northwestern States Portland Cement Co.* v. *Minnesota,* 358 U.S. 450 (1959); *General Motors Corp.* v. *Washington,* 377 U.S. 436 (1964); *Central R.R.* v. *Pennsylvania,* 370 U.S. 607 (1962); *Exxon Corp.* v. *Wisconsin Dept. of Revenue,* 447 U.S. 207 (1980); and *ASARCO* v. *Idaho,* 50 L.W. 4962 (1982).

GIBBONS *v.* OGDEN
9 Wheat 1; 6 L. Ed. 23 (1824)

[Robert Livingston and Robert Fulton were pioneers in the development of a practical steamboat. In 1807, their vessel made a successful trip from New York to Albany. The next year the New York State legislature granted the two men an exclusive thirty-year franchise to operate steamboats on New York waters. Under the terms of the monopoly, no person was to be allowed to navigate New York waters without first securing a license from Fulton and Livingston. Any unlicensed vessel found on New York waters was to be forfeited to them. Steamboat navigation developed very rapidly after 1808, and the New York monopoly became extremely unpopular. A number of states passed retaliatory measures: Connecticut, for example, prohibited vessels licensed by Fulton and Livingston from entering the state's waters; other states made exclusive grants similar to the New York monopoly. Thus, when the case of Gibbons *v.* Ogden *first arose, the states were engaged in bitter commercial warfare.*

Ogden, who had been licensed by Fulton and Livingston, operated boats from New York to New Jersey. Gibbons also operated boats between the two states in direct competition with Ogden under a coasting license issued by the federal authorities under the provisions of the Federal Coasting Act. Ogden began a suit to enjoin Gibbons from continuing in the interstate business. A decision written by Chancellor James Kent, perhaps the outstanding jurist of his day, sustained the steamboat monopoly and granted Ogden an injunction. The highest state court affirmed. Gibbons then appealed to the Supreme Court.]

[15] Justice Stone, in a note in *McGoldrick* v. *Berwind-White Coal Mining Co.,* 309 U.S. 33 (1940). See also *Dept. of Revenue v. Association of Washington Stevedoring Companies,* 435 U.S. 734 (1978); *Boston Stock Exchange* v. *State Tax Commission,* 429 U.S. 318 (1977).

MR. CHIEF JUSTICE MARSHALL delivered the opinion of the Court:

The appellant contends that this decree is erroneous, because the laws which purport to give the exclusive privilege it sustains, are repugnant to the Constitution and laws of the United States.

They are said to be repugnant—

1. To that clause in the Constitution which authorizes Congress to regulate commerce.

2. To that which authorizes Congress to promote the progress of science and useful arts. . . .

As preliminary to the very able discussions of the Constitution which we have heard from the bar, and as having some influence on its construction, reference has been made to the political situation of these States, anterior to its formation. It has been said, that they were sovereign, were completely independent, and were connected with each other only by a league. This is true. But, when these allied sovereigns converted their league into a government, when they converted their Congress of Ambassadors, deputed to deliberate on their common concerns, and to recommend measures of general utility, into a Legislature, empowered to enact laws on the most interesting subjects, the whole character in which the States appear underwent a change, the extent of which must be determined by a fair consideration of the instrument by which that changes was effected.

This instrument contains an enumeration of powers expressly granted by the people to their government. It has been said that these powers ought to be construed strictly. But why ought they to be so construed? Is there one sentence in the Constitution which gives countenance to this rule? In the last of the enumerated powers, that which grants, expressly, the means for carrying all others into execution, Congress is authorized "to make all laws which shall be necessary and proper" for the purpose. But this limitation on the means which may be used is not extended to the powers which are conferred; nor is there one sentence in the Constitution, which has been pointed out by the gentlemen of the bar, or which we have been able to discern that prescribes this rule. We do not, therefore, think ourselves justified in adopting it. What do gentlemen mean by a strict construction? If they contend only against that enlarged construction which would extend words beyond their natural and obvious import, we might question the application of the term, but should not controvert the principle. If they contend for that narrow construction which, in support of some theory not to be found in the Constitution, would deny to the government those powers which the words of the grant, as usually understood, import, and which are consistent with the general views and objects of the instrument; for that narrow construction, which would cripple the government, and render it unequal to the objects for which it is declared to be instituted, and to which the powers given, as fairly understood, render it competent; then we cannot perceive the propriety of this strict construction, nor adopt it as the rule by which the Constitution is to be expounded. As men whose intentions require no concealment generally employ the words which most directly and aptly express the ideas they intend to convey, the enlightened patriots who framed our Constitution, and the people who adopted it, must be understood to have employed words in their natural sense, and to have intended what they have said. If, from the imperfection of human language, there should be serious doubts respecting the extent of any given power, it is a well settled rule that the objects for which it was given, especially when those objects are expressed in the instrument itself, should have great influence in the construction. We know of no reason for excluding this rule from the present case. The grant does not convey power which might be beneficial to the grantor, if retained by himself, or which can enure solely to the benefit of the grantee; but is an investment of power for the general advantage, in the hands of agents selected for that purpose; which power can never be exercised by the people themselves, but must be placed in the hands of agents, or lie dormant. We know of no rule for construing the extent of such powers, other than is given by the language of the instrument which confers them, taken in connection with the purposes for which they were conferred.

The words are, "Congress shall have power to regulate commerce with foreign nations, and among the several States, and with the Indian tribes."

The subject to be regulated is commerce; and our Constitution being, as was aptly said at the bar, one of enumeration and not of definition, to ascertain the extent of the power it becomes necessary to settle the meaning of the word. The counsel for the appellee would limit it to traffic, to buying and selling, or the interchange of commodities, and do not admit that it comprehends navigation. This would restrict a general term, applicable to many objects, to one of its significations. Commerce, undoubtedly, is traffic, but it is something more; it is intercourse. It describes the commercial intercourse between nations, and parts of nations, in all its branches, and is regulated by prescribing rules for carrying on that intercourse. The mind can scarcely conceive a system for regulating commerce between nations which shall exclude all laws concerning navigation, which shall be silent on the admission of the vessels of one nation into the ports of the other, and be confined to prescribing rules for the conduct of individuals in the actual employment of buying or selling, or of barter.

If commerce does not include navigation, the government of the Union has no direct power over that subject, and can make no law prescribing what shall constitute American vessels, or requiring that they shall be navigated by American seamen. Yet this power has been exercised from the commencement of the government, has been understood by all to be a commercial regulation. All America understands, and has uniformly understood, the word *commerce* to comprehend navigation. It was so understood, and must have been so understood, when the Constitution was framed. The power over commerce, including navigation, was one of the primary objects for which the people of America adopted their government, and must have been contemplated in forming it. The convention must have used the word in that sense, because all have understood it in that sense; and the attempt to restrict it comes too late.

. . . The word used in the Constitution, then, comprehends, and has been always understood to comprehend, navigation within its meaning; and a power to regulate navigation is as expressly granted as if that term had been added to the word *commerce.*

To what commerce does this power extend? The Constitution informs us, to commerce "with the foreign nations, and among the several States, and with the Indian tribes."

It has, we believe, been universally admitted, that these words comprehend every species of commercial intercourse between the United States and foreign nations. No sort of trade can be carried on between this country and any other, to which this power does not extend. It has been truly said that commerce, as the word is used in the Constitution, is a unit, every part of which is indicated by the term.

If this be the admitted meaning of the word in its application to foreign nations, it must carry the same meaning throughout the sentence, and remain a unit, unless there be some plain intelligible cause which alters it.

The subject to which the power is next applied is to commerce "among the several States." The word *among* means intermingled with. A thing which is among others, is intermingled with them. Commerce among the States cannot stop at the external boundary line of each State, but may be introduced into the interior.

It is not intended to say that these words comprehend that commerce which is completely internal, which is carried on between man and man in a State, or between different parts of the same State, and which does not extend to or affect other States. Such a power would be inconvenient, and is certainly unnecessary.

Comprehensive as the word *among* is, it may very properly by restricted to that commerce which concerns more States than one. . . . The completely internal commerce of a State, then, may be considered as reserved for the State itself.

But, in regulating commerce with foreign nations, the power of Congress does not stop at the jurisdictional lines of the several States. It would be a very useless power if it could not pass those lines. The commerce of the United States with foreign nations is that of the whole United States. Every district has a right to participate in it. The deep streams which penetrate our country in every direction pass through the interior of almost every State in the Union, and furnish the means of exerting this right. If Congress has the power to regulate it, that power must be exercised whenever the subject exists. If it exists within the States, if a foreign voyage may commence or terminate at a port within a State, then the power of Congress may be exercised within a State.

This principle is, if possible, still more clear when applied to commerce "among the several States." They either join each other, in which case they are separated by a mathematical line, or they are remote from each other, in which case other States lie between them. What is commerce "among" them; and how is it to be conducted? Can a trading expedition between two adjoining States commence and terminate outside of each? And if the trading intercourse be between two States remote from each other, must it not commence in one, terminate in the other, and probably pass through a third? Commerce among the States must, of necessity, be commerce with the States. In the regulation of trade with the Indian tribes, the action of the law, especially when the Constitution was made, was chiefly within a State. The power of Congress, then, whatever it may be, must be exercised within the territorial jurisdiction of the several States.

. . . We are now arrived at the inquiry—What is this power?

It is the power to regulate; that is, to prescribe the rule by which commerce is to be governed. This power, like all others vested in Congress, is complete in itself, may be exercised to its utmost extent, and acknowledges no limitations other than are prescribed in the Constitution. These are expressed in plain terms, and do not affect the questions which arise in this case, or which have been discussed at the bar. If, as has always been understood, the sovereignty of Congress, though limited to specified objects, is plenary as to those objects, the power over commerce with foreign nations, and among the several States, is vested in Congress as absolutely as it would be in a single government, having in its constitution the same restrictions on the exercise of the power as are found in the Constitution of the United States. . . .

The power of Congress, then, comprehends navigation within the limits of every State in the Union; so far as that navigation may be, in any manner, connected with "commerce with foreign nations, or among the several States, or with the Indian tribes." It may, of consequence, pass the jurisdictional line of New York, and act upon the very waters to which the prohibition now under consideration applies.

But it has been urged with great earnestness that, although the power of Congress to regulate commerce with foreign nations, and among the several States, be co-extensive with the subject itself, and have no other limits than are prescribed in the Constitution, yet the States may severally exercise the same power within their respective jurisdictions. In support of this argument, it is said that they possessed it as an inseparable attribute of sovereignty before the formation of the Constitution, and still retain it, except so far as they have surrendered it by that instrument; that this principle results from the nature of the government, and is secured by the Tenth Amendment; that an affirmative grant of power is not exclusive, unless in its own nature it be such that the continued exercise of it by the former possessor is inconsistent with the grant, and that this is not of that description.

The appellant, conceding these postulates, except the last, contends that full power to regulate a particular subject implies the whole power, and leaves no residuum; that a grant of the whole is incompatible with the existence of a right in another to any part of it.

Both parties have appealed to the Constitution, to legislative acts, and judicial decisions; and have drawn arguments from all these sources to support and illustrate the proposition they respectively maintain.

. . . In discussing the question, whether this power is still in the States, in the case under consideration, we may dismiss from it the inquiry, whether it is surrendered by the mere grant to Congress, or is retained until Congress shall exercise the power. We may dismiss that inquiry, because it has been exercised, and the regulations which Congress deemed it proper to make are now in full operation. The sole question is, can a State regulate commerce with foreign nations and among the States, while Congress is regulating it? . . .

It has been said, that the act of August 7, 1789, acknowledges a concurrent power in the States to regulate the conduct of pilots, and hence is inferred an admission of their concurrent right with Congress to regulate commerce with foreign nations, and amongst the States. But this inference is not, we think, justified by the fact.

Although Congress cannot enable a State to legislate, Congress may adopt the provisions of a State on any subject. When the government of the Union was brought into existence, it found a system for the regulation of its pilots in full force in every State. The act which has been mentioned adopts this system and gives it the same validity as if its provisions had been specially made by Congress. But the act, it may be said, is prospective also, and the adoption of laws to be made in future, presupposes the right in the maker to legislate on the subject.

The act unquestionably manifests an intention to leave this subject entirely to the States, until Congress should think proper to interpose; but the very enactment of such a law indicates an opinion that it was necessary; that the existing system would not be applicable to the new state of things unless expressly applied to it by Congress. . . .

It has been contended by the counsel for the appellant that, as the word "to regulate" implies in its nature full power over the thing to be regulated, it excludes, necessarily, the action of all others that would perform the same operation on the same thing. That regulation is designed for the entire result, applying to those parts which remain as they were, as well as to those which are altered. It produces a uniform whole, which is as much disturbed and deranged by changing what the regulating power designs to leave untouched, as that on which it has operated.

There is great force in this argument, and the Court is not satisfied that it has been refuted.

Since, however, in exercising the power of regulating their own purely internal affairs, whether of trading or police, the States may sometimes enact laws, the validity of which depends on their interfering with, and being contrary to, an act of Congress passed in pursuance of the Constitution, the Court will enter upon the inquiry, whether the laws of New York, as expounded by the highest tribunal of that State, have, in their application to this case, come into collision with an act of Congress, and deprived a citizen of a right to which that act entitles him. Should this collision exist, it will be immaterial whether those laws were passed in virtue of a concurrent power "to regulate commerce with foreign nations and among the several States" or in virtue of a power to regulate their domestic trade and police. In one case and the other, the acts of New York must yield to the law of Congress; and the decision sustaining the privilege they confer, against a right given by a law of the Union, must be erroneous.

This opinion has been frequently expressed in this Court, and is founded as well on the nature of the government as on the words of the Constitution. In argument, however, it has been contended that if a law passed by a State, in the exercise of its acknowledged sovereignty, comes into conflict with a law passed by Congress in pursuance of the Constitution, they affect the subject, and each other, like equal opposing powers.

But the framers of our Constitution foresaw this state of things, and provided for it by declaring the supremacy not only of itself, but of the laws made in pursuance of it. The nullity of any act inconsistent with the Constitution is produced by the declaration that the Constitution is the supreme law. The appropriate application of that part of the clause which confers the same supremacy on laws and treaties, is to such acts of the State Legislatures as do not transcend their powers, but, though enacted in the execution of acknowledged State powers, interfere with or are contrary to the laws of Congress, made in pursuance of the Constitution, or some treaty made under the authority of the United States. In every such case, the act of Congress, or the treaty, is supreme; and the law of the State, though enacted in the exercise of powers not controverted, must yield to it.

. . . "An act [of Congress] for the enrolling and licensing of steamboats" . . . authorizes a steamboat employed, or intended to be employed, only in a river or bay of the United States, owned wholly or in part by an alien, resident within the United States, to be enrolled and licensed as if the same belonged to a citizen of the United States.

This act demonstrates the opinion of Congress that steamboats may be enrolled and licensed in common with vessels using sails. They are, of course, entitled to the same privileges, and can no more be restrained from navigating waters, and entering ports which are free to such vessels, than if they were wafted on their voyage by winds instead of being propelled by the agency of fire. The one element may be as legitimately used as the other for every commercial purpose authorized by the law of the Union; and the act of a State inhibiting the use of either to any vessel having a license under the act of Congress comes, we think, in direct collision with that act.

As this decides the cause, it is unnecessary to enter in an examination of that part of the Constitution which empowers Congress to promote the progress of science and the useful arts.

Reversed.

[Mr. Justice Johnson concurred on the ground that the power of Congress over interstate commerce was intended to be exclusive and that the licensing act did not affect the case.]

COOLEY *v.* BOARD OF WARDENS OF THE PORT OF PHILADELPHIA
12 How. 299; 13 L. Ed. 996 (1852)

[In 1803, the Pennsylvania legislature enacted a statute that set up various rules regarding pilotage in the port of Philadelphia. A particular section of the law required vessels to receive pilots for entering or leaving the port. A fine of half the pilotage fee was levied against any vessel that did not use a pilot. Cooley violated the law by refusing to pay the fines on two of his vessels, neither of which had employed a pilot. In a suit to recover the fees, judgments were rendered against Cooley in the state courts. Cooley then brought the cases to the Supreme Court on writs of error.]

MR. JUSTICE CURTIS delivered the opinion of the Court:

We think this particular regulation concerning half-pilotage fees is an appropriate part of a general system of regulations of this subject. Testing it by the practice of commercial States and countries legislating on this subject, we find it has usually been deemed necessary to make similar provisions. Numerous laws of this kind are cited in the learned argument of the counsel for the defendant in error; and their fitness, as a part of a system of pilotage, in many places, may be inferred from their existence in so many different States and countries. . . .

It remains to consider the objection that it is repugnant to the third clause of the eighth section of the first article. "The Congress shall have power to regulate commerce with foreign nations and among the several States, and with the Indian tribes."

That the power to regulate includes the regulation of navigation, we consider settled. And when we look to the nature of the service performed by pilots, to the relations which that service and its compensations bear to navigation between the several States, and between the ports of the United States and foreign countries, we are brought to the conclusion that the regulation of the qualifications of pilots, of the modes and times of offering and rendering their services, of the responsibilities which shall rest upon them, of the powers they shall possess, of the compensation they may demand, and of the penalities by which their rights and duties may be enforced, do constitute regulations of navigation, and consequently of commerce, within the just meaning of this clause of the Constitution.

The power to regulate navigation is the power to prescribe rules in conformity with which navigation must be carried on. It extends to the persons who conduct it, as well as to the instruments used. Accordingly, the first Congress assembled under the Constitution passed laws requiring the masters of ships and vessels of the United States to be citizens of the United States, and established many rules for the government and regulation of officers and seamen. . . . These have been from time to time added to and changed, and we are not aware that their validity has been questioned.

Now, a pilot, so far as respects the navigation of the vessel in that part of the voyage which is his pilotage-ground, is the temporary master charged with the safety of the vessel and cargo, and of the lives of those on board, and intrusted with the command of the crew. He is not only one of the persons engaged in navigation, but he occupies a most important and responsible place among those thus engaged. And if Congress has power to regulate the seamen who assist the pilot in the management of the vessel, a power never denied, we can perceive no valid reason why the pilot should be beyond the reach of the same power. It is true that, according to the usages of modern commerce on the ocean, the pilot is on board only during a part of the voyage between ports of different States, or between ports of the United States and foreign countries; but if he is on board for such a purpose and during so much of the voyage as to be engaged in navigation, the power to regulate navigation extends to him while thus engaged, as clearly as it would if he were to remain on board throughout the whole passage, from port to port. For it is a power which extends to every part of the voyage, and may regulate those who conduct or assist in conducting navigation in one part of a voyage as much as in another part, or during the whole voyage.

Nor should it be lost sight of that this subject of the regulation of pilots and pilotage has an intimate connection with, and an important relation to, the general subject of commerce with foreign nations and among the several States, over which it was one main object of the Constitution to create a national control. Conflicts between the laws of neighboring States and discriminations favorable or adverse to commerce with particular foreign nations might be created by State laws regulating pilotage, deeply affecting that equality of commercial rights, and that freedom from State interference, which those who formed the Constitution were so anxious to secure, and which the experience of more than half a century has taught us to value so highly. . . . And a majority of the Court are of opinion, that a regulation of pilots is a regulation of commerce within the grant to Congress of the commercial power, contained in the third clause of the eighth section of the first article of the Constitution.

It becomes necessary, therefore, to consider whether this law of Pennsylvania, being a regulation of commerce, is valid.

The act of Congress of the 7th of August, 1789, Section 4, is as follows:

"That all pilots in the bays, inlets, rivers, harbors, and ports of the United States shall continue to be regulated in conformity with the existing laws of the States, respectively, wherein such pilots may be, or with such laws as the States may respectively hereafter enact for the purpose, until further legislative provision shall be made by Congress."

. . . If the States were divested of the power to legislate on this subject by the grant of the commercial power to Congress, it is plain this act could not confer upon them power thus to legislate. If the Constitution excluded the States from making any law regulating commerce, certainly Congress cannot regrant, or in any manner reconvey to the States that power. . . . [W]e are brought directly and unavoidably to the consideration of the question, whether the grant of the commercial power to Congress did *per se* deprive the States of all power to regulate pilots. This question has never been decided by this Court, nor in our judgment, has any case depending upon all the considerations which must govern this one come before this Court. The grant of commercial power to Congress does not contain any terms which expressly exclude the States from exercising an authority over its subject matter. If they are excluded, it must be because the nature of the power thus granted to Congress requires that a similar authority should not exist in the States. If it were conceded on the one side, that the nature of this power, like that to legislate for the District of Columbia, is absolutely and totally repugnant to the existence of similar power in the States, probably no one would deny that the grant of the power to Congress as effectually and perfectly excludes the States from all future legislation on the subject as if express words had been used to exclude them. And on the other hand, if it were admitted that the existence of this power in Congress, like the power of taxation, is compatible with the existence of a similar power in the States, then it would be in conformity with the contemporary exposition of the Constitution *(Federalist, No.* 32) and with the judicial construction given from time to time by this Court, after the most deliberate consideration, to hold that the mere grant of such a power to Congress did not imply a prohibition on the States to exercise the same power; that it is not the mere existence of such a power, but its exercise by Congress, which may be incompatible with the exercise of the same power by the States, and that the States may legislate in the absence of congressional regulations. . . .

The diversities of opinion, therefore, which have existed on this subject, have arisen from the different views taken of the nature of this power. But when the nature of a power like this is spoken of, when it is said that the nature of the power requires that it should be exercised exclusively by Congress, it must be intended to refer to the subjects of that power, and to say they are of such a nature as to require exclusive legislation by Congress. Now the power to regulate commerce embraces a vast field, containing not only many, but exceedingly various subjects, quite unlike in their nature; some imperatively demanding a single uniform rule, operating equally on the commerce of the United States in every port, and some, like the subject now in question, as imperatively demanding that diversity, which alone can meet the local necessities of navigation.

Either absolutely to affirm or deny that the nature of this power requires exclusive legislation by Congress is to lose sight of the nature of the subjects of this power, and to assert concerning all of them what is really applicable but to a part. Whatever subjects of this power are in their nature national, or admit only of one uniform system or plan of regulation, may justly be said to be of such a nature as to require exclusive legislation by Congress. That this cannot be affirmed of laws for the regulation of pilots and pilotage is plain. The act of 1789 contains a clear and authoritative declaration by the first Congress, that the nature of this subject is such that, until Congress should find it necessary to exert its power, it should be left to the legislation of the States; that it is local and not national; that it is likely to be the best provided for, not by one system, or plan of regulations, but by as many as the legislative discretion of the several States should deem applicable to the local peculiarities of the ports within their limits.

Viewed in this light, so much of this act of 1789 as declares that pilots shall continue to be regulated "by such laws as the States may respectively hereafter enact for that purpose," instead of being held to be inoperative as an attempt to confer on the States a power to legislate, of which the Constitution had deprived them, is allowed an appropriate and important signification. It manifests the understanding of Congress, at the outset of the government, that the nature of this subject is not such as to require its exclusive legislation. The practice of the States, and of the national government, has been in conformity with this declaration from the origin of the national government to this time; and the nature of the subject when examined is such as to leave no doubt of the superior fitness and propriety, not to say the absolute necessity, of different systems of regulation, drawn from local knowledge and experience, and conformed to local wants. How then can we say, that by the mere grant of power to regulate commerce, the States are deprived of all the power to legislate on this subject, because from the nature of the power the legislation of Congress must be exclusive. This would be to affirm that the nature of the power is in any case something different from the nature of the subject to which, in such case, the power extends, and that the nature of the power necessarily demands, in all cases, exclusive legislation by Congress, while the nature of one of the subjects of that power not only does not require such exclusive legislation, but may be best provided for by many different systems enacted by the States in conformity with the circumstances of the ports within their limits. In construing an instrument designed for the formation of a government, and in determining the extent of one of its important grants of power to legislate, we can make no such distinction between the nature of the power and the nature of the subject on which that power was intended practically to operate, nor consider the grant more extensive by affirming of the power, what is not true of its subject now in question.

It is the opinion of a majority of the Court that the mere grant to Congress of the power to regulate commerce did not deprive the States of power to regulate pilots, and that although Congress has legislated on this subject, its legislation manifests an intention, with a single exception, not to regulate this subject, but to leave its regulation to the several States. To these precise questions, which are all we are called on to decide, this opinion must be understood to be confined. It does not extend to the question what other subjects, under the commercial power, are within the exclusive control of Congress, or may be regulated by the States in the absence of all congressional legislation; nor to the general question how far any regulation of a subject by Congress may be deemed to operate as an exclusion of all legislation by the States upon the same subject. We decide the precise questions before us, upon what we deem sound principles, applicable to this particular subject in the state in which the legislation of Congress has left it. We go no further.

. . . We are of opinion that this State law . . . is therefore valid, and the judgment of the Supreme Court of Pennsylvania in each case must be

Affirmed.

[Mr. Justice McLean and Mr. Justice Wayne dissented. Mr. Justice Daniel wrote a separate opinion concurring with the judgment of the Court, but differed in reasoning on the basis that the control of pilotage was an "original and inherent" state power not "subject to the sanction of the Federal Government."]

SOUTHERN PACIFIC COMPANY *v.* ARIZONA
325 U.S. 761; 65 Sup. Ct. 1515; 89 L. Ed. 1915 (1945)

[The Arizona Train Limit Law of 1912 made it unlawful for any person or corporation to operate within the state a railroad train with more than fourteen passenger cars or more than seventy freight cars. The law was a safety measure designed to avoid accidents resulting from the "slack action" of individual cars on long trains. Slack action is defined as the amount of free movement of one car before it transmits its motion to an adjoining coupled car. A fine was to be paid for each violation of the law. In 1940, Arizona tried to collect penalities from the Southern Pacific Company for violations of the law. The company admitted the violations but contended that the act was unconstitutional. The trial court rendered a judgment for the company, but the state supreme court reversed the judgment and upheld the constitutionality of the law. The company then brought the case to the Supreme Court on appeal.]

MR. CHIEF JUSTICE STONE delivered the opinion of the Court:

. . . The questions for decision are whether Congress has, by legislative enactment, restricted the power of the states to regulate the length of interstate trains as a safety measure and, if not, whether the statute contravenes the commerce clause of the Federal Constitution. . . .

Congress, in enacting legislation within its constitutional authority over interstate commerce, will not be deemed to have intended to strike down a state statute designed to protect the health and safety of the public unless its purpose to do so is clearly manifested. . . . or unless the state law, in terms or in its practical administration, conflicts with the Act of Congress, or plainly and palpably infringes its policy. . . .

Congress, although asked to do so, has declined to pass legislation specifically limiting trains to seventy cars. We are therefore brought to appellant's principal contention, that the state statute contravenes the commerce clause of the Federal Constitution.

Although the commerce clause conferred on the national government power to regulate commerce, its possession of the power does not exclude all state power of regulation. Ever since *Willson* v. *Blackbird Creek Marsh Co.,* 2 Pet. 245, and *Cooley* v. *Board of Wardens,* 12 How. 299, it has been recognized that, in the absence of conflicting legislation by Congress, there is a residuum of power in the state to make laws governing matters of local concern which nevertheless in some measure affect interstate commerce or even, to some extent, regulate it. . . . Thus the states may regulate matters which, because of their number and diversity, may never be adequately dealt with by Congress. . . . When the regulation of matters of local concern is local in character and effect, and its impact on the national commerce does not seriously interfere with its operation, and the consequent incentive to deal with them nationally is slight, such regulation has been generally held to be within state authority. . . .

But ever since *Gibbons* v. *Ogden* . . . the states have not been deemed to have authority to impede substantially the free flow of commerce from state to state, or to regulate those phases of the national commerce which, because of the need of national uniformity, demand that their regulation, if any, be prescribed by a single authority. . . . Whether or not this long-recognized distribution of power between the national and the state governments is predicated upon the implications of the commerce clause itself . . . or upon the presumed intention of Congress, where Congress has not spoken . . . the result is the same.

In the application of these principles, some enactments may be found to be plainly within and others plainly without state power. But between these extremes lies the infinite variety of cases in which regulation of local matters may also operate as a regulation of commerce, in which reconciliation of the conflicting claims of state and national power is to be attained only by some appraisal and accommodation of the competing demands of the state and national interests involved. . . .

For a hundred years it has been accepted constitutional doctrine that the commerce clause, without the aid of Congressional legislation, thus affords some protection from state legislation inimical to the national commerce, and that in such cases, where Congress has not acted, this Court, and not the state legislature, is under the commerce clause the final arbiter of the competing demands of state and national interests. . . .

Congress has undoubted power to redefine the distribution of power over interstate commerce. It may either permit the states to regulate the commerce in a manner which would otherwise not be permissible, . . . or exclude state regulation even of matters of peculiarly local concern which nevertheless affect interstate commerce. . . .

But in general Congress has left it to the courts to formulate the rules thus interpreting the commerce clause in its application, doubtless because it has appreciated the destructive consequences to the commerce of the nation if their protection were withdrawn, . . . and has been aware that in their application state laws will not be invalidated without the support of relevant factual material which will "afford a sure basis" for an informed judgment. . . . Meanwhile, Congress has accommodated its legislation, as have the states, to these rules as an established feature of our constitutional system. There has thus been left to the states wide scope for the regulation of matters of local state concern, even though it in some measure affects the commerce, provided it does not materially restrict the free flow of commerce across state lines, or interfere with it in matters with respect to which uniformity of regulation is of predominant national concern.

Hence the matters for ultimate determination here are the nature and extent of the burden which the state regulation of interstate trains, adopted as a safety measure, imposes on interstate commerce, and whether the relative weights of the state and national interests involved are such as to make inapplicable the rule, generally observed, that the free flow of interstate commerce and its freedom from local restraints in matters requiring uniformity of regulation are interests safeguarded by the commerce clause from state interference. . . .

The findings show that the operation of long trains, that is, trains of more than fourteen passenger and more than seventy freight cars, is standard practice over the main lines of the railroads of the United States, and that, if the length of trains is to be regulated at all, national uniformity in the regulation adopted, such as only Congress can prescribe, is practically indispensable to the operation of an efficient and economical national railway system. On many railroads passenger trains of more than fourteen cars and freight trains of more than seventy cars are operated, and on some systems freight trains are run ranging from 125 to 160 cars in length. Outside of Arizona, where the length of trains is not restricted, appellant runs a substantial proportion of long trains. . . .

The record shows a definite relationship between operating costs and the length of trains, the increase in length resulting in a reduction of operating costs per car. The additional cost of operation of trains complying with the Train Limit Law in Arizona amounts for the two railroads traversing that state to about $1,000,000 a year. The reduction in train lengths also impedes efficient operation. More locomotives and more manpower are required; the necessary conversion and reconversion of train lengths at terminals, and the delay caused by breaking up and remaking long trains upon entering and leaving the state in order to comply with the law, delays the traffic and diminishes its volume moved in a given time, especially when traffic is heavy. . . .

The unchallenged findings leave no doubt that the Arizona Train Limit Law imposes a serious burden on the interstate commerce conducted by appellant. It materially impedes the movement of appellant's interstate trains through that state and interposes a substantial obstruction to the national policy proclaimed by Congress, to promote adequate, economical, and efficient railway transportation service. . . . Enforcement of the law in Arizona, while train lengths remain unregulated or are regulated by varying standards in other states, must inevitably result in an impairment of uniformity of efficient railroad operation because the railroads are subjected to regulation which is not uniform in its application. Compliance with a state statute limiting train lengths requires interstate trains of a length lawful in other states to be broken up and reconstituted as they enter each state according as it may impose varying limitations upon train lengths. The alternative is for the carrier to conform to the lowest train limit restriction of any of the states through which its trains pass, whose laws thus control the carriers' operations both within and without the regulating state. . . .

If one state may regulate train lengths, so may all the others, and they need not prescribe the same maximum limitation. The practical effect of such regulation is to control train operations beyond the boundaries of the state exacting it because of the necessity of breaking up and reassembling long trains at the nearest terminal points before entering and after leaving the regulating state. The serious impediment to the free flow of commerce by the local regulation of train lengths and the practical necessity that such regulation, if any, must be prescribed by a single body having a nationwide authority are apparent.

The trial court found that the Arizona law had no reasonable relation to safety, and made train operation more dangerous. Examination of the evidence and the detailed findings makes it clear that this conclusion was rested on facts found which indicate that such increased danger of accident and personal injury as may result from the greater length of trains is more than offset by the increase in the number of accidents resulting from the larger number of trains when train lengths are reduced. In considering the effect of the statute as a safety measure, therefore, the factor of controlling significance for present purposes is not whether there is basis for the conclusion of the Arizona Supreme Court that the increase in length of trains beyond the statutory maximum has an adverse effect upon safety of operation. The decisive question is whether in the circumstances the total effect of the law as a safety measure in reducing accidents and casualties is so slight or problematical as not to outweigh the national interest in keeping interstate commerce free from interferences which seriously impede it and subject it to local regulation which does not have a uniform effect on the interstate train journey which it interrupts. . . .

We think, as the trial court found, that the Arizona Train Limit Law, viewed as a safety measure, affords at most slight and dubious advantage, if any, over unregulated train lengths. . . . Its undoubted effect on the commerce is the regulation, without securing uniformity, of the length of trains operated in interstate commerce, which lack is itself a primary cause of preventing the free flow of commerce by delaying it and by substantially increasing its cost and impairing its efficiency. In these respects the case differs from those where a state, by regulatory measures affecting the commerce, has removed or reduced safety hazards without substantial interference with the interstate movement of trains. . . .

The principle that, without controlling Congressional action, a state may not regulate interstate commerce so as substantially to affect its flow or deprive it of needed uniformity in its regulation is not to be avoided by "simply invoking the convenient apologetics of the police power."

. . . [W]e conclude that the state does go too far. Its regulation of train lengths, admittedly obstructive to interstate train operation, and having a seriously adverse effect on transportation efficiency and economy, passes beyond what is plainly essential for safety since it does not appear that it will lessen rather than increase the danger of accident. Its attempted regulation of the operation of interstate trains cannot establish nationwide control such as is essential to the maintenance of an efficient transportation system, which Congress alone can prescribe. The state interest cannot be preserved at the expense of the national interest by an enactment which regulates interstate train lengths without securing such control, which is a matter of national concern. To this the interest of the state here asserted is subordinate.

Appellees especially rely on the full train-crew cases, *Chicago, R.I. & P.R. Co.* v. *Arkansas* (219 U.S. 453) . . . and also on *South Carolina Highway Dept.* v. *Barnwell Bros.* (303 U.S. 177) . . . as supporting the state's authority to regulate the length of interstate trains. While the full train-crew laws undoubtedly placed an added financial burden on the railroads in order to serve a local interest, they did not obstruct interstate transportation or seriously impede it. They had no effects outside the state beyond those of picking up and setting down the extra employees at the state boundaries; they involved no wasted use of facilities or serious impairment of transportation efficiency, which are among the factors of controlling weight here. In sustaining those laws the Court considered the restriction a minimal burden on the commerce comparable to the law requiring the licensing of engineers as a safeguard against those of reckless and intemperate habits, sustained in *Smith* v. *Alabama,* 124 U.S. 465, or those afflicted with color blindness, upheld in *Nashville, C. & St. L. Ry.* v. *Alabama,* 128 U.S. 96, and other similar regulations. . . .

South Carolina Highway Dept. v. *Barnwell Bros. supra,* was concerned with the power of the state to regulate the weight and width of motor cars passing interstate over its highways, a legislative field over which the state has a far more extensive control than over interstate railroads. In that case . . . we were at pains to point out that there are few subjects of state regulations affecting interstate commerce which are so peculiarly of local concern as is the use of the state's highways. Unlike the railroads local highways are built, owned, and maintained by the state or its municipal subdivisions. The state is responsible for their safe and economical administration. Regulations affecting the safety of their use must be applied alike to intrastate and interstate traffic. The fact that they affect alike shippers in interstate and intrastate commerce in great numbers, within as well as without the state, is a safeguard against regulatory abuses. Their regulation is akin to quarantine measures, game laws, and like local regulations of rivers, harbors, piers, and docks, with respect to which the state has exceptional scope for the exercise of its regulatory power, and which, Congress not acting, have been sustained even though they materially interfere with interstate commerce. . . .

The contrast between the present regulation and the full train-crew laws in point of their effects on the commerce, and the like contrast with the highway safety regulations, in point of the nature of the subject of regulation and the state's interest in it, illustrate and emphasize the considerations which enter into a determination of the relative weights of state and national interests where state regulation affecting interstate commerce is attempted. Here examination of all the relevant factors makes it plain that the state interest is outweighed by the interest of the nation in an adequate, economical, and efficient railway transportation service, which must prevail.

Reversed.

MR. JUSTICE RUTLEDGE concurs in the result.

MR. JUSTICE BLACK, dissenting:

In *Hennington* v. *Georgia,* 163 U.S. 299, 304, a case which involved the power of a state to regulate interstate traffic, this Court said, "The whole theory of our government, federal and state, is hostile to the idea that questions of legislative authority may depend . . . upon opinions of judges as to the wisdom or want of wisdom in the enactment of laws under powers clearly conferred upon the legislature." What the Court decides today is that it is unwise governmental policy to regulate the length of trains. I am therefore constrained to note my dissent. . . .

. . . . [T]he determination of whether it is in the interest of society for the length of trains to be governmentally regulated is a matter of public policy. Someone must fix that policy—either the Congress, or the state, or the courts. A century and a half of constitutional history and government admonishes this Court to leave that choice to the elected legislative representatives of the people themselves. . . .

I think that legislatures, to the exclusion of courts, have the constitutional power to enact laws limiting train lengths for the purpose of reducing injuries brought about by "slack movements." Their power is not less because a requirement of short trains might increase grade-crossing accidents. This latter fact raises an entirely different element of danger which is itself subject to legislative regulation. For legislatures may, if necessary, require railroads to take appropriate steps to reduce the likelihood of injuries at grade crossings. . . . And the fact that grade-crossing improvements may be expensive is no sufficient reason to say that an unconstitutional "burden" is put upon a railroad even though it be an interstate road. . . .

. . . [E]ven the broadest exponents of judicial power in this field have not heretofore expressed doubt as to a state's power, absent a paramount congressional declaration, to regulate interstate trains in the interest of safety. For as early as 1913, this Court, speaking through Mr. Justice Hughes, later Chief Justice, referred to "the settled principle that, in the absence of legislation by Congress, the states are not denied the exercise of their power to secure safety in the physical operation of railroad trains within their territory, even though such trains are used in interstate commerce. That has been the law since the beginning of railroad transportation." *Atlantic Coast Line R. Co.* v. *Georgia,* 234 U.S. 280, 291. Until today, the oft-repeated principles of that case have never been repudiated in whole or in part. . . .

This record in its entirety leaves me with no doubt whatever that many employees have been seriously injured and killed in the past, and that many more are likely to be so in the future, because of "slack movement" in trains. Everyday knowledge, as well as direct evidence presented at the various hearings, substantiates the report of the Senate Committee that the danger from slack movement is greater in long trains than in short trains. It may be that offsetting dangers are possible in the operation of short trains. The balancing of these probabilities, however, is not in my judgment a matter for judicial determination, but one which calls for legislative consideration. Representatives elected by the people to make their laws, rather than judges appointed to interpret those laws, can best determine the policies which govern the people. That at least is the basic principle on which our democratic society rests. I would affirm the judgment of the Supreme Court of Arizona.

[Mr. Justice Douglas also wrote a dissenting opinion.]

EDWARDS *v.* CALIFORNIA

314 U.S. 160; 62 Sup. Ct. 164; 86 L. Ed. 119 (1941)

[Edwards, who was a citizen of the United States and a resident of Marysville, California, went to Texas in 1939 to bring his wife's brother, Frank Duncan, to Marysville. Duncan was an American citizen and a resident of Texas. When Edwards arrived in Texas, he learned that Duncan had last been employed by the Works Progress Administration. He thus was aware of the fact that Duncan was and continued to be an indigent person throughout the case. The two men went to California in Edwards's car. Duncan had about $20 when he left Texas, but by the time he reached Marysville it had all been spent. Duncan lived with Edwards's family for approximately ten days until he received financial help from the Farm Security Administration.

A complaint was filed against Edwards under Section 2615 of the Welfare and Institutions Code of California, which provided as follows: "Every person, firm or corporation or officer or agent thereof that brings or assists in bringing into the State any indigent person who is not a resident of the State, knowing him to be an indigent person, is guilty of a misdemeanor." Edwards was convicted of violating the law. He was sentenced to six months' imprisonment in the county jail, and sentence was suspended. The Superior Court of Yuba County, California, affirmed the conviction, holding the statute constitutional as a valid exercise of the state's police power. Edwards then brought an appeal to the Supreme Court requesting that the judgment of the Superior Court be reversed.]

MR. JUSTICE BYRNES delivered the opinion of the Court:

. . . Art. I, Section 8 of the Constitution delegates to the Congress the authority to regulate interstate commerce. And it is settled beyond question that the transportation of persons is "commerce," within the meaning of that provision. It is nevertheless true, that the States are not wholly precluded from exercising their police power in matters of local concern even though they may thereby affect interstate commerce. . . . The issue presented in this case, therefore, is whether the prohibition embodied in Section 2615 against the "bringing" or transportation of indigent persons into California is within the police power of that State. We think that it is not, and hold that it is an unconstitutional barrier to interstate commerce.

The grave and perplexing social and economic dislocation which this statute reflects is a matter of common knowledge and concern. We are not unmindful of it. We appreciate that the spectacle of large segments of our population constantly on the move has given rise to urgent demands upon the ingenuity of government. . . . The State asserts that the huge influx of migrants into California in recent years has resulted in problems of health, morals, and especially finance, the proportions of which are staggering. It is not for us to say that this is not true. We have repeatedly and recently affirmed, and we now reaffirm, that we do not conceive it our function to pass upon "the wisdom, need, or appropriateness" of the legislative efforts of the States to solve such difficulties. . . .

But this does not mean that there are no boundaries to the permissible area of State legislative activity. There are. And none is more certain than the prohibition against attempts on the part of any single State to isolate itself from difficulties common to all of them by restraining the transportation of persons and property across its borders. It is frequently the case that a State might gain a momentary respite from the pressure of events by the simple expedient of shutting its gates to the outside world. But, in the words of Mr. Justice Cardozo: "The Constitution was framed under the dominion of a political philosophy less parochial in range. It was framed upon the theory that the peoples of the several States must sink or swim together, and that in the long run prosperity and salvation are in union and not division." *Baldwin* v. *Seelig,* 294 U.S. 511, 523.

It is difficult to conceive of a statute more squarely in conflict with this theory than the Section challenged here. Its express purpose and inevitable effect is to prohibit the transportation of indigent persons across the California border. The burden upon interstate commerce is intended and immediate; it is the plain and sole function of the statute. Moreover, the indigent nonresidents who are the real victims of the statute are deprived of the opportunity to exert political pressure upon the California legislature in order to obtain a change in policy. . . . We think this statute must fail under any known test of the validity of State interference with interstate commerce.

It is urged, however, that the concept which underlies Section 2615 enjoys a firm basis in English and American history. This is the notion that each community should care for its own indigent, that relief is solely the responsibility of local government. Of this it must first be said that we are not now called upon to determine anything other than the propriety of an attempt by a State to prohibit the transportation of indigent nonresidents into its territory. The nature and extent of its obligation to afford relief to newcomers is not here involved. We do, however, suggest that the theory of the Elizabethan poor laws no longer fits the facts. Recent years, and particularly the past decade, have been marked by a growing recognition that in an industrial society the task of providing assistance to the needy has ceased to be local in character. The duty to share the burden, if not wholly to assume it, has been recognized not only by State governments, but by the Federal Government as well. The changed attitude is reflected in the Social Security laws under which the Federal and State Governments cooperate for the care of the aged, the blind, and dependent children. . . . It is reflected in the works programs under which work is furnished the unemployed, with the States supplying approximately 25 per cent and the Federal Government approximately 75 per cent of the cost. . . . It is further reflected in the Farm Security laws, under which the entire cost of the relief provisions is borne by the Federal Government. . . .

Indeed, the record in this very case illustrates the inadequate basis in fact for the theory that relief is presently a local matter. Before leaving Texas, Duncan had received assistance from the Works Progress Administration. After arriving in California he was aided by the Farm Security Administration, which, as we have said, is wholly financed by the Federal Government. This is not to say that our judgment would be different if Duncan had received relief from local agencies in Texas and California. Nor is it to suggest that the financial burden of assistance to indigent persons does not continue to fall heavily upon local and State governments. It is only to illustrate that in not inconsiderable measure the relief of the needy has become the common responsibility and concern of the whole nation.

What has been said with respect to financing relief is not without its bearing upon the regulation of the transportation of indigent persons. For the social phenomenon of large-scale interstate migration is as certainly a matter of national concern as the provision of assistance to those who have found a permanent or temporary abode. Moreover, and unlike the relief problem, this phenomenon does not admit to diverse treatment by the several States. The prohibition against transporting indigent nonresidents into one State is an open invitation of retaliatory measures, and the burdens upon the transportation of such persons become cumulative. Moreover, it would be a virtual impossibility for migrants and those who transport them to acquaint themselves with the peculiar rules of admission of many States. "The Court has repeatedly declared that the grant (the commerce clause) established the immunity of interstate commerce from the control of the States respecting all those subjects embraced within the grant which are of such a nature as to demand that, if regulated at all, their regulation must be prescribed by a single authority." . . . We are of the opinion that the transportation of indigent persons from State to State clearly falls within this class of subjects. The scope of Congressional power to deal with this problem we are not now called upon to decide.

There remains to be noticed only the contention that the limitation upon State power to interfere with the interstate transportation of persons is subject to an exception in the case of "Paupers." It is true that support for this contention may be found in early decisions of this Court. In *City of New York* v. *Miln,* 11 Pet. 102, . . . it was said that it is "as competent and as necessary for a State to provide precautionary measures against the moral pestilence of paupers, vagabonds, and possibly convicts, as it is to guard against the physical pestilence, which may arise from unsound and infectious articles imported. . . ." This language has been casually repeated in numerous later cases up to the turn of the century. . . . In none of these cases, however, was the power of a State to exclude "paupers" actually involved.

Whether an able-bodied but unemployed person like Duncan is a "pauper" within the historical meaning of the term is open to considerable doubt. . . . But assuming that the term is applicable to him and to persons similarly situated, we do not consider ourselves bound by the language referred to. *City of New York* v. *Miln* was decided in 1837. Whatever may have been the notion then prevailing, we do not think that it will now be seriously contended that because a person is without employment and without funds he constitutes a "moral pestilence." Poverty and immorality are not synonymous.

We are of the opinion that Section 2615 is not a valid exercise of the police power of California; that it imposes an unconstitutional burden upon interstate commerce, and that the conviction under it cannot be sustained. In the view we have taken, it is unnecessary to decide whether the Section is repugnant to other provisions of the Constitution.

Reversed.

MR. JUSTICE JACKSON, concurring:

I concur in the result reached by the Court, and I agree that the grounds of its decision are permissible ones under applicable authorities. But the migrations of a human being, of whom it is charged that he possesses nothing that can be sold and has no wherewithal to buy, do not fit easily into my notions as to what is commerce. To hold that the measure of his rights is the commerce clause is likely to result eventually either in distorting the commercial law or in denaturing human rights. I turn, therefore, away from principles by which commerce is regulated to that clause of the Constitution by virtue of which Duncan is a citizen of the United States and which forbids any State to abridge his privileges or immunities as such.

This clause was adopted to make United States citizenship the dominant and paramount allegiance among us. The return which the law had long associated with allegiance was protection. The power of citizenship as a shield against oppression was widely known from the example of Paul's Roman citizenship, which sent the centurion scurrying to his higher-ups with the message: "Take heed what thou doest: for this man is a Roman." I suppose none of us doubts that the hope of imparting to American citizenship some of this vitality was the purpose of declaring in the Fourteenth Amendment: "All persons born or naturalized in the United States, and subject to the jurisdiction thereof, are citizens of the United States and of the State wherein they reside. No State shall make or enforce any law which shall abridge the privileges or immunities of citizens of the United States. . . ."

But the hope proclaimed in such generality soon shriveled in the process of judicial interpretation. For nearly three quarters of a century this Court rejected every plea to the privileges and immunities clause. . . .

While instances of valid "privileges or immunities" must be but few, I am convinced that this is one. I do not ignore or belittle the difficulties of what has been characterized by this Court as an "almost forgotten" clause. But the difficulty of the task does not excuse us from giving these general and abstract words whatever of specific content and concreteness they will bear as we mark out their application, case by case. That is the method of the common law, and it has been the method of this Court with other no less general statements in our fundamental law. This Court has not been timorous about giving concrete meaning to such obscure and vagrant phrases as "due process," "general welfare," "equal protection," or even "commerce among the several States." But it has always hesitated to give any real meaning to the privileges and immunities clause lest it improvidently give too much.

This Court should, however, hold squarely that it is a privilege of citizenship of the United States, protected from state abridgment, to enter any state of the Union, either for temporary sojourn or for the establishment of permanent residence therein and for gaining resultant citizenship thereof. If national citizenship means less than this, it means nothing.

The language of the Fourteenth Amendment declaring two kinds of citizenship is discriminating. It is: "All persons born or naturalized in the United States, and subject to the jurisdiction thereof, are citizens of the United States and of the State wherein they reside." While it thus establishes national citizenship from the mere circumstances of birth within the territory and jurisdiction of the United States, birth within a state does not establish citizenship thereof. State citizenship is ephemeral. It results only from residence and is gained or lost therewith. That choice of residence was subject to local approval is contrary to the inescapable implications of the westward movement of our civilization.

Even as to an alien who had "been admitted to the United States under the Federal law," this Court, through Mr. Justice Hughes, declared that "He was thus admitted with the privilege of entering and abiding in the United States, and hence of entering and abiding in any State in the Union. . . ." Why we should hesitate to hold that federal citizenship implies rights to enter and abide in any state of the Union at least equal to those possessed by aliens passes my understanding. The world is even more upside down than I had supposed it to be, if California must accept aliens in deference to their federal privileges but is free to turn back citizens of the United States unless we treat them as subjects of commerce.

The right of the citizen to migrate from state to state which, I agree with Mr. Justice Douglas, is shown by our precedents to be one of national citizenship, is not, however, an unlimited one. In addition to being subject to all constitutional limitations imposed by the federal government, such citizen is subject to some control by state governments. He may not, if a fugitive from justice, claim freedom to migrate unmolested, nor may he endanger others by carrying contagion about. These causes, and perhaps others that do not occur to me now, warrant any public authority in stopping a man where it finds him and arresting his progress across a state line quite as much as from place to place within the state.

It is here that we meet the real crux of this case. Does "indigence" as defined by the application of the California statute constitute a basis for restricting the freedom of a citizen, as crime or contagion warrants its restriction? We should say now, and in no uncertain terms, that a man's mere property status, without more, cannot be used by a state to test, qualify, or limit his rights as a citizen of the United States. "Indigence" in itself is neither a source of rights or a basis for denying them. The mere state of being without funds is a neutral fact—constitutionally an irrelevance, like race, creed, or color. I agree with what I understand to be the holding of the Court that cases which may indicate the contrary are overruled.

Any measure which would divide our citizenry on the basis of property into one class free to move from state to state and another class that is poverty-bound to the place where it has suffered misfortune is not only at war with the habit and custom by which our country has expanded, but is also a short-sighted blow at the security of property itself. Property can have no more dangerous, even if unwitting, enemy than one who would make its possession a pretext for unequal or exclusive civil rights. Where those rights are derived from national citizenship no state may impose such a test, and whether the Congress could do so we are not called upon to inquire.

I think California had no right to make the condition of Duncan's purse, with no evidence of violation by him of any law or social policy which caused it, the basis of excluding him or of punishing one who extended him aid.

If I doubted whether his federal citizenship alone were enough to open the gates of California to Duncan, my doubt would disappear on consideration of the obligations of such citizenship. Duncan owes a duty to render military service, and this Court has said that this duty is the result of his citizenship. Mr. Chief Justice White declared in the *Selective Draft Law Cases,* 245 U.S. 366, . . . "It may not be doubted that the very conception of a just government and its duty to the citizen includes the reciprocal obligation of the citizen to render military service in case of need and the right to compel it." A contention that a citizen's duty to render military service is suspended by "indigence" would meet with little favor. Rich or penniless, Duncan's citizenship under the Constitution pledges his strength to the defense of California as a part of the United States, and his right to migrate to any part of the land he must defend is something she must respect under the same instrument. Unless this Court is willing to say that citizenship of the United States means at least this much to the citizen, then our heritage of constitutional privileges and immunities is only a promise to the ear to be broken to the hope, a teasing illusion like a munificent bequest in a pauper's will.

[Mr. Justice Douglas also wrote a concurring opinion, in which Mr. Justice Black and Mr. Justice Murphy joined. Justice Douglas agreed with Justice Jackson in maintaining that the right to move freely from state to state was an incident of national citizenship protected by the privileges and immunities clause of the Fourteenth Amendment.]

CHAPTER 9

The Commerce and Tax Powers of Congress

Despite Marshall's early broad interpretation of the Federal Government's commerce power in *Gibbons* v. *Ogden,* the development of the commerce clause as a grant of *positive* powers to Congress had no substantial development until the beginning of the twentieth century. Throughout the nineteenth century, decisions of the Supreme Court under the commerce clause dealt "almost entirely with the permissibility of state activity which it was claimed discriminated against or burdened interstate commerce. During this period there was perhaps little occasion for the affirmative exercise of the commerce power, and the *influence of the clause on American life and law was a negative one,* resulting almost wholly from its operation as a restraint upon the powers of the states." [1] After the Civil War, more and more economic activities were perceived as national in scope and as requiring national aid and regulation. For example, a unanimous decision of the

[1] *Wickard* v. *Filburn,* 317 U.S. 111 (1942). (Italics supplied.)

Supreme Court in the 1869 case of *Paul* v. *Virginia,* 8 Wall. 168, declared that a Virginia state statute did not offend the commerce clause because "issuing a policy of insurance is not a transaction of commerce." Seventy-five years later the Court held in *United States* v. *Southeastern Underwriters' Assoc.,* 322 U.S. 533 (1944), that the business of insurance is within the federal commerce power and, therefore, is subject to regulation under the Sherman Antitrust Act of 1890. In rendering the majority opinion, Justice Black remarked that no "commercial enterprise of any kind which conducts its activities across state lines" can be wholly beyond the commerce power of Congress. "We cannot make an exception of the business of insurance."

Perhaps nowhere is the change from local to national regulation better demonstrated than in the case of the railroads. In 1877, in a group of cases known as the Granger cases, the Supreme Court held that the states could fix minimum and maximum railroad and other rates in the absence of congressional legislation.[2] But only nine years later the Court felt compelled to repudiate its Granger decisions. In the Wabash case, *Wabash, St. Louis and Pacific Railroad Co.* v. *Illinois,* 118 U.S. 557 (1886), the Court struck down an Illinois statute that imposed penalties on railroads that charged lower rates per mile for long hauls than for short ones. Such long hauls, of course, nearly always extended beyond the borders of the state. The Court held that a state statute impinging to this extent on interstate railroad rates was in conflict with the commerce clause even though Congress had not legislated in this field. "Here was a matter that demanded single unified control. The interests of interstate movement could not be left to the individual policies of the states." [3] But if the states could not regulate, and Congress had not done so, how were railroad rates to be controlled? The answer came a few months after the *Wabash* case when Congress created the Interstate Commerce Commission (ICC) to fill the resulting gap. With the enactment of the Interstate Commerce Act of 1887, the commerce clause ". . . began to exert positive influence in American law and life. This first important federal resort to the commerce power was followed in 1890 by the Sherman Anti-Trust Act and, thereafter, mainly after 1903, by many others. These statutes ushered in new phases of adjudication, which required the Court to approach the interpretation of the commerce clause in the light of an actual exercise by Congress of its power thereunder." [4]

Some industrial and business interests of the country relied heavily on a narrow construction of the commerce clause as well as on the due process clause of the Fourteenth Amendment as constitutional weapons to resist govern-

[2] The first and most celebrated of the Granger cases was *Munn* v. *Illinois,* 94 U.S. 113 (1877), which is considered fully in Chapter 10. The Granger movement, which was influential particularly in the 1870s, was organized and led by western farmers who wished to curtail the abuses of the railroads. Their efforts resulted in the enactment of remedial legislation in a number of states. Some of this legislation was upheld in the Granger cases.

[3] Felix Frankfurter, *The Commerce Clause Under Marshall, Taney and Waite* (Chapel Hill: University of North Carolina Press, 1937), p. 100.

[4] *Wickard* v. *Filburn,* loc. cit.

mental control. The commerce clause had been the sole constitutional basis for the Sherman Act, which was intended to prevent combinations and conspiracies in restraint of trade. The Court first dealt with the Sherman Act [5] in *United States* v. *E. C. Knight Co.* (p. 264). It held that the Sherman Act could not be applied to a virtual monopoly of the sugar industry. In delivering the opinion, Chief Justice Fuller indicated clearly the Court's suspicion of any national legislation under the commerce clause that threatened the independence of the states and the nation's laissez-faire economic system. Justice Harlan, who was the lone dissenter in the case, remarked that "while the opinion of the Court does not declare the act of 1890 to be unconstitutional, it defeats the main object for which it was passed." During the same term the Court delivered two other extremely conservative opinions.

In *Pollock* v. *Farmers' Loan and Trust Co.* (p. 268), the Court held that taxes on income derived from land or personal property were direct taxes and therefore unconstitutional because they had not been properly levied. This case was overruled by the Sixteenth Amendment, which was ratified in 1913. In the case of In re *Debs,* 158 U.S. 564 (1895), the Court upheld a sweeping antilabor injunction issued in connection with the famous Pullman strike in Chicago during the summer of 1894. These three opinions brought storms of protest from large segments of the American people, who were now convinced that the judiciary had become the reactionary defender of entrenched economic interests.

"Even while important opinions in this line of restrictive authority were being written, however, other cases called forth broader interpretation of the commerce clause. . . ." [6] In *Swift and Co.* v. *United States,* 196 U.S. 375 (1905), the Court held that a combination of meat packers was an illegal monopoly under the Sherman Act on the ground that its activities were transactions in interstate commerce. Speaking for a unanimous Court, Justice Holmes stated the "commerce among the states is not a technical legal conception, but a practical one, drawn from the course of business. When cattle are sent for sale from a place in one state, with the expectation that they will end their transit, after purchase, in another, and when in effect they do so, with only the interruption necessary to find a purchaser at the stockyards, and when this is a typical, constantly recurring course, the current thus existing is a current of commerce among the states, and the purchase of the cattle is a part and incident of such commerce." [7]

[5] See Lawrence M. Friedman, *A History of American Law* (New York: Simon & Schuster, 1973), pp. 406–408.

[6] *Wickard* v. *Filburn,* loc. cit.

[7] Other prior cases also restricted the authority of the *Knight* case. In *Addyston Pipe and Steel Co.* v. *United States,* 175 U.S. 211 (1899), the Court held that a combination in the manufacture and sale of cast-iron pipe violated the Sherman Act. This was the first successful application of the Sherman Act to an industrial combination. In *Northern Securities Co.* v. *United States,* 193 U.S. 197 (1904), the Court held that the acquisition by a holding company of the stock of competing railroads was a violation of the Sherman Act.

In some later cases the Court continued to demonstrate its readiness to construe the commerce clause broadly. In the well-known Shreveport case [*Houston E. and W. Railroad Co.* v. *United States,* 234 U.S. 342 (1914)], the Court upheld the power of the ICC to fix intrastate railroad rates because of their effect on interstate commerce. Local or intrastate commerce could be regulated by the Federal Government in this situation because of its "close and substantial relation" to interstate commerce. And in the case of *Stafford* v. *Wallace,* 258 U.S. 495 (1922), the Court upheld, with only one dissenting vote, the Packers and Stockyards Act of 1921, which was designed to bring the activities of commission men and livestock dealers under federal control. In sustaining the statute, Chief Justice Taft relied heavily on the *Swift* decision and noted that the "application of the commerce clause of the Constitution in the *Swift* case was the result of the natural development of interstate commerce under modern conditions. It was the inevitable recognition of the great central fact that such streams of commerce from one part of the country to another, which are ever-flowing, are in their very essence the commerce among the states and with foreign nations which historically it was one of the chief purposes of the Constitution to bring under national protection and control."

Federal Police Powers

In a series of cases during the same period, the Court began to sustain the use of the commerce clause as a basis for the exercise of federal police powers. Theoretically, the power to legislate in the interest of the health, morals, safety, and the general welfare of the community is reserved to the states under the Tenth Amendment, because the Constitution does not grant such power to Congress. However, Congress has used some of its delegated powers, such as its commerce, taxing, and postal powers, to legislate for purely social and economic ends. In 1903, in the case of *Champion* v. *Ames,* 188 U.S. 321 (1903), the Court for the first time sustained a federal act based on the commerce clause that prohibited the interstate shipment of lottery tickets. Thus, the doctrine that Congress was empowered to exclude dangerous or evil objects from interstate commerce, the so-called "noxious products" doctrine, received judicial blessing. Shortly after the decision in the Lottery Case, Congress proceeded to enact a number of statutes that barred objectionable articles from interstate commerce or that forbade the use of interstate commerce facilities for immoral or criminal activities. The cases upholding these statutes are noted in *Hammer* v. *Dagenhart* (p. 272).

The Supreme Court's restrictive interpretation of the commerce clause appeared again in *Hammer* v. *Dagenhart.* In that case, the Court held that Congress could not prohibit from interstate commerce goods produced by child labor. The classic dissent of Justice Holmes in *Hammer* v. *Dagenhart* was used twenty-five years later by Justice Stone to overrule the majority opinion [*United States*

v. *Darby* (p. 284).] In the *Hammer* case, the Court relied heavily on its decision in the *United States* v. *E. C. Knight Co.*

Thus, when the Court was confronted with the constitutionality of the New Deal legislation under the commerce clause, two lines of precedent were available. The Court could construe the federal commerce power narrowly, as was done in *United States* v. *E. C. Knight Co.* and in *Hammer* v. *Dagenhart.* Or the Court could take a broad view of the commerce power, in line with the decisions in such cases as *Gibbons* v. *Ogden, Swift and Co.* v. *United States,* and *Stafford* v. *Wallace.*

CONGRESSIONAL TAXING POWER

Taxes are usually levied for the obvious purpose of raising money. But taxation inevitably is also a form of regulation. In the words of Justice Stone, "every tax is in some measure regulatory. To some extent it interposes an economic impediment to the activity taxed as compared with others not taxed." [8] Thus, the taxing power "becomes an instrument available to government for accomplishing objectives other than raising revenue." [9]

When tax laws are designed to produce income for the support of governmental activities, no constitutional questions are raised. Furthermore, the Supreme Court has generally sanctioned tax laws that are primarily regulatory or even destructive in nature when such laws are used to aid Congress in exercising some other power, such as the regulation of commerce or the control of the currency. In short, "regulatory or destructive taxation may properly be used as a means of doing anything falling within the delegated powers of Congress." [10] In 1866, for example, Congress levied an annual tax of 10 per cent on state bank notes. The purpose of the law was not revenue but rather to drive the state notes out of existence, thereby giving to the newly established national banks a monopoly of bank note circulation. The tax was upheld by the Supreme Court in *Veazie Bank* v. *Fenno,* 8 Wall. 533 (1869), on the ground that Congress could have achieved the same result by directly prohibiting the issuance of state bank notes under its power to regulate the currency.

On some occasions, however, Congress has used its taxing power to regulate matters that are *outside* the scope of any of its delegated powers. Such legislation raises much more difficult constitutional questions. In some early cases, the Supreme Court refused to look into the motives of Congress and sustained a number of regulatory or destructive tax laws. In *McCray* v. *United States,* 195 U.S. 27 (1904), the Court upheld an act which levied a ¼-cent per pound tax on uncolored oleomargarine and a tax of ten cents per pound on margarine colored yellow to resemble butter. The tax, which had been supported vigorously

[8] *Sonzinsky* v. *United States,* 300 U.S. 506 (1937).

[9] Roy Blough, *The Federal Taxing Process* (Englewood Cliffs, N.J.: Prentice-Hall, 1952), p. 410.

[10] Robert Cushman, "Social and Economic Control Through Taxation," *Minnesota Law Review,* Vol. 18 (1934), p. 759. Reprinted in *Selected Essays of Constitutional Law,* Vol. 3 (1938), p. 543.

by dairy farmers, was designed chiefly to discourage the consumption of margarine in favor of butter. Justice White, in delivering the majority opinion, quoted from a previous decision of Chief Justice Fuller, stating that "the act before us is on its face an act for levying taxes, and although it may operate in so doing to prevent deception in the sale of oleomargarine as and for butter, its primary object must be assumed to be the raising of revenue." Not until 1950 did the concerted efforts of margarine manufacturers, urban consumers, and others result in the repeal of all federal margarine taxes, over the vigorous opposition of the diary interests. Shortly after the *McCray* decision, when Congress was also in the process of expanding its federal police powers under the commerce clause, the taxing power was used to regulate the manufacture of white-phosphorous matches and narcotics. The match tax was never challenged in the courts, but the narcotics law was upheld in a 5-to-4 decision in *United States* v. *Doremus,* 249 U.S. 86 (1919).

In spite of these decisions, the Court announced a different doctrine in 1922 in the case of *Bailey* v. *Drexel Furniture Co.,* 259 U.S. 20, which declared the second Child Labor Law unconstitutional.[11] After *Hammer* v. *Dagenhart* had invalidated the Child Labor Law of 1916, the second Child Labor Law sought to accomplish the same objectives as the 1916 law by using the taxing power of Congress as the basis for regulation. A 10 per cent tax was imposed on the annual profits of mines and quarries that employed children under 16 and of mills and factories that employed children under the age of 14. But, again, the attempt to regulate child labor failed. The tax at issue in the *Bailey* case was declared to be a penalty rather than a true tax. In addition, the Court regarded the regulation of child labor as a function reserved to the states. The *Bailey* case thus established an important limitation on the congressional use of the taxing power for police power purposes.

Because the *Bailey* and *McCray* decisions were largely irreconcilable, the Court, after 1922, had two lines of reasoning that it could follow in dealing with tax as well as commerce statutes. The Court soon proceeded to make use of both precedents. For example, the doctrine of the *McCray* case was followed in *Magnano Co.* v. *Hamilton,* 292 U.S. 40 (1934), in which the Court upheld a state statute that taxed all butter substitutes in the state so heavily that they were driven out of the market. In the *Magnano* case the Court refused to examine the motives behind the tax. On the other hand, the Court followed the *Bailey* case in *United States* v. *Constantine,* 296 U.S. 287 (1935). In that case a special federal excise tax of $1,000 on retail liquor dealers who violated state laws was held to be a penalty rather than a tax and thereby an encroachment upon the police powers of the state.

By the time the New Deal statutes came before the Court, the two possible lines of reasoning had been established clearly. The Court's use of the two available precedents to 1935 has been well summarized as follows:

[11] On the same day the *Bailey* decision was rendered, the Court held void the Future Trading Act of 1921, which imposed a heavy tax on the sale of grain for future delivery. [*Hill* v. *Wallace,* 259 U.S. 44 (1922)]. The act was invalidated on the authority of the *Bailey* case.

> When it [the Supreme Court] wishes to uphold the statute, it utilizes the doctrine of the *McCray* and *Magnano* cases, which may be called the doctrine of judicial obtuseness, and refuses to see or know about the tax anything that does not appear in the language of the act. If, however, the act pushes too far and impinges upon interests that the Court feels are entitled to protection, it falls back upon the doctrine of the child-labor case *[Bailey]*, takes judicial notice of the palpable legislative intention to destroy rather than to raise money, and declares the act void on the ground that it is not a tax at all but a regulation.[12]

The Expanding National Commerce and Tax Powers

By 1936 the more restrictive views of commerce and tax powers had come into violent collision with the New Deal. In the process of invalidating a number of key New Deal measures, the Court majority had opposed vigorously any expansion of the federal commerce power. In fact, the Court seemed determined, in the *Schechter* case (p. 275), which invalidated the National Industrial Recovery Act (NIRA), to maintain the distinction between commerce and manufacturing as enunciated in *United States* v. *E. C. Knight* and *Hammer* v. *Dagenhart.* And in *Carter* v. *Carter Coal Co.,* 298 U.S. 238 (1936), which held void the Bituminous Coal Conservation Act of 1935 (Guffey Act), the Court emphasized that Congress could not regulate the relations between employers and workmen in the coal industry because such relations did not affect interstate commerce directly.[13] Justice Sutherland's vigorous defense of states' rights in the majority opinion in the *Carter* case appeared to doom the New Deal's efforts to control various aspects of industrial activity.[14]

Yet less than a year later, on April 12, 1937, the Supreme Court ruled that the *Schechter* and *Carter* precedents were "inapplicable" and upheld the National Labor Relations Act (Wagner Act) in a series of five separate cases. In the

[12] Robert Cushman, "Constitutional Law in 1933–34," *American Political Science Review,* Vol. 29 (Feb. 1935), p. 51.

[13] *Carter* and *Schechter* also rest on the alternate ground that the statutes at issue make unconstitutional delegations of congressional authority. Another anti-New Deal decision, *Panama Refining Co.* v. *Ryan,* 293 U.S. 388 (1935), principally rests on such a finding. All three have been severely criticized because both before and since the Court has approved broad delegation of congressional power to the President without concerning itself excessively with whether Congress has established clear standards limiting executive discretion. [See *Brig Aurora* v. *United States,* 7 Cr. 382 (1813); *Field* v. *Clark,* 143 U.S. 649 (1892); and *Yakus* v. *United States,* 321 U.S. 414 (1944).] Nevertheless, the further delegation of government power to private groups, for the "presidential codes" in *Schechter* were really price-fixing agreements among private businessmen, raises troubling problems that may yet lead to a revival of the reputation of that opinion. See Theodore Lowi, *The End of Liberalism* (New York: Norton, 1969), p. 298; Sotirios Barber, *The Constitution and the Delegation of Congressional Power* (Chicago: University of Chicago Press, 1975).

[14] During this same period, the case of *Kentucky Whip and Collar Co.* v. *Illinois Central R.R. Co.,* 299 U.S. 334 (1937), was also decided. Here the Court subscribed to a broader view of the commerce clause, as it refused to apply cases that had been most restrictive in the interpretation of the commerce power. The restrictive interpretation was also weakened by *Whitfield* v. *Ohio,* 297 U.S. 431 (1936). This case sustained the Hawes-Cooper Act of 1929, which provided that convict-made goods would be subject to the laws of the state on their arrival therein.

first and most important of these cases [*National Labor Relations Board* v. *Jones and Laughlin Steel Corp.* (p. 280)], the Court gave the federal interstate commerce power its maximum sweep. The "*Jones and Laughlin* case is the great modern case on the scope of federal power over interstate commerce. Other cases involving much smaller businesses were decided the same day with the same result. The way was open for general control of business by the Federal Government if the people so wished. The panoramic view of the *Jones and Laughlin* case emerges: the United States consists no longer of fifty separate economic entities. Economically we are one nation, and accordingly, in economic matters we stand or fall together." [15] Two facts must be noted about the Wagner Act cases: (1) The cases were decided by the same justices who had invalidated the key New Deal measures; this was made possible when Justice Roberts abandoned the conservatives and voted with the liberal group. (2) The decision came at a time when the Roosevelt court-packing proposal was being hotly debated, so that the President's proposed court reform now seemed unnecessary.

A comparable story can be told in the tax area. In January 1936, the Court held unconstitutional a major New Deal measure, the Agricultural Adjustment Act (AAA) of 1933, in *United States* v. *Butler,* 297 U.S. 1 (1936). This law was designed to increase the price of agricultural products, and thereby the farmers' purchasing power, by reducing the production of basic agricultural commodities. Provision was made for benefit payments to farmers who reduced the production of cotton, tobacco, wheat, and other items. The money for the payments was to be raised by levying a tax on the processors of agricultural commodities, such as meat packers and textile manufacturers. The Court followed the narrow construction of federal taxing power announced in the *Bailey* and *Constantine* cases by looking to the purpose of the tax, which was clearly the regulation of agriculture. The Court held agriculture to be a purely local matter beyond the reach of Congress. The New Deal lawyers had sought to justify the payments to farmers under the general welfare clause of the Constitution (Article I, Section 8), arguing that Congress had the power to spend and tax for the general welfare. For the first time, the Court interpreted this clause. Although the Court endorsed Hamilton's expansive version of the general welfare clause, its decision comes closer to Madison's narrower concept of the clause. For though it suggests that the clause does create an independent congressional power apart from the other congressional powers enumerated in Article I, the Court also holds that this power is limited by the reserved powers of the states. In effect, it limits the taxing power to the same scope as the commerce power. Just as Congress cannot reach agriculture under the commerce power because it is purely local, it cannot be reached under the tax power.

The decision in the *Butler* case undermined the Roosevelt farm program and raised serious doubts about the constitutionality of other important New Deal measures. Yet only sixteen months later, the *Butler* decision was narrowed greatly in *Steward Machine Co.* v. *Davis,* 301 U.S. 548 (1937), which upheld

[15] Jere Williams, *The Supreme Court Speaks* (Austin: University of Texas Press, 1956), p. 295.

a payroll tax on employers to finance the unemployment compensation provisions of the Social Security Act of 1935. On the same day the Court sustained the old-age pension phase of the Social Security program in *Helvering* v. *Davis,* 301 U.S. 619 (1937). In these cases, the Court employed a broader interpretation of the federal taxing power, among other things, as *Butler* had suggested, holding that there was an independent congressional power to tax and spend for the general welfare.

It is difficult to reconcile the *Butler* and *Steward Machine Company* decisions. Workers' retirement benefits, like agriculture, could have been viewed as a purely local matter beyond the delegated powers of Congress. As in *Jones and Laughlin,* Justice Roberts's vote was decisive. Even though he had written the *Butler* opinion, he now voted with the liberals. A Court majority was now ready to accept the New Deal. The Social Security Act cases mark the turn of the tide in the Court's attitude toward New Deal legislation. Since 1937, the expansion of national power under the commerce clause has opened the way for federal tax levies whose purpose is primarily regulation rather than revenue.

In *Mulford* v. *Smith,* 307 U.S. 38 (1939), the Court upheld the AAA of 1938 as it pertained to the fixing of marketing quotas for flue-cured tobacco. The act was based on the commerce clause. In *United States* v. *Darby* (p. 284), it upheld the application of a federal wages and hours statute to the employees of a Georgia lumber manufacturer. The doctrines that agriculture and manufacturing were local activities not in interstate commerce were dead. In the extreme case of *Wickard* v. *Filburn* (p. 286), the Court went a step farther. The unanimous opinion of the Court in the *Filburn* case represents one of the broadest holdings to date under the commerce clause.[16] That case has recently been reaffirmed in *Katzenbach* v. *McClung,* 379 U.S. 294 (1964), upholding the constitutionality, under the commerce clause, of the Civil Rights Act of 1964 as applied to restaurants that have no interstate customers but receive some of their foodstuffs from other states. It may well be that today "the federal commerce power is as broad as the economic needs of the nation," [17] and indeed must be broad enough to go far beyond purely economic needs.

Contemporary Commerce and Tax Powers

In recent years commerce clause questions have arisen far less in relation to pure economic regulation than in connection with new federal statutes aimed at criminal conspiracies, organized crime, and incitement to violence. With

[16] For other broad interpretations see *United States* v. *Sullivan,* 332 U.S. 689 (1948); *Lorain Journal Co.* v. *United States,* 342 U.S. 143 (1951); and *Perez* v. *United States,* 402 U.S. 146 (1971). In this last case the Court upheld a federal antiloan-sharking statute because "It appears . . . that loan sharking in its national setting is one way organized interstate crime holds its guns to the heads of the poor and the rich alike and syphons funds from numerous localities to finance its national operations."

[17] *American Power and Light Co.* v. *Securities and Exchange Commission,* 329 U.S. 90 (1946).

the exception of the *Perez* case just noted, few of these issues have as yet reached the Supreme Court. However, the key public accommodations sections of the civil rights legislation of the 1960s (see Chapter 5) were grounded in the commerce clause. We have already noted the *McClung* case. The key case is *Heart of Atlanta Motel* v. *United States* (p. 289), which reminds us that *Gibbons* v. *Ogden* continues to be part of the living Constitution. The Court uses the eighteenth-century wisdom of Marshall to uphold the power of Congress to desegregate a very twentieth-century motel. In *Daniel* v. *Paul,* 395 U.S. 298 (1969), the Court goes even further in holding that an amusement area used for boating and picnicking, located twelve miles from the nearest city, on county roads and far from any major interstate highway, is nevertheless within reach of Congress's commerce power and thus of the civil rights statutes.

The language of the more recent tax cases shows that the Supreme Court will allow wide use of the federal taxing power for the promotion of almost any general welfare program. In *United States* v. *Sanchez,* 340 U.S. 42 (1950), the Court sustained a federal regulatory tax on sales of marijuana. Speaking for the Court, Justice Clark said:

> It is beyond serious question that a tax does not cease to be valid merely because it regulates, discourages, or even definitely deters the activities taxed. The principle applies even though the revenue obtained is obviously negligible, or the revenue purpose of the tax may be secondary. Nor does a tax statute necessarily fall because it touches on activities which Congress might not otherwise regulate. The tax in question is a legitimate exercise of the taxing power despite its collateral regulatory purpose and effect.

The Court reconfirmed this broad position on federal regulation by taxation in another case involving federal laws on narcotics and marijuana, *Minor* v. *United States,* 396 U.S. (1969).

In *United States* v. *Kahriger,* 345 U.S. 22 (1953), the Court upheld a 1951 federal occupational tax on gambling that was designed to regulate as well as to produce some revenue. In *Marchetti* v. *United States,* 390 U.S. 39 (1968), the Supreme Court overruled Kahriger on self-incrimination grounds, but continued to approve the broad theory of taxation on which it had rested. In a companion case to *Marchetti,* the Court struck down a similar tax on gun dealers. Congress then amended the National Firearms Act to overcome self-incrimination objections. The Court upheld the amended act in *United States* v. *Freed,* 401 U.S. 601 (1971), holding that under the revised procedures "the information in the hands of the Internal Revenue Service, as a matter of practice, is not available to state or other federal authorities and, as a matter of law, cannot be used as evidence in a criminal proceeding with respect to a prior or concurrent violation of law."

The Burger Court has reentered the commerce clause–economic regulation area. In *National League of Cities* v. *Usery* (p. 146), for the first time since 1937 the Court struck down a federal statute as a violation of the commerce clause (see Chapter 5). In *Goldfarb* v. *Virginia State Bar Association,* 421 U.S.

773 (1975), however, it read the clause very expansively to allow application of the Sherman Act to the action of a county bar association in suggesting minimum fees for title searches performed by lawyers in conjunction with real estate sales. [See also *McLain* v. *Real Estate Board of New Orleans,* 444 U.S. 232 (1980).]

UNITED STATES *v.* E. C. KNIGHT CO.

156 U.S. 1; 15 Sup. Ct. 249; 39 L. Ed. 325 (1895)

[In 1892, the American Sugar Refining Company, a New Jersey corporation that controlled a majority of the sugar refining companies in the United States, obtained nearly complete control of the manufacture and distribution of refined sugar by purchasing the stock of the E. C. Knight Company and three other Philadelphia refineries. The government brought suit under the newly enacted Sherman Antitrust Act of 1890 to break up the company on the ground that it constituted a "combination . . . in restraint of trade and commerce among the several states." The lower federal courts held that the facts did not show a contract, combination, or conspiracy to restrain or monopolize trade or commerce. The United States then brought the case to the Supreme Court on appeal.]

MR. CHIEF JUSTICE FULLER, after stating the case, delivered the opinion of the Court:

. . . The fundamental question is, whether conceding that the existence of a monopoly in manufacture is established by the evidence, that monopoly can be directly suppressed under the act of Congress in the mode attempted by this bill.

It cannot be denied that the power of a State to protect the lives, health, and property of its citizens, and to preserve good order and the public morals, "the power to govern men and things within the limits of its dominion," is a power originally and always belonging to the States, not surrendered by them to the general government, nor directly restrained by the Constitution of the United States, and essentially exclusive. The relief of the citizens of each State from the burden of monopoly and the evils resulting from the restraint of trade among such citizens was left with the States to deal with, and this court has recognized their possession of that power even to the extent of holding that an employment or business carried on by private individuals, when it becomes a matter of such public interest and importance as to create a common charge or burden upon the citizen; in other words, when it becomes a practical monopoly, to which the citizen is compelled to resort and by means of which a tribute can be exacted from the community, is subject to regulation by state legislative power. On the other hand, the power of Congress to regulate commerce among the several States is also exclusive. The Constitution does not provide that interstate commerce shall be free, but, by the grant of this exclusive power to regulate it, it was left free except as Congress might impose restraints. Therefore it has been determined that the failure of Congress to exercise this exclusive power in any case is an expression of its will that the subject shall be free from restrictions or imposition upon it by the several States, and if a law passed by a State in the exercise of its acknowledged powers comes into conflict with that will, the Congress and the State cannot occupy the position of equal opposing sovereignities, because the Constitution declares its supremacy and that of the laws passed in pursuance thereof; and that which is not supreme must yield to that which is supreme. "Commerce, undoubtedly, is traffic," said Chief Justice Marshall, "but it is something more; it is intercourse. It describes the commercial intercourse between nations and parts of nations in all its branches, and is regulated by prescribing rules for carrying on that intercourse." That which belongs to commerce is within the jurisdiction of the United States, but that which does not belong to commerce is within the jurisdiction of the police power of the State. . . .

The argument is that the power to control the manufacture of refined sugar is a monopoly over a necessary of life, to the enjoyment of which by a large part of the population of the United States interstate commerce is indispensible, and that, therefore, the general government in the exercise of the power to regulate commerce may repress such monopoly directly and set aside the instruments which have created it. But this argument cannot be confined to necessaries of life merely, and must include all articles of general consumption. Doubtless the power to control the manufacture of a given thing involves in a certain sense the control of its disposition, but this is a secondary and not the primary sense; and although the exercise of that power may result in bringing the operation of commerce into play, it does not control it, and affects it only incidentally and indirectly. Commerce succeeds to manufacture, and is not a part of it. The power to regulate commerce is the power to prescribe the rule by which commerce shall be governed, and is a power independent of the power to suppress monopoly. But it may operate in repression of monopoly whenever that comes within the rules by which commerce is governed or whenever the transaction is itself a monopoly of commerce.

It is vital that the independence of the commercial power and of the police power, and the delimitation between them, however sometimes perplexing, should always be recognized and observed, for while the one furnishes the strongest bond of union, the other is essential to the preservation of the autonomy of the States as required by our dual form of government; and acknowledged evils, however grave and urgent they may appear to be, had better be borne, than the risk be run, in the effort to suppress them, of more serious consequences by resort to expedients of even doubtful constitutionality.

It will be perceived how far-reaching the proposition is that the power of dealing with a monopoly directly may be exercised by the general government whenever interstate or international commerce may be ultimately affected. The regulation of commerce applies to the subjects of commerce and not to matters of internal police. Contracts to buy, sell, or exchange goods to be transported among the several States, the transportation and its instrumentalities, and articles bought, sold, or exchanged for the purposes of such transit among the States, or put in the way of transit, may be regulated, but this is because they form part of interstate trade or commerce. The fact that an article is manufactured for export to another State does not of itself make it an article of interstate commerce, and the intent of the manufacturer does not determine the time when the article or product passes from the control of the State and belongs to commerce. . . .

Contracts, combinations, or conspiracies to control domestic enterprise in manufacture, agriculture, mining, production in all its forms, or to raise or lower prices or wages, might unquestionably tend to restrain external as well as domestic trade, but the restraint would be an indirect result, however inevitable and whatever its extent, and such result would not necessarily determine the object of the contract, combination, or conspiracy.

Again, all the authorities agree that in order to vitiate a contract or combination it is not essential that its result should be a complete monopoly; it is sufficient if it really tends to that end and to deprive the public of the advantages which flow from free competition. Slight reflection will show that if the national power extends to all contracts and combinations in manufacture, agriculture, mining, and other productive industries, whose ultimate result may affect external commerce, comparatively little of business operations and affairs would be left for state control.

It was in the light of well-settled principles that the act of July 2, 1890, was framed. Congress did not attempt thereby to assert the power to deal with monopoly directly as such; or to limit and restrict the rights of corporations created by the States or the citizens of the States, in the acquisition, control, or disposition of property; or to regulate or prescribe the price or prices at which such property or the products thereof should be sold; or to make criminal the acts of persons in the acquisition and control of property which the States of their residence or creation sanctioned or permitted. Aside from the provisions applicable where Congress might exercise municipal power, what the law struck at was combinations, contracts, and conspiracies to monopolize trade and commerce among the several States or with foreign nations; but the contracts and acts of the defendants related exclusively to the acquisition of the Philadelphia refineries and the business of sugar refining in Pennsylvania, and bore no direct relation to commerce between the States or with foreign nations. The object was manifestly private gain in the manufacture of the commodity, but not through the control of interstate or foreign commerce. It is true that the bill alleged that the products of these refineries were sold and distributed among the several States, and that all the companies were engaged in trade or commerce with the several States and with foreign nations; but this was no more than to say that trade and commerce served manufacture to fulfill its function. . . . There was nothing in the proofs to indicate any intention to put a restraint upon trade or commerce, and the fact, as we have seen, that trade or commerce might be indirectly affected was not enough to entitle complainants to a decree. . .

Decree affirmed.

MR. JUSTICE HARLAN, dissenting:

. . . In its consideration of the important constitutional question presented, this court assumes on the record before us that the result of the transactions disclosed by the pleadings and proof was the creation of a monopoly in the manufacture of a necessary of life. If this combination, so far as its operations necessarily or directly affect interstate commerce, cannot be restrained or suppressed under some power granted to Congress, it will be cause for regret that the patriotic statesmen who framed the Constitution did not foresee the necessity of investing the national government with power to deal with gigantic monopolies holding in their grasp, and injuriously controlling in their own interest, the entire trade among the States in food products that are essential to the comfort of every household in the land. . . .

What is commerce among the States? The decisions of this court fully answer the question. "Commerce, undoubtedly, is traffic, but it is something more; it is intercourse." It does not embrace the completely interior traffic of the respective States—that which is "carried on between man and man in a State, or between different parts of the same State and which does not extend to or affect other States"—but it does embrace "every species of commercial intercourse" between the United States and foreign nations and among the States, and, therefore, it includes such traffic or trade, buying, selling, and interchange of commodities, as directly affects or necessarily involves the interests of the People of the United States. "Commerce, as the word is used in the Constitution, is a unit," and "cannot stop at the external boundary line of each State, but may be introduced into the interior." "The genius and character of the whole government seem to be, that its action is to be applied to all the external concerns of the nation, and to those internal concerns which affect the States generally."

These principles were announced in *Gibbons* v. *Ogden,* and have often been approved. . . .

In the light of these principles, determining as well the scope of the power to regulate commerce among the States as the nature of such commerce, we are to inquire whether the act of Congress July 2, 1890, . . . entitled "An act to protect trade and commerce against unlawful restraints and monopolies," . . . is repugnant to the Constitution. . . .

It would seem to be indisputable that no combination of corporations or individuals can, of right, impose unlawful restraints upon interstate trade, whether upon transportation or upon such interstate intercourse and traffic as precede transportation, any more than it can, of right, impose unreasonable restraints upon the completely internal traffic of a State. The supposition cannot be indulged that this general proposition will be disputed. If it be true that a combination of corporations or individuals may, so far as the power of Congress is concerned, subject interstate trade, in any of its stages, to unlawful restraints, the conclusion is inevitable that the Constitution has failed to accomplish one primary object of the Union, which was to place commerce among the States under the control of the common government of all the people, and thereby relieve or protect it against burdens or restrictions imposed, by whatever authority, for the benefit of particular localities or special interest. . . .

The power of Congress covers and protects the absolute freedom of such intercourse and trade among the States as may or must succeed manufacture and precede transportation from place of purchase. This would seem to be conceded; for, the court in the present case expressly declare that "contracts to buy, sell, or exchange goods to be transported among the several States, the transportation and its instrumentalities, and articles bought, sold, or exchanged for the purpose of such transit among the States, or put in the way of transit, may be regulated, but this is because they form part of interstate trade or commerce." Here is a direct admission—one which the settled doctrines of this court justify—that contracts to buy and the purchasing of goods to be transported from one State to another, and transportation, with its instrumentalities, are all parts of interstate trade or commerce. Each part of such trade is then under the protection of Congress. And yet, by the opinion and judgment in this case, if I do not misapprehend them, Congress is without power to protect the commercial intercourse that such purchasing necessarily involves against the restraints and burdens arising from the existence of combinations that meet purchasers, from whatever State they come, with the threat—for it is nothing more or less than a threat—that they shall not purchase what they desire to purchase, except at the prices fixed by such combinations. A citizen of Missouri has the right to go in person, or send orders, to Pennsylvania and New Jersey for the purpose of purchasing refined sugar. But of what value is that right if he is confronted in those States by a vast combination which absolutely controls the price of that article by reason of its having acquired all the sugar refineries in the United States in order that they may fix prices in their own interest exclusively?

In my judgment, the citizens of the several States composing the Union are entitled, of right, to buy goods in the State where they are manufactured, or in any other State, without being confronted by an illegal combination whose business extends throughout the whole country, which by the law everywhere is an enemy to the public interests, and which prevents such buying, except at prices arbitrarily fixed by it. I insist that the free course of trade among the States cannot coexist with such combinations. When I speak of trade I mean the buying and selling of articles of every kind that are recognized articles of interstate commerce. Whatever improperly obstructs the free course of interstate intercourse and trade, as involved in the buying and selling of articles to be carried from one State to another, may be reached by Congress, under its authority to regulate commerce among the States. The exercise of that authority so as to make trade among the States, in all recognized articles of commerce, absolutely free from unreasonable or illegal restrictions imposed by combinations, is justified by an express grant of power to Congress and would redound to the welfare of the whole country. I am unable to perceive that any such result would imperil the autonomy of the States, especially as that result cannot be attained through the action of any one State. . . .

To the general government has been committed the control of commercial intercourse among the States, to the end that it may be free at all times from any restraints except such as Congress may impose or permit for the benefit of the whole country. The common government of all the people is the only one that can adequately deal with a matter which directly and injuriously affects the entire commerce of the country, which concerns equally all the people of the Union, and which, it must be confessed, cannot be adequately controlled by any one State. Its authority should not be so weakened by construction that it cannot reach and eradicate evils that, beyond all question, tend to defeat an object which that government is entitled, by the Constitution, to accomplish. . . .

I dissent from the opinion and judgment of the court.

POLLOCK *v.* FARMERS' LOAN AND TRUST CO.
158 U.S. 601; 15 Sup. Ct. 673; 39 L. Ed. 1108 (1895)

[Article I, Section 2, clause 3; and Article 1, Section 9, clause 4 provide that "direct taxes must be apportioned among the states according to population." Direct taxes (with the exception of income taxes) have seldom been used in the United States. In 1861, an income tax law was upheld by the Supreme Court in a unanimous decision in Springer *v.* United States, *102 U. S. 586 (1881). This statute expired in 1872, but in 1894 another, somewhat different, income tax law was passed by a Democratic Congress. It imposed a tax of 2 per cent on incomes above $4,000. Incomes from (1) real estate; (2) stocks, bonds, and other securities; (3) state and municipal bonds; and (4) wages, salaries, and professional earnings were subject to the tax. The law was widely supported by the Populist party, the South, and a scattering of agricultural states. Most opposition came from both Republicans and Democrats in the industrial states, where most of the tax would be collected. The law was tested before the Supreme Court in a most unorthodox way. The ordinary way to test the validity of a tax law is to pay the tax and then sue the government to get it back. But business leaders, who bitterly denounced the law as socialistic, wished to avoid any delay. A New York lawyer, therefore, arranged to have Charles Pollock, a Boston stockholder of the Farmer's Loan and Trust Company, demand that his company refuse to pay the tax. Pollock filed a bill in a federal circuit court to enjoin the trust company from paying the income tax.*

On April 8, 1895, the Court, with Justice Howell E. Jackson absent because of illness, declared the law invalid only insofar as it was applied to income from real estate and state and municipal bonds. The Court was divided on the other questions presented. Within a month, however, a rehearing was granted and the decision below rendered.]

MR. CHIEF JUSTICE FULLER delivered the opinion of the Court:

. . . [T]he Constitution divided Federal taxation into two great classes, the class of direct taxes, and the class of duties, imposts, and excise; and prescribed two rules which qualified the grant of power as to each class.

The power to lay direct taxes apportioned among the several States in proportion to their representation in the popular branch of Congress, a representation based on population as ascertained by the census, was plenary and absolute; but to lay direct taxes without apportionment was forbidden. The power to lay duties, imposts, and excises was subject to the qualification that the imposition must be uniform throughout the United States.

Our previous decision was confined to the consideration of the validity of the tax on the income from real estate, and on the income from municipal bonds. The question thus limited was whether such taxation was direct or not, in the meaning of the Constitution; and the court went no farther, as to the tax on the income from real estate, than to hold that it fell within the same class as the source whence the income was derived, that is, that a tax upon the realty and a tax upon the receipts therefrom were alike direct; while as to the income from municipal bonds, that could not be taxed because of want of power to tax the source, and no reference was made to the nature of the tax as being direct or indirect.

We are now permitted to broaden the field of inquiry, and to determine to which of the two great classes a tax upon a person's entire income, whether derived from rents, or products, or otherwise, of real estate, or from bonds, stocks, or other forms of personal property, belongs; and we are unable to conclude that the enforced subtraction from the yield of all the owner's real or personal property, in the manner prescribed, is so different from a tax upon the property itself, that it is not a direct, but an indirect tax, in the meaning of the Constitution. . . .

We know of no reason for holding otherwise than that the words "direct taxes," on the one hand, and "duties, imposts and excises," on the other, were used in the Constitution in their natural and obvious sense. Nor, in arriving at what those terms embrace, do we perceive any ground for enlarging them beyond, or narrowing them within, their natural and obvious import at the time the Constitution was framed and ratified. . . .

In the light of the struggle in the convention as to whether or not the new Nation should be empowered to levy taxes directly on the individual until after the States had failed to respond to requisitions—a struggle which did not terminate until the amendment to the effect, proposed by Massachusetts and concurred in by South Carolina, New Hampshire, New York, and Rhode Island, had been rejected—it would seem beyond reasonable question that direct taxation, taking the place as it did of requisitions, was purposely restrained to apportionment according to representation, in order that the former system as to ratio might be retained, while the mode of collection was changed. . . .

The reasons for the clauses of the Constitution in respect of direct taxation are not far to seek. The States, respectively, possessed plenary powers of taxation. They could tax the property of their citizens in such manner and to such extent as they saw fit; they had unrestricted powers to impose duties or imposts on imports from abroad, and excises on manufactures, consumable commodities, or otherwise. They gave up the great sources of revenue derived from commerce; they retained the concurrent power of levying excises, and duties covering anything other than excises; but in respect of them the range of taxation was narrowed by the power granted over interstate commerce, and by the danger of being put at disadvantage in dealing with excises on manufactures. They retained the power of direct taxation, and to that they looked as their chief resource; but even in respect of that, they granted the concurrent power, and if the tax were placed by both governments on the same subject, the claim of the United States had preference. Therefore, they did not grant the power of direct taxation without regard to their own condition and resources as States; but they granted the power of apportioned direct taxation, a power just as efficacious to serve the needs of the general government, but securing to the States the opportunity to pay the amount apportioned, and to recoup from their own citizens in the most feasible way, and in harmony with their systems of local self-government. If, in the changes of wealth and population in particular States, apportionment produced inequality, it was an inequality stipulated for, just as the equal representation of the States, however small, in the Senate, was stipulated for. The Constitution ordains affirmatively that each State shall have two members of that body, and negatively that no State shall by amendment be deprived of its equal suffrage in the Senate without its consent. The Constitution ordains affirmatively that representatives and direct taxes shall be apportioned among the several States according to numbers, and negatively that no direct tax shall be laid unless in proportion to the enumeration. . . . it seems to us to inevitably follow that in Mr. Hamilton's judgment at that time all internal taxes, except duties and excises on articles of consumption, fell into the category of direct taxes. . . .

Thus we find Mr. Hamilton . . . gives, . . . a definition which covers the question before us. A tax upon one's whole income is a tax upon the annual receipts from his whole property, and as such falls within the same class as a tax upon that property, and is a direct tax, in the meaning of the Constitution. And Mr. Hamilton in his report on the public credit, in referring to contracts with citizens of a foreign country, said: "This principle, which seems critically correct, would exempt as well the income as the capital of the property. It protects the use, as effectually as the thing. What, in fact, is property, but a fiction, without the beneficial use of it? In many cases, indeed, the income or annuity is the property itself."

. . . The Constitution prohibits any direct tax, unless in proportion to numbers as ascertained by the census; and in the light of the circumstances to which we have referred, is it not an evasion of the prohibition to hold that a general unapportioned tax, imposed upon all property owners as a body for or in respect of their property, is not direct, in the meaning of the Constitution, because confined to the income therefrom?

Whatever the speculative views of political economists or revenue reformers may be, can it be properly held that the Constitution, taken in its plain and obvious sense, and with due regard to the circumstances attending the formation of the government, authorizes a general unapportioned tax on the products of the farm and the rents of real estate, although imposed merely because of ownership and with no possible means of escape from payment, as belonging to a totally different class from that which includes the property from whence the income proceeds?

There can be but one answer, unless the constitutional restriction is to be treated as utterly illusory and futile, and the object of its framers defeated. We find it impossible to hold that a fundamental requisition, deemed so important as to be enforced by two provisions, one affirmative and one negative, can be refined away by forced distinctions between that which gives value to property, and the property itself.

Nor can we perceive any ground why the same reasoning does not apply to capital in personality held for the purpose of income or ordinarily yielding income, and to the income therefrom. All the real estate of the country, and all its invested personal property, are open to the direct operation of the taxing power if an apportionment be made according to the Constitution. The Constitution does not say that no direct tax shall be laid by apportionment on any other property than land; on the contrary, it forbids all unapportioned direct taxes; and we know of no warrant for excepting personal property from the exercise of the power, or any reason why an apportioned direct tax cannot be laid and assessed.

The stress of the argument is thrown, however, on the assertion that an income tax is not a property tax at all; that it is not a real estate tax, or a crop tax, or a bond tax; that it is an assessment upon the taxpayer on account of his money-spending power as shown by his revenue for the year preceding the . . . assessment; that rent received, crops harvested, interest collected, have lost all connection with their origin, and although once not taxable have become transmuted in their new form into taxable subject-matter; in other words, that income is taxable irrespective of the source from whence it is derived. . . .

We have unanimously held in this case that, so far as this law operates on the receipts from municipal bonds, it cannot be sustained, because it is a tax on the power of the States, and on their instrumentalities to borrow money, and consequently repugnant to the Constitution. But if, as contended, the interest when received has become merely money in the recipient's pocket, and taxable as such without reference to the source from which it came, the question is immaterial whether it could have been originally taxed at all or not. This was admitted by the Attorney General with characteristic candor; and it follows that, if the revenue derived from municipal bonds cannot be taxed because the source cannot be, the same rule applies to revenue from any other source not subject to the tax; and the lack of power to levy any but an apportioned tax on real and personal property equally exists as to the revenue therefrom.

Admitting that this act taxes the income of property irrespective of its source, still we cannot doubt that such a tax is necessarily a direct tax in the meaning of the Constitution. . . .

Our conclusions may, therefore, be summed up as follows:

First. We adhere to the opinion already announced, that, taxes on real estate being indisputably direct taxes, taxes on the rents or income of real estate are equally direct taxes.

Second. We are of opinion that taxes on personal property, or on the income of personal property, are likewise direct taxes.

Third. The tax imposed by Sections 27 to 37, inclusive, of the act of 1894, so far as it falls on the income of real estate and of personal property, being a direct tax within the meaning of the Constitution, and, therefore, unconstitutional and void because not apportioned according to representation, all those sections, constituting one entire scheme of taxation, are necessarily invalid.

The decrees herein before entered in this court will be vacated; the decrees below will be reversed, and the cases remanded, with instructions to grant the relief prayer.

MR. JUSTICE HARLAN, dissenting:

. . . In my judgment a tax on income derived from real property ought not to be, and until now has never been, regarded by any court as a direct tax on such property within the meaning of the Constitution. As the great mass of lands in most of the States do not bring any rents, and as incomes from rents vary in the different States, such a tax cannot possibly be apportioned among the States on the basis merely of numbers with any approach to equality of right among taxpayers, any more than a tax on carriages or other personal property could be so apportioned. And, in view of former adjudications, beginning with the *Hylton* case and ending with the *Springer* case, a decision now that a tax on income from real property can be laid and collected only by apportioning the same among the States, on the basis of numbers, may, not improperly, be regarded as a judicial revolution, that may sow the seeds of hate and distrust among the people of different sections of our common country. . . .

In determining whether a tax on income from rents is a direct tax, within the meaning of the Constitution, the inquiry is not whether it may in some way indirectly affect the land or the land owner, but whether it is a direct tax on the thing taxed, the land. The circumstance that such a tax may possibly have the effect to diminish the value of the use of the land is neither decisive of the question nor important. While a tax on the land itself, whether at a fixed rate applicable to all lands without regard to their value, or by the acre or according to their market value, might be deemed a direct tax within the meaning of the Constitution as interpreted in the *Hylton* case, a duty on rents is a duty on something distinct and entirely separate from, although issuing out of, the land. . . .

In my judgment, to say nothing of the disregard of the former adjudications of this court, and of the settled practice of the government—this decision may well excite the gravest apprehensions. It strikes at the very foundations of national authority, in that it denies to the general government a power which is, or may become, vital to the very existence and preservation of the Union in a national emergency, such as that of war with a great commercial nation, during which the collection of all duties upon imports will cease or be materially diminished. It tends to re-establish that condition of helplessness in which Congress found itself during the period of the Articles of Confederation, when it was without authority by laws operating directly upon individuals, to lay and collect, through its own agents, taxes sufficient to pay the debts and defray the expenses of government, but was dependent, in all such matters, upon the good will of the States, and their promptness in meeting requisitions made upon them by Congress.

Why do I say that the decision just rendered impairs or menaces the national authority? The reason is so apparent that it need only be stated. In its practical operation this decision withdraws from national taxation not only all incomes derived from real estate, but tangible personal property, "invested personal property, bonds, stocks, investments of all kinds," and the income that may be derived from such property. This results from the fact that by the decision of the court, all such personal property and all incomes from real estate and personal property, are placed beyond national taxation otherwise than by apportionment among the States on the basis simply of population. No such apportionment can possibly be made without doing gross injustice to the many for the benefit of the favored few in particular States. Any attempt upon the part of Congress to apportion among the States, upon the basis simply of their population, taxation of personal property or of incomes, would tend to arouse such indignation among the freemen of America that it would never be repeated. When, therefore, this court adjudges, as it does now adjudge, that Congress cannot impose a duty or tax upon personal property, or upon income arising either from rent of real estate or from personal property, including invested personal property, bonds, stocks, and investments of all kinds, except by apportioning the sum to be so raised among the States according to population, it practically decides that, without an amendment of the Constitution—two thirds of both Houses of Congress and three fourths of the States concurring—such property and incomes can never be made to contribute to the support of the national government. . . .

I cannot assent to an interpretation of the Constitution that impairs and cripples the just powers of the National Government in the essential matter of taxation, and at the same time discriminates against the greater part of the people of our country.

The practical effect of the decision today is to give to certain kinds of property a position of favoritism and advantage inconsistent with the fundamental principles of our social organization, and to invest them with power and influence that may be perilous to that portion of the American people upon whom rests the larger part of the burdens of the government, and who ought not to be subjected to the dominion of aggregated wealth any more than the property of the country should be at the mercy of the lawless.

I dissent from the opinion and judgment of the court.

[Justices Brown, Jackson, and White also delivered separate dissenting opinions.]

HAMMER *v.* DAGENHART

247 U.S. 251; 38 Sup. Ct. 529; 62 L. Ed. 1101 (1918)

[In 1916, Congress passed a law providing that goods produced by child labor should be excluded from shipment in interstate or foreign commerce. Dagenhart, the father of two children who were employed in a North Carolina cotton mill, brought suit in a district court to enjoin Hammer, United States District Attorney, from enforcing the act against his children. The district court granted Dagenhart the injunction, holding that the law was unconstitutional. Hammer then appealed to the Supreme Court.]

MR. JUSTICE DAY delivered the opinion of the Court:

. . . The attack upon the act rests upon three propositions:

First. It is not a regulation of interstate and foreign commerce.

Second. It contravenes the Tenth Amendment to the Constitution.

Third. It conflicts with the Fifth Amendment to the Constitution.

The controlling question for decision is: Is it within the authority of Congress in regulating commerce among the states to prohibit the transportation in interstate commerce of manufactured goods, the product of a factory in which, within thirty days prior to their removal therefrom, children under the age of 14 have been employed or permitted to work, or children between the ages of 14 and 16 years have been employed or permitted to work more than eight hours in any day, or more than six days in any week, or after the hour of 7 o'clock P.M. or before the hour of 6 o'clock A.M.?

The power essential to the passage of this act, the government contends, is found in the commerce clause of the Constitution, which authorizes Congress to regulate commerce with foreign nations and among the states.

In *Gibbons* v. *Ogden* . . . Chief Justice Marshall, speaking for this court, and defining the extent and nature of the commerce power, said: "It is the power to regulate—that is, to prescribe the rule by which commerce is to be governed." In other words, the power is one to control the means by which commerce is carried on, which is directly the contrary of the assumed right to forbid commerce from moving and thus destroy it as to particular commodities. But it is insisted that adjudged cases in this court establish the doctrine that the power to regulate given to Congress incidentally includes the authority to prohibit the movement of ordinary commodities, and therefore that the subject is not open for discussion. The cases demonstrate the contrary. They rest upon the character of the particular subjects dealt with and the fact that the scope of governmental authority, state or national, possessed over them, is such that the authority to prohibit is, as to them, but the exertion of the power to regulate.

The first of these cases is *Champion* v. *Ames,* 188 U.S. 321, the so-called Lottery Case, in which it was held that Congress might pass a law having the effect to keep the channels of commerce free from use in the transportation of tickets used in the promotion of lottery schemes. In *Hipolite Egg Co.* v. *United States,* 220 U.S. 45, this court sustained the power of Congress to pass the Pure Food and Drugs Act, which prohibited the introduction into the states by means of interstate commerce of impure foods and drugs. In *Hoke* v. *United States,* 227 U.S. 308, this court sustained the constitutionality of the so-called "White Slave Traffic Act," whereby transportation of a woman in interstate commerce for the purpose of prostitution was forbidden. . . .

In *Caminetti* v. *United States,* 242 U.S. 470, we held that Congress might prohibit the transportation of women in interstate commerce for the purposes of debauchery and kindred purposes. In *Clark Distilling Co.* v. *Western Maryland R. Co.,* 242 U.S. 311, the power of Congress over the transportation of intoxicating liquors was sustained. . . .

In each of these instances the use of interstate transportation was necessary to the accomplishment of harmful results. In other words, although the power over interstate transportation was to regulate, that could only be accomplished by prohibiting the use of the facilities of interstate commerce to effect the evil intended.

This element is wanting in the present case. The thing intended to be accomplished by this statute is the denial of the facilities of interstate commerce to those manufacturers in the states who employ children within the prohibited ages. The act in its effect does not regulate transportation among the states, but aims to standardize the ages at which children may be employed in mining and manufacturing within the states. The goods shipped are of themselves harmless. The act permits them to be freely shipped after thirty days from the time of their removal from the factory. When offered for shipment, and before transportation begins, the labor of their production is over, and the mere fact that they were intended for interstate commerce transportation does not make their production subject to Federal control under the commerce power.

Commerce "consists of intercourse and traffic . . . and includes the transportation of persons and property, as well as the purchase, sale, and exchange of commodities." The making of goods and the mining of coal are not commerce, nor does the fact that these things are to be afterwards shipped, or used in interstate commerce, make their production a part thereof. . . .

Over interstate transportation, or its incidents, the regulatory power of Congress is ample, but the production of articles intended for interstate commerce is a matter of local regulation. . . .

The grant of power to Congress over the subject of interstate commerce was to enable it to regulate such commerce, and not to give it authority to control the states in their exercise of the police power over local trade and manufacture.

The grant of authority over a purely Federal matter was not intended to destroy the local power always existing and carefully reserved to the states in the Tenth Amendment to the Constitution. . . .

That there should be limitations upon the right to employ children in mines and factories in the interest of their own and the public welfare, all will admit. That such employment is generally deemed to require regulation is shown by the fact that the brief of counsel states that every state in the Union has a law upon the subject, limiting the right to thus employ children. In North Carolina, the state wherein is located the factory in which the employment was had in the present case, no child under twelve years of age is permitted to work.

It may be desirable that such laws be uniform, but our Federal Government is one of enumerated powers. . . .

In interpreting the Constitution it must never be forgotten that the nation is made up of states, to which are intrusted the powers of local government. And to them and to the people the powers not expressly delegated to the national government are reserved . . . To sustain this statute would not be, in our judgment, a recognition of the lawful exertion of congressional authority over interstate commerce, but would sanction an invasion by the Federal power of the control of a matter purely local in its character, and over which no authority has been delegated to Congress in conferring the power to regulate commerce among the states.

We have neither authority nor disposition to question the motives of Congress in enacting this legislation. The purposes intended must be attained consistently with constitutional limitations upon the exercise of authority, Federal and state, to the end that each may continue to discharge, harmoniously with the other, the duties intrusted to it by the Constitution.

In our view the necessary effect of this act is, by means of a prohibition against the movement in interstate commerce of ordinary commercial commodities, to regulate the hours of labor of children in factories and mines within the states—a purely state authority. Thus the act in a twofold sense is repugnant to the Constitution. It not only transcends the authority delegated to Congress over commerce, but also exerts a power as to a purely local matter to which the Federal authority does not extend. The far-reaching result of upholding the act cannot be more plainly indicated than by pointing out that if Congress can thus regulate matters intrusted to local authority by prohibition of the movement of commodities in interstate commerce, all freedom of commerce will be at an end, and the power of the states over local matters may be eliminated, and thus our system of government be practically destroyed.

. . . We hold that this law exceeds the constitutional authority of Congress. It follows that the decree of the District Court must be

Affirmed.

MR. JUSTICE HOLMES, dissenting:

. . . [T]he statute in question is within the power expressly given to Congress, if considered only as to its immediate effects, and . . . if invalid it is so only upon some collateral ground. The statute confines itself to prohibiting the carriage of certain goods in interstate or foreign commerce. Congress is given power to regulate such commerce in unqualified terms. It would not be argued today that the power to regulate does not include the power to prohibit. Regulation means the prohibition of something, and when interstate commerce is the matter to be regulated I cannot doubt that the regulations may prohibit any part of such commerce that Congress sees fit to forbid. At all events it is established by the *Lottery Case* and others that have followed it that a law is not beyond the regulative power of Congress merely because it prohibits certain transportation out-and-out. . . .

The question, then, is narrowed to whether the exercise of its otherwise constitutional power by Congress can be pronounced unconstitutional because of its possible reaction upon the conduct of the states in a matter upon which I have admitted that they are free from direct control. I should have thought that the matter had been disposed of so fully as to leave no room for doubt. I should have thought that the most conspicuous decisions of this court had made it clear that the power to regulate commerce and other constitutional powers could not be cut down or qualified by the fact that it might interfere with the carrying out of the domestic policy of any state.

. . . It does not matter whether the supposed evil precedes or follows the transportation. It is enough that, in the opinion of Congress, the transportation encourages the evil. . . .

The notion that prohibition is any less prohibition when applied to things now thought evil I do not understand. But if there is any matter upon which civilized countries have agreed—far more unanimously than they have with regard to intoxicants and some other matters over which this country is now emotionally aroused—it is the evil of premature and excessive child labor. I should have thought that if we were to introduce our own moral conceptions where, in my opinion, they do not belong, this was preeminently a case for upholding the exercise of all its powers by the United States.

But I had thought that the propriety of the exercise of a power admitted to exist in some cases was for the consideration of Congress alone, and that this court always had disavowed the right to intrude its judgment upon questions of policy or morals. It is not for this court to pronounce when prohibition is necessary to regulation if it ever may be necessary—to say that it is permissible as against strong drink, but not as against the product of ruined lives.

The act does not meddle with anything belonging to the states. They may regulate their internal affairs and their domestic commerce as they like. But when they seek to send their products across the state line they are no longer within their rights. If there were no Constitution and no Congress their power to cross the line would depend upon their neighbors. Under the Constitution such commerce belongs not to the states, but to Congress to regulate. It may carry out its views of public policy whatever indirect effect they may have upon the activities of the states. Instead of being encountered by a prohibitive tariff at her boundaries, the state encounters the public policy of the United States, which it is for Congress to express. . . . The national welfare as understood by Congress may require a different attitude within its sphere from that of some self-seeking state. It seems to me entirely constitutional for Congress to enforce its understanding by all the means at its command.

[Mr. Justice McKenna, Mr. Justice Brandeis, and Mr. Justice Clark concur in this opinion.]

A. L. A. SCHECHTER POULTRY CORP. *et al.* *v.* UNITED STATES

295 U.S. 495; 55 Sup. Ct. 837; 79 L. Ed. 1570 (1935)

MR. CHIEF JUSTICE HUGHES delivered the opinion of the Court:

Petitioners . . . were convicted in the District Court of the United States for the Eastern District of New York on eighteen counts of an indictment charging violations of what is known as the "Live Poultry Code," and on an additional count for conspiracy to commit such violation. . . . [T]he defendants contended (1) that the Code had been adopted pursuant to an unconstitutional delegation by Congress of legislative power; (2) that it attempted to regulate intrastate transactions which lay outside the authority of Congress; and (3) that in certain provisions it was repugnant to the due process clause of the Fifth Amendment. . . .

New York City is the largest live-poultry market in the United States. Ninety-six per cent of the live poultry there marketed comes from other States. Three fourths of this amount arrives by rail and is consigned to commission men or receivers. . . . The commission men transact by far the greater part of the business on a commission basis, representing the shippers as agents, and remitting to them the proceeds of sale, less commissions, freight, and handling charges. Otherwise, they buy for their own account. They sell to slaughterhouse operators who are also called marketmen.

The defendants are slaughterhouse operators of the latter class. A. L. A. Schechter Poultry Corporation and Schechter Live Poultry Market are corporations conducting wholesale poultry slaughterhouse markets in Brooklyn, New York City. . . . They buy the poultry for slaughter and resale. After the poultry is trucked to their slaughterhouse markets in Brooklyn, it is there sold, usually within twenty-four hours, to retail poultry dealers and butchers who sell directly to consumers. . . . Defendants do not sell poultry in interstate commerce.

The "Live Poultry Code" was promulgated under Section 3 of the National Industrial Recovery Act. That section . . . authorizes the President to approve "codes of fair competition."

. . . The "Live Poultry Code" was approved by the President on April 13, 1934. . . .

. . . The Code is established as "a code of fair competition for the live-poultry industry of the metropolitan area in and about the City of New York." . . .

Of the eighteen counts of the indictment upon which the defendants were convicted, aside from the count for conspiracy, two counts charged violation of the minimum-wage and maximum-hour provisions of the Code, and ten counts were for violation of the requirement (found in the "trade practice provisions") of "straight killing." . . . The charges in the ten counts, respectively, were that the defendants in selling to retail dealers and butchers had permitted "selections of individual chickens taken from particular coops and half coops." . . .

First. Two preliminary points are stressed by the Government with respect to the appropriate approach to the important questions presented. We are told that the provision of the statute authorizing the adoption of codes must be viewed in the light of the grave national crisis with which Congress was confronted. Undoubtedly, the conditions to which power is addressed are always to be considered when the exercise of power is challenged. Extraordinary conditions may call for extraordinary remedies. But the argument necessarily stops short of an attempt to justify action which lies outside the sphere of constitutional authority. Extraordinary conditions do not create or enlarge constitutional power. The Constitution established a national government with powers deemed to be adequate, as they have proved to be both in war and peace, but these powers of the national government are limited by the constitutional grants. Those who act under these grants are not at liberty to transcend the imposed limits because they believe that more or different power is necessary. Such assertions of extraconstitutional authority were anticipated and precluded by the explicit terms of the Tenth Amendment—"The powers not delegated to the United States by the Constitution, nor prohibited by it to the States, are reserved to the States respectively, or to the people. . . ."

Second. The Question of the Delegation of Legislative Power. . . . The Constitution provides that "All legislative powers herein granted shall be vested in a Congress of the United States, which shall consist of a Senate and House of Representatives." Article I, Section 1. And the Congress is authorized "To make all laws which shall be necessary and proper for carrying into execution" its general powers. Article I, Section 8, par. 18. The Congress is not permitted to abdicate or to transfer to others the essential legislative functions with which it is thus vested. We have repeatedly recognized the necessity of adapting legislation to complex conditions involving a host of details with which the national legislature cannot deal directly. We pointed out in the *Panama Company* case that the Constitution has never been regarded as denying to Congress the necessary resources of flexibility and practicality, which will enable it to perform its function in laying down policies and establishing standards, while leaving to selected instrumentalities the making of subordinate rules within prescribed limits and the determination of facts to which the policy as declared by the legislature is to apply. But we said that the constant recognition of the necessity and validity of such provisions, and the wide range of administrative authority which has been developed by means of them, cannot be allowed to obscure the limitations of the authority to delegate, if our constitutional system is to be maintained. . . .

Accordingly, we look to the statute to see whether Congress has overstepped these limitations—whether Congress in authorizing "codes of fair competition" has itself established the standards of legal obligation, thus performing its essential legislative function, or, by the failure to enact such standards, has attempted to transfer that function to others. . . .

What is meant by "fair competition" as the term is used in the Act? Does it refer to a category established in the law, and is the authority to make codes limited accordingly? Or is it used as a convenient designation for whatever set of laws the formulators of a code for a particular trade or industry may propose and the President may approve (subject to certain restrictions), or the President may himself prescribe, as being wise and beneficient provisions for the government of the trade or industry in order to accomplish the broad purpose of rehabilitation, correction, and expansion which are stated in the first section of Title I?

The Act does not define "fair competition. . . ."

The Government urges that the codes

will "consist of rules of competition deemed fair for each industry by representative members of that industry—by the persons most vitally concerned and most familiar with its problems." Instances are cited in which Congress has availed itself of such assistance; as, for example, in the exercise of its authority over the public domain, with respect to the recognition of local customs or rules of miners as to mining claims, or, in matters of a more or less technical nature, as in designating the standard height of drawbars. But would it be seriously contended that Congress could delegate its legislative authority to trade or industrial associations or groups so as to empower them to enact the laws they deem to be wise and beneficient for the rehabilitation and expansion of their trade or industries? Could trade or industrial associations or groups be constituted legislative bodies for that purpose because such associations or groups are familiar with the problems of their enterprises? And, could an effort of that sort be made valid by such a preface of generalities as to permissible aims as we find in Section 1 of Title I? The answer is obvious. Such a delegation of legislative power is unknown to our law and is utterly inconsistent with the constitutional prerogatives and duties of Congress.

The question, then, turns upon the authority which Section 3 of the Recovery Act vests in the President to approve or prescribe. If the codes have standing as penal statutes, this must be due to the effect of the executive action. But Congress cannot delegate legislative power to the President to exercise an unfettered discretion to make whatever laws he thinks may be needed or advisable for the rehabilitation and expansion of trade or industry. . . .

. . . Section 3 of the Recovery Act is without precedent. It supplies no standards for any trade, industry, or activity. It does not undertake to prescribe rules of conduct to be applied to particular states of fact determined by appropriate administrative procedure. Instead of prescribing rules of conduct, it authorizes the making of codes to prescribe them. For the legislative undertaking, Section 3 sets up no standards, aside from the statement of the general aims of rehabilitation, correction, and expansion described in Section 1. In view of the scope of that broad declaration, and of the nature of the few restrictions that are imposed, the discretion of the President in approving or prescribing codes, and thus enacting laws for the government of trade and industry throughout the country, is virtually unfettered. We think that the code-making authority thus conferred is an unconstitutional delegation of legislative power.

Third. The Question of the Application of the Provisions of the Live Poultry Code to Intrastate Transactions. Although the validity of the codes (apart from the question of delegation) rests upon the commerce clause of the Constitution, Section 3(a) is not in terms limited to interstate and foreign commerce. From the generality of its terms, and from the argument of the Government at the bar, it would appear that Section 3(a) was designed to authorize codes without that limitation. But under Section 3(f) penalties are confined to violations of a code provision "in any transaction in or affecting interstate or foreign commerce." This aspect of the case presents the question whether the particular provisions of the Live Poultry Code, which the defendants were convicted for violating and for having conspired to violate, were within the regulating power of Congress.

These provisions relate to the hours and wages of those employed by defendants in their slaughterhouses in Brooklyn and to the sales there made to retail dealers and butchers.

(1) Were these transactions "*in*" interstate commerce? Much is made of the fact that almost all the poultry coming to New York is sent there from other States. But the code provisions, as here applied, do not concern the transportation of the poultry from other States to New York, or the transactions of the commission men or others to whom it is consigned, or the sales made by such consignees to defendants. When defendants had made their purchases, whether at the West Washington Market in New York City or at the railroad terminals serving the City, or elsewhere, the poultry was trucked to their slaughterhouses in Brooklyn for local disposition. The interstate transactions in relation to

that poultry then ended. Defendants held the poultry at their slaughterhouse markets for slaughter and local sale to retail dealers and butchers, who in turn sold directly to consumers. Neither the slaughtering nor the sales by defendants were transactions in interstate commerce. . . .

The undisputed facts thus afford no warrant for the argument that the poultry handled by defendants at their slaughterhouse markets was in a "*current*" or "*flow*" of interstate commerce and was thus subject to congressional regulation. The mere fact that there may be a constant flow of commodities into a State does not mean that the flow continues after the property has arrived and has become commingled with the mass of property within the State and is there held solely for local disposition and use. So far as the poultry here in question is concerned, the flow in interstate commerce had ceased. The poultry had come to a permanent rest within the State. It was not held, used, or sold by defendants in relation to any further transactions in interstate commerce and was not destined for transportation to other States. Hence, decisions which deal with a stream of interstate commerce—where goods come to rest within a State temporarily and are later to go forward to interstate commerce—and with the regulations of transactions involved in that practical continuity of movement, are not applicable here. . . .

(2) Did the defendants' transactions directly "*affect*" interstate commerce so as to be subject to federal regulation? The power of Congress extends not only to the regulation of transactions which are part of interstate commerce, but to the protection of that commerce from injury. It matters not that the injury may be due to the conduct of those engaged in intrastate operations. Thus, Congress may protect the safety of those employed in interstate transportation "no matter what may be the source of the dangers which threaten it. . . ."

. . . Defendants have been convicted, not upon direct charges of injury to interstate commerce or of interference with persons engaged in that commerce, but of violations of certain provisions of the Live Poultry Code and of conspiracy to commit these violations. Interstate commerce is brought in only upon the charge that violations of these provisions—as to hours and wages of employees and local sales "*affected*" interstate commerce.

In determining how far the federal government may go in controlling intrastate transactions upon the ground that they "affect" interstate commerce, there is a necessary and well-established distinction between direct and indirect effects. The precise line can be drawn only as individual cases arise, but the distinction is clear in principle. Direct effects are illustrated by the railroad cases, . . . as, for example, the effect of failure to use prescribed safety appliances on railroads which are the highways of both interstate and intrastate commerce, injury to an employee engaged in interstate transportation by the negligence of an employee engaged in intrastate movement, the fixing of rates for intrastate transportation which unjustly discriminate against interstate commerce. But where the effect of intrastate transactions upon interstate commerce is merely indirect, such transactions remain with the domain of state power. If the commerce clause were construed to reach all enterprises and transactions which could be said to have an indirect effect upon interstate commerce, the federal authority would embrace practically all the activities of the people, and the authority of the State over its domestic concerns would exist only by sufferance of the federal government. Indeed, on such a theory, even the development of the State's commercial facilities would be subject to federal control. . . .

. . . [T]he distinction between direct and indirect efforts of intrastate transactions upon interstate commerce must be recognized as a fundamental one, essential to the maintenance of our constitutional system. Otherwise, as we have said, there would be virtually no limit to the federal power and for all practical purposes we should have a completely centralized government. We must consider the provisions here in question in the light of this distinction.

The question of chief importance relates to the provisions of the Code as to the hours and wages of those employed in defendants' slaughterhouse markets. It is plain that these requirements are imposed in order to govern the details of defendants' management of their local business. The persons employed in slaughtering and selling in local trade are not employed in interstate commerce. Their hours and wages have no direct relation to interstate commerce.

. . . [T]he apparent implication is that the federal authority under the commerce clause should be deemed to extend to the establishment of rules to govern wages and hours in intrastate trade and industry generally throughout the country, thus overriding the authority of the States to deal with domestic problems arising from labor conditions in their internal commerce.

It is not the province of the Court to consider the economic advantages or disadvantages of such a centralized system. It is sufficient to say that the Federal Constitution does not provide for it. Our growth and development have called for wide use of the commerce power of the federal government in its control over the expanded activities of interstate commerce, and in protecting that commerce from burdens, interferences, and conspiracies to restrain and monopolize it. But the authority of the federal government may not be pushed to such an extreme as to destroy the distinction, which the commerce clause itself establishes, between commerce "among the several States" and the internal concerns of a State. The same answer must be made to the contention that is based upon the serious economic situation which led to the passage of the Recovery Act—the fall in prices, the decline in wages and employment, and the curtailment of the market for commodities. Stress is laid upon the great importance of maintaining wage distributions which would provide the necessary stimulus in starting "the cumulative forces making for expanding commercial activity." Without in any way disparaging this motive, it is enough to say that the recuperative efforts of the Federal Government must be made in a manner consistent with the authority granted by the Constitution.

We are of the opinion that the attempt through the provisions of the Code to fix the hours and wages of employees of defendants in their intrastate business was not a valid exercise of federal power.

The other violations for which defendants were convicted related to the making of local sales. Ten counts, for violation of the provisions as to "straight killing," were for permitting customers to make "selection of individual chickens taken from particular coops and half coops." Whether or not this practice is good or bad for the local trade, its effect, if any, upon interstate commerce was only indirect. The same may be said of violations of the Code by intrastate transactions consisting of the sale "of an unfit chicken" and of sales which were not in accord with the ordinances of the City of New York. The requirement of reports as to prices and volumes of defendants' sales was incident to the effort to control their intrastate business.

In view of these conclusions, we find it unnecessary to discuss other questions which have been raised as to the validity of certain provisions of the Code under the due process clause of the Fifth Amendment.

On both the grounds we have discussed, the attempted delegation of legislative power, and the attempted regulation of intrastate transactions which affect interstate commerce only indirectly, we hold the code provisions here in question to be invalid and that the judgment of conviction must be reversed. . . .

MR. JUSTICE CARDOZO, concurring:

[*Mr. Justice Stone joined in this opinion.*]

The delegated power of legislation which has found expression in this code is not canalized within banks that keep it from overflowing. It is unconfined and vagrant, if I may borrow my own words in an earlier opinion. . . .

. . . Here, in the case before us, is an attempted delegation not confined to any single act nor to any class or group of acts identified or described by reference to a standard. Here in effect is a roving commission to inquire into evils and upon discovery correct them.

I have said that there is no standard, definite or even approximate, to which legislation must conform. Let me make my meaning more precise. If codes of fair competition are codes eliminating "unfair" methods of competition ascertained upon inquiry to prevail in one industry or another, there is no unlawful delegation of legislative functions when the President is directed to inquire into such practices and denounce them when discovered. For many years a like power has been committed to the Federal Trade Commission with the approval of this court in a long series of decisions. . . . Delegation in such circumstances is born of the necessities of the occasion. The industries of the country are too many and diverse to make it possible for Congress, in respect of matters such as these, to legislate directly with adequate appreciation of varying conditions. Nor is the substance of the power changed because the President may act at the instance of trade or industrial associations having special knowledge of the facts. Their function is strictly advisory; it is the *imprimatur* of the President that begets the quality of law. . . .

But there is another conception of codes of fair competition, their significance and function, which leads to very different consequences, though it is one that is struggling now for recognition and acceptance. By this other conception a code is not to be restricted to the elimination of business practices that would be characterized by general acceptation as oppressive or unfair. It is to include whatever ordinances may be desirable or helpful for the well-being or prosperity of the industry affected. In that view, the function of its adoption is not merely negative, but positive; the planning of improvements as well as the extirpation of abuses. What is fair, as thus conceived, is not something to be contrasted with what is unfair or fraudulent or tricky. The extension becomes as wide as the field of industrial regulation. If that conception shall prevail, anything that Congress may do within the limits of the commerce clause for the betterment of business may be done by the President upon the recommendation of a trade association by calling it a code. This is delegation running riot. No such plenitude of power is susceptible of transfer. . . .

But there is another objection, far-reaching and incurable, aside from any defect of unlawful delegation.

If this code has been adopted by Congress itself, and not by the President on the advice of an industrial association, it would even then be void unless authority to adopt it is included in the grant of power "to regulate commerce with foreign nations and among the several states. . . ."

I find no authority in that grant for the regulation of wages and hours of labor in the intrastate transactions that make up the defendants' business. . . .

NATIONAL LABOR RELATIONS BOARD *v.* JONES AND LAUGHLIN STEEL CORPORATION

301 U.S. 1; 57 Sup. Ct. 615; 81 L. Ed. 893 (1937)

[The National Labor Relations Act of 1935 was designed to reduce the number of labor disputes that burdened interstate and foreign commerce. The motivation behind the act was the granting of the right of collective bargaining. The act forbids a number of unfair labor practices. The National Labor Relations Board was empowered to issue cease and desist orders against companies that engaged in any unfair practice prohibited by the act. In the instant case, the Jones and Laughlin Steel Corporation had discharged ten employees because of their labor union activities. After a proper hearing, the board ordered that the employees be reinstated. Upon the company's refusal to comply with the order, the board petitioned the circuit court of appeals to enforce the order in accordance with the act. The Court refused to enforce the board's action, stating that it "lay beyond the range of federal power." The Supreme Court granted certiorari.]

MR. CHIEF JUSTICE HUGHES delivered the opinion of the Court:

. . . The facts as to the nature and scope of the business of the Jones and Laughlin Steel Corporation have been found by the Labor Board. . . . The Labor Board has found: The corporation is organized under the laws of Pennsylvania and has its principal office at Pittsburgh. It is engaged in the business of manufacturing iron and steel in plants situated in Pittsburgh and nearby Aliquippa, Pennsylvania. It manufactures and distributes a widely diversified line of steel and pig iron, being the fourth largest producer of steel in the United States. With its subsidiaries—nineteen in number—it is a completely integrated enterprise, owning and operating ore, coal, and limestone properties, lake and river transportation facilities and terminal railroads located at its manufacturing plants. It owns or controls mines in Michigan and Minnesota. It operates four ore steamships on the Great Lakes used in the transportation of ore to its factories. It owns coal mines in Pennsylvania. It operates towboats and steam barges used in carrying coal to its factories. It owns limestone properties in various places in Pennsylvania and West Virginia. It owns the Monongahela connecting railroad, which connects the plants of the Pittsburgh works and forms an interconnection with the Pennsylvania, New York Central, and Baltimore and Ohio Railroad systems. It owns the Aliquippa and Southern Railroad Company, which connects the Aliquippa works with the Pittsburgh and Lake Erie, part of the New York Central system. Much of its product is shipped to its warehouses in Chicago, Detroit, Cincinnati, and Memphis—to the last two places by means of its own barges and transportation equipment. In Long Island City, New York, and in New Orleans it operates structural-steel fabricating shops in connection with the warehousing of semifinished materials sent from its works. Through one of its wholly-owned subsidiaries it owns, leases, and operates stores, warehouses, and yards for the distribution of equipment and supplies for drilling and operating oil and gas mills and for pipe lines, refineries, and pumping stations. It has sales offices in twenty cities in the United States and a wholly-owned subsidiary which is devoted exclusively to distributing its product in Canada. Approximately 75 per cent of its product is shipped out of Pennsylvania.

Summarizing these operations, the Labor Board concluded that the works in Pittsburgh and Aliquippa "might be likened to the heart of a self-contained, highly integrated body. They draw in the raw materials from Michigan, Minnesota, West Virginia, Pennsylvania in part through arteries and by means controlled by the respondent; they transform the materials and then pump them out of all parts of the nation through the vast mechanism which the respondent has elaborated. . . ."

The Scope of the Act. The Act is challenged in its entirety as an attempt to regulate all industry, thus invading the reserved powers of the States over their local concerns. It is asserted that the references in the Act to interstate and foreign commerce are colorable at best; that the Act is not a true regulation of such commerce or of matters which directly affect it but on the contrary has the fundamental object of placing under the compulsory supervision of the Federal Government all industrial labor relations within the nation. The argument seeks support in the broad words of the preamble (Section 1) and in the sweep of the provisions of the Act, and it is further insisted that its legislative history shows an essential universal purpose in the light of which its scope cannot be limited by either construction or by the application of the separability clause.

If this conception of terms, intent, and consequent inseparability were sound, the Act would necessarily fall by reason of the limitation upon the Federal power which inheres in the constitutional grant, as well as because of the explicit reservation of the Tenth Amendment. *Schechter Poultry Corp.* v. *United States.* . . . The authority of the Federal Government may not be pushed to such an extreme as to destroy the distinction, which the commerce clause itself establishes, between commerce "among the several States" and the internal concerns of a State. The distinction between what is national and what is local in the activities of commerce is vital to the maintenance of our Federal system. . . .

We think it clear that the National Labor Relations Act may be construed so as to operate within the sphere of constitutional authority. The jurisdiction conferred upon the Board, and invoked in this instance, is found in Section 10(a), which provides:

"Section 10 (a), The Board is empowered, as hereinafter provided, to prevent any person from engaging in any unfair labor practice (listed in Section 8) affecting commerce."

The critical words of this provision, prescribing the limits of the Board's authority in dealing with the labor practices, are "affecting commerce. . . ."

There can be no question that the commerce thus contemplated by the Act (aside from that within a Territory or the District of Columbia) is interstate and foreign commerce in the constitutional sense. The Act also defines the term "affecting commerce" Section 2(7):

"The term *affecting commerce* means in commerce, or burdening or obstructing commerce or the free flow of commerce, or having led or tending to lead to a labor dispute burdening or obstructing commerce or the free flow of commerce."

This definition is one of exclusion as well as inclusion. The grant of authority to the Board does not purport to extend to the relationship between all industrial employees and employers. Its terms do not impose collective bargaining upon all industry regardless of effects upon interstate or foreign commerce. It purports to reach only what may be deemed to burden or obstruct that commerce and, thus qualified, it must be construed as contemplating the exercise of control within constitutional bounds. It is a familiar principle that acts which directly burden or obstruct interstate or foreign commerce, or its free flow, are within the reach of the congressional power. Acts having that effect are not rendered immune because they grow out of labor disputes. . . . It is the effect upon commerce, not the source of the injury, which is the criterion. . . . Whether or not particular action does affect commerce in such a close and intimate a fashion as to be subject to Federal control, and hence to lie within the authority conferred upon the Board, is left by the statute to be determined as individual cases arise. We are thus to inquire whether in the instant case the constitutional boundary has been passed. . . .

The Application of the Act to Employees Engaged in Production—The Principle Involved. Respondent says that whatever may be said of employees engaged in interstate commerce, the industrial relations and activities in the manufacturing department of respondent's enterprise are not subject to Federal regulation. The argument rests upon the proposition that manufacturing in itself is not commerce. . . .

The various parts of respondent's enterprise are described (by the government) as interdependent and as thus involving "a great movement of iron ore, coal, and limestone along well-defined paths to the steel mills, thence through them, and thence in the form of steel products into the consuming centers of the country—a definite and well-understood course of business." It is urged that these activities constitute a "stream" or "flow" of commerce, of which the Aliquippa manufacturing plant is the focal point, and that industrial strife at that point would cripple the entire movement. . . .

We do not find it necessary to determine whether these features of defendant's business dispose of the asserted analogy to the "stream of commerce" cases. The instances in which that metaphor has been used are but particular, and not exclusive, illustrations of the protective power which the Government invokes in support of the present Act. The congressional authority to protect interstate commerce from burdens and obstructions is not limited to transactions which can be deemed to be an essential part of a "flow" of interstate or foreign commerce. Burdens and obstructions may be due to injurious action springing from other sources. The fundamental principle is that the power to regulate commerce is the power to enact "all appropriate legislation" for "its protection and advancement.". . . ; to adopt measures "to promote its growth and insure its safety". . . ; "to foster, protect, control, and restrain. . . ." That power is plenary and may be exerted to protect interstate commerce "no matter what the source of the dangers which threaten it. . . ." Although activities may be intrastate in character when separately considered, if they have such a close and substantial relation to interstate commerce that their control is essential or appropriate to protect that commerce from burdens and obstructions, Congress cannot be denied the power to exercise that control. . . . Undoubtedly the scope of this power must be considered in the light of our dual system of government and may not be extended so as to embrace effects upon interstate commerce so indirect and remote that to embrace them, in view of our complex society, would effectually obliterate the distinction between what is national and what is local and create a completely centralized government. . . . The question is necessarily one of degree. . . .

[T]he fact that the employees here concerned were engaged in production is not determinative. The question remains as to the effect upon interstate commerce of the labor practice involved. In the *Schechter Poultry Corp.* case, . . . we found that the effect there was so remote as to be beyond the Federal power. To find "immediacy of directness" there was to find it "almost everywhere," a result inconsistent with the maintenance of our Federal system. In the *Carter* case, . . . the Court was of the opinion that the provisions of the statute relating to production were invalid upon several grounds—that there was improper delegation of legislative power, and that the requirements not only went beyond any sustainable measure of protection of interstate commerce but were also inconsistent with due process. These cases are not controlling here. . . .

Effects of the Unfair Labor Practice in Respondent's Enterprise. Giving full weight to respondent's contention with respect to a break in the complete continuity of the "stream of commerce" by reason of respondent's manufacturing operations, the fact remains that the stoppage of those operations by industrial strife would have a most serious effect upon interstate commerce. In view of respondent's far-flung activities, it is idle to say that the effect would be indirect or remote. It is obvious that it would be immediate and might be catastrophic. We are asked to shut our eyes to the plainest facts of our national life and to deal with the question of direct and indirect effects in an intellectual vacuum. Because there may be but indirect and remote effects upon interstate commerce in connection with a host of local enterprises throughout the country, it does not follow that other industrial activities do not have such a close and intimate relation to interstate commerce as to make the presence of industrial strife a matter of the most urgent national concern. When industries organize themselves on a national scale, making their relation to interstate commerce the dominant factor in their activities, how can it be maintained that their industrial labor relations constitute a forbidden field into which Congress may not enter when it is necessary to protect interstate commerce from the paralyzing consequences of industrial war? We have often said that interstate commerce itself is a practical conception. It is equally true that interferences with that commerce must be appraised by a judgment that does not ignore actual experience.

Experience has abundantly demonstrated that the recognition of the right of employees to self-organization and to have representatives of their own choosing for the purpose of collective bargaining is often an essential condition of industrial peace. Refusal to confer and negotiate has been one of the most prolific causes of strife. . . .

It is not necessary again to detail the facts to respondent's enterprise. Instead of being beyond the pale, we think that it presents in a most striking way the close and intimate relation which a manufacturing industry may have to interstate commerce, and we have no doubt that Congress had constitutional authority to safeguard the right of respondent's employees to self-organization and freedom in the choice of representatives for collective bargaining. . . .

Our conclusion is that the order of the Board was within its competency and that the Act is valid as here applied. The judgment of the Circuit Court of Appeals is reversed and the cause is remanded for further proceedings in conformity with this opinion.

Reversed.

MR. JUSTICE MC REYNOLDS delivered the following dissenting opinion:

MR. JUSTICE VAN DEVANTER, MR. JUSTICE SUTHERLAND, MR. JUSTICE BUTLER and I are unable to agree with the decisions just announced. . . .

The Court, as we think, departs from well-established principles followed in *Schechter Poultry Corp.* v. *United States* . . . and *Carter* v. *Carter Coal Co.* . . . Upon the authority of these decisions . . . the power of Congress under the commerce clause does not extend to relations between employers and their employees engaged in manufacture, and therefore the Act conferred upon the National Relations Board no authority in respect of matters covered by the questioned orders. . . . No decision of judicial opinion to the contrary has been cited, and we find none. . . .

UNITED STATES *v.* DARBY

312 U.S. 100; 61 Sup. Ct. 451; 85 L. Ed. 609 (1941)

[Darby manufactured lumber for shipment in interstate commerce. He was indicted for violation of various sections of the Fair Labor Standards Act of 1938, which fixed minimum wages and maximum hours for employees engaged in producing goods for shipment in interstate commerce. A district court quashed the indictment, holding that the regulation of wages and hours of employment of persons engaged in the manufacture of goods for possible shipment in interstate commerce was not within the commerce power of Congress. The United States appealed directly to the Supreme Court.]

MR. JUSTICE STONE delivered the opinion of the Court:

The two principal questions raised by the record in this case are, first, whether Congress has constitutional power to prohibit the shipment in interstate commerce of lumber manufactured by employees whose wages are less than a prescribed minimum or whose weekly hours of labor at that wage are greater than a prescribed maximum, and, second, whether it has power to prohibit the employment of workmen in the production of goods "for interstate commerce" at other than prescribed wages and hours. . . .

The indictment charges that appellee is engaged, in the State of Georgia, in the business of acquiring raw materials, which he manufactures into finished lumber with the intent, when manufactured, to ship it in interstate commerce to customers outside the state, and that he does in fact so ship a large part of the lumber so produced. There are numerous counts charging appellee with the shipment in interstate commerce from Georgia to points outside the state of lumber in the production of which, for interstate commerce, appellee has employed workmen at less than the prescribed minimum wage or more than the prescribed maximum hours without payment to them of any wage for overtime. . . .

The case comes here on assignments by the Government that the district court erred in so far as it held that Congress was without constitutional power to penalize the acts set forth in the indictment, and appellee seeks to sustain the decision below on the grounds that the prohibition by Congress of those Acts is unauthorized by the Commerce Clause and is prohibited by the Fifth Amendment. . . . [W]e . . . confine our decision to the validity and construction of the statute. . . .

While manufacture is not of itself interstate commerce, the shipment of manufactured goods interstate is such commerce and the prohibition of such shipment by Congress is indubitably a regulation of the commerce. The power to regulate commerce is the power "to prescribe the rule by which commerce is governed." *Gibbons* v. *Ogden* . . . It extends not only to those regulations which aid, foster, and protect the commerce, but embraces those which prohibit it. . . . It is conceded that the power of Congress to prohibit transportation in interstate commerce includes noxious articles, *Lottery Case,* . . . stolen articles, *Brooks* v. *United States* . . . kidnapped persons, *Gooch* v. *United States* . . . and articles such as intoxicating liquor or convict-made goods, traffic in which is forbidden or restricted by the laws of the state of destination. *Kentucky Whip & Collar Co.* v. *Illinois Central R. Co.* . . .

But it is said that the present prohibition falls within the scope of none of these categories; that while the prohibition is nominally a regulation of the commerce its motive or purpose is regulation of wages and hours of persons engaged in manufacture, the control of which has been reserved to the states and upon which Georgia and some of the states of destination have placed no restriction; that the effect of the present statute is not to exclude the proscribed articles from interstate commerce in aid of state regulation as in *Kentucky Whip & Collar Co.* v. *Illinois Central R. Co.* . . . but instead, under the guise of a regulation of interstate commerce, it undertakes to regulate wages and hours within the state contrary to the policy of the state which has elected to leave them unregulated. . . .

The motive and purpose of the present regulation are plainly to make effective the Congressional conception of public policy that interstate commerce should not be made the instrument of competition in the distribution of goods produced under substandard labor conditions, which competition is injurious to the commerce and to the states from and to which the commerce flows. The motive and purpose of a regulation of interstate commerce are matters for the legislative judgment, upon the exercise of which the Constitution places no restriction and over which the courts are given no control. . . . Whatever their motive and purpose, regulations of commerce which do not infringe some constitutional prohibition are within the plenary power conferred on Congress by the Commerce Clause. Subject only to that limitation, presently to be considered, we conclude that the prohibition of the shipment interstate of goods produced under the forbidden substandard labor conditions is within the constitutional authority of Congress.

In the more than a century which has elapsed since the decision of *Gibbons* v. *Ogden*, these principles of constitutional interpretation have been so long and repeatedly recognized by this Court as applicable to the Commerce Clause, that there would be little occasion for repeating them now were it not for the decision of this Court twenty-two years ago in *Hammer* v. *Dagenhart*. . . . In that case it was held by a bare majority of the Court, over the powerful and now classic dissent of Mr. Justice Holmes setting forth the fundamental issues involved, that Congress was without power to exclude the products of child labor from interstate commerce. The reasoning and conclusion of the Court's opinion there cannot be reconciled with the conclusion which we have reached, that the power of Congress under the Commerce Clause is plenary to exclude any article from interstate commerce subject only to the specific prohibitions of the Constitution.

Hammer v. *Dagenhart* has not been followed. The distinction on which the decision was rested that Congressional power to prohibit interstate commerce is limited to articles which in themselves have some harmful or deleterious property—a distinction which was novel when made and unsupported by any provision of the Constitution—has long since been abandoned. . . .

The conclusion is inescapable that *Hammer* v. *Dagenhart* was a departure from the principles which have prevailed in the interpretation of the Commerce Clause both before and since the decision and that such vitality, as a precedent, as it then had has long since been exhausted. It should be and now is overruled.

Validity of the Wage and Hour Requirements. Section 15(a) (2) and Sections 6 and 7 require employers to conform to the wage and hour provisions with respect to all employees engaged in the production of goods for interstate commerce. As appellee's employees are not alleged to be "engaged in interstate commerce" the validity of the prohibition turns on the question whether the employment, under other than the prescribed labor standards, of employees engaged in the production of goods for interstate commerce is so related to the commerce and so affects it as to be within the reach of power of Congress to regulate it. . . .

Congress, having by the present Act adopted the policy of excluding from interstate commerce all goods produced for the commerce which do not conform to the specified labor standards, may choose the means reasonably adapted to the attainment of the permitted end, even though they involve control of intrastate activities. Such legislation has often been sustained with respect to powers, other than the commerce power granted to the national government, when the means chosen, although not themselves within the granted power, were nevertheless deemed appropriate aids to the accomplishment of some purpose within an admitted power of the national government. . . . A familiar like exercise of power is the regulation of intrastate transactions which are so commingled with or related to interstate commerce that all must be regulated if the interstate commerce is to be effectively controlled. . . . Similarly Congress may require inspection and preventive treatment of all cattle in a disease-infected area in order to prevent shipment in interstate commerce of some of the cattle without the treatment. . . . It may prohibit the removal, at destination, of labels required by the Pure Food and Drug Acts to be affixed to articles transported in interstate commerce. . . .

The Sherman Act and the National Labor Relations Act are familiar examples of the exertion of the commerce power to prohibit or control activities wholly intrastate because of their effect on interstate commerce. . . .

The means adopted by Section 15(a) (2) for the protection of interstate commerce by the suppression of the production of the condemned goods for interstate commerce is so related to the commerce and so affects it as to be within the reach of the commerce power. . . . Congress, to attain its objective in the suppression of nation-wide competition in interstate commerce by goods produced under substandard labor conditions, has made no distinction as to the volume or amount of shipments in the commerce or of production for commerce by any particular shipper or producer. It recognized that in present-day industry, competition by a small part may affect the whole and that the total effect of the competition of many small producers may be great. . . .

So far as *Carter* v. *Carter Coal Co.* . . . is inconsistent with this conclusion, its doctrine is limited in principle by the decisions under the Sherman Act and the National Labor Relations Act, which we have cited and which we follow. . . .

Our conclusion is unaffected by the Tenth Amendment which provides: "The powers not delegated to the United States by the Constitution, nor prohibited by it to the States, are reserved to the States respectively, or to the people." The amendment states but a truism that all is retained which has not been surrendered. There is nothing in the history of its adoption to suggest that it was more than declaratory of the relationship between the national and state governments as it had been established by the Constitution before the amendment or that its purpose was other than to allay fears that the new national government might seek to exercise powers not granted, and that the states might not be able to exercise fully their reserved powers. . . .

Validity of the Wage and Hour Provisions Under the Fifth Amendment: Both provisions are minimum-wage requirements compelling the payment of a minimum standard wage with a prescribed increased wage for overtime. . . . Since our decision in *West Coast Hotel Co.* v. *Parrish,* . . . it is no longer open to question that the fixing of a minimum wage is within the legislative power and that the bare fact of its exercise is not a denial of due process under the Fifth more than under the Fourteenth Amendment. Nor is it any longer open to question that it is within the legislative power to fix maximum hours. . . .

The Act is sufficiently definite to meet constitutional demands. One who employs persons, without conforming to the prescribed wage and hour conditions, to work on goods which he ships or expects to ship across state lines, is warned that he may be subject to the criminal penalties of the Act. No more is required. . . .

Reversed.

WICKARD, SECRETARY OF AGRICULTURE, *et al.* *v.* FILBURN
317 U.S. 111; 63 Sup. Ct. 82; 87 L. Ed. 122 (1942)

[Filburn, the appellee, owned and operated a small farm in Ohio. Under the terms of the Agricultural Adjustment Act of 1938, which was designed to stabilize agricultural production, Filburn was given a wheat acreage quota of 11.1 acres for his 1941 crop.

But he sowed twenty-three acres of wheat, claiming that the excess wheat was produced for use on his own farm rather than for shipment in interstate commerce. He refused to pay the penalty of $117.11 for producing the extra wheat and brought an action to enjoin the Secretary of Agriculture and others from enforcing the penalty. The proclamation of national quotas had been made by the Secretary as stipulated by the AAA. A three-judge district court issued the injunction on grounds that did not involve the major constitutional issue. The Secretary of Agriculture and others then appealed to the Supreme Court. The portions of the opinion printed here deal only with the major constitutional issue presented to the Court.]

MR. JUSTICE JACKSON delivered the opinion of the Court:

It is argued that under the commerce clause of the Constitution, Article I, Section 8, clause 3, Congress does not possess the power it has in this instance sought to exercise. The question would merit little consideration since our decision in *United States* v. *Darby* . . . sustaining the federal power to regulate production of goods for commerce, except for the fact that this Act extends federal regulation to production not intended in any part for commerce but wholly for consumption on the farm. The Act includes a definition of "market" and its derivatives, so that as related to wheat, in addition to its conventional meaning, it also means to dispose of "by feeding (in any form) to poultry or livestock which, or the products of which, are sold, bartered, or exchanged, or to be disposed of." Hence, marketing quotas not only embrace all that may be sold without penalty but also what may be consumed on the premises. Wheat produced on excess acreage is designated as "available for marketing" as so defined, and the penalty is imposed thereon. Penalties do not depend upon whether any part of the wheat, either within or without the quota, is sold or intended to be sold. The sum of this is that the Federal Government fixes a quota including all that the farmer may harvest for sale or for his own farm needs, and declares that wheat produced on excess acreage may neither be disposed of nor used except upon payment of the penalty, or except it is stored as required by the Act or delivered to the Secretary of Agriculture.

Appellee says that this is a regulation of production and consumption of wheat. Such activities are, he urges, beyond the reach of Congressional power under the commerce clause, since they are local in character, and their effects upon interstate commerce are at most "indirect." In answer the Government argues that the statute regulates neither production nor consumption, but only marketing; and, in the alternative, that if the Act does go beyond the regulation of marketing it is sustainable as a "necessary and proper" implementation of the power of Congress over interstate commerce.

The Government's concern lest the Act be held to be a regulation of production or consumption, rather than of marketing, is attributable to a few dicta and decisions of this Court which might be understood to lay it down that activities such as "production," "manufacturing," and "mining" are strictly "local" and, except in special circumstances which are not present here, cannot be regulated under the commerce power because their effects upon interstate commerce are, as matter of law, only "indirect." Even today, when this power has been held to have great latitude, there is no decision of this Court that such activities may be regulated where no part of the product is intended for interstate commerce or intermingled with the subjects thereof. We believe that a review of the course of decision under the commerce clause will make plain, however, that questions of the power of Congress are not to be decided by reference to any formula which would give controlling force to nomenclature such as "production" and "indirect" and foreclose consideration of the actual effects of the activity in question upon interstate commerce.

At the beginning Chief Justice Marshall described the federal commerce power with a breadth never yet exceeded. *Gibbons* v. *Ogden*. . . . He made emphatic the embracing and penetrating nature of this power by warning that effective restraints on its exercise must proceed from political rather than from judicial processes.

. . . Once an economic measure of the reach of the power granted to Congress in the commerce clause is accepted, questions of federal power cannot be decided simply by finding the activity in question to be "production," nor can consideration of its economic effects be forclosed by calling them "indirect." The present Chief Justice has said in summary of the present state of the law: "The commerce power is not confined in its exercise to the regulation of commerce among the states. It extends to those activities intrastate which so affect interstate commerce, or the exertion of the power of Congress over it, as to make regulation of them appropriate means to the attainment of a legitimate end, the effective execution of the granted power to regulate interstate commerce. . . . The power of Congress over interstate commerce is plenary and complete in itself, may be exercised to its utmost extent, and acknowledges no limitations other than are prescribed in the Constitution. . . . It follows that no form of state activity can constitutionally thwart the regulatory power granted by the commerce clause to Congress. Hence the reach of that power extends to those intrastate activities which in a substantial way interfere with or obstruct the exercise of the granted power." *United States* v. *Wrightwood Dairy Co.,* 315 U.S. 110. . . .

Whether the subject of the regulation in question was "production," "consumption," or "marketing" is, therefore, not material for purposes of deciding the question of federal power before us. That an activity is of a local character may help in a doubtful case to determine whether Congress intended to reach it. The same consideration might help in determining whether in the absence of congressional action it would be permissible for the state to exert its power on the subject matter, even though in so doing it to some degree affected interstate commerce. But even if appellee's activity be local and though it may not be regarded as commerce, it may still, whatever its nature, be reached by Congress if it exerts a substantial economic effect on interstate commerce, and this irrespective of whether such effect is what might at some earlier time have been defined as "direct" or "indirect."

. . . The maintenance by government regulation of a price for wheat undoubtedly can be accomplished as effectively by sustaining or increasing the demand as by limiting the supply. The effect of the statute before us is to restrict the amount which may be produced for market and the extent as well to which one may forestall resort to the market by producing to meet his own needs. That appellee's own contribution to the demand for wheat may be trivial by itself is not enough to remove him from the scope of federal regulation where, as here, his contribution, taken together with that of many others similarly situated, is far from trivial. . . .

It is well established by decision of this Court that the power to regulate commerce includes the power to regulate the prices at which commodities in that commerce are dealt in and practices affecting such prices. One of the primary purposes of the Act in question was to increase the market price of wheat, and to that end to limit the volume thereof that could affect the market. It can hardly be denied that a factor of such volume and variability as home-consumed wheat would have a substantial influence on price and market conditions. This may arise because being in marketable condition such wheat overhangs the market and, if induced by rising prices, tends to flow into the market and check price increases. But if we assume that it is never marketed, it supplies a need of the man who grew it which would otherwise be reflected by purchases in the open market. Home-grown wheat in this sense competes with wheat in commerce. The stimulation of commerce is a use of the regulatory function quite as definitely as prohibitions or restrictions thereon. This record leaves us in no doubt that Congress may properly have considered that wheat consumed on the farm where grown, if wholly outside the scheme of regulation, would have a substantial effect in defeating and obstructing its purpose to stimulate trade therein at increased prices.

It is said, however, that this Act, forcing some farmers into the market to buy what they could provide for themselves, is an unfair promotion of the markets and prices of specializing wheat growers. It is of the essence of regulation that it lays a restraining hand on the self-interest of the regulated and that advantages from the regulation commonly fall to others. The conflicts of economic interest between the regulated and those who advantage by it are wisely left under our system to resolution by the Congress under its more flexible and responsible legislative process. Such conflicts rarely lend themselves to judicial determination. And with the wisdom, workability, or fairness of the plan of regulation we have nothing to do. . . .

Reversed.

HEART OF ATLANTA MOTEL *v.* UNITED STATES

379 U.S. 241; 85 Sup. Ct. 348; 13 L. Ed. 2d 258 (1964)

MR. JUSTICE CLARK delivered the opinion of the Court:

This is a declaratory judgment action attacking the constitutionality of Title II of the Civil Rights Act of 1964. . . . Appellant owns and operates the Heart of Atlanta Motel which has 216 rooms available to transient guests. The motel is located on Courtland Street, two blocks from downtown Peachtree Street. It is readily accessible to interstate highways 75 and 85 and state highways 23 and 41. Appellant solicits patronage from outside the State of Georgia through various national advertising media, including magazines of national circulation; it maintains over fifty billboards and highway signs within the State, soliciting patronage for the motel; it accepts convention trade from outside Georgia and approximately 75 per cent of its registered guests are from out of State. Prior to passage of the Act the motel had followed a practice of refusing to rent rooms to Negroes, and it alleged that it intended to continue to do so. In an effort to perpetuate that policy this suit was filed.

The appellant contends that Congress in passing this Act exceeds its power to regulate commerce under Article I, Section 8, clause 3, of the Constitution of the United States. . . .

This Title is divided into seven sections beginning with Section 201 (a) which provides that:

> "All persons shall be entitled to the full and equal enjoyment of the goods, services, facilities, privileges, advantages, and accommodations of any place of public accommodation, as defined in this section, without discrimination or segregation on the ground of race, color, religion, or national origin."

There are listed in Section 201 (b) four classes of business establishments, each of which "serves the public" and "is a place of public accommodation" within the meaning of Section 201 (a) "if its operations affect commerce, or if discrimination or segregation by it is supported by State action." The covered establishments [include] (1) any inn, hotel, motel, or other establishment which provides lodging to transient guests. . . . Section 201 (c) . . . declares that "any inn, hotel, motel, or other establishment which provides lodging to transient guests" affects commerce per se. . . .

The sole question posed is, therefore, the constitutionality of the Civil Rights Act of 1964 as applied to these facts. The legislative history of the Act indicates that Congress based the Act on Section 5 and the Equal Protection Clause of the Fourteenth Amendment as well as its power to regulate interstate commerce under Article I, Section 8, clause 3 of the Constitution.

The Senate Commerce Committee made it quite clear that the fundamental object of Title II was to vindicate "the deprivation of personal dignity that surely accompanies denials of equal access to public establishments." At the same time, however, it noted that such an objective has been and could be readily achieved "by congressional action based on the commerce power of the Constitution.". . . Our study of the legislative record, made in the light of prior cases, has brought us to the conclusion that Congress possessed ample power in this regard, and we have therefore not considered the other grounds relied upon. This is not to say that the remaining authority upon which it acted was not adequate, a question upon which we do not pass, but merely that since the commerce power is sufficient for our decision here we have considered it alone. . . .

In light of our ground for decision, it might be well at the outset to discuss the Civil Rights Cases, which declared provisions of the Civil Rights Act of 1875 unconstitutional. We think that decision inapposite, and without precedential value in determining the constitutionality of the present Act. Unlike Title II of the present legislation, the 1875 Act broadly proscribed discrimination in "inns, public conveyances on land or water, theaters, and other public places of amusement," without limiting the categories of affected business to those impinging upon interstate commerce. In contrast, the applicability of Title II is carefully limited to enterprises having a direct and substantial relation to the interstate flow of goods and people, except where state action is involved. Further, the fact that certain kinds of businesses may not in 1875 have been sufficiently involved in interstate commerce to warrant bringing them within the ambit of the commerce power is not necessarily dispositive of the same question today. Our populace had not reached its present mobility, nor were facilities, goods and services circulating as readily in interstate commerce as they are today. Although the principles which we apply today are those first formulated by Chief Justice Marshall in *Gibbons* v. *Ogden* . . . , the conditions of transportation and commerce have changed dramatically, and we must apply those principles to the present state of commerce. The sheer increase in volume of interstate traffic alone would give discriminatory practices which inhibit travel a far larger impact upon the Nation's commerce than such practices had in the economy of another day. . . .

While the Act as adopted carried no congressional findings the record of its passage through each house is replete with evidence of the burdens that discrimination by race or color places upon interstate commerce. . . . This testimony included the fact that our people have become increasingly mobile with millions of people of all races traveling from State to State; that Negroes in particular have been the subject of discrimination in transient accommodations, having to travel great distances to secure the same; that often they have been unable to obtain accommodations and have had to call upon friends to put them up overnight . . . ; and that these conditions have become so acute as to require the listing of available lodging for Negroes in a special guidebook which was itself "dramatic testimony to the difficulties" Negroes encounter in travel. . . . These exclusionary practices were found to be nationwide, the Under Secretary of Commerce testifying that there is "no question that this discrimination in the North still exists to a large degree" and in the West and Midwest as well. . . . This testimony indicated a qualitative as well as quantitive effect on interstate travel by Negroes. The former was the obvious impairment of the Negro traveler's pleasure and convenience that resulted when he continually was uncertain of finding lodging. As for the latter, there was evidence that this uncertainty stemming from racial discrimination had the effect of discouraging travel on the part of a substantial portion of the Negro community. . . . This was the conclusion not only of the Under Secretary of Commerce but also of the Administrator of the Federal Aviation Agency who wrote the Chairman of the Senate Commerce Committee that it was his "belief that air commerce is adversely affected by the denial to a substantial segment of the traveling public of adequate and desegregated public accommodations.". . . We shall not burden this opinion with further details since the voluminous testimony presents overwhelming evidence that discrimination by hotels and motels impedes interstate travel.

The power of Congress to deal with these obstructions depends on the meaning of the Commerce Clause. Its meaning was first enunciated 140 years ago by the great Chief Justice Marshall in *Gibbons* v. *Ogden*. . . . The determinative test of the exercise of power by the Congress under the Commerce Clause is simply whether the activity sought to be regulated is "commerce which concerns more States than one" and has a real and substantial relation to the national interest. Let us now turn to this facet of the problem.

That the "intercourse" of which the Chief Justice spoke included the movement of persons through more States than one was settled as early as 1849, in the Passenger Cases . . . where Mr. Justice McLean stated: "That the transportation of passengers is a part of commerce is not now an open question.". . .

The same interest in protecting interstate commerce which led Congress to deal with segregation in interstate carriers and the white slave traffic has prompted it to extend the exercise of its power to gambling . . . to deceptive practices in the sale of products . . . to wages and hours . . . to crop control. . . .

That Congress was legislating against moral wrongs in many of these areas rendered its enactments no less valid. In framing Title II of this Act Congress was also dealing with what it considered a moral problem. But that fact does not detract from the overwhelming evidence of the disruptive effect that racial discrimination has had on commercial intercourse. It was this burden which empowered Congress to enact appropriate legislation, and, given this basis for the exercise of its power, Congress was not restricted by the fact that the particular obstruction to interstate commerce with which it was dealing was also deemed a moral and social wrong.

It is said that the operation of the motel here is of a purely local character. But, assuming this to be true, "[i]f it is interstate commerce that feels the pinch, it does not matter how local the operation which applies thc squeeze."

. . . As Chief Justice Stone put it in *United States* v. *Darby:* "The power of Congress over interstate commerce is not confined to the regulation of commerce among the states. It extends to those activities intrastate which so affect interstate commerce or the exercise of the power of Congress over it as to make regulation of them appropriate means to the attainment of a legitimate end, and exercise of the granted power of Congress to regulate interstate commerce. . . ."

Thus the power of Congress to promote interstate commerce also includes the power to regulate the local incidents thereof, including local activities in both the States of origin and destination, which might have a substantial and harmful effect upon that commerce. One need only examine the evidence which we have discussed above to see that Congress may—as it has—prohibit racial discrimination by motels serving travelers, however "local" their operations may appear . . .

We, therefore, conclude that the action of the Congress in the adoption of the Act as applied here to a motel which concededly serves interstate travelers is within the power granted it by the Commerce Clause of the Constitution, as interpreted by this Court for 140 years. It may be argued that Congress could have pursued other methods to eliminate the obstructions it found in interstate commerce caused by racial discrimination. But this is a matter of policy that rests entirely with the Congress not with the courts. How obstructions in commerce may be removed—what means are to be employed—is within the sound and exclusive discretion of the Congress. It is subject only to one caveat—that the means chosen by it must be reasonably adapted to the end permitted by the Constitution. We cannot say that its choice here was not so adapted. The Constitution requires no more.

Affirmed.

JUSTICES BLACK, DOUGLAS, and GOLDBERG concurred.

CHAPTER 10

The Fourteenth Amendment and the Regulation of Business

The Thirteenth, Fourteenth, and Fifteenth Amendments, which were adopted at the close of the Civil War, were designed to protect the newly won freedom of former slaves. The Thirteenth Amendment prohibited slavery and involuntary servitude except as a punishment for crime. The Fourteenth Amendment defined citizenship; provided that no state was to abridge privileges and immunities of citizens of the United States; forbade states to deprive persons of life, liberty, or property without due process of law; and forbade the states to deny anyone the equal protection of the laws. The Fourteenth Amendment also provided for a method of reduced representation in Congress as a punishment for states that denied the right to vote to adult male citizens. The Fifteenth Amendment stated that the right to vote could not be denied on the ground of race, color, or previous condition of servitude.

The Fourteenth Amendment emerged gradually as the most important of the Reconstruction amendments. In fact, this amendment has been the subject of more Supreme Court cases than *any* other provision of the Constitution. Much of the Court's present authority is based on its vague phrases.

Early Judicial Construction of the Fourteenth Amendment

The Fourteenth Amendment was ratified in 1868 and was first interpreted by the Supreme Court in the *Slaughterhouse* cases (p. 302). Interestingly enough, the *Slaughterhouse* cases had nothing to do with the rights of blacks, but despite the fact that the Court's narrow interpretation of privileges and immunities, due process, and equal protection "dwarfed and dulled" the civil rights protections intended by its framers, the decision constitutes a landmark in American constitutional law. The three key phrases of the amendment are, of course, extremely vague and ambiguous. There is much evidence to indicate that the authors of the Fourteenth Amendment used these vague terms deliberately to ensure its approval. Certainly, many of the Amendment's supporters sought to "define United States citizenship authoritatively, to make the restrictions of the first eight amendments applicable to the states, and to render the constitutionality of the Civil Rights Bill (1866) free from doubt. A fear on the part of the reconstructionists that an amendment baldly phrased to show these specific objects would not prove acceptable led to the use of vague and ambiguous phrases that, it was hoped, would accomplish the desired ends without too clearly indicating the purpose." [1]

But soon the Supreme Court was faced with the task of giving some meaning to the Fourteenth Amendment. In the *Slaughterhouse* cases, each of these phrases was interpreted very narrowly. What the Court said of each of these clauses had a great effect on the course of constitutional law.

PRIVILEGES AND IMMUNITIES

The Court's narrow construction of the privileges and immunities clause practically obliterated it from the Fourteenth Amendment. Since the *Slaughterhouse* cases, the Court's interpretation of privileges and immunities has not changed substantially.

Some attempts have been made to broaden the scope of privileges and immunities.[2] In *Hague* v. *Committee for Industrial Organization,* 307 U.S. 496 (1939), two justices (Roberts and Black) took the position that the rights of citizens to assemble and discuss their rights under the National Labor Relations Act was one of the privileges and immunities of citizens of the United States under the Fourteenth Amendment. We have already seen that in *Edwards* v.

[1] Ray A. Brown, "Due Process of Law, Police Power and the Supreme Court," *Columbia Law Review,* Vol. 13 (1913), p. 294.

[2] See *Colgate* v. *Harvey,* 296 U.S. 404 (1935), overruled in *Madden* v. *Kentucky,* 309 U.S. 83 (1940).

California (Chapter 8), four justices preferred to base their condemnation of the California "Anti-Okie Law" on privileges and immunities rather than the commerce clause. Again, in *Oyama* v. *California,* 332 U.S. 633 (1948), the Court agreed with the contention of petitioners that the California Alien Land Law deprived Oyama of the "equal protection of California's laws and of his privileges as an American citizen." However, the Court did not enlarge on this single statement. The right to travel mentioned as a possible privilege and immunity in the *Slaughterhouse* cases has been confirmed by the Court but not pegged to any specific clause of the Constitution. (See Chapter 6.) For many years, the privileges and immunities clause remained the "almost forgotten" clause of the Fourteenth Amendment.

Then two cases in the 1977 Term of the Court dealt with the clause. The first, *Hicklin v. Orbeck,* 437 U.S. 518 (1978), involved an Alaska statute that required that only Alaska residents be hired on certain construction projects. The Court might have invoked right to travel or commerce arguments. Instead it held the statute unconstitutional as a violation of the privileges and immunities clause. It said that the clause "establishes a norm of comity that is to prevail among the States with respect to their treatment of each other's residents." On the other hand in *Baldwin v. Montana Fish & Game Commission,* 435 U.S. 371 (1978) the Court upheld a state policy which required out-of-staters to pay higher fees for hunting licenses than those charged to state residents against arguments that it violated the privileges and immunities clause.

DUE PROCESS OF LAW AND EQUAL PROTECTION

A careful reading of the *Slaughterhouse* cases will disclose that both the due process and equal protection clauses were given very little attention and casually dismissed by Justice Miller. But, unlike its holding with respect to privileges and immunities, the Court's interpretation of due process and equal protection has been set aside completely. In fact, the dissenting opinions in the *Slaughterhouse* cases are more significant than the majority holding in terms of later developments. The dissenting opinions of both Justices Bradley and Swayne in the *Slaughterhouse* cases were based on the due process and equal protection clauses rather than privileges and immunities. Note that the vehement dissent of Justice Field is based on privileges and immunities; however, his dissenting opinion in *Munn* v. *Illinois* (p. 308) is grounded on the due process clause. In the short period between the two cases, Justice Field evidently found that the due process clause would serve as a more reliable tool for the protection of liberty and property.

Munn *v.* Illinois

The opinion of the Court in *Munn* v. *Illinois* constitutes another important expression of the doctrine of judicial noninterference during this period. *Munn* v. *Illinois* was the most important case in a series known as the Granger cases, so named because they were concerned with laws initiated by an organization of farmers known as the Patrons of Husbandry, or the Grange.[3]

The farmers had much to be unhappy about. The deflation following the Civil War had left them heavily indebted, because the value of the dollar had gone up while the demand for farm products had declined. The farmers were almost completely dependent on the railroads to ship their products to market. In addition, grain elevators were more often than not controlled by railroad managers.

To fight the entrenched power of the railroads, the farmers went into politics with a vengeance. Soon the Grangers elected a number of their own leaders to state governorships. They captured state legislatures in Illinois, Minnesota, Ohio, Michigan, Iowa, and other states. Before long a number of states had passed laws setting maximum rates for carrying and storing grain. Illinois had taken the lead in this respect. The following year the Granger-controlled legislature passed a law that made all grain elevators in cities of 100,000 inhabitants or more *public* elevators. The same law fixed the charges for storage in the elevators much lower than the then-existing rate. In addition, each operator of a grain elevator was required to obtain a license from a county court before transacting any business. Out of this legislation arose the *Munn* case.

In upholding the Illinois statute, Chief Justice Waite remarked, in an often-quoted statement, that "for protection against abuses by legislatures the people must resort to the polls, not to the courts." Waite's holding was supported by the Court for nearly a decade, but by 1890 the justices began to view the Fourteenth Amendment as an important tool for the protection of private property and vested interests. Shocked by Waite's majority opinion, the business interests had applauded Field's dissenting opinion and leveled a storm of criticism at the decision.

The change in the judicial construction of the Fourteenth Amendment was made possible by the Court's initial refusal to define authoritatively the due process and equal protection clauses. Even *Munn* suggests that business, other than that affected with a public interest, may enjoy judicial protection against unreasonable regulation. In *Davidson* v. *New Orleans,* 96 U.S. 97 (1878), the Court noted the difficulties in attempting to define due process of law and asserted that its meaning would have to evolve "by the gradual process of inclusion and exclusion, as the cases presented for decision shall require." Neither has it been possible to distinguish clearly between the protections afforded by the due process clause and those based on equal protection. Obviously, however, the two clauses overlap. "In many cases, laws which have been held invalid as denying due process of law might also have been so held as denying equal protection of the laws, or vice versa, and, in fact, in not a few cases the courts have referred to both prohibitions leaving it uncertain which prohibition was deemed the most pertinent and potent in the premises." [4]

[3] These materials are drawn from Rocco J. Tresolini, "Chief Justice Morrison R. Waite and the Public Interest," *Northwest Ohio Quarterly,* Vol. 34 (Summer 1962), pp. 124–37.

[4] Westel W. Willoughby, *The Constitutional Law of the United States* (New York: Baker, Voorhis and Co., 1929), Vol. 3, p. 1929.

Although both the due process and equal protection clauses were destined to grow, the development of due process as a constitutional deterrent to governmental action clearly overshadowed the equal protection clause until 1937.[5] The tremendous growth of that clause since 1937 is discussed in Chapters 13 and 14.

The Rise of Substantive Due Process

In the 1880s there were powerful forces at work that sought to break down the restricted meaning given to the Fourteenth Amendment in the *Slaughterhouse* cases and *Munn* v. *Illinois.* The United States was in the midst of a great Industrial Revolution. The legal system of the country was soon to be affected by big industry, big finance, the continued growth in population clustered largely in emerging urban centers, and the increased interdependence of activities. The new American corporate interests wanted to expand and grow without fear of governmental intervention. These powerful interests, which were represented by brilliant lawyers strongly committed to the laissez-faire doctrine, sought to forge the due process clause of the Fourteenth Amendment into a powerful tool for the protection of private property and vested interests against "unreasonable" social legislation.[6] Of course, a number of difficulties first had to be overcome.

Due process had never been defined precisely, but it was associated generally with procedural rights. "The generation that fought the Civil War usually identified due process with common-law procedure."[7] It believed that due process was designed principally to provide persons accused of crime with the right to counsel, protection against arrest without a warrant, and other procedural safeguards that are discussed in Chapter 15. The framers of the Fourteenth Amendment, too, thought that due process of law had "the customary meaning recognized by the courts," which was unquestionably procedural.[8]

However, even before the Civil War, the guarantee of due process of law had been used to protect vested property interests. We saw in Chapter 7 that the doctrine of vested rights had been associated closely with the contract clause. Also, in a series of New York State cases before the Civil War, due process of law was held to guarantee *substantive* as well as *procedural* rights. The

[5] See Edward S. Corwin, *Liberty Against Government* (Baton Rouge: Louisiana State U.P., 1948), p. 127; Walton H. Hamilton, "The Path of Due Process of Law," in Conyers Read, ed., *The Constitution Reconsidered* (New York: Columbia U.P., 1938), p. 167.

[6] Lawrence Friedman, *A History of American Law* (New York: Simon & Schuster, 1973), pp. 293–408.

[7] Charles M. Hough, "Due Process of Law—Today," *Harvard Law Review,* Vol. 32 (1918–19), p. 224.

[8] Joseph B. James, *The Framing of the Fourteenth Amendment* (Urbana: University of Illinois Press, 1956), pp. 86–87.

most important of these cases was *Wynehamer* v. *New York,* 13 N.Y. 378 (1856), where a state law regulating the manufacture of liquor was held invalid on the ground that it violated the due process clause in the state constitution. The state court noted that this clause was to be viewed as a general restriction on the power of the state legislature to interfere with private property.

The Supreme Court also began to accept the doctrine that due process of law could be used to protect substantive as well as procedural rights against legislative action.[9] The Court's revolutionary shift from a narrow to a broader conception of due process was gradual but unmistakable. In 1886, the Supreme Court held that corporations were persons within the meaning of the equal protection clause and were therefore entitled to the protection of the Fourteenth Amendment.[10] The Court based this holding on an argument advanced in a previous case by Roscoe Conkling, an influential New York lawyer who had played an important role in the drafting of the Fourteenth Amendment. Conkling maintained that he and members of the drafting committee had "conspired" to use the word *person* instead of *citizen* in the Amendment in order to extend its protection to corporations. Although later historical research indicated clearly that Conkling's "conspiracy" argument was largely fraudulent, it did have some effect on the Supreme Court. In numerous subsequent decisions the Court repeated the assertion that the word *person* in the Fourteenth Amendment included corporations. Of course, many important factors other than Conkling's so-called conspiracy argument contributed to a broader judicial conception of the Fourteenth Amendment. Nevertheless, Conkling's argument "sounded the death knell of the narrow 'Negro-race theory' of the Fourteenth Amendment" indicated in the *Slaughterhouse* cases. By so doing, the Court "cleared the way for the modern development of due process of law and the corresponding expansion of the Court's discretionary powers over social and economic legislation." [11]

The decisive case came in 1890. In *Chicago, Milwaukee and St. Paul R.R. Co.* v. *Minnesota,* 134 U.S. 418, the Court examined a Minnesota statute, which delegated the regulation of rates to a commission. The decision looks like *procedural* due process. The statute is held unconstitutional because it deprives the railroad of the procedural right to appeal from the commission to the courts. The Court actually takes the crucial step to *substantive* due process, however, because it holds that the reason why a judicial review procedure is essential is so that judges may review the reasonableness of the rates the commission has set. "The question of reasonableness of a rate of charge for transportation by a railroad company, involving as it does the element of reasonableness both as regards the company and as regards the public, *is eminently a question for judicial investigation, requiring due process of law for its determination.*" (Italics

[9] *Hepburn* v. *Griswold,* 8 Wall. 603 (1870); *Davidson* v. *New Orleans,* 96 U.S. 97 (1878).

[10] *Santa Clara County* v. *Southern Pacific R.R. Co.,* 118 U.S. 394 (1886).

[11] Howard J. Graham, "The 'Conspiracy Theory' of the Fourteenth Amendment," *Harvard Law Review,* Vol. 47 (1937–38), p. 372.

supplied.) If courts must be the ultimate judges of the reasonableness of rates—not only the reasonableness of the procedures for setting the rates but of the rates themselves—then the judges are making the substantive policy judgments about what rate is high enough to give the railroad a profit and low enough to protect the public interest. The Court thus converted the due process clause into a positive, judicially enforced restriction on state legislation. Justice Field's dissenting views in the earlier cases had won the day. After 1890, the Supreme Court was to become the "perpetual censor" of state legislation under the Fourteenth Amendment and federal laws under the Fifth Amendment. The victory of due process over the states' police power was discernible clearly in *Lochner* v. *New York* (p. 314), despite the famous dissent of Justice Holmes. "Even a casual examination of this new judicial attitude will indicate how thoroughgoing a revolution it wrought in our constitutional law. This new doctrine involved two things. First, it imposed upon the courts a new duty, the duty of applying to social legislation the limitations of due process of law and equal protection of the law. Secondly, this duty made it necessary for the courts to determine just how the guaranties of due process and equal protection of the law could be used as yardsticks for measuring the validity of social legislation." [12]

During this period when the Fourteenth Amendment was used with increasing frequency to protect economic rights, the Court interpreted the scope of procedural protections afforded by the Amendment rather narrowly. In a series of decisions, the Court held that the right of indictment by a grand jury, the right to trial by jury in both civil and criminal cases, and the right to be free from self-incrimination were *not* required in *state* judicial proceedings by the Fourteenth Amendment.[13] Each of these procedural safeguards is discussed in greater detail in Chapter 15.

REASONS FOR THE JUDICIAL REVOLUTION IN SUBSTANTIVE DUE PROCESS

A number of important factors contributed to the judicial revolution. Conkling's conspiracy argument and the dissenting opinions in the *Slaughterhouse* and *Munn* cases were of some influence. But there were two other factors that perhaps were of greater importance.

1. The Supreme Court was undoubtedly influenced by the prevailing economic philosophy of laissez-faire. This philosophy was supported vigorously by many Americans, particularly by the large corporate interests.

> Due process was fashioned from the most respectable ideological stuff of the later nineteenth century. The ideas out of which it was shaped were in full accord with the dominant thought of the age. In philosophy it was individualism, in government

[12] Robert E. Cushman, "The Social and Economic Interpretation of the Fourteenth Amendment," *Michigan Law Review*, Vol. 20 (1922), p. 737.

[13] *Hurtado* v. *California*, 110 U.S. 516 (1884); *Walker* v. *Sauvinet*, 92 U.S. 90 (1875); *Maxwell* v. *Dow*, 176 U.S. 581 (1900); and *Twining* v. *New Jersey*, 211 U.S. 78 (1908).

laissez faire, in economics the natural law of supply and demand, in law the freedom of contract. An impact that had been irresistible elsewhere should surely have won its way into constitutional law. Its coming seemed inevitable; the constitutional concept which it made its domicile was a mere matter of doctrinal accident.[14]

2. Important changes in the personnel of the Court from 1877 to 1890 also helped to bring about the new interpretation of the Fourteenth Amendment. During this period seven justices resigned or died. Of the judges who had decided the *Slaughterhouse* and *Munn* cases, only Justices Bradley and Field remained after the death of Justice Miller in 1890. Each of these justices had written vigorous dissents in the *Slaughterhouse* cases, and Justice Field had disssented in *Munn* v. *Illinois.* The majority of the new Court appointees had been influenced greatly by the propaganda campaign conducted by the American Bar Association in behalf of the laissez-faire doctrine. The association, which had been founded in 1878, "became a sort of juristic sewing circle for mutual education in the gospel of laissez-faire." [15] That the new justices wished to protect the property interests of the emerging business corporations was not surprising. "By 1890, sturdy individualists of the new monarchism, such as Fuller, Peckham, Brewer, and Field, dominated the Court, and the scope of judicial review was expanded by them. . . ." [16]

The Era of Substantive Due Process (1890–1937)

In the period between 1890 and 1937, the Court proceeded to read its own laissez-faire notions into the due process and equal protection clauses of the Fourteenth Amendment. Of course, there were numerous deviations and constant readjustments; but the Fourteenth Amendment and other constitutional provisions such as the interstate commerce clause often were used to strike down state and federal regulatory legislation. Under this new constitutional doctrine, the Court invalidated laws regulating minimum wages and maximum hours in employment, requiring workmen's compensation, regulating various business activities, and fixing prices. The major theme of the new constitutional doctrine was freedom of contract. This is demonstrated well in the *Lochner* case (p. 314), where the Court defined liberty to include freedom of contract. Thus legislative interference with freedom of contract constituted a deprivation of "liberty" without due process of law. The vigorous dissenting opinion of Justice Holmes in the *Lochner* case deserves careful attention, because it was destined to become the majority view of the Court after 1937.

[14] Hamilton, op cit., p. 189. See also Benjamin R. Twiss, *Lawyers and the Constitution* (Princeton, N.J.: Princeton U.P., 1942).

[15] Corwin, op. cit., p. 138.

[16] Alpheus T. Mason, "The Conservative World of Mr. Justice Sutherland, 1883–1910," *American Political Science Review,* Vol. 32 (1938), p. 476. See Robert McCloskey, *American Conservatism in the Age of Enterprise* (Chicago: University of Chicago Press, 1951).

Only three years after the *Lochner* decision, the Court seemed to adopt a much more liberal attitude toward social and economic legislation. In *Muller* v. *Oregon,* 208 U.S. 412 (1908), the Court unanimously sustained an Oregon statute that limited the employment of women to ten hours a day in almost any type of industrial establishment. The Court's more liberal attitude toward social and economic legislation resulted, in part, from the influence of the arguments presented by Louis D. Brandeis in defense of the Oregon law. Brandeis, who was then a prominent Boston lawyer, submitted an unusual brief that included only two pages of legal arguments. But over a hundred pages of the brief consisted of American and European facts and statistics designed to show that women needed protection from excessive hours of labor. Brandeis argued that his data, which was obtained from committee reports, commissions on hygiene, inspectors of factories, and various other bureaus, proved that Oregon was justified in reducing a woman's working day for both physiological and social reasons. The majority opinion of the Court, written by Justice Brewer, revealed clearly the influence of what came to be called the Brandeis brief. The Court noted that the legislation and data presented by Brandeis "may not be, technically speaking, authorities, and in them is little or no discussion of the constitutional question presented to us for determination, yet they are significant of a widespread belief that woman's physical structure, and the functions she performs in consequence thereof, justify special legislation restricting or qualifying the conditions under which she would be permitted to toil." Thus the Court approved, for the first time, the revolutionary Brandeis technique of using social and economic facts to support the reasonableness of social welfare legislation.

The Brandeis technique was used with success in subsequent cases before the Supreme Court. In *Bunting* v. *Oregon,* 243 U.S. 426 (1917), the Court upheld an Oregon ten-hour law that applied to both men and women, despite a broad statement in the *Muller* case that legislation designed for the protection of women may be sustained "even when like legislation is not necessary for men, and could not be sustained." *Lochner* v. *New York* was not even mentioned in the *Bunting* case. By implication, the *Lochner* case thus appeared to be silently overruled. In *Stettler* v. *O'Hara,* 243 U.S. 629 (1917), the Court divided 4 to 4 and thereby left standing a decision of the Oregon Supreme Court which had upheld the state minimum-wage law. (A decision of a lower court is sustained when there is a tie vote in the Court.)

Despite the apparent liberalism of the *Bunting* and *Stettler* cases, the *Lochner* precedent was far from dead. "Those who had assumed a permanent change in the Court's outlook were to be disappointed. Change in the Court's personnel and pressure of postwar economic and social views soon reflected themselves in decisions."[17] In the 1923 case of *Adkins* v. *Children's Hospital* (p. 318), the Court resurrected the *Lochner* precedent to invalidate a minimum-wage law for women and children in the District of Columbia. Justice Brandeis,

[17] Felix Frankfurter, ed., *Mr. Justice Holmes* (New York: Coward-McCann, 1931), p. 81.

who had been appointed to the Court in 1916, did not participate in the decision because his daughter was the Secretary of the District Minimum Wage Board. But Justice Holmes dissented, and even the conservative Chief Justice (Taft) felt impelled to write a dissenting opinion.

The *Adkins* case was criticized bitterly, but with little practical effect for over a decade. As late as 1936, the Supreme Court held void a New York minimum-wage statute for women and children as a violation of the due process clause of the Fourteenth Amendment by applying the *Adkins* reasoning (*Morehead* v. *New York* ex rel. *Tipaldo,* 298 U.S. 587).

The Decline of Substantive Due Process

Despite the *Tipaldo* holding, which was deplored by liberals and conservatives alike, the 1934 case of *Nebbia* v. *New York* (p. 323) was an indication that the Court would soon reject the due process philosophy enunciated in the *Lochner* and *Adkins* decisions. In the *Nebbia* case, the Court abandoned entirely the vague and elusive concept of business affected with the public interest announced in *Munn* v. *Illinois* and appeared reluctant to substitute its judgment for that of state legislators in social and economic policy matters.

The end came in *West Coast Hotel Co.* v. *Parrish* (p. 325), in which the Court expressly overruled the *Adkins* case by a 5-to-4 vote. The reversal of Justice Roberts's position in the *Tipaldo* case made the new majority holding possible. Since the *Parrish* decision, the Court has "consciously returned closer and closer to the earlier constitutional principle that states have power to legislate against what are found to be injurious practices in their internal commercial and business affairs, so long as their laws do not run afoul of some specific federal constitutional prohibition or of some valid federal law. Under this constitutional doctrine, the due process clause is no longer to be so broadly construed that the Congress and state legislatures are put in a strait jacket when they attempt to suppress business and industrial conditions which they regard as offensive to the public welfare." [18] Thus, the holdings against which Justice Holmes and Brandeis had for long contended have been rejected by the Court.

If by "substantive due process" we mean *only* the Court's use of the due process clause to protect business against government regulation, then the conclusion of a number of commentators that substantive due process died in the period between 1937 and 1946 is largely correct.[19] More broadly, however, substantive due process would seem to be composed of two elements. First is the enforcement of substantive as well as procedural rights. Second is the substitution of judicial for legislative judgment on issues of public policy. In Chapter

[18] *Lincoln Federal Labor Union* v. *Northwestern Iron and Metal Co.,* 335 U.S. 525 (1949).

[19] C. Herman Pritchett, *Civil Liberties and the Vinson Court* (Chicago: U. of Chicago, 1954), p. 3; Robert G. McCloskey, "Economic Due Process and the Supreme Court, an Exhumation and Reburial," *Supreme Court Review,* 1962, p. 34. See also Arthur S. Miller, *The Supreme Court and American Capitalism* (New York: Free Press, 1968).

15 we shall trace the "incorporation" of most of the procedural *and* substantive rights of the first eight Amendments into the due process clause of the Fourteenth Amendment and the impact of this incorporation on the rights of the accused. And though, for purposes of convenience, Chapter 11 will usually speak of the First Amendment, in fact a fair share of the freedom of speech and association cases it surveys involve the reading of substantive speech rights into the due process clause.

Then in Chapter 14 we shall discover that through the due process clause and/or through what may fairly be called "substantive equal protection," the contemporary Supreme Court is again very concerned with the protection of economic rights. But this time they are the economic rights of the poor, the black, the illegitimate and women rather than businessmen. (See particularly the section of Chapter 14 headed "Old Property—New Property.") In these areas the justices are quite willing to substitute their own policy decisions for those of the legislature. Finally, Chapter 16 indicates that in the largely nonconstitutional area of judicial review of administrative agency decisions, the Court continues to show considerable concern for business interests. That chapter also shows that in antitrust cases the Court continues to be a major economic policy maker.

Constitutional approaches such as substantive due process have considerable staying power.[20] As the comic cat of a great American humorist used to say: "There's life in the old gal yet."

THE SLAUGHTERHOUSE CASES
16 Wall. 36; 21 L. Ed. 394 (1873)

[Three separate cases that grew out of the same set of circumstances are known as the Slaughterhouse *cases. These cases resulted from a Louisiana statute, enacted in 1869, that granted a monopoly to a slaughterhouse company in New Orleans. The act provided that the slaughtering of all animals in the New Orleans area was to be carried on by a single company for a period of twenty-five years. When the statute was enacted, the Louisiana state legislature was dominated by Reconstruction, or carpetbag, elements and many legislative officers were under corrupt influences. The legislation had the effect of depriving some 1,000 butchers of work. Some of these butchers sought an injunction against the monopoly in the state courts, contending that they were deprived of the "right to exercise their trade, the business to which they have been trained and on which they depend for the support of themselves and their families." The Supreme Court of Louisiana decided in favor of the slaughterhouse company. The butchers then brought the cases to the Supreme Court on a writ of error.]*

MR. JUSTICE MILLER delivered the opinion of the court:

. . . The plaintiffs in error . . . allege that the statute is a violation of the Constitution of the United States in these several particulars:

[20] Martin Shapiro, "The Constitution and Economic Rights," in M. Judd Harmon, ed., *Essays on the Constitution of the United States* (Port Washington, N.Y.: Kennikat Press, 1978).

That it creates an involuntary servitude forbidden by the thirteenth article of amendment:

That it abridges the privileges and immunities of citizens of the United States:

That it denies to the plaintiffs the equal protection of the laws; and,

That it deprives them of their property without due process of law; contrary to the provisions of the first section of the fourteenth article of amendment.

This court is thus called upon for the first time to give construction to these articles.

. . . [O]n the most casual examination of the language of these amendments [the Thirteenth, Fourteenth, and Fifteenth], no one can fail to be impressed with the one pervading purpose found in them all, lying at the foundation of each, and without which none of them would have been even suggested; we mean the freedom of the slave race, the security and firm establishment of that freedom, and the protection of the newly-made freeman and citizen from the oppressions of those who had formerly exercised unlimited dominion over him. It is true that only the Fifteenth amendment, in terms, mentions the Negro by speaking of his color and his slavery. But it is just as true that each of the other articles was addressed to the grievances of that race, and designed to remedy them as the Fifteenth.

We do not say that no one else but the Negro can share in this protection. Both the language and spirit of these articles are to have their fair and just weight in any question of construction. Undoubtedly while Negro slavery alone was in mind of the Congress which proposed the thirteenth article, it forbids any other kind of slavery, now or hereafter. . . .

The first section of the fourteenth article, to which our attention is more specially invited, opens with a definition of citizenship—not only citizenship of the United States, but citizenship of the States. No such definition was previously found in the Constitution, nor had any attempt been made to define it by act of Congress. It had been the occasion of much discussion in the courts, by the executive departments, and in the public journals. It had been said by eminent judges that no man was a citizen of the United States, except as he was a citizen of one of the States composing the Union. Those, therefore, who had been born and resided always in the District of Columbia or in the Territories, though within the United States, were not citizens. Whether this proposition was sound or not had never been judicially decided. But it had been held by this court, in the celebrated *Dred Scott* case, only a few years before the outbreak of the Civil War, that a man of African descent, whether a slave or not, was not and could not be a citizen of a State or of the United States. This decision, while it met the condemnation of some of the ablest statesmen and constitutional lawyers of the country, had never been overruled; and if it was to be accepted as a constitutional limitation of the right of citizenship, then all the Negro race who had recently been made freemen, were still, not only not citizens, but were incapable of becoming so by anything short of an amendment to the Constitution.

To remove this difficulty primarily, and to establish a clear and comprehensive definition of citizenship which should declare what should constitute citizenship of the United States, and also citizenship of a State, the first clause of the first section was framed.

"All persons born or naturalized in the United States, and subject to the jurisdiction thereof, are citizens of the United States and of the State wherein they reside."

The first observation we have to make on this clause is, that it puts at rest both the questions which we stated to have been the subject of differences of opinion. It declares that persons may be citizens of the United States without regard to their citizenship of a particular State, and it overturns the *Dred Scott* decision by making *all persons* born within the United States and subject to its jurisdiction citizens of the United States. That its main purpose was to establish the citizenship of the Negro can admit of no doubt. The phrase, "subject to its jurisdiction," was intended to exclude from its operation children of ministers, consuls, and citizens or subjects of foreign States born within the United States.

The next observation is more important

in view of the arguments of counsel in the present case. It is, that the distinction between citizenship of the United States and citizenship of a State is clearly recognized and established. Not only may a man be a citizen of the United States without being a citizen of a State, but an important element is necessary to convert the former into the latter. He must reside within the State to make him a citizen of it, but it is only necessary that he should be born or naturalized in the United States to be a citizen of the Union.

It is quite clear, then, that there is a citizenship of the United States, and a citizenship of a State, which are distinct from each other, and which depend upon different characteristics or circumstances in the individual.

We think this distinction and its explicit recognition in this amendment of great weight in this argument, because the next paragraph of this same section, which is the one mainly relied on by the plaintiffs in error, speaks only of privileges and immunities of citizens of the United States, and does not speak of those of citizens of the several States. The argument, however, in favor of the plaintiffs rests wholly on the assumption that the citizenship is the same, and the privileges and immunities guaranteed by the clause are the same.

The language is, "No State shall make or enforce any law which shall abridge the privileges or immunities of citizens of *the United States.*" It is a little remarkable, if this clause was intended as a protection to the citizen of a State against the legislative power of his own State, that the word citizen of the State should be left out when it is so carefully used, and used in contradistinction to citizens of the United States, in the very sentence which precedes it. It is too clear for argument that the change in phraseology was adopted understandingly and with a purpose.

Of the privileges and immunities of the citizen of the United States, and of the privileges and immunities of the citizen of the State, and what they respectively are, we will presently consider; but we wish to state here that it is only the former which are placed by this clause under the protection of the Federal Constitution, and that the latter, whatever they may be, are not intended to have any additional protection by this paragraph of the amendment.

If, then, there is a difference between the privileges and immunities belonging to a citizen of the United States as such, and those belonging to the citizen of the State as such, the latter must rest for their security and protection where they have heretofore rested; for they are not embraced by this paragraph of the amendment.

The first occurrence of the words "privileges and immunities" in our constitutional history, is to be found in the fourth of the articles of the old Confederation.

It declares "that the better to secure and perpetuate mutual friendship and intercourse among the people of the different States in this Union, the free inhabitants of each of these States, paupers, vagabonds, and fugitives from justice excepted, shall be entitled to all the privileges and immunities of free citizens in the several States; and the people of each State shall have free ingress and egress to and from any other State, and shall enjoy therein all the privileges of trade and commerce, subject to the same duties, impositions, and restrictions as the inhabitants thereof respectively."

In the Constitution of the United States, which superseded the Articles of Confederation, the corresponding provision is found in section two of the fourth article, in the following words: "The citizens of each State shall be entitled to all the privileges and immunities of citizens of the several States."

There can be but little question that the purpose of both these provisions is the same, and that the privileges and immunities intended are the same in each. In the article of the Confederation we have some of these specifically mentioned, and enough perhaps to give some general idea of the class of civil rights meant by the phrase. . . .

The constitutional provision there alluded to did not create those rights, which it called privileges and immunities of citizens of the States. It threw around them in that clause no security for the citizen of the State in which they were claimed or exercised. Nor did it profess to control the power of the State governments over the rights of its own citizens.

Its sole purpose was to declare to the several States, that whatever those rights, as you grant or establish them to your own citizens, or as you limit or qualify, or impose restrictions on their exercise, the same, neither more nor less, shall be the measure of the rights of citizens of other States within your jurisdiction.

It would be the vainest show of learning to attempt to prove by citations of authority, that up to the adoption of the recent amendments, no claim or pretence was set up that those rights depended on the Federal Government for their existence or protection, beyond the very few express limitations which the Federal Constitution imposed upon the States—such, for instance, as the prohibition against ex post facto laws, bills of attainder, and laws impairing the obligation of contracts. But with the exception of these and a few other restrictions, the entire domain of the privileges and immunities of citizens of the States, as above defined, lay within the constitutional and legislative power of the States, and without that of the Federal Government. Was it the purpose of the Fourteenth Amendment, by the simple declaration that no State should make or enforce any law which shall abridge the privileges and immunities of *citizens of the United States,* to transfer the security and protection of all the civil rights which we have mentioned, from the States to the Federal Government? And where it is declared that Congress shall have the power to enforce that article, was it intended to bring within the power of Congress the entire domain of civil rights heretofore belonging exclusively to the States?

All this and more must follow, if the proposition of the plaintiffs in error be sound. For not only are these rights subject to the control of Congress whenever in its discretion any of them are supposed to be abridged by State legislation, but that body may also pass laws in advance, limiting and restricting the exercise of legislative power by the States, in their most ordinary and usual functions, as in its judgment it may think proper on all such subjects. And still further, such a construction followed by the reversal of the judgments of the Supreme Court of Louisiana in these cases, would constitute this court a perpetual censor upon all legislation of the States, on the civil rights of their own citizens, with authority to nullify such as it did not approve as consistent with those rights, as they existed at the time of the adoption of this amendment. The argument we admit is not always the most conclusive which is drawn from the consequences urged against the adoption of a particular construction of an instrument. But when, as in the case before us, these consequences are so serious, so far-reaching and pervading, so great a departure from the structure and spirit of our institutions; when the effect is to fetter and degrade the State governments by subjecting them to the control of Congress, in the exercise of powers heretofore universally conceded to them of the most ordinary and fundamental character; when in fact it radically changes the whole theory of the relations of the State and Federal governments to each other and of both these governments to the people; the argument has a force that is irresistible, in the absence of language which expresses such a purpose too clearly to admit doubt.

We are convinced that no such results were intended by the Congress which proposed these amendments, nor by the legislatures of the States which ratified them.

Having shown that the privileges and immunities relied on in the argument are those which belong to citizens of the States as such, and that they are left to the State governments for security and protection, and not by this article placed under the special care of the Federal Government, we may hold ourselves excused from defining the privileges and immunities of citizens of the United States which no State can abridge, until some case involving those privileges may make it necessary to do so.

But lest it should be said that no such privileges and immunities are to be found if those we have been considering are excluded, we venture to suggest some which owe their existence to the Federal Government, its National character, its Constitution, or its laws.

One of these . . . is said to be the right of the citizen of this great country, protected by implied guarantee of its Constitution, "to come to the seat of government to assert any claim he may have upon that government, to transact any business he may have with it, to seek its protection, to share its offices, to engage in administering its functions. He has the right of free access to its seaports, through which all operations of foreign commerce are conducted, to the sub-treasuries, land offices, and courts of justice in the several States." And quoting from the language of Chief Justice Taney . . . it is said "that *for all the great purposes for which the Federal Government* was established, we are one people, with one common country, *we are all citizens of the United States;*". . .

Another privilege of a citizen of the United States is to demand the care and protection of the Federal Government over his life, liberty, and property when on the high seas or within the jurisdiction of a foreign government. Of this there can be no doubt, nor that the right depends upon his character as a citizen of the United States. The right to peaceably assemble and petition for redress of grievances, the privilege of the writ of *habeas corpus,* are rights of the citizen guaranteed by the Federal Constitution. The right to use the navigable waters of the United States, however they may penetrate the territory of the several States, all rights secured to our citizens by treaties with foreign nations are dependent upon citizenship of the United States, and not citizenship of a State. One of these privileges is conferred by the very article under consideration. It is that a citizen of the United States can, of his own volition, become a citizen of any State of the Union by a *bona fide* residence therein, with the same rights as other citizens of that State. To these may be added the rights secured by the thirteenth and fifteenth articles of amendment, and by the other clause of the fourteenth, next to be considered.

But it is useless to pursue this branch of the inquiry, since we are of opinion that the rights claimed by these plaintiffs in error, if they have any existence, are not privileges and immunities of citizens of the United States within the meaning of the clause of the Fourteenth Amendment under consideration. . . .

The argument has not been much pressed in these cases that the defendant's charter deprives the plaintiffs of their property without due process of law, or that it denies to them the equal protection of the law. The first of these paragraphs has been in the Constitution since the adoption of the Fifth Amendment, as a restraint upon the Federal power. It is also to be found in some form of expression in the constitutions of nearly all the States, as a restraint upon the power of the States. This law, then, has practically been the same as it now is during the existence of the government, except so far as the present amendment may place the restraining power over the States in this matter in the hands of the Federal Government.

We are not without judicial interpretation, therefore, both State and National, of the meaning of this clause. And it is sufficient to say that under no construction of that provision that we have ever seen, or any that we deem admissible, can the restraint imposed by the State of Louisiana upon the exercise of their trade by the butchers of New Orleans be held to be a deprivation of property within the meaning of that provision.

"Nor shall any State deny to any person within its jurisdiction the equal protection of the laws."

In the light of the history of these amendments, and the pervading purpose of them, which we have already discussed, it is not difficult to give a meaning to this clause. The existence of laws in the States where the newly emancipated Negroes resided, which discriminated with gross injustice and hardship against them as a class, was the evil to be remedied by this clause, and by it such laws are forbidden.

If, however, the States did not conform their laws to its requirements, then by the fifth section of the article of amendment Congress was authorized to enforce it by suitable legislation. We doubt very much whether any action of a State not directed by way of discrimination against the Negroes as a class, or on account of their race, will ever be held to come within the purview of this provision. It is so clearly a provision for that race and that emergency, that a strong case would be necessary for its application to any other. But as it is a State that is to be dealt with, and not alone the validity of its laws, we may safely leave that matter until Congress shall have exercised its power, or some case of State oppression, by denial of equal justice in its courts, shall have claimed a decision at our hands. We find no such case in the one before us, and do not deem it necessary to go over the argument again, as it may have relation to this particular clause of the amendment. . . .

The judgments of the Supreme Court of Louisiana in these cases are

Affirmed.

MR. JUSTICE FIELD, dissenting:

. . . The question presented is . . . one of the gravest importance, not merely to the parties here, but to the whole country. It is nothing less than the question whether the recent amendments to the Federal Constitution protect the citizens of the United States against the deprivation of their common rights by State legislation. In my judgment the Fourteenth Amendment does afford such protection, and was so intended by the Congress which framed and the States which adopted it. . . .

The amendment does not attempt to confer any new privileges or immunities upon citizens, or to enumerate or define those already existing. It assumes that there are such privileges and immunities which belong of right to citizens as such, and ordains that they shall not be abridged by State legislation. If this inhibition has no reference to privileges and immunities of this character, but only refers, as held by the majority of the court in their opinion, to such privileges and immunities as were before its adoption specially designated in the Constitution or necessarily implied as belonging to citizens of the United States, it was a vain and idle enactment, which accomplished nothing, and most unnecessarily excited Congress and the people on its passage. With privileges and immunities thus designated or implied, no State could ever have interfered by its laws, and no new constitutional provision was required to inhibit such interference. The supremacy of the Constitution and the laws of the United States always controlled any State legislation of that character. But if the amendment refers to the natural and inalienable rights which belong to all citizens, the inhibition has a profound significance and consequence.

What, then, are the privileges and immunities which are secured against abridgment by State legislation? . . .

The terms, privileges and immunities, are not new in the amendment; they were in the Constitution before the amendment was adopted. They are found in the second section of the fourth article, which declares that "the citizens of each State shall be entitled to all privileges and immunities of citizens in the several States," and they have been the subject of frequent consideration in judicial decisions. In *Corfield* v. *Coryell,* Mr. Justice Washington said he had "no hesitation in confining these expressions to those privileges and immunities which were, in their nature, fundamental; which belong of right to citizens of all free governments, and which have at all times been enjoyed by the citizens of the several States which compose the Union, from the time of their becoming free, independent, and sovereign"; and, in considering what those fundamental privileges were, he said that perhaps it would be more tedious than difficult to enumerate them, but that they might be "all comprehended under the following general heads; protection by the government; the enjoyment of life and liberty, with the right to acquire and possess property of every kind, and to pursue and obtain happiness and safety, subject, nevertheless, to such restraints as the government may justly prescribe for the general good of the whole." This appears to me to be a sound construction of the clause in question. The privileges and immunities designated are those *which of right belong to the citizens of all free governments.* Clearly among these must be placed the right to pursue a lawful employment in a lawful manner, without other restraint than such as equally affects all persons. . . .

This equality of right, with exemption from all disparaging and partial enactments, in the lawful pursuits of life, throughout the whole country, is the distinguishing privilege of citizens of the United States. To them, everywhere, all pursuits, all professions, all avocations are open without other restrictions than such as are imposed equally upon all others of the same age, sex, and condition. The State may prescribe such regulations for every pursuit and calling of life as will promote the public health, secure the good order and advance the general prosperity of society, but when once prescribed, the pursuit or calling must be free to be followed by every citizen who is within the conditions designated, and will conform to the regulations. This is the fundamental idea upon which our institutions rest, and unless adhered to in the legislation of the country our government will be a republic only in name. The Fourteenth Amendment, in my judgment, makes it essential to the validity of the legislation of every State that this equality of right should be respected. How widely this equality has been departed from, how entirely rejected and trampled upon by the act of Louisiana, I have already shown. And it is to me a matter of profound regret that its validity is recognized by a majority of this court, for by it the right of free labor, one of the most sacred and imprescriptible rights of man, is violated. . . . [G]rants of exclusive privileges, such as is made by the act in question, are opposed to the whole theory of free government, and it requires no aid from any bill of rights to render them void. That only is a free government, in the American sense of the term, under which the inalienable right of every citizen to pursue his happiness is unrestrained, except by just, equal, and impartial laws.

I am authorized by the CHIEF JUSTICE, MR. JUSTICE SWAYNE, and MR. JUSTICE BRADLEY, to state that they concur with me in this dissenting opinion.

[Mr. Justice Bradley and Mr. Justice Swayne also wrote separate dissenting opinions.]

MUNN *v.* ILLINOIS
94 U.S. 113; 24 L. Ed. 77 (1877)

[Munn was convicted of operating a grain warehouse without a license and of charging higher rates than those established for the storage and handling of grain. Both practices were illegal under an Illinois statute that had been enacted in 1871 after the state constitution of 1870 had empowered the state legislature to regulate the storage of grain. The Illinois Supreme Court affirmed the judgment of a county court that had fined Munn and a partner $100 for the violation. Munn then brought the case to the Supreme Court on a writ of error.]

MR. CHIEF JUSTICE WAITE delivered the opinion of the court:

The question to be determined in this case is whether the general assembly of Illinois can, under the limitations upon the legislative power of the States imposed by the Constitution of the United States, fix by law the maximum of charges for the storage of grain in warehouses at Chicago and other places in the State having not less than 100,000 inhabitants, "in which grain is stored in bulk, and in which the grain of different owners is mixed together, or in which grain is stored in such a manner that the identity of different lots or parcels cannot be accurately preserved."

It is claimed that such a law is repugnant—

1. To that part of Section 8, Article I, of the Constitution of the United States which confers upon Congress the power "to regulate commerce with foreign nations and among the several States;"

2. To that part of Section 9 of the same article which provides that "no preference shall be given by any regulation of commerce or revenue to the ports of one State over those of another;" and

3. To that part of Amendment Fourteen which ordains that no State shall "deprive any person of life, liberty, or property, without due process of law, nor deny to any person within its jurisdiction the equal protection of the laws."

We will consider the last of these objections first.

Every statute is presumed to be constitutional. The courts ought not to declare one to be unconstitutional, unless it is clearly so. If there is doubt, the expressed will of the legislature should be sustained.

The Constitution contains no definition of the word *deprive,* as used in the Fourteenth Amendment. To determine its signification, therefore, it is necessary to ascertain the effect which usage has given it, when employed in the same or a like connection.

While this provision of the amendment is new in the Constitution of the United States, as a limitation upon the powers of the States, it is old as a principle of civilized government. It is found in Magna Carta, and, in substance if not in form, in nearly or quite all the constitutions that have been from time to time adopted by the several States of the Union. By the Fifth Amendment, it was introduced into the Constitution of the United States as a limitation upon the powers of the national government, and by the Fourteenth, as a guaranty against any encroachment upon an acknowledged right of citizenship by the legislatures of the States. . . .

When one becomes a member of society, he necessarily parts with some rights or privileges which, as an individual not affected by his relations to others, he might retain. "A body politic," as aptly defined in the preamble of the Constitution of Massachusetts, "is a social compact by which the whole people covenants with each citizen, and each citizen with the whole people, that all shall be governed by certain laws for the common good." This does not confer power upon the whole people to control rights which are purely and exclusively private, . . . but it does authorize the establishment of laws requiring each citizen to so conduct himself, and so use his own property, as not unnecessarily to injure another. This is the very essence of government. . . . From this source come the police powers, which, as was said by Mr. Chief Justice Taney in the *License* cases, 5 How. 583, "are nothing more or less than the powers of government inherent in every sovereignty, . . . that is to say, . . . the power to govern men and things." Under these powers the government regulates the conduct of its citizens one towards another, and the manner in which each shall use his own property, when such regulation becomes necessary for the public good. In their exercise it has been customary in England from time immemorial, and in this country from its first colonization, to regulate ferries, common carriers, hackmen, bakers, millers, wharfingers, innkeepers, etc., and in so doing to fix a maximum of charge to be made for services rendered, accommodations furnished, and articles sold. To this day, statutes are to be found in many of the States upon some or all these subjects; and we think it has never yet been successfully contended that such legislation came within any of the constitutional prohibitions against interference with private property. With the Fifth Amendment in force, Congress, in 1820, conferred power upon the city of Washington "to regulate . . . the rates of wharfage at private wharves, . . . the sweeping of chimneys, and to fix the rates of fees therefor, . . . and the weight and quality of bread". . . ; and, in 1848, "to make all necessary regulations respecting hackney carriages and the rates of fare of the same, and the rates of hauling by cartmen, wagoners, carmen, and draymen, and rates of commission of auctioneers.". . .

From this it is apparent that, down to the time of the adoption of the Fourteenth Amendment, it was not supposed that statutes regulating the use, or even the price of the use, of private property necessarily deprived an owner of his property without due process of law. Under some circumstances they may, but not under all. The amendment does not change the law in this particular: it simply prevents the States from doing that which will operate as such a deprivation.

This brings us to inquire as to the principles upon which this power of regulation rests, in order that we may determine what is within and what without its operative effect: Looking, then, to the common law, from whence came the right which the Constitution protects, we find that when private property is "affected with a public interest, it ceases to be *juris privati* only." This was said by Lord Chief Justice Hale more than 200 years ago . . . , and has been accepted without objection as an essential element in the law of property ever since. Property does become clothed with a public interest when used in a manner to make it of public consequence, and affect the community at large. When, therefore, one devotes his property to a use in which the public has an interest, he, in effect, grants to the public an interest in that use, and must submit to be controlled by the public for the common good, to the extent of the interest he has thus created. He may withdraw his grant by discontinuing the use; but, so long as he maintains the use, he must submit to the control. . . .

Enough has already been said to show that, when private property is devoted to a public use, it is subject to public regulation. It remains only to ascertain whether the warehouses of these plaintiffs in error, and the business which is carried on there, come within the operation of this principle.

For this purpose we accept as true the statements of fact contained in the elaborate brief of one of the counsel of the plaintiffs in error. From these it appears that "the great producing region of the West and North-west sends its grain by water and rail to Chicago, where the greater part of it is shipped by vessel for transportation to the seaboard by the Great Lakes, and some of it is forwarded by railway to the Eastern ports. . . . Vessels, to some extent, are loaded in the Chicago harbor, and sailed through the St. Lawrence directly to Europe. . . . The quantity (of grain) received in Chicago has made it the greatest grain market in the world. This business has created a demand for means by which the immense quantity of grain can be handled or stored, and these have been found in grain warehouses, which are commonly called elevators, because the grain is elevated from the boat or car, by machinery operated by steam, into bins prepared for its reception, and elevated from the bins, by a like process, into the vessel or car which is to carry it on. . . . In this way the largest traffic between the citizens of the country north and west of Chicago and the citizens of the country lying on the Atlantic coast north of Washington is in grain which passes through the elevators of Chicago. In this way the trade in grain is carried on by the inhabitants of seven or eight of the great States of the West with four or five of the States lying on the seashore, and forms the largest part of interstate commerce in these States. The grain warehouses or elevators in Chicago are immense structures, holding from 300,000 to 1,000,000 bushels at one time, according to size. They are divided into bins of large capacity and great strength. . . . They are located with the river harbor on one side and the railway tracks on the other; and the grain is run through them from car to vessel, or boat to car, as may be demanded in the course of business. It has been found impossible to preserve each owner's grain separate, and this has given rise to a system of inspection and grading, by which the grain of different owners is mixed, and receipts issued for the number of bushels which are negotiable, and redeemable in like kind, upon demand. This mode of conducting the business was inaugurated more than twenty years ago, and has grown to immense proportions. The railways have found it impracticable to own such elevators, and public policy forbids the transaction of such business by the carrier; the ownership has, therefore, been by private individuals, who have embarked their capital and devoted their industry to such business as a private pursuit.

In this connection it must also be borne in mind that, although in 1874 there were in Chicago fourteen warehouses adopted to this particular business, and owned by about thirty persons, nine business firms controlled them, and that the prices charged and received for storage were such "as have been from year to year agreed upon and established by the different elevators or warehouses in the city of Chicago, and which rates have been annually published in one or more newspapers printed in said city, in the month of January in each year, as the established rates for the year then next ensuing such publication." Thus it is apparent that all the elevating facilities through which these vast productions "of seven or eight great States of the West" must pass on the way "to four or five of the States on the sea-shore" may be a "virtual" monopoly.

Under such circumstances it is difficult

to see why, if the common carrier, or the miller, or the ferryman, or the innkeeper, or the wharfinger, or the baker, or the cartman, or the hackney-coachman, pursues a public employment and exercises "a sort of public office," these plaintiffs in error do not. They stand, to use again the language of their counsel, in the very "gateway of commerce," and take toll from all who pass. Their business most certainly "tends to a common charge, and is become a thing of public interest and use." Every bushel of grain for its passage "pays a toll, which is a common charge," and, therefore, according to Lord Hale, every such warehouseman "ought to be under public regulations, viz., that he . . . take but a reasonable toll." Certainly, if any business can be clothed "with a public interest, and cease to be *juris privati* only," this has been. It may not be made so by the operation of the Constitution of Illinois or this statute, but is by the facts.

We also are not permitted to overlook the fact that, for some reason, the people of Illinois, when they revised their Constitution in 1870, saw fit to make it the duty of the general assembly to pass laws "for the protection of producers, shippers, and receivers of grain and produce."

. . . Neither is it a matter of any moment that no precedent can be found for a statute precisely like this. It is conceded that the business is one of recent origin, that its growth has been rapid, and that it is already of great importance. And it must also be conceded that it is a business in which the whole public has a direct and positive interest. It presents, therefore, a case for the application of a long-known and well-established principle in social science, and this statute simply extends the law so as to meet this new development of commercial progress. There is no attempt to compel these owners to grant the public an interest in their property, but to declare their obligations, if they use it in this particular manner. . . .

It is insisted, however, that the owner of property is entitled to a reasonable compensation for its use, even though it be clothed with a public interest, and that what is reasonable is a judicial and not a legislative question.

As has already been shown, the practice has been otherwise. In countries where the common law prevails, it has been customary from time immemorial for the legislature to declare what shall be a reasonable compensation under such circumstances, or, perhaps more properly speaking, to fix a maximum beyond which any charge made would be unreasonable. Undoubtedly, in mere private contracts, relating to matters in which the public has no interest, what is reasonable must be ascertained judicially. But this is because the legislature has no control over such a contract. So, too, in matters which do affect the public interest, and as to which legislative control may be exercised, if there are no statutory regulations upon the subject, the courts must determine what is reasonable. The controlling fact is the power to regulate at all. If that exists, the right to establish the maximum of charge, as one of the means of regulation, is implied. In fact, the common-law rule, which requires the charge to be reasonable, is itself a regulation as to price. Without it the owner could make his rates at will, and compel the public to yield to his terms, or forego the use.

But a mere common-law regulation of trade or business may be changed by statute. A person has no property, no vested interest, in any rule of the common law. . . . Rights of property which have been created by the common law cannot be taken away without due process; but the law itself, as a rule of conduct, may be changed at the will, or even at the whim, of the legislature, unless prevented by constitutional limitations. Indeed, the great office of statutes is to remedy defects in the common law as they are developed, and to adapt it to the changes of time and circumstances. To limit the rate of charge for services rendered in a public employment, or for the use of property in which the public has an interest, is only changing a regulation which existed before. It establishes no new principle in the law, but only gives a new effect to an old one.

We know that this is a power which may be abused; but that is no argument against its existence. For protection against abuses by legislatures the people must resort to the polls, not to the courts.

. . . We come now to consider the effect upon this statute of the power of Congress to regulate commerce.

. . ."It is not everything that affects commerce that amounts to a regulation of it, within the meaning of the Constitution." The warehouses of these plaintiffs in error are situated and their business carried on exclusively within the limits of the State of Illinois. They are used as instruments by those engaged in State as well as those engaged in interstate commerce, but they are no more necessarily a part of commerce itself than the dray or the cart by which, but for them, grain would be transferred from one railroad station to another. Incidentally they may become connected with interstate commerce, but not necessarily so. Their regulation is a thing of domestic concern, and, certainly, until Congress acts in reference to their interstate relations, the State may exercise all the powers of government over them, even though in so doing it may indirectly operate upon commerce outside its immediate jurisdiction. We do not say that a case may not arise in which it will be found that a State, under the form of regulating its own affairs, has encroached upon the exclusive domain of Congress in respect to interstate commerce, but we do say that, upon the facts as they are represented to us in this record, that has not been done.

The remaining objection, to wit, that the statute in its present form is repugnant to Section 9, Article I, of the Constitution of the United States, because it gives preference to the ports of one State over those of another, may be disposed of by the single remark that this provision operates only as a limitation of the powers of Congress, and in no respect affects the States in the regulation of their domestic affairs.

We conclude, therefore, that the statute in question is not repugnant to the Constitution of the United States. . . .

Judgment Affirmed.

MR. JUSTICE FIELD:

I am compelled to dissent from the decision of the court in this case. . . . The principle upon which the opinion of the majority proceeds is, in my judgment, subversive of the rights of private property, heretofore believed to be protected by constitutional guaranties against legislative interference, and is in conflict with the authorities cited in its support. . . .

The question presented . . . is one of the greatest importance—whether it is within the competency of a State to fix the compensation which an individual may receive for the use of his own property in his private business, and for his services in connection with it.

. . . [I]t would seem from its opinion that the court holds that property loses something of its private character when employed in such a way as to be generally useful. The doctrine declared is that property "becomes clothed with a public interest when used in a manner to make it of public consequence, and affect the community at large"; and from such clothing the right of the legislature is deduced to control the use of the property, and to determine the compensation which the owner may receive for it. When Sir Matthew Hale, and the sages of the law in his day, spoke of property as affected by a public interest, and ceasing from that cause to be *juris privati* solely, that is, ceasing to be held merely in private right, they referred to property dedicated by the owner to public uses, or to property the use of which was granted by the government, or in connection with which special privileges were conferred. Unless the property was thus dedicated, or some right bestowed by the government was held with the property, . . . the property was not affected by any public interest so as to be taken out of the category of property held in private right. But it is not in any such sense that the terms "clothing property with a public interest" are used in this case. From the nature of the business under consideration—the storage of grain —which, in any sense in which the words can be used, is a private business, in which the public are interested only as they are interested in the storage of other products of the soil, or in articles of manufacture, it is clear that the court intended to declare that, whenever one devotes his property to a business which is useful to the public— "affects the community at large"—the legislature can regulate the compensation which the owner may receive for its use, and for his own services in connection with it. . . . The building used by the defendants was for the storage of grain: in such storage, says the court, the public has an interest; therefore the defendants, by devoting the building to that storage, have granted the public an interest in that use, and must submit to have their compensation regulated by the legislature.

If this be sound law, if there be no protection, either in the principles upon which our republican government is founded, or in the prohibitions of the Constitution against such invasion of private rights, all property and all business in the State are held at the mercy of a majority of its legislature. . . . The public is interested in the manufacture of cotton, woolen, and silken fabrics, in the construction of machinery, in the printing and publication of books and periodicals, and in the making of utensils of every variety, useful and ornamental; indeed, there is hardly an enterprise or business engaging the attention and labor of any considerable portion of the community, in which the public has not an interest in the sense in which that term is used by the court in its opinion; and the doctrine which allows the legislature to interfere with and regulate the charges which the owners of property thus employed shall make for its use, that is, the rates at which all these different kinds of business shall be carried on, has never before been asserted, so far as I am aware, by any judicial tribunal in the United States.

The doctrine of the State court, that no one is deprived of his property, within the meaning of the constitutional inhibitions, so long as he retains its title and possession, and the doctrine of this court, that, whenever one's property is used in such a manner as to affect the community at large, it becomes by that fact clothed with a public interest, and ceases to be *juris privati* only, appear to me to destroy, for all useful purposes, the efficacy of the constitutional guaranty. All that is beneficial in property arises from its use, and the fruits of that use; and whatever deprives a person of them deprives him of all that is desirable or valuable in the title and possession. . . .

No State "shall deprive any person of life, liberty, or property without due process of law," says the Fourteenth Amendment to the Constitution. . . .

By the term *liberty*, as used in the provision, something more is meant than mere freedom from physical restraint or the bounds of a prison. It means freedom to go where one may choose, and to act in such manner, not inconsistent with the equal rights of others, as his judgment may dictate for the promotion of his happiness; that is, to pursue such callings and avocations as may be most suitable to develop his capacities, and give to them their highest enjoyment.

The same liberal construction which is required for the protection of life and liberty, in all particulars in which life and liberty are of any value, should be applied to the protection of private property. If the legislature of a State, under pretence of providing for the public good, or for any other reason, can determine, against the consent of the owner, the uses to which private property shall be devoted, or the prices which the owner shall receive for its uses, it can deprive him of the property as completely as by a special act for its confiscation or destruction. If, for instance, the owner is prohibited from using his building for the purposes for which it was designed, it is of little consequence that he is permitted to retain the title possession; or, if he is compelled to take as compensation for its use less than the expenses to which he is subjected by its ownership, he is, for all practical purposes, deprived of the property as effectually as if the legislature had ordered his forcible dispossession. If it be admitted that the legislature has any control over the compensation, the extent of that compensation becomes a mere matter of legislative discretion. . . .

It is true that the legislation which secures to all protection in their rights, and the equal use and enjoyment of their property, embraces an almost infinite variety of subjects. Whatever affects the peace, good order, morals, and health of the community, comes within its scope; and every one must use and enjoy his property subject to the restrictions which such legislation imposes. What is termed the police power of the State, which, from the language often used respecting it, one would suppose to be an undefined and irresponsible element in government, can only interfere with the conduct of individuals in their intercourse with each other, and in the use of their property, so far as may be required to secure these objects. . . .

There is nothing in the character of the business of the defendants as warehousemen which called for the interference complained of in this case. Their buildings are not nuisances; their occupation of receiving and storing grain infringes upon no rights of others, disturbs no neighborhood, infects not the air, and in no respect prevents others from using and enjoying their property as to them may seem best. The legislation in question is nothing less than a bold assertion of absolute power by the State to control at its discretion the property and business of the citizen, and fix the compensation he shall receive. . . . The decision of the court in this case gives unrestrained license to legislative will. . . .

[Mr. Justice Strong concurred in the opinion of Mr. Justice Field.]

LOCHNER *v.* NEW YORK

198 U.S. 45; 25 Sup. Ct. 539; 49 L. Ed. 937 (1905)

[A New York statute known as the Labor Law made it unlawful for an employee in a bakery or confectionery establishment to work more than sixty hours in any one week or an average of over ten hours a day. Lochner, who owned a bakery in Utica, N.Y., was convicted in a county court of requiring one of his employees to work more than sixty hours in one week. His conviction was upheld by the New York appellate courts. Lochner then brought the case to the Supreme Court on a writ of error.]

MR. JUSTICE PECKHAM delivered the opinion of the Court:

. . . The statute necessarily interferes with the right of contract between the employer and employees, concerning the number of hours in which the latter may labor in the bakery of the employer. The general right to make a contract in relation to his business is part of the liberty of the individual protected by the Fourteenth Amendment of the Federal Constitution. . . . Under the provision no State can deprive any person of life, liberty, or property without due process of law. The right to purchase or to sell labor is part of the liberty protected by this amendment, unless there are circumstances which exclude the right. There are, however, certain powers, existing in the sovereignty of each State in the Union, somewhat vaguely termed police powers, the exact description and limitation of which have not been attempted by the courts. Those powers, broadly stated and without, at present, any attempt at a more specific limitation, relate to the safety, health, morals, and general welfare of the public. Both property and liberty are held on such reasonable conditions as may be imposed by the governing power of the State in the exercise of those powers, and with such conditions the Fourteenth Amendment was not designed to interfere. . . .

The State, therefore, has power to prevent the individual from making certain kinds of contracts, and in regard to them the Federal Constitution offers no protection. If the contract be one which the State, in the legitimate exercise of its police power, has the right to prohibit, it is not prevented from prohibiting it by the Fourteenth Amendment. Contracts in violation of a statute, either of the Federal or State government, or a contract to let one's property for immoral purposes, or to do any other unlawful act, could obtain no protection from the Federal Constitution, as coming under the liberty of person or of free contract. Therefore, when the State, by its legislature, in the assumed exercise of its police powers, has passed an act which seriously limits the right to labor or the right of contract in regard to their means of livelihood between persons who are *sui juris* (both employer and employee), it becomes of great importance to determine which shall prevail—the right of the individual to labor for such time as he may choose, or the right of the State to prevent the individual from laboring or from entering into any contract to labor, beyond a certain time prescribed by the State.

It must, of course, be conceded that there is a limit to the valid exercise of the police power by the State. There is no dispute concerning this general proposition. Otherwise the Fourteenth Amendment would have no efficacy and the legislatures of the States would have unbounded power, and it would be enough to say that any piece of legislation was enacted to conserve the morals, the health, or the safety of the people; such legislation would be valid, no matter how absolutely without foundation the claim might be. The claim of the police power would be a mere pretext—become another and delusive name for the supreme sovereignty of the State to be exercised free from constitutional restraint. This is not contended for. In every case that comes before this court, therefore, where legislation of this character is concerned and where the protection of the Federal Constitution is sought, the question necessarily arises: Is this a fair, reasonable and appropriate exercise of the police power of the State, or is it an unreasonable, unnecessary and arbitrary interference with the right of the individual to his personal liberty or to enter into those contracts in relation to labor which may seem to him appropriate or necessary for the support of himself and his family? Of course the liberty of contract relating to labor includes both parties to it. The one has as much right to purchase as the other to sell labor.

This is not a question of substituting the judgment of the court for that of the legislature. If the act be within the power of the State it is valid, although the judgment of the court might be totally opposed to the enactment of such a law. But the question would still remain: Is it within the police power of the State? and that question must be answered by the court.

The question whether this act is valid as a labor law, pure and simple, may be dismissed in a few words. There is no reasonable ground for interfering with the liberty of person or the right of free contract, by determining the hours of labor in the occupation of a baker. There is no contention that bakers as a class are not equal in intelligence and capacity to men in other trades or manual occupations, or that they are not able to assert their rights and care for themselves without the protecting arm of the State, interfering with their independence of judgment and of action. They are in no sense wards of the State. Viewed in the light of a purely labor law, with no reference whatever to the question of health, we think that a law like the one before us involves neither the safety, the morals, nor the welfare of the public, and that the interest of the public is not in the slightest degree affected by such an act. The law must be upheld, if at all, as a law pertaining to the health of the individual engaged in the occupation of a baker. It does not affect any other portion of the public than those who are engaged in that occupation. Clean and wholesome bread does not depend upon whether the baker works but ten hours per day or only sixty hours a week. The limitation of the hours of labor does not come within the police power on that ground.

It is a question of which of two powers or rights shall prevail—the power of the State to legislate or the right of the individual to liberty of person and freedom of contract. The mere assertion that the subject relates though but in a remote degree to the public health does not necessarily render the enactment valid. The act must have a more direct relation, as a means to an end, and the end itself must be appropriate and legitimate, before an act can be held to be valid which interferes with the general right of an individual to be free in his person and in his power to contract in relation to his own labor. . . .

We think the limit of the police power has been reached and passed in this case. There is, in our judgment, no reasonable foundation for holding this to be necessary or appropriate as a health law to safeguard the public health or the health of the individuals who are following the trade of a baker. If this statute be valid, and if, therefore, a proper case is made out in which to deny the right of an individual, *sui juris*, as employer or employee, to make contracts for the labor of the latter under the protection of the provisions of the Federal Constitution, there would seem to be no length to which legislation of this nature might not go. . . .

We think that there can be no fair doubt that the trade of a baker, in and of itself, is not an unhealthy one to that degree which would authorize the legislature to interfere with the right to labor, and with the right of free contract on the part of the individual, either as employer or employee. In looking through statistics regarding all trades and occupations, it may be true that the trade of a baker does not appear to be as healthy as some other trades, and is also vastly more healthy than still others. To the common understanding the trade of a baker has never been regarded as an unhealthy one. Very likely physicians would not recommend the exercise of that or of any other trade as a remedy for ill health. Some occupations are more healthy than others, but we think there are none which might not come under the power of the legislature to supervise and control the hours of working therein, if the mere fact that the occupation is not absolutely and perfectly healthy is to confer that right upon the legislative department of the Government. It might be safely affirmed that almost all occupations more or less affect the health. There must be more than the mere fact of the possible existence of some small amount of unhealthiness to warrant legislative interference with liberty. It is unfortunately true that labor, even in any department, may possibly carry with it the seeds of unhealthiness. But are we all, on that account, at the mercy of legislative majorities? A printer, a tinsmith, a locksmith, a carpenter, a cabinetmaker, a drygoods clerk, a bank's, a lawyer's or a physician's clerk, or a clerk in almost any kind of business, would all come under the power of the legislature on this assumption. No trade, no occupation, no mode of earning one's living, could escape this all-pervading power, and the acts of the legislature in limiting the hours of labor in all employments would be valid, although such limitation might seriously cripple the ability of the laborer to support himself and his family.

. . . It is also urged, pursuing the same line of argument, that it is to the interest of the State that its population should be strong and robust, and therefore any legislation which may be said to tend to make people healthy must be valid as health laws, enacted under the police power. If this be a valid argument and a justification for this kind of legislation, it follows that the protection of the Federal Constitution from undue interference with liberty of person and freedom of contract is visionary, wherever the law is sought to be justified as a valid exercise of the police power. Scarcely any law but might find shelter under such assumptions, and conduct, properly so called, as well as contract, would come under the restrictive sway of the legislature. Not only the hours of employees, but the hours of employers, could be regulated, and doctors, lawyers, scientists, all professional men, as well as athletes and artisans, could be forbidden to fatigue their brains and bodies by prolonged hours of exercise, lest the fighting strength of the State be impaired. We mention these extreme cases because the contention is extreme. We do not believe in the soundness of the views which uphold this law. On the contrary, we think that such a law as this, although passed in the assumed exercise of the police power, and as relating to the public health, or the health of the employees named, is not within that power, and is invalid. The act is not, within any fair meaning of the term, a health law, but is an illegal interference with the rights of individuals, both employers and employees, to make contracts regarding labor upon such terms as they may think best, or which they may agree upon with the other parties to such contracts. Statutes of the nature of that under review, limiting the hours in which grown and intelligent men may labor to earn their living, are mere meddlesome interferences with the rights of the individual, and they are not saved from condemnation by the claim that they are passed in the exercise of the police power and upon the subject of the health of the individual whose rights are interfered with, unless there be some fair ground, reasonable in and of itself, to say that there is material danger to the public health or to the health of the employees, if the hours of labor are not curtailed. . . .

It was further urged . . . that restricting the hours of labor in the case of bakers was valid because it tended to cleanliness on the part of the workers, as a man was more apt to be cleanly when not overworked, and if cleanly then his "output" was also more likely to be so. . . . In our judgment it is not possible in fact to discover the connection between the number of hours a baker may work in the bakery and the healthful quality of the bread made by the workman. The connection, if any exists, is too shadowy and thin to build any argument for the interference of the legislature. If the man works ten hours a day it is all right, but if ten and a half or eleven his health is in danger and his bread may be unhealthful, and, therefore, he shall not be permitted to do it. This, we think, is unreasonable and entirely arbitrary. . . .

. . . It seems to us that the real object and purpose were simply to regulate the hours of labor between the master and his employees (all being men, *sui juris*) in a private business, not dangerous in any degree to morals or in any real and substantial degree to the health of the employees. Under such circumstances the freedom of master and employee to contract with each other in relation to their employment, and in defining the same, cannot be prohibited or interfered with, without violating the Federal Constitution. . . .

Reversed.

MR. JUSTICE HARLAN, with whom MR. JUSTICE WHITE and MR. JUSTICE DAY concurred, dissenting:

. . . I find it impossible, in view of common experience, to say that there is no real or substantial relation between the means employed by the State and the end sought to be accomplished by its legislation. . . .

We judicially know that the question of the number of hours during which a workman should continuously labor has been, for a long period, and is yet, a subject of serious consideration among civilized peoples, and by those having special knowledge of the laws of health. Suppose the statute prohibited labor in bakery and confectionery establishments in excess of eighteen hours each day. No one, I take it, could dispute the power of the State to enact such a statute. But the statute before us does not embrace extreme or exceptional cases. It may be said to occupy a middle ground in respect to the hours of labor. What is the true ground for the State to take between legitimate protection, by legislation, of the public health and liberty of contract is not a question easily solved, nor one in respect of which there is or can be absolute certainty. There are very few, if any, questions in political economy about which entire certainty may be predicted. . . .

I do not stop to consider whether any particular view of this economic question presents the sounder theory. What the precise facts are it may be difficult to say. It is enough for the determination of this case, and it is enough for this court to know, that the question is one about which there is room for debate and for an honest difference of opinion. There are many reasons of a weighty, substantial character, based upon the experience of mankind, in support of the theory that, all things considered, more than ten hours' steady work each day, from week to week, in a bakery or confectionery establishment, may endanger the health, and shorten the lives of the workmen, thereby diminishing their physical and mental capacity to serve the State, and to provide for those dependent upon them.

If such reasons exist, that ought to be the end of this case, for the State is not amenable to the judiciary, in respect of its legislative enactments, unless such enactments are plainly, palpably, beyond all question, inconsistent with the Constitution of the United States. . . . Let the State alone in the management of its purely domestic affairs, so long as it does not appear beyond all question that it has violated the Federal Constitution. This view necessarily results from the principle that the health and safety of the people of a State are primarily for the State to guard and protect. . . .

The judgment in my opinion should be affirmed.

MR. JUSTICE HOLMES, dissenting:

. . . This case is decided upon an economic theory which a large part of the country does not entertain. If it were a question whether I agreed with that theory, I should desire to study it further and long before making up my mind. But I do not conceive that to be my duty, because I strongly believe that my agreement or disagreement has nothing to do with the right of a majority to embody their opinions in law. It is settled by various decisions of this court that state constitutions and state laws may regulate life in many ways which we as legislators might think as injudicious or if you like as tyrannical as this, and which equally with this interfere with the liberty to contract. Sunday laws and usury laws are ancient examples. A more modern one is the prohibition of lotteries. The liberty of the citizen to do as he likes so long as he does not interfere with the liberty of others to do the same, which has been a shibboleth for some well-known writers, is interfered with by school laws, by the Post Office, by every state or municipal institution which takes his money for purposes thought desirable, whether he like it or not. The Fourteenth Amendment does not enact Mr. Herbert Spencer's Social Statics. . . . United States and state statutes and decisions cutting down the liberty to contract by way of combination are familiar to this court. . . . Two years ago we upheld the prohibition of sales of stock on margins or for future delivery in the constitution of California. . . . The decision sustaining an eight-hour law for miners is still recent. . . . Some of these laws embody convictions or prejudices which judges are likely to share. Some may not. But a constitution is not intended to embody a particular economic theory, whether of paternalism and the organic relation of the citizen to the State or of *laissez faire.* It is made for people of fundamentally differing views, and the accident of our finding certain opinions natural and familiar or novel and even shocking ought not to conclude our judgment upon the question whether statutes embodying them conflict with the Constitution of the United States.

General propositions do not decide concrete cases. The decision will depend on a judgment or intuition more subtle than any articulate major premise. But I think that the proposition just stated, if it is accepted, will carry us far toward the end. Every opinion tends to become a law. I think that the word "liberty" in the Fourteenth Amendment is perverted when it is held to prevent the natural outcome of a dominant opinion, unless it can be said that a rational and fair man necessarily would admit that the statute proposed would infringe fundamental principles as they have been understood by the traditions of our people and our law. It does not need research to show that no such sweeping condemnation can be passed upon the statute before us. A reasonable man might think it a proper measure on the score of health. Men whom I certainly could not pronounce unreasonable would uphold it as a first installment of a general regulation of the hours of work. Whether in the latter aspect it would be open to the charge of inequality I think it unnecessary to discuss.

ADKINS *v.* CHILDREN'S HOSPITAL
261 U.S. 525; 43 Sup. Ct. 394; 67 L. Ed. 785 (1923)

[An Act of Congress of 1918 provided for the creation of a Minimum Wage Board authorized to set up minimum wages for women and children in the District of Columbia. The Children's Hospital, which employed several women at wages lower than those permitted by the board, obtained an injunction against enforcement of the Act by Adkins and two others who were members of the Wage Board. A second case decided and reported together with the Children's Hospital case raised the same questions. The trial court decrees granting the injunction were affirmed by a federal court of appeals. Adkins and the other board members then brought an appeal to the Supreme Court.]

MR. JUSTICE SUTHERLAND delivered the opinion of the Court:

The question presented for determination by these appeals is the constitutionality of the Act of September 19, 1918, providing for the fixing of minimum wages for women and children in the District of Columbia. . . .

The statute now under consideration is attacked upon the ground that it authorizes an unconstitutional interference with the freedom of contract included within the guaranties of the due process clause of the Fifth Amendment. That the right to contract about one's affairs is a part of the liberty of the individual protected by this clause is settled by the decisions of this court, and is no longer open to question. . . . Within this liberty are contracts of employment of labor. In making such contracts, generally speaking, the parties have an equal right to obtain from each other the best terms they can as the result of private bargaining. . . .

There is, of course, no such thing as absolute freedom of contract. It is subject to a great variety of restraints. But freedom of contract is, nevertheless, the general rule and restraint the exception; and the exercise of legislative authority to abridge it can be justified only by the existence of exceptional circumstances. Whether these circumstances exist in the present case constitutes the question to be answered. . . .

The essential characteristics of the statute now under consideration, which differentiate it from the laws fixing hours of labor, will be made to appear as we proceed. It is sufficient now to point out that the latter . . . deal with incidents of the employment having no necessary effect upon the heart of the contract; that is, the amount of wages to be paid and received. A law forbidding work to continue beyond a given number of hours leaves the parties free to contract about wages and thereby equalize whatever additional burdens may be imposed upon the employer as a result of the restrictions as to hours, by an adjustment in respect of the amount of wages. Enough has been said to show that the authority to fix hours of labor cannot be exercised except in respect of those occupations where work of long-continued duration is detrimental to health. This court has been careful in every case where the question has been raised, to place its decision upon this limited authority of the legislature to regulate hours of labor, and to disclaim any purpose to uphold the legislation as fixing wages, thus recognizing an essential difference between the two. It seems plain that these decisions afford no real support for any form of law establishing minimum wages.

If now, in the light furnished by the foregoing exceptions to the general rule forbidding legislative interference with freedom of contract, we examine and analyze the statute in question, we shall see that it differs from them in every material respect. . . . It is simply and exclusively a price-fixing law, confined to adult women (for we are not now considering the provisions relating to minors), who are legally as capable of contracting for themselves as men. It forbids two parties having lawful capacity—under penalties as to the employer—to freely contract with one another in respect to the price for which one shall render service to the other in a purely private employment where both are willing, perhaps anxious, to agree, even though the consequences may be to oblige one to surrender a desirable engagement, and the other to dispense with the services of a desirable employee. . . .

The standard furnished by the statute for the guidance of the board is so vague as to be impossible of practical application with any reasonable degree of accuracy. What is sufficient to supply the necessary cost of living for a woman worker and maintain her in good health and protect her morals is obviously not a precise or unvarying sum—not even approximately so. The amount will depend upon a variety of circumstances: the individual temperament; habits of thrift, care, ability to buy necessaries intelligently, and whether the woman lives alone or with her family. To those who practice economy, a given sum will afford comfort, while to those of contrary habit the same sum will be wholly inadequate. The cooperative economics of the family group are not taken into account, though they constitute an important consideration in estimating the cost of living, for it is obvious that the individual expense will be less in the case of a member of a family than in the case of one living alone. The relation between earnings and morals is not capable of standardization. It cannot be shown that well-paid women safeguard their morals more carefully than those who are poorly paid. Morality rests upon other considerations than wages; and there is, certainly, no such prevalent connection between the two as to justify a broad attempt to adjust the latter with reference to the former. . . .

The law takes account of the necessities of only one party to the contract. It ignores the necessities of the employer by compelling him to pay not less than a certain sum, not only whether the employee is capable of earning it, but irrespective of the ability of his business to sustain the burden, generously leaving him, of course, the privilege of abandoning his business as an alternative for going on at a loss. Within the limits of the minimum sum, he is precluded, under penalty of fine and imprisonment, from adjusting compensation to the differing merits of his employees. It compels him to pay at least the sum fixed in any event, because the employee needs it, but requires no service of equivalent value from the employee. It therefore undertakes to solve but one half of the problem. . . . To the extent that the sum fixed exceeds the fair value of the services rendered, it amounts to a compusory exaction from the employer for the support of a partially indigent person, for whose condition there rests upon him no peculiar responsibility, and therefore, in effect, arbitrarily shifts to his shoulders a burden which, if it belongs to anybody, belongs to society as a whole.

The feature of this statute which, perhaps more than any other, puts upon it the stamp of invalidity is that it exacts from the employer an arbitrary payment for a purpose and upon a basis having no causal connection with his business, or of the contract, or the work the employee engages to do. The declared basis . . . is not the value of the service rendered, but the extraneous circumstance that the employee needs to get a prescribed sum of money to insure her subsistence, health, and morals. The ethical right of every worker, man or woman, to a living wage, may be conceded. One of the declared and important purposes of trade organizations is to secure it. And with that principle and with every legitimate effort to realize it in fact, no one can quarrel; but the fallacy of the proposed method of attaining it is that it assumes that every employer is bound, at all events to furnish it. The moral requirement, implicit in every contract of employment, viz., that the amount to be paid and the service to be rendered shall bear to each other some relation of just equivalence, is completely ignored. . . . In principle, there can be no difference between the case of selling labor and the case of selling goods. If one goes to the butcher, the baker, or grocer to buy food, he is morally entitled to obtain the worth of his money, but he is not entitled to more. If what he gets is worth what he pays, he is not justified in demanding more simply because he needs more; and the shopkeeper, having dealt fairly and honestly in that transaction, is not concerned in any peculiar sense with the question of his customer's necessities. . . . [A] statute which prescribes payment without regard to any of these things, and solely with relation to circumstances apart from the contract of employment, the business affected by it, and the work done under it, is so clearly the product of a naked, arbitrary exercise of power, that it cannot be allowed to stand under the Constitution of the United States. . . .

It is said that great benefits have resulted from the operation of such statutes, not alone in the District of Columbia, but in the several states where they have been in force. A mass of reports, opinions of special observers and students of the subject, and the like, has been brought before us in support of this statement, all of which we have found interesting but only mildly persuasive. That the earnings of women now are greater than they were formerly, and that conditions affecting women have become better in other respects, may be conceded; but convincing indications of the logical relation of these desirable changes to the law in question are significantly lacking. They may be, and quite probably are, due to other causes. . . .

Finally, it may be said that if, in the interest of the public welfare, the police power may be invoked to justify the fixing of a minimum wage, it may, when the public welfare is thought to require it, be invoked to justify a maximum wage. The power to fix high wages connotes, by like course of reasoning, the power to fix low wages. If, in the face of the guaranties of the Fifth Amendment, this form of legislation shall be legally justified, the field for the operation of the police power will have been widened to a great and dangerous degree. If, for example, in the opinion of future lawmakers, wages in the building trades shall become so high as to preclude people of ordinary means from building and owning homes, an authority which sustains the minimum wage will be invoked to support a maximum wage for building laborers and artisans, and the same argument which has been here urged to strip the employer of his constitutional liberty of contract in one direction will be utilized to strip the employee of his constitutional liberty of contract in the opposite direction. A wrong decision does not end with itself: it is a precedent, and, with the swing of sentiment, its bad influence may run from one extremity of the arc to the other.

It has been said that legislation of the kind now under review is required in the interest of social justice, for whose ends freedom of contract may lawfully be subjected to restraint. The liberty of the individual to do as he pleases, even in innocent matters, is not absolute. It must frequently yield to the common good, and the line beyond which the power of interference may not be pressed is neither definite nor unalterable, but may be made to move, within limits not well defined, with changing need and circumstance. Any attempt to fix a rigid boundary would be unwise as well as futile. But, nevertheless, there are limits to the power, and when these have been passed, it becomes the plain duty of the courts, in the proper exercise of their authority, to so declare. To sustain the individual freedom of action contemplated by the Constitution is not to strike down the common good, but to exalt it; for surely the good of society as a whole cannot be better served than by the preservation against arbitrary restraint of the liberties of its constituent members.

It follows from what has been said that the act in question passes the limit prescribed by the Constitution, and, accordingly, the decrees of the court below are affirmed. . . .

MR. JUSTICE BRANDEIS took no part in the consideration or decision of these cases.

MR. CHIEF JUSTICE TAFT, dissenting:

. . . The boundary of the police power, beyond which its exercise becomes an invasion of the guaranty of liberty under the Fifth and Fourteenth Amendments to the Constitution, is not easy to mark. Our court has been laboriously engaged in pricking out a line in successive cases. We must be careful, it seems to me, to follow that line as well as we can, and not to depart from it by suggesting a distinction that is formal rather than real.

Legislatures, in limiting freedom of contract between employee and employer by a minimum wage, proceed on the assumption that employees in the class receiving least pay are not upon a full level of equality of choice with their employer, and in their necessitous circumstances are prone to accept pretty much anything that is offered. They are peculiarly subject to the overreaching of the harsh and greedy employer. The evils of the sweating system and of the long hours and low wages which are characteristic of it are well known. Now, I agree that it is a disputable question in the field of political economy how far a statutory requirement of maximum hours or minimum wages may be a useful remedy for these evils, and whether it may not make the case of the oppressed employee worse than it was before. But it is not the function of this court to hold congressional acts invalid simply because they are passed to carry out economic views which the court believes to be unwise or unsound. . . .

The right of the legislature under the Fifth and Fourteenth Amendments to limit the hours of employment on the score of the health of the employee, it seems to me, has been firmly established. . . .

. . . In *[Bunting v. Oregon]* this court sustained a law limiting the hours of labor of any person, whether man or woman, working in any mill, factory, or manufacturing establishment to ten hours a day with a proviso as to further hours to which I shall hereafter advert. The law covered the whole field of industrial employment and certainly covered the case of persons employed in bakeries. Yet the opinion in the *Bunting Case* does not mention the *Lochner Case.* No one can suggest any constitutional distinction between employment in a bakery and one in any other kind of a manufacturing establishment which should make a limit of hours in the one invalid, and the same limit in the other permissible. It is impossible for me to reconcile the *Bunting Case* and the *Lochner Case,* and I have always supposed that the *Lochner Case* was thus overruled *sub silentio.* Yet the opinion of the court herein in support of its conclusion quotes from the opinion in the *Lochner Case* as one which has been sometimes distinguished but never overruled. Certainly there was no attempt to distinguish it in the *Bunting Case.*

However, the opinion herein does not overrule the *Bunting Case* in express terms, and therefore I assume that the conclusion in this case rests on the distinction between a minimum of wages and a maximum of hours in the limiting of liberty to contract. I regret to be at variance with the court as to the substance of this distinction. In absolute freedom of contract the one term is as important as the other, for both enter equally into the consideration given and received, a restriction as to one is not any greater in essence than the other, and is of the same kind. One is the multiplier and the other the multiplicand. . . .

I am authorized to say that MR. JUSTICE SANFORD concurs in this opinion.

MR. JUSTICE HOLMES, dissenting:

The question in this case is the broad one, whether Congress can establish minimum rates of wages for women in the District of Columbia, with due provision for special circumstances, or whether we must say that Congress has no power to meddle with the matter at all. To me, notwithstanding the deference due to the prevailing judgment of the court, the power of Congress seems absolutely free from doubt. The end—to remove conditions leading to ill health, immorality, and the deterioration of the race—no one would deny to be within the scope of constitutional legislation. The means are means that have the approval of Congress, of many states, and of those governments from which we have learned our greatest lessons. When so many intelligent persons, who have studied the matter more than any of us can, have thought that the means are effective and are worth the price, it seems to me impossible to deny that the belief reasonably may be held by reasonable men. If the law encountered no other objection than that the means bore no relation to the end, or that they cost too much, I do not suppose that anyone would venture to say that it was bad. I agree, of course, that a law answering the foregoing requirements might be invalidated by specific provisions of the Constitution. For instance, it might take private property without just compensation. But, in the present instance, the only objection that can be urged is found within the vague contours of the Fifth Amendment, prohibiting the depriving [of] any person of liberty or property without due process of law. To that I turn.

The earlier decisions upon the same words in the Fourteenth Amendment began within our memory, and went no farther than an unpretentious assertion of the liberty to follow the ordinary callings. Later that innocuous generality was expanded into the dogma, Liberty of Contract. Contract is not specially mentioned in the text that we have to construe. It is merely an example of doing what you want to do, embodied in the word "liberty." But pretty much all law consists in forbidding men to do some things that they want to do, and contract is no more exempt from law than other acts. . . . women's hours of labor may be fixed. . . . And the principle was extended to men, with the allowance of a limited overtime, to be paid for "at the rate of time and one-half of the regular wage" in *Bunting* v. *Oregon,* 243 U.S. 426.

I confess that I do not understand the principle on which the power to fix a minimum for the wages of women can be denied by those who admit the power to fix a maximum for their hours of work. . . . The bargain is equally affected whichever half you regulate. *Muller* v. *Oregon,* I take it, is as good law today as it was in 1908. It will need more than the Nineteenth Amendment to convince me that there are no differences between men and women, or that legislation cannot take those differences into account. I should not hesitate to take them into account if I thought it necessary to sustain this act. . . . But after *Bunting* v. *Oregon* . . . , I had supposed that it was not necessary, and that *Lochner* v. *New York* . . . would be allowed a deserved repose. . . .

I am of opinion that the statute is valid and that the decree should be

Reversed.

NEBBIA *v.* NEW YORK

291 U.S. 502; 54 Sup. Ct. 505; 78 L. Ed. 940 (1934)

[In 1933, the New York State legislature passed a law that was designed to help stabilize the state's milk industry, which had been affected adversely by the economic depression of the 1930s. The law provided for the establishment of a Milk Control Board, which was empowered to fix minimum and maximum prices to be charged for milk. The board fixed the price of milk sold in stores at nine cents a quart. Nebbia, the proprietor of a grocery store in Rochester, N.Y., was convicted of selling two quarts of milk and a loaf of bread for only eighteen cents, in violation of the board's order. His conviction was sustained by the New York Court of Appeals. Nebbia then brought an appeal to the Supreme Court on the grounds that the Milk Control Law and the board's order contravened the equal protection clause and the due process clause of the Fourteenth Amendment.]

MR. JUSTICE ROBERTS delivered the opinion of the Court:

. . . *First.* The appellant urges that the order of the Milk Control Board denies him the equal protection of the laws. It is shown that the order requires him, if he purchases his supply from a dealer, to pay eight cents per quart and five cents per pint, and to resell at not less than nine and six, whereas the same dealer may buy his supply from a farmer at lower prices and deliver milk to consumers at ten cents the quart and six cents the pint. We think the contention that the discrimination deprives the appellant of equal protection is not well founded. For aught that appears, the appellant purchased his supply of milk from a farmer as do distributors, or could have procured it from a farmer if he so desired. There is therefore no showing that the order placed him at a disadvantage, or in fact affected him adversely, and this alone is fatal to the claim of denial of equal protection. But if it were shown that the appellant is compelled to buy from a distributor, the difference in the retail price he is required to charge his customers, from that prescribed for sales by distributors, is not on its face arbitrary or unreasonable, for there are obvious distinctions between the two sorts of merchants which may well justify a difference of treatment, if the legislature possess the power to control the prices to be charged for fluid milk. . . .

Second. The more serious question is whether, in the light of the conditions disclosed, the enforcement of [the price regulation] denied the appellant the due process secured to him by the Fourteenth Amendment. . . .

Under our form of government the use of property and the making of contracts are normally matters of private and not of public concern. The general rule is that both shall be free of governmental interference. But neither property rights nor contract rights are absolute; for government cannot exist if the citizen may at will use his property to the detriment of his fellows, or exercise his freedom of contract to work them harm. Equally fundamental with the private right is that of the public to regulate it in the common interest. . . .

The milk industry in New York has been the subject of long-standing and drastic regulation in the public interest. The legislative investigation of 1932 was persuasive of the fact that for this and other reasons unrestricted competition aggravated existing evils, and the normal law of supply and demand was insufficient to correct maladjustments detrimental to the community. The inquiry disclosed destructive and demoralizing competitive conditions and unfair trade practices which resulted in retail price-cutting and reduced the income of the farmer below the cost of production. We do not understand the appellant to deny that in these circumstances the legislature might reasonably consider further regulation and control desirable for protection of the industry and the consuming public. That body believed conditions could be improved by preventing destructive price-cutting by stores which, due to the flood of surplus milk, were able to buy at much lower prices than the larger distributors and to sell without incurring the delivery costs of the latter. In the order of which complaint is made, the Milk Control Board fixed a price of ten cents per quart for sales by a distributor to a consumer, and nine cents by a store to a consumer, thus recognizing the lower costs of the store, and endeavoring to establish a differential which would be just to both. In the light of the facts, the order appears not to be unreasonable or arbitrary, or without relation to the purpose to prevent ruthless competition from destroying the wholesale price structure on which the farmer depends for his livelihood, and the community for an assured supply of milk.

But we are told that because the law essays to control prices it denies due process. Notwithstanding the admitted power to correct existing economic ills by appropriate regulation of business, even though an indirect result may be a restriction of the freedom of contract or a modification of charges for services or the price of commodities, the appellant urges that direct fixation of prices is a type of regulation absolutely forbidden. His position is that the Fourteenth Amendment requires us to hold the challenged statute void for this reason alone. The argument runs that the public control of rate or prices is per se unreasonable and unconstitutional, save as applied to business affected with a public interest; that a business so affected is one in which property is devoted to an enterprise of a sort which the public itself might appropriately undertake, or one whose owner relies on a public grant or franchise for the right to conduct the business, or in which he is bound to serve all who apply; in short, such as is commonly called a utility; or a business in its nature a monopoly. The milk industry, it is said, possesses none of these characteristics, and, therefore, not being affected with a public interest, its charges may not be controlled by the state. Upon the soundness of this contention the appellant's case against the statute depends.

We may as well say at once that the dairy industry is not, in the accepted sense of the phrase, a public utility. We think the appellant is also right in asserting that there is in this case no suggestion of any monopoly or monopolistic practice. It goes without saying that those engaged in the business are in no way dependent upon public grants or franchises for the privilege of conducting their activities. But if, as must be conceded, the industry is subject to regulation in the public interest, what constitutional principle bars the state from correcting existing maladjustments by legislation touching prices? We think there is no such principle. The due process clause makes no mention of sales or of prices any more than it speaks of business or contracts or buildings or other incidents of property. The thought seems nevertheless to have persisted that there is something peculiarly sacrosanct about the price one may charge for what he makes or sells, and that, however able to regulate other elements of manufacture or trade, with incidental effect upon price, the state is incapable of directly controlling the price itself. This view was negatived many years ago. *Munn* v. *Illinois*. . . .

It is clear that there is no closed class or category of business affected with a public interest, and the function of courts in the application of the Fifth and Fourteenth Amendments is to determine in each case whether circumstances vindicate the challenged regulation as a reasonable exertion of governmental authority or condemn it as arbitrary or discriminatory. . . . The phrase "affected with a public interest" can, in the nature of things, mean no more than that an industry, for adequate reason, is subject to control for the public good. In several of the decisions of this court wherein the expressions "affected with a public interest," and "clothed with a public use," have been brought forward as the criteria of the validity of price control, it has been admitted that they are not susceptible of definition and form an unsatisfactory test of the constitutionality of legislation directed at business practices or prices. These decisions must rest, finally, upon the basis that the requirements of due process were not met because the laws were found arbitrary in their operation and effect. But there can be no doubt that upon proper occasion and by appropriate measures the state may regulate a business in any of its aspects, including the prices to be charged for the products or commodities it sells.

So far as the requirement of due process is concerned, and in the absence of other constitutional restriction, a state is free to adopt whatever economic policy may reasonably be deemed to promote public welfare, and to enforce that policy by legislation adapted to its purpose. The courts are without authority either to declare such policy, or, when it is declared by the legislature, to override it. If the laws passed are seen to have a reasonable relation to a proper legislative purpose, and are neither arbitrary nor discriminatory, the requirements of due process are satisfied. . . .

Price control, like any form of regulation, is unconstitutional only if arbitrary, discriminatory, or demonstrably irrelevant to the policy the legislature is free to adopt, and hence an unnecessary and unwarranted interference with individual liberty. . . .

The judgment is

Affirmed.

[Mr. Justice McReynolds dissented in an opinion concurred in by Mr. Justice Van Devanter, Mr. Justice Sutherland, and Mr. Justice Butler.]

WEST COAST HOTEL CO. *v.* PARRISH
300 U.S. 379; 57 Sup. Ct. 578; 81 L. Ed. 703 (1937)

[In 1913, the state of Washington enacted a minimum-wage law for women and minors. Under the terms of the statute, an administrative board known as the Industrial Welfare Commission was authorized to establish minimum wages and conditions of labor for women and minors in the state. Elsie Parrish was employed as a chambermaid by the West Coast Hotel Company. She and her husband brought suit to recover the difference between the wages paid her by the hotel company and the minimum wage fixed by the commission. (The minimum wage for her job was $14.50 for a forty-eight-hour week.) The trial court decided against Mrs. Parrish, but the Supreme Court of Washington reversed the trial court and sustained the statute. The hotel company then brought the case to the Supreme Court on appeal.]

MR. CHIEF JUSTICE HUGHES delivered the opinion of the Court:

This case presents the question of the constitutional validity of the minimum-wage law of the State of Washington. . . .

The appellant relies upon the decision of this Court in *Adkins* v. *Children's Hospital,* 261 U.S. 525, which held invalid the District of Columbia Minimum Wage Act, which was attacked under the due process clause of the Fifth Amendment. On the argument at bar, counsel for the appellees attempted to distinguish the *Adkins* case upon the ground that the appellee was employed in a hotel and that the business of an innkeeper was affected with a public interest. That effort at distinction is obviously futile, as it appears that in one of the cases ruled by the *Adkins* opinion the employee was a woman employed as an elevator operator in a hotel. . . .

The Supreme Court of Washington has upheld the minimum-wage statute of that State. It has decided that the statute is a reasonable exercise of the police power of the State. In reaching that conclusion the state court has invoked principles long established by this Court in the application of the Fourteenth Amendment. The state court has refused to regard the decision in the *Adkins* case as determinative and has pointed to our decisions both before and since that case as justifying its position. We are of the opinion that this ruling of the state court demands on our part a reexamination of the *Adkins* case. The importance of the question, in which many States having similar laws are concerned, the close division by which the decision in the *Adkins* case was reached, and the economic conditions which have supervened, and in the light of which the reasonableness of the exercise of the protective power of the State must be considered, make it not only appropriate, but we think imperative, that in deciding the present case the subject should receive fresh consideration. . . .

The principle which must control our decision is not in doubt. The constitutional provision invoked is in the due process clause of the Fourteenth Amendment governing the States, as the due process clause invoked in the *Adkins* case governed Congress. In each case the violation alleged by those attacking minimum-wage regulation for women is deprivation of freedom of contract. What is this freedom? The Constitution does not speak of freedom of contract. It speaks of liberty and prohibits the deprivation of liberty without due process of law. In prohibiting that deprivation the Constitution does not recognize an absolute and uncontrollable liberty. Liberty in each of its phases has its history and connotation. But the liberty safeguarded is liberty in a social organization which requires the protection of law against the evils which menace the health, safety, morals, and welfare of the people. Liberty under the Constitution is thus necessarily subject to the restraints of due process, and regulation which is reasonable in relation to its subject and is adopted in the interests of the community is due process. . . .

This power under the Constitution to restrict freedom of contract has had many illustrations. That it may be exercised in the public interest with respect to contracts between employer and employee is undeniable. . . .

The point that has been strongly stressed that adult employees should be deemed competent to make their own contracts was decisively met nearly forty years ago in *Holden* v. *Hardy,* where we pointed out the inequality in the footing of the parties. We said . . . :

"The legislature has also recognized the fact, which the experience of legislators in many States has corroborated, that the proprietors of these establishments and their operatives do not stand upon an equality, and that their interests are, to a certain extent, conflicting. The former naturally desire to obtain as much labor as possible from their employees, while the latter are often induced by the fear of discharge to conform to regulations which their judgment, fairly exercised, would pronounce to be detrimental to their health or strength. In other words, the proprietors lay down the rules and the laborers are practically constrained to obey them. In such cases self-interest is often an unsafe guide, and the legislature may properly interpose its authority."

And we added that the fact "that both parties are of full age and competent to contract does not necessarily deprive the State of the power to interfere where the parties do not stand upon an equality, or where the public health demands that one party to the contract shall be protected against himself. . . ."

It is manifest that this established principle is peculiarly applicable in relation to the employment of women, in whose protection the State has a special interest. That phase of the subject received elaborate consideration in *Muller* v. *Oregon* (1908), 208 U.S. 412, where the constitutional authority of the State to limit the working hours of women was sustained. . . .

This array of precedents and the principles they applied were thought by the dissenting Justices in the *Adkins* case to demand that the minimum-wage statute be sustained. The validity of the distinction made by the Court between a minimum wage and a maximum of hours in limiting liberty of contract was especially challenged. . . . That challenge persists and is without any satisfactory answer. . . .

The minimum wage to be paid under the Washington statute is fixed after full consideration by representatives of employers, employees, and the public. It may be assumed that the minimum wage is fixed in consideration of the services that are performed in the particular occupations under normal conditions. Provision is made for special licenses at less wages in the case of women who are incapable of full service. The statement of Mr. Justice Holmes in the *Adkins* case is pertinent: "This statute does not compel anybody to pay anything. It simply forbids employment at rates below those fixed as the minimum requirement of health and right living. It is safe to assume that women will not be employed at even the lowest wages allowed unless they earn them, or unless the employer's business can sustain the burden. In short the law in its character and operation is like hundreds of so-called police laws that have been upheld." . . . And Chief Justice Taft forcibly pointed out the consideration which is basic in a statute of this character: "Legislatures which adopt a requirement of maximum hours or minimum wages may be presumed to believe that when sweating employers are prevented from paying unduly low wages by positive law they will continue their business, abating that part of their profits, which were wrung from the necessities of their employees, and will concede the better terms required by the law; and that while in individual cases hardships may result, the restriction will enure to the benefit of the general class of employees in whose interest the law is passed and so to that of the community at large. . . ."

We think that the views thus expressed are sound and that the decision in the *Adkins* case was a departure from the true application of the principles governing the regulation by the State of the relation of employer and employed. . . .

With full recognition of the earnestness and vigor which characterize the prevailing opinion in the *Adkins* case, we find it impossible to reconcile that ruling with these well-considered declarations. What can be closer to the public interest than the health of women and their protection from unscrupulous and overreaching employers? And if the protection of women is a legitimate end of the exercise of the state power, how can it be said that the requirement of the payment of a minimum wage fairly fixed in order to meet the very necessities of existence is not an admissible means to that end? The legislature of the State was clearly entitled to consider the situation of women in employment, the fact that they are in the class receiving the least pay, that their bargaining power is relatively weak, and that they are the ready victims of those who would take advantage of their necessitous circumstances. The legislature was entitled to adopt measures to reduce the evils of the "sweating system," the exploiting of workers at wages so low as to be insufficient to meet the bare cost of living, thus making their very helplessness the occasion of a most injurious competition. The legislature had the right to consider that its minimum-wage requirements would be an important aid in carrying out its policy of protection. The adoption of similar requirements by many States evidences a deep-seated conviction both as to the presence of the evil and as to the means adapted to check it. Legislative response to that conviction cannot be regarded as arbitrary or capricious, and that is all we have to decide. Even if the wisdom of the policy be regarded as debatable and its effects uncertain, still the legislature is entitled to its judgment.

There is an additional and compelling consideration which recent economic experience has brought into a strong light. The exploitation of a class of workers who are in an unequal position with respect to bargaining power and are thus relatively defenseless against the denial of a living wage is not only detrimental to their health and well-being but casts a direct burden for their support upon the community. What these workers lose in wages the taxpayers are called to pay. The bare cost of living must be met. We may take judicial notice of the unparalleled demands for relief which arose during the recent period of depression and still continue to an alarming extent despite the degree of economic recovery which has been achieved. It is unnecessary to cite official statistics to establish what is of common knowledge through the length and breadth of the land. While in the instant case no factual brief has been presented, there is no reason to doubt that the State of Washington has encountered the same social problem that is present elsewhere. The community is not bound to provide what is in effect a subsidy for unconscionable employers. The community may direct its lawmaking power to correct the abuse which springs from their selfish disregard of the public interest. The argument that the legislation in question constitutes an arbitrary discrimination, because it does not extend to men, is unavailing. This Court has frequently held that the legislative authority, acting within its proper field, is not bound to extend its regulation to all cases which it might possibly reach. The legislature "is free to recognize degrees of harm and it may confine its restrictions to those classes of cases where the need is deemed to be clearest." If "the law presumably hits the evil where it is most felt, it is not to be overthrown because there are other instances to which it might have been applied." There is no "doctrinaire requirement" that the legislation should be couched in all-embracing terms. . . .

Our conclusion is that the case of *Adkins* v. *Children's Hospital* . . . should be, and it is, overruled. The judgment of the Supreme Court of the State of Washington is

Affirmed.

[Mr. Justice Sutherland, joined by Mr. Justice Van Devanter, Mr. Justice McReynolds, and Mr. Justice Butler, dissented.]

PART III

Political and Civil Rights

"Although freedom cannot be maintained by expositions alone, in the end they furnish the main strength of liberty. A people gets sooner or later as much freedom as it wants. This want is partly created by prophets on or off the bench, but partly by constant discussion from plain citizens like us. The best safeguard against inroads on freedom of speech lies in the ferment in the thoughts of the young and of those who will not let themselves grow old."

Zechariah Chafee, Jr.

From a lecture entitled, "Thirty-five Years with Freedom of Speech," delivered at Columbia University, March 12, 1952.

CHAPTER 11

Freedom of Speech, Press, and Assembly

Along with freedom of religion, the First Amendment provides for freedom of speech and press. The First Amendment concludes by providing that the people have the right to assemble peaceably and petition the government for redress of grievances.

In the discussion that follows, two major points should be kept in mind:

1. The First Amendment restrictions applied *only* to Congress for many years. Only after the Supreme Court's expansion of the Fourteenth Amendment could the denial of First Amendment rights by the states be challenged in the federal courts.
2. Despite the fact that the First Amendment states categorically that Congress shall make *no* law abridging freedom of speech, the Court has never held that an individual is always entitled to say anything he pleases, any way he pleases, in any place he pleases, under any circumstances he pleases.

Whether one adopts the most "absolute" interpretation of the First Amendment, as Justices Black and Douglas frequently did, or reads almost all meaning out of the amendment, as Justices Frankfurter and Judge Learned Hand sometimes did,[1] the issue is always just how much freedom of speech the Court is willing to read into the amendment.

The literature and court decisions on freedom of speech, press, and assembly are exceedingly vast and complex.[2] Cases dealing with the right to assemble peaceably are discussed under the major freedom of speech and press headings.

Early Development

The first congressional limitation on freedom of speech was made in the Sedition Act of 1798, only seven years after the adoption of the First Amendment. But the Sedition Act never came directly before the Supreme Court. In fact, no important case involving freedom of speech or press was decided by the Supreme Court prior to World War I. After that war, an important group of cases came before the Court as the result of convictions obtained under the Espionage Act of 1917 and the amendments to that law enacted in 1918 and known as the Sedition Act. These statutes were enacted because of the fears engendered by the war with Germany and by the Russian Revolution of 1917.

CLEAR AND PRESENT DANGER

The first Supreme Court decision growing out of these prosecutions was *Schenck* v. *United States* (p. 355). In this case, Justice Holmes enunciated the famous "clear and present danger" test for determining the boundary between speech that can be protected by the Constitution and speech that can be punished. He stated:

> The question in every case is whether the words used are used in such circumstances and are of such a nature as to create a clear and present danger that they will bring about the substantive evils that Congress has a right to prevent. It is a question of proximity and degree. When a nation is at war many things that might be said in time of peace are such a hindrance to its effort that their utterance will not be endured so long as men fight and that no Court could regard them as protected by any constitutional right.

The clear and present danger test was used subsequently to justify convictions under the Espionage Act for the publication of twelve newspaper articles attack-

[1] See Learned Hand, *The Bill of Rights* (Cambridge: Harvard U.P., 1958).

[2] In general see Martin Shapiro, *Freedom of Speech: The Supreme Court and Judicial Review* (Englewood Cliffs, N.J.: Prentice-Hall, 1966); Henry Abraham, *Freedom and the Court,* 2nd ed. (London: Oxford U.P., 1973); and Thomas I. Emerson, *The System of Freedom of Expression* (New York: Random, 1970).

ing the war [3] and for a speech attacking American participation in the war.[4] In three subsequent cases in which the Court upheld the convictions of speakers, Justices Holmes and Brandeis dissented because they felt that the words used by the defendants had not created a clear and present danger to the United States. [*Abrams* v. *United States,* 250 U.S. 616 (1919); *Schaefer* v. *United States,* 251 U.S. 466 (1920); and *Pierce* v. *United States,* 252 U.S. 239 (1920).]

BAD TENDENCY TEST

In *Gitlow* v. *New York,* 268 U.S. 652 (1925), the Court propounded the "remote possibility" or "bad tendency" test, which was unfavorable to freedom of speech and press. Under the bad tendency test, a legislative body can suppress speech that might *tend* to injure the government some time in the future even though there is no evidence that it will do so at any particular time or to any particular degree. The Court argued that a state "cannot reasonably be required to defer the adoption of measures for its own peace and safety until the revolutionary utterances lead to actual disturbances of the public peace or imminent and immediate danger of its own destruction; but it may, in the exercise of its judgment, suppress the threatened danger in its incipiency." After 1925, the Court could apply either the clear and present danger or the bad tendency test in cases involving First Amendment freedoms.

In the long run, the most lasting effect of *Gitlow* resulted from its statement: "For present purposes we may and do assume that freedom of speech and of the press—which are protected by the First Amendment from abridgment by Congress—are among the fundamental personal rights and liberties protected by the due process clause of the Fourteenth Amendment from impairment by the states." Subsequently, the Court has repeatedly held that *Gitlow* incorporated the First Amendment into the Fourteenth.[5]

In *Whitney* v. *California* (p. 356), in which a conviction was sustained on grounds similar to those in the *Gitlow* case, Justice Brandeis wrote a concurring opinion espousing clear and present danger that is undoubtedly one of the most powerful statements in behalf of freedom of expression ever written by a justice. After 1937, the clear and present danger doctrine emerged as a more acceptable standard for judging the constitutionality of restrictions of freedom of speech, press, and assembly.

CRITICISM OF THE CLEAR AND PRESENT DANGER TEST

Although the clear and present danger test retains some of its vitality, it had been criticized severely by judges and scholars. The reasons for Justice Frankfurter's rejection of clear and present danger are outlined in his concurring opinion in *Dennis* v. *United States* (p. 359).

[3] *Frohwerk* v. *United States,* 249 U.S. 204 (1919).

[4] *Debs* v. *United States,* 249 U.S. 211 (1919).

[5] Richard C. Cortner, *The Supreme Court and the Second Bill of Rights* (Madison, Wisc.: University of Wisconsin Press, 1981), Chs. 3 and 4.

Perhaps the most severe critic of the clear and present danger doctrine—from a quite different point of view—has been the distinguished educator and philosopher, Alexander Meiklejohn. He criticized the Holmes test as a "peculiarly inept and unsuccessful attempt to formulate an exception to the principle of the freedom of speech." [6] This criticism was premised on Meiklejohn's conviction that freedom of speech on public issues is an *absolute* concept admitting no exceptions. Nevertheless, even Meiklejohn felt that incitement to riot statutes would be constitutional when applied to language that directly and immediately caused serious violence.

Freedom of Speech and Press After 1930

In 1930, President Hoover named Charles Evans Hughes to replace Chief Justice Taft, who had resigned. "It was a crucial moment in the development of constitutional safeguards for civil liberty when Hughes returned to the bench. . . . His decision to push . . . vigorously forward is one of the most significant facts in our recent constitutional history." [7]

In three decisions rendered in 1931, the new Chief Justice revealed clearly his desire to uphold freedom of speech and press against governmental action. "Something new and astonishing had happened. What had been the lonely views of Justices Holmes and Brandeis were becoming the views of the majority of the Supreme Court." [8] The most important of the three decisions was *Near* v. *Minnesota,* 283 U.S. 1 (1931), for it was the Court's first great decision on censorship of publications.[9] In the *Near* case, the Court for the first time obliterated *completely* a state law under the guaranty of liberty clause of the Fourteenth Amendment. In the process it delivered a ringing denunciation of prior restraint.

PRIOR RESTRAINT

The prior restraint doctrine announced in *Near* has subsequently been very important. It is based on the rationale that preventing speech before it can be uttered is a far greater danger to freedom of speech than punishing the speaker after he has spoken. Prior restraint is worse than subsequent punishment because

[6] Alexander Meiklejohn, *Free Speech and Its Relation to Self-Government* (New York: Harper, 1948), p. 50.

[7] Merlo J. Pusey, *Charles Evans Hughes* (New York: Macmillan, Inc., 1951), Vol. 2, pp. 717–18.

[8] Zechariah Chafee, Jr., *Free Speech in the United States* (Cambridge: Harvard U.P., 1942), p. 362.

[9] See Fred Friendly, *The Minnesota Rag* (New York: Random House, 1981). The two other decisions are *Stromberg* v. *California,* 283 U.S. 359 (1931), and *United States* v. *Macintosh,* a citizenship case (see Chapter 6). Chief Justice Hughes wrote the majority opinion in the *Stromberg* case. He wrote the dissenting opinion in the *Macintosh* case. Justices Holmes, Brandeis, and Stone joined him in that opinion.

where the state seeks to prosecute a speaker, at least the public finds out from the trial what kind of speech is being suppressed, and the state has to get a jury to go along with the suppression. Under a system of prior restraint, where a government censor privately decides what can be published and what cannot, the public does not even know what kinds of things it is forbidden to see or hear.

Although the court has stated that the prohibition on prior restraint is not absolute (see *Freedman* v. *Maryland,* discussed later in this chapter), it has struck down a number of such restraints on the grounds that only the most compelling state interests could justify a prior restraint. (See *Nebraska Press Association* v. *Stuart,* discussed later in this chapter, and *New York Times Co.* v. *United States,* which appears in Chapter 6.)

PREFERRED-POSITION DOCTRINE

After 1937, the Court became reluctant to declare laws regulating business unconstitutional. On the other hand it reactivated the clear and present danger doctrine which led it to declare some laws regulating speech unconstitutional. How could it justify its judicial activism in the realm of speech, while it practiced judicial self-restraint in the economic realm? In his famous footnote four of *United States* v. *Carolene Products Co.,* 304 U.S. 144 (1938), Justice Stone provided a solution that became known as the preferred-position doctrine. He argued that certain fundamental rights like freedom of speech held a preferred place in the Constitution because they were necessary to the basic functioning of democracy. Thus laws restricting freedom of speech, press, religion, and assembly were not to fall under the New Deal justices' doctrine that laws passed by Congress and the state legislatures are to be presumed valid. The preferred-position doctrine shifted the burden of proof to those who defended legislation restricting First Amendment freedoms. They had to convince the Court that the restrictive legislation was indispensable or justified by some clear and present danger to the public security.

Perhaps the most extreme statement of the doctrine was made by Justice Rutledge in *Thomas* v. *Collins,* 323 U.S. 516 (1945), in which the Court held that a state law that required all labor organizers to secure permits before soliciting members for their unions violated the First and Fourteenth Amendments.

> This case confronts us again with the duty our system places on this Court to say where the individual's freedom ends and the State's power begins. Choice on that border, now as always delicate, is perhaps more so where the usual presumption supporting legislation is balanced by the preferred place given in our scheme to the great, the indispensable democratic freedoms secured by the First Amendment. That priority gives these liberties a sanctity and a sanction not permitting dubious intrusions.
>
> For these reasons any attempt to restrict those liberties must be justified by clear public interest, threatened not doubtfully or remotely, but by clear and present danger.

> The rational connection between the remedy provided and the evil to be curbed, which in other contexts might support legislation against attack on due process grounds, will not suffice. These rights rest on firmer foundation.

For more than a decade after 1937, the Supreme Court continued to strike down governmental restrictions on First Amendment rights. The Court brought peaceful picketing in labor disputes under the protection of the First Amendment in *Thornhill* v. *Alabama,* 310 U.S. 88 (1940) and in several subsequent decisions. A notable victory for freedom of assembly came in *Hague* v. *Committee for Industrial Organization,* 307 U.S. 496 (1939), in which the Court invalidated a Jersey City ordinance that forbade all public assemblies in streets and parks without a permit from the local director of public safety. The Court reasoned that the ordinance did not make "comfort or convenience in the use of streets or parks the standard of official action. It enables the Director of Safety to refuse a permit on his mere opinion that such refusal will prevent riots, disturbances, or disorderly assemblage. It can thus be made the instrument of arbitrary suppression of free expression of views on national affairs, for the prohibition of all speaking will undoubtedly 'prevent' such eventualities. But uncontrolled official suppression of the privilege cannot be made a substitute for the duty to maintain order in connection with the exercise of the right."

In *Bridges* v. *California,* 314 U.S. 252 (1941), the Court reversed convictions for contempt of court imposed on a labor leader and several newspaper editors because they had published critical comments concerning pending litigation involving a labor dispute. The Court reasoned that the publications did not present a clear and present danger to the orderly administration of justice. Therefore, they were within the permissible limits of free discussion. A similar decision was reached in *Pennekamp* v. *Florida.* 328 U.S. 331 (1946).

The Court's use of the clear and present danger test during this period is demonstrated well by the controversial holdings in *Terminiello* v. *Chicago,* 337 U.S. 1 (1949) and *Feiner* v. *New York,* 340 U.S. 315 (1951). Terminiello delivered an anti-Semitic and racist speech in an auditorium outside of which, in spite of a cordon of police, about a thousand angry and turbulent persons committed a number of disturbances. In a street corner speech, listened to by a handful of people, Feiner called then President Truman a bad name, which inspired an onlooker to say angry words about the speaker to a policeman. Using the clear and present danger rule, the Court struck down Terminiello's conviction for breach of the peace and upheld Feiner's. These cases also illustrate the "hostile audience" or "heckler's veto" problem. If speakers may be silenced by police whenever an audience threatens them and thus creates a clear and present danger of violence, then anyone can strip speakers of their First Amendments rights by threatening them in the presence of a police officer. Shouldn't the police arrest the threatener rather than the speaker? On the other hand what about a Nazi speaker who deliberately chooses to give a speech in favor of concentration camps or lynching in a Jewish or black neighborhood precisely because he hopes his audience will react violently against him and thus get him media attention? Should the police be required to arrest hundreds of angry people or the National Guard be called out to tear-gas the neighborhood in order to protect the speaker's rights?

The Balancing Approach and National Security

Feiner marks the beginning of the period when Justice Frankfurter's philosophy of judicial self-restraint dominated the Court. He rejected the preferred-position doctrine after an exhaustive review of its history.[10] With the deaths of Justices Murphy and Rutledge in 1949 and their subsequent replacement by Justices Clark and Minton, only Justices Black and Douglas remained as active supporters of the preferred-position doctrine. After 1949 the constitutionality of a statute came to be determined by balancing the social interests protected by the statute, such as national security, against the extent of infringement on speech. If the other interests were sufficiently weighty, the speech might be suppressed.

A low point of the Court's concern for freedom of speech came with two balancing cases: *Dennis* v. *United States* (p. 359), in which the justices undercut the clear and present danger rule while professing to follow it; and *Barenblatt* v. *United States* (p. 374), in which the Court, in effect, held that Congress could infringe on freedom of speech rights if it had a good reason to.

The Smith Act provisions, which are noted in *Dennis,* became the major weapon for the federal prosecution of American Communist party leaders after World War II. In addition, both the states and the Federal Government enacted new legislation designed to help achieve national security. The most stringent of the nation's Communist control laws came into being in 1950, with the enactment of the long and involved Internal Security Act. This law, popularly known as the McCarran Act, placed many restrictions on Communists and their supporters. Among other things, Communist and pro-Communist organizations were required to register with the Justice Department, Communists were barred from federal employment and from work in any "defense facility," the penalties for espionage were increased, Communists were denied passports, and the deportation of "subversives" was made easier. Later Congress enacted the uncertain and ambiguous Communist Control Act of 1954, which was designed to outlaw the Communist party.

These and other federal enactments were supplemented by a wave of state legislation also designed to protect the nation against subversion and espionage. These included antianarchy, criminal syndicalism and sedition laws, and statutes barring subversives from public employment, barring "subversive" political organizations from appearing on the ballot, and laws denying the use of public school buildings as meeting places for "subversive" groups.

Other methods were employed after World War II to control communism.

[10] Concurring opinion in *Kovacs* v. *Cooper,* 336 U.S. 77 (1949).

Both the Senate and the House of Representatives created numerous investigatory committees that sought to track down and expose Communists and their sympathizers. Several states set up their own legislative committees to combat subversion. Loyalty and security programs designed to ferret out disloyal governmental employees were instituted by the Federal Government and a majority of the states. The first important subversion case before the Court grew out of a provision of the Taft-Hartley Act of 1947 that required non-Communist oaths on the part of labor union officers. No union could take advantage of the act's provisions unless each of its officers filed an affidavit stating that (1) he was not a member of or affiliated with the Communist party and (2) that he did not believe in and was neither a member of nor supported any organization that believes in the violent overthrow of the government. In *American Communications Association* v. *Douds,* 339 U.S. 382 (1950), the Court held that the oath requirement did not violate the First Amendment and was therefore constitutional. Chief Justice Vinson, delivering the majority opinion, reasoned that the non-Communist oath was not intended to punish belief but rather was designed to regulate the conduct of union affairs. Congress could control union activities under its power to regulate interstate commerce in order to prevent union leaders from calling political strikes designed to interfere with the free flow of commerce and weaken the American people. Only Justice Black dissented from the basic holding of the Court. Justice Douglas and two other members of the Court did not participate in the decision.

In the *Dennis* case, the Court considered the validity of the important Smith Act of 1940 for the first time. There the Court sustained the convictions of eleven top Communist party leaders under the Smith Act for conspiracy to advocate overthrow of the government by revolution and violence. But the five opinions of the *Dennis* case demonstrate clearly the difficulties experienced by the Court in arriving at clear-cut decisions during this chaotic period. They reveal also the diversity of views among the justices regarding the real meaning of the clear and present danger test.

In addition to the *Douds* and *Dennis* cases, the Vinson Court rendered a number of other decisions dealing with loyalty and subversion. Many of these cases were also characterized by multiple concurring and dissenting opinions that indicated a lack of unity on fundamental concepts among the members of the Court. In general, the Court upheld the measures adopted by legislative bodies against the claims of individual freedoms.[11] In fact, the Vinson Court

[11] Important cases include *Adler* v. *Board of Education,* 342 U.S. 485 (1952), *Garner* v. *Board of Public Works,* 341 U.S. 716 (1951), and *Gerende* v. *Board of Supervisors,* 341 U.S. 56 (1951). In the *Garner* case, the Court upheld a Los Angeles ordinance that required all city employees to take a loyalty oath. In the *Gerende* case, the Court sustained unanimously a Maryland statute that required candidates for public office to take a loyalty oath. Individual rights were supported in a few cases. Thus, in *Wieman* v. *Updegraff,* 344 U.S. 183 (1952), a poorly drawn Oklahoma statute that required all state officers and employees to take a loyalty oath was struck down because it made simple membership in one of the listed "subversive" organizations a bar to public employment. The Court noted that, under the Oklahoma law "the fact of association alone determines

operated largely on the principle that legislative bodies should not be hampered in their efforts to stamp out subversion. The balancing test served as a useful vehicle for this principle because it allowed the Court to find that in each particular case the government's interest in protecting itself against subversion far outweighed the infringements on freedom of speech necessary to achieve internal security. The test also allowed the Court to do this without openly abandoning its role as protector of the First Amendment; it was always possible that in some cases it would strike the balance in favor of free speech.

The Warren Court and Subversion

In 1953, the Supreme Court entered a new phase. For example, in *Pennsylvania* v. *Nelson,* 350 U.S. 497 (1956), the Court held that the states could not prosecute persons who advocate the violent overthrow of the government, because the field of antisubversive activities had been preempted by the Federal Government. In *Cole* v. *Young,* 351 U.S. 536 (1956), the Court limited the federal security program to persons in "sensitive" jobs.

A series of decisions rendered during the closing months of the Court's 1956–1957 term indicated unmistakably the new direction of the Court under Chief Justice Warren. In *Watkins* v. *United States,* 354 U.S. 178 (1957), while confirming the power of Congress to investigate for a valid legislative purpose that had been proclaimed in *McGrain* v. *Daugherty,* 273 U.S. 135 (1927), Chief Justice Warren went out of his way to read a sharp lecture to Congress on the abuses of its investigating function.[12] An important sequel to the *Dennis* case was the decision in *Yates* v. *United States* (p. 369). There the Court limited the application of the Smith Act of 1940.

Many commentators and legal scholars felt that the Court had finally come to the rescue of constitutional rights that had been abridged for too long by overzealous legislative and executive officers. Others charged that the decisions seriously weakened the internal security of the country. *Yates* does, in fact, require such strict standards of proof for conviction for "advocacy" under the Smith Act that a prosecutor in a position to prove violation of the act would also be in a position to prove criminal conspiracy or sedition punishable under other federal statutes and so would not need the act to send Communists to jail. In this sense, *Yates* deprives the Smith Act of much of its meaning. *Watkins,* however, in spite of its rhetoric, did not place any serious limitations on the investigating power.

---

disloyalty and disqualification. It matters not whether association existed innocently or knowingly. Indiscriminate classification of innocent with knowing activity must fall as an assertion of arbitrary power." A decision favorable to individual freedom was rendered in *Joint Anti-Fascist Refugee Committee* v. *McGrath,* which is examined in Chapter 16.

[12] In the companion case of *Sweezy* v. *New Hampshire,* 354 U.S. 234 (1957), the Court placed constitutional restrictions on investigations by state legislative committees, but it did not establish any definite rules. The *Sweezy* case was practically obliterated by *Uphaus* v. *Wyman,* 360 U.S. 72 (1959), which upheld a contempt conviction of a pacifist minister for refusing to give to the Attorney General of New Hampshire the names of persons attending a "world fellowship" camp.

In fact, the Warren Court made a "tactical withdrawal" in a number of cases linked with subversion. It limited the scope and impact of the *Watkins* case in *Barenblatt* v. *United States* (p. 374), which upheld a conviction for contempt of the House Un-American Activities Committee (HUAC) by invoking the balancing test. In two additional cases in 1961, the Court held by a vote of 5 to 4 that the refusal of a witness to tell the HUAC whether he was a member of the Communist party was punishable as contempt.[13] These cases are the high-water mark of the antisubversive campaign and still probably constitutionally legitimize the extremely broad use of the investigatory weapon in the area of subversion. In retrospect, however, they may be most important for their unanimous and specific holdings by the Court that the congressional investigations at issue did infringe on First Amendment rights.

Immediately thereafter, by 5-to-4 decisions, the Court upheld against First Amendment pleas the registration provisions of the McCarran Act, *Communist Party* v. *Subversive Activities Control Board,* 367 U.S. 1 (1961), and the clause of the Smith Act making criminal membership in an organization that advocates overthrow of the government by force and violence, *Scales* v. *United States* (p. 380). The *Subversive Activities Control Board* case, however, left open the question of whether the party and its members could plead self-incrimination to avoid registration, because the Communist Control Act had made membership in the party a crime, and registration is a confession of membership. Government efforts to require the party as an entity to register were thwarted when no officer of the party would step forward to register it. Then, when the government sought to force individual members to register, the Supreme Court held, in *Albertson* v. *Subversive Activities Control Board,* 382 U.S. 70 (1965), that they might refuse to do so because of the possibility of self-incrimination. Similarly, the *Scales* requirement of active, knowing membership with specific intent, like *Yates,* requires such a high level of proof that if the government can satisfy its demands, it can successfully prosecute under the normal criminal law and would not have to resort to Smith Act "membership" prosecutions.

The Court has also exerted greater control over loyalty and security programs in recent years. It has struck down the blanket prohibitions on the issuance of passports to Communists, in the process acknowledging a constitutional right to travel linked to the First and Fifth Amendments, *Aptheker* v. *Secretary of State,* 378 U.S. 500 (1964). The court struck down another provision of the McCarran Act in *United States* v. *Robel,* 389 U.S. 258 (1967). The provision made it unlawful for any member of a "Communist-action organization" to work in a "defense facility." The Court argued that the statute failed to take into consideration the degree of the worker's commitment to the illegal aims

[13] *Wilkinson* v. *United States,* 365 U.S. 399 (1961); and *Braden* v. *United States,* 365 U.S. 431 (1961). However, in *Russell* v. *United States,* 369 U.S. 749 (1962), the Court set aside convictions for contempt of two congressional committees on the ground that the subject under inquiry was not clearly identified at the time of the defendants' refusal to answer questions. In *Deutsch* v. *United States,* 367 U.S. 456 (1961), a conviction for contempt of HUAC was set aside because answers were required to questions that were not pertinent to its inquiry.

of communism and whether he was in the sort of job in which he could damage our defense efforts. Thus, the statute was not narrowly drawn to protect our defense effort without infringing on the political freedoms of government workers. Undercutting *American Communications Association* v. *Douds,* it has declared a statute barring Communists from holding union office to be an unconstitutional bill of attainder, *United States* v. *Brown,* 381 U.S. 437 (1965). And in a series of cases culminating in *Keyishian* v. *Board of Regents* (p. 389), which in effect overrules the *Adler* decision, the Court has struck down state loyalty oaths and employment provisions on the grounds that they were vague and/or condemned membership in general rather than only active, knowing membership with specific intent of the sort described in *Scales.*

In *Gibson* v. *Florida Legislative Investigation Comm.* (p. 384), the Court has imposed serious limitations on legislative investigations that threaten political freedoms, although it has still left a broader leeway in the subversion areas than in others. In *Lamont* v. *Postmaster General,* 381 U.S. 301 (1965), the Supreme Court for the first time struck down a congressional statute on First Amendment grounds.

NEW PROBLEMS AND ECLECTIC DOCTRINES

In the course of the 1960s, new freedom of speech problems began to displace subversion in the Court's attention. Both the clear and present danger test and the preferred-position doctrine reappeared in majority opinions: the former in *Brandenburg* v. *Ohio* (p. 399), which overruled *Whitney* and vindicated Justice Brandeis's concurrence; and the latter in the form of requiring that the state show a "compelling state interest" to justify infringement on speech. (See *Gibson* v. *Florida Legislative Investigation Comm.*)

The Warren Court also showed a strong inclination to strike down statutes interfering with speech if they were so vaguely worded as to make unclear what speech was or was not prohibited, or so broadly worded that they might be used to punish speech that posed no threat to the purposes that the statute sought to achieve. It also struck down statutes on the grounds that they might have achieved their purposes by means that interfered less with freedom of speech or that did not interfere with speech at all. In all these instances, the Court might hold that the statute was invalid "on its face" because the very existence of the statute and the consequent risk of prosecution had a "chilling effect" on potential speakers. Thus the "vagueness," "overbreadth," "least means," "chilling effect," and "facially invalid" doctrines were included in the Court's repertoire. At the same time the balancing doctrine continued in active use. Thus, although it did not arrive at a firm position on freedom of speech of the kind that it developed in the segregation and apportionment areas, the Court did have a whole armory of doctrines with which to face its diverse cases.

Freedom of speech problems arose most acutely in connection with the civil rights movement and other social protest demonstrations. The Court had little difficulty striking down crude Southern attempts to block sit-ins and other demonstrations through disturbing-the-peace prosecutions. [See *Garner* v. *Louisiana,* 368 U.S. 157 (1961) and *Edwards* v. *South Carolina,* 372 U.S. 229 (1963).] Subsequently, it was able to avoid crucial issues raised by sit-ins as, in a series of cases, it found that new federal and local statutes desegregating public facilities undercut prosecutions that had been begun before the new laws were passed. [See *Bell* v. *Maryland,* 378 U.S. 226 (1964) and *Hamm* v. *Rock Hill,* 379 U.S. 306 (1964).] However, the Court was eventually faced squarely with the major issue of whether demonstrators might be barred from state and private property; that is, whether freedom of speech entitled the speaker to trespass and obstruct the normal operations of business and government. In *Cox* v. *Louisiana,* 379 U.S. 536, 559 (1965), the Court upheld a state law forbidding demonstrations near a courthouse, although it managed to find grounds for reversing the convictions of the picketers. In *Adderley* v. *Florida* (p. 395), it holds that the state need not open all its property to demonstrators who may disrupt its lawful operations. And, in *Walker* v. *Birmingham,* 388 U.S. 307 (1967), it confirmed earlier dicta to the effect that the First Amendment did not protect those who deliberately violated valid laws as a means of social protest. In *Tinker* v. *Des Moines School District* (p. 420), *Grayned* v. *City of Rockford,* 408 U.S. 104 (1972), and *Board of Education* v. *Pico,* 50 L.W. 4831 (1982), however, the Court held that public school students may exercise some measure of freedom of speech on school campuses.

In this whole area, where the right of the individual to be protected from tresspassers and the interest of the government in operating its various facilities without disruption intersects with freedom of speech, Justice Black, an ardent defender of the First Amendment, played a crucial role, with his vote sometimes being decisive in holding against speakers who violated others' rights to make use of their property. It is best to let him speak for himself:

> Their argument comes down to this: that . . . they had a perfect constitutional right to assemble and remain in the restaurant, over the owner's continuing objections, for the purpose of expressing themselves by language and "demonstrations" bespeaking their hostility to Hooper's refusal to serve Negroes. . . . Unquestionably, petitioners had a constitutional right to express these views wherever they had an unquestioned legal right to be. But there is the rub. . . . The right to freedom of expression is a right to express views—not a right to force other people to supply a platform or a pulpit.
>
> A great purpose of freedom of speech and press is to provide a forum for settlement of acrimonious disputes peaceably, without resort to intimidation, force, or violence. The experience of ages points to the inexorable fact that people are frequently stirred to violence when property which the law recognizes as theirs is forcibly invaded or occupied by others. Trespass laws are born of this experience. . . . The Constitution does not confer upon any group the right to substitute rule by force for rule by law. Force leads to violence, violence to mob conflicts, and these to rule by the strongest groups with control of the most deadly weapons.[14]

[14] Dissenting in *Bell* v. *Maryland,* 378 U.S. 343, 344–46 (1964).

Out of these and earlier cases, constitutional commentators shaped the "public forum" doctrine which holds that in certain publicly owned places, such as streets and parks, the government must give all speakers equal access rather than favoring some over others. The protections that this doctrine offer for freedom of speech are often undercut by the longstanding doctrine that government may make reasonable regulations of the time, place, and manner of speech even in the public forum. Often the dispute before the Court is whether a particular ordinance is such a reasonable regulation designed to avoid traffic congestion or excessive noise or whether it is really an attempt to ban speakers the government does not like.

The Burger Court

In many areas of constitutional law the Burger Court has shown some inclination to trim, or at least refuse to further extend, Warren Court holdings. For instance, in *Amalgamated Food Employees Local 509* v. *Logan Valley Plaza, Inc.,* 395 U.S. 575 (1969), the Warren Court seemed to extend freedom of speech rights into shopping centers, malls, and plazas even though they were privately owned. But in *Lloyd Corp.* v. *Tanner,* 407 U.S. 551 (1972), and *Hudgens* v. *N.L.R.B.,* 424 U.S. 507 (1976), the Burger Court specifically blocked the technique of viewing shopping centers as analogous to business districts and overruled *Logan Valley Plaza.* Thus, the Court seemed to close a promising avenue of extending general freedom of speech rights into areas where more and more Americans spend more and more of their leisure time. It has allowed state supreme courts to continue to follow the *Logan Valley* approach if they wish to cite independent state constitutional grounds for doing so [*Pruneyard Shopping Center* v. *Robins,* 447 U.S. 74 (1980)].

The remnants of the Warren Court continued to use the "least means" or "overbreadth" approach to strike down statutes that swept more broadly against speakers than was necessary to achieve their purposes. Thus, in *Coates* v. *Cincinnati,* 402 U.S. 611 (1971), the Court struck down a city ordinance that made it illegal for "three or more persons to assemble . . . on any of the sidewalks and there conduct themselves in a manner annoying to persons passing by," on the grounds that it might be used to prosecute those whose speech simply annoyed their listeners. Justice White and the Nixon appointees began to protest against what they considered excessively liberal use of the overbreadth doctrine. By 1973, in the process of upholding federal and state laws limiting the political activities of public employees, they were successful in arguing that statutes should only be struck down on their face for "substantial overbreadth." [*U.S. Civil Service Comm.* v. *National Association of Letter Carriers,* 413 U.S. 548 (1973); and *Broadrick* v. *Oklahoma,* 413 U.S. 601 (1973).]

In *Lewis* v. *New Orleans,* 415 U.S. 130 (1974), the Court did strike down as unconstitutionally vague a statute forbidding "wantonly to curse or revile or to use obscene or opprobrious language toward" a policeman. But Justice

Powell concurred separately and Justices Blackmun, Burger, and Rehnquist dissented, again attacking excessive use of vagueness and overbreadth doctrines to strike down statutes on their face. In *Arnett* v. *Kennedy,* 416 U.S. 134 (1974), six justices upheld a federal statute that allowed firing of federal employees for "such cause as will promote the efficiency of the service," including such causes as criticizing a superior, against claims that it was vague and overbroad. And in *Parker* v. *Levy,* 417 U.S. 733 (1974), a majority refused to extend the vagueness, overbreadth, and "chilling effects" doctrines to military law. The Court sustained provisions of the Uniform Code of Military Justice that forbade "conduct unbecoming an officer."

We have noted *Laird* v. *Tatum* in Chapter 4. There, on grounds of lack of standing, the Court rejected the plea of anti-Vietnam war groups that surveillance by Army Intelligence had a chilling effect on their freedom of speech. And in *Kleindienst* v. *Mandel,* 408 U.S. 753 (1972), after acknowledging that First Amendment rights were involved, the Court nonetheless upheld the government's refusal to allow a Belgian Marxist to enter the United States to lecture. The Court simply cited the line of earlier cases recognizing the "plenary power" of Congress to exclude aliens. In one of a long line of state loyalty oath cases, *Cole* v. *Richardson,* 405 U.S. 676 (1972), a 4-to-3 majority upheld the Massachusetts oath for public employees, arguing that it was drawn narrowly enough to meet the constitutional standards prescribed in earlier cases.

Yet, in other cases, the Burger Court proved receptive to First Amendment claims. In *Organization for a Better Austin* v. *Keefe,* 402 U.S. 415 (1971), the Court invalidated a state court injunction prohibiting the distribution of literature attacking a realtor for "blockbusting" and "panic peddling." Chief Justice Burger wrote for a unanimous Court: "so long as the means are peaceful, the communication need not meet standards of acceptability." In *Police Department of Chicago* v. *Mosley,* 408 U.S. 92 (1972), the Court struck down a statute prohibiting picketing within 150 feet of a school, with the exception of labor dispute picketing, on the grounds that the state could not pick and choose which kinds of speech it would permit in the public forum. [See also *Carey* v. *Brown,* 447 U.S. 455 (1980).]

The Court unanimously struck down disturbing-the-peace convictions where the jury had been instructed that defendants are guilty if their speech "offends, disturbs, incites, or tends to incite" others gathered in the same area. [*Bachellar* v. *Maryland,* 397 U.S. 564 (1970).] And in a vagueness holding, it struck down a municipal ordinance regulating door-to-door political campaigning. [*Hynes* v. *Mayor and Council of Borough of Oradell,* 425 U.S. 610 (1976).] In *Wooley* v. *Maynard,* 430 U.S. 705 (1977), the Court held that New Hampshire could not force its citizens to display the state motto "Live Free or Die" on their license plates. In *N.A.A.C.P.* v. *Claiborne,* 50 L.W. 5122 (1982), the court held that consumer boycotts were protected by the First Amendment.

The mixed responses of the Burger Court to various minor clashes between the First Amendment and government regulations obviously designed to serve legitimate interests can be seen in three recent cases. In *United States Postal*

Service v. *Council of Greenburgh Civic Associations,* 101 S.Ct. 2676 (1981), the Court upheld a post office regulation against placing unstamped mail in mailboxes against the claim that mailboxes ought to be considered a "public forum" open equally to all speakers. In *Heffron* v. *International Society for Krishna Consciousness,* 101 U.S. 2559 (1981), the Court upheld a state fairgrounds rule that all organizations must distribute their literature only from a fixed site rather than by wandering through the grounds against a sect's claims that its religious ritual required its members to move about distributing their literature. But in *Village of Schaumburg* v. *Citizens for a Better Environment,* 444 U.S. 620 (1980), with only Justice Rehnquist dissenting, the Court held that an ordinance prohibiting door-to-door or on-street solicitation of contributions by charitable organizations not using at least 75 per cent of their receipts for "charitable purposes" was a constitutionally overbroad invasion of First Amendment rights.

In *Flower* v. *United States,* 407 U.S. 197 (1972), the Court reversed disturbing-the-peace convictions where peace leaflets were distributed on the streets of an Army post that was open to the public. But in *Greer* v. *Spock,* 424 U.S. 828 (1976), it denied that there was any generalized constitutional right to make political speeches or distribute leaflets on a military reservation. [See also *Brown* v. *Glines,* 444 U.S. 348 (1980).] In Chapter 6 we noted *The Pentagon Papers* case, in which the Court refused to forbid the publication of certain government documents. In *Healy* v. *James,* 408 U.S. 169 (1972), the Court unanimously struck down a state college's refusal to recognize a chapter of Students for a Democratic Society (SDS) as an official campus group. Justice Powell wrote: "As repugnant as [their] views may have been, . . . the mere expression of them would not justify the denial of First Amendment rights."

In *Miami Herald Publishing Co.* v. *Tornillo,* 418 U.S. 241 (1974), the Court struck down a Florida statute that required newspapers to print replies from persons they had attacked editorially. The justices saw a statute under which the government could dictate what would be printed by a newspaper as a clear violation of the First Amendment. The decision will prove a roadblock to the development of a First Amendment "right of access,"—that is, to the argument that true freedom of speech does not exist unless persons who do not control newspapers and TV and radio stations are guaranteed access to the mass media that are the only effective means of speaking to the whole American people. [See also *Lehman* v. *City of Shaker Heights,* discussed in Chapter 17.]

Access to TV and radio are, however, a somewhat different problem than access to newspapers because the electronic media have always been licensed by the federal government. In *Red Lion Broadcasting Co.* v. *Federal Communications Commission,* 395 U.S. 367 (1969) the Warren Court had upheld the FCC's fairness doctrine which required stations to present balanced coverage of public issues and provide reply time to those who had been attacked by or disagreed with the editorial positions taken by a station. In *Columbia Broadcasting System* v. *Democratic National Committee,* 412 U.S. 94 (1973), the Burger Court emphasized the editorial discretion that must be left to the stations in providing fair coverage. It rejected a claim of the Democratic National Committee that broadcasters' refusal to sell any public issue advertising time violated the fairness doctrine. In *C.B.S., Inc.* v. *Federal Communications Commission,* 101 S.Ct. 2813 (1981), the Court reduced its emphasis on broadcasters' discretion, reaffirmed *Red Lion*'s justification of federal regulation, and balanced the First Amendment rights of candidates, the public and broadcasters in upholding an FCC order to the networks to provide time to federal election candidates.

The Burger Court has continued to use "imminence" language, stemming from the clear and present danger rule and *Brandenburg* v. *Ohio,* in such cases as *Eaton* v. *Tulsa,* 415 U.S. 697 (1974), *Communist Party of Indiana* v. *Whitcomb,* 414 U.S. 441 (1974), which struck down yet another state loyalty oath and *Landmark Communications Inc. v. Virginia,* 435 U.S. 829 (1978).

In *Elrod* v. *Burns,* 427 U.S. 347 (1976), an opinion of the Court signed by only three justices held that noncivil service government employees, who had been hired when their party won an election, could not then be fired after the other party won the next election simply because they belonged to the losing party. The Court interpreted the First Amendment as forbidding the patronage system. [See also *Branti* v. *Finkel,* 445 U.S. 507 (1980).]

By far the most important freedom of speech decision of the Burger Court has been *Buckley* v. *Valeo* (p. 400). Like the rest of the Burger Court record in this area, it is mixed. It adopts a balancing approach to strike down some and uphold other provisions of the Campaign Financing Act against First Amendment attack. *Buckley* firmly reestablishes balancing as the Court's central First Amendment doctrine. In a subsequent case, *Citizens Against Rent Control* v. *City of Berkeley,* 102 S.Ct. 434 (1981), the Court found that First Amendment rights outweighed the city's interest in limiting contributions in campaigns on ballot measures submitted to a popular vote.

The Excluded Areas

In the 1940s and early 1950s, several justices, in the course of trying to show that freedom of speech is not absolutely unlimited, rather casually and often in dicta, argued that obscene or libelous statements are not protected by the First Amendment. They also added "fighting words" to the excluded categories. (See pp. 435–36.) More recently, in line with evolving social standards, the Court has been more tolerant of four-letter words. (See *Cohen* v. *California,* 403 U.S. 15 (1971); *Papish* v. *Board of Curators,* 410 U.S. 667 (1973).] In *Federal Communications Commission* v. *Pacifica Foundation,* 438 U.S. 726 (1978), however, the Court upheld a ban on the broadcasting of certain four-letter words arguing that broadcasting pervasively intruded its speech into the privacy of family life. The Court has had a great deal of difficulty, however, with statutes that forbid the use of opprobrious words or abusive language. In *Gooding* v. *Wilson,* 405 U.S. 518 (1972), the majority found such a statute unconstitutionally vague because the state courts had not narrowed its application to cover only "fighting words." But Chief Justice Burger and Justice Blackmun dissented in that case, and Justices Powell and Rehnquist did not participate. *Lewis* v. *New Orleans,* discussed above, is a closely parallel case with parallel results. The quarrel is not about whether the fighting words exclusion from freedom of speech protection should continue but about whether state statutes aimed at offensive language have drawn the line between fighting words and protected words with sufficient precision.

OBSCENITY

The early exclusion holdings paved the way for the Court's decision, in *Roth* v. *United States,* 354 U.S. 476 (1957), that obscene speech is not protected because it is "utterly without redeeming social importance." The test to determine if a given work is obscene was "whether to the average person, applying contemporary community standards, the dominant theme of the material taken as a whole appeals to prurient interest" (that is, material having a tendency to excite "lustful thought").

After announcing this test, which authorizes the government to engage in thought control, the Court has faced a long series of obscenity decisions, none of which were particularly logical or enlightening. At one point it tacitly abandoned the *Roth* test of obscenity for something close to a hard-core pornography standard, although the justices could not agree on exactly what that standard was. Although the high point of confusion seemed to be *Jacobellis* v. *Ohio,* 378 U.S. 184 (1964), in which no more than two justices could agree on any given test, the Court topped itself in three cases decided in 1966: *Memoirs* v. *Massachusetts,* 383 U.S. 413; *Mishkin* v. *New York,* 383 U.S. 502; and *Ginzburg* v. *United States,* 383 U.S. 463. In the latter case the Court seemed to say that, even if the works he sold were not quite obscene, a man might be sent to jail as a smut peddler if he advertised and sold works as if they were obscene. The Court also held that states may place greater restrictions on materials sold to minors than those sold to adults. [*Ginsberg* v. *New York,* 390 U.S. 629 (1968). *Note:* Do not confuse this case with *Ginzburg* v. *United States.*] It also held that mere private possession of obscene materials cannot be a crime. [*Stanley* v. *Georgia,* 394 U.S. 557 (1969).] The doctrinal confusion in this area does not seem to have been alleviated by *Miller* v. *California* (p. 408), which is now the leading case.

In *Burstyn, Inc.* v. *Wilson,* 343 U.S. 495 (1952), the Court reversed a long-standing decision and ruled that motion pictures are within the free speech and free press guarantees of the First and Fourteenth Amendments—but it has since turned out that the justices did not quite mean it. We have noted the Court's particular concern for prior restraint. Yet it has authorized prior restraint of motion pictures, albeit under strict standards requiring prompt judicial review of the censor's decisions, in *Freedman* v. *Maryland,* 380 U.S. 51 (1965). It has also upheld zoning regulations that require "adult" motion picture theaters to be at least 1,000 feet apart. [*Young* v. *American Mini Theatres,*

Inc., 427 U.S. 50 (1976). Cf. *Schad* v. *Borough of Mount Ephraim,* 101 S.Ct. 2177 (1981).] In *Erznozik* v. *City of Jacksonville,* 422 U.S. 205 (1975), however, the Court struck down an ordinance forbidding the showing of films containing nudity by drive-in theaters whose screens could be seen from a public street. "Child pornography," the visual depiction of children engaged in sexual acts, is excluded from First Amendment protection even when it is not obscene under the *Roth-Miller* standard. [*New York* v. *Ferber,* 50 L.W. 5077 (1982).]

LIBEL

The other major excluded area is libel. [See *Beauharnais* v. *Illinois,* 343 U.S. 250 (1952), which upholds a group libel statute forbidding derogatory statements about racial, religious, or other similar groups.] But in the important case of the *New York Times Co.* v. *Sullivan* (p. 415), certain kinds of libelous speech are held to be protected by the First Amendment. Where the speech is directed against a public official, it is protected and so may not be punished under the libel laws unless it was uttered with knowledge that it was false or with reckless disregard of whether it was true or false. *Sullivan* incorporates much of Professor Meiklejohn's approach to absolute freedom of public speech. (See p. 334.) Indeed, it goes out of its way to declare the unconstitutionality of the old Alien and Sedition acts. It can be argued that *Sullivan* signaled a new commitment to freedom of speech by the justices, although subsequent speech cases hardly make this clear. In a series of decisions since the *New York Times* case, the Court has indicated that the decision applies not only to elected officials, but to appointed ones who make governmental policy (although not to the lowest ranges of civil servants) and to certain figures of public interest, even those who hold no official governmental position. The Court has also indicated that the question of "reckless disregard" may rest on judicial evaluation of whether there was serious deviation from normal news gathering and editorial practices. [See *Rosenblatt* v. *Baer,* 383 U.S. 75 (1966); *Garrison* v. *Louisiana,* 379 U.S. 64 (1964); *Curtis Publishing Co.* v. *Butts,* 388 U.S. 130 (1967); *Time, Inc.* v. *Hill,* 385 U.S. 374 (1967); and *Rosenbloom* v. *Metromedia, Inc.,* 403 U.S. 29 (1971).]

The Burger Court, here as in so many other areas, is showing a tendency to blunt the further development of Warren Court doctrines. The Warren Court seemed to be extending the *New York Times* rule to more and more persons who were further and further away from being public officials. In *Gertz* v. *Robert Welch, Inc.,* 418 U.S. 323 (1974), the Burger Court held that a lawyer representing the family of a victim murdered by a policeman was not a public person. Thus libelous statements made about him by the press were not protected by the *New York Times* rule. Because a lawyer is an "officer of the court" and the litigation in which this lawyer was involved was receiving a great deal of public attention, the Court could easily have ruled that he did fall under the *New York Times* rule. The Court did hold, however, that even where a purely private person was libeled, state courts might not constitutionally award punitive or presumed damages nor impose liability without fault. Here again we encounter a familiar Burger Court pattern. In the very act of refusing to extend what it regards as too absolute a Warren Court constitutional principle, it has taken on itself a roving commission to supervise each state libel litigation to ensure that only those libel verdicts survive that do not do too much damage to freedom of speech. [See also *Time, Inc.* v. *Firestone,* 424 U.S. 448 (1976), which held that a socially prominent woman, engaged in a divorce action that inspired much newspaper coverage and *Hutchison* v. *Proxmire,* 443 U.S. 111 (1979) holding that a scientist engaged in federally funded research were not public figures.]

COMMERCIAL AND CORPORATE SPEECH

Commercial speech traditionally was an area excluded from First Amendment protection. Here, too, the Burger Court has broadened its policy-making role. In a series of decisions, the most important of which was *Virginia State Board of Pharmacy* v. *Virginia Citizens Consumer Council, Inc.,* 425 U.S. 748 (1976), the Court has now held that commercial speech is protected by the First Amendment. It does not, however, necessarily enjoy the same degree of protection as other speech. [*Friedman* v. *Rogers* (p. 419). See also *Bates* v. *State Bar of Arizona,* 433 U.S. 350 (1977); *In re Primus,* 436 U.S. 412 (1978); *Ohralik* v. *Ohio State Bar Association,* 436 U.S. 447 (1978); *Village of Hoffman Estates* v. *Flipside, Hoffman Estates,* 102 S.Ct. 1186 (1982); *In the Matter of R.M.J.* 102 S.Ct. 929 (1982).] *In Metromedia, Inc.* v. *San Diego,* 101 S.Ct. 2882 (1981), a badly divided Court struck down a billboard regulation ordinance. The majority had no objections to the provisions regulating commercial speech, but found unconstitutional those provisions which regulated noncommercial billboards such as public issue and election advertising.

In *First National Bank* v. *Bellotti,* 436 U.S. 765 (1978), the Court confirmed that corporations as well as natural persons have free speech rights. In *Consolidated Edison Co.* v. *Public Service Commission of New York,* 447 U.S. 530 (1980) and *Central Hudson Gas and Electric Corp.* v. *Public Service Commission of New York,* 447 U.S. 557 (1980) the Court struck down state regulations prohibiting utility companies from inserting discussions of controversial public policy issues in their monthly billing envelopes and from all advertising promoting the use of electricity.

MILITARY AND INTELLIGENCE OPERATIONS

The Burger Court has recently announced a new excluded area. In 1931 when the Court announced the rule against prior restraint in the *Near* case discussed earlier in this chapter, it said that prior restraints would be justified in a few instances such as preventing "publication of the sailing dates of transports or the number and location of troops." In *Haig* v. *Agee,* 101 S.Ct. 2706 (1981), more fully discussed in Chapter 6, the Court held that "Agee's disclosures

. . . have the declared purpose of obstructing intelligence operations and the recruiting of intelligence personnel. They are clearly not protected by the Constitution."

Symbolic Expression

The line between speech and action is not always easy to draw, as the clear and present danger cases indicate. Even more difficulties are involved when First Amendment protection is claimed for "symbolic" actions designed to convey a message. Many symbolic expression cases involve flags, which are themselves, after all, symbols whose ideological content is far more important than their cloth content. In *Stromberg* v. *California,* 283 U.S. 359 (1931), the Court held unconstitutional a California statute prohibiting the flying of a red flag "as a sign, symbol or emblem of opposition to organized government." In *West Virginia Board of Education* v. *Barnette* (p. 447), a World War II case, the Court upheld the right of school children not to salute the American flag if saluting was contrary to their religious principles. Recently, in the context of Vietnam, the Court was confronted by a state statute making it an offense to "publicly mutilate, deface, defile, or defy, trample upon, or cast contempt upon either by words or act" an American flag. In *Street* v. *New York,* 394 U.S. 576 (1969), the Court avoided the symbolic expression issue. It focused on the statutory language forbidding "words" and quashed the offender's conviction on the grounds that it might have rested on his words—a clear violation of his freedom of speech rights.

A Massachusetts flag misuse law was struck down as unconstitutionally vague in *Smith* v. *Goguen,* 415 U.S. 566 (1974). The Court also struck down the conviction of a Washington man who taped a peace symbol to his flag, in an opinion which openly acknowledged that his action constituted symbolic speech protected by the First Amendment. [*Spence* v. *Washington,* 418 U.S. 405 (1974)]. However, even in this case it carefully avoided holding that desecration or destruction of the flag was constitutionally protected.

United States v. *O'Brien,* 391 U.S. 367 (1968) is a parallel case. In 1965, as draft-card burning became a popular expression of protest against the war in Vietnam, Congress amended the draft statute to forbid destroying a draft card. The Court seemed to admit that the act of burning a draft card might be symbolic expression protected by the First Amendment. But it held that where speech and nonspeech elements were combined, government regulation of the nonspeech element might be justified even if it incidentally infringed on speech. Using a balancing approach, the Court found that the government had a compelling interest in insuring that each draft registrant had a draft card in his possession. Such an interest was sufficient to justify whatever infringement on speech might be involved in the prohibition on burning.

The Court has also dealt with other, more passive, forms of symbolic expression. In *Brown* v. *Louisiana,* 383 U.S. 131 (1966), the Court seemed to hold that where blacks stood silently in a public library to protest its racial segregation, they were protected by the First Amendment. Then, in *Tinker* v. *Des Moines School District* (p. 420), the Court held that the suspension from school of students who wore black arm bands to protest the Vietnam war was a violation of their First Amendment rights. This would seem to be a clear incorporation of at least some forms of symbolic expression into freedom of speech.

Freedom of Speech and the Judicial Process

The old issue of press coverage and comment on trials raised in the *Bridges* and *Pennekamp* cases mentioned earlier returned to the Court in *Craig* v. *Harney*, 331 U.S. 367 (1947). In that case, the Court followed the earlier cases and decided that abusive newspaper commentary on a trial did not constitute a clear and present danger to the judge's impartiality. Then, in *Wood* v. *Georgia*, 370 U.S. 375 (1962), the Court held that a partisan, political attack on local judges by an elected county sheriff did not present a danger to the administration of justice in the particular circumstances. The problem that arose in a different context in the *Bridges* and *Pennekamp* cases returned to the Court in *Sheppard* v. *Maxwell*, 384 U.S. 333 (1966) and *Estes* v. *Texas*, 381 U.S. 532 (1965). In these cases, the Court reversed the convictions of two famous defendants, Dr. Samuel Sheppard and Billy Sol Estes, because of "disruptive" activities in the courtroom by newsmen *(Sheppard)* and television personnel *(Estes)*.

The Burger Court has followed the tradition of the Warren Court in finding that a defendant has a constitutional right to a trial sufficiently insulated from newspaper and television coverage to insure its fairness. [*Groppi* v. *Wisconsin*, 400 U.S. 505 (1971).] But in *Murphy* v. *Florida*, 421 U.S. 589 (1975), it took the view that extensive pretrial publicity did not render a trial fundamentally unfair so long as proper care was taken to impanel an unbiased jury.

In *Nebraska Press Association* v. *Stuart*, 427 U.S. 539 (1976), a state court had restrained the news media from reporting before the trial a defendant's confessions and other statements that strongly implicated him. The Supreme Court struck down this order as a prior restraint. The potential conflict between the rights of the press and a defendant's rights posed in this case is a serious one. For instance, let us suppose that the defendant's confession in this case had been obtained by the police illegally. The Court has held that the Fifth Amendment renders such confessions inadmissible as evidence at trial. (See Chapter 15.) Yet if prospective jurors had already read such a confession in their newspapers before the trial began, how effectively could the defendant's Fifth Amendment rights be protected by the formal exclusion of the confession from the trial evidence itself.[15] The Court did not absolutely forbid all pretrial gag orders in the *Nebraska* case. It left the door slightly open to such orders

[15] Martin Shapiro, "Freedom of Speech and Fair Trial," *Trial*, Vol. 12 (1976), pp. 32 ff.

where they did not prevent the publication of material already in the public record and where, considering all the circumstances, such an order might be the only effective way of protecting the defendant's rights.

One theme developed in *Nebraska Press Association* was that material already in a public record, for instance testimony at an open preliminary hearing, could not be subject to a gag order. For surely the press had a right to report to the public what they were entitled to see and hear for themselves. Similarly, in a case that is something of a blow to the right of privacy discussed in Chapter 17, the Court struck down an award of damages for invasion of privacy against a television station that broadcast the name of a rape victim. The Court argued that since the name of the victim was part of the public trial record, the media could hardly be prohibited from transmitting it to the public. [*Cox Broadcasting Corp.* v. *Cohn,* 420 U.S. 469 (1975). See also *Smith* v. *Daily Mail Publishing Co.,* 443 U.S. 97 (1979).] Then in *Houchins* v. *KQED, Inc.,* 438 U.S. 1 (1978), the Court held that journalists had no greater right of access to prisoners and prisons than did other persons. [See also *Pell* v. *Procunier,* 417 U.S. 817 (1974).] And in *Nixon* v. *Warner Communications, Inc.,* 435 U.S. 589 (1978), the Court denied television networks access to Presidential tape recordings that were in the custody of a federal district court and had not been released to the public. The Court said: "The First Amendment generally grants the press no right to information about a trial superior to that of the general public."

Thus a major theme of the Burger Court seems to have been that in their relations to legal processes and institutions, news media are entitled only to the same First Amendment rights enjoyed by any person or by the public at large. For instance in *Zurcher* v. *Stanford Daily,* 436 U.S. 1 (1978) the Court ruled that a newspaper office was no more or less subject to search for evidence of crime than were other people's offices.[16] In *Gannett Co.* v. *De Pasquale,* 443 U.S. 368 (1979), a newspaper challenged a judicial order barring the public, including the press, from a pretrial hearing on suppression of evidence. Trying to avoid the problems that we have just looked at in connection with *Nebraska Press Association,* prosecutor, defendant and judge agreed on a closed hearing. The very purpose of the hearing was to decide whether evidence had been illegally obtained and so must be kept from the jury. That purpose would be defeated if the excluded evidence were described in the newspapers that prospective jurors would see. The Court upheld the order, holding that the Sixth Amendment right to a public trial was a right of the accused, which he or she could waive, rather than a general right of the public, including the press, to attend trials. It also hinted that if there were some sort of First Amendment right of public access to actual trials, it was outweighed in preliminary suppression hearings of this sort by the fair trial rights of the defendant to have illegally seized evidence kept away from prospective jurors. Then in *Richmond Newspapers, Inc.* v. *Virginia,* 448 U.S. 555 (1980), the Court held that the public and

[16] Subsequent state and federal legislation has granted special protections from search warrants to news media offices.

thus the media did have a First Amendment right of access to criminal trials. In *Chandler* v. *Florida,* 101 S.Ct. 802 (1981), the Court reinterpreted *Estes* to allow TV broadcasting of criminal trials when broadcasting did not disrupt the proceedings or prejudice the jury. [See *Globe* v. *Court,* 50 L.W. 4759 (1982).]

Herbert v. *Lando,* 441 U.S. 153 (1979) involved a libel action against CBS by a "public figure" under the *New York Times* rule. In refusing to answer questions about whom he had talked to, how he had gathered the news, and why he had reached the conclusions he did, the producer of the TV show involved asserted a First Amendment privilege not to reveal the editorial process that went into a final news story. The Court denied him such a privilege essentially on the ground that media defendants were no more entitled than other defendants in civil cases to withhold crucial evidence. It would be fundamentally unfair to require a "public figure" libel plaintiff to prove that the media defendant had known that its story was false or acted with reckless disregard of its truth or falsity while at the same time forbidding the plaintiff to ask precisely those questions about the journalist's conduct that would reveal his or her state of mind at the time the story was produced.

The Supreme Court has now recognized that the planning and conducting of litigation is itself a political right protected by the First Amendment. [*NAACP* v. *Button,* 371 U.S. 415 (1963)]. The decision is interesting because of the Court's frank avowal that litigation is a political activity. *Cox* v. *Louisiana,* discussed earlier, should also be borne in mind in connection with the judicial process and freedom of speech, as should the problem of a judge's contempt power to punish demonstrators. The *Branzburg* case (p. 423) also involves the interrelation of free speech and fair trial.

The Right of Association

The right of association "is central to any serious conception of constitutional democracy. In the big states of modern times the individual cannot function politically with any measure of effectiveness unless he is free to associate with others without hindrance. In fact, most people find much of their identity, in either economic, social, political, professional, or confessional terms, in some form of group activity. . . . It follows that government has an obligation to protect the right of association from invasion, and to refrain from making inroads into that right through its own activities." [17] Even though the right of association has long been assumed to be protected by the First Amendment through the due process clause of the Fourteenth Amendment, there were very few cases on the subject until the 1950s, when associational rights began to be seriously challenged. The challenge came chiefly from federal statutes dealing with subver-

[17] David Fellman, *The Constitutional Right of Association* (Chicago: U. of Chicago, 1963), p. 104.

sive organizations and the attempt of many Southern states to impede the activities of the NAACP, which has spearheaded the drive of blacks for equal rights. Although the Court has not issued a direct First Amendment challenge to the registration and punishment of members of subversive organizations under the provisions of the various federal security statutes or to the exposure of subversives by legislative investigation, it has very narrowly circumscribed the kind of membership that may be punished, blocked registration by self-incrimination rulings, and severely limited investigating committee inquiry in all areas where subversion is not clearly and directly involved. The Court has blunted the attempts of the Southern states to cripple the NAACP and thereby defended important rights of association. See *NAACP* v. *Alabama* (p. 428).

After the decision in *NAACP* v. *Alabama,* the Warren Court generally defended freedom of association.[18] In holding void another more recent attempt by Virginia to curb the activities of the NAACP, Justice Brennan concluded that the Constitution "protects expression and association without regard to the race, creed, or political or religious affiliation of the members of the group which invokes its shield, or to the truth, popularity, or social utility of the ideas and beliefs which are offered." [19] In many of these cases, the key question was "anonymous" association—the right of individuals to engage in group political activities without having to tell the government what organization they do or do not belong to. This right to anonymity was also protected by the Court in *Talley* v. *California,* 362 U.S. 60 (1960), where the Court struck down an ordinance prohibiting the distribution of anonymously printed handbills.

The right of association has not fared so well, however, in more recent decisions by the Burger Court involving political parties. In the *Letter Carriers* and *Broadrick* cases discussed earlier in this chapter, the Court upheld limitations on civil servants' participation in political party activities. *Buckley* v. *Valeo* (p. 400) involves serious inroads on freedom of association, particularly anonymous association.

We shall see in Chapter 13 that the courts have been prepared to interfere with the freedom of association claimed by political organizations and parties where racial discrimination was involved. In nonracial discrimination contexts, the Supreme Court has been more reluctant to interfere with the internal affairs of political parties. In *O'Brien* v. *Brown,* 409 U.S. 1 (1972), *Cousins* v. *Wigoda,* 419 U.S. 477 (1975) and *Democratic Party* v. *La Follette,* 101 S.Ct. 1010 (1981) the justices avoided judicial involvement in disputes about the seating of delegates to national party conventions. In the latter case the Court held that a state could not dictate to the national parties their mode of choosing delegates. In *Marchioro* v. *Chaney,* 442 U.S. 191 (1979), however, the Court upheld a state statute requiring each major political party to have a state committee consisting of two persons from each county.

[18] *Bates* v. *City of Little Rock,* 361 U.S. 516 (1960); *Shelton* v. *Tucker,* 364 U.S. 479 (1960); and *Louisiana* ex rel. *Gremillion* v. *NAACP,* 366 U.S. 293 (1961).

[19] *NAACP* v. *Button,* 371 U.S. 415 (1963).

SCHENCK *v.* UNITED STATES
249 U.S. 47; 39 Sup. Ct. 247; 63 L. Ed. 470 (1919)

[Charles T. Schenck, the general secretary of the Socialist party, and another party member were indicted under the Espionage Act of 1917 for sending out, to men called to military service, 15,000 leaflets urging them to resist the draft. The impassioned language of the leaflets is noted in the subsequent opinion. After conviction in a federal district court, the case went to the Supreme Court on a writ of error.]

MR. JUSTICE HOLMES delivered the opinion of the Court:

. . . The defendants . . . set up the First Amendment to the Constitution, forbidding Congress to make any law abridging the freedom of speech or of the press, and, bringing the case here on that ground, have argued some other points also of which we must dispose. . . .

The document in question, upon its first printed side, recited the First section of the Thirteenth Amendment, said that the idea embodied in it was violated by the Conscription Act, and that a conscript is little better than a convict. In impassioned language it intimated that conscription was depotism in its worst form and a monstrous wrong against humanity, in the interest of Wall Street's chosen few. It said: "Do not submit to intimidation;" but in form at least confined itself to peaceful measures, such as a petition for the repeal of the act. The other and later printed side of the sheet was headed, "Assert Your Rights." It stated reasons for alleging that anyone violated the Constitution when he refused to recognize "your right to assert your opposition to the draft," and went on: "If you do not assert and support your rights, you are helping to deny or disparage rights which it is the solemn duty of all citizens and residents of the United States to retain." It described the arguments on the other side as coming from cunning politicians and a mercenary capitalist press, and even silent consent to the Conscription Law as helping to support an infamous conspiracy. It denied the power to send our citizens away to foreign shores to shoot up the people of other lands, and added that words could not express the condemnation such cold-blooded ruthlessness deserves, etc., etc., winding up, "You must do your share to maintain, support, and uphold the rights of the people of this country." Of course the document would not have been sent unless it had been intended to have some effect, and we do not see what effect it could be expected to have upon persons subject to the draft except to influence them to obstruct the carrying of it out. The defendants do not deny that the jury might find against them on this point.

But it is said, suppose that that was the tendency of this circular, it is protected by the First Amendment to the Constitution. Two of the strongest expressions are said to be quoted respectively from well-known public men. It well may be that the prohibition of laws abridging the freedom of speech is not confined to previous restraints, although to prevent them may have been the main purpose. . . . We admit that in many places and in ordinary times the defendants, in saying all that was said in the circular, would have been within their constitutional rights. But the character of every act depends upon the circumstances in which it is done. . . . The most stringent protection of free speech would not protect a man in falsely shouting fire in a theater, and causing a panic. It does not even protect a man from an injunction against uttering words that may have all the effect of force. . . . The question in every case is whether the words used are used in such circumstances and are of such a nature as to create a clear and present danger that they will bring about the substantive evils that Congress has a right to prevent. It is a question of proximity and degree. When a nation is at war many things that might be said in time of peace are such a hindrance to its effort that their utterance will not be endured so long as men fight, and that no court could regard them as protected by any constitutional right. It seems to be admitted that if an actual obstruction of the recruiting service were proved, liability for words that produced the effect might be enforced. The Statute of 1917, in Section 4, punishes conspiracies to obstruct as well as actual obstruction. If the act (speaking, or circulating a paper), its tendency and the intent with which it is done, are the same, we perceive no ground for saying that success alone warrants making the act a crime. . . .

Judgments affirmed.

WHITNEY *v.* CALIFORNIA

274 U.S. 357; 47 Sup. Ct. 641; 71 L. Ed. 1095 (1927)

[Charlotte Anita Whitney, a niece of Justice Stephen Field and a "renegade" member of the conservative and wealthy Field family, sought in various ways to promote the welfare of the poor. In 1919, she assisted in organizing the Communist Labor party of California during a convention in Oakland and was elected a member of its state executive committee. The constitution of the party provided that it be affiliated with the Communist Labor party of America and the Communist International of Moscow. Although she testified that she did not want her party to engage in terrorism or violence, Miss Whitney was convicted of a felony in a county court and sentenced to prison under the California Criminal Syndicalism Act of 1919, whose provisions are noted in the subsequent opinion. A state district court of appeals affirmed the conviction. After the state supreme court refused to review the case, it went to the Supreme Court on a writ of error.

Even though she again lost her case in the Supreme Court, Miss Whitney was later pardoned by the Governor of California, who was reported to have been greatly influenced by Justice Brandeis's eloquent concurring opinion.]

MR. JUSTICE SANFORD delivered the opinion of the court:

. . . The pertinent provisions of the Criminal Syndicalism Act are

"Section 1. The term *criminal syndicalism* as used in this act is hereby defined as any doctrine or precept advocating, teaching or aiding and abetting the commission of crime, sabotage (which word is hereby defined as meaning wilful and malicious physical damage or injury to physical property), or unlawful acts of force and violence or unlawful methods of terrorism as a means of accomplishing a change in industrial ownership or control, or effecting any political change.

"Section 2. Any person who: . . . (4) Organizes or assists in organizing, or is or knowingly becomes a member of, any organization, society, group or assemblage of persons organized or assembled to advocate, teach or aid and abet criminal syndicalism. . . .

"Is guilty of a felony and punishable by imprisonment.". . .

That the freedom of speech which is secured by the Constitution does not confer an absolute right to speak, without responsibility, whatever one may choose, or an unrestricted and unbridled license giving immunity for every possible use of language and preventing the punishment of those who abuse this freedom; and that a state in the exercise of its police power may punish those who abuse this freedom by utterances inimical to the public welfare, tending to incite to crime, disturb the public peace, or endanger the foundations of organized government and threaten its overthrow by unlawful means, is not open to question. *Gitlow* v. *New York*. . . .

By enacting the provisions of the Syndicalism Act the state has declared, through its legislative body, that to knowingly be or become a member of or assist in organizing an association to advocate, teach or aid and abet the commission of crimes or unlawful acts of force, violence or terrorism as a means of accomplishing industrial or political changes, involves such danger to the public peace and the security of the state, that these acts should be penalized in the exercise of its police power. That determination must be given great weight. Every presumption is to be indulged in favor of the validity of the statute. . . .

The essence of the offense denounced by the act is the combining with others in an association for the accomplishment of the desired ends through the advocacy and use of criminal and unlawful methods. It partakes of the nature of a criminal conspiracy. . . . That such united and joint action involves even greater danger to the public peace and security than the isolated utterances and acts of individuals, is clear. We cannot hold that, as here applied, the act is an unreasonable or arbitrary exercise of the police power of the state, unwarrantably infringing any right of free speech, assembly or association. . . .

MR. JUSTICE BRANDEIS, concurring:

. . . The felony which the statute created is a crime very unlike the old felony of conspiracy or the old misdemeanor of unlawful assembly. The mere act of assisting in forming a society for teaching syndicalism, of becoming a member of it, or of assembling with others for that purpose is given the dynamic quality of crime. There is guilt although the society may not contemplate immediate promulgation of the doctrine. Thus, the accused is to be punished, not for attempt, incitement or conspiracy, but for a step in preparation, which, if it threatens the public order at all, does so only remotely. The novelty in the prohibition introduced is that the statute aims, not at the practice of criminal syndicalism, nor even directly at the preaching of it, but at association with those who propose to preach it.

Despite arguments to the contrary which had seemed to me persuasive, it is settled that the due process clause of the Fourteenth Amendment applies to matters of substantive law as well as to matters of procedure. Thus all fundamental rights comprised within the term "liberty" are protected by the Federal Constitution from invasion by the states. The right of free speech, the right to teach, and the right of assembly are, of course, fundamental rights.

. . . These may not be denied or abridged. But, although the rights of free speech and assembly are fundamental, they are not in their nature absolute. Their exercise is subject to restriction, if the particular restriction proposed is required in order to protect the state from destruction or from serious injury, political, economic or moral. That the necessity which is essential to a valid restriction does not exist unless speech would produce, or is intended to produce, a clear and imminent danger of some substantive evil which the state constitutionally may seek to prevent has been settled. See *Schenck* v. *United States*. . . .

It is said to be the function of the legislature to determine whether at a particular time and under the particular circumstances the formation of, or assembly with, a society organized to advocate criminal syndicalism constitutes a clear and present danger of substantive evil; and that by enacting the law here in question the legislature of California determined that question in the affirmative. Compare *Gitlow* v. *New York*. . . . The legislature must obviously decide, in the first instance, whether a danger exists which calls for a particular protective measure. But where a statute is valid only in case certain conditions exist, the enactment of the statute cannot alone establish the facts which are essential to its validity. Prohibitory legislation has repeatedly been held invalid, because unnecessary, where the denial of liberty involved was that of engaging in a particular business. The powers of the courts to strike down an offending law are no less when the interests involved are not property rights, but the fundamental personal rights of free speech and assembly. . . .

Those who won our independence believed that the final end of the state was to make men free to develop their faculties; and that in its government the deliberative forces should prevail over the arbitrary. They valued liberty both as an end and as a means. They believed liberty to be the secret of happiness and courage to be the secret of liberty. They believed that freedom to think as you will and to speak as you think are means indispensible to the discovery and spread of political truth; that without free speech and assembly discussions would be futile; that with them, discussion affords ordinarily adequate protection against the dissemination of noxious doctrine; that the greatest menace to freedom is an inert people; that public discussion is a political duty; and that this should be a fundamental principle of the American government. They recognized the risks to which all human institutions are subject. But they knew that order cannot be secured merely through fear of punishment for its infraction; that it is hazardous to discourage thought, hope and imagination; that fear breeds repression; that repression breeds hate; that hate menaces stable government; that the path of safety lies in the opportunity to discuss freely supposed grievances and proposed remedies; and that the fitting remedy for evil counsels is good ones. Believing in the power of reason as applied through public discussion, they eschewed silence coerced by law—the argument of force in its worst form. Recognizing the occasional tyrannies of governing majorities, they amended the Constitution so that free speech and assembly should be guaranteed.

Fear of serious injury cannot alone justify suppression of free speech and assembly. Men feared witches and burned women. It is the function of speech to free men from the bondage of irrational fears. To justify suppression of free speech there must be reasonable ground to fear that serious evil will result if free speech is practiced. There must be reasonable ground to believe that the danger apprehended is imminent. There must be reasonable ground to believe that the evil to be prevented is a serious one. Every denunciation of existing law tends in some measure to increase the probability that there will be violation of it. Condonation of a breach enhances the probability. Expressions of approval add to the probability. Propagation of the criminal state of mind by teaching syndicalism increases it. Advocacy of lawbreaking heightens it still further. But even advocacy of violation, however reprehensible morally, is not a justification for denying free speech where the advocacy falls short of incitement and there is nothing to indicate that the advocacy would be immediately acted on. The wide difference between advocacy and incitement, between preparation and attempt, between assembling and conspiracy, must be borne in mind. In order to support a finding of clear and present danger it must be shown either that immediate serious violence was to be expected or was advocated, or that the past conduct furnished reason to believe that such advocacy was then contemplated.

Those who won our independence by revolution were not cowards. They did not fear political change. They did not exalt order at the cost of liberty. To courageous, self-reliant men, with confidence in the power of free and fearless reasoning applied through the processes of popular government, no danger flowing from speech can be deemed clear and present, unless the incidence of the evil apprehended is so imminent that it may befall before there is opportunity for full discussion. If there be time to expose through discussion the falsehood and fallacies, to avert the evil by the process of education, the remedy to be applied is more speech, not enforced silence. Only an emergency can justify repression. Such must be the rule if authority is to be reconciled with freedom. Such, in my opinion, is the command of the Constitution. It is, therefore, always open to Americans to challenge a law abridging free speech and assembly by showing that there was no emergency justifying it.

Moreover, even imminent danger cannot justify resort to prohibition of these functions essential to effective democracy, unless the evil apprehended is relatively serious. Prohibition of free speech and assembly is a measure so stringent that it would be inappropriate as the means for averting a relatively trivial harm to society. A police measure may be unconstitutional merely because the remedy, although effective as means of protection, is unduly harsh or oppressive. Thus, a state might, in the exercise of its police power, make any trespass upon the land of another a crime, regardless of the results of or the intent or purpose of the trespasser. It might, also, punish an attempt, a conspiracy, or an incitement to commit the trespass. But it is hardly conceivable that this court would hold constitutional a statute which punished as a felony the mere voluntary assembly with a society formed to teach that pedestrians had the moral right to cross unenclosed, unposted, waste lands and to advocate their doing so, even if there was imminent danger that advocacy would lead to a trespass. The fact that speech is likely to result in some violence or in destruction of property is not enough to justify its suppression. There must be the probability of serious injury to the state. Among freemen, the deterrents ordinarily to be applied to prevent crime are education and punishment for violations of the law, not abridgment of the rights of free speech and assembly. . . .

Whether, in 1919, when Miss Whitney did the things complained of, there was in California such clear and present danger of serious evil, might have been made the important issue in the case. She might have required that the issue be determined either by the court or the jury. She claimed below that the statute as applied to her violated the Federal Constitution; but she did not claim that it was void because there was no clear and present danger of serious evil, nor did she request that the existence of these conditions of a valid measure thus restricting the rights of free speech and assembly be passed upon by the court or a jury. On the other hand, there was evidence on which the court or jury might have found that such danger existed. I am unable to assent to the suggestion in the opinion of the court that assembling with a political party, formed to advocate the desirability of a proletarian revolution by mass action at some date necessarily far in the future, is not a right within the protection of the Fourteenth Amendment. In the present case, however, there was other testimony which tended to establish the existence of a conspiracy, on the part of members of the International Workers of the World, to commit present serious crimes; and likewise to show that such a conspiracy would be furthered by the activity of the society of which Miss Whitney was a member. Under these circumstances the judgment of the state court cannot be disturbed. . . .

MR. JUSTICE HOLMES joins in this opinion.

DENNIS v. UNITED STATES

341 U.S. 494; 71 Sup. Ct. 857; 95 L. Ed. 1137 (1951)

[Dennis and ten other leaders of the Communist party were charged with violating the conspiracy provisions of the Smith Act of 1940, which are reproduced here. They were convicted in a New York district court after a sensational and hectic trial that lasted over nine months. With one exception, each of the defendants was sentenced to imprisonment for five years and to a fine of $10,000 by Judge Medina, who presided at the trial. At the conclusion of the trial, Judge Medina also imposed sentences ranging from thirty days' to six months' imprisonment on the six defense attorneys for contemptuous conduct during the trial. President Truman promoted Judge Medina to the court of appeals shortly after the trial.

The convictions of the eleven Communist party leaders were affirmed by a court of appeals in an opinion by Judge Learned Hand. The defendants then sought to obtain review by the Supreme Court on all the grounds considered by the court of appeals. These included questions relating to the scope of freedom of speech, the legal composition of the jury, and the fairness of the trial. The Court granted certiorari, which was strictly limited to a review of whether Sections 2 and 3 of the Smith Act, as construed and applied, violated the First and Fifth Amendments and other provisions of the Bill of Rights.]

MR. CHIEF JUSTICE VINSON announced the judgment of the Court and an opinion in which MR. JUSTICE REED, MR. JUSTICE BURTON, and MR. JUSTICE MINTON join:

. . . Sections 2 and 3 of the Smith Act . . . provide as follows:

"Section 2. (a) It shall be unlawful for any person—

"(1) to knowingly or wilfully advocate, abet, advise, or teach the duty, necessity, desirability, or propriety of overthrowing or destroying any government in the United States by force or violence, or by the assassination of any officer of any such government;

"(2) with intent to cause the overthrow or destruction of any government in the United States, to print, publish, edit, issue, circulate, sell, distribute, or publicly display any written or printed matter advocating, advising, or teaching the duty, necessity, desirability, or propriety of overthrowing or destroying any government in the United States by force or violence;

"(3) to organize or help to organize any society, group, or assembly of persons who teach, advocate, or encourage the overthrow or destruction of any government in the United States by force, or violence; or to be or become a member of, or affiliate with, any such society, group, or assembly of persons, knowing the purposes thereof.

"(b) For the purposes of this section, the term 'government in the United States' means the Government of the United States, the government of any State, Territory, or possession of the United States, the government of the District of Columbia, or the government of any political subdivision of any of them.

"Section 3. It shall be unlawful for any person to attempt to commit, or to conspire to commit, any of the acts prohibited by the provisions of this title."

The indictment charged the petitioners with willfully and knowingly conspiring (1) to organize as the Communist Party of the United States of America a society, group, and assembly of persons who teach and advocate the overthrow and destruction of the Government of the United States by force and violence, and (2) knowingly and willfully to advocate and teach the duty and necessity of overthrowing and destroying the Government of the United States by force and violence. The indictment further alleged that Section 2 of the Smith Act proscribes these acts and that any conspiracy to take such action is a violation of Section 3 of the Act.

. . . Our limited grant of the writ of certiorari has removed from our consideration any question as to the sufficiency of the evidence to support the jury's determination that petitioners are guilty of the offense charged. Whether on this record petitioners did in fact advocate the overthrow of the Government by force and violence is not before us, and we must base any discussion of this point upon the conclusions stated in the opinion of the Court of Appeals, which treated the issue in great detail. That court held that the record in this case amply supports the necessary finding of the jury that petitioners, the leaders of the Communist Party in this country, were unwilling to work within our framework of democracy, but intended to initiate a violent revolution whenever the propitious occasion appeared. Petitioners dispute the meaning to be drawn from the evidence, contending that the Marxist-Leninist doctrine they advocated taught that force and violence to achieve a Communist form of government in an existing democratic state would be necessary only because the ruling classes of that state would never permit the transformation to be accomplished peacefully, but would use force and violence to defeat any peaceful political and economic gain the Communists could achieve. But the Court of Appeals held that the record supports the following broad conclusions: By virtue of their control over the political apparatus of the Communist Political Association, petitioners were able to transform that organization into the Communist Party; that the policies of the Association were changed from peaceful cooperation with the United States and its economic and political structure to a policy which had existed before the United States and the Soviet Union were fighting a common enemy, namely, a policy which worked for the overthrow of the Government by force and violence; that the Communist Party is a highly disciplined organization, adept at infiltration into strategic positions, use of aliases, and double-meaning language; that the Party is rigidly controlled; that Communists, unlike other political parties, tolerate no dissension from the policy laid down by the guiding forces, but that the approved program is slavishly followed by the members of the Party; that the literature of the Party and the statements and activities of its leaders, petitioners here, advocate, and the general goal of the Party was, during the period in question, to achieve a successful overthrow of the existing order by force and violence.

I

It will be helpful in clarifying the issue to treat the contention that the trial judge improperly interpreted the statute by charging that the statute required an unlawful intent before the jury could convict. . . .

. . . The structure and purpose of the statute demand the inclusion of intent as an element of the crime. Congress was concerned with those who advocate and organize for the overthrow of the Government. Certainly those who recruit and combine for the purpose of advocating overthrow intend to bring about the overthrow. We hold that the statute requires as an essential element of the crime proof of the intent of those who are charged with its violation to overthrow the Government by force and violence. . . .

II

The obvious purpose of the statute is to protect existing Government, not from change by peaceable, lawful, and constitutional means, but from change by violence, revolution, and terrorism. That it is within the *power* of the Congress to protect the Government of the United States from armed rebellion is a proposition which requires little discussion. Whatever theoretical merit there may be to the argument that there is a "right" to rebellion against dictatorial government is without force where the existing structure of the government provides for peaceful and orderly change. We reject any principle of governmental helplessness in the face of preparation for revolution, which principle, carried to its logical conclusion, must lead to anarchy. No one could conceive that it is not within the power of Congress to prohibit acts intended to overthrow the Government by force and violence. The question with which we are concerned here is not whether Congress has such *power,* but whether the *means* which it has employed conflict with the First and Fifth Amendments to the Constitution.

One of the bases for the contention that the means which Congress has employed are invalid takes the form of an attack on the face of the statute on the grounds that by its terms it prohibits academic discussion of the merits of Marxism-Leninism, that it stifles ideas and is contrary to all concepts of a free speech and a free press. Although we do not agree that the language itself has that significance, we must bear in mind that it is the duty of the federal courts to interpret federal legislation in a manner not inconsistent with the demands of the Constitution. . . .

The very language of the Smith Act negates the interpretation which petitioners would have us impose on that Act. It is directed at advocacy, not discussion. Thus, the trial judge properly charged the jury that they could not convict if they found that petitioners did "no more than pursue peaceful studies and discussions or teachings and advocacy in the realm of ideas." He further charged that it was not unlawful "to conduct in an American college or university a course explaining the philosophical theories set forth in the books which have been placed in evidence." Such a charge is in strict accord with the statutory language, and illustrates the meaning to be placed on those words. Congress did not intend to eradicate the free discussion of political theories, to destroy the traditional rights of Americans to discuss and evaluate ideas without fear of governmental sanction. Rather Congress was concerned with the very kind of activity in which the evidence showed these petitioners engaged.

III

But although the statute is not directed at the hypothetical cases which petitioners have conjured, its application in this case has resulted in convictions for the teaching and advocacy of the overthrow of the Government by force and violence, which, even though coupled with the intent to accomplish that overthrow, contains an element of speech. For this reason, we must pay special heed to the demands of the First Amendment marking out the boundaries of speech.

We pointed out in *Douds* . . . that

the basis of the First Amendment is the hypothesis that speech can rebut speech, propaganda will answer propaganda, free debate of ideas will result in the wisest governmental policies. It is for this reason that this Court has recognized the inherent value of free discourse. An analysis of the leading cases in this Court which have involved direct limitations on speech, however, will demonstrate that both the majority of the Court and the dissenters in particular cases have recognized that this is not an unlimited, unqualified right, but that the societal value of speech must, on occasion, be subordinated to other values and considerations.

No important case involving free speech was decided by this Court prior to *Schenck* v. *United States*. . . . Writing for a unanimous Court, Justice Holmes stated that the "question in every case is whether the words are used in such circumstances and are of such a nature as to create a clear and present danger that they will bring about the substantive evils that Congress has a right to prevent." *[The Court here discusses a number of other post-World War I cases that interpreted the clear and present danger test.]*

The rule we deduce from these cases is that where an offense is specified by a statute in nonspeech or nonpress terms, a conviction relying upon speech or press as evidence of violation may be sustained only when the speech or publication created a "clear and present danger" of attempting or accomplishing the prohibited crime, *e.g.*, interference with enlistment. The dissents, we repeat, in emphasizing the value of speech, were addressed to the argument of the sufficiency of the evidence.

The next important case before the Court in which free speech was the crux of the conflict was *Gitlow* v. *New York*. . . . There New York had made it a crime to advocate "the necessity or propriety of overthrowing . . . organized government by force. . . ." The evidence of violation of the statute was that the defendant had published a Manifesto attacking the Government and capitalism. The convictions were sustained, Justice Holmes and Brandeis dissenting. The majority refused to apply the "clear and present danger" test to the specific utterance. Its reasoning was as follows: The "clear and present danger" test was applied to the utterance itself in *Schenck* because the question was merely one of sufficiency of evidence under an admittedly constitutional statute. *Gitlow*, however, presented a different question. There a legislature had found that a certain kind of speech was, itself, harmful and unlawful. The constitutionality of such a state statute had to be adjudged by this Court just as it determined the constitutionality of any state statute, namely, whether the statute was "reasonable." Since it was entirely reasonable for a state to attempt to protect itself from violent overthrow, the statute was perforce reasonable. The only question remaining in the case became whether there was evidence to support the conviction, a question which gave the majority no difficulty. Justices Holmes and Brandeis refused to accept this approach, but insisted that whenever speech was the evidence of the violation, it was necessary to show that the speech created the "clear and present danger" of the substantive evil which the legislature had the right to prevent. Justice Holmes and Brandeis, then, made no distinction between a federal statute which made certain acts unlawful, the evidence to support the conviction being speech, and a statute which made speech itself the crime. This approach was emphasized in *Whitney* v. *California* . . . , where the Court was confronted with a conviction under the California Criminal Syndicalist statute. The Court sustained the conviction, Justices Brandeis and Holmes concurring in the result. In their concurrence they repeated that even though the legislature had designated certain speech as criminal, this could not prevent the defendant from showing that there was no danger that the substantive evil would be brought about.

Although no case subsequent to *Whitney* and *Gitlow* has expressly overruled the majority opinions in those cases, there is little doubt that subsequent opinions have inclined toward the Holmes-Brandeis rationale. . . .

In this case we are squarely presented with the application of the "clear and present danger" test, and must decide what that phrase imports. We first note that many of the cases in which this Court has reversed convictions by use of this or similar tests have been based on the fact that the interest which the State was attempting to protect was itself too insubstantial to warrant restriction of speech. . . . Overthrow of the Government by force and violence is certainly a substantial enough interest for the Government to limit speech. Indeed, this is the ultimate value of any society, for if a society cannot protect its very structure from armed internal attack, it must follow that no subordinate value can be protected. If, then, this interest may be protected, the literal problem which is presented is what has been meant by the use of the phrase "clear and present danger" of the utterances bringing about the evil within the power of Congress to punish.

Obviously, the words cannot mean that before the Government may act, it must wait until the putsch is about to be executed, the plans have been laid and the signal is awaited. If Government is aware that a group aiming at its overthrow is attempting to indoctrinate its members and to commit them to a course whereby they will strike when the leaders feel the circumstances permit, action by the Government is required. The argument that there is no need for Government to concern itself, for Government is strong, it possesses ample powers to put down a rebellion, it may defeat the revolution with ease needs no answer. For that is not the question. Certainly an attempt to overthrow the Government by force, even though doomed from the outset because of inadequate numbers or power of the revolutionists, is a sufficient evil for Congress to prevent. The damage which such attempts create both physically and politically to a nation makes it impossible to measure the validity in terms of the probability of success, or the immediacy of a successful attempt. In the instant case the trial judge charged the jury that they could not convict unless they found that petitioners intended to overthrow the Government "as speedily as circumstances would permit." This does not mean, and could not properly mean, that they would not strike until there was certainty of success. What was meant was that the revolutionists would strike when they thought the time was ripe. We must therefore reject the contention that success or probability of success is the criterion.

The situation with which Justices Holmes and Brandeis were concerned in *Gitlow* was a comparatively isolated event, bearing little relation in their minds to any substantial threat to the safety of the community. . . . They were not confronted with any situation comparable to the instant one—the development of an apparatus designed and dedicated to the overthrow of the Government, in the context of world crisis after crisis.

Chief Judge Learned Hand, writing for the majority below, interpreted the phrase as follows: "In each case (courts) must ask whether the gravity of the 'evil,' discounted by its improbability, justifies such invasion of free speech as is necessary to avoid the danger.". . . We adopt this statement of the rule. As articulated by Chief Judge Hand, it is as succinct and inclusive as any other we might devise at this time. It takes into consideration those factors which we deem relevant, and relates their significances. More we cannot expect from words.

Likewise, we are in accord with the court below, which affirmed the trial court's findings that the requisite danger existed. The mere fact that from the period 1945 to 1948 petitioners' activities did not result in an attempt to overthrow the Government by force and violence is of course no answer to the fact that there was a group that was ready to make the attempt. The formation by petitioners of such a highly organized conspiracy, with rigidly disciplined members subject to call when the leaders, these petitioners, felt that the time had come for action, coupled with the inflammable nature of world conditions, similar uprisings in other countries, and the touch-and-go nature of our relations with countries with whom petitioners were in the very least ideologically attuned, convince us that their convictions were justified on this score. And this analysis disposes of the contention that a conspiracy to advocate, as distinguished from the advocacy itself, cannot be constitutionally restrained, because it comprises only the preparation. It is the existence of the conspiracy which creates the danger. . . . If the ingredients of the reaction are present, we cannot bind the Government to wait until the catalyst is added.

IV

[The Court here considers whether the trial judge was correct in not submitting to the jury the issue of the existence of clear and present danger.]

. . . The argument that the action of the trial court is erroneous, in declaring as a matter of law that such violation shows sufficient danger to justify the punishment despite the First Amendment, rests on the theory that a jury must decide a question of the application of the First Amendment. We do not agree.

When facts are found that establish the violation of a statute, the protection against conviction afforded by the First Amendment is a matter of law. The doctrine that there must be a clear and present danger of substantive evil that Congress has a right to prevent is a judicial rule to be applied as a matter of law by the courts. The guilt is established by proof of facts. Whether the First Amendment protects the activity which constitutes the violation of the statute must depend upon a judicial determination of the scope of the First Amendment applied to the circumstances of the case. . . .

V

There remains to be discussed the question of vagueness—whether the statute as we have interpreted it is too vague, not sufficiently advising those who would speak of the limitations upon their activity. It is urged that such vagueness contravenes the First and Fourth Amendments. This argument is particularly nonpersuasive when presented by petitioners, who, the jury found intended to overthrow the Government as speedily as circumstances would permit. . . .

We agree that the standard as defined is not a neat, mathematical formulary. Like all verbalizations it is subject to criticism on the score of indefiniteness. But petitioners themselves contend that the verbalization "clear and present danger" is the proper standard. . . .

We hold that Sections 2(a) (1), 2(a) (3), and 3 of the Smith Act do not inherently, or as construed or applied in the instant case, violate the First Amendment and other provisions of the Bill of Rights, or the First and Fifth Amendments because of indefiniteness. Petitioners intended to overthrow the Government of the United States as speedily as the circumstances would permit. Their conspiracy to organize the Communist Party and to teach and advocate the overthrow of the Government of the United States by force and violence created a "clear and present danger" of an attempt to overthrow the Government by force and violence. They were properly and constitutionally convicted for violation of the Smith Act. The judgments of conviction are

Affirmed.

MR. JUSTICE CLARK took no part in the consideration or decision of this case.

MR. JUSTICE FRANKFURTER, concurring in affirmative of the judgment:

. . . Few questions of comparable import have come before this Court in recent years. The appellants maintain that they have a right to advocate a political theory, so long, at least, as their advocacy does not create an immediate danger of obvious magnitude to the very existence of our present scheme of society. On the other hand, the Government asserts the right to safeguard the security of the Nation by such a measure as the Smith Act. Our judgment is thus solicited on a conflict of interests of the utmost concern to the well-being of the country. This conflict of interests cannot be resolved by a dogmatic preference for one or the other, nor by a sonorous formula which is in fact only a euphemistic disguise for an unresolved conflict. If adjudication is to be a rational process, we cannot escape a candid examination of the conflicting claims with full recognition that both are supported by weighty title-deeds.

I

. . . The language of the First Amendment is to be read not as barren words found in a dictionary but as symbols of historic experience illumined by the presuppositions of those who employed them. Not what words did Madison and Hamilton use, but what was it in their minds which they conveyed? Free speech is subject to prohibition of those abuses of expression which a civilized society may forbid. As in the case of every other provision of the Constitution that is not crystallized by the nature of its technical concepts, the fact that the First Amendment is not self-defining and self-enforcing neither impairs its usefulness nor compels its paralysis as a living instrument.

. . . The demands of free speech in a democratic society as well as the interest in national security are better served by candid and informed weighing of the competing interests, within the confines of the judicial process, than by announcing dogmas too inflexible for the non-Euclidian problems to be solved.

But how are competing interests to be assessed? Since they are not subject to quantitative ascertainment, the issue necessarily resolves itself into asking: Who is to make the adjustment?—Who is to balance the relevant factors and ascertain which interest is in the circumstances to prevail? Full responsibility for the choice cannot be given to the courts. Courts are not representative bodies. They are not designed to be a good reflex of a democratic society. Their judgment is best informed, and therefore most dependable, within narrow limits. Their essential quality is detachment, founded on independence. History teaches that the independence of the judiciary is jeopardized when courts become embroiled in the passions of the day and assume primary responsibility in choosing between competing political, economic, and social pressures.

Primary responsibility for adjusting the interests which compete in the situation before us of necessity belongs to Congress. The nature of the power to be exercised by this Court has been delineated in decisions not charged with the emotional appeal of situations such as that now before us. We are to set aside the judgment of those whose duty it is to legislate only if there is no reasonable basis for it. . . . (W)e must scrupulously observe the narrow limits of judicial authority even though self-restraint is alone set over us. Above all we must remember that this Court's power of judicial review is not "an exercise of the powers of a superlegislature. . . ."

II

. . . *First.* Free-speech cases are not an exception to the principle that we are not legislators, that direct policy-making is not our province. How best to reconcile competing interests is the business of legislatures, and the balance they strike is a judgment not to be displaced by ours, but to be respected unless outside the pale of fair judgment. . . .

Second. A survey of the relevant decision indicates that the results which we have reached are on the whole those that would ensue from careful weighing of conflicting interests. The complex issues presented by regulation of speech in public places, by picketing, and by legislation prohibiting advocacy of crime have been resolved by scrutiny of many factors besides the imminence and gravity of the evil threatened. The matter has been well summarized by a reflective student of the Court's work. "The truth is that the clear and present danger test is an oversimplified judgment unless it takes account also of a number of factors: the relative seriousness of the danger in comparison with the value of the occasion for speech or political activity; the availability of more moderate controls than those which the state has imposed; and perhaps the specific intent with which the speech or activity is launched. No matter how rapidly we utter the phrase 'clear and present danger,' or how closely we hyphenate the words, they are not a substitute for the weighing of values. They tend to convey a delusion of certitude when what is most certain is the complexity of the strands in the web of freedoms which the judge must disentangle. . . ."

Bearing in mind that Mr. Justice Holmes regarded questions under the First Amendment as question of "proximity and degree," *Schenck* v. *United States* . . . it would be a distortion, indeed a mockery, of his reasoning to compare the "puny anonymities." . . . to which he was addressing himself in the *Abrams* case in 1919, or the publication that was "futile and too remote from possible consequences" . . . in the

Gitlow case in 1925, with the setting of events in this case in 1950. . . .

III

. . . It is not for us to decide how we would adjust the clash of interests which this case presents were the primary responsibility for reconciling it ours. Congress has determined that the danger created by advocacy of overthrow justifies the ensuing restriction on freedom of speech. The determination was made after due deliberation, and the seriousness of the congressional purpose is attested by the volume of legislation passed to effectuate the same ends.

Can we then say that the judgment Congress exercised was denied it by the Constitution? Can we establish a constitutional doctrine which forbids the elected representatives of the people to make this choice? Can we hold that the First Amendment deprives Congress of what it deemed necessary for the Government's protection?

To make validity of legislation depend on judicial reading of events still in the womb of time—a forecast, that is, of the outcome of forces at best appreciated only with knowledge of the topmost secrets of nations—is to charge the judiciary with duties beyond its equipment. . . .

MR. JUSTICE JACKSON, concurring:

II

. . . The "clear and present danger" test was an innovation by Mr. Justice Holmes in the *Schenck* case, reiterated and refined by him and Mr. Justice Brandeis in later cases, all arising before the era of World War II revealed the subtlety and efficacy of modernized revolutionary techniques used by totalitarian parties. In those cases, they were faced with convictions under so-called criminal syndicalism statutes aimed at anarchists but which, loosely construed, had been applied to punish socialism, pacifism, and left-wing ideologies, the charges often resting on far-fetched inferences which, if true, would establish only technical or trivial violations. They proposed a "clear and present danger" as a test for the sufficiency of evidence in particular cases.

I would save it, unmodified, for application as a "rule of reason" in the kind of case for which it was devised. When the issue is criminality of a hotheaded speech on a street corner, or circulation of a few incendiary pamphlets, or parading by some zealots behind a red flag, or refusal of a handful of school children to salute our flag, it is not beyond the capacity of the judicial process to gather, comprehend, and weigh the necessary materials for decision whether it is a clear and present danger of substantive evil or a harmless letting off of steam. It is not a prophecy, for the danger in such cases has matured by the time of trial or it was never present. The test applies and has meaning where a conviction is sought to be based on a speech or writing which does not directly or explicitly advocate a crime but to which such tendency is sought to be attributed by construction or by implication from external circumstances. The formula in such cases favors freedoms that are vital to our society, and, even if sometimes applied too generously, the consequences cannot be grave. But its recent expansion has extended, in particular to Communists, unprecedented immunities. Unless we are to hold our Government captive in a judge-made verbal trap, we must approach the problem of a well-organized, nationwide conspiracy, such as I have described, as realistically as our predecessors faced the trivialities that were being prosecuted until they were checked with a rule of reason. . . .

If we must decide that this Act and its application are constitutional only if we are convinced that petitioner's conduct creates a "clear and present danger" of violent overthrow, we must appraise imponderables, including international and national phenomena which baffle the best-informed foreign offices and our most experienced politicians. We would have to foresee and predict the effectiveness of Communist propaganda, opportunities for infiltration, whether, and when, a time will come that they consider propitious for action, and whether and how fast our existing government will deteriorate. And we would have to speculate as to whether an approaching Communist coup would not be anticipated by a nationalistic fascist movement. No doctrine can be sound whose application requires us to make a prophecy of that sort in the guise of a legal decision. The judicial process simply is not adequate to a trial of such far-flung issues. The answers given would reflect our own political predilections and nothing more.

The authors of the clear and present danger test never applied it to a case like this, nor would I. If applied as it is proposed here, it means that the Communist plotting is protected during its period of incubation; its preliminary stages of organization and preparation are immune from the law; the Government can move only after imminent action is manifest, when it would, of course, be too late. . . .

IV

What really is under review here is a conviction of conspiracy, after a trial for conspiracy, on an indictment charging conspiracy, brought under a statute outlawing conspiracy. With due respect to my colleagues, they seem to me to discuss anything under the sun except the law of conspiracy. One of the dissenting opinions even appears to chide me for "invoking the law of conspiracy." As that is the case before us, it may be more amazing that its reversal can be proposed without even considering the law of conspiracy. . . .

I do not suggest that Congress could punish conspiracy to advocate something, the doing of which it may not punish. Advocacy or exposition of the doctrine of communal property ownership, or any political philosophy unassociated with advocacy of its imposition by force or seizure of government by unlawful means could not be reached through conspiracy prosecution. But it is not forbidden to put down force or violence, it is not forbidden to punish its teaching or advocacy, and the end being punishable, there is no doubt of the power to punish conspiracy for the purpose. . . .

The law of conspiracy has been the chief means at the Goverment's disposal to deal with the growing problems created by such organizations. . . .

While I think there was power in Congress to enact this statute and that, as applied in this case, it cannot be held unconstitutional, I add that I have little faith in the long-range effectiveness of this conviction to stop the rise of the Communist movement. Communism will not go to jail with these Communists. No decision by this Court can forestall revolution whenever the existing government fails to command the respect and loyalty of the people and sufficient distress and discontent is allowed to grow up among the masses. Many failures by fallen governments attest that no government can long prevent revolution by outlawry. Corruption, ineptitude, inflation, oppressive taxation, militarization, injustice, and loss of leadership capable of intellectual initiative in domestic or foreign affairs are allies on which the Communists count to bring opportunity knocking to their door. Sometimes I think they may be mistaken. But the Communists are not building just for today—the rest of us might profit by their example.

MR. JUSTICE BLACK, dissenting:

. . . At the outset I want to emphasize what the crime involved in this case is, and what it is not. These petitioners were not charged with an attempt to overthrow the Government. They were not charged with overt acts of any kind designed to overthrow the Government. The charge was that they agreed to assemble and to talk and publish certain ideas at a later date. The indictment is that they conspired to organize the Communist Party and to use speech or newspapers and other publications in the future to teach and advocate the forcible overthrow of the Government. No matter how it is worded, this is a virulent form of prior censorship of speech and press, which I believe the First Amendment forbids. I would hold Section 3 of the Smith Act authorizing this prior restraint unconstitutional on its face and as applied. . . .

So long as this Court exercises the power of judicial review of legislation, I cannot agree that the First Amendment permits us to sustain laws suppressing freedom of speech and press on the basis of Congress' or our own notions of mere "reasonableness." Such a doctrine waters down the First Amendment so that it amounts to little more than an admonition to Congress. The Amendment as so construed is not likely to protect any but those "safe" or orthodox views which rarely need its protection. . . .

Public opinion being what it now is, few will protest the conviction of these Communist petitioners. There is hope, however, that in calmer times, when present pressures, passions, and fears subside, this or some later Court will restore the First Amendment liberties to the high preferred place where they belong in a free society.

MR. JUSTICE DOUGLAS, dissenting:

If this were a case where those who claimed protection under the First Amendment were teaching the techniques of sabotage, the assassination of the President, the filching of documents from public files, the planting of bombs, the art of street warfare, and the like, I would have no doubts. The freedom to speak is not absolute; the teaching of methods of terror and other seditious conduct should be beyond the pale along with obscenity and immorality. This case was argued as if those were the facts. The argument imported much seditious conduct into the record. That is easy and it has popular appeal, for the activities of Communists in plotting and scheming against the free world are common knowledge. But the fact is that no such evidence was introduced at the trial. There is a statute which makes a seditious conspiracy unlawful. Petitioners, however, were not charged with a "conspiracy to overthrow" the Government. They were charged with a conspiracy to form a party and groups and assemblies of people who teach and advocate the overthrow of our Government by force or violence and with a conspiracy to advocate and teach its overthrow by force and violence. It may well be that indoctrination in the techniques of terror to destroy the Government would be indictable under either statute. But the teaching which is condemned here is of a different character.

So far as the present record is concerned, what petitioners did was to organize people to teach and themselves teach the Marxist-Leninist doctrine contained chiefly in four books: Stalin, *Foundations of Leninism* (1924); Marx and Engels, *Manifesto of the Communist Party* (1848); Lenin, *The State and Revolution* (1917); *History of the Communist Party of the Soviet Union* (B.) (1939).

Those books are to Soviet Communism what *Mein Kampf* was to Nazism. If they are understood, the ugliness of Communism is revealed, its deceit and cunning are exposed, the nature of its activities becomes apparent, and the chances of its success less likely. That is not, of course, the reason why petitioners chose these books for their classrooms. They are fervent Communists to whom these volumes are gospel. They preached the creed with the hope that some day it would be acted upon.

The opinion of the Court does not outlaw these texts nor condemn them to the fire, as the Communists do literature offensive to their creed. But if the books themselves are not outlawed, if they can lawfully remain on library shelves, by what reasoning does their use in a classroom become a crime? It would not be a crime under the Act to introduce these books to a class, though that would be teaching what the creed of violent overthrow of the Government is. The Act, as construed, requires the element of intent—that those who teach the creed believe in it. The crime then depends not on what is taught but on who the teacher is. That is to make freedom of speech turn not on *what is said,* but on the *intent* with which it is said. Once we start down that road we enter territory dangerous to the liberties of every citizen. . . .

The First Amendment provides that "Congress shall make no law . . . abridging the freedom of speech." The Constitution provides no exception. This does not mean, however, that the Nation need hold its hand until it is in such weakened condition that there is no time to protect itself from incitement to revolution. Seditious conduct can always be punished. But the command of the First Amendment is so clear that we should not allow Congress to call a halt to free speech except in the extreme case of peril from the speech itself. The First Amendment makes confidence in the common sense of our people and in their maturity of judgment the great postulate of our democracy. Its philosophy is that violence is rarely, if ever, stopped by denying civil liberties to those advocating resort to force. The First Amendment reflects the philosophy of Jefferson "that it is time enough for the rightful purposes of civil government, for its officers to interfere when principles break out into overt acts against peace and good order." The political censor has no place in our public debates. Unless and until extreme and necessitous circumstances are shown, our aim should be to keep speech unfettered and to allow the processes of law to be invoked only when the provocateurs among us move from speech to action. . . .

. . . Our faith should be that our people will never give support to these advocates of revolution, so long as we remain loyal to the purposes for which our Nation was founded.

YATES *v.* UNITED STATES
354 U.S. 298; 77 Sup. Ct. 1064; 1 L. Ed. 2d 1356 (1957)

[Oleta O'Connor Yates and thirteen other leaders and organizers of the Communist party on the West Coast were charged with violation of the two sections of the Smith Act of 1940, which are reproduced, in part, in the preceding Dennis *case. As in the* Dennis *case, the fourteen leaders were charged with conspiracy to violate the Smith Act by knowingly and willfully (1) teaching and advocating the violent overthrow of the government of the United States and (2) organizing the Communist party, a society that teaches or advocates violent overthrow of the government. All fourteen leaders were convicted in a federal district court, and each was sentenced to five years' imprisonment and a fine of $10,000. The convictions were affirmed in a court of appeals. The Supreme Court then granted certiorari.]*

MR. JUSTICE HARLAN delivered the opinion of the Court:

We brought these cases here to consider certain questions arising under the Smith Act which have not heretofore been passed upon by this Court, and otherwise to review the convictions of these petitioners for conspiracy to violate that Act. Among other things, the convictions are claimed to rest upon an application of the Smith Act which is hostile to the principles upon which its constitutionality was upheld in *Dennis* v. *United States*. . . .

In the view we take of this case, it is necessary for us to consider only the following of petitioners' contentions: (1) that the term "organize" as used in the Smith Act was erroneously construed by the two lower courts; (2) that the trial court's instructions to the jury erroneously excluded from the case the issue of "incitement to action"; (3) that the evidence was so insufficient as to require the Court to direct the acquittal of these petitioners. . . . For reasons given hereafter, we concluded that these convictions must be reversed and the case remanded to the District Court with instructions to enter judgments of acquittal as to certain of the petitioners, and to grant a new trial as to the rest. . . .

Petitioners claim that "organize" means to "establish," "found," or "bring into existence," and that in this sense the Communist Party was organized by 1945 at the latest. On this basis petitioners contend that this part of the indictment, returned in 1951, was barred by the three-year statute of limitations. The Government, on the other hand, says that "organize" connotes a continuing process which goes on throughout the life of an organization, and that, in the words of the trial court's instructions to the jury, the term includes such things as "the recruiting of new members and the forming of new units, and the regrouping or expansion of existing clubs, classes, and other units of any society, party, group or other organization." The two courts below accepted the Government's position. We think, however, that petitioners' position must prevail. . . .

The statute does not define what is meant by "organize." Dictionary definitions are of little help, for, as those offered us sufficiently show, the term is susceptible of both meanings attributed to it by the parties here. The fact that the Communist Party comprises various components and activities, in relation to which some of the petitioners bore the title of "Organizer," does not advance us towards a solution of the problem. The charge here is that petitioners conspired to organize the Communist Party, and, unless "organize" embraces the continuing concept contended for by the Government, the establishing of new units within the Party and similar activities, following the Party's initial formation in 1945, have no independent significance or vitality so far as the "organizing" charge is involved. Nor are we here concerned with the quality of petitioners' activities as such, that is, whether particular activities may properly be categorized as "organizational." Rather, the issue is whether the term "organize" as used in this statute is limited by temporal concepts. Stated most simply, the problem is to choose between two possible answers to the question: when was the Communist Party "organized"? Petitioners contend that the only natural answer to the question is the formation date—in this case, 1945. The Government would have us answer the question by saying that the Party today is still not completely "organized"; that "organizing" is a continuing process that does not end until the entity is dissolved.

The legislative history of the Smith Act is no more revealing as to what Congress meant by "organize" than is the statute itself. . . .

We are thus left to determine for ourselves the meaning of this provision of the Smith Act, without any revealing guides as to the intent of Congress. In these circumstances we should follow the familiar rule that criminal statutes are to be strictly construed and give to "organize" its narrow meaning, that is, that the word refers only to acts entering into the creation of a new organization, and not to acts thereafter performed in carrying on its activities, even though such acts may loosely be termed "organizational." . . . Such indeed is the normal usage of the word "organize," and until the decisions below in this case the federal trial courts in which the question had arisen uniformly gave it that meaning. . . . We too think this statute should be read "according to the natural and obvious import of the language, without resorting to subtle and forced construction for the purpose of either limiting or extending its operation."

. . . We conclude, therefore, that since the Communist Party came into being in 1945, and the indictment was not returned until 1951, the three-year statute of limitations had run on the "organizing" charge, and required the withdrawal of that part of the indictment from the jury's consideration. . . .

II. Instructions to the Jury

Petitioners contend that the instructions to the jury were fatally defective in that the trial court refused to charge that, in order to convict, the jury must find that the advocacy which the defendants conspired to promote was of a kind calculated to "incite" persons to action for the forcible overthrow of the Government. It is argued that advocacy of forcible overthrow as mere *abstract doctrine* is within the free-speech protection of the First Amendment; that the Smith Act, consistently with that constitutional provision, must be taken as proscribing only the sort of advocacy which incites to illegal *action;* and that the trial court's charge, by permitting conviction for mere advocacy, unrelated to its tendency to produce forcible action, resulted in an unconstitutional application of the Smith Act. The Government, which at the trial also requested the court to charge in terms of "incitement," now takes the position, however, that the true constitutional dividing line is not between inciting and abstract advocacy of forcible overthrow, but rather between advocacy as such, irrespective of its inciting qualities, and the mere discussion or exposition of violent overthrow as an abstract theory. . . .

We are thus faced with the question whether the Smith Act prohibits advocacy and teaching of forcible overthrow as an abstract principle, divorced from any effort to instigate action to that end, so long as such advocacy or teaching is engaged in with evil intent. We hold that it does not.

The distinction between advocacy of abstract doctrine and advocacy directed at promoting unlawful action is one that has been consistently recognized in the opinions of this Court. . . .

We need not, however, decide the issue before us in terms of constitutional compulsion, for our first duty is to construe this statute. . . . The legislative history of the

Smith Act and related bills showed beyond all question that Congress was aware of the distinction between the advocacy or teaching of abstract doctrine and the advocacy or teaching of action, and that it did not intend to disregard it. The statute was aimed at the advocacy and teaching of concrete action for the forcible overthrow of the Government, and not of principles divorced from action.

The Government's reliance on this Court's decision in *Dennis* is misplaced. The jury instructions which were refused here were given there, and were referred to by this Court as requiring "the jury to find the facts *essential* to establish the substantive crime."

. . . In failing to distinguish between advocacy of forcible overthrow as an abstract doctrine and advocacy of action to that end, the District Court appears to have been led astray by the holding in *Dennis* that advocacy of violent action to be taken at some future time was enough. It seems to have considered that, since "inciting" speech is usually thought of as calculated to induce immediate action, and since *Dennis* held advocacy of action for future overthrow sufficient, this meant that advocacy, irrespective of its tendency to generate action, is punishable, provided only that it is uttered with a specific intent to accomplish overthrow. In other words, the District Court apparently thought that *Dennis* obliterated the traditional dividing line between advocacy of abstract doctrine and advocacy of action.

This misconceives the situation confronting the Court in *Dennis* and what was held there. Although the jury's verdict, interpreted in light of the trial court's instructions, did not justify the conclusion that the defendant's advocacy was directed at, or created any danger of, immediate overthrow, it did establish that the advocacy was aimed at building up a seditious group and maintaining it in readiness for action at a propitious time. In such circumstances, said Chief Justice Vinson, the Government need not hold its hand "until the putsch is about to be executed, the plans have been laid, and the signal is awaited. If Government is aware that a group aiming at its overthrow is attempting to indoctrinate its members and commit them to a course whereby they will strike when the leaders feel the circumstances permit, action by the Goverment is required." . . . The essence of the *Dennis* holding was that indoctrination of a group in preparation for future violent action, as well as exhortation to immediate action, by advocacy found to be directed to "action for the accomplishment" of forcible overthrow, to violence "as a rule or principle of action," and employing "language of incitement," . . . is not constitutionally protected when the group is of sufficient size and cohesiveness, is sufficiently oriented towards action, and other circumstances are such as reasonably to justify apprehension that action will occur. This is quite a different thing from the view of the District Court here that mere doctrinal justification of forcible overthrow, is punishable *per se* under the Smith Act. That sort of advocacy, even though uttered with the hope that it may ultimately lead to violent revolution, is too remote from concrete action to be regarded as the kind of indoctrination preparatory to action which was condemned in *Dennis*. . . .

We recognize that distinctions between advocacy or teaching of abstract doctrines, with evil intent, and that which is directed to stirring people to action, are often subtle and difficult to grasp, for in a broad sense, as Mr. Justice Holmes said in his dissenting opinion in *Gitlow*, . . . "Every idea is an incitement." But the very subtlety of these distinctions required the most clear and explicit instructions with reference to them, for they concerned an issue which went to the very heart of the charges against these petitioners. The need for precise and understandable instructions on this issue is further emphasized by the equivocal character of the evidence in this record, with which we deal in Part III of this opinion. Instances of speech that could be considered to amount to "advocacy of action" are so few and far between as to be almost completely overshadowed by the hundreds of instances in the record in which overthrow, if mentioned at all, occurs in the course of doctrinal disputation so remote from action as to be almost wholly lacking in probative value. Vague references to "revolutionary" or "militant" action of an unspecified character, which are found in the evidence, might in addition be given too great weight by the jury in the absence of more precise instructions. Particularly in light of this record, we must regard the trial court's charge in this respect as furnishing wholly inadequate guidance to the jury on this central point in the case. We cannot allow a conviction to stand on such "an equivocal direction to the jury on a basic issue." . . .

III. The Evidence

The determination already made require a reversal of these convictions. Nevertheless, . . . we have conceived it to be our duty to scrutinize this lengthy record with care, in order to determine whether the way should be left open for a new trial of all or some of these petitioners. Such a judgment, we think, should, on the one hand, foreclose further proceedings against those of the petitioners as to whom the evidence in this record would be palpably insufficient upon a new trial, and should, on the other hand, leave the Government free to retry the other petitioners under proper legal standards, especially since it is by no means clear that certain aspects of the evidence against them could not have been clarified to the advantage of the Government had it not been under a misapprehension as to the burden cast upon it by the Smith Act.

. . . when it comes to Party advocacy or teaching in the sense of a call to forcible action at some future time we cannot but regard this record as strikingly deficient. At best this voluminous record shows but a half dozen or so scattered incidents which, even under the loosest standards, could be deemed to show such advocacy. Most of these were not connected with any of the petitioners, or occurred many years before the period covered by the indictment. We are unable to regard this sporadic showing as sufficient to justify viewing the Communist Party as the nexus between these petitioners and the conspiracy charged. . . .

We must, then, look elsewhere than to the evidence concerning the Communist Party as such for the existence of the conspiracy to advocate charged in the indictment. As to the petitioners Connelly, Kusnitz, Richmond, Spector, and Steinberg we find no adequate evidence in the record which would permit a jury to find that they were members of such a conspiracy. For all purposes relevant here, the sole evidence as to them was that they had long been members, officers, or functionaries of the Communist Party of California; and that standing alone, as Congress has enacted in Section 4(f) of the Internal Security Act of 1950, makes out no case against them. So far as this record shows, none of them has engaged in or been associated with any but what appear to have been wholly lawful activities, or has ever made a single remark or been present when someone else made a remark, which would tend to prove the charges against them. . . .

Moreover, apart from the inadequacy of the evidence to show, at best, more than the abstract advocacy and teaching of forcible overthrow by the Party, it is difficult to perceive how the requisite specific intent to accomplish such overthrow could be deemed proved by a showing of mere membership or the holding of office in the Communist Party. We therefore think that as to these petitioners the evidence was entirely too meagre to justify putting them to a new trial, and that their acquittal should be ordered.

As to the nine remaining petitioners, we consider that a different conclusion should be reached. . . . [W]hile the record contains evidence of little more than a general program of educational activity by the Communist Party which included advocacy of violence as a theoretical matter, we are not prepared to say, at this stage of the case, that it would be impossible for a jury . . . to find that advocacy of action was also engaged in when the group involved was thought particularly trustworthy, dedicated, and suited for violent tasks.

Nor can we say that the evidence linking these nine petitioners to that sort of advocacy, with the requisite specific intent, is so tenuous as not to justify their retrial under proper legal standards. . . . [A]ll of these nine petitioners were shown either to have made statements themselves, or apparently approved statements made in their presence, which a jury might take as some evidence of their participation with the requisite intent in a conspiracy to advocate illegal action.

As to these nine petitioners, then, we shall not order an acquittal. . . .

Since there must be a new trial, we have not found it necessary to deal with the contention of the petitioners as to the fairness of the trial already held. The judgment of the Court of Appeals is reversed, and the case remanded to the District Court for further proceedings consistent with this opinion.

It is so ordered.

MR. JUSTICE BURTON, concurring in the result:

I agree with the result reached by the Court, and with the opinion of the Court except as to its interpretation of the term "organize" as used in the Smith Act. . . .

MR. JUSTICE BRENNAN and MR. JUSTICE WHITTAKER took no part in the consideration or decision of this case. . . .

MR. JUSTICE BLACK, with whom MR. JUSTICE DOUGLAS joins, concurring in part and dissenting in part:

I

I would reverse every one of these convictions and direct that all the defendants be acquitted. In my judgment the statutory provisions on which these prosecutions are based abridge freedom of speech, press, and assembly in violation of the First Amendment to the United States Constitution. . . .

First. I agree with Part I of the Court's opinion that deals with the statutory term *organize,* and holds that the organizing charge in the indictment was barred by the three-year statute of limitations.

Second. I also agree with the Court in so far as it holds that the trial judge erred in instructing that persons could be punished under the Smith Act for teaching and advocating forceful overthrow as an abstract principle. But on the other hand, I cannot agree that the instruction which the Court indicates it might approve is constitutionally permissible. The Court says that persons can be punished for advocating action to overthrow the Government by force and violence, where those to whom the advocacy is addressed are urged "to *do* something, now or in the future, rather than merely to *believe* in something." Under the Court's approach, defendants could still be convicted simply for agreeing to talk as distinguished from agreeing to act. I believe the First Amendment forbids Congress to punish people for talking about public affairs, whether or not such discussion incites to action, legal or illegal. . . .

Second. I also agree with the Court that petitioners, Connelly, Kusnitz, Richmond, Spector, and Steinberg, should be ordered acquitted since there is no evidence that they have ever engaged in anything but "wholly lawful activities." But in contrast to the Court, I think the same action should also be taken as to the remaining nine defendants. The Court's opinion summarizes the strongest evidence offered against these defendants. This summary reveals a pitiful inadequacy of proof to show beyond a reasonable doubt that the defendants were guilty of conspiring to incite persons to act to overthrow the Government. . . .

In essence, petitioners were tried upon the charge that they believe in and want to foist upon this country a different and to us a despicable form of authoritarian government in which voices criticizing the existing order are summarily silenced. I fear that the present type of prosecutions are more in line with the philosophy of authoritarian government than with that expressed by our First Amendment.

Doubtlessly, dictators have to stamp out causes and beliefs which they deem subversive to their evil regimes. But governmental suppression of causes and beliefs seem to me to be the very antithesis of what our Constitution stands for. The choice expressed in the First Amendment in favor of free expression was made against a turbulent background by men such as Jefferson, Madison, and Mason—men who believed that loyalty to the provisions of this Amendment was the best way to assure a long life for this new nation and its Government. Unless there is complete freedom for expression of all ideas, whether we like them or not, concerning the way government should be run and who shall run it. I doubt if any views in the long run can be secured against the censor. The First Amendment provides the only kind of security system that can preserve a free government—one that leaves the way wide open for people to favor, discuss advocate, or incite causes and doctrines however obnoxious and antagonistic such views may be to the rest of us. . . .

MR. JUSTICE CLARK, dissenting:

I would affirm the convictions. However, the Court has freed five of the convicted petitioners and ordered new trials for the remaining nine. As to the five, it says that the evidence is "clearly insufficient." I agree with the Court of Appeals, the District Court, and the jury that the evidence showed guilt beyond a reasonable doubt. . . .

. . . I agree with my Brother Burton that the Court has incorrectly interpreted the term *organize* as used in the Smith Act. . . .

. . . As I see it, the trial judge charged in essence all that was required under the *Dennis* opinions. . . . Apparently what disturbs the Court now is that the trial judge here did not give the *Dennis* charge although both the prosecution and the defense asked that it be given. Since he refused to grant these requests I suppose the majority feels that there must be some difference between the two charges, else the one that was given in *Dennis* would have been followed here. While there may be some distinctions between the charges, as I view them they are without material difference. I find, as the majority intimates, that the distinctions are too "subtle and difficult to grasp." *[Author's Note: See Brandenburg v. Ohio (p. 399).]*

BARENBLATT *v.* UNITED STATES

360 U.S. 109; 79 Sup. Ct. 1081; 3 L. Ed. 2d 1115 (1959)

[Lloyd Barenblatt, a former instructor in psychology at Vassar College, refused to tell a subcommittee of the House Un-American Activities Committee whether or not he had been a member of the Communist party during 1947–1950 while pursuing graduate work at the University of Michigan; he also refused to reveal his current associations with the Communist party. He maintained that the subcommittee had no right to inquire into his political, religious, and personal affairs or "associated activities," arguing vehemently that the Committee had violated his constitutional rights "by abridging freedom of speech, thought, press, and association, and by conducting legislative trials of known or suspected Communists which trespassed on the exclusive power of the judiciary."

For refusing to answer the questions, Barenblatt was placed in contempt and upon conviction in a district court was sentenced to six months in prison and fined $250. His conviction was affirmed by a unanimous court of appeals. However, the Supreme Court granted certiorari, vacated the court of appeals' judgment, and remanded the case back to that court for further consideration in the light of Watkins *v.* United States, *which had been recently decided. A sharply divided court of appeals reaffirmed the conviction. The Supreme Court then granted certiorari a second time.]*

MR. JUSTICE HARLAN delivered the opinion of the Court:

Once more the Court is required to resolve the conflicting constitutional claims of congressional power and of an individual's right to resist its exercise. The congressional power in question concerns the internal process of Congress in moving within its legislative domain; it involves the utilization of its committees to secure "testimony needed to enable it efficiently to exercise a legislative function belonging to it under the Constitution." . . . The power of inquiry has been employed by Congress throughout our history, over the whole range of the national interests concerning which Congress might legislate or decide upon due investigation not to legislate; it has similarly been utilized in determining what to appropriate from the national purse, or whether to appropriate. The scope of the power of inquiry, in short, is as penetrating and far-reaching as the potential power to enact and appropriate under the Constitution.

Broad as it is, the power is not, however, without limitations. Since Congress may only investigate into those areas in which it may potentially legislate or appropriate, it cannot inquire into matters which are within the exclusive province of one or the other branch of the Government. Lacking the judicial power given to the Judiciary, it cannot inquire into matters that are exclusively the concern of the Judiciary. Neither can it supplant the Executive in what exclusively belongs to the Executive. And the Congress, in common with all branches of the Government, must exercise its powers subject to the limitations placed by the Constitution on governmental action, more particularly in the context of this case the relevant limitations of the Bill of Rights. . . .

Our function, at this point, is purely one of constitutional adjudication in the particular case and upon the particular record before us, not to pass judgment upon the general wisdom of efficacy of the activities of this Committee in a vexing and complicated field.

The precise constitutional issue confronting us is whether the Subcommittee's inquiry into petitioner's past or present membership in the Communist Party transgressed the provisions of the First Amendment, which of course reach and limit congressional investigations. . . .

The Court's past cases established sure guides to decision. Undeniably, the First Amendment in some circumstances protects an individual from being compelled to disclose his associational relationships. However, the protections of the First Amendment, unlike a proper claim of the privilege against self-incrimination under the Fifth Amendment, do not afford a witness the right to resist inquiry in all circumstances. Where First Amendment rights are asserted to bar governmental interrogation, resolution of the issue always involves a balancing by the courts of the competing private and public interests at stake in the particular circumstances shown. These principles were recognized in the *Watkins* case, where, in speaking of the First Amendment in relation to congressional inquiries, we said . . . : "It is manifest that despite the adverse effects which follow upon compelled disclosure of private matters, not all such inquiries are barred. . . . The critical element is the existence of, and the weight to be ascribed to, the interest of the Congress in demanding disclosures from an unwilling witness." . . .

The first question is whether this investigation was related to a valid legislative purpose, for Congress may not constitutionally require an individual to disclose his political relationships or other private affairs except in relation to such a purpose. . . .

That Congress has wide power to legislate in the field of Communist activity in this Country, and to conduct appropriate investigations in aid thereof, is hardly debatable. This existence of such power has never been questioned by this Court, and it is sufficient to say, without particularization, that Congress has enacted or considered in this field a wide range of legislative measures, not a few of which have stemmed from recommendations of the very Committee whose actions have been drawn in question here. In the last analysis this power rests on the right of self-preservation, "the ultimate value of any society." . . . Justification for its exercise in turn rests on the long and widely accepted view that the tenets of the Communist Party include the ultimate overthrow of the Government of the United States by force and violence, a view which has been given formal expression by the Congress.

On these premises, this Court in its constitutional adjudications has consistently refused to view the Communist Party as an ordinary political party, and has upheld federal legislation aimed at the Communist problem which in a different context would certainly have raised constitutional issues of the gravest character. . . . To suggest that because the Communist Party may also sponsor peaceable political reforms the constitutional issues before us should now be judged as if that Party were just an ordinary political party from the standpoint of national security, is to ask this Court to bind itself to world affairs which have determined the whole course of our national policy since the close of World War II. . . .

We think that investigatory power in this domain is not to be denied Congress solely because the field of education is involved. . . . Indeed we do not understand petitioner here to suggest that Congress in no circumstances may inquire into Communist activity in the field of education. Rather, his position is in effect that this particular investigation was aimed not at the revolutionary aspects but at the theoretical classroom discussion of communism.

In our opinion the position rests on a too constricted view of the nature of the investigatory process, and is not supported by a fair assessment of the record before us. An investigation of advocacy of or preparation for overthrow certainly embraces the right to identify a witness as a member of the Communist Party . . . and to inquire into the various manifestations of the Party's tenets. The strict requirements of a prosecution under the Smith Act, see *Dennis* v. *United States* . . . and *Yates* v. *United States* . . . , are not the measure of the permissible scope of a congressional investigation into "overthrow," for of necessity the investigatory process must proceed step by step. Nor can it fairly be concluded that this investigation was directed at controlling what is being taught at our universities rather than at overthrow. The statement of the Subcommittee Chairman at the opening of the investigation evinces no such intention, and so far as this record reveals nothing thereafter transpired which would justify our holding that the thrust of the investigation later changed. The record discloses considerable testimony concerning the foreign domination and revolutionary purposes and efforts of the Communist Party. That there was also testimony on the abstract philosophical level does not detract from the dominant theme of this investigation—Communist infiltration furthering the alleged ultimate purpose of overthrow. And certainly the conclusion would not be justified that the questioning of petitioner would have exceeded permissible bounds had he not shut off the Subcommittee at the threshold.

Nor can we accept the further contention that this investigation should not be deemed to have been in furtherance of a legislative purpose because the true objective of the Committee and of the Congress was purely "exposure." So long as Congress acts in pursuance of its constitutional power, the judiciary lacks authority to intervene on the basis of the motives which spurred the exercise of that power. . . . [I]n stating in the Watkins case . . . that "there is no congressional power to expose for the sake of exposure," we at the same time declined to inquire into the "motives of committee members," and recognized that their "motives alone would not vitiate an investigation which had been instituted by a House of Congress if that assembly's legislative purpose is being served." Having scrutinized this record we cannot say that the unanimous panel of the Court of Appeals which first considered this case was wrong in concluding that "the primary purposes of the inquiry were in aid of legislative processes." . . . Certainly this is not a case like *Kilbourn* v. *Thompson* . . . where "the House of Representatives not only exceeded the limit of its own authority, but assumed a power which could only be properly exercised by another branch of the government, because it was in its nature clearly judicial." . . . The constitutional legislative power of Congress in this instance is beyond question.

Finally, the record is barren of other factors which in themselves might sometimes lead to the conclusion that the individual interests at stake were not subordinate to those of the state. There is no indication in this record that the Subcommittee was attempting to pillory witnesses. Nor did petitioner's appearance as a witness follow from indiscriminate dragnet procedures, lacking in probable cause for belief that he possessed information which might be helpful to the Subcommittee. And the relevancy of the question put to him by the Subcommittee is not open to doubt.

We conclude that the balance between the individual and the governmental interests here at stake must be struck in favor of the latter, and that therefore the provisions of the First Amendment have not been offended.

We hold that petitioner's conviction for

contempt of Congress discloses no infirmity, and that the judgment of the Court of Appeals must be

Affirmed.

MR. JUSTICE BLACK, with whom THE CHIEF JUSTICE and MR. JUSTICE DOUGLAS concur, dissenting:

The First Amendment says in no equivocal language that Congress shall pass no law abridging freedom of speech, press, assembly or petition. The activities of this Committee, authorized by Congress, do precisely that, through exposure, obloquy and public scorn. . . . The Court does not really deny this fact but relies on a combination of three reasons for permitting the infringement: (1) The notion that despite the First Amendment's command Congress can abridge speech and association if this Court decides that the governmental interest in abridging speech is greater than an individual's interest in exercising that freedom, (2) the Government's right to "preserve itself," (3) the fact that the Committee is only after Communists or suspected Communists in this investigation.

1. I do not agree that laws directly abridging First Amendment freedoms can be justified by a congressional or judicial balancing process. There are, of course, cases suggesting that a law which primarily regulates conduct but which might also indirectly affect speech can be upheld if the effect on speech is minor in relation to the need for control of the conduct. . . .

To apply the Court's balancing test under such circumstances is to read the First Amendment to say "Congress shall pass no law abridging freedom of speech, press, assembly and petition, unless Congress and the Supreme Court reached the joint conclusion that on balance the interests of the Government in stifling these freedoms is greater than the interest of the people in having them exercised." This is closely akin to the notion that neither the First Amendment nor any other provision of the Bill of Rights should be enforced unless the Court believes it is reasonable to do so. Not only does this violate the genius of our written Constitution, but it runs expressly counter to the injunction of Court and Congress made by Madison when he introduced the Bill of Rights. "If they (the first ten amendments) are incorporated into the Constitution, independent tribunals of justice will consider themselves in a peculiar manner the guardians of those rights; they will be an impenetrable bulwark against every assumption of power in the Legislative or Executive; they will be naturally led to resist every encroachment upon rights expressly stipulated for in the Constitution by the declaration of rights." Unless we return to this view of our judicial function, unless we once again accept the notion that the Bill of Rights means what it says and that this Court must enforce that meaning, I am of the opinion that our great charter of liberty will be more honored in the breach than in the observance.

But even assuming what I cannot assume, that some balancing is proper in this case, I feel that the Court after stating the test ignores it completely. At most it balances the right of the Government to preserve itself, against Barenblatt's right to refrain from revealing Communist affiliations. Such a balance, however, mistakes the factors to be weighed. In the first place, it completely leaves out the real interest in Barenblatt's silence, the interest of the people as a whole in being able to join organizations, advocate causes and make political "mistakes" without later being subjected to governmental penalties for having dared to think for themselves. It is this right, the right to err politically, which keeps us strong as a Nation. For no number of laws against communism can have as much effect as the personal conviction which comes from having heard its arguments and rejected them, or from having once accepted its tenets and later recognized their worthlessness. Instead, the obloquy which results from investigations such as this not only stifles "mistakes" but prevents all but the most courageous from hazarding any views which might at some later time become disfavored. This result, whose importance cannot be overestimated, is doubly crucial when it affects the universities, on which we must largely rely for the experimentation and development of new ideas essential to our country's welfare. It is these interests of society, rather than Barenblatt's own right to silence, which I think the Court should put on the balance against the demands of the Government, if any balancing process is to be tolerated. Instead they are not mentioned, while on the other side the demands of the government are vastly overstated and called "self-preservation." . . . Such a result reduces "balancing" to a mere play on words and is completely inconsistent with the rules this Court has previously given for applying a "balancing test," where it is proper: "(T)he courts should be astute to examine the effect of the challenged legislation. Mere legislative preferences or beliefs . . . may well support regulation directed at other personal activities, but be insufficient to justify such as diminishes the exercise of rights so vital to the maintenance of democratic institutions." . . .

2. Moreover, I cannot agree with the Court's notion that First Amendment freedoms must be abridged in order to "preserve" our country. That notion rests on the unarticulated premise that this Nation's security hangs upon its power to punish people because of what they think, speak or write about, or because of those with whom they associate for political purposes. The Government, in its brief, virtually admits this position when it speaks of the "communication of unlawful ideas." I challenge this premise, and deny that ideas can be proscribed under our Constitution. I agree that despotic governments cannot exist without stifling the voice of opposition to their oppressive practices. The First Amendment means to me, however, that the only constitutional way our Government can preserve itself is to leave its people the fullest possible freedom to praise, criticize or discuss, as they see fit, all governmental policies and to suggest, if they desire, that even its most fundamental postulates are bad and should be changed; "Therein lies the security of the Republic, the very foundation of constitutional government." On that premise this land was created, and on that premise it has grown to greatness. Our Constitution assumes that the common sense of the people and their attachment to our country will enable them, after free discussion, to withstand ideas that are wrong. To say that our patriotism must be protected against false ideas by means other than these is, I think, to make a baseless charge. Unless we can rely on these qualities—if, in short, we begin to punish speech—we cannot honestly proclaim ourselves to be a free Nation and we have lost what the Founders of this land risked their lives and their sacred honors to defend.

3. The Court implies, however, that the ordinary rules and requirements of the Constitution do not apply because the Committee is merely after Communists and they do not constitute a political party but only a criminal gang. "(T)he long and widely accepted view," the Court says, is "that the tenets of the Communist Party include the ultimate overthrow of the Government of the United States by force and violence." This justifies the investigation undertaken. By accepting this charge and allowing it to support treatment of the Communist Party and its members which would violate the Constitution if applied to other groups, the Court, in effect, declares that Party outlawed. It has been only a few years since there was a practically unanimous feeling throughout the country and in our courts that this could not be done in our free land. Of course it has always been recognized that members of the Party who, either individually or in combination, commit acts in violation of valid laws can be prosecuted. But the Party as a whole and innocent members of it could not be attainted merely because it had some illegal aims and because some of its members were lawbreakers. . . .

[N]o matter how often or how quickly we repeat the claim that the Communist Party is not a political party, we cannot outlaw it, as a group, without endangering the liberty of all of us. The reason is not hard to find, for mixed among those aims of communism which are illegal are perfectly normal political and social goals. And muddled with its revolutionary tenets is a drive to achieve power through the ballot, if it can be done. These things necessarily make it a political party whatever other, illegal aims it may have. . . . Significantly until recently the Communist Party was on the ballot in many States. When that was so, many Communists undoubtedly hoped to accomplish its lawful goals through support of Communist candidates. Even now some such may still remain. To attribute to them, and to those who have left the Party, the taint of the group is to ignore both our traditions that guilt, like belief, is "personal and not a matter of mere association" and the obvious fact that "men adhering to a political party or other organization notoriously do not subscribe unqualifiedly to all of its platforms or asserted principles." . . .

The fact is that once we allow any group which has some political aims or ideas to be driven from the ballot and from the battle for men's minds because some of its members are bad and some of its tenets are illegal, no group is safe. Today we deal with Communists or suspected Communists. In 1920, instead, the New York Assembly suspended duly elected legislators on the ground that, being Socialists, they were disloyal to the country's principles. In the 1830s the Masons were hunted as outlaws and subversives, and abolitionists were considered revolutionaries of the most dangerous kind in both North and South. Earlier still, at the time of the universally unlamented alien and sedition laws, Thomas Jefferson's party was attacked and its members were derisively called "Jacobins." Fisher Ames described the party as a "French faction" guilty of "subversion" and "officered, regimented and formed to subordination." Its members, he claimed, intended to "take arms against the laws as soon as they dare." History should teach us then, that in times of high emotional excitement minority parties and groups which advocate extremely unpopular social or governmental innovations will always be typed as criminal gangs and attempts will always be made to drive them out. It was knowledge of this fact, and of its great dangers, that caused the Founders of our land to enact the First Amendment as a guaranty that neither Congress nor the people would do anything to hinder or destroy the capacity of individuals and groups to seek converts and votes for any cause, however radical or unpalatable their principles might seem under the accepted notions of the time. Whatever the States were left free to do, the First Amendment sought to leave Congress devoid of any kind or quality of power to direct any type of national laws against the freedom of individuals to think what they please, advocate whatever policy they choose, and join with others to bring about the social, religious, political and governmental changes which seem best to them. Today's holding, in my judgment, marks another major step in the progressively increasing retreat from the safeguards of the First Amendment. . . .

Finally, I think Barenblatt's conviction violates the Constitution because the chief aim, purpose and practice of the House Un-American Activities Committee, as disclosed by its many reports, is to try witnesses and punish them because they are or have been Communists or because they refuse to admit or deny Communist affiliations. The punishment imposed is generally punishment by humiliation and public shame. There is nothing strange or novel about this kind of punishment. It is in fact one of the oldest forms of governmental punishment known to mankind; branding, the pillory, ostracism and subjection to public hatred being but a few examples of it. . . .

I do not question the Committee's patriotism and sincerity in doing all this. I merely feel that it cannot be done by Congress under our Constitution. For, even assuming that the Federal Government can compel witnesses to testify as to Communist affiliations in order to subject them to ridicule and social and economic retaliation, I cannot agree that this is a legislative function. Such publicity is merely punishment, and the Constitution allows only one way in which people can be convicted and punished. . . . [I]f communism is to be made a crime, and Communists are to be subjected to "pains and penalties," I would still hold this conviction bad, for the crime of communism, like all others, can be punished only by court and jury after a trial with all judicial safeguards.

It is no answer to all this to suggest that legislative committees should be allowed to punish if they grant the accused some rules of courtesy or allow him counsel. For the Constitution proscribes all bills of attainder by State or Nation, not merely those which lack counsel or courtesy. It does this because the Founders believed that punishment was too serious a matter to be entrusted to any group other than an independent judiciary and a jury of twelve men . . . It is the protection from arbitrary punishments through the right to a judicial trial with all these safeguards which over the years has distinguished America from lands where drum-head courts and other similar "tribunals" deprive the weak and the unorthodox of life, liberty and property without due process of law. It is this same right which is denied to Barenblatt, because the Court today fails to see what is here for all to see—that exposure and punishment is the aim of this Committee and the reason for its existence. To deny this aim is to ignore the Committee's own claims and the reports it has issued ever since it was established. I cannot believe that the nature of our judicial office requires us to be so blind, and must conclude that the Un-American Activities Committee's "identification" and "exposure" of Communists and suspected Communists . . . amount to an encroachment on the judiciary which bodes ill for the liberties of the people of this land.

Ultimately all the questions in this case really boil down to one—whether we as a people will try fearfully and futilely to preserve Democracy by adopting totalitarian methods, or whether in accordance with our traditions and our Constitution we will have the confidence and courage to be free.

I would reverse this conviction.

MR. JUSTICE BRENNAN, dissenting:

I would reverse this conviction. It is sufficient that I state my complete agreement with my Brother Black that no purpose for the investigation of Barenblatt is revealed by the record except exposure purely for the sake of exposure. This is not a purpose to which Barenblatt's rights under the First Amendment can validly be subordinated. An investigation in which the processes of lawmaking and law evaluating are submerged entirely in exposure of individual behavior—in adjudication, or a sort, through the exposure process—is outside the constitutional pale of congressional inquiry. . . .

SCALES *v.* UNITED STATES

367 U.S. 203; 81 Sup. Ct. 1469; 6 L. Ed. 2d. 782 (1961)

[Scales was chairman of the North and South Carolina Districts of the Communist party and in that capacity recruited new members for the party, directed a secret school where the principles of communism were taught, and sought to strengthen the party in various other ways. In 1955, he was convicted in a federal district court for violation of the "membership clause" of the Smith Act, which makes membership in any organization that advocates the overthrow of the Federal Government by force a felony punishable by up to twenty years' imprisonment and a fine of $20,000. A court of appeals upheld the conviction, but the Supreme Court granted certiorari and reversed the decision when the Solicitor General agreed that the Court's intervening decision in Jencks *v.* United States, *353 U.S. 657 (1956), entitled Scales to a new trial.*

Scales was retried, convicted again, and sentenced to a six-year prison term. A court of appeals again affirmed, and the Supreme Court granted certiorari a second time.]

MR. JUSTICE HARLAN delivered the opinion of the Court:

. . . It will bring the constitutional issues into clearer focus to notice first the premises on which the case was submitted to the jury. The jury was instructed that in order to convict it must find that within the three-year limitations period (1) the Communist Party advocated the violent overthrow of the Government, in the sense of present "advocacy of action" to accomplish that end as soon as circumstances were propitious; and (2) petitioner was an "active" member of the Party, and not merely "a nominal, passive, inactive or purely technical" member, with knowledge of the Party's illegal advocacy and a specific intent to bring about violent overthrow "as speedily as circumstances would permit."

The constitutional attack upon the membership clause, as thus construed, is that the statute offends (1) the Fifth Amendment, in that it impermissibly imputes guilt to an individual merely on the basis of his associations and sympathies, rather than because of some concrete personal involvement in criminal conduct; and (2) the First Amendment, in that it infringes free political expression and association. . . .

Fifth Amendment

In our jurisprudence guilt is personal, and when the imposition of punishment on a status or on conduct can only be justified by reference to the relationship of that status or conduct to other concededly criminal activity (here advocacy of violent overthrow), that relationship must be sufficiently substantial to satisfy the concept of personal guilt in order to withstand attack under the Due Process Clause of the Fifth Amendment. Membership, without more, in an organization engaged in illegal advocacy, it is now said, has not heretofore been recognized by this Court to be such a relationship. This claim stands, and we shall examine it, independently of that made under the First Amendment.

Any thought that due process puts beyond the reach of the criminal law all individual associational relationships, unless accompanied by the commission of specific acts of criminality, is dispelled by familiar concepts of the law of conspiracy and complicity. While both are commonplace in the landscape of the criminal law, they are not natural features. Rather they are particular legal concepts manifesting the more general principle that society, having the power to punish dangerous behavior, cannot be powerless against those who work to bring about that behavior. The fact that Congress has not resorted to either of these familiar concepts means only that the enquiry here must direct itself to an analysis of the relationship between the fact of membership and the underlying substantive illegal conduct, in order to determine whether that relationship is indeed too tenuous to permit its use as the basis of criminal liability. In this instance it is an organization which engages in criminal activity, and we can perceive no reason why one who actively and knowingly works in the ranks of that organization, intending to contribute to the success of those specifically illegal activities, should be any more immune from prosecution than he to whom the organization has assigned the task of carrying out the substantive criminal act. Nor should the fact that Congress has focused here on "membership," the characteristic relationship between an individual and the type of conspiratorial quasipolitical associations with the criminal aspect of whose activities Congress was concerned, of itself require the conclusion that the legislature has traveled outside the familiar and permissible bounds of criminal imputability. In truth, the specificity of the proscribed relationship is not necessarily a vice; it provides instruction and warning.

What must be met, then, is the argument that membership, even when accompanied by the elements of knowledge and specific intent, affords an insufficient quantum of participation in the organization's alleged criminal activity, that is, an insufficiently significant form of aid and encouragement to permit the imposition of criminal sanctions on that basis. It must indeed be recognized that a person who merely becomes a member of an illegal organization, by that "act" alone need be doing nothing more than signifying his assent to its purposes and activities on one hand, and providing, on the other, only the sort of moral encouragement which comes from the knowledge that others believe in what the organization is doing. It may indeed be argued that such assent and encouragement do fall short of the concrete, practical impetus given to a criminal enterprise which is lent for instance by a commitment on the part of a conspirator to act in furtherance of that enterprise. A member, as distinguished from a conspirator, may indicate his approval of a criminal enterprise by the very fact of his membership without thereby necessarily committing himself to further it by any act or course of conduct whatever.

In an area of the criminal law which this Court has indicated more than once demands its watchful scrutiny . . . these factors have weight and must be found to be overborne in a total constitutional assessment of the statute. We think, however, they are duly met when the statute is found to reach only "active" members having also a guilty knowledge and intent, and which therefore presents a conviction on what otherwise might be regarded as merely an expression of sympathy with the alleged criminal enterprise, unaccompanied by any significant action in its support or any commitment to undertake such action.

Thus, given the construction of the membership clause already discussed, we think the factors called for in rendering members criminally responsible for the illegal advocacy of the organization fall within established, and therefore presumably constitutional standards of criminal imputability.

First Amendment

Little remains to be said concerning the claim that the statute infringes First Amendment freedoms. It was settled in *Dennis* that the advocacy with which we are here concerned is not constitutionally protected speech, and it was further established that a combination to promote such advocacy, albeit under the aegis of what purports to be a political party, is not such association as is protected by the First Amendment. We can discern no reason why membership, when it constitutes a purposeful form of complicity in a group engaging in this same forbidden advocacy, should receive any greater degree of protection from the guaranties of the Amendment.

If it is said that the mere existence of such an enactment tends to inhibit the exercise of constitutionally protected rights, in that it engenders an unhealthy fear that one may find himself unwittingly embroiled in criminal liability, the answer surely is that the statute provides that a defendant must be proven to have knowledge of the proscribed advocacy before he may be convicted. It is, of course, true that quasi-political parties or other groups that may embrace both legal and illegal aims differ from a technical conspiracy, which is defined by its criminal purpose, so that all-knowing association with the conspiracy is a proper subject for criminal proscription as far as First Amendment liberties are concerned. If there were similar blanket prohibition of association with a group having both legal and illegal aims, there would indeed be a real danger that legitimate political expression or association would be impaired, but the membership clause, as here construed, does not cut deeper into the freedom of association than is necessary to deal with "the substantive evils that Congress has a right to prevent." *Schenck* v. *United States*. . . . The clause does not make criminal all association with an organization, which has been shown to engage an illegal advocacy. There must be clear proof that a defendant "specifically intend(s) to accomplish (the aims of the organization) by resort to violence." . . . Thus the member for whom the organization is a vehicle for the advancement of legitimate aims and policies does not fall within the ban of the statute: he lacks the requisite specific intent "to bring about the overthrow of the government as speedily as circumstances would permit." Such a person may be foolish, deluded, or perhaps merely optimistic, but he is not by this statute made a criminal.

We conclude that petitioner's constitutional challenge must be overuled. . . .

The judgment of the Court of Appeals must be

Affirmed.

MR. JUSTICE BLACK, dissenting:

. . . My reasons for dissenting from this decision are primarily those set out by Mr. Justice Brennan . . . and Mr. Justice Douglas. . . .

I think it is important to point out the manner in which this case reemphasizes the freedom-destroying nature of the "balancing test" presently in use by the Court to justify its refusal to apply specific constitutional protections of the Bill of Rights. In some of the recent cases in which it has "balanced" away the protections of the First Amendment, the Court has suggested that it was justified in the application of this "test" because no direct abridgment of First Amendment freedoms was involved, the abridgment in each of these cases being, in the Court's opinion, nothing more than "an incident of the informed exercise of a valid governmental function." A possible implication of that suggestion was that if the Court were confronted with what it would call a direct abridgment of speech, it would not apply the "balancing test" but would enforce the protections of the First Amendment according to its own terms. This case causes me to doubt that such an implication is justified. Petitioner is being sent to jail for the express reason that he has associated with people who have entertained unlawful ideas and said unlawful things, and that of course is a direct abridgment of his freedoms of speech and assembly—under any definition that has ever been used for that term. Nevertheless, even as to this admittedly direct abridgment, the Court relies upon its prior decisions to the effect that the Government has power to abridge speech and assembly if its interest in doing so is sufficient to outweigh the interest in protecting these First Amendment freedoms.

This, I think, demonstrates the unlimited breadth and danger of the "balancing test" as it is currently being applied by a majority of this Court. Under the "test," the question in every case in which a First Amendment right is asserted is not whether there has been an abridgment of that right, not whether the abridgment of the right was intentional on the part of the Government, and not whether there is any other way in which the Government could accomplish a lawful aim without an invasion of the constitutionally guaranteed rights of the people. It is, rather, simply whether the Government has an interest in abridging the right involved and, if so, whether that interest is of sufficient importance, in the opinion of a majority of this Court, to justify the Government's action in doing so. This doctrine, to say the very least, is capable of being used to justify almost any action Government may wish to take to suppress First Amendment freedoms.

MR. JUSTICE DOUGLAS, dissenting:

When we allow petitioner to be sentenced to prison for six years for being a "member" of the Communist Party, we make a sharp break with traditional concepts of First Amendment rights and make serious Mark Twain's lighthearted comment that "It is by the goodness of God that in our Country we have those three unspeakably precious things: freedom of speech, freedom of conscience, and the prudence never to practice either of them." . . . There is here no charge of conspiracy, no charge of any overt act to overthrow the Government by force and violence, no charge of any other criminal act. The charge is being a "member" of the Communist Party "well-knowing" that it advocated the overthrow of the Government by force and violence, "said defendant intending to bring about such overthrow by force and violence as speedily as circumstances would permit." That falls far short of a charge of conspiracy. Conspiracy rests not in intention alone but in an agreement with one or more others to promote an unlawful project. . . . No charge of any kind or sort of agreement hitherto embraced in the concept of a conspiracy is made here.

We legalize today guilt by association, sending a man to prison when he committed no unlawful act. . . .

The case is not saved by showing that petitioner was an active member. None of the activity constitutes a crime. . . .

Not one single illegal act is charged to petitioner. That is why the essence of the crime covered by the indictment is merely belief—belief in the proletarian revolution, belief in Communist creed. . . .

Nothing but beliefs are on trial in this case. They are unpopular and to most of us revolting. But they are nonetheless ideas or dogma or faith within the broad framework of the First Amendment. . . .

MR. JUSTICE BRENNAN, with whom THE CHIEF JUSTICE and MR. JUSTICE DOUGLAS join, dissenting:

I think that in Section 4 (f) of the Internal Security Act Congress legislated immunity from prosecution under the membership clause of the Smith Act. The first sentence of Section 4 (f) is: "Neither the holding of office nor membership in any Communist organization by any person shall constitute per se a violation of subsection (a) or subsection (c) of this section or of any other criminal statute." The immunity granted by that sentence is not in my view restricted, as the Court holds, to mere membership, that is to membership which is nominal, passive or theoretical. . . .

GIBSON *v.* FLORIDA LEGISLATIVE INVESTIGATION COMMITTEE
372 U.S. 539; 83 Sup. Ct. 889; 9 L. E. 2d 929 (1963)

MR. JUSTICE GOLDBERG delivered the opinion of the Court:

The petitioner, then president of the Miami branch of the NAACP, was ordered to appear before the respondent Committee on November 4, 1959. . . . Prior to interrogation of any witnesses the Committee chairman read the text of the statute creating the Committee and declared that the hearings would be "concerned with the activities of various organizations which have been or are presently operating in this State in the fields of, first, race relations; second, the coercive reform of social and educational practices and mores by litigation and pressured administrative action; third, of labor; fourth, of education; fifth, and other vital phases of life in this State." The chairman also stated that the inquiry would be directed to Communists and Communist activities, including infiltration of Communists into organizations operating in the described fields.

Upon being called to the stand, the petitioner admitted that he was custodian of his organization's membership records. . . . The petitioner told the Committee that he had not brought these records with him to the hearing and announced that he would not produce them for the purpose of answering questions concerning membership in the NAACP. . . . The petitioner's refusal to produce his organization's membership lists was based on the ground that to bring the lists to the hearing and to utilize them as the basis of his testimony would interfere with the free exercise of Fourteenth Amendment association rights of members and prospective members of the NAACP.

In accordance with Florida procedure, the petitioner was brought before a state court and, after a hearing, was adjudged in contempt. . . . The Florida Supreme Court sustained the judgment below. . . .

We are here called upon once again to resolve a conflict between individual rights of free speech and association and governmental interest in conducting legislative investigations. Prior decisions illuminate the contending principles. This Court has repeatedly held that rights of association are within the ambit of the constitutional protections afforded by the First and Fourteenth Amendments. *NAACP* v. *Alabama.* . . . "It is beyond debate that freedom to engage in association for the advancement of beliefs and ideas is an inseparable aspect of the 'liberty' assured by the Due Process Clause of the Fourteenth Amendment, which embraces freedom of speech.". . . And it is equally clear that the guarantee encompasses protection of privacy of association in organizations such as that of which the petitioner is president; indeed, in both the Bates and Alabama cases, this Court held NAACP membership lists of the very type here in question to be beyond the States' power of discovery in the circumstances there presented. . . . And, as declared in *NAACP* v. *Alabama,* "It is hardly a novel perception that compelled disclosure of affiliation with groups engaged in advocacy may constitute [an] . . . effective . . . restraint on freedom of association. . . . This Court has recognized the vital relationship between freedom to associate and privacy in one's associations. . . . Inviolability of privacy in group association may in many circumstances be indispensable to preservation of freedom of association, particularly where a group espouses dissident beliefs." So it is here.

At the same time, however, this Court's prior holdings demonstrate that there can be no question that the State has power adequately to inform itself—through legislative investigation, if it so desires—in order to act and protect its legitimate and vital interests. As this Court said in considering the propriety of the congressional inquiry challenged in *Watkins* v. *United States,* . . . "The power . . . to conduct investigations is inherent in the legislative process. That power is broad. It encompasses inquiries concerning the administration of existing laws as well as proposed or possibly needed statutes. It includes surveys of defects in our social, economic or political system for the purpose of enabling the Congress to remedy them". . . It is no less obvious, however, that the legislative power to investigate, broad as it may be, is not without limit. The fact that the general scope of the inquiry is authorized and permissible does not compel the conclusion that the investigatory body is free to inquire into or demand all forms of information. Validation of the broad subject matter under investigation does not necessarily carry with it automatic and wholesale validation of all individual questions, subpoenas, and documentary demands. . . . When, as in this case, the claim is made that particular legislative inquiries and demands infringe substantially upon First and Fourteenth Amendment associational rights of individuals, the courts are called upon to, and must, determine the permissibility of the challenged actions. . . . "[T]he delicate and difficult task falls upon the courts to weigh the circumstances and to appraise the substantiality of the reasons advanced in support of the regulation of the free enjoyment of the rights.". . . The interests here at stake are of significant magnitude, and neither their resolution nor impact is limited to, or dependent upon, the particular parties here involved. Freedom and viable government are both, for this purpose, indivisible concepts; whatever affects the rights of the parties here, affects all. . . . It is an essential prerequisite to the validity of an investigation which intrudes into the area of constitutionally protected rights of speech, press, association, and petition that the State convincingly show a substantial relation between the information sought and a subject of overriding and compelling state interest. Absent such a relation between the NAACP and conduct in which the State may have a compelling regulatory concern, the Committee has not "demonstrated so cogent an interest in obtaining and making public" the membership information sought to be obtained as to "justify the substantial abridgment of associational freedom which such disclosures will effect." *Bates* v. *Little Rock*. . . . "Where there is a significant encroachment upon personal liberty, the State may prevail only upon showing a subordinating interest which is compelling." Ibid.

Applying these principles to the facts of this case, the respondent Committee contends that the prior decisions of this Court . . . compel a result here upholding the legislative right of inquiry. In *Barenblatt, Wilkinson,* and *Braden,* however, it was a refusal to answer a question or questions concerning the witness' *own* past or present membership in *the Communist Party* which supported his conviction. It is apparent that the necessary preponderating governmental interest and, in fact, the very result in those cases were founded on the holding that the Communist Party is not an ordinary or legitimate political party, as known in this country, and that, because of its particular nature, membership therein is *itself* a permissible subject of regulation and legislative scrutiny. Assuming the correctness of the premises on which those cases were decided, no further demonstration of compelling governmental interests was deemed necessary, since the direct object of the challenged questions there was discovery of membership in the Communist Party, a matter held pertinent to a proper subject then under inquiry.

Here, however, it is not alleged Communists who are the witnesses before the Committee and it is not discovery of their membership in that party which is the object of the challenged inquiries. Rather, it is the NAACP itself which is the subject of the investigation, and it is its local president, the petitioner, who was called before the Committee and held in contempt because he refused to divulge the contents of its membership records. There is no suggestion that the Miami branch of the NAACP or the national organization with which it is affiliated was, or is, itself a subversive organization. Nor is there any indication that the activities or policies of the NAACP were either Communist dominated or influenced. . . .

Moreover, even to say, as in *Barenblatt,* . . . that it is permissible to inquire into the subject of Communist infiltration of educational or other organizations does not mean that it is permissible to demand or require from such other groups disclosure of their membership by inquiry into their records when such disclosure will seriously inhibit or impair the exercise of constitutional rights and has not itself been demonstrated to bear a crucial relation to a proper governmental interest or to be essential to fulfillment of a proper governmental purpose. The prior holdings that governmental interest in controlling subversion and the particular character of the Communist Party and its objectives outweigh the right of individual Communists to conceal party membership or affiliations by no means require the wholly different conclusion that other groups—concededly legitimate—automatically forfeit their rights to privacy of association simply because the general subject matter of the legislative inquiry is Communist subversion or infiltration. . . .

. . . We rest our result on the fact that the record in this case is insufficient to show a substantial connection between the Miami branch of the NAACP and Communist *activities* which the respondent Committee itself concedes is an essential prerequisite to demonstrating the immediate, substantial, and subordinating state interest necessary to sustain its right of inquiry into the membership lists of the association. . . .

Nothing we say here impairs or denies the existence of the underlying legislative right to investigate or legislate with respect to subversive activities by Communists or anyone else; our decision today deals only with the manner in which such power may be exercised and we hold simply that groups which themselves are neither engaged in subversive or other illegal or improper activities nor demonstrated to have any substantial connections with such activities are to be protected in their rights of free and private association. As declared in *Sweezy* v. *New Hamsphire* . . . (opinion of the Chief Justice), "It is particularly important that the exercise of the power of compulsory process be carefully circumscribed when the investigative process tends to impinge upon such highly sensitive areas as freedom of speech or press, freedom of political association, and freedom of communication of ideas.". . .

To permit legislative inquiry to proceed on less than an adequate foundation would be to sanction unjustified and unwarranted intrusions into the very heart of the constitutional privilege to be secure in associations in legitimate organizations engaged in the exercise of First and Fourteenth Amendment rights; to impose a lesser standard than we here do would be inconsistent with the maintenance of those essential conditions basic to the preservation of our democracy.

The judgment below must be and is

Reversed.

MR. JUSTICE BLACK, *concurring:*

. . . Since, as I believe, the National Association for the Advancement of Colored People and its members have a constitutional right to choose their own associates, I cannot understand by what constitutional authority Florida can compel answers to questions which abridge that right. Accordingly, I would reverse here on the ground that there has been a direct abridgment of the right of association of the National Association for the Advancement of Colored People and its members. But, since the Court assumes for purposes of this case that there was not direct abridgment of First Amendment freedoms, I concur in the Court's opinion, which is based on constitutional principles laid down in *Schneider* v. *Irvington* . . . and later cases of this Court following *Schneider.*

MR. JUSTICE DOUGLAS, concurring:

I join the opinion of the Court, because it is carefully written within the framework of our current decisions. But since the matters involved touch constitutional rights and since I see the Constitution in somewhat different dimensions than are reflected in our decisions, it seems appropriate to set out my views. . . .

When the constitutional limits of lawmaking are passed, investigation is out of bounds. . . . That is to say, investigations by a legislative commitee which "could result in no valid legislation on the subject" are beyond the pale. . . . In my view, government is not only powerless to legislate with respect to membership in a lawful organization; it is also precluded from probing the intimacies of spiritual and intellectual relationships in the myriad of such societies and groups that exist in this country, regardless of the legislative purpose sought to be served. "[T]he provisions of the First Amendment . . . of course reach and limit . . . investigations." *Barenblatt* v. *United States.* . . . If this is not true I see no barrier to investigation of newspapers, churches, political parties, clubs, societies, unions, and any other association for their political, economic, social, philosophical, or religious views. If, in its quest to determine whether existing laws are being enforced or new laws are needed, an investigating committee can ascertain whether known Communists or criminals are members of an organization not shown to be engaged in conduct properly subject to regulation, it is but a short and inexorable step to the conclusion that it may also probe to ascertain what effect they have had on the other members. For how much more "necessary and appropriate" this information is to the legislative purpose being pursued!

It is no answer to the conclusion that all such investigations are illegal to suggest that the committee is pursuing a lawful objective in the manner it has determined most appropriate. For, as Laurent Frantz, "The First Amendment in the Balance," 71 *Yale L.J.* 1424, 1441, has so persuasively shown, "it does not follow that any objective can ever be weighed against an express limitation on the means available for its pursuit. The public interest in the suppression of crime, for example, cannot be weighed against a constitutional provision that accused persons may not be denied the right to counsel." When otherwise valid legislation is sought to be applied in an unconstitutional manner we do not sustain its application. A different test should not obtain for legislative investigations. "[A]ny constitutional limitation serves a significant function only insofar as it stands in the way of something which government thinks ought to be done. Nothing else needs to be prohibited." Frantz, supra, at 1445. . . .

There is no other course consistent with the Free Society envisioned by the First Amendment. For the views a citizen entertains, the beliefs he harbors, the utterances he makes, the ideology he embraces and the people he associates with are no concern of government. That article of faith marks indeed the main difference between the Free Society which we espouse and the dictatorships both on the Left and on the Right. . . .

Government can intervene only when belief, thought, or expression moves into the realm of action that is inimical to society. . . .

MR. JUSTICE HARLAN, whom MR. JUSTICE CLARK, MR. JUSTICE STEWART, and MR. JUSTICE WHITE join, dissenting:

The difficulties with this decision will become apparent once the case is deflated to its true size.

The essential facts are these. For several years before petitioner was convicted of this contempt, the respondent, a duly authorized Committee of the Florida Legislature, had been investigating alleged Communist "infiltration" into various organizations in Dade County, Florida, including the Miami Branch of the National Association for the Advancement of Colored People. There was no suggestion that the branch itself had engaged in any subversive or other illegal activity, but the Committee had developed information indicating that fourteen of the fifty-two present or past residents of Dade County, apparently at one time or another members of the Communist Party or connected organizations, were or had been members or had "participated in the meetings and other affairs" of this local branch of the NAACP.

Having failed to obtain from prior witnesses, other than its own investigator, any significant data as to the truth or falsity of this information, the Committee, in 1959, summoned the petitioner to testify, also requiring that he bring with him the membership records of the branch. Petitioner, a Negro clergyman, was then and for the past five years had been president of the local branch, and his custodianship of the records stands conceded.

On his appearance before the Committee petitioner was asked to consult these records himself and, after doing so, to inform the Committee which, if any, of the fifty-two individually identified persons were or had been members of the NAACP Miami Branch. He declined to do this. . . .

I

This Court rests reversal on its finding that the Committee did not have sufficient justification for including the Miami Branch of the NAACP within the ambit of its investigation—that, in the language of our cases *(Uphaus* v. *Wyman, . . .)* an adequate "nexus" was lacking between the NAACP and the subject matter of the Committee's inquiry.

The Court's reasoning is difficult to grasp. I read its opinion as basically proceeding on the premise that the governmental interest in investigating Communist infiltration into admittedly nonsubversive organizations, as distinguished from investigating organizations themselves suspected of subversive activities, is not sufficient to overcome the countervailing right to freedom of association. . . . On this basis "nexus" is seemingly found lacking because it was never claimed that the NAACP Miami Branch had itself engaged in subversive activity . . . and because none of the Committee's evidence relating to any of the fifty-two alleged Communist Party members was sufficient to attribute such activity to the local branch or to show that it was dominated, influenced, or used "by Communists.". . .

But, until today, I had never supposed that any of our decisions relating to state or federal power to investigate in the field of Communist subversion could possibly be taken as suggesting any difference in the degree of governmental investigatory interest as between Communist infiltration *of* organizations and Communist activity *by* organizations. See, e.g., *Barenblatt* v. *United States* . . . (infiltration into education); *Wilkinson* v. *United States* and *Braden* v. *United States,* . . . (infiltration into basic industries). . . .

Given the unsoundness of the basic premise underlying the Court's holding as to the absence of "nexus," this decision surely falls of its own weight. For unless "nexus" requires an investigating agency to prove in advance the very things it is trying to find out, I do not understand how it can be said that the information preliminarily developed by the Committee's investigator was not sufficient to satisfy, under any reasonable test, the requirement of "nexus."

II

I also find it difficult to see how this case really presents any serious question as to interference with freedom of association. Given the willingness of the petitioner to testify from recollection as to individual memberships in the local branch of the NAACP, the germaneness of the membership records to the subject matter of the Committee's investigation, and the limited purpose for which their use was sought—as an aid to refreshing the witness' recollection, involving their divulgence only to the petitioner himself. . . —this case of course bears no resemblance whatever to *NAACP* v. *Alabama* or *Bates* v. *Little Rock.* . . . In both of those cases the State had sought general divulgence of local NAACP membership lists without any showing of a justifying state interest. In effect what we are asked to hold here is that the petitioner had a constitutional right to give only partial or inaccurate testimony, and that indeed seems to me the true effect of the Court's holding today. . . .

I would affirm.

MR. JUSTICE WHITE, dissenting:

In my view, the opinion of the Court represents a serious limitation upon the Court's previous cases dealing with this subject matter and upon the right of the legislature to investigate the Communist Party and its activities. Although one of the classic and recurring activities of the Communist Party is the infiltration and subversion of other organizations, either openly or in a clandestine manner, the Court holds that even where a legislature has evidence that a legitimate organization is under assault and even though that organization is itself sounding open and public alarm, an investigating committee is nevertheless forbidden to compel the organization or its members to reveal the fact, or not, of membership in that organization of named Communists assigned to the infiltrating task. . . .

The net effect of the Court's decision is, of course, to insulate from effective legislative inquiry and preventive legislation the time-proven skills of the Communist Party in subverting and eventually controlling legitimate organizations. Until such a group, chosen as an object of Communist Party action, has been effectively reduced to vassalage, legislative bodies may seek no information from the organization under attack by duty-bound Communists. When the job has been done and the legislative committee can prove it, it then has the hollow privilege of recording another victory for the Communist Party, which both Congress and this Court have found to be an organization under the direction of a foreign power, dedicated to the overthrow of the Government if necessary by force and violence.

I respectfully dissent.

KEYISHIAN *v.* BOARD OF REGENTS OF THE UNIVERSITY OF THE STATE OF NEW YORK

385 U.S. 589; 87 Sup. Ct. 675; 17 L. Ed. 2d 629 (1967)

MR. JUSTICE BRENNAN delivered the opinion of the Court:

Appellants were members of the faculty of the privately owned and operated University of Buffalo, and became state employees when the University was merged in 1962 into the State University of New York, an institution of higher education owned and operated by the State of New York. As faculty members of the State University their continued employment was conditioned upon their compliance with a New York plan, formulated partly in statutes and partly in administrative regulations, which the State utilizes to prevent the appointment or retention of "subversive" persons in state employment. . . .

Appellants brought this action for declaratory and injunctive relief alleging that the state program violated the Federal Constitution in various respects.

We considered some aspects of the constitutionality of the New York plan fifteen years ago in *Adler* v. *Board of Education*. . . .

Adler was a declaratory judgment suit in which the Court held, in effect, that there was no constitutional infirmity in former Section 12 (a) or in the Feinberg Law on their faces and that they were capable of constitutional application. But the contention urged in this case that both Sections 3021 and 105 are unconstitutionally vague was not heard or decided. Section 3021 of the Education Law was challenged in *Adler* as unconstitutionally vague, but because the challenge had not been made in the pleadings or in the proceedings in the lower courts, this Court refused to consider it. Nor was any challenge on grounds of vagueness made in *Adler* as to subsections (1) (a) and (b) of Section 105 of the Civil Service Law. Subsection (3) of Section 105 was not added until 1958. Appellants in this case timely asserted below the unconstitutionality of all these sections on grounds of vagueness and that question is now properly before us for decision. Moreover, to the extent that *Adler* sustained the provision of the Feinberg Law constituting membership in an organization advocating forceful overthrow of government a ground for disqualification, pertinent constitutional doctrines have since rejected the premises upon which that conclusion rested. *Adler* is therefore not dispositive of the constitutional issues we must decide in this case. . . .

Section 3021 requires removal for "treasonable or seditious" utterances or acts. The 1958 amendment to Section 105 of the Civil Service Law, now subsection 3 of that section, added such utterances or acts as a ground for removal under that law also. The same wording is used in both statutes—that "the utterance of any treasonable or seditious word or words or the doing of any treasonable or seditious act or acts" shall be ground for removal. . . . Our experience under the Sedition Act of 1798 taught us that dangers fatal to First Amendment freedoms inhere in the word "seditious." See *New York Times Co.* v. *Sullivan*. . . . The teacher cannot know the extent, if any, to which a "seditious" utterance must transcend mere statement about abstract doctrine, the extent to which it must be intended to and tend to indoctrinate or incite to action in furtherance of the defined doctrine. The crucial consideration is that no teacher can know just where the line is drawn between "seditious" and nonseditious utterances and acts.

Other provisions of Section 105 also have

the same defect of vagueness. Subsection (1) (a) of Section 105 bars employment of any person who "by word of mouth or writing wilfully and deliberately advocates, advises or teaches the doctrine" of forceful overthrow of government. This provision is plainly susceptible to sweeping and improper application. It may well prohibit the employment of one who merely advocates the doctrine in the abstract without any attempt to indoctrinate others, or incite others to action in furtherance of unlawful aims. . . . And in prohibiting "advising" and "doctrine" of unlawful overthrow does the statute prohibit mere "advising" and "advising" of the existence of the doctrine, or advising another to support the doctrine? Since "advocacy" of the doctrine of forceful overthrow is separately prohibited, need the person "teaching" or "advising" this doctrine himself "advocate" it? Does the teacher who informs his class about the precepts of Marxism or the Declaration of Independence violate this prohibition?

Similar uncertainty arises as to the application of subsection (1) (b) of Section 105. That subsection requires the disqualification of an employee involved with the distribution of written material "containing or advocating, advising or teaching the doctrine" of forceful overthrow, and who himself "advocates, advises, teaches, or embraces the duty, necessity or propriety of adopting the doctrine contained therein." Here again, mere advocacy of abstract doctrine is apparently included. And does the prohibition of distribution of matter "containing" the doctrine bar histories of the evolution of Marxist doctrine or tracing the background of the French, American, and Russian revolutions? The additional requirement, that the person participating in distribution of the material be one who "advocates, advises, teaches, or embraces the duty, necessity or propriety of adopting the doctrine" of forceful overthrow, does not alleviate the uncertainty in the scope of the section, but exacerbates it. Like the language of Section 105 (1) (a), this language may reasonably be construed to cover mere expression of belief. For example, does the university librarian who recommends the reading of such materials thereby "advocate the propriety of adopting the doctrine contained therein?"

We do not have the benefit of a judicial gloss by the New York courts enlightening us as to the scope of this complicated plan. In light of the intricate administrative machinery for its enforcement, this is not surprising. The very intricacy of the plan and the uncertainty as to the scope of its proscriptions make it a highly efficient *in terrorem* mechanism. It would be a bold teacher who would not stay as far as possible from utterance or acts which might jeopardize his living by enmeshing him in this intricate machinery. The uncertainty as to the utterances and acts proscribed increases that caution in "those who believe the written law means what it says." *Baggett* v. *Bullitt.* . . . The result must be to stifle "that free play of the spirit which all teachers ought especially to cultivate and practice. . . ." That probability is enhanced by the provisions requiring an annual review of every teacher to determine whether any utterance or act of his, inside the classroom or out, came within the sanctions of the laws. For a memorandum warns employees that under the statutes "subversive" activities may take the form of "the writing of articles, the distribution of pamphlets, the endorsement of speeches made or articles written or acts performed by others," and reminds them "that it is the primary duty of the school authorities in each school district to take positive action to eliminate from the school system any teacher in whose case there is evidence that he is guilty of subversive activity. School authorities are under obligation to proceed immediately and conclusively in every such case."

There can be no doubt of the legitimacy of New York's interest in protecting its education system from subversion. But "even though the government purpose be legitimate and substantial, that purpose cannot be pursued by means that broadly stifle fundamental personal liberties when the end can be more narrowly achieved." *Shelton* v. *Tucker*. . . . The principle is not inapplicable because the legislation is aimed at keeping subversives out of the teaching ranks. In *DeJonge* v. *State of Oregon* . . . the Court said:

> "The greater the importance of safeguarding the community from incitements to the overthrow of our institu-

tions by force and violence, the more imperative is the need to preserve inviolate the constitutional rights of free speech, free press and free assembly in order to maintain the opportunity for free political discussion, to the end that government may be responsive to the will of the people and that changes, if desired, may be obtained by peaceful means. Therein lies the security of the Republic, the very foundation of constitutional government."

Our Nation is deeply committed to safeguarding academic freedom, which is of transcendent value to all of us and not merely to the teachers concerned. That freedom is therefore a special concern of the First Amendment, which does not tolerate laws that cast a pall of orthodoxy over the classroom. "The vigilant protection of constitutional freedoms is nowhere more vital than in the community of American schools." *Shelton* v. *Tucker*. . . . The classroom is peculiarly the "marketplace of ideas." The Nation's future depends upon leaders trained through wide exposure to that robust exchange of ideas which discovers truth "out of a multitude of tongues, [rather] than through any kind of authoritative selection.". . . In *Sweezy* v. *State of New Hampshire,* we said:

> "The essentiality of freedom in the community of American universities is almost self-evident. No one should underestimate the vital role in a democracy that is played by those who guide and train our youth. To impose any strait jacket upon the intellectual leaders in our colleges and universities would imperil the future of our Nation. No field of education is so thoroughly comprehended by man that new discoveries cannot yet be made. Particularly is that true in the social sciences, where few, if any, principles are accepted as absolutes. Scholarship cannot flourish in an atmosphere of suspicion and distrust. Teachers and students must always remain free to inquire, to study and to evaluate, to gain new maturity and understanding; otherwise our civilization will stagnate and die."

We emphasize once again that "[p]recision of regulation must be the touchstone in an area so closely touching our most precious freedoms." *NAACP* v. *Button*. . . . "For standards of permissible statutory vagueness are strict in the area of free expression. . . . Because First Amendment freedoms need breathing space to survive, government may regulate in the area only with narrow specificity.". . . New York's complicated and intricate scheme plainly violates that standard. When one must guess what conduct or utterance may lose him his position, one necessarily will 'steer far wider of the unlawful zone. . . ." *Speiser* v. *Randall*. . . . For "The threat of sanctions may deter . . . almost as potently as the actual application of sanctions." *NAACP* v. *Button*. . . . The danger of that chilling effect upon the exercise of vital First Amendment rights must be guarded against by sensitive tools which clearly inform teachers what is being sanctioned. . . .

The regulatory maze created by New York is wholly lacking in "terms susceptible of objective measurement." *Cramp* v. *Board of Public Instruction*. . . . It has the quality of "extraordinary ambiguity" found to be fatal to the oaths considered in *Cramp* and *Baggett* v. *Bullitt*. "[M]en of common intelligence must necessarily guess at its meaning and differ as to its application. . . ." *Baggett* v. *Bullitt*. . . . Vagueness of wording is aggravated by prolixity and profusion of statutes, regulations, and administrative machinery, and by manifold cross-references to interrelated enactments and rules.

We therefore hold that Section 3021 of the Education Law and subsections (1) (a), (1) (b) and (3) of Section 105 of the Civil Service Law as implemented by the machinery created pursuant to Section 3022 of the Education Law are unconstitutional.

Appellants have also challenged the constitutionality of the discrete provisions of subsection (1) (c) of Section 105 and subsection (2) of the Feinberg Law, which make Communist Party membership, as such, prima facie evidence of disqualification. . . . Subsection (2) of the Feinberg Law was, however, before the Court in *Adler* and its *constitutionality* was sustained. But constitutional doctrine which has emerged since that decision has rejected its major premise. That premise was that public employment, including academic employment, may be conditioned upon the surrender of constitutional rights which could not be abridged by direct government action. . . . the Court said in *Adler* . . . that a teacher denied employment because of membership in a listed organization "is not thereby denied the right of free speech and assembly. His freedom of choice between membership in the organization and employment in the school system might be limited, but not his freedom of speech or assembly, except in the remote sense that limitation is inherent in every choice."

However, the Court of Appeals for the Second Circuit correctly said in an earlier stage of this case, ". . . the theory that public employment which may be denied altogether may be subjected to any conditions, regardless of how unreasonable, has been uniformly rejected.". . . Indeed, that theory was expressly rejected in a series of decisions following *Adler.* See *Wieman* v. *Updergraff*. . . *Cramp* v. *Board of Public Instruction; Baggett* v. *Bullitt; Shelton* v. *Tucker; Speiser* v. *Randall.* In *Sherbert* v. *Verner,* . . . we said: "It is too late in the day to doubt that the liberties of religion and expression may be infringed by the denial of or placing of conditions upon a benefit or privilege."

We proceed then to the question of the validity of the provisions of subsection (c) of Section 105 and subsection (2) of Section 3022, barring employment to members of listed organizations. Here again constitutional doctrine has developed since *Adler.* Mere knowing membership without a specific intent to further the unlawful aims of an organization is not a constitutionally adequate basis for exclusion from such positions as those held by appellants.

In *Elfbrandt* v. *Russell,* . . . we said, "Those who join an organization but do not share its unlawful purposes and who do not participate in its unlawful activities surely pose no threat, either as citizens or as public employees." We there struck down a statutorily required oath binding the state employee not to become a member of the Communist Party with knowledge of its unlawful purpose, on threat of discharge and perjury prosecution if the oath were violated. We found that "[a]ny lingering doubt that proscription of mere knowing membership, without any showing of 'specific intent,' would run afoul of the Constitution was set at rest by our decision in *Aptheker* v. *Secretary of State.* . . ." In *Aptheker* we held that Party membership, without knowledge of the Party's unlawful purposes *and* specific intent to further its unlawful aims, could not constitutionally warrant deprivation of the right to travel abroad. As we said in *Schneidermann* v. *United States* . . . "[U]nder our traditions beliefs are personal and not a matter of mere association, and . . . men in adhering to a political party or other organization notoriously do not subscribe unqualifiedly to all of its platforms or asserted principles." "A law which applies to membership without the 'specific intent' to further the illegal aims of the organization infringes unnecessarily on protected freedoms. It rests on the doctrine of 'guilt by association' which has no place here.". . . Thus mere Party membership, even with knowledge of the Party's unlawful goals, cannot suffice to justify criminal punishment, see *Scales* v. *United States* . . . ; *Yates* v. *United States;* nor may it warrant a finding of moral unfitness justifying disbarment. *Schware* v. *Board of Bar Examiners.* . . .

These limitations clearly apply to a provision, like Section 105(1) (c), which blankets all state employees, regardless of the "sensitivity" of their positions. But even the Feinberg Law provision, applicable primarily to activities of teachers, who have captive audiences of young minds, are subject to these limitations in favor of freedom of expression and association; the stifling effect on the academic mind from curtailing freedom of association in such manner is manifest, and has been documented in recent studies. *Elfbrandt* and *Aptheker* state the governing standard: legislation which sanctions membership unaccompanied by specific intent to further the unlawful goals of the organization or which is not active membership violates constitutional limitations.

Measured against this standard, both Civil Service Law Section 105(1) (c) and Education Law Section 3022(2) sweep overbroadly into association which may not be sanctioned. . . .

They seek to bar employment both for

association which legitimately may be sanctioned and for association which may not be sanctioned consistently with First Amendment rights. Where statutes have an overbroad sweep, just as where they are vague, "the hazard of loss or substantial impairment of those precious rights may be critical," *Dombrowski* v. *Pfister,* since those covered by the statute are bound to limit their behavior to that which is unquestionably safe. As we said in *Shelton* v. *Tucker,* "The breadth of legislative abridgment must be viewed in the light of less drastic means for achieving the same basic purpose."

We therefore hold that Civil Service Law Section 105(1) (c) and Education Law Section 3022(2) are invalid insofar as they sanction mere knowing membership without any showing of specific intent to further the unlawful aims of the Communist Party of the United States or of the State of New York.

The judgment of the District Court is reversed and the case is remanded for further proceedings consistent with this opinion.

Reversed and remanded.

MR. JUSTICE CLARK, with whom MR. JUSTICE HARLAN, MR. JUSTICE STEWART and MR. JUSTICE WHITE join, dissenting:

The blunderbuss fashion in which the majority couches "its artillery of words" together with the morass of cases it cites as authority and the obscurity of their application to the question at hand makes it difficult to grasp the true thrust of its decision. At the outset, it is therefore necessary to focus on its basis.

This is a declaratory judgment action testing the *application* of thc Feinberg Law to appellants. The certificate and statement once required by the Board and upon which appellants base their attack were, before the case was tried, abandoned by the Board and are no longer required to be made. Despite this fact the majority proceeds to its decision striking down New York's Feinberg Law and other of its statutes as applied to appellants on the basis of the old certificate and statement. It does not explain how the statute can be applied to appellants under procedures which have been for over two years a dead letter. The issues posed are, therefore, purely abstract and entirely speculative in character. The Court under such circumstances has in the past refused to pass upon constitutional questions. In addition, the appellants have neither exhausted their administrative remedies, nor pursued the remedy of judicial review of agency action as provided earlier by subdivision (d) of Section 12 (a) of the Civil Service Law. Finally, one of the sections stricken, Section 105 (3), has been amended and under its terms will not become effective until September 1, 1967, L.1965, Ch. 1030.)

I

The old certificate upon which the majority operates required all of the appellants, save Starbuck, to answer the query whether they were Communists, and if they were, whether they had communicated that fact to the President of the University. Starbuck was required to answer whether he had ever advised, taught, or been a member of a group which taught or advocated the doctrine that the Government of the United States, or any of its political subdivisions, should be overthrown by force, violence, or any unlawful means. All refused to comply. It is in this nonexistent frame of reference that the majority proceeds to act.

It is clear that the Feinberg Law, in which this Court found "no constitutional infirmity" in 1952, has been given its death blow today. Just as the majority here finds that there "can be no doubt of the legitimacy of New York's interest in protecting its education system from subversion" there can also be no doubt that "the be-all and end-all" of New York's effort is here. And regardless of its correctness neither New York nor the several States that have followed the teaching of *Adler* for some fifteen years, can ever put the pieces together again. No court has ever reached out so far to destroy so much with so little.

II

This court has again and again, since at least 1951, approved procedures either identical or at the least similar to the ones the Court condemns today. In *Garner* v. *Board of Works of Los Angeles,* we held that a public employer was not precluded, simply because it was an agency of the

State, "from inquiring of its employees as to matters that may prove relevant to their fitness and suitability for the public service." 341 U.S., at p. 720. The oath there used practically the same language as the Starbuck statement here and the affidavit reflects the same type of inquiry as was made in the old certificate condemned here. Then in 1952, in *Adler* v. *Board of Education,* this Court passed upon the identical statute condemned here. It, too, was a declaratory judgment action—as in this case. However, there the issues were not so abstractly framed. Our late Brother Minton wrote for the Court:

> "A teacher works in a sensitive area in a schoolroom. There he shapes the attitude of young minds towards the society in which they live. In this, the state has a vital concern. It must preserve the integrity of the schools. That the school authorities have the right and the duty to screen the officials, teachers, and employees as to their fitness to maintain the integrity of the schools as a part of ordered society cannot be doubted." At 493 of 342 U.S.

And again in 1958 the problem was before us in *Beilan* v. *Board of Education,* School District of Philadelphia. There our late Brother Barton wrote for the Court:

> "By engaging in teaching in the public schools, petitioner did not give up his right to freedom of belief, speech or association. He did, however, undertake obligations of frankness, candor and cooperation in answering inquiries made of him by his employing Board examining into his fitness to serve it as a public school teacher."

And on the same day in *Lerner* v. *Casey* . . . our Brother Harlan again upheld the severance of a public employee for the refusal to answer questions concerning his loyalty, and in the same Term my Brother Brennan himself cited *Garner* with approval in *Speiser* v. *Randall.* . . .

Since that time the *Adler* line of cases have been cited again and again with approval: *Shelton* v. *Tucker* . . . in which both *Adler* and *Beilan* were quoted with approval and *Garner* and *Lerner* were cited in a like manner; likewise in *Cramp* v. *Board of Public Instruction,* . . . Adler was quoted twice with approval, and, in a related field where the employee was discharged for refusal to answer questions as to his loyalty after being ordered to do so, the Court cited with approval all of the cases which today it says have been rejected, *i.e., Garner, Adler, Beilan* and *Lerner. Nelson* v. *Los Angeles County.* . . . Later *Konigsberg* v. *State Bar* . . . likewise cited with approval both *Beilan* and *Garner.* And in our decision in In re *Anastaplo* (1961), . . . *Garner, Beilan* and *Lerner* were all referred to. Finally, only two Terms ago my Brother White relied upon *Cramp* which in turn quoted *Adler* with approval twice. See *Baggett* v. *Bullitt.* . . .

In view of this long list of decisions covering over fifteen years of this Court's history, in which no opinion of this Court even questioned the validity of the *Adler* line of cases, it is strange to me that the Court now finds that the "constitutional doctrine which has emerged since . . . has rejected *[Adler's]* major premise." With due respect, as I read them, our cases have done no such thing.

III

Likewise subsection (1) (3) of Section 105 is also inapplicable. It was derived from Section 23 (a) of the Civil Service Law. The latter provision was on the books at the time of the Feinberg Law as well as when *Adler* was decided. The Feinberg Law referred only to Section 12 (a) of the Civil Service Law, not Section 23 (a). Section 12 (a) was later recodified, as subsections (1) (a) and (b) of Section 105 of the Civil Service Law. Section 23 (a) (now Section 105(3)) deals only with the civil divisions of the Civil Service of the State. As the Attorney General tells us, the law before us has to do with the qualifications of college level personnel not covered by Civil Service. The Attorney General also advises that no superintendent, teacher, or employee of the educational system has ever been charged with violating Section 105(3). The Court seems to me to be building straw men.

The majority also says that no challenge or vagueness points were passed upon in *Adler.* A careful examination of the briefs in that case casts considerable doubt on this conclusion.

IV

But even if *Adler* did not decide these questions I would be obliged to answer them in the same way. The only portion of the Feinberg Law which the majority says was not covered there and is applicable to appellants is Sections 105(1) (a), (1) (b) and (1) (c). These have to do with teachers who advocate, advise, or teach the doctrine of overthrow of our Government by force and violence, either orally or in writing. This was the identical conduct that was condemned in *Dennis* v. *United States,* supra. There the Court found the exact verbiage not to be unconstitutionally vague, and that finding was of course not affected by the decision of this Court in *Yates* v. *United States.* The majority makes much over the horribles that might arise from subsection (1) (b) of Section 105 which condemns the printing, publishing, selling etc., of matter containing such doctrine. But the majority fails to state that this action is condemned only *when and if* the teacher also personally advocates, advises, teaches, etc., the necessity or propriety of adopting such doctrine. This places this subsection on the same footing as (1) (a). And the same is true of subsection (1) (c) where a teacher organizes, helps to organize or becomes a member of an organization which teaches or advocates such doctrine, for scienter would also be a necessary ingredient under our opinion in *Garner,* supra. Moreover, membership is only prima facie evidence of disqualification and could be rebutted, leaving the burden of proof on the State. Furthermore, all of these procedures are protected by an adversary hearing with full judicial review.

In the light of these considerations the strained and unbelievable suppositions that the majority poses could hardly occur. As was said in *Dennis,* supra, "we are not convinced that because there may be borderline cases" the State should be prohibited the protection it seeks. Where there is doubt as to one's intent or the nature of his activities we cannot assume that the administrative boards will not give those offended full protection. Furthermore, the courts always sit to make certain that this is done.

The majority says that the Feinberg Law is bad because it has an "overbroad sweep." I regret to say—and I do so with deference—that the majority has by its broadside swept away one of our most precious rights, namely, the right of self-preservation. Our public educational system is the genius of our democracy. The minds of our youth are developed there and the character of that development will determine the future of our land. Indeed, our very existence depends upon it. The issue here is a very narrow one. It is not freedom of speech, freedom of thought, freedom of press, freedom of assembly, or of association, even in the Communist Party. It is simply this: May the State provide that one who after a hearing with full judicial review, is found to wilfully and deliberately advocate, advise, or teach that our Government should be overthrown by force or violence or other unlawful means; or who wilfully and deliberately prints, publishes, etc., any book or paper that so advocates *and who personally* advocates such doctrine himself; or who wilfully and deliberately becomes a member of an organization that advocates such doctrine, is prima facie disqualified from teaching in its university? My answer, in keeping with all of our cases up until today, is "Yes"!

I dissent.

ADDERLEY *v.* FLORIDA

385 U.S. 39; 87 Sup. Ct. 242; 17 L. Ed. 2d 149 (1966)

MR. JUSTICE BLACK delivered the opinion of the Court:

Petitioners, Harriett Louise Adderley and thirty-one other persons, were convicted by a jury in a joint trial in the County Judge's Court of Leon County, Florida, on a charge of "trespass with a malicious and mischievous intent" upon the premises of the county jail contrary to Section 821.18 of the Florida statutes.

. . . Petitioners, apparently all students of the Florida A & M University in Tallahassee, had gone from the school to the jail about a mile away, along with many other students, to "demonstrate" at the jail their protests because of arrests of other protesting students the day before, and perhaps to protest more generally against state and local policies and practices of racial segregation, including segregation of the jail. The county sheriff, legal custodian of the jail and jail grounds, tried to persuade the students to leave the jail grounds. When this did not work, he . . . notified them that they must leave or he would arrest them for trespassing. . . . Some of the students left, but others, including petitioners, remained and they were arrested. . . .

I

Petitioners have insisted from the beginning of these cases that they are controlled and must be reversed because of our prior cases of *Edwards* v. *South Carolina* [1963] and *Cox* v. *Louisiana* [1965]. We cannot agree.

The *Edwards* case, like this one, did come up when a number of persons demonstrated on public property against their State's segregation policies. They also sang hymns and danced, as did the demonstrators in this case. But here the analogies to this case end. In Edwards, the demonstrators went to the South Carolina State Capitol grounds to protest. In this case they went to the jail. Traditionally, state capitol grounds are open to the public. Jails, built for security purposes, are not. The demonstrators at the South Carolina Capitol went in through a public driveway and as they entered they were told by state officials there that they had a right as citizens to go through the State House grounds as long as they were peaceful. Here the demonstrators entered the jail grounds through a driveway used only for jail purposes and without warning to or permission from the sheriff. More importantly, South Carolina sought to prosecute its State Capitol demonstrators by charging them with the common-law crime of breach of the peace. This Court in Edwards took pains to point out at length the indefinite, loose, and broad nature of this charge; indeed, this Court pointed out . . . that the South Carolina Supreme Court had itself declared that the "breach of the peace charge" is "not susceptible of exact definition." South Carolina's power to prosecute, it was emphasized . . ., would have been different had it proceeded under a "precise and narrowly drawn regulatory statute evincing a legislative judgment that certain specific conduct be limited or proscribed" such as, for example, "limiting the periods during which the State House grounds were open to the public . . ." The South Carolina breach-of-the-peace statute was thus struck down as being so broad and all-embracing as to jeopardize speech, press, assembly and petition, under the constitutional doctrine enunciated in *Cantwell* v. *Connecticut* [1940], and followed in many subsequent cases. And it was on this same ground of vagueness that in *Cox* v. *Louisiana* the Louisiana breach-of-the-peace law used to prosecute Cox was invalidated.

The Florida trespass statute under which these petitioners were charged cannot be challenged on this ground. It is aimed at conduct of one limited kind, that is for one person or persons to trespass upon the property of another with a malicious and mischievous intent. There is no lack of notice in this law, nothing to entrap or fool the unwary.

Petitioners seem to argue that the Florida trespass law is void for vagueness because it requires a trespass to be "with a malicious and mischievous intent . . ." But these words do not broaden the scope of trespass so as to make it cover a multitude of types of conduct as does the common-law breach-of-the-peace charge. On the contrary, these words narrow the scope of the offense. . . . The use of these terms in the statute, instead of contributing to uncertainty and misunderstanding, actually makes its meaning more understandable and clear. . . . Disturbed and upset by the arrest of their schoolmates the day before, a large number of Florida A & M students assembled on the school grounds and decided to march down to the county jail. Some apparently wanted to get themselves put in jail too, along with the students already there. A group of around two hundred marched from the school and arrived at the jail singing and clapping. They went directly to the jail door entrance where they were met by a deputy sheriff, evidently surprised by their arrival. He asked them to move back, claiming they were blocking the entrance to the jail and fearing that they might attempt to enter the jail. They moved back part of the way, where they stood or sat, singing, clapping and dancing, on the jail driveway and on an adjacent grassy area upon the jail premises. This particular jail entrance and driveway were not normally used by the public, but by the sheriff's department for transporting prisoners to and from the courts several blocks away and by commercial concerns for servicing the jail. Even after their partial retreat, the demonstrators continued to block vehicular passage over this driveway up to the entrance of the jail.* Someone called the sheriff who was at the moment apparently conferring with one of the state court judges about incidents connected with prior arrests for demonstrations. When the sheriff returned to the jail, he immediately inquired if all was safe inside the jail and was told it was. He then engaged in a conversation with two of the leaders. He told them that they were trespassing upon jail property and that he would give them ten minutes to leave or he would arrest them. Neither of the leaders did anything to disperse the crowd, and one of them told the sheriff that they wanted to get arrested. A local minister talked with some of the demonstrators and told them not to enter the jail, because they could not arrest themselves, but just to remain where they were. After about ten minutes, the sheriff, in a voice loud enough to be heard by all, told the demonstrators that he was the legal custodian of the jail and its premises, that they were trespassing on county property in violation of the law, that they should all leave forthwith or he would arrest them, and that if they attempted to resist arrest, he would charge them with that as a separate offense. Some of the group then left. Others, including all petitioners, did not leave. Some of them sat down. In a few minutes, realizing that the remaining demonstrators had no intention of leaving, the sheriff ordered his deputies to surround those remaining on jail premises and placed them, 107 demonstrators, under arrest. The sheriff unequivocally testified that he did not arrest any person other than those who were on the jail premises. Of the three petitioners testifying, two insisted that they were arrested before they had a chance to leave, had they wanted to, and one testified that she did not intend to leave. The sheriff again explicitly testified that he did not arrest any person who was attempting to leave.

Under the foregoing testimony the jury was authorized to find that the State had proven every essential element of the crime, as it was defined by the state court. That interpretation is, of course, binding on us, leaving only the question of whether conviction of the state offense, thus defined, unconstitutionally deprives petitioners of their rights to freedom of speech, press, assembly or petition. We hold it does not. The sheriff, as jail custodian, had power, as the state courts have here held, to direct that this large crowd of people get off the grounds. There is not a shred of evidence in this record that this power was exercised, or that its exercise was sanctioned by the lower courts, because the sheriff objected to what was being sung or said by the demonstrators or because he disagreed with the objectives of their protest. The record reveals that he objected only to their presence on that part of the jail grounds reserved for jail uses. There is no evidence at all that on any other occasion similarly large groups of the public had been permitted to gather on this portion of the jail grounds

* Although some of the petitioners testified that they had no intention of interfering with vehicular traffic to and from the jail entrance and that they noticed no vehicle trying to enter or leave the driveway, the deputy sheriff testified that it would have been impossible for automobiles to drive up to the jail entrance and that one serviceman, finished with his business in the jail, waited inside because the demonstrators were sitting around and leaning against his truck parked outside. The sheriff testified that the time the demonstrators were there, between 9:30 and 10 A.M. Monday morning, was generally a very busy time for using the jail entrance to transport weekend inmates to the courts and for tradesmen to make service calls on the jail.

for any purpose. Nothing in the Constitution of the United States prevents Florida from even-handed enforcement of its general trespass statute against those refusing to obey the sheriff's order to remove themselves from what amounted to the curtilage of the jailhouse. The State, no less than a private owner of property, has power to preserve the property under its control for the use to which it is lawfully dedicated. For this reason there is no merit to the petitioners' argument that they had a constitutional right to stay on the property, over the jail custodian's objections, because this "area chosen for the peaceful civil rights demonstration was not only 'reasonable' but also particularly appropriate. . . ." Such an argument has as its major unarticulated premise the assumption that people who want to propagandize protests or views have a constitutional right to do so whenever and however and wherever they please. That concept of constitutional law was vigorously and forthrightfully rejected in two of the cases petitioners rely on, *Cox* v. *Louisiana,* supra, at 554–555 and 563–564. We reject it again. The United States Constitution does not forbid a State to control the use of its own property for its own lawful nondiscriminatory purpose.

These judgments are

Affirmed

MR. JUSTICE DOUGLAS, with whom THE CHIEF JUSTICE, MR. JUSTICE BRENNAN, and MR. JUSTICE FORTAS concur, dissenting:

. . . the Court errs in treating the case as if it were an ordinary trespass case or an ordinary picketing case.

The jailhouse, like an executive mansion, a legislative chamber, a courthouse, or the statehouse itself (*Edwards* v. *South Carolina*) is one of the seats of government whether it be the Tower of London, the Bastille, or a small county jail. And when it houses political prisoners or those whom many think are unjustly held, it is an obvious center for protest. The right to petition for the redress of grievances has an ancient history and is not limited to writing a letter or sending a telegram to a congressman; it is not confined to appearing before the local city council, or writing letters to the President or Governor or Mayor. . . . Conventional methods of petitioning may be, and often have been, shut off to large groups of our citizens. Legislators may turn deaf ears; formal complaints may be routed endlessly through a bureaucratic maze; courts may let the wheels of justice grind very slowly. Those who do not control television and radio, those who cannot afford to advertise in newspapers or circulate elaborate pamphlets may have only a more limited type of access to public officials. Their methods should not be condemned as tactics of obstruction and harassment as long as the assembly and petition are peaceable, as these were.

There is no question that petitioners had as their purpose a protest against the arrest of Florida A & M students for trying to integrate public theatres. The sheriff's testimony indicates that he well understood the purpose of the rally. The petitioners who testified unequivocally stated that the group was protesting the arrests, and state and local policies of segregation, including segregation of the jail. This testimony was not contradicted or even questioned. The fact that no one gave a formal speech, that no elaborate handbills were distributed, and that the group was not laden with signs would seem to be immaterial. Such methods are not the *sine qua non* of petitioning for the redress of grievances. The group did sing "freedom" songs. And history shows that a song can be a powerful tool of protest. . . . There was no violence; no threats of violence; no attempted jail break; no storming of a prison; no plan or plot to do anything but protest. The evidence is uncontradicted that the petitioners' conduct did not upset the jailhouse routine; things went on as they normally would. None of the group entered the jail. Indeed, they moved back from the entrance as they were instructed. There was no shoving, no pushing, no disorder or threat of riot. It is said that some of the group blocked part of the driveway leading to the jail entrance. The chief jailer to be sure testified that vehicles would not have been able to use the driveway. Never did the students locate themselves so as to cause interference with persons or vehicles going to or coming from the jail. Indeed, it is undisputed that the sheriff and deputy sheriff, in separate cars, were able to drive up the driveway to the parking places near the entrance and that no one obstructed their path. Further, it is undisputed that the entrance to the jail was not blocked. And wherever the students were requested to move they did so. If there was congestion, the solution was a further request to move to lawns or parking areas, not complete ejection and arrest. The claim is made that a tradesman waited inside the jail because some of the protestants were sitting around and leaning on his truck. The only evidence supporting such a conclusion is the testimony of a deputy sheriff that the tradesman "came to the door and then did not leave." His remaining is just as consistent with a desire to satisfy his curiosity as it is with a restraint. Finally the fact that some of the protestants may have felt their cause so just that they were willing to be arrested for making their protest outside the jail seems wholly irrelevant. A petition is nonetheless a petition, though its futility may make martyrdom attractive.

We do violence to the First Amendment when we permit this "petition for redress of grievances" to be turned into a trespass action. . . . In the first place the jailhouse grounds were not marked with "No Trespassing!" signs, nor does respondent claim that the public was generally excluded from the grounds. Only the sheriff's fiat transformed lawful conduct into an unlawful trespass. To say that a private owner could have done the same if the rally had taken place on private property is to speak of a different case, as an assembly and a petition for redress of grievances run to government not to private proprietors.

. . . When we allow Florida to construe her "malicious trespass" statute to bar a person from going on property knowing it is not his own and to apply that prohibition to public property, we discard *Cox* and *Edwards.* Would the case be any different if, as is common, the demonstration took place outside a building which housed both the jail and the legislative body? I think not.

There may be some public places which are so clearly committed to other purposes that their use for the airing of grievances is anomalous. There may be some instances in which assemblies and petitions for redress of grievances are not consistent with other necessary purposes of public property. A noisy meeting may be out of keeping with the serenity of the statehouse or the quiet of the courthouse. No one, for example, would suggest that the Senate gallery is the proper place for a vociferous protest rally. And, in other cases it may be necessary to adjust the right to petition for redress of grievances to the other interests inhering in the uses to which the public property is normally put. . . . But this is quite different than saying that all public places are off-limits to people with grievances. . . . And it is farther yet from saying that the "custodian" of the public property in his discretion can decide when public places shall be used for the communication of ideas, especially the constitutional right to assemble and petition for redress of grievances. . . . For to place such discretion in any public official, be he the "custodian" of the public property, or the local police commissioner . . . is to place those who assert their First Amendment rights at his mercy.

BRANDENBURG *v.* OHIO

395 U.S. 444; 89 Sup. Ct. 1827; 23 L. Ed. 2d 430 (1969)

[Brandenburg was arrested after he invited a local television station to film a Klan rally at which a few rifles and pistols were waved, hoods were worn, and speeches were made—of which the most exciting seems to have been the following: "We're not a revengent organization, but if our President, our Congress, our Supreme Court, continues to suppress the white, Caucasian race, it's possible that there might have to be some revengence taken."

The Noto *case referred to in the opinion is* Noto *v.* United States, *367 U.S. 290 (1961), in which the Court reversed the conviction of a Communist worker because the evidence consisted almost entirely of the abstract teachings of the Communist party and almost no specific actions by* Noto.].

Per Curiam

The appellant, a leader of a Ku Klux Klan group, was convicted under the Ohio Criminal Syndicalism statute. . . .

The Ohio Criminal Syndicalism Statute was enacted in 1919. From 1917 to 1920, identical or quite similar laws were adopted by twenty States and two territories. In 1927, this Court sustained the constitutionality of California's Criminal Syndicalism Act, the text of which is quite similar to that of the laws of Ohio. *Whitney* v. *California.* The Court upheld the statute on the ground that, without more, "advocating" violent means to effect political and economic change involves such danger to the security of the State that the State may outlaw it. But *Whitney* has been thoroughly discredited by later decisions. These later decisions have fashioned the principle that the constitutional guarantees of free speech and free press do not permit a State to forbid or proscribe advocacy of the use of force or of law violation except where such advocacy is directed to inciting or producing imminent lawless action and is likely to incite or produce such action. As we said in *Noto,* "the mere abstract teaching . . . of the moral propriety or even moral necessity for a resort to force and violence, is not the same as preparing a group for violent action and steeling it to such action." A statute which fails to draw this distinction impermissibly intrudes upon the freedoms guaranteed by the First and Fourteenth Amendments. It sweeps within its condemnation speech which our Constitution has immunized from governmental control. [Cf. *Yates* v. *United States.*]

Measured by this test, Ohio's Criminal Syndicalism Act cannot be sustained. The Act punishes persons who "advocate or teach the duty, necessity, or propriety" of violence "as a means of accomplishing industrial or political reform"; or who publish or circulate or display any book or paper containing such advocacy; or who "justify" the commission of violent acts "with intent to exemplify, spread or advocate the propriety of the doctrines of criminal syndicalism"; or who "voluntarily assemble" with a group formed "to teach or advocate the doctrines of criminal syndicalism." Neither the indictment nor the trial judge's instructions to the jury in any way refined the statute's bald definition of the crime in terms of mere advocacy not distinguished from incitement to imminent lawless action.

Accordingly, we are here confronted with a statute which, by its own words and as applied, purports to punish mere advocacy and to forbid, on pain of criminal punishment, assembly with others merely to advocate the described type of action. Such a statute falls within the condemnation of the First and Fourteenth Amendments. The contrary teaching of *Whitney* cannot be supported, and that decision is therefore overruled.

Reversed.

MR. JUSTICE BLACK, concurring:

I agree with the views expressed by Mr. Justice Douglas in his concurring opinion in this case that the "clear and present danger" doctrine should have no place in the interpretation of the First Amendment. I join the Court's opinion, which, as I understand it, simply cites *Dennis,* but does not indicate any agreement on the Court's part with the "clear and present danger" doctrine on which *Dennis* purported to rely. *[Mr. Justice Douglas concurred.]*

BUCKLEY *v.* VALEO

424 U.S. 1; 96 Sup. Ct. 612; 46 L. Ed. 2d (1976)

[The Federal Elections Campaign Act of 1971 as amended in 1974 contained a large number of provisions:

1. *Contribution Limitations—Individuals and groups may spend no more than $1,000 each and political committees no more than $5,000 each for any single candidate in any single election, and no individual may make more than $25,000 in total annual political contributions.*
2. *Independent Expenditure Limitations—No individual or group may independently spend more than $1,000 per election, "relative to a clearly identified candidate."*
3. *Personal Expenditures—Limits are set on the amount a candidate and his family may spend on his own campaign.*
4. *Campaign Expenditures—Limits are placed on overall spending in primary and general elections.*
5. *Reporting and Disclosure—Public disclosure of the identity of contributors and the nature of campaign expenditures is required.*
6. *Public Financing—Public financing of primary and general elections is provided with major party candidates to receive "full" funding, and "minor" and "new" party candidates to receive federal funds to match funds raised privately.*
7. *Federal Election Commission—A commission is created to enforce these regulations.]*

Per Curiam.

I. Contribution and Expenditure Limitations

The intricate statutory scheme adopted by Congress to regulate federal election campaigns includes restrictions on political contributions and expenditures that apply broadly to all phases of and all participants in the election process. The major contribution and expenditure limitations in the Act prohibit individuals from contributing more than $25,000 in a single year or more than $1,000 to any single candidate for an election campaign and from spending more than $1,000 a year "relative to a clearly identified candidate." Other provisions restrict a candidate's use of personal and family resources in his campaign and limit the overall amount that can be spent by a candidate in campaigning for federal office.

In upholding the constitutional validity of the Act's contribution and expenditure provisions on the ground that those provisions should be viewed as regulating conduct, not speech, the Court of Appeals relied upon *United States* v. *O'Brien*, . . .

We cannot share the view that the present Act's contribution and expenditure limitations are comparable to the restrictions on conduct upheld in *O'Brien*. The expenditure of money simply cannot be equated with such conduct as destruction of a draft card. . . . [T]his Court has never suggested that the dependence of a communication on the expenditure of money operates itself to introduce a nonspeech element or to reduce the exacting scrutiny required by the First Amendment. . . .

A restriction on the amount of money a person or group can spend on political communication during a campaign necessarily reduces the quantity of expression by restricting the number of issues discussed, the depth of their exploration, and the size of the audience reached. This is because virtually every means of communicating ideas in today's mass society requires the expenditure of money.

The electorate's increasing dependence on television, radio, and other mass media for news and information has made these expensive modes of communication indispensible instruments of effective political speech.

The expenditure limitations contained in the Act represent substantial rather than merely theoretical restraints on the quantity and diversity of political speech. . . .

By contrast [a] limitation on the amount of money a person may give to a candidate or campaign organization . . . involves little direct restraint on his political communication, for it permits the symbolic expression of support evidenced by a contribution but does not in any way infringe the contributor's freedom to discuss candidates and issues. While contributions may result in political expression if spent by a candidate or an association to present views to the voters, the transformation of contributions into political debate involves speech by someone other than the contributor. . . .

There is no indication that the contribution limitations imposed by the Act would have any dramatic adverse effect on the funding of campaigns and political associations. The overall effect by the Act's contribution ceilings is merely to require candidates and political committees to raise funds from a greater number of persons and to compel people who would otherwise contribute amounts greater than the statutory limits to expend such funds on direct political expression, rather than to reduce the total amount of money potentially available to promote political expression.

The Act's contribution and expenditure limitations also impinge on protected associational freedoms. Making a contribution, like joining a political party, serves to affiliate a person with a candidate. In addition, it enables like-minded persons to pool their resources in furtherance of common political goals. The Act's contribution ceilings thus limit one important means of associating with a candidate or committee, but leave the contributor free to become a member of any political association and to assist personally in the association's efforts on behalf of candidates. And the Act's contribution limitations permit associations and candidates to aggregate large sums of money to promote effective advocacy. By contrast, the Act's $1,000 limitation on independent expenditures "relative to a clearly identified candidate" precludes most associations from effectively amplifying the voice of their adherents, the original basis for the recognition of First Amendment protection of the freedom of association. . . .

In sum, although the Act's contribution and expenditure limitations both implicate fundamental First Amendment interests, its expenditure ceilings impose significantly more severe restrictions on protected freedoms of political expression and association than do its limitations on financial contributions.

B. Contribution Limitations

. . . In view of the fundamental nature of the right to associate, governmental "action which may have the effect of curtailing the freedom to associate is subject to the closest scrutiny." *NAACP* v. *Alabama*. Yet, it is clear that "[n]either the right to associate nor the right to participate in political activities is absolute." *United States Civil Service Comm'n* v. *National Association of Letter Carriers*. Even a " 'significant interference' with protected rights of political association" may be sustained if the State demonstrates a sufficiently important interest and employs means closely drawn to avoid unnecessary abridgment of associational freedoms. . . .

It is unnecessary to look beyond the Act's primary purpose—to limit the actuality and appearance of corruption resulting from large individual financial contributions—in order to find a constitutionally sufficient justification for the $1,000 contribution limitation. . . . To the extent that large contributions are given to secure political *quid pro quos* from current and potential office holders, the integrity of our system of representative democracy is undermined. Although the scope of such pernicious practices can never be reliably ascertained, the deeply disturbing examples surfacing after the 1972 election demonstrate that the problem is not an illusory one.

Of almost equal concern as the danger of actual *quid pro quo* arrangements is the impact of the appearance of corruption stemming from public awareness of the opportunities for abuse inherent in a regime of large individual financial contributions. . . .

Appellants contend that the contribution limitations must be invalidated because bribery laws and narrowly-drawn disclosure requirements constitute a less restrictive means of dealing with "proven and suspected *quid pro quo* arrangements." But laws making criminal the giving and taking of bribes deal with only the most blatant and specific attempts of those with money to influence governmental action. And while disclosure requirements serve the many salutary purposes discussed elsewhere in this opinion, Congress was surely entitiled to conclude that disclosure was only a partial measure, and that contribution ceilings were a necessary legislative concomitant to deal with the reality or appearance of corruption inherent in a system permitting unlimited financial contributions, even when the identities of the contributors and the amounts of their contributions are fully disclosed.

The Act's $1,000 contribution limitation focuses precisely on the problem of large campaign contributions—the narrow aspect of political association where the actuality and potential for corruption have been identified. . . . Significantly, the Act's contribution limitations in themselves do not undermine to any material degree the potential for robust and effective discussion of candidates and campaign issues by individual citizens, associations, the institutional press, candidates, and political parties.

We find that, under the rigorous standard of review established by our prior decisions, the weighty interests served by restricting the size of financial contributions to political candidates are sufficient to justify the limited effect upon First Amendment freedoms caused by the $1,000 contribution ceiling. . . .

C. Expenditure Limitations

1. The $1,000 Limitation on Expenditures "Relative to a Clearly Identified Candidate."

Section 608(e)(1) provides that "[n]o person may make any expenditure . . . relative to a clearly identified candidate during a calendar year which, when added to all other expenditures made by such person during the year advocating the election or defeat of such candidate, exceeds $1,000." The plain effect of section 608(e)(1) is to prohibit all individuals, who are neither candidates nor owners of institutional press facilities, and all groups, except political parties and campaign organizations, from voicing their views "relative to a clearly identified candidate" through means that entail aggregate expenditures of more than $1,000 during a calendar year. The provision, for example, would make it a federal criminal offense for a person or association to place a single one-quarter page advertisement "relative to a clearly identified candidate" in a major metropolitan newspaper. . . .

We find that the governmental interest in preventing corruption and the appearance of corruption is inadequate to justify section 608(e)(1)'s ceiling on independent expenditures. First, assuming *arguendo* that large independent expenditures pose the same dangers of actual or apparent *quid pro quo* arrangements as do large contributions, section 608(e)(1) does not provide an answer that sufficiently relates to the elimination of those dangers. Unlike the contribution limitations' total ban on the giving of large amounts of money to candidates, section 608(e)(1) prevents only some large expenditures. So long as persons and groups eschew expenditures that in express terms advocate the election or defeat of a clearly identified candidate, they are free to spend as much as they want to promote the candidate and his views. . . . It would naively underestimate the ingenuity and resourcefulness of persons and groups desiring to buy influence to believe that they would have much difficulty devising expenditures that skirted the restriction on express advocacy of election or defeat but nevertheless benefited the candidate's campaign. Yet no substantial societal interest would be served by a loophole-closing provision designed to check corruption that permitted unscrupulous persons and organizations to expend unlimited sums of money in order to obtain improper influence over candidates for elective office. . . .

. . . While the independent expenditure ceiling thus fails to serve any substantial governmental interest in stemming the reality or appearance of corruption in the electoral process, it heavily burdens core First Amendment expression. For the First Amendment right to " 'speak one's mind . . . on all public institutions' " includes the right to engage in " 'vigorous advocacy' no less than 'abstract discussion.' " Advocacy of the election or defeat of candidates for federal office is no less entitled to protection under the First Amendment than the discussion of political policy generally or advocacy of the passage or defeat of legislation.

It is argued, however, that the ancillary governmental interest in equalizing the relative ability of individuals and groups to influence the outcome of elections serves to justify the limitation on express advocacy of the election or defeat of candidates imposed by section 608(e)(1)'s expenditure ceiling. But the concept that government may restrict the speech of some elements of our society in order to enhance the relative voice of others is wholly foreign to the First Amendment, which was designed "to secure 'the widest possible dissemination of information from diverse and antagonistic sources,' " and " 'to assure unfettered interchange of ideas for the bringing about of political and social changes desired by the people.' ". . .

The ceiling on personal expenditures by candidates on their own behalf, like the limitations on independent expenditures contained in section 608(e)(1), imposes a substantial restraint on the ability of persons to engage in protected First Amendment expression. The candidate, no less than any other person, has a First Amendment right to engage in the discussion of public issues and vigorously and tirelessly to advocate his own election and the election of other candidates. . . .

The primary governmental interest served by the Act—the prevention of actual and apparent corruption of the political process—does not support the limitation on the candidate's expenditure of his own personal funds. . . . Indeed, the use of personal funds reduces the candidate's dependence on outside contributions and thereby counteracts the coercive pressures and attendant risks of abuse to which the Act's contribution limitations are directed.

The ancillary interest in equalizing the relative financial resources of candidates competing for elective office, therefore, provides the sole relevant rationale for [an] . . . expenditure ceiling. That interest is clearly not sufficient to justify the provision's infringement of fundamental First Amendment rights. . . . The First Amendment simply cannot tolerate . . . [a] restriction upon the freedom of a candidate to speak without legislative limit on behalf of his own candidacy. We therefore hold that . . . restrictions on a candidate's personal expenditures is unconstitutional.

. . . In sum, the provisions of the Act that impose a $1,000 limitation on contributions to a single candidate, section 608(b)(1), a $5,000 limitation on contributions by a political committee to a single candidate, section 608(b)(2), and a $25,000 limitation on total contributions by an individual during any calendar year, section 608(b)(3), are constitutionally valid. . . . The contribution ceilings . . . serve the basic governmental interest in safeguarding the integrity of the electoral process without directly impinging upon the rights of individual citizens and candidates to engage in political debate and discussion. By contrast, the First Amendment requires the invalidation of the Act's independent expenditure ceiling, section 608(e)(1), its limitation on a candidate's expenditures from his own personal funds, section 608(a), and its celings on overall campaign expenditures, section 608(c). These provisions place substantial and direct restrictions on the ability of candidates, citizens, and associations to engage in protected political expression, restrictions that the First Amendment cannot tolerate.

II. Reporting and Disclosure Requirements

A. General Principles

. . . Unlike the overall limitations on contributions and expenditures, the disclosure requirements impose no ceiling on campaign-related activities. But we have repeatedly found that compelled disclosure, in itself, can seriously infringe on privacy of association and belief guaranteed by the First Amendment, *NAACP* v. *Alabama*. . . .

We long have recognized that significant encroachments on First Amendment rights of the sort that compelled disclosure imposes cannot be justified by a mere showing of some legitimate governmental interest. Since *Alabama* we have required that the subordinating interests of the State must survive exacting scrutiny. . . .

The governmental interests sought to be vindicated by the disclosure requirements . . . fall into three categories. First, disclosure provides the electorate with information "as to where political campaign money comes from and how it is spent by the candidate" in order to aid the voters in evaluating those who seek Federal office. . . .

Second, disclosure requirements deter actual corruption and avoid the appearance of corruption by exposing large contributions and expenditures to the light of publicity. . . .

Third, and not least significant, recordkeeping, reporting and disclosure requirements are an essential means of gathering the data necessary to detect violations of the contribution limitations described above. . . .

It is undoubtedly true that public disclosure of contributions to candidates and political parties will deter some individuals who otherwise might contribute. In some instances, disclosure may even expose contributors to harassment or retaliation. These are not insignificant burdens on individual rights, and they must be weighed carefully against the interests which Congress has sought to promote by this legislation. In this process, we note and agree with appellants' concession that disclosure requirements—certainly in most applications—appear to be the least restrictive means of curbing the evils of campaign ignorance and corruption that Congress found to exist. Appellants argue, however, that the balance tips against disclosure when it is required of contributors to certain [minor] parties and candidates. We turn now to this contention.

B. Application to Minor Parties and Independents

. . . Appellants agree that "the record here does not reflect the kind of focused and insistent harassment of contributors and members that existed in the NAACP cases." They argue, however, that a blanket exemption for minor parties is necessary lest irreparable injury be done before the required evidence can be gathered.

. . . We recognize that unduly strict requirements of proof could impose a heavy burden, but it does not follow that a blanket exemption for minor parties is necessary. Minor parties must be allowed sufficient flexibility in the proof of injury to assure a fair consideration of their claim. . . .

Where it exists the type of chill and harassment identified in *Alabama* can be shown. We cannot assume that courts will be insensitive to similar showings when made in future cases. We therefore conclude that a blanket exemption is not required. . . .

[W]e sustain . . . the disclosure and reporting provisions, . . .

III. Public Financing of Presidential Election Campaigns

[The Court upheld the public financing provisions against claims that they violated the general welfare and due process clauses. The Court argued that Congress was the proper judge of whether such expenditures were in the general welfare and that the statute's differing treatment of major and minor parties did not unfairly or unnecessarily burden the political opportunity of any party or candidate.]

IV. The Federal Election Commission

[The Court struck down the provision of the statute providing that, of the six voting members of the Federal Election Commission, two should be appointed by the President, two by the House, and two by the Senate, on the grounds that under the separation of powers all appointments to such an executive agency must be made by the President.]

[Congress subsequently amended this portion of the act to meet the Court's constitutional objections.]

MR. JUSTICE STEVENS took no part in the consideration or decision of these cases.

MR. CHIEF JUSTICE BURGER, concurring in part and dissenting in part:

. . . I dissent from those parts of the Court's holding sustaining the Act's provisions (a) for disclosure of small contributions, (b) for limitations on contributions, and (c) for public financing of Presidential campaigns. . . . The Act's system for public financing of Presidential campaigns is, in my judgment, an impermissible intrusion by the Government into the traditionally private political process.

More broadly, the Court's result does

violence to the intent of Congress in this comprehensive scheme of campaign finance. By dissecting the Act bit by bit, and casting off vital parts, the Court fails to recognize that the whole of this Act is greater than the sum of its parts. Congress intended to regulate all aspects of federal campaign finances, but what remains after today's holding leaves no more than a shadow of what Congress contemplated. I question whether the residue leaves a workable program.

Disclosure Provisions

[G]iven the objectives to which disclosure is directed, I agree that the need for disclosure outweighs individual constitutional claims.

Disclosure is, however, subject to First Amendment limitations which are to be defined by looking to the relevant public interests. The legitimate public interest is the elimination of the appearance and reality of corrupting influences. Serious dangers to the very processes of government justify disclosure of contributions of such dimensions reasonably thought likely to purchase special favors. . . .

The Court's theory, however, goes beyond permissible limits. Under the Court's view, disclosure serves broad informational purposes, enabling the public to be fully informed on matters of acute public interest. Forced disclosure of one aspect of a citizen's political activity, under this analysis, serves the public right-to-know. This open-ended approach is the only plausible justification for the otherwise irrationally low ceilings of $10 and $100 for anonymous contributions. The burdens of these low ceilings seem to me obvious, and the Court does not try to question this. . . . Examples come readily to mind. Rank-and-file union members or rising junior executives may now think twice before making even modest contributions to a candidate who is disfavored by the union or management hierarchy. Similarly, potential contributors may well decline to take the obvious risks entailed in making a reportable contribution to the opponent of a well-entrenched incumbent. . . .

The public right-to-know ought not be absolute when its exercise reveals private political convictions. . . . In other contexts, this Court has seen to it that governmental power cannot be used to force a citizen to disclose his private affiliations. . . . For me it is far too late in the day to recognize an ill-defined "public interest" to breach the historic safeguards guaranteed by the First Amendment.

. . . The balancing test used by the Court requires that fair recognition be given to competing interests. With respect, I suggest the Court has failed to give the traditional standing to some of the First Amendment values at stake here. "In the area of First Amendment freedoms government has the duty to confine itself to *the least* intrusive regulations which are adequate for the purpose.". . .

In light of these views, it seems to me that the threshold limits fixed at $10 and $100 for anonymous contributions are constitutionally impermissible on their face. . . . To argue that a 1976 contribution of $10 or $100 entails a risk of corruption or its appearance is simply too extravagant to be maintained. No public right-to-know justifies the compelled disclosure of such contributions, at the risk of discouraging them. There is, in short, no relation whatever between the means used and the legitimate goal of ventilating possible undue influence. Congress has used a shotgun to kill wrens as well as hawks.

In saying that the lines drawn by Congress are "not wholly without rationality," the Court plainly fails to apply the traditional test:

"Precision of regulation must be the touchstone in an area so closely touching on our most precious freedoms. . . ."

Contribution and Expenditure Limits

I agree fully with that part of the Court's opinion that holds unconstitutional the limitations the Act puts on campaign expenditures which "place substantial and direct restrictions on the ability of candidates, citizens, and associations to engage in protected political expression, restrictions that the First Amendment cannot tolerate. . . . Yet when it approves similarly stringent limitations on contributions, the Court ignores the reasons it finds so persuasive in he context of expenditures. For me contributions and expenditures are two sides of the same First Amendment coin.

By limiting campaign contributions, the Act restricts the amount of money that will be spent on political activity—and does so directly. . . . In treating campaign expenditure limitations, the Court says that the "First Amendment denies government the power to determine that spending to promote one's political views is wasteful, excessive, or unwise. . . ." Limiting contributions, as a practical matter, will limit expenditures and will put an effective ceiling on the amount of political activity and debate that the Government will permit to take place. . . .

At any rate, the contribution limits are a far more severe restriction on First Amendment activity than the sort of "chilling" legislation for which the Court has shown such extraordinary concern in the past. . . . There are many prices we pay for the freedoms secured by the First Amendment; the risk of undue influence is one of them, confirming what we have long known: freedom is hazardous, but some restraints are worse.

MR. JUSTICE WHITE, concurring in part and dissenting in part:

. . . In the interest of preventing undue influence that large contributors would have or that the public might think they would have, the Court upholds the provision that an individual may not give to a candidate, or spend on his behalf if requested or authorized by the candidate to do so, more than $1,000 in any one election. . . .

It would make little sense to me, and apparently made none to Congress, to limit the amounts an individual may give to a candidate or spend with his approval but fail to limit the amounts that could be spent on his behalf. Yet the Court permits the former while striking down the latter limitation. No more than $1,000 may be given to a candidate or spent at his request or with his approval or cooperation; but otherwise, apparently, a contributor is to be constitutionally protected in spending unlimited amounts of money in support of his chosen candidate or candidates.

Let us suppose that each of two brothers spends one million dollars on TV spot announcements that he has individually prepared and in which he appears, urging the election of the same named candidate in identical words. One brother has sought and obtained the approval of the candidate; the other has not. The former may validly be prosecuted under section 608(e); under the Court's view, the latter may not, even though the candidate could scarcely help knowing about and appreciating the expensive favor. For constitutional purposes it is difficult to see the difference between the two situations. I would take the word of those who know—that limiting independent expenditures is essential to prevent transparent and widespread evasion of the contribution limits. . . .

Proceeding from the maxim that "money talks," the Court finds that the expenditure limitations will seriously curtail political expression by candidates and interfere substantially with their chances for election. . . . The record before us no more supports the conclusion that the communicative efforts of congressional and Presidential candidates will be crippled by the expenditure limitations than it supports the contrary. The judgment of Congress was that reasonably effective campaigns could be conducted within the limits established by the Act and that the communicative efforts of these campaigns would not seriously suffer. In this posture of the case, there is no sound basis for invalidating the expenditure limitations, so long as the purposes they serve are legitimate and sufficiently substantial, which in my view they are. . . .

By limiting the importance of personal wealth, section 608(a) helps to assure that only individuals with a modicum of support from others will be viable candidates. This in turn would tend to discourage any notion that the outcome of elections is primarily a function of money. Similarly, section 608(a) tends to equalize access to the political arena, encouraging the less wealthy, unable to bankroll their own campaigns, to run for political office.

As with the campaign expenditure limits, Congress was entitled to determine that personal wealth ought to play a less important role in political campaigns than it has in the past. Nothing in the First Amendment stands in the way of that determination.

MR. JUSTICE REHNQUIST, concurring in part and dissenting in part:

. . . I join in all of the Court's opinion except Subpart III–B–1, which sustains, against appellants' First and Fifth Amendment challenges, the disparities found in the congressional plan for financing general Presidential elections between the two major parties, on the one hand and minor parties and candidates on the other. . . .

Congress, of course, does have an interest in not "funding hopeless candidacies with large sums of public money,". . . and may for that purpose legitimately require " 'some preliminary showing of a significant modicum of support,' *Jenness* v. *Fortson,* as an eligibility requirement for public funds." . . . But Congress in this legislation has done a good deal more than that. It has enshrined the Republican and Democratic Parties in a permanently preferred position, and has established requirements for funding minor party and independent candidates to which the two major parties are not subject. . . . I find it impossible to subscribe to the Court's reasoning that because no third party has posed a credible threat to the two major parties in Presidential elections since 1860, Congress may by law attempt to assure that this pattern will endure forever.

MILLER *v.* CALIFORNIA
413 U.S. 5; 93 Sup. Ct. 2607; 37 L. Ed. 2d 419 (1973)

[Miller had conducted a mass mailing campaign to advertise the sale of illustrated "adult" books. The advertising brochures contained some printed material but primarily they consisted of "pictures and drawings very explicitly depicting men and women in groups of two or more engaging in a variety of sexual activities, with genitals often prominently displayed." In the companion case, Paris Adult Theatre I *v.* Slaton, *413 U.S. 49 (1973), Georgia had instituted an obscenity prosecution against "a conventional, inoffensive theatre entrance, without any pictures, but with signs indicating that the theatres exhibited 'Atlanta's Finest Mature Feature Films.' On the door itself is a sign saying: 'Adult Theatre—You must be 21 and able to prove it. If viewing the nude body offends you, Please Do Not Enter.'" The films shown depicted scenes of simulated sex acts. The majority opinion is from* Miller. *The dissents are from* Paris Adult Theatre.

The case the Court refers to as Memoirs *is* A Book Named "John Cleland's Memoirs of a Woman of Pleasure," et al. *v.* Attorney General of Massachusetts, *often called* The Fanny Hill Case. Stanley *v.* Georgia, *which is noted in the introduction to this chapter as permitting the private possession of obscene materials, also emphasized the state's right to keep obscenity away from juveniles and unwilling adults. It and* Redrup *v.* New York, *386 U.S. 767 (1967), are referred to frequently in these opinions.* Redrup *was a* per curiam *in which the Court admitted that the justices could not agree on obscenity standards but were in agreement that the particular works in question were not obscene.]*

MR. CHIEF JUSTICE BURGER delivered the opinion of the Court:

This is one of a group of "obscenity-pornography" cases being reviewed by the Court in a re-examination of standards enunciated in earlier cases involving what Mr. Justice Harlan called "the intractable obscenity problem." . . .

I

This case involves the application of a State's criminal obscenity statute to a situation in which sexually explicit materials have been thrust by aggressive sales action upon unwilling recipients who had in no way indicated any desire to receive such materials. This Court has recognized that the States have a legitimate interest in prohibiting dissemination or exhibition of obscene material when the mode of dissemination carries with it a significant danger of offending the sensibilities of unwilling recipients or of exposure to juveniles. *[Stanley]*. It is in this context that we are called on to define the standards which must be used to identify obscene material that a State may regulate. . . .

[I]t is useful for us to focus on two of the landmark cases. . . . While *Roth* presumed "obscenity" to be "utterly without redeeming social value," *Memoirs* required that to prove obscenity it must be affirmatively established that the material is "*utterly* without redeeming social value." Thus, even as they repeated the words of *Roth,* the *Memoirs* plurality produced a drastically altered test that called on the prosecution to prove a negative, i.e., that the material was "*utterly* without redeeming social value"—a burden virtually impossible to discharge under our criminal standards of proof. . . .

Apart from the initial formulation in the *Roth* case, no majority of the Court has at any given time been able to agree on a standard to determine what constitutes obscene, pornographic material subject to regulation under the States' police power. [This] is not remarkable, for in the area of freedom of speech and press the courts must always remain sensitive to any infringement on genuinely serious literary, artistic, political, or scientific expression. This is an area in which there are few eternal verities.

This much has been categorically settled by the Court, that obscene material is unprotected by the First Amendment. . . . We acknowledge, however, the inherent dangers of undertaking to regulate any form of expression. State statutes designed to regulate obscene materials must be carefully limited. As a result, we now confine the permissible scope of such regulation to works which depict or describe sexual conduct. That conduct must be specifically defined by the applicable state law, as written or authoritatively construed. A state offense must also be limited to works which, taken as a whole, appeal to the prurient interest in sex, which portray sexual conduct in a patently offensive way, and which, taken as a whole, do not have serious literary, artistic, political, or scientific value.

The basic guidelines for the trier of fact must be: (1) whether "the average person, applying contemporary community standards" would find that the work, taken as a whole, appeals to the prurient interest *[Roth],* (2) whether the work depicts or describes, in a patently offensive way, sexual conduct specifically defined by the applicable state law, and (3) whether the work, taken as a whole, lacks serious literary, artistic, political, or scientific value. We do not adopt as a constitutional standard the "*utterly* without redeeming social value" test of *[Memoirs]*. If a state law that regulates obscene material is thus limited, as written or construed, [First Amendment values] are adequately protected by the ultimate power of appellate courts to conduct an independent review of constitutional claims when necessary. . . .

We emphasize that it is not our function to propose regulatory schemes for the States. That must await their concrete legislative efforts. It is possible, however, to give a few plain examples of what a state statute could define for regulation under the second part (2) of the standard announced in this opinion:

1. Patently offensive representations or descriptions of ultimate sexual acts, normal or perverted, actual or simulated.

2. Patently offensive representations or descriptions of masturbation, excretory functions, and lewd exhibition of the genitals.

Sex and nudity may not be exploited without limit by films or pictures exhibited or sold in places of public accommodation any more than live sex and nudity can be exhibited or sold without limit in such public places. At a minimum, prurient, patently offensive depiction or description of sexual conduct must have serious literary, artistic, political, or scientific value to merit First Amendment protection. . . . For example, medical books for the education of physicians and related personnel necessarily use graphic illustrations and descriptions of human anatomy. In resolving the inevitably sensitive questions of fact and law, we must continue to rely on the jury system, accompanied by the safeguards that judges, rules of evidence, presumption of innocence and other protective features provide, as we do with rape, murder and a host of other offenses against society and its individual members.

Mr. Justice Brennan . . . has abandoned his former positions and now maintains that no formulation of this Court, the Congress, or the States can adequately distinguish obscene material unprotected by the First Amendment from protected expression. Paradoxically, [he] indicates that suppression of unprotected obscene material is permissible to avoid exposure to unconsenting adults, as in this case, and to juveniles, although he gives no indication of how the division between protected and nonprotected materials may be drawn with greater precision for these purposes than for regulation of commercial exposure to consenting adults only. Nor does he indicate where in the Constitution he finds the authority to distinguish between a willing "adult" one month past the law age of majority and a willing "juvenile" one month younger.

Under the holdings announced today, no one will be subject to prosecution for the sale or exposure of obscene materials unless these materials depict or describe patently offensive "hard core" sexual conduct specifically defined by the regulating state law, as written or construed. We are satisfied that these specific prerequisites will provide fair notice to a dealer in such materials that his public commercial activities may bring prosecution. . . . If the inability to define regulated materials with ultimate, god-like precision altogether removes the power of the States or the Congress to regulate, then "hard core" pornography may be exposed without limit to the juvenile, the passerby, and the consenting adult alike, as, indeed, Mr. Justice Douglas contends. . . . In this belief, however, Mr. Justice Douglas now stands alone.

Mr. Justice Brennan also emphasizes "institutional stress" in justification of his change of view. . . . It is certainly true that the absence, since *Roth,* of a single majority view of this Court as to proper standards for testing obscenity has placed a strain on both state and federal courts. But today, for the first time since *Roth* was decided in 1957, a majority of this Court has agreed on concrete guidelines to isolate "hard core" pornography from expression protected by the First Amendment. Now we may abandon the casual practice of *[Redrup]* and attempt to provide positive guidance to the federal and state courts alike.

This may not be an easy road, free from difficulty. But no amount of "fatigue" should lead us to adopt a convenient "institutional" rationale—an absolutist, "anything goes" view of the First Amendment—because it will lighten our burdens. . . . Nor should we remedy "tension between state and federal courts" by arbitrarily depriving the States of a power reserved to them under the Constitution. . . .

Under a national Constitution, fundamental First Amendment limitations on the powers of the States do not vary from community to community, but this does not mean that there are, or should or can be, fixed, uniform national standards of precisely what appeals to the "prurient interest" or is "patently offensive." These are essentially questions of fact, and our nation is simply too big and too diverse for this Court to reasonably expect that such standards could be articulated for all fifty States in a single formulation, even assuming the prerequisite consensus exists. . . . To require a State to structure obscenity proceedings around evidence of a *national* "community standard" would be an exercise in futility.

. . . It is neither realistic nor constitutionally sound to read the First Amendment as requiring that the people of Maine or Mississippi accept public depiction of conduct found tolerable in Las Vegas, or New York City. . . . People in different States vary in their tastes and attitudes, and this diversity is not to be strangled by the absolutism of imposed uniformity. . . .

IV

The dissenting Justices sound the alarm of repression. But, in our view, to equate the free and robust exchange of ideas and political debate with commercial exploitation of obscene material demeans the grand conception of the First Amendment and its high purposes in the historic struggle for freedom. . . . "The protection given speech and press was fashioned to assure unfettered interchange of *ideas* for the bringing about of political and social changes desired by the people," *[Roth*—emphasis added.] But the public portrayal of hard core sexual conduct for its own sake, and for the ensuing commercial gain, is a different matter.

There is no evidence, empirical or historical, that the stern nineteenth-century American censorship of public distribution and display of material relating to sex in any way limited or affected expression of serious literary, artistic, political, or scientific ideas. On the contrary, it is beyond any question that the era following Thomas Jefferson to Theodore Roosevelt was an "extraordinarily vigorous period" not just in economics and politics, but in *belles-lettres* and in "the outlying fields of social and political philosophies." We do not see the harsh hand of censorship of ideas—good or bad, sound or unsound—and "repression" of political liberty lurking in every state regulation of commercial exploitation of human interest in sex.

MR. JUSTICE BRENNAN finds "it is hard to see how state-ordered regimentation of our minds can ever be forestalled." These doleful anticipations assume that courts cannot distinguish commerce in ideas, protected by the First Amendment, from commercial exploitation of obscene material. . . . One can concede that the "sexual revolution" of recent years may have had useful byproducts in striking layers of prudery from a subject long irrationally kept from needed ventilation. But it does not follow that no regulation of patently offensive "hard core" materials is needed or permissible; civilized people do not allow unregulated access to heroin because it is a derivative of medicinal morphine.

In sum we (1) reaffirm the *Roth* holding that obscene material is not protected by the First Amendment, (2) hold that such material can be regulated by the States, subject to the specific safeguards enunciated above, without a showing that the material is "*utterly* without redeeming social value," and (3) hold that obscenity is to be determined by applying "contemporary community standards,". . . not "national standards.". . .

MR. JUSTICE BRENNAN, with whom MR. JUSTICE STEWART and MR. JUSTICE MARSHALL join, dissenting:

. . . I am convinced that the approach initiated fifteen years ago in *[Roth],* and culminating in the Court's decision today, cannot bring stability to this area of the law without jeopardizing fundamental First Amendment values, and I have concluded that the time has come to make a significant departure from that approach. . . .

The decision of the Georgia Supreme Court rested squarely on its conclusion that the State could constitutionally suppress these films even if they were displayed only to persons over the age of 21 who were aware of the nature of their contents and who had consented to viewing them. [I] am convinced of the invalidity of that conclusion of law, and I would therefore vacate [the judgment]. I have no occasion to consider the extent of state power to regulate the distribution of sexually oriented materials to juveniles or to unconsenting adults. Nor am I required, for the purposes of this appeal, to consider whether or not these petitioners had, in fact, taken precautions to avoid exposure of films to minors or unconsenting adults. . . .

The essence of our problem in the obscenity area is that we have been unable to provide "sensitive tools" to separate obscenity from other sexually oriented but constitutionally protected speech, so that efforts to suppress the former do not spill over into the suppression of the latter. . . . Today a majority of the Court offers a slightly altered formulation of the basic *Roth* test, while leaving entirely unchanged the underlying approach.

Our experience with the *Roth* approach has certainly taught us that the outright suppression of obscenity cannot be reconciled with the fundamental principles of the First and Fourteenth Amendments. For we have failed to formulate a standard that sharply distinguishes protected from unprotected speech, and out of necessity, we have resorted to the *Redrup* approach, which resolves cases as between the parties, but offers only the most obscure guidance to legislation, adjudication by other courts, and primary conduct. By disposing of cases [summarily] we have deliberately and effectively obscured the rationale underlying the decision. It comes as no surprise that judicial attempts to follow our lead conscientiously have often ended in hopeless confusion.

Of course, the vagueness problem would be largely of our own creation if it stemmed primarily from our failure to reach a consensus on any one standard. But after fifteen years of experimentation and debate I am reluctantly forced to the conclusion that none of the available formulas, including the one announced today, can reduce the vagueness to a tolerable level while at the same time striking an acceptable balance between the protections of the First and Fourteenth Amendments, on the one hand, and on the other the asserted state interest in regulating the dissemination of certain sexually oriented materials. Any effort to draw a constitutionally acceptable boundary on state power must resort to such indefinite concepts as "prurient interest," "patent offensiveness," "serious literary value," and the like. The meaning of these concepts necessarily varies with the experience, outlook, and even idiosyncrasies of the person defining them. Although we have assumed that obscenity does exist and that we "know it when [we] see it," . . . we are manifestly unable to describe it in advance except by reference to concepts so elusive that they fail to distinguish clearly between protected and unprotected speech. [N]o one definition, no matter how precisely or narrowly drawn, can possibly suffice for all situations, or carve out fully suppressible expression from all media without also creating a substantial risk of encroachment upon the guarantees of the Due Process Clause and the First Amendment.

The vagueness of the standards in the obscenity area produces a number of separate problems, and any improvement must rest on understanding that the problems are to some extent distinct. First, a vague statute fails to provide adequate notice to persons who are engaged in the type of conduct that the statute could be thought to proscribe. . . . In addition to problems that arise when any criminal statute fails to afford fair notice of what it forbids, a vague statute in the areas of speech and press creates a second level of difficulty. [Justice Brennan then discusses the "chilling effect" on speakers of a vaguely worded statute.] . . . a vague statute in this area creates a third, although admittedly more subtle, set of problems. These problems concern the institutional stress that inevitably results where the line separating protected from unprotected speech is excessively vague. Almost every case is "marginal." And since the "margin" marks the point of separation between protected and unprotected speech, we are left with a system in which almost every obscenity case presents a constitutional question of exceptional difficulty. . . .

As a result of our failure to define standards with predictable application to any given piece of material, there is no probability of regularity in obscenity decisions by state and lower federal courts. That is not to say that these courts have performed badly in this area or paid insufficient attention to the principles we have established. The problem is, rather, that one cannot say with certainty that material is obscene until at least five members of this Court, applying inevitably obscure standards, have pronounced it so. The number of obscenity cases on our docket gives ample testimony to the burden that has been placed upon this Court.

. . . quite apart from the number of cases involved and the need to make a fresh constitutional determination in each case, we are tied to the "absurd business of perusing and viewing the miserable stuff that pours into the Court." . . . While the material may have varying degrees of social importance, it is hardly a source of edification to the members of this Court who are compelled to view it before passing on its obscenity. . . .

Moreover, we have managed the burden of deciding scores of obscenity cases by relying on per curiam reversals or denials of certiorari—a practice which conceals the rationale of decision and gives at least the appearance of arbitrary action by this Court. . . . the practice effectively censors protected expression by leaving lower court determinations of obscenity intact even though the status of the allegedly obscene material is entirely unsettled until final review here. In addition, the uncertainty of the standards creates a continuing source of tension between state and federal courts, since the need for an independent determination by this Court seems to render superfluous even the most conscientious analysis by state tribunals. And our inability to justify our decisions with a persuasive rationale—or indeed, any rationale at all—necessarily creates the impression that we are merely second-guessing state court judges.

The severe problems arising from the lack of fair notice, from the chill on protected expression, and from the stress imposed on the state and federal judicial machinery persuade me that a significant change in direction is urgently required.

The alternative adopted by the Court today recognizes that a prohibition against any depiction or description of human sexual organs could not be reconciled with the guarantees of the First Amendment. But the Court does retain the view that certain sexually oriented material can be considered obscene and therefore unprotected by the First and Fourteenth Amendments. To describe that unprotected class of expression, the Court adopts a restatement of the *Roth-Memoirs* definition of obscenity. . . .

The differences between this formulation and the . . . *Memoirs* test are, for the most part, academic. . . . In my view, the restatement leaves unresolved the very difficulties that compel our rejection of the underlying *Roth* approach, while at the same time contributing substantial difficulties of its own. The modification of the *Memoirs* test may prove sufficient to jeopardize the analytic underpinnings of the entire scheme. And today's restatement will likely have the effect, whether or not intended, of permitting far more sweeping suppression of sexually oriented expression, including expression that would almost surely be held protected under our current formulation.

. . . The Court's approach necessarily assumes that some works will be deemed obscene—even though they clearly have *some* social value—because the State was able to prove that the value, measured by some unspecified standard, was not sufficiently "serious" to warrant constitutional protection. That result is not merely inconsistent with our holding in *Roth;* it is nothing less than a rejection of the fundamental First Amendment premises and rationale of the *Roth* opinion and an invitation to widespread suppression of sexually oriented speech. Before today, the protections of the First Amendment have never been thought limited to expression of *serious* literary or political value.

. . . One should hardly need to point out that under the third component of the Court's test the prosecution is still required to "prove a negative" . . . Whether it will be easier to prove that material lacks "serious" value than to prove that it lacks any value at all remains, of course, to be seen. In any case, even if the Court's approach left undamaged the conceptual framework of *Roth,* and even if it clearly barred the suppression of works with at least some social value, I would nevertheless be compelled to reject it. For it is beyond dispute that the approach can have no ameliorative impact on the cluster of problems that grow out of the vagueness of our current standards. . . .

The Court surely demonstrates little sensitivity to our own institutional problems, much less the other vagueness-related difficulties, in establishing a system that requires us to consider whether a description of human genitals is sufficiently "lewd" to deprive it of constitutional protection; whether a sexual act is "ultimate"; whether the conduct depicted in materials before us fits within one of the categories of conduct whose depiction the state or federal governments have attempted to suppress; and a host of equally pointless inquiries. . . .

Our experience since *Roth* requires us not only to abandon the effort to pick out obscene materials on a case-by-case basis, but also to reconsider a fundamental postulate of *Roth:* that there exists a definable class of sexually oriented expression that may be totally suppressed by the Federal and State Governments. . . .

Because we assumed—incorrectly, as experience has proven—that obscenity could be separated from other sexually oriented expression without significant costs . . . , we had no occassion in *Roth* to probe the asserted state interest in curtailing unprotected, sexually oriented speech. . . .

The opinions in *Redrup* and *[Stanley]* reflected our emerging view that the state interests in protecting children and in protecting unconsenting adults may stand on a different footing from the other asserted state interests. It may well be, as one commentator has argued, that "exposure to [erotica] is for some persons an intense emotional experience. A communication of this nature, imposed upon a person contrary to his wishes, has all the characteristics of a physical assault. [It] constitutes an invasion of his privacy." . . . the State may have a substantial interest in precluding the flow of obscene materials even to consenting juveniles.

. . . But the State's interest in regulating morality by suppressing obscenity, while often asserted, remains essentially unfocused and ill-defined. . . . the effort to suppress obscenity is predicated on unprovable, although strongly held assumptions about human behavior, morality, sex, and religion. The existence of these assumptions cannot validate a statute that substantially undermines the guarantees of the First Amendment. . . . For if a State may, in an effort to maintain or create a particular moral tone, prescribe what its citizens cannot read or cannot see, then it would seem to follow that in pursuit of that same objective a State could decree that its citizens must read certain books or must view certain films. . . . Even a legitimate, sharply focused state concern for the morality of the community cannot, . . . justify an assault on the protections of the First Amendment. Where the state interest in regulation of morality is vague and ill-defined, interference with the guarantees of the First Amendment is even more difficult to justify.

In short, while I cannot say that the interest of the State—apart from the question of juveniles and unconsenting adults—are trivial or nonexistent, I am compelled to conclude that these interests cannot justify the substantial damage to constitutional rights and to this Nation's judicial machinery that inevitably results from state efforts to bar the distribution even of unprotected material to consenting adults. I would hold, therefore, that at least in the absence of distribution to juveniles or obtrusive exposure to unconsenting adults, the First and Fourteenth Amendments prohibit the state and federal governments from attempting wholly to suppress sexually oriented materials on the basis of their allegedly "obscene" contents.

. . . I do not pretend to have found a complete and infallible answer. . . . Difficult questions must still be faced, notably in the areas of distribution to juveniles and offensive exposure to unconsenting adults. Whatever the extent of state power to regulate in those areas, it should be clear that the view I espouse today would introduce a large measure of clarity to this troubled area, would reduce the institutional pressure on this Court and the rest of the State and Federal judiciary, and would guarantee fuller freedom of expression while leaving room for the protection of legitimate governmental interests. . . .

MR. JUSTICE DOUGLAS, dissenting:

. . . I have expressed on numerous occasions my disagreement with the basic decision that held that "obscenity" was not protected by the First Amendment. I disagreed also with the definitions that evolved. [I] became convinced that the creation of the "obscenity" exception to the First Amendment was a legislative and judicial tour de force; that if we were to have such a regime of censorship and punishment, it should be done by constitutional amendment.

. . . Life in this crowded modern technological world creates many offensive statements and many offensive deeds. There is no protection against offensive ideas, only against offensive conduct.

"Obscenity" at most is the expression of offensive ideas. . . . I am sure I would find offensive most of the books and movies charged with being obscene. But in a life that has not been short, I have yet to be trapped into seeing or reading something that would offend me. I never read or see the materials coming to the Court under charges of "obscenity," because I have thought the First Amendment made it unconstitutional for me to act as a censor. I see ads in bookstores and neon lights over theatres that resemble bait for those who seek vicarious exhilaration. As a parent or a priest or as a teacher I would have no compulsion in edging my children or wards away from the books and movies that did no more than excite man's base instincts. But I never supposed that government was permitted to sit in judgment on one's tastes or beliefs—save as they involved action within the reach of the police power of government.

I applaud the effort of my Brother Brennan to forsake the low road which the Court has followed in this field. The new regime he would inaugurate is much closer than the old to the policy of abstention which the First Amendment proclaims. But since we do not have here the unique series of problems raised by government imposed or government approved captive audiences . . . I see no constitutional basis for fashioning a rule that makes a publisher, producer, bookseller, librarian, or movie house criminally responsible, when he or she fails to take affirmative steps to protect the consumer against literature or books offensive to those who temporarily occupy the seats of the mighty.

POSTNOTE TO *MILLER* v. *CALIFORNIA*

Justice Brennan has since repeated his *Miller* position that a statute barring oscenity violates the constitutional prohibition against vagueness and is "clearly overbroad and unconstitutional on its face." [*Pinkus* v. *United States,* 436 U.S. 293, 306 (1978) (dissenting).] Justices Stewart and Marshall have also consistently taken this position in their post *Miller* opinions. In *Pinkus,* Justice Stevens says explicitly that he too would take this position if it could be a majority one.

The current majority, however, has been moving toward a firmer anti-obscenity position. In *Hamling* v. *United States,* 418 U.S. 87 (1974), it holds that local community standards apply even in prosecutions under a federal statute of national applicability. *Pinkus, Hamling* and *Splawn* v. *California,* 431 U.S. 595 (1977) reaffirm the *Ginzburg* v. *United States* holding that advertising may be taken into account to tip a work of doubtful obscenity over the line. The Court has not really taken the one liberalizing facet of *Miller* seriously. It continues to uphold convictions under state statutes that do not specify exactly what depictions are patently offensive. [See *Ward* v. *Illinois,* 431 U.S. 767 (1977).] It also reaffirmed in *Pinkus* that where the material is intended for a deviant group, its appeal to the prurient interest of that group as well as to the average person is relevant.

NEW YORK TIMES CO. *v.* SULLIVAN
376 U.S. 254; 84 Sup. Ct. 710; 11 L. Ed. 686 (1964)

MR. JUSTICE BRENNAN delivered the opinion of the Court:

We are required for the first time in this case to determine the extent to which the constitutional protections for speech and press limit a State's power to award damages in a libel action brought by a public official against critics of his official conduct.

Respondent L. B. Sullivan is one of the three elected Commissioners of the City of Montgomery, Alabama. He testified that he was "Commissioner of Public Affairs and the duties are supervision of the Police Department, Fire Department, Department of Cemetery and Department of Scales." He brought this civil libel action against the four individual petitioners, who are Negroes and Alabama clergymen, and against petitioner the New York Times Company, a New York corporation which publishes the *New York Times,* a daily newspaper. A jury in the Circuit Court of

Montgomery County awarded him damages of $500,000, the full amount claimed, against all the petitioners, and the Supreme Court of Alabama affirmed.

Respondent's complaint alleged that he had been libeled by statements in a full-page advertisement that was carried in *The New York Times* on March 29, 1960. . . .

It is uncontroverted that some of the statements contained in the [advertisement] were not accurate descriptions of events which occurred in Montgomery. . . .

The trial judge submitted the case to the jury under instructions that the statements in the advertisement were "libelous per se." . . . The jury was instructed that, because the statements were libelous per se . . . "falsity and malice are presumed" . . . and the judge charged that "mere negligence or carelessness is not evidence of actual malice or malice in fact, and does not justify an award of exemplary or punitive damages." He refused to charge, however, that the jury must be "convinced" of malice, in the sense of "actual intent" to harm or "gross negligence and recklessness," to make such an award, and he also refused to require that a verdict for respondent differentiate between compensatory and punitive damages. . . .

Under Alabama law as applied in this case . . . once "libel per se" has been established, the defendant has no defense as to stated facts unless he can persuade the jury that they were true in all their particulars. . . . His privilege of "fair comment" for expressions of opinion depends on the truth of the facts upon which the comment is based. . . . Unless he can discharge the burden of proving truth, general damages are presumed, and may be awarded without proof of pecuniary injury. A showing of actual malice is apparently a prerequisite to recovery of punitive damages, and the defendant may in any event forestall these by a retraction meeting the statutory requirements. Good motives and belief in truth do not negate an inference of malice, but are relevant only in mitigation of punitive damages if the jury chooses to accord them weight. . . .

The question before us is whether this rule of liability, as applied to an action brought by a public official against critics of his official conduct, abridges the freedom of speech and of the press that is guaranteed by the First and Fourteenth Amendments.

Respondent relies heavily, as did the Alabama courts, on statements of this Court to effect that the Constitution does not protect libelous publications. Those statements do not foreclose our inquiry here. None of the cases sustained the use of libel laws to impose sanctions upon expression critical of the official conduct of public officials. The dictum in *Pennekamp* v. *Florida,* 328 U.S. 331 . . . that "when the statements amount to defamation, a judge has such remedy in damages for libel as do other public servants," implied no view as to what remedy might constitutionally be afforded to public officials. In *Beauharnais* v. *Illinois,* 343 U.S. 250 . . . the Court sustained an Illinois criminal libel statute as applied to a publication held to be both defamatory of a racial group and "liable to cause violence and disorder." But the Court was careful to note that it "retains and exercises authority to nullify action which encroaches on freedom of utterance under the guise of punishing libel"; for "public men, are, as it were, public property," and "discussion cannot be denied and the right, as well as the duty, of criticism must not be stifled." In the only previous case that did present the question of constitutional limitations upon the power to award damages for libel of a public official, the Court was equally divided and the question was not decided. *Schenectady Union Pub. Co.* v. *Sweeney,* 316 U.S. 642. . . . In deciding the question now, we are compelled by neither precedent nor policy to give any more weight to the epithet "libel" than we have to other "mere labels" of state law. Like "insurrection," contempt, advocacy of unlawful acts, breach of the peace, obscenity, solicitation of legal business, and the various other formulae for the repression of expression that have been challenged in this Court, libel can claim no talismanic immunity from constitutional limitations. It must be measured by standards that satisfy the First Amendment.

The general proposition that freedom of expression upon public questions is secured by the First Amendment has long been settled by our decisions. The constitutional safeguard, we have said, "was fashioned to assure unfettered interchange of ideas for the bringing about of political and social changes desired by the people." . . . *Roth* v. *United States.* . . . "The maintenance of the opportunity for free political discussion to the end that government may be responsive to the will of the people and that changes may be obtained by lawful means, an opportunity essential to the security of the Republic, is a fundamental principle of our constitutional system." *Stromberg* v. *California,* 283 U.S. 359. . . . "[I]t is a prized American privilege to speak one's mind, although not always with perfect good taste, on all public institutions," *Bridges* v. *California,* 314 U.S. 252, . . . and this opportunity is to be afforded for "vigorous advocacy" no less than "abstract discussion." *NAACP* v. *Button.* The First Amendment, said Judge Learned Hand, "presupposes that right conclusions are more likely to be gathered out of a multitude of tongues, than through any kind of authoritative selection. To many this is, and always will be, folly; but we have staked upon it our all." *United States* v. *Associated Press,* 52 F. Supp. 362, 372 (D.C.S.D.-N.Y. 1943). Mr Justice Brandeis, in his concurring opinion in *Whitney* v. *California* . . . gave the principle its classic formulation.

Thus we consider this case against the background of a profound national commitment to the principle that debate on public issues should be uninhibited, robust, and wide-open, and that it may well include vehement, caustic, and sometimes unpleasantly sharp attacks on government and public officials. See *Terminiello* v. *Chicago.* . . . The present advertisement, as an expression of grievance and protest of our time, would seem clearly to qualify for the constitutional protection. The question is whether it forfeits that protection by the falsity of some of its factual statements and by its alleged defamation of respondent.

Authoritative interpretations of the First Amendment guarantees have consistently refused to recognize an exception for any test of truth, whether administered by judges, juries, or administrative officials—and especially not one that puts the burden of proving truth on the speaker. . . .

That erroneous statement is inevitable in free debate, and that it must be protected if the freedoms of expression are to have the "breathing space" that they "need . . . to survive," *NAACP* v. *Button,* was also recognized by the Court of Appeals for the District of Columbia Circuit in *Sweeny* v. *Patterson,* 128 F. 2d 457, 458 (1942). Judge Edgerton spoke for a unanimous court which affirmed the dismissal of a Congressman's libel suit based upon a newspaper article charging him with anti-Semitism in opposing a judicial appointment. He said:

"Cases which impose liability for erroneous reports of the political conduct of officials reflect the obsolete doctrine that the governed must not criticize their governors. . . . The interest of the public here outweighs the interest of appellant or any other individual. The protection of the public requires not merely discussion, but information. Political conduct and views which some respectable people approve, and others condemn, are constantly imputed to Congressmen. Errors of fact, particularly in regard to a man's mental states and processes, are inevitable. . . . Whatever is added to the field of libel is taken from the field of free debate."

Just as factual error affords no warrant for repressing speech that would otherwise be free, the same is true of injury to official reputation. Where judicial officers are involved, this Court has held that concern for the dignity and reputation of the courts does not justify the punishment as criminal contempt of criticism of the judge or his decision. *Bridges* v. *California.* This is true even though the utterance contains "half-truths" and "misinformation." *Pennekamp* v. *Florida;* such repression can be justified, if at all, only by a clear and present danger of the obstruction of justice. . . .

If neither factual error nor defamatory content suffices to remove the constitutional shield from criticism of official conduct, the combination of the two elements is no less inadequate. This is the lesson to be drawn from the great controversy over the Sedition Act of 1798, 1 Stat. 596, which first crystallized a national awareness of the central meaning of the First Amendment. That statute made it a crime, punishable by a $5,000 fine and five years in prison, "if any person shall write, print, utter or publish . . . any false, scandalous and malicious writing or writings against the government of the United States, or either house of the Congress . . . or the President. . . , with the intent to defame . . . or to bring them or either of them, into contempt or disrepute; or to excite against them, or either or any of them, the hatred of the good people of the United States." The Act allowed the defendant the defense of truth, and provided that the jury were to be judges both of the law and the facts. Despite these qualifications, the Act was vigorously condemned as unconstitutional in an attack joined in by Jefferson and Madison. . . .

Although the Sedition Act was never tested in this Court, the attack upon its validity has carried the day in the court of history. Fines levied in its prosecution were repaid by Act of Congress on the ground that it was unconstitutional. . . . Jefferson, as President, pardoned those who had been convicted and sentenced under the Act and remitted their fines, stating: "I discharged every person under punishment or prosecution under the Sedition Law because I considered, and now consider, that law to be a nullity as absolute and palpable as if Congress had ordered us to fall down and worship a golden image." . . .

The state rule of law is not saved by its allowance of the defense of truth. . . . A rule compelling the critic of official conduct to guarantee the truth of all his factual assertions—and to do so on pain of libel judgments virtually unlimited in amount—leads to . . . "self-censorship." Allowance of the defense of truth, with the burden of proving it on the defendant, does not mean that only false speech will be deterred. Even courts accepting this defense as an adequate safeguard have recognized the difficulties of adducing legal proofs that the alleged libel was true in all its factual particulars. . . . Under such a rule, would-be critics of official conduct may be deterred from voicing their criticism, even though it is believed to be true and even though it is in fact true, because of doubt whether it can be proved in court or fear of the expense of having to do so. They tend to make only statements which "steer far wider of the unlawful zone." . . . The rule thus dampens the vigor and limits the variety of public debate. It is inconsistent with the First and Fourteenth Amendments.

The constitutional guarantees require, we think, a federal rule that prohibits a public official from recovering damages for a defamatory falsehood relating to his official conduct unless he proves that the statement was made with "actual malice"—that is, with knowledge that it was false or with reckless disregard of whether it was false or not. . . .

Such a privilege for criticism of official conduct is appropriately analogous to the protection accorded a public official when *he* is sued for libel by a private citizen. In *Barr* v. *Matteo,* 360 U.S. 564 . . . this Court held the utterance of a federal official to be absolutely privileged if made "within the outer perimeter" of his duties. The States accord the same immunity to statements of their highest officers, although some differentiate their lesser officials and qualify the privilege they enjoy. But all hold that all officials are protected unless actual malice can be proved. The reason for the official privilege is said to be that the threat of damage suits would otherwise "inhibit the fearless, vigorous, and effective administration of policies of government" and "dampen the ardor of all but the most resolute, or the most irresponsible, in the unflinching discharge of their duties." . . . Analogous considerations support the privilege for the citizen-critic of government. It is as much his duty to criticize as it is the official's duty to administer. See *Whitney* v. *California* (concurring opinion of Mr. Justice Brandeis). As Madison said, "the censorial power is in the people over the Government, and not in the Government over the people." It would give public servants an unjustified preference over the public they serve, if critics of official conduct did not have a fair equivalent of the immunity granted to the officials themselves.

We conclude that such a privilege is required by the First and Fourteenth Amendments.

We hold today that the Constitution delimits a State's power to award damages for libel in actions brought by public officials against critics of their official conduct. Since this is such an action, the rule requiring proof of actual malice is applicable. While Alabama law apparently requires proof of actual malice for an award of punitive damages, where general damages are concerned malice is "presumed." Such a presumption is inconsistent with the federal rule. "The power to create presumptions is not a means of escape from constitutional restrictions," *Bailey* v. *Alabama,* 219 U.S. 219. . . . Since the trial judge did not instruct the jury to differentiate between general and punitive damages, it may be that the verdict was wholly an award of one or the other. But it is impossible to know, in view of the general verdict returned. Because of this uncertainty, the judgment must be reversed and the case remanded. . . .

[Justices Black and Douglas concurred.]

FRIEDMAN *v.* ROGERS

440 U.S. 1; 99 Sup. Ct. 887; 59 L. Ed. 2d 100 (1979)

[Section 5.13(d) of the Texas Optometry Act prohibited engaging in the practice of optometry under a trade name. Rogers, an optometrist who practiced under the name "Texas State Optical" challenged this and other provisions of the act on various constitutional grounds. Only the free speech issues are considered in the excerpts of the opinion presented here.]

MR. JUSTICE POWELL delivered the opinion of the Court:

In holding that § 5.13(d) infringes First Amendment rights, the District Court relied primarily on this Court's decisions in *Bates* v. *State Bar of Arizona,* 433 U.S. 350 (1977), and *Virginia Pharmacy Board* v. *Virginia Citizens Consumer Council,* 425 U.S. 748 (1976). . . .

At issue in *Virginia Pharmacy* was the validity of Virginia's law preventing advertising by pharmacists of the prices of prescription drugs. After establishing that the economic nature of the pharmacists' interest in the speech did not preclude First Amendment protection for their advertisements, the Court discussed the other interests in the advertisements that warranted First Amendment protection. To individual consumers, information about prices of prescription drugs at competing pharmacies "could mean the alleviation of physical pain or the enjoyment of basic necessities." Society also has a strong interest in the free flow of commercial information, both because the efficient allocation of resources depends upon informed consumer choices and because "even an individual advertisement, though entirely 'commercial,' may be of general public interest." The Court acknowledged the important interest of the State in maintaining high standards among pharmacists, but concluded that this interest could not justify the ban on truthful price advertising when weighed against the First Amendment interests in the information conveyed.

In the next Term, the Court applied the rationale of *Virginia Pharmacy* to the advertising of certain information by lawyers. After weighing the First Amendment interests identified in *Virginia Pharmacy* against the State's interests in regulating the speech in question, the Court concluded that the truthful advertising of the prices at which routine legal services will be performed also is protected by the First Amendment. *Bates* v. *State Bar of Arizona.*

In both *Virginia Pharmacy* and *Bates,* we were careful to emphasize that "[s]ome forms of commercial speech regulation are surely permissible." For example, restrictions on the time, place, or manner of expression are permissible provided that "they are justified without reference to the content of the regulated speech, that they serve a significant governmental interest, and that in so doing they leave open ample alternative channels for communication of the information." *Virginia Pharmacy,* at 771. Equally permissible are restrictions on false, deceptive, and misleading commercial speech.

"Untruthful speech, commercial or otherwise, has never been protected for its own sake. Obviously, much commercial speech is not provably false, or even wholly false, but only deceptive or misleading. We foresee no obstacle to a State's dealing effectively with this problem. The First Amendment, as we construe it today, does not prohibit the State from insuring that the stream of commercial information flow cleanly as well as freely." *Id.*, at 771–772. Regarding the permissible extent of commercial-speech regulation, the Court observed in *Virginia Pharmacy* that certain features of commercial speech differentiate it from other varieties of speech in ways that suggest that "a different degree of protection is necessary to insure that the flow of truthful and legitimate commercial information is unimpaired." Because it relates to a particular product or service, commercial speech is more objective, hence more verifiable, than other varieties of speech. Commercial speech, because of its importance to business profits, and because it is carefully calculated, is also less likely than other forms of speech to be inhibited by proper regulation. These attributes, the Court concluded, indicate that it is "appropriate to require that a commercial message appear in such a form . . . as [is] necessary to prevent its being deceptive. . . . They may also make inapplicable the prohibition against prior restraints." . . .

The use of trade names in connection with optometrical practice . . . is a form of commercial speech and nothing more. . . . A trade name conveys no information about the price and nature of the services offered by an optometrist until it acquires meaning over a period of time by associations formed in the minds of the public between the name and some standard of price or quality. Because these ill-defined associations of trade names with price and quality information can be manipulated by the users of trade names, there is a significant possibility that trade names will be used to mislead the public. . . .

By using different trade names at shops under his common ownership, an optometrist can give the public the false impression of competition among the shops. The use of a trade name also facilitates the advertising essential to large-scale commercial practices with numerous branch offices, conduct the State rationally may wish to discourage while not prohibiting commercial optometrical practice altogether. . . .

It is clear that the State's interest in protecting the public from the deceptive and misleading use of optometrical trade names is substantial and well demonstrated. We are convinced that § 5.13(d) is a constitutionally permissible state regulation in furtherance of this interest. We emphasize, in so holding, that the restriction on the use of trade names has only the most incidental effect on the content of the commercial speech of Texas optometrists. . . . Since the Act does not prohibit or limit the type of informational advertising held to be protected in *Virginia Pharmacy* and *Bates*, the factual information associated with trade names may be communicated freely and explicitly to the public. An optometrist may advertise the type of service he offers, the prices he charges, and whether he practices as a partner, associate, or employee with other optometrists. Rather than stifling commercial speech, § 5.13(d) ensures that information regarding optometrical services will be communicated more fully and accurately to consumers than it had been in the past when optometrists were allowed to convey the information through unstated and ambiguous associations with a trade name. In sum, Texas has done no more than require that commercial information about optometrical services "appear in such a form . . . as [is] necessary to prevent its being deceptive." *Virginia Pharmacy*. . . . The case is remanded with instruction to dissolve the injunction against the enforcement of Sec. 5.13(d).

[Mr. Justice Blackmun, with whom Mr. Justice Marshall joined, concurred in part and dissented in part.]

TINKER *v.* DES MOINES SCHOOL DISTRICT

393 U.S. 503; 89 Sup. Ct. 733; 21 L. Ed. 2d 731 (1969)

[A number of Des Moines children were suspended from school for wearing black armbands to class to protest against the war in Vietnam. Parents went to the federal courts to challenge the constitutionality of the suspensions.]

MR. JUSTICE FORTAS delivered the opinion of the Court:

The problem posed by the present case does not relate to regulation of the length of skirts or the type of clothing, to hair style, or deportment. Cf. *Ferrell* v. *Dallas Independent School District,* 392 F. 2d 697 (1968); *Pugsley* v. *Sellmeyer,* 158 Ark. 247, 250 S. W. 538 (1923). It does not concern aggressive, disruptive action or even group demonstrations. Our problem involves direct, primary First Amendment rights akin to "pure speech."

The school officials banned and sought to punish petitioners for a silent, passive expression of opinion, unaccompanied by any disorder or disturbance on the part of petitioners. There is here no evidence whatever of petitioners' interference, actual or nascent, with the schools' work or of collision with the rights of other students to be secure and to be let alone. Accordingly, this case does not concern speech or action that intrudes upon the work of the schools or the rights of other students.

The District Court concluded that the action of the school authorities was reasonable because it was based upon their fear of a disturbance from the wearing of the armbands. But, in our system, undifferentiated fear or apprehension of disturbance is not enough to overcome the right to freedom of expression.

In order for the State in the person of school officials to justify prohibition of a particular expression of opinion, it must be able to show that its action was caused by something more than a mere desire to avoid the discomfort and unpleasantness that always accompany an unpopular viewpoint. Certainly where there is no finding and no showing that engaging in the forbidden conduct would "materially and substantially interfere with the requirements of appropriate discipline in the operation of the school," the prohibition cannot be sustained.

In the present case, the District Court made no such finding, and our independent examination of the record fails to yield evidence that the school authorities had reason to anticipate that the wearing of the armbands would substantially interfere with the work of the school or impinge upon the rights of other students. Even an official memorandum prepared after the suspension that listed the reasons for the ban on wearing the armbands made no reference to the anticipation of such disruption.

On the contrary, the action of the school authorities appears to have been based upon an urgent wish to avoid the controversy which might result from the expression, even by the silent symbol of armbands, of opposition to this Nation's part in the conflagration in Vietnam.

It is also relevant that the school authorities did not purport to prohibit the wearing of all symbols of political or controversial significance. The record shows that students in some of the schools wore buttons relating to national political campaigns, and some even wore the Iron Cross, traditionally a symbol of Nazism. The order prohibiting the wearing of armbands did not extend to these. Instead, a particular symbol—black armbands worn to exhibit opposition to this Nation's involvement in Vietnam—was singled out for prohibition. Clearly, the prohibition of expression of one particular opinion, at least without evidence that it is necessary to avoid material and substantial interference with schoolwork or discipline, is not constitutionally permissible.

As we have discussed, the record does not demonstrate any facts which might reasonably have led school authorities to forecast substantial disruption of or material interference with school activities, and no disturbances or disorders on the school premises in fact occurred. These petitioners merely went about their ordained rounds in school. Their deviation consisted only in wearing on their sleeve a band of black cloth, not more than two inches wide. They wore it to exhibit their disapproval of the Vietnam hostilities and their advocacy of a truce, to make their views known, and, by their example, to influence others to adopt them. They neither interrupted school activities nor sought to intrude in the school affairs or the lives of others. They caused discussion outside of the classrooms, but no interference with work and no disorder. In the circumstances, our Constitution does not permit officials of the State to deny their form of expression.

Reversed and remanded.

MR. JUSTICE STEWART, concurring:

Although I agree with much of what is said in the Court's opinion, and with its judgment in this case, I cannot share the Court's uncritical assumption that, school discipline aside, the First Amendment rights of children are co-extensive with those of adults.

MR. JUSTICE BLACK, dissenting:

Assuming that the Court is correct in holding that the conduct of wearing armbands for the purpose of conveying political ideas is protected by the First Amendment, compare, *e.g., Giboney* v. *Empire Storage & Ice Co.,* 336 U.S. 490 (1949), the crucial remaining questions are whether students and teachers may use the schools at their whim as a platform for the exercise of free speech—"symbolic" or "pure"—and whether the courts will allocate to themselves the function of deciding how the pupils' school day will be spent. While I have always believed that under the First and Fourteenth Amendments neither the State nor the Federal Government has any authority to regulate or censor the content of a speech, I have never believed that any person has a right to give speeches or engage in demonstrations where he pleases and when he pleases. This Court has already rejected such a notion. In *Cox* v. *Louisiana,* 379 U.S. 536, 554 (1965), for example, the Court clearly stated that the rights of free speech and assembly "do not mean that everyone with opinions or beliefs to express may address a group at any public place and at any time."

While the record does not show that any of these armband students shouted, used profane language, or were violent in any manner, detailed testimony by some of them shows their armbands caused comments, warnings by other students, the poking of fun at them, and a warning by an older football player that other, nonprotesting students had better let them alone. There is also evidence that a teacher of mathematics had his lesson period practically "wrecked" chiefly by disputes with Beth Tinker, who wore her armband for her "demonstration." Even a casual reading of the record shows that this armband did divert students' minds from their regular lessons, and that talk, comments, etc., made John Tinker "self-conscious" in attending school with his armband. While the absence of obscene remarks or boisterous and loud disorder perhaps justifies the Court's statement that the few armband students did not actually "disrupt" the classwork, I think the record overwhelmingly shows that the armbands did exactly what the elected school officials and principals foresaw they would, that it took the students' minds off their classwork and diverted them to thoughts about the highly emotional subject of the Vietnam war. And I repeat that if the time has come when pupils of state-supported schools, kindergartens, grammar schools, or high schools, can defy and flout orders of school officials to keep their minds on their own schoolwork, it is the beginning of a new revolutionary era of permissiveness in this country fostered by the judiciary. The next logical step, it appears to me, would be to hold unconstitutional laws that bar pupils under 21 or 18 from voting, or from being elected members of the boards of education.

Change has been said to be truly the law of life but sometimes the old and the tried and true are worth holding. The schools of this Nation have undoubtedly contributed to giving us a more law-abiding people. Uncontrolled and uncontrollable liberty is an enemy to domestic peace. We cannot close our eyes to the fact that some of the country's greatest problems are crimes committed by the youth, too many of school age. They have picketed schools to force students not to cross their picket lines and have too often violently attacked earnest but frightened students who wanted an education that the pickets did not want them to get. Students engaged in such activities are apparently confident that they know far more about how to operate public school systems than do their parents, teachers, and elected school officials. It is no answer to say that the particular students here have not yet reached such high points in their demands to attend classes in order to exercise their political pressures. Turned loose with lawsuits for damages and injunctions against their teachers as they are here, it is nothing but wishful thinking to imagine that young, immature students will not soon believe it is their right to control the schools rather than the right of the States that collect the taxes to hire the teachers for the benefit of the pupils. This case, therefore, wholly without constitutional reasons in my judgment, subjects all the public schools in the country to the whims and caprices of their loudest-mouthed, but maybe not their brightest, students. I, for one, am not fully persuaded that school pupils are wise enough, even with this Court's expert help from Washington, to run the 23,390 public school systems in our fifty States. I wish, therefore, wholly to disclaim any purpose on my part to hold that the Federal Constitution compels the teachers, parents, and elected school officials to surrender control of the American public school system to public school students. I dissent.

MR. JUSTICE HARLAN, dissenting:

I certainly agree that state public school authorities in the discharge of their responsibilities are not wholly exempt from the requirements of the Fourteenth Amendment respecting the freedoms of expression and association. At the same time I am reluctant to believe that there is any disagreement between the majority and myself on the proposition that school officials should be accorded the widest authority in maintaining discipline and good order in their institutions. To translate that proposition into a workable constitutional rule, I would, in cases like this, cast upon those complaining the burden of showing that a particular school measure was motivated by other than legitimate school concerns—for example, a desire to prohibit the expression of an unpopular point of view, while permitting expression of the dominant opinion.

Finding nothing in this record which impugns the good faith of respondents in promulgating the armband regulation, I would affirm the judgment below.

BRANZBURG *v.* HAYES

408 U.S. 665; 92 Sup. Ct. 2646; 33 L. Ed. 2d 626 (1972)

[This case and its two companions each involve reporters. Branzburg had written articles about drug activities he had observed. He refused to testify to a state grand jury about those activities. Pappas was allowed to remain in Black Panther headquarters on the condition that he would not disclose what he observed. He refused to answer state grand jury questions about what went on at the headquarters during a riot. Caldwell was a black reporter who had been covering the Black Panthers. He refused to testify before a federal grand jury inquiring into the possible violation of federal statutes forbidding threatening the life of the President and crossing state lines for the purpose of inciting to riot.]

Opinion of the Court by MR. JUSTICE WHITE . . . :

The issue in these cases is whether requiring newsmen to appear and testify before State or federal grand juries abridges the freedom of speech and press guaranteed by the First Amendment. We hold that it does not.

[The newsmen] press First Amendment claims that may be simply put: that to gather news it is often necessary to agree either not to identify the source of information published or to publish only part of the facts revealed, or both; that if the reporter is nevertheless forced to reveal these confidences to a grand jury, the source so identified and other confidential sources of other reporters will be measurably deterred from furnishing publishable information, all to the detriment of the free flow of information protected by the First Amendment. . . . The heart of the claim is that the burden on news gathering resulting from compelling reporters to disclose confidential information outweighs any public interest in obtaining the information.

We do not [hold] that news gathering does not qualify for First Amendment protection; without some protection for seeking out the news, freedom of the press could be eviscerated. But this case involves no intrusions upon speech or assembly, [and] no penalty, civil or criminal, related to the content of published material is at issue here. The use of confidential sources by the press is not forbidden or restricted; reporters remain free to seek news from any source by means within the law. No attempt is made to require the press to publish its sources of information or indiscriminately to disclose them on request.

The sole issue before us is the obligation of reporters to respond to grand jury subpoenas as other citizens do and to answer questions relevant to an investigation into the commission of crime. . . .

It is clear that the First Amendment does not invalidate every incidental burdening of the press that may result from the enforcement of civil or criminal statutes of general applicability. . . . It has generally been held that the First Amendment does not guarantee the press a constitutional right of special access to information not available to the public generally. . . . Despite the fact that news gathering may be hampered, the press is regularly excluded from grand jury proceedings, our own conferences, the meetings of other official bodies gathered in executive session, and the meeting of private organizations. Newsmen have no constitutional right of access to the scenes of crime or disaster when the general public is excluded, and they may be prohibited from attending or publishing information about trials if such restrictions are necessary to assure a defendant a fair trial before an impartial tribunal. . . . It is thus not surprising that the great weight of authority is that newsmen are not exempt from the normal duty of appearing before a grand jury and answering questions relevant to a criminal investigation. . . .

The prevailing constitutional view of the newsman's privilege is very much rooted in the ancient role of the grand jury. . . . Because its task is to inquire into the existence of possible criminal conduct and to return only well-founded indictments, its investigative powers are necessarily broad. . . . Although the powers of the grand jury are not unlimited and are subject to the supervision of a judge, the long standing principle that "the public has a right to every man's evidence," except for those persons protected by a constitutional, common law, or statutory privilege, is particularly applicable to grand jury proceedings.

A number of States have provided newsmen a statutory privilege of varying breadth, but the majority have not done so, and none has been provided by federal statute. . . . We are asked to [interpret] the First Amendment to grant newsmen a testimonial privilege that other citizens do not enjoy. This we decline to do. . . . On the records now before us, we perceive no basis for holding that the public interest in law enforcement and in ensuring effective grand jury proceedings is insufficient to override the consequential, but uncertain, burden on news gathering which is said to result from insisting that reporters, like other citizens, respond to relevant questions put to them in the course of a valid grand jury investigation or criminal trial.

This conclusion [does not] threaten the vast bulk of confidential relationships between reporters and their sources. Grand juries address themselves to the issues of whether crimes have been committed and who committed them. Only where news sources themselves are implicated in crime or possess information relevant to the grand jury's task need they or the reporter be concerned about grand jury subpoenas. Nothing before us indicates that a large number or percentage of *all* confidential news sources fall into either category and would in any way be deterred by our holding. . . .

The preference for anonymity of those confidential informants involved in actual criminal conduct is presumably a product of their desire to escape criminal prosecution, and this preference, while understandable, is hardly deserving of constitutional protection. It would be frivolous to assert—and no one does in these cases—that the First Amendment, in the interest of securing news or otherwise, confers a license on either the reporter or his news sources to violate otherwise valid criminal laws. Although stealing documents or private wiretapping could provide noteworthy information, neither reporter nor source is immune from conviction for such conduct, whatever the impact on the flow of news. . . . [W]e cannot seriously entertain the notion that the First Amendment protects a newsman's agreement to conceal the criminal conduct of his source, or evidence thereof, on the theory that it is better to write about crime than to do something about it. . . .

There remain those situations where a source is not engaged in criminal conduct but has information suggesting illegal conduct by others. . . . The argument that the flow of news will be diminished by compelling reporters to aid the grand jury in a criminal investigation is not irrational, nor are the records before us silent on the matter. But we remain unclear how often and to what extent informers are actually deterred from furnishing information when newsmen are forced to testify before a grand jury. The available data indicate that some newsmen rely a great deal on confidential sources and that some informants are particularly sensitive to the threat of exposure and may be silenced if it is held by this Court that, ordinarily, newsmen must testify pursuant to subpoenas, but the evidence fails to demonstrate that there would be a significant constriction of the flow of news to the public if this Court reaffirms the prior common law and constitutional rule regarding the testimonial obligations of newsmen. Estimates of the inhibiting effect of such subpoenas on the willingness of informants to make disclosures to newsmen are widely divergent and to a great extent speculative. It would be difficult to canvass the views of the informants themselves; surveys of reporters on this topic are chiefly opinions of predicted informant behavior and must be viewed in the light of the professional self-interest of the interviewees. Reliance by the press on confidential informants does not mean that all such sources will in fact dry up because of the later possible appearance of the newsman before a grand jury. The reporter may never be called and if he objects to testifying, the prosecution may not insist. Also, the relationship of many informants to the press is a symbiotic one which is unlikely to be greatly inhibited by the threat of subpoena: quite often, such informants are members of a minority political or cultural group which relies heavily on the media to propagate its views, publicize its aims, and magnify its exposure to the public. Moreover, grand juries characteristically conduct secret proceedings, and law enforcement officers are themselves experienced in dealing with informers and have their own methods for protecting them without interference with the effective administration of justice. There is little before us indicating that informants whose interest in avoiding exposure is that it may threaten job security, personal safety, or peace of mind, would in fact, be in a worse position, or would think they would be, if they risked placing their trust in public officials as well as reporters. . . .

Accepting the fact, however, that an undetermined number of informants not themselves implicated in crime will nevertheless, for whatever reason, refuse to talk to newsmen if they fear identification by a reporter in an official investigation, we cannot accept the argument that the public interest in possible future news about crime from undisclosed, unverified sources must take precedence over the public interest in pursuing and prosecuting those crimes reported to the press by informants and in thus deterring the commission of such crimes in the future. . . .

We are admonished that refusal to provide a First Amendment reporter's privilege will undermine the freedom of the press to collect and disseminate news. But this is not the lesson history teaches us. [T]he common law recognized no such privilege, and the constitutional argument was not even asserted until 1958. From the beginning of our country the press has operated without constitutional protection for press informants, and the press has flourished. . . .

It is said that currently press subpoenas have multiplied, that mutual distrust and tension between press and officialdom have increased, that reporting styles have changed, and that there is now more need for confidential sources, particularly where the press seeks news about minority cultural and political groups or dissident organizations suspicious of the law and public officials. These developments, even if true, are treacherous grounds for a far-reaching interpretation of the First Amendment fastening a nationwide rule on courts, grand juries, and prosecuting officials everywhere. . . .

The argument for such a constitutional privilege rests heavily on those cases holding that the infringement of protected First

Amendment rights must be no broader than necessary to achieve a permissible governmental purpose. We do not deal, however, with a governmental institution that has abused its proper function. . . . Nothing in the record indicates that these grand juries were "prob[ing] at will and without relation to existing need." Also, there is no attempt here by the grand juries to invade protected First Amendment rights by forcing wholesale disclosures of names and organizational affiliations for a purpose which is not germane to the determination of whether crime has been committed, and the characteristic secrecy of grand jury proceedings is a further protection against the undue invasion of such rights.

The requirements of those cases which hold that a State's interest must be "compelling" or "paramount" to justify even an indirect burden on First Amendment rights, are also met here. . . . it is quite apparent (1) that the State has the necessary interest in extirpating the traffic in illegal drugs, in forestalling assassination attempts on the President, and in preventing the community from being disrupted by violent disorders endangering both persons and property; and (2) that, based on the stories Branzburg and Caldwell wrote and Pappas' admitted conduct, the grand jury called these reporters as they would others—because it was likely that they could supply information to help the Government determine whether illegal conduct had occurred and, if it had, whether there was sufficient evidence to return an indictment.

. . . The administration of a constitutional newsman's privilege would present practical and conceptual difficulties of a high order. Sooner or later, it would be necessary to define those categories of newsmen who qualified for the privilege, a questionable procedure in light of the traditional doctrine that liberty of the press is the right of the lonely pamphleteer who uses carbon paper or a mimeograph just as much as of the large metropolitan publisher who utilizes the latest photocomposition methods. . . . The informative function asserted by representatives of the organized press in the present cases is also performed by lecturers, political pollsters, novelists, academic researchers, and dramatists. . . .

In addition, there is much force in the pragmatic view that the press has at its disposal powerful mechanisms of communication and is far from helpless to protect itself from harassment or substantial harm. Furthermore, if what the newsmen urged in these cases is true—that law enforcement cannot hope to gain and may suffer from subpoenaing newsmen before grand juries—prosecutors will be loath to risk so much for so little. Thus, at the federal level the Attorney General has already fashioned a set of rules for federal officials in connection with subpoenaing members of the press to testify before grand juries or at criminal trials. These rules are a major step in the direction petitioners desire to move. They may prove wholly sufficient to resolve the bulk of disagreements and controversies between press and federal officials.

. . . grand jury investigations if instituted or conducted other than in good faith, would pose wholly different issues for resolution under the First Amendment. Official harassment of the press undertaken not for purposes of law enforcement but to disrupt a reporter's relationship with his news sources would have no justification. Grand juries are subject to judicial control and subpoenas to motions to quash. We do not expect courts will forget that grand juries must operate within the limits of the First Amendment as well as the Fifth.

MR. JUSTICE POWELL, concurring in the opinion of the Court.

I add this brief statement to emphasize what seems to me to be the limited nature of the Court's holding. The Court does not hold that newsmen, subpoenaed to testify before a grand jury, are without constitutional rights with respect to the gathering of news or in safeguarding their sources. Certainly, we do not hold, as suggested in the dissenting opinion, that state and federal authorities are free to "annex" the news media as "an investigative arm of government." . . .

As indicated in the concluding portion of the opinion, the Court states that no harassment of newsmen will be tolerated. . . .

In short, the courts will be available to newsmen under circumstances where legitimate First Amendment interests require protection.

MR. JUSTICE STEWART, with whom MR. JUSTICE BRENNAN and MR. JUSTICE MARSHALL join, dissenting:

The Court's crabbed view of the First Amendment reflects a disturbing insensitivity to the critical role of an independent press in our society. The question whether a reporter has a constitutional right to a confidential relationship with his source is of first impression here, but the principles which should guide our decision are as basic as any to be found in the Constitution. While Mr. Justice Powell's enigmatic concurring opinion gives some hope of a more flexible view in the future, the Court in these cases holds that a newsman has no First Amendment right to protect his sources when called before a grand jury. The Court thus invites state and federal authorities to undermine the historic independence of the press by attempting to annex the journalistic profession as an investigative arm of government. Not only will this decision impair performance of the press' constitutionally protected functions, but it will, I am convinced, in the long run, harm rather than help the administration of justice. . . .

The right to gather news implies, in turn, a right to a confidential relationship between a reporter and his source. This proposition follows as a matter of simple logic once three factual predicates are recognized: (1) newsmen require informants to gather news; (2) confidentiality—the promise or understanding that names or certain aspects of communications will be kept off-the-record—is essential to the creation and maintenance of a news-gathering relationship with informants; and (3) the existence of an unbridled subpoena power—the absence of a constitutional right protecting, in *any* way, a confidential relationship from compulsory process—will either deter sources from divulging information or deter reporters from gathering and publishing information. After today's decision, the potential [informant must] choose between risking exposure by giving information or avoiding the risk by remaining silent. The reporter must speculate about whether contact with a controversial source or publication of controversial material will lead to a subpoena.

[T]he common sense understanding that [deterrence] will occur is buttressed by concrete evidence. . . . Individual reporters and commentators have noted such effects. Surveys have verified that unbridled subpoena power will substantially impair the flow of news to the public, especially in sensitive areas involving governmental officials, financial affairs, political figures, dissidents, or minority groups that require in-depth, investigative reporting. . . . No evidence contradicting the existence of such deterrent effects was offered at the trials or in the briefs here. . . .

The impairment of the flow of news cannot, of course, be proven with scientific precision, as the Court seems to demand. Obviously, not every news-gathering relationship requires confidentiality. And it is difficult to pinpoint precisely how many relationships do require a promise or understanding of nondisclosure. But we have never before demanded that First Amendment rights rest on elaborate empirical studies demonstrating beyond any conceivable doubt that deterrent effects exist; we have never before required proof of the exact number of people potentially affected by governmental action, who would actually be dissuaded from engaging in First Amendment activity.

. . . Thus, we cannot escape the conclusion that when neither the reporter nor his source can rely on the shield of confidentiality against unrestrained use of the grand jury's subpoena power, valuable information will not be published and the public dialogue will inevitably be impoverished.

Posed against the First Amendment's protection of the newsman's confidential relationships in these cases is society's interest in the use of the grand jury to administer justice fairly and effectively. [T]he longstanding rule making every person's evidence available to the grand jury is not absolute. The rule has been limited by the Fifth Amendment, the Fourth Amendment, and the evidentiary privileges of the common law. [The Court has] observed that any exemption from the duty to testify before the grand jury "presupposes a very real interest to be protected." Such an interest must surely be the First Amendment protection of a confidential relationship that I have discussed above.

In striking the proper balance, [we] must begin with the basic proposition [that] First Amendment rights require special safeguards. This Court has erected such safeguards when government, by legislative investigation or other investigative means, has attempted to pierce the shield of privacy inherent in freedom of association. . . .

The established method of "carefully" circumscribing investigative powers is to place a heavy burden of justification on government officials when First Amendment rights are impaired. *[NAACP* v. *Button; Gibson.]* Thus, when an investigation impinges on First Amendment rights, the government must not only show that the inquiry is of "compelling and overriding importance" but it must also "convincingly" demonstrate that the investigation is "substantially related" to the information sought. . . .

[T]he vices of vagueness and overbreadth which legislative investigations may manifest are also exhibited by grand jury inquiries, [since] standards of materiality and relevance are greatly relaxed. For, as the United States notes in its brief in *Caldwell,* the grand jury "need establish no factual basis for commencing an investigation, and can pursue rumors which further investigation may prove groundless."

Accordingly, when a reporter is asked to appear before a grand jury and reveal confidences, I would hold that the government must (1) show that there is probable cause to believe that the newsman has information which is clearly relevant to a specific probable violation of law; (2) demonstrate that the information sought cannot be obtained by alternative means less destructive of First Amendment rights; and (3) demonstrate a compelling and overriding interest in the information. . . .

[It] is obviously not true that the only persons about whom reporters will be forced to testify [under the Court's decision] will be those "confidential informants involved in actual criminal conduct" and those having "information suggesting illegal conduct by others." [G]iven the grand jury's extraordinarily broad investigative powers and the weak standards of relevance and materiality that apply during such inquiries, reporters, if they have no testimonial privilege, will be called to give information about informants who have neither committed crimes nor have information about crime. It is to avoid deterrence of such sources and thus to prevent needless injury to First Amendment values that I think the government must be required to show probable cause that the newsman has information which is clearly relevant to a specific probable violation of criminal law. . . .

Both the "probable cause" and "alternative means" requirements [would] serve the vital function of mediating between the public interest in the administration of justice and the constitutional protection of the full flow of information. These requirements would avoid a direct conflict between these competing concerns, and they would generally provide adequate protection for newsmen. . . .The sad paradox of the Court's position is [that] the newsman will not only cease to be a useful grand jury witness; he will cease to investigate and publish information about issues of public import. I cannot subscribe to such an anomalous result, for, in my view, the interests protected by the First Amendment are not antagonistic to the administration of justice. . . .

[Mr. Justice Douglas also dissented.]

NATIONAL ASSOCIATION FOR THE ADVANCEMENT OF COLORED PEOPLE *v.* ALABAMA

357 U.S. 449; 78 Sup. Ct. 1163; 2 L. Ed. 2d 1488 (1958)

[The controversy over the desegregation of public schools and other accommodations resulted in a number of attempts to curb the activities of the NAACP, a nonprofit membership corporation chartered in New York State, which had long sought to improve the lot of the Negro. This significant case arose from the efforts of Alabama to halt the work of the organization.

Like many other states, Alabama has a statute requiring out-of-state corporations to register and meet certain other requirements before conducting business in the state. The NAACP opened a regional office in Alabama in 1951, but it never complied with the statute, because it considered itself exempt. In 1956, the state Attorney General brought court action to enjoin the NAACP from conducting further activities within the state and to oust it from Alabama. A state circuit court issued an order restraining the association from engaging in any further activities and forbidding it to take any steps to qualify itself to do business within the state. The court also ordered that the association produce its records and papers, including the names and addresses of all of the group's members and agents in Alabama. After a brief delay, the NAACP produced all the records called for by the production order except the membership lists, the disclosure of which it resisted on constitutional grounds. For refusing to submit its membership lists, the organization was held in contempt and fined $100,000. Petitions for certiorari to review the contempt judgment were twice dismissed by the Supreme Court of Alabama. The Supreme Court then granted certiorari.]

MR. JUSTICE HARLAN delivered the opinion of the Court:

. . . The question presented is whether Alabama, consistently with the Due Process Clause of the Fourteenth Amendment, can compel petitioner to reveal to the State's Attorney General the names and addresses of all its Alabama members and agents, without regard to their positions or functions in the Association. . . .

The Association both urges that it is constitutionally entitled to resist official inquiry into its membership lists, and that it may assert, on behalf of its members, a right personal to them to be protected from compelled disclosure by the State of their affiliation with the Association as revealed by the membership lists. We think that petitioner argues more appropriately the rights of its members, and that its nexus with them is sufficient to permit that it act as their representative before this Court. In so concluding, we reject respondent's argument that the Association lacks standing to assert here constitutional rights pertaining to the members, who are not of course parties to the litigation.

To limit the breadth of issues which must be dealt with in particular litigation, this Court has generally insisted that parties rely only on constitutional rights which are personal to themselves. . . . This rule is related to the broader doctrine that constitutional adjudication should where possible be avoided. . . . The principle is not disrespected where constitutional rights of persons who are not immediately before the Court could not be effectively vindicated except through an appropriate representative before the Court. . . .

If petitioner's rank-and-file members are constitutionally entitled to withhold their connection with the Association despite the production order, it is manifest that this right is properly assertable by the Association. To require that it be claimed by the members themselves would result in nullification of the right at the very moment of its assertion. Petitioner is the appropriate party to assert these rights, because it and its members are in every practical sense identical. The Association, which provides in its constitution that "any person who is in accordance with [its] principles and policies . . ." may become a member, is but the medium through which its individual members seek to make more effective the expression of their own views. The reasonable likelihood that the Association itself through diminished financial support and membership may be adversely affected if production is compelled is a further factor pointing towards our holding that petitioner has standing to complain of the production order on behalf of its members. . . .

We thus reach petitioner's claim that the production order in the state litigation trespasses upon fundamental freedoms protected by the Due Process Clause of the Fourteenth Amendment. Petitioner argues that in view of the facts and circumstances shown in the record, the effect of compelled disclosure of the membership lists will be to abridge the rights of its rank-and-file members to engage in lawful association in support of their common beliefs. It contends that governmental action which, although not directly suppressing association, nevertheless carries this consequence, can be justified only upon some overriding valid interest of the State.

Effective advocacy of both public and private points of view, particularly controversial ones, is undeniably enhanced by group association, as this Court has more than once recognized by remarking upon the close nexus between the freedoms of speech and assembly. . . . It is beyond debate that freedom to engage in association for the advancement of beliefs and ideas is an inseparable aspect of the "liberty" assured by the Due Process Clause of the Fourteenth Amendment, which embraces freedom of speech. . . . Of course, it is immaterial whether the beliefs sought to be advanced by association pertain to political, economic, religious or cultural matters, and state action which may have the effect of curtailing the freedom to associate is subject to the closest scrutiny. . . .

It is hardly a novel perception that compelled disclosure of affiliation with groups engaged in advocacy may constitute as effective a restraint on freedom of association as the forms of governmental action in the case above were thought likely to produce upon the particular constitutional rights there involved. This Court has recognized the vital relationship between freedom to associate and privacy in one's associations. When referring to the varied forms of governmental action which might interfere with freedom of assembly, it said in *American Communications Assn.* v. *Douds* . . . : "A requirement that adherents of particular religious faiths or political parties wear identifying arm-bands, for example, is obviously of this nature." Compelled disclosure of membership in an organization engaged in advocacy of particular beliefs is of the same order. Inviolability of privacy in group association may in many circumstances be indispensable to preservation of freedom of association, particularly where a group espouses dissident beliefs. . . .

We think that the production order, in the respects here drawn in question, must be regarded as entailing the likelihood of a substantial restraint upon the exercise by petitioner's members of their right to freedom of association. Petitioner has made an uncontroverted showing that on past occasions revelation of the identity of its rank-and-file members has exposed these members to economic reprisal, loss of employment, threat of physical coercion, and other manifestations of public hostility. Under these circumstances, we think it apparent that compelled disclosure of petitioner's Alabama membership is likely to affect adversely the ability of petitioner and its members to pursue their collective effort to foster beliefs which they admittedly have the right to advocate, in that it may induce members to withdraw from the Association and dissuade others from joining it because of fear of exposure of their beliefs shown through their associations and of the consequences of this exposure.

It is not sufficient to answer, as the State does here, that whatever repressive effect compulsory disclosure of names of petitioner's members may have upon participation by Alabama citizens in petitioner's activities follows not from state action but from private community pressures. The crucial factor is the interplay of governmental and private action, for it is only after the initial exertion of state power represented by the production order that private action takes hold.

We turn to the final question whether Alabama has demonstrated an interest in obtaining the disclosures it seeks from petitioner which is sufficient to justify the deterrent effect which we have concluded these disclosures may well have on the free exercise by petitioner's members of their constitutionally protected right of association. . . . It is not of moment that the State has here acted solely through its judicial branch, for whether legislative or judicial, it is still the application of state power which we are asked to scrutinize.

It is important to bear in mind that petitioner asserts no right to absolute immunity from state investigation, and no right to disregard Alabama's laws. As shown by its substantial compliance with the production order, petitioner does not deny Alabama's right to obtain from it such information as the State desires concerning the purposes of the Association and its activities within the State. Petitioner has not objected to divulging the identity of its members who are employed by or hold official positions with it. It has urged the rights solely of its ordinary rank-and-file members. This is therefore not analogous to a case involving the interest of a State in protecting its citizens in their dealings with paid solicitors or agents of foreign corporations by requiring identification. . . .

We hold that the immunity from state scrutiny of membership lists which the Association claims on behalf of its members is here so related to the right of the members to pursue their lawful private interest privately and to associate freely with others in so doing as to come within the protection of the Fourteenth Amendment. And we conclude that Alabama has fallen short of showing a controlling justification for the deterrent effect on the free enjoyment of the right to associate which disclosure of membership lists is likely to have. Accordingly, the judgment of civil contempt and the $100,000 fine which resulted from petitioner's refusal to comply with the production order in this respect must fall. . . .

For the reasons stated, the judgment of the Supreme Court of Alabama must be reversed and the case remanded for proceedings not inconsistent with this opinion.

Reversed.

CHAPTER 12

Freedom of Religion

The First Amendment provides in clear and positive terms that Congress cannot pass laws respecting an establishment of religion or prohibiting its free exercise.

The religious freedom clause of the First Amendment was the product of the Colonists' bitter memories of established state churches, religious wars, and various forms of religious persecution. The First Amendment launched a unique American experiment in the development of religious freedom and the separation of church and state. "The experiment rested upon the principle that government has no power to legislate in the field of religion either by restricting its free exercise or providing for its support." [1] This was a radical departure indeed from the firmly established tradition that the "relationship between man and God was a matter of legitimate concern of political government." [2] The religious freedom provision of the First Amendment confirmed

[1] Leo Pfeffer, *The Liberties of an American* (Boston: Beacon Press, 1956), p. 33.

[2] Ibid., p. 32.

the feelings of the overwhelming majority of Americans, who looked upon religion as a private matter. This attitude was reflected in Congress, where very few laws dealing with religion were enacted. Thus very few cases testing the meaning of the religion clause of the First Amendment were brought to the Supreme Court.

State action affecting religion could be challenged in the Supreme Court on constitutional grounds only after the development of the doctrine that the First Amendment restrictions applied to the states through the Fourteenth Amendment. We have already seen that the process of bringing the First Amendment freedoms under the protection of the Fourteenth Amendment did not begin until 1925, with Justice Sanford's remark in *Gitlow* v. *New York*. Finally, in 1940, the Supreme Court held, in *Cantwell* v. *Connecticut* (p. 444), that the freedom of religion provision of the First Amendment constituted a restriction upon the states through the Fourteenth Amendment. In 1947, the Court completed the process of incorporating the First Amendment into the "liberty" of the Fourteenth Amendment by holding, in *Everson* v. *Board of Education* (p. 452), that the establishment of religion clause also restricted state action.

As regards religion, the First Amendment contains *two* prohibitions; it forbids laws that prohibit the free exercise of religion as well as laws respecting an establishment of religion. Although in many cases the Supreme Court considers the free exercise and the separation of church and state as parts of the same principle, a basic paradox in the relation of the two prohibitions to one another should be noted. The case of *Sherbert* v. *Verner*, 374 U.S. 398 (1963), provides a good illustration. A Seventh Day Adventist, in a town whose factories worked a Monday through Saturday week, was denied unemployment benefits because she was not available for work on every working day as required by the statute. The Court held that such a denial placed an unconstitutional burden on the free exercise of her religion, which forbade her to work on Saturday—her Sabbath. (Compare this holding with the *Sunday law* decisions rendered earlier by the Court, p. 483.) But to protect her free exercise, the Court had to carve out a special, religiously based exemption to the state's general unemployment statute—an exemption that resulted in better treatment for those who refuse to work on Saturday for a religious reason than for those who refuse for some other reason. Thus, in order to protect free exercise, the Court has to require establishment at least in the sense of demanding governmental recognition of a particular religious group as enjoying a special exemption from a statute that all others must obey. It is not easy to see how this dilemma can be resolved. [See *Thomas* v. *Review Board*, 101 S.Ct. 1425 (1981).]

The same problem was involved in the conscientious objection provision of the Selective Service Act, which provided draft exemptions for those whose objection to war was based on a "belief in a relation to a Supreme Being involving duties superior to those arising from any human relation, [rather than] essentially political, sociological, or philosophical views or a merely personal moral code." In order to protect the free exercise of the orthodox, religious pacifist, this statute exempted members of some religions from the general legal obligations that bind members of other religions and the nonreligious.

The Court avoided the problem in *United States* v. *Seeger,* 380 U.S. 163 (1965) by expanding the statutory language to cover those like the defendant who had no formal religious affiliation but did have a "belief that is sincere and meaningful [and] occupies a place in the life of its possessor parallel to that filled by the orthodox belief in God." In *Welsh* v. *United States,* 398 U.S. 333 (1970), it extended the *Seeger* protection to all who believed deeply in pacifism and whose belief was based on "moral, ethical, or religious principles." Finally, in *Gillette* v. *United States,* 401 U.S. 437 (1971), the Court ruled against the constitutional claims of those who had been refused exemption because they objected to the particular war in Vietnam rather than war in general. The Court held that the statutory distinction between thoroughgoing pacifists and selective conscientious objectors was based on the "neutral, secular" purpose of creating a standard for draft boards that could be easily and fairly administered.

Free Exercise of Religion

The meaning of the First Amendment in the field of religion was considered for the first time by the Supreme Court in *Reynolds* v. *United States,* 98 U.S. 145 (1878). At that time Mormons had a religious duty, when circumstances permitted, to practice polygamy. Reynolds, a Mormon living in the Territory of Utah, had two wives, in conformity with the religious doctrine of his church. However, Congress had enacted a law that made polygamy a crime in the territories of the United States. Reynolds was tried and convicted of violating the federal law. In his appeal to the Supreme Court, he maintained that because polygamy was a part of his religious belief, the act of Congress violated his free exercise of religion under the First Amendment. Nevertheless, the Court upheld the statute in a unanimous opinion.

> Laws are made for the government of actions, and while they cannot interfere with mere religious belief and opinions, they may with practices. Suppose that one believed that human sacrifices were a necessary part of religious worship, would it be seriously contended that the civil government under which he lived could not interfere to prevent a sacrifice? Or, if a wife religiously believed it was her duty to burn herself upon the funeral pyre of her dead husband, would it be beyond the power of the civil government to prevent her carrying her belief into practice? So here, as a law of the organization of society under the exclusive dominion of the United States, it is provided that plural marriages shall not be allowed. Can a man excuse his practices to the contrary because of his religious belief? To permit this would be to make the professed doctrines of religious belief superior to the law of the land, and in effect to permit every citizen to become a law unto himself. Government could exist only in name under such circumstances.

The *Reynolds* decision established clearly that freedom of religion, like other freedoms, is not absolute or unlimited. The constitutional limits of the free exercise of religion are defined ultimately by the Supreme Court.

JEHOVAH'S WITNESSES

The issue of religious freedom has been raised often by a small religious sect known as Jehovah's Witnesses. The Witnesses attracted little attention in the United States until the 1930s, when they began a vigorous nationwide campaign to spread their religious doctrines and prepare the world for the second coming of the Lord.[3]

Jehovah's Witnesses have fought vigorously every legal attempt to curb their activities. As a result, they have contributed more to the development of a constitutional law concerning First Amendment liberties than any other group in our history. They have all the attributes necessary for political success: manpower, money, organization, tenacity, and a taste for political action—in this instance litigation, or lobbying the Supreme Court.

Many of the Supreme Court cases involving Jehovah's Witnesses have been decided under the freedom of speech, press, and assembly guaranties rather than the religion clause. In *Lovell* v. *City of Griffin,* 303 U.S. 444 (1938), they won the right to distribute religious handbills without having first to secure a license from a local official. The Court decided also, in *Martin* v. *City of Struthers,* 319 U.S. 141 (1943), that Witnesses cannot be forbidden to knock on doors or ring doorbells in order to give out handbills and literature. In *Cantwell* v. *Connecticut* (p. 444) they won another notable victory.

On the other hand, the Witnesses' claims were denied by the Supreme Court in a few cases. In *Cox* v. *New Hampshire,* 312 U.S. 569 (1941), the Court ruled that Witnesses can be required to secure a permit before holding a parade or procession on public streets. From *Cox* there flows a whole line of cases that establish the right of government to make reasonable regulations governing the time, place, and manner of speech so long as those regulations are not used to prevent speech or favor some speakers over others. [See *Walker* v. *City of Birmingham,* 388 U.S. 307 (1967); and *Shuttlesworth* v. *Birmingham,* 394 U.S. 147 (1969).] And in *Chaplinsky* v. *New Hampshire,* 315 U.S. 568 (1942), the Court held that a Witness could be punished for a breach of the peace for using "fighting words" in a public place. (See Chapter 11.) In this instance, Chaplinsky called the city marshal of a New Hampshire community "a goddamned racketeer" and a "damned Fascist" because of the marshal's interference with his preaching.

The conflict between religious liberty and governmental authority was most dramatically presented to the Supreme Court by the refusal of the Witnesses to permit their children to salute the flag. In *Minersville School District* v. *Gobitis,* 310 U.S. 586 (1940), the Court sustained the constitutionality of a Pennsylvania school board regulation that required school children to salute the flag despite contentions that the compulsory flag salute violated freedom of religion. Because the case was decided during the country's preparation for

[3] Hollis W. Barber, "Religious Liberty v. Police Power: Jehovah's Witnesses," *American Political Science Review,* Vol. 41 (1947), p. 227.

possible war, "time and circumstances" very probably played an important role in the Court's opinion, which was delivered by Justice Frankfurter. At the time the decision was handed down, there was intense alarm in the United States because the Nazis were sweeping through France and the Low Countries almost without opposition. Only Justice Stone dissented.

The *Gobitis* opinion was criticized severely by the overwhelming majority of responsible commentators. But some people looked at the Court's approval of the compulsory flag salute as a signal for the use of more repressive measures against the Witnesses. Shortly after the decision, Witnesses were beaten and driven from several communities. Many local school officials enforced the flag-salute requirement with increased vigor. "In several states the lower courts treated recalcitrant Witnesses' children as delinquents and confined them to state reform schools. The Court itself thus became a weapon in the struggle for men's minds." [4]

Several members of the Court were disturbed deeply by the nation's reaction to the *Gobitis* decision. In June, 1942, in connection with another case *(Jones* v. *City of Opelika,* 316 U.S. 584), Justices Black, Douglas, and Murphy, who had voted with the majority in the *Gobitis* case, stated jointly that they had become convinced that *Gobitis* was "wrongly decided." These three justices and Justices Rutledge and Jackson, who were appointed after the *Gobitis* decision, joined Justice Stone to reverse the *Gobitis* holding in *West Virginia Board of Education* v. *Barnette* (p. 447). Thus, in one of the most dramatic reversals in the Court's history, Justice Stone's lone dissent became the majority opinion only three years later. Justice Jackson relied heavily on the *Gobitis* dissent in writing the eloquent opinion in the *Barnette* case. Justice Frankfurter's dissent in the *Barnette* case is largely a defense of his *Gobitis* opinion and should be read with care because it reveals clearly his philosophy concerning the nature of the judicial function. From time to time that philosophy has had the support of numerous justices.[5]

Separation of Church and State

During most of our history the establishment of religion clause of the First Amendment has provoked few controversies. A few early cases were concerned with various aspects of church-state relationships before recent years, but these did not necessitate an interpretation of the establishment clause. For example, in *Pierce* v. *Society of Sisters,* 268 U.S. 510 (1925), the Court invalidated an Oregon law that required all children to attend the public schools and thus, in effect, abolished private schools. The Court rested its opinion on the right of parents to direct the upbringing and education of their children and on the principle that the Oregon law deprived private schools of business and property

[4] Mason, *Harlan Fiske Stone,* op. cit., p. 533.

[5] A most detailed analysis of the *Gobitis and Barnette* cases is found in David R. Manwaring, *Render Unto Caesar* (Chicago: U. of Chicago, 1962).

without due process of law in violation of the Fourteenth Amendment. A case more closely related to the basic issues was that of *Cochran* v. *Louisiana State Board of Education,* 281 U.S. 370 (1930), in which the Court upheld a state law that authorized the distribution of free textbooks to children in *both* public and private schools. In the *Cochran* case the Court proceeded on the theory that the textbooks, which had been purchased by the state for free distribution with public funds, were designed to help children rather than private schools.

Not until 1947, in *Everson* v. *Board of Education* (p. 452), was the meaning of the establishment clause spelled out by the Supreme Court. This case drew the Court into sharp and bitter controversy, "where any action it took was bound to be bitterly attacked." [6] The great difficulties faced by the Court in attempting to define the proper relationship between church and state can be perceived by the various opinions of the *Everson* case, as well as by subsequent decisions to be reproduced here.

The problem will not be resolved easily by the Supreme Court or any other agency of government. There is too much disagreement over fundamental matters. For example, the Roman Catholic Church and other groups have campaigned vigorously for federal aid to private as well as public schools. The Roman Catholic bishops of the United States have declared on several occasions that private and parochial schools have "full right" to receive government aid. The bishops argue that students of such schools "have the right to benefit from those measures, grants, or aids, which are manifestly designed for the health, safety, and welfare of American youth, irrespective of the school attended." [7] On the other hand, many Protestant groups oppose the use of public funds for the support of private or church-related schools. They argue that those who desire "to maintain private schools in which general education and religious education are brought together in one institution are appropriately free to do so." However, "the full support for such private schools should be provided by those who choose to maintain them. Asking for the support of church schools by tax funds on the grounds that they contribute to the national welfare is not different in principle from asking for the support of churches by tax funds, for churches surely contribute to the national welfare. Such support would in both cases be contrary to the separation of church and state." [8]

The controversy over church-state relationship was fanned anew by the case of *Illinois* ex rel. *McCollum* v. *Board of Education* (p. 455), where a released-time program of religious instruction in the Illinois public schools was held unconstitutional. The decision was greeted by a wave of bitter criticism, because

[6] C. Herman Pritchett, *Civil Liberties and the Vinson Court* (Chicago: U. of Chicago, 1954), p. 11.

[7] From the text of the Roman Catholic bishops' statement on church-related schools, *The New York Times,* Nov. 20, 1955, p. 84.

[8] From the text of a statement issued by the National Council of Churches of Christ, which is the largest organization of Protestant churches in the United States. *U.S. News and World Report* (Dec. 16, 1955), p. 121. Both sides of the controversy are presented ably in a symposium on religion and the state appearing in *Law and Contemporary Problems,* Vol. 14 (1949), pp. 1–159. See also Philip B. Kurland, *Religion and the Law* (Chicago: Aldine, 1962).

many church groups in various states had developed similar released-time programs. In addition, the *McCollum* decision "was announced when the nation was on the threshold or in the early stages of a period of religious revival. Periods of great fear drive men toward religion, and the steadily advancing threat of atomic destruction made the mid-century a period of great fear. Religion, moreover, had become a staunch ally of nationalism, for in the eyes of many the major difference between Americanism and communism was acceptance or rejection of God. It was thus scarcely surprising that the *McCollum* decision, which in effect held that the public schools must be not only nonsectarian but secular or godless, should evoke a storm of acrimonious criticism." The voices of many who supported the Court's decision "were drowned in the strident chorus of disapproval." [9]

Against this background of acrimonious criticism, the Court again considered the released-time issue in *Zorach* v. *Clauson* (p. 459). As the dissenters pointed out in the *Zorach* case, some will find it difficult to perceive that a *real* distinction exists between the two released-time programs at issue in the *McCollum* and *Zorach* cases. The majority opinion in the *Zorach* case may have been intended principally "to quiet the storm caused by the *McCollum* decision." [10]

In 1968, the Court upheld another state textbook distribution program using the same arguments used in the *Cochran* case (see p. 437) but also emphasizing that the state might aid only secular education in religious schools *[Board of Education* v. *Allen,* 392 U.S. 236 (1968)].

The Court has also stressed the distinction between secular and religious questions in the work of the courts themselves. *Presbyterian Church in the United States* v. *Mary Elizabeth Blue Hull Memorial Presbyterian Church,* 393 U.S. 440 (1969) involved a Georgia statute requiring that, in the awarding of disputed church property, courts determine whether one of the rival claimants had departed from the true doctrines of the denomination. The Court held this statute unconstitutional because it required a state court to decide a purely religious question. [See also *Serbian Eastern Orthodox Diocese* v. *Milojevick,* 426 U.S. 696 (1976); *Jones* v. *Wolf,* 443 U.S. 595 (1979).]

SCHOOL PRAYERS AND BIBLE READING

The nationwide controversy set off by the decision in *Engel* v. *Vitale* (p. 463) and the reaction to the outlawing of Bible reading and the recitation of the Lord's Prayer in *Abington School District* v. *Schempp* (p. 468) were discussed in Chapter 3. In each case the Court held that the particular religious practice at issue was unconstitutional because it violated the establishment clause of the First Amendment as made applicable to the states by the Fourteenth Amendment. Despite the furor over these cases, the issues involved were not new or novel. As early as the 1870s several states had outlawed Bible reading in the

[9] Pfeffer, op. cit., p. 44.
[10] Pritchett, op. cit., p. 14.

public schools. The problem was presented to the Supreme Court in *Doremus* v. *Board of Education,* 342 U.S. 429 (1952), which challenged Bible reading in the public schools of New Jersey; but the Court refused to decide the issue, instead resorting to the technical ground that the plaintiff lacked standing to maintain the suit.

The Court held in *Epperson* v. *Arkansas,* 393 U.S. 97 (1968), that the state's forbidding the teaching of evolution in the public schools constituted a violation of the establishment clause because that clause "forbids alike the preference of a religious doctrine or the prohibition of theory which is deemed antagonistic to a particular dogma. . . . The state has no legitimate interest in protecting any or all religions from views distasteful to them." In the course of this opinion, the Court repeated its earlier statement that the "study of religions and of the Bible, from a literary and historic viewpoint, presented objectively as part of a secular program of education, need not collide with the First Amendment's prohibition . . ." of establishment. But it is not enough for the state merely to profess a secular purpose. In *Stone* v. *Graham,* 101 S.Ct. 192 (1980), the Court struck down a Kentucky law requiring the posting of the Ten Commandments in all classrooms even though the state said it wanted the children to see the Commandments because they were the basis of the laws of Western society rather than because they were religious teachings.

Religion and the Burger Court

In recent years the establishment controversy has become more and more heated as parochial schools have encountered financial crises that have threatened to throw their students into already terribly burdened public school systems unless the government gives assistance. The problem has, however, acquired racial overtones. White, urban, blue-collar workers, many of whom are Catholic ethnics, and indeed many whites who are not ethnic, urban, blue collar or Catholic, began to see nonpublic schools as a haven from the methods of integration employed by public schools under court order. (See Chapter 13.)

The Burger Court handled the easiest problem first in *Walz* v. *Tax Commission,* 397 U.S. 664 (1970), which upheld state tax exemptions for religious property devoted wholly to worship. In the course of the opinion, Chief Justice Burger announced an approach that has come to characterize his Court in a number of areas: to move away from broadly stated rules toward sweeping case-by-case judicial discretion. If the Warren Court was "activist" in the sense of declaring new constitutional rules and pushing them toward absolute prohibitions or commands, the Burger Court has been activist in avoiding absolute rules while vesting broad policy-making discretion in itself. *Walz* announced what might be called the doctrines of "substantive free exercise" and "substantive no establishment," if we mean by "substantive" a technique in which the Court becomes the final, case-by-case arbiter of the wisdom of each particular piece of legislation, largely unconstrained by constitutional language and precedent. The Chief Justice said:

> The Court has struggled to find a neutral course between the two Religion Clauses, both of which are cast in absolute terms; and either of which, if expanded to a logical extreme, would tend to clash with the other. . . . The course of constitutional neutrality in this area cannot be an absolutely straight line; rigidity could well defeat the basic purpose of these provisions, which is to insure that no religion be sponsored or favored, none commanded, and none inhibited. The general principle deducible . . . is this: that we will not tolerate either governmentally established religion or governmental interference with religion. Short of those expressly proscribed governmental acts there is room for play in the joints productive of a benevolent neutrality which will permit religious exercise to exist without sponsorship and without interference. . . . No perfect or absolute separation is really possible.

The "benevolent" added before "neutrality" is particularly interesting. Does *benevolent neutrality* mean that government may act somewhat more in favor of religion than it could if it had to engage in just plain *neutrality?*

This substantive approach is charted by the Court's subsequent decisions. The meaning of "benevolent" became clearer in *Wisconsin* v. *Yoder,* 406 U.S. 205 (1972). Wisconsin's compulsory school attendance law required children to attend school until the age of sixteen. It was a law of general application with no hint in its origins or application of a motive of discrimination against any religious group. And it was within the very center of the state's authority. Amish parents refused to obey the law because their religious beliefs did not countenance sending children to school beyond the age of fourteen. *Reynolds* v. *United States,* discussed earlier in this chapter, would seem to be clearly applicable. Yet Justice Burger, speaking for the Court, found for the Amish, largely on the basis that they were splendid people who were preparing their children so well in the virtues of self-reliance and self-sufficiency that there was no compelling need for the state to intervene and require further schooling. Chief Justice Burger makes it absolutely explicit that the Court's holding is based on the justices' assessment of the Amish as a particularly fine, traditional religious sect and that it would not apply to "progressive" groups. Whether or not one agrees with the Chief Justice's policy conclusions, it is clear that *Yoder* raises in almost insoluble form the conflict between free exercise and establishment discussed earlier in connection with *Sherbert* v. *Verner.* For either the state must compel the Amish to act against their religious convictions or it must allow a special exemption from the general law for certain religious groups.

The central arena of constitutional conflict was, as might have been expected, government aid to parochial schools. The Burger Court's first major entry into this arena was in two cases that seem to have been deliberately paired in order to make the justices' new doctrinal position clear.

The first was *Lemon* v. *Kurtzman,* 403 U.S. 602 (1971). It involved Rhode Island and Pennsylvania legislation that provided state funds for the payment of the salaries of teachers of secular subjects in nonpublic (and, in practice, largely parochial) elementary and secondary schools. Both states carefully incorporated provisions for strict state monitoring of the schools to insure that none of the money was spent on religious instruction. The Rhode Island statute even contained elaborate audit procedures to insure that schools were not using the state money devoted to secular instruction to free up their own money for greater spending on religious instruction.

The second was *Tilton* v. *Richardson,* 403 U.S. 672 (1971), which involved grants under Title I of the federal Higher Educational Facilities Act of 1963 to church-related colleges and universities for the construction of buildings to be used exclusively for secular educational purposes. The act provided for federal on-site inspections to insure that the secular-use provisions were obeyed.

The Court struck down the state and upheld the federal statute. In the course of doing so, it introduced the "no excessive entanglements" doctrine as the true meaning of the "no establishment clause." That clause was not to be taken as absolutely barring government relations with religion, but only as forbidding excessive entanglement between the two—as well as forbidding statutes whose "purpose and effect" was to directly advance religion. It was, of course, the Court that was to decide what was or was not "excessive."

The Court offered a number of reasons for its finding that the entanglement was excessive in *Lemon.* First was the "substantial religious character" of "church-related . . . precollege education." Second, in differentiating this case from earlier Court approval of state textbook programs, the Court said: "Unlike a book, a teacher cannot be inspected once" to determine if he or she is purely secular. Then the Court focused on the very elaborate state audit and inspection requirements as entangling the state deeply in the affairs of religious schools. Here the Court engages in a favorite tactic of the justices who defended substantive economic due process at the turn of the century. The justices seize on the very provisions that the legislature introduced to limit the statute and keep it out of constitutional trouble and hold that they are the very heart of the unconstitutionality. A legislature that provided aid to parochial schools without insuring that the funds were not spent for religious purposes would surely be violating the no establishment clause. A legislature that does provide elaborate restrictions to insure secular use of funds will have involved itself in "excessive entanglement."

In *Lemon* the Court also based its finding of excessive entanglement on a political analysis so remarkably candid that it deserves extended quotation.

> A broader base of entanglement of yet a different character is presented by the divisive political potential of these state programs. In a community where such a large number of pupils are served by church-related schools, it can be assumed that state assistance will entail considerable political activity. . . . Candidates will be forced to declare and voters to choose. It would be unrealistic to ignore the fact that many people confronted with issues of this kind will find their votes aligned with their faith.
>
> Ordinarily, political debate and division, however vigorous or even partisan, are

> normal and healthy manifestations of our democratic system of government, but political division along religious lines was one of the principal evils against which the First Amendment was intended to protect. . . . Here . . . we are confronted with successive and very likely permanent annual appropriations which benefit relatively few religious groups. Political fragmentation and divisiveness on religious lines is thus likely to be intensified. The potential for political divisiveness related to religious belief and practice is aggravated in these two statutory programs by the need for continuing annual appropriations and the likelihood of larger and larger demands as costs and populations grow.

And, finally, the Court found excessive entanglement in the possibility that programs like those at issue might be first steps down the slippery slope to more and more aid to parochial schools precisely because the parochial schools needed the money so badly and had so much political support.

In *Tilton,* on the other hand, no excessive entanglement was found because (1) "religious indoctrination" is not a substantial purpose or activity of church-related colleges and universities (at least the ones involved in this litigation) as it is of primary and secondary schools; (2) the buildings, unlike the teachers in parochial schools, are religiously neutral; and (3) as these are one-time, single-purpose construction grants, "there is no continuing financial relationships or . . . audits."

Of course, there had to be continuing federal inspection of the buildings to insure their secular use. Church-related colleges might use the money they did not have to spend on a new federally aided science building to build a new chapel. Further congressional appropriations might be involved in continuing the effectiveness of the Higher Education Act. Congressional debate on aid to religious elementary and secondary schools had already begun at the time of the Act's passage and continued thereafter. Indeed the fear that the Act might be the first step down the road to federal aid to parochial schools had been voiced in Congress. But none of these factors seemed as significant to Chief Justice Burger in *Tilton* as similar factors had in *Lemon.*

At the time, *Walz, Yoder, Lemon,* and *Tilton* seemed to suggest that the Chief Justice was going to lead the Court toward a pragmatic and supportive position of government action favorable at least to orthodox, well-established religious groups. The future looked especially bright for "pass through" proposals in which the government made tuition grants or allowed tuition tax deduction to parents who then chose for themselves whether to send their children to public or private schools. It would be the parent then and not the government that gave money to the private school. Such provisions might avoid "excessive entanglement."

As the dissent in *Committee for Public Ed. & Religious Lib.* v. *Nyquist* (p. 474) indicates, the Chief Justice may indeed have been leading; but as the majority opinion of Justice Powell shows, the Court apparently has not been following. *Nyquist* was a major blow to the hopes of those who wanted to move tax money into private education by building a political coalition of those concerned about the financial crisis in parochial schools, those who wanted to get their children out of the integration turmoil in the public schools, and those who hoped to improve educational methods by creating innovative, private competitors to the quasimonopoly of the public schools.

After *Nyquist* the Court has wavered on supplementary aid to parochial schools. *Meek* v. *Pittenger,* 421 U.S. 349 (1975), involved three state programs. One was a textbook program substantially identical to the one the Court had upheld in *Board of Education* v. *Allen,* discussed earlier in this chapter. The second provided for the loan of state-owned audiovisual and other instructional materials to the schools. The third provided for state employees to provide "auxiliary" services such as psychological testing and speech therapy to students in private schools. The constitutional defense of all these programs was that, like the ones in *Allen* and *Tilton,* they were purely secular; and because, by their very nature, they could not be turned from secular to religious use, they required no state monitoring that might constitute excessive entanglement. Though the Court admitted the self-policing, secular nature of all three programs, it upheld only the first. It fastened on the fact that the textbooks were provided to the students but that the instructional and auxiliary services went directly to the schools. It concluded that where services costing the state millions of dollars were poured directly into schools that played a predominantly religious role, the Establishment Clause was violated.

In *Wolman* v. *Walter,* 433 U.S. 406 (1977) the Court upheld state programs for lending textbooks, administering standardized academic tests, providing speech and hearing and psychological diagnostic services, and providing certain remedial services to students of parochial schools while striking down programs for loaning instructional equipment to the schools and paying them for field trip transportation.

In *Roemer* v. *Board of Public Works,* 426 U.S. 736 (1976), the Court did uphold a program that poured large sums of money directly into sectarian colleges, apparently following the *Tilton* rationale that colleges more neatly separated sectarian from secular instruction than did primary and secondary schools. Although the state statute required elaborate accounting and auditing procedures to insure that the money was spent on secular purposes, the Court found no "excessive entanglement."

From *Meek* and *Wolman* some judges tried to derive the rule that while the states might provide supplemental, purely secular educational services *to the students* of parochial schools, they might not provide direct cash assistance *to the schools.* In *Committee for Public Education* v. *Regan,* 444 U.S. 646 (1980), however, the Court upheld direct cash "reinbursements" to parochial schools for their performance of various state-mandated services such as administration of statewide testing requirements. Justice Blackmun, who had written the principal opinion in *Wolman,* dissented, as did three other justices.

Meek, Wolman, and *Roemer* also generated a great many dissenting and concurring opinions. Neither *Meek* nor *Wolman* had a clear majority opinion. The "wall of separation" seems as difficult to construct as ever.

Widman v. *Vincent,* 102 S.Ct. 269 (1981), involved a state university which had established a public forum open to all student groups except religious groups. The university feared that opening its forum to religious groups would violate the establishment clause. The Court held that opening the forum to religious as well as all other groups would not have as its primary purpose or effect the advancement of religion nor create an excessive government entanglement with religion and so would not violate the establishment clause. On the other hand, banning only religious speech from the forum would be a content-based discrimination forbidden by the free speech provisions of the First Amendment.

SUNDAY CLOSING LAW

In four cases decided together and known as the *Sunday Closing Law Cases* (p. 483), the Court was faced with the difficult task of deciding if Sunday "blue laws" violate both the establishment and free exercise of religion clauses of the First Amendment as applied to the states by the Fourteenth Amendment. In deciding that they do not, the Court wrote more than 150 pages of carefully reasoned opinions. The decision reproduced here has been greatly condensed.

RELIGIOUS TEST FOR PUBLIC OFFICIALS

In the unusual case of *Torcaso* v. *Watkins* [367 U.S. 488 (1961)], the Court, by unanimous vote, held that a Maryland religious test for public office constituted an invasion of freedom of belief and religion. [See also *McDaniel* v. *Patty,* 435 U.S. 618 (1978).

CANTWELL *v.* CONNECTICUT

310 U.S. 296; 60 Sup. Ct. 900; 84 L. Ed. 1213 (1940)

[Cantwell and his two sons, members of Jehovah's Witnesses, went from house to house in a predominantly Roman Catholic residential district of New Haven, Connecticut, soliciting money and subscriptions for their religious cause. They were charged in five counts with statutory and common law offenses. All of them were convicted on the third count under a state statute that provided that no person could solicit money for alleged religious purposes without first obtaining a certificate of approval from the secretary of the Public Welfare Council. The Cantwells had not obtained the required permit, claiming that their religious activities did not come within the statute. The Cantwells also were convicted on the fifth count, that of inciting others to breach of the peace, because a phonograph record was played that violently attacked Roman Catholicism. The state supreme court affirmed the convictions of all three on the third count but affirmed the conviction of only one of the Cantwells on the fifth count. The Cantwells brought their case to the Supreme Court on appeal. The Court also granted a writ of certiorari to review the breach of peace conviction.]

MR. JUSTICE ROBERTS delivered the opinion of the Court:

. . . *First.* We hold that the statute, as construed and applied to the appellants, deprives them of their liberty without due process of law in contravention of the Fourteenth Amendment. The fundamental concept of liberty embodied in that Amendment embraces the liberties guaranteed by the First Amendment. The First Amendment declares that Congress shall make no law respecting an establishment of religion or prohibiting the free exercise thereof. The Fourteenth Amendment has rendered the legislatures of the states as incompetent as Congress to enact such laws. The constitutional inhibition of legislation on the subject of religion has a double aspect. On the one hand, it forestalls compulsion by law of the acceptance of any creed or the practice of any form of worship. Freedom of conscience and freedom to adhere to such religious organization or form of worship as the individual may choose cannot be restricted by law. On the other hand, it safeguards the free exercise of the chosen form of religion. Thus the Amendment embraces two concepts—freedom to believe and freedom to act. The first is absolute but, in the nature of things, the second cannot be. Conduct remains subject to regulation for the protection of society. The freedom to act must have appropriate definition to preserve the enforcement of that protection. In every case the power to regulate must be so exercised as not, in attaining a permissible end, unduly to infringe the protected freedom. No one would contest the proposition that a State may not, by statute, wholly deny, the right to preach or to disseminate religious views. Plainly such a previous and absolute restraint would violate the terms of the guaranty. It is equally clear that a State may by general and nondiscriminatory legislation regulate the times, the places, and the manner of soliciting upon its streets, and of holding meetings thereon; and may in other respects safeguard the peace, good order, and comfort of the community, without unconstitutionally invading the liberties protected by the Fourteenth Amendment. The appellants are right in their insistence that the Act in question is not such a regulation. If a certificate is procured, solicitation is permitted without restraint, but in the absence of a certificate solicitation is altogether prohibited. . . .

It will be noted . . . that the Act requires an application to the secretary of the public welfare council of the State; that he is empowered to determine whether the cause is a religious one, and that the issue of a certificate depends upon his affirmative action. If he finds that the cause is not that of religion, to solicit for it becomes a crime. He is not to issue a certificate as a matter of course. His decision to issue or refuse it involves appraisal of facts, the exercise of judgment, and the formation of an opinion. He is authorized to withhold his approval if he determines that the cause is not a religious one. Such a censorship of religion as the means of determining its right to survive is a denial of liberty protected by the First Amendment and included in the liberty which is within the protection of the Fourteenth.

The State asserts that if the licensing officer acts arbitrarily, capriciously, or corruptly, his action is subject to judicial correction. Counsel refer to the rule prevailing in Connecticut that the decision of a commission or an administrative official will be reviewed upon a claim that "it works material damage to individual or corporate rights, or invades or threatens such rights, or is so unreasonable as to justify judicial intervention, or is not consonant with justice, or that a legal duty has not been performed." It is suggested that the statute is to be read as requiring the officer to issue a certificate unless the cause in question is clearly not a religious one; and that if he violates his duty his action will be corrected by a court.

To this suggestion there are several sufficient answers. The line between a discretionary and a ministerial act is not always easy to mark, and the statute has not been construed by the state court to impose a mere ministerial duty on the secretary of the welfare council. Upon his decision as to the nature of the cause, the right to solicit depends. Moreover, the availability of a judicial remedy for abuses in the system of licensing still leaves that system one of previous restraint which, in the field of free speech and press, we have held inadmissible. A statute authorizing previous restraint upon the exercise of the guaranteed freedom by judicial decision after trial is as obnoxious to the Constitution as one providing for like restraint by administrative action.

Nothing we have said is intended even remotely to imply that, under the cloak of religion, persons may, with impunity, commit frauds upon the public. Certainly penal laws are available to punish such conduct. Even the exercise of religion may be at some slight inconvenience in order that the State may protect its citizens from injury. Without doubt a State may protect its citizens from fraudulent solicitation by requiring a stranger in the community, before permitting him publicly to solicit funds for any purpose, to establish his identity and his authority to act for the cause which he purports to represent. The State is likewise free to regulate the time and manner of solicitation generally, in the interest of public safety, peace, comfort, or convenience. But to condition the solicitation of aid for the perpetuation of religious views or systems upon a license, the grant of which rests in the exercise of a determination by state authority as to what is a religious cause, is to lay a forbidden burden upon the exercise of liberty protected by the Constitution.

Second. The offense known as breach of the peace embraces a great variety of conduct destroying or menacing public order and tranquility. It includes not only violent acts but acts and words likely to produce violence in others. No one would have the hardihood to suggest that the principle of freedom of speech sanctions incitement to riot or that religious liberty connotes the privilege to exhort others to physical attack upon those belonging to another sect. When clear and present danger of riot, disorder, interference with traffic upon the public streets, or other threat to public safety, peace, or order appears, the power of the State to prevent or punish is obvious. Equally obvious is it that a State may not unduly suppress free communication of views, religious or other, under the guise of conserving desirable conditions. Here we have a situation analogous to a conviction under a statute sweeping in a great variety of conduct under a general and indefinite characterization, and leaving to the executive and judicial branches too wide a discretion in its application. . . .

The record played by Cantwell embodies a general attack on all organized religious systems as instruments of Satan and injurious to man; it then singles out the Roman Catholic Church for strictures couched in terms which naturally would offend not only persons of that persuasion, but all others who respect the honestly-held religious faith of their fellows. The hearers were in fact highly offended. One of them said he felt like hitting Cantwell and the other that he was tempted to throw Cantwell off the street. The one who testified he felt like hitting Cantwell said, in answer to the question "Did you do anything else or have any other reaction?" "No, sir, because he said he would take the victrola and he went." The other witness testified that he told Cantwell he had better get off the street before something happened to him, and that was the end of the matter as Cantwell picked up his books and walked up the street.

Cantwell's conduct, in the view of the court below, considered apart from the effect of his communication upon his hearers, did not amount to a breach of the peace. One may, however, be guilty of the offense if he commit acts or make statements likely to provoke violence and disturbance of good order, even though no such eventuality be intended. Decisions to this effect are many, but examination discloses that, in practically all, the provocative language which was held to amount to a breach of the peace consisted of profane, indecent, or abusive remarks directed to the person of the hearer. Resort to epithets or personal abuse is not in any proper sense communication of information or opinion safeguarded by the Constitution, and its punishment as a criminal act would raise no question under that instrument.

We find in the instant case no assault or threatening of bodily harm, no truculent bearing, no intentional discourtesy, no personal abuse. On the contrary, we find only an effort to persuade a willing listener to buy a book or to contribute money in the interest of what Cantwell, however misguided others may think him, conceived to be true religion.

In the realm of religious faith, and in that of political belief, sharp differences arise. In both fields the tenets of one man may seem the rankest error to his neighbor. To persuade others to his own point of view, the pleader, as we know, at times, resorts to exaggeration, to vilification of men who have been, or are, prominent in church or state, and even to false statement. But the people of this nation have ordained in the light of history, that, in spite of the probability of excesses and abuses, these liberties are, in the long view, essential to enlightened opinion and right conduct on the part of the citizens of a democracy.

The essential characteristic of these liberties is, that under their shield many types of life, character, opinion, and belief can develop unmolested and unobstructed. Nowhere is this shield more necessary than in our own country for a people composed of many races and of many creeds. There are limits to the exercises of these liberties. The danger in these times from the coercive activities of those who in the delusion of racial or religious conceit would incite violence and breaches of the peace in order to deprive others of their equal right to the exercise of their liberties, is emphasized by events familiar to all. These and other transgressions of those limits the States appropriately may punish.

Although the contents of the record not unnaturally aroused animosity, we think that, in the absence of a statute narrowly drawn to define and punish specific conduct as constituting a clear and present danger to a substantial interest of the State, the petitioner's communication, considered in the light of the constitutional guaranties, raised no such clear and present menace to public peace and order as to render him liable to conviction of the common-law offense in question.

The judgment affirming the convictions on the third and fifth counts is reversed, and the cause is remanded for further proceedings not inconsistent with this opinion.

Reversed.

WEST VIRGINIA STATE BOARD OF EDUCATION v. BARNETTE
319 U.S. 624; 62 Sup. Ct. 1178; 87 L. Ed. 1628 (1943)

[After the decision in Minersville School District *v.* Gobitis, *the West Virginia Board of Education adopted a resolution requiring all public school teachers and pupils to salute the flag. Refusal to salute the flag was made an act of insubordination that was punishable by expulsion. Readmission was possible only if the expelled child agreed to render the salute; meanwhile, the expelled child was considered unlawfully absent and therefore delinquent. His parents or guardians could be prosecuted and if convicted could be made subject to a $50 fine and thirty days in jail.*

A number of the Witnesses' children were expelled from various public schools in West Virginia for refusal to salute the flag. State officials threatened to send these children to reformatories and to prosecute their parents for causing delinquency. Barnette and other Witnesses brought suit in a federal district court to enjoin the enforcement of the board's regulation. They claimed that the board's regulation, as applied to them, violated their religious freedom and freedom of speech under the First and Fourteenth Amendments. The district court granted the injunction. The board of education then brought the case to the Supreme Court by direct appeal.]

MR. JUSTICE JACKSON delivered the opinion of the Court:

. . . The freedom asserted by these appellees does not bring them into collision with rights asserted by any other individual. It is such conflicts which most frequently require intervention of the State to determine where the rights of one end and those of another begin. But the refusal of these persons to participate in the ceremony does not interfere with or deny rights of others to do so. Nor is there any question in this case that their behavior is peaceable and orderly. The sole conflict is between authority and rights of the individual. The State asserts power to condition access to public education on making a prescribed sign and profession and at the same time to coerce attendance by punishing both parent and child. The latter stand on a right of self-determination in matters that touch individual opinion and personal attitude.

As the present Chief Justice said in dissent in the *Gobitis* case, the State may "require teaching by instruction and study of all in our history and in the structure and organization of our government, including the guaranties of civil liberty, which tend to inspire patriotism and love of country." . . . Here, however, we are dealing with a compulsion of students to declare a belief. They are not merely made acquainted with the flag salute so that they may be informed as to what it is or even what it means. The issue here is whether this slow and easily neglected route to aroused loyalties constitutionally may be short-cut by substituting a compulsory salute and slogan. . . .

There is no doubt that, in connection with the pledges, the flag salute is a form of utterance. Symbolism is a primitive but effective way of communicating ideas. The use of an emblem or flag to symbolize some system, idea, institution, or personality, is a short cut from mind to mind. Causes and nations, political parties, lodges, and ecclesiastical groups seek to knit the loyalty of their followings to a flag or banner, a color or design. The State announces rank, function, and authority through crowns and maces, uniforms and black robes; the church speaks through the Cross, the Crucifix, the altar and shrine, and clerical raiment. Symbols of State often convey political ideas just as religious symbols come to convey theological ones. Associated with many of these symbols are appropriate gestures of acceptance or respect: a salute, a bowed or bared head, a bended knee. A person gets from a symbol the meaning he puts into it, and what is one man's comfort and inspiration is another's jest and scorn.

Over a decade ago Chief Justice Hughes led this Court in holding that the display of a red flag as a symbol of opposition by peaceful and legal means to organized government was protected by the free-speech guaranties of the Constitution. *Stromberg* v. *California,* 283 U.S. 359. Here it is the State that employs a flag as a symbol of adherence to government as presently organized. It requires the individual to communicate by word and sign his acceptance of the political ideas it thus bespeaks. Objection to this form of communication when coerced is an old one, well known to the framers of the Bill of Rights.

It is also to be noted that the compulsory flag salute and pledge requires affirmation of a belief and an attitude of mind. It is not clear whether the regulation contemplates that pupils forego any contrary convictions of their own and become unwilling converts to the prescribed ceremony, or whether it will be acceptable if they stimulate assent by words without belief and by a gesture barren of meaning. It is now a commonplace that censorship or suppression of expression of opinion is tolerated by our Constitution only when the expression presents a clear and present danger of action of a kind the State is empowered to prevent and punish. It would seem that involuntary affirmation could be commanded only on even more immediate and urgent grounds than silence. But here the power of compulsion is invoked without any allegation that remaining passive during a flag-salute ritual creates a clear and present danger that would justify an effort even to muffle expression. To sustain the compulsory flag salute we are required to say that a Bill of Rights which guards the individual's right to speak his own mind, left it open to public authorities to compel him to utter what is not in his mind.

Whether the First Amendment to the Constitution will permit officials to order observance of ritual of this nature does not depend upon whether as a voluntary exercise we would think it to be good, bad, or merely innocuous. Any credo of nationalism is likely to include what some disapprove or to omit what others think essential, and to give off different overtones as it takes on different accents or interpretations. If official power exists to coerce acceptance of any patriotic creed, what it shall contain cannot be decided by courts, but must be largely discretionary with the ordaining authority, whose power to prescribe would no doubt include power to amend. Hence validity of the asserted power to force an American citizen publicly to profess any statement of belief or to engage in any ceremony of assent to one, presents questions of power that must be considered independently of any idea we may have as to the utility of the ceremony in question.

Nor does the issue as we see it turn on one's possession of particular religious views or the sincerity with which they are held. While religion supplies appellees' motive for enduring the discomforts of making the issue in this case, many citizens who do not share these religious views hold such a compulsory rite to infringe constitutional liberty of the individual. It is not necessary to inquire whether nonconformist beliefs will exempt from the duty to salute unless we first find power to make the salute a legal duty.

The *Gobitis* decision, however, *assumed,* as did the argument in that case and in this, that power exists in the State to impose the flag-salute discipline upon school children in general. The Court only examined and rejected a claim based on religious beliefs of immunity from an unquestioned general rule. The question which underlies the flag-salute controversy is whether such a ceremony so touching matters of opinion and political attitude may be imposed upon the individual by official authority under powers committed to any political organization under our Constitution. We examine rather than assume existence of this power and, against this broader definition of issues in this case, re-examine specific grounds assigned for the *Gobitis* decision.

1. It was said that the flag-salute controversy confronted the Court with "the problem which Lincoln cast in memorable dilemma: 'Must a government of necessity be too *strong* for the liberties of its people, or too *weak* to maintain its own existence?' " and that the answer must be in favor of strength. . . .

We think these issues may be examined free of pressure or restraint growing out of such considerations.

It may be doubted whether Mr. Lincoln would have thought that the strength of government to maintain itself would be impressively vindicated by our confirming the power of the State to expel a handful of children from school. Such over-simplification, so handy in political debate, often lacks the precision necessary to postulates of judicial reasoning. If validly applied to this problem, the utterance cited would resolve every issue of power in favor of those in authority and would require us to override every liberty thought to weaken or delay execution of their policies.

Government of limited power need not be anemic government. Assurance that rights are secure tends to diminish fear and jealousy of strong government, and by making us feel safe to live under it makes for its better support. Without promise of a limiting Bill of Rights it is doubtful if our Constitution could have mustered enough strength to enable its ratification. To enforce those rights today is not to choose weak government over strong government. It is only to adhere as a means of strength to individual freedom of mind in preference to officially disciplined uniformity, for which history indicates a disappointing and disastrous end.

The subject now before us exemplifies this principle. Free public education, if faithful to the ideal of secular instruction and political neutrality, will not be partisan or enemy of any class, creed, party, or faction. If it is to impose any ideological discipline, however, each party or denomination must seek to control, or failing that, to weaken the influence of the educational system. Observance of the limitations of the Constitution will not weaken government in the field appropriate for its exercise.

2. It was also considered in the *Gobitis* case that functions of educational officers in States, counties, and school districts were such that to interfere with their authority "would in effect make us the school board for the country. . . ."

The Fourteenth Amendment, as now applied to the States, protects the citizens against the State itself and all of its creatures—Boards of Education not excepted. These have of course, important, delicate, and highly discretionary functions, but none that they may not perform within the limits of the Bill of Rights. That they are educating the young for citizenship is reason for scrupulous protection of constitutional freedoms of the individual, if we are not to strangle the free mind at its source and teach youth to discount important principles of our government as mere platitudes.

Such Boards are numerous and their territorial jurisdiction often small. But small and local authority may feel less sense of responsibility to the Constitution, and agencies of publicity may be less vigilant in calling it to account. The action of Congress in making flag observance voluntary and respecting the conscience of the objector in a matter so vital as raising the Army contrasts sharply with these local regulations in matters relatively trivial to the welfare of the nation. . . .

3. The *Gobitis* opinion reasoned that this is a field "where courts possess no marked and certainly no controlling competence," that it is committed to the legislatures as well as the courts to guard cherished liberties and that it is constitutionally appropriate to "fight out the wise use of legislative authority in the forum of public opinion and before legislative assemblies rather than to transfer such a contest to the judicial arena," since all the "effective means of inducing political changes are left free. . . ."

The very purpose of a Bill of Rights was to withdraw certain subjects from the vicissitudes of political controversy, to place them beyond the reach of majorities and officials and to establish them as legal principles to be applied by the courts. One's right to life, liberty, and property, to free speech, a free press, freedom of worship and assembly, and other fundamental rights may not be submitted to vote; they depend on the outcome of no elections.

In weighing arguments of the parties it is important to distinguish between the due process clause of the Fourteenth Amendment as an instrument for transmitting the principles of the First Amendment and those cases in which it is applied for its own sake. The test of legislation which collides with the Fourteenth, because it also collides with the principles of the First, is much more definitive than the test when only the Fourteenth is involved. Much of the vagueness of the due process clause disappears when the specific prohibitions of the First become its standard. The right of a State to regulate, for example, a public utility may well include, so far as the due process test is concerned, power to impose all of the restrictions which a legislature may have a "rational basis" for adopting. But freedoms of speech and of press, of assembly, and of worship may not be infringed on such slender grounds. They are susceptible of restriction only to prevent grave and immediate danger to interests which the State may lawfully protect. It is important to note that while it is the Fourteenth Amendment which bears directly upon the State, it is the more specific limiting principles of the First Amendment that finally govern this case.

Nor does our duty to apply the Bill of Rights to assertions of official authority depend upon our possession of marked competence in the field where the invasion of rights occurs. True, the task of translating the majestic generalities of the Bill of Rights, conceived as part of the pattern of liberal government in the eighteenth century, into concrete restraints on officials dealing with the problems of the twentieth century, is one to disturb self-confidence. These principles grew in soil which also produced a philosophy that the individual was the center of society, that his liberty was attainable through mere absence of governmental restraints, and that government should be entrusted with few controls and only the mildest supervision over men's affairs. We must transplant these rights to a soil in which the laissez-faire concept or principle of noninterference has withered at least as to economic affairs, and social advancements are increasingly sought through closer integration of society and through expanded and strengthened governmental controls. These changed conditions often deprive precedents of reliability and cast us more than we would choose upon our own judgment. But we act in these matters not only by authority of our competence but by force of our commissions. We cannot, because of modest estimates of our competence in such specialties as public education, withhold the judgment that history authenticates as the function of this Court when liberty is infringed.

4. Lastly, and this is the very heart of the *Gobitis* opinion, it reasons that "National unity is the basis of national security," that the authorities have "the right to select appropriate means for its attainment," and hence reaches the conclusion that such compulsory measures toward "national unity" are constitutional. . . . Upon the verity of this assumption depends our answer in this case.

National unity as an end which officials may foster by persuasion and example is not in question. The problem is whether under our Constitution compulsion as here employed is a permissible means for its achievement.

Struggles to coerce uniformity of sentiment in support of some end thought essential to their time and country have been waged by many good as well as by evil men. Nationalism is a relatively recent phenomenon, but at other times and places the ends have been racial or territorial security, support of a dynasty or regime, and particular plans for saving souls. As first and moderate methods to attain unity have failed, those bent on its accomplishment must resort to an ever-increasing severity. . . . Ultimate futility of such attempts to compel coherence is the lesson of every such effort from the Roman drive to stamp out Christianity as a disturber of its pagan unity, the Inquisition, as a means to religious and dynastic unity, Siberian exiles as a means to Russian unity, down to the fast-failing efforts of our present totalitarian enemies. Those who begin coercive elimination of dissent soon find themselves exterminating dissenters. Compulsory unification of opinion achieves only the unanimity of the graveyard.

It seems trite but necessary to say that the First Amendment to our Constitution was designed to avoid these ends by avoiding these beginnings. There is no mysticism in the American concept of the State or of the nature or origin of its authority. We set up government by consent of the governed, and the Bill of Rights denies those in power any legal opportunity to coerce that consent. Authority here is to be controlled by public opinion, not public opinion by authority.

The case is made difficult not because the principles of its decision are obscure but because the flag involved is our own. Nevertheless, we apply the limitations of the Constitution with no fear that freedom to be intellectually and spiritually diverse or even contrary will disintegrate the social organization. To believe that patriotism will not flourish if patriotic ceremonies are voluntary and spontaneous instead of a compulsory routine is to make an unflattering estimate of the appeal of our institutions to free minds. We can have intellectual diversities that we owe to exceptional minds only at the price of occasional eccentricity and abnormal attitudes. When they are so harmless to others or to the State as those we deal with here, the price is not too great. But freedom to differ is not limited to things that do not matter much. That would be a mere shadow of freedom. The test of its substance is the right to differ as to things that touch the heart of the existing order.

If there is any fixed star in our constitutional constellation, it is that no official, high or petty, can prescribe what shall be orthodox in politics, nationalism, religion, or other matters of opinion or force citizens to confess by word or act their faith therein. If there are any circumstances which permit an exception, they do not now occur to us.

We think the action of the local authorities in compelling the flag salute and pledge transcends constitutional limitations on their power and invades the sphere of intellect and spirit which it is the purpose of the First Amendment to our Constitution to reserve from all official control.

The decision of this Court in *Minersville School District* v. *Gobitis* [is] overruled, and the judgment enjoining enforcement of the West Virginia Regulation is

Affirmed.

[Mr. Justice Black, Mr. Justice Douglas, and Mr. Justice Murphy concurred.]

MR. JUSTICE FRANKFURTER, dissenting:

One who belongs to the most vilified and persecuted minority in history is not likely to be insensible to the freedoms guaranteed by our Constitution. Were my purely personal attitude relevant I should wholeheartedly associate myself with the general libertarian views in the Court's opinion, representing as they do the thought and action of a lifetime. But as judges we are neither Jew nor Gentile, neither Catholic nor agnostic. We owe equal attachment to the Constitution and are equally bound by our judicial obligations whether we derive our citizenship from the earliest or the latest immigrants to these shores. As a member of this Court I am not justified in writing my private notions of policy into the Constitution, no matter how deeply I may cherish them or how mischievous I may deem their disregard. The duty of a judge who must decide which of two claims before the Court shall prevail, that of a State to enact and enforce laws within its general competence or that of an individual to refuse obedience because of the demands of his conscience, is not that of the ordinary person. It can never be emphasized too much that one's own opinion about the wisdom or evil of a law should be excluded altogether when one is doing one's duty on the bench. The only opinion of our own even looking in that direction that is material is our opinion whether legislators could in reason have enacted such a law. In the light of all the circumstances, including the history of this question in this Court, it would require more daring than I possess to deny that reasonable legislators could have taken the action which is before us for review. Most unwillingly, therefore, I must differ from my brethren with regard to legislation like this. I cannot bring my mind to believe that the "liberty" secured by the Due Process Clause gives this Court authority to deny to the State of West Virginia the attainment of that which we all recognize as a legitimate legislative end, namely, the promotion of good citizenship, by employment of the means here chosen.

. . . When Mr. Justice Holmes, speaking for this Court, wrote that "it must be remembered that legislatures are ultimate guardians of the liberties and welfare of the people in quite as great a degree as the courts," . . . he went to the very essence of our constitutional system and the democratic conception of our society. He did not mean that for only some phases of civil government this Court was not to supplant and sit in judgment upon the right or wrong of a challenged measure. He was stating the comprehensive judicial duty and role of this Court in our constitutional scheme whenever legislation is sought to be nullified on any ground, namely that responsibility for legislation lies with legislatures, answerable as they are directly to the people, and this Court's only and very narrow function is to determine whether within the broad grant of authority vested in legislatures they have exercised a judgment for which reasonable justification can be offered.

. . . The reason why from the beginning even the narrow judicial authority to nullify legislation has been viewed with a jealous eye is that it serves to prevent the full play of the democratic process. The fact that it may be an undemocratic aspect of our scheme of government does not call for its rejection or its disuse. But it is the best of reasons, as this Court has frequently recognized, for the greatest caution in its use.

. . . If the function of this Court is to be essentially no different from that of a legislature, if the considerations governing constitutional construction are to be substantially those that underlie legislation, then indeed judges should not have life tenure and they should be made directly responsible to the electorate. . . .

[Mr. Justice Roberts and Mr. Justice Reed also dissented.]

EVERSON *v.* BOARD OF EDUCATION

330 U.S. 1; 67 Sup. Ct. 504; 91 L. Ed. 711 (1947)

[A New Jersey statute enacted in 1941 authorized school boards to make rules and contracts for the transportation of school children, including those attending nonprofit private and parochial schools. Under this law, a township board of education (Ewing, N.J.) authorized

reimbursement to parents of money spent for school transportation expenses to Catholic parochial schools as well as public schools. Everson, who was a taxpayer in the school district, challenged the right of the board to reimburse parents of parochial school students. A state court agreed with Everson and held that the New Jersey legislature did not have the power to authorize such payments under the state constitution. However, the highest state court (New Jersey Court of Errors and Appeals) reversed the lower court's decision. Everson then brought the case to the Supreme Court on appeal.]

MR. JUSTICE BLACK delivered the opinion of the Court:

. . . The New Jersey statute is challenged as a "law respecting an establishment of religion." The First Amendment, as made applicable to the states by the Fourteenth . . . commands that a state "shall make no law respecting an establishment of religion, or prohibiting the free exercise thereof.". . . These words of the First Amendment reflected in the minds of early Americans a vivid mental picture of conditions and practices which they fervently wished to stamp out in order to preserve liberty for themselves and for their posterity. Doubtless their goal has not been entirely reached; but so far has the Nation moved toward it that the expression "law respecting an establishment of religion," probably does not so vividly remind present-day Americans of the evils, fears, and political problems that caused that expression to be written into our Bill of Rights. Whether this New Jersey law is one respecting an "establishment of religion" requires an understanding of the meaning of that language, particularly with respect to the imposition of taxes. . . .

The "establishment of religion" clause of the First Amendment means at least this: Neither a state nor the Federal Government can set up a church. Neither can pass laws which aid one religion, aid all religions, or prefer one religion over another. Neither can force nor influence a person to go to or to remain away from church against his will or force him to profess a belief or disbelief in any religion. No person can be punished for entertaining or professing religious beliefs or disbeliefs, for church attendance or non-attendance. No tax in any amount, large or small, can be levied to support any religious activities or institutions, whatever they may be called, or whatever form they may adopt to teach or practice religion. Neither a state nor the Federal Government can, openly or secretly, participate in the affairs of any religious organizations or groups and *vice versa.* In the words of Jefferson, the clause against establishment of religion by law was intended to erect "a wall of separation between church and State. . . ."

Measured by these standards, we cannot say that the First Amendment prohibits New Jersey from spending tax-raised funds to pay the bus fares of parochial-school pupils as a part of a general program under which it pays the fares of pupils attending public and other schools. It is undoubtedly true that children are helped to get to church schools. There is even a possibility that some of the children might not be sent to the church schools if the parents were compelled to pay their children's bus fares out of their own pockets when transportation to a public school would have been paid for by the State. The same possibility exists where the state requires a local transit company to provide reduced fares to school children, including those attending parochial schools, or where a municipally-owned transportation system undertakes to carry all school children free of charge. Moreover, state-paid policemen, detailed to protect children going to and from church schools from the very real hazards of traffic, would serve much the same purpose and accomplish much the same result as state provisions intended to guarantee free transportation of a kind which the state deems to be best for the school children's welfare. And parents might refuse to risk their children to the serious danger of traffic accidents going to and from parochial schools, the approaches to which were not protected by policemen. Similarly, parents might be reluctant to permit their children to attend schools which the state had cut off from such general government services as ordinary police and fire protection, connection for sewage disposal, public highways and sidewalks. Of course, cutting off church schools from these services, so separate and so indisputably marked off from the religious function, would make it far more difficult for the schools to operate. But such is obviously not the purpose of the First Amendment. The Amendment requires the state to be a neutral in its relations with groups of religious believers and nonbelievers; it does not require the state to be their adversary. State power is no more to be used so as to handicap religions than it is to favor them.

This Court has said that parents may, in the discharge of their duty under state compulsory education laws, send their children to a religious rather than a public school if the school meets the secular educational requirements which the state power has to impose. . . . It appears that these parochial schools meet New Jersey's requirements. The States contributes no money to the schools. It does not support them. Its legislation, as applied, does no more than provide a general program to help parents get their children, regardless of their religion, safely and expeditiously to and from accredited schools.

The First Amendment has erected a wall between church and state. That wall must be kept high and impregnable. We could not approve the slightest breach. New Jersey has not breached it here.

Affirmed.

MR. JUSTICE JACKSON dissented.

MR. JUSTICE FRANKFURTER joined MR. JUSTICE JACKSON'S dissent. MR. JUSTICE RUTLEDGE, with whom MR. JUSTICE FRANKFURTER, MR. JUSTICE JACKSON, and MR. JUSTICE BURTON agree, dissenting:

This case forces us to determine squarely for the first time what was "an establishment of religion" in the First Amendment's conception; and by that measure to decide whether New Jersey's action violates its command. . . .

The Amendment's purpose was not to strike merely at the official establishment of a single sect, creed, or religion, outlawing only a formal relation such as had prevailed in England and some of the colonies. Necessarily it was to uproot all such relationships. But the object was broader than separating church and state in this narrow sense. It was to create a complete and permanent separation of spheres of religious activity and civil authority by comprehensively forbidding every form of public aid or support for religion. In proof the Amendment's wording and history unite with this Court's consistent utterances whenever attention has been fixed directly upon the question.

[Mr. Justice Rutledge follows with the history of the First Amendment, which he states reveals clearly that the Amendment was designed to forbid the use of any public funds to aid or support religious exercises.]

. . . Does New Jersey's action furnish support for religion by use of the taxing power? Certainly it does, if the test remains undiluted as Jefferson and Madison made it, that money taken by taxation from one is not to be used or given to support another's religious training or belief, or indeed one's own. Today as then the furnishing of "contributions of money for the propagation of opinions which he disbelieves" is the forbidden exaction; and the prohibition is absolute for whatever measure brings that consequence and whatever amount may be sought or given to that end.

The funds used here were raised by taxation. The Court does not dispute, nor could it, that their use does in fact give aid and encouragement to religious instruction. It only concludes that this aid is not "support" in law. . . . Here parents pay money to send their children to parochial schools and funds raised by taxation are used to reimburse them. This not only helps the children to get to school and the parents to send them. It aids them in a substantial way to get the very thing which they are sent to the particular school to secure, namely, religious training and teaching. . . .

New Jersey's action therefore exactly fits the type of exaction and the kind of evil at which Madison and Jefferson struck. Under the test they framed it cannot be said that the cost of transportation is no part of the cost of education or of the religious instruction given. That it is a substantial and a necessary element is shown most plainly by the continuing and increasing demand for the state to assume it. . . .

But we are told that the New Jersey statute is valid in its present application because the appropriation is for a public, not a private purpose, namely, the promotion of education, and the majority accept this idea in the conclusion that all we have here is "public welfare legislation." If that is true and the Amendment's force can be thus destroyed, what has been said becomes all the more pertinent. For then there could be no possible objections to more extensive support of religious education by New Jersey.

. . . Our constitutional policy is exactly the opposite. It does not deny the value or the necessity for religious training, teaching or observance. Rather it secures their free exercise. But to that end it does deny that the state can undertake or sustain them in any form or degree. For this reason the sphere of religious activity, as distinguished from the secular intellectual liberties, has been given the twofold protection and, as the state cannot forbid, neither can it perform or aid in performing the religious function. The dual prohibition makes that function altogether private. It cannot be made a public one by legislative act. . . .

It is not because religious teaching does not promote the public or the individual's welfare, but because neither is furthered when the state promotes religious education, that the Constitution forbids it to do so. Both legislatures and courts are bound by that distinction. In failure to observe it lies the fallacy of the "public function"-"social legislation" argument. . . . Public money devoted to payment of religious costs, educational or other, brings the quest for more. It brings too the struggle of sect against sect for the larger share or for any. Here one by numbers alone will benefit most, there another. That is precisely the history of societies which have had an established religion and dissident groups. The end of such strife cannot be other than to destroy the cherished liberty. The dominating group will achieve the dominant benefit; or all will embroil the state in their dissensions. . . .

No one conscious of religious values can be unsympathetic toward the burden which our constitutional separation puts on parents who desire religious instruction mixed with secular for their children. They pay taxes for others' children's education, at the same time the added cost of instruction for their own. Nor can one happily see benefits denied to children which others receive, because in conscience they or their parents for them desire a different kind of training others do not demand.

But if those feelings should prevail, there would be an end to our historic constitutional policy and command. No more unjust or discriminatory in fact is it to deny attendants at religious schools the cost of their transportation than it is to deny them tuitions, sustenance for their teachers, or any other educational expense which others receive at public cost. Hardship in fact there is, which none can blink. But, for assuring for those who undergo it the greater, the most comprehensive freedom, it is one written by design and firm intent into our basic law.

The judgment should be

Reversed.

ILLINOIS ex rel. McCOLLUM *v.* BOARD OF EDUCATION
333 U.S. 203; Sup. Ct. 461; 92 L. Ed. 648 (1948)

[Mrs. Vashti McCollum, whose child was enrolled in the Champaign, Illinois, public school system, tried to obtain a writ of mandamus to prohibit the use of the local school facilities for religious instruction. She contended that the religious program conducted in the schools violated the First and Fourteenth Amendments. A county court denied her petition for mandamus. On appeal the state supreme court affirmed. Mrs. McCollum then brought the case to the Supreme Court on appeal. The details of the religious instruction program are given in the Court's opinion.]

MR. JUSTICE BLACK delivered the opinion of the Court:

This case relates to the power of a state to utilize its tax-supported public school system in aid of religious instruction in so far as that power may be restricted by the First and Fourteenth Amendments to the Federal Constitution. . . .

Appellant's petition for mandamus alleged that religious teachers, employed by private religious groups, were permitted to come weekly into the school buildings during the regular hours set apart for secular teaching, and then and there for a period of thirty minutes substitute their religious teaching for the secular education provided under the compulsory education law.

Although there are disputes between the parties as to various inferences that may or may not properly be drawn from the evidence concerning the religious program, the following facts are shown by the record without dispute. In 1940, interested members of the Jewish, Roman Catholic, and a few of the Protestant faiths formed a voluntary association called the Champaign Council on Religious Education. They obtained permission from the Board of Education to offer classes in religious instruction to public school pupils in grades four to nine inclusive. Classes were made up of pupils whose parents signed printed cards requesting that their children be permitted to attend; they were held weekly, thirty minutes for the lower grades, forty-five minutes for the higher. The council employed the religious teachers at no expense to the school authorities, but the instructors were subject to the approval and supervision of the superintendent of schools. The classes were taught in three separate religious groups by Protestant teachers, Catholic priests, and a Jewish rabbi, although for the past several years there have apparently been no classes instructed in the Jewish religion. Classes were conducted in the regular classrooms of the school building. Students who did not choose to take the religious instruction were not released from public school duties; they were required to leave their classrooms and go to some other place in the school building for pursuit of their secular studies. On the other hand, students who were released from secular study for the religious instructions were required to be present at the religious classes. Reports of their presence or absence were to be made to their secular teachers.

The foregoing facts, without reference to others that appear in the record, show the use of tax-supported property for religious instruction carried on by separate religious sects. Pupils compelled by law to go to school for secular education are released in part from their legal duty upon the condition that they attend the religious classes. This is beyond all question a utilization of the tax-established and tax-supported public school system to aid religious groups to spread their faith. And it falls squarely under the ban of the First Amendment (made applicable to the States by the Fourteenth) as we interpreted it in *Everson* v. *Board of Education*. . . .

To hold that a state cannot consistently with the First and Fourteenth Amendments utilize its public school system to aid any or all religious faiths or sects in the dissemination of their doctrines and ideals does not, as counsel urge, manifest a government hostility to religion or religious teachings. A manifestation of such hostility would be at war with our national tradition as embodied in the First Amendment's guaranty of the free exercise of religion. For the First Amendment rests upon the premise that both religion and government can best work to achieve their lofty aims if each is left free from the other within its respective sphere. Or, as we said in the *Everson* case, the First Amendment has erected a wall between Church and State which must be kept high and impregnable.

Here not only are the State's tax-supported public school buildings used for the dissemination of religious doctrines. The State also affords secretarian groups an invaluable aid in that it helps to provide pupils for their religious classes through the use of the State's compulsory public school machinery. This is not separation of Church and State.

The cause is reversed and remanded to the State Supreme Court for proceedings not inconsistent with this opinion

Reversed and remanded.

[Mr. Justice Rutledge and Mr. Justice Burton also concurred in the Court's opinion.]

MR. JUSTICE FRANKFURTER delivered the following opinion, in which MR. JUSTICE JACKSON, MR. JUSTICE RUTLEDGE, and MR. JUSTICE BURTON join:

We dissented in *Everson* v. *Board of Education*. . . because in our view the constitutional principle requiring separation of Church and State compelled invalidation of the ordinance sustained by the majority. Illinois has here authorized the commingling of sectarian with secular instruction in the public schools. The Constitution of the United States forbids this. . . .

Agreement, in the abstract, that the First Amendment was designed to erect a "wall of separation between church and state," does not preclude a clash of views as to what the wall separates. Involved is not only the constitutional principle but the implications of judicial review in its enforcement. Accommodation of legislative freedom and constitutional limitations upon that freedom cannot be achieved by a mere phrase. We cannot illuminatingly apply the "wall-of-separation" metaphor until we have considered the relevant history of religious education in America, the place of the "released-time" movement in that history, and its precise manifestation in the case before us. . . .

The evolution of colonial education, largely in the service of religion, into the public school system of today is the story of changing conceptions regarding the American democratic society, of the functions of State-maintained education in such a society, and of the role therein of the free exercise of religion by the people. The modern public school derived from a philosophy of freedom reflected in the First Amendment. . . . As the momentum for popular education increased and in turn evoked strong claims for State support of religious education, contests not unlike that which in Virginia had produced Madison's Remonstrance appeared in various forms in other States. New York and Massachusetts provide famous chapters in the history that established dissociation of religious teaching from State-maintained schools. In New York, the rise of the common schools led, despite fierce sectarian opposition, to the barring of tax funds to church schools, and later to any school in which sectarian doctrine was taught. In Massachusetts, largely through the efforts of Horace Mann, all sectarian teachings were barred from the common school to save it from being rent by denominational conflict. The upshot of these controversies, often long and fierce, is fairly summarized by saying that long before the Fourteenth Amendment subjected the States to new limitations, the prohibition of furtherance by the State of religious instruction became the guiding principle, in law and feeling, of the American people. . . .

Separation in the field of education, then was not imposed upon unwilling States by force of superior law. In this respect the Fourteenth Amendment merely reflected a principle then dominant in our national life. To the extent that the Constitution thus made it binding upon the States, the basis of the restriction is the whole experience of our people. Zealous watchfulness against fusion of secular and religious activities by Government itself, through any of its instruments but especially through its education agencies, was the democratic response of the American community to the particular needs of a young and growing nation, unique in the composition of its people. A totally different situation elsewhere, as illustrated for instance by the English provisions for religious education in State-maintained schools, only serves to illustrate that free societies are not cast on one mold. . . . Different institutions evolve from different historic circumstances.

. . . [T]he intrusion of religious instruction into the public school system of Champaign [cannot] be minimized by saying that it absorbs less than an hour a week; in fact, that affords evidence of a design constitutionally objectionable. If it were merely a question of enabling a child to obtain religious instruction with a receptive mind, the thirty or forty-five minutes could readily be found on Saturday or Sunday. If that were all, Champaign might have drawn upon the French system, known in its American manifestation as "dismissed time," whereby one school day is shortened to allow all children to go where they please, leaving those who so desire to go to a religious school. The momentum of the whole school atmosphere and school planning is presumably put behind religious instruction, as given in Champaign, precisely in order to secure for the religious instruction such momentum and planning. To speak to "released time" as being only half or three-quarters of an hour is to draw a thread from a fabric. . . .

Separation means separation, not something less. Jefferson's metaphor in describing the relation between Church and State speaks of a "wall of separation," not of a fine line easily overstepped. The public school is at once the symbol of our democracy and the most pervasive means for promoting our common destiny. In no activity of the State is it more vital to keep out divisive forces than in its schools, to avoid confusing, not to say fusing, what the Constitution sought to keep strictly apart. "The great American principle of eternal separation"—Elihu Root's phrase bears repetition—is one of the vital reliances of our Constitutional system for assuring unities among our people stronger than our diversities. It is the Court's duty to enforce this principle in its full integrity. . . .

MR. JUSTICE REED, dissenting:

. . . The phrase "an establishment of religion" may have been intended by Congress to be aimed only at a state church. When the First Amendment was pending in Congress in substantially its present form, "Mr. Madison said, he apprehended the meaning of the words to be, that Congress should not establish a religion, and enforce the legal observation of it by law, nor compel men to worship God in any manner contrary to their conscience." Passing years, however, have brought about acceptance of a broader meaning, although never until today, I believe, has this Court widened its interpretation to any such degree as holding that recognition of the interest of our nation in religion, through the granting, to qualified representatives of the principal faiths, of opportunity to present religion as an optional, extracurricular subject during released school time in public school buildings, was equivalent to an establishment of religion. A reading of the general statements of eminent statesmen of former days, referred to in the opinions in this case and in *Everson* v. *Board of Education,* . . . will show that circumstances such as those in this case were far from the minds of the authors. The words and spirit of those statements may be wholeheartedly accepted without in the least impugning the judgment of the State of Illinois. . . .

It seems clear to me that the "aid" referred to by the Court in the *Everson* case could not have been those incidental advantages that religious bodies, with other groups similarly situated, obtain as a byproduct of organized society. This explains the well-known fact that all churches receive "aid" from government in the form of freedom from taxation. The *Everson* decision itself justified the transportation of children to church schools by New Jersey for safety reasons. It accords with *Cochran* v. *Louisiana State Board of Education,* . . . , where this Court upheld a free textbook statute of Louisiana against a charge that it aided private schools on the ground that books were for the education of the children, not to aid religious schools. Likewise the National School Lunch Act aids all school children attending tax-exempt schools. In *Bradfield* v. *Roberts,* 175 U.S. 291, this Court held proper the payment of money by the Federal Government to build an addition to a hospital, chartered by individuals who were members of a Roman Catholic sisterhood, and operated under the auspices of the Roman Catholic Church. This was done over the objection that it aided the establishment of religion. While obviously in these instances the respective churches, in a certain sense, were aided, this Court has never held that such "aid" was in violation of the First or Fourteenth Amendment. . . .

The practices of the Federal Government offer many examples of this kind of "aid" by the state to religion. The Congress of the United States has a chaplain for each House who daily invokes divine blessings and guidance for the proceedings. The armed forces have commissioned chaplains from early days. They conduct the public services in accordance with the liturgical requirements of their respective faiths, ashore and afloat, employing for the purpose property belonging to the United

States and dedicated to the services of religion. Under the Servicemen's Readjustment Act of 1944, eligible Veterans may receive training at government expense for the ministry in denominational schools. The schools of the District of Columbia have opening exercises which "include a reading from the Bible without note or comment, and the Lord's Prayer."

In the United States Naval Academy and the United States Military Academy, schools wholly supported and completely controlled by the federal government, there are a number of religious activities. Chaplains are attached to both schools. Attendance at church services on Sunday is compulsory at both the Military and Naval Academies. At West Point the Protestant services are held in the Cadet Chapel, the Catholic in the Catholic Chapel, and the Jewish in the Old Cadet Chapel; at Annapolis only Protestant services are held on the reservation, midshipmen of other religious persuasions attend the churches of the city of Annapolis. These facts indicate that both schools since their earliest beginnings have maintained and enforced a pattern of participation in formal worship.

With the general statements in the opinions concerning the constitutional requirement that the nation and the states, by virtue of the First and Fourteenth Amendments, may "make no law respecting an establishment of religion," I am in agreement. But, in the light of the meaning given to these words by the precedents, customs, and practices which I have detailed above, I cannot agree with the Court's conclusion that when pupils compelled by law to go to school for secular education are released from school so as to attend the religious classes, churches are unconstitutionally aided. Whatever may be the wisdom of the arrangement as to the use of the school buildings made with the Champaign Council of Religious Education, it is clear to me that past practice shows such cooperation between the schools and a non-ecclesiastical body is not forbidden by the First Amendment. . . . The prohibition of enactments respecting the establishment of religion do not bar every friendly gesture between church and state. It is not an absolute prohibition against every conceivable situation where the two may work together, any more than the other provisions of the First Amendment—free speech, free press—are absolutes. . . . Devotion to the great principle of religious liberty should not lead us into a rigid interpretation of the constitutional guaranty that conflicts with accepted habits of our people. This is an instance where, for me, the history of past practices is determinative of the meaning of a constitutional clause, not a decorous introduction to the study of its text. The judgment should be affirmed.

ZORACH *v.* CLAUSON

343 U.S. 306; 72 Sup. Ct. 679; 96 L. Ed. 954 (1952)

[Zorach and another New York City resident challenged the constitutionality of the City's released-time program, which is described in the Court's opinion. They contended that the program violated the establishment of religion and free exercise of religion clauses of the First Amendment by reason of the Fourteenth Amendment. The highest state court sustained the released-time program. The case was then brought to the Supreme Court on appeal. (Clauson was a member of the New York City Board of Education.)]

MR. JUSTICE DOUGLAS delivered the opinion of the Court:

New York City has a program which permits its public schools to release students during the school day so that they may leave the school buildings and school grounds and go to religious centers for religious instruction or devotional exercises. A student is released on written request of his parents. Those not released stay in the classrooms. The churches make weekly reports to the schools, sending a list of children who have been released from public school but who have not reported for religious instruction.

This "released-time" program involves neither religious instruction in public-school classrooms nor the expenditure of public funds. All costs, including the application blanks, are paid by the religious organizations. The case is therefore unlike *McCollum* v. *Board of Education*. . . . In that case the classrooms were turned over to religious instructors. We accordingly held that the program violated the First Amendment which (by reason of the Fourteenth Amendment) prohibits the states from establishing religion or prohibiting its free exercise. . . .

[Our] problem reduces itself to whether New York by this system has either prohibited the "free exercise" of religion or has made a law "respecting an establishment of religion" within the meaning of the First Amendment.

It takes obtuse reasoning to inject any issue of the "free exercise" of religion to the present case. No one is forced to go to the religious classroom and no religious exercise or instruction is brought to the classrooms of the public schools. A student need not take religious instruction. He is left to his own desires as to the manner or time of his religious devotions, if any.

There is a suggestion that the system involves the use of coercion to get public-school students into religious classrooms. There is no evidence in the record before us that supports that conclusion. The present record indeed tells us that the school authorities are neutral in this regard and do no more than release students whose parents so request. If in fact coercion were used, if it were established that any one or more teachers were using their office to persuade or force students to take the religious instruction, a wholly different case would be presented. Hence we put aside that claim of coercion both as respects the "free exercise" of religion and "an establishment of religion" within the meaning of the First Amendment.

Moreover, apart from that claim of coercion, we do not see how New York by this type of "released-time" program has made a law respecting an establishment of religion within the meaning of the First Amendment. There is much talk of the separation of Church and State in the history of the Bill of Rights and in the decisions clustering around the First Amendment. See *Everson* v. *Board of Education*. . . . There cannot be the slightest doubt that the First Amendment reflects the philosophy that Church and State should be separated. And so far as interference with the "free exercise" of religion and an "establishment" of religion are concerned, the separation must be complete and unequivocal. The First Amendment within the scope of its coverage permits no exception; the prohibition is absolute. The First Amendment, however, does not say that in every and all respects there shall be a separation of Church and State. Rather, it studiously defines the manner, the specific ways, in which there shall be no concert or union or dependency one on the other. That is the common sense of the matter. Otherwise the state and religion would be aliens to each other—hostile, suspicious, and even unfriendly. Churches could not be required to pay even property taxes. Municipalities would not be permitted to render police or fire protection to religious groups. Policemen who helped parishioners into their places of worship would violate the Constitution. Prayers in our legislative halls; the appeals to the Almighty in the messages of the Chief Executive; the proclamations making Thanskgiving Day a holiday; "so help me God" in our courtroom oaths—these and all other references to the Almighty that run through our laws, our public rituals, our ceremonies would be flouting the First Amendment. A fastidious atheist or agnostic could even object to the supplication with which the Court opens each session: "God save the United States and this Honorable Court."

We would have to press the concept of separation of Church and State to these extremes to condemn the present law on constitutional grounds. . . .

We are a religious people whose institutions presuppose a Supreme Being. We guarantee the freedom to worship as one chooses. We make room for as wide a variety of beliefs and creeds as the spiritual needs of man deem necessary. We sponsor an attitude on the part of government that shows no partiality to any one group and that lets each flourish according to the zeal of its adherents and the appeal of its dogma. When the state encourages religious instruction or cooperates with religious authorities by adjusting the schedule of public events to sectarian needs, it follows the best of our traditions. For it then respects the religious nature of our people and accommodates the public service to their spiritual needs. To hold that it may not would be to find in the Constitution a requirement that the government show a callous indifference to religious groups. That would be preferring those who believe in no religion over those who do believe. Government may not finance religious groups nor undertake religious instruction nor blend secular and sectarian education nor use secular institutions to force one or some religion on any person. But we find no constitutional requirement which makes it necessary for government to be hostile to religion and to throw its weight against efforts to widen the effective scope of religious influence. The government must be neutral when it comes to competition between sects. It may not thrust any sect on any person. It may not make a religious observance compulsory. It may not coerce anyone to attend church, to observe a religious holiday, or to take religious instruction. But it can close its doors or suspend its operations as to those who want to repair to their religious sanctuary for worship or instruction. No more than that is undertaken here. . . .

In the *McCollum* case the classrooms were used for religious instruction and the force of the public school was used to promote that instruction. Here, as we have said, the public schools do no more than accommodate their schedules to a program of outside religious instruction. We follow the *McCollum* case. But we cannot expand it to cover the present released-time program unless separation of Church and State means that public institutions can make no adjustments of their schedules to accommodate the religious needs of the people. We cannot read into the Bill of Rights such a philosophy of hostility to religion.

Affirmed.

MR. JUSTICE BLACK, dissenting:

. . . I see no significant difference between the invalid Illinois system and that of New York here sustained. Except for the use of the school buildings in Illinois, there is no difference between the systems which I consider even worthy of mention. In the New York program, as in that of Illinois, the school authorites release some of the children on the condition that they attend the religious classes, get reports on whether they attend, and hold the other children in the school building until the religious hour is over. As we attempted to make categorically clear, the *McCollum* decision would have been the same if the religious classes had not been held in the school building. . . .

I am aware that our *McCollum* decision on separation of Church and State has been subjected to a most searching examination throughout the country. Probably few opinions from this Court in recent years have attracted more attention or stirred wider debate. Our insistence on "a wall between Church and State which must be kept high and impregnable" has seemed to some a correct exposition of the philosophy and a true interpretation of the language of the First Amendment to which we should strictly adhere. With equal conviction and sincerity, others have thought the *McCollum* decision fundamentally wrong and have pledged continuous warfare against it. . . .

Here the sole question is whether New York can use its compulsory education laws to help religious sects get attendants presumably too unenthusiastic to go unless moved to do so by the pressure of this state machinery. That this is the plan, purpose, design, and consequence of the New York program cannot be denied. The state thus makes religious sects beneficiaries of its power to compel children to attend secular schools. Any use of such coercive power by the state to help or hinder some religious sects or to prefer all religious sects over nonbelievers or vice versa is just what I think the First Amendment forbids. . . .

The Court's validation of the New York system rests in part on its statement that Americans are "a religious people whose institutions presuppose a Supreme Being." This was at least as true when the First Amendment was adopted; and it was just as true when eight Justices of this Court invalidated the released-time system in *McCollum* on the premise that a state can no more "aid all religions" than it can aid one. It was precisely because eighteenth-century Americans were a religious people divided into many fighting sects that we were given the constitutional mandate to keep Church and State completely separate. . . .

MR. JUSTICE FRANKFURTER dissented.

MR. JUSTICE JACKSON, dissenting:

This released time program is founded upon a use of the State's power of coercion, which, for me, determines its unconstitutionality. Stripped to its essentials, the plan has two stages: first, that the State compel each student to yield a large part of his time for public secular education; and, second, that some of it be "released" to him on condition that he devote it to sectarian religious purposes.

No one suggests that the Constitution would permit the State directly to require this "released" time to be spent "under the control of a duly constituted religious body." This program accomplishes that forbidden result by indirection. If public education were taking so much of the pupil's time as to injure the public or the students' welfare by encroaching upon their religious opportunity, simply shortening everyone's school day would facilitate voluntary and optional attendance at Church classes. But that suggestion is rejected upon the ground that if they are made free many students will not go to the Church. Hence, they must be deprived of freedom for this period, with Church attendance put to them as one of the two permissible ways of using it.

The greater effectiveness of this system over voluntary attendance after school hours is due to the truant officer who, if the youngster fails to go to the Church school, dogs him back to the public schoolroom. Here schooling is more or less suspended during the "released time" so the nonreligious attendants will not forge ahead of the church-going absentees. But it serves as a temporary jail for a pupil who will not go to Church. It takes more subtlety of mind than I possess to deny that this is governmental constraint in support of religion. It is as unconstitutional, in my view, when exerted by indirection as when exercised forthrightly.

As one whose children, as a matter of free choice, have been sent to privately supported Church schools, I may challenge the Court's suggestion that opposition to this plan can only be anti-religious, atheistic, or agnostic. My envangelistic brethren confuse an objection to compulsion with an objection to religion. It is possible to hold a faith with enough confidence to believe that what should be rendered to God does not need to be decided and collected by Caesar.

The day that this country ceases to be free for irreligion it will cease to be free for religion—except for the sect that can win political power. The same epithetical jurisprudence used by the Court today to beat down those who oppose pressuring children into some religion can devise as good epithets tomorrow against those who object to pressuring them into a favored religion. . . . We start down a rough road when we begin to mix compulsory public education with compulsory godliness.

A number of Justices just short of a majority of the majority that promulgates today's passionate dialectics joined in answering them in *Illinois* ex rel. *McCollum* v. *Board of Education*, . . . The distinction attempted between that case and this is trivial, almost to the point of cynicism, magnifying its nonessential details and disparaging compulsion which was the underlying reason for invalidity. A reading of the Court's opinion in that case along with its opinion in this case will show such differences of overtones and undertones as to make clear that the *McCollum* case has passed like a storm in a teacup. The wall which the Court was professing to erect between Church and State has become even more warped and twisted than I expected. Today's judgment will be more interesting to students of psychology and of the judicial processes than to students of constitutional law.

ENGEL *v.* VITALE

370 U.S. 421; 82 Sup. Ct. 1261; 8 L. Ed. 2d 601 (1962)

[In November 1951, the New York State Board of Regents, which controls and supervises the state's public school system, proposed a prayer for daily recitation in the public schools. The brief prayer was regarded by the board of regents as nonsectarian and read as follows: "Almighty God, we acknowledge our dependence upon Thee, and we beg Thy blessings upon us, our parents, our teachers and our country." The regents' proposal was by no means mandatory; it was simply a recommendation that local school boards were free to adopt or not as they saw fit, and only about 10 per cent of the local boards did adopt the prayer.

In 1958, the school board of New Hyde Park, a Long Island suburb of New York City, adopted the regents' prayer and directed the school district principal to cause the prayer "to be said aloud by each class in the presence of a teacher at the beginning of each school day." Steven Engel, who had two children enrolled in the New Hyde Park schools, and a group of other parents in the community brought suit in a state court with the help of the New York chapter of the American Civil Liberties Union. The parents argued that the use of the official prayer "was contrary to the beliefs, religions and religious practices of both themselves and their children," and hence constituted a violation of the First and Fourteenth Amendments. Specifically, Engel and the other parents asked the trial court for a mandamus to compel the school board to discontinue the use of the prayer, but it was denied. The trial court remanded the case to the school board so that measures could be taken, if necessary, to eliminate any possible coercion and "to protect those who objected to reciting the prayer." The trial court decision was affirmed by the appellate division. Upon appeal, the New York Court of Appeals (New York's highest court) also affirmed by a vote of 5 to 2, holding that the noncompulsory daily recitation of the prayer did not violate the constitutional guaranties concerning freedom of religion. The Supreme Court then granted certiorari.

The respondents are the members of the New Hyde Park school board. William J. Vitale, Jr., was the presiding officer of the board.]

MR. JUSTICE BLACK delivered the opinion of the Court:

. . . We think that by using its public school system to encourage recitation of the Regents' prayer, the State of New York has adopted a practice wholly inconsistent with the Establishment Clause. There can, of course, be no doubt that New York's program of daily classroom invocation of God's blessings as prescribed in the Regents' prayer is a religious activity. It is solemn avowal of divine faith and supplication for the blessings of the Almighty. The nature of such a prayer has always been religious, none of the respondents has denied this and the trial court expressly so found:

"The religious nature of prayer was recognized by Jefferson and has been concurred in by theological writers, the United States Supreme Court and State courts and administrative officials, including New York's Commissioner of Education. A committee of the New York Legislature has agreed.

"The Board of Regents as *amicus curiae,* the respondents and intervenors all concede the religious nature of prayer, but seek to distinguish this prayer because it is based on our spiritual heritage. . . ."

The petitioners contend among other things that the state laws requiring or permitting use of the Regents' prayer must be struck down as a violation of the Establishment Clause because that prayer was composed by governmental officials as a part of a governmental program to further religious beliefs. For this reason, petitioners argue, the State's use of the Regents' prayer in its public school system breaches the constitutional wall of separation between Church and State. We agree with that contention since we think that the constitutional prohibition against laws respecting an establishment of religion must at least mean that in this country it is no part of the business of government to compose offical prayers for any group of the American people to recite as a part of a religious program carried on by government.

It is a matter of history that this very practice of establishing governmentally composed prayers for religious services was one of the reasons which caused many of our early colonists to leave England and seek religious freedom in America. The Book of Common Prayer, which was created under governmental direction and which was approved by Acts of Parliament in 1548 and 1549, set out in minute detail the accepted form and content of prayer and other religious ceremonies to be used in the established, tax-supported Church of England. The controversies over the Book and what should be its content repeatedly threatened to disrupt the peace of that country as the accepted forms of prayer in the established church changed with the views of the particular ruler that happened to be in control at the time. Powerful groups representing some of the varying religious views of the people struggled among themselves to impress their particular views upon the Government and obtain amendments of the Book more suitable to their respective notions of how religious services should be conducted in order that the official religious establishment would advance their particular religious beliefs. Other groups, lacking the necessary political power to influence the Government on the matter, decided to leave England and its established church and seek freedom in America from England's governmentally ordained and supported religion.

It is an unfortunate fact of history that when some of the very groups which had most strenuously opposed the established Church of England found themselves sufficiently in control of colonial governments in this country to write their own prayers into law, they passed laws making their own religion the official religion of their respective colonies. Indeed, as late as the time of the Revolutionary War, there were established churches in at least eight of the thirteen former colonies and established religions in at least four of the other five. But the successful Revolution against English political domination was shortly followed by intense opposition to the practice of establishing religion by law. This opposition crystalized rapidly into an effective political force in Virginia where the minority religious groups such as Presbyterians, Lutherans, Quakers and Baptists had gained such strength that the adherents to the established Episcopal Church were actually a minority themselves. In 1785–1786, those opposed to the established Church, led by James Madison and Thomas Jefferson, who, though themselves not members of any of these dissenting religious groups, opposed all religious establishments by law on grounds of principle, obtained the enactment of the famous "Virginia Bill for Religious Liberty" by which all religious groups were placed on equal footing so far as the State was concerned. Similar though less far-reaching legislation was being considered and passed in other States.

By the time of the adoption of the Constitution, our history shows that there was a widespread awareness among many Americans of the dangers of a union of Church and State. . . . The First Amendment was added to the Constitution to stand as a guaranty that neither the power nor the prestige of the Federal Government would be used to control, support or influence the kinds of prayer the American people can say—that the people's religions must not be subjected to the pressures of government for change each time a new political administration is elected to office. Under that Amendment's prohibition against governmental establishment of religion, as reinforced by the provisions of the Fourteenth Amendment, government in this country, be it state or federal, is without power to prescribe by law any particular form of prayer which is to be used as an official prayer in carrying on any program of governmentally sponsored religious activity.

There can be no doubt that New York's state prayer program officially establishes the religious beliefs embodied in the Regent's prayer. The respondents' argument to the contrary, which is largely based upon the contention that the Regents' prayer is "nondenominational" and the fact that the program, as modified and approved by state courts, does not require all pupils to recite the prayer but permits those who wish to do so to remain silent or be excused from the room, ignores the essential nature of the program's constitutional defects. Neither the fact that the prayer may be denominationally neutral, nor the fact that its observance on the part of the students is voluntary can serve to free it from the limitations of the Establishment Clause, as it might from the Free Exercise Clause, of the First Amendment, both of which are operative against the States by virtue of the Fourteenth Amendment. Although these two clauses may in certain instances overlap, they forbid two quite different kinds of governmental encroachment upon religious freedom. The Establishment Clause, unlike the Free Exercise Clause, does not depend upon any showing of direct governmental compulsion and is violated by the enactment of laws which establish an official religion whether those laws operate directly to coerce non-observing individuals or not. This is not to say, of course, that laws officially prescribing a particular form of religious worship do not involve coercion of such individuals. When the power, prestige and financial support of government is placed behind a particular religious belief, the indirect coercive pressure upon religious minorities to conform to the prevailing officially approved religion is plain. But the purposes underlying the Establishment Clause go much further than that. Its first and most immediate purpose rested on the belief that a union of government and religion tends to destroy government and to degrade religion. . . . Another purpose of the Establishment Clause rested upon an awareness of the historical fact that governmentally established religions and religious persecutions go hand in hand. The Founders knew that only a few years after the Book of Common Prayer became the only accepted form of religious services in the established Church of England, an Act of Uniformity was passed to compel all Englishmen to attend those services and to make it a criminal offense to conduct or attend religious gatherings of any other kind—a law which was consistently flouted by dissenting religious groups in England and which contributed to widespread persecutions of people like John Bunyan who persisted in holding "unlawful [religious] meetings . . . to the great disturbance and distraction of the good subjects of this kingdom. . . ." And they knew that similar persecutions had received the sanction of law in several of the colonies in this country soon after the establishment of official religions in those colonies. It was in large part to get completely away from this sort of systematic religious persecution that the Founders brought into being our Nation, our Constitution, and our Bill of Rights with its prohibition against any governmental establishment of religion. The New York laws officially prescribing the Regents' prayer are inconsistent with both the purposes of the Establishment Clause and with the Establishment Clause itself.

It has been argued that to apply the Constitution in such a way as to prohibit state laws respecting an establishment of religious services in public schools is to indicate a hostility toward religion or toward prayer. Nothing, of course, could be more wrong. The history of man is inseparable from the history of religion. And perhaps it is not too much to say that since the beginning of that history many people have devoutly believed that "More things are wrought by prayer than this world dreams of." It was doubtless largely due to men who believed this that there grew up a sentiment that caused men to leave the cross-currents of officially established state religions and religious persecution in Europe and come to this country filled with the hope that they could find a place in which they could pray when they pleased to the God of their faith in the language they chose. And there were men of this same faith in the power of prayer who led the fight for adoption of our Constitution and also for our Bill of Rights with the very guaranties of religious freedom that forbid the sort of governmental activity which New York has attempted here. These men knew that the First Amendment, which tried to put an end to governmental control of religion and of prayer, was not written to destroy either. They knew rather that it was written to quiet well-justified fears which nearly all of them felt arising out of an awareness that governments of the past had shackled men's tongues to make them speak only the religious thoughts that government wanted them to speak and to pray only to the God that government wanted them to pray to. It is neither sacrilegious nor antireligious to say that each separate government in this country should stay out of the business of writing or sanctioning official prayers and leave that purely religious function to the people themselves and to those the people choose to look to for religious guidance.

It is true that New York's establishment of its Regents' prayer as an officially approved religious doctrine of that State does not amount to a total establishment of one particular religious sect to the exclusion of all others—that, indeed, the governmental endorsement of that prayer seems relatively insignificant when compared to the governmental encroachments upon religion which were commonplace 200 years ago. To those who may subscribe to the view that because the Regents' official prayer is so brief and general there can be no danger to religious freedom in its governmental establishment, however, it may be appropriate to say in the words of James Madison, the author of the first Amendment:

> "[I]t is proper to take alarm at the first experiment on our liberties. . . . Who does not see that the same authority which can establish Christianity, in exclusion of all other Religions, may establish with the same ease any particular sect of Christians, in exclusion of all other Sects? That the same authority which can force a citizen to contribute three pence only of his property for the support of any one establishment, may force him to conform to any other establishment in all cases whatsoever?"

The judgment of the Court of Appeals of New York is reversed and the cause remanded for further proceedings not inconsistent with this opinion.

Reversed and remanded.

MR. JUSTICE FRANKFURTER took no part in the decision of this case.

MR. JUSTICE WHITE took no part in the consideration or decision of this case.

MR. JUSTICE DOUGLAS, concurring:

. . . The point for decision is whether the Government can constitutionally finance a religious exercise. Our system at the federal and state levels is presently honeycombed with such financing. Nevertheless, I think it is an unconstitutional undertaking whatever form it takes. . . .

What New York does on the opening of its public schools is what we do when we open court. Our Marshal has from the beginning announced the convening of the Court and then added "God save the United States and this honorable court." That utterance is supplication, a prayer in which we, the judges, are free to join, but which we need not recite any more than the students need recite the New York prayer.

What New York does on the opening of its public schools is what each House of Congress does at the opening of each day's business. . . .

In New York the teacher who leads in prayer is on the public payroll; and the time she takes seems minuscule as compared with the salaries appropriated by state legislatures and Congress for chaplains to conduct prayers in the legislative halls. Only a bare fraction of the teacher's time is given to reciting this short twenty-two-word prayer, about the same amount of time that our Marshal spends announcing the opening of our sessions and offering a prayer for this Court. Yet for me the principle is the same, no matter how briefly the prayer is said, for in each of the instances given the person praying is a public official on the public payroll, performing a religious exercise in a governmental institution.

. . . once government finances a religious exercise it inserts a divisive influence into our communities. . . .

My problem today would be uncomplicated but for *Everson* v. *Board of Education,* . . . which allowed taxpayers' money to be used to pay "the bus fares of parochial school pupils as a part of a general program under which" the fares of pupils attending public and other schools were also paid. The *Everson* case seems in retrospect to be out of line with the First Amendment. Its result is appealing, as it allows aid to be given to needy children. Yet by the same token, public funds could be used to satisfy other needs of children in parochial schools—lunches, books, and tuition being obvious examples.

MR. JUSTICE STEWART, dissenting:

. . . The Court does not hold, nor could it, that New York has interfered with the free exercise of anybody's religion. For the state courts have made clear that those who object to reciting the prayer must be entirely free of any compulsion to do so, including any "embarrassments and pressures.". . . But the Court says that in permitting school children to say this simple prayer, the New York authorities have established "an official religion."

With all respect, I think the Court has misapplied a great constitutional principle. I cannot see how an "official religion" is established by letting those who want to say a prayer say it. On the contrary, I think that to deny the wish of these school children to join in reciting this prayer is to deny them the opportunity of sharing in the spiritual heritage of our Nation.

The Court's historical review of the quarrels over the Book of Common Prayer in England throws no light for me on the issue before us in this case. England had then and has now an established church. Equally unenlightening, I think, is the history of the early establishment and later rejection of an official church in our own States. For we deal here not with the establishment of a state church, which would, of course, be constitutionally impermissible, but with whether school children who want to begin their day by joining in prayer must be prohibited from doing so. Moreover, I think that the Court's task, in this as in all areas of constitutional adjudication, is not responsibly aided by the uncritical invocation of metaphors like the "wall of separation," a phrase nowhere to be found in the Constitution. What is relevant to the issue here is not the history of an established church in sixteenth-century England or in eighteenth-century America, but the history of the religious traditions of our people, reflected in countless practices of the institutions and officials of our government.

At the opening of each day's Session of this Court we stand, while one of our officials invokes the protection of God. Since the days of John Marshall our Crier has said, "God save the United States and this Honorable Court." Both the Senate and the House of Representatives open their daily Sessions with prayer. Each of our Presidents, from George Washington to John F. Kennedy, has upon assuming his Office asked the protection and help of God.

The Court today says that the state and federal governments are without constitutional power to prescribe any particular form of words to be recited by any group of the American people on any subject touching religion. The third stanza of "The Star-Spangled Banner," made our National Anthem by Act of Congress in 1931, contains these verses:

"Blest with victory and peace,
may the heav'n rescued land
Praise the Pow'r that hath made
and preserved us as a nation!
Then conquer we must,
when our cause it is just,
And this be our motto,
'In God is our Trust.' "

In 1954, Congress added a phrase to the Pledge of Allegiance to the Flag so that it now contains the words "one Nation under God, indivisible, with liberty and justice for all." In 1952, Congress enacted legislation calling upon the President each year to proclaim a National Day of Prayer. Since 1865, the words "In God We Trust" have been impressed on our coins.

Countless similar examples could be listed, but there is no need to belabor the obvious. . . .

I do not believe that this Court, or the Congress, or the President has by the actions and practices I have mentioned established an "official religion" in violation of the Constitution. And I do not believe the State of New York has done so in this case. What each has done has been to recognize and to follow the deeply entrenched and highly cherished spiritual traditions of our Nation—traditions which come down to us from those who almost two hundred years ago avowed their "firm reliance on the Protection of Divine Providence" when they proclaimed the freedom and independence of this brave new world.

I dissent.

ABINGTON SCHOOL DISTRICT *v.* SCHEMPP
MURRAY *v.* CURLETT
374 U.S. 203; 83 Sup. Ct. 1560; 10 L. Ed. 2d 844 (1963)

[These companion cases deal with Bible reading and the recitation of the Lord's Prayer in the public schools. The Schempp *case originated in Pennsylvania, where a state law required that "at least ten verses from the Holy Bible shall be read, without comments, at the opening of each public school on each day." The statute further provided that any child could be excused from attending the Bible reading with the written request of his parent or guardian. The Schempp family—husband, wife, and two children, who attended one of the Abington district schools—was Unitarian and brought suit to enjoin the practice of daily Bible readings, contending that it violated their rights under the Establishment Clause of the First Amendment as applied to the states by the due process clause of the Fourteenth Amendment. A three-judge district court in Pennsylvania found the statute unconstitutional. The case then went to the Supreme Court on appeal.*

The Murray *case originated in Baltimore, Md., where the Board of School Commissioners, relying on an appropriate state statute, adopted a rule providing for opening exercises in the Baltimore public schools consisting primarily of the "reading, without comment, of a chapter in the Holy Bible and/or the use of the Lord's Prayer." Mrs. Murray and her son, a student in one of the city schools, were both professed atheists who found the Bible "nauseating, historically inaccurate, replete with the ravings of madmen." They felt that the public schools should "prepare children to face the problems on earth, not to prepare for heaven—which is a delusional dream of the unsophisticated minds of the ill-educated clergy." The Murrays filed for a mandamus to compel Curlett, the president of the Board of School Commissioners, to rescind the rule requiring Bible reading or the recitation of the Lord's Prayer. The trial court ruled against the Murrays. The Maryland Court of Appeals, the state's highest court, affirmed by a close 4-to-3 vote. The case then went to the Supreme Court on certiorari.]*

MR. JUSTICE CLARK delivered the opinion of the Court:

Once again we are called upon to consider the scope of the provision of the First Amendment to the United States Constitution which declares that "Congress shall make no law respecting an establishment of religion or prohibiting the free exercise thereof. . . ." These companion cases present the issues in the context of state action requiring that schools begin each day with readings from the Bible. While raising the basic questions under slightly different factual situations, the cases permit of joint treatment. In light of the history of the First Amendment and of our cases interpreting and applying its requirements, we hold that the practices at issue and the laws requiring them are unconstitutional under the Establishment Clause, as applied to the states through the Fourteenth Amendment. . . .

It is true that religion has been closely identified with our history and government. As we said in *Engel* v. *Vitale* . . . "The history of man is inseparable from the history of religion. And . . . since the beginning of that history many people have devoutly believed that 'More things are wrought by prayer than this world dreams of.' " In *Zorach* v. *Clauson* . . . we gave specific recognition to the proposition that "we are a religious people whose institutions presuppose a Supreme Being." The fact that the Founding Fathers believed devotedly that there was a God and that the unalienable rights of man were rooted in Him is clearly evidenced in their writings, from the Mayflower Compact to the Constitution itself. This background is evidenced today in our public life through the continuance in our oaths of office from the Presidency to the Alderman of the final supplication, "So help me God." Likewise each House of the Congress provides through its Chaplain an opening prayer, and the sessions of this Court are declared open by the crier in a short ceremony, the final phrase of which invokes the grace of God. Again, there are such manifestations in our military forces, where those of our citizens who are under the restrictions of military service wish to engage in voluntary worship. Indeed, only last year an official survey of the country indicated that 64 per cent of our people have church membership . . . while less than 3 per cent profess no religion whatever. . . . It can be truly said, therefore, that today, as in the beginning, our national life reflects a religious people. . . .

This is not to say, however, that religion has been so identified with our history and government that religious freedom is not likewise as strongly imbedded in our public and private life. Nothing but the most telling of personal experiences in religious persecution suffered by our forebears . . . could have planted our belief in liberty of religious opinion any more deeply in our heritage. It is true that this liberty frequently was not realized by the Colonists, but this is readily accountable to their close ties to the Mother Country. However, the views of Madison and Jefferson, preceded by Roger Williams, came to be incorporated not only in the Federal Constitution but likewise in those of most of our States. This freedom to worship was indispensable in a country whose people came from the four quarters of the earth and brought with them a diversity of religious bodies, . . .

[T]his Court has decisively settled that the First Amendment's mandate that "Congress shall make no law respecting an establishment of religion, or prohibiting the free exercise thereof" has been made wholly applicable to the states by the Fourteenth Amendment. . . . In a series of cases since *Cantwell* the Court has repeatedly reaffirmed that doctrine, and we do so now. . . .

[T]his Court has rejected unequivocally the contention that the establishment clause forbids only governmental preference of one religion over another. Almost twenty years ago in *Everson* . . . the Court said that "neither a state nor the Federal Government can set up a church. Neither can pass laws which aid one religion, or prefer one religion over another.". . . Further, Mr. Justice Rutledge, joined by Justices Frankfurter, Jackson and Burton, declared:

> "The [First] Amendment's purpose was not to strike merely at the official establishment of a single sect, creed or religion, outlawing only a formal relation such as had prevailed in England and some of the Colonies. Necessarily it was to uproot all such relationships. But the object was broader than separating church and state in this narrow sense. It was to create a complete and permanent separation of the spheres of religious activity and civil authority by comprehensively forbidding every form of public aid or support for religion. . . ."

The same conclusion has been firmly maintained ever since that time . . . and we reaffirm it now.

While none of the parties to either of these cases has questioned these basic conclusions of the Court, both of which have been long established, recognized and consistently reaffirmed, others continue to question their history, logic and efficacy. Such contentions, in the light of the consistent interpretation in cases of this Court, seem entirely untenable and of value only as academic exercises. . . .

[I]n *Engel* v. *Vitale,* only last year, these principles were so universally recognized that the Court without the citation of a single case and over the sole dissent of Mr. Justice Stewart reaffirmed them. The Court found the twenty-two-word prayer used in "New York's program of daily classroom invocation of God's blessings as prescribed in the Regents' prayer . . . [to be] a religious activity.". . . It held that "it is no part of the business of government to compose official prayers for any group of the American people to recite as a part of a religious program carried on by the government.". . . [T]he Court found that the "first and most immediate purpose [of the Establishment Clause] rested on a belief that a union of government and religion tends to destroy government and to degrade religion.". . . When government, the Court said, allies itself with one particular form of religion, the inevitable result is that it incurs "the hatred, disrespect and even contempt of those who held contrary beliefs."

. . . The wholesome "neutrality" of which this Court's cases speak thus stems from a recognition of the teachings of history that powerful sects or groups might bring about a fusion of governmental and religious functions or a concert or dependency of one upon the other to the end that official support of the State or Federal Government would be placed behind the tenets of one or of all orthodoxies. This the Establishment Clause prohibits. And a further reason for neutrality is found in the Free Exercise Clause, which recognizes the value of religious training, teaching and observance and more particularly, the right of every person to freely choose his own course with reference thereto, free of any compulsion from the state. This the Free Exercise Clause guarantees. Thus . . . the two clauses may overlap. . . . [T]he Establishment Clause has been directly considered by this Court eight times in the past score of years and, with only one Justice dissenting on the point, it has consistently held that the clause withdrew all legislative power respecting religious belief or the expression thereof. The test may be stated as follows: what are the purpose and the primary effect of the enactment? If either is the advancement or inhibition of religion then the enactment exceeds the scope of legislative power as circumscribed by the Constitution. That is to say that to withstand the strictures of the Establishment Clause there must be a secular legislative purpose and a primary effect that neither advances nor inhibits religion. . . . The Free Exercise Clause, likewise considered many times here, withdraws from legislative power, state and federal, the exertion of any restraint on the free exercise of religion. Its purpose is to secure religious liberty in the individual by prohibiting any invasions thereof by civil authority. Hence it is necessary in a free exercise case for one to show the coercive effect of the enactment as it operates against him in the practice of his religion. The distinction between the two clauses is apparent—a violation of the Free Exercise Clause is predicated on coercion while the Establishment Clause violation need not be so intended.

Applying the Establishment Clause principles to the cases at bar we find that the States are requiring the selection and reading at the opening of the school day of verses from the Holy Bible and the recitation of the Lord's Prayer by the students in unison. These exercises are prescribed as part of the curricular activities of students who are required by law to attend school. They are held in the school buildings under the supervision and with the participation of teachers employed in those schools. None of these factors, other than compulsory school attendance, was present in the program upheld in *Zorach* v. *Clauson.*

The conclusion follows that in both cases the laws require religious exercises and such exercises are being conducted in direct violation of the rights of the appellees and petitioners. Nor are these required exercises mitigated by the fact that individual students may absent themselves upon parental request, for that fact furnishes no defense to a claim of unconstitutionality under the Establishment Clause. . . . Further, it is no defense to urge that the religious practices here may be relatively minor encroachments on the First Amendment. The breach of neutrality that is today a trickling stream may all too soon become a raging torrent and, in the words of Madison, "it is proper to take alarm at the first experiment on our liberties."

. . . It is insisted that unless these religious exercises are permitted a "religion of secularism" is established in the schools. We agree of course that the State may not establish a "religion of secularism" in the sense of affirmatively opposing or showing hostility to religion, thus "preferring those who believe in no religion over those who do believe.". . . We do not agree, however, that this decision in any sense has that effect. In addition, it might well be said that one's education is not complete without a study of comparative religion or the history of religion and its relationship to the advancement of civilization. It certainly may be said that the Bible is worthy of study for its literary and historic qualities. Nothing we have said here indicates that such study of the Bible or of religion, when presented objectively as part of a secular program of education, may not be effected consistent with the First Amendment. But the exercises here do not fall into those categories. They are religious exercises, required by the States in violation of the command of the First Amendment that the Government maintain strict neutrality, neither aiding nor opposing religion.

Finally, we cannot accept that the concept of neutrality, which does not permit a State to require a religious exercise even with the consent of the majority of those affected, collides with the majority's right to free exercise of religion. While the Free Exercise Clause clearly prohibits the use of State action to deny the rights of free exercise to anyone, it has never meant that a majority could use the machinery of the State to practice its beliefs. Such a contention was effectively answered by Mr. Justice Jackson for the Court in *West Virginia Board of Education* v. *Barnette* . . . :

> "The very purpose of a Bill of Rights was to withdraw certain subjects from the vicissitudes of political controversy, to place them beyond the reach of majorities and officials and to establish them as legal principles to be applied by the courts. One's right to . . . freedom of worship . . . and other fundamental rights may not be submitted to vote; they depend on the outcome of no elections."

The place of religion in our society is an exalted one, achieved through a long tradition of reliance on the home, the church and the inviolable citadel of the individual heart and mind. We have come to recognize through bitter experience that it is not within the power of government to invade that citadel, whether its purpose or effect be to aid or oppose, to advance or retard. In the relationship between man and religion, the State is firmly committed to a position of neutrality. Though the application of that rule requires interpretation of a delicate sort, the rule itself is clearly and concisely stated in the words of the First Amendment. Applying that rule to the facts of these cases, we affirm the judgment in [the *Schempp* case]. In *[Murray* v. *Curlett]* the judgment is reversed and the cause remanded to the Maryland Court of Appeals for further proceedings consistent with this opinion.

It is so ordered.

MR. JUSTICE DOUGLAS, concurring:

In these cases we have no coercive religious exercise aimed at making the students conform. The prayers announced are not compulsory, though some may think they have that indirect effect because the nonconformist student may be induced to participate for fear of being called an "oddball." But that coercion, if it be present, has not been shown; so the vices of the present regimes are different.

The regimes violate the Establishment Clause in two different ways. In each case the State is conducting a religious exercise; and, as the Court holds, that cannot be done without violating the "neutrality" required of the State by the balance of power between individual, church and state that has been struck by the First Amendment. But the Establishment Clause is not limited to precluding the State itself from conducting religious exercises. It also forbids the State to employ its facilities or funds in a way that gives any church, or all churches, greater strength in our society than it would have by relying on its members alone. Thus, the present regimes must fall under that clause for the additional reason that public funds, though small in amount, are being used to promote a religious exercise. Through the mechanism of the State, all of the people are being required to finance a religious exercise that only some of the people want and that violates the sensibilities of others.

The most effective way to establish any institution is to finance it; and this truth is reflected in the appeals by church groups for public funds to finance their religious schools. Financing a church either in its strictly religious activities or in other activities is equally unconstitutional, as I understand the Establishment Clause. Budgets for one activity may be technically separable from budgets for others. But the institution is an inseparable whole, a living organism, which is strengthened in proselytizing when it is strengthened in any department by contributions from other than its own members.

Such contributions may not be made by

the State even in a minor degree without violating the Establishment Clause. It is not the amount of public funds expended; as this case illustrates, it is the use to which public funds are put that is controlling. For the First Amendment does not say that some forms of establishment are allowed; it says that "no law respecting an establishment of religion" shall be made. What may not be done directly may not be done indirectly lest the Establishment Clause become a mockery.

MR. JUSTICE BRENNAN, concurring:

. . . The religious nature of the exercises here challenged seems plain. Unless *Engel* v. *Vitale* is to be overruled, or we are to engage in wholly disingenuous distinction, we cannot sustain these practices. Daily recital of the Lord's Prayer and the reading of passages of Scripture are quite as clearly breaches of the command of the Establishment Clause as was the daily use of the rather bland Regents' Prayer in the New York public schools. Indeed, I would suppose that if anything the Lord's Prayer and the Holy Bible are more clearly sectarian, and the present violations of the First Amendment consequently more serious.

[In the next twenty-seven pages of his opinion Justice Brennan reviews the long history of Bible reading and daily prayer in the public schools and concludes that "these practices standing by themselves constitute an impermissible breach of the Establishment Clause."]

. . . These considerations bring me to a final contention of the school officials in these cases: that the invalidation of the exercises at bar permits this Court no alternative but to declare unconstitutional every vestige, however slight, of cooperation or accommodation between religion and government. I cannot accept that contention. While it is not, of course, appropriate for this Court to decide questions not presently before it, I venture to suggest that religious exercises in the public schools present a unique problem. For not every involvement of religion in public life violates the Establishment Clause. Our decision in these cases does not clearly forecast anything about the constitutionality of other types of interdependence between religious and other public institutions. . . .

I think a brief survey of certain of these forms of accommodation will reveal that the First Amendment commands not official hostility toward religion, but only a strict neutrality in matters of religion. Moreover, it may serve to suggest that the scope of our holding today is to be measured by the special circumstances under which these cases have arisen, and by the particular dangers to church and state which religious exercises in the public schools present. . . .

1. *The Conflict Between Establishment and Free Exercise.* There are certain practices, conceivably violative of the Establishment Clause, the striking down of which might seriously interfere with certain religious liberties also protected by the First Amendment. Provisions for churches and chaplains at military establishments for those in the armed services may afford one such example. The like provision by state and federal governments for chaplains in penal institutions may afford another example. It is argued that such provisions may be assumed to contravene the Establishment Clause, yet be sustained on constitutional grounds as necessary to secure to the members of the Armed Forces and prisoners those rights of worship guaranteed under the Free Exercise Clause. Since government has deprived such persons of the opportunity to practice their faith at places of their choice, the argument runs, government may, in order to avoid infringing the free exercise guaranties, provide substitutes where it requires such persons to be. Such a principle might support, for example, the constitutionality of draft exemptions for ministers and divinity students . . . ; of the excusal of children from school on their respective religious holidays; and of the allowance by government of temporary use of public buildings by religious organizations when their own churches have become unavailable because of a disaster or emergency.

Such activities and practices seem distinguishable from the sponsorship of daily Bible reading and prayer recital. For one thing, there is no element of coercion present in the appointment of military or prison chaplains; the soldier or convict who declines the opportunities for worship would not ordinarily subject himself to the suspicion or obloquy of his peers. Of special significance to this distinction is the fact that we are here usually dealing with adults, not with impressionable children as in the public schools. Moreover, the school exercises are not designed to provide the pupils with general opportunities for worship denied them by the legal obligation to attend school. The student's compelled presence in school for five days a week in no way renders the regular religious facilities of the community less accessible to him than they are to others. The situation of the school child is therefore plainly unlike that of the isolated soldier or the prisoner. . . .

2. *Establishment and Exercises in Legislative Bodies.* The saying of invocational prayers in legislative chambers, state or federal, and the appointment of legislative chaplains, might well represent no involvements of the kind prohibited by the Establishment Clause. Legislators, federal and state, are mature adults who may presumably absent themselves from such public and ceremonial exercises without incurring any penalty, direct or indirect. It may also be significant that, at least in the case of the Congress, Article I, Section 5, of the Constitution makes each House the monitor of the "Rules of its Proceedings" so that it is at least arguable whether such matters present "political questions" the resolution of which is exclusively confided to Congress. . . . Finally, there is the difficult question of who may be heard to challenge such practices. . . .

3. *Nondevotional Use of the Bible in the Public Schools.* The holding of the Court today plainly does not foreclose teaching about the Holy Scriptures or about the differences between religious sects in classes in literature or history. Indeed, whether or not the Bible is involved, it would be impossible to teach meaningfully many subjects in the social sciences or the humanities without some mention of religion. To what extent, and at what points in the curriculum religious materials should be cited, are matters which the courts ought to entrust very largely to the experienced officials who superintend our Nation's public schools. They are experts in such matters, and we are not. . . .

4. *Uniform Tax Exemptions Incidentally Available to Religious Institutions.* Nothing we hold today questions the propriety of certain tax deductions or exemptions which incidentally benefit churches and religious institutions, along with many secular charities and nonprofit organizations. If religious institutions benefit, it is in spite of rather than because of their religious character. For religious institutions simply share benefits which government makes generally available to educational, charitable, and eleemosynary groups. There is no indication that taxing authorities have used such benefits in any way to subsidize worship or foster belief in God. And as among religious beneficiaries, the tax exemption or deduction can be truly nondiscriminatory, available on equal terms to small as well as large religious bodies, to popular and unpopular sects, and to those organizations which reject as well as those which accept a belief in God.

5. *Religious Considerations in Public Welfare Programs.* Since government may not support or directly aid religious activities without violating the Establishment Clause, there might be some doubt whether nondiscriminatory programs of governmental aid may constitutionally include individuals who become eligible wholly or partially for religious reasons. For example, it might be suggested that where a State provides unemployment compensation generally to those who are unable to find suitable work, it may not extend such benefits to persons who are unemployed by reason of religious beliefs or practices without thereby establishing the religion to which those persons belong. Therefore, the argument runs, the State may avoid an establishment only by singling out and excluding such persons on the ground that religious beliefs or practices have made them potential beneficiaries. Such a construction would, it seems to me, require government to impose religious discriminations and disabilities, thereby jeopardizing the free exercise of religion, in order to avoid what is thought to constitute an establishment.

The inescapable flaw in the argument, I suggest, is its quite unrealistic view of the aims of the Establishment Clause. The Framers were not concerned with the effects of certain incidental aids to individual worshippers which come about as by-products of general and nondiscriminatory welfare programs. If such benefits serve to make easier or less expensive the practice of a particular creed, or of all religions, it can hardly be said that the purpose of the program is in any way religious, or that the consequence of its nondiscriminatory application is to create the forbidden degree of interdependence between secular and sectarian institutions. I cannot therefore accept the suggestion, which seems to me implicit in the argument outlined here, that every judicial or administrative construction which is designed to prevent a public welfare program from abridging the free exercise of religious beliefs, is for that reason *ipso facto* an establishment of religion.

6. *Activities Which, Though Religious in Origin, Have Ceased to Have Religious Meaning.* As we noted in our *Sunday Law* decisions, nearly every criminal law on the books can be traced to some religious principle or inspiration. But that does not make the present enforcement of the criminal law in any sense an establishment of religion, simply because it accords with widely held religious principles. . . . This rationale suggests that the use of the motto "In God We Trust" in currency, on documents and public buildings and the like may not offend the clause. It is not that the use of those four words can be dismissed as "de minimis"—for I suspect there would be intense opposition to the abandonment of that motto. The truth is that we have simply interwoven the motto so deeply into the fabric of our civil polity that its present use may well not present that type of involvement which the First Amendment prohibits.

This general principle might also serve to insulate the various patriotic exercises and activities used in the public schools and elsewhere which, whatever may have been their origins, no longer have a religious purpose or meaning. The reference to divinity in the revised pledge of allegiance, for example, may merely recognize the historical fact that our Nation was believed to have been founded "under God." Thus reciting the pledge may be no more of a religious exercise than the reading aloud of Lincoln's Gettysburg Address, which contains an allusion to the same historical fact. . . .

MR. JUSTICE GOLDBERG, with whom MR. JUSTICE HARLAN joined, concurred. MR. JUSTICE STEWART dissented.

COMMITTEE FOR PUBLIC ED. & RELIGIOUS LIB. *v.* NYQUIST
413 U.S. 756; 93 Sup. Ct. 2955; 37 L. Ed. 2d 948 (1973)

MR. JUSTICE POWELL delivered the opinion of the Court.

. . . It has never been thought either possible or desirable to enforce a regime of total separation, and as a consequence cases arising under these Clauses have presented some of the most perplexing questions to come before this Court. Those cases have occasioned thorough and thoughtful scholarship by several of this Court's most respected former Justices, including Justices Black, Frankfurter, Harlan, Jackson, Rutledge, and Chief Justice Warren.

As a result of these decisions and opinions, it may no longer be said that the Religion Clauses are free of "entangling" precedents. Neither, however, may it be said that Jefferson's metaphoric "wall of separation" between Church and State has become "as winding as the famous serpentine wall" he designed for the University of Virginia. *McCollum* v. *Board of Education.* (Jackson, J., separate opinion.) Indeed, the controlling constitutional standards have become firmly rooted and the broad contours of our inquiry are now well defined. Our task, therefore, is to assess New York's several forms of aid in the light of principles already delineated. . . .

In May 1972, the Governor of New York signed into law several amendments to the State's Education and Tax Laws. The first five sections of these amendments established three distinct financial aid programs for nonpublic elementary and secondary schools.

The first section of the challenged enactment, entitled "Health and Safety Grants for Nonpublic School Children," provides for direct money grants from the state to "qualifying" nonpublic schools to be used for the "maintenance and repair of . . . school facilities and equipment to ensure the health, welfare and safety of enrolled pupils." A "qualifying" school is any nonpublic nonprofit elementary or secondary school which "has been designated during the [immediately preceding] year as serving a high concentration of pupils from low-income families for purposes of Title IV of the Federal Higher Education Act of 1965." . . . This section is prefaced by a series of legislative findings which shed light on the State's purpose in enacting the law. The findings conclude that the State "has a primary responsibility to ensure the health, welfare and safety of children attending . . . nonpublic schools"; that the "fiscal crisis in nonpublic education . . . has caused a diminution of proper maintenance and repair programs, threatening the health, welfare and safety of nonpublic school children" in low-income urban areas; and that "a healthy and safe school environment" contributes "to the stability of urban neighborhoods." For these reasons, the statute declares that "the state has the right to make grants for maintenance and repair expenditures which are clearly secular, neutral and nonideological in nature."

The remainder of the challenged legislation—Section 2 through 5—is a single package captioned the "Elementary and Secondary Education Opportunity Program." It is composed, essentially, of two parts, a tuition grant program and a tax-benefit program. Section 2 establishes a limited plan providing tuition reimbursements to parents of children attending elementary or secondary nonpublic schools. To qualify under this section the parent must have an annual taxable income of less than $5,000. . . .

This section, like Section 1, is prefaced by a series of legislative findings designed to explain the impetus for the State's action. Expressing a dedication to the "vitality of our pluralistic society," the findings state that a "healthy competitive and diverse alternative to public education is not only desirable but indeed vital to a state and nation that have continually reaffirmed the value of individual differences." The findings further emphasize that the right to select among alternative educational systems "is diminished or even denied to children of lower-income families, whose parents, of all groups, have the least options in determining where their children are to be educated." Turning to the public schools, the findings state that any "precipitous decline in the number of nonpublic school pupils would cause a massive increase in public school enrollment and costs," an increase that would "aggravate an already serious fiscal crisis in public education" and would "seriously jeopardize the quality of education for all children." Based on these premises, the statute asserts the State's right to relieve the financial burden of parents who send their children to nonpublic schools through this tuition reimbursement program. Repeating the declaration contained in Section 1, the findings conclude that such assistance is early "secular, neutral and nonideological."

The remainder of the "Elementary and Secondary Education Opportunity Program," contained in Section 3, 4, and 5 of the challenged law, is designed to provide a form of tax relief to those who fail to qualify for tuition reimbursement. . . . Comparable tax benefits pick up at approximately the point at which tuition reimbursement benefits leave off. . . .

Plaintiffs argued below that because of the substantially religious character of the intended beneficiaries, each of the State's three enactments offended the Establishment Clause. . . .

. . . a law may be one "respecting the establishment of religion" even though its consequence is not to promote a "state religion," *Lemon* v. *Kurtzman,* and even though it does not aid one religion more than another but merely benefits all religions alike. *Everson* v. *Board of Education.* It is equally well established, however, that not every law that confers an "indirect," "remote," or "incidental" benefit upon religious institutions is, for that reason alone, constitutionally invalidated. Ibid.; *McGowan* v. *Maryland, Walz* v. *Tax Commission* (1970). What our cases require is careful examination of any law challenged on establishment grounds with a view to ascertaining whether it furthers any of the evils against which that Clause protects. Primary among those evils have been "sponsorship, financial support, and active involvement of the sovereign in religious activity." *Walz* v. *Tax Commission; Lemon* v. *Kurtzman.*

. . . the now well defined three-part test that has emerged from our decisions is a product of considerations derived from the full sweep of the Establishment Clause cases. Taken together these decisions dictate that to pass muster under the Establishment Clause the law in question first must reflect a clearly secular legislative purpose, e.g., *Epperson* v. *Arkansas,* 393 U.S. 97 (1968), second, must have a primary effect that neither advances nor inhibits religion, e.g., *McGowan* v. *Maryland; School District of Abington Township* v. *Schempp,* and, third, must avoid excessive government entanglement with religion, e.g., *Walz* v. *Tax Commission.* See *Lemon* v. *Kurtzman.* *

In applying these criteria to the three distinct forms of aid involved in this case, we need touch only briefly on the requirement of a "secular legislative purpose." As the recitation of legislative purposes appended to New York's law indicates, each measure is adequately supported by legitimate, nonsectarian state interests. We do not question the propriety, and fully secular content, of New York's interest in preserving a healthy and safe educational environment for all of its school children. And we do not doubt—indeed, we fully recognize—the validity of the State's interest in promoting pluralism and diversity among its public and nonpublic schools. Nor do we hesitate to acknowledge the reality of its concern for an already overburdened public school system that might suffer in the event that a significant percentage of children presently attending nonpublic schools should abandon those schools in favor of the public schools.

But the propriety of a legislature's purposes may not immunize from further scrutiny a law which either has a primary effect that advances religion, or which fosters excessive entanglements between Church and State. Accordingly, we must weigh each of the three aid provisions challenged here against these criteria of effect and entanglement.

A

The "maintenance and repair" provisions of Section 1 authorize direct payments to nonpublic schools, virtually all of which are Roman Catholic schools in low income areas. The grants, totaling $30 or $40 per pupil depending on the age of the institution, are given largely without restriction on usage. So long as expenditures do not exceed 50 per cent of comparable expenses in the public school system, it is possible for a sectarian elementary or secondary school to finance its entire "maintenance and repair" budget from state tax-raised funds. No attempt is made to restrict payments to those expenditures related to the upkeep of facilities used exclusively for secular purposes, nor do we think it possible within the context of these religion-oriented institutions to impose such restrictions. Nothing in the statute, for instance, bars a qualifying school from paying out of state funds the salary of employees who maintain the school chapel, or the cost of renovating classrooms in which religion is taught, or the cost of heating and lighting those same facilities. Absent appropriate restrictions on expenditures for these and similar purposes, it simply cannot be denied that this section has a primary effect that advances religion in that it subsidizes directly the religious

* In discussing the application of these "tests," Mr. Chief Justice Burger noted in *Tilton* v. *Richardson,* supra, that "there is no single constitutional caliper that can be used to measure the precise degree" to which any one of them is applicable to the state action under scrutiny. Rather, these tests or criteria should be "viewed as guidelines" within which to consider "the cumulative criteria developed over many years and applying to a wide range of governmental action challenged as violative of the Establishment Clause."

activities of sectarian elementary and secondary schools.

The state officials nevertheless argue that these expenditures for "maintenance and repair" are similar to other financial expenditures approved by the Court. Primarily they rely on *Everson* v. *Board of Education; Board of Education* v. *Allen;* and *Tilton* v. *Richardson.* In each of those cases it is true that the Court approved a form of financial assistance which conferred undeniable benefits upon private, sectarian schools. But a close examination of those cases illuminates their distinguishing characteristics. In *Everson,* the Court, in a 5-to-4 decision, approved a program of reimbursements to parents of public as well as parochial school children for bus fares paid in connection with transportation to and from school, a program which the Court characterized as approaching the "verge" of impermissible state aid. In *Allen,* decided some twenty years later, the Court upheld a New York law authorizing the provision of *secular* textbooks for all children in grades seven through twelve attending public and nonpublic schools. Finally, in *Tilton,* the Court upheld federal grants of funds for the construction of facilities to be used for clearly *secular* purposes by public and nonpublic institutions of higher learning.

These cases simply recognize that sectarian schools perform secular, educative functions as well as religious functions, and that some forms of aid may be channelled to the secular without providing direct aid to the sectarian. But the channel is a narrow one, as the above cases illustrate. Of course it is true in each case that the provision of such neutral, nonideological aid, assisting only the secular functions of sectarian schools, served indirectly and incidentally to promote the religious function by rendering it more likely that children would attend sectarian schools and by freeing the budgets of those schools for use in other nonsecular areas. But an indirect and incidental effect beneficial to religious institutions has never been thought a sufficient defect to warrant the invalidation of a state law. In *McGowan* v. *Maryland,* Sunday Closing Laws were sustained even though one of their undeniable effects was to render it somewhat more likely that citizens would respect religious institutions and even attend religious services. Also, in *Walz* v. *Tax Commission,* property tax exemptions for church property were held not violative of the Establishment Clause despite the fact that such exemptions relieved churches of fianancial burden.

Tilton draws the line most clearly. While a bare majority was there persuaded, for the reasons stated in the plurality opinion and in Mr. Justice White's concurrence, that carefully limited construction grants to colleges and universities could be sustained, the Court was unanimous in its rejection of one clause of the federal statute in question. Under that clause, the Government was entitled to recover a portion of its grant to a sectarian institution in the event that the constructed facility was used to advance religion by, for instance, converting the building to a chapel or otherwise allowing it to be "used to promote religious interests." But because the statute provided that the condition would expire at the end of twenty years, the facilities would thereafter be available for use by the institution for any sectarian purpose. In striking down this provision, the plurality opinion emphasized that "[l]imiting the prohibition for religious use of the structure to twenty years obviously opens the facility to use for any purpose at the end of that period." And in that event, "the original federal grant will in part have the effect of advancing religion." See also Douglas, J., dissenting, Brennan, J., dissenting, White, J., concurring in the judgment. If tax-raised funds may not be granted to institutions of higher learning where the possibility exists that those funds will be used to construct a facility utilized for sectarian activities twenty years hence, a fortiori they may not be distributed to elementary and secondary sectarian schools † for the maintenance and repair of facilities without any limitations on their use. If the State may not erect buildings in which religious

† The plurality in *Tilton* was careful to point out that there are "significant differences between the religious aspects of church-related institutions of higher learning and parochial elementary and secondary schools."

activities are to take place, it may not maintain such buildings or renovate them when they fall into disrepair.

B

New York's tuition reimbursement program also fails the "effect" test, for much the same reasons that govern its maintenance and repair grants. The state program is designed to allow direct, unrestricted grants of $50 to $100 per child (but no more than 50 per cent of tuition actually paid) as reimbursement to parents in low-income brackets who send their children to non-public schools. To qualify, a parent must have earned less than $5,000 in taxable income and must present a receipted tuition bill from a nonpublic school, the bulk of which are concededly sectarian in orientation.

There can be no question that these grants could not, consistently with the Establishment Clause, be given directly to sectarian schools, since they would suffer from the same deficiency that renders invalid the grants for maintenance and repair. In the absence of an effective means of guaranteeing that the state aid derived from public funds will be used exclusively for secular, neutral, and nonideological purposes, it is clear from our cases that direct aid in whatever form is invalid. As Mr. Justice Black put it quite simply in *Everson:* "No tax in any amount, large or small, can be levied to support any religious activities or institutions, whatever they may be called, or whatever form they may adopt to teach or practice religion." The controlling question here, then, is whether the fact that the grants are delivered to parents rather than schools is of such significance as to compel a contrary result. The State and intervenor-appellees rely on *Everson* and *Allen* for their claim that grants to parents, unlike grants to institutions, respect the "wall of separation" required by the Constitution. It is true that in those cases the Court upheld laws that provided benefits to children attending religious schools and to their parents: As noted above, in *Everson* parents were reimbursed for bus fares paid to send children to parochial schools, and in *Allen* textbooks were loaned directly to the children. But those decisions make clear that, far from providing a per se immunity from examination of the substance of the State's program, the fact that aid is disbursed to parents rather than to the schools is only one among many factors to be considered.

In *Everson,* the Court found the bus fare program analogous to the provision of services such as police and fire protection, sewage disposal, highways, and sidewalks for parochial schools. Such services, provided in common to all citizens, are "so separate and so indisputably marked off from the religious function," that they may fairly be viewed as reflections of a neutral posture toward religious institutions. *Allen* is founded upon a similar principle. The Court there repeatedly emphasized that upon the record in that case there was no indication that textbooks would be provided for anything other than purely secular courses. "Of course books are different from buses. Most bus rides have no inherent religious significance, while religious books are common. However, the language of [the law under consideration] does not authorize the loan of religious books, and the State claims no right to distribute religious literature. . . . Absent evidence, we cannot assume that school authorities . . . are unable to distinguish between secular and religious books or that they will not honestly discharge their duties under the law."

The tuition grants here are subject to no such restrictions. There has been no endeavor "to guarantee the separation between secular and religious educational functions and to ensure that State financial aid supports only the former." *Lemon* v. *Kurtzman.* Indeed, it is precisely the function of New York's law to provide assistance to private schools, the great majority of which are sectarian. By reimbursing parents for a portion of their tuition bill, the State seeks to relieve their financial burdens sufficiently to assure that they continue to have the option to send their children to religion-oriented schools. And while the other purposes for that aid—to perpetuate a pluralistic educational environment and to protect the fiscal integrity of overburdened public schools—are certainly unexceptionable, the effect of the aid is unmistakably to provide desired financial support for nonpublic, sectarian institutions.‡

Mr. Justice Black, dissenting in *Allen,* warned that,

> "[i]t requires no prophet to foresee that on the argument used to support this law others could be upheld providing for state or Federal Government funds to buy property on which to erect religious school buildings or to erect the buildings themselves, to pay the salaries of the religious school teachers, and finally to have the sectarian religious groups cease to rely on voluntary contributions of members of their sects while waiting for the government to pick up all the bills for the religious schools."

His fears regarding religious buildings and religious teachers have not come to pass, *Tilton* v. *Richardson; Lemon* v. *Kurtzman,* and insofar as tuition grants constitute a means of "pick[ing] up . . . the bills for the religious schools," neither has his greatest fear materialized. But the ingenious plans for channeling state aid to sectarian schools that periodically reach this Court abundantly support the wisdom of Justice Black's prophecy. . . .

Finally, the State argues that its program of tuition grants should survive scrutiny because it is designed to promote the free exercise of religion. The State notes that only "low-income parents" are aided by this law, and without state assistance their right to have their children educated in a religious environment "is diminished or even denied." It is true, of course, that this Court has long recognized and maintained the right to choose nonpublic over public education. *Pierce* v. *Society of Sisters,* 268 U.S. 510 (1925). It is also true that a state law interfering with a parent's right to have his child educated in a sectarian school would run afoul of the Free Exercise Clause. But this Court repeatedly has recognized that tension inevitably exists between the Free Exercise and the Establishment Clauses, and that it may often not be possible to promote the former without offending the latter. As a result of this tension, our cases require the State to maintain an attitude of "neutrality," neither "advancing" nor "inhibiting" religion. In its attempt to enhance the opportunities of the poor to choose between public and nonpublic education, the State has taken a step which can only be regarded as one "advancing" religion. However great our sympathy for the burdens experienced by those who must pay public school taxes at the same time that they support other schools because of the constraints of "conscience and discipline," ibid., and notwithstanding the "high social importance" of the State's purposes, *Wisconsin* v. *Yoder,* neither may justify an eroding of the limitations of the Establishment Clause now firmly emplanted.

C

Sections 3, 4, and 5 establish a system for providing income tax benefits to parents of children attending New York's nonpublic schools. . . .

In practical terms there would appear to be little difference, for purposes of determining whether such aid has the effect of advancing religion, between the tax benefit allowed here and the tuition grant allowed under Section 2. The qualifying parent under either program receives the same form of encouragement and reward for sending his children to nonpublic schools. The only difference is that one parent receives an actual cash payment while the other is allowed to reduce by an arbitrary amount the sum he would otherwise be obliged to pay over to the State. We see no answer to Judge Hays' dissenting statement below that "[i]n both instances the money in-

‡ Appellees, focusing on the term "principal or primary effect" which this Court has utilized in expressing the second prong of the three-part test, e.g., *Lemon* v. *Kurtzman,* have argued that the Court must decide in this case whether the "primary" effect of New York's tuition grant program is to subsidize religion or to promote these legitimate secular objectives. Mr. Justice White's dissenting opinion similarly suggests that the Court today fails to make this "ultimate judgment." We do not think that such metaphysical judgments are either possible or necessary. Our cases simply do not support the notion that a law found to have a "primary" effect to promote some legitimate end under the State's police power is immune from further examination to ascertain whether it also has the direct and immediate effect of advancing religion.

volved represents a charge made upon the state for the purpose of religious education.". . .

. . . appellees place their strongest reliance on *Walz* v. *Tax Commission,* supra, in which New York's property tax exemption for religious organizations was upheld. We think that *Walz* provides no support for appellees' position. Indeed, its rationale plainly compels the conclusion that New York's tax package violates the Establishment Clause. . . .

The Court in *Walz* surveyed the history of tax exemptions and . . . concluded that "[f]ew concepts are more deeply embedded in the fabric of our national life, beginning with pre-Revolutionary Colonial times, than for the government to exercise at the very least this kind of benevolent neutrality toward churches and religious exercise generally." We know of no historical precedent for New York's recently promulgated tax relief program. Indeed, it seems clear that tax benefits for parents whose children attend parochial schools are a recent innovation, occasioned by the growing financial plight of such nonpublic institutions and designed, albeit unsuccessfully, to tailor state aid in a manner not incompatible with the recent decisions of this Court. . . . Special tax benefits, however, cannot be squared with the principle of neutrality established by the decisions of this Court. To the contrary, insofar as such benefits render assistance to parents who send their children to sectarian schools, their purpose and inevitable effect are to aid and advance those religious institutions.

Apart from its historical foundations, *Walz* is a product of the same dilemma and inherent tension found in most government-aid-to-religion controversies. To be sure, the exemption of church property from taxation conferred a benefit, albeit an indirect and incidental one. Yet that "aid" was a product not of any purpose to support or to subsidize, but of a fiscal relationship designed to minimize involvement and entanglement between Church and State. "The exemption," the Court emphasized, "tends to complement and reinforce the desired separation insulating each from the other." Furthermore, "[e]limination of the exemption would tend to expand the involvement of government by giving rise to tax valuation of church property, tax liens, tax foreclosures, and the direct confrontations and conflicts that follow in the train of those legal processes." The granting of the tax benefits under the New York statute, unlike the extension of an exemption, would tend to increase rather than limit the involvement between Church and State.

Because we have found that the challenged sections have the impermissible effect of advancing religion, we need not consider whether such aid would result in entanglement of the State with religion in the sense of "[a] comprehensive, discriminating, and continuing state surveillance." *Lemon* v. *Kurtzman.* But the importance of the competing societal interests implicated in this case prompts us to make the further observation that, apart from any specific entanglement of the State in particular religious programs, assistance of the sort here involved carries grave potential for entanglement in the broader sense of continuing political strife over aid to religion.

Few would question most of the legislative findings supporting this statute. We recognized in *Board of Education* v. *Allen,* 392 U.S., at 247, that "private education has played and is playing a significant and valuable role in raising levels of knowledge, competenc[y], and experience," and certainly private parochial schools have contributed importantly to this role. Moreover, the tailoring of the New York statute to channel the aid provided primarily to afford low-income families the option of determining where their children are to be educated is most appealing. There is no doubt that the private schools are confronted with increasingly grave fiscal problems, that resolving these problems by increasing tuition charges forces parents to turn to the public schools, and that this in turn—as the present legislation recognizes—exacerbates the problems of public education at the same time that it weakens support for the parochial schools.

These, in briefest summary, are the underlying reasons for the New York legislation and for similar legislation in other States. They are substantial reasons. Yet they must be weighed against the relevant provisions and purposes of the First Amendment, which safeguard the separation of Church from State and which have been regarded from the beginning as among the most cherished features of our constitutional system.

One factor of recurring significance in this weighing process is the potentially divisive political effect of an aid program. As Mr. Justice Black's opinion in *Everson* v. *Board of Education,* supra, emphasizes, competition among religious sects for political and religious supremacy has occasioned considerable civil strife, "generated in large part" by competing efforts to gain or maintain the support of government. As Mr. Justice Harlan put it, "[w]hat is at stake as a matter of policy in Establishment Clause cases is preventing that kind and degree of government involvement in religious life that, as history teaches us, is apt to lead to strife and frequently strain a political system to the breaking point." *Walz* v. *Tax Commission.* . . .

The Court recently addressed this issue specifically and fully in *Lemon* v. *Kurtzman.* After describing the political activity and bitter differences likely to result from the state programs there involved, the Court said:

> "The potential for political divisiveness related to religious belief and practice is aggravated in these two statutory programs by the need for continuing annual appropriations and the likelihood of larger and larger demands as costs and population grow."

The language of the Court applies with peculiar force to the New York statute now before us. Section 1 (grants for maintenance) and Section 2 (tuition grants) will require continuing annual appropriations. Sections 3, 4, and 5 (income tax relief) will not necessarily require annual re-examination, but the pressure for frequent enlargement of the relief is predictable. All three of these programs start out at modest levels: . . . But we know from long experience with both Federal and State Governments that aid programs of any kind tend to become entrenched, to escalate in cost, and to generate their own aggressive constituencies. And the larger the class of recipients, the greater the pressure for accelerated increases. . . .

In this situation, where the underlying issue is the deeply emotional one of Church-State relationships, the potential for serious divisive political consequences needs no elaboration. And while the prospect of such divisiveness may not alone warrant the invalidation of state laws that otherwise survive the careful scrutiny required by the decisions of this Court, it is certainly a "warning signal" not to be ignored.

Our examination of New York's aid provisions, in light of all relevant considerations, compels the judgment that each, as written, has a "primary effect that advances religion" and offends the constitutional prohibition against laws "respecting the establishment of religion."

MR. JUSTICE REHNQUIST, with whom THE CHIEF JUSTICE and MR. JUSTICE WHITE concur, dissenting in part:

Differences of opinion are undoubtedly to be expected when the Court turns to the task of interpreting the meaning of the Religious Clauses of the First Amendment, since our previous cases arising under these clauses, as the Court notes, "have presented some of the most perplexing questions to come before [the] Court." I dissent from those portions of the Court's opinion which strike down Sections 2 through 5, c 414, 1972 N.Y. Laws. Section 2 grants limited state aid to low-income parents sending their children to nonpublic schools and Sections 3 through 5 make roughly comparable benefits available to middle-income parents through the use of tax deductions. I find both the Court's reasoning and result all but impossible to reconcile with *Walz* v. *Tax Commission,* decided only three years ago, and with *Board of Education* v. *Allen* and *Everson* v. *Board of Education.*

The opinions in *Walz* make it clear that tax deductions and exemptions, even when directed to religious institutions, occupy quite a different constitutional status under the Religion Clauses of the First Amendment than do outright grants to such institutions. Chief Justice Burger, speaking for the Court in *Walz,* said:

> "The grant of a tax exemption is not sponsorship since the government does not transfer part of its revenue to churches but simply abstains from demanding that the church support the state. No one has ever suggested that tax exemption has converted libraries,

art galleries, or hospitals into arms of the state or put employees 'on the public payroll.' *There is no genuine nexus between tax exemption and establishment of religion.*"

Mr. Justice Brennan in his concurring opinion amplified the distinction between tax benefits and direct payments in these words:

"Tax exemptions and general subsidies, however, are qualitatively different. Though both provide economic assistance, they do so in fundamentally different ways. A subsidy involves the direct transfer of public monies to the subsidized enterprise and uses resources exacted from taxpayers as a whole. An exemption, on the other hand, involves no such transfer. . . . Tax exemptions, accordingly, constitute mere passive state involvement with religion and not the affirmative involvement characteristic of outright government subsidy."

Here the effect of the tax benefit is trebly attenuated as compared with the outright exemption considered in *Walz.* There the result was a complete forgiveness of taxes, while here the result is merely a reduction in taxes. There the ultimate benefit was available to an actual house of worship, while here even the ultimate benefit redounds only to a religiously sponsored school. There the churches themselves received the direct reduction in the tax bill, while here it is only the parents of the children who were sent to religiously sponsored schools who receive the direct benefit. . . .

While it is true that the Court reached its result in *Walz* in part by examining the unbroken history of property tax exemptions for religious organizations in this country, there is no suggestion in the opinion that only those particular tax exemption schemes that have roots in pre-Revolutionary days are sustainable against an Establishment Clause challenge. . . .

The Court's statement that "special tax benefits, however, cannot be squared with the principle of neutrality established by the decisions of this Court," and that "insofar as such benefits render assistance to parents who send their children to sectarian schools, their purpose and inevitable effect are to aid and advance those religious institutions," are impossible to reconcile with *Walz.* Who can doubt that the tax exemptions which that case upheld were every bit as much of a "special tax benefit" as the New York tax deduction plan here, or that the benefits resulting from the exemption in *Walz* had every bit as much tendency to "aid and advance . . . religious institutions" as did New York's plan here? . . .

. . . It would take more of a record than is present in this case to prove the possibility of a slightly lower aggregate tax bill accorded New York taxpayers who send their dependents to nonpublic schools provides any more incentive to send children to such schools than personal exemptions provide for getting married or having children. That parents might incidentally find it easier to send children to nonpublic schools has not heretofore been held to require invalidation of a state statute. *Board of Education* v. *Allen, Everson* v. *Board of Education.* . . .

Regardless of what the court chooses to call the New York plan, it is still abstention from taxation, and that abstention stands on no different theoretical footing, in terms of running afoul the Establishment Clause, from any other deduction or exemption currently allowable for religious contributions or activities. . . .

II

In striking down both plans, the Court places controlling weight on the fact that the State has not purported to restrict to secular purposes either the reimbursements or the money which it has not taxed. This factor assertedly serves to distinguish *Board of Education* v. *Allen* and *Everson* v. *Board of Education,* and compels the result that inevitably the primary effect of the plans is to provide financial support for sectarian schools.

In *Everson,* the Court sustained the constitutional validity of a New Jersey statute and resulting school board regulation that provided, in part, for the direct reimbursement to parents of children attending sectarian schools of amounts expended in providing public transportation to and from such schools. Expressly noting that the challenged regulation undoubtedly helped children to get to church schools and that:

"There is even a possibility that some of the children might not be sent to the church schools if the parents were compelled to pay their children's bus fares out of their own pockets when transportation to a public school would have been paid for by the State. . . ."

the majority, in an opinion written by Mr. Justice Black, held that the state scheme did not violate the Establishment clause. And it was emphasized that the State in that case contributed no money to the schools, rather it did no more than effectuate a secular purpose—the transportation of children safely and expeditiously to and from accredited schools.

Similarly in *Allen,* a state program whereby secular textbooks were loaned to all children in accredited schools was approved as consistent with the Establishment Clause, even though the court recognized that free books made it more likely that some children would choose to attend a sectarian school. It was again emphasized that "no funds or books [were] furnished to parochial schools," and that therefore "the financial benefit [was] to parents and children, not to schools." This factor was considered crucial in *Lemon* v. *Kurtzman,* where the court stated:

"The Pennsylvania statute, moreover, has the further defect of providing state financial aid directly to the church-related school. *This factor distinguishes both* Everson *and* Allen, *for in both cases the Court was careful to point out that State aid was provided to the student and his parents—not to the church-related school.* . . ." (Emphasis added.)

Both *Everson* and *Allen* gave significant recognition to the "benevolent neutrality" concept, and the Court was guided by the fact that any effect from state aid to parents has a necessarily attenuated impact on religious institutions when compared to direct aid to such institutions.

The reimbursement and tax benefit plans today struck down, no less than the plans in *Everson* and *Allen,* are consistent with the principle of neutrality. New York has recognized that parents who are sending their children to nonpublic schools are rendering the State a service by decreasing the costs of public education and by physically relieving an already overburdened public school system. Such parents are nonetheless compelled to support public school services unused by them and to pay for their own children's education. Rather than offering "an incentive to parents to send their children to sectarian schools," as the majority suggests, New York is effectuating the secular purpose of the equalization of the costs of educating New York children that are borne by parents who send their children to nonpublic schools. As in *Everson* and *Allen,* the impact, if any, on religious education from the aid granted is significantly diminished by the fact that the benefits go to the parents rather than to the institutions.

The increasing difficulties faced by private schools in our country are no reason at all for this Court to readjust the admittedly rough hewn limits on governmental involvement with religion which are found in the first and Fourteenth Amendments. But quite understandably these difficulties can be expected to lead to efforts on the part of those who wish to keep alive pluralism in education to obtain through legislative channels forms of permissible public assistance which were not thought necessary a generation ago. Within the limits permitted by the Constitution, these decisions are quite rightly hammered out on the legislative anvil. If the Constitution does indeed allow for play in the legislative joints, *Walz,* the Court must distinguish between a new exercise of power within constitutional limits and an exercise of legislative power which transgresses those limits. I believe the Court has failed to make that distinction here, and I therefore dissent.

SUNDAY CLOSING LAW CASES

366 U.S. 420; 81 Sup. Ct. 1101; 6 L. Ed. 2d. 393 (1961)

[The Sunday blue laws of Maryland, Massachusetts, and Pennsylvania were examined by the Supreme Court in four cases decided together and known as the Sunday Closing Law Cases. In two cases, the Sunday closing laws of Maryland and Pennsylvania were

challenged by regular commercial establishments. The two other cases were brought in Massachusetts and Pennsylvania by Jewish merchants who argued that because their religion required that their shops be closed on Saturdays, the Sunday Closing laws limited them to a five-day week. In all the cases, the statutes were challenged on the ground that they violated the equal protection clause of the Fourteenth Amendment because they contained so many exceptions for certain kinds of commercial activities. The Supreme Court agreed unanimously that equal protection had not been violated because the Fourteenth Amendment permits the states a "wide scope of discretion in enacting laws which affect some groups of citizens differently from others. State legislators are presumed to have acted within their constitutional power despite the fact that, in practice, their laws result in some inequality." The argument on the issue of equal protection is not reproduced here, except for the brief opinion of Justice Stewart, which concisely raises the free exercise, as opposed to the establishment, problem.

The other opinions that follow are from McGowan *v.* Maryland, *the most important of the four cases. Margaret McGowan and other employees of a large discount department store located on a highway in Maryland were indicted for selling goods on Sunday in violation of the state's Sunday closing laws. The laws prohibited the sale on Sunday of all merchandise except such items as tobacco products, milk, bread, fruit, gasoline, drugs, and newspapers. The employees were convicted in a state court, and each was fined $5 and costs, and the convictions were affirmed by the Maryland Court of Appeals. The case then went to the Supreme Court on appeal.]*

MR. CHIEF JUSTICE WARREN delivered the opinion of the Court:

. . . The . . . questions for decision are whether the Maryland Sunday Closing Laws conflict with the Federal Constitution's provision for religious liberty. First, appellants contend here that the statutes applicable to Anne Arundel County violate the constitutional guaranty of freedom of religion in that the statute's effect is to prohibit the free exercise of religion in contravention of the First Amendment, made applicable to the States by the Fourteenth Amendment. But appellants allege only economic injury to themselves; they do not allege any infringement of their own religious freedoms due to Sunday closing. In fact, the record is silent as to what appellants' religious beliefs are. Since the general rule is that "a litigant may only assert his own constitutional rights or immunities," . . . we hold that appellants have no standing to raise this contention. . . .

Secondly, appellants contend that the statutes violate the guaranty of separation of church and state in that the statutes are laws respecting an establishment of religion contrary to the First Amendment, made applicable to the states by the Fourteenth Amendment. . . . Appellants here concededly have suffered direct economic injury, allegedly due to the imposition on them of the tenets of the Christian religion. We find that, in these circumstances, these appellants have standing to complain that the statutes are laws respecting an establishment of religion.

The essence of appellant's "establishment" argument is that Sunday is the Sabbath day of the predominant Christian sects; that the purpose of the enforced stoppage of labor on that day is to facilitate and encourage church attendance; that the purpose of setting Sunday as a day of universal rest is to induce people with no religion or people with marginal religious beliefs to join the predominant Christian sects; that the purpose of the atmosphere of tranquility created by Sunday closing is to aid the conduct of church services and religious observance of the sacred day. . . . There is no dispute that the original laws which dealt with Sunday labor were motivated by religious forces. But what we must decide is whether present Sunday legislation, having undergone extensive changes from the earliest forms, still retains its religious character.

Sunday Closing Laws go far back into American history, having been brought to the Colonies with a background of English legislation dating to the thirteenth century. . . . [C]learly . . . the English Sunday legislation was in aid of the established church.

The American Colonial Sunday restrictions arose soon after settlement. Starting in 1650, the Plymouth Colony proscribed servile work, unnecessary travelling, sports, and the sale of alcoholic beverages on the Lord's day and enacted laws concerning church attendance. The Massachusetts Bay Colony and the Connecticut and New Haven Colonies enacted similar prohibitions, some even earlier in the seventeenth century. The religious orientation of the Colonial statutes was equally apparent. . . .

But, despite the strongly religious origin of these laws, beginning before the eighteenth century, nonreligious arguments for Sunday closing began to be heard more distinctly and the statutes began to lose some of their totally religious flavor. In the middle 1700s, Blackstone wrote, "[T]he keeping one day in the seven holy, as a time of relaxation and refreshment as well as for public worship, is of admirable service to a state considered merely as a civil institution. It humanizes, by the help of conversation and society, the manners of the lower classes; which would otherwise degenerate into a sordid ferocity and savage selfishness of spirit; it enables the industrious workman to pursue his occupation in the ensuing week with health and cheerfulness.". . . The preamble to a 1679 Rhode Island enactment stated that the reason for the ban on Sunday employment was that "persons being evil minded, have presumed to employ in servile labor, more than necessity requireth, their servants. . . ." With the advent of the First Amendment, the Colonial provisions requiring church attendance were soon repealed. . . .

More recently, further secular justifications have been advanced for making Sunday a day of rest, a day when people may recover from the labors of the week just passed and may physically and mentally prepare for the week's work to come. . . .

The proponents of Sunday closing legislation are no longer exclusively representatives of religious interests. Recent New Jersey Sunday legislation was supported by the labor groups and trade associations. . . .

Almost every State in our country presently has some type of Sunday regulation and over forty possess a relatively comprehensive system. . . . Some of our States now enforce their Sunday legislation through Departments of Labor. . . . Thus have Sunday laws evolved from the wholly religious sanctions that originally were enacted. . . .

[I]n order to dispose of the case before us, we must consider the standards by which the Maryland statutes are to be measured. . . .

[T]he First Amendment, in its final form, did not simply bar a congressional enactment establishing a church; it forbade all laws respecting an establishment of religion. Thus, this Court has given the Amendment a "broad interpretation". . . "in the light of its history and the evils it was designed forever to suppress. . . ." It has found that the First and Fourteenth amendments afford protection against religious establishment far more extensive than merely to forbid a national or state church. . . .

However, it is equally true that the "Establishment" Clause does not ban federal or state regulation of conduct whose reason or effect merely happens to coincide or harmonize with the tenets of some or all religions. In many instances, the Congress or state legislatures conclude that the general welfare of society, wholly apart from any religious considerations, demands such regulation. Thus, for temporal purposes, murder is illegal. And the fact that this agrees with the dictates of the Judaeo-Christian religions while it may disagree with others does not invalidate the regulation. So too with the questions of adultery and polygamy. . . .

In light of the evolution of our Sunday Closing Laws through the centuries, and of their more or less recent emphasis upon secular considerations, it is not difficult to discern that as presently written and administered, most of them, at least, are of a secular rather than of a religious character, and that presently they bear no relationship to establishment of religion as those words are used in the Constitution of the United States.

Throughout this century and longer, both the federal and state governments have oriented their activities very largely toward improvement of the health, safety, recreation and general well-being of our citizens. Numerous laws affecting public health, safety factors in industry, hours and conditions of labor of women and children, week-end diversion at parks and beaches, and cultural activities of various kinds, now point the way toward the good life for all. Sunday Closing Laws, like those before us, have become part and parcel of this great governmental concern wholly apart from their original purposes or connotations. The present purpose and effect of most of them is to provide a uniform day of rest for all citizens; the fact that this day is Sunday, a day of particular significance for the dominant Christian sects, does not bar the State from achieving its secular goals. To say that the States cannot prescribe Sunday as a day of rest for these purposes solely because centuries ago such laws had their genesis in religion would give a constitutional interpretation of hostility to the public welfare rather than one of mere separation of church and State. . . .

But, this does not answer all of appellant's contentions. We are told that the State has other means at its disposal to accomplish its secular purpose, other courses that would not even remotely or incidentally give state aid to religion. . . . It is true that if the State's interest were simply to provide for its citizens a periodic respite from work, a regulation demanding that everyone rest one day in seven, leaving the choice of the day to the individual, would suffice.

However, the State's purpose is not merely to provide a one-day-in-seven work stoppage. In addition to this, the State seeks to set one day apart from all others as a day of rest, repose, recreation and tranquility—a day which all members of the family and community have the opportunity to spend and enjoy together, a day in which there exists relative quiet and disassociation from the everyday intensity of commercial activities, a day in which people may visit friends and relatives who are not available during working days.

Obviously, a state is empowered to determine that a rest-one-day-in-seven statute would not accomplish this purpose; that it would not provide for a general cessation of activity, a special atmosphere of tranquility, a day which all members of the family or friends and relatives might spend together. Furthermore, it seems plain that the problems involved in enforcing such a provision would be exceedingly more difficult than those in enforcing a common-day-of-rest provision.

Moreover, it is common knowledge that the first day of the week has come to have special significance as a rest day in this country. People of all religions and people with no religion regard Sunday as a time for family activity, for visiting friends and relatives, for late-sleeping, for passive and active entertainments, for dining out and the like. . . . Sunday is a day apart from all others. The cause is irrelevant; the fact exists. It would seem unrealistic for enforcement purposes and perhaps detrimental to the general welfare to require a state to choose a common-day-of-rest other than that which most persons would select of their own accord. For these reasons, we hold that the Maryland statutes are not laws respecting an establishment of religion. . . .

Accordingly, the decision is

Affirmed.

MR. JUSTICE DOUGLAS, dissenting *[in all four cases]:*

. . . I do not see how a State can make protesting citizens refrain from doing innocent acts on Sunday because the doing of those acts offends sentiments of their Christian neighbors.

The institutions of our society are founded on the belief that there is an authority higher than the authority of the State; that there is a moral law which the state is powerless to alter; that the individual possesses rights, conferred by the Creator, which government must respect. . . .

[T]hose who fashioned the Constitution decided that if and when God is to be served, His service will not be motivated by coercive measures of government. . . . The First Amendment by its "establishment" clause prevents, of course, the selection by government of an "official" church. Yet the ban plainly extends farther than that. . . . The "establishment" clause protects citizens also against any law which selects any religious custom, practice, or ritual, puts the force of government behind it, and fines, imprisons, or otherwise penalizes a person for not observing it. The Government plainly could not join forces with one religious group and decree a universal and symbolic circumcision. Nor could it require all children to be baptized or give tax exemptions only to those whose children were baptized.

Could it require a fast from sunrise to sunset throughout the Moslem month of Ramadan? I should think not. Yet how then can it make criminal the doing of other acts, as innocent as eating, during the day that Christians revere?

Sunday is a word heavily overlaid with connotations and traditions deriving from the Christian roots of our civilization that color all judgments concerning it. . . .

The issue of these cases would therefore be in better focus if we imagined that a state legislature, controlled by orthodox Jews and Seventh Day Adventists, passed a law making it a crime to keep a shop open on Saturdays. Would a Baptist, Catholic, Methodist, or Presbyterian be compelled to obey that law or go to jail or pay a fine? Or suppose Moslems grew in political strength here and got a law through a state legislature making it a crime to keep a shop open on Fridays? Would the rest of us have to submit under the fear of criminal sanctions? . . .

The Court picks and chooses language from various decisions to bolster its conclusion that these Sunday Laws in the modern setting are "civil regulations." No matter how much is written, no matter what is said, the parentage of these laws is the Fourth Commandment; and they serve and satisfy the religious predispositions of our Christian communities. After all, the labels a State places on its laws are not binding on us when we are confronted with a constitutional decision. We reach our own conclusion as to the character, effect, and practical operation of the regulation in determining its constitutionality. . . .

It seems to me plain that by these laws the States compel one, under sanction of law, to refrain from work or recreation on Sunday because of the majority's religious views about that day. . . .

These laws are sustained because, it is said, the First Amendment is concerned with religious convictions or opinion, not with conduct. But it is a strange Bill of Rights that makes it possible for the dominant religious group to bring the minority to heel because the minority, in the doing of acts which intrinsically are wholesome and not antisocial, does not defer to the majority's beliefs. . . .

The Court balances the need of the people for rest, recreation, late-sleeping, family visiting and the like against the command of the First Amendment that no one need bow to the religious beliefs of another. There is in this realm no room for balancing. I see no place for it in the constitutional scheme. A legislature of Christians can no more make minorities conform to their weekly regime than a legislature of Moslems, or a legislature of Hindus. The religious regime of every group must be respected—unless it crosses the line of criminal conduct. But no one can be forced to come to a halt before it, or refrain from doing things that would offend it. That is my reading of the Establishment Clause and the Free Exercise Clause. . . .

MR. JUSTICE STEWART dissenting [in *Braunfeld* v. *Brown]:*

Pennsylvania has passed a law which compels an orthodox Jew to choose between his religious faith and his economic survival. That is a cruel choice. It is a choice which I think no State can constitutionally demand. For me this is not something that can be swept under the rug and forgotten in the interest of enforced Sunday togetherness. I think the impact of this law upon these appellants grossly violates their constitutional right to the free exercise of their religion.

Separate opinion of MR. JUSTICE FRANKFURTER, whom MR. JUSTICE HARLAN joined *[in all four cases]:*

[In this separate concurring opinion Justice Frankfurter set forth in detail the long history of Sunday legislation. The opinion is eighty-six pages long; sixteen additional pages of appendices include tables and other supporting data.]

CHAPTER 13

Race Discrimination

Racial discrimination, which has penetrated so many aspects of American life, has been attacked in the courts on the basis of a wide variety of constitutional and statutory claims. These include the "badges of servitude" implications of the Thirteenth Amendment; the due process, equal protection and privileges, and immunities clauses of the Fourteenth Amendment; the voting provisions of the Fifteenth Amendment; the due process clause of the Fifth Amendment; the interstate commerce clause; and various civil rights statutes enacted by Congress under the necessary and proper clause and the enforcement clauses of the Thirteenth, Fourteenth, and Fifteenth Amendments. In addition, many rights of accused and freedom of speech and association cases arise out of situations involving racial discrimination and protests against it. Thus, materials on discrimination can be found in Chapters 5 (civil rights statutes), 8 and 9 (commerce), 11 (speech and association), and 15 (rights of accused).

This chapter is devoted largely to discrimination in education, public facilities, housing, voting, employment and the selection of juries challenged under the Thirteenth and Fifteenth Amendments and the equal protection and due process clauses of the Fourteenth Amendment. Although the cases in this chapter invoke all of these constitutional provisions, the dominant constitutional mandate behind them is the equal protection clause: "No state shall . . . deny to any person within its jurisdiction the equal protection of the laws."

We have seen in Chapter 10 that the wide use of the due process clause of the Fourteenth Amendment to protect private property rights pushed the equal protection clause of that Amendment into the background for many years. After 1937, however, the Court relied more and more on the equal protection clause. As a result, that clause has had a dramatic and unparalleled growth, particularly in the cause of rights for blacks.

The term *equal protection of the laws* is impossible to define with any degree of precision. Nevertheless, the clause was obviously designed to guarantee the newly freed Negroes* equality of treatment in the enjoyment of basic civil and political rights. Justice Miller noted in the *Slaughterhouse Cases* (Chapter 10) that, in the light of the historical background of the Civil War amendments, there was no difficulty in giving meaning to the equal protection clause. "The existence of laws in the States where the newly emancipated Negroes resided, which discriminated with gross injustice and hardship against them as a class, was the evil to be remedied by this clause, and by it such laws are forbidden." Despite these fine words, the Court interpreted the Fourteenth Amendment very narrowly in the *Slaughterhouse Cases* and thereby helped to make it an ineffective instrument for the protection of Negro rights.

The Civil War was hardly over before the newly won civil and political rights of Negroes began to be curtailed by state legislation. The radical Congress attempted to halt these efforts through the enactment of a series of civil rights acts to implement the Civil War amendments. A final serious attempt to establish civil and legal rights for Negroes was made in the Civil Rights Act of 1875. There Congress provided that all persons, regardless of race or color, were entitled to the "full and equal enjoyment of the accommodations, advantages, facilities, and privileges of inns, public conveyances on land or water, theaters and other places of public amusement." Denial of these rights to others by any person was made a federal crime punishable by fine or imprisonment. This law extended the protection of the federal government to many areas of civil rights that had traditionally been under state protection. However, with only Justice Harlan dissenting, the Supreme Court held the Civil Rights Act of 1875 unconstitutional in the *Civil Rights Cases* (p. 154). In the majority opinion, Justice Bradley reasoned that the Fourteenth Amendment only prohibited discrimination by state governments. Congress could not penalize *private* persons for discriminating against Negroes. The decision in the *Civil Rights Cases* further

* In this chapter the words *Negro* and *black* are used to correspond with the accepted usage of the historical period being described.

prevented the Fourteenth Amendment from becoming an effective barrier against racial discrimination. The opinion "served notice that the Federal Government could not lawfully protect the Negro against the discrimination which private individuals might choose to exercise against him. This was another way of saying that the system of 'white supremacy' was mainly beyond federal control." [1]

In this period the one major building block to the Court's later racial discrimination decisions is *Yick Wo* v. *Hopkins,* 118 U.S. 356 (1886). San Francisco had granted permits to operate laundries in wooden buildings to all but one non-Chinese applicant. It had not granted even one to the two hundred Chinese applicants. The Court held that although the laundry permit law did not contain a racial provision, discrimination in its administration was unconstitutional state action.

Separate but Equal Doctrine

By the turn of the century, the Southern states had adopted a maze of restrictions against the Negro that consigned him largely to his pre-Civil War caste status. The segregation pattern developed in the South was approved by the Supreme Court in *Plessy* v. *Ferguson* (p. 512), upholding a Louisiana statute that required railroads to provide separate but equal accommodations for white and colored races. Only Justice Harlan dissented.

In the years after *Plessy,* case after case invoked the separate but equal doctrine without reexamining it. Actually, the doctrine had no real meaning, for the Supreme Court refused to look beyond lower court holdings to find if the segregated facilities for Negroes were, in fact, equal to those provided for whites. As a result, many Negro accommodations were said to be equal when it was a matter of common knowledge that they were decidedly inferior. The President's Committee on Civil Rights remarked aptly that the separate but equal doctrine "is one of the outstanding myths of American history, for it is almost always true that while indeed separate, these facilities are far from equal. Throughout the segregated public institutions, Negroes have been denied an equal share of tax-supported services and facilities." [2]

Beginning in the late 1930s the Court became much stricter about the equality requirement. The first important decision was *Missouri* ex rel. *Gaines* v. *Canada,* 305 U.S. 337 (1938). In that case, the state refused to admit a Negro to the Law School of the University of Missouri. There was no law school for Negroes

[1] Alfred H. Kelly and Winfred A. Harbison, *The American Constitution, Its Origins and Development* (New York: Norton, 1948), p. 491. The *Civil Rights Cases* are analyzed thoroughly in Milton R. Konvitz, *The Constitution and Civil Rights* (New York: Columbia U.P., 1946), Ch. 2.

[2] President's Committee, *To Secure These Rights* (Washington, D.C.: Government Printing Office, 1947), pp. 81–82. See also Rocco J. Tresolini, "John Marshall Harlan and Desegregation," *The Quarterly Review of Higher Education Among Negroes,* Vol. 30 (Jan. 1962), p. 1.

in the state, but a Missouri statute provided for the payment of tuition charges for Negro residents of Missouri at law schools in adjacent states. Missouri argued that this provision satisfied the separate but equal requirement. The Court ruled, however, that if facilities were provided for the legal education of white students within the state, equal facilities were also to be made available in the state for Negroes desiring a law degree. Delivering the majority opinion of the Court, Chief Justice Hughes stated:

> By the operation of the laws of Missouri a privilege has been created for white law students which is denied to Negroes by reason of their race. The white resident is afforded legal education within the State; the Negro resident having the same qualifications is refused it there and must go outside the State to obtain it. That is a denial of the equality of legal right to the enjoyment of the privilege which the State has set up, and the provision for the payment of tuition fees in another State does not remove the discrimination.

In subsequent cases the Court continued to insist on equal facilities for Negroes. In *Sipuel* v. *University of Oklahoma,* 332 U.S. 631 (1948), the Court held that qualified Negroes must be admitted to the state law school or be provided with equal educational facilities within the state. In *McLaurin* v. *Oklahoma State Regents,* 339 U.S. 637 (1950), it ruled that Negroes may not be segregated within a university after they have been admitted to its graduate school. The Court reasoned that the equal protection clause required that Negroes receive the same treatment as other students upon admission to a state-supported graduate school.[3] On the same day the *McLaurin* decision was announced, the Court rendered its important opinion in *Sweatt* v. *Painter* (p. 515), which paved the way for the 1954 decisions on segregation in the public schools. Although the Court did not hold that segregation per se was unconstitutional in the *Sweatt* case, the decision indicated clearly that it was virtually impossible for a state to comply with the separate but equal doctrine in the area of professional and graduate education.

The broadest challenge to racial discrimination came in 1952, when the Supreme Court was asked to outlaw segregation in the public schools in four states and the District of Columbia. The Court heard arguments during its 1952 term but adjourned without rendering an opinion and called for rearguments during the next term. The Court was obviously moving cautiously, clearly aware of the full implications of any decision it might render in this explosive area. In 1952, seventeen states and the District of Columbia required segregation by law. Four other states permitted segregation by local option. More than 8,000,000 white students and more than 2,500,000 colored pupils, representing about 4 per cent of the nation's public school enrollment, were required to

[3] In *Henderson* v. *United States,* 339 U.S. 816 (1950), the Court held that segregation of Negroes in dining cars under rules of the ICC was incompatible with equality of treatment. This decision had the effect of outlawing segregation in common carriers, but *Plessy* v. *Ferguson* was not even mentioned in the Court's decision.

attend segregated schools. Obviously, the overruling of the separate but equal doctrine would bring drastic changes in American education in many parts of the country. In addition, the death knell would be sounded for the entire pattern of segregation if the separate but equal concept could not be applied to public education.

John W. Davis, the Democratic candidate for President in 1924, headed the staff of lawyers who argued the case for the states. He relied principally on *Plessy* v. *Ferguson* in presenting his arguments for continued segregation in the public schools. He pointed out that when Congress and the states adopted the Fourteenth Amendment, there was no intention of abolishing segregation in public education. Davis further contended that under the Constitution the states were empowered to educate their children as they saw fit without interference from the Federal Government.

The arguments against segregation were presented by Thurgood Marshall, counsel for the NAACP. Marshall had already appeared before the Court in numerous important cases such as *Sweatt* v. *Painter* and *Shelley* v. *Kraemer* (p. 534) and had won some notable legal victories. He argued that the Fourteenth Amendment had been adopted to strike down the discriminatory legislation passed by many of the Southern states after the Civil War. Marshall urged the Court to reject completely the separate but equal doctrine. He contended that segregation stamped the Negro as an inferior and that it produced detrimental psychological effects on whites and Negroes alike.

On May 17, 1954, the Court concluded, in *Brown* v. *Board of Education* (p. 517), that "in the field of public education the doctrine of 'separate but equal' has no place." Shortly after the decision was rendered, a leading newspaper noted that "it is fifty-eight years since the Supreme Court, with Justice Harlan dissenting, established the doctrine of 'separate but equal' provision for the white and Negro races on interstate carriers. It is forty-three years since John Marshall Harlan passed from this earth. Now the words he used in his lonely dissent in an 8-to-1 decision in the case of *Plessy* v. *Ferguson* in 1896 have become a part of the law of the land." The *Brown* decision "dealt solely with segregation in the public schools, but there was not one word in Chief Justice Warren's opinion that was inconsistent with the earlier views of Justice Harlan. This is an instance in which the voice crying in the wilderness finally becomes the expression of a people's will and in which justice overtakes and thrusts aside a timorous expediency." [4]

The *Brown* decision was a momentous one indeed. Its impact on many phases of American life will be felt for decades to come. That the Court was keenly aware of its heavy responsibilities in rendering a decision that cut so deeply into long-established laws and customs is indicated by the following unusual aspects of its opinion.

1. *The Court was unanimous.* Only one opinion was written. Thus, the Court appeared united before the country and the world on a question of fundamental importance.

[4] *The New York Times,* May 23, 1954, p. 10E.

2. *The Court postponed a decision on the application of its decision until a later date.* This was done by restoring the case to the docket for argument at the next term and inviting all interested parties to present their views as to how the decision could be carried out. One of the chief merits of this action "was that it would afford a period for reflection in which sentiment in some of the most vitally affected areas might moderate. Some integration of schools could take place, and those who saw the system in operation might feel better about it." [5] In 1955, the Court ordered that the states make "a prompt and reasonable start toward full compliance" with its segregation ruling [*Brown* v. *Board of Education,* 2nd Case (p. 520)].

At the same time the *Brown* decision was handed down, the Court invalidated racial segregation in the public schools of the District of Columbia in *Bolling* v. *Sharpe,* 347 U.S. 497 (1954). Because the equal protection clause of the Fourteenth Amendment cannot be applied to the Federal Government, the *Bolling* decision was based on the due process clause of the Fifth Amendment. A similar "reading back" of the equal protection clause into the Fifth occurs in *Jiminez* v. *Weinberger,* 417 U.S. 628 (1974). The Court bars federal discrimination against certain illegitimate children which would violate equal protection if undertaken by the states but here is said instead to violate due process.

The *Brown* case did not explicitly overrule *Plessy* v. *Ferguson,* but it did indicate that segregation in areas other than public education would be difficult to maintain. Only a week after the *Brown* decision, the Court sent three racial segregation cases back to lower courts with orders that they be reexamined in the light of the *Brown* holding. The cases involved racial segregation in the amphitheater of a public park, a municipal housing project, and a city golf course.

The later pattern of Supreme Court affirmances and reversals in brief *per curiam* opinions has made clear that discrimination is forbidden in all public facilities. But the Court has never explained why. Instead, it merely cites *Brown.* But does *Brown* really explain why segregation in general (as opposed to segregation in education) is unconstitutional?

Before venturing any further, one more dimension of the legal problem of discrimination must be explored. Discrimination may refer to purpose and intent. Did someone purposely treat blacks or other minorities less well than he treated whites? Did he intend to discriminate? Discrimination may also refer to impact or result. A rule or policy may not have been adopted with the intention of hurting minorities, but it may in fact do so. For instance a rule that only those with a year of high school chemistry can go to the state pharmacy school may have a differential impact on blacks and whites if only 20 per cent of black students take chemistry in high school while 40 per cent of whites do so. Is this rule a discriminatory one even if it is clear that students who have had some chemistry are better qualified for pharmacy training than those who

[5] Luther A. Huston, "Segregation: Warren Role in Case," *The New York Times,* May 23, 1954, p. 5E.

have not? And how do we know whether the state adopted the rule because it wanted better-qualified pharmacy students or because it wanted fewer black pharmacists? In all the areas of discrimination to be considered in this and the next chapter, the Court struggles with the issue of whether to bar only intentional discrimination or to strike at racially differential impacts as well.

Implementing Brown

It was inevitable that the *Public School Segregation Cases,* which were of such vital national importance, would generate mixed reactions. The Court has been both highly praised and roundly denounced for those decisions. In the South itself, reactions have ranged all the way from open defiance of the Court to complete acceptance of its holding.

The difficulties encountered in enforcing the *Brown* decision in the face of opposition by state authorities are illustrated by *Cooper* v. *Aaron,* 358 U.S. 1 (1958), in which the Court ordered integration of the Little Rock, Arkansas, schools in the face of open defiance by the state government so severe that it was overcome only when President Eisenhower sent federal troops to the city. The Court said: "The constitutional rights of respondents are not to be sacrificed or yielded to the violence and disorder which have followed upon the actions of the Governor and Legislature. . . . Thus, law and order are not here to be preserved by depriving the Negro children of their constitutional rights."

In the defiant states, a number of programs designed to circumvent the Court's mandate were adopted. The post-*Brown* judicial record came to look like a continuous guerilla war between the Southern authorities and the lower federal courts, with occasional interventions by the Supreme Court. In *Griffin* v. *County School Board of Prince Edward County,* 377 U.S. 218 (1964), the Court struck down a county program of closing public schools altogether and giving grants to white children to attend private schools. The Court said, the "public schools were closed and private schools operated in their place with state and county assistance, for one reason, and one reason only: to insure . . . that white and colored children in Prince Edward County would not, under any circumstances, go to the same school. Whatever nonracial grounds might support a State's allowing a county to abandon public schools, the object must be a constitutional one, and grounds of race and opposition to desegregation do not qualify as constitutional."

First in *Goss* v. *Board of Education,* 373 U.S. 683 (1963), and then in *Green* v. *County School Board,* 391 U.S. 430 (1968), the Court struck down "freedom of choice" plans whose effects were to maintain a dual school system. In both these cases and in a number of others throughout the mid-1960s, the Court voiced impatience at desegregation delays that school authorities sought to justify under the "all deliberate speed" formula.

At the same time the lower federal courts, in decisions often affirmed by the Supreme Court, began to speak more and more in terms of an affirmative duty to integrate on the part of authorities who had earlier erected dual school systems.

In 1969, in a brief *per curiam, Alexander* v. *Holmes County Board of Education,* 396 U.S. 19 (1969), the Court announced: "continued operation of segregated schools under a standard of allowing 'all deliberate speed' for desegregation is no longer constitutionally permissible. Under explicit holdings of this Court the obligation of every school district is to terminate dual school systems at once and to operate now and hereafter only unitary schools." Up to this time the Court had maintained a united front in school desegregation cases. Now, when the time had come to actually require integration, splits began to occur. In *Carter* v. *West Feliciana Parish School Board,* 396 U.S. 290 (1970), a majority said that the "at once" in *Alexander* meant "at once" and ordered an integration plan into immediate effect. Only five justices composed the majority. Justices Harlan and White concurred but qualified the "at once." Chief Justice Burger and Justice Stewart dissented, indicating that they would still allow some delay.

By the late 1960s three major, and overlapping, problems confronted the Court. The first involved the positive duty to integrate. *Brown* had imposed a negative duty on the state: the duty to abolish the laws and regulations requiring a segregated, dual school system. But the rationale of *Brown* had been positive. The justices had not simply argued that blacks were harmed by the existence of official Jim Crow policies, that is, by being legally prevented from attending the schools of their choice. Instead they had argued that the harm lay in the loss of educational opportunities for black children that stemmed from not being in classrooms with white children. The order in *Brown* seemed to create a state duty to desegregate in the sense of abolishing legal barriers. But the Court's rationale might be read as creating a state duty to integrate—that is, to take positive steps to insure that blacks were in classrooms with whites.

Such a positive duty led to the second problem—busing—which became a major political issue. Given patterns of residential segregation, simply abolishing Jim Crow laws would not necessarily put blacks and whites into the same classrooms, particularly in cities. So if the state had a positive duty to integrate, then busing students from one neighborhood to another might be necessary. Yet, antibusing sentiment became so strong that it led not only to local resistance, but to congressional antibusing legislation of doubtful constitutionality.

The third major problem was "*de facto*" segregation. Southern school segregation by law did not raise "state action" problems of the sort that will be discussed in the next section of this chapter. For segregation by law was clearly action by the state of the sort contemplated by the wording of the Fourteenth Amendment: "No state shall . . ." However, in the North, school segregation, although not required by law, nevertheless occurred as a result of discrimination in housing and employment. Segregation occurred in fact *(de facto)* if not by law *(de jure)*. Did the *Brown* holding apply to *de facto* as well as *de jure* segregation?

Given these three problems, a number of alternative strategies were available to the Supreme Court:

1. It could abandon the positive thrust of *Brown* and require only that school segregation laws be abolished. The results would be the abolition of official Jim Crow in the South, no busing, and no movement against Northern segregation—or for that matter *de facto* segregation in the South.

2. It could hold that where legally segregated schools existed in the past, school authorities were under a duty to "dismantle" the dual school system by taking positive action to create an integrated school system. The result would be to require integration including busing in the South, but to leave the North alone.

3. The Court could implement (2). Then, in addition, it could find that some Northern school authorities had acted to support patterns of residential segregation by the way they drew attendance boundaries, assigned teachers, and located new schools. These actions by government would turn *de facto* into *de jure* segregation. Some, many, or all Northern school districts would then be under a positive duty to integrate, depending on just how much *de jure* segregation the Court wished to see in the North. Busing would undoubtedly be necessary in many Northern cities if they were under a positive duty to integrate.

4. The Court could hold that *de facto* segregation was just as unconstitutional as *de jure* segregation. The result would be that the same demands, including busing, would be made on the North and the South and that all Northern schools would have to integrate.

5. The Court could adopt positions (2), (3), or (4) but hold that the need to integrate must be balanced against other educational needs and values. This alternative would allow the Court to press for some integration but would enable it to go slow on busing, new school construction, and the like, and to avoid imposing strict racial quotas. Districts would be allowed to plead that such factors as the expense of busing, time spent in travel, preservation of neighborhood schools, creation of special educational opportunities, and creation of incentives to whites to stay in the city sometimes justified slowing the speed and extent of integration.

Thus, observers began to watch the Court's school segregation opinions of the 1970s closely to divine toward which strategy the Court was leaning.

Swann v. *Charlotte-Mecklenburg Board of Education,* (p. 520), affirmed a very thoroughgoing district court desegregation order for Charlotte, North Carolina. It imposed a positive duty to integrate and required considerable busing. But the decision did not reveal too much about the Court's inclinations. Charlotte was a Southern city that had practiced legal segregation in the past. Chief Justice Burger tended to put the positive duty to integrate in terms of the need "to eliminate from the public schools all vestiges of state-imposed segregation." Thus, the applicability to the North was not at all clear. Nor does *Swann* constitute a blanket endorsement of busing, although in a companion case, *North Carolina State Board of Education* v. *Swann,* 402 U.S. 43 (1971), the Court struck down a North Carolina antibusing statute. The district court order

required very thorough integration. The Supreme Court affirmed this order but spoke at length against the need for strictly mathematical racial quotas.

A crucial question facing many school authorities at the time was whether central cities and suburbs ought to be, or had to be, thrown together into unified districts in order to achieve integration. Because *Swann* involved an area that had been created by combining city and suburban districts long before segregation issues arose, the case said nothing about whether such unification might be constitutionally required to end segregation. Finally, after various broad hints early in the opinion that the Court might in the future find *de jure* segregation even where no official school segregation laws had existed, the Chief Justice ended with even broader hints that the Court is *not* prepared to find *de facto* segregation unconstitutional.

Wright v. *Emporia City Council,* 407 U.S. 451 (1972), raises indirectly the city-suburb question not met in *Swann.* Emporia, Virginia, had become a city in 1967 but remained in the county school district. When the county district came under an integration order, Emporia sought to withdraw and establish its own system. Justice Stewart for a majority of five sought to decide the case on the narrow ground that the district court could exercise its equitable discretion to prevent the withdrawal of Emporia, because such a withdrawal "would actually impede the process of dismantling the existing dual system."

The realistic crux of the matter was that if Emporia did not withdraw, the school district would be 34 per cent white and 66 per cent black. If it withdrew, the county would be 28 per cent white and 72 per cent black and Emporia would be 48 per cent white and 52 per cent black. Chief Justice Burger, for the four dissenters, felt that the district court order forbidding withdrawal was invalid because it was motivated by a desire to achieve the kind of exact mathematical balances that he had denounced in *Swann.* For the Chief Justice and the other Nixon appointees, the object was the dismantling of dual schools not achieving "racial balancing." In the companion case of *United States* v. *Scotland Neck Board of Education,* 407 U.S. 484 (1972), the Chief Justice and the other dissenters in *Emporia* concurred with the majority because in this instance the carving out of a new school system would in fact "preclude meaningful desegregation."

The city-suburb problem was finally raised directly in *School Board of Richmond* v. *State Board of Education,* 412 U.S. 92 (1973). There a federal district judge had required Richmond, Virginia, and two adjoining counties to create a unified integration plan to achieve a "viable racial mix" by overcoming the great concentration of blacks in Richmond. Obviously, such steps are crucial in many instances to achieving truly integrated education. Otherwise big-city school districts, already substantially black, will be "desegregated": the remaining whites will flee to the suburbs and the desegregated schools will be all black. On the other hand, to allow a federal court to order bona fide, politically independent entities to merge is to allow federal courts to dictate the internal political structures of the states—a matter that it would seem should fall within the powers of the states and not the central government. [See *Gomillion* v. *Lightfoot* (discussed later in this chapter) and the discussions of reapportionment in Chapters 4 and 14.] The court of appeals reversed the district court and the Supreme Court affirmed the court of appeals by a 4-to-4 vote without opinion. Justice Powell did not participate because he had formerly been a member of the Richmond school board.

Similarly inconclusive results appear in *Keyes* v. *School District No. 1, Denver, Colorado,* 413 U.S. 189 (1973). This was the Court's first Northern school desegregation case. It involved the Denver, Colorado, schools. It was claimed that although school authorities had not followed a general policy of segregation, they had intentionally clumped about a third of the city's children in one school located in a black, suburban residential area. Justices Powell and Douglas, in separate opinions, argued for scrapping the *de jure–de facto* distinction and announcing a national right to integrated schools. Justice White did not participate. Chief Justice Burger concurred in the majority result, but not in its opinion. Justice Rehnquist dissented, apparently finding decisive the fact that racial segregation had never been required by law in Denver.

The majority opinion by Justice Brennan seems to opt for strategy (3) described on p. 496. The decision is not entirely clear because the case was remanded for further action in the district court. However, Justice Brennan held that where a Northern school board had acted with "purpose or intent to segregate," it had created *de jure* segregation even in the absence of school segregation laws. Moreover, even where such *de jure* segregation had been created in only one or a few of a district's schools, the entire district might be considered a dual school system under the same duties and subject to the same remedies as Southern districts. Where one school was segregated *de jure,* the finding of the existence of a dual school system could only be avoided if "other segregated schools within the system are not also the result of intentionally segregative actions." But the burden of proof was on the school authorities to show that they had not intended segregation in the other schools.

The Court added: "We have no occasion to consider in this case whether a 'neighborhood school policy' of itself will justify racial or ethnic concentrations in the absence of a finding that school authorities have committed acts constituting *de jure* segregation."

In *Dayton Board of Education* v. *Brinkman,* 433 U.S. 406 (1977), the Court shed a little more light on the *Keyes* problem. It disapproved a court of appeals order for systemwide desegregation in Dayton, Ohio, saying, "only if there has been a system-wide impact [of earlier *de jure* discrimination] may there be a system-wide remedy."

The city-suburb problem raised in the Richmond case came to a head in *Milliken* v. *Bradley* (p. 524). A federal district court found that school and other government authorities in Detroit had acted to create and support patterns of segregation in housing and schools, thus involving themselves in *de jure* segregation, even though no school segregation laws existed. It ordered a massive busing program involving not only Detroit schools but those of a large number of surrounding school districts. The Detroit court felt that the only way to ensure that white and black children would actually go to school together would be to throw city and suburbs together for school attendance purposes. The

Supreme Court rejected this approach. (But see the discussion of *Hills* v. *Gautreaux* later in this chapter.)

The Detroit case shows the ultimate tension within *Brown* v. *Board,* a tension that the Court has never been willing to face up to directly. Does *Brown* mean that the Constitution forbids segregation, or does *Brown* mean that the Constitution requires integration? The *Brown* ruling, that legally segregated, dual school systems must be abolished, looks to desegregation. The *Brown* rationale, that blacks educated in all-black classrooms receive inherently unequal educations, looks to integration.

The general tendency of the Warren Court was to move very, very gradually toward the integration position. The Detroit case clearly moves toward the desegregation position. In effect, it says that Detroit runs a dual school system. Detroit must therefore abolish that system. But the majority of the Court is unwilling to concern itself with the possibility that official desegregation may result in nonintegration—that is, in schools in which all or nearly all students are black. It emphasizes the legal obligation of officials to stop acting illegally, to stop *de jure* segregation, rather than any direct judicial concern for achieving a racial balance in the schools.

In the political context of the time, there is little doubt that the Court's decision was a severe blow to integration forces. It provided support to the antibusing movement. It blocked, at least temporarily, the only feasible method of integrating the schools of large northern cities in the absence of positive action by the state governments to themselves redraw school district boundaries.

In the longer run, the decision set the stage for a new, extensive, expensive, time-consuming litigational campaign by integration forces. For the crux of the Court's decision was that suburban districts could not be thrown in with the city because the district court had not found that either the state government or the suburban districts themselves had engaged in *de jure* segregation. So remedies were confined to the one governmental unit that actually had been found to be practicing *de jure* segregation—the City of Detroit. Clearly, the next stage is litigation designed to show that a city *and* either state authorities or suburban governments or both are engaged in *de jure* segregation.

The Detroit Case returned to the Court in *Milliken* v. *Bradley,* 433 U.S. 267 (1977), in which the Court upheld a district court order requiring remedial educational programs as part of its desegregation decree. *Milliken II* is important because in the course of enforcing desegregation decrees, federal courts have often become deeply involved in making educational policies for the school districts concerned. This case is the Supreme Court's first approval of remedies that go not only to which children go to which school but to the substance of the educational program.

In *Pasadena City Board of Education* v. *Spangler,* 427 U.S. 424 (1976), however, the Court found that the district court had gone too far. Subsequent to a first student reassignment plan, shifts in population had resulted in some schools' becoming more black or more white than originally required. The district court ordered that students be reassigned annually in order to achieve the desired goal of no school in which a majority of the students were black.

The Supreme Court, relying on *Swann,* held that the district court could not require such reassignments. The decision rested on two grounds. First *Swann* had explicitly forbidden the district courts to require any "particular degree of racial balance or mixing" such as the Pasadena requirement that no school in the district contain a majority of students from a race that constituted a minority in the overall school population. Second, *Swann* had said that once dual schools had been dismantled, subsequent changes in the racial composition of particular schools caused by population shifts, and in no way due to segregatory actions by school officials, could not justify further district court reassignment orders.

In three cases in the 1976–1977 term,[6] the Court disapproved systemwide busing orders and referred to the *Washington* v. *Davis, Arlington Heights* "purpose and intent" standard discussed later in this chapter. The Court seems to be saying again that the goal is not integration but desegregation. Where school authorities have purposely segregated in the past, the effects of those segregations must be removed. But the mere fact that some schools are all black and others are all white, in the absence of a showing of segregatory intent, ought not to trigger district court busing orders to achieve completely racially integrated student bodies. Two years later the Court spoke again in *Columbus Board of Education* v. *Penick,* 443 U.S. 449 (1979), and *Dayton Board of Education* v. *Brinkman,* 443 U.S. 526 (1979). These decisions reveal deep divisions among the justices, particularly on the issue of busing. Nevertheless a majority endorsed two system-wide busing orders on the basis that the lower courts had found that the districts involved had engaged in deliberate segregation in the past and that their discriminatory policies had affected their whole educational systems rather than only a few isolated schools. The justices quarreled bitterly about what the standards and procedures ought to be for deciding whether a district had been engaged in *de jure* segregation and whether that *de jure* segregation had been pervasive enough to justify district-wide remedies. The Court continues to use strategy (3) outlined earlier in this chapter and then leaves to the district courts and the courts of appeal almost unlimited discretion to either find or not find *de jure* segregation in all or part of any Northern school district. In 1982 the Court struck down one state anti-busing measure and approved another. [*Washington* v. *Seattle School District No. 1,* 50 L.W. 4998; *Crawford* v. *Los Angeles Board of Education,* 50 L.W. 5016.]

STATE ACTION, PUBLIC FACILITIES, AND CLAIMS OF DISCRIMINATION

Many of the most harmful forms of racial discrimination are not governmental, such as in school segregation, but are the private discrimination by one person, or business, or private group against another in hiring, housing, and the provision

[6] *Dayton Board of Education* v. *Brinkman,* 433 U.S. 406 (1977); *Austin Ind. School Dist.* v. *United States,* 429 U.S. 990 (1976); *School Dist.* v. *United States,* 433 U.S. 667 (1977).

were exercised in a discriminatory way, courts might not enforce those rights, however legal, because court enforcement would constitute discriminatory state action. The notion that one has a private right to discriminate, but that private rights employed discriminatorily are not enforceable in court, just about destroys the distinction between private and state action. Private rights do not really exist unless they can be legally enforced. Under *Shelley,* could a policeman remove a trespasser from the living room sofa in a private house once the owner admitted that he wanted the man out because he did not want anyone of another race in his house?

Reitman returns us to problems of positive versus negative duties found in the school cases. The Fourteenth Amendment does not seem to require the states to pass laws against private discrimination. If a state does pass such a law and then repeals it, is the repeal an unconstitutional state action because it aids future private discrimination? How can a state have a constitutional duty not to repeal a state law that it had no duty to pass in the first place? In *Reitman* the Court manages to invalidate a California repeal of a state antidiscrimination in housing law without directly confronting these problems.

The positive-duty problem also arises in connection with discrimination in state facilities other than schools. We have seen that per curiams after *Brown* prohibited discrimination in other state facilities. In *Palmer* v. *Thompson,* 403 U.S. 217 (1971), in a 5-to-4 decision, the Court held that Jackson, Mississippi, had not acted unconstitutionally in closing down its municipal swimming pools, which were under court desegregation orders. In *Griffin* v. *Prince Edward County,* 377 U.S. 218 (1964), the Court was careful to say that the state was not constitutionally required to operate public schools. But it had held that closing public schools in the context of aiding whites to go to private schools and with the purpose of preserving discrimination was unconstitutional. In *Palmer* the closing of public pools was not coupled with state aid to private ones—although, in fact, after the closing, private pools would be available to whites and not blacks. The Court was obviously reluctant to impose a constitutional duty on the state to provide swimming pools or to declare that once the city had opened a pool, it was required to keep it open forever.

The Court might have used the purpose of the city government to avoid integration as decisive. But the city pleaded other purposes, and the Court has traditionally been reluctant to look to the motives of government—although it obviously does so in many instances. Indeed, in the *Emporia* and *Scotland Neck* cases discussed earlier, four of the justices, led by Chief Justice Burger, had wanted to base their distinction between the two creations of new districts on their finding that one did have a discriminatory purpose and the other did not.

Perhaps behind the *Palmer* decision lurks the notion that although the state may not shut down fundamental services such as schools, it may shut down peripheral ones such as swimming pools. It is easier to proclaim a fundamental right to education than to summer recreation. We shall return to the problem of fundamental rights in the next chapter.

of goods and services. Yet, the Supreme Court traditionally has he Fourteenth Amendment prohibits only "state action," not private discr In Chapter 5 we saw the reflection of this state-action concept, fi adverse treatment of civil rights statutes by the Supreme Court and the "under color of law" decisions. The Court now also holds that w act constitutes "state action" under the 14th Amendment, it is an a "under color of law" for purposes of Sec. 1983 of the civil rights st [*Rendell-Baker* v. *Kohn,* 50 L.W. 4825 (1982).] Particularly in the per which Congress did not act, and in which there were constitutional d about whether it could act, against private discrimination, "state action" extremely important. It governed the extent to which the Supreme Court c intervene directly against discrimination. State action remains important in those instances in which individuals want the courts to vindicate their clai in areas in which they have no statutory protection and must rely directly the Constitution. Many of the state-action cases seem more like logical puzzl than public policy disputes. However, behind the surface questions usually lurk the issue of whether the boundaries of state action are to be drawn narrowly or expanded to allow greater judicial intervention against private discrimination. Thus, *Burton* v. *Wilmington Parking Authority,* 365 U.S. 715 (1961), involved restaurant space in a state-owned parking lot rented by the state to a private concessionaire. The Court found unconstitutional state action in the restaurant's refusal to serve blacks.

Evans v. *Newton,* 382 U.S. 296 (1966), and *Pennsylvania* v. *Board of Trusts,* 353 U.S. 230 (1957), both involve situations in which private persons died leaving property—a park and a school, respectively—and naming the state as trustee to administer it. Both had specified that the property be used for whites only. In both instances, the Supreme Court ruled that state action was involved in the discriminatory operation of the property even though the state was only acting as a trustee carrying out the wishes of a deceased individual for his private property.

State-action arguments were pressed in a number of the sit-in cases discussed in Chapter 11. The argument at its broadest is that when private operators of restaurants in the South discriminated against blacks, they were engaged in state action either because (1) they were obeying the general customs of the community or because (2) they had state business and health licenses necessary to run a restaurant. These arguments were not decisive, and the cases wen off on other grounds. In *Moose Lodge* v. *Irvis,* 407 U.S. 163 (1972), the Suprem Court held that discrimination by a private club did not become state acti simply because the club held a state liquor license. [See also *Blum* v. *Yaret* 50 L.W. 4859 (1982).] State-action issues are crucial to the white primary c to be discussed later in this chapter.

Perhaps the most puzzling of all the state-action cases are *Shelley* v. *Kr* (p. 534) and *Reitman* v. *Mulkey,* 387 U.S. 369 (1967). In the former, the Su Court reached the odd conclusion that a contract might be legally va unenforceable in court. It seemed to hold that where private propert

In *Gilmore* v. *City of Montgomery,* 417 U.S. 556 (1974), the Court struck down a district court ban on the use of city recreational facilities by segregated private groups. The Court argued that "mere use" by such groups might not involve state action.

After avoiding the issue for many years, the Supreme Court finally struck down state miscegenation statutes in *McLaughlin* v. *Florida,* 379 U.S. 184 (1964), and *Loving* v. *Virginia,* 388 U.S. 1 (1967)—probably the most aptly named case ever to reach the Court.

Racial Discrimination in Housing

Racial discrimination in schools and housing are closely connected, because residential segregation that forces blacks or other groups to live in limited areas results in segregated schools. The barring of racial discrimination in housing might permit a greater dispersal of populations and break down public school segregation in many areas of the North as well as the South.

In their efforts to break out of crowded racial ghettos into unsegregated residential areas, blacks have relied heavily on the Fourteenth Amendment. The Supreme Court early held in *Buchanan* v. *Warley,* 245 U.S. 60 (1917), that municipal residential-segregation ordinances violate the Fourteenth Amendment. Because the *Buchanan* case made it impossible to prevent Negroes from moving into white neighborhoods by law, restrictive covenants were employed widely after 1917 to effect the same purpose. Restrictive covenants are simply private agreements whereby owners of property agree not to sell or lease their property to Negroes or other groups. In *Corrigan* v. *Buckley,* 271 U.S. 323 (1926), the Court unanimously upheld the use of private restrictive covenants. The Court noted that the Fourteenth Amendment restricts only state action and not the action of private individuals. For approximately twenty years after *Corrigan* v. *Buckley,* the Supreme Court refused to review subsequent restrictive-covenant cases. However, in the 1948 case of *Shelley* v. *Kraemer* (p. 534), the Court held that private restrictive covenants could not be validly enforced by the state courts because this would violate the equal protection clause of the Fourteenth Amendment.[7] At the same time the Court held, in *Hurd* v. *Hodge,* 334 U.S. 24 (1948), that the enforcement of restrictive covenants in the District of Columbia was prohibited by federal statutes.

After the *Shelley* and *Hurd* cases, attempts were made to enforce racial restrictive covenants by allowing signers of the covenant to sue those who had broken it by selling or leasing property to Negroes or other groups. But in *Barrows* v. *Jackson,* 346 U.S. 249 (1953), the Court ruled that a restrictive covenant may not be enforced by a suit for damages against a party who broke the contract. In delivering the majority opinion of the Court, Justice Minton re-

[7] The painstaking strategy of the NAACP in this case is noted in Chapter 3 and is described fully in Clement E. Vose, *Caucasians Only: The Supreme Court, the NAACP, and the Restrictive Covenant Cases* (Berkeley and Los Angeles: University of California Press, 1959), p. 213.

marked that if a state upheld such damage suits, it would be encouraging the use of restrictive covenants.

Many states have now passed various forms of open-housing legislation. In *Reitman* v. *Mulkey,* 387 U.S. 369 (1967), the Supreme Court held that the state might not insert into its constitution a provision barring future antidiscrimination statutes.

In 1968, Congress passed legislation that required the end of discrimination in the rental and sale of most federally aided housing. In the same year, the Supreme Court went even further by ruling that an obscure provision of the Civil Rights Act of 1866 prohibited private discrimination in the sale or rental of property. [*Jones* v. *Alfred H. Mayer Co.* (p. 159).]

Those concerned with racial discrimination in housing have shifted much of their fire to zoning ordinances, which they claim often have the effect of closing middle-class suburbs to the poor and particularly the black by barring the kinds of housing they can afford. In *Village of Arlington Heights* v. *Metropolitan Housing Development Corp.* (p. 547), the Court upheld the refusal of a town to rezone land from single family to apartment use so that low and medium income housing could be built there. Invoking the doctrine of *Washington* v. *Davis* (p. 544), it held that though the ultimate effect of the zoning might be to contribute to the preservation of racial segregation in housing, refusals to change it were valid so long as their "purpose or intent" was not discriminatory. The Court has also limited the standing of those not directly involved to challenge zoning ordinances. (See Chapter 4.)

In *Hills* v. *Gautreaux,* 425 U.S. 284 (1976), where the Court found that the U.S. Department of Housing and Urban Development and the Chicago Housing Authority had cooperated in racial segregation in public housing in the City of Chicago, the Court ordered an interdistrict remedy. It required that public housing available to blacks be provided in suburban areas around Chicago. The Court argued that, unlike the suburban school districts in *Milliken* v. *Bradley,* HUD had been proved to be directly involved in the discrimination. Therefore, it might be ordered to cure the discrimination within its jurisdiction, which extended beyond the boundaries of the city.

Suffrage

The original Constitution left the regulation of suffrage almost entirely in the hands of the states. Article I (Section 2, clause 1) provides simply that all persons who are qualified to vote for members of the most numerous house of the state legislature are eligible to vote for members of the House of Representatives. This same rule governs the election of senators, because a like provision was included in the Seventeenth Amendment. The Constitution provides also that the President and Vice-President are to be chosen by presidential electors. These electors are selected in each state "in such manner as the legislature thereof may direct." (Article II, Section 1.) Nevertheless, the states must fix the qualifications for voting in both national and state elections within the limits set by the Fourteenth, and Nineteenth Amendments. The equal protection clause of the Fourteenth Amendment prohibits the states from making unreasonable classifications or discriminations affecting the right to vote. The Fourteenth Amendment also contains a penalty clause that authorizes Congress to reduce the congressional representation of a state that has disfranchised a proportion of the adult male population. This penalty provision was designed to guarantee to the newly freed Negroes the right to vote, but it has never been enforced. The Fifteenth Amendment forbids the states to deny or abridge the right to vote because of race, color, or previous condition of servitude; and the Nineteenth Amendment prohibits discrimination because of sex.

The Fourteenth and Fifteenth Amendments were resisted vigorously by the Southern states, and not long after Union troops were withdrawn in 1877, Negroes were effectively disfranchised. A number of legal devices, such as poll taxes, literacy tests, and the white primary, were employed to deny Negroes the right to vote. The President's Committee on Civil Rights noted, in 1947, that in addition to the "formal, legal methods of disfranchisement, there are the long-standing techniques of terror and intimidation, in the face of which great courage is required of the Negro who tries to vote. In the regions most characterized by generalized violence against Negroes, little more than 'advice' is often necessary to frighten them away from the polls. They have learned, through the years, to discover threats in mood and atmosphere." [8]

GRANDFATHER CLAUSE

As time went on, the legality of a number of the devices developed for the disfranchisement of the Negro were challenged in the Supreme Court. One of these was the interesting and novel "grandfather clause" that had been adopted in several states. The Oklahoma grandfather clause, for example, which was enacted as an amendment to the state constitution in 1910, required a literacy test (ability to read and write *any* section of the Oklahoma constitution) for voting. However, it provided that the test need not be taken by persons or descendants of anyone who was entitled to vote under any form of government or who resided in a foreign nation prior to January 1, 1866. Because Negroes could not vote prior to 1866 in Oklahoma, as well as in most other states, the required literacy test was used to deny most of them the right to vote. But in the 1915 case of *Guinn* v. *United States,* 238 U.S. 347, the Supreme Court held that the Oklahoma grandfather clause violated the Fifteenth Amendment.

In 1916, Oklahoma enacted a new suffrage law that omitted the ancestral

[8] President's Committee, *To Secure These Rights* (Washington, D.C.: Government Printing Office, 1947), p. 40.

exemptions held invalid in the *Guinn* case, but which provided that all persons who had voted in the general election of 1914, when the grandfather clause was still in effect, were permanently qualified to vote without taking a literacy test. All other persons, except those given a short extension because of sickness or absence from the state, were required to register during a twelve-day period or be *permanently disfranchised.* In *Lane* v. *Wilson,* 307 U.S. 268 (1939), the Supreme Court held the statute invalid as a violation of the Fifteenth Amendment. Speaking for the Court, Justice Frankfurter pointed out that the Fifteenth Amendment "nullifies sophisticated as well as simple-minded modes of discrimination. It hits onerous procedural requirements that effectively handicap exercise of the franchise by the colored race although the abstract right to vote may remain unrestricted as to race."

THE WHITE PRIMARY

For many years the most effective "legal" method for denying blacks the right to vote was the white primary. This device simply excluded blacks from voting in the Democratic party primary elections. For all practical purposes, this action disfranchised the colored race, because the dominance of the Democratic party in the South made victory in a primary tantamount to election.

The white primary appeared to be legal for two major reasons. In the first place, the Constitution prohibits discrimination against the Negro by the state, but not by private individuals or organizations. Theoretically, the Democratic party "acted as a purely private organization. So long as the fiction of party as private association could be maintained, all could agree on the legality of its exclusion of the Negro from the Democratic primary." [9] Secondly, it seemed, for a long time, that Congress had no control over primaries. Article I, Section 4, of the Constitution provides that Congress may make or alter the times, places, and manner of holding congressional elections. But in *Newberry* v. *United States,* 256 U.S. 232 (1921), the Supreme Court held that a primary was not an election within the meaning of that article. Consequently, Congress could not regulate primaries.

The Texas white primary law, enacted in 1923, which was held void in *Nixon* v. *Herndon,* 273 U.S. 536 (1927), seems to have been inspired by the *Newberry* doctrine. The *Nixon* case is discussed in *Smith* v. *Allwright* (p. 537), where the Supreme Court held the Texas white primary unconstitutional after a long and tortuous process of litigation. The case of *United States* v. *Classic,* 313 U.S. 299 (1941), which helped pave the way for the downfall of the white primary by resolving the doubts raised by the *Newberry* case, is also discussed in *Smith* v. *Allwright.*

In a number of Southern states where the *Allwright* decision was accepted with little or no resistance, black participation in the political process was increased gradually. However, in some states efforts were made almost immediately

[9] V. O. Key, Jr., *Southern Politics* (New York: Knopf, 1950), p. 621.

to circumvent the *Allwright* holding by various ingenious methods. All of these attempts met with disaster in the federal courts. See *Schnell* v. *Davis,* 336 U.S. 933 (1949). The most novel attempt to offset the consequences of *Smith* v. *Allwright* was made in a Texas county where blacks were barred from voting through the use of a preprimary primary. Blacks were excluded from the primaries of an organization known as the Jaybird Democratic Association on the ground that the group was a self-governing voluntary club. However, it was shown that, with very few exceptions, candidates endorsed by the Jaybird Association were unopposed in the regular Democratic party primaries and general elections. Every countrywide official elected to office since 1889 had first been endorsed in a Jaybird primary. With only Justice Minton dissenting, the Supreme Court relied on the *Allwright* decision in holding, in *Terry* v. *Adams,* 345 U.S. 461 (1953), that the Jaybird scheme violated the Fifteenth Amendment. The Court said that the Democratic party primary and the general election "have become no more than the perfunctory ratifiers of the choice that has already been made in Jaybird elections from which Negroes have been excluded. The Jaybird primary has become an integral part, indeed the only effective part, of the elective process that determines who shall rule and govern in the county. The effect of the whole procedure is to do precisely that which the Fifteenth Amendment forbids."

The *Allwright* decision and the subsequent federal court cases noted here have destroyed the legal basis of the white primary in the South. Nevertheless, *Smith* v. *Allwright* and subsequent decisons did not prevent numerous local officials from excluding blacks from the polls. Provisions to protect the voting rights of blacks were included in the Civil Rights Acts of 1957, 1960, and 1964; but the strongest provisions are contained in the Voting Rights Act of 1965,[10] which is explained and upheld in *South Carolina* v. *Katzenbach* (p. 541). See also *Katzenbach* v. *Morgan,* discussed in Chapter 14.

RACE AND DISTRICTING

Gomillion v. *Lightfoot,* 364 U.S. 339 (1960), involved a redrawing of the city boundaries of Tuskegee, Alabama, so that most of the Negro residents would no longer live in the city and so no longer be eligible to vote in city elections. The case arose before *Baker* v. *Carr* (see Chapter 4), so that the Court might well have considered it as presenting a "political question" unsuitable for judicial decision. Instead, the Court held that a redrawing of electoral district lines designed to deprive Negroes of their vote violated the Fifteenth Amendment.[11]

[10] The key provisions of these acts can be found in Martin Shapiro, ed., *The Constitution of the United States and Related Documents* (Northbrook, Ill.: AHM Publishing Corp., 1973).

[11] Jo Desha Lucas, "Dragon in the Thicket: A Perusal of *Gomillion* v. *Lightfoot,*" *the Supreme Court Review* (1961), p. 243. For a readable step-by-step report on the case, see Bernard Taper, *Gomillion* v. *Lightfoot, the Tuskegee Gerrymander Case* (New York: McGraw-Hill, 1962).

Gomillion was decided in the relatively clear context of white majority discrimination against a black minority. By the 1970s the problems appeared more complex. We shall discuss many of them in the next few sections of this introduction. But electoral districting involves some special ones. First, nearly any set of district boundaries will help some economic, social, ethnic, religious, or racial voting blocs and hurt others. For any boundaries will split up some blocs into a number of districts in none of which they are in a majority and concentrate others in such strength that they control their district and elect whom they please. But may legislatures deliberately draw boundaries to give some of these blocs, particularly racial ones, one or more districts of their own?

If we admit as a constitutional matter that legislatures are permitted to take race into account in drawing voting district boundaries, when and how may they do so? May they choose to favor some racial or ethnic groups in this way and not others? May they choose to concentrate a racial group in one district to "help" it but not to "hurt" it? If it does not want to be concentrated or only if it wants to be? Does it really help a racial group more to concentrate it or disperse it? If concentrated in one district, it names its own spokesman to the legislature. But none of the other legislators care much about it. If split between a number of districts, a minority elects no spokesman of its own. But then a number of legislators may concern themselves with the minority's interests because each wants the votes of the minority members in his or her district. If blacks constitute 30 per cent of the population of a state, are they best off with a legislature that has 30 per cent black legislators and 70 per cent white ones who have no black voters in their district? Or are they better off with an all-white legislature in which every legislator knows that unless he or she helps blacks, he or she risks loosing 30 per cent of the votes in his or her district? No doubt, something in between would be best, with some black legislators to push black interests and many white legislators dependent on black voting support in their home districts. But does the Constitution require or allow such a mix and, if so, what mix? And how do we tell whether any particular change in the mix was designed to "help" or "hurt"?

Some of these problems are well illustrated by *United Jewish Organizations of Williamsburgh, Inc.* v. *Carey,* 430 U.S. 114 (1977). Certain counties of New York State fell under Section 5 of the Voting Rights Act of 1965. It requires that, where there is a past history of discrimination, state reapportionment plans be approved by the Attorney General or a federal district court in order to insure that they do not "deny or abridge the right to vote on account of race or color." Under pressure from the Attorney General, New York redrew boundaries to increase nonwhite majorities in four electoral districts so that there would be a better chance that nonwhites would be elected to the state legislature from those districts. In order to achieve this increase for nonwhites, the 30,000 Hasidic Jews who live in the Williamsburgh section of Brooklyn and who formerly all voted in one assembly and one Senate district would be split into two assembly districts and two Senate districts, thus having their voting strength diluted. From a powerful minority voting bloc in one assembly and one senate district, they would become weak voting blocs in two. The Jewish organizations argued that the new plan assigned voters to districts on the basis of race and thus violated the Fourteenth Amendment.

No clear majority position of the Court emerges. The general thrust seems to run in two directions. First, because whites were not fenced out of the electoral process altogether as blacks were in *Gomillion,* but only moved from one district to another, they have not been deprived of their vote in violation of the Fourteenth and Fifteenth Amendments. Second, New York used racial classification of voters as part of a bona fide effort to comply with the Voting Rights Act. Because all the Civil Rights Acts necessarily deal with race in the context of seeking to achieve racial equality, racial classifications may be used in their enforcement so long as the classifications are designed to achieve the purposes of the acts rather than to foster racial inequality. Thus the plan was upheld.

Justice Marshall did not participate, but presumably he would have joined with Justices White, Stevens, Brennan, and Blackmun, who held that "the permissible use of racial criteria is not confined to eliminating the effects of past discriminat[ion]." Only White and Stevens seem to commit themselves completely to affirmative government action that deliberately favors minorities over whites. Justices Stewart and Blackmun seem to evidence some hesitation at "benign discrimination" in view of the difficulty of determining when it is really benign and in the light of the racial ill will it may arouse among whites who are disfavored. Justice Rehnquist concurred on narrow grounds. Only Chief Justice Burger dissented.

The Court now seems to have held that while Section 1 of the Fifteenth Amendment only forbids purposeful discrimination against minority voters, Section 2 of the Amendment allows Congress to outlaw state election laws that do not purposefully discriminate but do have a disparate impact on minorities. [See *City of Mobile* v. *Bolden,* 446 U.S. 55 (1980) and *City of Rome* v. *United States,* 446 U.S. 156 (1980).]

One of the most complex problems facing the Court at the moment is that of multimember districts and at-large local elections. These systems raise the same problem of vote dilution as raised by the *Williamsburgh* case. If minority voters living clustered in a small area get a single-member district, they can easily elect a minority legislator or city council member. If they are thrown into a large multi-member district with a white majority, or their candidate must run in a city-wide election where most of the city is white, the chances of electing minority legislators and council members decline. This is an area where two bodies of law meet. One is the "one person one vote" rule of the Equal Protection Clause of the Fourteenth Amendment as enforced by court orders. The other is the Fifteenth Amendment's prohibition on racial discrimination in voting as enforced by the Voting Rights Act. It is also an area in which many electoral systems which may not have been chosen with the purpose of discriminating nevertheless have an adverse impact on minority voters. The Court has decided a fairly long string of cases but has not come to any clear policy in this area. [See *White* v. *Regester,* 412 U.S. 755 (1973); *Wise* v. *Lipscomb,* 437 U.S. 535 (1978); *City of Mobile* v. *Bolden,* 446 U.S. 55 (1980); *Uvalde School District* v. *United States,* 101 S.Ct. 2341 (1981); *Rogers* v. *Lodge,* 50 L.W. 5041 (1982).]

Race and Employment

In Chapter 5 we noted that the various civil rights statutes interact in subtle ways with the Thirteenth, Fourteenth, and Fifteenth Amendments. In looking at the *Williamsburgh Case,* we see that again, for a number of the justices seek to avoid the difficult problem of whether the amendments authorize or require "reverse discrimination" by emphasizing that New York's racial classifications were authorized and indeed necessitated by the Voting Rights Act.

In the employment area, a similar interaction occurs. The Court has generally refused to reach private discriminations by direct application of the Fourteenth Amendment. But as we have seen, it has upheld congressional regulation of private economic discrimination through the Civil Rights Acts. Where a public employer like a city government discriminates, it is, of course, subject directly to the Fourteenth Amendment. Where a private employer discriminates, it is subject to the provisions of various civil rights acts. As we have seen, the Act of 1866 (now 42 U.S.C. Sec. 1981 and 1982) is based on the Thirteenth Amendment and forbids discrimination in contracts that may include employment contracts. Title VII of the 1964 Act is based on the interstate commerce power of Congress and forbids racial discrimination in employment.

The interaction between constitutional and statutory provisions is illustrated and explained in *Washington* v. *Davis* (p. 544). This decision is important not only for its implications for various affirmative action employment programs (see Chapter 14) but also for its more general doctrine on how "purpose and intent" and "impact" are to be used in determining whether unconstitutional discrimination has occurred. As we have already seen earlier in this chapter, these doctrines are applicable in all areas of discrimination, not only in employment. A short excerpt from *Village of Arlington Heights* v. *Metropolitan Housing Development Corp.* (p. 547) is included, which sheds some additional light on these important doctrines. [See also *City of Memphis* v. *Greene,* 101 S.Ct. 1584 (1981).]

Two other important employment cases should be noted. In *Griggs* v. *Duke Power Co.,* 401 U.S. 424 (1971), the Court held that employment tests that result in disproportionate employment or promotions of whites must be shown to be job-related; that is, they must accurately indicate skills that are really necessary to performing the job for which the applicant is being considered. Otherwise, they violate Title VII. *McDonald* v. *Santa Fe Trail Trans. Co.,* 427 U.S. 272 (1976), involved three employees who allegedly stole cargo. The two whites were fired. The black was not. The Court found discrimination against the whites and found that that discrimination violated both Title VII and Sec. 1981.

The Court is currently experiencing great difficulty in working out a set of rules for deciding Title VII race and sex discrimination in employment cases. The rules are so unsettled that no concise description of them can be offered. In general the Court has been concerned with the following questions. Does the employment policy seem to deliberately discriminate—that is, purposely treat minorities and/or women less well than it treats others? If so, can the employer show that what appears to be discrimination is really not discriminatory but is a policy reasonably related to a legitimate business purpose? If the employment policy does not appear to directly discriminate, does it nevertheless have an adverse impact on the employment of minorities or women? If so, can the employer show that his policy is justified by business necessity? Must the plaintiff show that the employer intended to discriminate? Can the employer show that he didn't? How much evidence of discrimination does the plaintiff have to show before the burden of proof shifts to the employer to show that he had a legitimate purpose or business necessity? So far the justices remain in disagreement about who has to prove how much under Title VII. They are particularly unclear on just how far Title VII makes it illegal to use employment tests that are not intended to discriminate but that lead to a disproportionately low share of minority employment because minorities do poorly on the tests.[12] This issue is, of course, closely related to the problems of affirmative action. Because affirmative action involves sex as well as racial discrimination, it is the point where the old equal protection meets the new. Accordingly, consideration of affirmative action is postponed until the end of the introduction to Chapter 14.

Jury Selection

Many rights of the accused received constitutional vindication in contexts where the presence of racial discrimination was an important factor in triggering judicial intervention. (See the discussion of *Powell* v. *Alabama* and *Furman* v. *Georgia* in Chapter 15.) The area showing the clearest interrelationship of the equal protection and due process clauses is jury selection. In one of the earliest equal protection cases, *Strauder* v. *West Virginia,* 100 U.S. 303 (1880), the Court reversed the conviction of a Negro because state law required all-white juries. Since then the Court has been faced repeatedly with situations in which the administration of various jury-selection methods has allegedly resulted in discrimination—although Negro participation was not expressly prohibited. The Court has held that juries need not mathematically reflect the ratios of blacks to whites in the general population. In *Avery* v. *Georgia,* 345 U.S. 559 (1953),

[12] See *McDonnell Douglas Corp.* v. *Green,* 411 U.S. 792 (1973); *Albemarle Paper Co.* v. *Moody,* 422 U.S. 405 (1975); *Furnco Construction Corp.* v. *Waters,* 438 U.S. 567 (1978); *Board of Trustees* v. *Sweeney,* 439 U.S. 25 (1978).

the Court struck down a jury-selection system in which the names of whites were put on white tickets and Negroes on yellow. Both races were available for jury service, but in the panel of sixty persons drawn from these tickets for Avery's jury, none were Negro.

In *Swain* v. *Alabama,* 380 U.S. 202 (1965), blacks had actually served on grand juries, but none had served on trial juries during the preceding fifteen years. It was alleged that this was because the prosecutor consistently used his peremptory challenges to exclude blacks from trial juries. The Court refused to invalidate Swain's conviction, arguing that the presence of some Negroes on the panels, and the failure to offer sufficient evidence to prove that prosecutors consistently challenged all blacks, left the Court unable to conclude that discrimination had occurred.

In a number of recent cases, the Court has invalidated convictions where fairly clear proof of discrimination was offered. [See *Alexander* v. *Louisiana,* 405 U.S. 625 (1972).] *Swain,* however, is a reminder that covert discrimination in jury selection can be extremely difficult for the justices to reach so long as the Court does not require that juries mathematically reflect the racial composition of the community.

PLESSY *v.* FERGUSON

163 U.S. 537; 16 Sup. Ct. 1138; 41 L. Ed. 256 (1896)

[A Louisiana statute enacted in 1890 required railroads to provide "separate but equal" accommodations for white and colored passengers. A section of the statute further stipulated that train officials were to assign each passenger to "the coach or compartment used for the race to which such passenger belongs." Plessy, who was one-eighth Negro but appeared to be white, took a vacant seat in a railway coach reserved for white persons. He refused to give up his seat and was subsequently imprisoned to answer a charge of violating the statute. The Supreme Court of Louisiana held the statute valid. Plessy then brought the case to the Supreme Court on a writ of error. Ferguson was the judge of a local court in Louisiana that had ordered Plessy's imprisonment.]

MR. JUSTICE BROWN delivered the opinion of the Court:

The constitutionality of this act is attacked upon the ground that it conflicts both with the Thirteenth Amendment of the Constitution, abolishing slavery, and the Fourteenth Amendment, which prohibits certain restrictive legislation on the part of the States.

1. That it does not conflict with the Thirteenth Amendment, which abolished slavery and involuntary servitude, except as a punishment for crime, is too clear for argument. . . .

A statute which implies merely a legal distinction between the white and colored races—a distinction which is founded in the color of the two races, and which must always exist so long as white men are distinguished from the other race by color—has no tendency to destroy the legal equality of the two races, or reestablish a state of involuntary servitude. Indeed, we do not understand that the Thirteenth Amendment is strenuously relied upon by the plaintiff in error in this connection.

2. By the Fourteenth Amendment, all persons born or naturalized in the United

States, and subject to the jurisdiction thereof, are made citizens of the United States and of the State wherein they reside; and the States are forbidden from making or enforcing any law which shall abridge the privileges or immunities of citizens of the United States, or shall deprive any person of life, liberty, or property without due process of law, or deny to any person within their jurisdiction the equal protection of the laws. . . .

The object of the amendment was undoubtedly to enforce the absolute equality of the two races before the law, but in the nature of things it could not have been intended to abolish distinctions based upon color, or to enforce social, as distinguished from political equality, or a commingling of the two races upon terms unsatisfactory to either. Laws permitting, and even requiring, their separation in places where they are liable to be brought into contact do not necessarily imply the inferiority of either race to the other, and have been generally, if not universally, recognized as within the competency of the state legislatures in the exercise of their police power. The most common instance of this is connected with the establishment of separate schools for white and colored children, which has been held to be a valid exercise of the legislative power even by courts of States where the political rights of the colored race have been longest and most earnestly enforced.

. . . It is claimed by the plaintiff in error that, in any mixed community, the reputation of belonging to the dominant race, in this instance the white race, is *property,* in the same sense that a right of action, or of inheritance, is property. Conceding this to be so, for the purposes of this case, we are unable to see how this statute deprives him of, or in any way affects his rights to, such property. If he be a white man and assigned to a colored coach, he may have his action for damages against the company for being deprived of his so-called property. Upon the other hand, if he be a colored man and be so assigned, he has been deprived of no property, since he is not lawfully entitled to the reputation of being a white man.

In this connection, it is also suggested by the learned counsel for the plaintiff in error that the same argument that will justify the state legislature in requiring railways to provide separate accommodation for the two races will also authorize them to require separate cars to be provided for people whose hair is of a certain color, or who are aliens, or who belong to certain nationalities, or to enact laws requiring colored people to walk upon one side of the street, and white people upon the other, or requiring white men's houses to be painted white, and colored men's black, or their vehicles or business signs to be of different colors, upon the theory that one side of the street is as good as the other, or that a house or vehicle of one color is as good as one of another color. The reply to all this is that every exercise of the police power must be reasonable, and extend only to such laws as are enacted in good faith for the promotion of the public good, and not for the annoyance or oppression of a particular class. . . .

So far, then, as a conflict with the Fourteenth Amendment is concerned, the case reduces itself to the question whether the statute of Louisiana is a reasonable regulation, and with respect to this there must necessarily be a large discretion on the part of the legislature. In determining the question of reasonableness it is at liberty to act with reference to the established usages, customs, and traditions of the people, and with a view to the promotion of their comfort, and the preservation of the public peace and good order. Gauged by this standard, we cannot say that a law which authorizes or even requires the separation of the two races in public conveyances is unreasonable, or more obnoxious to the Fourteenth Amendment than the acts of Congress requiring separate schools for colored children in the District of Columbia, the constitutionality of which does not seem to have been questioned, or the corresponding acts of state legislatures.

We consider the underlying fallacy of the plaintiff's argument to consist in the assumption that the enforced separation of the two races stamps the colored race with a badge of inferiority. If this be so, it is not by reason of anything found in the act, but solely because the colored race chooses to put that construction upon it. The argument necessarily assumes that if, as has been more than once the case, and is not unlikely to be so again, the colored race should become the dominant power in the state legislature, and should enact a law in precisely similar terms, it would thereby relegate the white race to an inferior position. We imagine that the white race, at least, would not acquiesce in this assumption. The argument also assumes that social prejudices may be overcome by legislation, and that equal rights cannot be secured to the Negro except by an enforced commingling of the two races. We cannot accept this proposition. If the two races are to meet upon terms of social equality, it must be the result of natural affinities, a mutual appreciation of each other's merits, and a voluntary consent of individuals. . . . Legislation is powerless to eradicate racial instincts or to abolish distinctions based upon physical differences, and the attempt to do so can only result in accentuating the difficulties of the present situation. If the civil and political rights of both races be equal one cannot be inferior to the other civilly or politically. If one race be inferior to the other socially, the Constitution of the United States cannot put them upon the same plane.

. . . The judgment of the court below is therefore,

Affirmed.

MR. JUSTICE HARLAN, dissenting:

. . . It was said in argument that the statute of Louisiana does not discriminate against either race, but prescribes a rule applicable alike to white and colored citizens. But this argument does not meet the difficulty. Everyone knows that the statute in question had its origin in the purpose, not so much to exclude white persons from railroad cars occupied by blacks, as to exclude colored people from coaches occupied by or assigned to white persons. Railroad corporations of Louisiana did not make discrimination among whites in the matter of accommodation for travelers. The thing to accomplish was, under the guise of giving equal accommodation for whites and blacks, to compel the latter to keep to themselves while travelling in railroad passenger coaches. No one would be so wanting in candor as to assert the contrary. The fundamental objection, therefore, to the statute is that it interferes with the personal freedom of citizens . . . If a white man and a black man choose to occupy the same public conveyance on a public highway, it is their right to do so, and no government, proceeding alone on grounds of race, can prevent it without infringing the personal liberty of each.

. . . The white race deems itself to be the dominant race in this country. And so it is, in prestige, in achievements, in education, in wealth, and in power. So I doubt not, it will continue to be for all time, if it remains true to its great heritage and holds fast to the principles of constitutional liberty. But in view of the Constitution, in the eye of the law, there is in this country no superior, dominant, ruling class of citizens. There is no caste here. Our Constitution is color-blind, and neither knows nor tolerates classes among citizens. In respect of civil rights, all citizens are equal before the law. The humblest is the peer of the most powerful. The law regards man as man, and takes no account of his surroundings or of his color when his civil rights as guaranteed by the supreme law of the land are involved. It is, therefore, to be regretted that this high tribunal, the final expositor of the fundamental law of the land, has reached the conclusion that it is competent for a state to regulate the enjoyment by citizens of their civil rights solely upon the basis of race.

. . . The sure guaranty of the peace and security of each race is the clear, distinct, unconditional recognition by our governments, National and State, of every right that inheres in civil freedom, and of the equality before the law of all citizens of the United States without regard to race. State enactments regulating the enjoyment of civil rights upon the basis of race, and cunningly devised to defeat legitimate results of the war, under the pretence of recognizing equality of rights, can have no other result than to render permanent peace impossible, and to keep alive a conflict of races, the continuance of which must do harm to all concerned. . . .

The arbitrary separation of citizens on the basis of race, while they are on a public highway, is a badge of servitude wholly inconsistent with the civil freedom and the equality before the law established by the Constitution. It cannot be justified upon any legal grounds.

If evils will result from the commingling of the two races upon public highways established for the benefit of all, they will be infinitely less than those that will surely come from state legislation regulating the enjoyment of civil rights upon the basis of race. We boast of the freedom enjoyed by our people above all other peoples. But it is difficult to reconcile that boast with a state of the law which, practically, puts the brand of servitude and degradation upon a large class of our fellow-citizens, our equals before the law. The thin disguise of "equal" accommodations for passengers in railroad coaches will not mislead any-one, nor atone for the wrong this day done. . . .

I am of the opinion that the statute of Louisiana is inconsistent with the personal liberty of citizens, white and black, in that State, and hostile to both the spirit and letter of the Constitution of the United States. . . .

For the reasons stated, I am constrained to withhold my assent from the opinion and judgment of the majority.

MR. JUSTICE BREWER did not hear the argument or participate in the decision of this case.

SWEATT *v.* PAINTER

339 U.S. 629; 70 Sup. Ct. 848; 94 L. Ed. 1114 (1950)

[Sweatt was denied admission to the University of Texas Law School solely because he was colored, admission of Negroes to the school being prohibited by state law even though there was no law school for Negroes in Texas at the time. Sweatt brought a suit for mandamus against Painter and other school officials to compel his admission. A trial court recognized that Sweatt was denied the equal protection of the laws guaranteed by the Fourteenth Amendment because he had no opportunity for the study of law. However, the court refused to issue the mandamus; instead, the case was continued for six months to give Texas time to provide equal training facilities in law for Negroes. After the six months' period, the university revealed that a law school for Negroes would be opened within two months. The court then denied the writ of mandamus. However, Sweatt refused to enter the new law school and continued his original action for mandamus. The Texas courts denied the mandamus on the ground that substantially equal facilities were provided in the Negro law school. Sweatt then brought the case to the Supreme Court on a writ of certiorari.]

MR. CHIEF JUSTICE VINSON delivered the opinion of the Court:

This case and *McLaurin* v. *Oklahoma State Regents* . . . present different aspects of this general question: To what extent does the Equal Protection Clause of the Fourteenth Amendment limit the power of a state to distinguish between students of different races in professional and graduate education in a state university? Broader issues have been urged for our consideration, but we adhere to the principle of deciding constitutional questions only in the context of the particular case before the Court. We have frequently reiterated that this Court will decide constitutional questions only when necessary to the disposition of the case at hand, and that such decisions will be drawn as narrowly as possible. . . .

The University of Texas Law School, from which petitioner was excluded, was staffed by a faculty of sixteen full-time and three part-time professors, some of whom are nationally recognized authorities in their field. Its student body numbered 850. The library contained over 65,000 volumes. Among the other facilities available to the students were a law review, moot-court facilities, scholarship funds, and Order of the Coif affiliation. The school's alumni occupy the most distinguished positions in the private practice of the law and in the public life of the State. It may properly be considered one of the nation's ranking law schools.

The law school for Negroes which was to have opened in February, 1947, would have had no independent faculty or library. The teaching was to be carried on by four members of the University of Texas Law School faculty, who were to maintain their offices at the University of Texas while teaching at both institutions. Few of the 10,000 volumes ordered for the library had arrived; nor was there any full-time librarian. The school lacked accreditation.

Since the trial of this case, respondents report the opening of a law school at the Texas State University for Negroes. It is apparently on the road to full accreditation. It has a faculty of five full-time professors; a student body of twenty-three; a library of some 16,500 volumes serviced by a full-time staff; a practice court and legal aid association; and one alumnus who has become a member of the Texas bar.

Whether the University of Texas Law School is compared with the original or the new law school for Negroes, we cannot find substantial equality in the educational opportunities offered white and Negro law students by the State. In terms of number of the faculty, variety of courses and opportunity for specialization, size of the student body, scope of the library, availability of law review and similar activities, the University of Texas Law School is superior. What is more important, the University of Texas Law School possesses to a far greater degree those qualities which are incapable of objective measurement but which make for greatness in a law school. Such qualities, to name but a few, include reputation of the faculty, experience of the administration, position and influence of the alumni, standing in the community, traditions and prestige. It is difficult to believe that one who had a free choice between these law schools would consider the question close.

Moreover, although the law is a highly learned profession, we are well aware that it is an intensely practical one. The law school, the proving ground for legal learning and practice, cannot be effective in isolation from the individuals and institutions with which the law interacts. Few students and no one who has practiced law would choose to study in an academic vacuum, removed from the interplay of ideas and the exchange of views with which the law is concerned. The law school to which Texas is willing to admit petitioner excludes from its student body members of the racial groups which number 85 per cent of the population of the State and include most of the lawyers, witnesses, jurors, judges, and other officials with whom petitioner will inevitably be dealing when he becomes a member of the Texas bar. With such a substantial and significant segment of society excluded, we cannot conclude that the education offered petitioner is substantially equal to that which he would receive if admitted to the University of Texas Law School.

It may be argued that excluding petitioner from that school is no different from excluding white students from the new law school. This contention overlooks realities. It is unlikely that a member of a group so decisively in the majority, attending a school with rich traditions and prestige which only a history of consistently maintained excellence could command, would claim that the opportunities afforded him for legal education were unequal to those held open to petitioner. That such a claim, if made, would be dishonored by the State, is no answer. "Equal protection of the laws is not achieved through indiscriminate imposition of inequalities."

. . . [P]etitioner may claim his full constitutional right: legal education equivalent to that offered by the State to students of other races. Such education is not available to him in a separate law school as offered by the State. We cannot, therefore, agree with respondents that the doctrine of *Plessy* v. *Ferguson* . . . requires affirmance of the judgment below. Nor need we reach petitioner's contention that *Plessy* v. *Ferguson* should be re-examined in the light of contemporary knowledge respecting the purposes of the Fourteenth Amendment and the effects of racial segregation. . . .

We hold that the Equal Protection Clause of the Fourteenth Amendment requires that petitioner be admitted to the University of Texas Law School. The judgment is reversed and the case is remanded for proceedings not inconsistent with this opinion.

Reversed.

BROWN et al. *v.* BOARD OF EDUCATION
347 U.S. 483; 74 Sup. Ct. 693; 98 L. Ed. 591 (1954)

MR. CHIEF JUSTICE WARREN delivered the opinion of the Court:

These cases come to us from the States of Kansas, South Carolina, Virginia, and Delaware. They are premised on different facts and different local conditions, but a common legal question justifies their consideration together in this consolidated opinion.

In each of the cases, minors of the Negro race, through their legal representatives, seek the aid of the courts in obtaining admission to the public schools of their community on a nonsegregated basis. In each instance, they had been denied admission to schools attended by white children under laws requiring or permitting segregation according to race. This segregation was alleged to deprive the plaintiffs of the equal protection of the laws under the Fourteenth Amendment. In each of the cases other than the Delaware case, a three-judge federal district court denied relief to the plaintiffs on the so-called "separate but equal" doctrine announced by this Court in *Plessy* v. *Ferguson*. . . .

The plaintiffs contend that segregated public schools are not "equal" and cannot be made "equal," and that hence they are deprived of the equal protection of the laws. Because of the obvious importance of the question presented, the Court took jurisdiction. Argument was heard in the 1952 Term, and reargument was heard this Term on certain questions propounded by the Court.

Reargument was largely devoted to the circumstances surrounding the adoption of the Fourteenth Amendment in 1868. It covered exhaustively consideration of the Amendment in Congress, ratification by the states, then existing practices in racial segregation, and the view of the proponents and opponents of the Amendment.This discussion and our own investigation convince us that, although these sources cast some light, it is not enough to resolve the problem with which we are faced. At best, they are inconclusive. The most avid proponents of the postwar Amendments undoubtedly intended them to remove all legal distinctions among "all persons born or naturalized in the United States." Their opponents, just as certainly, were antagonistic to both the letter and the spirit of the Amendments and wished them to have the most limited effect. What others in Congress and the state legislatures had in mind cannot be determined with any degree of certainty.

An additional reason for the inclusive nature of the Amendment's history, with respect to segregated schools, is the status of public education at that time. In the South, the movement toward free common schools, supported by general taxation, had not yet taken hold. Education of white children was largely in the hands of private groups. Education of Negroes was almost nonexistent, and practically all of the race were illiterate. In fact, any education of Negroes was forbidden by law in some states. Today, in contrast, many Negroes have achieved outstanding success in the arts and science as well as in the business and professional world. It is true that public education had already advanced further in the North, but the effect of the Amendment on northern states was generally ignored in the congressional debates. Even in the North, the conditions of public education did not approximate those existing today. The curriculum was usually rudimentary; ungraded schools were common in rural areas; the school term was but three months a year in many states; and compulsory school attendance was virtually unknown. As a consequence, it is not surprising that there should be so little in the history of the Fourteenth Amendment relating to its intended effect on public education.

In the first cases in this Court construing the Fourteenth Amendment, decided shortly after its adoption, the Court interpreted it as proscribing all state-imposed discriminations against the Negro race. The doctrine of "separate but equal" did not make its appearance in this Court until 1896 in the case of *Plessy* v. *Ferguson, supra,* involving not education but transportation. American courts have since labored with the doctrine for over half a century. In this Court, there have been six cases involving the "separate but equal" doctrine in the field of public education. In *Cummings* v. *County Board of Education,* 175 U.S. 528, and *Gong Lum* v. *Rice,* 275 U.S. 78, the validity of the doctrine itself was not challenged. In more recent cases, all on the graduate-school level, inequality was found in that specific benefits enjoyed by white students were denied to Negro students of the same educational qualifications. *Missouri* ex rel. *Gaines* v. *Canada,* 305 U.S. 337; *Sipuel* v. *Oklahoma,* 332 U.S. 631; *Sweatt* v. *Painter,* 339 U.S. 629; *McLaurin* v. *Oklahoma State Regents,* 339 U.S. 637. In none of these cases was it necessary to re-examine the doctrine to grant relief to the Negro plaintiff. And in *Sweatt* v. *Painter,* . . . the Court expressly reserved decision on the question whether *Plessy* v. *Ferguson* should be held inapplicable to public education.

In the instant cases, that question is directly presented. Here, unlike *Sweatt* v. *Painter,* there are findings below that the Negro and white schools involved have been equalized, or are being equalized, with respect to buildings, curricula, qualifications and salaries of teachers, and other "tangible" factors. Our decision, therefore, cannot turn on merely a comparison of these tangible factors in the Negro and white schools involved in each of the cases. We must look instead to the effect of segregation itself on public education.

In approaching this problem, we cannot turn the clock back to 1868 when the Amendment was adopted, or even to 1896 when *Plessy* v. *Ferguson* was written. We must consider public education in the light of its full development and its present place in American life throughout the Nation. Only in this way can it be determined if segregation in public schools deprives these plaintiffs of the equal protection of the laws.

Today, education is perhaps the most important function of state and local governments. Compulsory school-attendance laws and the great expenditures for education both demonstrate our recognition of the importance of education to our democratic society. It is required in the performance of our most basic public responsibilities, even service in the armed forces. It is the very foundation of good citizenship. Today it is a principal instrument in awakening the child to cultural values, in preparing him for later professional training, and in helping him to adjust normally to his environment. In these days, it is doubtful any child may reasonably be expected to succeed in life if he is denied the opportunity of an education. Such an opportunity, where the state has undertaken to provide it, is a right which must be made available to all on equal terms.

We come then to the question presented: Does segregation of children in public schools solely on the basis of race, even though the physical facilities and other "tangible" factors may be equal, deprive the children of the minority group of equal educational opportunities? We believe that it does.

In *Sweatt* v. *Painter,* . . . in finding that a segregated law school for Negroes could not provide them equal educational opportunities, this Court relied in large part on "those qualities which are incapable of objective measurement but which make for greatness in a law school." In *McLaurin* v. *Oklahoma State Regents,* . . . the Court, in requiring that a Negro admitted to a white graduate school be treated like all other students, again resorted to intangible considerations: ". . . his ability to study, to engage in discussions and exchange views with other students, and, in general, to learn his profession." Such considerations apply with added force to children in grade and high schools. To separate them from others of similar age and qualifications solely because of their race generates a feeling of inferiority as to their status in the community that may affect their hearts and minds in a way unlikely ever to be undone. The effect of this separation on their educational opportunities was well stated by a finding in the Kansas case by a court which nevertheless felt compelled to rule against the Negro plaintiffs:

> "Segregation of white and colored children in public schools has a detrimental effect upon the colored children. The impact is greater when it has the sanction of the law; for the policy of separating the races is usually interpreted as denoting the inferiority of the Negro group. A sense of inferiority affects the motivation of a child to learn. Segregation with the sanction of law, therefore, has a tendency to retard the educational and mental development of Negro children and to deprive them of some of the benefits they would receive in a racially integrated school system."

Whatever may have been the extent of psychological knowledge at the time of *Plessy* v. *Ferguson,* this finding is amply supported by modern authority. Any language in *Plessy* v. *Ferguson* contrary to this finding is rejected.

We conclude that in the field of public education the doctrine of "separate but equal" has no place. Separate educational facilities are inherently unequal. Therefore, we hold that the plaintiffs and others similarly situated for whom the actions have been brought are, by reason of the segregation complained of, deprived of the equal protection of the laws guaranteed by the Fourteenth Amendment. This disposition makes unnecessary any discussion whether such segregation also violates the Due Process Clause of the Fourteenth Amendment.

Because these are class actions, because of the wide applicability of this decision, and because of the great variety of local conditions, the formulation of decrees in these cases presents problems of considerable complexity. On reargument, the consideration of appropriate relief was necessarily subordinated to the primary question—the constitutionality of segregation in public education. We have now announced that such segregation is a denial of the equal protection of the laws. In order that we may have the full assistance of the parties in formulating decrees, the cases will be restored to the docket, and the parties are requested to present further argument on Questions 4 and 5 previously propounded by the Court for the reargument this Term.* The Attorney General of the United States is again invited to participate. The Attorneys General of the states requiring or permitting segregation in public education will also be permitted to appear as *amici curiae* [friends of the Court who give advice on matters pending before it] upon request to do so by September 15, 1954, and submission of briefs by October 1, 1954.

It is so ordered.

* "4. Assuming it is decided that segregation in public shools violates the Fourteenth Amendment.

"(a) would a decree necessarily follow providing that, within the limits set by normal geographic school districting, Negro children should forthwith be admitted to schools of their choice, or

"(b) may this Court, in the exercise of its equity powers, permit an effective gradual adjustment to be brought about from existing segregated systems to a system not based on color distinctions?

"5. On the assumption on which questions 4(a) and (b) are based, and assuming further that this Court will exercise its equity powers to the end described in question 4(b),

"(a) should this Court formulate detailed decrees in these cases;

"(b) if so, what specific issues should decrees reach;

"(c) should this Court appoint a special master to hear evidence with a view to recommending specific terms for such decrees;

"(d) should this Court remand to the courts of first instance with directions to frame decrees in these cases, and if so, what general directions should the decrees of this Court include and what procedures should the courts of first instance follow in arriving at the specific terms of more detailed decrees?"

BROWN *v.* BOARD OF EDUCATION (Second Case)
349 U.S. 294; 75 Sup. Ct. 753; 99 L. Ed. 1083 (1955)

MR. CHIEF JUSTICE WARREN delivered the opinion of the Court:

These cases were decided on May 17, 1954. The opinions of that date, declaring the fundamental principle that racial discrimination in public education is unconstitutional, are incorporated herein by reference. All provisions of federal, state, or local law requiring or permitting such discrimination must yield to this principle. There remains for consideration the manner in which relief is to be accorded. . . .

Full implementation of these constitutional principles may require solution of varied local school problems. School authorities have the primary responsibility for elucidating, assessing, and solving these problems; courts will have to consider whether the action of school authorities constitutes good faith implementation of the governing constitutional principles. Because of their proximity to local conditions and the possible need for further hearings, the courts which originally heard these cases can best perform this judicial appraisal. Accordingly, we believe it appropriate to remand the cases to those courts.

In fashioning and effectuating the decrees, the courts will be guided by equitable principles. Traditionally, equity has been characterized by a practical flexibility in shaping its remedies and by a facility for adjusting and reconciling public and private needs. These cases call for the exercise of these traditional attributes of equity power. At stake is the personal interest of the plaintiffs in admission to public schools as soon as practicable on a nondiscriminatory basis. To effectuate this interest may call for elimination of a variety of obstacles in making the transition to school systems operated in accordance with the constitutional principles set forth in our May 17, 1954, decision. Courts of equity may properly take into account the public interest in the elimination of such obstacles in a systematic and effective manner. But it should go without saying that the vitality of these constitutional principles cannot be allowed to yield simply because of disagreement with them.

While giving weight to these public and private considerations, the courts will require that the defendants make a prompt and reasonable start toward full compliance with our May 17, 1954, ruling. Once such a start has been made, the courts may find that additional time is necessary to carry out the ruling in an effective manner. The burden rests upon the defendants to establish that such time is necessary in the public interest and is consistent with good faith compliance at the earliest practicable date. To that end, the courts may consider problems related to administration, arising from the physical condition of the school plant, the school transportation system, personnel, revision of school district and attendance areas into compact units to achieve a system of determining admission to the public schools on a nonracial basis, and revision of local laws and regulations which may be necessary in solving the foregoing problems. They will also consider the adequacy of any plans the defendants may propose to meet these problems and to effectuate a transition to a racially nondiscriminatory school system. During this period of transition, the courts will retain jurisdiction of these cases. . . .

The . . . cases are remanded to the district courts to take such proceedings and enter such orders and decrees consistent with this opinion as are necessary and proper to admit to public schools on on a racially nondiscriminatory basis with all deliberate speed the parties to these cases. . . .

It is so ordered.

SWANN *v.* CHARLOTTE-MECKLENBURG BOARD OF EDUCATION
402 U.S. 1; 91 Sup. Ct. 1267; 28 L. Ed. 2d 554 (1971)

[The City of Charlotte is in Mecklenburg County, North Carolina. City and county operate a unified school system. Litigation had gone on for many years before this case reached

the Supreme Court. The district court had rejected a number of desegregation plans proposed by the school board. Convinced that the board was not acting in good faith, the court appointed its own expert and accepted the plan he proposed. The fourth circuit set aside the district court plan and ordered further proceedings. Several new plans were proposed, but the school board was not willing to accept any of them. The district court then reimposed its own plan.]

MR. CHIEF JUSTICE BURGER delivered the opinion of the Court:

This case . . . arose in states having a long history of maintaining two sets of schools in a single school system deliberately operated to carry out a governmental policy to separate pupils in schools solely on the basis of race. That was what *Brown* v. *Board of Education* was all about. These cases present us with the problem of defining in more precise terms than heretofore the scope of the duty of school authorities and district courts in implementing *Brown I*. . . .

The problems encountered by the district courts and courts of appeals make plain that we should now try to amplify guidelines, however incomplete and imperfect, for the assistance of school authorities and courts. The failure of local authorities to meet their constitutional obligations aggravated the massive problem of converting from the state-enforced discrimination of racially separate school systems. This process has been rendered more difficult by changes since 1954 in the structure and patterns of communities, the growth of student population, movement of families, and other changes, some of which had marked impact on school planning, sometimes neutralizing or negating remedial action before it was fully implemented. Rural areas accustomed for half a century to the consolidated school systems implemented by bus transportation could make adjustments more readily than metropolitan areas with dense and shifting population, numerous schools, congested and complex traffic patterns.

The objective today remains to eliminate from the public schools all vestiges of state-imposed segregation. . . . If school authorities fail in their affirmative obligations under [our earlier] holdings, judicial authority may be invoked. Once a right and a violation have been shown, the scope of a district court's equitable powers to remedy past wrongs is broad, for breadth and flexibility are inherent in equitable remedies. . . .In seeking to define even in broad and general terms how far this remedial power extends it is important to remember that judicial powers may be exercised only on the basis of a constitutional violation. . . . Judicial authority enters only when local authority defaults.

School authorities are traditionally charged with broad power to formulate and implement educational policy and might well conclude, for example, that in order to prepare students to live in a pluralistic society each school should have a prescribed ratio of Negro to white students reflecting the proportion for the district as a whole. To do this as an educational policy is within the broad discretionary powers of school authorities; absent a finding of a constitutional violation, however, that would not be within the authority of a federal court. . . .

The basis of our decision must be the prohibition of the Fourteenth Amendment that no State shall "deny to any person within its jurisdiction the equal protection of the laws."

We turn now to the problem of defining with more particularity the responsibilities of school authorities in desegregating a state-enforced dual school system in light of the Equal Protection Clause. Although the several related cases before us are primarily concerned with problems of student assignment, it may be helpful to begin with a brief discussion of other aspects of the process.

. . . Independent of student assignment, where it is possible to identify a "white school" or a "Negro school" simply by reference to the racial composition of teachers and staff, the quality of school buildings and equipment, or the organization of sports activities, a prima facie case of violation of substantive constitutional rights under the Equal Protection Clause is shown. . . . In the companion *Davis* case, the Mobile school board has argued that the Constitution requires that teachers be assigned on a "color blind" basis. It also argues that the Constitution prohibits district courts from using their equity power to order assignment of teachers to achieve a particular degree of faculty desegregation. We reject that contention. . . .

The construction of new schools and the closing of old ones is one of the most important functions of local school authorities and also one of the most complex. . . . The result of this will be a decision which, when combined with one technique or another of student assignment, will determine the racial composition of the student body in each school in the system. . . . The location of schools [may] influence the patterns of residential development of a metropolitan area and have important impact on composition of inner city neighborhoods. In the past, choices in this respect have been used as a potent weapon for creating or maintaining a state-segregated school system. . . . Upon a proper showing a district court may consider this in fashioning a remedy. . . . In devising remedies where legally imposed segregation has been established, it is the responsibility of local authorities and district courts to see to it that future school construction and abandonment is not used and does not serve to perpetuate or re-establish the dual system. . . .

The central issue in this case is that of student assignment, and there are essentially four problem areas: . . .

1. *Racial Balances or Racial Quotas* . . .

We are concerned in these cases with the elimination of the discrimination inherent in the dual school systems, not with myriad factors of human existence which can cause discrimination in a multitude of ways on racial, religious, or ethnic grounds. The target of the cases from *Brown I* to the present was the dual school system. The elimination of racial discrimination in public schools is a large task and one that should not be retarded by efforts to achieve broader purposes lying beyond the jurisdiction of school activities. One vehicle can carry only a limited amount of baggage. It would not serve the important objective of *Brown I* to seek to use school desegregation cases for purposes beyond their scope, although desegregation of schools ultimately will have impact on other forms of discrimination. We do not reach in this case the question whether a showing that school segregation is a consequence of other types of state action, without any discriminatory action by the school authorities, is a constitutional violation requiring remedial action by a school desegregation decree. This case does not present that question and we therefore do not decide it. . . .

In this case it is urged that the District Court has imposed a racial balance requirement of 71 to 29 per cent on individual schools. [Its decision] contains intimations that the "norm" is a fixed mathematical racial balance reflecting the pupil constituency of the system. If we were to read the holding of the District Court to require, as a matter of substantive constitutional right, any particular degree of racial balance or mixing, that approach would be disapproved and we would be obliged to reverse. The constitutional command to desegregate schools does not mean that every school in every community must always reflect the racial composition of the school system as a whole.

[Here] the use made of mathematical ratios was no more than a starting point in the process of shaping a remedy, rather than an inflexible requirement. . . . As we said in *Green,* a school authority's remedial plan or a district court's remedial decree is to be judged by its effectiveness. Awareness of the racial composition of the whole school system is likely to be a useful starting point in shaping a remedy to correct past constitutional violations. In sum, the very limited use made of mathematical ratios was within the equitable remedial discretion of the District Court.

2. *One-Race Schools*

The record in this case reveals the familiar phenomenon that in metropolitan areas minority groups are often found concentrated in one part of the city. In some circumstances, certain schools may remain all or largely of one race until new schools can be provided or neighborhood patterns change. Schools all or predominantly of one race in a district of mixed population will require close scrutiny to determine that school assignments are not part of state-enforced segregation.

In light of the above, it should be clear

that the existence of some small number of one-race, or virtually one race, schools within a district is not in and of itself the mark of a system which still practices segregation by law. [But the] court should scrutinize such schools, and the burden upon the school authorities will be to satisfy the court that their racial composition is not the result of present or past discriminatory action on their part.

An optional majority-to-minority transfer provision has long been recognized as a useful part of every desegregation plan. Provision for optional transfer of those in the majority racial group of a particular school to other schools where they will be in the minority is an indispensable remedy for those students willing to transfer to other schools in order to lessen the impact on them of the state-imposed stigma of segregation. In order to be effective, such a transfer arrangement must grant the transferring student free transportation and space must be made available in the school to which he desires to move. . . .

3. *Remedial Altering of Attendance Zones*

The maps submitted in these cases graphically demonstrate that one of the principal tools employed by school planners and by courts to break up the dual school system has been a frank—and sometimes drastic—gerrymandering of school districts and attendance zones. An additional step was pairing, "clustering," or "grouping" of schools with attendance assignments made deliberately to accomplish the transfer of Negro students out of formerly segregated Negro schools and transfer of white students to formerly all-Negro schools. More often than not, these zones are neither compact nor contiguous; indeed they may be on opposite ends of the city. As an interim corrective measure, this cannot be said to be beyond the broad remedial powers of a court.

Absent a constitutional violation there would be no basis for judicially ordering assigment of students on a racial basis. All things being equal, with no history of discrimination, it might well be desirable to assign pupils to schools nearest their homes. But all things are not equal in a system that has been deliberately constructed and maintained to enforce racial segregation. The remedy for such segregation may be administratively awkward, inconvenient and even bizarre in some situations and may impose burdens on some; but all awkwardness and inconvenience cannot be avoided in the interim period when remedial adjustments are being made to eliminate the dual school systems.

No fixed or even substantially fixed guidelines can be established as to how far a court can go, but it must be recognized that there are limits. The objective is to dismantle the dual school system. "Racially neutral" assignment plans proposed by school authorities to a district court may be inadequate; such plans may fail to counteract the continuing effects of past school segregation resulting from discriminatory location of school sites or distortion of school size in order to achieve or maintain an artificial racial separation. When school authorities present a district court with a "loaded game board," affirmative action in the form of remedial altering of attendance zones is proper to achieve truly nondiscriminatory assignments. . . . We hold that the pairing and grouping of noncontiguous school zones is a permissible tool and such action is to be considered in light of the objectives sought. . . .

4. *Transportation of Students*

[It is not possible to construct rigid standards] of permissible transportation of students as an implement of a remedial decree. . . . Bus transportation has been an integral part of the public education system for years. . . . Eighteen million of the nation's public school children, approximately 39 per cent, were transported to their schools by bus in 1969–1970 in all parts of the country.

The importance of bus transportation as a normal and accepted tool of educational policy is readily discernible in this and the companion case. . . . The decree provided that the . . . trips for elementary school pupils average about seven miles and the District Court found that they would take "not over 35 minutes at the most." This system compares favorably with the transportation plan previously operated in Charlotte under which each day 23,600 students on all grade levels were transported an average of 15 miles one way for an average trip requiring over an hour. In these circumstances, we find no basis for holding that the local school authorities may not be required to employ bus transportation as one tool of school desegregation. Desegregation plans cannot be limited to the walk-in school.

An objection to transportation of students may have validity when the time or distance of travel is so great as to risk either the health of the children or significantly impinge on the educational process. District courts must weigh the soundness of any transportation plan in light of what is said in subdivisions (1), (2), and (3) above. . . . The reconciliation of competing values in a desegregation case is, of course, a difficult task with many sensitive facets but fundamentally no more so than remedial measures courts of equity have traditionally employed.

. . . On the facts of this case, we are unable to conclude that the order of the District Court is not reasonable, feasible and workable. However, in seeking to define the scope of remedial power or the limits on remedial power of courts in an area as sensitive as we deal with here, words are poor instruments to convey the sense of basic fairness inherent in equity. Substance, not semantics, must govern, and we have sought to suggest the nature of limitations without frustrating the appropriate scope of equity.

At some point, these school authorities and others like them should have achieved full compliance with this Court's decision in *Brown I.* The systems will then be "unitary" in the sense required by our decisions in *Green* and *Alexander.*

It does not follow that the communities served by such systems will remain demographically stable, for in a growing, mobile society, few will do so. Neither school authorities nor district courts are constitutionally required to make year-by-year adjustments of the racial composition of student bodies once the affirmative duty to desegregate has been accomplished and racial discrimination through official action is eliminated from the system. This does not mean that federal courts are without power to deal with future problems, but in the absence of a showing that either the school authorities or some other agency of the State has deliberately attempted to fix or alter demographic patterns to affect the racial composition of the schools, further intervention by a district court should not be necessary.

MILLIKEN *v.* BRADLEY

418 U.S. 717; 94 Sup. Ct. 3112; 41 L. Ed. 2d 1069 (1974)

[Milliken was governor of Michigan; and Bradley, the parent of a Detroit school child.]

MR. CHIEF JUSTICE BURGER delivered the opinion of the Court.

We granted certiorari in these consolidated cases to determine whether a federal court may impose a multidistrict, areawide remedy to a single district *de jure* segregation problem absent any finding that the other included school districts have failed to operate unitary school systems within their districts, absent any claim or finding that the boundary lines of any affected school district were established with the purpose of fostering racial segregation in public schools, [and] absent any finding that the included districts committed acts which affected segregation within the other districts, . . .

I

The action was commenced in August of 1970 by the respondents, the Detroit Branch of the National Association for the Advancement of Colored People and individual parents and students, on behalf of a class . . . defined . . . to include "all school children of the City of Detroit and all Detroit resident parents who have children of school age." . . .

. . . The complaint alleged that the Detroit Public School System was and is segregated on the basis of race as a result of the official policies and actions of the defendants and their predecessors in office, and called for the implementation of a plan that would eliminate "the racial identity of every school in the [Detroit] system and . . . maintain now and hereafter a unitary nonracial school system." . . . On September 27, 1971, the District Court issued its findings and conclusions on the issue of segregation finding that "Government actions and inactions at all levels, federal, state and local, have combined, with those of private organizations, such as loaning institutions and real estate associations and brokerage firms, to establish and to maintain the pattern of residential segregation throughout the Detroit metropolitan area." *Bradley* v. *Milliken,* 338 F. Supp. 582, 587 (ED Mich. 1971). While still addressing a Detroit-only violation, the District Court reasoned:

> "While it would be unfair to charge the present defendants with what other governmental officers or agencies have done, it can be said that the actions or the failure to act by the responsible school authorities, both city and state, were linked to that of these other governmental units. When we speak of governmental action we should not view the different agencies as a collection of unrelated units. Perhaps the most that can be said is that all of them, including the school authorities, are, in part, responsible for the segregated conditions which exist. And we note that just as there is an interaction between residential patterns and the racial composition of the schools, so there is a corresponding effect on the residential pattern by the racial composition of the schools." 338 F. Supp., at 587. . . .

The District Court found that the Detroit Board of Education created and maintained optional attendance zones within Detroit neighborhoods undergoing racial transition and between high school attendance areas of opposite predominant racial compositions. These zones, the court found, had the "natural, probable, foreseeable and actual effect" of allowing White pupils to escape identifiably Negro schools. Similarly, the District Court found that Detroit school attendance zones had been drawn along north-south boundary lines despite the Detroit Board's awareness that drawing boundary lines in an east-west direction would result in significantly greater desegregation. Again, the District Court concluded, the natural and actual effect of these acts was the creation and perpetuation of school segregation within Detroit.

The District Court found that in the operation of its school transportation program, which was designed to relieve overcrowding, the Detroit Board had admittedly bused Negro Detroit pupils to predominantly Negro schools which were beyond or away from closer White schools with available space. . . . This practice was found to have continued in recent years despite the Detroit Board's avowed policy, adopted in 1967, of utilizing transportation to increase desegregation. . . .

With respect to the Detroit Board of Education's practices in school construction, the District Court found that Detroit school construction generally tended to have segregative effect. . . . Thus, of the 14 schools which opened for use in 1970–1971, 11 opened over 90% Negro and one opened less than 10% Negro.

The District Court also found that the State of Michigan had committed several constitutional violations with respect to the exercise of its general responsibility for, and supervision of, public education. The State, for example, was found to have failed, until the 1971 Session of the Michigan Legislature, to provide authorization or funds for the transportation of pupils within Detroit regardless of their poverty or distance from the school to which they were assigned; during this same period the State provided many neighboring, mostly White, suburban districts the full range of state supported transportation. . . .

The District Court also held that the acts of the Detroit Board of Education, as a subordinate entity of the State, were attributable to the State of Michigan, thus creating a vicarious liability on the part of the State. Under Michigan law, Mich. Stat. Ann. § 15, 1961, for example, school building construction plans had to be approved by the State Board of Education, and prior to 1962, the State Board had specific statutory authority to supervise school site selection. The proofs concerning the effect of Detroit's school construction program were, therefore, found to be largely applicable to show State responsibility for the segregative results. . . .

During the period from March 28, 1972 to April 14, 1972, the District Court conducted hearings on a metropolitan plan. . . . The plan was to be based on 15 clusters, each containing part of the Detroit system and two or more suburban districts, and was to "achieve the greatest degree of actual desegregation to the end that, upon implementation, no school, grade or classroom [would be] substantially disproportionate to the overall pupil racial composition. . . ."

On June 12, 1973, a divided Court of Appeals, sitting en banc, affirmed in part, vacated in part and remanded for further proceedings. 484 F. 2d 215 (CA6 1973). . . the Court of Appeals concluded that "the only feasible desegregation plan involves the crossing of the boundary lines between the Detroit School District and adjacent or nearby school districts for the limited purpose of providing an effective desegregation plan." 484 F. 2d, at 249. It reasoned that such a plan would be appropriate because of the State's violations, and could be implemented because of the State's authority to control local school districts. Without further elaboration, and without any discussion of the claims that no constitutional violation by the outlying districts had been shown and that no evidence on that point had been allowed, the Court of Appeals held:

> "[T]he State has committed *de jure* acts of segregation and . . . the State controls the instrumentalities whose action is necessary to remedy the harmful effects of the State acts." *Ibid.*

An inter-district remedy was thus held to be "within the equity powers of the District Court." 484 F. 2d, at 250.

II

In *Brown* v. *Board of Education,* 349 U.S. 294 (1955) *(Brown II),* the Court's first encounter with the problem of remedies in school desegregation cases, the Court noted that:

> "In fashioning and effectuating the decrees the courts will be guided by equitable principles. Traditionally, equity has been characterized by a practical flexibility in shaping its remedies and by a facility for adjusting and reconciling public and private needs."

In further refining the remedial process, *Swann* held, the task is to correct, by a balancing of the individual and collective interests, "the condition that offends the Constitution." A federal remedial power may be exercised "only on the basis of a constitutional violation" and, "[a]s with any equity case, the nature of the violation determines the scope of the remedy." 402 U.S., at 15, 16.

Proceeding from these basic principles, we first note that in the District Court the complainants sought a remedy aimed at the *condition* alleged to offend the Constitution—the segregation within the Detroit City school district.* The court acted on this theory of the case and in its initial ruling on the "Desegregation Area" stated:

> "The task before this court, therefore, is now, and . . . has always been, how to desegregate the Detroit public schools."

Thereafter, however, the District Court abruptly rejected the proposed Detroit-only plans on the ground that "while it would provide a racial mix more in keeping with the Black-White proportions of the student population, [it] would accentuate the racial identifiability of the [Detroit] district as a Black school system, and would not accomplish desegregation." [T]he racial composition of the student body is such," said the court, "that the plan's implementation would clearly make the entire Detroit public school system racially identifiable" "leav[ing] many of its schools 75 to 90 percent Black."

While specifically acknowledging that the District Court's findings of a condition

* Although the list of issues presented for review in petitioners' briefs and petitions for writs of certiorari do not include arguments on the findings on segregatory violations on the part of the Detroit defendants, two of the petitioners argue in brief that these findings constitute error. Supreme Court Rules 23 (1) (c) and 40 (1) (d) (2), at a minimum, limit our review of the Detroit violation findings to "plain error," and under our decision last Term in *Keyes* v. *School District No. 1, Denver, Colorado,* 413 U.S. 189, the findings appear to be correct.

of segregation were limited to Detroit, the Court of Appeals approved the use of a metropolitan remedy largely on the grounds that it is:

> "impossible to declare 'clearly erroneous' the District Judge's conclusion that any Detroit only segregation plan will lead directly to a single segregated Detroit school district overwhelmingly black in all of its schools, surrounded by a ring of suburbs and suburban school districts overwhelmingly white in composition in a state in which the racial composition is 87 percent white and 13 percent black." 484 F. 2d, at 249.

Viewing the record as a whole, it seems clear that the District Court and the Court of Appeals shifted the primary focus from a Detroit remedy to the metropolitan area only because of their conclusion that total desegregation of Detroit would not produce the racial balance which they perceived as desirable. Both courts proceeded on an assumption that the Detroit schools could not be truly desegregated—in their view of what constituted desegregation—unless the racial composition of the student body of each school substantially reflected the racial composition of the population of the metropolitan area as a whole. The metropolitan area was then defined as Detroit plus 53 of the outlying school districts. . . . In *Swann,* which arose in the context of a single independent school district, the Court held:

> "If we were to read the holding of the District Court to require as a matter of substantive constitutional right, any particular degree of racial balance or mixing, that approach would be disapproved and we would be obliged to reverse." 402 U.S., at 24.

The clear import of this language from *Swann* is that desegregation, in the sense of dismantling a dual school system, does not require any particular racial balance in each "school, grade or classroom." †

Here the District Court's approach to what constituted "actual desegregation" raises the fundamental question, not presented in *Swann,* as to the circumstances in which a federal court may order desegregation relief that embraces more than a single school district. The court's analytical starting point was its conclusion that school district lines are no more than arbitrary lines on a map "drawn for political convenience." Boundary lines may be bridged where there has been a constitutional violation calling for inter-district relief, but, the notion that school district lines may be casually ignored or treated as a mere administrative convenience is contrary to the history of public education in our country. No single tradition in public education is more deeply rooted than local control over the operation of schools; local autonomy has long been thought essential both to the maintenance of community concern and support for public schools and to quality of the educational process. . . .

The Michigan educational structure involved in this case, in common with most States, provides for a large measure of local control, and a review of the scope and character of these local powers indicates the extent to which the inter-district remedy approved by the two courts could disrupt and alter the structure of public education in Michigan. The metropolitan remedy would require, in effect, consolidation of 54 independent school districts historically administered as separate units into a vast

† Disparity in the racial composition of pupils within a single district may well constitute a "signal" to a district court at the outset, leading to inquiry into the causes accounting for a pronounced racial identifiability of schools within one school system. In *Swann,* for example, we were dealing with a large but single, independent school system and a unanimous Court noted: "Where the proposed plan for conversion from a dual to a unitary system contemplates the continued existence of some schools that are all or predominantly of one race [the school authority has] the burden of showing that such school assignments are genuinely nondiscriminatory." *Id.,* p. 26. See also *Keyes,* 413 U.S. 189 at 208. However, the use of significant racial imbalance in schools within an autonomous school district as a signal which operates simply to shift the burden of proof, is a very different matter from equating racial imbalance with a constitutional violation calling for a remedy. *Keyes, supra,* also involved a remedial order within a single autonomous school district.

new super school district. Entirely apart from the logistical and other serious problems attending large-scale transportation of students, the consolidation would give rise to an array of other problems in financing and operating this new school system. Some of the more obvious questions would be: What would be the status and authority of the present popularly elected school boards? Would the children of Detroit be within the jurisdiction and operating control of a school board elected by the parents and residents of other districts? What board or boards would levy taxes for school operations in these 54 districts constituting the consolidated metropolitan area? . . .

. . . it is obvious from the scope of the inter-district remedy itself that absent a complete restructuring of the laws of Michigan relating to school districts the District Court will become first, a *de facto* "legislative authority" to resolve these complex questions, and then the "school superintendent" for the entire area. This is a task which few, if any, judges are qualified to perform and one which would deprive the people of control of schools through their elected representatives.

Of course, no state law is above the Constitution. School district lines and the present laws with respect to local control, are not sacrosanct and if they conflict with the Fourteenth Amendment federal courts have a duty to prescribe appropriate remedies. But our prior holdings have been confined to violations and remedies within a single school district. We therefore turn to address, for the first time, the validity of a remedy mandating cross-district or inter-district consolidation to remedy a condition of segregation found to exist in only one district.

The controlling principle consistently expounded in our holdings is that the scope of the remedy is determined by the nature and extent of the constitutional violation. *Swann.* Before the boundaries of separate and autonomous school districts may be set aside by consolidating the separate units for remedial purposes or by imposing a cross-district remedy, it must first be shown that there has been a constitutional violation within one district that produces a significant segregative effect in another district. Specifically it must be shown that racially discriminatory acts of the state or local school districts, or of a single school district have been a substantial cause of inter-district segregation. Thus an inter-district remedy might be in order where the racially discriminatory acts of one or more school districts caused racial segregation in an adjacent district, or where district lines have been deliberately drawn on the basis of race. In such circumstances an inter-district remedy would be appropriate to eliminate the inter-district segregation directly caused by the constitutional violation. Conversely, without an inter-district violation and inter-district effect, there is no constitutional wrong calling for an inter-district remedy.

The record before us, voluminous as it is, contains evidence of *de jure* segregated conditions only in the Detroit schools; indeed, that was the theory on which the litigation was initially based and on which the District Court took evidence. With no showing of significant violation by the 53 outlying school districts and no evidence of any inter-district violation or effect, the court went beyond the original theory of the case as framed by the pleadings and mandated a metropolitan area remedy. To approve the remedy ordered by the court would impose on the outlying districts, not shown to have committed any constitutional violation, a wholly impermissible remedy based on a standard not hinted at in *Brown I* and *II* or any holding of this Court.

In dissent MR. JUSTICE WHITE and MR. JUSTICE MARSHALL undertake to demonstrate that agencies having statewide authority participated in maintaining the dual school system found to exist in Detroit. They are apparently of the view that once such participation is shown, the District Court should have a relatively free hand to reconstruct school districts outside of Detroit in fashioning relief. Our assumption, *arguendo,* that state agencies did participate in the maintenance of the Detroit system, should make it clear that it is not on this point that we part company. The difference between us arises instead from established doctrine laid down by our cases, *Brown, Green, Swann, Scotland Neck,* and

Emporia, each addressed the issue of constitutional wrong in terms of an established geographic and administrative school system populated by both Negro and White children. In such a context, terms such as "unitary" and "dual" systems, and "racially identifiable schools," have meaning, and the necessary federal authority to remedy the constitutional wrong is firmly established. But the remedy is necessarily designed, as all remedies are, to restore the victims of discriminatory conduct to the position they would have occupied in the absence of such conduct. Disparate treatment of White and Negro students occurred within the Detroit school system, and not elsewhere, and on this record the remedy must be limited to that system. *Swann* at 16.

The constitutional right of the Negro respondents residing in Detroit is to attend a unitary school system in that district. Unless petitioners drew the district lines in a discriminatory fashion, or arranged for White students residing in the Detroit district to attend schools in Oakland and Macomb Counties, they were under no constitutional duty to make provisions for Negro students to do so. The view of the dissenters, that the existence of a dual system in *Detroit* can be made the basis for a decree requiring cross-district transportation of pupils cannot be supported on the grounds that it represents merely the devising of a suitably flexible remedy for the violation of rights already established by our prior decisions. It can be supported only by drastic expansion of the constitutional right itself, an expansion without any support in either constitutional principle or precedent.‡

. . . The Court of Appeals . . . held the State derivatively responsible for the Detroit Board's violations on the theory that actions of Detroit as a political subdivision of the State were attributable to the State. Accepting, *arguendo*, the correctness of this finding of State responsibility for the segregated conditions within the city of Detroit, it does not follow that an inter-district remedy is constitutionally justified or required. . . . there has been no showing that either the State or any of the 85 outlying districts engaged in activity that had a cross-district effect. . . . Where the schools of only one district have been affected, there is no constitutional power in the courts to decree relief balancing the racial composition of that district's schools with those of the surrounding districts. . . .

We conclude that the relief ordered by the District Court and affirmed by the Court of Appeals was based upon an erroneous standard and was unsupported by record evidence that acts of the outlying districts affected the discrimination found to exist in the schools of Detroit. Accordingly, the judgment of the Court of Appeals is vacated and the case is remanded for further proceedings consistent with this opinion leading to prompt formulation of a decree directed to eliminating the segregation found to exist in Detroit city schools, a remedy which has been delayed since 1970.

Reversed and remanded.

MR. JUSTICE STEWART, concurring:

In joining the opinion of the Court, I

‡ The suggestion in the dissent of MR. JUSTICE MARSHALL that schools which have a majority of Negro students are not "desegregated," whatever the racial makeup of the school district's population and however neutrally the district lines have been drawn and administered, finds no support in our prior cases. In *Green* v. *County School Board of New Kent County*, 391 U.S. 430 (1968), for example, this Court approved a desegregation plan which would have resulted in each of the schools within the district having a racial composition of 57% Negro and 43% White. In *Wright* v. *Council of the City of Emporia*, 407 U.S. 451 (1972), the optimal desegregation plan would have resulted in the schools being 66% Negro and 34% White, substantially the same percentages as could be obtained under one of the plans involved in this case. And in *United States* v. *Scotland Neck Board of Education*, 407 U.S. 484, 491, n. 5 (1972), a desegregation plan was implicitly approved for a school district which had a racial composition of 77% Negro and 22% White. In none of these cases was it even intimated that "actual desegregation" could not be accomplished as long as the number of Negro students was greater than the number of White students. . . .

think it appropriate, in view of some of the extravagant language of the dissenting opinions, to state briefly my understanding of what it is that the Court decides today. . . .

In this case, no inter-district violation was shown. Indeed, no evidence at all concerning the administration of schools outside the city of Detroit was presented other than the fact that these schools contained a higher proportion of white pupils than did the schools within the city. Since the mere fact of different racial compositions in contiguous districts does not itself imply or constitute a violation of the Equal Protection Clause in the absence of a showing that such disparity was imposed, fostered, or encouraged by the State or its political subdivisions, it follows that no inter-district violation was shown in this case.* The formulation of an inter-district remedy was thus simply not responsive to the factual record before the District Court and was an abuse of that court's equitable powers. . . .

[Mr. Justice Douglas dissented.]

MR. JUSTICE WHITE, with whom MR. JUSTICE DOUGLAS, MR. JUSTICE BRENNAN, and MR. JUSTICE MARSHALL join, dissenting:

. . . Regretfully, and for several reasons, I can join neither the Court's judgment nor its opinion. The core of my disagreement is that deliberate acts of segregation and their consequences will go unremedied, not because a remedy would be infeasible or unreasonable in terms of the usual criteria governing school desegregation cases, but because an effective remedy would cause what the Court considers to be undue administrative inconvenience to the State. The result is that the State of Michigan, the entity at which the Fourteenth Amendment is directed, has successfully insulated itself from its duty to provide effective desegregation remedies by vesting sufficient power over its public schools in its local school districts. If this is the case in Michigan, it will be the case in most States.

. . . The task is not to devise a system of pains and penalties to punish constitutional violations brought to light. Rather, it is to desegregate an *educational* system in which the races have been kept apart, without, at the same time, losing sight of the central *educational* function of the schools.

Viewed in this light, remedies calling for school zoning, pairing, and pupil assignments, become more and more suspect as they require that school children spend more and more time in buses going to and from school and that more and more educational dollars be diverted to transportation systems. Manifestly, these considerations are of immediate and urgent concern when the issue is the desegregation of a city

* My Brother MARSHALL seems to ignore this fundamental fact when he states that "the most essential finding [made by this District Court] was that Negro children in Detroit had been confined by intentional acts of segregation to a growing core of Negro schools surrounded by a receding ring of white schools." This conclusion is simply not substantiated by the record presented in this case. The record here does support the claim made by the respondents that white and Negro students within Detroit who otherwise would have attended school together were separated by acts of the State or its subdivision. However, segregative acts within the city alone cannot be presumed to have produced—and no factual showing was made that they did produce—an increase in the number of Negro students *in the city as a whole.* It is this essential fact of a predominantly Negro school population in Detroit—caused by unknown and perhaps unknowable factors such as in-migration, birth rates, economic changes, or cumulative acts of private racial fears—that accounts for the "growing core of Negro schools," a "core" that has grown to include virtually the entire city. The Constitution simply does not allow federal courts to attempt to change that situation unless and until it is shown that the State, or its political subdivisions, have contributed to cause the situation to exist. No record has been made in this case showing that the racial composition of the Detroit school population or that residential patterns within Detroit and in the surrounding areas were in any significant measure caused by governmental activity, and it follows that the situation over which my dissenting Brothers express concern cannot serve as the predicate for the remedy adopted by the District Court and approved by the Court of Appeals.

school system where residential patterns are predominantly segregated and the respective areas occupied by blacks and whites are heavily populated and geographically extensive. Thus, if one postulates a metropolitan school system covering a sufficiently large area, with the population evenly divided between whites and Negroes and with the races occupying identifiable residential areas, there will be very real practical limits on the extent to which racially identifiable schools can be eliminated within the school district. It is also apparent that the larger the proportion of Negroes in the area, the more difficult it would be to avoid having a substantial number of all-black or nearly all-black schools.

The Detroit school district is both large and heavily populated. It covers 139.6 square miles, encircles two entirely separate cities and school districts, and surrounds a third city on three sides. Also, whites and Negroes live in identifiable areas in the city. . . . [Under a Detroit-only plan] transportation on a "vast scale" would be required; 900 buses would have to be purchased for the transportation of pupils who are not now bussed. . . . the plan "would change a school system which is now Black and White to one that would be perceived as Black, thereby increasing the flight of Whites from the city and the system, thereby increasing the Black student population." For the District Court, "[t]he conclusion, under the evidence in this case, is inescapable that relief of segregation in the public schools of the City of Detroit cannot be accomplished within the corporate geographical limits of the city."

The District Court therefore considered extending its remedy to the suburbs. After hearings, it concluded that a much more effective desegregation plan could be implemented if the suburban districts were included. In proceeding to design its plan on the basis that student bus rides to and from school should not exceed 40 minutes each way as a general matter, the court's express finding was that "[f]or all the reasons stated heretofore—including time, distance, and transportation factors—desegregation within the area described is physically easier and more practicable and feasible, than desegregation efforts limited to the corporate geographic limits of the city of Detroit."

Despite the fact that a metropolitan remedy, if the findings of the District Court accepted by the Court of Appeals are to be credited, would more effectively desegregate the Detroit schools, would prevent resegregation, and would be easier and more feasible from many standpoints, the Court fashions out of whole cloth an arbitrary rule that remedies for constitutional violations occurring in a single Michigan school district must stop at the school district line. . . .

Until today, the permissible contours of the equitable authority of the district courts to remedy the unlawful establishment of a dual school system have been extensive, adaptable, and fully responsive to the ultimate goal of achieving "the greatest possible degree of actual desegregation." There are indeed limitations on the equity powers of the federal judiciary, but until now the Court has not accepted the proposition that effective enforcement of the Fourteenth Amendment could be limited by political or administrative boundary lines demarcated by the very State responsible for the constitutional violation and for the disestablishment of the dual system.

MR. JUSTICE MARSHALL, with whom MR. JUSTICE DOUGLAS, MR. JUSTICE BRENNAN, and MR. JUSTICE WHITE join, dissenting:

. . . Our precedents, in my view, firmly establish that where, as here, state-imposed segregation has been demonstrated, it becomes the duty of the State to eliminate root and branch all vestiges of racial discrimination and to achieve the greatest possible degree of actual desegregation. I agree with both the District Court and the Court of Appeals that, under the facts of this case, this duty cannot be fulfilled unless the State of Michigan involves outlying metropolitan area school districts in its desegregation remedy. Furthermore, I perceive no basis either in law or in the practicalities of the situation justifying the State's interposition of school district boundaries as absolute barriers to the implementation of an effective desegregation remedy. Under established and frequently used Michigan procedures, school district lines are both flexible and permeable for a wide variety of pur-

reads these words in a manner which perverts their obvious meaning. The nature of a violation determines the scope of the remedy simply because the function of any remedy is to cure the violation to which it is addressed. In school segregation cases, as in other equitable causes, a remedy which effectively cures the violation is what is required. No more is necessary, but we can tolerate no less. To read this principle as barring a District Court from imposing the only effective remedy for past segregation and remitting the court to a patently ineffective alternative is, in my view, to turn a simple commonsense rule into a cruel and meaningless paradox. Ironically, by ruling out an inter-district remedy, the only relief which promises to cure segregation in the Detroit public schools, the majority flouts the very principle on which it purports to rely.

Nor should it be of any significance that the suburban school districts were not shown to have themselves taken any direct action to promote segregation of the races. Given the State's broad powers over local school districts, it was well within the State's powers to require those districts surrounding the Detroit school district to participate in a metropolitan remedy. . . .

. . . it is plain that one of the basic emotional and legal issues underlying these cases concerns the propriety of transportation of students to achieve desegregation . . . the metropolitan plan would not involve the busing of substantially more students than already ride buses . . . with regard to both the number of students transported and the time and distances involved, the outlined desegregation plan "compares favorably with the transportation plan previously operated. . . ."

As far as economics are concerned, a metropolitan remedy would actually be more sensible than a Detroit-only remedy . . . a Detroit-only plan was estimated to require the purchase of 900 buses to effectuate the necessary transportation . . . in the inter-district remedy, the District Court found that only 350 additional buses would probably be needed. . . .

Today's holding, I fear, is more a reflection of a perceived public mood that we have gone far enough in enforcing the Constitution's guarantee of equal justice than it is the product of neutral principles of law. In the short run, it may seem to be the easier course to allow our great metropolitan areas to be divided up each into two cities—one white, the other black—but it is a course, I predict, our people will ultimately regret. I dissent.

SHELLEY *v.* KRAEMER

334 U.S. 1; 68 Sup. Ct. 836; 92 L. Ed. 1161 (1948)

[Two instances of private agreements known as restrictive covenants are involved in this case. These separate but similar agreements barred the Negro ownership of residential property in certain areas of St. Louis and Detroit. Only the facts relating to the St. Louis case are given here, because the circumstances surrounding each case are similar.]

MR. CHIEF JUSTICE VINSON delivered the opinion of the Court:

These cases present for our consideration questions relating to the validity of court enforcement of private agreements, generally described as restrictive covenants, which have as their purpose the exclusion of persons of designated race or color from the ownership or occupancy of real property. Basic constitutional issues of obvious importance have been raised.

The first of these cases comes to this Court on certiorari to the Supreme Court of Missouri. On February 16, 1911, thirty out of a total of thirty-nine owners of property fronting both sides of Labadie Avenue between Taylor and Cora Avenue in the city of St. Louis, signed an agreement, which was subsequently recorded, providing in part:

"the said property is hereby restricted to the use and occupancy for the term of Fifty (50) years from this date, so that it shall be a condition all the time and whether recited and referred to as *(sic)* not in subsequent conveyances and shall attach to the land as a condition precedent to the sale of the same, that hereafter no part of said property or any portion thereof shall be, for said term of Fifty years, occupied by any person not of the Caucasian race, it being intended hereby to restrict the use of said property for said period of time against the occupancy as owners or tenants of any portion of said property for resident or other purpose by people of the Negro or Mongolian Race."

. . . On August 11, 1945, pursuant to a contract for sale, petitioners Shelley, who are Negroes, for valuable consideration received from one Fitzgerald a warranty deed to the parcel in question. The trial court found that petitioners had no actual knowledge of the restrictive agreement at the time of purchase.

On October 9, 1945, respondents, as owners of other property subject to the terms of the restrictive covenant, brought suit in the Circuit Court of the city of St. Louis praying that petitioners Shelley be restrained from taking possession of the property and that judgment be entered divesting title out of petitioners Shelley and revesting title in the immediate grantor or in such other person as the court should direct. The trial court denied the requested relief on the ground that the restrictive agreement, upon which respondents based their action, had never become final and complete because it was the intention of the parties to that agreement that it was not to become effective until signed by all property owners in the district, and signatures of all the owners had never been obtained. The Supreme Court of Missouri sitting *en banc* reversed and directed the trial court to grant relief for which the respondents had prayed.

Petitioners have placed primary reliance on their contentions, first raised in the state courts, that judicial enforcement of the restrictive agreements in these cases has violated rights guaranteed to petitioners by the Fourteenth Amendment of the Federal Constitution and Acts of Congress passed pursuant to that Amendment. Specifically, petitioners urge that they have been denied the equal protection of the laws, deprived of property without due process of law, and have been denied privileges and immunities of citizens of the United States. We pass to a consideration of those issues.

I

Whether the equal protection clause of the Fourteenth Amendment inhibits judicial enforcement by state courts of restrictive covenants based on race or color is a question which this Court has not heretofore been called upon to consider. . . .

It is well, at the outset, to scrutinize the terms of the restrictive agreements involved in these cases. In the Missouri case, the covenant declares that no part of the affected property shall be "occupied by any person not of the Caucasian race, it being intended hereby to restrict the use of said property . . . against the occupancy as owners or tenants of any portion of said property for resident or other purpose by people of the Negro or Mongolian Race." Not only does the restriction seek to proscribe use and occupancy of the affected properties by members of the excluded class, but as construed by the Missouri courts, the agreement requires that title of any person who uses his property in violation of the restriction shall be divested. . . .

It cannot be doubted that among the civil rights intended to be protected from discriminatory state action by the Fourteenth Amendment are the rights to acquire, enjoy, own, and dispose of property. Equality in the enjoyment of property rights was regarded by the framers of that Amendment as an essential precondition to the realization of other basic civil rights and liberties which the Amendment was intended to guarantee. . . .

It is likewise clear that restrictions on the right of occupancy of the sort sought to be created by the private agreements in these cases could not be squared with the requirements of the Fourteenth Amendment if imposed by state statute or local ordinance. . . .

But the present cases . . . do not involve action by state legislatures or city councils. Here the particular patterns of discrimination and the areas in which the restrictions are to operate, are determined, in the first instance, by the terms of agreements among private individuals. Participation of the State consists in the enforcement of the restriction so defined. The crucial issue with which we are here confronted is whether this distinction removes these cases from the operation of the prohibitory provisions of the Fourteenth Amendment.

Since the decision of this Court in the *Civil Rights Cases,* 109 U.S. 3 (1883), the principle has become firmly embedded in our constitutional law that the action inhibited by the first section of the Fourteenth Amendment is only such action as may fairly be said to be that of the States. That Amendment erects no shield against merely private conduct, however discriminatory or wrongful.

We conclude, therefore, that the restrictive agreements standing alone cannot be regarded as violative of any rights guaranteed to petitioners by the Fourteenth Amendment. So long as the purposes of those agreements are effectuated by voluntary adherence to their terms, it would appear clear that there has been no action by the State and the provisions of the Amendment have not been violated. . . .

But here there was more. These are cases in which the purposes of the agreements were secured only by judicial enforcement by state courts of the restrictive terms of the agreements. The respondents urge that judicial enforcement of private agreements does not amount to state action; or, in any event, the participation of the State is so attenuated in character as not to amount to state action within the meaning of the Fourteenth Amendment. Finally, it is suggested, even if the States in these cases may be deemed to have acted in the constitutional sense, their action did not deprive petitioners of rights guaranteed by the Fourteenth Amendment. We move to a consideration of these matters.

II

That the action of state courts and judicial officers in their official capacities is to be regarded as action of the State within the meaning of the Fourteenth Amendment, is a proposition which has long been established by decisions of this Court. That principle was given expression in the earliest cases involving the construction of the terms of the Fourteenth Amendment. . . .

But the examples of state judicial action which have been held by this Court to violate the Amendments' commands are not restricted to situations in which the judicial proceedings were found in some manner to be procedurally unfair. It has been recognized that the action of state courts in enforcing a substantive common-law rule formulated by those courts, may result in the denial of rights guaranteed by the Fourteenth Amendment, even though the judicial proceedings in such cases may have been in complete accord with the most rigorous conceptions of procedural due process. . . .

The short of the matter is that from the time of the adoption of the Fourteenth Amendment until the present, it has been the consistent ruling of this Court that the action of the States to which the Amendment has reference includes action of state courts and state judicial officials. Although, in construing the terms of the Fourteenth Amendment, differences have from time to time been expressed as to whether particular types of state action may be said to offend the Amendment's prohibitory provisions, it has never been suggested that state court action is immunized from the operation of those provisions simply because the act is that of the judicial branch of the state government.

III

Against this background of judicial construction, extending over a period of some three quarters of a century, we are called upon to consider whether enforcement by state courts of the restrictive agreements in these cases may be deemed to be the acts of those States; and, if so, whether that action has denied these petitioners the equal protection of the laws which the Amendment was intended to insure.

We have no doubt that there has been state action in these cases in the full and complete sense of the phrase. The undisputed facts disclose that petitioners were willing purchasers of properties upon which they desired to establish homes. The owners of the properties were willing sellers; and contracts of sale were accordingly consummated. It is clear that but for the active intervention of the state courts, supported by the full panoply of state power, petitioners would have been free to occupy the properties in question without restraint.

These are not cases, as has been suggested, in which the States have merely abstained from action, leaving private individuals free to impose such discriminations as they see fit. Rather, these are cases in which the States have made available to such individuals the full coercive power of government to deny to petitioners, on the grounds of race or color, the enjoyment of property rights in premises which petitioners are willing and financially able to acquire and which the grantors are willing to sell. The difference between judicial enforcement and nonenforcement of the restrictive covenants is the difference to petitioners between being denied rights of property available to other members of the community and being accorded full enjoyment of those rights on an equal footing. . . .

We hold that in granting judicial enforcement of the restrictive agreements in these cases, the States have denied petitioners the equal protection of the laws and that, therefore, the action of the state courts cannot stand. We have noted that freedom from discrimination by the States in the enjoyment of property rights was among the basic objectives sought to be effectuated by the framers of the Fourteenth Amendment. That such discrimination has occurred in these cases is clear. Because of the race or color of these petitioners they have been denied rights of ownership or occupancy enjoyed as a matter of course by other citizens of different race or color. . . .

Respondents urge, however, that since the state courts stand ready to enforce restrictive covenants excluding white persons from the ownership or occupancy of property covered by such agreements, enforcement of covenants excluding colored persons may not be deemed a denial of equal protection of the laws to the colored persons who are thereby affected. This contention does not bear scrutiny. The parties have directed our attention to no case in which a court, state or federal, has been called upon to enforce a covenant excluding members of the white majority from ownership or occupancy of real property on grounds of race or color. But there are more fundamental considerations. The rights created by the first section of the Fourteenth Amendment are, by its terms, guaranteed to the individual. The rights established are personal rights. It is, therefore, no answer to these petitioners to say that the courts may also be induced to deny white persons rights of ownership and occupancy on grounds of race or color. Equal protection of the laws is not achieved through indiscriminate imposition of inequalities. . . .

The historical context in which the Fourteenth Amendment became a part of the Constitution should not be forgotten. Whatever else the framers sought to achieve, it is clear that the matter of primary concern was the establishment of equality in the enjoyment of basic civil and political rights and the preservation of those rights from discriminatory action on the part of the States based on considerations of race or color. Seventy-five years ago this Court announced that the provisions of the Amendment are to be construed with this fundamental purpose in mind. Upon full consideration, we have concluded that in these cases the States have acted to deny petitioners the equal protection of the laws guaranteed by the Fourteenth Amendment. Having so decided, we find it unnecessary to consider whether petitioners have also been deprived of property without due process of law or denied privileges and immunities of citizens of the United States. . . .

Reversed.

[Mr. Justice Reed, Mr. Justice Jackson, and Mr. Justice Rutledge took no part in the consideration or decision of these cases.]

SMITH *v.* ALLWRIGHT

321 U.S. 649; 64 Sup. Ct. 757; 88 L. Ed. 987 (1944)

[A Negro citizen of Texas named Smith tried to vote in the Democratic party primary election of 1940, in which candidates for state and national offices were to be chosen. Allwright, a precinct election judge, and other election officials refused to give Smith a

ballot. They contended that a state Democratic party convention resolution adopted in 1932 limited membership in the party to white persons. Smith brought suit for damages against Allwright in a federal district court. He claimed that Allwright and other election officials had deprived him of his voting rights under the Constitution. The district court ruled against Smith and a court of appeals affirmed the district court's ruling on the authority of Grovey *v.* Townsend, *which is discussed in the opinion here. Smith then brought the case to the Supreme Court on a writ of certiorari.]*

MR. JUSTICE REED delivered the opinion of the Court:

. . . The State of Texas by its Constitution and statutes provides that every person, if certain other requirements are met which are not here in issue, qualified by residence in the district or county "shall be deemed a qualified elector." . . . Primary election for United States Senators, Congressmen, and state officers are provided for by Chapters Twelve and Thirteen of the statutes. Under these chapters, the democratic party was required to hold the primary which was the occasion of the alleged wrong to petitioner. . . . These nominations are to be made by the qualified voters of the party. . . .

Texas is free to conduct her elections and limit her electorate as she may deem wise, save only as her action may be affected by the prohibitions of the United States Constitution or in conflict with powers delegated to and exercised by the National Government. The Fourteenth Amendment forbids a State from making or enforcing any law which abridges the privileges or immunities of citizens of the United States, and the Fifteenth Amendment specifically interdicts any denial or abridgment by a State of the right of citizens to vote on account of color. Respondents appeared in the District Court and the Circuit Court of Appeals and defended on the ground that the Democratic party of Texas is a voluntary organization with members banded together for the purpose of selecting individuals of the group representing the common political beliefs as candidates in the general election. As such a voluntary organization, it was claimed, the Democratic party is free to select its own membership and limit to whites participation in the party primary. Such action, the answer asserted, does not violate the Fourteenth, Fifteenth, or Seventeenth Amendment, as officers of government cannot be chosen at primaries and the Amendments are applicable only to general elections where governmental officers are actually elected. Primaries, it is said, are political party affairs, handled by party, not governmental, officers. . . .

The right of a Negro to vote in the Texas primary has been considered heretofore by this Court. The first case was *Nixon* v. *Herndon,* 273 U.S. 536. At that time, 1924, the Texas statute . . . declared, "in no event shall a Negro be eligible to participate in a Democratic Party primary election in the State of Texas." Nixon was refused the right to vote in a Democratic primary and brought a suit for damages against the election officers. . . . It was urged to this Court that the denial of the franchise to Nixon violated his Constitutional rights under the Fourteenth and Fifteenth Amendments. Without consideration of the Fifteenth, this Court held that the action of Texas in denying the ballot to Negroes by statute was in violation of the equal protection clause of the Fourteenth Amendment and reversed the dismissal of the suit.

The legislature of Texas re-enacted the article but gave the State Executive Committee of a party the power to prescribe the qualifications of its members for voting or other participation. This article remains in the statutes. The State Executive Committee of the Democratic party adopted a resolution that white Democrats and none other might participate in the primaries of that party. Nixon was refused again the privilege of voting in a primary and again brought suit for damages. . . . This Court again reversed the dismissal of the suit for the reason that the Committee action was deemed to be state action and invalid as discriminatory under the Fourteenth

Amendment. The test was said to be whether the Committee operated as representative of the State in the discharge of the State's authority. *Nixon* v. *Condon,* 286 U.S. 73. The question of the inherent power of a political party in Texas "without restraint by any law to determine its own membership" was left open. . . .

In *Grovey* v. *Townsend,* 295 U.S. 45, this Court had before it a suit for damages for the refusal in a primary of a county clerk, a Texas officer with only public functions to perform, to furnish petitioner, a Negro, an absentee ballot. The refusal was solely on the ground of race. This case differed from *Nixon* v. *Condon* . . . in that a state convention of the Democratic party had passed the resolution of May 24, 1932, hereinbefore quoted. It was decided that the determination by the state convention of the membership of the Democratic party made a significant change from a determination by the Executive Committee. The former was party action, voluntary in character. The latter, as had been held in the *Condon* case, was action by authority of the State. The managers of the primary election were therefore declared not to be state officials in such sense that their action was state action. A state convention of a party was said not to be an organ of the State. This Court went on to announce that to deny a vote in a primary was a mere refusal of party membership with which "the State need have no concern," . . . while for a State to deny a vote in a general election on the ground of race or color violated the Constitution. Consequently, there was found no ground for holding that the county clerk's refusal of a ballot because of racial ineligibility for party membership denied the petitioner any right under the Fourteenth or Fifteenth Amendment.

Since *Grovey* v. *Townsend* and prior to the present suit, no case from Texas involving primary elections has been before this Court. We did decide, however, *United States* v. *Classic,* 313 U.S. 299. We there held that Section 4 of Article I of the Constitution authorized Congress to regulate primary as well as general elections . . . "where the primary is by law made an integral part of the election machinery." . . . Consequently, in the *Classic* case, we upheld the applicability to frauds in a Louisiana primary of Sections 19 and 20 of the Criminal Code. Thereby corrupt acts of election officers were subjected to Congressional sanctions because that body had power to protect rights of federal suffrage secured by the Constitution in primary as in general elections. . . . This decision depended, too, on the determination that under the Louisiana statutes the primary was a part of the procedure for choice of federal officials. By this decision the doubt as to whether or not such primaries were a part of "elections" subject to federal control, which had remained unanswered since *Newberry* v. *United States* . . . was erased. . . . *[Editor's Note: Despite this statement by the Court, the* Newberry *case was generally regarded as holding that Congress could not regulate primaries.]* The fusing by the *Classic* case of the primary and general elections into a single instrumentality for choice of officers has a definite bearing on the permissibility under the Constitution of excluding Negroes from primaries. This is not to say that the *Classic* case cuts directly into the rationale of *Grovey* v. *Townsend.* This latter case was not mentioned in the opinion. *Classic* bears upon *Grovey* v. *Townsend* not because exclusion of Negroes from primaries is any more or less state action by reason of the unitary character of the electoral process but because the recognition of the place of the primary in the electoral scheme makes clear that state delegation to a party of the power to fix the qualifications of primary elections is delegation of a state function that may make the party's action the action of the State. When *Grovey* v. *Townsend* was written, the Court looked upon the denial of a vote in a primary as a mere refusal by a party of party membership. . . . As the Louisiana statutes for holding primaries are similar to those of Texas, our ruling in *Classic* as to the unitary character of the electoral process calls for a re-examination as to whether or not the exclusion of Negroes from a Texas party primary was state action. . . .

It may now be taken as a postulate that the right to vote in such a primary for the nomination of candidates without discrimination by the State, like the right to vote in a general election, is a right secured by the Constitution. . . . By the terms of the Fifteenth Amendment that right may not be abridged by any State on account of race. Under our Constitution that great privilege of the ballot may not be denied a man by the State because of his color.

We are thus brought to an examination of the qualifications for Democratic primary electors in Texas, to determine whether state action or private action has excluded Negroes from participation. Despite Texas' decision that the exclusion is produced by private or party action . . . federal courts must for themselves appraise the facts leading to that conclusion. It is only by the performance of this obligation that a final and uniform interpretation can be given to the Constitution, the "supreme Law of the Land."

We think that this statutory system for the selection of party nominees for inclusion on the general election ballot makes the party which is required to follow these legislative directions an agency of the State insofar as it determines the participants in a primary election. The party takes its character as a state agency from the duties imposed upon it by state statutes; the duties do not become matters of private law because they are performed by a political party. The plan of the Texas primary follows substantially that of Louisiana, with the exception that in Louisiana the State pays the cost of the primary while Texas assesses the cost against candidates. In numerous instances, the Texas statutes fix or limit the fees to be charged. Whether paid directly by the State or through state requirements, it is state action which compels. When primaries become a part of the machinery for choosing officials, state and national, as they have here, the same tests to determine the character of discrimination or abridgment should be applied to the primary as are applied to the general election. If the State requires a certain electoral procedure, prescribes a general election ballot made up of party nominees so chosen and limits the choice of the electorate in general elections for state offices, practically speaking, to those whose names appear on such a ballot, it endorses, adopts, and enforces the discrimination against Negroes practiced by a party entrusted by Texas law with the determination of the qualifications of participants in the primary. This is state action within the meaning of the Fifteenth Amendment. . . .

The United States is a constitutional democracy. Its organic law grants to all citizens a right to participate in the choice of elected officials without restriction by any State because of race. This grant to the people of the opportunity for choice is not to be nullified by a State through casting its electoral process in a form which permits a private organization to practice racial discrimination in the election. Constitutional rights would be of little value if they could be thus indirectly denied. . . .

The privilege of membership in a party may be, as this Court said in *Grovey* v. *Townsend* . . . no concern of a State. But when, as here, that privilege is also the essential qualification for voting in a primary to select nominees for a general election, the State makes the action of the party the action of the State. In reaching this conclusion we are not unmindful of the desirability of continuity of decision in constitutional questions. However, when convinced of former error, this Court has never felt constrained to follow precedent. In constitutional questions, where correction depends upon amendment and not upon legislative action, this Court throughout its history has freely exercised its power to re-examine the basis of its constitutional decisions. This has long been accepted practice, and this practice has continued to this day. This is particularly true when the decision believed erroneous is the application of a constitutional principle rather than an interpretation of the Constitution to extract the principle itself. Here we are applying, contrary to the recent decision in *Grovey* v. *Townsend*, the well-established principle of the Fifteenth Amendment, forbidding the abridgement by a State of a citizen's right to vote. *Grovey* v. *Townsend* is overruled.

Judgment reversed.

[Mr. Justice Frankfurter concurred in the result. Mr. Justice Roberts dissented.]

SOUTH CAROLINA *v.* KATZENBACH

383 U.S. 301; 86 Sup. Ct. 803; 15 L. Ed. 2d 769 (1966)

MR. CHIEF JUSTICE WARREN delivered the opinion of the Court:

By leave of the Court, South Carolina has filed a bill of complaint, seeking a declaration that selected provisions of the Voting Rights Act of 1965 violate the Federal Constitution, and asking for an injunction against enforcement of these provisions by the Attorney General. Original jurisdiction is founded on the presence of a controversy between a State and a citizen of another State under Article III, Section 2, of the Constitution. . . .

The Voting Rights Act was designed by Congress to banish the blight of racial discrimination in voting, which has infected the electoral process in parts of our country for nearly a century. The Act creates stringent new remedies for voting discrimination where it persists on a pervasive scale, and in addition the statute strengthens existing remedies for pockets of voting discrimination elsewhere in the country. Congress assumed the power to prescribe these remedies from Section 2 of the Fifteenth Amendment, which authorizes the national legislature to effectuate by "appropriate" measures the constitutional prohibition against racial discrimination in voting. We hold that the sections of the Act which are properly before us are an appropriate means for carrying out Congress' constitutional responsibilities and are consonant with all other provisions of the Constitution. We therefore deny South Carolina's request that enforcement of these sections of the Act be enjoined.

The constitutional propriety of the Voting Rights Act of 1965 must be judged with reference to the historical experience which it reflects. Before enacting the measure, Congress explored with great care the problem of racial discrimination in voting. . . .

In recent years, Congress has repeatedly tried to cope with the problem by facilitating case-by-case litigation against voting discrimination. The Civil Rights Act of 1957 authorized the Attorney General to seek injunctions against public and private interference with the right to vote on racial grounds. Perfecting amendments in the Civil Rights Act of 1960 permitted the joinder of States as party defendants, gave the Attorney General access to local voting records, and authorized courts to register voters in areas of systematic discrimination. Title I of the Civil Rights Act of 1964 expedited the hearing of voting cases before three-judge courts and outlawed some of the tactics used to disqualify Negroes from voting in federal elections.

Despite the earnest efforts of the Justice Department and of many federal judges, these new laws have done little to cure the problem of voting discrimination. According to estimates by the Attorney General during hearings on the Act, registration of voting age Negroes in Alabama rose only from 10.2 per cent to 19.4 per cent between 1958 and 1964; in Louisiana it barely inched ahead from 31.7 per cent to 31.8 per cent between 1956 and 1965; and in Mississippi it increased only from 4.4 per cent to 6.4 per cent between 1954 and 1964. In each instance, registration of voting age whites ran roughly fifty percentage points or more ahead of Negro registration.

The previous legislation has proved ineffective for a number of reasons. Voting suits are unusually onerous to prepare, sometimes requiring as many as 6,000 man-hours spent combing through registration records in preparation for trial. Litigation has been exceedingly slow, in part because of the ample opportunities for delay afforded voting officials and others involved in the proceedings. Even when favorable decisions have finally been obtained, some of the States affected have merely switched to discriminatory devices not covered by the federal decrees or have enacted difficult new tests designed to prolong the existing disparity between white and Negro registration. Alternatively, certain local officials have defied and evaded court orders or have simply closed their registration offices to freeze the voting rolls. The provision of the 1960 law authorizing registration by federal officers has had little impact on local maladministration because of its procedural complexities. . . .

The Voting Rights Act of 1965 reflects

Congress' firm intention to rid the country of racial discrimination in voting. The heart of the Act is a complex scheme of stringent remedies aimed at areas where voting discrimination has been most flagrant. . . .

At the outset, we emphasize that only some of the many portions of the Act are properly before us. . . .

These provisions of the Voting Rights Act of 1965 are challenged on the fundamental ground that they exceed the powers of Congress and encroach on an area reserved to the States by the Constitution. . . .

Has Congress exercised its powers under the Fifteenth Amendment in an appropriate manner with relation to the States?

The ground rules for resolving this question are clear. The language and purpose of the Fifteenth Amendment, the prior decisions construing its several provisions, and the general doctrines of constitutional interpretation, all point to one fundamental principle. As against the reserved powers of the States, Congress may use any rational means to effectuate the constitutional prohibition of racial discrimination in voting. Cf. our rulings last Term, sustaining Title II of the Civil Rights Act of 1964, in *Heart of Atlanta Motel* v. *United States,* and *Kazenbach* v. *McClung.* . . . We turn now to a more detailed description of the standards which govern our review of the Act.

Section 1 of the Fifteenth Amendment declares that "the right of citizens of the United States to vote shall not be denied or abridged by the United States or by any State on account of race, color, or previous condition of servitude." This declaration has always been treated as self-executing and has repeatedly been construed, without further legislative specification, to invalidate state voting qualifications or procedures which are discriminatory on their face or in practice. . . . The gist of the matter is that the Fifteenth Amendment supersedes contrary exertions of state power. . . .

South Carolina contends that the cases cited above are precedents only for the authority of the judiciary to strike down state statutes and procedures—that to allow an exercise of this authority by Congress would be to rob the courts of their rightful constitutional role. On the contrary, Section 2 of the Fifteenth Amendment expressly declares that "Congress shall have the power to enforce this article by appropriate legislation." By adding this authorization, the Framers indicated that Congress was to be chiefly responsible for implementing the rights created in Section 1. . . .

Congress has repeatedly exercised these powers in the past, and its enactments have repeatedly been upheld. For recent examples, see the Civil Rights Act of 1957, which was sustained in *United States* v. *Raines,* 362 U.S. 17. . . .

The basic test to be applied in a case involving Section 2 of the Fifteenth Amendment is the same as in all cases concerning the express powers of Congress with relation to the reserved powers of the States. Chief Justice Marshall laid down the classic formulation, fifty years before the Fifteenth Amendment was ratified:

> "Let the end be legitimate, let it be within the scope of the constitution, and all means which are appropriate, which are plainly adapted to that end, which are not prohibited, but consist with the letter and spirit of the constitution, are constitutional." *McCulloch* v. *Maryland.* . . .

We therefore reject South Carolina's argument that Congress may appropriately do no more than to forbid violations of the Fifteenth Amendment in general terms—that the task of fashioning specific remedies or of applying them to particular localities must necessarily be left entirely to the courts. Congress is not circumscribed by any such artificial rules under Section 2 of the Fifteenth Amendment. In the oft-repeated words of Chief Justice Marshall, referring to another specific legislative authorization in the Constitution, "This power, like all others vested in Congress, is complete in itself, may be exercised to its utmost extent, and acknowledges no limitations, other than are prescribed in the constitution." *Gibbons* v. *Ogden.*

Congress exercised its authority under the Fifteenth Amendment in an inventive manner when it enacted the Voting Rights Act of 1965.

First: The measure prescribes remedies for voting discrimination which go into effect without any need for prior adjudication. This was clearly a legitimate response to the problem, for which there is ample precedent under other constitutional provisions. . . . Congress had found that case-by-case litigation was inadequate to combat widespread and persistent discrimination in voting, because of the inordinate amount of time and energy required to overcome the obstructionist tactics invariably encountered in these lawsuits. After enduring nearly a century of systematic resistance to the Fifteenth Amendment, Congress might well decide to shift the advantage of time and inertia from the perpetrators of the evil to its victims. The question remains, of course, whether the specific remedies prescribed in the Act were an appropriate means of combating the evil, and to this question we shall presently address ourselves.

Second: The Act intentionally confines these remedies to a small number of States and political subdivisions which in most instances were familiar to Congress by name. This, too, was a permissible method of dealing with the problem. Congress had learned that substantial voting discrimination presently occurs in certain sections of the country, and it knew no way of accurately forecasting whether the evil might spread elsewhere in the future. In acceptable legislative fashion, Congress chose to limit its attention to the geographic areas where immediate action seemed necessary. . . . The doctrine of the equality of States, invoked by South Carolina, does not bar this approach, for that doctrine applies only to the terms upon which States are admitted to the Union, and not to the remedies for local evils which have subsequently appeared. . . .

We now consider the related question of whether the specific States and political subdivisions within Section 4 (b) of the Act were an appropriate target for the new remedies. Congress began work with reliable evidence of actual voting discrimination in a great majority of the States and political subdivisions affected by the new remedies of the Act. The formula eventually evolved to describe these areas was relevant to the problem of voting discrimination. . . . It was therefore permissible to impose the new remedies on the few remaining States and political subdivisions covered by the formula, at least in the absence of proof that they have been free of substantial voting discrimination in recent years. . . .

It is irrelevant that the coverage formula excludes certain localities which do not employ voting tests and devices but for which there is evidence of voting discrimination by other means. Congress had learned that widespread and persistent discrimination in voting during recent years has typically entailed the misuse of tests and devices, and this was the evil for which the new remedies were specifically designed. . . . Legislation need not deal with all phases of a problem in the same way, so long as the distinctions drawn have some basis in practical experience. . . . There are no States or political subdivisions exempted from coverage under Section 4 (b) in which the record reveals recent racial discrimination involving tests and devices. This fact confirms the rationality of the formula. . . .

We now arrive at consideration of the specific remedies prescribed by the Act for areas included within the coverage formula. South Carolina assails the temporary suspension of existing voting qualifications. . . . The record shows that in most of the States covered by the Act, including South Carolina, various tests and devices have been instituted with the purpose of disenfranchising Negroes, have been framed in such a way as to facilitate this aim, and have been administered in a discriminatory fashion for many years. Under these circumstances, the Fifteenth Amendment has clearly been violated. . . .

The Act suspends literacy tests and similar devices for a period of five years from the last occurrence of substantial voting discrimination. This was a legitimate response to the problem, for which there is ample precedent in Fifteenth Amendment cases. . . .

The Act *[Sec. 5]* suspends new voting regulations pending scrutiny by federal authorities to determine whether their use would violate the Fifteenth Amendment. This may have been an uncommon exercise of congressional power, as South Carolina contends, but the Court has recognized that exceptional conditions can justify legislative measures not otherwise appropriate. . . . Congress knew that some of the States covered by Section 4 (b) of the Act had resorted to the extraordinary strategem of contriving new rules of various kinds for the sole purpose of perpetuating voting discrimination in the face of adverse federal decrees. Congress had reason to suppose that these States might try similar maneuvers in the future, in order to evade the remedies for voting discrimination contained in the Act itself. Under the compulsion of these unique circumstances, Congress responded in a permissibly decisive manner. . . .

The Act authorizes the appointment of federal examiners to list qualified applicants who are thereafter entitled to vote, subject to an expeditious challenge procedure. This was clearly an appropriate response to the problem, closely related to remedies authorized in the prior cases. . . . In many of the political subdivisions covered by Section 4 (b) of the Act, voting officials have persistently employed a variety of procedural tactics to deny Negroes the franchise, often in direct defiance or evasion of federal decrees. Congress realized that merely to suspend voting rules which have been misused or are subject to misuse might leave this localized evil undisturbed. As for the briskness of the challenge procedure, Congress knew that in some of the areas affected, challenges had been persistently employed to harass registered Negroes. It chose to forestall this abuse, at the same time providing alternative ways for removing persons listed through error or fraud. . . .

After enduring nearly a century of widespread resistance to the Fifteenth Amendment, Congress has marshalled an array of potent weapons against the evil, with authority in the Attorney General to employ them effectively. Many of the areas directly affected by this development have indicated their willingness to abide by any restraints legitimately imposed upon them. We here hold that the portions of the Voting Rights Act properly before us are a valid means for carrying out the commands of the Fifteenth Amendment. Hopefully, millions of non-white Americans will now be able to participate for the first time on an equal basis in the government under which they live. We may finally look forward to the day when truly "the right of citizens of the United States to vote shall not be denied or abridged by the United States or by any State on account of race, color, or previous condition of servitude."

The bill of complaint is

Dismissed.

[Mr. Justice Black concurred except as to the validity of Section 5.]

WASHINGTON *v.* DAVIS

426 U.S. 229; 96 S. Ct. 2040; 48 L. Ed. 2d 597 (1976)

[Unsuccessful applicants to the Washington, D.C., police department challenged its use of a verbal aptitude test as a violation of the Fifth Amendment and of Title VII of the Civil Rights (Equal Employment Opportunities) Act of 1964. The district court upheld the use of the tests. The Court of Appeals for the District of Columbia reversed the District Court. The city then brought the case to the Supreme Court. The party named Washington is not the city but Walter Washington, the then recently elected black mayor. The electorate of the city was overwhelmingly black and the police recruitment program at issue in this case was an important part of the program of municipal reform introduced by the new, black city administration.]

MR. JUSTICE WHITE delivered the opinion of the Court:

This case involves the validity of a qualifying test administered to applicants for positions as police officers in the District of Columbia Metropolitan Police Department. The test was sustained by the District Court but invalidated by the Court of Appeals. . . .

. . . to be accepted by the Department

. . . the police recruit was required to satisfy certain physical and character standards, to be a high school graduate or its equivalent and to receive a grade of at least 40 on "Test 21," which is "an examination that is used generally throughout the federal service," . . . and which was "designed to test verbal ability, vocabulary, reading and comprehension."

. . . Petitioners' evidence, the District Court said, warranted three conclusions, "(a) The number of black police officers, while substantial, is not proportionate to the population mix of the city. (b) A higher percentage of blacks fail the Test than whites. (c) The Test has not been validated to establish its reliability for measuring subsequent job performance." . . . [The Court of Appeals held] that lack of discriminatory intent in designing and administering Test 21 was irrelevant; the critical fact was rather that a far greater proportion of blacks—four times as many—failed the test than did whites. This disproportionate impact, standing alone and without regard to whether it indicated a discriminatory purpose, was held sufficient to establish a constitutional violation, absent proof by petitioners that the test was an adequate measure of job performance in addition to being an indicator of probable success in the training program, a burden which the court ruled petitioners had failed to discharge.

. . . our cases have not embraced the proposition that a law or other official act, without regard to whether it reflects a racially discriminatory purpose, is unconstitutional *solely* because it has a racially disproportionate impact.

Almost 100 years ago, *Strauder* established that the exclusion of Negroes from grand and petit juries in criminal proceedings violated the Equal Protection Clause, but the fact that a particular jury or a series of juries does not statistically reflect the racial composition of the community does not in itself make out an invidious discrimination forbidden by the Clause. "A purpose to discriminate must be present which may be proven by systematic exclusion of eligible jurymen of the prescribed race or by an unequal application of the law to such an extent as to show intentional discrimination."

The rule is the same in other contexts. *Wright v. Rockefeller,* 376 U.S. 52; 84 S. Ct. 603; 11 L. Ed. 2d 512 (1964), upheld a New York congressional apportionment statute against claims that district lines had been racially gerrymandered. The challenged districts were made up predominantly of whites or of minority races, and their boundaries were irregularly drawn. The challengers did not prevail because they failed to prove that the New York legislature "was either motivated by racial considerations or in fact drew the districts on racial lines." . . .

The school desegregation cases have also adhered to the basic equal protection principle that the invidious quality of a law claimed to be racially discriminatory must ultimately be traced to a racially discriminatory purpose. That there are both predominantly black and predominantly white schools in a community is not alone violative of the Equal Protection Clause. The essential element of de jure segregation is "a current condition of segregation resulting from intentional state action . . . the differentiating factor between de jure segregation and so-called de facto segregation . . . is *purpose* or *intent* to segregate." *Keyes v. School Dist.* . . .

This is not to say that the necessary discriminatory racial purpose must be express or appear on the face of the statute, or that a law's disproportionate impact is irrelevant in cases involving Constitution-based claims of racial discrimination. A statute, otherwise neutral on its face, must not be applied so as invidiously to discriminate on the basis of race. *Yick Wo.* It is also clear from the cases dealing with racial discrimination in the selection of juries that the systematic exclusion of Negroes is itself such an "unequal application of the law . . . as to show intentional discrimination." A prima facie case of discriminatory purpose may be proved as well by the absence of Negroes on a particular jury combined with the failure of the jury commissioners to be informed of eligible Negro jurors in a community, or with racially non-neutral selection procedures. With a prima facie case made out, "the burden of proof shifts to the State to rebut the presumption of unconstitutional action by showing that permissible racially neutral selection criteria and procedures have produced the monochromatic result."

Necessarily, an invidious discriminatory purpose may often be inferred from the totality of the relevant facts, including the fact, if it is true, that the law bears more heavily on one race than another. It is also not infrequently true that the discriminatory impact—in the jury cases for example, the total or seriously disproportionate exclusion of Negroes from jury venires—may for all practical purposes demonstrate unconstitutionality because in various circumstances the discrimination is very difficult to explain on nonracial grounds. Nevertheless, we have not held that a law, neutral on its face and serving ends otherwise within the power of government to pursue, is invalid under the Equal Protection Clause simply because it may affect a greater proportion of one race than of another. . . .

There are some indications to the contrary in our cases. In *Palmer v. Thompson,* the city of Jackson, Miss., following a court decree to this effect, desegregated all of its public facilities save five swimming pools which had been operated by the city and which, following the decree, were closed by ordinance pursuant to a determination by the city council that closure was necessary to preserve peace and order and that integrated pools could not be economically operated. Accepting the finding that the pools were closed to avoid violence and economic loss, this Court rejected the argument that the abandonment of this service was inconsistent with the outstanding desegregation decree and that the otherwise seemingly permissible ends served by the ordinance could be impeached by demonstrating that racially invidious motivations had prompted the city council's action. The holding was that the city was not overtly or covertly operating segregated pools and was extending identical treatment to both whites and Negroes. The opinion warned against grounding decision on legislative purpose or motivation, thereby lending support for the proposition that the operative effect of the law rather than its purpose is the paramount factor. But the holding of the case was that the legitimate purposes of the ordinance—to preserve peace and avoid deficits—were not open to impeachment by evidence that the councilmen were actually motivated by racial considerations. Whatever dicta the opinion may contain, the decision did not involve, much less invalidate, a statute or ordinance having neutral purposes but disproportionate racial consequences. . . .

[The Test used here] seeks to ascertain whether those who take it have acquired a particular level of verbal skill; and it is untenable that the Constitution prevents the government from seeking modestly to upgrade the communicative abilities of its employees rather than to be satisfied with some lower level of competence, particularly where the job requires special ability to communicate orally and in writing. Respondents, as Negroes, could no more successfully claim that the test denied them equal protection than could white applicants who also failed. The conclusion would not be different in the face of proof that more Negroes than whites had been disqualified by Test 21. . . .

Nor on the facts of the case before us would the disproportionate impact of Test 21 warrant the conclusion that it is a purposeful device to discriminate against Negroes. . . . As we have said, the test is neutral on its face and rationally may be said to serve a purpose the government is constitutionally empowered to pursue. Even agreeing with the District Court that the differential racial effect of Test 21 called for further inquiry, we think the District Court correctly held that the affirmative efforts of the Metropolitan Police Department to recruit black officers, the changing racial composition of the recruit classes and of the force in general, and the relationship of the test to the training program negated any inference that the Department discriminated on the basis of race or that "a police officer qualifies on the color of his skin rather than ability."

Under Title VII . . . Congress provided that when hiring and promotion practices disqualifying substantially disproportionate numbers of blacks are challenged, discriminatory purpose need not be proved, and that it is an insufficient response to demonstrate some rational basis for the challenged practices. It is necessary, in addition, that they be "validated" in terms of job performance. . . . However this process proceeds, it involves a more probing judicial review of, and less deference to, the seemingly reasonable acts of administrators and executives than is appropriate under the Constitution where special racial impact, without discriminatory purpose, is claimed. We are not disposed to adopt this more rigorous standard for the purposes of applying the Fifth and the Fourteenth Amendments in cases such as this.

A rule that a statute designed to serve neutral ends is nevertheless invalid, absent compelling justification, if in practice it benefits or burdens one race more than another would be far reaching and would raise serious questions about, and perhaps invalidate, a whole range of tax, welfare, public service, regulatory, and licensing statutes that may be more burdensome to the poor and to the average black than to the more affluent white.

Given that rule, such consequences would perhaps be likely to follow. However, in our view, extension of the rule beyond those areas where it is already applicable by reason of statute, such as in the field of public employment, should await legislative prescription. . . .

As we have indicated, it was error to direct summary judgment for respondents based on the Fifth Amendment.

We also hold that the Court of Appeals should have affirmed the judgment of the District Court granting the motions for summary judgment filed by petitioners and the federal parties. Respondents were entitled to relief on neither constitutional nor statutory grounds.

[The Court then proceeds to uphold the District Court's finding that the test was "validated" within the meaning of Title VII because it was directly related to the ability of applicants to successfully complete the police training program. It rejects the holding of the Court of Appeals that in order to meet the statutory validation standard, the test must be directly related to the on the job performance of the police.]

The judgment of the Court of Appeals accordingly is reversed.

[Mr. Justice Stewart joined in the Court's Fifth Amendment holding. Mr. Justice Stevens concurred. Mr. Justice Brennan and Mr. Justice Marshall dissented.]

VILLAGE OF ARLINGTON HEIGHTS *v.* METROPOLITAN HOUSING DEV. CORP.

429 U.S. 252; 97 S. Ct. 555; 50 L. Ed. 2d 450 (1977)

[This case is described more fully in the introduction to this chapter. The excerpts here are presented only to further explain the "purpose and intent" holding in the immediately preceding case of Washington *v.* Davis.]

MR. JUSTICE POWELL delivered the opinion of the Court:

Davis does not require a plaintiff to prove that the challenged action rested solely on racially discriminatory purposes. . . .

When there is proof that a discriminatory purpose has been a motivating factor in the decision, . . . judicial deference is no longer justified.

Determining whether invidious discriminatory purpose was a motivating factor demands a sensitive inquiry into such circumstantial and direct evidence of intent as may be available. The impact of the official action [may] provide an important starting point. Sometimes a clear pattern, unexplainable on grounds other than race, emerges from the effect of the state action even when the governing legislation appears neutral on its face. . . . The evidentiary inquiry is then relatively easy. But such cases are rare. Absent a pattern as stark as that in *Gomillion* or *Yick Wo,* impact alone is not determinative, and the Court must look to other evidence.

The historical background of the decision is one evidentiary source, particularly if it reveals a series of official actions taken for invidious purposes. . . . The specific sequence of events leading up to the challenged decisions also may shed some light on the decision-maker's purposes. . . .

Departures from the normal procedural sequence also might afford evidence that improper purposes are playing a role. Substantive departures too may be relevant, particularly if the factors usually considered important by the decisionmaker strongly favor a decision contrary to the one reached.

The legislative or administrative history may be highly relevant, especially where there are contemporary statements by members of the decisionmaking body, minutes of its meetings, or reports. In some extraordinary instances the members might be called to the stand at trial to testify concerning the purpose of the official action, . . .

The foregoing summary identifies, without purporting to be exhaustive, subjects of proper inquiry in determining whether racially discriminatory intent existed. . . .

CHAPTER 14

The New Equal Protection

The most dramatic political interventions of the Warren Court—school desegregation and reapportionment—were accomplished under the equal protection clause. And although its criminal law reforms were typically dressed in the language of due process or such specific guarantees as right to counsel, they too essentially reflected equal protection concerns. For most of them were designed to provide equal justice for the poor. It was natural that having raised the banner of equal protection, the Court should begin hearing a wider and wider variety of equal protection claims.

The equal protection clause allows as broad or even broader a scope than the due process clause for substantive interpretation—that is, for the injection of the policy preferences of the justices. "Equal" may appear to mean "equal," but that is only an illusion of certainty. There are three reasons for the ambiguity of the word "equal" in the constitutional context.

First of all, the very purpose of most statutes

is to single out some class or group for special treatment—to "discriminate" for or against them. For instance, the federal statute providing additional assistance for welfare families with dependent children does not treat all children equally. It gives money to poor children and "discriminates" against wealthy children. Suppose we defend this inequality by saying it gives money to children who need it and not those who don't. In so doing, we encounter our second reason.

The statute, like most, is underinclusive, overinclusive, or both. It does not treat need *equally.* It is underinclusive because it fails to include the children of those poor who work and do not collect welfare but who also are in need. It is overinclusive because it gives money to some children on welfare who are not needy because they are actually supported by prosperous friends or relatives. Given the complexity of the real world, it is almost impossible to write a statute that can be effectively administered to fit exactly each and every situation so that they all come out equal.

The third reason nearly all statutes are unequal stems from the limited resources of government. Should government wait until it has the money, the political support, and the administrative capacity to introduce a sweeping, absolutely complete program before it introduces any program? If government is capable of aiding some children now, should it refuse to do so until it can aid all children equally? Is it not better to give aid to needy welfare children now rather than let them suffer until the government finally creates a comprehensive children's assistance program that will assure decent care for every child in America? Our normal style of government action is piecemeal; it takes care of one problem at a time, the most pressing first. Yet this style of legislation, as opposed to absolutely comprehensive social and economic planning, is always unequal in the sense that it shapes benefits for only a few people at a time, leaving many outside the scope of government action.

Thus, a court may find that nearly any statute it looks at violates the equal protection clause. Traditionally, the Supreme Court held that because all statutes inherently treat some people differently from others, they violate equal protection only when they create "unreasonable" classifications. A classification is unreasonable when it is not reasonably related to a legitimate purpose of the statute. Thus, a fire prevention statute requiring all green houses but no red houses to install fire extinguishers would violate equal protection. Classification by color bears no reasonable relation to the purpose of fire prevention because fire is no more or less likely to break out in one color house than another. It was the judges, of course, who would decide what was and was not reasonable.

The post-Civil War Court had fastened on the due process clause as its vehicle for judging the reasonableness of business regulation statutes. (See Chapter 10.) So there were few "old" equal protection cases, but the few there were tended to be laissez-faire judicial interventions in favor of business and against government regulation. Thus, the post-New Deal Court invoked the same deference to legislative economic judgments in the equal protection area as it did in due process and interstate commerce. (See Chapters 8, 9, and 10.)

Just as with due process, however, equal protection began to take on a new life in civil liberties and "human rights," as opposed to "economic rights." So long as the equal protection clause was used essentially to end racial discrimination, few problems of constitutional logic or boundaries arose. Racial classifications were almost always clearly invidious and unrelated to any legitimate statutory purpose. The Court argued that, although it would exercise judicial deference to economic classifications made by legislatures, racial classifications were automatically "suspect" and subject to "close scrutiny" by the judiciary.

When the Court entered the reapportionment area (See Chapter 4 and this chapter, pp 552–554), the difficulties began. Aside from *Gomillion* v. *Lightfoot,* 364 U.S. 339 (1960), the electoral districting cases did not involve the suspect classification of race. The Court began to present a new rationale for judicial activism in favor of equal protection—the fundamental rights rationale. Whenever legislation impinged on a fundamental right such as voting, judicial deference to legislative classification was out of order.

Given the egalitarian enthusiasms of the Warren Court, once started down the road of fundamental rights, there seemed to be no stopping point. *Shapiro* v. *Thompson* (p. 570) was a key turning point. It struck down state residency requirements for welfare recipients. No matter how much it covers itself in the language of fundamental human rights, it is a case about economic interests. There is nothing more economic than receiving or not receiving a welfare check. Furthermore, the state classification—resident versus nonresident—is at least arguably reasonable. Certainly, it is not automatically invidious and suspect in the way racial classification is. In *Shapiro* the Court seeks to cover over its substitution of its own judgment for that of the legislature on the reasonableness of an economic classification by introducing a federal right to travel. It argues that if residents of one state cannot be assured of receiving welfare when they move to a new state, their travel will be inhibited. Once the case is put as one in which a state law infringes on a federal right to travel (see Chapter 6), it becomes a civil rights, rather than an economic rights, decision. The issue of judicial deference to legislative judgments in the economic sphere no longer arises. Nevertheless, although in the short term *Shapiro* was seen as a fundamental right *to travel* case, in the long run it looks like a fundamental right *to welfare* case.

To *Shapiro* must be added the racial discrimination cases involving education and housing. (See Chapter 13.) Just as in *Shapiro* right to travel provides an entering wedge into welfare, so in many other cases the right against racial discrimination provides an entering wedge for the Court into education and housing. If we put them all together, we can build a set of precedents that might create a fundamental constitutional right to a decent life: adequate amounts of food, clothing, housing, and education. Such an argument is appealing because these are, after all, fundamental human needs. Thus, many groups whose alleged mistreatment by society could be ascribed to factors other than racial discrimination could now come forward to claim a "new equal protection" for a new set of economic rights.

In its later years the Warren Court began the development of a new and elaborate equal protection position that may be called substantive equal protection, or the two-tiered approach to equal protection.[1] Where a classification fell in the traditional realm of business regulation, the Court would defer to legislative judgment. Where the statute involved either a "suspect classification" or an infringement on "fundamental rights," it would be subject to "close scrutiny" by the Court.

By the end of the Warren Court, however, the list of fundamental rights had not been greatly expanded beyond speech, voting, travel, and the like—that is, the traditional Bill of Rights freedoms. Food, housing, and education still stood on the sidelines. And the list of suspect classifications still had not been expanded much beyond race. Here it was poverty that hovered at the sidelines.

In this area, as in others, the Burger Court has shown little disposition to roll back the Warren Court's position. But it also has shown a strong inclination not to move a great deal beyond that Court's position. It has been fairly firm in not expanding the list of fundamental rights with the exception of the right to privacy discussed in Chapter 17. An important signal of the Burger Court's approach is a short *per curiam* opinion in *Ortwein* v. *Schwab,* 410 U.S. 656 (1973). The Court held that the interest in welfare payments "has far less constitutional significance" than other interests earlier given constitutional protection and that welfare lies "in the area of economic and social welfare," rather than in fundamental rights.

There is also some evidence that the Burger Court may abandon the two-tiered approach for an intermediate standard under which it would afford most legislative classifications some deference but nonetheless would hold them up to a reasonableness standard. Such an approach would be in harmony with the general style of the Burger Court, which seems to aim at maximizing judicial discretion while avoiding the imposition of major new constitutional limitations on government action.

These tendencies of the Warren and Burger Courts can be seen by examining a number of cases out of whose overlapping subject matters the new equal protection has been built.

Elections

The principal reapportionment cases were examined in Chapter 4 because they grew out of an elaborate debate about the scope of judicial review and the political questions doctrine. Yet once the propriety of judicial intervention was established, reapportionment—with its slogan of "one man, one vote"—became one of the key areas of Warren Court egalitarianism. As the last two reapportionment cases discussed in Chapter 4 indicate, the Burger Court has

[1] Gerald Gunther, "In Search of Evolving Doctrine on a Changing Court: A Model for a Newer Equal Protection," *Harvard Law Review,* vol. 86 (1972), pp. 1–48.

shown the same distaste for mathematical exactitude in reapportionment as it has in dealing with racial quotas. (See *Swann* v. *Charlotte-Mecklenburg,* p. 520.) In 1973, the Court seemed to hold that it would not concern itself at all with variations of less than 10 per cent in state legislative districting. [*Gaffney* v. *Cummings,* 412 U.S. 735; *White* v. *Regester,* 412 U.S. 755.] In *Mahan* v. *Howell,* 410 U.S. 315 (1973), the Court upheld a deviation of at least 16.4 per cent in the populations of state legislative districts because the disparity resulted from a state policy of drawing district boundaries in conformity with the boundaries of local government units. Nevertheless, in national elections it has essentially stuck to the Warren Court position. And in *Connor* v. *Finch,* 431 U.S. 407 (1977), it disapproved a reapportionment scheme that did not provide a sufficient justification for deviations comparable to those in *Mahan.*

Elections to local governments have always created a special set of problems in the application of the one-person-one-vote standard. In *Avery* v. *Midland County,* 390 U.S. 474 (1968), the Warren Court held the one-person-one-vote standard applicable to such elections and, in *Kramer* v. *Union Free School District,* 395 U.S. 621 (1969) and *Hadley* v. *Junior College District,* 397 U.S. 50 (1970), extended it to elections for special-purpose boards and districts. The same standard was applied to a municipal bond election in *Cipriano* v. *City of Houma,* 395 U.S. 701 (1969). In 1973, however, the Burger Court held that a water storage district's board of trustees might reflect the value of land held. Some landowners, therefore, received more votes than others, and nonowners were entirely unrepresented. [*Salyer Land Co.* v. *Tulare Lake Basin Water Stor. Dist.,* 410 U.S. 719 (1973). See also *Bell* v. *James,* 101 S.Ct. 1811 (1981).] The Court has also held the one-person-one-vote standard inapplicable to judicial elections. [*Wells* v. *Edwards,* 409 U.S. 1095 (1973).] And in *Gordon* v. *Lance,* 403 U.S. 1 (1971), the Court upheld a state requirement that new taxes and bonds be approved by a 60 per cent, rather than a simple majority, vote. [See also *Lockport* v. *Citizens for Community Action,* 430 U.S. 259 (1977), upholding special voting provisions for a referendum on a new county charter.]

The Court has continued to refuse to examine the constitutionality of gerrymanders. [But see the discussions of *Gomillion* v. *Lightfoot,* the *Williamsburgh* case, and vote dilution in Chapter 13.]

In *Katzenbach* v. *Morgan,* 384 U.S. 641 (1966), the Court had upheld a congressional civil rights act provision suspending state literacy tests that, even when fairly administered, were preventing many Spanish-speaking citizens from voting.

The Court has also had a number of cases involving registration requirements for primary elections and the access of independent candidates and third parties to the ballot. All of them seem to involve balancing the public interest in maintaining the strength of the two-party system and excluding frivolous candidates against the rights of individuals to run for office and change their party affiliations. These rights are sometimes expressed in First Amendment and sometimes in equal protection terms. No clear pattern emerges from the cases, the Court essentially basing itself on what seems to be wise public policy in each instance. [See *Williams* v. *Rhodes,* 393 U.S. 23 (1968); *Rosario* v. *Rockefeller,* 410 U.S. 752 (1973); *Kusper* v. *Pontikes,* 414 U.S. 51 (1973); *Jennes* v. *Fortson,* 403 U.S. 431 (1971); *Storer* v. *Brown,* 415 U.S. 724 (1974); *American Party of Texas* v. *White,* 415 U.S. 767 (1974); *Illinois State Board of Elections* v. *Socialist Workers Party,* 440 U.S. 173 (1979).]

THE POOR AND ELECTIONS

In Chapter 13 we dealt with the intersection of race and voting. The Court has also dealt with the intersection of poverty and voting—and, more generally, with equal protection of voting rights. The Twenty-fourth Amendment eliminated state poll tax requirements for federal elections, and the Supreme Court has struck down such taxes, even for state elections, as a violation of equal protection [*Harper* v. *Virginia State Board of Elections,* 383 U.S. 663 (1966)]. The poll tax decisions were based on the burden they placed on voting by the poor. In a number of other cases, the Court has struck down property qualifications for voters and filing fee requirements for candidates that have handicapped the access of the poor to the electoral process. [*Bullock* v. *Union Free School District,* 405 U.S. 134 (1972); *Kramer* v. *School District,* 395 U.S. 621 (1969); *Cipriano* v. *City of Houma,* 395 U.S. 701 (1969); and *Lubin* v. *Panish,* 415 U.S. 709 (1974).]

THE POOR, RESIDENCY REQUIREMENTS, AND ELECTIONS

We have already noted that the leading case of *Shapiro* v. *Thompson* eliminated state residency requirements for recipients of welfare. *Shapiro* led to an attack on other state residency requirements. Using an approach almost identical to *Shapiro,* the Court struck down a residency requirement for county-provided nonemergency hospitalization and medical care. [*Memorial Hospital* v. *Maricopa County,* 415 U.S. 250 (1974).] In *Dunn* v. *Blumstein,* 405 U.S. 331 (1972), the Court invalidated a state voting law requiring a one-year residence in the state and a three-month residency in the county. Even earlier it had struck down a provision of the Texas constitution that prohibited members of the military services from establishing state residency for voting purposes. [*Carrington* v. *Rash,* 380 U.S. 89 (1965).] But in *Marston* v. *Lewis,* 410 U.S. 679 (1973), a divided Court upheld a fifty-day residence and registration requirement. And in *Rosario* v. *Rockefeller,* 410 U.S. 752 (1973), it upheld, 5 to 3, a state statute providing that to vote in a party primary, a voter must have registered his party affiliation at least thirty days before the previous general election. [Cf. *Kusper* v. *Pontikes,* 414 U.S. 51 (1973).]

In *Vlandis* v. *Kline,* 412 U.S. 441 (1973), the Court refused to follow the *Shapiro* rationale and did not strike down state residency requirements for favorable tuition status at state universities. In *Sosna* v. *Iowa,* 419 U.S. 393 (1975), the Court upheld a one-year state residency requirement for divorce.

Due Process, Equal Protection, and the Poor

In the *Vlandis* case, however, the Court actually struck down the Connecticut statute that provided for higher tuition for nonresident students on the grounds that it did not provide fair proceedings for determining who was and who was not a resident.

In Chapter 13, which was basically about the equal protection clause and the rights of blacks, it was necessary to have a brief look at due process because the Court sometimes used due process as a substitute for, or in combination with, equal protection rulings favorable to blacks. Similarly, in this chapter there must be a discussion of due process because the Court sometimes uses due process in the same way to protect the interests of the poor. The clearest examples are, of course, in criminal law. In order to assure that rich and poor receive equal justice, the Court has insisted on such procedural rights for the ignorant and indigent as state-provided counsel, legal fees and transcripts, and police warnings about their rights. (See Chapter 15.) In *Williams* v. *Illinois,* 399 U.S. 235 (1970), and *Tate* v. *Short,* 401 U.S. 395 (1971), the Court invalidated the imprisonment of indigent defendants who, had they been wealthier, could have substituted the payment of fines for days in jail.

The Court has also used a *Vlandis* approach to provide the poor with greater protection in non-criminal law areas. The decisions relating to divorce, bankruptcy, termination of parental rights, and establishment of parental responsibility are discussed in Chapter 15. It has held that welfare benefits cannot be cut off without at least an evidentiary, administrative hearing [*Goldberg* v. *Kelly,* (p. 719)] and that a judicial hearing is required before salaries can be garnisheed for debt. [*Sniadach* v. *Family Finance Corp,* 95 U.S. 337 (1969). But compare *Lindsey* v. *Normet,* 405 U.S. 56 (1972), upholding summary judicial proceedings for eviction for nonpayment of rent.]

In *Fuentes* v. *Shevin,* 407 U.S. 67 (1972), the Court seemed to require a judicial hearing before property might be repossessed for debt, but it has largely backtracked on the *Fuentes* decision in *Mitchell* v. *W. T. Grant Co.,* 416 U.S. 600 (1974). [See also *Flagg Bros.* v. *Brooks,* 436 U.S. 149 (1978).] The Court still insists that debtors are entitled to some sort of due process but not necessarily a full hearing. The Court, in effect, says it will decide case by case whether any given state procedure properly balances debtor and creditor interests. For instance in *Memphis Light, Gas and Water Division* v. *Craft,* 436 U.S. 1 (1978) the Court held that notice and hearing were constitutionally required before termination of utility services. In *Matthews* v. *Eldridge,* 424 U.S. 319 (1976), the Court seemed to trim back the potential reach of *Goldberg* v. *Kelly* by holding that an evidentiary hearing is not required before the termination of disability benefits. (On due process hearing requirements in connection with public employment, see the sections on the new property and public employment later in this chapter.)

In general the Court has developed a "variable" due process standard for non-criminal proceedings. In determining just how much due process is required for a particular proceeding, it considers how severe the loss to the individual will be if he or she loses, how great the government's interest is in making a speedy, inexpensive determination, and what the risk is that simple, quick procedures will lead to wrong decisions. As a result it is impossible to predict exactly what level of free legal services the Court will require to be provided to the poor in any particular kind of proceeding.

Welfare and Family Services

The Court's intervention in *Goldberg* was highly significant. Welfare and related social services have become a major and highly controversial government program with a vast bureaucracy administering an incredibly complex set of rules and procedures. To import judicial, constitutional supervision into this realm of government activity is to invite a whole new range of claims for Supreme Court attention. We will note in Chapter 15 that the Court has refused to label social worker home visitation of welfare clients unreasonable search. But it did intervene to protect the poor in the administration of the food stamp program in ways remarkably reminiscent of those pursued by the pre-1937 Court in its protection of the economic rights of business. [*Dept. of Agriculture* v. *Moreno,* 413 U.S. 528 (1973).] Its *Shapiro* v. *Thompson* decision was a step toward nationalizing welfare at a time when both political parties, Congress, and President Nixon were deeply interested in creating uniform national standards for dealing with poverty.

As might have been expected, the procedural due process claims in cases such as *Goldberg* v. *Kelly* soon turned into demands for what was in reality substantive due process or, really, substantive equal protection. Thus, a number of cases have challenged state and federal regulations that reduced welfare and other social payments below the levels the recipients desired. The leading case is *Dandridge* v. *Williams* (p. 576), which certainly does not indicate that the Court will act as a champion of the poor against government. However, it does show little disposition to retreat into a position of total judicial self-restraint. In *Richardson* v. *Belcher,* 404 U.S. 78 (1971), a 4-to-3 decision upheld the Social Security Act provisions that reduce disability payments to a worker who also receives workmen's compensation. *Jefferson* v. *Hackney,* 406 U.S. 535 (1972), upheld a state policy that provided only 75 per cent of the standard of need for those participating in Aid to Families with Dependent Children (AFDC) while it provided 100 per cent of need for the aged and 95 per cent for the blind.

HOUSING, EDUCATION, AND THE LOCAL COMMUNITY

James v. *Valtierra* (p. 581) and *San Antonio Independent School District* v. *Rodriguez* (p. 582) show two quite different intersections between the interests of the poor and the interests of local communities. *Valtierra* concerns a provision of the California constitution requiring that before a low-rent public-housing project can be developed in any community, the voters of the community must approve it by majority vote in a local election. This would seem to be democracy at work, giving local communities a say in their own destinies. But it also was likely to impede public housing for the poor, particularly in the suburbs. Were the poor denied equal protection because the construction they wanted was subject to the special hurdle of local elections while other state construction was not? The Court concluded that no denial of equal protection had occurred. [But see the discussion of *Hills* v. *Gautreaux* in Chapter 13. In that case, however, the Court continued to indicate its acceptance of statutes requiring local approval of public housing projects.]

Rodriguez presents almost the opposite problem. Here local communities that were poor challenged the state method of supporting schools through the local property tax. School districts with low assessed valuation and large numbers of children had far less to spend on their children's education than did rich districts—or at least they would have to burden their taxpayers far more heavily than would wealthy districts in order to achieve the same per-pupil expenditure. The property tax method of school financing had been under attack for many years. Indeed this tax had become so burdensome that many communities faced taxpayer revolts in which property owners would not approve increased school expenditures even for absolutely essential services. In a number of states property tax reform was a major political campaign issue. Two state supreme courts had declared their states' property tax arrangements unconstitutional. Of course, there was a strong element of racial tension in the conflict, for rich districts with a few students were almost invariably white, whereas among the school systems in the worst financial shape were those of the cities with large concentrations of low-income blacks.

On the other hand, one could hardly imagine a matter more typically of state rather than federal concern than the state tax system and its impact on local schools. If the Court had invalidated the Texas tax system, it would probably have been invalidating the similar systems of all the other states and would have created chaos in state finances. More fundamentally, it would have been attacking basic American political arrangements that have maintained great local autonomy, and with that autonomy widely different levels of municipal services in rich and poor communities.

Alienage

In *Graham* v. *Richardson,* 403 U.S. 365 (1971), the Court announced that alienage was a suspect classification in the course of striking down state laws denying welfare benefits to aliens. In *Sugarman* v. *Dougall,* 413 U.S. 634 (1973), it struck down a state law excluding aliens from its civil service and in *Nyquist* v. *Mauclet,* 432 U.S. 1 (1977), a statute excluding them from state higher education loans. In *Hampton* v. *Mow Sun Wong,* 426 U.S. 88 (1976), the Court struck down a federal Civil Service Commission regulation barring aliens from the federal civil service. It left the door open, however, to the argument that the federal government's plenary powers in the areas of immigration, citizenship, and national defense would allow it more leeway than the states in employing alienage classifications. For instance, the Court upheld a provision of a federal Medicare program that excluded certain classes of aliens from benefits. [*Mathews* v. *Diaz,* 426 U.S. 67 (1976).] In *Foley v. Connelie,* 435 U.S. 291 (1978) the Court upheld a state statute limiting appointments to the state police force to U.S. citizens. In *Ambach* v. *Norwick,* 441 U.S. 68 (1979), a 5-to-4 Court drew out of the *Sugarman* decision a "governmental functions" exception to the rule that classifications based on alienage require strict scrutiny. Where the state excludes aliens from offices that "perform functions that go the heart of representative government," the statute need only meet the rational basis standard. The Court upheld a New York statute forbidding certain aliens from serving as public school teachers. See also *Cabell* v. *Chavez-Salido,* 102 S.Ct. 735 (1982), which ruled that aliens may be forbidden to serve as state probation officers.

Illegitimacy

Racial minorities and the poor are not the only classes of persons making equal protection claims. The Court has recently heard a series of cases involving less favorable legal treatment of illegitimate than legitimate children. *Levy* v. *Louisiana,* 391 U.S. 68 (1968), concerned a suit on behalf of five illegitimate children for damages as a result of the death of their mother. Louisiana courts read the state wrongful death statute as authorizing the recovery of damages only by legitimate children. The Court held:

> While a state has broad power when it comes to making classifications, it may not draw a line which constitutes an invidious discrimination against a particular class. Though the test has been variously stated, the end result is whether the line drawn is a rational one. . . .
>
> Legitimacy or illegitimacy of birth has no relation to the nature of the wrong allegedly inflicted on the mother by appellees. These children, though illegitimate, were dependent on her; she cared for them and nurtured them; they were indeed hers in the biological and in the spiritual sense; in her death they suffered wrong in the sense that any dependent would.
>
> We conclude that it is invidious to discriminate against them when no action, conduct, or demeanor of theirs is possibly relevant to the harm that was done the mother.

Then in *Labine* v. *Vincent,* 401 U.S. 532 (1971), the Court upheld a state intestate succession statute under which illegitimate children did not have the same inheritance rights as legitimate children when the parent died without leaving a will.

Thus, in deciding the third of our illegitimacy trilogy, *Weber* v. *Aetna Casualty & Surety Company* (p. 596), the Court faced a situation familiar to students of the pre-1937 Court. It enjoyed two equal and opposite precedents, and it was absolutely free to decide a case of economic rights either way. The opinion is included here because the language of Justice Powell is also so magnificently reminiscent of the Court circa 1900. He finds for the economic interests of the individual against the government; and he does so after his sweeping, legislative-style analysis concludes that some of the policies the state might be pursuing in its statute are unwise and that whatever wise policies it may be pursuing, the statute is ill-designed to attain them.

In *Jiminez* v. *Weinberger,* 417 U.S. 628 (1974), the Court, voting 8 to 1, struck down a federal statute barring disability benefit payments to nonlegitimated illegitimates born after the onset of disability of their parent. Nevertheless, in *Mathews* v. *Lucas,* 427 U.S. 495 (1976), the Court held that legitimacy classifications did not necessarily trigger strict scrutiny. Justice Blackmun upheld provisions of the Social Security Act that required certain classes of illegitimate children to meet particularly strict standards of proof of dependency in order to collect survivors benefits. The provisions were found to be a "possibly rational" means of insuring that survivor benefits were not paid to children not dependent on their deceased parents.

Then in *Trimble* v. *Gordon,* 430 U.S. 762 (1977), the Court declared that, although illegitimacy was not a suspect classification, this did not mean that it would treat such classifications with the total deference of New Deal times. It would not uphold a statute simply because the legislature could offer some minimally rational defense of it. Thus it struck down an Illinois statute that allowed illegitimate children to inherit only from their mothers. Justice Powell repeats his performance in *Weber.* He finds that the classification enjoys too "attenuated" a relationship to any legitimate state goal to be constitutionally approved. [See also *Fiallo* v. *Bell,* 430 U.S. 787 (1977), in which the Court was extremely deferential to an illegitimacy classification in federal immigration law because of Congress's special powers over immigration.]

In three subsequent cases, the Court found that various illegitimacy classifications were constitutional. [*Lalli* v. *Lalli,* 439 U.S. 259 (1979); *Califano* v. *Boles,* 443 U.S. 282 (1979); *Parham* v. *Hughes,* 441 U.S. 347 (1979).] In 1982, however, it invalidated requirements that the state sought to defend on the grounds of important state interests, holding that they were really excuses for denying parental support rights to illegitimate children that were extended to legitimate ones. [*Mills v. Habluetzel,* 50 L.W. 4372 (1982).]

Family Life

Under various due process, equal protection and privacy rationales, the Court has now undertaken to provide constitutional standards for family law. In *Stanley v. Illinois,* 405 U.S. 645 (1972), the Court held that the state could not take the custody of his child from an unwed father without a hearing to determine whether he was a fit parent. In *Quilloin v. Walcott,* 434 U.S. 246 (1978) the Court tested a Georgia adoption against various constitutional standards and found that a natural father had not been deprived of his rights when the state allowed a stepfather to adopt the child over the natural father's protest. In *Zablocki v. Redhall,* 434 U.S. 374 (1978), the Court held unconstitutional a Wisconsin statute that required a person under court order to make child support payments to ask that court's permission to remarry. In *Smith v. Organization of Foster Families,* 431 U.S. 816 (1977), the Court upheld New York procedures for removing children from foster homes. See also *Parham* v. *J. R.,* 442 U.S. 584 (1979); *Secretary of Public Welfare* v. *Institutionalized Juveniles,* 442 U.S. 640 (1979); *Bellotti* v. *Baird,* 443 U.S. 622 (1979).]

Sex Discrimination

Similar echoes of the past arise when we examine the cases on sex discrimination. The time was when liberals applauded as proper exercises of judicial self-restraint the early Court cases upholding state wages and hours regulations for women. They hissed at other decisions striking down such laws as judicial activism that poured the justices' own laissez-faire economic philosophy into the due process clause. This was the dreaded substantive economic due process. Now many of those same kinds of statutes are ringingly denounced as unconstitutional by women's groups. And just in case these statutes do not turn out to be unconstitutional under substantive equal protection, a women's rights amendment has been before the states that would provide the Court with new and more specific constitutional grounds for striking them down. Of course, statutes that singled out women for protection during the first half of the century may be inappropriate in contemporary social and economic circumstances. But should the Court repeal them rather than leaving that judgment to the legislatures?

Prior to this recent revival of interest, the last major women's rights case the Court handled was *Goesaert* v. *Cleary,* 335 U.S. 464 (1948). It sustained a Michigan statute providing that no woman could obtain a bartender's license unless she was the wife or daughter of the owner of a saloon. It was challenged by women not so genetically or romantically favored. The Court thought it was doing its self-restrained post-New Deal best in refusing an equal protection challenge of this kind to a state economic regulation.

Since then a provision of the Civil Rights Act of 1964 has come into effect prohibiting employment discrimination on the basis of sex. As late as 1961 the Court upheld a state jury selection method under which women, unlike men, were not called unless they voluntarily registered [*Hoyt* v. *Florida,* 368 U.S. 57 (1961)].

In 1971, however, the Court struck down an Idaho probate code provision that gave preference to men over women to serve as administrators of estates. [*Reed* v. *Reed,* 404 U.S. 71 (1971).] *Reed* held that statutory sexual classifications were "subject to scrutiny under the Equal Protection Clause."

A leading case is *Frontiero* v. *Richardson* (p. 599). In considering it, the student should bear in mind the holding in *Eisenstadt* v. *Baird,* 405 U.S. 438 (1972). There the Court held that a Massachusetts statute that forbade providing birth control supplies to unmarried, but not to married, women violated the equal protection clause. In *Stanton* v. *Stanton,* 421 U.S. 7 (1975), the Court struck down a state court ruling that resulted in child support payments ending for a girl at age eighteen when they would have continued for a male until he was twenty-one. In *Craig* v. *Boren,* 429 U.S. 190 (1976), the Court struck down a state statute that allowed females to purchase 3.2 beer at age eighteen but prohibited males from doing so until they were twenty-one. The Court said: "classifications by gender must serve important governmental objectives and must be substantially related to achievement of those objectives." In a number of subsequent cases, the Court has struck down statutes that followed traditional steroetypes about sex roles, by treating wives and husbands or mothers and fathers differently. [*Orr* v. *Orr,* 440 U.S. 268 (1979); *Califano* v. *Westcott,* 443 U.S. 76 (1979); *Caban* v. *Mohammed,* 441 U.S. 380 (1979); *Wengler* v. *Druggists Mutual Insurance Co.,* 446 U.S. 142 (1980); *Kirchberg* v. *Feenstra,* 101 S.Ct. 1195 (1981).]

In *Geduldig* v. *Aiello,* 417 U.S. 484 (1974), the Court upheld a California disability insurance program that exempted from coverage loss of wages resulting from normal pregnancy. Justice Stewart, for the majority, argued that the classification was rationally supportable and that the state might choose to insure against some risks such as injury without insuring against all risks including pregnancy. Justices Brennan, Douglas, and Marshall argued in dissent that where the sole major risk the state chose not to insure against was one that only befell women, unconstitutional sex discimination was involved. In *Personnel Administrator* v. *Feeney,* 442 U.S. 256 (1979), the Court followed the familiar path of distinguishing between discriminatory purpose and adverse impact. It upheld a statute giving preference to veterans in state employment on the grounds that its purpose was to favor veterans over non-veterans, not men over women, even though its actual impact would be adverse to women as a class.

On the other hand, using due process arguments, the Court struck down a school board rule that required maternity leave to begin five months before the expected birth on the ground that it bore no rational relationship to any legitimate state interest in health and safety or continuity of instruction. [*Cleveland Board of Education* v. *LaFleur,* 414 U.S. 632 (1974).] In three recent cases the Court has found a rational basis for the sexual classifications at issue. It upheld draft registration for men and not women [*Rostker* v. *Goldberg,* 101 S.Ct. 2646 (1981)]; a statutory rape law that punished only men [*Michael M.* v. *Superior Court,* 101 S.Ct. 1200 (1981)]; and a state statute that allowed any mother to sue for the wrongful death of her child but only fathers of legitimate or legitimated children. [*Parham* v. *Hughes,* 441 U.S. 347 (1979).]

"BENEVOLENT" CLASSIFICATIONS

In *Kahn* v. *Shevin,* 416 U.S. 351 (1974), the Court upheld a Florida statute providing widows but not widowers a property tax exemption. The majority could see a reasonable basis for the classification. The dissenters, using the two-tiered approach, argued that sex was a suspect classification, and so the statute required careful scrutiny. Such scrutiny revealed that it did not truly provide equal protection because it gave the exemption to some widows who did not need it and withheld it from some widowers who did.

Kahn is the first of a series of cases that uphold more favorable statutory treatment of women than men, based on the argument that such treatment is a compensation for past economic discrimination. Perhaps the best example is *Schlesinger* v. *Ballard,* 419 U.S. 498 (1975). It involved a regulation that allowed women naval officers to remain on active duty after they had been passed over twice for promotion. Male officers in the same situation were required to leave the service. A group of them challenged the regulation. The Court held that it was reasonable for Congress to conclude that normal chances for promotion in the navy were better for men than for women and that as a result it was reasonable to give women more leeway under "up or out" procedures.

In three cases dealing with Social Security Act provisions that appeared on their face to treat women better than men, the Court demonstrated that ultimately it would decide which unequal treatments were truly benevolent and which were not. It upheld two of the regulations and struck down the third. [*Weinberger* v. *Wiesenfeld,* 420 U.S. 636 (1975); *Califano* v. *Goldfarb,* 430 U.S. 199 (1977); *Califano* v. *Webster,* 430 U.S. 313 (1977).]

Particularly interesting is the following footnote in *Craig* v. *Boren,* 429 U.S. 190 (1976): "*Kahn* v. *Shevin* and *Schlesinger* v. *Ballard,* upholding the use of gender-based classifications, rested upon the Court's perception of the laudatory purposes of those laws as remedying disadvantageous conditions suffered by women in economic and military life. Needless to say, in this case Oklahoma does not suggest that the age-sex differential was enacted to ensure the availability of 3.2% beer for women as compensation for previous deprivations."

These approvals of "benevolent" gender classifications are important forerunners of the problems of affirmative action discussed later in this chapter.

STATUTORY PROTECTIONS

Title VII of the Civil Rights Act of 1964 prohibits sexual as well as racial discrimination in employment. In *Phillips* v. *Martin Marietta Corp.,* 400 U.S. 542 (1971), the Court found that the statute was violated by a company policy that forbade the hiring of women with children but not men with children. In *Dothard* v. *Rawlinson,* 433 U.S. 321 (1977), the Court struck down height and weight requirements for prison guards but upheld regulations barring the hiring of women guards for "contact positions" in all male penitentiaries.

In *Los Angeles Dept. of Water and Power v. Manhart,* 435 U.S. 702 (1978), the Court held that a retirement plan that required women to make higher contributions than men violated Title VII even though the longer life expectancies of women meant that they would probably draw more benefits than men. In *General Electric Co. v. Gilbert,* 429 U.S. 125 (1977), the Court followed

Geduldig reasoning in upholding against Title VII attack an employer exclusion of pregnancy from his disability benefit plan. In spite of *Gilbert* and *Geduldig,* however, it remains quite unclear exactly which treatments of pregnancy in leave and disability programs will be found to violate Title VII and which will be upheld. See *Nashville Gas Co. v. Satty,* 434 U.S. 136 (1977).

In *County of Washington* v. *Gunther,* 101 S.Ct. 2242 (1981), the Court dealt with a complex tangle of federal legislation in such a way as to to open an important new field of sex discrimination in employment cases. It held, 5 to 4, that women may not only sue when women and men who do the same jobs get unequal pay but also when a whole category of jobs mostly held by women—such as secretarial jobs—is paid less well than some other category of jobs requiring less skill.

SUSPECT CLASSIFICATIONS AND THE E.R.A.

Earlier we noted the disinclination of the Burger Court to add to the list of fundamental rights begun by the Warren Court. Similarly it has been reluctant to expand the list of suspect classifications. Alienage has been added, but as we have seen, the Court has introduced an exception even to that addition. Illegitimacy and sex seemed to come close but have not quite made it onto the list. Moreover, where the impact of a legislative act on a class of persons is indirect and does not result from a purposive legislative intent to treat the class differently from others, the legislative act will not be subject to strict scrutiny even if the class is suspect. [*Schweiker* v. *Wilson,* 101 S.Ct. 1074 (1981).] One effect of the proposed Equal Rights Amendment would be to make sex a suspect classification.

Old Property—New Property

One way of looking at the various approaches to equal protection used by the Warren and Burger Courts is in terms of the old and the new property. The New Deal experience led the Court toward total deference to the legislature where statutes regulated traditional economic interests such as owning property or operating a business. Recently, the Court again underlined that in this sphere it continues to be totally deferent. In *New Orleans* v. *Dukes,* 427 U.S. 297 (1976), it upheld a city ordinance that banned all hot dog vendors from a part of the city except two who had been there the longest. The rest of the vendors had claimed, of course, that they were not being given equal treatment. Either all the hot dog stands should go, or all should be allowed to stay. As if to emphasize that its decision rested solely on New Deal deference rather than on any real evaluation of the reasonableness of the statute, the Court specifically overruled *Morey* v. *Doud,* 354 U.S. 457 (1957), the one post-1937

Where the Court denotes the classification being tested as purely economic—that is, as a regulation of the old property—it adopts a New Deal deference standard. The Court upholds the statute so long as *any* rational relation of the classification can be *imagined* to any *conceivable* legitimate state purpose. [See *New Orleans* v. *Dukes,* 427 U.S. 297 (1976). Cf *Zobel* v. *Williams,* 50 L.W. 4613 (1982).]

In most instances involving the new property, the test supposedly remains that of "mere" rationality rather than whether the statute embodies the best possible policy. But the Court will not go out of its way to imagine rational relations or conceive legitimate purposes that are not really there and are not articulated in the statute. In other words, the Court will really examine whether a rational argument can be made for the classification in the light of the real situation and the actual legislative purpose. It will strike down some statutes because it cannot find such rationality. It will uphold others where it may disagree with the policy but nevertheless finds the classification one that rational persons could adopt. This approach is broad and variable. It is bounded at one extreme by the "relatively relaxed" standard of review in *Massachusetts Board of Retirement* v. *Murgia* (p. 601). At the other extreme, it is bounded by cases involving the almost "suspect" classifications of sex and legitimacy like *Weber* (p. 596), where the Court is far more prone to find irrationality than rationality.

The third approach is the "two-tiered" one of the race cases and *Shapiro* v. *Thompson* (p. 570). Here the Court chooses to find that a statute invades a fundamental right or employs a suspect classification, that is, one bearing on a "discrete and insular" group that historically has been so disadvantaged as to "command extraordinary protection from the majoritarian political process." Where such a finding is made, the Court subjects the statute to "strict scrutiny." Under strict scrutiny, any classification can be declared unconstitutional, and the Court, in fact, only upholds those that embody policies that it wholeheartedly approves.

Irrebuttable Presumptions

Another way to look at many of the equal protection cases is in terms of "irrebuttable presumptions." Does the classification presume that something is true that may or may not be true and then prevent the person so classified from proving what is really true? For instance, in *Vlandis* v. *Kline,* discussed earlier in this chapter, the Court's reason for striking down a durational residency requirement was that it did not allow students a chance to prove that even though they had not been in the state very long, they really had become residents. In *Cleveland Board of Education* v. *La Fleur,* also discussed earlier in this chapter, the Court held that presuming that every woman teacher who reached her fifth month of pregnancy could no longer safely teach school was such an unconstitutional presumption. [See also *Dept. of Agriculture* v. *Murry,* 413 U.S. 508 (1973).]

Like all the other equal protection approaches, this one has not been followed consistently by the Court. For instance, the regulation upheld in *Murgia* (p. 601) does create an irrebuttable presumption that policemen over fifty are physically unfit for duty. And in *Weinberger* v. *Salfi*, 422 U.S. 749 (1975), the Court upheld a Social Security regulation that denies survivors benefits to wives and stepchildren where the marriage has taken place less than nine months prior to the death of the wage earner. The Court might have found this regulation to create an irrebuttable presumption that the woman had married the man just to get his benefits. Instead, it finds that it is an administratively convenient way of sorting those women who married for bona fide reasons and are thus deserving of benefits from those who married in the expectation that the man would soon die and leave them something. [See also *Califano* v. *Jobst*, 434 U.S. 47 (1978).]

In the modern welfare state, which must handle millions of transactions, it would involve incredible costs and delays to make specific determinations in every instance as to whether the individual involved really deserved the benefit. Persons must often be lumped into classifications by general rules if we are to administer the system with any degree of efficiency. Apparently, the Court will decide when a classification creates an unconstitutional irrebuttable presumption and when it creates a reasonable rule of administrative convenience.

Benign Classification and Affirmative Action or Quotas and Reverse Discrimination?

The newest racial discrimination problem to reach the Court is that of affirmative action. The Supreme Court has never held that the Constitution was colorblind—that government might never take race into account. Instead, race is a "suspect classification" that triggers close judicial scrutiny. Obviously, in commanding school districts to dismantle their dual school systems, the Court was requiring them to use racial classification, for compliance necessarily depended on deliberately assigning children to schools according to their race in order to achieve mixed classrooms.

Following the Court's lead, Congress passed the various civil rights laws that also openly dealt with race as a relevant concern in making public policy. Administrative regulations implementing the laws mandated affirmative action programs that were designed to move minorities into the mainstream of American life. At one extreme, affirmative action might mean only that individuals and organizations simply declare that they welcomed minority persons. At the other extreme, it might mean that minority persons must be given preference over whites in access to all opportunities or that a specific share of all opportunities must be reserved for minorities only.

The *Williamsburgh, Washington,* and *Santa Fe* cases have introduced many of the problems and paradoxes of affirmative action. What seems to some to be compensation for decades of discrimination and injustice seems to others simply a new round of discrimination and injustice, this time directed against whites. The Court has been sparring with these problems, working toward some intermediate position that avoids rigid racial quotas and direct discrimination against whites but nevertheless approves policies that contribute to a quickened movement toward racial equality.

In several cases, the Court avoided direct confrontation with the new problems. In *De Funis* v. *Odegaard,* 416 U.S. 312 (1974), involving preferential admissions for minority applicants to law school, the Court held that the case was rendered moot by the complainant's graduation from law school. He had been admitted pending the outcome of his case. In *Morton* v. *Mancari,* 417 U.S. 535 (1974), the Court upheld employment preferences for Indians in the Bureau of Indian Affairs but on grounds that avoided racial issues.

Several cases dealing with sexual classifications implied that some legislative favoring of women to make up for past injustices might be constitutional. (See *Califano* v. *Goldfarb* and *Califano* v. *Webster,* discussed in this chapter.)

All of these cases are the forerunners of *Regents of the University of California* v. *Bakke* (p. 604), involving a racially preferential admissions procedure used by the U.C. Davis Medical School.

Because of the 4–1–4 vote in *Bakke,* it may help to summarize the Court's holdings here. All of them apply to higher education admissions decisions only, not to employment or other matters.

1. *Title VI of the Civil Rights Act of 1964.* A firm, five-man majority (Powell, Brennan, White, Marshall and Blackmun) holds that Title VI does not prohibit taking race into account.

2. *Racial Classifications Absent Past Discrimination.* The same firm, five-man majority holds that the equal protection clause permits considerations of race to play a part in some circumstances even when there is no evidence of past discrimination by the institution making the decisions. The other four justices did not commit themselves one way or the other on this question. Justice Stevens, however, had earlier silently joined an opinion in *Williamsburgh* that said that race might be taken into account absent past discrimination.

3. *Quotas Absent Past Discrimination.* The Davis program was one of the most extreme affirmative action programs in higher education. It reserved a specific number of places for minority candidates who did not have to compete in any way with other candidates for admission. In fact in the years at issue Davis admitted minority candidates to these reserved places whose grades and test scores were far below those of other successful applicants. Most of them not only would have had no chance of regular admission to Davis but would have fallen well below the normal minimums of most medical schools in the country. Four justices (Brennan, White, Marshall and Blackmun) found the Davis program constitutionally acceptable and so presumably would accept very high levels of reverse discrimination and certainly would accept quotas. Justice Powell rejects quotas. He insists that all candidates be considered competitively in the same pool where race along with other factors may be considered in arriving at individualized admissions decisions aimed at achieving a diverse

student body. Justices Burger, Stevens, Rehnquist and Stewart do not commit themselves on these questions. As a practical matter, given that Brennan, White, Marshall and Blackmun will probably vote for nearly any affirmative action admissions program no matter how extreme, future admissions programs that are challenged will have to be moderate enough to pick up one more vote, presumably Powell's. That is why the details of what he wants are so important. It is possible, however, that future cases will reveal that the added vote may be found among the uncommitted four or new appointees.

4. *Racial Classifications and Quotas as Remedies for Past Discrimination.* None of the justices took any position on racial classifications or quotas as remedies for past discrimination.

United Steelworkers v. *Weber,* 443 U.S. 193 (1979) involved an affirmative action plan entered into by a union and a steel company for on-the-job training to prepare low-paid workers for higher-paying craft jobs. One minority worker had to be admitted for each white worker admitted until the percentage of minority craft workers in the plant was equal to the percentage of minorities in the local labor force. Because the plan had been entered into voluntarily rather than after a court trial on discrimination charges, there was no allegation or proof of past discrimination. After it was initiated the program was challenged by a white as a violation of the prohibition against racial discrimination in employment found in Title VII of the Civil Rights Acts of 1964. (See the discussion of *McDonald* v. *Santa Fe Trail Transportation Co.* in Chapter 13.) Justices Brennan, Marshall, White, Stewart, and Blackmun formed the majority that upheld the program. They found that Congress had not intended the ban on racial discrimination in Title VII to prohibit all private, voluntary, race-conscious, affirmative action plans. Indeed they saw a congressional intent to encourage voluntary compliance with Title VII's command to end discrimination. They emphasized that to interpret Title VII as prohibiting all affirmative action would create an impossible situation. Employers were commanded by Title VII to remedy past racial discrimination. If Title VII also prohibited them from voluntary plans such as the one in this case, they would end up getting sued by minorities if they didn't do something about their past discrimination and being sued by whites if they did. The majority pointed to the moderation of the plan, that it left some room for white advancement and that the reverse discrimination or quota involved would end as soon as racial equality was achieved.

The most troubling point was that this reverse discrimination was not being employed to correct a proven, past discrimination against minorities. Yet the facts of the case strongly suggested that the steel companies were voluntarily agreeing to such plans because they were pretty sure that discrimination could be proved against them if Title VII actions were brought against them by minorities. Instead of requiring proof of past discrimination to justify voluntary affirmative action programs, the Court held that Title VII permitted voluntary affirmative action "to eliminate conspicuous racial imbalance in traditionally segregated job categories." Justices Powell and Stevens did not participate. Chief Justice

Burger and Justice Rehnquist in dissent pointed out that Title VII says clearly and unambiguously that "It shall be an unlawful employment practice for any employer, labor organization, or joint labor-management committee controlling . . . on-the-job training programs to discriminate against any individual because of his race . . . in admission to any program established to provide . . . training."

Subsequently a unanimous Court held that Title VII does not itself create an independent requirement that an employer always give preferential treatment to women or minorities or do its hiring in such a way as to maximize the number of women and minorities hired. [*Texas Department of Community Affairs* v. *Burdine,* 101 S.Ct. 1089 (1981).]

In the *Bakke* case the quota issue had been crucial to Justice Powell's pivotal opinion. *Weber* had approved a temporary quota entered into voluntarily by an employer and a union that represented both minority and white workers. Could government impose a quota? That is the question presented in *Fullilove* v. *Klutznick* (p. 618). Notice that *Fullilove* addresses only the constitutionality of quotas under the Fourteenth Amendment. It does not deal with whether Title VII does or does not forbid quotas.

New Adventures With the Intermediate Standard (see pp. 551–2, 565–6): In *Plyer* v. *Doe,* 50 L.W. 4650 (1982), the Court struck down a Texas statute denying free public education to the children of illegal aliens. In *Mississippi University for Women* v. *Hogan,* 50 L.W. 5068 (1982), it ordered the state to admit male applicants to a previously all female nursing school. In both instances the Court refused to find a "suspect classification" or a "fundamental right" but found the state action unconstitutional because the state had not provided an "exceedingly persuasive justification" in terms of a "substantial" or "important" government interest.

SHAPIRO *v.* THOMPSON

394 U.S. 618; 89 Sup. Ct. 1322; 22 L. Ed. 2d 600 (1969)

[This case involves challenges to welfare requirements in three states. Only the facts behind one of these challenges are included in the excerpt from the Court opinion provided here.]

MR. JUSTICE BRENNAN delivered the opinion of the Court:

In No. 9, the Connecticut Welfare Department invoked Section 17 (2d) of the Connecticut General Statutes to deny the application of appellee Vivian Marie Thompson for assistance under the program for Aid to Families with Dependent Children (AFDC). She was a 19-year-old unwed mother of one child and pregnant with her second child when she changed her residence in June 1966 from Dorchester, Massachusetts, to Hartford, Connecticut, to live with her mother, a Hartford resident. She moved to her own apartment in Hartford in August 1966, when her mother was no longer able to support her and her infant son. Because of her pregnancy, she was unable to work or enter a work training program. Her application for AFDC assistance, filed in August, was denied in November solely on the ground that, as required by Section 17 (2d), she had not lived in the State for a year before her application was filed. . . .

There is no dispute that the effect of the waiting-period requirement in each case is to create two classes of needy resident families indistinguishable from each other except that one is composed of residents who have resided a year or more, and the second of residents who have resided less than a year, in the jurisdiction. On the basis of this sole difference the first class is granted and the second class is denied welfare aid upon which may depend the ability of the families to obtain the very means to subsist—food, shelter, and other necessities of life. In each case, the District Court found that appellees met the test for residence in their jurisdictions, as well as all other eligibility requirements except the requirements of residence for a full year prior to their applications. On reargument, appellees' central contention is that the statutory prohibition of benefits to residents of less than a year creates a classification which constitutes an invidious discrimination denying them equal protection of the laws. We agree. The interests which appellants assert are promoted by the classification either may not constitutionally be promoted by government or are not compelling governmental interests.

Primarily, appellants justify the waiting-period requirement as a protective device to preserve the fiscal integrity of state public assistance programs. It is asserted that people who require welfare assistance during their first year of residence in a State are likely to become continuing burdens on state welfare programs. Therefore, the argument runs, if such people can be deterred from entering the jurisdiction by denying them welfare benefits during the first year, state programs to assist longtime residents will not be impaired by a substantial influx of indigent newcomers.

There is weighty evidence that exclusion from the jurisdiction of the poor who need or may need relief was the specific objective of these provisions. In the Congress, sponsors of federal legislation to eliminate all residence requirements have been consistently opposed by representatives of state and local welfare agencies who have stressed the fears of the States that elimination of the requirements would result in a heavy influx of individuals into States providing the most generous benefits. . . .

We do not doubt that the one-year waiting period device is well suited to discourage the influx of poor families in need of assistance. An indigent who desires to migrate, resettle, find a new job, start a new life will doubtless hesitate if he knows that he must risk making the move without the possibility of falling back on state welfare assistance during his first year of residence, when his need may be most acute. But the purpose of inhibiting migration by needy persons into the State is constitutionally impermissible.

This court long ago recognized that the nature of our Federal Union and our constitutional concepts of personal liberty unite to require that all citizens be free to travel throughout the length and breadth of our land uninhibited by statutes, rules, or regulations which unreasonably burden or restrict this movement. That proposition was early stated by Chief Justice Taney in the *Passenger Cases:*

> "For all the great purposes for which the Federal government was formed, we are one people, with one common country. We are all citizens of the United States; and, as members of the same community, must have the right to pass and repass through every part of it without interruption, as freely as in our own States."

We have no occasion to ascribe the source of this right to travel interstate to a particular constitutional provision. It suffices that, as Mr. Justice Stewart said for the Court in *United States* v. *Guest:*

> "The constitutional right to travel from one State to another . . . occupies a position fundamental to the concept of one Federal Union. It is a right that has been firmly established and repeatedly recognized.
>
> "[T]he right finds no explicit mention in the Constitution. The reason, it has been suggested, is that a right so elementary was conceived from the beginning to be a necessary concomitant of the stronger Union the Constitution created. In any event, freedom to travel through-

out the United States has long been recognized as a basic right under the Constitution."

Thus, the purpose of deterring the immigration of indigents cannot serve as justification for the classification created by the one-year waiting period, since that purpose is constitutionally impermissible. If a law has "no other purpose . . . than to chill the assertion of constitutional rights by penalizing those who choose to exercise them, then it [is] patently unconstitutional." *United States* v. *Jackson.*

Alternatively, appellants argue that even if it is impermissible for a State to attempt to deter the entry of all indigents, the challenged classification may be justified as a permissible state attempt to discourage those indigents who would enter the State solely to obtain larger benefits. We observe first that none of the statutes before us is tailored to serve that objective. Rather, the class of barred newcomers is all-inclusive, lumping the great majority who come to the State for other purposes with those who come for the sole purpose of collecting higher benefits. In actual operation, therefore, the three statutes enact what in effect are nonrebuttable presumptions that every applicant for assistance in his first year of residence came to the jurisdiction solely to obtain higher benefits. Nothing whatever in any of these records supplies any basis in fact for such a presumption.

More fundamentally, a State may no more try to fence out those indigents who seek higher welfare benefits than it may try to fence out indigents generally. Implicit in any such distinction is the notion that indigents who enter a State with the hope of securing higher welfare benefits are somehow less deserving than indigents who do not take this consideration into account. But we do not perceive why a mother who is seeking to make a new life for herself and her children should be regarded as less deserving because she considers, among other factors, the level of a State's public assistance. Surely such a mother is no less deserving than a mother who moves into a particular State in order to take advantage of its better educational facilities.

Appellants argue further that the challenged classification may be sustained as an attempt to distinguish between new and old residents on the basis of the contribution they have made to the community through the payment of taxes. . . . Appellant's reasoning would logically permit the State to bar new residents from schools, parks, or libraries or deprive them of police and fire protection. Indeed it would permit the State to apportion all benefits and services according to the past tax contributions of its citizens. The Equal Protection Clause prohibits such an apportionment of state services.

We recognize that a State has a valid interest in preserving the fiscal integrity of its programs. It may legitimately attempt to limit its expenditures, whether for public assistance, public education, or any other program. But a State may not accomplish such a purpose by invidious distinction between classes of its citizens. It could not, for example, reduce expenditure for education by barring indigent children from its schools. Similarly, in the cases before us, appellants must do more than show that denying welfare benefits to new residents saves money. The saving of welfare costs cannot be an independent ground for an invidious classification.

In sum, neither deterrence of indigents from migrating to the State nor limitation of welfare benefits to those regarded as contributing to the State is a constitutionally permissible state objective. . . .

MR. JUSTICE STEWART, concurring:

In joining the opinion of the Court, I add a word in response to the dissent of my Brother Harlan, who, I think, has quite misapprehended what the Court's opinion says.

The Court today does *not* "pick out particular human activities, characterize them as 'fundamental,' and give them added protection . . ." To the contrary, the Court simply recognizes, as it must, an established constitutional right, and gives to that right no less protection than the Constitution itself demands.

"The constitutional right to travel from one State to another . . . has been firmly established and repeatedly recognized." *United States* v. *Guest.* . . . This constitutional right, which, of course, includes the right of "entering and abiding in any state in the Union" . . . is *not* a mere conditional liberty subject to regulation and control under conventional due process or equal protection standards. "[T]he right to travel freely from State to State finds constitutional protection that is quite independent of the Fourteenth Amendment." *United States* v. *Guest.* It is a right broadly assertable against private interference as well as governmental action. Like the right of association, *NAACP* v. *Alabama,* . . . it is a virtually unconditional personal right, guaranteed by the Constitution to us all.

It follows, as the Court says, that "the purpose of deterring the in-migration of indigents cannot serve as justification for the classification created by the one-year waiting period, since that purpose is constitutionally impermissible." And it further follows, as the Court says, that any *other* purposes offered in support of a law that so clearly impinges upon the constitutional right of interstate travel must be shown to reflect a *compelling* governmental interest. This is necessarily true whether the impinging law be a classification statute to be tested against the Equal Protection Clause, or a state or federal regulatory law, to be tested against the Due Process Clause of the Fourteenth or Fifth Amendment. As Mr. Justice Harlan wrote for the Court more than a decade ago, "[T]o justify the deterrent effect . . . on the free exercise . . . of their constitutionally protected right . . . a 'subordinating interest of the State must be compelling.'" *NAACP* v. *Alabama.* . . .

The Court today, therefore, is not "contriving new constitutional principles." It is deciding these cases under the aegis of established constitutional law.

MR. CHIEF JUSTICE WARREN, with whom MR. JUSTICE BLACK joins, dissented.

MR. JUSTICE HARLAN, dissenting:

The Court today holds unconstitutional Connecticut, Pennsylvania, and District of Columbia statutes which restrict certain kinds of welfare benefits to persons who have lived within the jurisdiction for at least one year immediately preceding their applications. The Court has accomplished this result by an expansion of the comparatively new constitutional doctrine that some state statutes will be deemed to deny equal protection of the laws unless justified by a "compelling" governmental interest, and by holding that the Fifth Amendment's Due Process Clause imposes a similar limitation on federal enactments. Having decided that the "compelling interest" principle is applicable, the Court then finds that the governmental interests here asserted are either wholly impermissible or are not "compelling." For reasons which follow, I disagree both with the Court's result and with its reasoning. . . .

The "compelling interest" doctrine, which today is articulated more explicitly than ever before, constitutes an increasingly significant exception to the long-established rule that a statute does not deny equal protection if it is rationally related to a legitimate governmental objective. The "compelling interest" doctrine has two branches. The branch which requires that classifications based upon "suspect" criteria be supported by a compelling interest apparently had its genesis in cases involving racial classifications, which have at least since *Korematsu* v. *United States* . . . been regarded as inherently "suspect." The criterion of "wealth" apparently was added to the list of "suspects" as an alternative justification for the rationale in *Harper* v. *Virginia Bd. of Elections* . . . in which Virginia's poll tax was struck down. The criterion of political allegiance may have been added in *Williams* v. *Rhodes.* . . . Today the list apparently has been further enlarged to include classifications based upon recent interstate movement, and perhaps those based upon the exercise of *any* constitutional right, for the Court states *ante* . . . :

> "The waiting-period provision denies welfare benefits to otherwise eligible applicants solely because they have recently moved into the jurisdiction. But in moving . . . appellees were exercising a constitutional right, and any classification which serves to penalize the exercise of that right, unless shown to be necessary to promote a *compelling* governmental interest, is unconstitutional."

I think that this branch of the "compelling interest" doctrine is sound when applied to racial classifications, for historically the Equal Protection Clause was largely a product of the desire to eradicate legal distinctions founded upon race. However, I believe that the more recent extensions have been unwise. For the reasons stated in my dissenting opinion in *Harper* v. *Virginia Bd. of Elections* . . . I do not consider wealth a "suspect" statutory criterion. And when, as in *Williams* v. *Rhodes,* and the present case, a classification is based upon the exercise of rights guaranteed against state infringement by the federal Constitution, then there is no need for any resort to the Equal Protection Clause; in such instances, this Court may properly and straightforwardly invalidate any undue burden upon those rights under the Fourteenth Amendment's Due Process Clause. . . .

The second branch of the "compelling interest" principle is even more troublesome. For it has been held that a statutory classification is subject to the "compelling interest" test if the result of the classification may be to affect a "fundamental right," regardless of the basis of the classification. This rule was foreshadowed in *Skinner* v. *Oklahoma* . . . in which an Oklahoma statute providing for compulsory sterilization of "habitual criminals" was held subject to "strict scrutiny" mainly because it affected "one of the basic civil rights." After a long hiatus, the principle re-emerged in *Reynolds* v. *Sims* . . . in which state apportionment statutes were subjected to an unusually stringent test because "any alleged infringement of the right of citizens to vote must be carefully and meticulously scrutinized." . . . It has reappeared today in the Court's cryptic suggestion . . . that the "compelling interest" test is applicable merely because the result of the classification may be to deny the appellees "food, shelter, and other necessities of life," as well as in the Court's statement . . . that "[s]ince the classification here touches on the fundamental right of interstate movement, its constitutionality must be judged by the stricter standard of whether it promotes a *compelling* state interest."

I think this branch of the "compelling interest" doctrine particularly unfortunate and unnecessary. It is unfortunate because it creates an exception which threatens to swallow the standard equal protection rule. Virtually every state statute affects important rights. This Court has repeatedly held, for example, that the traditional equal protection standard is applicable to statutory classifications affecting such fundamental matters as the right to pursue a particular occupation, the right to receive greater or smaller wages or to work more or less hours, and the right to inherit property. Rights such as these are in principle indistinguishable from those involved here, and to extend the "compelling interest" rule to all cases in which such rights are affected would go far toward making this Court a "super-legislature." This branch of the doctrine is also unnecessary. When the right affected is one assured by the federal Constitution, any infringement can be dealt with under the Due Process Clause. But when a statute affects only matters not mentioned in the federal Constitution and is not arbitrary or irrational, I must reiterate that I know of nothing which entitles this Court to pick out particular human activities, characterize them as "fundamental," and give them added protection under an unusually stringent equal protection test.

I shall consider in the next section whether welfare residence requirements deny due process by unduly burdening the right of interstate travel. If the issue is regarded purely as one of equal protection, then for the reasons just set forth this nonracial classification should be judged by ordinary equal protection standards. The applicable criteria are familiar and well-established. A legislative measure will be found to deny equal protection only if "it is without any reasonable basis, and therefore is purely arbitrary." . . .

For reasons hereafter set forth . . . a legislature might rationally find that the imposition of a welfare residence requirement would aid in the accomplishment of at least four valid governmental ojectives. It might also find that residence requirements have advantages not shared by other methods of achieving the same goals. In light of this undeniable relation of residence requirements to valid legislative aims, it cannot be said that the requirements are "arbitrary" or "lacking in rational justification." Hence, I can find no objection to these residence requirements under the Equal Protection Clause of the Fourteenth Amendment or under the analogous standard embodied in the Due Process Clause of the Fifth Amendment.

The next issue, which I think requires fuller analysis than that deemed necessary by the Court under its equal protection rationale, is whether a one-year welfare residence requirement amounts to an undue burden upon the right of interstate travel. Four considerations are relevant:

First. What is the constitutional source and nature of the right to travel which is relied upon?

Second. What is the extent of the interference with that right?

Third. What governmental interests are served by welfare residence requirements?

Fourth. How should the balance of the competing considerations be struck?

. . . I conclude that the right to travel interstate is a "fundamental" right which, for present purposes, should be regarded as having its source in the Due Process Clause of the Fifth Amendment.

The next questions are: (1) To what extent does a one-year residence condition upon welfare eligibility interfere with this right to travel?; and (2) What are the governmental interests supporting such a condition? The consequence of the residence requirements is that persons who contemplate interstate changes of residence, and who believe that they otherwise would qualify for welfare payments, must take into account the fact that such assistance will not be available for a year after arrival. The number or proportion of persons who are actually deterred from changing residence by the existence of these provisions is unknown. If one accepts evidence put forward by the appellees, to the effect that there would be only a miniscule increase in the number of welfare applicants were existing residence requirements to be done away with, it follows that the requirements do not deter an appreciable number of persons from moving interstate.

Against this indirect impact on the right to travel must be set the interests of the States . . . in imposing residence conditions. There appear to be four such interests. First, it is evident that a primary concern of . . . the . . . Legislatures was to deny welfare benefits to persons who moved into the jurisdiction primarily in order to collect those benefits. This seems to me an entirely legitimate objective. A legislature is certainly not obliged to furnish welfare assistance to every inhabitant of the jurisdiction, and it is entirely rational to deny benefits to those who enter primarily in order to receive them, since this will make more funds available for those whom the legislature deems more worthy of subsidy.

A second possible purpose of residence requirements is the prevention of fraud. A residence requirement provides an objective and workable means of determining that an applicant intends to remain indefinitely within the jurisdiction. It therefore may aid in eliminating fraudulent collection of benefits by nonresidents and persons already receiving assistance in other States. There can be no doubt that prevention of fraud is a valid legislative goal. Third, the requirement of a fixed period of residence may help in predicting the budgetary amount which will be needed for public assistance in the future. While none of the appellant jurisdictions appears to keep data sufficient to permit the making of detailed budgetary predictions in consequence of the requirement, it is probable that in the event of a very large increase or decrease in the number of indigent newcomers the waiting period would give the legislature time to make needed adjustments in the welfare laws. Obviously, this is a proper objective. Fourth, the residence requirements conceivably may have been predicated upon a legislative desire to restrict welfare payments financed in part by state tax funds to persons who have recently made some contribution to the State's economy, through having been employed, having paid taxes, or having spent money in the State. This too would appear to be a legitimate purpose.

The next question is the decisive one: whether the governmental interests served by residence requirements outweigh the burden imposed upon the right to travel. In my view, a number of considerations militate in favor of constitutionality. First, as just shown, four separate, legitimate governmental interests are furthered by residence requirements. Second, the impact of the requirements upon the freedom of individuals to travel interstate is indirect and, according to evidence put forward by the appellees themselves, insubstantial. Third, these are not cases in which a State or States, acting alone, have attempted to interfere with the right of citizens to travel. . . . Fourth, the legislatures which enacted these statutes have been fully exposed to the arguments of the appellees as to why these residence requirements are unwise, and have rejected them. This is not, therefore, an instance in which legislatures have acted without mature deliberation.

Fifth, and of longer-range importance, the field of welfare assistance is one in which there is a widely recognized need for fresh solutions and consequently for experimentation. Invalidation of welfare residence requirements might have the unfortunate consequence of discouraging the Federal and State Governments from establishing unusually generous welfare programs in particular areas of an experimental basis, because of fears that the program would cause an influx of persons seeking higher welfare payments. Sixth and finally, a strong presumption of constitutionality attaches to statutes of the types now before us. Congressional enactments come to this Court with an extremely heavy presumption of validity. . . . A similar presumption of constitutionality attaches to state statutes, particularly when, as here, a State has acted upon a specific authorization from Congress. . . .

I conclude with the following observations. Today's decision, it seems to me, reflects to an unusual degree the current notion that this Court possesses a peculiar wisdom all its own whose capacity to lead this Nation out of its present troubles is contained only by the limits of judicial ingenuity in contriving new constitutional principles to meet each problem as it arises. For anyone who, like myself, believes that it is an essential function of this Court to maintain the constitutional division between state and federal authority and among the three branches of the Federal Government, today's decision is a step in the wrong direction. This resurgence of the expansive view of "equal protection" carries the seeds of more judicial interference with the state and federal legislative process, much more indeed than does the judicial application of "due process" according to traditional concepts. . . .

DANDRIDGE *v.* WILLIAMS
397 U.S. 471; 90 Sup. Ct. 1153, 25 L. Ed. 2d 491 (1970)

MR. JUSTICE STEWART delivered the opinion of the Court:

This case involves the validity of a method used by Maryland, in the administration of an aspect of its public welfare program, to reconcile the demands of its needy citizens with the finite resources available to meet those demands. Like every other State in the Union, Maryland participates in the Federal Aid to Families with Dependent Children (AFDC) program. Under this jointly financed program, a State computes the so-called "standard of need" of each eligible family unit within its borders. Some States provide that every family shall receive grants sufficient to meet fully the determined standard of need. Other States provide that each family unit shall receive a percentage of the determined need. Still others provide grants to most families in full accord with the ascertained standard of need, but impose an upper limit on the total amount of money any one family unit may receive. Maryland, through administrative adoption of a "maximum grant regulation," has followed this last course. This suit was brought by several AFDC recipients to enjoin the application of the Maryland maximum grant regulation on the ground that it is in conflict with the Social Security Act of 1935 and with the Equal Protection Clause of the Fourteenth Amendment. A three-judge District Court held that the Maryland regulation violates the Equal Protection Clause.

[Maryland] computes the standard of need for each eligible family based on the number of children in the family and the circumstances under which the family lives. In general, the standard of need increases with each additional person in the household, but the increments become proportionately smaller. The regulation here in issue imposes upon the grant that any single family may receive in upper limit of $250 per month in certain counties and Baltimore City, and of $240 per month elsewhere in the State. The appellees all have large families, so that their standards of need as computed by the State substantially exceed the maximum grants that they actually receive under the regulation. The appellees urged in the District Court that the maximum grant limitation operates to discriminate against them merely because of the size of their families. . . .

Maryland says that its maximum grant regulation is wholly free of any invidiously discriminatory purpose or effect, and that the regulation is rationally supportable on at least four entirely valid grounds. The regulation can be clearly justified, Maryland argues, in terms of legitimate state interests in encouraging gainful employment, in maintaining an equitable balance in economic status as between welfare families and those supported by a wage-earner, in providing incentives for family planning, and in allocating available public funds in such a way as fully to meet the needs of the largest possible number of families. The District Court, while apparently recognizing the validity of at least some of these state concerns, nonetheless held that the regulation "is invalid on its face for overreaching,"—that it violates the Equal Protection Clause "[b]ecause it cuts too broad a swath on an indiscriminate basis as applied to the entire group of AFDC eligibles to which it purports to apply. . . ."

If this were a case involving government action claimed to violate the First Amendment guarantee of free speech, a finding of "overreaching" would be significant and might be crucial. For when otherwise valid governmental regulation sweeps so broadly as to impinge upon activity protected by the First Amendment, its very overbreadth may make it unconstitutional. But the concept of "overreaching" has no place in this case. For here we deal with state regulation in the social and economic field, not affecting freedoms guaranteed by the Bill of Rights, and claimed to violate the Fourteenth Amendment only because the regulation results in some disparity in grants of welfare payments to the largest AFDC families.* For this Court to approve the invalidation of state economic or social regulation as "overreaching" would be far too reminiscent of an era when the Court thought the Fourteenth Amendment gave it power to strike down state laws "because they may be unwise, improvident, or out of harmony with a particular school of thought." That era long ago passed into history.

In the area of economics and social welfare, a State does not violate the Equal Protection Clause merely because the classifications made by its laws are imperfect. If the classification has some "resonable basis," it does not offend the Constitution simply because the classification "is not made with mathematical nicety or because in practice it results in some inequality." "A statutory discrimination will not be set aside if any state of facts reasonably may be conceived to justify it."

To be sure, [the cases] enunciating this fundamental standard under the Equal Protection Clause, have in the main involved state regulation of business or industry. The administration of public welfare assistance, by contrast, involves the most basic economic needs of impoverished human beings. We recognize the dramatically real factual difference between the cited cases and this one, but we can find no basis for applying a different constitutional standard. It is a standard that has consistently been applied to state legislation restricting the availability of employment opportunities. And it is a standard that is true to the principle that the Fourteenth Amendment gives the federal courts no power to impose upon the States their views of what constitutes wise economic or social policy.

Under this long-established meaning of the Equal Protection Clause, it is clear that the Maryland maximum grant regulation

* Cf. *Shapiro* v. *Thompson,* 394 U.S. 618, where, by contrast, the Court found state interference with the constitutionally protected freedom of interstate travel.

is constitutionally valid. We need not explore all the reasons that the State advances in justification of the regulation. It is enough that a solid foundation for the regulation can be found in the State's legitimate interest in encouraging employment and in avoiding discrimination between welfare families and the families of the working poor. By combining a limit on the recipient's grant with permission to retain money earned, without reduction in the amount of the grant, Maryland provides an incentive to seek gainful employment. And by keying the maximum family AFDC grants to the minimum wage a steadily employed head of a household receives, the State maintains some semblance of an equitable balance between families on welfare and those supported by an employed breadwinner.

It is true that in some AFDC families there may be no person who is employable. It is also true that with respect to AFDC families whose determined standard of need is below the regulatory maximum, and who therefore receive grants equal to the determined standard, the employment incentive is absent. But the Equal Protection Clause does not require that a State must choose between attacking every aspect of a problem or not attacking the problem at all. It is enough that the State's action be rationally based and free from invidious discrimination. The regulation before us meets that test.

We do not decide today that the Maryland regulation is wise, that it best fulfills the relevant social and economic objectives that Maryland might ideally espouse, or that a more just and humane system could not be devised. Conflicting claims of morality and intelligence are raised by opponents and proponents of almost every measure, certainly including the one before us. But the intractable economic, social, and even philosophical problems presented by public welfare assistance programs are not the business of this Court. The Constitution may impose certain procedural safeguards upon systems of welfare administration. But the Constitution does not empower this Court to second-guess state officials charged with the difficult responsibility of allocating limited public welfare funds among the myriad of potential recipients. . . .

[Justices Harlan and Black and Chief Justice Burger joined in the opinion of the Court with additional comments.]

MR. JUSTICE MARSHALL, whom MR. JUSTICE BRENNAN joins, dissenting: . . .

[A]s a general principle, individuals should not be afforded different treatment by the State unless there is a relevant distinction between them *[Morey* v. *Doud].* In the instant case, the only distinction between those children with respect to whom assistance is granted and those children who are denied such assistance is the size of the family into which the child permits himself to be born. The class of individuals with respect to whom payments are actually made (the first four or five eligible dependent children in a family), is grossly underinclusive in terms of the class that the AFDC program was designed to assist, namely, *all* needy dependent children. Such underinclusiveness manifests "a prima facie violation of the equal protection requirement of reasonable classification," compelling the State to come forward with a persuasive justification for the classification.

The Court never undertakes to inquire for such a justification; rather it avoids the task by focusing upon the abstract dichotomy between two different approaches to equal protection problems that have been utilized by this Court.

Under the so-called "traditional test," a classification is said to be permissible under the Equal Protection Clause unless it is "without any reasonable basis." . . . On the other hand, if the classification affects a "fundamental right," then the state interest in perpetuating the classification must be "compelling" in order to be sustained. . . .

This case simply defies easy characterization in terms of one or the other of these "tests." The cases relied on by the Court, in which a "mere rationality" test was actually used, . . . are most accurately described as involving the application of equal protection reasoning to the regulation of business interests. The extremes to which the Court has gone in dreaming up rational bases for state regulation in that area may in many instances be ascribed to a healthy revulsion from the Court's earlier excesses in using the Constitution to protect interests that have more than enough power to protect themselves in the legislative halls. This case, involving the literally vital interests of a powerless minority—poor families without breadwinners—is far removed from the area of business regulation, as the Court concedes. Why then is the standard used in those cases imposed here? We are told no more than that this case falls in "the area of economics and social welfare," with the implication that from there the answer is obvious.

In my view, equal protection analysis of this case is not appreciably advanced by the priori definition of a "right," fundamental or otherwise.† Rather, concentration must be placed upon the character of the classification in question, the relative importance to individuals in the class discriminated against of the governmental benefits that they do not receive, and the asserted state interests in support of the classification. . . .

As we said only recently, "In determining whether or not a state law violates the Equal Protection Clause, we must consider the facts and circumstances behind the law, the interests which the State claims to be protecting, and the interests of those who are disadvantaged by the classification." *Kramer* v. *Union School District,* 395 U.S. 621, 626 (1969), quoting *Williams* v. *Rhodes,* 393 U.S. 23, 30 (1968).

It is the individual interests here at stake that, as the Court concedes, most clearly distinguish this case from the business regulation" equal protection cases. AFDC support to needy dependent children provides the stuff that sustains those children's lives: food, clothing, shelter. And this Court has already recognized several times that when a benefit, even a "gratuitous" benefit, is necessary to sustain life, stricter constitutional standards, both procedural and substantive,§ are applied to the deprivation of that benefit.

Nor is the distinction upon which the deprivation is here based—the distinction between large and small families—one that readily commends itself as a basis for determining which children are to have support approximating subsistence and which are not. Indeed, governmental discrimination between children on the basis of a factor over which they have no control—the number of their brothers and sisters—bears some resemblance to the classification between legitimate and illegitimate children which we condemned as a violation of the Equal Protection Clause. . . .

The asserted state interests in the maintanance of the maximum grant regulation, on the other hand, are hardly clear. [Maryland] apparently abandoned reliance on the fiscal justification. In its place, there have now appeared several different rationales for the maximum grant regulation, prominent among them being those relied upon by the majority—the notions that imposition of the maximum serves as an incentive to welfare recipients to find and maintain employment and provides a semblance of equality with persons earning a minimum wage.

With regard to the latter, Maryland has urged that the maximum grant regulation serves to maintain a rough equality between wage earning families and AFDC families, thereby increasing the political support

† Appellees do argue that their "fundamental rights" are infringed by the maximum grant regulation. They cite, for example, *Skinner* v. *Oklahoma,* 316 U.S. 535 (1942), for the proposition that the "right of procreation" is fundamental. This statement is no doubt accurate as far as it goes, but the effect of the maximum grant regulation upon the right of procreation is marginal and indirect at best, totally unlike the compulsory sterilization law that was at issue in *Skinner.* At the same time the Court's insistence that equal protection analysis turns on the basis of a closed category of "fundamental rights" involves a curious value judgment. It is certainly difficult to believe that a person whose very survival is at stake would be comforted by the knowledge that his "fundamental" rights are preserved intact.

§ [Our] cases suggest that whether or not there is a constitutional "right" to subsistence . . . , deprivations of benefits necessary for subsistence will receive closer constitutional scrutiny, under both the Due Process and Equal Protection Clauses, than will deprivations of less essential forms of governmental entitlements.

for—or perhaps reducing the opposition to—the AFDC program. [W]hether elimination of the maximum would produce welfare incomes out of line with other incomes in Maryland is itself open to question on this record. [A]nd it is too late to argue that political expediency will sustain discrimination not otherwise supportable.

Vital to the employment-incentive basis found by the Court to sustain the regulation is of course, the supposition that an appreciable number of AFDC recipients are in fact employable. . . . In this connection, Maryland candidly notes that "only a very small percentage of the total universe of welfare recipients are employable." The State, however, urges us to ignore the "total universe" and to concentrate attention instead upon the heads of AFDC families. Yet the very purpose of the AFDC program since its inception has been to provide assistance for dependent *children.* The State's position is thus that the State may deprive certain needy children of assistance to which they would otherwise be entitled in order to provide an arguable work incentive for their parents. But the State may not wield its economic whip in this fashion when the effect is to cause a deprivation to needy dependent children in order to correct an arguable fault of their parents.

Even if the invitation of the State to focus upon the heads of AFDC families is accepted, the minimum rationality of the maximum grant regulation is hard to discern. [N]ot only has the State failed to establish that there is a substantial or even a significant proportion of AFDC heads of households as to whom the maximum grant regulation arguably serves as a viable and logical work incentive, but it is also indisputable that the regulation at best is drastically *overinclusive* since it applies with equal vigor to a very substantial number of persons who like appellees are completely disabled from working. Finally, it should be noted that, to the extent there is a legitimate state interest in encouraging heads of AFDC households to find employment, application of the maximum grant regulation is also grossly *underinclusive* because it singles out and affects only large families. . . .

The State has presented other arguments to support the regulation. However, they are not dealt with specifically by the Court, and the reason is not difficult to discern. The Court has picked the strongest available; the others suffer similar and greater defects.‖ . . . One need not speculate too far on the actual reason for the regulation, for in the early stages of this litigation the State virtually conceded that it set out to limit the total cost of the program along the path of least resistance. Now, however, we are told that other rationales can be manufactured to support the regulation and to sustain it against a fundamental constitutional challenge.

However, these asserted state interests, which are not insignificant in themselves, are advanced either not at all or by complete accident by the maximum grant regulation. Clearly they could be served by measures far less destructive of the individual interests at stake. Moreover, the device assertedly chosen to further them is at one and the same time both grossly underinclusive—because it does not apply at all to a much larger class in an equal position—and grossly overinclusive—because it applies so strongly against a substantial class as to which it can rationally serve no end. Were this a case of pure business regulation, these defects would place it beyond what has heretofore seemed a borderline case, and I do not believe that the regulation can be sustained even under the Court's "reasonableness" test.

In any event, it cannot suffice merely to invoke the spectre of the past to decide the case. Appellees are not a gas company or an optical dispenser; they are needy dependent children and families who are discriminated against by the State. The basis

‖ Thus, the State cannot single out a minuscule proportion of the total number of families in the State as in need of birth control incentives. Not only is the classification effected by the regulation totally underinclusive if this is its rationale, but it also arbitrarily punishes children for factors beyond their control, and overinclusively applies to families like appellees' that were already large before it became necessary to seek assistance. For similar reasons, the argument that the regulation serves as a disincentive to desertion does not stand scrutiny.

of that discrimination—the classification of individuals into large and small families—is too arbitrary and too unconnected to the asserted rationale, the impact on those discriminated against—the denial of even a subsistence existence—too great, and the supposed interests served too contrived and attenuated to meet the requirements of the Constitution. . . .

JAMES *v.* VALTIERRA

402 U.S. 137; 91 Sup. Ct. 1331; 28 L. Ed. 2d 678 (1971)

MR. JUSTICE BLACK delivered the opinion of the Court:

These cases raise but a single issue. It grows out of the United States Housing Act of 1937, which established a federal housing agency authorized to make loans and grants to state agencies for slum clearance and low-rent housing projects. . . . At the time the federal legislation was passed the California Constitution had for many years reserved to the State's people the power to initiate legislation and to reject or approve by referendum any Act passed by the state legislature. The same section reserved to the electors of counties and cities the power of initiative and referendum over acts of local government bodies. In 1950, however, the State Supreme Court held that local authorities' decisions on seeking federal aid public housing projects were "executive" and "administrative," not "legislative," and therefore the state constitution's referendum provisions did not apply to these actions. Within six months of that decision the California voters adopted Article XXXIV of the state constitution to bring public housing decisions under the State's referendum policy. The Article provided that no low-rent housing project should be developed, constructed or acquired in any manner by a state public body until the project was approved by a majority of those voting at a community election.

The present suits were brought by citizens of San Jose, California, and San Mateo County, localities where housing authorities could not apply for federal funds because low-cost housing proposals had been defeated in referendums. The plaintiffs, who are eligible for low-cost public housing, sought a declaration that Article XXXIV was unconstitutional. . . . A three-judge court held that [it] denied the plaintiffs equal protection of the laws. [W]e reverse.

[The District Court's] chief reliance plainly rested on *Hunter* v. *Erickson,* 393 U.S. 385 (1969). The court below erred. . . . Unlike the case before us, Hunter rested on the conclusion that Akron's referendum law denied equal protection by placing "special burdens on racial minorities within the governmental process." [I]t cannot be said that California's Article XXXIV rests on "distinctions based on race." The Article requires referendum approval for any low-rent public housing project, not only for projects which will be occupied by a racial minority. And the record here would not support any claim that a law seemingly neutral on its face is in fact aimed at a racial minority. Cf. *Gomillion* v. *Lightfoot,* . . . The present case could be affirmed only by extending Hunter, and this we decline to do.

California's entire history demonstrates the repeated use of referendums to give citizens a voice on questions of public policy. . . . Provisions for referendums demonstrate devotion to democracy, not to bias, discrimination, or prejudice. Nonetheless, appellees contend that Article XXXIV denies them equal protection because it demands a mandatory referendum while many other referendums only take place upon citizen initiative. They suggest that the mandatory nature of the Article XXXI referendum constitutes unconstitutional discrimination because it hampers persons desiring public housing from achieving their objective when no such roadblock faces other groups seeking to influence other public decisions to their advantage. But of course a law-making procedure that "disadvantages" a particular group does not always deny equal protection. Under any such holding, presumably a State would not be able to require referendums on any subject unless referendums were required on all, because they would always disadvantage some group. And this Court would be required to analyze governmental structures to determine whether a gubernatorial veto provision or a filibuster rule is likely to "disadvantage" any of the diverse and shifting groups that make up the American people.

Furthermore, an examination of California law reveals that persons advocating low-income housing have not been singled out for mandatory referendums while no other group must face that obstacle. Mandatory referendums are required for approval of state constitutional amendments, for the issuance of general obligation long-term bonds by local governments, and for certain municipal territorial annexations. California statute books contain much legislation first enacted by voter initiative, and no such law can be repealed or amended except by referendum. . . .

The people of California have also decided by their own vote to require referendum approval of low-rent public housing projects. This procedure ensures that all the people of a community will have a voice in a decision which may lead to large expenditures of local governmental funds for increased public services and to lower tax revenues. . . . This procedure for democratic decision-making does not violate the constitutional command that no State shall deny to any person "the equal protection of the laws." . . .

Reversed.

MR. JUSTICE DOUGLAS took no part in the consideration or decision of this case. MR. JUSTICE MARSHALL, whom MR. JUSTICE BRENNAN and MR. JUSTICE BLACKMUN join, dissenting:

[Article 34] explicitly singles out low-income persons to bear its burden. Publicly assisted housing developments designed to accommodate the aged, veterans, state employees, persons of moderate income, or any class of citizens other than the poor need not be approved by prior referenda.

In my view, Article 34 on its face constitutes invidious discrimination. . . . "The States, of course, are prohibited by the Equal Protection Clause from discriminating between 'rich' and 'poor' *as such* in the formulation and application of their laws." *Douglas* v. *California,* 372 U.S. 353, 361 (1963) (Mr. Justice Harlan, dissenting). Article 34 is neither "a law of general applicability that may affect the poor more harshly than it does the rich," ibid, nor an "effort to redress economic imbalances," ibid. It is rather an explicit classification on the basis of poverty—a suspect classification which demands exacting judicial scrutiny, . . .

The Court, however, chooses to subject the article to no scrutiny whatsoever and treats the provision as if it contained a totally benign, technical economic classification. . . . It is far too late in the day to contend that the Fourteenth Amendment prohibits only racial discrimination; and to me, singling out the poor to bear a burden not placed on any other class of citizens tramples the values that the Fourteenth Amendment was designed to protect. . . .

SAN ANTONIO INDEPENDENT SCHOOL DISTRICT *v.* RODRIGUEZ
411 U.S. 1; 93 Sup. Ct. 1278; 36 L. Ed. 2d 16 (1973)

[About half of the school funds for the state of Texas are provided by the "Minimum Foundation School Program." About 80 per cent of its funds are derived from state revenues and 20 per cent from local funds, called the Local Fund Assignment. The assignment is met from local property taxes and is calculated on a formula based on each district's assessed property valuation. The purpose of this financing formula is to have some equalizing effects, with the heaviest burdens placed on those local districts best able to pay, but with each local district having to contribute something. However, in comparing the least and most affluent districts in the San Antonio area, one overwhelmingly Mexican-American,

the other predominantly Anglo, the Court found that the wealthier district was taxed at $.85 per $100 valuation and spent $594 per pupil whereas the poorer district was taxed at $1.05 and spent $356 even after the addition of state and federal funds.]

MR. JUSTICE POWELLdelivered the opinion of the Court:

I and II

. . . We must decide, first, whether the Texas system of financing public education operates to the disadvantage of some suspect class or impinges upon a fundamental right explicitly or implicitly protected by the Constitution, thereby requiring strict judicial scrutiny. If so, the judgment of the District Court should be affirmed. If not, the Texas scheme must still be examined to determine whether it rationally furthers some legitimate, articulated state purpose and therefore does not constitute an invidious discrimination Clause of the Fourteenth Amendment.

[F]or the several reasons that follow, we find neither the suspect classification nor the fundamental interest analysis persuasive.

A

The wealth discrimination discovered by the District Court in this case, and by several other courts that have recently struck down school financing laws in other States, is quite unlike any of the forms of wealth discrimination heretofore reviewed by this Court. Rather than focusing on the unique features of the alleged discrimination, the courts in these cases have virtually assumed their findings of a suspect classification through a simplistic process of analysis: since, under the traditional systems of financing public schools, some poorer people receive less expensive educations than other more affluent people, these systems discriminate on the basis of wealth. This approach largely ignores the hard threshold questions, including whether it makes a difference for purposes of consideration under the Constitution that the class of disadvantaged "poor" cannot be identified or defined in customary equal protection terms, and whether the relative—rather than absolute—nature of the asserted deprivation is of significant consequence. Before a State's laws and the justifications for the classifications they create are subjected to strict judicial scrutiny, we think these threshold considerations must be analyzed more closely than they were in the court below.

[There are] at least three ways in which the discrimination claimed here might be described. The Texas system of school finance might be regarded as discriminating (1) against "poor" persons whose incomes fall below some identifiable level of poverty or who might be characterized as functionally "indigent," or (2) against those who are relatively poorer than others, or (3) against all those who, irrespective of their personal incomes, happen to reside in relatively poorer school districts. Our task must be to ascertain whether, in fact, the Texas system has been shown to discriminate on any of these possible bases and, if so, whether the resulting classification may be regarded as suspect.

The precedents of this Court provide the proper starting point. The individuals or groups of individuals who constituted the class discriminated against in our prior cases shared two distinguishing characteristics: because of their impecunity they were completely unable to pay for same desired benefit, and as a consequence, they sustained an absolute deprivation of a meaningful opportunity to enjoy that benefit. . . .

Only appellees' first possible basis for describing the class disadvantaged by the Texas school finance system—discrimination against a class of definably "poor" persons—might arguably meet the criteria established in these prior cases. Even a cursory examination, however, demonstrates that neither of the two distinguishing characteristics of wealth classifications can be found here. First, . . . appellees have made no effort to demonstrate that [the system] operates to the peculiar disadvantage of any class fairly definable as indigent, or as composed of persons whose incomes are beneath any designated poverty level. Indeed, there is reason to believe that the poorest families are not necessarily clustered in the poorest property districts. [A] Connecticut study found, not surprisingly, that the poor were clustered around commercial and industrial areas—those same areas that provide the most attractive sources of property tax income for school districts. Whether a similar pattern would be discovered in Texas is not known, but there is no basis on the record in this case for assuming that the poorest people—defined by reference to any level of absolute impecunity—are concentrated in the poorest districts.

Second, . . . unlike each of the foregoing cases, lack of personal resources has not occasioned an absolute deprivation of the desired benefit. [The state points out] that it now assures "every child in every school district an adequate education." No proof was offered at trial persuasively discrediting or refuting the State's assertion. For these two reasons . . . the disadvantaged class is not susceptible to identification in traditional terms.

[Appellee's argument] might be characterized as a theory of relative or comparative discrimination based on family income. Appellees sought to prove that a direct correlation exists between the wealth of families within each district and the expenditures therein for education. That is, along a continuum, the poorer the family the lower the dollar amount of education received by the family's children.

[Assuming the accuracy of this analysis, it] would still face serious unanswered questions, including whether . . . a class of this size and diversity could ever claim the special protection accorded "suspect" classes. But in fact the districts that spend next to the most money on education are populated by families having next to the lowest median family incomes while the districts spending the least have the highest median family income. . . .

This brings us, then, to the third way in which the classification scheme might be defined—*district* wealth discrimination. Since the only correlation indicated by the evidence is between district property wealth and expenditures, it may be argued that discrimination might be found without regard to the individual income characteristics of district residents. Assuming a perfect correlation between district property wealth and expenditures from top to bottom, the disadvantaged class might be viewed as encompassing every child in every district except the district that has the most assessable wealth and spends the most on education. Alternatively, as suggested in [Justice Marshall's dissent], the class might be defined more restrictively to include children in districts with assessable property which falls below the statewide average, or median, or below some other artificially defined level.

However described, it is clear that appellees' suit asks this Court to extend its most exacting scrutiny to review a system that allegedly discriminates against a large, diverse, and amorphous class, unified only by the common factor of residence in districts that happen to have less taxable wealth than other districts. The system of alleged discrimination and the class it defines have none of the traditional indicia of suspectness: the class is not saddled with such disabilities, or subjected to such a history of purposeful unequal treatment, or relegated to such a position of political powerlessness as to command extraordinary protection from the majoritarian political process.

We thus conclude that the Texas system does not operate to the peculiar disadvantage of any suspect class. But in recognition of the fact that this Court has never heretofore held that wealth discrimination alone provides an adequate basis for invoking strict scrutiny, appellees have not relied solely on this contention. They also assert that the State's system impermissibly interferes with the exercise of a "fundamental" right and that accordingly the prior decisions of this Court require the application of the strict standard of judicial review. . . . It is this question—whether education is a fundamental right, in the sense that it is among the rights and liberties protected by the Constitution—which has so consumed the attention of courts and commentators in recent years.

B

. . . Nothing this Court holds today in any way detracts from our historic dedication to public education. . . . But the importance of a service performed by the State does not determine whether it must be regarded as fundamental for purposes of examination under the Equal Protection Clause.

The lesson of *[Shapiro* v. *Thomson* and *Dandridge* v. *Williams]* . . . in addressing the question now before the Court is plain. It is not the province of this Court to create substantive constitutional rights in the name of guaranteeing equal protection of the laws. Thus the key to discovering whether education is "fundamental" is not to be found in comparisons of the relative societal significance of education as opposed to subsistence or housing. Nor is it to be found by weighing whether education is as important as the right to travel. Rather, the answer lies in assessing whether there is a right to education explicitly or implicitly guaranteed by the Constitution. *Eisenstadt* v. *Baird,* 405 U.S. 438 (1972); *Dunn* v. *Blumstein,* 405 U.S. 330 (1972); * *Chicago Police Dept.* v. *Mosley,* 408 U.S. 92 (1972); *Skinner* v. *Oklahoma,* 316 U.S. 535 (1942).†

Education, of course, is not among the rights afforded explicit protection under our Federal Constitution. Nor do we find any basis for saying it is implicitly so protected.

[Appellees claim] that education is distinguishable from other services and benefits provided by the State because it bears a peculiarly close relationship to other rights and liberties accorded protection under the Constitution. Specifically, they insist that education is itself a fundamental personal right because it is essential to the effective exercise of First Amendment freedoms and to intelligent utilization of the right to vote. In asserting a nexus between speech and education, appellees urge that the right to speak is meaningless unless the speaker is capable of articulating his thoughts intelligently and persuasively. . . .

A similar line of reasoning is pursued with respect to the right to vote . . . : a voter cannot cast his ballot intelligently unless his reading skills and thought processes have been adequately developed.

We need not dispute any of these propositions. . . . Yet we have never presumed to possess either the ability or the authority to guarantee to the citizenry the most *effective* speech or the most *informed* electoral choice. That these may be desirable goals of a system of freedom of expression and of a representative form of government is not to be doubted. . . . But they are not values to be implemented by judicial intrusion into otherwise legitimate state activities.

Even if it were conceded that some identifiable quantum of education is a constitutionally protected prerequisite to the meaningful exercise of either right, we have no indication that the present levels of educational expenditure in Texas provide an education that falls short. [N]o charge fairly could be made that the system fails to provide each child with an opportunity to acquire the basic minimal skills necessary for the enjoyment of the rights of speech and of full participation in the political process.

Furthermore, the logical limitations on appellees' nexus theory are difficult to perceive. How, for instance, is education to be distinguished from the significant personal interests in the basics of decent food and shelter? Empirical examination might well buttress an assumption that the ill-fed, ill-clothed, and ill-housed are among the most ineffective participants in the political process and that they derive the least enjoyment from the benefits of the First Amendment. If so appellees' thesis would cast serious doubt on the authority of *Dandridge* v. *Williams,* and *Lindsey* v. *Normet,* . . .

* Dunn fully canvasses this Court's voting rights cases and explains that "this Court has made clear that a citizen has a *constitutionally protected right* to participate in elections on an equal basis with other citizens in the jurisdiction." [Emphasis supplied.] The constitutional underpinnings of the right to equal treatment in the voting process can no longer be doubted even though, as the Court noted in *Harper* v. *Virginia Bd. of Elections,* 383 U.S. 663, 665 (1966), "the right to vote in state elections is nowhere expressly mentioned.". . .

† *Skinner* applied the standard of close scrutiny to a state law permitting forced sterilization of "habitual criminals." Implicit in the Court's opinion is the recognition that the right of procreation is among the rights of personal privacy protected under the Constitution.

. . . In one further respect we find this a particularly inappropriate case in which to subject state action to strict judicial scrutiny. . . . Each of our prior [strict scrutiny] cases involved legislation which "deprived," "infringed," or "interfered" with the free exercise of some such fundamental personal right or liberty. . . . A critical distinction between those cases and the one now before us lies in what Texas is endeavoring to do with respect to education. . . . The Texas system of school finance is not unlike the federal legislation involved in *[Katzenbach* v. *Morgan].* Every step leading to the establishment of the system Texas utilizes today—including the decisions permitting localities to tax and expend locally, and creating and continuously expanding state aid—was implemented in an effort to *extend* public education and to improve its quality. Of course, every reform that benefits some more than others may be criticized for what it fails to accomplish. But we think it plain that, in substance, the thrust of the Texas system is affirmative and reformatory and, therefore, should be scrutinized under judicial principles sensitive to the nature of the State's efforts and to the rights reserved to the States under the Constitution.

C

. . . We need not rest our decision, however, solely on the inappropriateness of the strict scrutiny test. A century of Supreme Court adjudication under the Equal Protection Clause affirmatively supports the application of the traditional standard of review, which requires only that the State's system be shown to bear some rational relationship to legitimate state purposes. This case represents far more than a challenge to the manner in which Texas provides for the education of its children. We have here nothing less than a direct attack on the way in which Texas has chosen to raise and disburse state and local tax revenues. We are asked to condemn the State's judgment in conferring on political subdivisions the power to tax local property to supply revenues for local interests. In so doing, appellees would have the Court intrude in an area in which it has traditionally deferred to state legislatures. This Court has often admonished against such interferences with the State's fiscal policies under the Equal Protection Clause. . . .

Thus we stand on familiar ground when we continue to acknowledge that the Justices of this Court lack both the expertise and the familiarity with local problems necessary to the making of wise decisions with respect to the raising and disposition of public revenues. Yet we are urged to direct the States either to alter drastically the present system or to throw out the property tax altogether in favor of some other form of taxation. No scheme of taxation, whether the tax is imposed on property, income, or purchases of goods and services, has yet been devised which is free of all discriminatory impact. In such a complex arena in which no perfect alternatives exist, the Court does well not to impose too rigorous a standard of scrutiny lest all local fiscal schemes become subjects of criticism under the Equal Protection Clause.‡

In addition to matters of fiscal policy, this case also involves the most persistent and difficult questions of educational policy, another area in which this Court's lack

‡ Those who urge that the present system be invalidated offer little guidance as to what type of school financing should replace it. The most likely result of rejection of the existing system would be statewide financing of all public education with funds derived from taxation of property or from the adoption or expansion of sales and income taxes. . . . The authors of *Private Wealth and Public Education,* [Coons, Clune, and Sugarman], suggest an alternative scheme, known as "district power equalizing." In simplest terms, the State would guarantee that at any particular rate of property taxation the district would receive a stated number of dollars regardless of the district's tax base. To finance the subsidies to "poorer" districts, funds would be taken away from the "wealthier" districts that, because of their higher property values, collect more than the stated amount at any given rate. This is not the place to weigh the arguments for and against "district power equalizing," beyond noting that commentators are in disagreement as to whether it is feasible, how it would work, and indeed whether it would violate the equal protection theory underlying appellees' case.

of specialized knowledge and experience counsels against premature interference with the informed judgments made at the state and local levels. . . . On even the most basic questions in this area the scholars and educational experts are divided. Indeed, one of the hottest sources of controversy concerns the extent to which there is a demonstrable correlation between educational expenditures and the quality of education—an assumed correlation underlying virtually every legal conclusion drawn by the District Court in this case. . . . [Moreover], it would be difficult to imagine a case having a greater potential impact on our federal system than the one now before us, in which we are urged to abrogate systems of financing public education presently in existence in virtually every State.

The foregoing considerations buttress our conclusion that Texas' system of public school finance is an inappropriate candidate for strict judicial scrutiny. These same considerations are relevant to the determination whether that system, with its conceded imperfections, nevertheless bears some rational relationship to a legitimate state purpose. It is to this question that we next turn our attention.

III

. . . Because of differences in expenditure levels occasioned by disparities in property tax income, appellees claim that children in less affluent districts have been made the subject of invidious discrimination. The District Court found that the State had failed even "to establish a reasonable basis" for a system that results in different levels of per pupil expenditure. We disagree.

In its reliance on state as well as local resources, the Texas system is comparable to the systems employed in virtually every other State. . . . While assuring a basic education for every child in the State, it permits and encourages a large measure of participation in and control of each district's schools at the local level. In an era that has witnessed a consistent trend toward centralization of the functions of government, local sharing of responsibility for public education has survived. . . .

Appellees do not question the propriety of Texas' dedication to local control of education. To the contrary, they attack the school finance system precisely because, in their view, it does not provide the same level of local control and fiscal flexibility in all districts. Appellees suggest that local control could be preserved and promoted under other financing systems that result in more equality in educational expenditures. While it is no doubt true that reliance on local property taxation for school revenues provides less freedom of choice with respect to expenditures for some districts than for others,§ the existence of "some inequality" in the manner in which the State's rationale is achieved is not alone a sufficient basis for striking down the entire system. . . . Nor must the financing system fail because, as appellees suggest, other methods of satisfying the State's interest, which occasion "less drastic" disparities in expenditures, might be conceived. Only where state action impinges on the exercise of fundamental constitutional rights or liberties must it be found to have chosen the least restrictive alternative. . . . It is also well to remember that even those districts that have reduced ability to make free decisions with respect to how much they spend on education still retain under the present system a large measure of authority as to how available funds will be allocated. They further enjoy the power to make numerous other decisions with respect to the opera-

§ Mr. Justice White suggests in his dissent that the Texas system violates the Equal Protection Clause because the means it has selected to effectuate its interest in local autonomy fail to guarantee complete freedom of choice to every district. He places special emphasis on the statutory provision that establishes a maximum rate of $1.50 per $100 valuation at which a local school district may tax for school maintenance. The maintenance rate in Edgewood when this case was litigated in the District Court was $.55 per $100, barely one-third of the allowable rate. . . . Appellees do not claim that the ceiling presently bars desired tax increases in Edgewood or in any other Texas district. Therefore, the constitutionality of that statutory provision is not before us and must await litigation in a case in which it is properly presented. . . .

tion of the schools. || The people of Texas may be justified in believing . . . that along with increased control of the purse strings at the state level will go increased control over local policies.

Appellees further urge that the Texas system is unconstitutionally arbitrary because it allows the availability of local taxable resources to turn on "happenstance." They see no justification for a system that allows, as they contend, the quality of education to fluctuate on the basis of the fortuitous positioning of the boundary lines of political subdivisions and the location of valuable commercial and industrial property. But any scheme of local taxation—indeed the very existence of identifiable local governmental units—requires the establishment of jurisdictional boundaries that are inevitably arbitrary. It is equally inevitable that some localities are going to be blessed with more taxable assets than others. Nor is local wealth a static quantity. . . .

Moreover, if local taxation for local expenditure is an unconstitutional method of providing for education then it may be an equally impermissible means of providing other necessary services customarily financed largely from local property taxes, including local police and fire protection, public health and hospitals, and public utility facilities of various kinds. We perceive no justification for such a severe denigration of local property taxation and control as would follow from appellees' contentions. . . .

In sum, to the extent that the Texas system of school finance results in unequal expenditures between children who happen to reside in different districts, we cannot say that such disparities are the product of a system that is so irrational as to be invidiously discriminatory.

[I]t is important to remember that at every stage of its development it has constituted a "rough accommodation" of interests in an effort to arrive at practical and workable solutions. . . . One also must remember that the system here challenged is not peculiar to Texas or to any other State. In its essential characteristics the Texas plan for financing public education reflects what many educators for a half century have thought was an enlightened approach to a problem for which there is no perfect solution. We are unwilling to assume for ourselves a level of wisdom superior to that of legislators, scholars, and educational authorities in forty-nine States, especially where the alternatives proposed are only recently conceived and nowhere yet tested. The constitutional standard under the Equal Protection Clause is whether the challenged state action rationally furthers a legitimate state purpose or interest. . . . We hold that the Texas plan abundantly satisfies this standard.

IV

In light of the considerable attention that has focused on the District Court opinion in this case and on its California predecessor *[Serrano* v. *Priest]*, a cautionary post-

|| Mr. Justice Marshall states in his dissenting opinion that the State's asserted interest in local control is a "mere sham," and that it has been offered not as a legitimate justification but "as an excuse . . . for interdistrict inequality." In addition to asserting that local control would be preserved and possibly better served under other systems—a consideration that we find irrelevant for purpose of deciding whether the system may be said to be supported by a legitimate and reasonable basis—the dissent suggests that Texas' lack of good faith may be demonstrated by examining the extent to which the State already maintains considerable control. The State, we are told, regulates "the most minute details of local public education," including text-book selection, teacher qualifications, and the length of the school day. This assertion, that genuine local control does not exist in Texas, simply cannot be supported. It is abundantly refuted by the elaborate statutory division of responsibilities set out in the Texas Education Code. Although policy decision-making and supervision in certain areas are reserved to the State, the day-to-day authority over the "management and control" of all public elementary and secondary schools is squarely placed on the local school boards. . . . It cannot be seriously doubted that in Texas education remains largely a local function, and that the preponderating bulk of all decisions affecting the schools are made and executed at the local level, guaranteeing the greatest participation by those most directly concerned.

script seems appropriate. [A decision for the appellees] would occasion in Texas and elsewhere an unprecedented upheaval in public education. Some commentators have concluded that, whatever the contours of the alternative financing programs that might be devised and approved, the result could not avoid being a beneficial one. But [those] who have devoted the most thoughtful attention to the practical ramifications of these cases have found no clear or dependable answers and their scholarship reflects no such unqualified confidence in the desirability of completely uprooting the existing system.

The complexity of these problems is demonstrated by the lack of consensus with respect to whether it may be said with any assurance that the poor, the racial minorities, or the children in overburdened core-city school districts would be benefited by abrogation of traditional modes of financing education. Unless there is to be a substantial increase in state expenditures on education across the board—an event the likelihood of which is open to considerable question—these groups stand to realize gains in terms of increased per pupil expenditures only if they reside in districts that presently spend at relatively low levels, i.e., in those districts that would benefit from the redistribution of existing resources. Yet recent studies have indicated that the poorest families are not invariably clustered in the most impecunious school districts. Nor does it now appear that there is any more than a random chance that racial minorities are concentrated in property-poor districts. Additionally, several research projects have concluded that any financing alternative designed to achieve a greater equality of expenditures is likely to lead to higher taxation and lower educational expenditures in the major urban centers, a result that would exacerbate rather than ameliorate existing conditions in those areas.

These practical considerations, of course, play no role in the adjudication of the constitutional issues presented here. But they serve to highlight the wisdom of the traditional limitations on this Court's function. . . . We hardly need add that this Court's action today is not to be viewed as placing its judicial imprimatur on the status quo. The need is apparent for reform in tax systems which may well have relied too long and too heavily on the local property tax. And certainly innovative new thinking as to public education, its methods and its funding, is necessary to assure both a higher level of quality and greater uniformity of opportunity. . . . But the ultimate solutions must come from the lawmakers and from the democratic pressures of those who elect them.

Reversed.

[Mr. Justice Steward concurred.]

MR. JUSTICE WHITE, with whom MR. JUSTICE DOUGLAS and MR. JUSTICE BRENNAN join, dissenting: . . .

The Equal Protection Clause permits discriminations between classes but requires that the classification bear some rational relationship to a permissible object sought to be attained by the statute. It is not enough that the Texas system before us seeks to achieve the valid, rational purpose of maximizing local initiative; the means chosen by the State must also be rationally related to the end sought to be achieved. . . .

Neither Texas nor the majority heeds this rule. If the State aims at maximizing local initiative and local choice, by permitting school districts to resort to the real property tax if they choose to do so, it utterly fails in achieving its purpose in districts with property tax bases so low that there is little if any opportunity for interested parents, rich or poor, to augment school district revenues. Requiring the State to establish only that unequal treatment is in furtherance of a permissible goal, without also requiring the State to show that the means chosen to effectuate that goal are rationally related to its achievement, makes equal protection analysis no more than an empty gesture.* In my view,

* The State of Texas appears to concede that the choice of whether or not to go beyond the state-provided minimum "is easier for some districts than for others. Those districts with large amounts of taxable property can produce more revenue at a lower tax rate and will provide their children with more expensive education." Brief for Appellants, p. 35. The State nevertheless in-

(Continued)

the parents and children in Edgewood, and in like districts, suffer from an invidious discrimination violative of the Equal Protection Clause.

This does not, of course, mean that local control may not be a legitimate goal of a school financing system. Nor does it mean that the State must guarantee each district an equal per-pupil revenue from the state school financing system. Nor does it mean, as the majority appears to believe, that, by affirming the decision below, this Court would be "interposing on the States inflexible constitutional restraints. . . ." On the contrary, it would merely mean that the State must fashion a financing scheme which provides a rational basis for the maximization of local control, if local control is to remain a goal of the system, and not a scheme with "different treatment be[ing] accorded to persons placed by a statute into different classes on the basis of criteria wholly unrelated to the objective of that statute." *Reed* v. *Reed*, . . .

MR. JUSTICE MARSHALL, with whom MR. JUSTICE DOUGLAS concurs, dissenting:

I

. . . [H]owever praiseworthy Texas' equalizing efforts, the issue in this case is not whether Texas is doing its best to ameliorate the worst features of a discriminatory scheme, but rather whether the scheme itself is in fact unconstitutionally discriminatory in the face of the Fourteenth Amendment's guarantee of equal protection of the laws. . . . The necessary effect of the Texas local property tax is, in short, to favor property rich districts and to disfavor property poor ones. . . .

[The state argues] that whatever the differences in per pupil spending among Texas districts, there are no discriminatory consequences for the children of the disadvantaged districts. [They] reject the suggestion that the quality of education in any particular district is determined by money—beyond some minimal level of funding which they believe to be assured. . . .

In my view, though, even an unadorned restatement of this contention is sufficient to reveal its absurdity. . . . It is an inescapable fact that if one district has more funds available per pupil than another district, the former will have greater choice in educational planning than will the latter. . . .

[T]he appellants and the majority may believe that the Equal Protection Clause cannot be offended by substantially unequal state treatment of persons who are similarly situated so long as the State provides everyone with some unspecified amount of education which evidently is "enough." The basis for such a novel view is far from clear. . . . The Equal Protection Clause is not addressed to the minimal sufficiency but rather to the unjustifiable inequalities of state action. . . . Neither the majority nor appellants inform us how judicially manageable standards are to be derived for determining how much education is "enough" to excuse constitutional discrimination. One would think that the majority would heed its own fervent affirmation of judicial self-restraint before undertaking the complex task of determining at large what level of education is constitutionally sufficient. . . .

Despite the evident discriminatory effect of the Texas financing scheme, both the appellants and the majority raise substantial questions concerning the precise character of the disadvantaged class in this case. [T]he conclusion that the school children of property-poor districts constitute a sufficient class for our purposes seems indisputable to me. . . .

I believe it is sufficient that the overarching form of discrimination in this case is between the school children of Texas on

sists that districts have a choice and that the people in each district have exercised that choice by providing some real property tax money over and above the minimum funds guaranteed by the State. Like the majority, however, the State fails to explain why the Equal Protection Clause is not violated or how its goal of providing local government with realistic choices as to how much money should be expended on education is implemented where the system makes it much more difficult for some than for others to provide additional educational funds and where as a practical and legal matter it is impossible for some districts to provide the educational budgets that other districts can make available from real property tax revenues.

the basis of the taxable property wealth of the districts in which they happen to live. . . . [C]onsistent with the guarantee of equal protection of the laws, "the quality of public education may not be a function of wealth, other than the wealth of the state as a whole." Under such a principle, the children of a district are excessively advantaged if that district has more taxable property per pupil than the average amount of taxable property per pupil considering the State as a whole. By contrast, the children of a district are disadvantaged if that district has less taxable property per pupil than the state average. The majority attempts to disparage such a definition of the disadvantaged class as the product of an "artificially defined level" of district wealth. But such is clearly not the case, for this is the definition unmistakably dictated by the constitutional principle for which appellees have argued throughout the course of this litigation. . . . Whether this discrimination, against the school children of property-poor districts, inherent in the Texas financing scheme is violative of the Equal Protection Clause is the question to which we must now turn.

II

A

To begin, I must once more voice my disagreement with the Court's rigidified approach to equal protection analysis. . . . The Court apparently seeks to establish today that equal protection cases fall into one of two neat categories which dictate the appropriate standard of review—strict scrutiny or mere rationality. But this Court's decisions in the field of equal protection defy such easy categorization. A principled reading of what this Court has done reveals that it has applied a spectrum of standards in reviewing discrimination allegedly violative of the Equal Protection Clause. This spectrum clearly comprehends variations in the degree of care with which the Court will scrutinize particular classifications, depending, I believe, on the constitutional and societal importance of the interest adversely affected and the recognized invidiousness of the basis upon which the particular classification is drawn. I find in fact that many of the Court's recent decisions embody the very sort of reasoned approach to equal protection analysis for which I previously argued *[Dandridge* v. *Williams].*

I therefore cannot accept the majority's labored efforts to demonstrate that fundamental interests, which call for strict scrutiny of the challenged classification, encompass only established rights which we are somehow bound to recognize from the text of the Constitution itself. To be sure, some interests which the Court has deemed to be fundamental for purposes of equal protection analysis are themselves constitutionally protected rights. . . . But it will not do to suggest that the "answer" to whether an interest is fundamental for purposes of equal protection analysis is *always* determined by whether that interest "is a right . . . explicitly or implicitly guaranteed by the Constitution."†

I would like to know where the Constitution guarantees the right to procreate *[Skinner],* or the right to vote in state elections, or the right to an appeal from a criminal conviction, . . .

The majority is, of course, correct when it suggests that the process of determining which interests are fundamental is a difficult one. But I do not think the problem is insurmountable. And I certainly do not accept the view that the process need necessarily degenerate into an unprincipled, subjective "picking-and-choosing" between various interests or that it must involve this Court in creating "substantive constitutional rights in the name of guaranteeing equal protection of the laws." Although not all fundamental interests are constitutionally guaranteed, the determination of which interests are fundamental should be firmly rooted in the text of the Constitution. The task in every case should be to determine the extent to which constitutionally guaranteed rights are dependent on interests not mentioned in the Constitution. As the

† Indeed, the Court's theory would render the established concept of fundamental interests in the context of equal protection analysis superfluous, for the substantive constitutional right itself requires that this Court strictly scrutinize any asserted state interest for restricting or denying access to any particular guaranteed right. . . .

nexus between the specific constitutional guarantee and the nonconstitutional interest draws closer, the nonconstitutional interest becomes more fundamental and the degree of judicial scrutiny applied when the interest is infringed on a discriminatory basis must be adjusted accordingly. Thus, it cannot be denied that interests such as procreation, the exercise of the state franchise, and access to criminal appellate processes are not fully guaranteed to the citizen by our Constitution. But these interests have nonetheless been afforded special judicial consideration in the face of discrimination because they are, to some extent, interrelated with constitutional guarantees. Procreation is now understood to be important because of its interaction with the established constitutional right of privacy. The exercise of the state franchise is closely tied to basic civil and political rights inherent in the First Amendment. And access to criminal appellate processes enhances the integrity of the range of rights implicit in the Fourteenth Amendment guarantee of due process of law. Only if we closely protect the related interests from state discrimination do we ultimately ensure the integrity of the constitutional guarantee itself. This is the real lesson that must be taken from our previous decisions involving interests deemed to be fundamental.

The effect of the interaction of individual interests with established constitutional guarantees upon the degree of care exercised by this Court in reviewing state discrimination affecting such interests is amply illustrated by our decision last Term in *[Eisenstadt* v. *Baird]*. [I]n *Baird* the Court clearly did not adhere to [the standards it purported to apply—the] highly tolerant standards of traditional rational review. For although there were conceivable state interests intended to be advanced by the statute—e.g., deterrence of premarital sexual activity; regulation of the dissemination of potentially dangerous articles—the Court was not prepared to accept these interests on their face, but instead proceeded to test their substantiality by independent analysis. Such close scrutiny of the State's interests was hardly characteristic of the deference shown state classifications in the context of economic interests. . . . Yet I think the Court's action was entirely appropriate, for access to and use of contraceptives bears a close relationship to the individual's constitutional right of privacy. . . .

A similar process of analysis with respect to the invidiousness of the basis on which a particular classification is drawn has also influenced the Court as to the appropriate degree of scrutiny to be accorded any particular case. . . . It may be that all of [the] considerations which make for particular judicial solicitude in the face of discrimination on the basis of race, nationality, or alienage, do not coalesce—or at least not to the same degree—in other forms of discrimination. Nevertheless, these considerations have undoubtedly influenced the care with which the Court has scrutinized other forms of discrimination. . . .

In *[Reed* v. *Reed]*, the Court . . . was unwilling to consider a theoretical and unsubstantiated basis for distinction—however reasonable it might appear—sufficient to sustain a statute discriminating on the basis of sex.

James and *Reed* can only be understood as instances in which the particularly invidious character of the classification caused the Court to pause and scrutinize with more than traditional care the rationality of state discrimination. . . . Still, the Court's sensitivity to the invidiousness of the basis for discrimination is perhaps most apparent in its decisions protecting the interests of children born out of wedlock from discriminatory state action. See *[Weber* and *Levy]*. . . .

In summary, it seems to me inescapably clear that this Court has consistently adjusted the care with which it will review state discrimination in light of the constitutional significance of the interests affected and the invidiousness of the particular classification. In the context of economic interests we find that discriminatory state action is almost always sustained, for such interests are generally far removed from constitutional guarantees. . . . But the situation differs markedly when discrimination against important individual interests with constitutional implications and against particularly disadvantaged or powerless classes is involved. The majority suggests, however, that a variable standard of review would give this Court the appearance of a "super-legislature." I cannot agree. Such an approach seems to me a part of the guarantees of our Constitution and of the historic experiences with oppression of and discrimination against discrete, powerless minorities which underlie that Document. In truth, the Court itself will be open to the criticism raised by the majority so long as it continues on its present course of effectively selecting in private which cases will be afforded special consideration without acknowledging the true basis of its action. Opinions such as those in *Reed* . . . seem drawn more as efforts to shield rather than to reveal the true basis of the Court's decisions. Such obfuscated action may be appropriate to a political body such as a legislature, but it is not appropriate to this Court. Open debate of the bases for the Court's action is essential to the rationality and consistency of our decisionmaking process. Only in this way can we avoid the label of legislature and ensure the integrity of the judicial process.

Nevertheless, the majority today attempts to force this case into the same category for purposes of equal protection analysis as decisions involving discrimination affecting commercial interests. By so doing, the majority singles this case out for analytic treatment at odds with what seems to me to be the clear trend of recent decisions in this Court, and thereby ignores the constitutional importance of the interest at stake and the invidiousness of the particular classification, factors that call for far more than the lenient scrutiny of the Texas financing scheme which the majority pursues. Yet if the discrimination inherent in the Texas scheme is scrutinized with the care demanded by the interest and classification present in this case, the unconstitutionality of that scheme is unmistakable.

B

[T]he Court concludes that public education is not constitutionally guaranteed. It is true that this Court has never deemed the provision of free public education to be required by the Constitution. Nevertheless, the fundamental importance of education is amply indicated by the prior decisions of this Court, by the unique status accorded public education by our society, and by the close relationship between education and some of our most basic constitutional values. . . .

Education directly affects the ability of a child to exercise his First Amendment interests both as a source and as a receiver of information and ideas, whatever interests he may pursue in life. . . . Of particular importance is the relationship between education and the political process. . . . [O]f most immediate and direct concern must be the demonstrated effect of education on the exercise of the franchise by the electorate. . . . It is this very sort of intimate relationship between a particular personal interest and specific constitutional guarantees that has heretofore caused the Court to attach special significance, for purposes of equal protection analysis, to individual interests such as procreation and the exercise of the state franchise. ‡

[These] compel us to recognize the fun-

‡ I believe that the close nexus between education and our established constitutional values with respect to freedom of speech and participation in the political process makes this a different case than our prior decisions concerning discrimination affecting public welfare, see, e.g., *[Dandrige* v. *Williams],* or housing, see, e.g., *[Lindsey* v. *Normet].* There can be no question that, as the majority suggests, constitutional rights may be less meaningful for someone without enough to eat or without decent housing. But the crucial difference lies in the closeness of the relationship. Whatever the severity of the impact of insufficient food or inadequate housing on a person's life, they have never been considered to bear the same direct and immediate relationship to constitutional concerns for free speech and for our political processes as education has long been recognized to bear. Perhaps the best evidence of this fact is the unique status which has been accorded public education as the single public service nearly unanimously guaranteed in the constitutions of our States. Education, in terms of constitutional values, is much more analogous, in my judgment, to the right to vote in state elections than to public welfare or public housing. Indeed, it is not without significance that we have long recognized education as an essential step in providing the disadvantaged with the tools necessary to achieve economic self-sufficiency.

damentality of education and to scrutinize with appropriate care the bases for state discrimination affecting equality of educational opportunity in Texas school districts—a conclusion which is only strengthened when we consider the character of the classification in this case.

C

[Harper, Griffin, and *Douglas* (see Chapter 15)] refute the majority's contention that we have in the past required an absolute deprivation before subjecting wealth classifications to strict scrutiny. . . .

As the Court points out, no previous decision has deemed the presence of just a wealth classification to be sufficient basis to call forth "rigorous judicial scrutiny" of allegedly discriminatory state action. . . . That wealth classifications alone have not necessarily been considered to bear the same high degree of suspectness as have classifications based on, for instance, race or alienage may be explainable on a number of grounds. The "poor" may not be seen as politically powerless as certain discrete and insular minority groups. Personal poverty may entail much the same social stigma as historically attached to certain racial or ethnic groups. But personal poverty is not a permanent disability; its shackles may be escaped. Perhaps, most importantly, though, personal wealth may not necessarily share the general irrelevance as basis for legislative action that race or nationality is recognized to have. . . . Thus, we have generally gauged the invidiousness of wealth classifications with an awareness of the importance of the interests being affected and the relevance of personal wealth to those interests. . . .

When evaluated with these considerations in mind, it seems to me that discrimination on the basis of group wealth in this case likewise calls for careful judicial scrutiny. . . . In the final analysis, then, the invidious characteristics of the group wealth classification present in this case merely serves to emphasize the need for careful judicial scrutiny of the State's justifications for the resulting interdistrict discrimination in the educational opportunity afforded to the school children of Texas.

D

The nature of our inquiry into the justifications for state discrimination is essentially the same in all equal protection cases. We must consider the substantiality of the state interests sought to be served, and we must scrutinize the reasonableness of the means by which the State has sought to advance its interests. Differences in the application of this test are, in my view, a function of the constitutional importance of the interests at stake and the invidiousness of the particular classification. [W]hen interests of constitutional importance are at stake, the Court does not stand ready to credit the State's classification with any conceivable legitimate purpose, but demands a clear showing that there are legitimate state interests which the classification was in fact intended to serve. Beyond the question of the adequacy of the state's purpose for the classification, the Court traditionally has become increasingly sensitive to the means by which a State chooses to act as its action affects more directly interests of constitutional significance. . . . Thus, by now, "less restrictive alternatives" analysis is firmly established in equal protection jurisprudence. . . . Here both the nature of the interest and the classification dictate close judicial scrutiny of the purposes which Texas seeks to serve with its present educational financing scheme and of the means it has selected to serve that purpose.

The only justification offered by appellants to sustain the discrimination in educational opportunity caused by the Texas financing scheme is local educational control. [T]rue state dedication to local control would present, I think, a substantial justification to weigh against simple interdistrict variations in the treatment of a State's school children. But I need not now decide how I might ultimately strike the balance were we confronted with a situation where the State's sincere concern for local control inevitably produced educational inequality. For on this record, it is apparent that the State's purported concern with local control is offered primarily as an excuse rather than as a justification for interdistrict inequality.

In Texas statewide laws regulate in fact the most minute details of local public education. . . . Moreover, even if we accept Texas' general dedication to local control in educational matters, it is difficult to find any evidence of such dedication with respect to fiscal matters. . . . If Texas had a system truly dedicated to local fiscal control one would expect the quality of the educational opportunity provided in each district to vary with the decision of the voters in that district as to the level of sacrifice they wish to make for public education. In fact, the Texas scheme produces precisely the opposite result. Local school districts cannot choose to have the best education in the State by imposing the highest tax rate. Instead, the quality of the educational opportunity offered by any particular district is largely determined by the amount of taxable property located in the district—a factor over which local voters can exercise no control. The study introduced in the District Court showed a direct inverse relationship between equalized taxable district property wealth and district tax effort with the result that the property poor districts making the highest tax effort obtained the lowest per pupil yield. . . .

In my judgment, any substantial degree of scrutiny of the operation of the Texas financing scheme reveals that the State has selected means wholly inappropriate to secure its purported interest in assuring its school districts local fiscal control.§ If, for the sake of local education control, this Court is to sustain interdistrict discrimination in the educational opportunity afforded Texas school children, it should require that the State present something more than the mere sham now before us.

III

In conclusion it is essential to recognize that an end to the wide variations in taxable district property wealth inherent in the Texas financing scheme would entail none of the untoward consequences suggested by the Court or by the appellants.

First, affirmance of the District Court's decisions would hardly sound the death knell for local control of education. Nor does the District Court's decision even necessarily eliminate local control of educational funding. Both centralized and decentralized plans for educational funding not involving interdistrict discrimination have been put forward. ‖ The choice among these

§ My Brother White, in concluding that the Texas financing scheme runs afoul of the Equal Protection Clause, likewise finds on analysis that the means chosen by Texas—local property taxation depended upon local taxable wealth—is completely unsuited in its present form to the achievement of the asserted goal of providing local fiscal control. Although my Brother White purports to reach this result by application of that lenient standard of mere rationality traditionally applied in the context of commercial interests, it seems to me that the care with which he scrutinizes the practical effectiveness of the present local property tax as a device for affording local fiscal control reflects the application of a more stringent standard of review, a standard which at the least is influenced by the constitutional significance of the process of public education.

‖ Centralized educational financing is, to be sure, one alternative. On analysis, though, it is clear that even centralized financing would leave in local hands the entire gamut of local educational policy-making—teachers, curriculum, school sites, the whole process of allocating resources among alternative educational objectives.

A second possibility is the much discussed theory of district power equalization put forth by Professors Coons, Clune, and Sugarman in their seminal work, *Private Wealth and Public Education* 201–242 (1970). Such a scheme would truly reflect a dedication to local fiscal control. Under their system, each school district would receive a fixed amount of revenue per pupil for any particular level of tax effort regardless of the level of local property tax base. . . .

District wealth reapportionment is yet another alternative which would accomplish directly essentially what district power equalization would seek to do artificially. . . .

A fourth possibility would be to remove commercial, industrial, and mineral property from local tax rolls, to tax this property on a statewide basis, and to return the resulting revenues to the local districts in a fashion that would compensate for remaining variations in the local tax bases.

None of these particular alternatives [is] nec-

(Continued)

personal rights might the classification endanger?

As was said in *Glona:* ". . . we see no possible rational basis . . . for assuming that if the natural mother is allowed recovery for the wrongful death of her illegitimate child, the cause of illegitimacy will be served. It would, indeed, be farfetched to asssume that women have illegitimate children so that they can be compensated in damages for their death."

. . . Nor can it be thought here that persons will shun illicit relations because the off-spring may not one day reap the benefits of workmen's compensation. . . .

The state interest in legitimate family relationships is not served by the statute; the state interest in minimizing problems of proof is not significantly disturbed by our decision. The inferior classification of dependent unacknowledged illegitimates bears, in this instance, no significant relationship to those recognized purposes of recovery which workmen's compensation statutes commendably serve.

The status of illegitimacy has expressed through the ages society's condemnation of irresponsible liaisons beyond the bonds of marriage. But visiting this condemnation on the head of an infant is illogical and unjust.

. . . Obviously, no child is responsible for his birth and penalzing the illegitimate child is an ineffectual—as well as an unjust—way of deterring the parent. Courts are powerless to prevent the social opprobrium suffered by these hapless children, but the Equal Protection Clause does enable us to strike down discriminatory laws relating to status of birth where—as in this case—the classification is justified by no legitimate state interest, compelling or otherwise.

[Mr. Justice Blackmun, concurred.]

MR. JUSTICE REHNQUIST, dissenting:

The Court in today's opinion, recognizing that two different standards have been applied in equal protection cases, apparently formulated a hybrid standard which is the basis of decision here. The standard is a two-pronged one:

> "What legitimate state interest does the classification promote? What fundamental personal rights might the classification endanger?"

Surely there could be no better nor more succinct guide to sound legislation than that suggested by these two questions. They are somewhat less useful, however, as guides to constitutional adjudication. . . .

While the Court's opinion today is by no means a sharp departure from the precedents on which it relies, it is an extraordinary departure from what I conceive to be the interest of the framers of the Fourteenth Amendment and the import of the traditional presumption of constitutionality accorded to legislative enactments. Nowhere in the text of the Constitution, or in its plain implications, is there any guide for determining what is a "legitimate" state interest, or what is a "fundamental personal right." The traditional police power of the States has been thought to embrace any measure thought to further the well-being of the State in question, subject only to the specific prohibitions contained in the Federal Constitution. That Constitution of course contains numerous guarantees of individual liberty, which I would have no trouble describing as "fundamental personal liberties," but the right of illegitimate children to sue in state court to recover workmen's compensation benefits is not among them. . . .

In the instant case I cannot condemn as irrational Louisiana's distinction between legitimate and illegitimate children. In a statutory compensation scheme such as this, the State must inevitably draw rather fine and arbitrary lines. For example, Louisiana declares that parents will have priority in this scheme over first-cousins, regardless of the degree of dependency or affection in any given case. Surely, no one would condemn this classification as violative of the Fourteenth Amendment, since it is likely to reflect fairly the unarticulated intent of the decedent. Similarly, the State might rationally presume that the decedent would have preferred the compensation to go to his legitimate children, rather than those illegitimates whom he has not acknowledged.

Although the majority argues that "the state interest in minimizing problems of proof is not *significantly* disturbed by our decision," [emphasis added] it clearly recognizes, as it must, that under its decision additional and sometimes more difficult problems of proof of paternity and dependency may be raised.

. . . Louisiana, like many other states, has a wide variety of laws designed to . . . discourage formation of illicit family relationships. Whether this is a wise state policy, or whether this particular statute will be particularly effective in advancing it, are not matters for this Court's determination.

Levy and today's decision . . . are quite inconsistent with *Dandridge* v. *Williams,* decided the year after *Levy.* If state welfare legislation involving "the most basic economic needs of impoverished human beings" is to be judged by the traditional "reasonable basis" standard, I am at a loss to see why that standard should not likewise govern legislation determining eligibility for state workmen's compensation benefits.

All legislation involves classification and line drawing of one kind or another. When this Court expands the traditional "reasonable basis" standard for judgment under the Equal Protection Clause into a search for "legitimate" state interests which the legislation may "promote," and "for fundamental personal rights" which it might "endanger," it is doing nothing less than passing policy judgments upon the acts of every state legislature in the country.

FRONTIERO *v.* RICHARDSON

411 U.S. 677; 93 Sup. Ct. 1764; 36 L. Ed. 2d 583 (1973)

[Richardson was Secretary of Defense at the time of this suit.]

MR. JUSTICE BRENNAN announced the judgment of the Court in an opinion in which MR. JUSTICE DOUGLAS, MR. JUSTICE WHITE, and MR. JUSTICE MARSHALL join:

The question before us concerns the right of a female member of the uniformed services to claim her spouse as a "dependent" for the purposes of obtaining increased quarters allowances and medical and dental benefits under 37 U.S.C. Sections 401, 403, and 10 U.S.C. Sections 1072, 1076, on an equal footing with male members. Under these statutes, a serviceman may claim his wife as a "dependent" without regard to whether she is in fact dependent upon him for any part of her support. . . . A servicewoman, on the other hand, may not claim her husband as a "dependent" under these programs unless he is in fact dependent upon her for over one half of his support. . . . Thus, the question for decision is whether this difference in treatment constitutes an unconstitutional discrimination against servicewomen in violation of the Due Process Clause of the Fifth Amendment. A three-judge [court] rejected this contention. . . .

Appellant Sharron Frontiero, a lieutenant in the United States Air Force, sought increased quarters allowances, and housing and medical benefits for her husband, appellant Joseph Frontiero, on the ground that he was her "dependent." Although such benefits would automatically have been granted with respect to the wife of a male member of the uniformed services, appellant's application was denied because she failed to demonstrate that her husband was dependent on her for more than one-half of his support. Appellants then commenced this suit, contending that, by making this distinction, the statutes unreasonably discriminate on the basis of sex in violation of the Due Process Clause of the Fifth Amendment. In essence, appellants asserted that the discriminatory impact of the statutes is two-fold: first, as a procedural matter, a female member is required to demonstrate her spouse's dependency, while no such burden is imposed upon male members; and second, as a substantive matter, a male member who does not provide more than one-half of his wife's support receives benefits, while a similarly situated female member is denied such benefits. . . .

At the outset, appellants contend that classifications based upon sex, like classifications based upon race, alienage, and national origin, are inherently suspect and must therefore be subjected to close judicial scrutiny. We agree and, indeed, find at least implicit support for such an approach in our unanimous decision only last Term in *Reed* v. *Reed,* 404 U.S. 71 (1971).

[T]he Court [in Reed] implicitly rejected

appellee's apparently rational explanation of the statutory scheme, and concluded that, by ignoring the individual qualifications of particular applicants, the challenged statute provided "dissimilar treatment for men and women who are . . . similarly situated." . . . This departure from "traditional" rational basis analysis with respect to sex-based classifications is clearly justified.

There can be no doubt that our Nation has had a long and unfortunate history of sex discrimination. Traditionally, such discrimination was rationalized by an attitude of "romantic paternalism" which, in practical effect, put women not on a pedestal, but in a cage.

As a result of notions such as these, our statute books gradually became laden with gross, stereotypical distinctions between the sexes and, indeed, throughout much of the nineteenth century the position of women in our society was, in many respects, comparable to that of blacks under the pre-Civil War slave codes. Neither slaves nor women could hold office, serve on juries, or bring suit in their own names, and married women traditionally were denied the legal capacity to hold or convey property or to serve as legal guardians of their own children. . . . And although blacks were guaranteed the right to vote in 1870, women were denied even that right—which is itself "preservative of other basic civil and political rights"—until adoption of the Nineteenth Amendment half a century later.

It is true, of course, that the position of women in America has improved markedly in recent decades. Nevertheless, it can hardly be doubted that, in part because of the high visibility of the sex characteristic, women still face pervasive, although at times more subtle, discrimination in our educational institutions, on the job market and, perhaps most conspicuously, in the political arena.* . . .

Moreover, since sex, like race and national origin, is an immutable characteristic determined solely by the accident of birth, the imposition of special disabilities upon the members of a particular sex because of their sex would seem to violate "the basic concept of our system that legal burdens should bear some relationship to individual responsibility. . . ." *Weber v. Aetna Casualty & Surety Company* . . . And what differentiates sex from such nonsuspect statuses as intelligence or physical disability, and aligns it with the recognized suspect criteria, is that the sex characteristic frequently bears no relation to ability to perform or contribute to society. As a result, statutory distinctions between the sexes often have the effect of invidiously relegating the entire class of females to inferior legal status without regard to the actual capabilities of its individual members. . . .

With these considerations in mind, we can only conclude that classifications based upon sex, like classifications based upon race, alienage, or national origin, are inherently suspect, and must therefore be subjected to strict judicial scrutiny. Applying the analysis mandated by that stricter standard of review, it is clear that the statutory scheme now before us is constitutionally invalid.

. . . [T]he Government concedes that the differential treatment accorded men and women under these statutes serves no purpose other than mere "administrative convenience." In essence, the Government maintains that, as an empirical matter, wives in our society frequently are dependent upon their husbands, while husbands rarely are dependent upon their wives. Thus, the Government argues that Congress might reasonably have concluded that it would be both cheaper and easier simply conclusively to presume that wives of male members are financially dependent upon their husbands, while burdening female

* It is true, of course, that when viewed in the abstract, women do not constitute a small and powerless minority. Nevertheless, in part because of past discrimination, women are vastly underrepresented in this Nation's decisionmaking councils. There has never been a female President, nor a female member of this Court. Not a single woman presently sits in the United States Senate, and only 14 women hold seats in the House of Representatives. And, as appellants point out, this underrepresentation is present throughout all levels of our State and Federal Government. . . .

members with the task of establishing dependency in fact.

The Government offers no concrete evidence, however, to support its view that such differential treatment in fact saves the Government any money. In order to satisfy the demands of strict judicial scrutiny, the Government must demonstrate, for example, that it is actually cheaper to grant increased benefits with respect to *all* male members, than it is to determine which male members are in fact entitled to such benefits and to grant increased benefits only to those members whose wives actually meet the dependency requirement. Here, however, there is substantial evidence that, if put to the test, many of the wives of male members would fail to qualify for benefits. And in light of the fact that the dependency determination with respect to the husbands of female members is presently made solely on the basis of affidavits, rather than through the more costly hearing process, the Government's explanation of the statutory scheme is, to say the least, questionable.

In any case, our prior decisions make clear that, although efficacious administration of governmental programs is not without some importance, "the Constitution recognizes higher values than speed and efficiency." *Stanley* v. *Illinois,* 405 U.S. 645, 656 (1972). And when we enter the realm of "strict judicial scrutiny," there can be no doubt that "administrative convenience" is not a shibboleth, the mere recitation of which dictates constitutionality. See *Shapiro* v. *Thompson; Carrington* v. *Rash,* 380 U.S. 89 (1965). On the contrary, any statutory scheme which draws a sharp line between the sexes, *solely* for the purpose of achieving administrative convenience, necessarily commands "dissimilar treatment for men and women who are . . . similarly situated," and therefore involves the "very kind of arbitrary legislative choice forbidden by the [Constitution]. . . ." *Reed* v. *Reed,* supra, at 77, 76. We therefore conclude that, by according differential treatment to male and female members of the uniformed services for the sole purpose of achieving administrative convenience, the challenged statutes violate the Due Process Clause of the Fifth Amendment insofar as they require a female member to prove the dependency of her husband.

MR. JUSTICE POWELL, with whom THE CHIEF JUSTICE [BURGER] and MR. JUSTICE BLACKMUN join, concurring in the judgment:

I agree that the challenged statutes constitute an unconstitutional discrimination against service women in violation of the Due Process Clause of the Fifth Amendment, but I cannot join the opinion of Mr. Justice Brennan. . . . It is unnecessary for the Court in this case to characterize sex as a suspect classification, with all of the far-reaching implications of such a holding. *Reed* v. *Reed* . . . which abundantly supports our decision today, did not add sex to the narrowly limited group of classifications which are inherently suspect. In my view, we can and should decide this case on the authority of *Reed* and reserve for the future any expansion of its rationale. *[Mr. Justice Rehnquist dissented.]*

MR. JUSTICE STEWART concurs in the judgment, agreeing that the statutes before us work an invidious discrimination in violation of the Constitution. *Reed* v. *Reed.*

MASSACHUSETTS BD. OF RETIREMENT *v.* MURGIA
427 U.S. 307; 96 S. Ct. 2562, 49; L. Ed. 2d 520 (1976)

Per Curiam.

This case presents the question whether the provision of a state statute requiring that a uniformed State Police Officer "shall be retired . . . upon his attaining age fifty" denies appellee police officer equal protection of the laws in violation of the Fourteenth Amendment.

Appellee Robert Murgia was an officer in the Uniformed Branch of the Massachusetts State Police. The Massachusetts Board of Retirement retired him upon his 50th birthday. . . . uniformed state officers [must] pass a comprehensive physical examination biennially until age 40. After that, until mandatory retirement at age 50, uniformed officers must pass annually a more rigorous examination. . . . Appellee Murgia had passed such an examination four months before he was retired, and there is no dispute that, when he retired, his excellent physical and mental health still rendered him capable of performing the duties of a uniformed officer. . . . The testimony clearly established that the risk of physical failure, particularly in the cardiovascular system, increases with age, and that the number of individuals in a given age group incapable of performing stress functions increases with the age of the group. The testimony also recognized that particular individuals over 50 could be capable of safely performing the functions of uniformed officers. . . . evaluating the risk of cardiovascular failure in a given individual would require a detailed number of studies. . . .

Rationality is the proper standard by which to test whether compulsory retirement at age 50 violates equal protection.

We need state only briefly our reasons for agreeing that strict scrutiny is not the proper test for determining whether the mandatory retirement provision denies appellee equal protection. . . . *[San Antonio Independent School District* v. *Rodriguez]* reaffirmed that equal protection analysis requires strict scrutiny of a legislative classification only when the classification impermissibly interferes with the exercise of a fundamental right or operates to the peculiar disadvantage of a suspect class. Mandatory retirement at age 50 under the Massachusetts statute involves neither situation. This Court's decisions give no support to the proposition that a right of governmental employment per se is fundamental. . . .

Nor does the class of uniformed state police officers over 50 constitute a suspect class for purposes of equal protection analysis. *Rodriguez* observed that a suspect class is one "saddled with such disabilities, or subjected to such a history of purposeful unequal treatment, or relegated to such a position of political powerlessness as to command extraordinary protection from the majoritarian political process." While the treatment of the aged in this Nation has not been wholly free of discrimination, such persons, unlike, say, those who have been discriminated against on the basis of race or national origin, have not experienced a "history of purposeful unequal treatment" or been subjected to unique disabilities on the basis of stereotyped characteristics not truly indicative of their abilities. The class subject to the compulsory retirement feature of the Massachusetts statute consists of uniformed state police officers over the age of 50. It cannot be said to discriminate only against the elderly. Rather, it draws the line at a certain age in middle life. But even old age does not define a "discrete and insular" group, *United States* v. *Carolene Products Co.,* n. 4 (1938), in need of "extraordinary protection from the majoritarian political process." Instead, it marks a stage that each of us will reach if we live out our normal span. Even if the statute could be said to impose a penalty upon a class defined as the aged, it would not impose a distinction sufficiently akin to those classifications that we have found suspect to call for strict judicial scrutiny. . . .

We turn then to examine this state classification under the rational basis standard. This inquiry employs a relatively relaxed standard reflecting the Court's awareness that the drawing of lines that create distinctions is peculiarly a legislative task and an unavoidable one. Perfection in making the necessary classifications is neither possible nor necessary. Such action by a legislature is presumed to be valid.

In this case, the Massachusetts statute clearly meets the requirements of the Equal Protection Clause, for the State's classification rationally furthers the purpose identified by the State: Through mandatory retirement at age 50, the legislature seeks to protect the public by assuring physical preparedness of its uniformed police. Since physical ability generally declines with age, mandatory retirement at 50 serves to remove from police service those whose fitness for uniformed work presumptively has diminished with age. This clearly is rationally related to the State's objective. There is no indication that [this requirement] has the effect of excluding from service so few officers who are in fact unqualified as to render age 50 a criterion wholly unrelated to the objective of the statute.

That the State chooses not to determine fitness more precisely through individualized testing after age 50 is not to say that the objective of assuring physical fitness is not rationally furthered by a maximum age limitation. It is only to say that with regard to the interest of all concerned, the State perhaps has not chosen the best means to accomplish this purpose. But where rationality is the test, a State "does not violate the Equal Protection Clause merely because the classifications made by its laws are imperfect." *Dandridge* v. *Williams*. . . .

Reversed.

MR. JUSTICE STEVENS took no part in the consideration or decision of this case.

MR. JUSTICE MARSHALL, dissenting:

I. Although there are signs that its grasp on the law is weakening, the rigid two-tier model still holds sway as the Court's articulated description of the equal protection test. Again, I must object to its perpetuation. The model's two fixed modes of analysis, strict scrutiny and mere rationality, simply do not describe the inquiry the Court has undertaken—or should undertake—in equal protection cases. Rather, the inquiry has been much more sophisticated and the Court should admit as much. It has focused upon the character of the classification in question, the relative importance to individuals in the class discriminated against of the governmental benefits that they do not receive, and the state interests asserted in support of the classification. . . . Although the Court outwardly adheres to the two-tier model, it has apparently lost interest in recognizing further "fundamental" rights and "suspect" classes. . . . In my view, this result is the natural consequence of the limitations of the Court's traditional equal protection analysis. If a statute invades a "fundamental" right or discriminates against a "suspect" class, it is subject to strict scrutiny. If a statute is subject to strict scrutiny, the statute always, or nearly always . . . is struck down. Quite obviously, the only critical decision is whether strict scrutiny should be invoked at all. It should be no surprise, then, that the Court is hesitant to expand the number of categories of rights and classes subject to strict scrutiny, when each expansion involves the invalidation of virtually every classification bearing upon a newly covered category.

But however understandable the Court's hesitancy to invoke strict scrutiny, all remaining legislation should not drop into the bottom tier, and be measured by the mere rationality test. For that test, too, when applied as articulated, leaves little doubt about the outcome; the challenged legislation is always upheld. It cannot be gainsaid that there remain rights, not now classified as "fundamental," that remain vital to the flourishing of a free society, and classes, not now classified as "suspect," that are unfairly burdened by invidious discrimination unrelated to the individual worth of their members. Whatever we call these rights and classes, we simply cannot forgo all judicial protection against discriminatory legislation bearing upon them, but for the rare instances when the legislative choice can be termed "wholly irrelevant" to the legislative goal. *McGowan* v. *Maryland.*

While the Court's traditional articulation of the rational basis test does suggest just such an abdication, happily the Court's deeds have not matched its words. Time and again, met with cases touching upon the prized rights and burdened classes of our society, the Court has acted only after a reasonably probing look at the legislative goals and means, and at the significance of the personal rights and interests invaded. *Stanton* v. *Stanton; Weinberger* v. *Weisenfeld; United States Dept. of Agriculture* v. *Moreno; Frontiero* v. *Richardson* (Powell, J., concurring in the judgment); *James* v. *Strange; Weber* v. *Aetna Casualty & Surety Co.; Eisenstadt* v. *Baird; Reed* v. *Reed*. . . . These cases make clear that the Court has rejected, albeit sub silentio, its most deferential statements of the rationality standard in assessing the validity under the Equal Protection Clause of much noneconomic legislation.

. . . All interests not "fundamental" and all classes not "suspect" are not the same; and it is time for the Court to drop the pretense that, for purposes of the Equal Protection Clause, they are.

The danger of the Court's verbal adherence to the rigid two-tier test, despite its effective repudiation of that test in the cases, is demonstrated by its efforts here. There is simply no reason why a statute that tells able-bodied police officers, ready and willing to work, that they no longer have the right to earn a living in their chosen profession merely because they are 50 years old should be judged by the same minimal standards of rationality that we use to test economic legislation that discriminates against business interests.

Whether "fundamental" or not, "the right of the individual . . . to engage in any of the common occupations of life" has been repeatedly recognized by this Court as falling within the concept of liberty guaranteed by the Fourteenth Amendment. *Board of Regents* v. *Roth,* quoting *Meyer* v. *Nebraska.* . . . While depriving any government employee of his job is a significant deprivation, it is particularly burdensome when the person deprived is an older citizen. Once terminated, the elderly cannot readily find alternative employment. The lack of work is not only economically damaging, but emotionally and physically draining. . . . Not only are the elderly denied important benefits when they are terminated on the basis of age, but the classification of older workers is itself one that merits judicial attention. Whether older workers constitute a "suspect" class or not, it cannot be disputed that they constitute a class subject to repeated and arbitrary discrimination in employment. . . .

Of course, the Court is quite right in suggesting that distinctions exist between the elderly and traditional suspect classes such as Negroes, and between the elderly and "quasi-suspect" classes such as women or illegitimates. The elderly are protected not only by certain anti-discrimination legislation, but by legislation that provides them with positive benefits not enjoyed by the public at large. Moreover, the elderly are not isolated in society, and discrimination against them is not pervasive but is centered primarily in employment. The advantage of a flexible equal protection standard, however, is that it can readily accommodate such variables. The elderly are undoubtedly discriminated against, and when legislation denies them an important benefit—employment—I conclude that to sustain the legislation the Commonwealth must show a reasonably substantial interest and a scheme reasonably closely tailored to achieving that interest. . . .

Turning, then, to the Commonwealth's arguments, I agree that the purpose of the mandatory retirement law is legitimate, and indeed compelling. The Commonwealth has every reason to assure that its state police officers are of sufficient physical strength and health to perform their jobs. In my view, however, the means chosen, the forced retirement of officers at age 50, is so overinclusive that it must fall.

. . . The Commonwealth does not seriously assert that its testing is no longer effective at age 50, nor does it claim that continued testing would serve no purpose because officers over 50 are no longer physically able to perform their jobs. Thus the Commonwealth is in the position of already individually testing its police officers for physical fitness, conceding that such testing is adequate to determine the physical ability of an officer to continue on the job, and conceding that that ability may continue after age 50. In these circumstances, I see no reason at all for automatically terminating those officers who reach the age of 50; indeed, that action seems the height of irrationality.

Accordingly, I conclude that the Commonwealth's mandatory retirement law cannot stand when measured against the significant deprivation the Commonwealth's action works upon the terminated employees. . . .

REGENTS OF THE UNIVERSITY OF CALIFORNIA *v.* BAKKE

438 U.S. 265; 98 S.Ct. 2733; 57 L. Ed. 2nd 750 (1978)

[The Medical School at University of California, Davis opened in 1968. By 1973 it was admitting sixteen disadvantaged, minority students by a special procedure separate from that used in selecting other students. In that year the eighty-four regular admittees had

a median science grade point average of 3.51, median quantitative MCAT scores of 76th percentile, and median science MCAT scores of 83rd percentile. Special admittees had corresponding scores of 2.62, 24th percentile and 35th percentile. In that year white applicant Bakke had scores of 3.44, 94th and 97th percentiles. He was not admitted. Subsequently he filed suit in the California Superior Court. The Superior Court found that the special admissions program violated the federal constitution, the state constitution and Title VI (Sec. 601) of the Civil Rights Act of 1964, but nevertheless refused to order Bakke admitted. He appealed to the California Supreme Court which held that, while the University might take economic and social disadvantage into account, taking race into account in admissions decisions violated the equal protection clause of the 14th Amendment. It ordered Bakke admitted. The University then successfully sought certiorari *in the U.S. Supreme Court.]*

MR. JUSTICE POWELL announced the judgment of the Court:

For the reasons stated in the following opinion, I believe that so much of the judgment of the California court as holds petitioner's special admissions program unlawful and directs that respondent be admitted to the Medical School must be affirmed. For the reasons expressed in a separate opinion, my Brothers THE CHIEF JUSTICE, MR. JUSTICE STEWART, MR. JUSTICE REHNQUIST, and MR. JUSTICE STEVENS concur in this judgment.

I also conclude for the reasons stated in the following opinion that the portion of the court's judgment enjoining petitioner from according any consideration to race in its admissions process must be reversed. For reasons expressed in separate opinions, my Brothers MR. JUSTICE BRENNAN, MR. JUSTICE WHITE, MR. JUSTICE MARSHALL, and MR. JUSTICE BLACKMUN concur in this judgment.

The language of § 601, like that of the Equal Protection Clause, is majestic in its sweep:

> "No person in the United States shall, on the ground of race, color, or national origin, be excluded from participation in, be denied the benefits of, or be subjected to discrimination under any program or activity receiving Federal financial assistance."

The concept of "discrimination," like the phrase "equal protection of the laws," is susceptible to varying interpretations, . . . Although isolated statements of various legislators, taken out of context, can be marshalled in support of the proposition that § 601 enacted a purely color-blind scheme, without regard to the reach of the Equal Protection Clause, these comments must be read against the background of both the problem that Congress was addressing and the broader view of the statute that emerges from a full examination of the legislative debates.

The problem confronting Congress was discrimination against Negro citizens at the hands of recipients of federal moneys. . . .

In addressing that problem, supporters of Title VI repeatedly declared that the bill enacted constitutional principles. For example, Representative Celler, the Chairman of the House Judiciary Committee and floor manager of the legislation in the House, emphasized this in introducing the bill: "It would, in short, *assure the existing right to equal treatment* in the enjoyment of Federal funds. It would not destroy any rights of private property or freedom of association." (emphasis added). . . .

In view of the clear legislative intent, Title VI must be held to proscribe only those racial classifications that would violate the Equal Protection Clause or the Fifth Amendment. . . .

En route to [the] crucial battle over the scope of judicial review, the parties fight a sharp preliminary action over the proper characterization of the special admissions program. Petitioner prefers to view it as establishing a "goal" of minority representation in the medical school. Respondent, echoing the courts below, labels it a racial quota.

This semantic distinction is beside the point: the special admissions program is undeniably a classification based on race and ethnic background. To the extent that there existed a pool of at least minimally qualified minority applicants to fill the 16 special admissions seats, white applicants could compete only for 84 seats in the entering class, rather than the 100 open to minority applicants. Whether this limitation is described as a quota or a goal, it is a line drawn on the basis of race and ethnic status. . . .*

It is settled beyond question that the "rights created by the first section of the Fourteenth Amendment are, by its terms, guaranteed to the individual. They are personal rights," *Shelley* v. *Kraemer*. . . . The guarantee of equal protection cannot mean one thing when applied to one individual and something else when applied to a person of another color. If both are not accorded the same protection, then it is not equal.

Nevertheless, petitioner argues that the court below erred in applying strict scrutiny to the special admissions programs because white males, such as respondent, are not a "discrete and insular minority" requiring extraordinary protection from the majoritarian political process. *Carolene Products Co.,* n. 4. This rationale, however, has never been invoked in our decisions as a prerequisite to subjecting racial or ethnic distinctions to strict scrutiny. Nor has this Court held that discreteness and insularity constitute necessary preconditions to a holding that a particular classification is invidious. See, *e.g., Skinner* v. *Oklahoma,* . . . Racial and ethnic classifications . . . are subject to stringent examination without regard to these additional characteristics. We declared as much in the first cases explicitly to recognize racial distinctions as suspect: . . .

". . . [A]ll legal restrictions which curtail the rights of a single racial group are immediately suspect. That is not to say that all such restrictions are unconstitutional. It is to say that courts must subject them to the most rigid scrutiny." *Korematsu,* 323 U.S., at 216. . . .

. . . it [. . . is . . .] no longer possible to peg the guarantees of the Fourteenth Amendment to the struggle for equality of one racial minority. During the dormancy of the Equal Protection Clause, the United States had become a nation of minorities. Each had to struggle—and to some extent struggles still—to overcome the prejudices not of a monolithic majority, but of a "majority" composed of various minority groups of whom it was said—perhaps unfairly in many cases—that a shared characteristic was a willingness to disadvantage other groups. As the Nation filled with the stock of many lands, the reach of the Clause was gradually extended to all ethnic groups seeking protection from official discrimination.

Although many of the Framers of the Fourteenth Amendment conceived of its primary function as bridging the vast distance between members of the Negro race and the white "majority," the Amendment itself was framed in universal terms, without reference to color, ethnic origin, or condition of prior servitude. As this Court recently remarked in interpreting the 1866 Civil Rights Act to extend to claims of racial discrimination against white persons, "the 39th Congress was intent upon establishing in federal law a broader principle than would have been necessary to meet the particular and immediate plight of the newly freed Negro slaves." *McDonald* v. *Santa Fe Trail Transp. Co.,* 427 U.S. 273, 296 (1976).

Petitioner urges us to adopt for the first time a more restrictive view of the Equal Protection Clause and hold that discrimination against members of the white "majority" cannot be suspect if its purpose can be characterized as "benign." † The clock

* Moreover, the University's special admissions program involves a purposeful, acknowledged use of racial criteria. This is not a situation in which the classification on its face is racially neutral, but has a disproportionate racial impact. In that situation, plaintiff must establish an intent to discriminate. *Village of Arlington Heights* v. *Metropolitan Housing Devel. Corp., Washington* v. *Davis.*

† In the view of MR. JUSTICE BRENNAN, MR. JUSTICE WHITE, MR. JUSTICE MARSHALL, and MR. JUSTICE BLACKMUN, the pliable notion of "stigma" is the crucial element in analyzing racial classifications. The Equal Protection Clause is not framed in terms of "stigma." Certainly

(Continued)

of our liberties, however, cannot be turned back to 1868. It is far too late to argue that the guarantee of equal protection to *all* persons permits the recognition of special wards entitled to a degree of protection greater than that accorded others.§

As observed above, the white "majority" itself is composed of various minority groups, most of which can lay claim to a history of prior discrimination at the hands of the state and private individuals. Not all of these groups can receive preferential treatment and corresponding judicial tolerance of distinctions drawn in terms of race and nationality, for then the only "majority" left would be a new minority of White Anglo-Saxon Protestants. There is no principled basis for deciding which groups would merit "heightened judicial solicitude" and which would not.‖ . . .

the word has no clearly defined constitutional meaning. It reflects a subjective judgment that is standardless. *All* state-imposed classifications that rearrange burdens and benefits on the basis of race are likely to be viewed with deep resentment by the individuals burdened. The denial to innocent persons of equal rights and opportunities may outrage those so deprived and therefore may be perceived as invidious. These individuals are likely to find little comfort in the notion that the deprivation they are asked to endure is merely the price of membership in the dominant majority and that its imposition is inspired by the supposedly benign purpose of aiding others. One should not lightly dismiss the inherent unfairness of, and the perception of mistreatment that accompanies, a system of allocating benefits and privileges on the basis of skin color and ethnic origin. Moreover, MR. JUSTICE BRENNAN, MR. JUSTICE WHITE, MR. JUSTICE MARSHALL, and MR. JUSTICE BLACKMUN offer no principle for deciding whether preferential classifications reflect a benign remedial purpose of a malevolent stigmatic classification, since they are willing in this case to accept mere *post hoc* declarations by an isolated state entity—a medical school faculty—unadorned by particularized findings of past discrimination, to establish such a remedial purpose.

§ Professor Bickel noted the self-contradiction of that view: "The lesson of the great decisions of the Supreme Court and the lesson of contemporary history have been the same for at least a generation: discrimination on the basis of race is illegal, immoral, unconstitutional, inherently wrong, and destructive of democratic society. Now this is to be unlearned and we are told that this is not a matter of fundamental principle but only a matter of whose ox is gored. Those for whom racial equality was demanded are to be more equal than others. Having found support in the Constitution for equality, they now claim support for inequality under the same Constitution." A. Bickel, The Morality of Consent 133 (1975).

‖ As I am in agreement with the view that race may be taken into account as a factor in an admissions program, I agree with my Brothers BRENNAN, WHITE, MARSHALL, and BLACKMUN that the portion of the judgment that would proscribe all consideration of race must be reversed. But I disagree with much that is said in their opinion.

They would require as a justification for a program such as petitioner's, only two findings: (i) that there has been some form of discrimination against the preferred minority groups "by society at large," (it being conceded that petitioner had no history of discrimination), and (ii) that "there is reason to believe" that the disparate impact sought to be rectified by the program is the "product" of such discrimination:

"If it was reasonable to conclude—as we hold that it was—that the failure of Negroes to qualify for admission at Davis under regular procedures was due principally to the effects of past discrimination, then there is a reasonable likelihood that, but for pervasive racial discrimination, respondent would have failed to qualify for admission even in the absence of Davis's special admission program."

The breadth of this hypothesis is unprecedented in our constitutional system. The first step is easily taken. No one denies the regrettable fact that there has been societal discrimination in this country against various racial and ethnic groups. The second step, however, involves a speculative leap; but for this discrimination by society at large, Bakke "would have failed to qualify for admission" because Negro applicants—nothing is said about Asians,—would have made better scores. Not one word in the record supports this conclusion, and the plurality offers no standard for courts to use in applying such a presumption of causation to other racial

(Continued)

If it is the individual who is entitled to judicial protection against classifications based upon his racial or ethnic background because such distinctions impinge upon personal rights, rather than the individual only because of his membership in a particular group, then constitutional standards may be applied consistently. . . . [A]n individual is entitled to a judicial determination that the burden he is asked to bear on [a racial] . . . basis is precisely tailored to serve a compelling governmental interest. The Constitution guarantees that right to every person regardless of his background.

Petitioner contends that on several occasions this Court has approved preferential classifications without applying the most exacting scrutiny. . . .

The school desegregation cases are inapposite. Each involved remedies for clearly determined constitutional violations. . . . Racial classifications thus were designed as remedies for the vindication of constitutional entitlement. . . . Here, there was no judicial determination of constitutional violation as a predicate for the formulation of a remedial classification. . . . we have never approved preferential classifications in the absence of proven constitutional or statutory violations. . . .

In a similar vein, petitioner contends that our recent decision in *United Jewish Organizations* v. *Carey,* 430 U.S. 144 (1977), indicates a willingness to approve racial classifications designed to benefit certain minorities, without denominating the classifications as "suspect.". . . *United Jewish Organizations,* . . . properly is viewed as a case in which the remedy for an administrative finding of discrimination encompassed measures to improve the previously disadvantaged group's ability to participate, without excluding individuals belonging to any other group from enjoyment of the relevant opportunity—meaningful participation in the electoral process.

In this case, unlike . . . *United Jewish Organizations,* there has been no determination by the legislature or a responsible administrative agency that the University engaged in a discriminatory practice requiring remedial efforts. Moreover, the operation of petitioner's special admissions program is quite different from the remedial measures approved in [that] case. It prefers the designated minority groups at the expense of other individuals who are totally foreclosed from competition for the 16 special admissions seats in every medical school class. Because of that foreclosure, some individuals are excluded from enjoyment of a state-provided benefit—admission to the medical school—they otherwise would receive. When a classification denies an individual opportunities or benefits enjoyed by others solely because of his race or ethnic background, it must be regarded as suspect.

. . . The special admissions program purports to serve the purposes of: (i) "reducing the historic deficit of traditionally disfavored minorities in medical schools and the medical profession," Brief for Petitioner 32; (ii) countering the effects of societal discrimination; (iii) increasing the number of physicians who will practice in communities currently underserved; and (iv) obtaining the educational benefits that flow from an ethnically diverse student body. It is necessary to decide which, if any, of these purposes is substantial enough to support the use of a suspect classification.

If petitioner's purpose is to assure within its student body some specified percentage of a particular group merely because of its race or ethnic origin, such a preferential purpose must be rejected not as insubstantial but as facially invalid. Preferring members of any one group for no reason other than race or ethnic origin is discrimination for its own sake. This the Constitution forbids. *E.g., Loving* v. *Virginia.* . . .

The State certainly has a legitimate and substantial interest in ameliorating, or eliminating where feasible, the disabling effects of identified discrimination. The line of school desegregation cases, commencing with *Brown,* attests to the importance of this state goal and the commitment of the judiciary to affirm all lawful means towards

or ethnic classifications. This failure is a grave one, since if it may be concluded *on this record* that each of the minority groups preferred by the petitioner's special program is entitled to the benefit of the presumption, it would seem difficult to determine that any of the dozens of minority groups that have suffered "societal discrimination" cannot also claim it, in any area of social intercourse.

its attainment. In the school cases, the States were required by court order to redress the wrongs worked by specific instances of racial discrimination. That goal was far more focused than the remedying of the effects of "societal discrimination," an amorphous concept of injury that may be ageless in its reach into the past.

We have never approved a classification that aids persons perceived as members of relatively victimized groups at the expense of other innocent individuals in the absence of judicial, legislative, or administrative findings of constitutional or statutory violations. . . . Without such findings of constitutional or statutory violations,# it cannot be said that the government has any greater interest in helping one individual than in refraining from harming another. Thus, the government has no compelling justification for inflicting such harm. . . .

Petitioner does not purport to have made, and is in no position to make, such findings. Its broad mission is education, not the formulation of any legislative policy or the adjudication of particular claims of illegality. . . . [I]solated segments of our vast governmental structures are not competent to make those decisions, at least in the absence of legislative mandates and legislatively determined criteria. . . . Lacking this capability, petitioner has not carried its burden of justification on this issue.

Hence, the purpose of helping certain groups whom the faculty of the Davis Medical School perceived as victims of "societal discrimination" does not justify a classification that imposes disadvantages upon persons like respondent, who bear no responsibility for whatever harm the beneficiaries of the special admissions program are thought to have suffered. To hold otherwise would be to convert a remedy heretofore reserved for violations of legal rights into a privilege that all institutions throughout the Nation could grant at their pleasure to whatever groups are perceived as victims of societal discrimination. That is a step we have never approved.

Petitioner identifies, as another purpose of its program, improving the delivery of health care services to communities currently underserved. . . . But there is virtually no evidence in the record indicating that petitioner's special admissions program is either needed or geared to promote that goal.

The fourth goal asserted by petitioner is the attainment of a diverse student body. This clearly is a constitutionally permissible goal for an institution of higher education. Academic freedom, though not a specifically enumerated constitutional right, long has been viewed as a special concern of the First Amendment. The freedom of a university to make its own judgments as to education includes the selection of its student body. . . . The atmosphere of "speculation, experiment and creation"—so essential to the quality of higher education—is widely believed to be promoted by a diverse student body.

Thus, in arguing that its universities

MR. JUSTICE BRENNAN, MR. JUSTICE WHITE, MR. JUSTICE MARSHALL, and MR. JUSTICE BLACKMUN misconceive the scope of this Court's holdings under Title VII when they suggest that "disparate impact" alone is sufficient to establish a violation of that statute and, by analogy, other civil rights measures. That this was not the meaning of Title VII was made quite clear in the seminal decision in this area, *Griggs* v. *Duke Power Co.,* 401 U.S. 424 (1971):

"*Discriminatory preference* for any group, minority or majority, is precisely and only what Congress has proscribed. What is required by Congress is the removal of *artificial, arbitrary, and unnecessary barriers* to employment when the barriers operate invidiously to discriminate on the basis of racial or other impermissible classification." *Id.,* at 431 (emphasis added).

Thus, disparate impact is a basis for relief under Title VII only if the practice in question is not founded on "business necessity," *ibid.,* or lacks "a manifest relationship to the employment in question," *id.,* at 432. See also *McDonnell Douglas Corp.* v. *Green,* 411 U.S. 792, 802–803, 805–806 (1973). Nothing *in this record*—as opposed to some of the general literature cited by MR. JUSTICE BRENNAN, MR. JUSTICE WHITE, MR. JUSTICE MARSHALL, and MR. JUSTICE BLACKMUN—even remotely suggests that the disparate impact of the general admissions program at Davis Medical School, resulting primarily from . . . disparate test scores and grades . . . is without educational justification.

must be accorded the right to select those students who will contribute the most to the "robust exchange of ideas," petitioner invokes a countervailing constitutional interest, that of the First Amendment. In this light, petitioner must be viewed as seeking to achieve a goal that is of paramount importance in the fulfillment of its mission. . . .

Ethnic diversity, however, is only one element in a range of factors a university properly may consider in attaining the goal of a heterogeneous student body. Although a university must have wide discretion in making the sensitive judgments as to who should be admitted, constitutional limitations protecting individual rights may not be disregarded. Respondent urges—and the courts below have held—that petitioner's dual admissions program is a racial classification that impermissibly infringes his rights under the Fourteenth Amendment. As the interest of diversity is compelling in the context of a university's admissions program, the question remains whether the program's racial classification is necessary to promote this interest.

It may be assumed that the reservation of a specified number of seats in each class for individuals from the preferred ethnic groups would contribute to the attainment of considerable ethnic diversity in the student body. But petitioner's argument that this is the only effective means of serving the interest of diversity is seriously flawed. In a most fundamental sense the argument misconceives the nature of the state interest that would justify consideration of race or ethnic background. It is not an interest in simple ethnic diversity, in which a specified percentage of the student body is in effect guaranteed to be members of selected ethnic groups, with the remaining percentage an undifferentiated aggregation of students. The diversity that furthers a compelling state interest encompasses a far broader array of qualifications and characteristics of which racial or ethnic origin is but a single though important element. Petitioner's special admissions program, focused *solely* on ethnic diversity, would hinder rather than further attainment of genuine diversity. . . .

The experience of other university admissions programs, which take race into account in achieving the educational diversity valued by the First Amendment, demonstrates that the assignment of a fixed number of places to a minority group is not a necessary means toward that end. An illuminating example is found in the Harvard College program:

> "In recent years Harvard College has expanded the concept of diversity to include students from disadvantaged economic, racial and ethnic groups. Harvard College now recruits not only Californians or Louisianans but also blacks and Chicanos and other minority students.
>
> "When the Committee on Admissions reviews the large middle group of applicants who are 'admissible' and deemed capable of doing good work in their courses, the race of an applicant may tip the balance in his favor just as geographic origin or a life spent on a farm may tip the balance in other candidates' cases. A farm boy from Idaho can bring something to Harvard College that a Bostonian cannot offer. Similarly, a black student can usually bring something that a white person cannot offer. . . .
>
> "In Harvard College admissions the Committee has not set target-quotas for the number of blacks, or of musicians, football players, physicists or Californians to be admitted in a given years. . . . It means only that in choosing among thousands of applicants who are not only 'admissible' academically but have other strong qualities, the Committee, with a number of criteria in mind, pays some attention to distribution among many types and categories of students.". . .

This kind of program treats each applicant as an individual** in the admissions process. The applicant who loses out on the last available seat to another candidate

** The denial to respondent of this right to individualized consideration without regard to his race is the principal evil of petitioner's special admissions program. Nowhere in the opinion of MR. JUSTICE BRENNAN, MR. JUSTICE WHITE, MR. JUSTICE MARSHALL, and MR. JUSTICE BLACKMUN is this denial even addressed.

receiving a "plus" on the basis of ethnic background will not have been foreclosed from all consideration for that seat simply because he was not the right color or had the wrong surname. It would mean only that his combined qualifications, which may have included similar nonobjective factors, did not outweigh those of the other applicant. His qualifications would have been weighed fairly and competitively, and he would have no basis to complain of unequal treatment under the Fourteenth Amendment.

It has been suggested that an admissions program which considers race only as one factor is simply a subtle and more sophisticated—but no less effective—means of according racial preference than the Davis program. A facial intent to discriminate, however, is evident in petitioner's preference program and not denied in this case. No such facial infirmity exists in an admissions program where race or ethnic background is simply one element—to be weighed fairly against other elements—in the selection process. . . . And a Court would not assume that a university, professing to employ a facially nondiscriminatory admissions policy, would operate it as a cover for the functional equivalent of a quota system. In short, good faith would be presumed in the absence of a showing to the contrary in the manner permitted by our cases. See, *e.g., Arlington Heights* v. *Metropolitan Housing Development Corp.,* 429 U.S. 252 (1977); *Washington* v. *Davis,* 426 U.S. 229 (1976).

In summary, it is evident that the Davis special admission program involves the use of an explicit racial classification never before countenanced by this Court. It tells applicants who are not Negro, Asian, or "Chicano" that they are totally excluded from a specific percentage of the seats in an entering class. No matter how strong their qualifications, quantitative and extracurricular, including their own potential for contribution to educational diversity, they are never afforded the chance to compete with applicants from the preferred groups for the special admission seats. At the same time, the preferred applicants have the opportunity to compete for every seat in the class.

The fatal flaw in petitioner's preferential program is its disregard of individual rights as guaranteed by the Fourteenth Amendment. Such rights are not absolute. But when a State's distribution of benefits or imposition of burdens hinges on the color of a person's skin or ancestry, that individual is entitled to a demonstration that the challenged classification is necessary to promote a substantial state interest. Petitioner has failed to carry this burden. For this reason, that portion of the California court's judgment holding petitioner's special admissions program invalid under the Fourteenth Amendment must be affirmed.

In enjoining petitioner from ever considering the race of any applicant, however, the courts below failed to recognize that the State has a substantial interest that legitimately may be served by a properly devised admissions program involving the competitive consideration of race and ethnic origin. For this reason, so much of the California court's judgment as enjoins petitioner from any consideration of the race of any applicant must be reversed.

With respect to respondent's entitlement to an injunction directing his admission to the Medical School, petitioner has conceded that it could not carry its burden of proving that, but for the existence of its unlawful special admissions program, respondent still would not have been admitted. Hence, respondent is entitled to the injunction, and that portion of the judgment must be affirmed.

MR. JUSTICE STEVENS, with whom THE CHIEF JUSTICE, MR. JUSTICE STEWART, and MR. JUSTICE REHNQUIST join, concurring in the judgment in part and dissenting in part: . . .

Both petitioner and respondent have asked us to determine the legality of the University's special admissions program by reference to the Constitution. Our settled practice, however, is to avoid the decision of a constitutional issue if a case can be fairly decided on a statutory ground. . . .

Section 601 of the Civil Rights Act of 1964 provides:

> "No person in the United States shall, on the ground of race, color, or national origin, be excluded from participation in, be denied the benefits of, or be sub-

jected to discrimination under any program or activity receiving Federal financial assistance."

The University, through its special admissions policy, excluded Bakke from participation in its program of medical education because of his race. The University also acknowledges that it was, and still is, receiving federal financial assistance. The plain language of the statute therefore requires affirmance of the judgment below. . . .

Title VI is an integral part of the far-reaching Civil Rights Act of 1964. No doubt, when this legislation was being debated, Congress was not directly concerned with the legality of "reverse discrimination" or "affirmative action" programs. Its attention was focused on the problem at hand, "the glaring . . . discrimination against Negroes which exists throughout our Nation," and, with respect to Title VI, the federal funding of segregated facilities. The genesis of the legislation, however, did not limit the breadth of the solution adopted. Just as Congress responded to the problem of employment discrimination by enacting a provision that protects all races, see *McDonald* v. *Santa Fe Trail Transportation Co.,* 427 U.S. 273, 279, so too its answer to the problem of federal funding of segregated facilities stands as a broad prohibition against the exclusion of *any* individual from a federally funded program "on the ground of race." In the words of the House Report, Title VI stands for "the general principle that *no person* . . . be excluded from participation . . . on the ground of race, color or national origin under any program or activity receiving Federal financial assistance." (emphasis added). This same broad view of Title VI and § 601 was echoed throughout the congressional debate and was stressed by every one of the major spokesmen for the Act. . . .

Petitioner contends, however, that exclusion of applicants on the basis of race does not violate Title VI if the exclusion carries with it no racial stigma. No such qualification or limitation of § 601's categorical prohibition of "exclusion" is justified by the statute or its history. The language of the entire section is perfectly clear; . . .

The legislative history reinforces this reading. . . . The opponents feared that the term "discrimination" would be read as mandating racial quotas and "racially balanced" colleges and universities, and they pressed for a specific definition of the term in order to avoid this possibility. In response, the proponents of the legislation gave repeated assurances that the Act would be "colorblind" in its application. . . .

In short, nothing in the legislative history justifies the conclusion that the broad language of § 601 should not be given its natural meaning. . . . As succinctly phrased during the Senate debate, under Title VI it is not "permissible to say 'yes' to one person, but to say 'no' to another person, only because of the color of his skin.". . . To date, the courts, including this Court, have unanimously concluded or assumed that a private action may be maintained under Title VI. . . .

The University's special admissions program violated Title VI of the Civil Rights Act of 1964 by excluding Bakke from the medical school because of his race. It is therefore our duty to affirm the judgment ordering Bakke admitted to the University.

Accordingly, I concur in the Court's judgment insofar as it affirms the judgment of the Supreme Court of California. To the extent that it purports to do anything else, I respectfully dissent.

Opinion of MR. JUSTICE BRENNAN, MR. JUSTICE WHITE, MR. JUSTICE MARSHALL, and MR. JUSTICE BLACKMUN, concurring in the judgment in part and dissenting:

The threshold question we must decide is whether Title VI of the Civil Rights Act of 1964 bars recipients of federal funds from giving preferential consideration to disadvantaged members of racial minorities as part of a program designed to enable such individuals to surmount the obstacles imposed by racial discrimination. . . .

The history of Title VI—from President Kennedy's request that Congress grant executive departments and agencies authority to cut off federal funds to programs that discriminate against Negroes through final enactment of legislation incorporating his proposals—reveals one fixed purpose: to give the Executive Branch of Government clear authority to terminate federal funding of private programs that use race as a means of disadvantaging minorities in a manner that would be prohibited by the Constitution if engaged in by government. . . .

The debates reveal that . . . Congress recognized that Negroes, in some cases with congressional acquiescence, were being discriminated against in the administration of programs and denied the full benefits of activities receiving federal financial support. It was aware that there were many federally funded programs and institutions which discriminated against minorities in a manner inconsistent with the standards of the Fifth and Fourteenth Amendments but whose activities might not involve sufficient state or federal action so as to be in violation of these Amendments. Moreover, Congress believed that it was questionable whether the Executive Branch possessed legal authority to terminate the funding of activities on the ground that they discriminated racially against Negroes in a manner violative of the standards contained in the Fourteenth and Fifth Amendments. Congress' solution was to end the Government's complicity in constitutionally forbidden racial discrimination by providing the Executive Branch with the authority and the obligation to terminate its financial support of any activity which employed racial criteria in a manner condemned by the Constitution. . . .

The legislative history of Title VI, as well as the statute itself, reveals a desire to induce voluntary compliance with the requirement of nondiscriminatory treatment. See § 602 of the Act, 42 U.S.C. § 2000d–1 (no funds shall be terminated unless and until it has been "determined that compliance cannot be secured by voluntary means"); H. R. Rep. No. 914, 88th Cong., 1st Sess., 25 (1963); 110 Cong. Rec. 13700 (Sen. Pastore); *id.,* at 6546 (Sen. Humphrey). It is inconceivable that Congress intended to encourage voluntary efforts to eliminate the evil of racial discrimination while at the same time forbidding the voluntary use of race-conscious remedies to cure acknowledged or obvious statutory violations. . . .†

Just last year Congress enacted legislation explicitly requiring that no grants shall be made "for any local public works project unless the applicant gives satisfactory assurance to the Secretary that at least 10 per centum of the amount of each grant shall be expended for minority business enterprises.". . . The term "minority group members" is defined in explicitly racial terms: "citizens of the United States who are Negroes, Spanish-speaking, Orientals, Indians, Eskimos, and Aleuts.". . .

The Court has . . . declined to adopt a "colorblind" interpretation of other statutes containing nondiscrimination provisions similar to that contained in Title VI . . . the Court has required that preferences be given by employers to members of racial minorities as a remedy for past violations of Title VII, even where there has been no finding that the employer has acted with a discriminatory intent. Finally, we have construed the Voting Rights Act of 1965, 42 U.S.C. § 1973, which contains a provision barring any voting procedure or qualification that denies or abridges "the right of any citizens of the United States to vote on account of race or color," as permitting States to voluntarily take race into account in a way that fairly represents the voting strengths of different racial groups in order to comply with the commands of the statute, even where the result is a gain for one racial group at the expense of others.§

We turn, therefore, to our analysis of the Equal Protection Clause of the Fourteenth Amendment.

The assertion of human equality is closely associated with the proposition that differences in color or creed, birth or status, are neither significant nor relevant to the way in which persons should be treated.

† Our Brother Stevens finds support for a colorblind theory of Title VI in its legislative history, but his interpretation gives undue weight to a few isolated passages from among the thousands of pages of the legislative history of Title VI.

§ *United Jewish Organizations of Williamsburgh* v. *Carey.*

Nonetheless, the position that such factors must be "[c]onstitutionally an irrelevance," *Edwards* v. *California,* 314 U.S. 160, 185 (1941) (Jackson, J., concurring), summed up by the shorthand phrase "[o]ur Constitution is color-blind," *Plessy* v. *Ferguson,* 163 U.S. 537, 559 (1896) (Harlan, J., dissenting), has never been adopted by this Court as the proper meaning of the Equal Protection Clause. Indeed, we have expressly rejected this proposition on a number of occasions. . . .

We conclude, therefore, that racial classifications are not *per se* invalid under the Fourteenth Amendment. Accordingly, we turn to the problem of articulating what our role should be in reviewing state action that expressly classifies by race.

. . . a number of considerations—developed in gender discrimination cases but which carry even more force when applied to racial classifications—lead us to conclude that racial classifications designed to further remedial purposes " 'must serve important governmental objectives and must be substantially related to achievement of those objectives.' ". . .

First, race, like "gender-based classifications too often [has] been inexcusably utilized to stereotype and stigmatize politically powerless segments of society.". . .

Second, race, like gender and illegitimacy, see *Weber* v. *Aetna Cas. & Surety Co.,* is an immutable characteristic which its possessors are powerless to escape or set aside. . . .

. . . because of the significant risk that racial classifications established for ostensibly benign purposes can be misused, causing effects not unlike those created by invidious classifications, it is inappropriate to inquire only whether there is any conceivable basis that might sustain such a classification. Instead, to justify such a classification an important and articulated purpose for its use must be shown. In addition, any statute must be stricken that stigmatizes any group or that singles out those least well represented in the political process to bear the brunt of a benign program. Thus our review under the Fourteenth Amendment should be strict. . . .

At least since *Green* v. *County School Board,* 391 U.S. 430 (1968), it has been clear that a public body which has itself been adjudged to have engaged in racial discrimination cannot bring itself into compliance with the Equal Protection Clause simply by ending its unlawful acts and adopting a neutral stance. . . .

Moreover, we stated that school boards, even in the absence of a judicial finding of past discrimination, could voluntarily adopt plans which assigned students with the end of creating racial pluralism by establishing fixed ratios of black and white students in each school. *Charlotte-Mecklenburg,* at 16. In each instance, the creation of unitary school systems, in which the effects of past discrimination had been "eliminated root and branch," *Green,* at 438, was recognized as a compelling social goal justifying the overt use of race.

Finally, the conclusion that state educational institutions may constitutionally adopt admissions programs designed to avoid exclusion of historically disadvantaged minorities, even when such programs explicitly take race into account, finds direct support in our cases construing congressional legislation designed to overcome the present effects of past discrimination. . . .

These cases cannot be distinguished simply by the presence of judicial findings of discrimination, for race-conscious remedies have been approved where such findings have not been made. *United Jewish Organizations of Williamsburgh* v. *Carey (UJO).*

Indeed, the requirement of a judicial determination of a constitutional or statutory violation as a predicate for race-conscious remedial actions would be self-defeating. Such a requirement would severely undermine efforts to achieve voluntary compliance with the requirements of law.

Nor can our cases be distinguished on the ground that the entity using explicit racial classifications had itself violated § 1 of the Fourteenth Amendment or an antidiscrimination regulation, for again race-conscious remedies have been approved where this is not the case. See *UJO,* 430 U.S., at 157 (opinion of WHITE, BLACKMUN, REHNQUIST, and STEVENS, J.J.); . . .

Moreover, the presence or absence of past discrimination by universities or employers is largely irrelevant to resolving respondent's constitutional claims. The claims of those burdened by the race-conscious actions of a university or employer who has never been adjudged in violation of an antidiscrimination law are not any more or less entitled to deference than the claims of the burdened nonminority workers in *Franks* v. *Bowman,* 424 U.S. 47 (1976), in which the employer had violated Title VII, for in each case the employees were innocent of past discrimination. And, although it might be argued that, where an employer has violated an antidiscrimination law, the expectations of nonminority workers are themselves products of discrimination and hence "tainted," see *Franks,* at 776, and therefore more easily upset, the same argument can be made with respect to respondent. If it was reasonable to conclude—as we hold that it was—that the failure of minorities to qualify for admission at Davis under regular procedures was due principally to the effects of past discrimination, then there is a reasonable likelihood that, but for pervasive racial discrimination, respondent would have failed to qualify for admission even in the absence of Davis' special admissions program.‖ . . .

. . . [O]ur cases under Title VII of the Civil Rights Act . . . compel the conclusion that States also may adopt race-conscious programs designed to overcome substantial, chronic minority underrepresentation where there is reason to believe that the evil addressed is a product of past racial discrimination.**

We therefore conclude that . . . Davis' goal of admitting minority students disadvantaged by the effects of past discrimination is sufficiently important to justify use of race-conscious admissions criteria.

. . . Davis clearly could conclude that the serious and persistent underrepresentation of minorities in medicine is the result of handicaps under which minority applicants labor as a consequence of a background of deliberate, purposeful discrimination against minorities in education and in society generally, as well as in the medical profession. . . .

The second prong of our test—whether the Davis program stigmatizes any discrete group or individual and whether race reasonably used in light of the program's objectives—is fairly satisfied by the Davis program. . . .

. . . [I]ts purpose is to overcome the effects of segregation by bringing the races together. True, whites are excluded from participation in the special admissions pro-

‖ Our cases cannot be distinguished by suggesting, as our Brother Powell does, that in none of them was anyone deprived of "the relevant benefit." Our school cases have deprived whites of the neighborhood school of their choice; our Title VII cases have deprived nondiscriminating employees of their settled seniority expectations; and *UJO* deprived the Hassidim of bloc voting strength. Each of these injuries was constitutionally cognizable as is respondent's here.

** We do not understand Mr. Justice Powell to disagree that providing a remedy for past racial prejudice can constitute a compelling purpose sufficient to meet strict scrutiny. Yet, because petitioner is a university, he would not allow it to exercise such power in the absence of "judicial, legislative, or administrative findings of constitutional or statutory violations." While we agree that reversal in this case would follow *a fortiori* had Davis been guilty of invidious racial discrimination or if a federal statute mandated that universities refrain from applying any admissions policy that had a disparate and unjustified racial impact, see, *e.g., McDaniel* v. *Barresi,* 402 U.S. 39 (1971); *Franks* v. *Bowman Transp. Co.,* 424 U.S. 747 (1976), we do not think it of constitutional significance that Davis has not been so adjudged.

. . . California, by constitutional provision, has chosen to place authority over the operation of the University of California in the Board of Regents. Control over the University is to be found not in the legislature, but rather in the Regents who have been vested with full legislative (including policymaking), administrative, and adjudicative powers by the citizens of California. . . . we, unlike our Brother Powell, find nothing in the Equal Protection Clause that requires us to depart from established principle by limiting the scope of power the Regents may exercise more narrowly than the powers that may constitutionally be wielded by the Assembly.

gram, but this fact only operates to reduce the number of whites to be admitted in the regular admissions program in order to permit admission of a reasonable percentage—less than their proportion of the California population—of otherwise underrepresented qualified minority applicants. . . . Nor was Bakke in any sense stamped as inferior by the Medical School's rejection of him. . . .

Nor can the program reasonably be regarded as stigmatizing the program's beneficiaries or their race as inferior. The Davis program does not simply advance less qualified applicants; rather, it compensates applicants, whom it is uncontested are fully qualified to study medicine, for educational disadvantage which it was reasonable to conclude was a product of state-fostered discrimination. . . . Since minority graduates cannot justifiably be regarded as less well qualified than nonminority graduates by virtue of the special admissions program, there is no reasonable basis to conclude that minority graduates at schools using such programs would be stigmatized as inferior by the existence of such programs.

We disagree with the lower courts' conclusion that the Davis program's use of race was unreasonable in light of its objectives. First, as petitioner argues, there are no practical means by which it could achieve its ends in the foreseeable future without the use of race-conscious measures. With respect to any factor (such as poverty or family educational background) that may be used as a substitute for race as an indicator of past discrimination, whites greatly outnumber racial minorities simply because whites make up a far larger percentage of the total population and therefore far outnumber minorities in absolute terms at every socioeconomic level. For example, of a class of recent medical school applicants from families with less than $10,000 income, at least 71% were white. Of all 1970 families headed by a person *not* a high school graduate which included related children under 18, 80% were white and 20% were racial minorities. Moreover, while race is positively correlated with differences in GPA and MCAT scores, economic disadvantage is not. Thus, it appears that economically disadvantaged whites do not score less well than economically advantaged whites, while economically advantaged blacks score less well than do disadvantaged whites. These statistics graphically illustrate that the University's purpose to integrate its classes by compensating for past discrimination could not be achieved by a general preference for the economically disadvantaged or the children of parents of limited education unless such groups were to make up the entire class. . . .

Finally, Davis' special admissions program cannot be said to violate the Constitution simply because it has set aside a predetermined number of places for qualified minority applicants rather than using minority status as a positive factor to be considered in evaluating the applications of disadvantaged minority applicants. For purposes of constitutional adjudication, there is no difference between the two approaches. In any admissions program which accords special consideration to disadvantaged racial minorities, a determination of the degree of preference to be given is unavoidable, and any given preference that results in the exclusion of a white candidate is no more or less constitutionally acceptable than a program such as that at Davis. Furthermore, the extent of the preference inevitably depends on how many minority applicants the particular school is seeking to admit in any particular year so long as the number of qualified minority applicants exceeds that number. There is no sensible, and certainly no constitutional, distinction between, for example, adding a set number of points to the admissions rating of disadvantaged minority applicants as an expression of the preference with the expectation that this will result in the admission of an approximately determined number of qualified minority applicants and setting a fixed number of places for such applicants as was done here.‡

The "Harvard" program, as those employing it readily concede, openly and suc-

‡ The excluded white applicant, despite Mr. Justice Powell's contention to the contrary, receives no more or less "individualized consideration" under our approach than under his.

cessfully employs a racial criterion for the purpose of ensuring that some of the scarce places in institutions of higher education are allocated to disadvantaged minority students. That the Harvard approach does not also make public the extent of the preference and the precise workings of the system while the Davis program employs a specific, openly stated number, does not condemn the latter plan for purposes of Fourteenth Amendment adjudication. It may be that the Harvard plan is more acceptable to the public than is the Davis "quota." If it is, any State, including California, is free to adopt it in preference to a less acceptable alternative, just as it is generally free, as far as the Constitution is concerned, to abjure granting any racial preferences in its admissions program. But there is no basis for preferring a particular preference program simply because in achieving the same goals that the Davis Medical School is pursuing, it proceeds in a manner that is not immediately apparent to the public.

Accordingly, we would reverse the judgment of the Supreme Court of California holding the Medical School's special admissions program unconstitutional and directing respondent's admission, as well as that portion of the judgment enjoining the Medical School from according any consideration to race in the admissions process.

MR. JUSTICE BLACKMUN, concurring in part and dissenting in part:

I, of course, accept the proposition that . . . the Fourteenth Amendment has expanded beyond its original 1868 conception and now is recognized to have reached a point where, as MR. JUSTICE POWELL states, quoting from the Court's opinion in *McDonald* v. *Santa Fe Trail Transp. Co.*, 427 U.S. 273, 296 (1976), it embraces a "broader principle."

This enlargement does not mean for me, however, that the Fourteenth Amendment has broken away from its moorings and its original intended purposes. Those original aims persist. And that, in a distinct sense, is what "affirmative action," in the face of proper facts, is all about. If this conflicts with idealistic equality, that tension is original Fourteenth Amendment tension, constitutionally conceived and constitutionally imposed, and it is part of the Amendment's very nature until complete equality is achieved in the area. . . .

MR. JUSTICE MARSHALL, concurring in part and dissenting in part:

. . . [I]t must be remembered that, during most of the past 200 years, the Constitution as interpreted by this Court did not prohibit the most ingenious and pervasive forms of discrimination against the Negro. Now, when a State acts to remedy the effects of that legacy of discrimination, I cannot believe that this same Constitution stands as a barrier. . . .

The position of the Negro today in America is the tragic but inevitable consequence of centuries of unequal treatment. Measured by any benchmark of comfort or achievement, meaningful equality remains a distant dream for the Negro. . . . I do not believe that the Fourteenth Amendment requires us to accept that fate. . . .

While I applaud the judgment of the Court that a university may consider race in its admissions process, it is more than a little ironic that, after several hundred years of class-based discrimination against Negroes, the Court is unwilling to hold that a class-based remedy for that discrimination is permissible. In declining to so hold, today's judgment ignores the fact that for several hundred years Negroes have been discriminated against, not as individuals, but rather solely because of the color of their skins. It is unnecessary in 20th century America to have individual Negroes demonstrate that they have been victims of racial discrimination; the racism of our society has been so pervasive that none, regardless of wealth or position, has managed to escape its impact. The experience of Negroes in America has been different in kind, not just in degree, from that of other ethnic groups. It is not merely the history of slavery alone but also that a whole people were marked as inferior by the law. And that mark has endured. The dream of America as the great melting pot has not been realized for the Negro; because of his skin color he never even made it into the pot.

These differences in the experience of the Negro make it difficult for me to accept that Negroes cannot be afforded greater protection under the Fourteenth Amendment where it is necessary to remedy the effects of past discrimination.

It is because of a legacy of unequal treatment that we now must permit the institutions of this society to give consideration to race in making decisions about who will hold the positions of influence, affluence and prestige in America. For far too long, the doors to those positions have been shut to Negroes. If we are ever to become a fully integrated society, one in which the color of a person's skin will not determine the opportunities available to him or her, we must be willing to take steps to open those doors. I do not believe that anyone can truly look into America's past and still find that a remedy for the effects of that past is impermissible.

FULLILOVE *v.* KLUTZNICK
448 U.S. 448; 100 Sup. Ct. 2758; 65 L. Ed. 2d 902 (1980)

MR. CHIEF JUSTICE BURGER announced the judgment of the Court and delivered an opinion in which MR. JUSTICE WHITE and MR. JUSTICE POWELL joined.

In May 1977, Congress enacted the Public Works Employment Act of 1977, Pub. L. 95–28, 91 Stat. 116, which amended the Local Public Works Capital Development and Investment Act of 1976. The 1977 amendments authorized an additional $4 billion appropriation for federal grants to be made . . . to state and local governmental entities for use in local public works projects. . . . Section 103(f)(2) of the 1977 Act, referred to as the "minority business enterprise" or "MBE" provision, requires that:

". . . no grant shall be made under this Act for any local public works project unless the applicant gives satisfactory assurance to the Secretary that at least 10 per centum of the amount of each grant shall be expended for minority business enterprises. For purposes of this paragraph, the term 'minority business enterprise' means a business at least 50 per centum of which is owned by minority group members. . . . For the purposes of the preceding sentence minority group members are citizens of the United States who are Negroes, Spanish-speaking, Orientals, Indians, Eskimos, and Aleuts.". . .

The 1976 Act was intended as a short-term measure to alleviate the problem of national unemployment and to stimulate the national economy by assisting state and local governments to build needed public facilities. . . . The 1977 Act . . . retained the underlying objective to direct funds into areas of high unemployment. The 1977 Act also added new restrictions on applicants seeking to qualify for federal grants; among these was the MBE provision. . . .

. . . A program that employs racial or ethnic criteria, even in a remedial context, calls for close examination; yet we are bound to approach our task with appropriate deference to the Congress, a co-equal branch. . . . In *Columbia Broadcasting System, Inc.* v. *Democratic National Committee,* 412 U.S. 94, 102 (1973), we accorded "great weight to the decisions of Congress" even though the legislation implicated fundamental constitutional rights guaranteed by the First Amendment. The rule is not different when a congressional program raises equal protection concerns.

The clear objective of the MBE provision is disclosed by our . . . review of its legislative and administrative background. The program was designed to ensure that, to the extent federal funds were granted under the Public Works Employment Act of 1977, grantees who elect to participate would not employ procurement practices that Congress had decided might result in perpetuation of the effects of prior discrimination which had impaired or foreclosed access by minority businesses to public contracting opportunities. The MBE program does not mandate the allocation of federal funds according to inflexible percentages solely based on race or ethnicity.

In enacting the MBE provision, it is clear

that Congress employed an amalgam of its specifically delegated powers. The Public Works Employment Act of 1977, by its very nature, is primarily an exercise of the Spending Power. . . .

The legislative history of the MBE provision shows that there was a rational basis for Congress to conclude that the subcontracting practices of prime contractors could perpetuate the prevailing impaired access by minority businesses to public contracting opportunities, and that this inequity has an effect on interstate commerce. Thus Congress could take necessary and proper action to remedy the situation. . . .

In certain contexts, there are limitations on the reach of the Commerce Power to regulate the actions of state and local governments. . . . To avoid such complications, we look to § 5 of the Fourteenth Amendment for the power to regulate the procurement practices of state and local grantees of federal funds. A review of our cases persuades us that the objectives of the MBE program are within the power of Congress under § 5 "to enforce by appropriate legislation" the equal protection guarantees of the Fourteenth Amendment.

With respect to the MBE provision, Congress had abundant evidence from which it could conclude that minority businesses have been denied effective participation in public contracting opportunities by procurement practices that perpetuated the effects of prior discrimination. . . . Although much of this history related to the experience of minority businesses in the area of federal procurement, there was direct evidence before the Congress that this pattern of disadvantage and discrimination existed with respect to state and local construction contracting as well. In relation to the MBE provision, Congress acted within its competence to determine that the problem was national in scope. . . . Insofar as the MBE program pertains to the actions of state and local [governments], Congress could have achieved its objectives by use of its power under § 5 of the Fourteenth Amendment. . . .

We now turn to the question whether, as a *means* to accomplish these plainly constitutional objectives, Congress may use racial and ethnic criteria, in this limited way, as a condition attached to a federal grant. We are mindful that "[i]n no matter should we pay more deference to the opinion of Congress than in its choice of instrumentalities to perform a function that is within its power." However, Congress may employ racial or ethnic classifications in exercising its Spending or other legislative Powers only if those classifications do not violate the equal protection component of the Due Process Clause of the Fifth Amendment. We recognize the need for careful judicial evaluation to assure that any congressional program that employs racial or ethnic criteria to accomplish the objective of remedying the present effects of past discrimination is narrowly tailored to the achievement of that goal. . . .

Our review of the regulations and guidelines governing administration of the MBE provision reveals that Congress enacted the program as a strictly remedial measure; moreover, it is a remedy that functions prospectively, in the manner of an injunctive decree. Pursuant to the administrative program, grantees and their prime contractors are required to seek out all available, qualified, bona fide MBE's; they are required to provide technical assistance as needed, to lower or waive bonding requirements where feasible, to solicit the aid of the Office of Minority Business Enterprise, the Small Business Administration or other sources for assisting MBE's to obtain required working capital, and to give guidance through the intricacies of the bidding process. The program assumes that grantees who undertake these efforts in good faith will obtain at least 10% participation by minority business enterprises. It is recognized that, to achieve this target, contracts will be awarded to available, qualified, bona fide MBE's even though they are not the lowest competitive bidders, so long as their higher bids, when challenged, are found to reflect merely attempts to cover costs inflated by the present effects of prior disadvantage and discrimination. There is available to the grantee a provision authorized by Congress for administrative waiver on a case-by-case basis should there be a demonstration that, despite affirmative efforts, this level of participation cannot be achieved without departing from the objectives of the program. There is also an administrative mechanism, including a complaint procedure, to ensure that only bona fide MBE's are encompassed by the remedial program, and to prevent unjust participation in the program by those minority firms whose access to public contracting opportunities is not impaired by the effects of prior discrimination. . . .

As a threshold matter, we reject the contention that in the remedial context the Congress must act in a wholly "color-blind" fashion. In *Swann* v. *Charlotte-Mecklenburg Board of Education* we rejected this argument in considering a court-formulated school desegregation remedy on the basis that examination of the racial composition of student bodies was an unavoidable starting point and that racially based attendance assignments were permissible so long as no absolute racial balance of each school was required. . . .

Here we deal, as we noted earlier, not with the limited remedial powers of a federal court, for example, but with the broad remedial powers of Congress. It is fundamental that in no organ of government, state or federal, does there repose a more comprehensive remedial power than in the Congress, expressly charged by the Constitution with competence and authority to enforce equal protection guarantees. Congress not only may induce voluntary action to assure compliance with existing federal statutory or constitutional antidiscrimination provisions, but also, where Congress has authority to declare certain conduct unlawful, it may, as here, authorize and induce state action to avoid such conduct.

A more specific challenge to the MBE program is the charge that it impermissibly deprives nonminority businesses of access to at least some portion of the government contracting opportunities generated by the Act. It must be conceded that by its objective of remedying the historical impairment of access, the MBE provision can have the effect of awarding some contracts to MBE's which otherwise might be awarded to other businesses, who may themselves be innocent of any prior discriminatory actions. Failure of nonminority firms to receive certain contracts is, of course, an incidental consequence of the program, not part of its objective. . . .

It is not a constitutional defect in this program that it may disappoint the expectations of nonminority firms. When effectuating a limited and properly tailored remedy to cure the effects of prior discrimination, such "a sharing of the burden" by innocent parties is not impermissible. The actual "burden" shouldered by nonminority firms is relatively light in this connection when we consider the scope of this public works program as compared with overall construction contracting opportunities. Moreover, although we may assume that the complaining parties are innocent of any discriminatory conduct, it was within congressional power to act on the assumption that in the past some nonminority businesses may have reaped competitive benefit over the years from the virtual exclusion of minority firms from these contracting opportunities. . . .

The history of governmental tolerance of practices using racial or ethnic criteria for the purpose or with the effect of imposing an invidious discrimination must alert us to the deleterious effects of even benign racial or ethnic classifications when they stray from narrow remedial justifications. Even in the context of a facial challenge such as is presented in this case, the MBE provision cannot pass muster unless, with due account for its administrative program, it provides a reasonable assurance that application of racial or ethnic criteria will be limited to accomplishing the remedial objectives of Congress and that misapplications of the program will be promptly and adequately remedied administratively.

It is significant that the administrative scheme provides for waiver and exemption. Two fundamental congressional assumptions underlie the MBE program: (1) that the present effects of past discrimination have impaired the competitive position of businesses owned and controlled by members of minority groups; and (2) that affirmative efforts to eliminate barriers to minority-firm access, and to evaluate bids with adjustment for the present effects of past discrimination, would assure that at least 10% of the federal funds granted under the Public Works Employment Act of 1977 would be accounted for by contracts with available, qualified, bona fide minority business enterprises. Each of these assumptions may be rebutted in the administrative process.

The administrative program contains measures to effectuate the congressional objective of assuring legitimate participation by disadvantaged MBE's. Administrative definition has tightened some less definite aspects of the statutory identification of the minority groups encompassed by the program. There is administrative scrutiny to identify and eliminate from participation in the program MBE's who are not "bonafide" within the regulations and guidelines; for example, spurious minority-front entities can be exposed. A significant aspect of this surveillance is the complaint procedure available for reporting "unjust participation by an enterprise or individuals in the MBE program." And even as to specific contract awards, waiver is available to avoid dealing with an MBE who is attempting to exploit the remedial aspects of the program by charging an unreasonable price, *i.e.*, a price not attributable to the present effects of past discrimination. We must assume that Congress intended close scrutiny of false claims and prompt action on them.

Grantees are given the opportunity to demonstrate that their best efforts will not succeed or have not succeeded in achieving the statutory 10% target for minority firm participation within the limitations of the program's remedial objectives. In these circumstances a waiver or partial waiver is available once compliance has been demonstrated. A waiver may be sought and granted at any time during the contracting process, or even prior to letting contracts if the facts warrant.

That the use of racial and ethnic criteria is premised on assumptions rebuttable in the administrative process gives reasonable assurance that application of the MBE program will be limited to accomplishing the remedial objectives contemplated by Congress and that misapplications of the racial and ethnic criteria can be remedied. . . .

Any preference based on racial or ethnic criteria must necessarily receive a most searching examination to make sure that it does not conflict with constitutional guarantees. This case is one which requires, and which has received, that kind of examination. This opinion does not adopt, either expressly or implicitly, the formulas of analysis articulated in such cases as *University of California Regents* v. *Bakke.* However, our analysis demonstrates that the MBE provision would survive judicial review under either "test" articulated in the several *Bakke* opinions. The MBE provision of the Public Works Employment Act of 1977 does not violate the Constitution.

MR. JUSTICE POWELL, concurring.

Although I would place greater emphasis than the Chief Justice on the need to articulate judicial standards of review in conventional terms, I view his opinion announcing the judgment as substantially in accord with my own views. Accordingly, I join that opinion and write separately to apply the analysis set forth by my opinion in *University of California* v. *Bakke.* . . . Section 103(f)(2) employs a racial classification that is constitutionally prohibited unless it is a necessary means of advancing a compelling governmental interest. . . .

Racial preference never can constitute a compelling state interest. . . . Thus, if the set-aside merely expresses a congressional desire to prefer one racial or ethnic group over another, § 103(f)(2) violates the equal protection component in the Due Process Clause of the Fifth Amendment.

The Government does have a legitimate interest in ameliorating the disabling effects of identified discrimination. The existence of illegal discrimination justifies the imposition of a remedy that will "make persons whole for injuries suffered on account of unlawful discrimination." *Albemarle Paper Co.* v. *Moody,* 422 U.S. 405, 418 (1975). A critical inquiry, therefore, is whether § 103(f)(2) was enacted as a means of redressing such discrimination. . . . this Court has never approved race-conscious remedies absent judicial, administrative, or legislative findings of constitutional or statutory violations.

Because the distinction between permissible remedial action and impermissible racial preference rests on the existence of a constitutional or statutory violation, the legitimate interest in creating a race-conscious remedy is not compelling unless an appropriate governmental authority has found that such a violation has occurred. In other words, two requirements must be met. First, the governmental body that attempts to impose a race-conscious remedy must have the authority to act in response to identified discrimination. Second, the governmental body must make findings that demonstrate the existence of illegal discrimination. In *Bakke,* the Regents failed both requirements. They were entrusted only with educational functions, and they made no findings of past discrimination. Thus, no compelling governmental interest was present to justify the use of a racial quota in medical school admissions.

Our past cases also establish that even if the government proffers a compelling interest to support reliance upon a suspect classification, the means selected must be narrowly drawn to fulfill the governmental purpose. In *Bakke,* for example, the state university did have a compelling interest in the attainment of a diverse student body. But the method selected to achieve that end, the use of a fixed admissions quota, was not appropriate. The Regents' quota system eliminated some nonminority applicants from all consideration for a specified number of seats in the entering class, although it allowed minority applicants to compete for all available seats. In contrast, an admissions program that recognizes race as a factor, but not the sole factor, in assessing an applicant's qualifications serves the University's interest in diversity while ensuring that each applicant receives fair and competitive consideration.

In reviewing the constitutionality of § 103(f)(2), we must decide: (i) whether Congress is competent to make findings of unlawful discrimination; (ii) if so, whether sufficient findings have been made to establish that unlawful discrimination has affected adversely minority business enterprises, and (iii) whether the 10% set-aside is a permissible means for redressing identifiable past discrimination. None of these questions may be answered without explicit recognition that we are reviewing an Act of Congress.

. . . Unlike the Regents of the University of California, Congress properly may—and indeed must—address directly the problems of discrimination in our society. . . .

It is beyond question that Congress has the authority to identify unlawful discriminatory practices, to prohibit those practices, and to prescribe remedies to eradicate their continuing effects. The next inquiry is whether Congress has made findings adequate to support its determination that minority contractors have suffered extensive discrimination.

In my view, the legislative history of § 103(f)(2) demonstrates that Congress reasonably concluded that private and governmental discrimination had contributed to the negligible percentage of public contracts awarded minority contractors.

Under this Court's established doctrine, a racial classification is suspect and subject to strict judicial scrutiny. . . . [T]he Government may employ such a classification only when necessary to accomplish a compelling governmental purpose. The conclusion that Congress found a compelling governmental interest in redressing identified discrimination against minority contractors therefore leads to the inquiry whether use of a 10% set-aside is a constitutionally appropriate means of serving that interest. In the past, this "means" test has been virtually impossible to satisfy. Only two of this Court's modern cases have held the use of racial classifications to be constitutional. See *Korematsu* v. *United States,* (1944); *Hirabayshi* v. *United States,* (1943). Indeed, the failure of legislative action to survive strict scrutiny has led some to wonder whether our review of racial classifications has been strict in theory, but fatal in fact. . . .

Enactment of the set-aside is designed to serve the compelling governmental interest in redressing racial discrimination. As this Court has recognized, the implementation of any affirmative remedy for redress of racial discrimination is likely to affect persons differently depending upon their race. Although federal courts may not order or approve remedies that exceed the scope of a constitutional violation, this Court has not required remedial plans to be limited to the least restrictive means of implementation. We have recognized that the choice of remedies to redress racial discrimination is "a balancing process left, within appropriate constitutional or statutory limits, to the sound discretion of the trial court."

I believe that the enforcement clauses of the Thirteenth and Fourteenth Amendments give Congress a similar measure of discretion to choose a suitable remedy for the redress of racial discrimination. . . . But that authority must be exercised in a manner that does not erode the guarantees of these Amendments. The Judicial Branch has the special responsibility to make a searching inquiry into the justification for employing a race-conscious remedy. Courts must be sensitive to the possibility that less intrusive means might serve the compelling state interest equally as well. I believe that Congress' choice of a remedy should be upheld, however, if the means selected are equitable and reasonably necessary to the redress of identified discrimination. Such a test allows the Congress to exercise necessary discretion but preserves the essential safeguard of judicial review of racial classifications.

When reviewing the selection by Congress of a race-conscious remedy, it is instructive to note the factors upon which the Courts of Appeals have relied in a closely analogous area. Courts reviewing the proper scope of race-conscious hiring remedies have considered (i) the efficacy of alternative remedies, (ii) the planned duration of the remedy, (iii) the relationship between the percentage of minority workers to be employed and the percentage of minority group members in the relevant population or work force, and (iv) the availability of waiver provisions if the hiring plan could not be met.

By the time Congress enacted § 103(f)(2) in 1977, it knew that other remedies had failed to ameliorate the effects of racial discrimination in the construction industry. Although the problem had been addressed by antidiscrimination legislation, executive action to remedy employment discrimination in the construction industry, and federal aid to minority businesses, the fact remained that minority contractors were receiving less than 1% of federal contracts. Congress also knew that economic recession threatened the construction industry as a whole. Section 103(f)(2) was enacted as part of a bill designed to stimulate the economy by appropriating $4 billion in federal funds for new public construction. Since the emergency public construction funds were to be distributed quickly, any remedial provision designed to prevent those funds from perpetuating past discrimination also had to be effective promptly. Moreover, Congress understood that any effective remedial program had to provide minority contractors the experience necessary for continued success without federal assistance. And Congress knew that the ability of minority group members to gain experience had been frustrated by the difficulty of entering the construction trades. The set-aside program adopted as part of this emergency legislation serves each of these concerns because it takes effect as soon as funds are expended under PWEA and because it provides minority contractors with experience that could enable them to compete without governmental assistance.

The § 103(f)(2) set-aside is not a permanent part of federal contracting requirements. As soon as the PWEA program concludes, this set-aside program ends. The temporary nature of this remedy ensures that a race-conscious program will not last longer than the discriminatory effects it is designed to eliminate. It will be necessary for Congress to re-examine the need for a race-conscious remedy before it extends or re-enacts § 103(f)(2).

The percentage chosen for the set-aside is within the scope of congressional discretion. The Courts of Appeals have approved temporary hiring remedies insuring that the percentage of minority group workers in a business or governmental agency will be reasonably related to the percentage of minority group members in the relevant population. Only 4% of contractors are members of minority groups, see *Fullilove* v. *Kreps*, 584 F.2d 600, 608 (CA2 1978), although minority group members constitute about 17% of the national population. The choice of a 10% set-aside thus falls roughly halfway between the present percentage of minority contractors and the percentage of minority group members in the Nation.

Although the set-aside is pegged at a reasonable figure, its effect might be unfair if it were applied rigidly in areas of the country where minority group members constitute a small percentage of the population. To meet this concern, Congress enacted a waiver provision into § 103(f)(2). The factors governing issuance of a waiver include the availability of qualified minority contractors in a particular geographic area, the size of the locale's minority population, and the efforts made to find minority contractors. . . .

A race-conscious remedy should not be approved without consideration of an additional crucial factor—the effect of the set-aside upon innocent third parties. In this case, the petitioners contend with some force that they have been asked to bear the burden of the set-aside even though they are innocent of wrongdoing. I do not believe, however, that their burden is so great that the set-aside must be disapproved. As noted above, Congress knew that minority contractors were receiving only 1% of federal contracts at the time the set-aside was enacted. The PWEA appropriated $4 billion for public work projects, of which it could be expected that approximately $400 million would go to minority contractors. The Court of Appeals calculated that the set-aside would reserve about .25% of all the funds expended yearly on construction work in the United States for approximately 4% of the Nation's contractors who are members of a minority group. The set-aside would have no effect on the ability of the remaining 96% of contractors to compete for 99.75% of construction funds. In my view, the effect of the set-aside is limited and so widely dispersed that its use is consistent with fundamental fairness.

Consideration of these factors persuades me that the set-aside is a reasonably necessary means of furthering the compelling governmental interest in redressing the discrimination that affects minority contractors. Any marginal unfairness to innocent nonminority contractors is not sufficiently significant—or sufficiently identifiable—to outweigh the governmental interest served by § 103(f)(2). When Congress acts to remedy identified discrimination, it may exercise discretion in choosing a remedy that is reasonably necessary to accomplish its purpose. Whatever the exact breadth of that discretion, I believe that it encompasses the selection of the set-aside in this case. . . .

Distinguishing the rights of all citizens to be free from racial classifications from the rights of some citizens to be made whole is a perplexing, but necessary, judicial task. When we first confronted such an issue in *Bakke,* I concluded that the Regents of the University of California were not competent to make, and had not made, findings sufficient to uphold the use of the race-conscious remedy they adopted. As my opinion made clear, I believe that the use of racial classifications, which are fundamentally at odds with the ideals of a democratic society implicit in the Due Process and Equal Protection Clauses, cannot be imposed simply to serve transient social or political goals, however worthy they may be. But the issue here turns on the scope of congressional power, and Congress has been given a unique constitutional role in the enforcement of the post-Civil War Amendments. In this case, where Congress determined that minority contractors were victims of purposeful discrimination and where Congress chose a reasonably necessary means to effectuate its purpose, I find no constitutional reason to invalidate § 103(f)(2).

MR. JUSTICE MARSHALL, with whom MR. JUSTICE BRENNAN and MR. JUSTICE BLACKMUN join, concurring in the judgment.

My resolution of the constitutional issue in this case is governed by the separate opinion I coauthored in *University of California Regents* v. *Bakke*. . . .

In *Bakke,* I joined my Brothers Brennan, White, and Blackmun in articulating the view that "racial classifications are not *per se* invalid under [the Equal Protection Clause of] the Fourteenth Amendment." *(opinion of Brennan, White, Marshall and Blackmun, J. J., concurring in the judgment in part and dissenting in part) (hereinafter cited as joint separate opinion).* We acknowledged that "a government practice or statute which contains 'suspect classifications' is to be subjected to 'strict scrutiny' and can be justified only if it furthers a compelling government purpose and, even then, only if no less restrictive alternative is available." Thus, we reiterated the traditional view that racial classifications are prohibited if they are irrelevant. In addition, we firmly adhered to "the cardinal principle that racial classifications that stigmatize—because they are drawn on the presumption that one race is inferior to another or because they put the weight of government behind racial hatred and separatism—are invalid without more."

We recognized, however, that these principles outlawing the irrelevant or pernicious use of race were inapposite to racial classifications that provide benefits to minorities for the purpose of remedying the present effects of past racial discrimination. Such classifications may disadvantage some whites, but whites as a class lack the " 'traditional indicia of suspectness: the class is not saddled with such disabilities, or subjected to such a history of purposeful unequal treatment, or relegated to such a position of political powerlessness as to command extraordinary protection from the majoritarian political process.' " Because the consideration of race is relevant to remedying the continuing effects of past racial discrimination, and because governmental programs employing racial classifications for remedial purposes can be crafted to avoid stigmatization, we concluded that such programs should not be subjected to conventional "strict scrutiny"—scrutiny that is strict in theory, but fatal in fact.

Nor did we determine that such programs should be analyzed under the minimally rigorous rational-basis standard of review. . . . We recognized that race has often been used to stigmatize politically powerless segments of society, and that efforts to ameliorate the effects of past discrimination could be based on paternalistic stereotyping, not on a careful consideration of modern social conditions. In addition, we acknowledged that governmental classification on the immutable characteristic of race runs counter to the deep national belief that state-sanctioned benefits and burdens should bear some relationship to individual merit and responsibility.

We concluded, therefore, that because a racial classification ostensibly designed for remedial purposes is susceptible to misuse, it may be justified only by showing "an important and articulated purpose for its use." "In addition any statute must be stricken that stigmatizes any group or that singles out those least well represented in the political process to bear the brunt of a benign program." . . . In our view, then, the proper inquiry is whether racial classifications designed to further remedial purposes serve important governmental objectives and are substantially related to achievement of those objectives.

Judged under this standard, the 10% minority set-aside provision at issue in this case is plainly constitutional. Indeed, the question is not even a close one.

MR. JUSTICE STEWART, with whom MR. JUSTICE REHNQUIST joins, dissenting.

"Our Constitution is color-blind, and neither knows nor tolerates classes among citizens. . . . The law regards man as man, and takes no account of his surroundings or of his color . . ." Those words were written by a Member of this Court 84 years ago. *Plessy* v. *Ferguson,* (Harlan, J., dissenting). His colleagues disagreed with him, and held that a statute that required the separation of people on the basis of their race was constitutionally valid because it was a "reasonable" exercise of legislative power and had been "enacted in good faith for the promotion [of] the public good. . . ." . . . Today, the Court upholds a statute that accords a preference to citizens who are "Negroes, Spanish-speaking, Orientals, Indians, Eskimos, and Aleuts," for much the same reasons. I think today's decision is wrong for the same reason that *Plessy* v. *Ferguson* was wrong, and I respectfully dissent.

The equal protection standard of the Constitution has one clear and central meaning—it absolutely prohibits invidious discrimination by government. That standard must be met by every State under the Equal Protection Clause of the Fourteenth Amendment.

And that standard must be met by the United States itself under the Due Process Clause of the Fifth Amendment. Under our Constitution, any official action that treats a person differently on account of his race or ethnic origin is inherently suspect and presumptively invalid. . . . Under our Constitution, the government may never act to the detriment of a person solely because of that person's race.* . . . In short, racial discrimination is by definition invidious discrimination.

The rule cannot be any different when the persons injured by a racially biased law are not members of a racial minority. The guarantee of equal protection is "universal in [its] application, to all persons . . . without regard to any differences of race, of color, or of nationality." *Yick Wo* v. *Hopkins.* The command of the equal protection guarantee is simple but unequivocal: In the words of the Fourteenth Amendment, "No State shall . . . deny to *any* person . . . the equal protection of the laws." Nothing in this language singles out some "persons" for more "equal" treatment than others. Rather, as the Court made clear in *Shelley* v. *Kraemer* the benefits afforded by the Equal Protection Clause "are, by its terms, guaranteed to the individual. [They] are personal rights." From the perspective of a person detrimentally affected by a racially discriminatory law, the arbitrariness and unfairness is entirely the same, whatever his skin color and whatever the law's purpose, be it purportedly "for the promotion of the public good" or otherwise. . . .

On its face, the minority business enterprise (MBE) provision at issue in this case denies the equal protection of the law. The Public Works Employment Act of 1977 directs that all project construction shall be performed by those private contractors who submit the lowest competitive bids and who meet established criteria of responsibility. One class of contracting firms—defined solely according to the racial and ethnic attributes of their owners—is, however, excepted from the full rigor of these requirements with respect to a percentage of each federal grant. The statute, on its face and in effect, thus bars a class to which the petitioners belong from having the opportunity to receive a government benefit, and bars the members of that class solely on the basis of their race or ethnic background. This is precisely the kind of law that the guarantee of equal protection forbids.

The Court's attempt to characterize the law as a proper remedial measure to counteract the effects of past or present racial discrimination is remarkably unconvincing. The Legislative Branch of government is not a court of equity. It has neither the dispassionate objectivity nor the flexibility that are needed to mold a race-conscious remedy around the single objective of eliminating the effects of past or present discrimination. . . .

Certainly, nothing in the Constitution gives Congress any greater authority to impose detriments on the basis of race than is afforded the Judicial Branch. And a judicial decree that imposes burdens on the basis of race can be upheld only where its sole purpose is to eradicate the actual effects of illegal race discrimination.

The provision at issue here does not satisfy this condition. Its legislative history suggests that it had at least two other objectives in addition to that of counteracting the effects of past or present racial discrimination in the public works construction industry. One such purpose appears to have been to assure to minority contractors a certain percentage of federally funded public works contracts. But, since the guarantee of equal protection immunizes from capricious governmental treatment "persons"—not "races," it can never countenance laws that seek racial balance as a goal in and of itself. "Preferring members of any one group for no reason other than race or ethnic origin is discrimination for its own sake. This the Constitution forbids." *Regents of the University of California* v. *Bakke, (opinion of Powell, J.).* Second, there are indications that the MBE provision may have been enacted to compensate for the effects of social, educational, and economic "disadvantage." No race,

* A court of equity may, of course, take race into account in devising a remedial decree to undo a violation of a law prohibiting discrimination on the basis of race. But such a judicial decree, following litigation in which a violation of law has been determined, is wholly different from generalized legislation that awards benefits and imposes detriments dependent upon the race of the recipients. . . .

however, has a monopoly on social, educational, or economic disadvantage, and any law that indulges in such a presumption clearly violates the constitutional guarantee of equal protection. Since the MBE provision was in whole or in part designed to effectuate objectives other than the elimination of the effects of racial discrimination, it cannot stand as a remedy that comports with the strictures of equal protection, even if it otherwise could.

The Fourteenth Amendment was adopted to ensure that every person must be treated equally by each State regardless of the color of his skin. . . . Today, the Court derails this achievement and places its imprimatur on the creation once again by government of privileges based on birth.

The Court, moreover, takes this drastic step without, in my opinion, seriously considering the ramifications of its decision. Laws that operate on the basis of race require definitions of race. Because of the Court's decision today, our statute books will once again have to contain laws that reflect the odious practice of delineating the qualities that make one person a Negro and make another white. Moreover, racial discrimination, even "good faith" racial discrimination, is inevitably a two-edged sword. "[P]referential programs may only reinforce common stereotypes holding that certain groups are unable to achieve success without special protection based on a factor having no relationship to individual worth." *University of California Regents* v. *Bakke (opinion of Powell, J.).* Most importantly, by making race a relevant criterion once again in its own affairs, the Government implicitly teaches the public that the apportionment of rewards and penalties can legitimately be made according to race—rather than according to merit or ability—and that people can, and perhaps should, view themselves and others in terms of their racial characteristics. Notions of "racial entitlement" will be fostered, and private discrimination will necessarily be encouraged.

There are those who think that we need a new Constitution, and their views may someday prevail. But under the Constitution we have, one practice in which government may never engage is the practice of racism—not even "temporarily" and not even as an "experiment."

For these reasons, I would reverse the judgment of the Court of Appeals.

MR. JUSTICE STEVENS, dissenting.

The 10% set-aside contained in the Public Works Employment Act of 1977, 91 Stat. 116 ("the Act") creates monopoly privileges in a $400,000,000 market for a class of investors defined solely by racial characteristics. The direct beneficiaries of these monopoly privileges are the relatively small number of persons within the racial classification who represent the entrepreneurial subclass—those who have, or can borrow, working capital. . . .

The legislative history of the Act discloses that there is a group of legislators in Congress identified as the "Black Caucus" and that members of that group argued that if the Federal Government was going to provide $4,000,000,000 of new public contract business, their constituents were entitled to "a piece of the action.". . .

. . . [A]n absolute preference that is unrelated to a minority firm's ability to perform a contract inevitably will engender resentment on the part of competitors excluded from the market for a purely racial reason and skepticism on the part of customers and suppliers aware of the statutory classification. . . . [A] statute of this kind inevitably is perceived by many as resting on an assumption that those who are granted this special preference are less qualified in some respect that is identified purely by their race. Because that perception—especially when fostered by the Congress of the United States—can only exacerbate rather than reduce racial prejudice, it will delay the time when race will become a truly irrelevant, or at least insignificant, factor. . . .

This Act has a character that is fundamentally different from a carefully drafted remedial measure like the Voting Rights Act of 1965. A consideration of some of the dramatic differences between these two legislative responses to racial injustice reveals not merely a difference in legislative craftsmanship but a difference of constitutional significance. Whereas the enactment of the Voting Rights Act was preceded by exhaustive hearings and debates concerning discriminatory denial of access to the electoral process, and became effective in specific States only after specific findings were made, this statute authorizes an automatic nationwide preference for all members of a diverse racial class regardless of their possible interest in the particular geographic areas where the public contracts are to be performed. Just why a wealthy Negro or Spanish-speaking investor should have a preferred status in bidding on a construction contract in Alaska—or a citizen of Eskimo ancestry should have a preference in Miami or Detroit—is difficult to understand in light of either the asserted remedial character of the set-aside or the more basic purposes of the public works legislation.

The Voting Rights Act addressed the problem of denial of access to the electoral process. By outlawing specific practices, such as poll taxes and special tests, the statute removed old barriers to equal access; by requiring preclearance of changes in voting practices in covered States, it precluded the erection of new barriers. The Act before us today does not outlaw any existing barriers to access to the economic market and does nothing to prevent the erection of new barriers. On the contrary, it adopts the fundamentally different approach of creating a new set of barriers of its own. . . .

Unlike Mr. Justice Stewart and Mr. Justice Rehnquist, however, I am not convinced that the Clause contains an absolute prohibition against any statutory classification based on race. I am nonetheless persuaded that it does impose a special obligation to scrutinize any governmental decisionmaking process that draws nationwide distinctions between citizens on the basis of their race and incidentally also discriminates against noncitizens in the preferred racial classes. For just as procedural safeguards are necessary to guarantee impartial decisionmaking in the judicial process, so can they play a vital part in preserving the impartial character of the legislative process.

In both its substantive and procedural aspects this Act is markedly different from the normal product of the legislative decisionmaking process. The very fact that Congress for the first time in the Nation's history has created a broad legislative classification for entitlement to benefits based solely on racial characteristics identifies a dramatic difference between this Act and the thousands of statutes that preceded it. This dramatic point of departure is not even mentioned in the statement of purpose of the Act or in the reports of either the House or the Senate Committee that processed the legislation, and was not the subject of any testimony or inquiry in any legislative hearing on the bill that was enacted. It is true that there was a brief discussion on the floor of the House as well as in the Senate on two different days, but only a handful of legislators spoke and there was virtually no debate. This kind of perfunctory consideration of an unprecedented policy decision of profound constitutional importance to the Nation is comparable to the accidental malfunction of the legislative process that led to what I regarded as a totally unjustified discrimination in *Delaware Tribal Business Committee* v. *Weeks*, . . . 430 U.S., at 97.

Although it is traditional for judges to accord the same presumption of regularity to the legislative process no matter how obvious it may be that a busy Congress has acted precipitately, I see no reason why the character of their procedures may not be considered relevant to the decision whether the legislative product has caused a deprivation of liberty or property without due process of law. Whenever Congress creates a classification that would be subject to strict scrutiny under the Equal Protection Clause of the Fourteenth Amendment if it had been fashioned by a state legislature, it seems to me that judicial review should include a consideration of the procedural character of the decisionmaking process. A holding that the classification was not adequately preceded by a consideration of less drastic alternatives or adequately explained by a statement of legislative purpose would be far less intrusive than a final determination that the substance of the decision is not "narrowly tailored to the achievement of that goal." . . .

In all events, rather than take the substantive position expressed in Mr. Justice Stewart's dissenting opinion, I would hold this statute unconstitutional on a narrower ground. It cannot fairly be characterized as a "narrowly tailored" racial classification because it simply raises too many serious questions that Congress failed to answer or even to address in a responsible way. . . . It is up to Congress to demonstrate that its unique statutory preference is justified by a relevant characteristic that is shared by the members of the preferred class. In my opinion, because it has failed to make that demonstration, it has also failed to discharge its duty to govern impartially embodied in the Fifth Amendment to the United States Constitution.

I respectfully dissent.

CHAPTER 15

Criminal Procedure

In our federal system, the administration of criminal justice is principally a function of the states. See *Barron* v. *Baltimore* (p. 138). In this regard, we should recall that the Fourteenth Amendment does not necessarily make *all* the procedural safeguards of the Bill of Rights applicable to the states. Justice Frankfurter noted in *Wolf* v. *Colorado,* 338 U.S. 25 (1949), that "the notion that the 'due process of law' guaranteed by the Fourteenth Amendment is shorthand for the first eight amendments of the Constitution and thereby incorporates them has been rejected by this Court again and again after impressive consideration." In *Palko* v. *Connecticut* (p. 663), Justice Cardozo undertook to draw a line between those portions of the Bill of Rights that are protected against state abridgment and those that are not so protected by classifying rights into essential and nonessential categories. Only the essential rights were protected. Thus, the states were left free to administer criminal justice without federal interference unless in so doing they offended some fundamental principle of justice.

In *Adamson* v. *California* (p. 666), the Court held, by a 5-to-4 vote, that the due process clause does not require state courts to give accused persons the protection against self-incrimination as provided by the Fifth Amendment. In his long dissenting opinion, Justice Black argued that the Fourteenth Amendment was designed to make all the guarantees of the Bill of Rights applicable to the states. However, this view has never been openly accepted by a Court majority.

Since 1937, when the *Palko* case was decided, all of the First Amendment; all of the Fourth; all of the Fifth, except grand jury indictment; most of the Sixth; and the Eighth, except excessive bail, have been declared binding on the states by "selective incorporation" into the Fourteenth.[1] In making these Bill of Rights requirements binding on the states, the Court has continued to use the language of *Palko,* speaking in terms of fundamental rights. Therefore, it can be argued that technically the Court has not been "incorporating" the Bill of Rights into the due process clause, but only defining more and more rights as fundamental. Certainly, this approach has spared the Court the necessity of ever offering a general explanation of why incorporation is appropriate, and it allows the justices to stage their interventions against the states one at a time. Perhaps it also allows the Court to allow the states a bit more leeway than federal law enforcement agencies when that seems wise. It may well be that in the end the only reason to maintain the *Palko* rule will be to avoid imposing the obsolete grand jury indictment system on the states. Indeed, the Court has now overruled the specific holding in *Palko* itself and has found that the double-jeopardy provisions of the Fifth are binding on the states. [*Benton* v. *Maryland,* 395 U.S. 784 (1969).]

Search and Seizure

THE EXCLUSIONARY RULE

The Fourth Amendment forbids "unreasonable search and seizure." The central meaning of that phrase has always been that the police may not search premises without a search warrant issued by a magistrate upon probable cause. In *Weeks* v. *United States,* 232 U.S. 383 (1914), the Supreme Court held that where evidence was the product of an unreasonable search by federal officers, it might not be admitted by a federal court. At the time it was not clear whether this "exclusionary rule" was a constitutional rule required by the Fourth Amendment or simply a rule of evidence imposed on the lower federal courts by the Supreme Court as supervisor of the federal court system.

The uncertainty made little difference until *Wolf* v. *Colorado,* 338 U.S. 25 (1949), in which the Court held that unreasonable search and seizure guarantees were also applicable against the states under the due process clause. As we

[1] Richard Cortner, *The Supreme Court and the Second Bill of Rights* (Madison: University of Wisconsin Press, 1981).

have already noted, the opinion was by Justice Frankfurter and followed the *Palko* approach of something less than full "incorporation." In *Wolf,* the Court refused to apply the exclusionary rule to the states. That refusal might be rationalized either on the ground that the Fourteenth only incorporated the "core" of the Fourth and the exclusionary rule is not part of the core or alternatively on the ground that the exclusionary rule was not part of the Fourth at all but only a rule of evidence. Although the Supreme Court has the authority to fashion procedural rules, such as rules of evidence, for the lower federal courts, it has no such authority over state courts. Thus, it could be argued, the Supreme Court could not impose the exclusionary rule on the states.

Whichever rationale is chosen, the result of *Wolf* was that the guarantees against unreasonable search and seizure were binding on both federal and state governments, but the exclusionary rule only on federal courts and not state. There were two basic reasons for the reluctance of the Supreme Court to extend the exclusionary rule to the states. The first was the Court's traditional respect for the autonomy of the states in criminal law matters—which, after all, fall at the center of the "police power." The second is a basic paradox of the rule itself. For, by excluding evidence of guilt gathered by the police, we attack the unconstitutional action of the policeman not by punishing him but by letting the guilty criminal go.

Following *Wolf,* even Justice Frankfurter occasionally permitted the exclusionary rule to operate against the states in extraordinary circumstances. Thus, in *Rochin* v. *California,* 342 U.S. 165 (1952), where the police forcibly stomach-pumped the accused in order to get at capsules he had swallowed, the capsules were held inadmissible as evidence in an opinion by Justice Frankfurter. He argued that this "breaking into the privacy" of the accused was "conduct that shocks the conscience." A similar result was reached in *Irvine* v. *California,* 347 U.S. 128 (1954), where police had keys made to a suspect's house and used them to enter and plant listening apparatus in the hall and bedroom.

Then, in *Elkins* v. *United States,* 364 U.S. 206 (1960), the Court overturned the old "silver-platter doctrine." Under that doctrine state officers engaged in a search without a warrant who discovered evidence of a federal crime could hand it over to federal authorities "on a silver platter." The evidence had been admissible in subsequent federal proceedings on the theory that *Weeks* only applied to the misdeeds of federal officers and here the federal officers had done nothing wrong. The Court now argued in *Elkins* that the silver-platter doctrine had been introduced before *Wolf* ruled that a warrantless search by state officers was unconstitutional. It was logically anomalous after *Wolf* because it allowed unconstitutionally gathered evidence into a federal court, contrary to *Weeks.*

Elkins, with its close tying of *Wolf* to *Weeks* and its plugging of one of the last loopholes for the admission of unconstitutionally seized evidence into federal courts, might have warned acute observers of things to come. After all, federal officers could not get unconstitutionally seized evidence into federal courts, federal officers were forbidden to obtain and turn over such evidence for use by state officers in state courts, and state officers might not turn over such evidence to federal officers for use in federal courts. About all that was left was state officers in state courts.

In spite of *Elkins,* most constitutional scholars and practitioners were surprised by *Mapp* v. *Ohio* (p. 672), which finally held that the exclusionary rule did apply to the states. Indeed, *Wolf* seemed so settled that the counsel for Mrs. Mapp did not even brief the illegally seized evidence point but instead concentrated on the obscenity aspects of the case.

Problems of federalism still exist, even after *Mapp.* Thus, in *Ker* v. *California,* 374 U.S. 23 (1963), the Court held that evidence was admissible in state courts that had been obtained by state officers through a method of search—unannounced or "no knock"—that was barred to federal officers by a federal statute at that time. The Court returned to the "supervisory powers" rationale. It held that federal courts must ban evidence whose seizure was illegal under federal law because of their responsibility to support federal law. The Supreme Court enforced the ban on lower federal courts because it is the head of the federal court system. That this kind of evidence was inadmissible for these reasons in federal courts did not make it inadmissible in state courts.

SEARCH WARRANTS

A warrant issues only on "probable cause." The Court has ruled that the probable-cause standards are the same for state and federal magistrates. [*Aguilar* v. *Texas,* 378 U.S. 108 (1964).] The justices have not shown any great desire to supervise local judges as to whether they truly had probable cause to issue a warrant. [See, however, *Franks* v. *Delaware,* 438 U.S. 154 (1978).] The few cases that have reached the Court have been concerned mostly with probable cause established by informers' tips and are discussed later in this chapter in the section on informers.

The traditional federal rule was that search warrants would not issue for "mere evidence of a crime," but only where the police could show they were seeking for contraband, such as the loot from a robbery. After *Mapp* imposed a stringent warrant requirement on the police, the Supreme Court, in *Warden* v. *Hayden,* 387 U.S. 294 (1967), abolished the mere-evidence rule. This opinion made it far easier for police to get warrants, but it was noticed little by those who were shouting about the Court handcuffing the police.

Although the central meaning of the Fourth Amendment is tied to the distinction between searches with and without a warrant, the amendment condemns not warrantless searches but unreasonable searches. The Court has long recognized a number of exceptions to the warrant requirement.

SEARCH INCIDENT TO ARREST AND "PLAIN-VIEW" SEIZURES

The most important of these exceptions to the warrant requirement is that for search incident to a lawful arrest. The Court has held that the arresting officer may make an immediate search without a warrant. The rationale for the "arrest exception" is that as a practical matter the police officer must be free to search the accused and his immediate vicinity for weapons that might endanger the officer and to keep items of evidence out of the range of the arrested person who might otherwise immediately destroy them. In spite of this rationale, the Court tended to approve broader and broader areas of search incident to arrest, sometimes permitting the search of rooms a substantial distance from the place in which the suspect had been arrested. Particularly after *Mapp*, search incident to arrest became a favorite police procedure for meeting the demands of the Fourth Amendment. In *Chimel* v. *California* (p. 696), the Court more carefully limited the scope of searches incident to arrest. Even after *Chimel*, however, the police could, as an incident to arrest, seize instrumentalities of crime if they were in "plain view," even if they were not within the zone of control of the person arrested.

Of course, for the search to be constitutional, the arrest has to be legal. There are two modes of legal arrest. The first is arrest with an arrest warrant that has been issued by a magistrate. The second is arrest without an arrest warrant. If a police officer has "probable cause" to believe that a crime has been committed and has probable cause to believe that the suspect is the perpetrator of the crime, he can arrest the perpetrator immediately without waiting to obtain an arrest warrant.[2] And if the arrest is legal, then generally so is his subsequent search. Thus, the key question in many search and seizure cases is whether the police officer had probable cause to make the arrest. [See *Draper* v. *United States*, 358 U.S. 307 (1959).]

The various warrant and probable cause requirements are confusing. The student must become accustomed to making distinctions among them and carefully labeling in thought, speech, and writing whether he or she is talking about a search warrant or an arrest warrant or about probable cause for obtaining a search warrant or probable cause for making an arrest without an arrest warrant.

VEHICULAR SEARCH

It is clear that a police officer may not normally make a search without a search warrant simply because he has probable cause to believe that he will find evidence of a crime. In such circumstances he must take his probable cause to a magistrate and get a warrant. But there is a major exception even to this rule—the vehicle exception. Police can search a vehicle they have lawfully intercepted if they have probable cause to believe that evidence of a crime is present. [*Carroll* v. *United States*, 267 U.S. 132 (1925); *Brinegar* v. *United States*, 338 U.S. 160 (1949); and *Henry* v. *United States*, 361 U.S. 98 (1959).] But their initial interception of the vehicle must be a lawful one before the search of the car without a warrant can become lawful.

Thus, before he or she can search a car without a warrant, the police

[2] This is the common law rule. It is confirmed as to public places by *United States* v. *Watson*, 423 U.S. 411 (1976).

officer must ask several questions: Can I find a specific reason, beyond mere suspicion, for stopping the car? Or can I find a traffic violation, or observe some faulty safety equipment that will allow me to stop the car in order to give a warning or citation? [See *Chambers* v. *Maroney,* 399 U.S. 42 (1970).] Once I have stopped it, can I find a probable cause to believe that evidence of a crime is present sufficient to justify a search? [*Wong Sun* v. *United States,* 371 U.S. 471 (1963).] Or can I make a lawful arrest that would legitimate a search? Can I manage to see an instrumentality of crime in plain sight in the car? Once I have made a lawful stop, can I get the driver to "consent" to a search?

CONSENT SEARCHES

A person can "waive" his Fourth Amendment rights just as he can waive his right against self-incrimination. So consent searches are another exception to the search warrant requirement and to the probable cause requirement for vehicular searches. The federal courts have generally been reluctant to believe a police officer's story that a suspect freely and willingly consented to an otherwise illegal search. The state courts have been far more willing to find consent. But it is clear that consent is not simply a matter of the suspect saying yes at the time of the search. The court will consider all of the actual circumstances, such as the number and behavior of the police, in determining whether consent was given consciously and freely or obtained by police tricks or coercion. The Supreme Court has said little about consent searches. [See *Schneckloth* v. *Bustamonte,* 412 U.S. 218 (1973).]

HOT PURSUIT

The police may enter premises without an arrest or search warrant when in "hot pursuit" of a fleeing suspect. Having entered, they may seize evidence encountered in the search for the suspect. [See *Warden* v. *Hayden,* 387 U.S. 294 (1967).] Today the Court often speaks of "exigent circumstances" to cover hot pursuit and other emergencies that might justify a warrantless entry or search.

STOP AND FRISK

Another exception to the warrant requirement is the stop-and-frisk situation. The Court fairly obviously chose *Mapp,* which involved an outrageous invasion of a residence, as its vehicle for imposing the exclusionary rule on the states because basically it was concerned with house searches, where the police could easily obtain a warrant. Their failure to do so was clearly an unjustified invasion of privacy. But *Mapp* was an impractical decision in the context of police needs on the street.

Even where a police officer saw highly suspicious goings-on in the street, such as a known dope pusher heading down a dark alley followed by a shaking junky waving his cash, the officer was legally powerless to intervene. Absent fairly concrete evidence that the pusher was "holding," the officer did not have probable cause to make an arrest. The evidence was in the pusher's pocket. The officer could not go into the pusher's pocket without a search warrant. The pusher would be gone by the time he got one. So the officer could not search the pusher unless he could do so incident to a valid arrest, and he could not find probable cause to make a valid arrest until he had searched the pusher. Faced with this assault on their common sense, many police officers resorted to "dropsie" evidence. They arrested the pusher, took the junk out of his pocket, and when the lawfulness of the search and arrest was challenged in court, they testified that upon approaching the subject he had dropped the evidence, they had picked it up, seen that it was dope, and then had probable cause to make an arrest. This testimony was fairly credible because a criminal is likely to throw away the evidence against him when he sees the police.

The Court partially confronted this situation in *Terry* v. *Ohio,* 392 U.S. 1 (1968), which upheld police stop-and-frisk procedures. The Court held that where authorized by state law, the police can conduct a "field interrogation" on a reasonable suspicion that falls below probable cause to make an arrest. In the course of such interrogation, the Court held, "there must be a narrowly drawn authority to permit a reasonable search for weapons for the protection of the police officer, where he has reason to believe that he is dealing with an armed and dangerous individual, regardless of whether he had probable cause to arrest the individual for a crime."

The Court concluded that a "frisk"—in which the officer pats down the clothing of the suspect and then enters his clothing if the "pat search" revealed a weapon—is constitutionally justified. Of course, just as in a search for weapons incident to a lawful arrest, not just weapons but anything encountered in the course of the lawful search is admissible as evidence.

Now the officer can approach the suspected peddler going down the alley and interrogate him. The peddler's words or actions during the interrogation may generate probable cause to make an arrest, as well as a subsequent search incident to arrest that will uncover the dope in his pocket. Alternatively, the police officer can conduct a pat search that may reveal a suspiciously hard lump that may be a weapon and so lead the officer to enter the suspect's pocket where, lo and behold, not a weapon but the dope will be discovered. The police have been in a better position since *Terry.* And no doubt the smart peddlers stopped carrying hard things in their pockets. If they kept cool, they still had the police in a legal quandary.

THE PERSON OF THE ACCUSED

The face, fingerprints, blood, voice, handwriting, and other personal attributes of the accused constitute special problems of search and seizure. The Court might have held that requiring an individual to submit himself, or part of himself, for identification was to require him to incriminate himself in violation of the Fifth Amendment. Such a holding would have greatly obstructed the police because the right against self-incrimination is almost absolute. (See p. 645.) Instead, the Court held that these matters fall under the search-and-seizure provisions. Therefore, the police can make identifications so long as they do not unreasonably seize. Thus, in *Schmerber* v. *California,* 384 U.S. 757 (1966), the Court upheld a state requirement of compulsory blood tests in drunken driver inquiries. And in *United States* v. *Wade,* 388 U.S. 218 (1967), it upheld compulsory lineups. Although occasionally it has struck down a peculiarly unreasonable police identification method, the Court has generally refused the claims of persons seeking to avoid identification. [See *Davis* v. *Mississippi,* 394 U.S. 721 (1969); see also the warning against rigged lineups in *Kirby* v. *Illinois,* 406 U.S. 682 (1972).]

ELECTRONIC SURVEILLANCE

Another special problem of search and seizure is electronic surveillance. For many years the Supreme Court was handicapped by the horse-and-buggy analogy that because eavesdropping by the police at an open window had never been considered an unreasonable search and seizure, neither should electronic eavesdropping. In *Olmstead* v. *United States,* 277 U.S. 438 (1928), the Court held that telephone taps did not violate the Fourth Amendment. In 1934, a federal statute made wiretapping a crime. In *Nardone* v. *United States,* 302 U.S. 379 (1937), the Court held that the statute applied to federal and state officers and excluded illegally obtained wiretap evidence from federal proceedings.

In the interval before *Mapp,* the statute led to problems of federalism, with the Court permitting the admission of wiretap evidence in state but not federal proceedings but then knocking out "silver-platter" tactics. Finally, in *Lee* v. *Florida,* 392 U.S. 378 (1968), the Court applied the exclusionary rule to state courts as well.

However, in that same year the wiretap provisions of the Crime Control Act of 1968 came into force, providing in effect for a search warrant procedure for federal wiretaps comparable to search warrant procedures for other types of searches. The Crime Control Act provides that the Attorney General may apply for an authorizing order to a federal judge. The President, however, is authorized to conduct taps without judicial authorization in national security and foreign intelligence-gathering matters. The statute provides that evidence from both court-ordered and presidential taps be admissible. The constitutionality of the presidential portion of the act is in some doubt. The act also provides that tapping is lawful when done with the consent of one of the parties even without a court order. The provision seems to have been constitutionally authorized by earlier Supreme Court decisions. [See *Rathbun* v. *United States,* 355 U.S. 107 (1957).]

Much electronic surveillance involves means other than telephone taps. For these, drawing on *Olmstead,* the Court eventually worked out a "trespass" doctrine. If the surveillance were done without trespassing on private premises—

for instance, by a detectaphone placed against an outside wall [*Goldman* v. *United States,* 316 U.S. 129 (1942)] or by wiring an informant who was invited onto the premises [*On Lee* v. *United States,* 343 U.S. 747 (1952)]—then there was no unreasonable search and seizure. Where trespass occurred, then the search and seizure—at least if there were no search warrant—was unlawful. The bizarre nature of this approach was revealed by *Silverman* v. *United States,* 365 U.S. 505 (1961), in which the Court unanimously struck down the admission of evidence gained by a "spike mike" stuck *into* a wall, while refusing to overrule *Goldman* where the mike had been stuck *onto* a wall.

In *Berger* v. *New York,* 388 U.S. 41 (1967), the Court repudiated *Olmstead* and held that conversation was protected by the Fourth Amendment and that the use of electronic devices to capture it was a search. *Katz* v. *United States* (p. 694) summed up the position that the Warren Court reached on electronic surveillance.

INFORMERS AND SECRET AGENTS

The use of informers and undercover agents by the police creates a wide range of interlocking search-and-seizure problems, as well as others involving self-incrimination and right to counsel. In *On Lee; Lopez* v. *United States,* 373 U.S. 427 (1963); and *Osborn* v. *United States,* 385 U.S. 323 (1966), the Court ruled admissible the evidence of conversations gathered through the use of electronically rigged agents to whom the accused thought they were speaking privately. The general rationale was that the accused could hardly claim that he had a constitutional right to secrecy for things he had already told to someone else—namely, the informer. *Hoffa* v. *United States* (p. 692) takes up a number of problems created by the use of "nonelectronic" informers.

In *Aguilar* v. *Texas,* 378 U.S. 108 (1964), and *Spinelli* v. *United States,* 393 U.S. 410 (1969), the Court took up the use of informer evidence to establish probable cause for the issuance of search warrants. The justices did not attempt a detailed code of specifics. They held that affidavits requesting warrants must do more than recite "mere conclusions" by the police that the warrant is justified. When informer information is used to justify the warrant, the magistrate must have facts showing the informer to have been "reliable" in the past and indicating that "underlying circumstances" in the present case support his tip.

THE FRUIT OF THE POISONOUS TREE

In *Silverthorne Lumber Co.* v. *United States,* 251 U.S. 385 (1920), the Supreme Court held that where evidence has been obtained by the government through an unconstitutional search and seizure, not only is the evidence inadmissible but any further evidence developed as a consequence of the illegal seizure is also inadmissible. [See *Wong Sun* v. *United States,* 371 U.S. 471 (1963).] But in *United States* v. *Calandra,* 414 U.S. 338 (1974), the Court held that a witness may not refuse to answer grand jury questions that are based on evidence obtained from unlawful search. And in *United States* v. *Crews,* 445 U.S. 463 (1980) the Court held that in-court identification of an unlawfully arrested defendant by his victim did not have to be suppressed as the fruit of the unlawful arrest. [See also *United States* v. *Ceccolini,* 435 U.S. 268 (1978).]

The Burger Court and Search and Seizure

The Warren Court's rights-of-accused decisions, and particularly its extension of the exclusionary rule to the states, came under a great deal of public fire and even became an issue in the presidential campaign of 1968. Chief Justice Burger owed his appointment by President Nixon in large part to his opposition to various extensions of the rights of the accused while serving as a judge on the circuit court for the District of Columbia. As in other areas, however, a gigantic rollback of Warren Court decisions has not occurred in the search-and-seizure field. But change is sufficiently evident to justify taking up the major Burger Court decisions as a separate unit.

EXCLUSION

On the central issue of the exclusionary rule, the Chief Justice has announced his total opposition to the *Mapp* decision. However, he has sometimes indicated that change in the rule should come from Congress, not the Court. [*Bivens* v. *Six Unknown Named Agents,* 403 U.S. 388 (1971).] Justice Blackmun has supported the argument that "the Fourth Amendment supports no exclusionary rule." [*Coolidge* v. *New Hampshire,* 403 U.S. 443 (1971).] And Justices Powell and Rehnquist have indicated similar views. [*Schneckloth* v. *Bustamonte,* 412 U.S. 218 (1973).] In *Stone* v. *Powell,* 428 U.S. 465 (1976), this critical attitude has spread to seven justices. Though still upholding the exclusionary rule, the Court holds that where the state courts have concluded that the accused's Fourth Amendment rights have not been violated, federal courts should not exercise habeas corpus jurisdiction to review their findings. The Court has also refused to extend the exclusionary rule to federal civil proceedings. [*United States* v. *Janis,* 428 U.S. 433 (1976).] In *United States* v. *Peltier,* 422 U.S. 531 (1975), and *Michigan* v. *De Fillippo,* 443 U.S. 31 (1979), the Court held that where an officer acted in good-faith conformity to law which subsequent court decisions found unconstitutional, the evidence collected need not be excluded. In *United States* v. *Havens,* 446 U.S. 620 (1980), the Court held that illegally seized evidence was admissible to impeach the testimony of a defendant. The evidence could not be used to prove the defendant was guilty of the crime for which he was being tried, but it could be used to show that he was lying when he testified in his own defense.

The Chief Justice's basic position is that *Mapp* sought to deter police misconduct at the cost of letting criminals go, that this cost is high, that the evidence suggests that the police have continued in their misconduct since *Mapp,* and that the solution is to get rid of the exclusionary rule and to invent new ways of protecting individuals from police misconduct.

SEARCH WARRANTS, SEARCH INCIDENT TO ARREST, AND VEHICULAR SEARCHES

Coolidge v. *New Hampshire,* 403 U.S. 443 (1971), is almost a catalogue of search-and-seizure problems. The Attorney General of New Hampshire, in the course of investigating a murder case, put on his other hat as a state justice of the peace and issued a search warrant for the inspection of a car belonging to a murder suspect. The Court held that the warrant was invalid because it was not issued by a "neutral magistrate." [See also *Shadwick* v. *Tampa,* 407 U.S. 345 (1972) (so long as magistrate is "neutral and detached and . . . capable of determining whether probable cause exists . . ." he need not be a lawyer or judge).]

The state then sought to justify the search of the defendant's car under various exceptions to the search warrant requirement. Some time after Coolidge's arrest at his home, his car, which had been parked in the driveway, was towed to a police station where a vacuuming turned up evidence of gunpowder. The Court rejected an "incidental to lawful arrest" justification. Arguably, under *Chimel,* the police might have searched the car at the time and place of arrest. But *Chimel* could not be stretched to cover searching it hours after, and at an entirely different place from the arrest. Nor would the Court allow the vehicular exception. Although a car was involved, the situation was not one envisioned by the vehicular exception—namely, one where car and driver were on a highway and might disappear before a search warrant could be obtained. Finally, the Court rejected a "plain-view" rationale for the search. For although the car was in plain view of the arresting officers, evidence of a crime certainly was not in plain view and indeed turned up only after vacuuming and close scrutiny.

The Court was deeply divided on every issue from the exclusionary rule on down in *Coolidge,* indicating that in the future the exceptions doctrines would be read with greater favor to the police. For instance, even earlier, in *Chambers* v. *Maroney,* 399 U.S. 42 (1970), the Court had allowed the vehicle exception in a case in which the car was not searched until after it had been taken to a police station.

This division is clearly reflected in *Cardwell* v. *Lewis,* 417 U.S. 583 (1974), in which police had arrested the suspect, taken his car keys, towed his car from a public parking lot to a police impound lot, and then taken paint scrapings and tire impressions without obtaining a search warrant. The majority held this to be a valid probable-cause, warrantless search of a vehicle. The vehicle exception was initially based on the rationale that the vehicle might move on before the search warrant arrived. *Cardwell* makes clear that the majority is abandoning the original rationale and substituting a privacy rationale, that one is entitled to less privacy from police search of one's car than one's house. The dissenters point out that through this change of rationale the Court is allowing warrantless searches even when the police have plenty of time to get a warrant. A similar clash occurred in *Rakas* v. *Illinois,* 439 U.S. 128 (1978), in which Justice Rehnquist held for a bare majority that passengers had shown no expectation of privacy in the glove compartment of the car in which they were riding and so suffered no Fourth Amendment injury from a warrentless search of the glove compartment. In *United States* v. *Chadwick,* 433 U.S. 1 (1977), the Court refused to extend the *Chambers* rule to the warrantless search of luggage lawfully seized in the trunk of a parked taxi and taken to a government building. The Court argued that there was more privacy interest in luggage than in autos. In *Arkansas* v. *Sanders,* 442 U.S. 753 (1979) and *Robbins* v. *California,* 101 S.Ct. 2841 (1981), the Court held that the police might not conduct a warrantless search of luggage found in the trunk of an automobile, treating the cases as "luggage" cases, not as "vehicle exception" cases. In *New York* v. *Belton,* 101 S.Ct. 2860 (1981), and *United States* v. *Ross,* 50 L.W. 4580 (1982), in a voting reallignment triggered by Justice Stewart's retirement, a new majority held that police, incident to a lawful arrest, or upon probable cause but without a search warrant, might search any part of a lawfully stopped vehicle and any container or luggage in it that might contain the object of the search. *Sanders* and *Robbins* were overruled.

In *United States* v. *Edwards,* 415 U.S. 800 (1974), the police lawfully arrested the defendant and believed that his clothing was itself material evidence. But he was jailed late at night, and no change of clothing was available for him. Some ten hours after his arrest the police gave him a newly purchased change of clothing and searched and seized his original clothing. The majority held that a search which might have been made at the time of arrest may be made subsequently at the place of confinement and that a custodial search and seizure may validly be made at the time the prisoner is placed in a cell. Justices Stewart, Douglas, Brennan, and Marshall in dissent pointed out that here again the majority is destroying the narrow rationale that initially both justified and limited a narrow exception to the warrant requirement. The original rationale for approving warrantless searches incident to lawful arrests was that they were necessary to discover hidden weapons that might endanger the arresting officers and evidence that the suspect might destroy if left on his person. A search conducted ten hours after arrest can hardly be for those purposes. Justice Stewart gained a majority for this point of view in *Mincey* v. *Arizona,* 437 U.S. 385 (1978) which declared unconstitutional a warrantless four-day search of a suspect's apartment after he had been arrested and confined.

The Court was divided with Chief Justice Burger and Justice Blackmun in dissent in *Whiteley* v. *Warden,* 401 U.S. 560 (1971). There the only probable cause for stopping a car, arresting its occupants, and then conducting a search of the car without a search warrant and incident to arrest was a wanted bulletin from another county. The sheriff of the other county had issued the bulletin on the basis of an informer's tip and his own conclusions. The Court held that the tip plus the conclusions did not justify a magistrate issuing an arrest warrant. Thus, they did not justify the sheriff in finding a probable cause to make an arrest without a warrant. Therefore, he was not constitutionally justified in issuing a wanted bulletin. In turn, the police of the next county had no probable cause to stop the car or make the arrest because their only cause was the unjustified wanted bulletin.

In *United States* v. *Robinson,* 414 U.S. 218 (1973), however, the Court held that the police might lawfully search incident to a valid traffic arrest. Although the majority saw this as a routine application to the search incident to arrest rule, the dissenters argued that the police might now use the traffic laws as an excuse to search nearly anyone without a warrant and without probable cause.

In *Zurcher* v. *Stanford Daily,* 436 U.S. 547 (1978), the Court held that a search warrant might issue for papers in the hands of non-suspects which might have been acquired by subpoena.

Consent Searches

This division in the Court was also reflected in *Schneckloth* v. *Bustamonte, supra,* in which Justice Stewart found consent for a search even though the suspect had not been informed by the police that he did not have to consent to the search and there was nothing in the record to indicate that he knew he had a right to refuse to be searched. Justices Brennan, Douglas, and Marshall dissented. In *United States* v. *Matlock,* 415 U.S. 164 (1974), the same three justices dissented when the Court held that consent to search of premises given by a woman with whom the suspect was cohabiting was sufficient to render the warrantless search reasonable. [See also *United States* v. *Mendenhall,* 446 U.S. 544 (1980).]

Stop and Frisk and Arrest

In *Adams* v. *Williams* (p. 702) the Burger Court seems to open the stop-and-frisk exception even wider than in *Terry.* It is also more tolerant than previously of probable cause established by an informer. [See also *United States* v. *Harris,* 403 U.S. 573 (1971), which also is receptive to the use of informers to establish probable cause for search warrants.] In *Pennsylvania* v. *Mimms,* 434 U.S. 106 (1977), the Court held that stop-and-frisk searches incidental to halting a car for a traffic offense were constitutional and in *United States* v. *Martinez-Fuente,* 428 U.S. 543 (1976), and *United States* v. *Brignoni-Ponce,* 422 U.S. 873 (1976), the Court gave the Border Patrol broad power to stop cars near the border in their search for illegal aliens. Shortly afterward, however, the Court began to work out a special standard for stops comparable to, but less demanding than, the "probable cause" requirement for making an arrest. It held that traffic stops must rest upon "at least articulable and reasonable suspicion" that a vehicular offense has occurred. Random "spot-check" stops were constitutionally impermissible. [*Delaware* v. *Prouse,* 440 U.S. 648 (1979).] *Brown* v. *Smith,* 443 U.S. 47 (1979), involved an officer who observed two men walking away from one another in an alley in an area where there was a lot of drug traffic. The officer concluded that the situation "looked suspicious" and asked one of the men to identify himself. He refused to do so and was arrested under a Texas statute that makes it a criminal act for a person to refuse to give identification to an officer "who has lawfully stopped him and requested the information." The Court held that the application of the Texas statute to the man was unconstitutional because the "stop" was not justified by "a reasonable suspicion" that a crime had been committed, "based on . . . specific, objective facts. . . ." The Court said in *Ybarra* v. *Illinois,* 444 U.S. 85 (1979), that the "narrow scope of the *Terry* exception does not permit a frisk for weapons on less than reasonable belief or suspicion" by the officer that the person involved is "armed and dangerous" and that *Terry* did not permit any search at all except for the purpose of finding weapons. [See also *Reid* v. *Georgia,* 448 U.S. 438 (1980).]

At the same time the Burger Court was drawing some boundaries for street investigation, it sharply emphasized both the privacy of the home and the limitations on confining a person on the basis of mere suspicion. In *Dunaway* v. *New York,* 442 U.S. 200 (1979), the Court banned the practice of "picking up" a suspect "for questioning" at the police station. It held that, no matter what it was called, such a procedure was an arrest that could not be justified except upon probable cause that the person had committed a crime. It acted more favorably toward the police in *Michigan* v. *Summers,* 101 S.Ct. 2587 (1981), holding that it is permissible to detain a person at his residence while a search of the residence is conducted under a valid search warrant. Thus a new kind of "stop," one in the home, is constitutionally approved over the protests of three dissenting justices. On the other hand in 1979 the Court held 6 to 3 that while it had earlier approved "probable cause" arrests without arrest warrants in public places, police may not forcibly enter a private residence to make a routine felony arrest on the basis of probable cause alone and without an arrest warrant. [*Payton* v. *New York,* 445 U.S. 573 (1979).] And in *Steagald* v. *United States,* 101 S.Ct. 1642 (1981), the Court held that in the absence of an emergency situation, police could not legally search for someone for whom they had an arrest warrant in the home of a third party unless they obtained a search warrant for the home.

Person of the Accused

United States v. *Dionisio,* 410 U.S. 1 (1973), follows earlier cases in rejecting objections grounded in the Fourth and Fifth Amendments to compelling suspects to provide voice and handwriting exemplars to a grand jury. [See *United States* v. *Euge,* 444 U.S. 407 (1980).]

ELECTRONIC SURVEILLANCE

The Court was unanimous, however (Justice Rehnquist not participating), in finding against the Nixon administration in "domestic security" wiretaps undertaken without warrants. The Court held in *United States* v. *District Court,*

407 U.S. 297 (1972), that the Crime Control Act had not intended to allow such warrantless taps for domestic security purposes. The Court explicitly left open the question of "the scope of the President's surveillance power with respect to the activities of foreign powers, within or without this country." However, the Court divided 6 to 3 in holding that, where a court order authorizing a phone tap named a husband but not his wife, intercepted conversations between the wife and third parties were admissible at her trial. [*United States* v. *Kahn,* 415 U.S. 143 (1974).] [See also *United States* v. *New York Telephone Co.,* 434 U.S. 159 (1977).] The Burger Court has approved phone taps conducted according to the warrant procedures of the Crime Control Act [*Scott* v. *United States,* 436 U.S. 128 (1978); *Dalia* v. *United States,* 441 U.S. 238 (1979)] and has held that the use of a "pen register" that records the numbers dialed from a particular phone is not a search within the meaning of the Fourth Amendment. [*Smith* v. *Maryland,* 442 U.S. 735 (1979).]

Electronic Surveillance and Informers

Deep divisions reappeared when the question of whether *Katz* (p. 694) overruled *On Lee* (discussed on p. 638) arose in the context of yet another instance in which the government collected evidence by bugging an informer sent to engage in conversation with a suspect. In *United States* v. *White,* 401 U.S. 745 (1971), the Chief Justice and Justices White, Stewart, and Blackmun found that *Katz,* which had struck down the bugging of a telephone booth, did not overrule *On Lee,* which had approved bugging an informer. Justices Brennan, Douglas, Harlan, and Marshall in dissent concluded the opposite. Justice Black concurred on the basis of his dissent in *Katz* to give the Chief Justice's side the majority.

Adams v. *Williams* (p. 702) seems to be quite tolerant of informer statements as a basis for building up the "reasonable suspicion" that justifies a "stop." *United States* v. *Harris,* 403 U.S. 573 (1971), is another of the many cases involving informers' information to justify the issuance of a search warrant. A federal tax investigator filed an affidavit requesting a warrant. It stated that the suspect had a reputation with the investigator as a bootlegger. It stated, too, that a local constable had found some of the suspect's whiskey. It also stated that the investigator had received a sworn statement from an informer who demanded to remain anonymous out of fear for his life. The informer had told the investigator that he had purchased and consumed illicit whiskey from the suspect and had personal knowledge that others did so. The Court was widely scattered in its opinions, but the Chief Justice and Justices Black, White, Blackmun, and Stewart found the affidavit sufficient—even though there was no showing of previous reliability of the informer. Justices Harlan, Douglas, Brennan, and Marshall dissented on the ground that the affidavit did not meet the reliability of the informer standard of *Aguilar-Spinelli.*

On the other hand, returning to the kind of problem raised in *Hoffa* (p. 692), in *United States* v. *Henry,* 497 U.S. 264 (1980), the justices ruled that the admission of incriminating statements by a prisoner to his cellmate, who was an informer whom the government had instructed to be alert for such statements, violated the prisoner's right to receive *Miranda* warnings before the government deliberately elicited statements from him.

ADMINISTRATIVE SEARCHES

In *Wyman* v. *James,* 400 U.S. 309 (1971), the Court upheld case-worker home visits to families receiving state aid to dependent children. Against a privacy claim, the Court held that such visitation was either not a search at all within the meaning of the Fourth Amendment or alternatively was a reasonable search within the context of the welfare program. Justices Douglas, Marshall, and Brennan dissented.

In *Air Pollution Board of Colorado* v. *Western Alfalfa Corporation,* 416 U.S. 861 (1974), a health inspector entered outdoor premises without knowledge or consent of the owner to observe smoke plumes coming from the company's chimneys. The Court upheld the warrantless search on the basis of an "open-fields" exception to the warrant requirement, arguing that the inspector only saw what anyone standing anywhere within miles could have seen.

Then in *Marshall* v. *Barlow's, Inc.,* 436 U.S. 307 (1978), the Court seemed to change direction. It held that provisions of the Occupational Safety and Health Act of 1970 that purported to authorize warrantless safety inspections of factories and mines violated the Fourth Amendment. In *Donovan* v. *Dewey,* 101 S.Ct. 2534 (1981), however, the Court upheld the warrantless inspection provisions of the Mine Safety Act of 1977 apparently because mine inspections are regularly scheduled four times a year while OSHA inspections may occur at any time and are thus more intrusive on privacy. The Court also argued that mines, unlike the wide range of facilities inspected by OSHA, have a long history of government inspection and thus have less expectation of privacy.

EXPECTATION OF PRIVACY

The general principle that the Warren and Burger Courts have evolved is clear enough. Any place or thing in which an individual has an "expectation of privacy" may not be searched by a government official except under a valid search warrant, incident to a lawful arrest, by consent, under the narrow stop-and-frisk exception or under "exigent circumstances." That principle with its exceptions is, however, extremely difficult to apply to the myriad circumstances of modern life. [See *Walter* v. *United States,* 447 U.S. 649 (1980); *Rawlings* v. *Kentucky,* 448 U.S. 98 (1980).]

Self-incrimination

The Fifth Amendment contains a number of provisions for the protection of persons accused of crime. One of the most important of these protections is found in the clause that "no person . . . shall be compelled in any criminal case to be witness against himself." Today this right is embodied in the laws or constitutions of every state as well as in the Fifth Amendment. Although the Fifth Amendment states that the privilege against self-incrimination applies to criminal cases alone, it can be invoked before any official body that has the power to compel testimony under oath. Thus, the protection can be invoked before a grand jury, a legislative committee, or a coroner's inquest.

"FIFTH AMENDMENT COMMUNISTS"

Much public hostility toward this privilege emerged while anti-Communist sentiment in the United States was at its peak in the early 1950s and alleged Communists frequently were taking the Fifth before congressional committees.

The Supreme Court has sustained the right of individuals to invoke the privilege against self-incrimination before congressional committees in a number of cases. In *Blau* v. *United States,* 340 U.S. 159 (1950), the Court ruled that a witness may refuse to answer questions before a grand jury about possible Communist connections, because he could reasonably fear that his testimony might result in a criminal prosecution under the Smith Act. A more difficult problem was presented by *Ullmann* v. *United States,* 350 U.S. 422 (1955). There the Court upheld a federal immunity act that authorized congressional committees to grant immunity from criminal prosecution to witnesses who refused to testify in a proceeding involving national security. The Court has also held that where an immunity act can be applied, the witness can still exercise his privilege to refuse to answer unless he is assured against prosecution by both federal and state authorities. [See *Murphy* v. *Waterfront Commission,* 378 U.S. 52 (1964).]

Two weeks after the *Ullmann* case, the Court rendered another important decision in *Slochower* v. *Board of Higher Education,* 350 U.S. 551 (1956). In that case, Slochower, a professor of twenty-seven years' experience in a college (Brooklyn) operated by the city of New York, was dismissed summarily for invoking the self-incrimination clause in refusing to testify before a congressional committee about his past Communist party membership. Slochower's dismissal was based on a provision of the New York City charter that required the automatic removal of any city employee who utilized the privilege against self-incrimination in refusing to answer legally authorized questions. In a 5-to-4 opinion, the Court held that, as applied to Slochower, the municipal charter provision violated the due process clause of the Fourteenth Amendment. In the majority opinion, Justice Clark revealed clearly the Court's objection to terms—such as Fifth Amendment Communist—that imply that the assertion of the privilege against self-incrimination constitutes an admission of guilt. Justice Clark stated: "We must condemn the practice of imputing sinister meaning to the exercise of a person's constitutional right under the Fifth Amendment. The privilege against self-incrimination would be reduced to a hollow mockery if its exercise could be taken as equivalent either to a confession of guilt or a conclusive presumption of perjury." Slochower was reinstated as a faculty member after the Court's decision, but he was then suspended by the college president on new charges of "untruthfulness and perjury."

COERCED CONFESSIONS

The Supreme Court had consistently overturned state convictions based on coerced confessions, although just what constituted coercion had always been subject to dispute.[3] The coerced-confession doctrine is a segment of the fair-trial rule announced in *Palko.* Rather than hold that any confession obtained in violation of the self-incrimination provisions of the Constitution was inadmissible as evidence against the defendant at his trial, for many years the Supreme Court insisted that only those confessions that were actually coerced were inadmissible. Whether a confession was voluntary or coerced was to be determined from the "totality of circumstances." The rationale for the inadmissibility of coerced confessions was that a confession wrung from a defendant by torture was likely to be untrustworthy. [See *Brown* v. *Mississippi,* 297 U.S. 278 (1936).] Thus, initially, inadmissibility—or the exclusionary rule, as we have called it in the search-and-seizure discussion—had been motivated not by the purpose of deterring police misconduct but by the suspicion that coerced confessions might be untrue.

Nevertheless, by the late 1940s the Court was excluding confessions even if there was no reason to believe them to be untrue. [See *Watts* v. *Indiana,* 338 U.S. 499 (1949).] Then, in *Spano* v. *New York,* 360 U.S. 315 (1960), Chief Justice Warren openly referred to the Court's abhorrence of police misconduct as another reason for excluding coerced confessions.

The Court began to move farther and farther from its initial focus on torture and held, in an increasing number of cases, that psychological pressure was sufficient to justify a finding that the confession had been coerced. As in other uses of the fair-trial rule, the Court's decisions became almost totally discretionary. Because all police interrogation exerts some psychological pressure on the accused, the cases became debates about how much is too much, or just how polite the police have to be.

THE MCNABB-MALLORY RULE

Just as in search and seizure, the Court imposed a fair-trial rule on the states but was much more rigorous in its demands on federal officers. And just as in search and seizure, it was not absolutely clear whether the greater demands on federal officers stemmed from the Court's supervisory powers or from the Fifth Amendment. Under one or the other or both, the Court imposed the *McNabb-Mallory* rule on federal officers. [*McNabb* v. *United States,* 318 U.S. 332 (1943); *Mallory* v. *United States,* 354 U.S. 449 (1957).] A federal statute required that federal prisoners be brought before a magistrate within seven hours of arrest. The *McNabb-Mallory* rule excluded confessions made by prisoners illegally held away from a magistrate beyond that time limit even where the confessions were otherwise voluntary. More generally, the federal authorities were held to whatever the Court conceived the letter of the Fifth

[3] See *Chambers* v. *Florida,* 309 U.S. 227 (1940); and *Leyra* v. *Denno,* 347 U.S. 556 (1954).

Amendment to be. Confessions gained in violation of the prisoner's constitutional rights were not admissible in federal courts even if they were not coerced.

INCORPORATION OF SELF-INCRIMINATION

In the key case of *Malloy* v. *Hogan* (p. 672), the Court reconsidered a number of prior decisions and held that the privilege against self-incrimination is safeguarded against state action by the Fourteenth Amendment. This decision did not clearly abolish all the earlier differences between the rules for state and federal officers. Some rules the Court imposed on federal officers may have stemmed from its supervisory powers rather than its enforcement of the Constitution. But rather than move in the direction of more detailed rules for the states on all prisoner-related matters, the Warren Court moved largely in one new direction.

THE WARREN COURT AND SELF-INCRIMINATION: WARNINGS AND COUNSEL

As we will note later in the section on right to counsel, the right to counsel and the right against self-incrimination are functionally related. For if counsel can get to the prisoner soon enough, he will advise him not to incriminate himself. And, conversely, if the prisoner confesses before he gets counsel, there may be little counsel can do for him once he arrives. A reflection of this tie between counsel and the right against self-incrimination is the police warning that the prisoner has the right to remain silent and the right to an attorney.

In *Massiah* v. *United States,* 377 U.S. 201 (1964), the Court held that admissions elicited by federal officers from the defendant, after he had been indicted and in the absence of his counsel, were inadmissible. Then, in the same term, the Court decided the landmark case of *Escobedo* v. *Illinois,* 378 U.S. 478 (1964). The Court had already extended the Sixth Amendment's right-to-counsel provisions to the states in *Gideon* v. *Wainwright* (p. 684), which will be discussed later in this chapter. On that basis it holds that Escobedo's confession was not admissible in a state court because it was made after he had asked for and been refused counsel and in the absence of any warning by the police that he had a right to remain silent. Shortly after, *Miranda* v. *Arizona* (p. 686) reconfirmed *Escobedo* and specified that the accused must be advised of both his right to remain silent and his right to counsel.

Thus, *Escobedo* and *Miranda* were the major holdings giving substance to *Malloy* v. *Hogan.* In addition, in *Griffin* v. *California,* 381 U.S. 957 (1965), the Court held that state prosecutors may not comment on a defendant's refusal to testify. *Spevack* v. *Klein,* 385 U.S. 511 (1967), holds that disbarment may not be based solely on refusal to testify at state bar proceedings.

There was also some Court activity on the federal side. Congress had passed legislation requiring gamblers and marijuana dealers to register and pay a tax, even though registering and paying such taxes would obviously be tantamount to confessing a crime. Nevertheless, the Supreme Court at first upheld such provisions by focusing on their purported purpose of raising tax revenues. The Court has subsequently overturned convictions under both statutes on Fifth Amendment grounds.[4]

The Burger Court and Self-incrimination

EXCLUSION, MCNABB-MALLORY, AND MIRANDA

The exclusionary rule for confessions provoked about as much unfavorable public and congressional reaction as its counterpart in the search-and-seizure area. The Crime Control Act of 1968 contains provisions purporting to repeal both the *McNabb-Mallory* rule and *Miranda.*

The Burger Court has very seriously reduced the scope of *Miranda.* In a 5-to-4 decision in *Harris* v. *New York,* 401 U.S. 22 (1971), it held that a confession obtained without the *Miranda* warnings might be introduced in evidence for purposes of impeaching a defendant's testimony should he choose to take the stand in his own defense. This means that the confession may be offered as evidence that the accused is now lying on the witness stand, but not as evidence that he committed the crime to which he confessed. Juries will not be capable of governing their thoughts by this subtle distinction. If they hear a confession, they will certainly be influenced by it in drawing conclusions about whether the defendant is guilty or not. Thus, in practice, most defendants who have confessed prior to receiving *Miranda* warnings will have to choose between their constitutional right to have the confession excluded and the opportunity to testify in their own behalf. *Harris* constitutes a major Burger Court assault on the constitutional position of the Warren Court.

Oregon v. *Hass,* 420 U.S. 714 (1975), applied *Harris* to statements made by a suspect who was issued *Miranda* warnings, refused to answer until his lawyer came, and continued to be questioned. The dissenters argued that the result would be to encourage police to respond to a refusal to answer by stepping up their questioning in the hope that they could break the suspect before his lawyer arrived. But in *Doyle* v. *Ohio,* 426 U.S. 610 (1976), the Court held a prosecutor might not use the defendant's post-*Miranda*-warnings silence to impeach his trial testimony. In this instance, the prosecutor had sought to cast doubt on the defendant's testimony during the trial by asking why, if he really had such a good explanation of his conduct, he had not given it to the police immediately after arrest. [But see *Fletcher* v. *Weir,* 102 S.Ct. 1309 (1982).] And in *Mincey* v. *Arizona,* 437 U.S. 385 (1978), the Court held that a defendant's statements made under conditions that rendered them untrustworthy, such as torture or other physical and mental distress, were inadmissible even for im-

[4] *Marchetti* v. *United States,* 390 U.S. 39 (1968); and *Leary* v. *United States,* 395 U.S. 6 (1969).

peachment purposes. In *Estelle* v. *Smith,* 101 S.Ct. 1866 (1981) the Court held unanimously that where a prisoner had not been given *Miranda* warnings before a court-ordered psychiatric examination, the psychiatrist's testimony was inadmissible at a death-penalty hearing.

TAX AND POLICE STATUTES

The Burger Court has shown some tendency to backtrack on those Warren Court cases that held that federal tax statutes, actually intended as police measures, created self-incrimination situations. In *United States* v. *Freed,* 401 U.S. 601 (1971), it upheld amendments to the National Fire Arms Act passed by Congress in response to an earlier Supreme Court holding that provisions of the act were unconstitutional; and in *California* v. *Byers,* 402 U.S. 424 (1971), in a 5-to-4 decision, it upheld against self-incrimination objections a state law requiring drivers to stay at the scene of an accident and identify themselves.

IMMUNITY

The Warren Court tended to increase the constitutional protections of those required to waive their self-incrimination rights in return for immunity from prosecution. But it never reached the question of exactly what the scope of the immunity must be. For years a debate raged about whether the Constitution required "transactional" immunity or only "use" immunity. Transactional immunity is immunity from future prosecution for the crime about which one is being compelled to testify. Use immunity is far narrower. It provides only that the actual testimony given under an immunity grant may not be used in future prosecutions. Government would still be free to prosecute for the offense about which the witness was forced to testify if it could find enough independent evidence, other than his testimony, to sustain a conviction. In *Kastigar* v. *United States,* 406 U.S. 441 (1972), the Burger Court sustained a federal use immunity statute.

NEGOTIATED GUILTY PLEAS

The Burger Court also opened up a new self-incrimination area, plea bargaining. It gave constitutional approval to at least the most typical forms of plea bargaining in *Brady* v. *United States,* 397 U.S. 742 (1970). Justice White wrote: ". . . We decline to hold that a guilty plea is compelled and invalid under the Fifth Amendment whenever motivated by the defendant's desire to accept the certainty or probability of a lesser penalty rather than face a wider range of possibilities extending from acquittal to conviction and a higher penalty authorized by law for the crime charged. . . . We cannot hold that it is unconstitutional for the State to extend a benefit to a defendant who in turn extends a substantial benefit to the State. . . ."

In *North Carolina* v. *Alford,* 400 U.S. 25 (1970), he amplified this holding:

"a plea of guilty which would not have been entered except for the defendant's desire to avoid a death penalty and to limit the maximum punishment to . . . a term of years was not for that reason compelled within the meaning of the Fifth Amendment." The justice argued that even when protesting his innocence all the way, a defendant may "voluntarily, knowingly, and understandingly consent to the imposition of a prison sentence when, as in the instant case, he intelligently concludes that his interests require entry of a guilty plea and the record before the judge contains strong evidence of actual guilt." This last qualification may be a fruitful source of future litigation. [See also *Corbitt* v. *New Jersey,* 439 U.S. 212 (1978).]

In *Bordenkircher* v. *Hayes,* 434 U.S. 357 (1978), the prosecutor threatened to prosecute the defendant under an habitual criminal act, which carried a stiffer penalty, unless he pleaded guilty to forgery. He was plainly subject to either prosecution. The Court held, in a 5 to 4 decision, that the prosecutor had not violated due process when he carried out his threat.

Santobello v. *New York,* 404 U.S. 257 (1971), involved a defendant who pleaded guilty on the basis of a promise that the prosecutor would make no recommendation as to sentence. Only months later did the defendant appear for sentencing. A new prosecutor, apparently not knowing about the bargain, recommended the maximum sentence, which the judge imposed. In vacating the sentence, Chief Justice Burger wrote: "when a plea rests in any significant degree on a promise or agreement of the prosecutor, so that it can be said to be a part of the inducement or consideration, such promise must be fulfilled."

COMMENTS TO THE JURY

A number of the early cases about incorporating the Fifth Amendment into the Fourteenth dealt with the question of what comments judges and lawyers might make to the jury about the defendant's failure to testify. After incorporation it became clear that inferences of guilt might not be drawn from such failure. In recent cases the Burger Court has held that a judge must instruct the jury not to infer guilt from refusal to testify if the defendant asks for such an instruction [*Carter* v. *Kentucky,* 101 S.Ct. 1112 (1981)], that the judge may give such an instruction even if the defendant doesn't want it [*Lakeside* v. *Oregon,* 435 U.S. 33 (1978)], and that a prosecutor's remarks to the jury that the state's evidence is "unrefuted" and "uncontradicted" is not an unconstitutional comment on the defendant's failure to testify. [*Lockett* v. *Ohio,* 438 U.S. 586 (1978).]

Right to Counsel

For many years, a corollary to the *Palko* doctrine was the fair-trial rule. Even though federal courts were held to the letter of all provisions of the Bill of Rights, a state court might violate some of its provisions so long as the conduct of the trial as a whole was fundamentally fair. As the Court has held more and more provisions of the first ten amendments directly binding on the states, the fair-trial rule has dwindled. For a long time, however, its most important application was in the area of right to counsel.

The right to counsel was first discussed at length by the Supreme Court in *Powell* v. *Alabama,* 287 U.S. 45 (1932). In 1931, Powell and six other Negroes were convicted in Alabama for the rape of two white girls. Their trial lasted one day, and they were all sentenced to death. They had been arrested, tried, and sentenced in an atmosphere of tense, hostile, and excited public sentiment. Neither were they represented by counsel; the trial judge had only vaguely appointed all members of the bar to represent the defendants. The Alabama Supreme Court affirmed the convictions, with its chief justice writing a strong dissent on the grounds that the defendants had not been given a fair trial. The U.S. Supreme Court said:

> It never has been doubted by this court, or any other so far as we know, that notice and hearing are preliminary steps essential to the passing of an enforceable judgment, and that they, together with a legally competent tribunal having jurisdiction of the case, constitute basic elements of the constitutional requirement of due process of law. . . .
>
> What, then, does a hearing include? Historically and in practice, in our own country at least, it has always included the right to the aid of counsel when desired and provided by the party asserting the right. The right to be heard would be, in many cases, of little avail if it did not comprehend the right to be heard by counsel. Even the intelligent and educated layman has small and sometimes no skill in the science of law. If charged with crime, he is incapable, generally, of determining for himself whether the indictment is good or bad. He is unfamiliar with the rules of evidence. Left without the aid of counsel he may be put on trial without a proper charge, and convicted upon incompetent evidence, or evidence irrelevant to the issue or otherwise inadmissible. He lacks both the skill and knowledge adequately to prepare his defense, even though he have a perfect one. He requires the guiding hand of counsel at every step in the proceedings against him. Without it, though he be not guilty, he faces the danger of conviction because he does not know how to establish his innocence. If that be true of men of intelligence, how much more true is it of the ignorant and illiterate, or those of feeble intellect. If in any case, civil or criminal, a state or federal court were arbitrarily to refuse to hear a party by counsel, employed by and appearing for him, it reasonably may not be doubted that such a refusal would be a denial of a hearing, and, therefore, of due process in the constitutional sense. . . .
>
> In the light of the facts . . . —the ignorance and illiteracy of the defendants, their youth, the circumstances of public hostility, the imprisonment and the close surveillance of the defendants by the military forces, the fact that their families were all in other states and communication with them necessarily difficult, and above all that they stood in deadly peril of their lives—we think the failure of the trial court to give them reasonable time and opportunity to secure counsel was a clear denial of due process.
>
> But passing that, and assuming their inability, even if opportunity has been given, to employ counsel, as the trial court evidently did assume, we are of opinion that,

> under the circumstances just stated, the necessity of counsel was so vital and imperative that the failure of the trial court to make an effective appointment of counsel was likewise a denial of due process within the meaning of the Fourteenth Amendment.

For some time *Powell* v. *Alabama* was assumed to mean that the assistance of counsel was required in *all* state criminal proceedings under the due process clause of the Fourteenth Amendment. However, in *Betts* v. *Brady,* 316 U.S. 455 (1942), the Court reasoned that the principle of the *Powell* case was limited to capital offenses alone. In the majority opinion, Justice Roberts noted that "we are unable to say that the concept of due process incorporated in the Fourteenth Amendment obligates the states, whatever may be their own views, to furnish counsel" in every criminal case. "Every court has power, if it deems proper, to appoint counsel where that course seems to be required in the interest of fairness." After *Betts* v. *Brady,* the Court held in numerous cases that counsel is required in noncapital cases only "where a person convicted in a state court has not intelligently and understandingly waived the benefit of counsel and where the circumstances show that his rights could not have been fairly protected without counsel."[5] However, in *Gideon* v. *Wainwright* (p. 684), the Court squarely overruled *Betts* v. *Brady* and held that a state's failure to appoint counsel in a noncapital criminal case deprived the indigent defendant of due process of law under the Fourteenth Amendment. In his majority opinion, Justice Black concluded that in *Betts* v. *Brady* the Court had "departed from the sound wisdom upon which the Court's holding *Powell* v. *Alabama* rested."

Gideon and subsequent cases provided for free legal counsel and ancillary services for indigents at the time of trial and appeal. A crucial question, however, was how early in the investigation and arrest process counsel must be provided. In *Massiah* v. *United States* (see p. 648); *Escobedo* v. *Illinois* (see p. 648); and *Miranda* v. *Arizona* (p. 686), the Court ruled that the defendant must be provided with counsel from the time of arrest and indictment or once the police investigation has focused on him as the probable culprit. Furthermore, the Court ruled that the police must, at these points in their investigation, notify the suspect as to his right to counsel and right to remain silent. Otherwise, confessions obtained by the police would be inadmissible as evidence. The Court subsequently extended this right to counsel to persons subjected to police lineups: *United States* v. *Wade* (see p. 637); *Gilbert* v. *California,* 388 U.S. 263 (1967). The Supreme Court has also made right to counsel and other Bill of Rights protections applicable to juvenile court proceedings [In re *Gault,* 387 U.S. 1 (1967)] and has taken the first steps toward doing so in commitment proceedings for the mentally ill. [*O'Connor* v. *Donaldson,* 422 U.S. 563 (1975).]

In a number of instances noted in this introduction, the Burger Court has

[5] *Pennsylvania* ex rel. *Herman* v. *Claudy,* 350 U.S. 116 (1956). A complete review of the right to counsel is found in William M. Beaney, *The Right to Counsel in American Courts* (Ann Arbor: University of Michigan Press, 1955). Each of the criminal protections of the Sixth Amendment is examined in Francis H. Heller, *The Sixth Amendment of the Constitution* (Lawrence: University of Kansas Press, 1951).

been inclined to cut back on Warren Court rights-of-accused holdings. The *Wade* and *Gilbert* decisions were subject to heated criticism in Congress, and a provision of the Crime Control Act of 1968 was designed to reverse them by providing that the "testimony of a witness that he saw the accused commit or participate in the commission of the crime . . . shall be admissible in evidence" in federal criminal proceedings. Then the Burger Court, by a 5-to-4 decision, narrowed the *Wade-Gilbert* requirements to post-indictment or preliminary hearing lineups and allowed the admission of testimony based on identification made at the police station before the defendant had been "formally charged with any criminal offense." However, even in this decision [*Kirby* v. *Illinois,* 406 U.S. 682 (1972)] the Court noted that a due process challenge would be available against lineups that were "unnecessarily suggestive and conducive to irreparable mistaken identification." Then, in *United States* v. *Ash,* 413 U.S. 300 (1973), the Court held that no right to counsel existed for a post-indictment, pretrial identification of a suspect from photographs.

On the other hand, the Burger Court has extended the *Gideon* rule to nonfelony cases by holding that "no person may be imprisoned for any offense unless he was represented by counsel at his trial." [*Argersinger* v. *Hamlin,* 407 U.S. 25 (1972).] In *Faretta* v. *California,* 422 U.S. 806 (1975), the Court held that a defendant has a right to proceed without counsel if he elects to do so.

The general rule is that counsel must be available at every "critical stage of the prosecution." In *Coleman* v. *Alabama,* 399 U.S. 1 (1970), for instance, the Court held that counsel must be provided even at a preliminary hearing prior to indictment. But in *Gagnon* v. *Scarpelli,* 411 U.S. 778 (1973), the Court held that the right to counsel did not necessarily include counsel at hearings on revocation of probation or parole.

In recent years the Burger Court has spent much of its energies in this area on details of police behavior. For instance, in *Brewer* v. *Williams,* 430 U.S. 387 (1977), Williams called a Des Moines attorney, who advised him to remain silent. He surrendered in Davenport and was arraigned by a judge there. The police promised his lawyer that they would not question him until he was back in Des Moines. On the 160-mile car trip, a police officer managed to persuade Williams to guide the police to the body of the child he had allegedly attacked. The Court overturned his subsequent conviction on the ground that *Massiah* had required a right to counsel at least from the time that judicial proceedings are initiated and Williams had been interrogated subsequent to arraignment without his counsel being present. This case, by the way, confirmed the dire warnings that someday the very body of a murder victim would be excluded from evidence under the exclusionary rule.

Rhode Island v. *Innis,* 446 U.S. 291 (1980) involves a very similar set of facts but reaches the opposite conclusion on admissibility. In *Brewer* the police had talked in the suspect's presence about how sad it was that a child was left lying in the snow. The murder suspect had then led them to the body. In *Innis* the police had talked about how dangerous it was to leave a shotgun lying around in an area where handicapped children played. The armed robbery suspect then led them to the gun. The Court held the gun admissible. In both cases the police claimed that they had not "interrogated" the arrestee after he had requested council but had only engaged in conversation among themselves that had triggered the suspect's voluntary cooperation. For an individual may waive his right to counsel and his right against self-incrimination after *Miranda* warnings are given and choose voluntarily to give information to the police. [See *Fare* v. *Michael,* 442 U.S. 707 (1970).]

Many Burger Court cases turn on just how truly voluntary a particular confession or waiver of rights was after *Miranda* warnings have been given. [See *North Carolina* v. *Butler,* 441 U.S. 369 (1979).] For instance in *Edwards* v. *Arizona,* 101 S.Ct. 1881 (1981) a prisoner had been given *Miranda* warnings. He asked for counsel, whereupon interrogation ceased. The next day the police again sought to interrogate him and again gave him *Miranda* warnings, after which he said he was willing to talk and confessed. The Court held the confession inadmissible, saying that after a suspect has once requested counsel, no subsequent interrogation may be conducted by the police in the absense of counsel unless the suspect has himself initiated further communication with the police.

In *Michigan* v. *Mosley,* 423 U.S. 96 (1975), Mosley was given the *Miranda* warnings after arrest for some robberies and refused to talk. Two hours later, in a different office on a different floor, a different interrogator gave him the *Miranda* warnings and then questioned him about a murder-robbery unconnected with the robberies for which he had been arrested. He then made an incriminating statement about the murder. The Court held the statement admissible. The dissenters complained that the decision encouraged the police to respond to a suspect's refusal to talk by holding a series of separate questioning sessions. *Edwards* and *Mosley* when read together mean that if a suspect simply refuses to talk after his *Miranda* warnings, the police may requestion him subsequently so long as they give the *Miranda* warnings again, but that once a suspect has requested counsel, he may not be requestioned unless counsel is present.

In *Brown* v. *Illinois,* 422 U.S. 590 (1975), Brown was illegally arrested, but the state courts found his confession to be voluntary per se and thus admissible because he had subsequently been given the *Miranda* warnings before he talked. Citing the *Wong Sun* case, noted in the earlier section entitled "The Fruit of the Poisonous Tree," the Supreme Court reversed. It held that *Miranda* warnings alone are not enough to remove "the taint of an unconstitutional arrest." Only if the confession were really "an act of free will unaffected by the initial illegality" would the confession be admissible.

In *Beckwith* v. *United States,* 425 U.S. 341 (1976), the Court sought to further explain what *Escobedo* and *Miranda* had meant in holding that the right to counsel began as soon as the investigation "focused" on the suspect. The Court emphasized that "focus" began "*after* a person has been taken into custody or otherwise deprived of his freedom of action in any significant way."

In quite a different line of cases, combining equal protection, due process, and right-to-counsel arguments, the Supreme Court has dealt with the problem of the expenses incurred in the course of pursuing legal proceedings. In *Griffin*

v. *Illinois,* 351 U.S. 12 (1956), and *Douglas* v. *California,* 372 U.S. 353 (1963), the Court ruled that the state must provide indigent defendants with copies of trial transcripts and other papers necessary to filing at least the first appeal as of right and also with counsel on appeal.

The Burger Court has had some difficulty with attempts to extend the *Griffin-Douglas* line of decisions beyond the criminal process. In *Boddie* v. *Connecticut,* 401 U.S. 371 (1971), it sustained welfare recipients in their demands that the state allow them access to divorce proceedings even though they could not pay the court fees required in filing for divorce. But in *United States* v. *Kras,* 409 U.S. 434 (1973), the Court refused to extend the *Boddie* rationale to indigent debtors and rejected the claim that they should be allowed to file for bankruptcy without paying the required fees.

Indeed the Burger Court seems bent on blocking further development of *Gideon-Griffin-Douglas.* In *Ross* v. *Moffitt,* 417 U.S. 600 (1974), the Court refused to extend the rule requiring appointment of counsel for indigents in their first state appeal as of right to subsequent discretionary state appeals and/or application for review by the U.S. Supreme Court. [See also *United States* v. *MacCollom,* 426 U.S. 317 (1976).] The Court has also begun to look favorably on state attempts to recoup the cost of counsel through subsequent repayment of legal fees by the defendant and on attempts to police the system against false claims by defendants that they are indigent. [*Fuller* v. *Oregon,* 417 U.S. 40 (1974); *United States* v. *Kahan,* 415 U.S. 239 (1974).]

Nevertheless in 1981 the Court conclusively broke through into a new area of indigent due process rights in noncriminal litigation. In *Little* v. *Streater,* 101 S.Ct. 2202 (1981) a unanimous Court held that where the state brought an action for child support against the putative father of a child receiving welfare benefits, the state must pay the costs of the blood tests which could prove that he was not the father if he could not afford to do so. In *Lassiter* v. *Dept. of Public Services,* 101 S.Ct. 2153 (1981) a 5-to-4 Court held that failure of the state to provide counsel to indigent parents for a judicial hearing in which the state sought to deprive them of parental control over their child was not a denial of due process. But all nine justices agreed that counsel would have to be provided in some cases of this kind. What emerges from these two cases is a new fair-trial rule. At least where the government is an adverse party, and the interest of the indigent party is a very important one, due process has been denied if the failure to provide counsel or other legal services renders the proceedings fundamentally unfair. [See also *Santosky* v. *Kramer,* 102 S.Ct. 1388 (1982).]

Other Rights of Accused

CONFRONTATION

In *Pointer* v. *Texas,* 380 U.S. 400 (1965), the "confrontation" clause of the Sixth Amendment was held applicable to the states. The major body of state law in potential conflict with the right to confrontation is the "hearsay" rule of evidence. The hearsay rule is a central rule of evidence invoked in many trials. It is not a single, simple rule, but a large body of rules prescribing what kinds of evidence are "best evidence" admissible at trial and what evidence is merely "hearsay" and thus nonadmissible. For instance, if what we want to establish in court is that *X* crossed the street, the testimony of *X* that he crossed the street is best evidence. The testimony of *Y* that *Z* told *Y* that he saw *X* cross the street is hearsay. Hearsay rules vary greatly from state to state, and in many states they are in the process of rapid change. In *Chambers* v. *Mississippi,* 410 U.S. 284 (1973), the Court held that where a mechanical application of the hearsay rule by a state trial judge had prevented the defense from getting vital testimony to the jury, the defendant's constitutional right to confrontation had been violated. *Chambers* and other cases like it promise a thriving new business for the Supreme Court in the supervision of state criminal proceedings. See also *Davis* v. *Alaska,* 415 U.S. 308 (1974); *Ohio* v. *Roberts,* 448 U.S. 56 (1980).

The Court has held also that a defendant who disrupts trial proceedings can lose his right to be present at trial, which is normally protected by the Sixth Amendment. [*Allen* v. *Illinois,* 397 U.S. 337 (1970).]

SPEEDY TRIAL

Both federal and state prisoners have a right to a speedy trial. In *Barker* v. *Wingo,* 407 U.S. 514 (1972), the Court indicated that it would not set rigid time limits but instead would consider all the circumstances to determine whether the delay that had occurred was justified.

THE "NO-EVIDENCE" RULE AND VAGUENESS

Although higher courts do not normally reevaluate trial court findings of fact to see if the evidence proves the guilt of the accused, the Supreme Court ruled in *Thompson* v. *Louisville,* 362 U.S. 199 (1960), that a conviction based on no evidence at all violated due process. Thompson, a Negro, had been convicted of disturbing the peace on the sole evidence that he had done a dance in a saloon. There was no evidence that anyone had objected or that there had been any disturbance. The Court invalidated Thompson's conviction. In *Jackson* v. *Virginia,* 443 U.S. 307 (1979), the Court went beyond the no evidence rule. It held that federal courts might examine the sufficiency of evidence in state criminal convictions. The federal court is to view the evidence in the light most favorable to the prosecutor. Then, if it finds that no reasonable trier of fact could have found the defendant guilty beyond a reasonable doubt on the basis of the evidence, it is to declare that the state conviction violates the due process clause.

Criminal statutes are unconstitutional if so vaguely worded that the individual is "forced to speculate . . . whether his conducted is prohibited." *Duncan* v. *United States,* 442 U.S. 100 (1979).

TRIAL BY JURY

Even though it has extended most procedural rights to juvenile proceedings, the Court has refused to hold that jury trial is a constitutional right in juvenile courts. [*McKeiver* v. *Pennsylvania,* 403 U.S. 528 (1971).]

The Court has been deeply divided over whether contempt-of-court cases and petty offenses can be tried without juries—and just how petty a petty offense must be to escape the jury requirement. [See *Frank* v. *United States,* 395 U.S. 147 (1969).] In 1970, it held the New York City system of trying misdemeanors without a jury unconstitutional. In *Groppi* v. *Leslie,* 404 U.S. 496 (1972), the Court struck down a punishment for contempt of the legislature imposed directly by the legislature but did not comment on its earlier holdings that judges might punish for contempt without a jury trial.

In *Mayberry* v. *Pennsylvania,* 400 U.S. 455 (1971), at the end of the trial, the judge imposed an eleven-to-twenty-two-year sentence for contempt on the defendant who had defended himself and in the process frequently abused the court. The Supreme Court reversed but carefully hedged its opinion so as not to require jury trials. Instead, it held that where a judge does not act on a contempt the instant it is committed, "it is generally wise where the marks of the unseemly conduct have left personal stings to ask a fellow judge to take his place" and conduct a separate contempt hearing.

In *Codispoti* v. *Pennsylvania,* 418 U.S. 506 (1974), the Court followed an earlier ruling in *Bloom* v. *Illinois,* 391 U.S. 194 (1968), in holding that where the aggregate sentence for contempts during a single trial was more than six months, a jury trial was required.

In *Williams* v. *Florida,* 399 U.S. 78 (1970), the Court held that a twelve-person jury was not required by the Sixth Amendment. *Williams* had upheld a six-person jury. In *Ballew* v. *Georgia,* 435 U.S. 223 (1978), the Court held that a five-person jury was too small to satisfy the constitutional requirement. In *Apodaca* v. *Oregon,* 406 U.S. 404 (1972), the Court sustained the constitutionality of state criminal convictions by a nonunanimous jury. The crucial vote was Justice Powell's. He held that the Sixth Amendment required unanimous verdicts by federal juries, but he returned to the *Palko* and selective incorporation rationales to hold that the unanimity rule did not apply to the states through the Fourteenth Amendment. Thus, the meaning of *Duncan* v. *Louisiana,* 391 U.S. 145 (1968), which seemed to incorporate the Sixth Amendment jury trial clause into the Fourteenth, is no longer entirely clear. (In *Apodaca,* eight justices believed that *Duncan* fully incorporated the Sixth, but only four of the eight believed that the Sixth required unanimous verdicts. Justice Powell joined the other four to determine the outcome. In *Ballew,* Justices Burger and Rehnquist joined Justice Powell's view that the Fourteenth did not fully incorporate the Sixth.) In *Burch* v. *Louisiana,* 441 U.S. 130 (1979), the Court held that where six-person juries are used in criminal cases their verdicts must be unanimous.

THE EFFECT OF GUILTY PLEAS

The Court has long held that "when a criminal defendant has solemnly admitted in open court that he is in fact guilty of the offense with which he is charged, he may not thereafter raise independent claims relating to the deprivation of constitutional rights that occurred prior to the entry of the guilty plea." [*Tollett* v. *Henderson,* 411 U.S. 258 (1973).] Given that most persons convicted of a crime in this country plead guilty, this holding insulates much of the criminal law process from constitutional review.

THE HARMLESS ERROR RULE

Appellate courts have generally refused to reverse the court below solely on the basis of minor technical errors that do not seem to have affected the outcome of a trial. How minor an error must be to be "harmless" is, of course, a matter of judicial discretion. Should the Burger Court wish to roll back Warren Court criminal proceedings holdings without attacking them directly, it could liberally apply the harmless error rule to excuse state violations of rights of the accused. The dissenters accuse the majority of such a tactic in *Milton* v. *Wainwright,* 407 U.S. 371 (1972), in which the accused made four confessions, all of which were admitted at trial. The admission of three was not challenged by the defense. The Court held that the admission of the fourth, an arguably inadmissible confession, was "harmless beyond a reasonable doubt."

Double Jeopardy

Under the double jeopardy provision of the Fifth Amendment, a person who has been tried for a crime in a federal court cannot be tried again for the same offense by the Federal Government. However, as the Court noted in *United States* v. *Lanza,* 260 U.S. 377 (1922), an act "denounced as a crime by both national and state sovereignties is an offense against the peace and dignity of both and may be punished by each" without violation of the double jeopardy provision. Even though it has been criticized, the *Lanza* rule still stands. The problem was explored fully by a sharply divided Court in *Bartkus* v. *Illinois,* 359 U.S. 121 (1959), which reaffirmed the *Lanza* doctrine. However, in *Benton* v. *Maryland,* 395 U.S. 784 (1969), the Court held the double jeopardy provisions applicable to the states. And in the *Murphy* case (see p. 646), the Court held that immunity statutes may not be used to compel self-incriminatory testimony unless the witness is assured protection against both federal and state prosecution. These decisions seem to undermine the logic of *Lanza,* but it has not been overruled. Indeed in *United States* v. *Wheeler,* 435 U.S. 313 (1978) the Court again specifically upholds the "dual sovereignties" doctrine of *Lanza.* The Department of Justice usually forbids U.S. Attorneys to initiate federal prosecutions where the same acts have already been prosecuted by the state.

The major double jeopardy problem in recent years has arisen from situations in which a defendant has won an appeal or a mistrial that has resulted in a new trial. The general rule is that such a retrial does not constitute double jeopardy. However, in certain circumstances—for instance, when an accused receives a greater sentence at his second than at his first trial or when the appeals court has in effect said that the defendant should have been acquitted at his first trial—the Court will sometimes find a violation of the double jeopardy clause. [See *North Carolina* v. *Pearce,* 395 U.S. 711 (1969); *Price* v. *Georgia,* 398 U.S. 323 (1970); *Chaffin* v. *Stynchcombe,* 412 U.S. 17 (1973); *Colten* v. *Kentucky,* 407 U.S. 104 (1972); *Illinois* v. *Somerville,* 410 U.S. 458 (1973); *Blackledge* v. *Perry,* 417 U.S. 21 (1974); *Arizona* v. *Washington,* 434 U.S. 497 (1978).]

In recent years the Court has also faced a number of instances in which the defendant has been discharged through a motion made before, during, or after trial. The prosecutor has then appealed the trial judge's ruling on the motion. Where an appeals court has found that the trial judge made an error of law in granting the defendant's motion, may he or she be retried? [See *Breed* v. *Jones,* 421 U.S. 519 (1975); *United States* v. *Wilson,* 420 U.S. 332 (1975); *United States* v. *Scott,* 437 U.S. 82 (1978).] Other cases involve state statutes that allow the government to seek higher penalties on appeal than those initially imposed by the trier of facts. Are such penalty appeals second trials? The Court's general position seems to be that, so long as appellate reversal of the motion or increase in penalties would not result in subjecting the defendant to a second round of fact-finding by a second jury or judge, no double jeopardy problem arises. But the state of the doctrine is so unsatisfactory that the Court will eventually have to undertake a major reconstruction of it. The Court has long held that a single transaction may give rise to multiple violations of the law, each of which may be tried and punished separately. [*Gore* v. *United States,* 357 U.S. 386 (1958); *Albernaz* v. *United States,* 101 S.Ct. 1137 (1981).]

The complex double jeopardy law being made in the federal area by the cases noted above and such cases as *Lee* v. *United States,* 432 U.S. 23 (1977), now seems to be increasingly applicable to the states as well. In *Crist* v. *Bretz,* 437 U.S. 28 (1978), the Court repeated earlier holdings that double jeopardy was incorporated into the Fourteenth Amendment. In that case and in *Greene* v. *Massey,* 437 U.S. 19 (1978), it seemed to be starting down the same confusing paths it is following in dealing with federal cases. Between 1978 and 1982 the Court issued twelve opinions in cases involving the problems described in the two preceding paragraphs without significantly clarifying them.

Commitment

Because of the insanity defense, commitment to a mental institution rather than imprisonment is sometimes the outcome of a criminal trial. Civil commitment, that is a proceeding in which a person not accused of a crime is confined to a mental institution, involves a serious deprivation of liberty. Indeed commitment is frequently more serious than imprisonment for a criminal offense because commitment usually is for an indefinite period and will end only when medical experts are prepared to release the person commited. The Supreme Court has now begun to bring certain due process requirements to commitment, but it is feeling its way very cautiously. [See *Addington* v. *Texas,* 441 U.S. 418 (1979); *Parham* v. *J. R.,* 442 U.S. 584 (1979); *Vitek* v. *Jones,* 445 U.S. 480 (1980); *Pennhurst State School and Hospital* v. *Halderman,* 101 S.Ct. 1531 (1981).]

Cruel and Unusual Punishment

Until very recently, very few cases arose under the cruel and unusual punishment provision of the Eighth Amendment. In *Witherspoon* v. *Illinois,* 391 U.S. 510 (1968), the Court held that the exclusion of all those who conscientiously opposed capital punishment from juries in capital cases would invalidate death penalties in such cases. That the Court was concerned with this constitutional provision can be seen in *Trop* v. *Dulles,* discussed on p. 175; *Robinson* v. *California,* 370 U.S. 660 (1962), which ruled that the state could not punish narcotics addiction as a crime; and *Powell* v. *Texas,* 392 U.S. 514 (1968), in which the justices were unable to agree on the precise line between drunkenness, which the state might punish as a crime, and alcoholism, which must be treated as a disease rather than punished as a crime.

In *Furman* v. *Georgia,* 408 U.S. 238 (1972), the Court finally directly confronted the issue of whether capital punishment constituted cruel and unusual punishment. In a 5-to-4 decision, the justices invalidated the Georgia death penalty statute and presumably those of all the other states. But only two justices, Brennan and Marshall, flatly argued that all capital punishment was unconstitutional. For the other three members of the majority, the wide discretion granted judges and juries, the infrequency of use, and the potential for racial and other types of discrimination seemed to be key factors.

After *Furman,* many states enacted new death penalty statutes designed to meet the justices' objections. In *Gregg* v. *Georgia,* 428 U.S. 153 (1976), the Court made clear that the death penalty per se was not unconstitutional by upholding the new Georgia death statute. The Court held that where proper procedures concentrated the jury's attention on the particular crime and the particular criminal and provided it with general rules for when the death penalty should be invoked, no cruel and unusual punishment occurred. On the other hand, where statutes made the death penalty mandatory for all perpetrators of certain categories of murder, the Court struck them down. [*Woodson* v. *North Carolina,* 428 U.S. 280 (1976); *Roberts* v. *Louisiana,* 428 U.S. 325 (1976); *Roberts* v. *Louisiana,* 431 U.S. 633 (1977); *Lockett* v. *Ohio,* 438 U.S. 586 (1978).] It struck down an Ohio statute because it did not permit sufficient individualized consideration of mitigating factors. [*Bell* v. *Ohio,* 438 U.S. 637 (1978).] Then in *Godfrey* v. *Georgia,* 446 U.S. 420 (1980), it held that the Georgia statute, which provided the death penalty for offenses that are "outrageously or wantonly vile, horrible or inhuman," was unconstitutional as construed by the state supreme court because it did not provide standards that would prevent the arbitrary and capricious infliction of the death penalty. In five other cases between 1978 and 1982 it found reasons to void capital sentences and in a number of other cases refused certiorari in circumstances where refusal would further delay executions. As Justice Rehnquist pointed out in a memorandum in 1981 (101 S.Ct. 2994), since *Gregg* thirty-odd states have had death penalty statutes, and hundreds of juries have sentenced persons to death, but only one defendant who persistently attacked his sentence has been executed.

In *Coker* v. *Georgia* (p. 705) the Court held the death penalty for rape to be cruel and unusual punishment. Until *Coker,* the Court's death penalty cases could be rationalized as essentially centered on procedural rather than substantive concerns. The Court might have been saying only that where the death penalty is invoked, especially good criminal justice procedures must be employed, such as a separate sentencing hearing at which the jury heard about all possible mitigating and extenuating circumstances and was given detailed information about the background and character of the accused. But in *Coker* the Court flatly says the death penalty is not appropriate to rape because the seriousness of the punishment does not match the seriousness of the crime. If death is too serious for rape, then why is not fifty years in prison too serious for burglary? *Furman* may well turn out to be a case like *Powell* v. *Alabama.* Once the Court had applied the right-to-counsel clause of the Sixth Amendment to capital cases, it eventually went on to apply it to all criminal prosecutions. *Coker* hints that, having applied the cruel and unusual punishment clause to capital cases in *Furman,* the Court will eventually apply it to all criminal penalties. In *Rummel* v. *Estelle,* 445 U.S. 263 (1980) four dissenters were prepared to invoke the clause against a Texas recidivist statute that required a sentence of life imprisonment for someone whose third offense was a felony conviction for obtaining $120.75 by false pretenses. See also *Hutto* v. *Davis,* 102 S.Ct. 703 (1982). (See the discussion of felony murder on p. 663.)

In *Ingraham* v. *Wright,* 430 U.S. 651 (1977), the Court holds that the cruel and unusual punishment clause does not apply to "traditional disciplinary practices in the public schools" such as paddling.

Prisoners

The Burger Court has not been bashful about moving into all sorts of new areas. One of these is prison administration. Prisoners have raised a whole host of due process, equal protection, First Amendment, and right-to-counsel claims quite apart from those involved in challenging the validity of their convictions. The Court has held that under some circumstances denying absentee ballots to prisoners is unconstitutional. [*O'Brien* v. *Skinner,* 414 U.S. 524 (1974).] It has held that due process hearings must be held before parole or probation can be revoked [*Morrissey* v. *Brewer,* 408 U.S. 471 (1972); *Gagnon* v. *Scarpelli,* 411 U.S. 778 (1973)] and at least a minimal hearing before an inmate may be deprived of "good time" credits. [*Wolff* v. *McDonnell,* 418 U.S. 539 (1974).] It has required less due process for refusal to grant parole than for revocation and no due process at all for refusals to commute life sentences. [*Greenholtz* v. *Inmates,* 442 U.S. 1 (1979); *Connecticut Board of Pardons* v. *Dumschat,*

101 S.Ct. 2460 (1981).] The Court unanimously struck down California prison regulations requiring censorship of prisoners' mail and banning the use of law students and legal paraprofessionals to conduct attorney-client interviews with prisoners. [*Procunier* v. *Martinez,* 416 U.S. 396 (1974).] Earlier it had struck down a prison regulation prohibiting any inmate from giving legal assistance to another. [*Johnson* v. *Avery,* 393 U.S. 483 (1969).] *Wolff* and *Procunier* quite clearly move the Burger Court into active supervision of many day-to-day aspects of running the prisons.

In *Bounds* v. *Smith,* 430 U.S. 817 (1977), the Court required that prison authorities provide prisoners with law libraries or adequate assistance from persons trained in the law to assist them in the preparation and filing of legal papers. In *Jones* v. *North Carolina Prisoner's Labor Union, Inc.,* 433 U.S. 119 (1977), however, the Court emphasized that prison authorities must have broad discretion in upholding prison regulations that limited the organizing of prisoners' unions.

In *Houchins v. KQED, Inc.,* 438 U.S. 1 (1978), the Court held that journalists have no greater rights of access to prisons and prisoners than do other persons.

In *Hutto v. Finney,* 437 U.S. 678 (1968) the Court held that holding a prisoner in an isolation cell for a long period might constitute cruel and unusual punishment. A number of lower federal courts have been actively intervening to correct what they view as unduely harsh prison conditions by invoking the cruel and unusual punishment clause and a number of other provisions of the Bill of Rights. The Burger Court has not been very receptive to such interventions. [See *Bell* v. *Wolfish,* 441 U.S. 520 (1979); *Rhodes* v. *Chapman,* 101 S.Ct. 2392 (1981).] It has, however, announced a limited right to minimum restraint and treatment for the institutionalized retarded. [*Youngberg* v. *Romeo,* 50 L.W. 4681 (1982).]

In *Enmund* v. *Florida,* 50 L.W. 5087 (1982), the Court confirmed some of the tendencies described on p. 662. It held that state "felony murder" statutes were unconstitutional when applied to defendants who participated in a felony in the course of which a murder occurred but in which they themselves did not kill, attempt to kill, or intend that lethal force be used. In such instances the defendant could not constitutionally be sentenced to death.

PALKO v. CONNECTICUT

302 U.S. 319; 58 Sup. Ct. 149; 82 L. Ed. 288 (1937)

[Palko was indicted and tried for murder in the first degree, but a jury found him guilty of second-degree murder, and he was given a life sentence. However, a Connecticut statute permitted the state to appeal rulings and decision "upon all questions of law arising on the trial of criminal cases." The state appealed, and a new trial was ordered. Palko was tried again, found guilty, and sentenced to death. The second conviction was affirmed

by the highest state court. Palko then brought the case to the Supreme Court on appeal, contending that he was being placed in jeopardy twice in violation of the Fifth and Fourteenth Amendments.]

MR. JUSTICE CARDOZO delivered the opinion of the Court:

. . . 1. The execution of the sentence will not deprive appellant of his life without the process of law assured to him by the Fourteenth Amendment of the Federal Constitution.

The argument for appellant is that whatever is forbidden by the Fifth Amendment is forbidden by the Fourteenth also. The Fifth Amendment, which is not directed to the states, but solely to the federal government, creates immunity from double jeopardy. No person shall be "subject for the same offense to be twice put in jeopardy of life or limb." The Fourteenth Amendment ordains, "nor shall any state deprive any person of life, liberty, or property, without due process of law." To retry a defendant, though under one indictment and only one, subjects him, it is said, to double jeopardy in violation of the Fifth Amendment, if the prosecution is one on behalf of the United States. From this the consequence is said to follow that there is a denial of life or liberty without due process of law, if the prosecution is one on behalf of the People of a State. . . .

We have said that in appellant's view the Fourteenth Amendment is to be taken as embodying the prohibitions of the Fifth. His thesis is even broader. Whatever would be a violation of the original Bill of Rights (Amendments 1 to 8), if done by the federal government, is now equally unlawful by force of the Fourteenth Amendment if done by a state. There is no such general rule.

The Fifth Amendment provides, among other things, that no person shall be held to answer for a capital or otherwise infamous crime unless on presentment or indictment of a grand jury. This court has held that, in prosecutions by a state, presentment or indictment by a grand jury may give way to informations at the instance of a public officer. *Hurtado* v. *California,* 110 U.S. 516. . . . The Fifth Amendment provides also that no person shall be compelled in any criminal case to be a witness against himself. This court has said that, in prosecutions by a state, the exemption will fail if the state elects to end it. *Twining* v. *New Jersey,* 211 U.S. 78. . . . The Sixth Amendment calls for a jury trial in criminal cases and the Seventh for a jury trial in civil cases at common law where the value in controversy shall exceed twenty dollars. This court has ruled that, consistently with those amendments, trial by jury may be modified by a state or abolished altogether. *Walker* v. *Sauvinet,* 92 U.S. 90. . . . *Maxwell* v. *Dow,* 176 U.S. 581.

. . . On the other hand, the due process clause of the Fourteenth Amendment may make it unlawful for a state to abridge by its statutes the freedom of speech which the First Amendment safeguards against encroachment by the Congress *(De Jonge* v. *Oregon,* 299 U.S. 353, 364, . . . *Herndon* v. *Lowry,* 301 U.S. 242, 259 . . .), or the like freedom of the press *(Grosjean* v. *American Press Co.,* 297 U.S. 233, . . . *Near* v. *Minnesota,* 283 U.S. 697, 707 . . .), or the free exercise of religion *(Hamilton* v. *University of California,* 293 U.S. 245, 262 . . .), or the right of peaceable assembly, without which speech would be unduly trammeled *(De Jonge* v. *Oregon* . . .), or the right of one accused of crime to the benefit of counsel *(Powell* v. *Alabama,* 287 U.S. 45 . . .). In these and other situations immunities that are valid as against the federal government by force of the specific pledges of particular amendments have been found to be implicit in the concept of ordered liberty, and thus, through the Fourteenth Amendment, become valid as against the states.

The line of division may seem to be wavering and broken if there is a hasty catalogue of the cases on the one side and the other. Reflection and analysis will induce a different view. There emerges the perception of a rationalizing principle which gives to discrete instances a proper order and coherence. The right to trial by jury and the immunity from prosecution except as the result of an indictment may have value and importance. Even so, they are not of the very essence of a scheme of ordered liberty. To abolish them is not to violate a "principle of justice so rooted in the traditions and conscience of our people as to be ranked as fundamental.". . . Few would be so narrow or provincial as to maintain that a fair and enlightened system of justice would be impossible without them. What is true of jury trials and indictments is true also, as the cases show, of the immunity from compulsory self-incrimination. . . . This too might be lost, and justice still be done. Indeed, today as in the past there are students of our penal system who look upon the immunity as a mischief rather than a benefit, and who would limit its scope or destroy it altogether. No doubt there would remain the need to give protection against torture, physical or mental. . . . Justice, however, would not perish if the accused were subject to a duty to respond to orderly inquiry. The exclusion of these immunities and privileges from the privileges and immunities protected against the action of the states has not been arbitrary or casual. It has been dictated by a study and appreciation of the meaning, the essential implications, of liberty itself.

We reach a different plane of social and moral values when we pass to the privileges and immunities that have been taken over from the earlier articles of the federal Bill of Rights and brought within the Fourteenth Amendment by a process of absorption. These in their origin were effective against the federal government alone. If the Fourteenth Amendment has absorbed them, the process of absorption has had its source in the belief that neither liberty nor justice would exist if they were sacrificed. . . . This is true, for illustration, of freedom of thought and speech. Of that freedom one may say that it is the matrix, the indispensable condition, of nearly every other form of freedom. With rare aberrations, a pervasive recognition of that truth can be traced in our history, political and legal. So it has come about that the domain of liberty, withdrawn by the Fourteenth Amendment from encroachment by the states, has been enlarged by latter-day judgments to include liberty of the mind as well as liberty of action. The extension became, indeed, a logical imperative when once it was recognized, as long ago it was, that liberty is something more than exemption from physical restraint, and that even in the field of substantive rights and duties the legislative judgment, if oppressive and arbitrary, may be overridden by the courts. . . .

Our survey of the cases serves, we think, to justify the statement that the dividing line between them, if not unfaltering throughout its course, has been true for the most part to a unifying principle. On which side of the line the case made out by the appellant has appropriate location must be the next inquiry and the final one. Is that kind of double jeopardy to which the statute has subjected him a hardship so acute and shocking that our polity will not endure it? Does it violate those "fundamental principles of liberty and justice which lie at the base of all our civil and political institutions?" . . . the answer surely must be "no." What the answer would have to be if the state were permitted after a trial free from error to try the accused over again or to bring another case against him, we have no occasion to consider. We deal with the statute before us and no other. The state is not attempting to wear the accused out by a multitude of cases with accumulated trials. It asks no more than this, that the case against him shall go on until there shall be a trial free from the corrosion of substantial legal error. . . . This is not cruelty at all, nor even vexation in any immoderate degree. If the trial had been infected with error adverse to the accused, there might have been review at his instance, and as often as necessary to purge the vicious taint. A reciprocal privilege, subject at all times to the discretion of the presiding judge . . . has now been granted to the state. There is here no seismic innovation. The edifice of justice stands, in its symmetry, to many, greater than before.

2. The conviction of appellant is not in derogation of any privileges or immunities that belong to him as a citizen of the United States. . . .

Affirmed.

MR. JUSTICE BUTLER dissents.

ADAMSON v. CALIFORNIA
332 U.S. 46; 67 Sup. Ct. 1672; 91 L. Ed. 1903 (1947)

[Adamson was convicted of murder without recommendation of mercy by the jury and sentenced to death. The sentence was affirmed by the Supreme Court of California. Adamson then brought his case to the Supreme Court on appeal. He argued that a California statute that permitted the prosecutor and judge to make adverse comments to the jury upon the failure of a defendant to take the witness stand to explain or deny evidence against him was invalid under the Fifth and Fourteenth Amendments. In his trial, Adamson, who had been previously convicted for burglary, larceny, and robbery, chose not to take the stand. As a result, both the prosecuting attorney and the court made adverse comments. Adamson argued that this practice put him in an impossible situation. If he did testify, the previous convictions would be revealed to the jury. If he did not testify (as in this case), he would be prejudiced by the comments of the prosecutor and judge. The California procedure was not permissible in federal courts and in the overwhelming majority of state jurisdictions.]

MR. JUSTICE REED delivered the opinion of the Court:

. . . In the first place, appellant urges that the provision of the Fifth Amendment that no person "shall be compelled in any criminal case to be a witness against himself" is a fundamental national privilege or immunity protected against state abridgment by the Fourteenth Amendment or a privilege or immunity secured, through the Fourteenth Amendment, against deprivation by state action because it is a personal right, enumerated in the federal Bill of Rights.

Secondly, appellant relies upon the due process of law clause of the Fourteenth Amendment to invalidate the provisions of the California law . . . as applied (a) because comment on failure to testify is permitted, (b) because appellant was forced to forego testimony in person because of danger of disclosure of his past convictions through cross-examination, and (c) because the presumption of innocence was infringed by the shifting of the burden of proof to appellant in permitting comment on his failure to testify.

We shall assume, but without any intention thereby of ruling upon the issue, that permission by law to the court, counsel and jury to comment upon and consider the failure of defendant "to explain or to deny by his testimony any evidence or facts in the case against him" would infringe defendant's privilege against self-incrimination under the Fifth Amendment if this were a trial in a court of the United States under a similar law. Such an assumption does not determine appellant's rights under the Fourteenth Amendment. It is settled law that the clause of the Fifth Amendment, protecting a person against being compelled to be a witness against himself, is not made effective by the Fourteenth Amendment as a protection against state action on the ground that freedom from testimonial compulsion is a right of national citizenship, or because it is a personal privilege or immunity secured by the Federal Constitution as one of the rights of man that are listed in the Bill of Rights.

The reasoning that leads to those conclusions starts with the unquestioned premise that the Bill of Rights, when adopted, was for the protection of the individual against the federal government and its provisions were inapplicable to similar actions done by the states . . . With the adoption of the Fourteenth Amendment, it was suggested that the dual citizenship recognized by its first sentence secured for citizens federal protection for their elemental privileges and immunities of state citizenship. The *Slaughterhouse Cases* decided, contrary to the suggestion, that these rights, as privileges and immunities of state citizenship, remained under the sole protection of the state governments. This Court, without the expression of a contrary view upon the phase of the issues before the Court, has approved this determination. . . . The power to free defendants in state trials from self-incrimination was specifically determined to be beyond the scope of the privileges and immunities clause of the Fourteenth Amendment in *Twining* v. *New Jersey,* 211 U.S. 78. . . . "The privilege against self-incrimination may be withdrawn and the accused put upon the stand as a witness for the state." The *Twining* case likewise disposed of the contention that freedom from testimonial compulsion, being specifically granted by the Bill of Rights, is a federal privilege or immunity that is protected by the Fourteenth Amendment against state invasion. This Court held that the inclusion in the Bill of Rights of this protection against the power of the national government did not make the privilege a federal privilege or immunity secured to citizens by the Constitution against state action. . . . After declaring that state and national citizenship co-exist in the same person, the Fourteenth Amendment forbids a state from abridging the privileges and immunities of citizens of the United States. As a matter of words, this leaves a state free to abridge, within the limits of the due process clause, the privileges and immunities flowing from state citizenship. This reading of the Federal Constitution has heretofore found favor with the majority of this Court as a natural and logical interpretation. It accords with the constitutional doctrine of federalism by leaving to the states the responsibility of dealing with the privileges and immunities of their citizens except those inherent in national citizenship. It is the construction placed upon the amendment by justices whose own experience had given them contemporaneous knowledge of the purposes that led to the adoption of the Fourteenth Amendment. This construction has become embedded in our federal system as a functioning element in preserving the balance between national and state power. We reaffirm the conclusion of the *Twining* and *Palko* cases that protection against self-incrimination is not a privilege or immunity of national citizenship.

Appellant secondly contends that if the privilege against self-incrimination is not a right protected by the privileges and immunities clause of the Fourteenth Amendment against state action, this privilege, to its full scope under the Fifth Amendment, inheres in the right to a fair trial. A right to a fair trial is a right admittedly protected by the due process clause of the Fourteenth Amendment. Therefore, appellant argues, the due process clause of the Fourteenth Amendment protects his privilege against self-incrimination. The due process clause of the Fourteenth Amendment, however, does not draw all the rights of the federal Bill of Rights under its protection. That contention was made and rejected in *Palko* v. *Connecticut.* . . . It was rejected with citation of the cases excluding several of the rights, protected by the Bill of Rights, against infringement by the National Government. Nothing has been called to our attention that either the framers of the Fourteenth Amendment or the states that adopted it intended its due process clause to draw within its scope the earlier amendments to the Constitution. *Palko* held that such provisions of the Bill of Rights as were "implicit in the concept of ordered liberty" became secure from state interference by the clause. But it held nothing more.

Specifically, the due process clause does not protect, by virtue of its mere existence, the accused's freedom from giving testimony by compulsion in state trials that is secured to him against federal interference by the Fifth Amendment. . . . For a state to require testimony from an accused is not necessarily a breach of a state's obligation to give a fair trial. . . .

Generally, comment on the failure of an accused to testify is forbidden in American jurisdictions. This arises from state constitutional or statutory provisions similar in character to the federal provisions. . . . California, however, is one of a few states that permit limited comment upon a defendant's failure to testify. That permission is narrow. The California law . . . authorizes comment by court and counsel upon the "failure of the defendant to explain or to deny by his testimony any evidence or facts in the case against him." This does not involve any presumption, rebuttable or irrebuttable, either of guilt or of the truth of any fact, that is offered in evidence. . . . It allows inferences to be drawn from proven facts. Because of this clause, the court can direct the jury's attention to whatever evidence there may be that a defendant could deny and the prosecution can argue as to inferences that may be drawn from the accused's failure to testify. . . . There is here no lack of power in the trial court to adjudge and no denial of a hearing. California has prescribed a method for advising the jury in the search of truth. However sound may be the legislative conclusion that an accused should not be compelled in any criminal case to be a witness against himself, we see no reason why comment should not be made upon his silence. It seems quite natural that when a defendant has opportunity to deny or explain facts and determines not to do so, the prosecution should bring out the strength of the evidence by commenting upon defendant's failure to explain or deny it. The prosecution evidence may be of facts that may be beyond the knowledge of the accused. If so, his failure to testify would have little if any weight. But the facts may be such as are necessarily in the knowledge of the accused. In that case a failure to explain would point to an inability to explain. . . .

It is true that if comment were forbidden, an accused in this situation could remain silent and avoid evidence of former crimes and comment upon his failure to testify. We are of the view, however, that a state may control such a situation in accordance with its own ideas of the most efficient administration of criminal justice. The purpose of due process is not to protect an accused against a proper conviction but against an unfair conviction. When evidence is before a jury that threatens conviction, it does not seem unfair to require him to choose between leaving the adverse evidence unexplained and subjecting himself to impeachment through disclosure of former crimes. Indeed, this is a dilemma with which any defendant may be faced. If facts, adverse to the defendant, are proven by the prosecution, there may be no way to explain them favorably to the accused except by a witness who may be vulnerable to impeachment on cross-examination. The defendant must then decide whether or not to use such a witness. The fact that the witness may also be the defendant makes the choice more difficult but a denial of due process does not emerge from the circumstances. . . .

We find no other error that gives ground for our intervention in California's administration of criminal justice.

Affirmed.

MR. JUSTICE FRANKFURTER, concurring:

Less than ten years ago, Mr. Justice Cardozo announced as settled constitutional law that while the Fifth Amendment, "which is not directed to the states, but solely to the federal government," provides that no person shall be compelled in any criminal case to be a witness against himself, the process of law assured by the Fourteenth Amendment does not require such immunity from self-incrimination: "in prosecutions by a state, the exemption will fail if the state elects to end it." *Palko* v. *Connecticut.* . . . Mr. Justice Cardozo spoke for the Court, consisting of Mr. Chief Justice Hughes, and (Justices) McReynolds, Brandeis, Sutherland, Stone, Roberts, Black. (Mr. Justice Butler dissented.) The matter no longer called for discussion; a reference to *Twining* v. *New Jersey* . . . decided thirty years before the *Palko* case, sufficed.

Decisions of this Court do not have equal intrinsic authority. The *Twining* case shows the judicial process at its best—comprehensive briefs and powerful arguments on both sides, followed by long deliberation, resulting in an opinion by Mr. Justice Moody which at once gained and has ever since retained recognition as one of the outstanding opinions in the history of the Court. After enjoying unquestioned prestige for forty years, the *Twining* case should not now be diluted, even unwittingly, either in its judicial philosophy or in its particulars. As the surest way of keeping the *Twining* case intact, I would affirm this case on its authority. . . .

The short answer to the suggestion that the provision of the Fourteenth Amendment, which ordains "nor shall any State deprive any person of life, liberty, or property, without due process of law," was a way of saying that every State must thereafter initiate prosecutions through indictment by a grand jury, must have a trial by a jury of twelve in criminal cases, and must have trial by such a jury in common-law suits where the amount in controversy exceeds twenty dollars, is that it is a strange way of saying it. It would be extraordinarily strange for a Constitution to convey such specific commands in such a roundabout and inexplicit way. After all, an amendment to the Constitution should be read in a " 'sense most obvious to the common understanding at the time of its adoption.'. . . For it was for public adoption that it was proposed.". . . Those reading the English language with the meaning which it ordinarily conveys, those conversant with the political and legal history of the concept of due process, those sensitive to the relations of the States to the central government as well as the relation of some of the provisions of the Bill of Rights to the process of justice, would hardly recognize the Fourteenth Amendment as a cover for the various explicit provisions of the first eight Amendments. Some of these are enduring reflections of experience with human nature, while some express the restricted views of eighteenth-century England regarding the best methods for the ascertainment of facts. The notion that the Fourteenth Amendment was a covert way of imposing upon the States all the rules which it seemed important to eighteenth-century statesmen to write into the Federal Amendments, was rejected by judges who were themselves witnesses of the process by which the Fourteenth Amendment became part of the Constitution. Arguments that may now be adduced to prove that the first eight Amendments were concealed within the historic phrasing of the Fourteenth Amendment were not unknown at the time of its adoption. A surer estimate of their bearing was possible for judges at the time than distorting distance is likely to vouchsafe. Any evidence or design or purpose not contemporaneously known could hardly have influenced those who ratified the Amendment. Remarks of a particular proponent of the Amendment, no matter how influential, are not to be deemed part of the Amendment. What was submitted for ratification was his proposal, not his speech. Thus, at the time of the ratification of the Fourteenth Amendment the constitutions of nearly half of the ratifying States did not have the rigorous requirements of the Fifth Amendment for instituting criminal proceedings through a grand jury. It could hardly have occurred to these States that by ratifying the Amendment they uprooted their established methods for prosecuting crime and fastened upon themselves a new prosecutorial system.

Indeed, the suggestion that the Fourteenth Amendment incorporates the first eight Amendments as such is not unambiguously urged. Even the boldest innovator would shrink from suggesting to more than half the States that they may no longer initiate prosecutions without indictment by grand jury, or that thereafter all the States of the Union must furnish a jury of twelve for every case involving a claim above twenty dollars. There is suggested merely a selective incorporation of the first eight Amendments into the Fourteenth Amendment. Some are in and some are out, but we are left in the dark as to which are in and which stay out. Nor are we given the calculus for determining which go in and which stay out. If the basis of selection is merely that those provisions of the first eight Amendments are incorporated which commend themselves to individual justices as indispensable to the dignity and happiness of a free man, we are thrown back to a merely subjective test. The protection against unreasonable search and seizure might have primacy for one judge, while trial by a jury of twelve for every claim above twenty dollars might appear to another as an ultimate need in a free society. In the history of thought "natural law" has a much longer and much better-founded meaning and justification than such subjective selection of the first eight Amendments for incorporation into the Fourteenth. If all that is meant is that due process contains within itself certain minimal standards which are "of the very essence of a scheme of ordered liberty," *Palko* v. *Connecticut* . . . putting upon this Court the duty of applying these standards from time to time, then we have merely arrived at the insight which our predecessors long ago expressed. . . . As judges charged with the delicate task of subjecting the government of a continent to the Rule of Law we must be particularly mindful that it is "a constitution we are expounding," so that it should not be imprisoned in what are merely legal forms even though they have the sanction of the eighteenth century.

And so, when, as in a case like the present, a conviction in a State court is here for review under a claim that a right protected by the Due Process Clause of the Fourteenth Amendment has been denied, the issue is not whether an infraction of one of the specific provisions of the first eight Amendments is disclosed by the record. The relevant question is whether the criminal proceedings which resulted in conviction deprived the accused of the due process of law to which the United States Constitution entitled him. Judicial review of that guaranty of the Fourteenth Amendment inescapably imposes upon this Court an exercise of judgment upon the whole course of the proceedings in order to ascertain whether they offend those canons of decency and fairness which express the notions of justice of English-speaking peoples even toward those charged with the most heinous offenses. These standards of justice are not authoritatively formulated anywhere as though they were prescriptions in a pharmacopoeia. But neither does the application of the Due Process Clause imply that judges are wholly at large. The judicial judgment in applying the Due Process Clause must move within the limits of accepted notions of justice and is not to be based upon the idiosyncrasies of a merely personal judgment. The fact that judges among themselves may differ whether in a particular case a trial offends accepted notions of justice is not disproof that general rather than idiosyncratic standards are applied. An important safeguard against such merely individual judgment is an alert deference to the judgment of the State court under review.

MR. JUSTICE BLACK, dissenting:

. . . This decision reasserts a constitutional theory spelled out in *Twining* v. *New Jersey* . . . that this Court is endowed by the Constitution with boundless power under "natural law" periodically to expand and contract constitutional standards to conform to the Court's conception of what at a particular time constitutes "civilized decency" and "fundamental liberty and justice." Invoking this *Twining* rule, the Court concludes that although comment upon testimony in a federal court would violate the Fifth Amendment, identical comment in a state court does not violate today's fashion in civilized decency and fundamentals and is therefore not prohibited by the Federal Constitution as amended.

The *Twining* case was the first, as it is the only, decision of this Court which has squarely held that states were free, notwithstanding the Fifth and Fourteenth Amendments, to exort evidence from one accused of crime. I agree that if *Twining* be reaffirmed, the result reached might appropriately follow. But I would not reaffirm the *Twining* decision. I think that decision and the "natural law" theory of the Constitution upon which it relies degrade the constitutional safeguards of the Bill of Rights and simultaneously appropriate for this Court a broad power which we are not authorized by the Constitution to exercise. . . .

My study of the historical events that culminated in the Fourteenth Amendment, and the expressions of those who sponsored and favored, as well as those who opposed its submission and passage, persuades me that one of the chief objects that the provisions of the Amendment's first section, separately, and as a whole, were intended to accomplish was to make the Bill of Rights applicable to the states. With full knowledge of the import of the *Barron* decision, the framers and backers of the Fourteenth Amendment proclaimed its purpose to be to overturn the constitutional rule that case had announced. This historical purpose has never received full consideration or exposition in any opinion of this Court interpreting the Amendment. . . .

In my judgment. . . . history conclusively demonstrates that the language of the first section of the Fourteenth Amendment, taken as a whole, was thought by those responsible for its submission to the people, and by those who opposed its submission, sufficiently explicit to guarantee that thereafter no state could deprive its citizens of the privileges and protections of the Bill of Rights. Whether this Court ever will, or whether it now should, in the light of past decisions, give full effect to what the Amendment was intended to accomplish is not necessarily essential to a decision here. However that may be, our prior decisions, including *Twining,* do not prevent our carrying out that purpose, at least to the extent of making applicable to the states, not a mere part, as the Court has, but the full protection of the Fifth Amendment's provision against compelling evidence from an accused to convict him of crime. And I further contend that the "natural law" formula which the Court uses to reach its conclusion in this case should be abandoned as an incongruous excrescence on our Constitution. I believe that formula to be itself a violation of our Constitution, in that it subtly conveys to courts, at the expense of legislatures, ultimate power over public policies in fields where no specific provision of the Constitution limits legislative power. And my belief seems to be in accord with the views expressed by this Court, at least for the first two decades after the Fourteenth Amendment was adopted. . . .

I cannot consider the Bill of Rights to be an outworn eighteenth century "strait jacket" as the *Twining* opinion did. Its provisions may be thought outdated abstractions by some. And it is true that they were designed to meet ancient evils. But they are the same kind of human evils that have emerged from century to century wherever excessive power is sought by the few at the expense of the many. In my judgment the people of no nation can lose their liberty so long as a Bill of Rights like ours survives and its basic purposes are conscientiously interpreted, enforced and respected so as to afford continuous protection against old, as well as new, devices and practices which might thwart those purposes. I fear to see the consequences of the Court's practice of substituting its own concepts of decency and fundamental justice for the language of the Bill of Rights as its point of departure in interpreting and enforcing that Bill of Rights. If the choice must be between the selective process of the *Palko* decision applying some of the Bill of Rights to the States, or the *Twining* rule applying none of them, I would choose the *Palko* selective process. But rather than accept either of these choices, I would follow what I believe was the original purpose of the Fourteenth Amendment—to extend to all the people of the nation the complete protection of the Bill of Rights. To hold that this Court can determine what, if any, provisions of the Bill of Rights will be enforced, and if so to what degree, is to frustrate the great design of a written Constitution.

Conceding the possibility that this Court is now wise enough to improve on the Bill of Rights by substituting natural law concepts for the Bill of Rights, I think the possibility is entirely too speculative to agree to take that course. I would therefore hold in this case that the full protection of the Fifth Amendment's proscription against compelled testimony must be afforded by California. This I would do because of reliance upon the original purpose of the Fourteenth Amendment.

It is an illusory apprehension that literal application of some or all of the provisions of the Bill of Rights to the States would unwisely increase the sum total of the powers of this Court to invalidate state legislation. The Federal Government has not been harmfully burdened by the requirement that enforcement of federal laws affecting civil liberty conform literally to the Bill of Rights. Who would advocate its repeal? It must be conceded, of course, that the natural-law-due-process formula, which the Court today reaffirms, has been interpreted to limit substantially this Court's power to prevent state violations of the individual civil liberties guaranteed by the Bill of Rights. But this formula also has been used in the past, and can be used in the future, to license this Court, in considering regulatory legislation, to roam at large in the broad expanses of policy and morals and to trespass, all too freely, on the legislative domain of the States as well as the Federal Government. . . .

MR. JUSTICE DOUGLAS joins in this opinion.

MR. JUSTICE MURPHY, with whom MR. JUSTICE RUTLEDGE concurs, dissenting:

While in substantial agreement with the views of Mr. Justice Black, I have one reservation and one addition to make.

I agree that the specific guaranties of the Bill of Rights should be carried over intact into the first section of the Fourteenth Amendment. But I am not prepared to say that the latter is entirely and necessarily limited by the Bill of Rights. Occasions may arise where a proceeding falls so far short of conforming to fundamental standards of procedure as to warrant constitutional condemnation in terms of a lack of due process despite the absence of a specific provision in the Bill of Rights. . . .

MAPP *v.* OHIO

367 U.S. 643; 81 Sup. Ct. 1684; 6 L. Ed. 2d (1961)

[Mapp was convicted in Ohio of having obscene materials in her possession in violation of a state statute. After the Ohio Supreme Court upheld the conviction, Mapp brought an appeal to the Supreme Court. Additional facts are found in the opinion.]

MR. JUSTICE CLARK delivered the opinion of the Court:

. . . On May 23, 1957, three Cleveland police officers arrived at appellant's residence in that city pursuant to information that "a person (was) hiding out in the home who was wanted for questioning in connection with a recent bombing, and that there was a large amount of policy paraphernalia being hidden in the home." Miss Mapp and her daughter by a former marriage lived on the top floor of the two-family dwelling. Upon their arrival at that house, the officers knocked on the door and demanded entrance but appellant, after telephoning her attorney, refused to admit them without a search warrant. They advised their headquarters of the situation and undertook a surveillance of the house.

The officers again sought entrance some three hours later when four or more additional officers arrived on the scene. When Miss Mapp did not come to the door immediately, at least one of the several doors to the house was forcibly opened and the policemen gained admittance. Meanwhile Miss Mapp's attorney arrived, but the officers, having secured their own entry, and continuing in their defiance of the law, would permit him neither to see Miss Mapp nor to enter the house. It appears that Miss Mapp was halfway down the stairs from the upper floor to the front door when the officers, in this highhanded manner, broke into the hall. She demanded to see the search warrant. A paper, claimed to be a warrant, was held up by one of the officers. She grabbed the "warrant" and placed it in her bosom. A struggle ensued in which the officers recovered the piece of paper and as a result of which they handcuffed appellant because she had been "belligerent" in resisting their official rescue of the "warrant" from her person. Running roughshod over appellant, a policeman "grabbed" her, "twisted (her) hand," and she "yelled (and) pleaded with him" because "it was hurting." Appellant, in handcuffs, was then forcibly taken upstairs to her bedroom where the officers searched a dresser, a chest of drawers, a closet and some suitcases. They also looked into a photo album and through personal papers belonging to the appellant. The search spread to the rest of the second floor including the child's bedroom, the living room, the kitchen and a dinette. The basement of the building and a trunk found therein was also searched. The obscene materials for possession of which she was ultimately convicted were discovered in the course of that widespread search.

At the trial no search warrant was produced by the prosecution, nor was the failure to produce one explained or accounted for. At best, "there is, in the record, considerable doubt as to whether there ever was any warrant for the search of defendant's home." . . .

The State says that even if the search were made without authority, or otherwise unreasonably, it is not prevented from using the unconstitutionally seized evidence at trial, citing *Wolf* v. *Colorado*, . . . in which this Court did indeed hold "that in a prosecution in a State court for a State crime the Fourteenth Amendment does not forbid the admission of evidence obtained by an unreasonable search and seizure." . . .

I

Seventy-five years ago, in *Boyd* v. *United States,* 116 U.S. 616, 630 (1886), considering the Fourth and Fifth Amendments as running "almost into each other" on the facts before it, this Court held the doctrines of those Amendments

> "apply to all invasions on the part of the government and its employees of the sanctity of a man's home and the privacies of life. It is not the breaking of his doors, and the rummaging of his drawers, that constitutes the essence of the offense; but it is the invasion of his indefeasible right of personal security, personal liberty and private property. . . . Breaking into a house and opening boxes and drawers are circumstances of aggravation; but any forcible and compulsory extortion of a man's own testimony or of his private papers to be used as evidence to convict him of crime or to forfeit his goods, is within the condemnation . . . [of those Amendments]. . . ."

Less than thirty years after *Boyd,* this Court, in *Weeks* v. *United States,* 232 U.S. 383 (1914), stated that

> "the Fourth Amendment . . . put the courts of the United States and Federal officials, in the exercise of their power and authority, under limitations and restraints (and) . . . forever secure(d) the people, their persons, houses, papers and effects against all unreasonable searches and seizures under the guise of law . . . and the duty of giving to it force and effect is obligatory upon all entrusted under our Federal system with the enforcement of the laws. . . ."

Specifically dealing with the use of the evidence unconstitutionally seized, the Court concluded:

> "If letters and private documents can thus be seized and held and used in evidence against a citizen accused of an offense, the protection of the Fourth Amendment declaring his right to be secure against such searches and seizures is of no value, and, so far as those thus placed are concerned, might as well be stricken from the Constitution. The efforts of the courts and their officials to bring the guilty to punishment, praiseworthy as they are, are not to be aided by the sacrifice of those great principles established by years of endeavor and suffering which have resulted in their embodiment in the fundamental law of the land. . . ."

Finally, the Court in that case clearly stated that use of the seized evidence involved "a denial of the constitutional rights of the accused." . . . Thus, in the year 1914, in the *Weeks* case, this Court "for the first time" held that "in a federal prosecution the Fourth Amendment barred the use of evidence secured through an illegal search and seizure." . . . This Court has ever since required of federal law officers a strict adherence to that command which this Court has held to be a clear, specific, and constitutionally required—even if judicially implied—deterrent safeguard without insistence upon which the Fourth Amendment would have been reduced to "a form of words." . . . It meant, quite simply, that "conviction by means of unlawful seizures and enforced confessions . . . should find no sanction in the judgments of the courts. . . ."

There are in the cases of this Court some passing references to the *Weeks* rule as being one of evidence. But the plain and unequivocal language of *Weeks*—and its later paraphrase in *Wolf*—to the effect that the *Weeks* rule is of constitutional origin, remains entirely undisturbed. . . .

II

In 1949, thirty-five years after *Weeks* was announced, this Court, in *Wolf* v. *Colorado,* supra, again for the first time, discussed the effect of the Fourth Amendment upon the States through the operation of the Due Process Clause of the Fourteenth Amendment. It said:

> "[W]e have no hesitation in saying that were a State affirmatively to sanction such police incursion into privacy it would run counter to the guaranty of the Fourteenth Amendment. . . ."

Nevertheless, after declaring that the "security of one's privacy against arbitrary intrusion by the police" is "implicit in the 'concept of ordered liberty' and as such enforceable against the States through the Due Process Clause," cf. *Palko* v. *Connecticut,* 302 U.S. 319 (1937), and announcing that it "stoutly adhere(d)" to the *Weeks* decision, the Court decided that the *Weeks* exclusionary rule would not then be imposed upon the States as "an essential ingredient of the right." . . .

III

Some five years after *Wolf,* in answer to a plea made here term after term that we overturn its doctrine on applicability of the *Weeks* exclusionary rule, this Court indicated that such should not be done until the States had "adequate opportunity to adapt or reject the *(Weeks)* rule. . . ."

Today we once again examine *Wolf's* constitutional documentation of the right to privacy free from unreasonable state intrusion, and, after its dozen years on our books, are led by it to close the only courtroom door remaining open to evidence secured by official lawlessness in flagrant abuse of that basic right, reserved to all persons as a specific guaranty against that very same unlawful conduct. We hold that all evidence obtained by searches and seizures in violation of the Constitution is, by that same authority, inadmissible in a state court.

IV

Since the Fourth Amendment's right of privacy has been declared enforceable against the States through the Due Process Clause of the Fourteenth, it is enforceable against them by the same sanction of exclusion as is used against the Federal Government. Were it otherwise, then just as without the *Weeks* rule the assurance against unreasonable federal searches and seizures would be "a form of words," valueless and undeserving of mention in a perpetual character of inestimable human liberties, so too, without that rule the freedom from state invasions of privacy would be so ephemeral and so neatly severed from its conceptual nexus with the freedom from all brutish means of coercing evidence as not to merit this Court's high regard as a freedom "implicit in the concept of ordered liberty." At the time that the Court held in *Wolf* that the Amendment was applicable to the States through the Due Process Clause, the cases of this Court, as we have seen, had steadfastly held that as to federal officers the Fourth Amendment included the exclusion of the evidence seized in violation of its provisions. . . . [T]he admission of the new constitutional right by *Wolf* could not consistently tolerate denial of its most important constitutional privilege, namely, the exclusion of the evidence which an accused had been forced to give by reason of the unlawful seizure. To hold otherwise is to grant the right but in reality to withhold its privilege and enjoyment. Only last year the Court itself recognized that the purpose of the exclusionary rule "is to deter—to compel respect for the constitutional guaranty in the only effectively availabe way—by removing the incentive to disregard it. . . ."

Indeed, we are aware of no restraint, similar to that rejected today, conditioning the enforcement of any other basic constitutional right. The right to privacy, no less important than any other right carefully and particularly reserved to the people, would stand in marked contrast to all other rights declared as "basic to a free society." . . . The Court has not hesitated to enforce as strictly against the States as it does against the Federal Government the rights of free speech and of a free press, the rights to notice and to a fair, public trial, including, as it does, the right not to be convicted by use of a coerced confession, however logically relevant it be, and without regard to its reliability. . . . We find that, as to the Federal Government, the Fourth and Fifth Amendments and, as to the States, the freedom from unconscionable invasions of privacy and the freedom from convictions based upon coerced confessions do enjoy an "intimate relation" in their perpetuation of "principles of humanity and civil liberty (secured) . . . only after years of struggle. . . ."

V

Moreover, our holding that the exclusionary rule is an essential part of both the Fourth and Fourteenth Amendments is not only the logical dictate of prior cases, but it also makes very good sense. There is no war between the Constitution and common sense. Presently, a federal prosecutor may make no use of evidence illegally seized, but a State's attorney across the street may, although he supposedly is operating under the enforceable prohibitions of the same Amendment. Thus the State, by admitting evidence unlawfully seized, serves to encourage disobedience to the Federal Constitution which it is bound to uphold. . . . In nonexclusionary States, federal officers, being human, were by it invited to and did, as our cases indicate, step across the street to the State's attorney with their unconstitutionally seized evidence. Prosecution on the basis of that evidence was then had in a state court in utter disregard of the enforceable Fourth Amendment. If the fruits of an unconstitutional search had been inadmissible in both state and federal courts, this inducement to evasion would have been sooner eliminated. . . .

Federal-state cooperation in the solution of crime under constitutional standards will be promoted, if only by recognition of their now mutual obligation to respect the same fundamental criteria in their approaches. "However much in a particular case insistence upon such rules may appear as a technicality that inures to the benefit of a guilty person, the history of the criminal law proves that tolerance of shortcut methods in law enforcement impairs its enduring effectiveness." . . . Denying shortcuts to only one of two cooperating law enforcement agencies tends naturally to breed legitimate suspicion of "working arrangements" whose results are equally tainted. . . .

The ignoble shortcut to conviction left open to the State tends to destroy the entire system of constitutional restraints on which the liberties of the people rest. Having once recognized that the right to privacy embodied in the Fourth Amendment is enforceable against the States, and that the right to be secure against rude invasions of privacy by state officers is, therefore, constitutional in origin, we can no longer permit that right to remain an empty promise. Because it is enforceable in the same manner and to like effect as other basic rights secured by the Due Process Clause, we can no longer permit it to be revocable at the whim of any police officer who, in the name of law enforcement itself, chooses to suspend its enjoyment. Our decision, founded on reason and truth, gives to the individual no more than that which the Constitution guarantees him, to the police officer no less than that to which honest law enforcement is entitled, and to the courts, that judicial integrity so necessary in the true administration of justice.

The judgment of the Supreme Court of Ohio is reversed and the case remanded for further proceedings not inconsistent with the opinion.

Reversed and remanded.

MR. JUSTICE BLACK, concurring:

. . . I am still not persuaded that the Fourth Amendment, standing alone, would be enough to bar the introduction into evidence against an accused of papers and effects seized from him in violation of its commands. For the Fourth Amendment does not itself contain any provision expressly precluding the use of such evidence, and I am extremely doubtful that such . . . a provision could properly be inferred from nothing more than the basic command against unreasonable searches and seizures. Reflection on the problem, however, in the light of cases coming before the Court since *Wolf,* has led me to conclude that when the Fourth Amendment's ban against unreasonable searches and seizures is considered together with the Fifth Amendment's ban against compelled self-incrimination, a constitutional basis emerges which not only justifies but actually requires the exclusionary rule.

The close interrelationship between the Fourth and Fifth Amendments, as they apply to this problem, has long been recognized and, indeed, was expressly made the ground for this Court's holding in *Boyd* v. *United States.* There the Court fully discussed this relationship and declared itself "unable to perceive that the seizure of a man's private books and papers to be used in evidence against him is substantially different from compelling him to be a witness against himself." It was upon this ground that Mr. Justice Rutledge largely relied in his dissenting opinion in the *Wolf* case. And, although I rejected the argument at that time, its force has, for me at least, become compelling with the more thorough understanding of the problem brought on by recent cases. In the final analysis, it seems to be that the *Boyd* doctrine, though perhaps not required by the express language of the Constitution strictly construed, is amply justified from an historical standpoint, soundly based in reason, and entirely consistent with what I regard to be the proper approach to interpretation of our Bill of Rights. . . .

The Court's opinion, in my judgment, dissipates the doubt and uncertainty in this field of constitutional law and I am persuaded, for this and other reasons stated, to depart from my prior views, to accept the *Boyd* doctrine as controlling in this state case and to join the Court's judgment and opinion which are in accordance with that constitutional doctrine.

MR. JUSTICE DOUGLAS, concurring:

. . . *Wolf* v. *Colorado* . . . was decided in 1949. The immediate result was a storm of constitutional controversy which only today finds its end. I believe that this is an appropriate case in which to put an end to the asymmetry which *Wolf* imported into the law. . . . It is an appropriate case because the facts it presents show—as would few other cases—the casual arrogance of those who have the untrammelled power to invade one's home and to seize one's person. . . .

Memorandum of MR. JUSTICE STEWART:

Agreeing fully with Part I of Mr. Justice Harlan's dissenting opinion, I express no view as to the merits of the constitutional issue which the Court today decides. I would, however, reverse the judgment in this case, because I am persuaded that the provisions of Section 2905.34 of the Ohio Revised Code, upon which the petitioner's conviction was based is, in the words of Mr. Justice Harlan, not "consistent with the rights of free thought and expression assured against state action by the Fourteenth Amendment."

MR. JUSTICE HARLAN, whom MR. JUSTICE FRANKFURTER and MR. JUSTICE WHITTAKER join, dissenting:

In overruling the *Wolf* case the Court, in my opinion, has forgotten the sense of judicial restraint which, with due regard for stare decisis, is one element that should enter into deciding whether a past decision of this Court should be overruled. Apart from that I also believe that the *Wolf* rule represents sounder Constitutional doctrine than the new rule which now replaces it.

I

From the Court's statement of the case one would gather that the central, if not controlling, issue on this appeal is whether illegally state-seized evidence is Constitutionally admissible in a state prosecution, an issue which would of course face us with the need for reexamining *Wolf.* However, such is not the situation. For, although that question was indeed raised here and below among appellant's subordinate points, the new and pivotal issue brought to the Court by this appeal is whether Section 2905.34 of the Ohio Revised Code making criminal the mere knowing possession or control of obscene material, and under which appellant has been convicted, is consistent with the rights of free thought and expression assured against state action by the Fourteenth Amendment. That was the principal issue which was decided by the Ohio Supreme Court, which was tendered by appellant's Jurisdictional Statement, and which was briefed and argued in this Court.

In this posture of things, I think it fair to say that five members of this Court have simply "reached out" to overrule *Wolf.* . . .

Thus, if the Court was bent on reconsidering *Wolf,* I think that there would soon have presented itself an appropriate opportunity in which we could have had the benefit of full briefing and argument. In any event, at the very least, the present case should have been set down for reargument, in view of the inadequate briefing and argument we have received on the *Wolf* point. To all intents and purposes the Court's present action amounts to a summary reversal of *Wolf,* without argument.

I am bound to say that what has been done is not likely to promote respect either for the Court's adjudicatory process or for the stability of its decisions. Having been unable, however, to persuade any of the majority to a different procedural course, I now turn to the merits of the present decision.

II

. . . I would not impose upon the States this federal exclusionary remedy. The reasons given by the majority for now suddenly turning its back on *Wolf* seem to me notably unconvincing. . . .

Our concern here, as it was in *Wolf,* is not with the desirability of that rule but only with the question whether the States are Constitutionally free to follow it or not as they may themselves determine, and the relevance of the disparity of views among the States on this point lies simply in the fact that the judgment involved is a debatable one. . . .

The preservation of a proper balance between state and federal responsibility in the administration of criminal justice demands patience on the part of those who might like to see things move faster among the States in this respect. Problems of criminal law enforcement vary widely from State to State. One State, in considering the totality of its legal picture, may conclude that the need for embracing the *Weeks* rule is pressing because other remedies are unavailable or inadequate to secure compliance with the substantive Constitutional principle involved. Another, though equally solicitous of Constitutional rights, may choose to pursue one purpose at a time, allowing all evidence relevant to guilt to be brought into a criminal trial, and dealing with Constitutional infractions by other means. Still another may consider the exclusionary rule too rough and ready a remedy, in that it reaches only unconstitutional intrusions which eventuate in criminal prosecution of the victims. Further, a State after experimenting with the *Weeks* rule for a time may, because of unsatisfactory experience with it, decide to revert to a nonexclusionary rule. And so on. From the standpoint of Constitutional permissibility in pointing a State in one direction or another, I do not see at all why "time has set its face against" the considerations which led Mr. Justice Cardozo, then chief judge of the New York Court in *People* v. *Defore,* 242 N.Y. 13, to reject the *Weeks* exclusionary rule. For us the question remains, as it has always been, one of state power, not one of passing judgment on the wisdom of one state course or another. In my view this Court should continue to forbear from fettering the States with an adamant rule which may embarrass them in coping with their own peculiar problems in criminal law enforcement. . . .

Our role in promulgating the *Weeks* rule and extension . . . was quite a different one than it is here. There, in implementing the Fourth Amendment, we occupied the position of a tribunal having the ultimate responsibility for developing the standards and procedures of judicial administration within the judicial system over which it presides. Here we review State procedures whose measure is to be taken not against the specific substantive commands of the Fourth Amendment but under the flexible contours of the Due Process Clause. I do not believe that the Fourteenth Amendment empowers this Court to mold state remedies effectuating the right to freedom from "arbitrary intrusion by the police" to suit its own notions of how things should be done. . . .

A state conviction comes to us as the complete product of a sovereign judicial system. Typically a case will have been tried in a trial court, tested in some final appellate court, and will go no further. In the comparatively rare instance when a conviction is reviewed by us on due process grounds we deal then with a finished product in the creation of which we are allowed no hand, and our task, far from being one of over-all supervision, is, speaking generally, restricted to a determination of whether the prosecution was constitutionally fair. The specifics of trial procedure, which in every mature legal system will vary greatly in detail, are within the sole competence of the States. I do not see how it can be said that a trial becomes unfair simply because a State determines that evidence may be considered by the trier of fact, regardless of how it was obtained, if it is relevant to the one issue with which the trial is concerned, the guilt or innocence of the accused. Of course, a court may use its procedures as an incidental means of pursuing other ends than the correct resolution of the controversies before it. Such indeed is the *Weeks* rule, but if a State does not choose to use its courts in this way, I do not believe that this Court is empowered to impose this much-debated procedure on local courts, however efficacious we may consider the *Weeks* rule to be as a means of securing Constitutional rights. . . .

I regret that I find so unwise in principle and so inexpedient in policy a decision motivated by the high purpose of increasing respect for Constitutional rights. But in the last analysis I think this Court can increase respect for the Constitution only if it rigidly respects the limitations which the Constitution places upon it, and respects as well the principles inherent in its own processes. In the present case I think we exceed both, and that our voice becomes only a voice of power, not of reason.

MALLOY *v.* HOGAN

378 U.S. 1; 84 Sup. Ct. 1489; 12 L. Ed. 2d 653 (1964)

MR. JUSTICE BRENNAN delivered the opinion of the Court:

In this case we are asked to reconsider prior decisions holding that the privilege against self-incrimination is not safeguarded against state action by the Fourteenth Amendment. *Twining* v. *New Jersey, Adamson* v. *California.*

The petitioner was arrested during a gambling raid in 1959 by Hartford, Connecticut, police. He pleaded guilty to the crime of pool selling, a misdemeanor, and was sentenced to one year in jail and fined $500. The sentence was ordered to be suspended after ninety days, at which time he was to be placed on probation for two years. About sixteen months after his guilty plea, petitioner was ordered to testify before a referee appointed by the Superior Court of Hartford County to conduct an inquiry into alleged gambling and other criminal activities in the county. The petitioner was asked a number of questions related to events surrounding his arrest and conviction. He refused to answer any question "on the grounds it may tend to incriminate me." The Superior Court adjudged him in contempt and committed him to prison until he was willing to answer the questions. Petitioner's application for a writ of habeas corpus was denied by the Superior Court, and the Connecticut Supreme Court of Errors affirmed. 150 Conn. 220, 187 A.2d 744. The latter court held that the Fifth Amendment's privilege against self-incrimination was not available to a witness in a state proceeding, that the Fourteenth Amendment extended no privilege to him, and that the petitioner had not properly invoked the privilege available under the Connecticut Constitution. . . .

The Court has not hesitated to reexamine past decisions according the Fourteenth Amendment a less central role in the preservation of basic liberties than that which was contemplated by its Framers when they added the Amendment to our constitutional scheme. Thus, although the Court as late as 1922 said that "neither the Fourteenth Amendment nor any other provision of the Constitution of the United States imposes upon the States any restrictions about 'freedom of speech.' . . ." three years later *Gitlow* v. *New York*. . . initiated a series of decisions which today hold immune from state invasion every First Amendment protection for the cherished rights of mind and spirit—the freedoms of speech, press, religion, assembly, association, and petition for redress of grievances.

Similarly, *Palko* v. *Connecticut* . . . decided in 1937, suggested that the rights secured by the Fourth Amendment were not protected against state action, citing the statement of the Court in 1914 in *Weeks* v. *United States,* that "the Fourth Amendment is not directed to individual misconduct of [state] officials." In 1961, however, the Court held that in the light of later decisions, it was taken as settled that ". . . the Fourth Amendment's right of privacy has been declared enforceable against the States through the Due Process Clause of the Fourteenth. . . ." *Mapp* v. *Ohio*. . . . Again, although the Court held in 1942 that in a state prosecution for a noncapital offense, "appointment of counsel is not a fundamental right," *Betts* v. *Brady;* cf.

Powell v. *Alabama* . . . only last Term this decision was re-examined and it was held that provision of counsel in all criminal cases was "a fundamental right, essential to a fair trial," and thus was made obligatory on the States by the Fourteenth Amendment. *Gideon* v. *Wainwright*. . . .

We hold today that the Fifth Amendment's exception from compulsory self-incrimination is also protected by the Fourteenth Amendment against abridgment by the States. Decisions of the Court since Twining and Adamson have departed from the contrary view expressd in those cases. We discuss first the decisions which forbid the use of coerced confessions in state criminal prosecutions.

Brown v. *Mississippi* . . . was the first case in which the Court held that the Due Process Clause prohibited the States from using the accused's coerced confessions against him. The Court in Brown felt impelled, in light of Twining, to say that its conclusion did not involve the privilege against self-incrimination. "Compulsion by torture to extort a confession is a different matter." . . . But this distinction was soon abandoned, and today the admissibility of a confession in a state criminal prosecution is tested by the same standard applied in federal prosecutions since 1897, when, in *Bram* v. *United States*, . . . the Court held that "[i]n criminal trials, in the courts of the United States, wherever a question arises whether a confession is incompetent because not voluntary, the issue is controlled by that portion of the Fifth Amendment to the constitution of the United States commanding that no person 'shall be compelled in any criminal case to be a witness against himself.' " . . .

The marked shift to the federal standard in state cases began with *Lisenba* v. *California*, . . . where the Court spoke of the accused's "free choice to admit, to deny, or to refuse to answer." . . . See *Ashcraft* v. *Tennessee; Malinski* v. *New York; Spano* v. *New York; Lynumm* v. *Illinois; Haynes* v. *Washington*. . . . The shift reflects recognition that the American system of criminal prosecution is accusatorial, not inquisitorial, and that the Fifth Amendment privilege is its essential mainstay. *Rogers* v. *Richmond*. . . .

Governments, state and federal, are thus constitutionally compelled to establish guilt by evidence independently and freely secured, and may not by coercion prove a charge against an accused out of his own mouth. Since the Fourteenth Amendment prohibits the States from inducing a person to confess through "sympathy falsely aroused," *Spano* v. *New York*, . . . or other like inducement far short of "compulsion by torture," *Haynes* v. *Washington*, it follows *a fortiori* that it also forbids the States to resort to imprisonment, as here, to compel him to answer questions that might incriminate him. The Fourteenth Amendment secures against state invasion the same privilege that the Fifth Amendment guarantees against federal infringement—the right of a person to remain silent unless he chooses to speak in the unfettered exercise of his own will, and to suffer no penalty, as held in *Twining*, for such silence.

This conclusion is fortified by our recent decision in *Mapp* v. *Colorado*, . . . overruling *Wolf* v. *Colorado*, . . . which had held "that in a prosecution in a State court for a State crime the Fourteenth Amendment does not forbid the admission of evidence obtained by an unreasonable search and seizure." . . . *Mapp* held that the Fifth Amendment privilege against self-incrimination implemented the Fourth Amendment in such cases, and that the two guarantees of personal security conjoined in the Fourteenth Amendment to make the exclusionary rule obligatory upon the States. We relied upon the great case of *Boyd* v. *United States*, . . . decided in 1886, which, considering the Fourth and Fifth Amendments as running "almost into each other," . . . held that "Breaking into a house and opening boxes and drawers are circumstances of aggravation; but any forcible and compulsory extortion of a man's own testimony, or of his private papers to be used as evidence to convict him of crime, or to forfeit his goods, is within the condemnation of [those Amendments]. . . ." We said in *Mapp:*

> "We find that, as to the Federal Government Fourth and Fifth Amendments and, as to the States, the freedom from unconscionable invasions of privacy and the freedom from convictions based

upon coerced confessions do enjoy an 'intimate relation' in their perpetuation of 'principles of humanity and civil liberty [secured] . . . only after years of struggle.' . . . The philosophy of each Amendment and of each freedom is complementary to, although not dependent upon, that of the other in its sphere of influence—the very least that together they assure in either sphere is that no man is to be convicted on unconstitutional evidence." . . .

In thus returning to the *Boyd* view that the privilege is one of the "principles of a free government," . . . *Mapp* necessarily repudiated the *Twining* concept of the privilege as a mere rule of evidence "best defended not as an unchangeable principle of universal justice, but as a law proved by experience to be expedient." . . .

The State urges, however, that the availability of the federal privilege to a witness in a state inquiry is to be determined according to a less stringent standard than is applicable in a federal proceeding. We disagree. We have held that the guarantees of the First Amendment, *Gitlow* v. *New York; Cantwell* v. *Connecticut; Louisiana ex rel. Gremillion* v. *NAACP*, . . . the prohibition of unreasonable searches and seizures of the Fourth Amendment, *Ker* v. *California*, . . . and the right to counsel guaranteed by the Sixth Amendment, *Gideon* v. *Wainwright*, are all to be enforced against the States under the Fourteenth Amendment according to the same standards that protect those personal rights against federal encroachment. . . . The Court thus has rejected the notion that the Fourteenth Amendment applies to the States only a "watered-down, subjective version of the individual guarantees of the Bill of Rights." . . . If *Cohen* v. *Hurley* . . . and *Adamson* v. *California*, suggest such an application of the privilege against self-incrimination, that suggestion cannot survive recognition of the degree to which the *Twining* view of the privilege has been eroded. What is accorded is a privilege of refusing to incriminate one's self, and the feared prosecution may be by either federal or state authorities. *Murphy* v. *Waterfront Commission*. . . . It would be incongruous to have different standards determine the validity of a claim of privilege based on the same feared prosecution, depending on whether the claim was asserted in a state or federal court. Therefore, the same standards must determine whether an accused's silence in either a federal or state proceeding is justified.

It was admitted on behalf of the State at oral argument—and indeed it is obvious from the questions themselves—that the State desired to elicit from the petitioner the identity of the person who ran the pool-selling operation in connection with which he had been arrested in 1959. It was apparent that petitioner might apprehend that if this person were still engaged in unlawful activity, disclosure of his name might furnish a link in a chain of evidence sufficient to connect the petitioner with a more recent crime for which he might still be prosecuted. . . .

We conclude, therefore, that as to each of the questions, it was "evident from the implications of the question, in the setting in which it [was] asked, that a responsive answer to the question or an explanation of why it [could not] be answered might be dangerous because injurious disclosure could result," *Hoffman* v. *United States*. . . .

Reversed.

While MR. JUSTICE DOUGLAS joins the opinion of the Court, he also adheres to his concurrence in *Gideon* v. *Wainwright*. . . .

MR. JUSTICE HARLAN, whom MR. JUSTICE CLARK joins, dissenting:

. . . I can only read the Court's opinion as accepting in fact what it rejects in theory: the application to the States, via the Fourteenth Amendment, of the forms of federal criminal procedure embodied within the first eight Amendments to the Constitution. While it is true that the Court deals today with only one aspect of state criminal procedure, and rejects the wholesale "incorporation" of such federal constitutional requirements, the logical gap between the Court's premises and its novel constitutional conclusion can, I submit, be bridged only by the additional premise that the Due Process Clause of the Fourteenth Amendment is a shorthand directive to this Court to pick and choose among the provisions of the first eight Amendments and apply those chosen, freighted with their entire accompanying body of federal doctrine, to law enforcement in the States.

I accept and agree with the proposition that continuing re-examination of the constitutional conception of Fourteenth Amendment "due process" of law is required, and that development of the community's sense of justice may in time lead to expansion of the protection which due process affords. In particular in this case, I agree that principles of justice to which due process gives expression, as reflected in decisions of this Court, prohibit a State, as the Fifth Amendment prohibits the Federal Government, from imprisoning a person *solely* because he refuses to give evidence which may incriminate him under the laws of the State. I do not understand, however, how this process of re-examination, which must refer always to the guiding standard of due process of law, including, of course, reference to the particular guarantees of the Bill of Rights, can be shortcircuited by the simple device of incorporating into due process, without critical examination, the whole body of law which surrounds a specific prohibition directed against the Federal Government. The consequence of such an approach to due process as it pertains to the States is inevitably disregard of all relevant differences which may exist between state and federal criminal law and its enforcement. The ultimate result is compelled uniformity, which is inconsistent with the purpose of our federal system and which is achieved either by encroachment on the States' sovereign powers or by dilution in federal law enforcement of the specific protections found in the Bill of Rights.

As recently as 1961, this Court reaffirmed that "the Fifth Amendment's privilege against self-incrimination," . . . was not applicable against the States. *Cohen* v. *Hurley*. . . . The question had been most fully explored in *Twining* v. *New Jersey*. . . . Since 1908, when *Twining* was decided, this Court has adhered to the view there expressed that "the exemption from compulsory self-incrimination in the courts of the states is not secured by any part of the Federal Constitution" . . ; *Palko* v. *Connecticut; Adamson* v. *California; Knapp* v. *Schweitzer; Cohen,* supra. Although none of these cases involved a commitment to prison for refusing to incriminate oneself under state law, and they are relevantly distinguishable from this case on that narrow ground, it is perfectly clear from them that until today it has been regarded as settled law that the Fifth Amendment privilege did not, by any process of reasoning, apply *as such* to the States.

The Court suggests that this consistent line of authority has been undermined by the concurrent development of constitutional doctrine in the areas of coerced confessions and search and seizure. That is *post facto* reasoning at best. Certainly there has been no intimation until now that *Twining* has been tacitly overruled.

It was in *Brown* v. *Mississippi* that this Court first prohibited the use of a coerced confession in a state criminal trial. The petitioners in *Brown* had been tortured until they confessed. The Court was hardly making an artificial distinction when it said:

> "[T]he question of the right of the state to withdraw the privilege against self-incrimination is not here involved. The compulsion to which the quoted statements [from Twining and Snyder, supra,] refer is that of the *processes of justice* by which the accused may be called as a witness and required to testify. *Compulsion by torture* to extort a confession is a different matter." . . . (Emphasis supplied.)

The majority is simply wrong when it asserts that this perfectly understandable distinction "was soon abandoned," . . . In none of the cases cited, . . . in which was developed the full sweep of the constitutional prohibition against the use of coerced confessions at state trials, was there anything to suggest that the Fifth Amendment was being made applicable to state proceedings. In *Lisenba* v. *California* . . . the privilege against self-incrimination is not mentioned. The relevant question before the Court was whether "the evidence [of coercion] requires that we set aside the finding of two courts and a jury and adjudge the admission of the confessions so fundamentally unfair, so contrary to the common concept of ordered liberty as to amount to a taking of life without due process of law." . . . Finally, in *Rogers* v. *Richmond*, . . . although the Court did recognize that "ours is an accusatorial and not an inquisitorial system," . . . it is clear that the Court was concerned only with the problem of coerced confessions. . . ; the opinion includes nothing to support the Court's assertion here . . . that "the Fifth Amendment privilege is . . . [the] essential mainstay" of our system.

The coerced confession cases are relevant to the problem of this case not because they overruled *Twining sub silentio,* but rather because they applied the same standard of fundamental fairness which is applicable here. The recognition in them that federal supervision of state criminal procedures must be directly based on the requirements of due process is entirely inconsistent with the theory here espoused by the majority. The parallel treatment of federal and state cases involving coerced confessions resulted from the fact that the same demand of due process was applicable in both; it was not the consequence of the automatic engrafting of federal law construing constitutional provisions inapplicable to the States onto the Fourteenth Amendment.

The decision in *Mapp* v. *Ohio*, . . . that evidence unconstitutionally seized . . . may not be used in a state criminal trial furnishes no "fortification" . . . for today's decision. The very passage from the Mapp opinion which the Court quotes . . . makes explicit the distinct bases of the exclusionary rule as applied in federal and state courts:

> "We find that, as to the Federal Government, the Fourth and Fifth Amendments and, as to the States, the freedom from unconscionable invasions of privacy and the freedom from convictions based upon coerced confessions do enjoy an 'intimate relation' in their perpetuation of 'principles of humanity and civil liberty [secured] . . . only after years of struggle.' . . ."

Although the Court discussed *Boyd* v. *United States*, . . . a federal case involving both the Fourth and Fifth Amendments, nothing in *Mapp* supports the statement . . . that the Fifth Amendment was part of the basis for extending the exclusionary rule to the States. The elaboration of *Mapp* in *Ker* v. *California* . . . did in my view make the Fourth Amendment applicable to the States through the Fourteenth; but there is nothing in it to suggest that the Fifth Amendment went along as baggage.

The previous discussion shows that this Court's decisions do not dictate the "incorporation" of the Fifth Amendment's privilege against self-incrimination into the Fourteenth Amendment. Approaching the question more broadly, it is equally plain that the line of cases exemplified by *Palko* v. *Connecticut*, . . . in which this Court has reconsidered the requirements which the Due Process Clause imposes on the States in the light of current standards, furnishes no general theoretical framework for what the Court does today. . . .

Seen in proper perspective, therefore, the fact that First Amendment protections have generally been given equal scope in the federal and state domains or that in some areas of criminal procedure the Due Process Clause demands as much of the States as the Bill of Rights demands of the Federal Government, is only tangentially relevant to the question now before us. It is toying with constitutional principles to assert that the Court has "rejected the notion that the Fourteenth Amendment applies to the states only a 'watered-down, subjective version of the individual guarantees of the Bill of Rights' ". . . . What the Court has, with the single exception of the *Ker* case, . . . consistently rejected is the notion that the Bill of Rights, as such, applies to the States in any aspect at all.

If one attends to those areas to which the Court points, . . . in which the prohibitions against the state and federal governments have moved in parallel tracks, the cases in fact reveal again that the Court's usual approach has been to ground the prohibitions against state action squarely on due process, without intermediate reliance on any of the first eight Amendments. Although more recently the Court has referred to the First Amendment to describe the protection of free expression against state infringement, earlier cases leave no doubt that such references are "shorthand" for doctrines developed by another route.

In *Gitlow* v. *New York,* . . . for example, the Court said:

"For present purposes we may and do assume that freedom of speech and of the press—which are protected by the First Amendment from abridgment by Congress—are among the fundamental personal rights and 'liberties' protected by the due process clause of the Fourteenth Amendment from impairment by the States."

The coerced confession and search and seizure cases have already been considered. The former, decided always directly on grounds of fundamental fairness, furnish no support for the Court's present views. *Ker* v. *California,* did indeed incorporate the Fourth Amendment's protection against invasions of privacy into the Due Process Clause. But that case should be regarded as the exception which proves the rule. The right to counsel in state criminal proceedings, which this Court assured in *Gideon* v. *Wainwright*. . . does not depend on the Sixth Amendment. . . .

Although *Gideon* overruled *Betts,* the constitutional approach in both cases was the same. *Gideon* was based on the Court's conclusion, contrary to that reached in *Betts,* that the appointment of counsel for an indigent criminal defendant *was* essential to the conduct of a fair trial, and was therefore part of due process. . . .

The Court's approach in the present case is in fact nothing more or less than "incorporation" in snatches. If, however, the Due Process Clause *is* something more than a reference to the Bill of Rights and protects only those rights which derive from fundamental principles, as the majority purports to believe, it is just as contrary to precedent and just as illogical to incorporate the provisions of the Bill of Rights one at a time as it is to incorporate them all at once.

The Court's undiscriminating approach to the Due Process Clause carries serious implications for the sound working of our federal system in the field of criminal law.

The Court concludes, almost without discussion, that "the same standards must determine whether an accused's silence in either a federal or state proceeding is justified,". . . About all that the Court offers in explanation of this conclusion is the observation that it would be "incongruous" if different standards governed the assertion of a privilege to remain silent in state and federal tribunals. Such "incongruity," however, is at the heart of our federal system. The powers and responsibilities of the state and federal governments are not congruent; under our Constitution, they are not intended to be. Why should it be thought, as an *a priori* matter, that limitations on the investigative power of the States are in all respects identical with limitations on the investigative power of the Federal Government? . . .

As the Court pointed out in *Abbate* v. *United States,* . . . "the States under our federal system have the principal responsibility for defining and prosecuting crimes." The Court endangers this allocation of responsibility for the prevention of crime when it applies to the States doctrines developed in the context of federal law enforcement, without any attention to the special problems which the States as a group or particular States may face. If the power of the States to deal with local crime is unduly restricted, the likely consequence is a shift of responsibility in this area to the Federal Government, with its vastly greater resources. Such a shift, if it occurs, may in the end serve to weaken the very liberties which the Fourteenth Amendment safeguards by bringing us closer to the monolithic society which our federalism rejects. Equally dangerous to our liberties is the alternative of watering down protections against the Federal Government embodied in the Bill of Rights so as not unduly to restrict the powers of the States.

Rather than insisting, almost by rote, that the Connecticut court, in considering the petitioner's claim of privilege, was required to apply the "federal standard," the Court should have fulfilled its responsibility under the Due Process Clause by inquiring whether the proceedings below met the demands of fundamental fairness which due process embodies. Such an approach may not satisfy those who see in the Fourteenth Amendment a set of easily applied "absolutes" which can afford a haven from unsettling doubt. It is, however, truer to the spirit which requires this Court constantly to re-examine fundamental principles and at the same time enjoins it from reading its own preferences into the Constitution. . . . MR. JUSTICE WHITE, with whom MR. JUSTICE STEWART joins, dissenting:

The Fifth Amendment safeguards an important complex of values, but it is difficult for me to perceive how these values are served by the Court's holding that the privilege was properly invoked in this case. While purporting to apply the prevailing federal standard of incrimination—the same standard of incrimination that the Connecticut courts applied—the Court has all but stated that a witness' invocation of the privilege to any question is to be automatically, and without more, accepted. With deference, I prefer the rule permitting the judge rather than the witness to determine when an answer sought is incriminating.

The established rule has been that the witness' claim of the privilege is not final, for the privilege qualifies a citizen's general duty of disclosure only when his answers would subject him to danger from the criminal law. The privilege against self-incrimination or any other evidentiary privilege does not protect silence which is solely an expression of political protest, a desire not to inform, a fear of social obloquy or economic disadvantage or fear of prosecution for future crimes. *Smith* v. *United States.* . . . If the general duty to testify when subpoenaed is to remain and the privilege is to be retained as a protection against compelled incriminating answers, the trial judge must be permitted to make a meaningful determination of when answers tend to incriminate. . . .

GIDEON *v.* WAINWRIGHT

372 U.S. 335; 83 Sup. Ct. 792; 9 L. Ed. 2d 799 (1963)

MR. JUSTICE BLACK delivered the opinion of the Court:

Since 1942, when *Betts* v. *Brady,* 316 U.S. 455, was decided by a divided Court, the problem of a defendant's federal constitutional right to counsel in a state court has been a continuing source of controversy and litigation in both state and federal courts. To give this problem another review here, we granted certiorari. Since Gideon was proceeding in *forma pauperis,* we appointed counsel to represent him and requested both sides to discuss in their briefs and oral arguments the following: "Should this Court's holding in *Betts* v. *Brady* be reconsidered?"

The facts upon which Betts claimed that he had been unconstitutionally denied the right to have counsel appointed to assist him are strikingly like the facts upon which Gideon here bases his federal constitutional claim. Betts was indicted for robbery in a Maryland state court. On arraignment, he told the trial judge of his lack of funds to hire a lawyer and asked the court to appoint one for him. Betts was advised that it was not the practice in that county to appoint counsel for indigent defendants except in murder and rape cases. He then pleaded not guilty, had witnesses summoned, cross-examined the State's witnesses, examined his own, and chose not to testify himself. He was found guilty by the judge, sitting without a jury, and sentenced to eight years in prison. Like Gideon, Betts sought release by habeas corpus, alleging that he had been denied the right to assistance of counsel in violation of the Fourteenth Amendment. Betts was denied any relief, and on review this Court affirmed. It was held that a refusal to appoint counsel for an indigent defendant charged with a felony did not necessarily violate the Due Process Clause of the Fourteenth Amendment, which for reasons given the Court deemed to be the only applicable federal constitutional provision. The Court said:

> "Asserted denial [of due process] is to be tested by an appraisal of the totality of facts in a given case. That which may, in one setting, constitute a denial of fundamental fairness, shocking to the universal sense of justice, may, in other circumstances, and in the light of other considerations, fall short of such denial." 316 U.S. at 462.

Treating due process as "a concept less

rigid and more fluid than those envisaged in other specific and particular provisions of the Bill of Rights," the Court held that refusal to appoint counsel under the particular facts and circumstances in the *Betts* case was not so "offensive to the common and fundamental ideas of fairness" as to amount to a denial of due process. Since the facts and circumstances of the two cases are so nearly indistinguishable, we think the *Betts* v. *Brady* holding if left standing would require us to reject Gideon's claim that the Constitution guarantees him the assistance of counsel. Upon full reconsideration we conclude that *Betts* v. *Brady* should be overruled. . . .

We accept *Betts* v. *Brady's* assumption, based as it was in our prior cases, that a provision of the Bill of Rights which is "fundamental and essential to a fair trial" is made obligatory upon the States by the Fourteenth Amendment. We think the Court in *Betts* was wrong, however, in concluding that the Sixth Amendment's guarantee of counsel is not one of these fundamental rights. Ten years before *Betts* v. *Brady,* this Court, after full consideration of all the historical data examined in *Betts,* had unequivocally declared that "the right to the aid of counsel is of this fundamental character." *Powell* v. *Alabama,* 287 U.S. 45, 68 (1932). While the Court at the close of its Powell opinion did by its language, as this Court frequently does, limit its holding to the particular facts and circumstances of that case, its conclusions about the fundamental nature of the right to counsel are unmistakable. . . .

. . . The fact is that in deciding as it did—that "appointment of counsel is not a fundamental right, essential to a fair trial"—the Court in *Betts* v. *Brady* made an abrupt break with its own well-considered precedents. In returning to these old precedents, sounder we believe than the new, we but restore constitutional principles established to achieve a fair system of justice. Not only these precedents but also reason and reflection require us to recognize that in our adversary system of criminal justice any person haled into court, who is too poor to hire a lawyer, cannot be assured a fair trial unless counsel is provided for him. This seems to us to be an obvious truth. Governments, both state and federal, quite properly spend vast sums of money to establish machinery to try defendants accused of crime. Lawyers to prosecute are everywhere deemed essential to protect the public's interest in an orderly society.

Similarly, there are few defendants charged with crime, few indeed, who fail to hire the best lawyers they can get to prepare and present their defenses. That government hires lawyers to prosecute and defendants who have the money hire lawyers to defend are the strongest indications of the widespread belief that lawyers in criminal courts are necessities, not luxuries. The right of one charged with crime to counsel may not be deemed fundamental and essential to fair trials in some countries, but it is in ours. From the very beginning, our state and national constitutions and laws have laid great emphasis on procedural and substantive safeguards designed to assure fair trials before impartial tribunals in which every defendant stands equal before the law. This noble idea cannot be realized if the poor man charged with crime has to face his accusers without a lawyer to assist him. . . . The Court in *Betts* v. *Brady* departed from the sound wisdom upon which the Court's holding in *Powell* v. *Alabama* rested. Florida, supported by two other States, has asked that *Betts* v. *Brady* be left intact. Twenty-two States, as friends of the Court, argue that *Betts* was "an anachronism when handed down" and that it should now be overruled. We agree. . . .

Reversed.

MR. JUSTICE HARLAN, concurring:

I agree that *Betts* v. *Brady* should be overruled, but consider it entitled to a more respectful burial than has been accorded, at least on the part of those of us who were not on the Court when that case was decided.

I cannot subscribe to the view that *Betts* v. *Brady* represented "an abrupt break with its own well-considered precedents." In 1932, in *Powell* v. *Alabama,* a capital case, this Court declared that under the particular facts there presented—"the ignorance and illiteracy of the defendants, their youth, the circumstances of public hostility . . .

and above all that they stood in deadly peril of their lives". . . . the state court had a duty to assign counsel for the trial as a necessary requisite of due process of law. It is evident that these limiting facts were not added to the opinion as an afterthought; they were repeatedly emphasized . . . and were clearly regarded as important to the result.

Thus when this Court, a decade later, decided *Betts* v. *Brady,* it did no more than to admit of the possible existence of special circumstances in noncapital as well as capital trials, while at the same time to insist that such circumstances be shown in order to establish a denial of due process. . . .

The principles declared in *Powell* and in *Betts,* however, had a troubled journey throughout the years that have followed first the one case and then the other. . . . In the first decade after *Betts,* there were cases in which the Court found special circumstances to be lacking, but usually by a sharply divided vote. However, no such decision has been cited to us, and I have found none, after . . . 1950. At the same time, there have been not a few cases in which special circumstances were found in little or nothing more than the "complexity" of the legal questions presented, although those questions were often of only routine difficulty. The Court has come to recognize, in other words, that the mere existence of a serious criminal charge constituted in itself special circumstances requiring the services of counsel at trial. In truth the *Betts* v. *Brady* rule is no longer a reality.

. . . To continue a rule which is honored by this Court only with lip service is not a healthy thing and in the long run will do disservice to the federal system. . . .

. . . In what is done today I do not understand the Court to depart from the principles laid down in *Palko* v. *Connecticut,* 302 U.S. 319, or to embrace the concept that the Fourteenth Amendment "incorporates" the Sixth Amendment as such. . . .

MIRANDA *v.* ARIZONA

384 U.S. 436; 86 Sup. Ct. 1602; 16 L. Ed. 2d 694 (1966)

[Miranda consolidates for decision the cases of four persons convicted on the basis of confessions made after extended questioning in which they were not informed of their rights to counsel and to remain silent. The crimes of which they were found guilty included kidnapping, rape, robbery, and murder.]

MR. CHIEF JUSTICE WARREN delivered the opinion of the Court:

The cases before us raise questions which go to the roots of our concepts of American criminal jurisprudence: the restraints society must observe consistent with the Federal Constitution in prosecuting individuals for crime. More specifically, we deal with the admissibility of statements obtained from an individual who is subjected to custodial police interrogation and the necessity for procedures which assure that the individual is accorded his privilege under the Fifth Amendment to the Constitution not to be compelled to incriminate himself. . . .

Our holding will be spelled out with some specificity in the pages which follow but briefly stated it is this: the prosecution may not use statements, whether exculpatory or inculpatory, stemming from custodial interrogation of the defendant unless it demonstrates the use of procedural safeguards effective to secure the privilege against self-incrimination. By custodial interrogation, we mean questioning initiated by law enforcement officers after a person has been taken into custody or otherwise deprived of his freedom of action in any significant way.* As for the procedural safeguards to be employed, unless other fully effective means are devised to inform accused persons of their right of silence and to assure a continuous opportunity to exercise it, the following measures are required. Prior to any questioning, the person must

* This is what we meant in *Escobedo* when we spoke of an investigation which had focused on an accused.

be warned that he has a right to remain silent, that any statement he does make may be used as evidence against him, and that he has a right to the presence of an attorney, either retained or appointed. The defendant may waive effectuation of these rights, provided the waiver is made voluntarily, knowingly and intelligently. If, however, he indicates in any manner and at any stage of the process that he wishes to consult with an attorney before speaking there can be no questioning. Likewise, if the individual is alone and indicates in any manner that he does not wish to be interrogated, the police may not question him. The mere fact that he may have answered some questions or volunteered some statements on his own does not deprive him of the right to refrain from answering any further inquiries until he has consulted with an attorney and thereafter consents to be questioned.

I

The constitutional issue we decide in each of these cases is the admissibility of statements obtained from a defendant questioned while in custody and deprived of his freedom of action. In each, the defendant was questioned by police officers, detectives, or a prosecuting attorney in a room in which he was cut off from the outside world. In none of these cases was the defendant given a full and effective warning of his rights at the outset of the interrogation process. In all the cases, the questioning elicited oral admissions, and in three of them, signed statements as well which were admitted at their trials. They all thus share salient features—incommunicado interrogation of individuals in a police-dominated atmosphere, resulting in self-incriminating statements without full warnings of constitutional rights.

An understanding of the nature and setting of this in-custody interrogation is essential to our decisions today. The difficulty in depicting what transpires at such interrogations stems from the fact that in this country they have largely taken place incommunicado. From extensive factual studies undertaken in the early 1930s, including the famous Wickersham Report to Congress by a Presidential Commission, it is clear that police violence and the "third degree" flourished at that time. In a series of cases decided by this Court long after these studies, the police resorted to physical brutality—beatings, hanging, whipping—and to sustained and protracted questioning incommunicado in order to extort confessions. The 1961 Commission on Civil Rights found much evidence to indicate that "some policemen still resort to physical force to obtain confessions.". . . The use of physical brutality and violence is not, unfortunately, relegated to the past or to any part of the country. Only recently in Kings County, New York, the police brutally beat, kicked and placed lighted cigarette butts on the back of a potential witness under interrogation for the purpose of securing a statement incriminating a third party.

The examples given above are undoubtedly the exception now, but they are sufficiently widespread to be the object of concern. Unless a proper limitation upon custodial interrogation is achieved—such as these decisions will advance—there can be no assurance that practices of this nature will be eradicated in the foreseeable future. . . .

Again we stress that the modern practice of in-custody interrogation is psychologically rather than physically oriented. As we have stated before, "Since *Chambers* v. *Florida,* this Court has recognized that coercion can be mental as well as physical, and that the blood of the accused is not the only hallmark of an unconstitutional inquisition." *Blackburn* v. *Alabama.* Interrogation still takes place in privacy. Privacy results in secrecy and this in turn results in a gap in our knowledge as to what in fact goes on in the interrogation rooms. A valuable source of information about present police practices, however, may be found in various police manuals and texts which document procedures employed with success in the past, and which recommend various other effective tactics. These texts are used by law enforcement agencies themselves as guides. It should be noted that these texts professedly present the most enlightened and effective means presently used to obtain statements through custodial interrogation. By considering these texts, and other data, it is possible to describe procedures observed and noted around the country. . . .

From these representative samples of interrogation techniques, the setting prescribed by the manuals and observed in practice becomes clear. In essence, it is this: To be alone with the subject is essential to prevent distraction and to deprive him of any outside support. The aura of confidence in his guilt undermines his will to resist. He merely confirms the preconceived story the police seek to have him describe. Patience and persistence, at times relentless questioning, are employed. To obtain a confession, the interrogator must "patiently maneuver himself or his quarry into a position from which the desired object may be obtained." When normal procedures fail to produce the needed result, the police may resort to deceptive stratagems such as giving false legal advice. It is important to keep the subject off balance, for example, by trading on his insecurity about himself or his surroundings. The police then persuade, trick, or cajole him out of exercising his constitutional rights.

Even without employing brutality, the "third degree" or the specific stratagems described above, the very fact of custodial interrogation exacts a heavy toll on individual liberty and trades on the weakness of individuals. . . .

In the cases before us today, given this background, we concern ourselves primarily with this interrogation atmosphere and the evils it can bring. In No. 759, *Miranda* v. *Arizona,* the police arrested the defendant and took him to a special interrogation room where they secured a confession. In No. 760, *Vignera* v. *New York,* the defendant made oral admissions to the police after interrogation in the afternoon, and then signed an inculpatory statement upon being questioned by an assistant district attorney later the same evening. In No. 761, *Westover* v. *United States,* the defendant was handed over to the Federal Bureau of Investigation by local authorities after they had detained and interrogated him for a lengthy period, both at night and the following morning. After some two hours of questioning, the federal officers had obtained signed statements from the defendant. Lastly, in No. 584, *California* v. *Stewart,* the local police held the defendant five days in the station and interrogated him on nine separate occasions before they secured his inculpatory statement.

In these cases, we might not find the defendants' statements to have been involuntary in traditional terms. Our concern for adequate safeguards to protect precious Fifth Amendment rights is, of course, not lessened in the slightest. In each of the cases, the defendant was thrust into an unfamiliar atmosphere and run through menacing police interrogation procedures. The potentiality for compulsion is forcefully apparent for example, in *Miranda,* where the indigent Mexican defendant was a seriously disturbed individual with pronounced sexual fantasies, and in *Stewart,* in which the defendant was an indigent Los Angeles Negro who had dropped out of school in the sixth grade. To be sure, the records do not evince overt physical coercion or patented psychological ploys. The fact remains that in none of these cases did the officers undertake to afford appropriate safeguards at the outset of the interrogation to insure that the statements were truly the product of free choice.

It is obvious that such an interrogation environment is created for no purpose other than to subjugate the individual to the will of his examiner. This atmosphere carries its own badge of intimidation. To be sure, this is not physical intimidation, but it is equally destructive of human dignity. The current practice of incommunicado interrogation is at odds with one of our Nation's most cherished principles—that the individual may not be compelled to incriminate himself. Unless adequate protective devices are employed to dispel the compulsion inherent in custodial surroundings, no statement obtained from the defendant can truly be the product of his free choice.

From the foregoing, we can readily perceive an intimate connection between the privilege against self-incrimination and police custodial questioning. . . .

II

. . . As a "noble principle often transcends its origins," the privilege has come rightfully to be recognized in part as an individual's substantive right, a "right to a private enclave where he may lead a private life. That right is the hallmark of our democracy.". . . We have recently noted that the privilege against self-incrimination—the essential mainstay of our adversary system—is founded on a complex of values. . . . All these policies point to one overriding thought: the constitutional foundation underlying the privilege is the respect a government—state or federal—must accord to the dignity and integrity of its citizens. To maintain a "fair state-individual balance," to require the government "to shoulder the entire load,". . . to respect the inviolability of the human personality, our accusatory system of criminal justice demands that the government seeking to punish an individual produce the evidence against him by its own independent labors, rather than by the cruel, simple expedient of compelling it from his own mouth. . . . In sum, the privilege is fulfilled only when the person is guaranteed the right "to remain silent unless he chooses to speak in the unfettered exercise of his own will.". . .

The question in these cases is whether the privilege is fully applicable during a period of custodial interrogation. . . . We are satisfied that all the principles embodied in the privilege apply to informal compulsion exerted by law-enforcement officers during in-custody questioning. An individual swept from familiar surroundings into police custody, surrounded by antagonistic forces, and subjected to the techniques of persuasion described above cannot be otherwise than under compulsion to speak. As a practical matter, the compulsion to speak in the isolated setting of the police station may well be greater than in courts or other official investigations, where there are often impartial observers to guard against intimidation or trickery. . . .

Our decision in *Malloy* v. *Hogan,* necessitates an examination of the scope of the privilege in state cases as well. In *Malloy,* we squarely held the privilege applicable to the States, and held that the substantive standards underlying the privilege applied with full force to state court proceedings. There, as in *Murphy* v. *Waterfront Commission,* and *Griffin* v. *California,* we applied the existing Fifth Amendment standards to the case before us. Aside from the holding itself, the reasoning in *Malloy* made clear what had already become apparent—that the substantive and procedural safeguards surrounding admissibility of confessions in state cases had become exceedingly exacting, reflecting all the policies embedded in the privilege. The voluntariness doctrine in the state cases, as *Malloy* indicates, encompasses all interrogation practices which are likely to exert such pressure upon an individual as to disable him from making a free and rational choice. The implications of this proposition were elaborated in our decision in *Escobedo* v. *Illinois* decided one week after *Malloy* applied the privilege to the States.

Our holding there stressed the fact that the police had not advised the defendant of his constitutional privilege to remain silent at the outset of the interrogation and we drew attention to that fact at several points in the decision. This was no isolated factor, but an essential ingredient in our decision. The entire thrust of police interrogation there, as in all the cases today, was to put the defendant in such an emotional state as to impair his capacity for rational judgment. The abdication of the constitutional privilege—the choice on his part to speak to the police—was not made knowingly or competently because of the failure to apprise him of his rights; the compelling atmosphere of the in-custody interrogation, and not an independent decision on his part, caused the defendant to speak.

A different phase of the *Escobedo* decision was significant in its attention to the absence of counsel during the questioning. There, as in the cases today, we sought a protective device to dispel the compelling atmosphere of the interrogation. In *Escobedo,* however, the police did not relieve the defendant of the anxieties which they had created in the interrogation rooms. Rather, they denied his request for the assistance of counsel. This heightened his dilemma, and made his later statements the product of this compulsion. The denial of the defendant's request for his attorney thus undermined his ability to exercise the privilege—to remain silent if he chose or to speak without any intimidation, blatant or subtle. The presence of counsel, in all the cases before us today, would be the adequate protective device necessary to make the process of police interrogation conform to the dictates of the privilege. His presence would insure that statements made in the government-established atmosphere are not the product of compulsion.

It was in this manner that *Escobedo* explicated another facet of the pretrial privilege, noted in many of the Court's prior decisions: the protection of rights at trial. That counsel is present when statements are taken from an individual during interrogation obviously enhances the integrity of the fact-finding processes in court. The presence of an attorney, and the warnings delivered to the individual, enable the defendant under otherwise compelling circumstances to tell his story without fear, effectively, and in a way that eliminates the evils in the interrogation process. . . .

III

At the outset, if a person in custody is to be subjected to interrogation, he must first be informed in clear and unequivocal terms that he has the right to remain silent. For those unaware of the privilege, the warning is needed simply to make them aware of it—the threshold requirement for an intelligent decision as to its exercise. More important, such a warning is an absolute prerequisite in overcoming the inherent pressures of the interrogation atmosphere. It is not just the subnormal or woefully ignorant who succumb to an interrogator's imprecations, whether implied or expressly stated, that the interrogation will continue until a confession is obtained or that silence in the face of accusation is itself damning and will bode ill when presented to a jury. Further, the warning will show the individual that his interrogators are prepared to recognize his privilege should he choose to exercise it.

The Fifth Amendment privilege is so fundamental to our system of constitutional rule and the expedient of giving an adequate warning as to the availability of the privilege so simple, we will not pause to inquire in individual cases whether the defendant was aware of his rights without a warning being given. Assessments of the knowledge the defendant possessed, based on information as to his age, education, intelligence, or prior contact with authorities, can never be more than speculation; a warning is a clearcut fact. More important, whatever the background of the person interrogated, a warning at the time of the interrogation is indispensable to overcome its pressures and to insure that the individual knows he is free to exercise the privilege at that point in time.

The warning of the right to remain silent must be accompanied by the explanation that anything said can and will be used against the individual in court. This warning is needed in order to make him aware not only of the privilege, but also of the consequences of foregoing it. It is only through an awareness of these consequences that there can be any assurance of real understanding and intelligent exercise of the privilege. Moreover, this warning may serve to make the individual more acutely aware that he is faced with a phase of the adversary system—that he is not in the presence of persons acting solely in his interest.

The circumstances surrounding in-custody interrogation can operate very quickly to overbear the will of one merely made aware of his privilege by his interrogators. Therefore, the right to have counsel present at the interrogation is indispensable to the protection of the Fifth Amendment privilege under the system we delineate today. Our aim is to assure that the individual's right to choose between silence and speech remains unfettered throughout the interrogation process. A once-stated warning, delivered by those who will conduct the interrogation, cannot itself suffice to that end among those who most require knowledge of their rights. A mere warning given by the interrogators is not alone sufficient to accomplish that end. Prosecutors themselves claim that the admonishment of the right to remain silent without more "will benefit only the recidivist and the professional.". . . Even preliminary advice given to the accused by his own attorney can be swiftly overcome by the secret interrogation process. . . . Thus, the need for counsel to protect the Fifth Amendment privilege comprehends not merely a right to consult with counsel prior to questioning, but also to have counsel present during any questioning if the defendant so desires. . . .

An individual need not make a preinterrogation request for a lawyer. While such request affirmatively secures his right to have one, his failure to ask for a lawyer does not constitute a waiver. No effective waiver of the right to counsel during interrogation can be recognized unless specifically made after the warnings we here delineate have been given. The accused who does not know his rights and therefore does not make a request may be the person who most needs counsel. . . .

Accordingly we hold that an individual held for interrogation must be clearly informed that he has the right to consult with a lawyer and to have the lawyer with him during interrogation under the system for protecting the privilege we delineate today. As with the warnings of the right to remain silent and that anything stated can be used in evidence against him, this warning is an absolute prerequisite to interrogation. No amount of circumstantial evidence that the person may have been aware of his right will suffice to stand in its stead. Only through such a warning is there ascertainable assurance that the accused was aware of this right.

If an individual indicates that he wishes the assistance of counsel before any interrogation occurs, the authorities cannot rationally ignore or deny his request on the basis that the individual does not have or cannot afford a retained attorney. The financial ability of the individual has no relationship to the scope of the rights involved here. The privilege against self-incrimination secured by the Constitution applies to all individuals. The need for counsel in order to protect the privilege exists for the indigent as well as the affluent. In fact, were we to limit these constitutional rights to those who can retain an attorney, our decisions today would be of little significance. The cases before us as well as the vast majority of confession cases with which we have dealt in the past involve those unable to retain counsel. While authorities are not required to relieve the accused of his poverty, they have the obligation not to take advantage of indigence in the administration of justice. Denial of counsel to the indigent at the time of interrogation while allowing an attorney to those who can afford one would be no more supportable by reason or logic than the similar situation at trial and on appeal struck down in *Gideon* v. *Wainwright*. . . .

In order fully to apprise a person interrogated of the extent of his rights under this system then, it is necessary to warn him not only that he has the right to consult with an attorney, but also that if he is indigent a lawyer will be appointed to represent him. Without this additional warning, the admonition of the right to consult with counsel would often be understood as meaning only that he can consult with a lawyer if he has one or has the funds to obtain one. The warning of a right to counsel would be hollow if not couched in terms that would convey to the indigent—the person most often subjected to interrogation—the knowledge that he too has a right to have counsel present. As with the warnings of the right to remain silent and of the general right to counsel, only by effective and express explanation to the indigent of this right can there be assurance that he was truly in a position to exercise it.

Once warnings have been given, the subsequent procedure is clear. If the individual indicates in any manner, at any time prior to or during questioning, that he wishes to remain silent, the interrogation must cease. At this point he has shown that he intends to exercise his Fifth Amendment privilege; any statement taken after the person invokes his privilege cannot be other than the product of compulsion, subtle or otherwise. Without the right to cut off questioning, the setting of in-custody interrogation operates on the individual to overcome free choice in producing a statement after the privilege has been once invoked. If the individual states that he wants an attorney, the interrogation must cease until an attorney is present. At that time, the individual must have an opportunity to confer with the attorney and to have him present during any subsequent questioning. If the individual cannot obtain an attorney and he indicates that he wants one before speaking to police, they must respect his decision to remain silent. . . .

An express statement that the individual is willing to make a statement and does not want an attorney followed closely by a statement could constitute a waiver. But a valid waiver will not be presumed simply from the silence of the accused after warnings are given or simply from the fact that a confession was in fact eventually obtained. . . .

Whatever the testimony of the authorities as to waiver of rights by an accused, the fact of lengthy interrogation or incommunicado incarceration before a statement is made is strong evidence that the accused did not validly waive his rights. In these circumstances the fact that the individual eventually made a statement is consistent with the conclusion that the compelling influence of the interrogation finally forced him to do so. It is inconsistent with any notion of a voluntary relinquishment of the privilege. Moreover, any evidence that the accused was threatened, tricked, or cajoled into a waiver will, of course, show that the defendant did not voluntarily waive his privilege. The requirement of warnings and waiver of rights is a fundamental with respect to the Fifth Amendment privilege and not simply a preliminary ritual to existing methods of interrogation.

The warnings required and the waiver necessary in accordance with our opinion today are, in the absence of a fully effective equivalent, prerequisites to the admissibility of any statement made by a defendant. . . .

The principles announced today deal with the protection which must be given to the privilege against self-incrimination when the individual is first subjected to police interrogation while in custody at the station or otherwise deprived of his freedom of action in any way. It is at this point that our adversary system of criminal proceedings commences, distinguishing itself at the outset from the inquisitorial system recognized in some countries. Under the system of warnings we delineate today or under any other system which may be devised and found effective, the safeguards to be erected about the privilege must come into play at this point. . . .

In dealing with statements obtained through interrogation, we do not purport to find all confessions inadmissible. Confessions remain a proper element in law enforcement. Any statement given freely and voluntarily without any compelling influences is, of course, admissible in evidence. The fundamental import of the privilege while an individual is in custody is not whether he is allowed to talk to the police without the benefit of warnings and counsel, but whether he can be interrogated. There is no requirement that police stop a person who enters a police station and states that he wishes to confess to a crime, or a person who calls the police to offer a confession or any other statement he desires to make. Volunteered statements of any kind are not barred by the Fifth Amendment and their admissibility is not affected by our holding today. . . .

Because of the nature of the problem and because of its recurrent significance in numerous cases, we have to this point discussed the relationship of the Fifth Amendment privilege to police interrogation without specific concentration on the facts of the cases before us. We turn now to these facts to consider the application to these cases of the constitutional principles discussed above. In each instance, we have concluded that statements were obtained from the defendant under circumstances that did not meet constitutional standards for protection of the privilege.*[Mr. Justice Clark dissented in part. Mr. Justice Harlan, whom Mr. Justice Stewart and Mr. Justice White joined, dissented.*

Mr. Justice White, with whom Mr. Justice Harlan and Mr. Justice Stewart joined, dissented.]

HOFFA *v.* UNITED STATES

385 U.S. 293; 87 Sup. Ct. 408; 18 L. Ed. 2d 738 (1966)

MR. JUSTICE STEWART delivered the opinion of the Court:

Over a period of several weeks in the late autumn of 1962 there took place in a federal court in Nashville, Tennessee, a trial by jury in which James Hoffa was charged with violating a provision of the Taft-Hartley Act. That trial, known in the present record as the Test Fleet trial, ended with a hung jury. The petitioners now before us—James Hoffa, Thomas Parks, Larry Campbell, and Ewing King—were tried and convicted in 1964 for endeavoring to bribe members of that jury. The convictions were affirmed by the Court of Appeals. A substantial element in the Government's proof that led to the convictions of these four petitioners was contributed by a witness named Edward Partin, who testified to several incriminating statements which he said petitioners Hoffa and King had made in his presence during the course of the Test Fleet trial. Our grant of certiorari was limited to the single issue of whether the Government's use in this case of evidence supplied by Partin operated to invalidate these convictions. . . .

The controlling facts can be briefly stated. The Test Fleet trial, in which James Hoffa was the sole individual defendant, was in progress between October 22 and December 23, 1962, in Nashville, Tennessee. James Hoffa was president of the International Brotherhood of Teamsters. During the course of the trial he occupied a three-room suite in the Andrew Jackson Hotel in Nashville. One of his constant companions throughout the trial was the petitioner King, president of the Nashville local of the Teamsters Union. Edward Partin, a resident of Baton Rouge, Louisiana, and a local Teamsters Union official there, made repeated visits to Nashville during the period of the trial. On these visits he frequented the Hoffa hotel suite, and was continually in the company of Hoffa and his associates, including King, in and around the hotel suite, the hotel lobby, the courthouse, and elsewhere in Nashville. During this period Partin made frequent reports to a federal agent named Sheridan concerning conversations he said Hoffa and King had had with him and with each other, disclosing endeavors to bribe members of the Test Fleet jury. Partin's reports and his subsequent testimony at the petitioners' trial unquestionably contributed, directly or indirectly, to the convictions of all four of the petitioners. . . . we proceed upon the premise that Partin was a government informer from the time he first arrived in Nashville on October 22, and that the Government compensated him for his services as such. It is upon that premise that we consider the constitutional issues presented. . . .

It is contended that only by violating the petitioner's rights under the Fourth Amendment was Partin able to hear the petitioner's incriminating statements in the hotel suite, and that Partin's testimony was therefore inadmissible under the exclusionary rule of *Weeks* v. *United States*. . . . The argument is that Partin's failure to disclose his role as a government informer vitiated the consent that the petitioner gave to Partin's repeated entries into the suite, and that by listening to the petitioner's statements Partin conducted an illegal "search" for verbal evidence.

The preliminary steps of this argument are on solid ground. A hotel room can clearly be the object of Fourth Amendment protection as much as a home or an office. . . . The Fourth Amendment can certainly be violated by guileful as well as by forcible intrusions into a constitutionally protected area. . . . And the protections of the Fourth Amendment are surely not limited to tangibles, but can extend as well to oral statements. *Silverman* v. *United States*. . . .

In the present case, however, it is evident that no interest legitimately protected by the Fourth Amendment is involved. It is obvious that the petitioner was not relying on the security of his hotel suite when he made the incriminating statements to Partin or in Partin's presence. Partin did not enter the suite by force or by stealth. He was not a surreptitious eavesdropper. Partin was in the suite by invitation, and every conversation which he heard was either directed to him or knowingly carried on in his presence. The petitioner, in a word, was not relying on the security of the hotel room; he was relying upon his misplaced confidence that Partin would not reveal his wrongdoing. . . .

Neither this Court nor any member of it has ever expressed the view that the Fourth Amendment protects a wrongdoer's misplaced belief that a person to whom he voluntarily confides his wrongdoing will not reveal it. Indeed, the Court unanimously rejected that very contention less than four years ago in *Lopez* v. *United States*. . . . In that case the petitioner had been convicted of attempted bribery of an internal revenue agent named Davis. The Court was divided with regard to the admissibility in evidence of a surreptitious electronic recording of an incriminating conversation Lopez had had in the private office with Davis. But there was no dissent to the view that testimony about the conversation by Davis himself was clearly admissible. . . .

Adhering to these views, we hold that no right protected by the Fourth Amendment was violated in the present case.

The petitioner argues that his right under the Fifth Amendment not to "be compelled in any criminal case to be a witness against himself" was violated by the admission of Partin's testimony. The claim is without merit.

There have been sharply differing views within the Court as to the ultimate reach of the Fifth Amendment right against compulsory self-incrimination. Some of those differences were aired last Term in *Miranda* v. *State of Arizona*. . . . But since at least as long ago as 1807, when Chief Justice Marshall first gave attention to the matter in the trial of Aaron Burr, all have agreed that a necessary element of compulsory self-incrimination is some kind of compulsion. Thus, in the *Miranda* case, dealing with the Fifth Amendment's impact upon police interrogation of persons in custody, the Court predicated its decision upon the conclusion "that without proper safeguards the process of in-custody interrogation of persons suspected or accused of crime contains inherently compelling pressures which work to undermine the individual's will to resist and to compel him to speak where he would not otherwise do so freely.". . .

In the present case no claim has been or could be made that the petitioner's incriminating statements were the product of any sort of coercion, legal or factual. The petitioner's conversations with Partin and in Partin's presence were wholly voluntary. For that reason, if for no other, it is clear that no right protected by the Fifth Amendment privilege against compulsory self-incrimination was violated in this case.

The petitioner's second argument under the Sixth Amendment needs no extended discussion. That argument goes as follows: Not later than October 25, 1962, the Government had sufficient ground for taking the petitioner into custody and charging him with endeavors to tamper with the Test Fleet jury. Had the Government done so, it could not have continued to question the petitioner without observance of his Sixth Amendment right to counsel. *Massiah* v. *United States* . . . ; *Escobedo* v. *State of Illinois*. . . . Therefore, the argument concludes, evidence of statements made by the petitioner subsequent to October 25 was inadmissible, because the Government acquired that evidence only by flouting the petitioner's Sixth Amendment right to counsel.

Nothing in *Massiah,* in *Escobedo,* or in any other case that has come to our attention, even remotely suggests this novel and paradoxical constitutional doctrine, and we decline to adopt it now. There is no constitutional right to be arrested. The police are not required to guess at their peril the precise moment at which they have probable cause to arrest a suspect, risking a violation of the Fourth Amendment if they act too soon, and a violation of the Sixth Amendment if they wait too long. Law enforcement officers are under no constitutional duty to call a halt to a criminal investigation the moment they have the minimum evidence to establish probable cause, a quantum of evidence which may fall far short of the amount necessary to support a criminal conviction.

Affirmed.

[Mr. Justice White and Mr. Justice Fortas took no part. Mr. Chief Justice Warren dissented. Mr. Justice Clark and Mr. Justice Douglas would have dismissed the writ of certiorari as improvidently granted.]

KATZ *v.* UNITED STATES

389 U.S. 347; 88 Sup. Ct. 507; 19 L. Ed. 2d 576 (1967)

MR. JUSTICE STEWART delivered the opinion of the Court:

The petitioner was convicted in the District Court for the Southern District of California under an eight-count indictment charging him with transmitting wagering information by telephone from Los Angeles to Miami and Boston in violation of a federal statute. At trial the Government was permitted, over the petitioner's objection, to introduce evidence of the petitioner's end of telephone conversations, overheard by FBI agents who had attached an electronic listening and recording device to the outside of the public telephone booth from which he had placed his calls. In affirming his conviction, the Court of Appeals rejected the contention that the recordings had been obtained in violation of the Fourth Amendment, because "[t]here was no physical entrance into the area occupied by, [the petitioner]." The correct solution of Fourth Amendment problems is not necessarily promoted by incantation of the phrase "constitutionally protected area." Secondly, the Fourth Amendment cannot be translated into a general constitutional "right to privacy." That Amendment, protects individual privacy against certain kinds of governmental intrusion, but its protections go further, and often have nothing to do with privacy at all. Other provisions of the Constitution protect personal privacy from other forms of governmental invasion. But the protection of a person's *general* right to privacy—his right to be let alone by other people—is, like the protection of his property and of his very life, left largely to the law of the individual States. . . . The petitioner has strenuously argued that the booth was a "constitutionally protected area." The Government has maintained with equal vigor that it was not. But this effort to decide whether or not a given "area," viewed in the abstract, is "constitutionally protected" deflects attention from the problem presented by this case. For the Fourth Amendment protects people, not places. What a person knowingly exposes to the public, even in his own home or office, is not a subject of Fourth Amendment protection. . . . But what he seeks to preserve as private, even in an area accessible to the public, may be constitutionally protected. . . . No less than an individual in a business office, in a friend's apartment, or in a taxicab, a person in a telephone booth may rely upon the protection of the Fourth Amendment. One who occupies it, shuts the door behind him, and pays the toll that permits him to place a call, is surely entitled to assume that the words he utters into the mouthpiece will not be broadcast to the world. To read the Constitution more narrowly is to ignore the vital role that the public telephone has come to play in private communication.

The Government contends, however, that the activities of its agents in this case should not be tested by Fourth Amendment requirements, for the surveillance technique they employed involved no physical penetration of the telephone booth from which the petitioner placed his calls. It is true that the absence of such penetration was at one time thought to foreclose further Fourth Amendment inquiry, *Olmstead* v. *United States* . . . ; *Goldman* v. *United States,* for that Amendment was thought to limit only searches and seizures of tangible property. But "[t]he premise that property interests control the right of the Government to search and seize has been discredited." *Warden, Md. Penitentiary* v. *Hayden*. . . . Thus, although a closely divided Court supposed in *Olmstead* that surveillance without any trespass and without the seizure of any material object fell outside the ambit of the Constitution, we have since departed from the narrow view on which that decision rested. Indeed, we have expressly held that the Fourth Amendment governs not only the seizure of tangible items, but extends as well to the recording of oral statements overheard without any "technical trespass under . . . local property law." *Silverman* v. *United States.* . . . Once this much is acknowledged, and once it is recognized that the Fourth Amendment protects people—and not simply "areas"—against unreasonable searches and seizures it becomes clear that the reach of that Amendment cannot turn upon the presence or absence of a physical intrusion into any given enclosure.

We conclude that the underpinnings of *Olmstead* and *Goldman* have been so eroded by our subsequent decisions that the "trespass" doctrine there enunciated can no longer be regarded as controlling. The Government's activities in electronically listening to and recording the petitioner's words violated the privacy upon which he justifiably relied while using the telephone booth and thus constituted a "search and seizure" within the meaning of the Fourth

Amendment. The fact that the electronic device employed to achieve that end did not happen to penetrate the wall of the booth can have no constitutional significance. . . . It is clear that this surveillance was so narrowly circumscribed that a duly authorized magistrate, properly notified of the need for such investigation, specifically informed of the basis on which it was to proceed, and clearly apprised of the precise intrusion it would entail, could constitutionally have authorized, with appropriate safeguards, the very limited search and seizure that the Government asserts in fact took place. Only last Term we sustained the validity of such an authorization, holding that, under sufficiently "precise and discriminate circumstances," a federal court may empower government agents to employ a concealed electronic device "for the narrow and particularized purpose of ascertaining the truth of the . . . allegations" of a "detailed factual affidavit alleging the commission of a specific criminal offense." *Osborn* v. *United States*. . . . Discussing that holding, the Court, in *Berger* v. *State of New York*, . . . said that "the order authorizing the use of the electronic device" in *Osborn* "afforded similar protections to those . . . of conventional warrants authorizing the seizure of tangible evidence." Through those protections, "no greater invasion of privacy was permitted than was necessary under the circumstances.". . . Here, too, a similar judicial order could have accommodated "the legitimate needs of law enforcement" by authorizing the carefully limited use of electronic surveillance.

In the absence of such safeguards, this Court has never sustained a search upon the sole ground that officers reasonably expected to find evidence of a particular crime and voluntarily confined their activities to the least intrusive means consistent with that end. . . . The Government . . . urges the creation of a new exception to cover this case. It argues that surveillance of a telephone booth should be exempted from the usual requirement of advance authorization by a magistrate upon a showing of probable cause. We cannot agree. Omission of such authorization "bypasses the safeguards provided by an objective predetermination of probable cause, and substitutes instead the far less reliable procedure of an after-the-event justification for the . . . search, too likely to be subtly influenced by the familiar shortcomings of hindsight judgment." *Beck* v. *State of Ohio,* 379 U.S. 89, 96. . . . The government agents here ignored "the procedure of antecedent justification . . . that is central to the Fourth Amendment," a procedure that we hold to be a constitutional precondition of the kind of electronic surveillance involved in this case. Because the surveillance here failed to meet that condition, and because it led to the petitioner's conviction, the judgment must be reversed. *[Mr. Justice Marshall took no part. Justices Douglas, Brennan, Harlan, and White concurred. Mr. Justice Black dissented.]*

CHIMEL *v.* CALIFORNIA

395 U.S. 752; 89 Sup. Ct. 2034; 23 L. Ed. 2d 685 (1969)

MR. JUSTICE STEWART delivered the opinion of the Court:

This case raises basic questions concerning the permissible scope under the Fourth Amendment of a search incident to a lawful arrest.

The relevant facts are essentially undisputed. Late in the afternoon of September 13, 1965, three police officers arrived at the Santa Ana, California, home of the petitioner with a warrant authorizing his arrest for the burglary of a coin shop. The officers knocked on the door, identified themselves to the petitioner's wife, and asked if they might come inside. She ushered them into the house, where they waited ten or fifteen minutes until the petitioner returned home from work. When the petitioner entered the house, one of the officers handed him the arrest warrant and asked for permission to "look around." The petitioner objected, but was advised that "on the basis of the lawful arrest," the officers would nonetheless conduct a search. No search warrant had been issued.

Accompanied by the petitioner's wife, the officers then looked through the entire three-bedroom house, including the attic, the garage, and a small workshop. In some rooms the search was relatively cursory. In the master bedroom and sewing room, however, the officers directed the petitioner's wife to open drawers and "to physically move contents of the drawers from side to side so that [they] might view any items that would have come from [the] burglary." After completing the search, they seized numerous items—primarily coins, but also several medals, tokens, and a few other objects. The entire search took between forty-five minutes and an hour.

At the petitioner's subsequent state trial on two charges of burglary, the items taken from his house were admitted into evidence against him, over his objection that they had been unconstitutionally seized. . . .

Approval of a warrantless search incident to a lawful arrest seems first to have been articulated by the Court in 1914 as dictum in *Weeks* v. *United States* . . . in which the Court stated:

> "What then is the present case? Before answering that inquiry specifically, it may be well by a process of exclusion to state what it is not. It is not an assertion of the right on the part of the Government, always recognized under English and American law, to search the person of the accused when legally arrested to discover and seize the fruits or evidences of crime.". . .

That statement made no reference to any right to search the *place* where an arrest occurs, but was limited to a right to search the "person." Eleven years later the case of *Carroll* v. *United States,* brought the following embellishment of the *Weeks* statement:

> "When a man is legally arrested for an offense, whatever is found upon his person *or in his control* which it is unlawful for him to have and which may be used to prove the offense, may be seized and held as evidence in the prosecution."

Still, that assertion too was far from a claim that the "place" where one is arrested may be searched so long as the arrest is valid. Without explanation, however, the principle emerged in expanded form a few months later in *Agnello* v. *United States* . . . although still by way of dictum:

> "The right without a search warrant contemporaneously to search persons lawfully arrested while committing crime and to search the place where the arrest is made in order to find and seize things connected with the crime as its fruits or as the means by which it was committed, as well as weapons and other things to effect an escape from custody, is not to be doubted."

And in *Marron* v. *United States* . . . two years later, the dictum of *Agnello* appeared to be the foundation of the Court's decision. In that case federal agents had secured a search warrant authorizing the seizure of liquor and certain articles used in its manufacture. When they arrived at the premises to be searched, they saw "that the place was used for retailing and drinking intoxicating liquors.". . . They proceeded to arrest the person in charge and to execute the warrant. In searching a closet for the items listed in the warrant they came across an incriminating ledger, concededly not covered by the warrant, which they also seized. The Court upheld the seizure of the ledger by holding that since the agents had made a lawful arrest, "[t]hey had a right without a warrant contemporaneously to search the place in order to find and seize the things used to carry on the criminal enterprise.". . .

That the *Marron* opinion did not mean all that it seemed to say became evident, however, a few years later in *Go-Bart Importing Co.* v. *United States,* . . . and *United States* v. *Lefkowitz.* . . . In each of those cases the opinion of the Court was written by Mr. Justice Butler, who had authored the opinion in *Marron.* In *Go-Bart,* agents had searched the office of persons whom they had lawfully arrested, and had taken several papers from a desk, a safe, and other parts of the office. The Court noted that no crime had been committed in the agent's presence, and that although the agent in charge "had an abundance of information and time to swear out a valid [search] warrant, he failed to do so.". . .

In holding the search and seizure unlawful, the Court stated:

"Plainly the case before us is essentially different from *Marron* v. *United States*. . . . There, officers executing a valid search warrant for intoxicating liquors found and arrested one Birdsall who in pursuance of a conspiracy was actually engaged in running a saloon. As an incident to the arrest they seized a ledger in a closet where the liquor or some of it was kept and some bills beside the cash register. These things were visible and accessible and in the offender's immediate custody. There was no threat of force or general search or rummaging of the place."

This limited characterization of *Marron* was reiterated in *Lefkowitz,* a case in which the Court held unlawful a search of desk drawers and a cabinet despite the fact that the search had accompanied a lawful arrest. . . .

The limiting views expressed in *Go-Bart* and *Lefkowitz* were thrown to the winds, however, in *Harris* v. *United States,* decided in 1947. In that case, officers had obtained a warrant for Harris' arrest on the basis of his alleged involvement with the cashing and interstate transportation of a forged check. He was arrested in the living room of his four-room apartment, and in an attempt to recover two canceled checks thought to have been used in effecting the forgery, the officers undertook a thorough search of the entire apartment. Inside a desk drawer they found a sealed envelope marked "George Harris, personal papers." The envelope, which was then torn open, was found to contain altered selective service documents, and those documents were used to secure Harris' conviction for violating the Selective Training and Service Act of 1940. The Court rejected Harris' Fourth Amendment claim, sustaining the search as "incident to arrest.". . .

Only a year after *Harris,* however, the pendulum swung again. In *Trupiano* v. *United States* . . . agents raided the site of an illicit distillery, saw one of several conspirators operating the still, and arrested him, contemporaneously "seiz[ing] the illicit distillery." The Court held that the arrest and others made subsequently had been valid, but that the unexplained failure of the agents to procure a search warrant—in spite of the fact that they had had more than enough time before the raid to do so—rendered the search unlawful. The opinion stated: "It is a cardinal rule that, in seizing goods and articles, law enforcement agents must secure and use search warrants wherever reasonably practicable. . . . This rule rests upon the desirability of having magistrates rather than police officers determine when searches and seizures are permissible and what limitations whould be placed upon such activities. . . . To provide the necessary security against unreasonable intrusions upon the private lives of individuals, the framers of the Fourth Amendment required adherence to judicial processes wherever possible. And subsequent history has confirmed the wisdom of that requirement.

"A search or seizure without a warrant as an incident to a lawful arrest has always been considered to be a strictly limited right. It grows out of the inherent necessities of the situation at the time of the arrest. But there must be something more in the way of necessity than merely a lawful arrest.". . .

In 1950, two years after *Trupiano,* came *United States* v. *Rabinowitz,* the decision upon which California primarily relies in the case now before us. In *Rabinowitz,* federal authorities had been informed that the defendant was dealing in stamps bearing forged overprints. On the basis of that information they secured a warrant for his arrest, which they executed at his one-room business office. At the time of the arrest, the officers "searched the desk, safe, and file cabinets in the office for about an hour and a half,". . . and seized 573 stamps with forged overprints. The stamps were admitted into evidence at the defendant's trial, and this Court affirmed his conviction, rejecting the contention that the warrantless search had been unlawful. The Court held that the search in its entirety fell within the principle giving law enforcement authorities "[t]he right 'to search the place where the arrest is made in order to find and seize things connected with the crime. . . .' " *Harris* was regarded as "ample authority" for that conclusion. . . . The opinion rejected the rule of *Trupiano* that "in seizing goods and articles, law enforcement agents must secure and use search warrants wherever reasonably practicable." The test, said the Court, "is not whether it is reasonable to procure a search warrant, but whether the search was reasonable."

Rabinowitz has come to stand for the proposition, *inter alia,* that a warrantless search "incident to a lawful arrest" may generally extend to the area that is considered to be in the "possession" or under the "control" of the person arrested. And it was on the basis of that proposition that the California courts upheld the search of the petitioner's entire house in this case. That doctrine, however, at least in the broad sense in which it was applied by the California courts in this case, can withstand neither historical nor rational analysis.

Even limited to its own facts, the *Rabinowitz* decision was, as we have seen, hardly founded on an unimpeachable line of authority. As Mr. Justice Frankfurter commented in dissent in that case, the "hint" contained in *Weeks* was, without persuasive justification, "loosely turned into dictum and finally elevated to a decision.". . . And the approach taken in cases such as *Go-Bart, Lefkowitz,* and *Trupiano* was essentially disregarded by the *Rabinowitz* Court.

Nor is the rationale by which the State seeks here to sustain the search of the petitioner's house supported by a reasoned view of the background and purpose of the Fourth Amendment. Mr. Justice Frankfurter wisely pointed out in his *Rabinowitz* dissent that the Amendment's proscription of "unreasonable searches and seizures" must be read in light of "the history that gave rise to the words"—a history of "abuses so deeply felt by the Colonies as to be one of the potent causes of the Revolution. . . ." The Amendment was in large part a reaction to the general warrants and warrantless searches that had so alienated the colonists and had helped speed the movement for independence. In the scheme of the Amendment, therefore, the requirement that "no Warrants shall issue, but upon probable cause," plays a crucial part. As the Court put it in *McDonald* v. *United States.* . . .

> "We are not dealing with formalities. The presence of a search warrant serves a high function. Absent some grave emergency, the Fourth Amendment has interposed a magistrate between the citizen and the police. This was done not to shield criminals nor to make the home a safe haven for illegal activities. It was done so that an objective mind might weigh the need to invade that privacy in order to enforce the law. The right of privacy was deemed too precious to entrust to the discretion of those whose job is the detection of crime and the arrest of criminals. . . . And so the Constitution requires a magistrate to pass on the desires of the police before they violate the privacy of the home. We cannot be true to that constitutional requirement and excuse the absence of a search warrant without a showing by those who seek exemption from the constitutional mandate that the exigencies of the situation made that course imperative."

Even in the *Agnello* case the Court relied upon the rule that "[b]elief, however well founded, that an article sought is concealed in a dwelling house furnishes no justification for a search of that place without a warrant. And such searches are held unlawful notwithstanding facts unquestionably showing probable cause." Clearly, the general requirement that a search warrant be obtained is not lightly to be dispensed with, and "the burden is on those seeking [an] exemption [from the requirement] to show the need for it. . . .

Only last Term in *Terry* v. *Ohio* . . . we emphasized that "the police must, whenever practicable, obtain advance judicial approval of searches and seizures through the warrant procedure,". . . and that "[t]he scope of [a] search must be 'strictly tied to and justified by' the circumstances which rendered its initiation permissible.". . . The search undertaken by the officer in that "stop and frisk" case was sustained under that test, because it was no more than a "protective . . . search for weapons.". . . But in a companion case, *Sibron* v. *New York* . . . we applied the same standard to another set of facts and reached a contrary result, holding that a policeman's action in thrusting his hand into a suspect's pocket had been neither motivated by nor limited to the objective of protection. Rather, the search had been made in order to find narcotics, which were in fact found.

A similar analysis underlies the "search incident to arrest" principle, and marks its proper extent. When an arrest is made, it is reasonable for the arresting officer to search the person arrested in order to remove any weapons that the latter might seek to use in order to resist arrest or effect his escape. Otherwise, the officer's safety might well be endangered, and the arrest itself frustrated. In addition, it is entirely reasonable for the arresting officer to search for and seize any evidence on the arrestee's person in order to prevent its concealment or destruction. And the area into which an arrestee might reach in order to grab a weapon or evidentiary items must, of course, be governed by a like rule. A gun on a table or in a drawer in front of one who is arrested can be as dangerous to the arresting officer as one concealed in the clothing of the person arrested. There is ample justification, therefore, for a search of the arrestee's person and the area "within his immediate control"—construing that phrase to mean the area from within which he might gain possession of a weapon or destructible evidence.

There is no comparable justification, however, for routinely searching rooms other than that in which an arrest occurs—or, for that matter, for searching through all the desk drawers or other closed or concealed areas in that room itself. Such searches, in the absence of well-recognized exceptions, may be made only under the authority of a search warrant. The "adherence to judicial processes" mandated by the Fourth Amendment requires no less.

This is the principle that underlay our decision in *Preston* v. *United States*. . . . In that case three men had been arrested in a parked car, which had later been towed to a garage and searched by police. We held the search to have been unlawful under the Fourth Amendment, despite the contention that it had been incidental to a valid arrest. Our reasoning was straightforward:

> "The rule allowing contemporaneous searches is justified, for example, by the need to seize weapons and other things which might be used to assault an officer or effect an escape, as well as by the need to prevent the destruction of evidence of the crime—things which might easily happen where the weapon or evidence is on the accused's person or under his immediate control. But these justifications are absent where a search is remote in time or place from the arrest.". . .

The same basic principle was reflected in our opinion last Term in *Sibron*. That opinion dealt with *Peters* v. *New York* . . . as well as with Sibron's case, and *Peters* involved a search that we upheld as incident to a proper arrest. We sustained the search, however, only because its scope had been "reasonably limited" by the "need to seize weapons" and "to prevent the destruction of evidence," to which *Preston* had referred. We emphasized that the arresting officer "did not engage in an unrestrained and thoroughgoing examination of Peters and his personal effects. He seized him to cut short his flight, and he searched him primarily for weapons.". . .

It is argued in the present case that it is "reasonable" to search a man's house when he is arrested in it. But that argument is founded on little more than a subjective view regarding the acceptability of certain sorts of police conduct, and not on considerations relevant to Fourth Amendment interests. Under such an unconfined analysis, Fourth Amendment protection in this area would approach the evaporation point. It is not easy to explain why, for instance, it is less subjectively "reasonable" to search a man's house when he is arrested on his front lawn—or just down the street—than it is when he happens to be in the house at the time of arrest. As Mr. Justice Frankfurter put it:

> "To say that the search must be reasonable is to require some criterion of reason. It is no guide at all either for a jury or for district judges or the police to say that an 'unreasonable search' is forbidden—that the search must be reasonable. What is the test of reason which makes a search reasonable? The test is the reason underlying and expressed by the Fourth Amendment: the history and the experience which it embodies and the safeguards afforded by it against the

evils to which it was a response." *United States* v. *Rabinowitz.* . . .

Thus, although "[t]he recurring questions of the reasonableness of searches" depend upon "the facts and circumstances—the total atmosphere of the case," (opinion of the Court), those facts and circumstances must be viewed in the light of established Fourth Amendment principles.

It would be possible, of course, to draw a line between *Rabinowitz* and *Harris* on the one hand, and this case on the other. For *Rabinowitz* involved a single room, and *Harris* a four-room apartment, while in the case before us an entire house was searched. But such a distinction would be highly artificial. The rationale that allowed the searches and seizures in *Rabinowitz* and *Harris* would allow the searches and seizures in this case. No consideration relevant to the Fourth Amendment suggests any point of rational limitation, once the search is allowed to go beyond the area from which the person arrested might obtain weapons or evidentiary items. The only reasoned distinction is one between a search of the person arrested and the area within his reach on the one hand, and more extensive searches on the other.

The petitioner correctly points out that one result of decisions such as *Rabinowitz* and *Harris* is to give law enforcement officials the opportunity to engage in searches not justified by probable cause, by the simple expedient of arranging to arrest suspects at home rather than elsewhere. We do not suggest that the petitioner is necessarily correct in his assertion that such a strategy was utilized here, but the fact remains that had he been arrested earlier in the day, at his place of employment rather than at home, no search of his house could have been made without a search warrant. In any event, even apart from the possibility of such police tactics, the general point so forcefully made by Judge Learned Hand in *United States* v. *Kirschenblatt* . . . remains:

"After arresting a man in his house, to rummage at will among his papers in search of whatever will convict him, appears to us to be indistinguishable from what might be done under a warrant; indeed, the warrant would give more protection, for presumably it must be issued by a magistrate. True, by hypothesis the power would not exist, if the supposed offender were not found on the premises; but it is small consolation to know that one's papers are safe only so long as one is not at home."

Rabinowitz and *Harris* have been the subject of critical commentary for many years, and have been relied upon less and less in our own decisions. It is time, for the reasons we have stated, to hold that on their own facts, and insofar as the principles they stand for are inconsistent with those that we have endorsed today, they are no longer to be followed.

Application of sound Fourth Amendment principles to the facts of this case produces a clear result. The search here went far beyond the petitioner's person and the area from within which he might have obtained either a weapon or something that could have been used as evidence against him. There was no constitutional justification, in the absence of a search warrant, for extending the search beyond that area. The scope of the search was, therefore, "unreasonable" under the Fourth and Fourteenth Amendments, and the petitioner's conviction cannot stand.

MR. JUSTICE HARLAN, concurring:

I join the Court's opinion with these remarks concerning a factor to which the Court has not alluded.

The only thing that has given me pause in voting to overrule *Harris* and *Rabinowitz* is that as a result of *Mapp* v. *Ohio* . . . and *Ker* v. *California* . . . every change in Fourth Amendment law must now be obeyed by state officials facing widely different problems of local law enforcement. We simply do not know the extent to which cities and towns across the Nation are prepared to administer the greatly expanded warrant system which will be required by today's decision; nor can we say with assurance that in each and every local situation, the warrant requirement plays an essential role in the protection of those fundamental liberties protected against state infringement by the Fourteenth Amendment.

[Mr. Justice White, with whom Mr. Justice Black joins, dissented.]

ADAMS *v.* WILLIAMS

407 U.S. 143; 92 Sup. Ct. 1921; 32 L. Ed. 2d 612 (1972)

MR. JUSTICE REHNQUIST delivered the opinion of the Court:

Respondent Robert Williams was convicted in a Connecticut state court of illegal possession of a handgun found during a "stop and frisk," as well as of possession of heroin that was found during a full search incident to his weapons arrest.

Police Sgt. John Connolly was alone early in the morning on car patrol duty in a high-crime area of Bridgeport, Connecticut. At approximately 2:15 A.M. a person known to Sgt. Connolly approached his cruiser and informed him that an individual seated in a nearby vehicle was carrying narcotics and had a gun at his waist.

After calling for assistance on his car radio, Sgt. Connolly approached the vehicle to investigate the informant's report. Connolly tapped on the car window and asked the occupant, Robert Williams, to open the door. When Williams rolled down the window instead, the sergeant reached into the car and removed a fully loaded revolver from Williams' waistband. The gun had not been visible to Connolly from outside the car, but it was in precisely the place indicated by the informant. Williams was then arrested by Connolly for unlawful possession of the pistol. A search incident to that arrest was conducted after other officers arrived. They found substantial quantities of heroin on Williams' person and in the car, and they found a machete and a second revolver hidden in the automobile.

Respondent contends that the initial seizure of his pistol, upon which rested the later search and seizure of other weapons and narcotics, was not justified by the informant's tip to Sgt. Connolly. He claims that absent a more reliable informant, or some corroboration of the tip, the policeman's actions were unreasonable under the standards set forth in *Terry* v. *Ohio.*

In *Terry* this Court recognized that "a police officer may in appropriate circumstances and in an appropriate manner approach a person for purposes of investigating possibly criminal behavior even though there is no probable cause to make an arrest.". . . The Fourth Amendment does not require a policeman who lacks the precise level of information necessary for probable cause to arrest to simply shrug his shoulders and allow a crime to occur or a criminal to escape. On the contrary, *Terry* recognizes that it may be the essence of good police work to adopt an intermediate response.

A brief stop of a suspicious individual, in order to determine his identity or to maintain the status quo momentarily while obtaining more information, may be most reasonable in light of the facts known to the officer at the time.

The Court recognized in *Terry* that the policeman making a reasonable investigatory stop should not be denied the opportunity to protect himself from attack by a hostile suspect. "When an officer is justified in believing that the individual whose suspicious behavior he is investigating at close range is armed and presently dangerous to the officer or to others," he may conduct a limited protective search for concealed weapons. . . . The purpose of this limited search is not to discover evidence of crime, but to allow the officer to pursue his investigation without fear of violence, and thus the frisk for weapons might be equally necessary and reasonable, whether or not carrying a concealed weapon violated any applicable state law. So long as the officer is entitled to make a forcible stop,* and has reason to believe that the suspect is armed and dangerous, he may conduct a weapons search limited in scope to this protective purpose. . . .

Applying these principles to the present case, we believe that Sgt. Connolly acted justifiably in responding to his informant's tip. The informant was known to him personally and had provided him with information in the past. . . . The informant here came forward personally to give information that was immediately verifiable at the scene.

Thus, while the Court's decisions indi-

* Petitioner does not contend that Williams acted voluntarily in rolling down the window of his car.

cate that this informant's unverified tip may have been insufficient for a narcotics arrest or search warrant, see e.g., *Spinelli* v. *United States* . . . the information carried enough indicia of reliability to justify the officer's forcible stop of Williams. . . .

Some tips, completely lacking in indicia of reliability, would either warrant no police response or require further investigation before a forcible stop of a suspect would be authorized. But in some situations—for example, when the victim of a street crime seeks immediate police aid and gives a description of his assailant, or when a credible informant warns of a specific impending crime—the subtleties of the hearsay rule should not thwart an appropriate police response.

While properly investigating the activity of a person who was reported to be carrying narcotics and a concealed weapon and who was sitting alone in a car in a high-crime area at 2:15 in the morning, Sgt. Connolly had ample reason to fear for his safety. When Williams rolled down his window, rather than complying with the policeman's request to step out of the car so that his movements could more easily be seen, the revolver allegedly at Williams' waist became an even greater threat. Under these circumstances the policeman's action in reaching to the spot where the gun was thought to be hidden constituted a limited intrusion designed to insure his safety, and we conclude that it was reasonable. The loaded gun seized as a result of this intrusion was therefore admissible at Williams' trial. *Terry* v. *Ohio*. . . .

Once Sgt. Connolly had found the gun precisely where the informant had predicted, probable cause existed to arrest Williams for unlawful possession of the weapon. Probable cause to arrest depends "upon whether, at the moment the arrest was made . . . the facts and circumstances within [the arresting officers'] knowledge and of which they had reasonably trustworthy information were sufficient to warrant a prudent man in believing that the [suspect] had committed or was committing an offense." *Beck* v. *Ohio,* 379 U.S. 89 . . . (1964) . In the present case the policeman found Williams in possession of a gun in precisely the place predicted by the informant. This tended to corroborate the reliability of the informant's further report of narcotics and, together with the surrounding circumstances, certainly suggested no lawful explanation for possession of the gun. Probable cause does not require the same type of specific evidence of each element of the offense as would be needed to support a conviction. See *Draper* v. *United States.* . . . Under the circumstances surrounding Williams' possession of the gun seized by Sgt. Connolly, the arrest on the weapons charge was supported by probable cause, and the search of his person and of the car incident to that arrest was lawful. . . . The fruits of the search were therefore properly admitted at Williams' trial, and the Court of Appeals erred in reaching a contrary conclusion.

MR. JUSTICE DOUGLAS . . . dissented.

MR. JUSTICE BRENNAN, dissenting:

The crucial question on which this case turns, as the Court concedes, is whether, there being no contention that Williams acted voluntarily in rolling down the window of his car, the State had shown sufficient cause to justify Sgt. Connolly's "forcible" stop. . . . For the following reasons stated by Judge, now Chief Judge, Friendly, dissenting, [below] . . . the State did not make that showing:

"To begin, I have the gravest hesitancy in extending *Terry* v. *Ohio,* . . . to crimes like the possession of narcotics. . . . There is too much danger that, instead of the stop being the object and the protective frisk an incident thereto, the reverse will be true. Against that we have here the added fact of the report that Williams had a gun on his person. . . . [But] Connecticut allows its citizens to carry weapons, concealed or otherwise, at will, provided only they have a permit, . . . and gives its police officers no special authority to stop for the purpose of determining whether the citizen has one. . . .

"If I am wrong in thinking that *Terry* should not be applied at all to mere possessory offenses, . . . I would not find the combination of Officer Connolly's almost meaningless observation and the tip in this case to be sufficient justification for the intrusion. The tip suffered from a threefold defect, with each fold compounding the others. The informer was unnamed, he was not shown to have been reliable with respect to guns or narcotics, and he gave no information which demonstrated personal knowledge or—what is worse—could not readily have been manufactured by the officer after the event. To my mind, it has been sufficiently recognized that the difference between this sort of tip and the accurate prediction of an unusual event is as important on the latter score as on the former. In *Draper* v. *United States*, . . . Narcotics Agent Marsh would hardly have been at the Denver Station at the exact moment of the arrival of the train Draper had taken from Chicago unless *someone* had told him *something* important, although the agent might later have embroidered the details to fit the observed facts. . . . There is no such guarantee of a patrolling officer's veracity when he testifies to a 'tip' from an unnamed informer saying no more than that the officer will find a gun and narcotics on a man across the street, as he later does. If the state wishes to rely on a tip of that nature to validate a stop and frisk, revelation of the name of the informer or demonstration that his name is unknown and could not reasonably have been ascertained should be the price.

"*Terry* v. *Ohio* was intended to free a police officer from the rigidity of a rule that would prevent his doing anything to a man reasonably suspected of being about to commit or having just committed a crime of violence, no matter how grave the problem or impelling the need for swift action, unless the officer had what a court would later determine to be probable cause for arrest. It was meant for the serious cases of imminent danger or of harm recently perpetrated to persons or property, not the conventional ones of possessory offences. If it is to be extended to the latter at all, this should be only where observation by the officer himself or well authenticated information shows 'that criminal activity may be afoot.' . . . I greatly fear that if the [contrary view] should be followed, *Terry* will have opened the sluicegates for serious and unintended erosion of the protection of the Fourth Amendment."

MR. JUSTICE MARSHALL, dissenting:

We upheld the stop and frisk in *Terry* because we recognized that the realities of on-the-street law enforcement require an officer to act at times on the basis of strong evidence, short of probable cause, that criminal activity is taking place and that the criminal is armed and dangerous. Hence, *Terry* stands only for the proposition that police officers have a "narrowly drawn authority to . . . search for weapons" without a warrant.

In today's decision the Court ignores the fact that *Terry* begrudgingly accepted the necessity for creating an exception from the warrant requirement of the Fourth Amendment and treats this case as if warrantless searches were the rule rather than the "narrowly drawn" exception. This decision betrays the careful balance that Terry sought to strike between a citizen's right to privacy and his government's responsibility for effective law enforcement and expands the concept of warrantless searches far beyond anything heretofore recognized as legitimate. . . . This Court has squarely held that a search and seizure cannot be justified on the basis of conclusory allegations of an unnamed informant who is allegedly credible. . . . In the recent case of *Spinelli* v. *United States*, Mr. Justice Harlan made it plain beyond any doubt that where police rely on an informant to make a search and seizure, they must know that the informant is generally trustworthy and that he has obtained his information in a reliable way. . . . Since the testimony of the arresting officer in the instant case patently fails to demonstrate that the informant was known to be trustworthy and since it is also clear that the officer had no idea of the source of the informant's "knowledge," a search and seizure would have been illegal.

Assuming, arguendo, that this case truly involves, not an arrest and a search incident thereto, but a stop and frisk,† we must decide whether or not the information possessed by the officer justified this interference with respondent's liberty. . . .

† *Terry* v. *Ohio* . . . makes it clear that a stop and frisk is a search and seizure within the meaning of the Fourth Amendment. When I use the term stop and frisk herein, I merely intend to emphasize that it is, as *Terry* held, a lesser intrusion than a full-scale search and seizure.

Terry did not hold that whenever a policeman has a hunch that a citizen is engaging in criminal activity, he may engage in a stop and frisk. It held that if police officers want to stop and frisk, they must have specific facts from which they can reasonably infer that an individual is engaged in criminal activity and is armed and dangerous. It was central to our decision in *Terry* that the police officer acted on the basis of his own personal observations and that he carefully scrutinized the conduct of his suspects before interfering with them in any way. When we legitimated the conduct of the officer in *Terry* we did so because of the substantial *reliability* of the information on which the officer based his decision to act. . . .

As I read *Terry,* an officer may act on the basis of *reliable* information short of probable cause to make a stop, and ultimately a frisk, if necessary; but, the officer may not use unreliable, unsubstantiated, conclusory hearsay to justify an invasion of liberty. *Terry* never meant to approve the kind of knee-jerk police reaction that we have before us in this case. . . .

Even if I could agree with the Court that the stop and frisk in this case was proper, I could not go further and sustain the arrest, and the subsequent searches. It takes probable cause to justify an arrest and search and seizure incident thereto. . . .

Once the officer seized the gun from respondent, it is uncontradicted that he did not ask whether respondent had a license to carry it, or whether respondent carried it for any other legal reason under Connecticut law. Rather, the officer placed him under arrest immediately and hastened to search his person. Since Connecticut has not made it illegal for private citizens to carry guns, there is nothing in the facts of this case to warrant a man "of prudence and caution" to believe that any offense had been committed merely because respondent had a gun on his person. . . .

Mr. Justice Douglas was the sole dissenter in *Terry.* He warned of the "powerful hydraulic pressures throughout our history that bear heavily on the Court to water down constitutional guarantees. . . ." While I took the position then that we were not watering down rights, but were hesitantly and cautiously striking a necessary balance between the rights of American citizens to be free from government intrusion into their privacy and their government's urgent need for a narrow exception to the warrant requirement of the Fourth Amendment, today's decision demonstrates just how prescient Mr. Justice Douglas was.

COKER *v.* GEORGIA

433 U.S. 584; 97 Sup. Ct. 2861; 52 L. Ed. 2d 982 (1977)

[In 1971, Coker raped and murdered a young woman. Less than eight months later he kidnapped, raped, and severely beat a sixteen-year-old woman, leaving her for dead in a wooded area. In 1974, he escaped from the state prison and raped another sixteen-year-old. After his conviction for the 1974 offense, a sentencing hearing was conducted of the kind the Court had recommended in Gregg. *The jury found that Coker's previous conviction for a capital felony and the fact that the rape had occurred during the commission of a felony (the armed robbery of the victim's husband) constituted aggravating circumstances. They assigned the death penalty.]*

MR. JUSTICE WHITE delivered the opinion of the Court:

As advised by recent cases, we seek guidance in history and from the objective evidence of the country's present judgment concerning the acceptability of death as a penalty for rape of an adult woman. At no time in the last 50 years has a majority of the States authorized death as a punishment for rape.

. . . In reviving death penalty laws to satisfy *Furman's* mandate, none of the States that had not previously authorized death for rape chose to include rape among

the courts tend to be cautious about judicial review of agency decisions. Nevertheless, where agency action seems to deviate considerably from the words of the statute or to pursue an unwise policy, the courts may be tempted to intervene.

Citizens to Preserve Overton Park, Inc. v. *Volpe* (p. 721) involves rival interpretations of the words of a statute, the issue of how much the courts must defer to administrative fact finding, and the delicate question of how far the judges should substitute their discretion for that of the responsible administrator. Also *Volpe* illustrates another typical aspect of the "other" judicial review. Very frequently review is conducted not by a flat holding for or against the agency, but by returning the matter to the agency and giving it a chance to mend its ways—or at least make a better case for what it proposes to do.

The Supreme Court and Federal Statutory Law

The statutory interpretation that the Court does in reviewing agencies is only a part of its total statutory interpretation duties. Preoccupation with the Court's constitutional business has tended to obscure the fact that it is also the highest court in a federal court system charged with the enforcement of a large and ever-growing body of federal statutory law. For instance, the reader of this or nearly any constitutional law book will come upon the famous antitrust case of *United States* v. *E. C. Knight Co.* (p. 264) because at the time it was decided, the enforcement of antitrust law raised important constitutional issues. Paradoxically enough, after 1937, when the Court's broadened definition of the commerce power (see Chapter 9) allowed a fuller sweep for the enforcement of antitrust law, it drops out of the sight of most students precisely because it no longer raises constitutional issues. Yet, the Supreme Court has gone on hearing antitrust cases, some of them far more important for the business community than *E. C. Knight.*

By far the most important of the Supreme Court's modern antitrust decisions, *United States* v. *Du Pont* (p. 726), is included here not only for its great intrinsic interest but to remind the reader that the Supreme Court is directly responsible for the interpretation and enforcement of major bodies of federal law. These include not only antitrust but patent, copyright, admiralty, bankruptcy, and federal criminal law, as well as a complex body of law about the liability of federal employers for injuries suffered by their workers. In addition, a mass of federal civil statutes ranging from customs regulations to federal rules governing the retirement of railroad workers brings cases into the federal courts and sometimes up to the Supreme Court. All this must be added to the Court's major responsibilities in the areas of tax, labor, transportation, securities, immigration, natural resources, and banking, which it normally exercises through review of administrative agency proceedings.

Certainly, no Supreme Court justice confronted by a "reserved-gate picketing" or "auxiliary and supplementary railroad-owned trucking service" case can forget what students of constitutional law sometimes forget: the Supreme Court is far more than the constitutional Supreme Court.

VITARELLI *v.* SEATON
359 U.S. 535; 79 Sup. Ct. 968; 3 L. Ed. 2d. 1012 (1959)

[William Vitarelli, a Quaker and conscientious objector during World War II, resided in Bucks County, Pennsylvania. In 1933, he graduated from college and entered the teaching profession. In 1949, he receivd his Ph.D. from Teachers College, Columbia University, and subsequently took a job with the Department of the Interior as an educational and training specialist. He was assigned to the Palau District of the Trust Territory of the Pacific Islands, held by the United States under a United Nations trusteeship. In this post Vitarelli was responsible for organizing the school system and supervising necessary school construction.

On March 30, 1954, Secretary of the Interior Douglas McKay, Seaton's predecessor in office, suspended Vitarelli as a security risk. McKay charged that from 1941 to 1945 Vitarelli had been in "sympathetic association" with members of the Communist party and that he had concealed these associations from the government. It was also charged that Vitarelli had been a supporter of the American Labor party, said to be dominated by the Communists, and that he had subscribed to the USSR Information Bulletin. *Vitarelli replied that he had never been sympathetic to the Communist party and demanded reinstatement or a hearing. The hearing was granted, and Vitarelli appeared before a security hearing board in Washington. At the hearing the Department of Interior brought in no evidence in support of its charges. No witnesses were called to testify against Vitarelli. However, the members of the security board questioned Vitarelli at length, and he and four witnesses in his behalf were extensively cross-examined. On September 10, 1954, Vitarelli was dismissed "in the interest of national security" as set forth in the letter of March 30, 1954. A "Notification of Personnel Action," dated September 21, 1954, setting forth the dismissal action, was filed with Vitarelli's records.*

After failing to obtain reinstatement, Vitarelli filed suit in the federal district court for the District of Columbia seeking a judgment that his removal was illegal and a mandatory injunction that he be reinstated with back pay. On October 10, 1956, while the case was still pending, a copy of the "Notification of Personnel Action," also dated September 21, 1954, was filed in the district court by the Department of Interior. This notification was identical with the one already mentioned, except that it omitted any reference to the reasons for Vitarelli's discharge and to the authority under which it was done. The reasons for this action are noted in the case here. The district court ruled against Vitarelli, and the court of appeals affirmed, with one judge dissenting. Vitarelli then brought the case to the Supreme Court on a writ of certiorari.

After the decision reproduced here, Vitarelli was reinstated and he returned to the South Pacific. He also sued in the Court of Claims for back pay, legal fees, annual leave pay, and the like, and after a lengthy litigation, he recovered a substantial proportion in the sum of $21,517.42.]

MR. JUSTICE HARLAN delivered the opinion of the Court:

This case concerns the legality of petitioner's discharge as an employee of the Department of the Interior. . . .

The Secretary's letter of March 30, 1954, and notice of dismissal of September 2, 1954, both relied upon Exec. Order No. 10450 . . . the Act of August 26, 1950 . . . and Department of the Interior Order No. 2738, all relating to discharges of government employees on security or loyalty grounds, as the authority for petitioner's dismissal. In *Cole* v. *Young,* 351 U.S. 536, this Court held that the statutes referred to did not apply to government employees in positions not designated as "sensitive." Respondent takes the position that since petitioner's position in government service has at no time been designated as sensitive, the effect of *Cole,* which was decided after the 1954 dismissal of petitioner, was to render also inapplicable to petitioner Department of the Interior Order No. 2738, under which the proceedings relating to petitioner's dismissal were had. It is urged that in this state of affairs petitioner, who concededly was at no time within the protection of the Civil Service Act, Veterans' Preference Act, or any other statute relating to employment rights of government employees, and who . . . could have been summarily discharged by the Secretary at any time without the giving of a reason, under no circumstances could be entitled to more than that which he has already received—namely, an "expunging" from the record of his 1954 discharge of any reference to the authority or reasons therefor.

Respondent misconceives the effect of our decision in *Cole.* It is true that the Act of August 26, 1950, and the Executive Order did not alter the power of the Secretary to discharge summarily an employee in petitioner's status, without the giving of any reason. Nor did the Department's own regulations preclude such a course. Since, however, the Secretary gratuitously decided to give a reason, and that reason was national security, he was obligated to conform to the procedural standards he had formulated in Order No. 2738 for the dismissal of employees on security grounds. . . . That Order on its face applies to all security discharges in the Department of the Interior. . . . *Cole* v. *Young* established that the Act of August 26, 1950, did not permit the discharge of nonsensitive employees pursuant to procedures authorized by that Act if those procedures were more summary than those to which the employee would have been entitled by virtue of any pre-existing statute or regulation. That decision cannot, however, justify noncompliance by the Secretary with regulations promulgated by him in the departmental Order, which as to petitioner afford greater procedural protections in the case of a dismissal stated to be for security reasons than in the case of dismissal without any statement of reasons. Having chosen to proceed against petitioner on security grounds, the Secretary . . . was bound by the regulations which he himself had promulgated for dealing with such cases, even though without such regulations he could have discharged petitioner summarily.

Petitioner makes various contentions as to the constitutional invalidity of the procedures provided by Order No. 2738. He further urges that even assuming the validity of the governing procedures, his dismissal cannot stand because the notice of suspension and hearing given him did not comply with the Order. We find it unnecessary to reach the constitutional issues, for we think that petitioner's second position is well taken and must be sustained.

Preliminarily, it should be said that departures from departmental regulations in matters of this kind involve more than mere consideration of procedural irregularities. For in proceedings of this nature, in which the ordinary rules of evidence do not apply, in which matters involving the disclosure of confidential information are withheld, and where it must be recognized that counsel is under practical constraints in the making of objections and in the tactical handling of his case which would not obtain in a case being tried in a court of law before trained judges, scrupulous observance of departmental procedural safeguards is clearly of particular importance. In this instance an examination of the record, and of the transcript of the hearing before the departmental security board, discloses that petitioner's procedural rights under the applicable regulations were violated in at least three material respects in the proceedings which terminated in the final notice of his dismissal.

First. Section 15(a) of Order No. 2738 requires that the statement of charges served upon an employee at the time of his suspension on security grounds "shall be as specific and detailed as security considerations, including the need for protection of confidential sources of information, permit . . . and shall be subject to amendment within thirty days of issuance." Although the statement of charges furnished petitioner appears on its face to be reasonably specific, the transcript of hearing establishes that the statement, which was never amended, cannot conceivably be said in fact to be as specific and detailed as "security considerations . . . permit." For petitioner was questioned by the security officer and by the hearing board in great detail concerning his association with and knowledge of various persons and organizations nowhere mentioned in the statement of charges, and at length concerning his activities in Bucks County, Pennsylvania, and elsewhere after 1945, activities as to which the charges are also completely silent. These questions were presumably asked because they were deemed relevant to the inquiry before the board, and the very fact that they were asked and thus spread on the record is conclusive indication that "security considerations" could not have justified the omission of any statement concerning them in the charges furnished petitioner.

Second. Sections 21(a) and (e) require that hearings before security hearing boards shall be "orderly" and that "reasonable restrictions shall be imposed as to relevancy, competency, and materiality of matters considered." . . . [T]hese indispensable indicia of a meaningful hearing were not observed. It is not an overcharacterization to say that as the hearing proceeded it developed into a wide-ranging inquisition into this man's educational, social, and political beliefs, encompassing even a question as to whether he was "a religious man."

Third. Section 21(c) (4) gives the employee the right "to cross-examine any witness offered in support of the charges." It is apparent from an over-all reading of the regulations that it was not contemplated that this provision should require the Department to call witnesses to testify in support of any or all of the charges, because it was expected that charges might rest on information gathered from or by "confidential informants." We think, however, that Section 21(c) (4) did contemplate the calling by the Department of any informant not properly classifiable as "confidential," if information furnished by that informant was to be used by the board in assessing an employee's status. The transcript shows that this provision was violated on at least one occasion at petitioner's hearing, for the security officer identified by name a person who had given information apparently considered detrimental to petitioner, thus negating any possible inference that that person was considered a "confidential informant" whose identity it was necessary to keep secret, and questioned petitioner at some length concerning the information supplied from this source without calling the informant and affording petitioner the right to cross-examine.

Because the proceedings attendant upon petitioner's dismissal from government service on grounds of national security fell substantially short of the requirements of the applicable departmental regulations, we hold that such dismissal was illegal and of no effect.

Respondent urges that even if the dismissal of September 10, 1954, was invalid, petitioner is not entitled to reinstatement by reason of the fact that he was at all events validly dismissed in October 1956, when a copy of the second "Notification of Personnel Action," omitting all reference to any statute, order, or regulation relating to security discharges, was delivered to him. Granting that the Secretary could at any time after September 10, 1954, have validly dismissed petitioner without any statement of reasons, and independently of the proceedings taken against him under Order No. 2738, we cannot view the delivery of the new notification to petitioner as an exercise of that summary dismissal power. Rather, the fact that it was dated "9–21–54," contained a termination of employment date of "9–10–54," was designated as "a revision" of the 1954 notification, and was evidently filed in the District Court before its delivery to petitioner indicates that its sole purpose was an attempt to moot petitioner's suit in the District Court by an "expunging" of the grounds for the dismissal which brought Order No. 2738 into play. In these circumstances, we would not be justified in now treating the 1956 action, plainly intended by the Secretary as a grant of relief to petitioner in connection with the form of the 1954 discharge, as an exercise of the Secretary's summary removal power as of the date of its delivery to petitioner.

It follows from what we have said that

petitioner is entitled to the reinstatement which he seeks, subject, of course to any lawful exercise of the Secretary's authority hereafter to dismiss him from employment in the Department of the Interior.

Reversed.

MR. JUSTICE FRANKFURTER, with whom MR. JUSTICE CLARK, MR. JUSTICE WHITTAKER, and MR. JUSTICE STEWART join, concurring in part and dissenting in part:

An executive agency must be rigorously held to the standards by which its action is to be judged . . . . Accordingly, if dismissal from employment is based on a defined procedure, even though generous beyond the requirements that bind such agency, that procedure must be scrupulously observed. . . . This judicially evolved rule of administrative law is now firmly established and, if I may add, rightly so. He that takes the procedural sword shall perish with that sword. Therefore, I unreservedly join in the Court's main conclusion, that the attempted dismissal of Vitarelli in September 1954 was abortive and of no validity because the procedure under Department of the Interior Order No. 2738 was invoked but not observed.

But when an executive agency draws on the freedom that the law vests in it, the judiciary cannot deny or curtail such freedom. The Secretary of the Interior concededly had untrammelled right to dismiss Vitarelli out of hand, since he had no protected employment rights. He could do so as freely as a private employer who is not bound by procedural restrictions of a collective bargaining contract. The Secretary was under no law-imposed or self-imposed restriction in discharging an employee in Vitarelli's position without a hearing. And so the question is, did the Secretary take action, after the abortive discharge in 1954, dismissing Vitarelli?

In October 1956 there was served upon Vitarelli a copy of a new notice of dismissal which had been inserted in the Department's personnel records in place of the first notice. Another copy was filed with the District Court in this proceeding. This second notice contained no mention of grounds of discharge. If, instead of sending this second notice to Vitarelli, the Secretary had telephoned Vitarelli to convey the contents of the second notice, he would have said: "I note that you are contesting the validity of the dismissal. I want to make this very clear to you. If I did not succeed in dismissing you before, I now dismiss you, and I dismiss you retroactively, effective September 1954."

The Court disallows this significance to the second notice of discharge because it finds controlling meaning in the suggestion of the Government that the expunging from the record of any adverse comment, and the second notice of discharge, signified a reassertion of the effectiveness of the first attempt at dismissal. And so, the Court concludes, no intention of severance from service in 1956 could legally be found since the Secretary expressed no doubt that the first dismissal had been effective. But this document of 1956 was not a mere piece of paper in a dialectic. The paper was a record of a process, a manifestation of purpose and action. The intendment of the second notice, to be sure, was to discharge Vitarelli retroactively, resting this attempted dismissal on valid authority—the summary power to dismiss without reason. Though the second notice could not predate the summary discharge because the Secretary rested his 1954 discharge on an unsustainable ground, and Vitarelli could not be deprived of rights accrued during two years of unlawful discharge, the prior wrongful action did not deprive the Secretary of the power in him to fire Vitarelli prospectively. And if the intent of the Secretary be manifested in fact by what he did, however that intent be expressed—here, the intent to be rid of Vitarelli—the Court should not frustrate the Secretary's rightful exercise of this power as of October 1956. . . .

This is the common sense of it: In 1956 the Secretary said to Vitarelli: "This document tells you without any ifs, ands, or buts, you have been fired right along and of course that means you are not presently employed by this Department." Since he had not been fired successfully in 1954, the Court concludes he must still be employed. I cannot join in an unreal interpretation which attributes to governmental action the empty meaning of confetti throwing.

GOLDBERG *v.* KELLY

397 U.S. 254; 90 Sup. Ct. 1011; 25 L. Ed. 2d 287 (1970)

[This case was initially brought to the Court by New York welfare recipients whose aid had been, or was about to be, cut off without personal or evidentiary appellate hearings.]

MR. JUSTICE BRENNAN delivered the opinion of the Court:

The question for decision is whether a State which terminates public assistance payments to a particular recipient without affording him the opportunity for an evidentiary hearing prior to termination denies the recipient procedural due process in violation of the Due Process Clause of the Fourteenth Amendment. . . . [The state regulation] provides that the local procedure must include the giving of notice to the recipient of the reasons for a proposed discontinuance or suspension at least seven days prior to its effective date, with notice also that upon request the recipient may have the proposal reviewed by a local welfare official holding a position superior to that of the supervisor who approved the proposed discontinuance or suspension. . . . Appellees' challenge to this procedure emphasizes the absence of any provisions for the personal appearance of the recipient before the reviewing official, for oral presentation of evidence, and for confrontation and cross-examination of adverse witnesses. However, the letter does inform the recipient that he may request a post-termination "fair hearing." This is a proceeding before an independent state hearing officer at which the recipient may appear personally, offer oral evidence, confront and cross-examine the witnesses against him, and have a record made of the hearing. If the recipient prevails at the "fair hearing" he is paid all funds erroneously withheld. . . . A recipient whose aid is not restored by a "fair hearing" decision may have judicial review.

The constitutional issue to be decided, therefore, is the narrow one whether the Due Process Clause requires that the recipient be afforded an evidentiary hearing *before* the termination of benefits. The District Court held that only a pretermination evidentiary hearing would satisfy the constitutional command, and rejected the argument of the state and city officials that the combination of the post-termination "fair hearing" with the informal pretermination review disposed of all due process claims. . . .

Appellant does not contend that procedural due process is not applicable to the termination of welfare benefits. . . .

The constitutional challenge cannot be answered by an argument that public assistance benefits are "a 'privilege' and not a 'right.'" *Shapiro* v. *Thompson*. . . . Relevant constitutional restraints apply as much to the withdrawal of public assistance benefits as to disqualification for unemployment compensation, *Sherbert* v. *Verner*, 374 U.S. 398 (1963); or to denial of a tax exemption, *Speiser* v. *Randall*, 357 U.S. 513 (1958); or to discharge from public employment, *Slochower* v. *Board of Higher Education*, 350 U.S. 551 (1956). The extent to which procedural due process must be afforded the recipient is influenced by the extent to which he may be "condemned to suffer grievous loss," *Joint Anti-Fascist Refugee Committee* v. *McGrath*, 341 U.S. 123 (1951) (Frankfurter, J., concurring), and depends upon whether the recipient's interest in avoiding that loss outweighs the governmental interest in summary adjudication. Accordingly, as we said in *Cafeteria & Restaurant Workers Union*, etc. v. *McElroy*, 367 U.S. 886, 895 (1961), "consideration of what procedures due process may require under any given set of circumstances must begin with a determination of the precise nature of the government function involved as well as of the private interest that has been affected by governmental action.". . .

It is true, of course, that some governmental benefits may be administratively terminated without affording the recipient a pretermination evidentiary hearing. But we agree with the District Court that when welfare is discontinued, only a pretermination evidentiary hearing provides the recipient with procedural due process. Cf. *Sniadach* v. *Family Finance Corporation,* 395 U.S. 337 (1969). For qualified recipients, welfare provides the means to obtain essential food, clothing, housing, and medical care. . . . Thus the crucial factor in this context—a factor not present in the case of the blacklisted government contractor, the discharged government employee, the taxpayer denied a tax exemption, or virtually anyone else whose governmental largesse is ended—is that termination of aid pending resolution of a controversy over eligibility may deprive an *eligible* recipient of the very means by which to live while he waits. Since he lacks independent resources, his situation becomes immediately desperate. His need to concentrate upon finding the means for daily subsistence, in turn, adversly affects his ability to seek redress from the welfare bureaucracy.

Moreover, important governmental interests are promoted by affording recipients a pretermination evidentiary hearing. From its founding the Nation's basic commitment has been to foster the dignity and well-being of all persons within its borders. We have come to recognize that forces not within the control of the poor contribute to their poverty. This perception, against the background of our traditions, has significantly influenced the development of the contemporary public assistance system. Welfare, by meeting the basic demands of subsistence, can help bring within the reach of the poor the same opportunities that are available to others to participate meaningfully in the life of the community. At the same time, welfare guards against the societal malaise that may flow from a widespread sense of unjustified frustration and insecurity. Public assistance, then, is not mere charity, but a means to "promote the general Welfare, and secure the Blessings of Liberty to ourselves and our Posterity." The same governmental interests which counsel the provision of welfare, counsel as well its uninterrupted provision to those eligible to receive it; pretermination evidentiary hearings are indispensable to that end.

Appellant does not challenge the force of these considerations but argues that they are outweighed by countervailing governmental interests in conserving fiscal and administrative resources. These interests, the argument goes, justify the delay of any evidentiary hearing until after discontinuance of the grants. Summary adjudication protects the public fisc by stopping payments promptly upon discovery of reason to believe that a recipient is no longer eligible. Since most terminations are accepted without challenge, summary adjudication also conserves both the fisc and administrative time and energy by reducing the number of evidentiary hearings actually held.

We agree with the District Court, however, that these governmental interests are not overriding in the welfare context. The requirement of a prior hearing doubtless involves some greater expense, and the benefits paid to ineligible recipients pending decision at the hearing probably cannot be recouped, since these recipients are likely to be judgment-proof. But the State is not without weapons to minimize these increased costs. Much of the drain on fiscal and administrative resources can be reduced by developing procedures for prompt pretermination hearings and by skillful use of personnel and facilities. Indeed, the very provision for a post-termination evidentiary hearing in New York's Home Relief program is itself cogent evidence that the State recognizes the primacy of the public interest in correct eligibility determinations and therefore in the provision of procedural safeguards. Thus, the interest of the eligible recipient in uninterrupted receipt of public assistance, coupled with the State's interest that his payments not be erroneously terminated, clearly outweighs the State's competing concern to prevent any increase in its fiscal and administrative burdens. As the District Court correctly concluded, "[t]he stakes are simply too high for the welfare recipient, and the possibility for honest error or irritable misjudgment too great, to allow termination of aid without giving the recipient a chance, if he so desires, to be fully informed of the case against him so that he may contest its basis and produce evidence in rebuttal.". . .

We also agree with the District Court, however, that the pretermination hearing need not take the form of a judicial or quasi-judicial trial.

. . . a complete record and a comprehensive opinion, which would serve primarily to facilitate judicial review and to guide future decisions, need not be provided at the pretermination stage. We recognize, too, that both welfare authorities and recipients have an interest in relatively speedy resolution of questions of eligibility, that they are used to dealing with one another informally, and that some welfare departments have very burdensome caseloads. These considerations justify the limitation of the pretermination hearing to minimum procedural safeguards, adapted to the particular characteristics of welfare recipients, and to the limited nature of the controversies to be resolved. We wish to add that we, no less than the dissenters, recognize the importance of not imposing upon the States or the Federal Government in this developing field of law any procedural requirements beyond those demanded by rudimentary due process.

. . . the present context . . . require[s] that a recipient have timely and adequate notice detailing the reasons for a proposed termination, and an effective opportunity to defend by confronting any adverse witnesses and by presenting his own arguments and evidence orally.

The opportunity to be heard must be tailored to the capacities and circumstances of those who are to be heard. It is not enough that a welfare recipient may present his position to the decision maker in writing or secondhand through his caseworker. Written submissions are an unrealistic option for most recipients, who lack the educational attainment necessary to write effectively and who cannot obtain professional assistance. Moreover, written submissions do not afford the flexibility of oral presentations; they do not permit the recipient to mold his argument to the issues the decision maker appears to regard as important. Particularly where credibility and veracity are at issue, as they must be in many termination proceedings, written submissions are a wholly unsatisfactory basis for decision. . . . Therefore a recipient must be allowed to state his position orally. Informal procedures will suffice; in this context due process does not require a particular order of proof or mode of offering evidence. . . .

In almost every setting where important decisions turn on questions of fact, due process requires an opportunity to confront and cross-examine adverse witnesses. . . . Welfare recipients must therefore be given an opportunity to confront and cross-examine the witnesses relied on by the department.

"The right to be heard would be, in many cases, of little avail if it did not comprehend the right to be heard by counsel." *Powell* v. *Alabama,* 287 U.S. 45, 68–69 (1932). We do not say that counsel must be provided at the pretermination hearing, but only that the recipient must be allowed to retain an attorney if he so desires. . . . We do not anticipate that this assistance will unduly prolong or otherwise encumber the hearing.

Affirmed

MR. JUSTICE BLACK and the CHIEF JUSTICE [BURGER] dissented.

CITIZENS TO PRESERVE OVERTON PARK, INC. *v.* VOLPE

401 U.S. 402; 91 Sup. Ct. 814; 28 L. Ed. 2d 136 (1971)

[John A. Volpe was Secretary of Transportation at the time this case was litigated. De novo *review, to which the Court refers in its opinion, is a form of review in which the appellate court rehears the evidence in the case rather than depending on the evidentiary record developed in the initial trial or agency hearing as reviewing courts normally do. The Administrative Procedure Act (APA), which is one of the statutes involved in this case, is discussed in the introduction to this chapter.]*

MR. JUSTICE MARSHALL delivered the opinion of the Court:

The growing public concern about the quality of our natural environment has prompted Congress in recent years to enact legislation designed to curb the accelerating destruction of our country's natural beauty. We are concerned in this case with Section 4(f) of the Department of Transportation Act of 1966 and Section 138 of the Federal-Aid to Highway Act of 1968. These statutes prohibit the Secretary of Transportation from authorizing the use of federal funds to finance the construction of highways through public parks if a "feasible and prudent" alternative route exists. If no such route is available, the statutes allow him to approve construction through parks only if there has been "all possible planning to minimize harm" to the park. . . .

Overton Park is a 342-acre city park located near the center of Memphis. The park contains a zoo, a nine-hole municipal golf course, an outdoor theatre, nature trails, a bridle path, an art academy, picnic areas, and 170 acres of forest. The proposed highway, which is to be a six-lane, high-speed, expressway, will sever the zoo from the rest of the park. Although the roadway will be depressed below ground level except where it crosses a small creek, 26 acres of the park will be destroyed. . . .

Although the route through the park was approved by the Bureau of Public Roads in 1956 and by the Federal Highway Administrator in 1966, the enactment of Section 4(f) of the Department of Transportation Act prevented distribution of federal funds for the section of the highway designated to go through Overton Park until the Secretary of Transportation determined whether the requirements of Section 4(f) had been met. Federal funding for the rest of the project was, however, available; and the state acquired right-of-way on both sides of the park. In April 1968, the Secretary announced that he concurred in the judgment of local officials that I–40 should be built through the park. And in September 1969 the State acquired the right-of-way inside Overton Park from the city. Final approval for the project—the route as well as the design—was not announced until November 1969, after Congress had reiterated in Section 138 of the Federal-Aid Highway Act that highway construction through public parks was to be restricted. Neither announcement approving the route and design of I–40 was accompanied by a statement of the Secretary's factual findings. He did not indicate why he believed there were no feasible and prudent alternative routes or why design changes could not be made to reduce the harm to the park.

Petitioners contend that the Secretary's action is invalid without such formal findings and that the Secretary did not make an independent determination but merely relied on the judgment of the Memphis City Council. They also contend that it would be "feasible and prudent" to route I–40 around Overton Park either to the north or to the south. And they argue that if these alternative routes are not "feasible and prudent," the present plan does not include "all possible" methods for reducing harm to the park. Petitioners claim that I–40 could be built under the park by using either of two possible tunneling methods, and they claim that, at a minimum, by using advanced drainage techniques the expressway could be depressed below ground level along the entire route through the park including the section that crosses the small creek.

Respondents argue that it was unnecessary for the Secretary to make formal findings and, that he did, in fact, exercise his own independent judgment that was supported by the facts. In the District Court, respondents introduced affidavits, prepared specifically for this litigation, which indicated that the Secretary had made the decision and that the decision was supportable. These affidavits were contradicted by affidavits introduced by petitioners, who also sought to take the deposition of a former federal highway administrator who had participated in the decision to route I–40 through Overton Park.

The District Court and the Court of Appeals found that formal findings by the Secretary were not necessary and refused to order the deposition of the former Federal Highway Administrator because those courts believed that probing of the mental processes of an administrative decision-maker was prohibited. And, believing that the Secretary's authority was wide and reviewing courts' authority narrow in the approval of highway routes, the lower courts held that the affidavits contained no basis for a determination that the Secretary had exceeded his authority.

We agree that formal findings were not

required. But we do not believe that in this case judicial review based solely on litigation affidavits was adequate.

A threshold question—whether petitioners are entitled to any judicial review—is easily answered. Section 701 of the Administrative Procedure Act, 5 U.S.C. Section 701 (Supp. V), provides that the action of "each authority of the Government of the United States," which includes the Department of Transportation, is subject to judicial review except where there is a statutory prohibition on review or where "agency action is committed to agency discretion by law." 5 U.S.C. Section 701 (Supp. V). In this case, there is no indication that Congress sought to prohibit judicial review and there is most certainly no "showing of 'clear and convincing evidence' of a . . . legislative intent" to restrict access to judicial review. *Abbott Laboratories* v. *Gardner,* 387 U.S. 136, 141 (1967). . . .

Similarly, the Secretary's decision here does not fall within the exception for action "committed to agency discretion." This is a very narrow exception. . . . The legislative history of the Administrative Procedure Act indicates that it is applicable in those rare instances where "statutes are drawn in such broad terms that in a given case there is no law to apply." S. Rep. No. 758, Senate Committee on the Judiciary, 79th Cong., 1st Sess., 26 (1945).

Section 4(f) of the Department of Transportation Act and Section 138 of the Federal-Aid Highway Act are clear and specific directives. Both the Department of Transportation Act and the Federal-Aid to Highway Act provide that the Secretary "shall not approve any program or project" that requires the use of any public parkland "unless (1) there is no feasible and prudent alternative to the use of such land, and (2) such program includes all possible planning to minimize harm to such park . . . 23 U.S.C. Section 138 (Supp.V); 49 U.S.C. Section 1653 (f) (Supp.V). This language is a plain and explicit bar to the use of federal funds for construction of highways through parks—only the most unusual situations are exempted.

Despite the clarity of the statutory language, respondents argue that the Secretary has wide discretion. They recognize that the requirement that there be no "feasible" alternative route admits of little administrative discretion. For this exemption to apply the Secretary must find that as a matter of sound engineering it would not be feasible to build the highway along any other route. Respondents argue, however, that the requirement that there be no other "prudent" route requires the Secretary to engage in a wide-ranging balancing of competing interests. They contend that the Secretary should weigh the detriment resulting from the destruction of parkland against the cost of other routes, safety considerations, and other factors, and determine on the basis of the importance that he attaches to these other factors whether, on balance, alternative feasible routes would be "prudent."

But no such wide-ranging endeavor was intended. It is obvious that in most cases considerations of cost, directness of route, and community disruption will indicate that parkland should be used for highway construction whenever possible. Although it may be necessary to transfer funds from one jurisdiction to another, there will always be a smaller outlay required from the public purse when parkland is used since the public already owns the land and there will be no need to pay for the right-of-way. And since people do not live or work in parks, if a highway is built on parkland no one will have to leave his home or give up his business. Such factors are common to substantially all highway construction. Thus if Congress intended these factors to be on an equal footing with preservation of parkland there would have been no need for the statutes.

Congress clearly did not intend that cost and disruption of the community were to be ignored by the Secretary. But the very existence of the statute indicates that protection of parkland was to be given paramount importance. The few green havens that are public parks were not to be lost unless there were truly unusual factors present in a particular case or the cost or community disruption resulting from alternative routes reached extraordinary magnitudes. If the statutes are to have any meaning, the Secretary cannot approve the destruction of parkland unless he finds that alternative routes present unique problems.

Plainly, there is "law to apply" and thus

Separate opinion of MR. JUSTICE BLACK, with whom MR. JUSTICE BRENNAN joins:

I agree with the Court that the judgment of the Court of Appeals is wrong and that its action should be reversed. I do not agree that the whole matter should be remanded to the District Court. I think the case should be sent back to the Secretary of Transportation. It is apparent from the Court's opinion today that the Secretary of Transportation completely failed to comply with the duty imposed upon him by Congress. . . . The Act of Congress in connection with other Federal Highway Aid legislation, it seems to me, calls for hearings, hearings that a court can review, hearings that demonstrate more than mere arbitrary defiance by the Secretary. Whether the findings growing out of such hearings are labeled "formal" or "informal" appears to me to be no more than an exercise in semantics. Whatever the hearing requirements might be, the Department of Transportation failed to meet them in this case.

MR. JUSTICE BLACKMUN:

I fully join the Court in its opinion and in its judgment. I merely wish to state the obvious:

1. The case comes to this Court as the end product of more than a decade of endeavor to solve the interstate highway problem at Memphis.

2. The administrative decisions under attack here are not those of a single Secretary; some were made by the present Secretary's predecessor and, before him, by the Department of Commerce's Bureau of Public Roads.

3. The 1966 Act and the 1968 Act here, have imposed new standards and have cut across former methods and conditions upon a situation that already was largely developed. . . .

UNITED STATES *v.* DU PONT

353 U.S. 586; 77 Sup. Ct. 872; 1 L. Ed. 2d 872 (1957)

[The basic antitrust law is the Sherman Act of 1890, which was later strengthened by the Clayton Act. It is far easier to get convictions under the Clayton Act because the government does not need to prove, as it must under the Sherman Act, that monopolizing is actually occurring, but only that current actions will tend to produce monopolies in the future. Nevertheless, neither statute condemns the existence of monopolies as such, but only monopolizing—that is, positive business actions creating or tending to create restraint of trade. Thus, although the Du Pont case involves two of the largest corporations in America—each of which might be argued to have monopoly power by virtue of both its sheer size and its dominance over its smaller competitors—the government must prove anticompetitive action rather than simply offer evidence of the economic strength of the two firms.

The Court speaks of two kinds of mergers. A horizontal merger is one in which a number of firms in the same business are joined—for instance, when two automobile manufacturers are bought by a third. A vertical merger joins companies in different businesses that are linked to one another—for instance, when a steel manufacturer buys the mines from which it obtains the iron and coal necessary to make steel.

The Du Pont case had such a massive potential for disrupting American business that a second Du Pont decision by the Supreme Court was necessary in order to fashion "remedies"—that is, ways in which Du Pont and General Motors could end their illegal connections. United States *v.* Du Pont, *366 U.S. 316 (1961). The Court ordered Du Pont to sell its General Motors stock, but the decree contained a number of special provisions designed to prevent the sale of such a huge block of such an important stock from disrupting the stock market or creating unfair losses to the sellers. The financial impact of these arrangements was so great that Congress passed legislation providing for special tax treatment for the proceeds of the sale.]*

MR. JUSTICE BRENNAN delivered the opinion of the Court:

The primary issue is whether Du Pont's commanding position as General Motors' supplier of automotive finishes and fabrics was achieved on competitive merit alone, or because its acquisition of the General Motors' stock, and the consequent close intercompany relationship, led to the insulation of most of the General Motors' market from free competition, with the resultant likelihood, at the time of suit, of the creation of a monopoly of a line of commerce.

The first paragraph of Section 7 [of the Clayton Act], pertinent here, provides:

"That no corporation engaged in commerce shall acquire, directly or indirectly, the whole or any part of the stock or other share capital of another corporation engaged also in commerce, where the effect of such acquisition may be to substantially lessen competition between the corporation whose stock is so acquired and the corporation making the acquisition, or to restrain such commerce in any section or community, or tend to create a monopoly of any line of commerce." . . . The section is violated whether or not actual restraints or monopolies, or the substantial lessening of competition, have occurred or are intended. . . .

We are met at the threshold with the argument that Section 7 before its amendment in 1950, applied only to an acquisition of the stock of a competing corporation, and not to an acquisition by a supplier corporation of the stock of a customer corporation—in other words, that the statute applied only to horizontal and not to vertical acquisitions. This is the first case presenting the question in this Court. . . .

During the thirty-five years before this action was brought, the Government did not invoke Section 7 against vertical acquisitions. . . .

The first paragraph of Section 7, written in the disjunctive, plainly is framed to reach not only the corporate acquisition of stock of a competing corporation, where the effect may be substantially to lessen competition between them, but also the corporate acquisition of stock of any corporation, competitor or not, where the effect may . . . tend to create a monopoly of any line of commerce. . . .

We hold that any acquisition by one corporation of all or any part of the stock of another corporation, competitor or not, is within the reach of the section whenever the reasonable likelihood appears that the acquisition will result in a restraint of commerce or in the creation of a monopoly of any line of commerce. Thus, although Du Pont and General Motors are not competitors, a violation of the section has occurred if, as a result of the acquisition, there was at the time of suit a reasonable likelihood of a monopoly of any line of commerce. . . .

Appellees argue that there exists no basis for a finding of a probable restraint or monopoly within the meaning of Section 7 because the total General Motors market for finishes and fabrics constituted only a negligible percentage of the total market for these materials for all uses, including automotive uses. It is stated in the General Motors brief that in 1947 Du Pont's finish sales to General Motors constituted 3.5 per cent of all sales of finishes to industrial users, and that its fabrics sales to General Motors comprised 1.6 per cent of the total market for the type of fabric used by the automobile industry.

The record shows that automotive finishes and fabrics have sufficient peculiar characteristics and uses to constitute them products sufficiently distinct from all other finishes and fabrics to make them a "line of commerce" within the meaning of the Clayton Act. . . . The bounds of the relevant market for the purposes of this case are not coextensive with the total market for finishes and fabrics, but are coextensive with the automobile industry, the relevant market for automotive finishes and fabrics. . . . in order to establish a violation of Section 7 the Government must prove a likelihood that competition may be "foreclosed in a substantial share of . . . [that market]." Both requirements are satisfied in this case. The substantiality of a relevant market comprising the automobile industry is undisputed. The substantiality of General Motors' share of that market is fully established in the evidence. . . . Expressed in percentages, Du Pont supplied 67 per cent of General Motors' requirements for finishes in 1946 and 68 per cent in 1947. In fabrics Du Pont supplied 52.3 per cent of requirements in 1946, and 38.5 per cent in 1947. Because General Motors accounts for almost one half of the automobile industry's annual sales, its requirements for automobile finishes and fabrics must represent approximately one half of the relevant market for these materials. Because the record clearly shows that quantitatively and percentagewise du Pont supplies the largest part of General Motors' requirements, we must conclude that Du Pont has a substantial share of the relevant market. . . .

The Du Pont Company's commanding position as a General Motors supplier was not achieved until shortly after its purchase of a sizable block of General Motors stock in 1917. At that time its production for the automobile industry and its sales to General Motors were relatively insignificant. General Motors then produced only about 11 per cent of the total automobile production and its requirements, while relatively substantial, were far short of the proportions they assumed as it forged ahead to its present place in the industry.

At least ten years before the stock acquisition, the Du Pont Company, for over a century the manufacturer of military and commercial explosives, had decided to expand its business into other fields. . . . The first step taken was the Du Pont purchase in 1910 of the Fabrikoid Company, then the largest manufacturer of artificial leather, reconstituted as the Du Pont Fabrikoid Company in 1913. . . .

In June 1916, the Fairfield Rubber Company, producers of rubber-coated fabrics for automobile and carriage tops, was taken over by Du Pont Fabrikoid. In March 1917, purchase was made of Harrison Brothers and Company, manufacturers of paint, varnish, acids and certain inorganic chemicals used in paint manufacture. Shortly afterwards, Harrison absorbed Beckton Chemical Company, a color manufacturer, and, also in 1917, the Bridgeport Wood Finishing Company, a varnish manufacturer. . . .

Thus, before the first block of General Motors stock was acquired, Du Pont was seeking markets not only for its nitrocellulose, but also for the artificial leather, celluloid, rubber-coated goods, and paints and varnishes in demand by automobile companies. In that connection, the trial court expressly found that ". . . reports and other documents written at or near the time of the investment show that Du Pont's representatives were well aware that General Motors was a large consumer of products of the kind offered by Du Pont," and that John J. Raskob, Du Pont's treasurer and the principal promoter of the investment, "for one, thought that Du Pont would ultimately get all that business. . . ."

On December 19, 1917, Raskob submitted a Treasurer's Report to the Du Pont Finance Committee recommending a purchase of General Motors stock in the amount of $25,000,000. That report makes clear that more than just a profitable investment was contemplated. A major consideration was that an expanding General Motors would provide a substantial market needed by the burgeoning Du Pont organization. . . .

This background of the acquisition, particularly the plain implications of the contemporaneous documents, destroys any basis for a conclusion that the purchase was made "solely for investment." Moreover, immediately after the acquisition, Du Pont's influence growing out of it was brought to bear within General Motors to achieve primacy for Du Pont as General Motors' supplier of automotive fabrics and finishes. . . . J. A. Haskell, Du Pont's former sales manager and vice-president, became the General Motors vice-president in charge of the operations committee. . . .

Haskell frankly and openly set about gaining the maximum share of the General Motors market for Du Pont. . . .

Thus sprung from the barrier, Du Pont quickly swept into a commanding lead over its competitors, who were never afterwards in serious contention. Indeed, General Motors' then principal paint supplier, Flint Varnish and Chemical Works, early in 1918 saw the handwriting on the wall. The Flint president came to Durant asking to be bought out, telling Durant, as the trial judge found, that he "knew Du Pont had bought a substantial interest in General Motors and was interested in the paint industry; that . . . [he] felt he would lose a valuable customer, General Motors." . . . The Du Pont Company bought the Flint Works and later dissolved it. . . .

Competitors did obtain higher percentages of the General Motors business in later years, although never high enough at any time substantially to affect the dollar amount of Du Pont's sales. Indeed, it appears likely that General Motors probably turned to outside sources of supply at least in part because its requirements outstripped Du Pont's production, when General Motors proportion of total automobile sales grew greater and the company took its place as the sales leader of the automobile industry. . . . The fact that sticks out in this voluminous record is that the bulk of Du Pont's production has always supplied the largest part of the requirements of the one customer in the automobile industry connected to Du Pont by a stock interest. The inference is overwhelming that Du Pont's commanding position was promoted by its stock interest and was not gained solely on competitive merit.

. . . Du Pont purposely employed its stock to pry open the General Motors market to entrench itself as the primary supplier of General Motors' requirements for automotive finishes and fabrics. . . .

The statutory policy of fostering free competition is obviously furthered when no supplier has an advantage over his competitors from an acquisition of his customer's stock likely to have the effects condemned by the statute. We repeat, that the test of a violation of Section 7 is whether at the time of suit there is a reasonable probability that the acquisition is likely to result in the condemned restraints. The conclusion upon this record is inescapable that such likelihood was proved as to this acquisition. The fire that was kindled in 1917 continues to smolder. It burned briskly to forge the ties that bind the General Motors market to Du Pont, and if it has quieted down, it remains hot, and, from past performance, is likely at any time to blaze and make the fusion complete.

The judgment [of the District Court in favor of Du Pont] must therefore be reversed and the cause remanded to the District Court for a determination, after further hearing, of the equitable relief necessary and appropriate in the public interest to eliminate the effects of the acquisition offensive to the statute.

MR. JUSTICE CLARK, MR. JUSTICE HARLAN and MR. JUSTICE WHITTAKER took no part in the consideration or decision of this case.

MR. JUSTICE BURTON, whom MR. JUSTICE FRANKFURTER joins, dissenting:

The legislative history, administrative practice, and judicial interpretation of Section 7 provide the perspective in which the Government's present assertion that Section 7 applies to vertical acquisitions should be viewed. Seen as a whole, they offer convincing evidence that Section 7, properly construed, has reference only to horizontal acquisitions. . . .

In this case the Government is challenging, in 1949, a stock acquisition that took place in 1917–1919. The Court, without advancing reasons to support its conclusion, holds that in determining whether the effect of the stock acquisition is such as to violate Section 7, the time chosen by the Government in bringing its suit is controlling rather than the time of the acquisition of the stock. This seems to me to ignore the language and structure of Section 7, the purpose of the Clayton Act, and all existing administrative and judicial precedents.

The first paragraph of Section 7 provides that "no corporation . . . shall acquire . . . the stock . . . of another corporation . . . where the effect of such acquisition may be. . . ." Yet the Court construes this provision as if it read "no corporation . . . shall acquire *or continue to hold* . . . the stock . . . of another corporation . . . *whenever it shall appear that* the effect of such acquisition *or continued holding* may be. . . ." . . . the fact of continued holding does not allow the Government to dispense with the necessity of proving that the stock was unlawfully acquired. The offense described by Section 7 is the acquisition, not the holding or the use, of stock.

The Clayton Act was not intended to replace the Sherman Act in remedying actual restraints and monopolies. Its purpose was to supplement the Sherman Act by checking anticompetitive tendencies in their incipiency, before they reached the point at which the Sherman Act comes into play. If, at the time of the stock acquisition, a potential threat to competition is apparent, the acquisition is unlawful under Section 7. If, on the other hand, a potential threat to competition is not then apparent, an antitrust violation is not involved unless subsequent use of the stock constitutes a restraint of trade prohibited by the Sherman Act.

The Court ignores the all-important lawfulness or unlawfulness of the stock acquisition at or about the time it occurred, and limits its attention to the probable anticompetitive effects of the continued holding of the stock at the time of suit, some thirty years later. The result is to subject a good-faith stock acquisition, lawful when made, to the hazard that the continued holding of the stock may make the acquisition illegal through unforeseen developments. Such a view is not supported by the statutory language and violates elementary principles of fairness. . . .

The remaining issues are factual: (1) whether the record established the existence of a reasonable probability that Du Pont's competitors will be foreclosed from securing General Motors' trade, and (2) whether the record establishes that such foreclosure, if probable, involves a substantial share of the relevant market and significantly limits the competitive opportunities of others trading in that market.

A. Foreclosure of Competitors

In this case, the only connection between Du Pont, the supplier, and General Motors, the customer, is Du Pont's 23 per cent stock interest in General Motors. A conclusion that such a stock interest automatically forecloses Du Pont's competitors from selling to General Motors would be without justification. Whether a foreclosure has occurred in the past or is probable in the future is a question of fact turning on the evidence in the record.

. . . the [majority] overturns the District Court's unequivocal findings to the effect that Du Pont was a principal supplier to General Motors prior to the 1917–1919 stock purchases, that Du Pont maintained this position in the years following the stock purchases, and that for the entire thirty-year period preceding the suit, General Motors' purchases of Du Pont's products were based solely on the competitive merits of those products. . . .

The record discloses that each division buys independently, that the pattern of buying varies greatly from one division to another, and that within each division purchases from Du Pont have fluctuated greatly in response to price, quality, service and other competitive considerations. For example, Oldsmobile is the only division which buys antifreeze from Du Pont and one of the two car divisions which does not finish its cars with Duco. Buick alone buys Du Pont motor enamel, and Cadillac alone uses Du Pont's copper electroplating exclusively. Thus the alleged nefarious influence arising from Du Pont's stock interest apparently affects the Oldsmobile antifreeze buyer; but not the Oldsmobile paint buyer; the paint buyers at Chevrolet, Buick and Pontiac, but not the antifreeze or electroplating buyers; and the electroplating buyer at Cadillac, but not the Cadillac paint buyer. . . .

1. *Paints*

Although Du Pont has been General Motors' principal supplier of paint for many years, General Motors continues to buy about 30 per cent of its paint requirements from competitors of Du Pont. . . .

Two products account for a high proportion of Du Pont finish sales to General Motors: "Duco," a nitrocellulose lacquer invented and patented by Du Pont, and "Dulux," a synthetic resin enamel developed by Du Pont. . . .

The invention and development of Duco in the early 1920s represented a significant technological advance. Automobiles previously had been finished by applying numerous coats of varnish. The finishing process took from twelve to thirty-three days, and the storage space and working capital tied up in otherwise completed cars were immense. The life expectancy of varnish finishes was less than a year. . . . In 1920, a Du Pont employee invented a quick drying and durable lacquer which contained a large amount of film-forming solids. This patented finish, named Duco, was submitted to the General Motors Paint and Enamel Committee in 1922 to be tested along with finishes of other manufacturers.

After two years of testing and improvement, the Paint and Enamel Committee became satisfied that Duco was far superior to any other product or any other method of finishing automobiles then available.

The gradual adoption of Duco by some of the General Motors' car divisions, viewed in conjunction with its proved superiority as an auto finish, illustrates the independent buying of each division and demonstrates that Duco made its way on its own merits.

. . . the success of Duco has never been confined to the General Motors' car divisions. In 1924 and 1925, nearly all car manufacturers abandoned varnish for Duco. . . . Ford has purchased finishes from Du Pont in very substantial amounts. . . .

As the District Court found, "*In view of all the evidence of record, the only reasonable conclusion is that Du Pont has continued to sell Duco in substantial quantities to General Motors only because General Motors believes such purchases best fit its needs.*" (Emphasis supplied.)

The second largest item which General Motors buys from Du Pont is Dulux, a synthetic enamel finish used on refrigerators and other appliances. . . .

The District Court did not err in concluding that Dulux—"is apparently an ideal refrigerator finish and is widely used by a number of major manufacturers other than General Motors. Several representatives of competitive refrigerator manufacturers testified that they purchased 100 per cent of their requirements from Du Pont. *There is no evidence that General Motors purchased from Du Pont for any reason other than those that prompted its competitors to buy Dulux from Du Pont—excellence of product, fair price and continuing quality of service.*" (Emphasis supplied.)

2. *Fabrics*

Although there have been variations from year to year and from one car division to another in response to competitive considerations, Du Pont generally has maintained its pre-1917 position as the principal supplier of coated and combined fabrics to General Motors. . . .

In addition to the mass of evidence supporting the District Court's finding that "*such purchases of fabrics as the General Motors divisions have made from Du Pont from time to time were based upon each division's exercise of its business judgment and are not the result of Du Pont domination*" (italics supplied) . . . the record clearly indicates that Du Pont's fabrics can and have made their way in the automotive industry on their merits. . . . Du Pont has continued to be Ford's largest supplier for the material which it does not manufacture for itself. Du Pont likewise has supplied, over the years, a considerable part of the coated and combined fabrics of most of the smaller automobile companies. . . .

Evidence Relied on by the Court

The Court, disregarding the mass of evidence supporting the District Court's conclusion that General Motors purchased Du Pont paint and fabrics solely because of their competitive merit, relies for its contrary conclusion on passages drawn from several documents written during the years 1918–1926, and on the logical fallacy that because Du Pont over a long period supplied a substantial portion of General Motors' requirements of paint and fabrics, its position must have been obtained by misuse of its stock interest rather than competitive considerations.

The isolated instances of alleged pressure or intent to obtain noncompetitive preferences are four: (1) the Raskob report of December 1917; (2) several letters of J. A. Haskell, written during 1918–1920; (3) certain reports and letters of Pierre and Lammont Du Pont during 1921–1924; and (4) a 1926 letter of John L. Pratt. Passages drawn from these 1918–1926 documents do not justify the conclusion reached by the Court. Each of them is a matter of disputed significance which cannot be evaluated without passing on the motivation and intent of the author. Each failed to achieve its specific object. Read in the context of the situations to which they were addressed, each is entirely consistent with the finding of the District Court that, although Du Pont was trying to get as much General Motors' business as it could, there was no restriction on General Motors' freedom to buy as it chose, and that General Motors' buyers did not regard themselves as in any way limited. Moreover, even if isolated paragraphs in these documents, taken from their context, are given some significance, and the other evidence relating to the period from 1918–1926 is entirely ignored, *all* of the evidence after 1926 affirmatively establishes without essential contradiction that Du Pont did not use its stock interest to receive any preferenial treatment from General Motors.

B. Relevant Market

Finally, even assuming the correctness of the Court's conclusion that Du Pont's competitors have been or will be foreclosed from General Motors' paint and fabric trade, it is still necessary to resolve one more issue in favor of the Government in order to reverse the District Court. It is necessary to hold that the Government proved that this foreclosure involves a substantial share of the relevant market and that it significantly limits the competitive opportunities of others trading in that market. . . .

The Court holds that the relevant market in this case is the automotive market for finishes and fabrics, and not the total industrial market for these products. The Court reaches that conclusion because in its view "automotive finishes and fabrics have sufficient peculiar characteristics and uses to constitute them products distinct from all other finishes and fabrics. . . ." We are not told what these "peculiar characteristics" are. . . .

The record does not show that the fabrics and finishes used in the manufacture of automobiles have peculiar characteristics differentiating them from the finishes and fabrics used in other industries. . . .

Duco was first marketed not to General Motors, but to the auto refinishing trade and to manufacturers of furniture, brush handles and pencils. In 1927, 44 per cent of Du Pont's sales of colored Duco, and 51.5 per cent of its total sales, were to purchasers other than auto manufacturers. Although the record does not disclose exact figures for all years, it does show that a substantial portion of Du Pont's sales of Duco have continued to be for nonautomotive uses. . . .

Dulux has never been used in the manufacture of automobiles. It replaced Duco and other lacquers as a finish on refrigerators, washers, dryers, and other appliances, and continues to have wide use on metallic objects requiring a durable finish. Yet the Court includes it as a finish having the unspecified but "peculiar characteristics" distinctive of "automotive finishes."

In 1947, when Du Pont's sales of Duco and Dulux to General Motors totaled about $15,400,000, the total national market for paints and finishes was $1,248,000,000, of which about $552,000,000 was for varnishes, lacquers, enamels, japans, thinners and dopes, the kinds of finishes sold primarily to industrial users. There is no evidence in this record establishing that these industrial finishes are not competitive with Duco and Dulux. There is considerable evidence that many of them are. It is probable that Du Pont's total sales of finishes to General Motors in 1947 constituted less than 3.5 per cent of all sales of industrial finishes.

The record also shows that the types of fabrics used for automobile trim and convertible tops—imitation leather and coated fabrics—are used in the manufacture of innumerable products, such as luggage, furniture, railroad upholstery, books, brief cases, baby carriages, hassocks, bicycle saddles, sporting goods, footwear, belts and table mats. In 1947, General Motors purchased about $9,454,000 of imitation leather and coated fabrics. Of this amount, $3,639,000 was purchased from Du Pont (38.5 per cent) and $5,815,000 from over fifty Du Pont competitors. Since Du Pont produced about 10 per cent of the national market for these products in 1946, 1947 and 1948, and since only 20 per cent of its sales were to the automobile industry, the Du Pont sales to the automobile industry constituted only about 2 per cent of the total market. The Court ignores the record by treating this small fraction of the total market as a market of distinct products.

It will not do merely to stress the large size of these two corporations . . . The commerce involved here is . . . less than 3.5 per cent of the national market for industrial finishes, and only about 1.6 per cent of the national market for [fabrics]. . . .

The Court might be justified in holding that products sold to the automotive industry constitute the relevant market in the case of products such as carburetors or tires which are sold primarily to automobile manufacturers. But the sale of Duco, Dulux, imitation leather, and coated fabrics is not so limited.

The burden was on the Government to prove that a substantial share of the relevant market would, in all probability, be affected by Du Pont's 23 per cent stock interest in General Motors. The Government proved only that Du Pont's sales of finishes and fabrics to General Motors were large in volume, and that General Motors was the leading manufacturer of automobiles during the later years covered by the record. The Government did not show that the identical products were not used on a large scale for many other purposes in many other industries. Nor did the Government show that the automobile industry in general, or General Motors in particular, comprised a large or substantial share of the total market. . . . Accordingly, I would affirm the judgment of the District Court.

CHAPTER 17

Privacy

The case of *Griswold* v. *Connecticut* (p. 739) does not fit neatly into any of the traditional categories of constitutional law. Indeed, the Court experienced some difficulty in finding a specific constitutional provision on which to hang its decision. Its final position seems to be that there are some things just too intimate for government regulation. More broadly, there has been much concern in recent years about a "right to privacy" or the "right to be let alone." [1] *Griswold* may introduce such a right into constitutional law. It has been recognized in some of the states.

Griswold was the Court's first modern venture into birth control. [In *Buck* v. *Bell,* 274 U.S.

[1] See David O'Brien, *Privacy, Law and Public Policy* (New York: Praeger, 1979); Alan F. Westin, *Privacy and Freedom* (New York: Atheneum, 1967); and Morris L. Ernst and Alan U. Schwartz, *Privacy, the Right to Be Let Alone* (New York: Macmillan, 1962). The pioneering exposition is in Samuel D. Warren and Louis D. Brandeis, "The Right to Privacy," *Harvard Law Review,* Vol. 4 (1890), p. 193. Cf. Harry Kalven, "Privacy in Tort Law—Were Warren and Brandeis Wrong?" *Law and Contemporary Problems,* Vol. 31 (1966), p. 326.

200 (1927), Justice Holmes, in an opinion that many of his admirers have come to regret, upheld the right of a state to sterilize a feebleminded, institutionalized woman. She was the daughter of a feebleminded mother in the same institution, and the mother of an illegitimate feebleminded child. Justice Holmes concluded his opinion with: "Three generations of imbeciles are enough." Cf. *Skinner* v. *Oklahoma,* 316 U.S. 535 (1942).] Although it invoked "privacy," the Court's major concern may well have been the kind of equal protection problems examined in Chapter 14. For antibirth control statutes tend to keep birth control services away from the poor. In practice they prevent the open provision of such services by public health facilities and charitable agencies. The more well-to-do, on the other hand, usually find such services readily available from private physicians on a confidential basis.

In a subsequent case, *Eisenstadt* v. *Baird,* 405 U.S. 438 (1972), the Court seized upon the fact that a Massachusetts statute prohibited the distribution of contraceptives to the unmarried but not the married to declare it unconstitutional as involving an unreasonable classification in violation of the equal protection clause. (See Chapter 14.) It held the state could show no convincing reason for distinguishing between the married and unmarried. There was an alternative holding in terms of privacy:

> If under *Griswold* the distribution of contraceptives to married persons cannot be prohibited, a ban on distribution to unmarried persons would be equally impermissible. It is true that in *Griswold* the right of privacy in question inhered in the marital relationship. Yet, the marital couple is not an independent entity with a mind and heart of its own, but an association of two individuals each with a separate intellectual and emotional make-up. If the right of privacy means anything, it is the right of the *individual,* married or single, to be free from unwarranted government intrusion into matters so fundamentally affecting a person as the decision whether to bear or beget a child.

The birth control decisions paved the way for *Roe* v. *Wade* and *Doe* v. *Bolton* (p. 743), the abortion decisions of 1973. They rested even more explicitly on privacy grounds than had *Griswold*—although here again equal protection may have been the underlying consideration.

In *Zoblocki* v. *Redhail,* 434 U.S. 374 (1978), the Court held that the right to marry is a "privacy" right protected by the due process clause. It struck down a state statute forbidding a resident who was under a court order to support his or her minor children, not in his or her custody, from marrying without the court's permission. The case could have been decided purely on equal protection grounds, and the Supreme Court seemed to go out of its way to treat marriage as a privacy right. The statute involved was clearly part of a complex set of state statutes regulating marriage, divorce, alimony, and child support. This case announces that the justices are now ready to constitutionalize yet another area of law that traditionally was considered purely a matter of state concern.

The search-and-seizure, self-incrimination, and anonymous association cases examined earlier in this book also contribute to the notion of privacy. Part of the problem of free speech versus trespass is a concern for the individual's freedom not to be subjected to speech he does not want to hear and to be left in the enjoyment of his peace and quiet, as expressed by Justice Black in *Bell* v. *Maryland* (see p. 342) and by Justice Powell in *Lloyd Corp.* v. *Tanner* (see Chapter 11). That interest is also reflected in Justice Douglas' dissent in *Public Utilities Commission* v. *Pollak* 343, U.S. 451 (1952). In *Martin* v. *Struthers,* 319 U.S. 141 (1943), the Court struck down a local ordinance forbidding doorbell ringing by door-to-door solicitors because it interfered with the religious freedom of the Jehovah's Witnesses. But several of the justices expressed concern for the peace and quiet of the residents. Even in that case the Court held that the dweller could protect himself by using "No Trespassing" signs, and it upheld similar ordinances against the challenge of purely commercial solicitors. In *Saia* v. *New York,* 334 U.S. 558 (1948), the Court struck down an ordinance directed at sound trucks because it vested too much discretion in the police chief, but the justices did indicate that statutes regulating the volume of sound emitted by such trucks might be constitutional and later upheld a statute banning "raucous" sound trucks. [*Kovacs* v. *Cooper,* 336 U.S. 77 (1949).]

Justice Douglas saw his old dissent in *Public Utilities Commission* v. *Pollak* largely vindicated in *Lehman* v. *Shaker Heights,* 418 U.S. 298 (1974), when the Court upheld a refusal by the city to allow political candidates to buy space in its transit advertising, which it devoted entirely to commercial ads and public service messages. A majority held that transit advertising was not a forum protected by the First Amendment, in part because political messages could otherwise be thrust upon a captive audience which wanted only transportation.

The Court seems to have been especially concerned with privacy in the context of the obscenity laws. In *Stanley* v. *Georgia,* 394 U.S. 557 (1969), the Court proclaimed the right of private possession for private use of obscene materials. *Stanley* involved the search of a private home. The Court's decision obviously rested on its disapproval of police invasions of privacy to seek out obscenity rather than its approval of the private enjoyment of obscenity. It has upheld the right of the government to bar the importation of obscene material even if that material is destined for private use rather than commercial sale. [See *United States* v. *37 Photographs,* 402 U.S. 363 (1971).]

Obscenity also raises precisely the opposite privacy problem—the desire of persons *not* to be the recipients of unwanted obscenity. In *Rowan* v. *Post Office Dept.,* 397 U.S. 728 (1970), the Court upheld a federal mailing statute. It provides that a person who has received by mail "a pandering advertisement which offers for sale matter which the addressee in his sole discretion believes to be erotically arousing or sexually provocative" can obtain a Post Office order requiring the removal of the addressee's name from the advertiser's mailing lists and prohibiting all future mailings.

The advertiser argued that his First Amendment rights had been abridged because the statute did not require a court determination that the advertisement was obscene. Chief Justice Burger replied: "The right of every person to be let alone must be placed in the scales with the right of others to communicate. In today's complex society we are inescapably captive audiences for many purposes, but a sufficient measure of individual autonomy must survive to permit every householder to exercise control over unwanted mail. . . ."

Cohen v. *California,* 403 U.S. 15 (1971), illustrates the "inescapably captive audiences." There the Court overthrew a disturbing-the-peace conviction based on the wearing, in a courthouse corridor, of a jacket with a four-letter word painted on its back. The Court said in part:

> The ability of government, consonant with the Constitution, to shut off discourse solely to protect others from hearing it is, in other words, dependent upon a showing that substantial privacy interests are being invaded in an essentially intolerable matter. Any broader view of this authority would effectively empower a majority to silence dissidents simply as a matter of personal predilections.
>
> In this regard, persons confronted with Cohen's jacket were in a quite different posture than, say, those subjected to the raucous emissions of sound trucks blaring outside their residences. Those in the Los Angeles courthouse could effectively avoid further bombardment of their sensibilities simply by averting their eyes. And while it may be that one has a more substantial claim to a recognizable privacy interest when walking through a courthouse corridor than, for example, strolling through Central Park, surely it is nothing like the interest in being free from unwanted expression in the confines of one's own home.

Subsequently the Court upheld the FCC's ban on the broadcasting of four-letter words. The justices noted the pervasive intrusiveness into the home of the broadcast media. [*F.C.C.* v. *Pacifica Foundation,* 438 U.S. 726 (1978).]

More generally, one portion of the hard-core pornography standard specified that a work was not obscene unless it went substantially beyond the limits of candor in the community. Obviously, what was involved was judicial concern for the protection of individual sensitivities from unwanted invasion. Justice Brennan sought to build a whole new standard of obscenity regulation for adults on this privacy rationale in his dissent in *Paris Adult Theatre I.* v. *Slaton* (p. 408). And the majority, in the companion case of *Miller* v. *California* (p. 408), though dropping the "utterly without redeeming social importance" part of the hard-core pornography standard, retained the test of "patent offensiveness."

The right of anonymous association examined in Chapter 11 is a right to privacy as well as a right to freedom of speech. It protects the individual from having to tell others about his associations. *Laird* v. *Tatum,* 408 U.S. 1 (1972), involving Army Intelligence surveillance of war-protests groups, in which the Court denied standing, raises interesting privacy issues. If a government requirement that its employees file statements revealing the groups to which they belong is an unconstitutional invasion of their right of association [*Bates* v. *Little Rock,* 361 U.S. 516 (1960)], would it be unconstitutional also for a government to employ agents to follow its employees to discover their group affiliations? [See also *Buckley* v. *Valeo* (p. 400).]

The most extensive Supreme Court concern for privacy, of course, is to be found in the Fourth Amendment unreasonable search cases in Chapter 15. Increasingly, however, the privacy issue also arises in noncriminal areas such as health and housing inspections and in the welfare visitation discussed in Chapter 16. The welfare state may provide many services at the cost of invading the privacy of those served.

In the area of residential privacy, too, are the cases concerning single-family zoning laws. See the discussions of the *Belle Terre* and *Moore* cases in Chapter 14.

A troubling case in terms of an emerging right of privacy is *Time, Inc.* v. *Hill,* 385 U.S. 374 (1967), one in the sequence of cases following *New York Times Co.* v. *Sullivan* (p. 415). It involved a supermarket manager and his family who had been held captive by bandits. The family had shunned publicity. Some years later a fictionalized account of their experience became the basis for a play. The play, in turn, generated a picture story in a national magazine that conveyed a number of false impressions. The Hills won a verdict under a New York statute designed to prevent invasions of privacy. The Supreme Court reversed on the grounds that they were public figures covered by the *Sullivan* rule even though they had literally been forced at gun point into a situation of interest to the public. *Time, Inc.,* together with *Griswold,* may mean that a constitutional right to privacy exists against government but not necessarily against other individuals or the press.

However, the Burger Court seems to have reversed this tendency by holding that a lawyer, even though engaged in litigation that attracted much public attention, was a private person not subject to the *Sullivan* rule. [See also *Time, Inc.* v. *Firestone,* 424 U.S. 448 (1977).] In *Cox Broadcasting Corp.* v. *Cohn,* 420 U.S. 469 (1975), the Court held that publication of the name of a rape victim, at least where the name was obtained from public records, did not constitute an unlawful invasion of her family's privacy. Similarly it has held that the publication of the names of those charged with juvenile offenses is protected by the First Amendment. [*Smith* v. *Daily Mail Publishing Co.,* 443 U.S. 97 (1979).]

Closely related to the right to privacy is the right to reputation, which is sometimes referred to as a property or liberty right under the due process clause. Reputation is often raised as a supplementary issue by government employees who allege that their dismissals from government service violated due process. They argue that their unexplained dismissals damage their reputations. These claims have not been very successful. [Cf. *Board of Regents* v. *Roth,* 408 U.S. 564 (1972) with *Bishop* v. *Wood,* 426 U.S. 341 (1976).]

Where the issue of government injury to reputation by publicizing of past actions is raised, the results are more mixed. In *Wisconsin* v. *Constantineau,* 400 U.S. 433 (1971), the Court declared unconstitutional a state law providing that state officials might post lists of excessive drinkers in liquor stores, forbidding sale or gift of liquor to them for one year. But in *Paul* v. *Davis,* 424 U.S. 693

(1976), the Court refused a remedy to a person who had been falsely identified as an "active shoplifter" in a flyer circulated by the police to retail merchants. Referring to *Constantineau* and other cases, Justice Rehnquist said: "This line of cases does not establish the proposition that reputation standing alone, apart from some more tangible interests, such as employment, is either 'liberty' or 'property' by itself sufficient to invoke the procedural protection of the Due Process Clause."

In a related case, *Whalen* v. *Roe,* 429 U.S. 589 (1977), the Court upheld a state statute requiring that the names of persons receiving dangerous prescription drugs be kept in a computer file. Roe claimed that such lists violated his rights to privacy because of the risk that the information might become public. The Court emphasized that the statute contained provisions designed to prevent such publicity. But the Court also said: "We are not unaware of the threat to privacy implicit in the accumulation of vast amounts of personal information in computerized data banks or other massive government files."

Obviously, the scope of a right to privacy will have to be carried out step by step in the light of the real problems of modern, technologically complex, and basically urban societies, but a judicial concern for such a right will be a sign of the continuing vitality and growth of our Constitution.

GRISWOLD v. CONNECTICUT

381 U.S. 479; 85 Sup. Ct. 1678; 14 L. Ed. 2d 510 (1965)

[Connecticut's birth control laws had been challenged twice before this case, and in each instance the Supreme Court managed to turn aside from the major issue by resting its decisions on questions of standing. Connecticut had not generally enforced its laws against individual physicians, sellers, or married couples. The main impact of the laws was to prohibit the poor from receiving the same birth control information and supplies available to the middle class. After birth control clinics were opened in spite of the statute, the state sought to enforce its laws against them. This case reached the Supreme Court.]

MR. JUSTICE DOUGLAS delivered the opinion of the Court:

Appellant Griswold is Executive Director of the Planned Parenthood League of Connecticut. Appellant Buxton is a licensed physician and a professor at the Yale Medical School who served as Medical Director for the League at its Center in New Haven—a center open and operating from November 1 to November 10, 1961, when appellants were arrested.

They gave information, instruction, and medical advice to *married persons* as to the means of preventing conception. They examined the wife and prescribed the best contraceptive device or material for her use. . . .

The statutes whose constitutionality is involved in this appeal are Sections 53–32 and 54–196 of the General Statutes of Connecticut (1958 rev.). The former provides: "Any person who uses any drug, medicinal article or instrument for the purpose of preventing conception shall be fined not less than $50 or imprisoned not less than sixty days nor more than one year or be both fined and imprisoned."

Section 54–196 provides: "Any person who assists, abets, counsels, causes, hires, or commands another to commit any offense may be prosecuted and punished as if he were the principal offender."

The appellants were found guilty as accessories and fined $100 each, against the

enumerated in the first eight amendments and an intent that the list of rights included there not be deemed exhaustive. . . .

. . . In sum, the Ninth Amendment simply lends strong support to the view that the "liberty" protected by the Fifth and Fourteenth Amendments from infringement by the Federal Government or the States is not restricted to rights specifically mentioned in the first eight amendments. . . .

MR. JUSTICE HARLAN and MR. JUSTICE WHITE concurred.

MR. JUSTICE BLACK, with whom MR. JUSTICE STEWART joins, dissented:

The Court talks about a constitutional "right of privacy" as though there is some constitutional provision or provisions forbidding any law ever to be passed which might abridge the "privacy" of individuals. But there is not. There are, of course, guarantees in certain specific constitutional provisions which are designed in part to protect privacy at certain times and places with respect to certain activities. Such, for example, is the Fourth Amendment's guarantee against "unreasonable searches and seizures." But I think it belittles that Amendment to talk about it as though it protects nothing but "privacy." To treat it that way is to give it a niggardly interpretation, not the kind of liberal reading I think any Bill of Rights provision should be given. The average man would very likely not have his feelings soothed any more by having his property seized openly than by having it seized privately and by stealth. He simply wants his property left alone. And a person can be just as much, if not more, irritated, annoyed and injured by an unceremonious public arrest by a policeman as he is by a seizure in the privacy of his office or home.

One of the most effective ways of diluting or expanding a constitutionally guaranteed right is to substitute for the crucial word or words of a constitutional guarantee another word or words more or less flexible and more or less restricted in meaning. This fact is well illustrated by the use of the term "right of privacy" as a comprehensive substitute for the Fourth Amendment's guarantee against "unreasonable searches and seizures." "Privacy" is a broad, abstract and ambiguous concept which can easily be shrunken in meaning but which can also, on the other hand, easily be interpreted as a constitutional ban against many things other than searches and seizures. I have expressed the view many times that First Amendment freedoms, for example, have suffered from a failure of the courts to stick to the simple language of the First Amendment in construing it, instead of invoking multitudes of words substituted for those the Framers used. . . .

I realize that many good and able men have eloquently spoken and written, sometimes in rhapsodical strains, about the duty of this Court to keep the Constitution in tune with the times. The idea is that the Constitution must be changed from time to time and that this Court is charged with a duty to make those changes. For myself, I must with all deference reject that philosophy. The Constitution makers knew the need for change and provided for it. Amendments suggested by the people's elected representatives can be submitted to the people or their selected agents for ratification. That method of change was good for our Fathers, and being somewhat old-fashioned I must add it is good enough for me. And so, I cannot rely on the Due Process Clause or the Ninth Amendment or any mysterious and uncertain natural law concept as a reason for striking down this state law. The Due Process Clause with an "arbitrary and capricious" or "shocking to the conscience" formula was liberally used by this Court to strike down economic legislation in the early decades of this century, threatening many people thought, the tranquility and stability of the Nation. See, e.g., *Lochner* v. *New York.* That formula, based on subjective considerations of "natural justice," is no less dangerous when used to enforce this Court's views about personal right than those about economic rights. I had thought that we had laid that formula, as a means for striking down state legislation, to rest once and for all in cases like *West Coast Hotel Co.* v. *Parrish.*

[Mr. Justice Stewart wrote a dissenting opinion in which Mr. Justice Black joined.]

ROE v. WADE

410 U.S. 113; 93 Sup. Ct. 705; 35 L. Ed. 2d 147 (1973)

DOE v. BOLTON

410 U.S. 179; 93 Sup. Ct. 739; 35 L. Ed. 2d 201 (1973)

[Roe and Doe are fictitious names for the parties who brought these class actions. Roe was a pregnant single woman; Doe was a married couple. In Doe *a licensed physician joined the Does in challenging the Georgia abortion statute.* Roe *is a challenge to the Texas statute. The Texas statute was rather typical of the old-fashioned style of abortion statutes. Georgia had a modern, "reform" statute. Thus, two separate decisions were needed. Justice Blackmun wrote the opinion of the Court in both cases. Chief Justice Burger and Justices Douglas and Stewart concurred and Justices White and Rehnquist dissented in both cases.]*

MR. JUSTICE BLACKMUN delivered the opinion of the Court [in Roe]: . . .

We forthwith acknowledge our awareness of the sensitive and emotional nature of the abortion controversy, of the vigorous opposing views, even among physicians, and of the deep and seemingly absolute convictions that the subject inspires. One's philosophy, one's experiences, one's exposure to the raw edges of human existence, one's religious training, one's attitudes toward life and family and their values, and the moral standards one establishes and seeks to observe, are all likely to influence and to color one's thinking and conclusions about abortion. In addition, population growth, pollution, poverty, and racial overtones tend to complicate and not to simplify the problem.

Our task, of course, is to resolve the issue by constitution measurement free of emotion and of predilection. We seek earnestly to do this, and, because we do, we have inquired into, and in this opinion place some emphasis upon, medical and medical-legal history and what that history reveals about man's attitudes toward the abortive procedure over the centuries. We bear in mind, too, Mr. Justice Holmes' admonition in his now vindicated dissent in *Lochner* v. *New York,* 198 U.S. 45, 76 (1905):

> "It [the Constitution] is made for people of fundamentally differing views, and the accident of our finding certain opinions natural and familiar or novel and even shocking ought not to conclude our judgment upon the question whether statutes embodying them conflict with the Constitution of the United States." . . .

The principal thrust of appellant's attack on the Texas statutes is that they improperly invade a right, said to be possessed by the pregnant woman, to choose to terminate her pregnancy. . . . Before addressing this claim, we feel it desirable briefly to survey, in several aspects, the history of abortion, for such insight as that history may afford us. . . .

The Constitution does not explicitly mention any right of privacy. . . . the Court has recognized that a right of personal privacy, or a guarantee of certain areas or zones of privacy, does exist under the Constitution. In varying contexts the Court or individual Justices have indeed found at least the roots of that right in the First Amendment [*Stanley* v. *Georgia*]; in the Fourth and Fifth Amendments [e.g., *Terry* v. *Ohio*]; in the penumbras of the Bill of Rights [*Griswold* v. *Connecticut*]; in the Ninth Amendment [id.]; or in the concept of liberty guaranteed by the first section of the Fourteenth Amendment, see [*Meyer* v. *Nebraska*]. These decisions make it clear that only personal rights that can be deemed "fundamental" or "implicit in the concept of ordered liberty" [*Palko* v. *Connecticut*] are included in this guarantee of personal privacy. They also make it clear that the right has some extension to activities relating to marriage [*Loving* v. *Virginia*], procreation [*Skinner* v. *Oklahoma*], contraception [*Eisenstadt* v. *Baird*], family relationships [*Prince* v. *Massachusetts*], and child rearing and education [*Pierce* v. *Society of Sisters; Meyer* v. *Nebraska*].

The right of privacy, whether it be founded in the Fourteenth Amendment's concept of personal liberty and restrictions upon state action, as we feel it is, or, as the District Court determined, in the Ninth Amendment's reservation of rights to the people, is broad enough to encompass a woman's decision whether or not to terminate her pregnancy. The detriment that the State would impose upon the pregnant woman by denying this choice altogether is apparent. Specific and direct harm medically diagnosable even in early pregnancy may be involved. Maternity, or additional offspring, may force upon the woman a distressful life and future. Psychological harm may be imminent. Mental and physical health may be taxed by child care. There is also the distress, for all concerned, associated with the unwanted child, and there is the problem of bringing a child into a family already unable, psychologically and otherwise, to care for it. In other cases, as in this one, the additional difficulties and continuing stigma of unwed motherhood may be involved. All these factors the woman and her responsible physician necessarily will consider in consultation.

On the basis of elements such as these, appellants and some *amici* argue that the woman's right is absolute and that she is entitled to terminate her pregnancy at whatever time, in whatever way, and for whatever reason she alone chooses. With this we do not agree. . . . The Court's decisions recognizing a right of privacy also acknowledge that some state regulation in areas protected by that right is appropriate. [A] state may properly assert important interests in safeguarding health, in maintaining medical standards, and in protecting potential life. At some point in pregnancy, these respective interests become sufficiently compelling to sustain regulation of the factors that govern the abortion decision. . . . In fact, it is not clear to us that the claim asserted by some *amici* that one has an unlimited right to do with one's body as one pleases bears a close relationship to the right of privacy previously articulated in the Court's decisions. The Court has refused to recognize an unlimited right of this kind in the past. [*Jacobson* v. *Massachusetts*] (vaccination); [*Buck* v. *Bell*] (sterilization).

We therefore conclude that the right of personal privacy includes the abortion decision, but that this right is not unqualified and must be considered against important state interests in regulation. . . .

Where certain "fundamental rights" are involved, the Court has held that regulation limiting these rights may be justified only by a "compelling state interest" . . . and that legislative enactments must be narrowly drawn to express only the legitimate state interests at stake. . . .

A.

The appellee and certain *amici* argue that the fetus is a "person" within the language and meaning of the Fourteenth Amendment. In support of this they outline at length and in detail the well-known facts of fetal development. If this suggestion of personhood is established, the appellant's case of course, collapses, for the fetus' right to life would then be guaranteed specifically by the Amendment. . . . On the other hand, the appellee conceded on reargument that no case could be cited that holds that a fetus is a person within the meaning of the Fourteenth Amendment.

The Constitution does not define "person" in so many words. . . . In nearly all these instances, [in which the Constitution employs the word] the use of the word is such that it has application only postnatally. None indicates, with any assurance, that it has any possible prenatal application.*

* When Texas urges that a fetus is entitled to Fourteenth Amendment protection as a person, it faces a dilemma. Neither in Texas nor in any other State are all abortions prohibited. Despite broad proscription, an exception always exists. The exception . . . for an abortion procured or attempted by medical advice for the purpose of saving the life of the mother is typical. But if the fetus is a person who is not to be deprived of life without due process of law, and if the mother's condition is the sole determinant, does not the Texas exception appear to

All this, together with our observation . . . that throughout the major portion of the nineteenth century prevailing legal abortion practices were far freer than they are today, persuades us that the word *person,* as used in the Fourteenth Amendment, does not include the unborn. . . . This conclusion, however, does not of itself fully answer the contentions raised by Texas, and we pass on to other considerations.

B.

The pregnant woman cannot be isolated in her privacy. She carries an embryo and, later, a fetus. . . . The situation therefore is inherently different from marital intimacy, or bedroom possession of obscene material, or marriage, or procreation, or education, with which *Eisenstadt, Griswold, Stanley, Loving, Skinner, Pierce,* and *Meyer* were respectively concerned. [I]t is reasonable and appropriate for a State to decide that at some point in time another interest, that of health of the mother or that of potential human life, becomes significantly involved. The woman's privacy is no longer sole and any right of privacy she possesses must be measured accordingly.

Texas urges that, apart from the Fourteenth Amendment, life begins at conception and is present throughout pregnancy, and that, therefore, the State has a compelling interest in protecting that life from and after conception. We need not resolve the difficult question of when life begins. When those trained in the respective disciplines of medicine, philosophy, and theology are unable to arrive at any consensus, the judiciary, at this point in the development of man's knowledge, is not in a position to speculate as to the answer. It should be sufficient to note briefly the wide divergence of thinking on this most sensitive and difficult question. . . .

In areas other than criminal abortion the law has been reluctant to endorse any theory that life, as we recognize it, begins before live birth or to accord legal rights to the unborn except in narrowly defined situations and except when the rights are contingent upon live birth. . . . In short, the unborn have never been recognized in the law as persons in the whole sense. In view of all this, we do not agree that, by adopting one theory of life, Texas may override the rights of the pregnant woman that are at stake. We repeat, however, that the State does have an important and legitimate interest in preserving and protecting the health of the pregnant woman, whether she be a resident of the State or a nonresident who seeks medical consultation and treatment there, and that it has still *another* important and legitimate interest in protecting the potentiality of human life. These interests are separate and distinct. Each grows in substantiality as the woman approaches term and, at a point during pregnancy, each becomes "compelling."

With respect to the State's important and legitimate interest in the health of the mother, the "compelling" point, in the light of present medical knowledge, is at approximately the end of the first trimester. This is so because of the now established medical fact . . . that until the end of the first trimester mortality in abortion is less than mortality in normal childbirth. It follows that, from and after this point, a State may regulate the abortion procedure to the extent that the regulation reasonably relates to the preservation and protection of maternal health. Examples of permissible state regulation in this area are requirements as to the qualifications of the person who is to perform the abortion; as to the licensure of that person; as to the facility in which the procedure is to be performed, that is, whether it must be a hospital or may be a clinic or some other place of less-than-hospital status; as to the licensing of the facility; and the like.

This means, on the other hand, that, for

be out of line with the Amendment's command?

There are other inconsistencies between Fourteenth Amendment status and the typical abortion statute. [I]n Texas the woman is not a principal or an accomplice with respect to an abortion upon her. If the fetus is a person, why is the woman not a principal or an accomplice? Further, the penalty for criminal abortion . . . is significantly less than the maximum penalty for murder. . . . If the fetus is a person, may the penalties be different?

the period of pregnancy prior to this "compelling" point, the attending physician, in consultation with his patient, is free to determine, without regulation by the State, that in his medical judgment the patient's pregnancy should be terminated. If that decision is reached, the judgment may be effectuated by an abortion free of interference by the State.

With respect to the State's important and legitimate interest in potential life, the "compelling" point is at viability. This is so because the fetus then presumably has the capability of meaningful life outside the mother's womb. State regulation protective of fetal life after viability thus has both logical and biological justifications. If the State is interested in protecting fetal life after viability, it may go so far as to proscribe abortion during that period except when it is necessary to preserve the life or health of the mother.

Measured against these standards, [the law] sweeps too broadly. The statute makes no distinction between abortions performed early in pregnancy and those performed later, and it limits to a single reason, "saving" the mother's life, the legal justification for the procedure. . . .

To summarize and to repeat:

1. A state criminal statute of the current Texas type, that excepts from criminality only a *life-saving* procedure on behalf of the mother, without regard to pregnancy stage and without recognition of the other interests involved, is violative of the Due Process Clause of the Fourteenth Amendment.

a. For the stage prior to approximately the end of the first trimester, the abortion decision and its effectuation must be left to the medical judgment of the pregnant woman's attending physician.

b. For the stage subsequent to approximately the end of the first trimester, the State, in promoting its interest in the health of the mother, may, if it chooses, regulate the abortion procedure in ways that are reasonably related to maternal health.

c. For the stage subsequent to viability the State, in promoting its interest in the potentiality of human life, may, if it chooses, regulate, and even proscribe abortion except where it is necessary in appropriate medical judgment, for the preservation of the life or health of the mother.

2. The State may define the term *physician* . . . to mean only a physician currently licensed by the State, and may proscribe any abortion by a person who is not a physician as so defined.

In *Doe* v. *Bolton,* post, procedural requirements contained in one of the modern abortion statutes are considered. That opinion and this one, of course, are to be read together.†

This holding, we feel, is consistent with the relative weights of the respective interests involved, with the lessons and example of medical and legal history, with the lenity of the common law, and with the demands of the profound problems of the present day. The decision leaves the State free to place increasing restrictions on abortion as the period of pregnancy lengthens, so long as those restrictions are tailored to the recognized state interests. The decision vindicates the right of the physician to administer medical treatment according to his professional judgment up to the points where important state interests provide compelling justifications for intervention. Up to those points the abortion decision in all its aspects is inherently, and primarily, a medical decision, and basic responsibility for it must rest with the physician. If an individual practitioner abuses the privilege of exercising proper medical judgment, the usual remedies, judicial and intraprofessional, are available. . . .

It is so ordered.

MR. JUSTICE STEWART, concurring: [in *Roe* v. *Wade*]

In 1963, this Court, in [*Ferguson* v. *Skrupa*], purported to sound the death knell for the doctrine of substantive due process. . . . Barely two years later, in [*Griswold* v. *Connecticut*], the Court held a Connecticut birth control law unconstitutional. In view of what had been so recently said in *Skrupa,* the Court's opinion in *Griswold* understandably did its best to avoid reliance on the Due Process Clause.

† Neither in this opinion nor in *Doe* v. *Bolton,* post, do we discuss the father's rights, if any exist in the constitutional context, in the abortion decision.

. . . Yet, the Connecticut law did not violate [any] specific provision of the Constitution. So it was clear to me then, and it is equally clear to me now, that the *Griswold* decision can be rationally understood only as a holding that the Connecticut statute substantively invaded the "liberty" that is protected by the Due Process Clause of the Fourteenth Amendment. As so understood *Griswold* stands as one in a long line of pre-*Skrupa* cases decided under the doctrine of substantive due process, and I now accept it as such.

[T]he "liberty" protected by the Due Process Clause of the Fourteenth Amendment covers more than those freedoms explicitly named in the Bill of Rights. As Mr. Justice Harlan once wrote: "[Liberty] is not a series of isolated points pricked out in terms of the taking of property; the freedom of speech, press, and religion; the right to keep and bear arms; the freedom from unreasonable searches and seizures; and so on. It is a rational continuum which, broadly speaking, includes a freedom from all substantial arbitrary impositions and purposeless restraints, . . . and which also recognizes, what a reasonable and sensitive judgment must, that certain interests require particularly careful scrutiny of the state needs asserted to justify their abridgment." [*Poe* v. *Ullman,* dissenting.]

Several decisions of this Court make clear that freedom of personal choice in matters of marriage and family life is one of the liberties protected by the Due Process Clause of the Fourteenth Amendment. . . . As recently as last Term, in [*Eisenstadt* v. *Baird*], we recognized "the right of the *individual,* married or single, to be free from unwarranted governmental intrusion into matters so fundamentally affecting a person as the decision whether to bear or beget a child." That right necessarily includes the right of a woman to decide whether or not to terminate her pregnancy. . . .

It is evident that the Texas abortion statute infringes that right directly. . . . The question then becomes whether the state interests advanced to justify this abridgment can survive the "particularly careful scrutiny" that the Fourteenth Amendment here requires.

The asserted state interests . . . are legitimate objectives, amply sufficient to permit a State to regulate abortions as it does other surgical procedures, and perhaps sufficient to permit a State to regulate abortions more stringently or even to prohibit them in the late stages of pregnancy. But such legislation is not before us, and I think the Court today has thoroughly demonstrated that these state interests cannot constitutionally support the broad abridgment of personal liberty worked by the existing Texas law. Accordingly, I join the Court's opinion holding that that law is invalid under the Due Process Clause of the Fourteenth Amendment.

MR. JUSTICE DOUGLAS, concurring [in *Doe* v. *Bolton* as well as in *Roe* v. *Wade*]:

While I join the opinion of the Court [except as to the dismissal of Dr. Hallford's complaint in the *Roe* case], I add a few words.

The questions presented [in these cases] involve the right of privacy, one aspect of which we considered in [*Griswold* v. *Connecticut*], when we held that various guarantees in the Bill of Rights create zones of privacy. . . .

The Ninth Amendment obviously does not create federally enforceable rights. It merely says, "The enumeration in the Constitution of certain rights shall not be construed to deny or disparage others retained by the people." But a catalogue of these rights includes customary, traditional, and time-honored rights, amenities, privileges, and immunities that come within the sweep of "the Blessings of Liberty" mentioned in the preamble to the Constitution. Many of them in my view come within the meaning of the term "liberty" as used in the Fourteenth Amendment.

First is the autonomous control over the development and expression of one's intellect, interests, tastes, and personality.

These are rights protected by the First Amendment and in my view they are absolute, permitting of no exceptions. . . .

Second is freedom of choice in the basic decisions of one's life respecting marriage, divorce, procreation, contraception, and the education and upbringing of children.

These ["fundamental"] rights, unlike

those protected by the First Amendment, are subject to some control by the police power. . . .

Third is the freedom to care for one's health and person, freedom from bodily restraint or compulsion, freedom to walk, stroll, or loaf.

These rights, though fundamental, are likewise subject to regulation on a showing of "compelling state interest." . . .

[A] woman is free to make the basic decision whether to bear an unwanted child. Elaborate argument is hardly necessary to demonstrate that childbirth may deprive a woman of her preferred life style and force upon her a radically different and undesired future. Such a holding is, however, only the beginning of the problem. The State has interests to protect. . . . While childbirth endangers the lives of some women, voluntary abortion at any time and place regardless of medical standards would impinge on a rightful concern of society. The woman's health is part of that concern; as is the life of the fetus after quickening. These concerns justify the State in treating the procedure as a medical one. . . .

MR. JUSTICE WHITE, with whom MR. JUSTICE REHNQUIST joins, dissenting [in *Doe* v. *Bolton* as well as in *Roe* v. *Wade*]:

At the heart of the controversy in these cases are those recurring pregnancies that pose no danger whatsoever to the life or health of the mother but are nevertheless unwanted for any one or more of a variety of reasons—convenience, family planning, economics, dislike of children, the embarrassment of illegitimacy, etc. The common claim before us is that for any one of such reasons, or for no reason at all, and without asserting or claiming any threat to life or health, any woman is entitled to an abortion as her request if she is able to find a medical advisor willing to undertake the procedure.

The Court for the most part sustains this position. During the period prior to the time the fetus becomes viable, the Constitution of the United States values the convenience, whim or caprice of the putative mother more than the life or potential life of the fetus; the Constitution, therefore, guarantees the right to an abortion as against any state law or policy seeking to protect the fetus from an abortion not prompted by more compelling reasons of the mother.

With all due respect, I dissent. I find nothing in the language or history of the Constitution to support the Court's judgment. The Court simply fashions and announces a new constitutional right for pregnant mothers and, with scarcely any reason or authority for its action, invests that right with sufficient substance to override most existing state abortion statutes. The upshot is that the people and the legislatures of the fifty States are constitutionally disentitled to weigh the relative importance of the continued existence and development of the fetus on the one hand against a spectrum of possible impacts on the mother on the other hand. As an exercise of raw judicial power, the Court perhaps has authority to do what it does today; but in my view its judgment is an improvident and extravagant exercise of the power of judicial review which the Constitution extends to this Court.

The Court apparently values the convenience of the pregnant mother more than the continued existence and development of the life or potential life which she carries. Whether or not I might agree with that marshalling of values, I can in no event join the Court's judgment because I find no constitutional warrant for imposing such an order of priorities on the people and legislatures of the States. In a sensitive area such as this, involving as it does issues over which reasonable men may easily and heatedly differ, I cannot accept the Court's exercise of its clear power of choice by interposing a constitutional barrier to state efforts to protect human life and by investing mothers and doctors with the constitutionally protected right to exterminate it. This issue, for the most part, should be left with the people and to the political processes the people have devised to govern their affairs.

It is my view, therefore, that the Texas statute is not constitutionally infirm because it denies abortions to those who seek to serve only their convenience rather than to protect their life or health. . . .

MR. JUSTICE REHNQUIST, dissenting: . . .

I have difficulty in concluding, as the Court does, that the right of "privacy" is involved in this case. [Texas] bars the performance of a medical abortion by a licensed physician on a plaintiff such as *Roe.* A transaction resulting in an operation such as this is not "private" in the ordinary usage of that word. Nor is the "privacy" which the Court finds here even a distant relative of the freedom from searches and seizures. . . .

If the Court means by the term *privacy* no more than that the claim of a person to be free from unwanted state regulation of consensual transactions may be a form of "liberty" protected by the Fourteenth Amendment, there is no doubt that similar claims have been upheld in our earlier decisions on the basis of that liberty. I agree [that "liberty"] embraces more than the rights found in the Bill of Rights. But that liberty is not guaranteed absolutely against deprivation, but only against deprivation without due process of law. The test traditionally applied in the area of social and economic legislation is whether or not a law such as that challenged has a rational relation to a valid state objective. [*Williamson* v. *Lee Optical Co.*] The Due Process Clause of the Fourteenth Amendment undoubtedly does place a limit on legislative power to enact laws such as this, albeit a broad one. If the Texas statute were to prohibit an abortion even where the mother's life is in jeopardy, I have little doubt that such a statute would lack a rational relation to a valid state objective under the test stated in [*Williamson*]. But the Court's sweeping invalidation of any restrictions on abortion during the first trimester is impossible to justify under that standard, and the conscious weighing of competing factors which the Court's opinion apparently substitutes for the established test is far more appropriate to a legislative judgment than to a judicial one. . . .

While the Court's opinion quotes from the dissent of Mr. Justice Holmes in [*Lochner* v. *New York*], the result it reaches is more closely attuned to the majority opinion of Mr. Justice Peckham in that case. As in *Lochner* and similar cases applying substantive due process standards to economic and social welfare legislation, the adoption of the compelling state interest standard will inevitably require this Court to examine the legislative policies and pass on the wisdom of these policies in the very process of deciding whether a particular state interest put forward may or may not be "compelling." The decision here to break the term of pregnancy into three distinct terms and to outline the permissible restrictions the State may impose in each one, for example, partakes more of judicial legislation than it does of a determination of the intent of the drafters of the Fourteenth Amendment.

The fact that a majority of the States, reflecting after all the majority sentiment in those States, have had restrictions on abortions for at least a century seems to me as strong an indication [as] there is that the asserted right to an abortion is not "so rooted in the traditions and conscience of our people as to be ranked as fundamental" [*Snyder* v. *Massachusetts*]. Even today, when society's views on abortion are changing, the very existence of the debate is evidence that the "right" to an abortion is not so universally accepted as the appellants would have us believe.

There apparently was no question concerning the validity of this provision or of any of the other state statutes when the Fourteenth Amendment was adopted. The only conclusion possible from this history is that the drafters did not intend to have the Fourteenth Amendment withdraw from the States the power to legislate with respect to this matter. . . .

MR. JUSTICE BLACKMUN delivered the opinion of the Court [in *Doe*]:

In this appeal the criminal abortion statutes recently enacted in Georgia are challenged on constitutional grounds, . . . we today have struck down, as constitutionally defective, the Texas criminal abortion statutes that are representative of provisions long in effect in a majority of our States. The Georgia legislation, however, is different and merits separate consideration. . . . The 1968 statutes are patterned upon the American Law Institute's Model Penal Code. The ALI proposal has served as the model for recent legislation in approximately one-fourth of our States. . . . The predecessor statute paralleled the Texas legislation considered in *Roe* v. *Wade, ante,* and made all abortions criminal except those necessary "to preserve the life" of the pregnant woman. . . .

Section 26–1201, with a referenced exception, makes abortion a crime, and Section 26–1203 provides that a person convicted of that crime shall be punished by imprisonment for not less than one nor more than ten years. Section 26–1202(a) states the exception and removes from Section 1201's definition of criminal abortion, and thus makes noncriminal, an abortion "performed by a physician duly licensed" in Georgia when, "based upon his best clinical judgment . . . an abortion is necessary . . .

"1. A continuation of the pregnancy would endanger the life of the pregnant woman or would seriously and permanently injure her health; or

"2. The fetus would very likely be born with a grave, permanent, and irremediable mental or physical defect; or

"3. The pregnancy resulted from forcible or statutory rape.". . .

The net result of the District Court's decision is that the abortion determination, so far as the physician is concerned, is made in the exercise of his professional, that is, his "best clinical" judgment in the light of *all* the attendant circumstances. He is not now restricted to the three situations originally specified. Instead, he may range farther afield wherever his medical judgment, properly and professionally exercised, so dictates and directs him.

We agree with the District Court, 319 F. Supp., at 1058, that the medical judgment may be exercised in the light of all factors—physical, emotional, psychological, familial, and the woman's age—relevant to the well-being of the patient. All these factors may relate to health. This allows the attending physician the room he needs to make his best medical judgment. And it is room that operates for the benefit, not the disadvantage, of the pregnant woman.

The appellants next argue that the District Court should have declared unconstitutional three procedural demands of the Georgia statute: (1) that the abortion be performed in a hospital accredited by the Joint Commission on Accreditation of Hospitals: (2) that the procedure be approved by the hospital staff abortion committee; and (3) that the performing physician's judgment be confirmed by the independent examinations of the patient by two other licensed physicians. . . .

1. *JCAH Accreditation.* The Joint Commission on Accreditation of Hospitals is an organization without governmental sponsorship or overtones. No question whatever is raised concerning the integrity of the organization or the high purpose of the accreditation process. That process, however, has to do with hospital standards generally and has no present particularized concern with abortion as a medical or surgical procedure. In Georgia there is no restriction of the performance of nonabortion surgery in a hospital not yet accredited by the JCAH so long as other requirements imposed by the State, such as licensing of the hospital and of the operating surgeon, are met. . . .

We hold that the JCAH accreditation requirement does not withstand constitutional scrutiny in the present context. It is a requirement that simply is not "based on differences that are reasonably related to the purposes of the Act in which it is found." *Morey* v. *Doud,* 354 U.S. 457, 465 . . . (1957).

This is not to say that Georgia may not or should not, from and after the end of the first trimester, adopt standards for licensing all facilities where abortions may be performed so long as those standards are legitimately related to the objectives the State seeks to accomplish. The appellants contend that such a relationship should be lacking even in a lesser requirement that an abortion be performed in a licensed hospital, as opposed to a facility, such as a clinic, that may be required by the State to possess all the staffing and services necessary to perform an abortion safely (including those adequate to handle serious complications or other emergency, or arrangements with a nearby hospital to provide such services). Appellants and various *amici* have presented us with a mass of data purporting to demonstrate that some facilities other than hospitals are entirely adequate to perform abortions if they possess these qualifications. The State, on the other hand, has not presented persuasive data to show that only hospitals meet its acknowledged interest in insuring the quality of the operation and the full protection of the patient. We feel compelled to agree with appellants that the State must show more than it has in order to prove that only the full resources of a licensed hospital, rather than those of some other appropriately licensed institution, satisfy these health interests. We hold that the hospital requirement of the Georgia law, because it fails to exclude the first trimester of pregnancy, see *Roe* v. *Wade* . . . is also invalid. In so holding we naturally express no opinion on the medical judgment involved in any particular case, that is, whether the patient's situation is such that an abortion should be performed in a hospital rather than in some other facility. . . .

Viewing the Georgia statute as a whole, we see no constitutionally justifiable pertinence in the structure for the advance approval by the abortion committee. With regard to the protection of potential life, the medical judgment is already completed prior to the committee stage, and review by a committee once removed from diagnosis is basically redundant. We are not cited to any other surgical procedure made subject to committee approval as a matter of state criminal law. . . .

We conclude that the interposition of the hospital abortion committee is unduly restrictive of the patient's rights and needs that, at this point, have already been medically delineated and substantiated by her personal physician. To ask more serves neither the hospital nor the State. . . .

It should be manifest that our rejection of the accredited hospital requirement and, more important, of the abortion committee's advance approval eliminates the major grounds of the attack based on the system's delay and the lack of facilities. There remains, however, the required confirmation by two Georgia-licensed physicians in addition to the recommendation of the pregnant woman's own consultant (making under the statute, a total of six physicians involved, including the three on the hospital's abortion committee). We conclude that this provision, too, must fall.

The statute's emphasis, as has been repetitively noted, is on the attending physician's "best clinical judgment that an abortion is necessary." That should be sufficient. The reasons for the presence of the confirmation step in the statute are perhaps apparent, but they are insufficient to withstand constitutional challenge. Again, no other voluntary medical or surgical procedure for which Georgia requires confirmation by two other physicians has been cited to us. If a physician is licensed by the State, he is recognized by the State as capable of exercising acceptable clinical judgment. If he fails in this, professional censure or deprivation of his license are available remedies. Required acquiescence by co-practitioners has no rational connection with a patient's needs and unduly infringes on the physician's right to practice. . . .

The appellants attack the residency requirement of the Georgia law . . . as violative of the right to travel stressed in *Shapiro* v. *Thompson*. . . .

A requirement of this kind, of course, could be deemed to have some relationship to the availability of postprocedure medical care for the aborted patient.

Nevertheless, we do not uphold the constitutionality of the residence requirement. . . . A contrary holding would mean that a State could limit to its own residents the general medical care available within its borders. This we could not approve.

In summary, we hold that the JCAH accredited hospital provision and the requirements as to approval by the hospital abortion committee, as to confirmation by two independent physicians, and as to residence in Georgia are all violative of the Fourteenth Amendment.

MR. CHIEF JUSTICE BURGER, concurring in both cases:

I agree that, under the Fourteenth Amendment to the Constitution, the abortion statutes of Georgia and Texas impermissibly limit the performance of abortions necessary to protect the health of pregnant women, using the term health in its broadest medical context. . . . I am somewhat troubled that the Court has taken notice of various scientific and medical data in reaching its conclusion; however, I do not believe that the Court has exceeded the scope of judicial notice accepted in other contexts.

In oral argument, counsel for the State of Texas informed the Court that early abortive procedures were routinely permitted in certain exceptional cases, such as nonconsensual pregnancies resulting from rape and incest. In the face of a rigid and narrow statute, such as that of Texas, no one in these circumstances should be placed in a posture of dependence on a prosecutorial policy or prosecutorial discretion. Of course, States must have broad power, within the limits indicated in the opinions, to regulate the subject of abortions, but where the consequences of state intervention are so severe, uncertainty must be avoided as much as possible. For my part, I would be inclined to allow a State to require the certification of two physicians to support an abortion, but the Court holds otherwise. I do not believe that such a procedure is unduly burdensome, as are the complex steps of the Georgia statute, which require as many as six doctors and the use of a hospital certified by the JCAH.

I do not read the Court holding today as having the sweeping consequences attributed to it by the dissenting Justices; the dissenting views discount the reality that the vast majority of physicians observe the standards of their profession, and act only on the basis of carefully deliberated medical judgments relating to life and health. Plainly, the Court today rejects any claim that the Constitution requires abortion on demand.

A NOTE ON SUBSEQUENT BIRTH CONTROL AND ABORTION DECISIONS

In *Planned Parenthood* v. *Danforth,* 428 U.S. 52 (1976), the Court dealt with a Missouri abortion statute passed in response to *Roe* and *Doe.* The Court accepted the state's definition of "viability" of a fetus as "that stage of fetal development when the life of the unborn child may be continued indefinitely outside the womb by natural or artificial life support systems." It also upheld a requirement that the woman provide written consent to the proposed abortion.

For the rest, the Court continued down paths it had committed itself to earlier. The Court struck down the requirement that the spouse consent to nontherapeutic abortions. His interests were treated as those of a husband in the family relation, not as those of the contributor of 50 per cent of the genetic materials to the fetus.

The Court struck down the parental consent requirement for abortions performed on minors. It says "minors, as well as adults . . . possess constitutional rights," citing *Goss* v. *Lopez, Tinker* v. *Des Moines* and *In re Gault,* all discussed elsewhere in this book. This holding is, however, the first time that the Court has found that minors have constitutional rights *as against their parents.* It raises a number of interesting questions. For instance, may an Amish parent forbid his fourteen-year-old child to attend Catholic religious services? May a Republican parent prohibit his twelve-year-old child from reading Communist tracts—or delivering Democratic campaign speeches on his front lawn? Though standing problems will keep most such questions out of the courts in the short run, this decision is likely in the long run to involve the Court deeply in yet another sphere of American life—family discipline.

The Court also struck down a provision of the statute that forbade the use of a particular abortive technique after the first twelve weeks of pregnancy. To do so, it had to engage in a learned medical disquisition on the merits of various techniques. Such a holding dramatizes the basic lack of judicial expertise and thus the weakness of the Court's claim to legitimacy in this area. The root of this holding, however, was not really a dispute about medical science. Instead, it was the Court's perception that Missouri was really attempting to forbid all abortions after the first trimester by banning the one technique then readily available for safely conducting second-trimester abortions.

Finally, the Court neatly skirted what may yet be its most serious problem, that of the fate of the viable fetus. It held the provision on preserving the health of the fetus unconstitutionally vague,[2] yet the basic question remains. In late-stage abortions, where a viable fetus is removed, is a failure to maintain it murder or simply abortion? And if it must be maintained until birth, what is the moral, biological, or legal rationale for allowing it to be separated in the first place from its optimum biological environment? In general the decision signals the Court's unwillingness to allow a state to erect a complex legislative scheme designed to thwart women's exercise of the rights announced in *Doe* and *Roe.*

In *Bellotti* v. *Baird,* 443 U.S. 622 (1979), the justices again took up the question of parental consent to abortions for minors. Eight of them agreed to strike down a Massachusetts parental consent law and four of the eight provided a set of instructions to state legislatures. A parental consent law would be valid if (1) it required the consent of either or both parents unless one or both were unavailable or an emergency existed and (2) provided a procedure by which an independent state official might determine that (a) the minor was mature enough and well informed enough to make her own abortion decision *or* (b) that it was in the best interest of the minor to have the abortion. If the official found *either* (a) *or* (b) the statute must provide for abortion without parental notification or consent. The justices' general argument was that the abortion decision was so much more crucial to a minor than other decisions traditionally requiring parental consent that it must not be subjected to an arbitrary veto by parents or state officials. [See also *H. L.* v. *Matheson,* 101 S.Ct. 1164 (1981).]

In *Carey* v. *Population Services Int'l.,* 431 U.S. 678 (1977), the Court invalidated New York statutes prohibiting the distribution of contraceptives except through pharmacies and prohibiting anyone other than a physician from distributing contraceptives to those under sixteen. The Court argued that the first provision burdened the fundamental right to make individual decisions about childbearing and that the state could offer no compelling interest for doing so. It offered in support of its second holding the argument that "State restrictions inhibiting the privacy rights of minors are valid only if they serve a significant state interest . . . not present in the case of an adult."

In both *Planned Parenthood* and *Carey,* only four justices signed the opinion of the Court, with various combinations of concurrences making up the majority. As a result, it is not clear how the Court will react in the future, particularly to more narrowly drawn statutes concerning minors.

The original *Roe* and *Doe* cases labeled abortion a privacy rather than an

[2] It adopted the same tactic in *Colautti* v. *Franklyn,* 439 U.S. 379 (1979).

equal protection issue. One consequence of that labeling is seen in *Maher* v. *Roe,* 432 U.S. 464 (1977). Privacy is essentially a negative right *against* government intervention in one's personal life. Equal protection often involves a positive claim to government services. In *Maher,* the Court holds that a state's refusal to provide Medicaid payments for nontherapeutic abortions, though providing such payments for childbirth, does not violate equal protection. It holds that indigent women do not form a "suspect class." Then using the more relaxed standard of equal protection (see Chapter 14), the majority holds that the state is under no obligation to pay any medical expenses and so may choose what it will and will not cover. (Cf. *Geduldig* v. *Aiello,* discussed in Chapter 14.) The justices conclude that though the state may not forbid abortion, it may choose to encourage "an alternative activity consonant with legislative policy."

Since 1976 Congress has attached some version of the "Hyde Amendment" to the annual appropriations act for the Department of Health and Human Services (formerly Health, Education and Welfare). It provides that the states may not spend federal medical care grant funds for most abortions. In *Harris* v. *McRae,* 448 U.S. 297 (1980), and a companion case, the Court upheld the amendment. The majority of five followed the line of argument established in *Maher.* In essence it said that Congress might choose to value the potential life of the fetus and to spend or not spend its money in support of that value. The dissenters said that the provision of government funds to the indigent for all other medical expenses, combined with the refusal to do so for abortion, constituted an invasion of indigent women's privacy rights to abortion. They argued that what legislatures were constitutionally forbidden to do by direct prohibition, they were also forbidden to do indirectly by withholding funds. Thus, in the context of funding, the Court returns to the unresolvable conflict raised in the initial abortion cases, the right of a woman to control the most intimate aspects of her own life versus the right to life of the fetus.

Both *Maher* and *Harris* acknowledged that legislatures are entitled to value the potential life of the fetus when making funding decisions. Are they in conflict with the older decisions that allow legislatures to take that life into account only during the third trimester of pregnancy?

APPENDIX I

Constitution of the United States of America

Adopted September 17, 1787
Effective March 4, 1789

PREAMBLE

We, the People of the United States, in Order to form a more perfect Union, establish Justice, insure domestic Tranquility, provide for the common defence, promote the general Welfare, and secure the Blessings of Liberty to ourselves and our Posterity, do ordain and establish this Constitution for the United States of America.

ARTICLE I

Section 1. All legislative Powers herein granted shall be vested in a Congress of the United States, which shall consist of a Senate and House of Representatives.

Section 2. The House of Representatives shall be composed of Members chosen every second Year by the People of the several States, and the Electors in each State shall have the Qualifications requisite for Electors of the most numerous Branch of the State Legislature.

No Person shall be a Representative who shall not have attained to the Age of twenty-five Years, and been seven Years a Citizen of the United States, and who shall not, when elected, be an Inhabitant of that State in which he shall be chosen.

Representatives and *direct Taxes shall be apportioned* [1] among the several States which may be included within this Union, according to their respective Numbers, *which shall be determined by adding to the whole Number of free Persons, including those bound to Service for a Term of Years,* and excluding Indians not taxed, *three-fifths of all other Persons.*[2] The actual Enumeration shall be made within three Years after the first Meeting of the Congress of the United States, and within every subsequent Term of ten Years, in such Manner as they shall by Law direct. The Number of Representatives shall not exceed one for every thirty Thousand, but each State shall have at Least one Representative; *and until such enumeration shall be made, the State of New Hampshire shall be entitled to choose three, Massachusetts eight, Rhode-Island and Providence Plantations one, Connecticut five, New York six, New Jersey four, Pennsylvania eight, Delaware one, Maryland six, Virginia ten, North Carolina five, South Carolina five, and Georgia three.*[3]

When vacancies happen in the Representation from any State, the Executive Authority thereof shall issue Writs of Election to fill such Vacancies.

The House of Representatives shall choose their Speaker and other Officers; and shall have the sole Power of Impeachment.

Section 3. The Senate of the United States shall be composed of two Senators from each State, *chosen by the Legislature thereof,*[4] for six Years; and each Senator shall have one Vote.

Immediately after they shall be assembled in Consequence of the first Election, they shall be divided as equally as may be into three Classes. The Seats of the Senators of the first Class shall be vacated at the Expiration of the second Year, of the second Class at the Expiration of the fourth Year, and of the third Class at the Expiration of the sixth Year, so that one-third may be chosen every second Year; *and if Vacancies happen by Resignation, or otherwise, during the Recess of the Legislature of any State, the Executive thereof may make temporary Appointment until the next Meeting of the Legislature, which shall then fill such Vacancies.*[5]

No Person shall be a Senator who shall not have attained to the Age of thirty Years, and been nine Years a Citizen of the United States, and who shall not, when elected, be an Inhabitant of that State for which he shall be chosen.

The Vice-President of the United States shall be President of the Senate, but shall have no Vote, unless they be equally divided.

The Senate shall choose their other Officers, and also a President pro tempore, in the Absence of the Vice-President, or when he shall exercise the Office of President of the United States.

The Senate shall have the sole Power to try all Impeachments. When sitting for that Purpose, they shall be on Oath or Affirmation. When the President of the United States is tried, the Chief Justice shall preside: And no Person shall be convicted without the Concurrence of two-thirds of the Members present.

Judgment in Cases of Impeachment shall not extend further than to removal from Office, and disqualification to hold and enjoy any Office of honor, Trust or Profit under

[1] Modified by the Sixteenth Amendment.

[2] Modified by the Fourteenth Amendment.

[3] Temporary provision.

[4] Modified by the Seventeenth Amendment.

[5] Ibid.

the United States: but the Party convicted shall nevertheless be liable and subject to Indictment, Trial, Judgment and Punishment, according to Law.

Section 4. The Times, Places and Manner of holding Elections for Senators and Representatives, shall be prescribed in each State by the Legislature thereof; but the Congress may at any time by Law make or alter such Regulations, except as to the Places of choosing Senators.

The Congress shall assemble at least once in every Year, and such Meeting shall be on the first Monday of December, unless they shall by Law appoint a different Day.[6]

Section 5. Each House shall be the Judge of the Elections, Returns and Qualifications of its own Members, and a Majority of each shall constitute a Quorum to do Business; but a smaller Number may adjourn from day to day, and may be authorized to compel the Attendance of absent Members, in such Manner, and under such Penalties as each House may provide.

Each House may determine the Rules of its Proceedings, punish its Members for disorderly Behavior, and, with the Concurrence of two-thirds, expel a Member.

Each House shall keep a Journal of its Proceedings, and from time to time publish the same, excepting such Parts as may in their Judgment require Secrecy; and the Yeas and Nays of the Members of either House on any question shall, at the Desire of one-fifth of those Present, be entered on the Journal.

Neither House, during the Session of Congress, shall, without the Consent of the other, adjourn for more than three days, nor to any other Place than that in which the two Houses shall be sitting.

Section 6. The Senators and Representatives shall receive a Compensation for their Services, to be ascertained by Law, and paid out of the Treasury of the United States. They shall in all Cases, except Treason, Felony and Breach of the Peace, be privileged from Arrest during their Attendance at the Session of their respective Houses, and in going to and returning from the same; and for any Speech or Debate in either House, they shall not be questioned in any other Place.

No Senator or Representative shall, during the Time for which he was elected, be appointed to any civil Office under the Authority of the United States, which shall have been created, or the Emoluments whereof shall have been increased during such time; and no Person holding any Office under the United States, shall be a Member of either House during his Continuance in Office.

Section 7. All Bills for raising Revenue shall originate in the House of Representatives; but the Senate may propose or concur with Amendments as on other Bills.

Every Bill which shall have passed the House of Representatives and the Senate shall, before it becomes a Law, be presented to the President of the United States; if he approve, he shall sign it, but if not, he shall return it, with his Objections, to that House in which it shall have originated, who shall enter the Objections at large on their Journal, and proceed to reconsider it. If after such Reconsideration two-thirds of the House shall agree to pass the Bill, it shall be sent, together with the Objections, to the other House, by which it shall likewise be reconsidered, and if approved by two-thirds of that House, it shall become a Law. But in all such Cases the Votes of both Houses shall be determined by Yeas and Nays, and the Names of the Persons voting for and against the Bill shall be entered on the Journal of each House respectively. If any Bill shall not be returned by the President within ten Days (Sundays excepted) after it shall have been presented to him, the Same shall be a Law, in like Manner as

[6] Modified by the Twentieth Amendment.

if he had signed it, unless the Congress by their Adjournment prevent its Return, in which Case it shall not be a law.

Every Order, Resolution, or Vote to which the Concurrence of the Senate and House of Representatives may be necessary (except on a question of Adjournment) shall be presented to the President of the United States; and before the Same shall take Effect, shall be approved by him, or being disapproved by him, shall be repassed by two-thirds of the Senate and House of Representatives, according to the Rules and Limitations prescribed in the Case of a Bill.

Section 8. The Congress shall have Power: To lay and collect Taxes, Duties, Imposts and Excises, to pay the Debts and provide for the common Defense and general Welfare of the United States; but all Duties, Imposts and Excises shall be uniform throughout the United States.

To borrow Money on the credit of the United States;

To regulate Commerce with foreign Nations, and among the several States, and with the Indian Tribes;

To establish a uniform Rule of Naturalization, and uniform Laws on the subject of Bankruptcies throughout the United States;

To coin Money, regulate the Value thereof, and of foreign Coin, and fix the Standard of Weights and Measures;

To provide for the Punishment of counterfeiting the Securities and current Coin of the United States;

To establish Post Offices and post Roads;

To promote the Progress of Science and useful Arts, by securing for limited Times to Authors and Inventors the exclusive Right to their respective Writings and Discoveries;

To constitute Tribunals inferior to the Supreme Court;

To define and punish Piracies and Felonies committed on the high Seas, and Offences against the Law of Nations;

To declare War, grant Letters of Marque and Reprisal, and make Rules concerning captures on Land and Water;

To raise and support Armies, but no Appropriation of Money to the Use shall be for a longer Term than two Years;

To provide and maintain a Navy;

To make Rules for the Government and Regulation of the land and naval Forces;

To provide for calling forth the Militia to execute the Laws of the Union, suppress Insurrections and repel Invasions;

To provide for organizing, arming, and disciplining the Militia, and for governing such Part of them as may be employed in the Service of the United States, reserving to the States respectively, the Appointment of the Officers, and the Authority of training the Militia according to the discipline prescribed by Congress;

To exercise exclusive Legislation in all Cases whatsoever, over such District (not exceeding ten Miles square) as may, by Cession of particular States, and the Acceptance of Congress, become the Seat of Government of the United States, and to exercise like Authority over all Places purchased by the Consent of the Legislature of the State in which the Same shall be, for the Erection of Forts, Magazines, Arsenals, dock-Yards, and other needful Buildings;—And

To make all Laws which shall be necessary and proper for carrying into Execution the foregoing Powers, and all other Powers vested by this Constitution in the Government of the United States, or in any Department or Officer thereof.

Section 9. *The Migration or Importation of such Persons as any of the States now existing shall think proper to admit, shall not be prohibited by the Congress prior to the Year one thousand eight hundred and eight, but a Tax or duty may be imposed on such Importation, not exceeding ten dollars for each Person.*[7]

The Privilege of the Writ of Habeas Corpus shall not be suspended, unless when in Cases of Rebellion or Invasion the public Safety may require it.

No Bill of Attainder or ex post facto Law shall be passed.

No Capitation, or other direct, Tax shall be laid, unless in Proportion to the Census or Enumeration herein before directed to be taken.[8]

No Tax or Duty shall be laid on Articles exported from any State.

No Preference shall be given by any Regulation of Commerce or Revenue to the Ports of one State over those of another: nor shall Vessels bound to, or from, one State, be obliged to enter, clear, or pay Duties in another.

No Money shall be drawn from the Treasury, but in Consequence of Appropriations made by Law; and a regular Statement and Account of the Receipts and Expenditures of all public Money shall be published from time to time.

No Title of Nobility shall be granted by the United States; And no Person holding any Office of Profit or Trust under them, shall, without the Consent of the Congress, accept of any present, Emolument, Office, or Title, of any kind whatever, from any King, Prince, or foreign State.

Section 10. No State shall enter into any Treaty, Alliance, or Confederation; grant Letters of Marque and Reprisal; coin Money; emit Bills of Credit; make any Thing but gold and silver Coin a Tender in Payment of Debts; pass any Bill of Attainder, ex post facto Law, or Law impairing the Obligation of Contracts, or Grant any Title of Nobility.

No State shall, without the Consent of the Congress, lay any Imposts or Duties on Imports or Exports, except what may be absolutely necessary for executing its inspection Laws; and the net Produce of all Duties and Imposts, laid by any State on Imports or Exports, shall be for the Use of the Treasury of the United States; and all such Laws shall be subject to the Revision and Control of the Congress.

No State shall, without the Consent of Congress, lay any Duty of Tonnage, keep Troops, or Ships of War in time of Peace, enter into any Agreement or Compact with another State, or with a foreign Power, or engage in War, unless actually invaded, or in such imminent Danger as will not admit of delay.

ARTICLE II

Section 1. *The executive Power shall be vested in a President of the United States of America. He shall hold his Office during the Term of four Years, and, together with the Vice-President, chosen for the same Term, be elected, as follows:*[9]

Each State shall appoint, in such Manner as the Legislature thereof may direct, a Number of Electors, equal to the whole Number of Senators and Representatives to which the State may be entitled in the Congress: but no Senator or Representative, or Person holding an Office of Trust or Profit under the United States, shall be appointed an Elector.

The Electors shall meet in their respective States, and vote by Ballot for two Persons,

[7] Temporary Provision.

[8] Modified by the Sixteenth Amendment.

[9] The number of terms is limited to two by the Twenty-second Amendment.

of whom one at least shall not be an Inhabitant of the same State with themselves. And they shall make a List of all the Persons voted for, and of the Number of Votes for each; which List they shall sign and certify, and transmit sealed to the Seat of the Government of the United States, directed to the President of the Senate. The President of the Senate shall, in the Presence of the Senate and House of Representatives, open all the Certificates, and the Votes shall then be counted. The Person having the greatest Number of Votes shall be the President, if such Number be a Majority of the whole Number of Electors appointed; and if there be more than one who have such Majority, and have an equal Number of Votes, then the House of Representatives shall immediately choose by Ballot one of them for President; and if no Person have a Majority, then from the five highest on the List the said House shall in like Manner choose the President. But in choosing the President, the Votes shall be taken by States, the Representation from each State having one Vote. A quorum for this Purpose shall consist of a Member or Members from two-thirds of the States, and a Majority of all the States shall be necessary to a Choice. In every Case, after the Choice of the President, the Person having the greatest Number of Votes of the Electors shall be the Vice-President. But if there should remain two or more who have equal Votes, the Senate shall choose from them by Ballot the Vice-President.[10]

The Congress may determine the Time of choosing the Electors, and the Day on which they shall give their Votes; which Day shall be the same throughout the United States.

No Person except a natural born Citizen, or a Citizen of the United States, at the time of the Adoption of this Constitution, shall be eligible to the Office of President; neither shall any Person be eligible to that Office who shall not have attained to the Age of thirty-five Years, and been fourteen Years a Resident within the United States.

In Case of the Removal of the President from Office, or of his Death, Resignation, or Inability to discharge the Powers and Duties of the said Office, the Same shall devolve on the Vice-President, and the Congress may by Law provide for the Case of Removal, Death, Resignation or Inability, both of the President and Vice-President, declaring what Officer shall then act as President, and such Officer shall act accordingly, until the Disability be removed, or a President shall be elected.[11]

The President shall, at stated Times, receive for his Services, a Compensation which shall neither be increased or diminished during the Period for which he shall have been elected, and he shall not receive within that Period any other Emolument from the United States, or any of them.

Before he enter on the Execution of his Office, he shall take the following Oath or Affirmation:—"I do solemnly swear (or affirm) that I will faithfully execute the office of President of the United States, and will, to the best of my Ability, preserve, protect and defend the Constitution of the United States."

Section 2. The President shall be Commander in Chief of the Army and Navy of the United States, and of the Militia of the several States, when called into actual Service of the United States; he may require the Opinion, in writing, of the principal Officer in each of the executive Departments, upon any Subject relating to the Duties of their respective Offices, and he shall have Power to grant Reprieves and Pardons for Offences against the United States, except in Cases of Impeachment.

[10] Superseded by the Twelfth Amendment, which, in turn, is modified by the Twentieth Amendment.

[11] See the Twenty-fifth Amendment.

He shall have Power, by and with the Advice and Consent of the Senate, to make Treaties, provided two-thirds of the Senators present concur; and he shall nominate, and by and with the Advice and Consent of the Senate, shall appoint Ambassadors, other public Ministers and Consuls, Judges of the Supreme Court, and all other Officers of the United States, whose Appointments are not herein otherwise provided for, and which shall be established by Law: but the Congress may by Law vest the Appointment of such inferior Officers, as they think proper, in the President alone, in the Courts of Law, or in the Heads of Departments.

The President shall have Power to fill up all Vacancies that may happen during the Recess of the Senate, by granting Commissions which shall expire at the End of their next Session.

Section 3. He shall from time to time give to the Congress Information of the State of the Union, and recommend to their Consideration such Measures as he shall judge necessary and expedient; he may, on extraordinary Occasions, convene both Houses, or either of them, and in Case of Disagreement between them, with Respect to the Time of Adjournment, he may adjourn them to such Time as he shall think proper; he shall receive Ambassadors and other public Ministers; he shall take Care that the Laws be faithfully executed, and shall Commission all the Officers of the United States.

Section 4. The President, Vice-President and all civil Officers of the United States, shall be removed from Office on Impeachment for, and Conviction of, Treason, Bribery, or other high Crimes and Misdemeanors.

Article III

Section 1. The judicial Power of the United States shall be vested in one Supreme Court, and in such inferior Courts as the Congress may from time to time ordain and establish. The Judges, both of the Supreme and inferior Courts, shall hold their Offices during good Behavior, and shall, at stated Times, receive for their Services, a Compensation, which shall not be diminished during their Continuance in Office.

Section 2. The judicial Power shall extend to all Cases, in Law and Equity, arising under this Constitution, the Laws of the United States, and Treaties made, or which shall be made, under their Authority;—to all Cases affecting Ambassadors, other public Ministers and Consuls;—to all Cases of admiralty and maritime Jurisdiction;—to Controversies to which the United States shall be a Party;—to Controversies between two or more States;—*between a State and Citizens of another State*;—between Citizens of different States;—between Citizens of the same State claiming Lands under Grants of different States, *and between a State, or the Citizens thereof, and foreign States, Citizens or Subjects.*[12]

In all Cases affecting Ambassadors, other public Ministers and Consuls, and those in which a State shall be a Party, the Supreme court shall have original Jurisdiction. In all the other Cases before mentioned, the Supreme Court shall have appellate Jurisdiction, both as to Law and Fact, with such Exceptions, and under such Regulations as the Congress shall make.

The Trial of all Crimes, except in Cases of Impeachment, shall be by Jury; and such Trial shall be held in the State where the said Crimes shall have been committed; but when not committed within any State, the Trial shall be at such Place or Places as the Congress may by Law have directed.

[12] Limited by the Eleventh Amendment.

Section 3. Treason against the United States, shall consist only in levying War against them, or in adhering to their Enemies, giving them Aid and Comfort. No Person shall be convicted of Treason unless on the Testimony of two Witnesses to the same overt Act, or on Confession in open Court.

The Congress shall have Power to declare the Punishment of Treason, but no Attainder of Treason shall work Corruption of Blood, or Forfeiture except during the Life of the Person attained.

Article IV

Section 1. Full Faith and Credit shall be given in each State to the public Acts, Records and judicial Proceedings of every other State. And the Congress may be general Laws prescribe the Manner in which such Acts, Records and Proceedings shall be proved, and the Effect thereof.

Section 2. The Citizens of each State shall be entitled to all Privileges and Immunities of Citizens in the several States.

A Person charged in any State with Treason, Felony, or other Crime, who shall flee from Justice, and be found in another State, shall on Demand of the executive Authority of the State from which he fled, be delivered up, to be removed to the State having Jurisdiction of the Crime.

No Person held to Service or Labour in one State, under the Laws thereof, escaping into another, shall, in Consequence of any Law or Regulation therein, be discharged from such Service or Labour, but shall be delivered up on Claim of the Party to whom such Service or Labour may be due.[13]

Section 3. New states may be admitted by the Congress into this Union; but no new States shall be formed or erected within the Jurisdiction of any other state; nor any state be formed by the Junction of two or more States, or Parts of States, without the Consent of the Legislatures of the States concerned as well as of the Congress.

The Congress shall have Power to dispose of and make all needful Rules and Regulations respecting the Territory or other Property belonging to the United States; and nothing in this Constitution shall be so construed as to Prejudice any Claims of the United States, or of any particular State.

Section 4. The United States shall guarantee to every State in the Union a Republican Form of Government, and shall protect each of them against Invasion; and on Application of the Legislature, or of the Executive (when the Legislature cannot be convened) against domestic Violence.

Article V

The Congress, whenever two-thirds of both Houses shall deem it necessary, shall propose Amendments to this Constitution, or, on the Application of the Legislatures of two-thirds of the several States, shall call a Convention for proposing Amendments, which, in either Case, shall be valid to all Intents and Purposes, as Part of this Constitution, when ratified by the Legislatures of three-fourths of the several States, or by Conventions in three-fourths thereof, as the one or the other Mode of Ratification may be proposed by the Congress; Provided *that no Amendment which may be made prior to the Year*

[13] Superseded by the Thirteenth Amendment.

One thousand eight hundred and eight shall in any Manner affect the first and fourth Clauses in the Ninth Section of the first Article; [14] and that no State, without its Consent, shall be deprived of its equal Suffrage in the Senate.

Article VI

All Debts contracted and Engagements entered into, before the Adoption of this Constitution, shall be as valid against the United States under this Constitution, as under the Confederation.

This Constitution, and the Laws of the United States which shall be made in Pursuance thereof and all Treaties made, or which shall be made, under the Authority of the United States, shall be the supreme Law of the Land; and the Judges in every State shall be bound thereby, any Thing in the constitution or Laws of any State to the Contrary notwithstanding.

The Senators and Representatives before mentioned, and the Members of the several State Legislatures, and all executive and judicial Officers, both of the United States and of the several States, shall be bound by Oath or Affirmation, to support this Constitution; but no religious Test shall ever be required as a Qualification to any Office or public Trust under the United States.

Article VII

The Ratification of the Conventions of nine States, shall be sufficient for the Establishment of this Constitution between the States so ratifying the Same.

DONE in Convention by the Unanimous Consent of the States present the Seventeenth Day of September in the Year of our Lord one thousand seven hundred and Eighty-seven and of the Independence of the United States of America the Twelfth. In witness whereof We have hereunto subscribed our Names, Attest
William Jackson
Secretary

G. Washington, Presidt.
and deputy from Virginia

ARTICLES IN ADDITION TO, AND AMENDMENT OF, THE CONSTITUTION OF THE UNITED STATES OF AMERICA, PROPOSED BY CONGRESS, AND RATIFIED BY THE SEVERAL STATES, PURSUANT TO THE FIFTH ARTICLE OF THE ORIGINAL CONSTITUTION

Amendment I

(*First Ten Amendments proposed by Congress on September 25, 1789; ratified and adoption certified on December 15, 1791*)

Congress shall make no law respecting an establishment of religion, or prohibiting the free exercise thereof; or abridging the freedom of speech, or of the press; or the

[14] Modified by the Twentieth Amendment.

right of the people peaceably to assemble, and to petition the Government for a redress of grievances.

AMENDMENT II

A well-regulated Militia, being necessary to the security of a free State, the right of the people to keep and bear Arms, shall not be infringed.

AMENDMENT III

No Soldier shall, in time of peace be quartered in any house, without the consent of the Owner, nor in time of war, but in a manner to be prescribed by law.

AMENDMENT IV

The right of the people to be secure in their persons, houses, papers, and effects, against unreasonable searches and seizures, shall not be violated, and no Warrants shall issue, but upon probable cause, supported by Oath or affirmation, and particularly describing the place to be searched, and the persons or things to be seized.

AMENDMENT V

No person shall be held to answer for a capital, or other infamous crime, unless on a presentment or indictment of a Grand Jury, except in cases arising in the land or naval forces, or in the Militia, when in actual service in time of War or public danger; nor shall any person be subject for the same offence to be twice put in jeopardy of life or limb; nor shall be compelled in any criminal case to be a witness against himself, nor be deprived of life, liberty, or property, without due process of law; nor shall private property be taken for public use, without just compensation.

AMENDMENT VI

In all criminal prosecutions, the accused shall enjoy the right to a speedy and public trial, by an impartial jury of the State and district wherein the crime shall have been committed, which district shall have been previously ascertained by law, and to be informed of the nature and cause of the accusation; to be confronted with the witnesses against him; to have compulsory process for obtaining witnesses in his favor, and to have the Assistance of Counsel for his defence.

AMENDMENT VII

In Suits at common law, where the value in controversy shall exceed twenty dollars, the right of trial by jury shall be preserved, and no fact tried by a jury, shall be otherwise re-examined in any Court of the United States, than according to the rules of the common law.

Amendment VIII

Excessive bail shall not be required, nor excessive fines imposed, nor cruel and unusual punishments inflicted.

Amendment IX

The enumeration in the Constitution, of certain rights, shall not be construed to deny or disparage others retained by the people.

Amendment X

The powers not delegated to the United States by the Constitution, nor prohibited by it to the States, are reserved to the States respectively, or to the people.

Amendment XI

(January 8, 1798) [15]

The judicial power of the United States shall not be construed to extend to any suit in law or equity, commenced or prosecuted against one of the United States by Citizens of another State, or by Citizens or Subjects of any Foreign State.

Amendment XII

(September 25, 1804)

The Electors shall meet in their respective states, and vote by ballot for President and Vice-President, one of whom, at least, shall not be an inhabitant of the same state with themselves; they shall name in their ballots the person voted for as President, and in distinct ballots the person voted for as Vice-President, and they shall make distinct lists of all persons voted for as President, and of all persons voted for as Vice-President, and of the number of votes for each, which lists they shall sign and certify, and transmit sealed to the seat of the government of the United States, directed to the President of the Senate;—The President of the Senate shall, in the presence of the Senate and House of Representatives, open all the certificates and the votes shall then be counted;—The person having the greatest number of votes for President, shall be the President, if such number be a majority of the whole number of Electors appointed, and if no person have such majority, then from the persons having the highest numbers not exceeding

[15] The dates noted under Amendments XI through XXVI are dates of ratification.

three on the list of those voted for as President, the House of Representatives shall choose immediately, by ballot, the President. But in choosing the President, the votes shall be taken by states, the representation from each state having one vote; a quorum for this purpose shall consist of a member or members from two-thirds of the states, and a majority of all the states shall be necessary to a choice. *And if the House of Representatives shall not choose a President whenever the right of choice shall devolve upon them, before the fourth day of March next following,*[16] then the Vice-President shall act as President, as in the case of the death or other constitutional disability of the President.—The person having the greatest number of votes as Vice-President, shall be the Vice-President, if such number be a majority of the whole number of Electors appointed, and if no person have a majority, then from the two highest numbers on the list, the Senate shall choose the Vice-President; a quorum for the purpose shall consist of two-thirds of the whole number of Senators, and a majority of the whole number shall be necessary to a choice. But no person constitutionally ineligible to the office of President shall be eligible to that of Vice-President of the United States.

Amendment XIII

(December 18, 1865)

Section 1. Neither slavery nor involuntary servitude, except as a punishment for crime whereof the party shall have been duly convicted, shall exist within the United States, or any place subject to their jurisdiction.

Section 2. Congress shall have power to enforce this article by appropriate legislation.

Amendment XIV

(July 28, 1868)

Section 1. All persons born or naturalized in the United States, and subject to the jurisdiction thereof, are citizens of the United States and of the State wherein they reside. No State shall make or enforce any law which shall abridge the privileges or immunities of citizens of the United States; nor shall any State deprive any person of life, liberty, and property, without due process of law; nor deny to any person within its jurisdiction the equal protection of the laws.

Section 2. Representatives shall be apportioned among the several States according to their respective numbers, counting the whole number of persons in each State, excluding Indians not taxed. But when the right to vote at any election for the choice of electors for President and Vice-President of the United States, Representatives in Congress, the Executive and Judicial officers of a State, or the members of the Legislature thereof, is denied to any of the male members of such State, being twenty-one years of age, and citizens of the United States, or in any way abridged, except for participation in rebellion, or other crime, the basis of representation therein shall be reduced in the proportion which the number of such male citizens shall bear to the whole number of male citizens twenty-one years of age in such State.

[16] Modified by the Twentieth Amendment.

Section 3. No person shall be a Senator or Representative in Congress, or elector of President and Vice-President, or hold any office, civil or military, under the United States, or under any State, who, having previously taken an oath, as a member of Congress, or as an officer of the United States, or as a member of any State legislature, or as an executive or judicial officer of any State, to support the Constitution of the United States, shall have engaged in insurrection or rebellion against the same, or given aid or comfort to the enemies thereof. But Congress may by a vote of two-thirds of each House, remove such disability.

Section 4. The validity of the public debt of the United States, authorized by law, including debts incurred for payment of pensions and bounties for services in suppressing insurrection or rebellion, shall not be questioned. But neither the United States nor any State shall assume or pay any debt or obligation incurred in aid of insurrection or rebellion against the United States, or any claim for the loss or emancipation of any slave; but all such debts, obligations and claims shall be held illegal and void.

Section 5. The Congress shall have power to enforce, by appropriate legislation, the provisions of this article.

Amendment XV

(March 30, 1870)

Section 1. The right of citizens of the United States to vote shall not be denied or abridged by the United States or by any State on account of race, color, or previous condition of servitude.

Section 2. The Congress shall have power to enforce this article by appropriate legislation.

Amendment XVI

(February 25, 1913)

The Congress shall have power to lay and collect taxes on incomes, from whatever sources derived, without apportionment among the several States, and without regard to any census or enumeration.

Amendment XVII

(May 31, 1913)

The Senate of the United States shall be composed of two Senators from each State, elected by the people thereof, for six years; and each Senator shall have one vote. The electors in each State shall have the qualifications requisite for electors of the most numerous branch of the State legislatures.

When vacancies happen in the representation of any State in the Senate, the executive authority of such State shall issue writs of election to fill such vacancies: *Provided,* That the legislature of any State may empower the executive thereof to make temporary appointments until the people fill the vacancies by election as the legislature may direct.

This amendment shall not be so construed as to affect the election or term of any Senator chosen before it becomes valid as part of the Constitution.

AMENDMENT XVIII

(January 29, 1919)

Section 1. *After one year from the ratification of this article the manufacture, sale, or transportation of intoxicating liquors within, the importation thereof into, or the exportation thereof from the United States and all territory subject to the jurisdiction thereof for beverage purposes is hereby prohibited.*

Section 2. *The Congress and the several States shall have concurrent power to enforce this article by appropriate legislation.*

Section 3. *This article shall be inoperative unless it shall have been ratified as an amendment to the Constitution by the legislatures of the several States, as provided in the Constitution, within seven years from the date of the submission hereof to the States by the Congress.*[17]

AMENDMENT XIX

(August 26, 1920)

The right of citizens of the United States to vote shall not be denied or abridged by the United States or by any State on account of sex.

Congress shall have power to enforce this article by appropriate legislation.

AMENDMENT XX

(February 6, 1933)

Section 1. The terms of the President and Vice-President shall end at noon on the 20th day of January, and the terms of Senators and Representatives at noon on the 3d day of January, of the years in which such terms would have ended if this article had not been ratified; and the terms of their successors shall then begin.

Section 2. The Congress shall assemble at least once in every year, and such meeting shall begin at noon on the 3d of January, unless they shall by law appoint a different day.

Section 3. If, at the time fixed for the beginning of the term of the President, the President elect shall have died, the Vice-President elect shall become President. If a President shall not have been chosen before the time fixed for the beginning of his term, or if the President elect shall have failed to qualify, then the Vice-President elect shall act as President until a President shall have qualified; and the Congress may by law provide for the case wherein neither a President elect nor a Vice-President elect

[17] Repealed by the Twenty-first Amendment.

shall have qualified, declaring who shall then act as President, or the manner in which one who is to act shall be selected, and such person shall act accordingly until a President or Vice-President shall have qualified.

Section 4. The Congress may by law provide for the case of the death of any of the persons from whom the House of Representatives may choose a President whenever the right of choice shall have devolved upon them, and for the case of the death of any of the persons from whom the Senate may choose a Vice-President whenever the right of choice shall have devolved upon them.

Section 5. Sections 1 and 2 shall take effect on the 15th day of October following the ratification of this article.

Section 6. This article shall be inoperative unless it shall have been ratified as an amendment to the Constitution by the legislatures of three-fourths of the several States within seven years from the date of its submission.

Amendment XXI [18]

(December 5, 1933)

Section 1. The eighteenth article of amendment to the Constitution of the United States is hereby repealed.

Section 2. The transportation or importation into any State, Territory, or Possession of the United States for delivery or use therein of intoxicating liquors, in violation of the laws thereof, is hereby prohibited.

Section 3. This article shall be inoperative unless it shall have been ratified as an amendment to the Constitution by conventions in the several States, as provided in the Constitution, within seven years from the date of the submission hereof to the States by the Congress.

Amendment XXII

(February 27, 1951)

Section 1. No person shall be elected to the office of the President more than twice, and no person who has held the office of President, or acted as President, for more than two years of a term to which some other person was elected President shall be elected to the office of President more than once. But this Article shall not apply to any person holding the office of President when this Article was proposed by the Congress, and shall not prevent any person who may be holding the office of President, or acting as President, during the term within which this Article becomes operative from holding the office of President or acting as President during the remainder of such term.

Section 2. This article shall be inoperative unless it shall have been ratified as an amendment to the Constitution by the legislatures of three-fourths of the several States within seven years from the date of its submission to the States by the Congress.

[18] This is the only amendment that has thus far been ratified by state conventions.

Amendment XXIII

(March 29, 1961)

Section 1. The District constituting the seat of Government of the United States shall appoint in such manner as the Congress may direct:

A number of electors of President and Vice-President equal to the whole number of Senators and Representatives in Congress to which the District would be entitled if it were a State, but in no event more than the least populous State; they shall be in addition to those appointed by the States, but they shall be considered, for the purposes of the election of President and Vice-President, to be electors appointed by a State; and they shall meet in the District and perform such duties as provided by the twelfth article of amendment.

Section 2. The Congress shall have power to enforce this article by appropriate legislation.

Amendment XXIV

(January 23, 1964)

The right of citizens of the United States to vote in any primary or other election for President or Vice-President, for electors for President or Vice-President, or for Senator or Representative in Congress shall not be denied or abridged by the United States or any State by reason of failure to pay any poll tax or other tax.

Amendment XXV

(February 23, 1967)

Section 1. In case of the removal of the President from office or of his death or resignation, the Vice President shall become President.

Section 2. Whenever there is a vacancy in the office of the Vice President, the President shall nominate a Vice President who shall take office upon confirmation by a majority vote of both Houses of Congress.

Section 3. Whenever the President transmits to the President pro tempore of the Senate and the Speaker of the House of Representatives his written declaration that he is unable to discharge the powers and duties of his office, and until he transmits to them a written declaration to the contrary, such powers and duties shall be discharged by the Vice President as Acting President.

Section 4. Whenever the Vice President and a majority of either the principal officers of the executive departments or of such other body as Congress may by law provide, transmit to the President pro tempore of the Senate and the Speaker of the House of Representatives their written declaration that the President is unable to discharge the powers and duties of his office, the Vice President shall immediately assume the powers and duties of the office as Acting President.

Thereafter, when the President transmits to the President pro tempore of the Senate and the Speaker of the House of Representatives his written declaration that no inability exists, he shall resume the powers and duties of his office unless the Vice President and a majority of either the principal officers of the executive department or of such other body as Congress may by law provide, transmit within four days to the President pro tempore of the Senate and the Speaker of the House of Representatives their written declaration that the President is unable to discharge the powers and duties of his office. Thereupon Congress shall decide the issue, assembling within forty-eight hours for that purpose if not in session. If the Congress, within twenty-one days after receipt of the latter written declaration, or, if Congress is not in session, within twenty-one days after Congress is required to assemble, determines by two-thirds vote of both Houses that the President is unable to discharge the powers and duties of his office, the Vice President shall continue to discharge the same as Acting President; otherwise, the President shall resume the powers and duties of his office.

AMENDMENT XXVI

(Ratified on June 30, 1971)

Section 1. The right of citizens of the United States, who are eighteen years of age, or older, to vote shall not be denied or abridged by the United States or by any State on account of age.

Section 2. The Congress shall have power to enforce this article by appropriate legislation.

APPENDIX **II**

United States Supreme Court Justices

(Capital letters indicate Chief Justices.)

Name	*Term of Office*	*Name*	*Term of Office*
JOHN JAY	1789–1795	Joseph Story	1811–1845
John Rutledge	1789–1791	Gabriel Duval	1812–1835
William Cushing	1789–1810	Smith Thompson	1823–1843
James Wilson	1789–1798	Robert Trimble	1826–1828
John Blair	1789–1796	John McLean	1829–1861
Robert H. Harrison	1789–1790	Henry Baldwin	1830–1844
James Iredell	1790–1799	James M. Wayne	1835–1867
Thomas Johnson	1791–1793	ROGER B. TANEY	1836–1864
William Paterson	1793–1806	Philip B. Barbour	1836–1841
JOHN RUTLEDGE	1795 [1]	John Catron	1837–1865
Samuel Chase	1796–1811	John McKinley	1837–1852
OLIVER ELLSWORTH	1796–1799	Peter V. Daniel	1841–1860
Bushrod Washington	1798–1829	Samuel Nelson	1845–1872
Alfred Moore	1799–1804	Levi Woodbury	1845–1851
JOHN MARSHALL	1801–1835	Robert C. Grier	1846–1870
William Johnson	1804–1834	Benj. R. Curtis	1851–1857
Brockholst Livingston	1806–1823	John A. Campbell	1853–1861
Thomas Todd	1807–1826	Nathan Clifford	1858–1881

[1] John Rutledge's appointment as Chief Justice in 1795 was not confirmed by Congress.

Name	*Term of Office*
Noah H. Swayne	1862–1881
Samuel F. Miller	1862–1890
David Davis	1862–1877
Stephen J. Feild	1863–1897
SALMON P. CHASE	1864–1873
William Strong	1870–1880
Joseph P. Bradley	1870–1892
Ward Hunt	1873–1882
MORRISON R. WAITE	1874–1888
John M. Harlan	1877–1911
William B. Woods	1881–1887
Stanley Matthews	1881–1889
Horace Gray	1882–1902
Samuel Blatchford	1882–1893
Lucius Q. C. Lamar	1888–1893
MELVILLE W. FULLER	1888–1910
David J. Brewer	1890–1910
Henry B. Brown	1891–1906
George Shiras, Jr.	1892–1903
Howell E. Jackson	1893–1895
Edward D. White	1894–1910
Rufus W. Peckham	1896–1909
Joseph McKenna	1898–1925
Oliver W. Holmes, Jr.	1902–1932
William R. Day	1903–1922
William H. Moody	1906–1910
Horace H. Lurton	1910–1914
Charles E. Hughes	1910–1916
Willis Van Devanter	1911–1937
Joseph R. Lamar	1911–1916
EDWARD D. WHITE	1910–1921
Mahlon Pitney	1912–1922
James C. McReynolds	1914–1941
Louis D. Brandeis	1916–1939
John H. Clarke	1916–1922
WILLIAM H. TAFT	1921–1930
George Sutherland	1922–1938
Pierce Butler	1922–1939
Edward T. Sanford	1923–1930
Harlan F. Stone	1925–1941
CHARLES E. HUGHES	1930–1941
Owen J. Roberts	1930–1945
Benjamin N. Cardozo	1932–1938
Hugo L. Black	1937–1970
Stanley F. Reed	1938–1957
Felix Frankfurter	1939–1962
William O. Douglas	1939–1975
Frank Murphy	1940–1949
HARLAN F. STONE	1941–1946
James F. Byrnes	1941–1942
Robert H. Jackson	1941–1954
Wiley B. Rutledge	1943–1949
Harold H. Burton	1945–1958
FRED M. VINSON	1946–1953
Tom C. Clarke	1949–1967
Sherman Minton	1949–1956
EARL WARREN	1953–1969
John M. Harlan	1954–1970
William J. Brennan	1956–
Charles E. Whittaker	1957–1962
Potter Stewart	1958–1981
Byron R. White	1962–
Arthur J. Goldberg	1962–1965
Abe Fortas	1965–1969
Thurgood Marshall	1967–
WARREN BURGER	1969–
Harry A. Blackmun	1970–
Lewis F. Powell, Jr.	1972–
William H. Rehnquist	1972–
John Paul Stevens	1975–
Sandra Day O'Connor	1981–

APPENDIX III

Selected Readings

I. The Supreme Court, the Constitution, and Constitutional Law

Abraham, Henry J. *Freedom and the Court.* 4th ed. New York: Oxford University Press, 1982.

———. *Justices and Presidents.* New York: Oxford, 1974.

Beard, Charles A. *The Supreme Court and the Constitution.* New York: Macmillan, 1912.

Becker, Theodore L., and Malcolm M. Feeley, eds. *The Impact of Supreme Court Decisions.* 2d ed. New York: Oxford University Press, 1973.

Berger, Raoul. *Congress Versus Supreme Court.* Cambridge: Harvard University Press, 1969.

Berkson, Larry. *The Supreme Court and Its Publics: The Communication of Policy Decisions.* Lexington, Mass.: Lexington, 1978.

Bickel, Alexander M. *The Least Dangerous Branch, the Supreme Court at the Bar of Politics.* Indianapolis: Bobbs-Merrill, 1962.

———. *Politics and the Warren Court.* New York: Harper & Row, 1965.

———. *The Supreme Court and the Idea of Progress.* New York: Harper & Row, 1970.

Black, Charles L., Jr. *The People and the Court.* New York: Macmillan, 1960.

Cahill, Fred V., Jr. *Judicial Legislation.* New York: Ronald Press, 1952.

Cahn, Edmond (ed.). *Supreme Court and Supreme Law.* Bloomington: Indiana University Press, 1954.

Carr, Robert K. *The Supreme Court and Judicial Review.* New York: Holt, Rinehart and Winston, 1942.

Casper, Jonathan D. *Lawyers Before the Warren Court.* Urbana: University of Illinois Press, 1972.

Choper, Jesse. *Judicial Review and the National Political Process.* Chicago: University of Chicago Press, 1980.

Corwin, Edward S. (ed.). *The Constitution of the United States of America, Analysis and Interpretation.* Washington, D.C.: Government Printing Office, 1953.

———. *Court over Constitution.* Princeton: Princeton University Press, 1938.

———. *The Doctrine of Judicial Review.* Princeton: Princeton University Press, 1914.

———. *The Twilight of the Supreme Court.* New Haven: Yale University Press, 1934.

Cox, Archibald. *The Role of the Supreme Court in American Government.* New York: Oxford, 1976.

———. *The Warren Court.* Cambridge: Harvard University Press, 1968.

Crosskey, William W. and William Jeffrey. *Politics and the Constitution in the History of the United States.* 3 vols. Chicago: University of Chicago Press, 1953, 1980.

Danelski, David. *A Supreme Court Justice Is Appointed.* New York: Random House, 1964.

Dolbeare, Kenneth, and Philip E. Hammond. *The School Prayer Decisions.* Chicago: University of Chicago Press, 1971.

Ely, John Hart. *Democracy and Distrust: A Theory of Judicial Review.* Cambridge: Harvard University Press, 1980.

Fairman, Charles. *Reconstruction and Reunion, 1864–88.* New York: Macmillan, 1971.

Frank, John P. *Marble Palace.* New York: Knopf, 1958.

Frankfurter, Felix. *Of Law and Men, Paper and Addresses, 1939–1956.* Philip Elman (ed.). New York: Harcourt, Brace & World, 1956.

Frankfurter, Felix, and James M. Landis. *The Business of the Supreme Court.* New York: Macmillan, 1928.

Freund, Paul A. *On Understanding the Supreme Court.* Boston: Little, Brown, 1949.

———. *The Supreme Court of the United States, Its Business, Purposes, Performance.* Cleveland and New York: World, 1961.

Funston, Richard. *Constitutional Counter-Revolution? The Warren Court and the Burger Court.* New York: Schenkman Publishing Co., 1977.

Garvey, Gerald. *Constitutional Bricolage.* Princeton: Princeton University Press, 1971.

Gray, David L. *The Supreme Court and the News Media.* Evanston: North-western University Press, 1968.

Haines, Charles G. *The American Doctrine of Judicial Supremacy.* 2nd. ed. Berkeley: University of California Press, 1959.

———. *The Role of the Supreme Court in American Government and Politics, 1789–1835.* Berkeley and Los Angeles: University of California Press, 1944.

Haines, Charles G., and Foster H. Sherwood. *The Role of the Supreme Court in American Government and Politics, 1835–1864.* Berkeley and Los Angeles: University of California Press, 1957.

Harmon, H. Judd (ed.). *Essays in Constitutional Law.* Port Washington, N.Y.: Kennikat Press, 1978.

Haskins, George L., and Herbert A. Johnston. *A History of the Supreme Court of the United States: The Foundations of Power: John Marshall, 1801–1815.* New York: Macmillan, 1981.

Henkin, Louis. *Foreign Affairs and the Constitution.* Mineola, N.Y.: Foundation Press, 1972.

Hughes, Charles E. *The Supreme Court of the United States.* New York: Columbia University Press, 1928.

Hurst, Willard. *The Growth of American Law, the Law Makers.* Boston: Little, Brown, 1950.

Hyneman, Charles S. *The Supreme Court on Trial.* New York: Atherton Press, 1963.

Jackson, Robert H. *The Struggle for Judicial Supremacy.* New York: Knopf, 1941.

———. *The Supreme Court in the American System of Government.* Cambridge: Harvard University Press, 1955.

Krislov, Samuel. *The Supreme Court and Political Freedom.* New York: The Free Press, 1968.

Kurland, Philip B. *Politics, the Constitution, and the Warren Court.* Chicago: University of Chicago Press, 1970.

——— (ed.). *Supreme Court Review.* Chicago: University of Chicago Press. Annually.

Kutler, Stanley. *Privilege and Creative Destruction: The Charles River Bridge Case.* New York: Norton, 1978.

McCloskey, Robert G. *The American Supreme Court.* Chicago: University of Chicago Press, 1960.

——— (ed.). *Essays in Constitutional Law.* New York: Knopf, 1957.

———. *The Modern Supreme Court.* Cambridge: Harvard University Press, 1972.

Magrath, C. Peter. *Yazoo.* Providence: Brown University Press, 1966.

Mason, Alpheus T. *The Supreme Court from Taft to Burger.* Baton Rouge: Louisiana State University Press, 1979.

Miller, Arthur S. *The Supreme Court and American Capitalism.* New York: Free Press, 1968.

Miller, Charles A. *The Supreme Court and the Uses of History.* Cambridge: Harvard University Press, 1969.

Murphy, Paul L. *Constitution in Crisis Times, 1918–1969.* New York: Harper & Row, 1972.

Murphy, Walter F. *Elements of Judicial Strategy.* Chicago: University of Chicago Press, 1973.

———. *Congress and the Court.* Chicago: University of Chicago Press, 1962.

Paul, Arnold M. *Conservative Crisis and Rule of Law: Attitudes of Bar and Bench, 1887–1895.* Ithaca: Cornell University Press, 1960.

Peltason, Jack W. *Federal Courts in the Political Process.* Garden City, N.Y.: Doubleday, 1955.

Pfeffer, Leo. *This Honorable Court: A History of the Supreme Court of the United States.* Boston: Beacon Press, 1965.

Pollak, Louis. *The Constitution and the Supreme Court: A Documentary History.* 2 vols. Cleveland: World Publishing Co., 1966.

Pritchett, C. Herman. *The Political Offender and the Warren Court.* Boston: Boston University Press, 1958.

———. *Congress Versus the Supreme Court.* Minneapolis: University of Minnesota Press, 1961.

———. *The Roosevelt Court.* New York: Macmillan, 1948.

Read, Conyers (ed.). *The Constitution Reconsidered.* New York: Columbia University Press, 1938.

Rodell, Fred. *Nine Men: A Political History of the Supreme Court from 1790–1955.* New York: Random House, 1955.

Roettinger, Ruth L. *The Supreme Court and State Police Power.* Washington, D.C.: Public Affairs Press, 1957.

Rosen, Paul L. *The Supreme Court and Social Science.* Urbana: University of Illinois Press, 1972.

Rossiter, Clinton. *1787: The Grand Convention.* New York: Macmillan, 1966.

Rostow, Eugene V. *The Sovereign Prerogative: The Supreme Court and the Quest for Law.* New Haven: Yale University Press, 1962.

Rottschaefer, Henry. *The Constitution and Socio-Economic Change.* Ann Arbor: University of Michigan Law School, 1948.

Schmidhauser, John R. *The Supreme Court: Its Politics, Personalities, and Procedures.* New York: Holt, Rinehart and Winston, 1960.

———, and Larry L. Berg. *The Supreme Court and Congress.* New York: Free Press, 1972.

Schubert, Glendon. *The Constitutional Polity.* Boston: Boston University Press, 1970.

———. *The Judicial Mind: Attitudes and Ideologies of Supreme Court Justices.* Evanston, Ill.: Northwestern University Press, 1965.

Schwartz, Bernard. *A Commentary on the Constitution of the United States.* New York: Macmillan, 1963–. Multiple vols.

Scigliano, Robert. *The Supreme Court and the Presidency.* New York: Free Press, 1972.

Selected Essays on Constitutional Law. 4 vols. Published under the auspices of the Association of American Law Societies. Brooklyn: Foundation Press, 1938. Vol. 5, 1963.

Shapiro, Martin. *Freedom of Speech, the Supreme Court, and Judicial Review.* Englewood Cliffs, N.J.: Prentice-Hall, 1966.

———. *Law and Politics in the Supreme Court.* New York: The Free Press, 1964.

——— (ed.). *The Pentagon Papers and the Courts.* San Francisco: Chandler, 1972.

———. *The Supreme Court and Administrative Agencies.* New York: The Free Press, 1968.

——— (ed.). *The Supreme Court and Constitutional Rights.* Chicago: Scott, Foresman, 1967.

——— (ed.). *The Supreme Court and Public Policy.* Chicago: Scott, Foresman, 1969.

Siegan, Bernard. *Economic Liberties and the Constitution.* Chicago: University of Chicago Press, 1980.

Sprague, John. *Voting Patterns of the United States Supreme Court.* Indianapolis: Bobbs-Merrill, 1968.

Steamer, Robert J. *Supreme Court in Crisis.* Amherst: University of Massachusetts Press, 1971.

Stites, Francis. *Private Interest and Public Gain: The Dartmouth College Case, 1819.* Amherst, Mass.: The University of Massachusetts Press, 1972.

Strum, Phillippa. *The Supreme Court and "Political Questions."* University, Ala.: University of Alabama Press, 1974.

Sutherland, Arthur. *Constitutionalism in America.* New York: Blaisdell Publishing Co., 1965.

Swisher, Carl B. *The Growth of Constitutional Power in the United States.* Chicago: University of Chicago Press, 1946.

———. *The Supreme Court in Modern Role.* New York: New York University Press, 1958.

———. *The Taney Period, 1835–64.* New York: Macmillan, 1974.

Tribe, Lawrence. *American Constitutional Law.* Mineola, N.Y.: Foundation Press, 1978.

Vose, Clement E. *Caucasians Only: The Supreme Court, the NAACP, and the Restrictive Covenant Cases.* Berkeley: University of California Press, 1959.

———. *Constitutional Change.* Lexington, Mass.: D. C. Heath, 1972.

Warren, Charles. *The Supreme Court in United States History.* Boston: Little, Brown, 1928.

Wasby, Stephen L. *Continuity and Change: From the Warren Court to the Burger Court.* Pacific Palasades, Calif.: Goodyear Publishing Co., 1977.

———. *The Impact of the U.S. Supreme Court.* Homewood, Ill.: Dorsey Press, 1970.

Westin, Allan F. (ed.). *The Anatomy of a Constitutional Law Case.* New York: Macmillan, 1958.

———. *An Autobiography of the Supreme Court.* New York: Macmillan, 1963.

———. *The Supreme Court: Views from Inside.* New York: W. W. Norton, 1961.

Wilkinson, J. Harvie III. *Serving Justice: A Supreme Court Clerk's View.* New York: Charterhouse, 1974.

Wright, Benjamin F. *The Growth of American Constitutional Law.* Boston: Houghton Mifflin, 1942.

II. Political and Civil Rights

Abernathy, Glenn. *The Right of Assembly and Association.* Columbia: South Carolina University Press, 1961.

Ackerman, Bruce. *Private Property and the Constitution.* New Haven: Yale University Press, 1977.

Becker, Carl L. *Freedom and Responsibility in the American Way of Life.* New York: Knopf, 1945.

Berns, Walter. *Freedom, Virtue, and the First Amendment.* Baton Rouge: Louisiana State University Press, 1957.

Blaustein, Albert P., and Clarence C. Ferguson, Jr. *Desegregation and the Law.* New Brunswick, N.J.: Rutgers University Press, 1957.

Brant, Irving. *The Bill of Rights.* Indianapolis: Bobbs-Merrill, 1965.

Cahn, Edmond (ed.). *The Great Rights.* New York: Macmillan, 1963.

Carr, Robert K. *Federal Protection of Civil Rights: Quest for a Sword.* Ithaca, N.Y.: Cornell University Press, 1949.

Chafee, Zechariah, Jr. *The Blessings of Liberty.* Philadelphia: J. B. Lippincott, 1956.

———. *Free Speech in the United States.* Cambridge: Harvard University Press, 1942.

———. *How Human Rights Got into the Constitution.* Boston: Boston University Press, 1952.

Chase, Harold W. *Security and Liberty, the Problem of Native Communists, 1947–1955.* Garden City, N.Y.: Doubleday, 1955.

Commager, Henry S. *Freedom, Loyalty, Dissent.* New York: Oxford University Press, 1954.

Cortner, Richard C. *The Supreme Court and the Second Bill of Rights.* Madison: Wisconsin University Press, 1981.

Corwin, Edward S. *Liberty Against Government.* Baton Rouge: Louisiana State University Press, 1948.

Cushman, Robert E. *Civil Liberties in the United States.* Ithaca, N.Y.: Cornell University Press, 1956.

Dixon, Robert G., Jr. *Democratic Representation: Reapportionment in Law and Politics.* New York: Oxford University Press, 1969.

Dorsen, Norman, Paul Bender, and Burt Neuborne. *Emerson, Haber, and Dorsen's Political and Civil Rights in the United States.* 2 vols. & supplements. Boston: Little Brown, 1976, 1977.

Elliott, Ward E. Y. *The Rise of Guardian Democracy: The Supreme Court's Role in Voting Rights Disputes, 1845–1969.* Cambridge: Harvard University Press, 1974.

Emerson, Thomas I. *The System of Freedom of Expression.* New York: Random House, 1970.

Fellman, David. *The Constitutional Right of Association.* Chicago: University of Chicago Press, 1963.

———. *Defendants' Rights Today.* Madison, Wisc.: University of Wisconsin Press, 1976.

Fraenkel, Osmond K. *The Supreme Court and Civil Liberties.* New York: Oceana, 1960.

Freund, Paul. *Religion and the Public Schools.* Cambridge: Harvard University Press, 1965.

Gellhorn, Walter. *American Rights: The Constitution in Action.* New York: Macmillan, 1960.

———. *Individual Freedom and Governmental Restraints.* Baton Rouge: Louisiana State University Press, 1956.

Graglia, Linus. *Disaster by Decrees: The Supreme Court Decisions on Race and the Schools.* Ithica: Cornell University Press, 1976.

Graham, Fred P. *Self-Inflicted Wound.* New York: Macmillan, 1970.

Grant, James A. C. *Our Common Law Constitution.* Boston: Boston University Press, 1960.

Greenberg, Jack. *Race Relations and American Law.* New York: Columbia University Press, 1959.

Hand, Learned. *The Bill of Rights.* Cambridge: Harvard University Press, 1958.

Hanson, Royce. *The Political Thicket: Reapportionment and Constitutional Democracy.* Englewood Cliffs, N.J.: Prentice-Hall, 1966.

Harris, Robert J. *The Quest for Equality: The Constitution, Congress, and the Supreme Court.* Baton Rouge: Louisiana State University Press, 1960.

Howe, Mark De Wolfe. *Garden and the Wilderness. Religion and Government in American Constitutional History.* Chicago: University of Chicago Press, 1965.

Hudon, Edward. *Freedom of Speech and Press in America.* Washington, D.C.: Public Affairs Press, 1963.

Kalven, Harry. *The Negro and the First Amendment.* Columbus: Ohio State University Press, 1965.

Kauper, Paul G. *Civil Liberties and the Constitution.* Ann Arbor: University of Michigan Press, 1962.

———. *Frontiers of Constitutional Liberty.* Ann Arbor: University of Michigan Law School, 1956.

———. *Religion and the Constitution.* Baton Rouge: Louisiana State University Press, 1964.

Kluger, Richard. *Simple Justice: The History of Brown v. Board of Education.* New York: Knopf, 1975.

Konvitz, Milton R. *The Constitution and Civil Rights.* New York: Columbia University Press, 1946.

———. *Expanding Liberties.* New York: Viking Press, 1966.
———. *Fundamental Liberties of a Free People: Religion, Speech, Press, Assembly.* Ithaca, N.Y.: Cornell University Press, 1957.
Konvitz, Milton R., and J. Leskes. *A Century of Civil Rights.* New York: Columbia University Press, 1961.
Kurland, Philip B. *Religion and the Law.* Chicago: Aldine Pub. Co., 1962.
Levy, Leonard. *Jefferson and Civil Liberties: The Darker Side.* Cambridge: Harvard University Press, 1963.
———. *Legacy of Suppression, Freedom of Speech and Press in Early American History.* Cambridge: Harvard University Press, 1960.
Lewis, Anthony. *Gideon's Trumpet.* New York: Random House, 1960.
Longaker, Richard P. *The Presidency and Civil Liberties.* Ithaca, N.Y.: Cornell University Press, 1961.
McKay, Robert. *Reapportionment: The Law and Politics of Equal Representation.* New York: Twentieth Century Fund, 1965.
Manwaring, David R. *Render unto Ceasar, the Flag-Salute Controversy.* Chicago: University of Chicago Press, 1962.
Meiklejohn, Alexander. *Free Speech and Its Relation to Self-government.* New York: Harper & Row, 1948.
———. *Political Freedom: The Constitutional Powers of the People.* New York: Harper & Row, 1960.
Morgan, Richard E. *The Supreme Court and Religion.* New York: Free Press, 1972.
O'Brian, John L. *National Security and Individual Freedom.* Cambridge: Harvard University Press, 1955.
O'Brien, David. *Privacy, Law and Public Policy.* New York: Praeger, 1979.
———. *The Public's Right to Know: The Supreme Court and the First Amendment.* New York: Praeger, 1981.
Peltason, Jack W. *Fifty-Eight Lonely Men, Southern Federal Judges and School Desegregation.* New York: Harcourt, Brace & World, 1961.
Pfeffer, Leo. *The Liberties of an American.* Boston: Beacon Press, 1956.
Pound, Roscoe. *The Development of Constitutional Guarantees of Liberty.* New Haven: Yale University Press, 1957.
President's Committee on Civil Rights. *To Secure These Rights.* Washington, D.C.: Government Printing Office, 1947.
Preston, William Jr. *Aliens and Dissenters, Federal Suppression of Radicals.* Cambridge: Harvard University Press, 1963.
Pritchett, C. Herman. *Civil Liberties and the Vinson Court.* Chicago: University of Chicago Press, 1954.
———. *The Political Offender and the Warren Court.* Boston: Boston University Press, 1958.
Rutland, Robert A. *The Birth of the Bill of Rights, 1776–1791.* Chapel Hill: University of North Carolina Press, 1955.
Stephens, Otis H. *The Supreme Court and Confessions of Guilt.* Nashville: University of Tennessee Press, 1973.
Superintendent of Documents. *The Report of the United States Commission on Civil Rights.* Washington, D.C.: Government Printing Office, 1959.
Taper, Bernard. *Gomillion v. Lightfoot, the Tuskegee Gerrymander Case.* New York: McGraw-Hill, 1962.
Tresolini, Rocco J. *Justice and the Supreme Court.* Philadelphia: J. B. Lippincott, 1963.

Vose, Clement E. *Caucasians Only: The Supreme Court, the NAACP, and the Restrictive Covenant Cases.* Berkeley: University of California Press, 1959.

Wasby, Stephen, Anthony D'Amato, and Rosemary Metrailer. *Desegregation From Brown to Alexander: An Exploration of Supreme Court Strategies.* Carbondale, Ill.: Southern Illinois University Press, 1977.

Westin, Alan. *Privacy and Freedom.* New York: Atheneum, 1967.

Wilkinson, J. Harvie, III. *From Brown to Bakke.* Oxford: Oxford University Press, 1979.

Williams, Edward B. *One Man's Freedom.* New York: Atheneum, 1962.

III. Judicial Biography

Baker, Leonard, *John Marshall. A Life in Law.* New York: Macmillan, 1974.

Beveridge, Albert J. *The Life of John Marshall.* 4 vols. Boston: Houghton Mifflin, 1919.

Bickel, Alexander M. *The Unpublished Opinions of Mr. Justice Brandeis; The Supreme Court at Work.* Cambridge: Harvard University Press, 1957.

Bowen, Catherine Drinker. *Yankee from Olympus.* Boston: Little, Brown, 1945.

Christman, Henry M. (ed.). *The Public Papers of Chief Justice Earl Warren.* New York: Simon and Schuster, 1959.

Corwin, Edward S. *John Marshall and the Constitution.* New Haven: Yale University Press, 1919.

Countryman, Vern. *The Judicial Record of Justice William O. Douglas.* Cambridge: Harvard University Press, 1974.

Danelski, D., and J. Tulchin (eds.). *Autobiographical Notes of Charles Evans Hughes.* Cambridge: Harvard University Press, 1973.

Dilliard, Irving (ed.). *One Man's Stand for Freedom, Mr. Justice Black and the Bill of Rights.* New York: Knopf, 1963.

Douglas, William O. *Court Years: The Autobiography of William O. Douglas.* New York: Random House, 1980.

Dunham, Allison, and Philip Kurland (eds.). *Mr. Justice.* Chicago: University of Chicago Press, 1956.

Dunne, G. T. *Hugo Black and the Judicial Revolution.* New York: Simon & Schuster, 1977.

———. *Justice Joseph Story and the Rise of the Supreme Court.* New York: Simon & Schuster, 1971.

Ewing, Cortez A. M. *The Judges of the Supreme Court, 1789–1937.* Minneapolis: University of Minnesota Press, 1938.

Fairman, Charles. *Mr. Justice Miller and the Supreme Court.* Cambridge: Harvard University Press, 1939.

Faulkner, Robert K. *The Jurisprudence of John Marshall.* Princeton: Princeton University Press, 1968.

Frank, John P. *Mr. Justice Black: The Man and His Opinions.* New York: Knopf, 1949.

———. *Justice Daniel Dissenting, A Biography of Peter V. Daniel, 1784–1860.* Cambridge: Harvard University Press, 1964.

Frankfurter, Felix. *Mr. Justice Holmes and the Supreme Court.* Cambridge: Harvard University Press, 1938.

Friedman, Leon, and Fred L. Israel. *The Justices of the United States Supreme Court, 1789–1969: Their Lives and Major Opinions.* 4 vols. New York: Chelsea House, 1969.

Gerhart, Eugene C. *America's Advocate: Robert H. Jackson.* Indianapolis: Bobbs-Merrill, 1957.

Hamilton, Virginia. *Hugo Black: The Alabama Years.* Baton Rouge: Louisiana State University Press, 1972.

Harper, Fowler V. *Justice Rutledge and the Bright Constellation.* Indianapolis: Bobbs-Merrill, 1965.

Hendel, Samuel. *Charles Evans Hughes and the Supreme Court.* New York: King's Crown Press, 1951.

Hirsch, H. N. *The Enigma of Felix Frankfurter.* New York: Basic Books, 1981.

Howard, J. Woodford. *Mr. Justice Murphy: A Political Biography.* Princeton: Princeton University Press, 1968.

Howe, Mark DeWolfe. *Justice Oliver Wendell Holmes, the Shaping Years, 1841–1870.* Cambridge: Harvard University Press, 1957.

———. *Justice Oliver Wendell Holmes, the Proving Years, 1870–1882.* Cambridge: Harvard University Press, 1963.

Jacobs, Clyde E. *Justice Frankfurter and Civil Liberties.* Berkeley: University of California Press, 1961.

Jones, W. Melville (ed.). *Chief Justice John Marshall, a Reappraisal.* Ithaca, N.Y.: Cornell University Press, 1956.

King, Willard L. *Melville Weston Fuller.* New York: Macmillan, 1950.

Konefsky, Samuel J. *Chief Justice Stone and the Supreme Court.* New York: Macmillan, 1945.

———. *The Legacy of Holmes and Brandeis.* New York: Macmillan, 1956.

———. *John Marshall and Alexander Hamilton, Architects of the American Constitution.* New York: Macmillan, 1964.

Lask, J. P. (ed.). *From the Diaries of Felix Frankfurter.* New York: W. W. Norton, 1975.

Lerner, Max. *The Mind and Faith of Mr. Justice Holmes.* New York: Random House, 1943.

Levy, Leonard W. *The Law of the Commonwealth and Chief Justice Shaw.* Cambridge: Harvard University Press, 1957.

Lewis, Walker. *Without Fear or Favor: A Biography of Roger Brooke Taney.* Boston: Houghton Mifflin, 1965.

McClellan, James. *Joseph Story and the American Constitution.* Norman, Okla.: University of Oklahoma Press, 1971.

McLean, Joseph E. *William Rufus Day.* Baltimore: John Hopkins Press, 1946.

Magee, James. *Mr. Justice Black: Absolutist on the Court.* Charlottesville, Va.: University of Virginia Press, 1980.

Magrath, C. Peter. *Morrison R. Waite: The Triumph of Character.* New York: Macmillan, 1963.

Marke, Julius J. (ed.). *The Holmes Reader.* New York: Oceana, 1955.

Mason, Alpheus T. *Brandeis—A Free Man's Life.* New York: Viking Press, 1956.

———. *Harlan Fiske Stone, Pillar of the Law.* New York: Viking Press, 1956.

———. *William Howard Taft—Chief Justice.* New York: Simon and Schuster, 1965.

Mendelson, Wallace. *Justices Black and Frankfurter: Conflict in the Court.* Chicago: University of Chicago Press, 1961.

Morgan, Donald G. *Justice William Johnson, the First Dissenter.* Columbia: University of South Carolina Press, 1954.

Murphy, Bruce. *The Brandeis-Frankfurter Connection.* New York: Oxford University Press, 1982.

Norris, Harold. *Mr. Justice Murphy and the Bill of Rights,* Dobbs Ferry, N.Y.: Oceana Pubs., 1965.

O'Brien, William. *Justice Reed and the First Amendment: The Religious Clauses.* Washington, D.C.: Georgetown University Press, 1958.

Paschal, Joel F. *Mr. Justice Sutherland: A Man Against the State.* Princeton: Princeton University Press, 1951.

Perkins, Dexter. *Charles Evans Hughes and American Democratic Statesmanship.* Boston: Little, Brown, 1956.

Phillips, H. B. (ed.). *Felix Frankfurter Reminisces.* New York: Reynal, 1960.

Pringle, Henry F. *The Life and Times of William Howard Taft.* 2 vols. New York: Farrar and Rinehart, 1939.

Pusey, Merlo J. *Charles Evans Hughes.* 2 vols. New York: Macmillan, 1951.

Schubert, Glendon. *The Dispassionate Justice: Judicial Opinions of Robert Jackson.* Indianapolis: Bobbs-Merrill, 1969.

Simon, James F. *Independent Journey: The Life of William O. Douglas.* New York: Harper & Row, 1980.

Stites, Francis M. *John Marshall: Defender of the Constitution.* Boston: Little, Brown, 1981.

Swindler, William F. *The Constitution and Chief Justice Marshall.* New York: Dodd, 1977.

Swisher, Carl B. *Roger B. Taney.* New York: Macmillan, 1935.

———. *Stephen J. Field.* Washington, D.C.: The Brookings Institute, 1930.

Thomas, Helen S. *Felix Frankfurter: Scholar on the Bench.* Baltimore: Johns Hopkins Press, 1960.

Todd, Alden L. *Justice on Trial: The Case of Louis D. Brandeis.* New York: McGraw-Hill, 1964.

Umbreit, Kenneth B. *Our Eleven Chief Justices: A History of the Supreme Court in Terms of Their Personalities.* New York: Harper & Row, 1940.

Warner, H. L. *The Life of Mr. Justice Clarke: A Testimony to the Power of Liberal Dissent in America.* Cleveland: Western Reserve University Press, 1959.

Williams, Charlotte. *Hugo L. Black, a Study in the Judicial Process.* Baltimore: Johns Hopkins Press, 1950.